COLLECTED BOOKS

ALSO BY ALLEN AHEARN

Book Collecting: A Comprehensive Guide

COLLECTED BOOKS

The Guide to Values

ALLEN AND PATRICIA AHEARN

G. P. PUTNAM'S SONS

New York

Published by G. P. Putnam's Sons,
200 Madison Avenue, New York, NY 10016.
Published simultaneously in Canada

The text of this book is set in Times Roman.
Designed by MaryJane DiMassi

Library of Congress Cataloging-in-Publication Data

Ahearn, Allen.
Collected books : the guide to values / Allen and Patricia Ahearn.
p.   cm.
Includes bibliographical references (p. 621).
ISBN 0-399-13663-0
1. Book collecting—United States—Handbooks, manuals, etc.
2. Books—Prices.   I. Ahearn, Patricia.   II. Title.
Z987.5.U6A36 1991   90-14559 CIP
002′.075—dc20

Printed in the United States of America
9   10

ACKNOWLEDGMENTS

First and foremost we wish to thank Bill Reese and Terry Halladay (William Reese Company, New Haven, Connecticut) for contributions above and beyond any we could have reasonably expected. The Americana titles included herein represent a broader selection with more accurate first edition identification and price estimates than would have been possible without their assistance.

Next we would like to thank Bob Fleck (Oak Knoll Books, New Castle, Delaware), a specialist in Books on Books, for suggesting a large selection of books in his field that he believed should be included in this guide; Larry Dingman (Dinkytown Antiquarian Bookstore, Minneapolis, Minnesota) for his suggestions on Western fiction; Robert W. Smith (martial arts); and Ralph Hirschtritt and Lee C. Dieter (golf).

We would also like to thank all those dealers who keep us on their mailing lists, which is the only way we can try (a vain attempt) to keep current on prices; and those that furnished us some specific advice or assistance in preparing this guide: Dan and Etta Adams, Tony and Nora Aldridge, Peter Allen, Bart Auerbach, Bert Babcock, John Ballinger, John Bell, Steve Bernard, George Bixby, Taylor Bowie, Marilyn Braiterman, Chris Bready, Andreas Brown, Jackson Bryer, John Butterworth, Bev Chaney, Tom Congalton, John Crichton, Lloyd Currey, John Curtis, Joe Dermont, Bill Dunn, Beth and Paul Garon, Rick Gekoski, Chan Gordon, Oscar Graham, Cliff Graubart, Mike Greenbaum, Carl Hahn, David Holmes, Glenn Horowitz, George Houle, Peter Howard, James Jaffe, Helen Kelly, John Knott, Drew Lebby, Ken Lopez, Steve Loewentheil, Bob Madle, Jeff Marks, David Mason, David Mayou, Ian McKelvie, Edmond Miller, George Minkoff, Larry

Moskowitz, Ed and Judy Myers, Julian Nangle, Frannie Ness, Maurice Neville, Gene O'Neil, James O'Neil, Gary Oleson, Otto Penzler, James Pepper, Phil Pirages, David Rees, Lin & Tucker Respess, Bertram Rota, Joel Sattler, Richard Shuh, Joel Silver, Ralph Sipper, R.S. Speck, Peter L. Stern, Don Stine, Allan Stypeck, Steve Temple, Harvey and Linda Tucker, Henry Turlington, Jeffrey Weinberg, Martin Weinkle, Jerry Weinstein, Burton Weiss, Bob Wilson, Clarence Wolf, Linda Wooley, Howard Woolmer, John Wronoski, and Herb Yellin.

A special thanks goes to Beth Ahearn, our new daughter-in-law, who spent hundreds of hours at the computer working on this and also to our daughters, Dyanne Ahearn, Beth Jones, and Sue Kalk, for their help.

And last but not least, we must acknowledge the work of Van Allen Bradley, who not only provided a starting point with the last edition of his *Handbook of Values,* but also created a strong market for a general price guide such as this.

FOR
ESTHERE

CONTENTS

COLLECTED BOOKS

INTRODUCTION

Our intent is to provide a basis for identifying and pricing the English-language first editions of books by collected authors.

We are much more concerned with assuring that the bibliographical information is correct than that the price estimates are perfect. We believe the prices herein are representative of the current retail prices for most of the titles; however, the most common titles will certainly show up at lower prices occasionally and the truly scarce titles may be priced far above these estimates when they finally appear on the market. The latter is reasonable because the estimates on these scarce books are, in many cases, based on very few appearances—and may not have been offered or appeared at auction for many years.

We hope eventually to cover books by collected authors in all fields. This was not possible in this first effort, but we intend to continue to branch out in later editions.

This book is similar in intent to Van Allen Bradley's *Handbook of Values,* but there are some differences that we believe are important:

This volume includes books published before 1800.

It is intended that this volume include sufficient information to allow the reader to identify first editions of a book in hand.

The prices are current (1991) rather than projections.

The number of press books has been reduced substantially, as it seems to us that the majority of the press books appear at auction often enough to make *American Book Prices Current* (ABPC) a more current source of price information than a guide such as this. We would recommend ABPC for the following presses: Ashendene, Book Club of California, Cuala, Doves, Derrydale, Eragny, Golden Cockerel, Grabhorn, Grolier Club, Kelmscott, Limited Editions Club, and Nonesuch.

We have used auction and catalog prices, or projections therefrom, over the last ten years to estimate the prices in this listing. In comparing it to the listings in Bradley, we should caution that it would be wise to hold on to the last edition, as there are thousands of entries in Bradley's last edition that are not in this volume. Conversely, there are thousands of entries herein that were not in Bradley. In addition, it should be noted that for each entry that appeared in the last edition of Bradley's book and also appears here, the bibliographical information has been verified and corrected if necessary.

We have tried to be bibliographically accurate, but we realize that errors are normal in works such as this and would encourage correspondence on errors or omissions.

USING THIS GUIDE

All books listed herein are first editions/first printings of the individual titles unless otherwise stated.

The estimated values are believed to be accurate plus or minus 20 percent and are based on:

Books published in 1839 or earlier being rebound at some date later than the date of publication unless otherwise stated.

Books being in original cloth (cloth-covered boards) or boards (paper-covered boards) unless otherwise stated for all books published in 1840 or later.

Books being in original dustwrappers if published in 1920 or later, except for limited editions in slipcases, which normally would not have dustwrappers, and those books issued in wraps (bound with paper covers), which would not have been issued in dustwrappers (unless noted).

All books being in very good or better condition as detailed below.

Note:

Persons interested in offering books listed within this book for sale to bookdealers must understand that the prices included here represent the estimated retail price one might expect to pay to a bookdealer to purchase a particular book when the book is in the condition noted below. Lesser copies are worth less. Exceptional copies of notable rarities are worth more. Bookdealers are classic examples of small independent businesses, and they cannot be expected to pay the estimated value for copies of books listed here. The percentage of value one can expect in sale to a dealer will vary, but one should not anticipate more than 40 to 50 percent of estimated value for other than prime items from a dealer. One alternative to consider is acceptance in trade of books the dealer owns; the percentage of return most likely will come closer to 60 percent or more, depending on what you are offering and what you wish to swap for. Most dealers are also not interested in accepting several lower-value books in exchange for higher-value titles. They will usually be happy to accept them for similarly priced books. Understand further that even though you may own books listed in this volume, that is no guarantee that a dealer will automatically be interested in buying or trading for them. Most dealers specialize in particular areas and are not interested in less than prime titles outside their fields. On the other hand, most responsible dealers would be glad to suggest dealers in other fields for books that he or she has no interest in purchasing; this is usually done as a courtesy and not as a payable service.

The entries are composed of:

Author, title, place of publication, date of publication, and only that additional information needed to identify the issue, state or edition, and the value.

All entries are first editions (first printings) unless otherwise stated. "Trade" is used to indicate the first general edition available for public sale after a limited edition has been issued. Usually the same sheets are used for both the limited and trade editions.

If the author's name does not appear on the title page, the entry will start with the title. If the author used a pseudonym, the pseudonym will appear first and the entry will include the author's name in parentheses.

Occasionally, the entry will reference VAB (Van Allen Bradley's *Handbook of Values* 1982–1983) if there were points in VAB that could not be found in any other reference work and we thought they should not be left out. In addition, some entries include reference to specific bibliographies such as *Bibliography of American Literature* (BAL), *Modern First Editions* by Merle Johnson (Johnson), etc. Full titles of these and other bibliographies used to develop this guide can be found at the end of this book.

If the place of publication or date does not appear on the title page, this information will be in parentheses ( ). This is *particularly significant* because the presence of a date on the title page may be the only way to differentiate between first and later printings.

First-Edition Identification

It is obvious, in looking over the entries, that the first key in starting to determine whether or not a particular book is a first edition is the date on the title page. This seems particularly true in the case of titles before 1900: whether the titles be fiction or nonfiction, it would appear that the vast majority of the first editions listed herein before 1900 had the date on the title page. After 1900, there are a number of publishers that did or currently do not put the date on the title page, but you can determine first editions of these titles by using the identification by publisher below.

If there is no date on the title page, checking to see if the publisher is one of the following reprint publishers would immediately tell you the book is not a first edition (with a few exceptions specifically noted in the entries): Blakiston, A.L. Burt, Grosset & Dunlap, Hurst, Modern Library, Sun Dial or Tower Books (World). If the book was not published by one of these, you should check the lists below for the purpose of identifying the first edition of the book.

It should be noted that most of the Book-of-the-Month-Club editions look exactly like the true first editions and may actually state "First Edition," but have a small black circle or a blind stamp (either in a circular, square or maple leaf pattern) on the lower right corner of the back cover. These books are not first editions.

The following publishers in the last few decades may have used a series of numbers including a "1" on the copyright page of the first edition. Prior to this they stated "First Edition," "First Printing," "First Impression," "First published" (month and year, or just year), "Published" (month and year, or just year), or put their logo or colophon on the copyright page of the first edition. Later printings would normally be noted on the copyright page. Exceptions will be noted in the entry:

Atheneum
Ballantine Books
Bobbs-Merrill (Since 1920. Prior to that, they used a bow-and-arrow design in some cases)
Bodley Head
Book Supply Co.
Brentano's (1928–33)
E.R. Burroughs, Inc.
Jonathan Cape
Cassell & Co.
Crime Club (U.S.)
Delacorte Press
George H. Doran (GHD logo on copyright page), but no indication on later printings.
Doubleday, Doran (but no statement on later printings)
Doubleday and Co. (but no statement on later printings)
Duell, Sloan (used "1" on copyright page)
E.P. Dutton
Editions Poetry
Eyre & Spottiswoode (since late 1940s)
Faber & Faber
Fantasy Press
Farrar, Rinehart (FR logo on copyright page but no statement on later printings)
Farrar, Straus (FS initials on copyright page but no statement on later printings)
Farrar, Straus & Cudahy
Farrar, Straus & Giroux
Fawcett
Funk & Wagnalls (used "1")
Gambit
Bernard Geis

Gnome Press

Grove Press

Robert Hale

Hamish Hamilton

Harcourt, Brace (& World) (since 1930 but no indication on later printings. More recently used "First Edition/BCDE." and in the last few years "First Edition/ABCDE.")

Harper & Bros. (Harper & Row) (since 1922, except for a period in the late 1960s and early 1970s when they put the series of numbers on the last blank leaf of the book on the first printing and failed to remove "First edition" from the copyright page on later printings but did adjust the numbers on the last blank leaf)

Rupert Hart-Davis

Hart-Davis MacGibbon

Heinemann (since the 1920s)

Henry Holt (since 1945)

Houghton, Mifflin (did not state "First Printing" until recently but always put date on title page and deleted the date in all later printings, but did not include a statement on later printings)

Michael Joseph (since mid 1930s)

John Lane (since 1925)

Little, Brown (since 1940)

Longmans

McBride

A.C. McClurg ("Published in [year]")

McGraw-Hill (since 1956)

Macmillan

Methuen & Co.

William Morrow (since 1973)

New English Library

Norton

Pantheon (since 1964)

Random House (until changing to "First Edition/23456789." On the second printing the "First Edition" was deleted. The only publisher that does not use a "1" on its first editions.)

Rinehart & Co. ("R" in a circle on copyright page, but no indication on later printings)

Scribners (since 1930 have put an "A" on copyright page on first
   printings, but no indication on later printings)
Secker & Warburg
Simon & Schuster (since 1952)
Viking Press ("First Published by Viking in [year]" or "Published
   by Viking in [year]")
Walker ("First Published By Walker in [year]")
Weidenfeld & Nicolson
Wesleyan University
John C. Winston

In the last few decades the following publishers may have used a series
of numbers including a "1" on their first editions, but prior to this did
not include any indication of the printings on the copyright page of the
first edition/first printing. Most university presses follow this method.
Normally later printings were indicated on the copyright page, although very occasionally they did put "First . . ." on the copyright
page—and these would be first editions.

Appleton-Century (used a numerical identification: (1)=first
   printing, (2)=second printing, etc., at the foot of the last page
   of the book)
Arkham House (very rarely reprinted titles. There is a colophon
   at the back of each book)
Avalon Books
Robert A. Ballou
A.S. Barnes
Ernest Benn
William Blackwood
Bobbs-Merrill (until 1920)
A. & C. Boni
Boni & Liveright
Brentano's (until 1928)
Calder & Boyars
Jonathan Cape & Harrison Smith
Cassell & Windus
Caxton Printers
Chapman & Hall

Chatto & Windus (sometimes "Published by . . ." but did not
    include date)

Clarke, Irwin

Collier

Contact Editions

Covici-Friede

Covici McGee

Pascal Covici

Coward-McCann

Creative Age

Crime Club (U.K.)

Crowell

John Day (established 1928 and stated "First" the first few years)

Devin-Adair

Dial Press

Dillingham

Dodd Mead

Doubleday, Page

Egoist Press

Eyre & Spottiswoode (until late 1940s)

Four Seas

Lee Furman

Gollancz

Harcourt, Brace (until 1930)

Harper & Brothers (until 1922)

Harvard University Press

William Heinemann (until the 1920s)

Hogarth Press

Henry Holt (prior to 1945)

B.W. Huebsch

Hutchinson & Co.

J.B. Lippincott

Little, Brown (prior to 1940 either did not state or showed month
    and year of publication on copyright page. Later printings were
    normally indicated)

Liveright

John Long

John Lovell

Lovell, Crowell
Macaulay
McClure, Phillips
McDowell, Obolensky
McGraw-Hill (until 1956)
Metropolitan Books
William Morrow (until 1973)
Museum of Modern Art
George Newnes
Oxford University Press
Peter Owen
Pantheon (until 1964)
Payson & Clarke
G.P. Putnam's Sons
Rapp & Whiting
Reynal & Hitchcock
Grant Richards
Scribners (until 1930)
Simon & Schuster (until 1952)
Small, Maynard
Harrison Smith & Robert Haas
Smith, Elder
Stokes
Alan Swallow
Trident Press
United Book
T. Fisher Unwin
Vanguard
Ward, Lock (normally dropped date from title page on later print-
ings but did not indicate later printings in any other way)

Condition

1970 to 1990: These are really "modern" first editions. Ninety-nine
percent of these books are fiction or poetry. Because they have been
published so recently, the prices listed herein would be for very fine
copies in DUSTWRAPPERS (unless in wraps or a limited edition

in slipcase) with *NO DEFECTS* (including such minor things as price-clipped dustwrappers, former owners' names written in, bookplates, remainder marks on bottom page edges, or closed tears (no tape repairs) in the dustwrappers—even though there may be no actual loss of paper on the dustwrappers).

1945 to 1969: These books are a little older, but still copies must be in ORIGINAL DUSTWRAPPERS (unless in wraps or a limited edition in slipcase) with no major defects. These books do not have to look as new as the foregoing (1970–90). Also, the price-clipped dustwrapper and closed tears would be more acceptable, but the book has to be fine with the dustwrapper showing only minor wear, fading, or soiling. The absence of the dustwrapper decreases the estimated price of fiction or poetry titles by about 75 percent of the value shown. For nonfiction titles, the absence of the dustwrapper probably decreases the estimated price shown by 20 percent.

1920 to 1944: The book must be very good to fine with only minimal (if any) soiling, IN A DUSTWRAPPER (unless in wraps or a limited edition in slipcase) that is clean with only minimal soiling or fading and only a few small chips (⅛ inch or less) and closed tears. Again, as in the above grouping, the absence of a dustwrapper on fiction or poetry titles would greatly reduce the value of the first edition (75 percent on fiction and 20 percent on nonfiction).

1880 to 1919: The book must be clean and bright with no loss or tears on the edges. The estimated prices are for copies without dustwrappers. It should be noted that books published in multiple volumes, (usually three volumes, but also two- and four-volume editions) are rare and prices here are for very good copies in matching condition. Fine to very fine copies would probably bring much more.

1840 to 1879: The book is good to very good with minor edge wear or loss but still tight and clean. If the title is nonfiction, particularly with maps or plates, the condition of the maps or plates is more important than the condition of the binding. The comment above on multiple-volume editions also applies here.

1839 and prior: The book would be rebound (probably sometime late in the nineteenth century) unless otherwise stated, in a clean binding. If the book in question is fiction, poetry, or an extremely important nonfiction work, the original binding would greatly increase the value above the estimated prices shown herein. However, if the title is a nonfiction work, especially with maps and plates, the original or contemporary binding increases the value—but only by a small percentage, perhaps 10 to 20 percent. It is the condition and color (if applicable) of the plates and maps that would determine the value.

COLLECTED BOOKS
AND THEIR VALUES

ALL books listed herein are
FIRST EDITIONS/FIRST PRINTINGS
OF THE INDIVIDUAL TITLES
unless otherwise stated

---

*Retail price estimates are considered to be accurate within
plus or minus 20 percent. A range such as the ones
shown below might be appropriate:*

Estimated price	*Normal Range for very good to fine copies*
$ 100	$ 75 to $ 125
$ 300	$250 to $ 350
$ 500	$400 to $ 600
$ 750	$600 to $ 900
$1,000	$800 to $1,200

A

A. Strayed Reveller (The), and Other Poems. London, 1849. By A. (Matthew Arnold.) Dark green cloth. 500 copies, most withdrawn soon after publication. $500.

A., T. B. *The Bells: A Collection of Chimes.* By T.B.A. New York, 1855. By Thomas Bailey Aldrich, his first book. $200.

ABBEY, Edward. *Appalachian Wilderness.* New York, 1970. With photographs by Eliot Porter. $150.

ABBEY, Edward. *The Brave Cowboy.* New York (1956). $500.

ABBEY, Edward. *Desert Images.* New York, 1979. With photographs by David Muench. In slipcase. $175.

ABBEY, Edward. *Fire on the Mountain.* New York, 1962. $200.

ABBEY, Edward. *Jonathan Troy.* New York, 1954. Author's first book. $400.

ABBEY, Edward. *Slickrock.* San Francisco (1971). With photographs by Philip Hyde. Cloth. $150. Wraps. $40.

ABBEY, James. *California. A Trip Across the Plains in the Spring of 1850.* New Albany, Ind., 1850. 64 pp., printed wraps. $5,000.

ABBEY, J.R. *Scenery of Great Britain and Ireland in Aquatint and Lithography, 1770–1860...* London, 1952–53, 56–57. 4 vols. Limited to 400 or 500. In dustwrapper. $2,500.

ABBOT, Anthony. *About the Murder of Geraldine Foster.* New York, 1930. By Charles Fulton Oursler, his first book. $125.

ABBOTSFORD, and Newstead Abbey. London, 1835. By the Author of "The Sketch-Book" (Washington Irving). In original boards. $600. Philadelphia, 1835. In original blue or green cloth, paper labels. With copyright notices on both pages (2) and (4). $500.

ABBOTT, Berenice. *The World of Atget.* New York, 1964. $200.

ABBOTT, Charles D. *Howard Pyle, A Chronicle.* New York, 1925. $75.

ABBOTT, E. C. (Teddy Blue), and SMITH, Helena Huntington. *We Pointed Them North.* New York (1939). $150.

A'BECKETT, Gilbert Abbott. *The Comic History of England.* London, 1846–48. Illustrated in color by John Leech. 20 parts in 19, blue wraps. $750. London, 1847–48. 2 vols. First edition in book form. $350.

ABRAHAMS, Peter. *A Blackman Speaks of Freedom.* Durban, 1938. Author's first book. $150.

ABRAHAMS, Peter. *Dark Testament.* London, 1942. $125.

AB-SA-RA-KA, Home of the Crows. Philadelphia, 1868. (By Mrs. Henry B. Carrington.) Folding map. Cloth. $250.

ABSE, Dannie. *After Every Green Thing.* London, 1949. Author's first book. $100.

ABSTRACT of Land Claims Compiled from the Records of the General Land Office of the State of Texas . . . Galveston, 1852. By John Burlage and J.P. Hollingsworth. Third edition. The first, 1838, is virtually unobtainable, while the second, 1841, is only slightly less rare. $1,750.

ABSTRACT or The Leavves Of Nevvy England, As They Are Novv Established. London, 1641. This is the first Anglo-American law code. $8,500.

ACELDAMA, a Place to Bury Strangers In. London, 1898. By a Gentleman of the University of Cambridge. (Aleister Crowley.) Author's first book. Wraps. $750.

ACHEBE, Chinua. *Things Fall Apart.* London, 1958. Author's first book. $100. New York, 1958. $40.

ACKERLEY, J. R. *My Dog Tulip.* London, 1956. $75.

ACKERLEY, J. R. *Poems By Four Authors.* London, 1923. Author's first book. $150.

ACKERLEY, J. R. *The Prisoners of War.* London, 1925. Wraps. $125.

ACKERMANN, Rudolph (publisher). *A History of the University of Cambridge.* London, 1815. Illustrated with color plates. 2 vols. $6,000.

ACKERMANN, Rudolph (publisher). *A History of the University of Oxford.* London, 1814. Illustrated with colored plates. $4,000.

ACKERMANN, Rudolph. *The Microcosm of London.* London (1808–10). 104 colored aquatint plates by Pugin and Rowlandson. 3 vols. $10,000. London, 1904. 3 vols., parchment and boards. $250.

ACKLEY, Mary E. *Crossing the Plains and Early Days in California.* San Francisco, 1928. Illustrated. Boards, printed label on spine. $350.

ACKROYD, Peter. *London Lickpenny.* London, 1973. Wraps, 500 copies. $150.

ACKROYD, Peter. *Ouch.* London, 1971. (About 200 copies.) Entire issue of *The Curiously Strong,* vol IV, no. 2, 10/31/71. Author's first book. Wraps. $300.

ACTON, Harold. *Aquarium.* London, 1923. Author's first book. Plain dustwrapper. $400.

ACTON, Harold. *The Last of the Medici.* Florence, Italy, 1930. Introduction by Norman Douglas. Portrait. Boards. One of 365 signed. $175.

ACTS, Resolutions and Memorials, Adopted by the Second Legislative Assembly of the Territory of Arizona. Prescott, Ariz., 1866. $500. Prescott, 1867. *Acts,* etc., for 3d Assembly. $350.

ADAIR, James. *The History of the American Indians; Particularly Those Nations Adjoining to the Mississippi, East and West Florida, Georgia, South and North Carolina, and Virginia . . . Also an Appendix Containing a Description of the Floridas, and the Mississippi Lands . . .* London, 1775. Folding map. $2,500.

ADAM, G. M. (editor). *Sandow's System of Physical Training.* New York, 1894. 8½ by 10 inches. $125.

ADAMS, Alice. *Careless Love.* New York, 1966. Author's first book. $250.

ADAMS, Andy. *The Log of a Cowboy.* Boston, 1903. Map, 6 plates. Brown pictorial cloth. First issue, with map at page 28 not in list of illustrations. Author's first book. $150. With dustwrapper $600.

ADAMS, Andy. *Texas Matchmaker.* Boston, 1904. $75. With dustwrapper $300.

ADAMS, Ansel. See Mary Austin.

ADAMS, Ansel (photographer). *Images: 1923–1974.* New York, 1974. $200. One of 1,000, with original signed print. $2,000.

ADAMS, Ansel (photographer). *Making a Photograph.* London (1939). $300. London (1948). $200.

ADAMS, Ansel (photographer). *My Camera in Yosemite Valley.* Yosemite and Boston, 1949. Wraps. $600.

ADAMS, Ansel (photographer). *Sierra Nevada . . .* Berkeley, 1938. One of 500 signed. Issued without dustwrapper. $1,750.

ADAMS, Charles F., Jr., and ADAMS, Henry. *Chapters of Erie, and Other Essays.* Boston, 1871. $200.

ADAMS, Henry. See Adams, Charles F., Jr. See also *Democracy; Mont Saint Michel and Chartres.*

ADAMS, Henry. *Civil Service Reform.* Boston, 1869. Author's first book. Wraps. $2,000.

ADAMS, Henry. *The Education of Henry Adams.* Washington, 1907. Blue cloth, leather spine label. One of 100. $6,000. Boston, 1918. Revised and edited by Henry Cabot Lodge. First trade edition. In dustwrapper. $500. Without. $100. Limited Editions Club. New York, 1942. Etchings by Samuel Chamberlain. In slipcase. $75.

ADAMS, Henry. *A Letter to American Teachers of History.* Washington, 1910. $200.

ADAMS, J. C. *Life of J.C Adams.* (Cover title.) (New York, 1860.) 29 pp., printed wraps. $2,000. Lacking covers, and with caption title only: *The Hair-Breadth Escapes and Adventures of "Grizzly Adams."* $1,500.

ADAMS, James Truslow. *Memorials of Bridgehampton.* 1916. Author's first book. $100.

ADAMS, John Quincy. *Oration on the Life and Character of Gilbert Motier de Lafayette.* Washington, 1835. Original wraps, bound in. $150. One of a few on thick paper, specially bound in morocco. $600.

ADAMS, Leonie. *High Falcon and Other Poems.* New York (1929). $200.

ADAMS, Leonie. *Those Not Elect.* New York, 1925. Author's first book. $350.

ADAMS, Ramon F., and BRITZMAN, Homer E. *Charles M. Russell, The Cowboy Artist. A Biography* with *Charles M. Russell, The Cowboy Artist. A Bibliography.* By

Karl Yost with a note by Homer E. Britzman and Frederic G. Renner. Pasadena (1948). 2 vols. Slipcase. $200.

ADAMS, Ramon F. *Cowboy Lingo.* Boston, 1936. Author's first book. $200.

ADAMS, Ramon. *The Rampaging Herd.* Norman, Okla., 1959. $175.

ADAMS, Richard. *Watership Down.* London, 1972. Author's first book. $600. New York, 1974. $60.

ADAMS, Thomas. *Typographia: Or The Printer's Instructor . . .* Philadelphia, 1853. Fourth edition with numerous emendations and additions (first was issued in 1837). $200.

ADAMS, Will. *Errata: or, The Works of Will Adams.* New York, 1823. (By John Neal.) 2 vols. $175.

ADAMS, William Taylor. See Ashton, Warren T.; Optic, Oliver.

ADDAMS, Charles. *Drawn and Quartered.* New York, 1942. Author's first book. $125.

ADE, George. *Artie.* Chicago, 1896. Cloth. Author's first regularly published book. $75.

ADE, George. *Circus Day.* Chicago, 1896. Author's first book. (5 previous anonymous offprints from Chicago quarterly.) $400.

ADE, George. *One Afternoon with Mark Twain.* (Chicago) 1939. Stiff wraps. One of 350. $100.

ADE, George. *Revived Remarks on Mark Twain.* Chicago, 1936. 36 pp., wraps. One of 500 signed. $150. Also, 500 copies unsigned. $75.

ADELER, Max. *Out of the Hurly-Burly.* Illustrated by A.B. Frost and others. Decorated cloth. Philadelphia, 1874. (By Charles Heber Clark.) Author's first book and first book illustrated by Frost. $75.

ADVENTURES of a Brownie (The), as Told to My Child. London, 1872. By the Author of *John Halifax, Gentleman* (Dinah M. Craik). $250.

ADVENTURES of Harry Franco (The). New York, 1839. 2 vols. (By Charles Frederick Briggs.) Author's first book. $200.

ADVENTURES of a Post Captain . . . (The). London (1817). By a Naval Officer (Alfred Thornton). 25 colored plates. $500.

ADVENTURES of Robin Day (The). Philadelphia, 1839 (By Robert Montgomery Bird.) 2 vols., in original purple cloth, paper label on spine. $300.

ADVENTURES of Timothy Peacock, Esquire (The). Middlebury, Vt., 1835. By a Member of the Vermont Bar. (Daniel Pierce Thompson, his first novel.) $400.

ADVENTURES of Ulysses (The). London, 1808. Frontispiece, engraved title page. (By Charles Lamb.) $250.

ADVENTURES of a Younger Son (The). London, 1831. 3 vols., in original boards. (By Edward John Trelawny.) Author's first book. $350.

AESCHYLUS. *Agamemnon: A Tragedy.* (London, 1865.) Translated by Edward Fitz-Gerald. Wraps. $200. London, 1876. Half leather. One of 250. $150.

AESOP. *Fables.* London, 1936. Sir Roger L'Estrange translation. Illustrated by Stephen Gooden. Vellum. One of 500 signed by Gooden. In slipcase. $1,000. Limited Editions Club. New York, 1933. Samuel Croxall translation. Illustrated by Bruce Rogers. Boards and vellum. In slipcase. $175.

AGASSIZ, Louis. *Lake Superior.* Boston, 1850. 16 plates. $300.

AGATE, James. *Ego: The Autobiography of James Agate.* London (1935). $60.

AGATE, James. *L. of C. (Lines of Communication).* London, 1917. Author's first book. $100.

AGATE, James. *A Shorter Ego: The Autobiography of James Agate.* London (1945). 2 vols., half morocco. One of 100 signed. $150.

AGE of Bronze (The). London, 1823. (By George Gordon Noel, Lord Byron.) $400.

AGEE, G. W. *Rube Burrows, King of Outlaws.* (Cincinnati, 1890.) 194 pp., wraps. $200.

AGEE, James. *A Death in the Family.* New York (1957). Blue cloth. First issue, with title page printed in blue, "walking" for "waking" on page 80. $125. Second issue, "waking." $60.

AGEE, James. *Four Early Stories.* West Branch, Iowa, 1964. 285 numbered copies. In handmade paper dustwrapper. $300.

AGEE, James. *Let Us Now Praise Famous Men.* Boston, 1941. Walker Evans photographs. Black cloth. $450. Boston (1960). $75. London, 1965. $75.

AGEE, James. *The Morning Watch.* Rome, 1950. Wraps. (Offprint from Botteghe Oscure.) $200. Boston, 1951. $200. London, 1952. $125.

AGEE, James. *Permit Me Voyage.* New Haven, 1934. Author's first book. $600.

AGNER, Dwight. *The Books of WAD, A Bibliography of the Books Designed by W.A. Dwiggins.* Baton Rouge, 1974. Limited to 206 numbered copies. 190 in cloth and boards. $150. 16 copies on large paper in half morocco. $350.

AGRICOLA, Georgius. See Hoover, Herbert C. and Henry, Lou.

AIKEN, Conrad. *Blue Voyage.* New York, 1927. $150. One of 125 signed. $300.

AIKEN, Conrad. *Bring! Bring!* New York, 1925. $150.

AIKEN, Conrad. *The Coming Forth by Day of Osiris Jones.* New York, 1931. Bluish green cloth. With Scribner "A" on copyright page and "The Music" in capital letters on page 37. $125.

AIKEN, Conrad. *Costumes by Eros.* New York, 1928. $150.

AIKEN, Conrad. *Earth Triumphant and Other Tales in Verse.* New York, 1914. Author's first book. $250.

AIKEN, Conrad. *Great Circle.* New York, 1933. $150.

AIKEN, Conrad. *A Heart for the Gods.* London, 1939. $500.

AIKEN, Conrad. *The Jig of Forslin: A Symphony.* Boston, 1916. $100.

AIKEN, Conrad. *King Coffin.* New York, 1935. Vivid greenish cloth, lettered in purple-blue. (Few copies.) $300. Grayish purple-blue, stamped in gold on spine. $150.

AIKEN, Conrad. *Preludes for Memnon.* New York, 1931. $150.

AIKEN, Conrad. *Punch: The Immortal Liar.* New York, 1921. In dustwrapper. $125.

AIKEN, Conrad. *Scepticisms.* New York, 1919. First binding. Green cloth, lettered in red. In dustwrapper. $125.

AIKEN, Conrad. *Turns and Movies and Other Tales in Verse.* Boston, 1916. Printed wraps over boards. $150.

AINSWORTH, William Harrison. See *Sir John Chiverton.*

AINSWORTH, William Harrison. *Cardinal Pole.* London, 1863. 3 vols., $400.

AINSWORTH, W. Harrison. *Jack Sheppard.* London, 1839. Portrait and illustrations by George Cruikshank. 3 vols., in original green cloth. $500.

AINSWORTH, W. Harrison. *The Leaguer of Lathom.* London, 1876. 3 vols. $500.

AINSWORTH, W. Harrison. *Merry England or Nobles and Serfs.* London, 1874. 3 vols., green cloth with "Merrie" on spines. $500.

AINSWORTH, W. Harrison. *The Miser's Daughter.* London, 1842. Illustrated by George Cruikshank. 3 vols., black cloth. $500.

AINSWORTH, W. Harrison. *The Tower of London.* London, 1840. Illustrated by George Cruikshank. 13 parts in 12, wraps. $1,000. London, 1840. Purple cloth. First book edition. $750.

AKEN, David. *Pioneers of the Black Hills.* (Milwaukee, 1920.) Pictorial wraps. $100.

AKERLY, Lewis F. *The Geology of the Hudson River.* New York, 1820. Colored map. $200.

ALARIC at Rome: A Prize Poem. Recited in Rugby School. June XII, MDCCCXL. Rugby (England), 1840. (By Matthew Arnold.) 12 pp., pink pictorial and printed wraps. Author's first book. $7,500.

ALBEE, Edward. *The American Dream.* New York (1961). Cloth. $125. Wraps. $25. London (1962). Wraps. $40.

ALBEE, Edward. *Tiny Alice.* New York, 1965. First edition not stated. $60. London (1966). $50.

ALBEE, Edward. *Who's Afraid of Virginia Woolf?* New York, 1962. Cloth. $200. Wraps. $35. London (1964). $100. Charlestown, W.Va. (1980). 100 signed, numbered copies (broadside with drawing by e.e. cummings). $75.

ALBEE, Edward. *The Zoo Story and the Sandbox.* (New York, 1960.) Author's first book. Wraps. $150.

ALBEE, Edward. *The Zoo Story. The Death of Bessie Smith. The Sandbox: Three Plays.* New York (1960). $125. London (1962). $75.

ALBEE, Edward. *The Wounding: An Essay on Education.* Charleston, W.Va. (1981). 50 signed, numbered copies. Simulated leather, in dustwrapper. $125. 200 signed, numbered copies. Wraps. $50.

ALBERT, James. *A Narrative of the Most Remarkable Particulars in the Life of James Albert, Akawsaw, Cranwasa; as Dictated by Himself.* Catskill, 1810. Paper over birch boards. $900.

ALCOTT, Amos Bronson. *Observations on the Principles and Methods of Infant Instruction.* Boston, 1830. Author's first book. Wraps. $850.

ALCOTT, Amos Bronson. *Sonnets and Canzonets.* Boston, 1882. Illustrated with photographs. One of 50 signed. $500. Trade edition, lacking photographs. $75.

ALCOTT, Louisa May. *Flower Fables.* Boston, 1855. Frontispiece and 5 plates. Cloth. $1,750.

ALCOTT, Louisa May. *Hospital Sketches.* Boston, 1863. Ad on back announcing Wendell Phillips' *Speeches* at $2.50 (not $2.25 [VAB]). BAL—Boards with ad for "Speeches" on book cover, no price mentioned. Johnson had cloth first because ad for "Speeches" had "as ready for September," and stated boards had "reviews" of "Speeches" on back, whereas BAL stated cloth had advertisement for fourth edition of "Speeches." Assume BAL is correct. $150.

ALCOTT, Louisa May. *Little Men.* London, 1871. Frontispiece. Blue cloth. $250. Boston, 1871. Green cloth. First American edition, first issue, with ads at front listing *Pink and White Tyranny* as nearly ready. $150.

ALCOTT, Louisa May. *Little Women.* Boston, 1868–69. Frontispiece and 3 plates, 2 vols. First edition, without "Part One" on spine of vol. I and with vol. 2 having no notice of *Little Women, Part First,* on page iv. $4,000. London, 1869. Blue cloth. First English edition. $750. Limited Editions Club, New York, 1967. In slipcase. $75.

ALCOTT, Louisa May. *An Old-Fashioned Girl.* Boston, 1870. Double frontispiece and 2 plates. Cloth. First issue, no ads on copyright page. $150. Second printing, with ads on copyright page. $75.

ALCOTT, Louisa May. *The Rose Family.* Boston, 1864. 47 pp., printed wraps. $300. Johnson stated this was also published in cloth, but BAL disputes this.

ALCUIN: A Dialogue. (By Charles B. Brown.) New York, 1798. Author's first book. $500.

ALDINGTON, Richard. *A. E. Housman and W. B. Yeats, Two Lectures.* Peacocks Press. (Hurst, England), 1955. One of 350. In glassine dustwrapper. $125.

ALDINGTON, Richard. *All Men Are Enemies.* London, 1933. One of 110 signed. $175.

ALDINGTON, Richard. *The Colonel's Daughter: A Novel.* London, 1931. One of 210 signed. Issued without dustwrapper. $125. Trade edition in dustwrapper. $60.

ALDINGTON, Richard. *Death of a Hero.* London, 1929. $200. Paris, 1930. 2 vols., printed wraps. Unexpurgated text. One of 300. $450.

ALDINGTON, Richard. *Ezra Pound and T.S. Eliot: A Lecture.* London, 1954. Peacocks Press. One of 350. $125. Full morocco. One of 10 trial copies on Azure paper, signed. $300.

ALDINGTON, Richard. *Images (1910–1915).* (Cover title.) (London, 1915.) Pictorial wraps. Author's first book. $300. Boston, 1916. Wraps. $125.

ALDINGTON, Richard. *Images of War.* London, 1919. Illustrated. Boards and cloth. One of 120 on paper. $125. One of 50 with hand-colored illustrations. $300. One of 30 on vellum, signed. $750.

ALDINGTON, Richard. *Images—Old and New.* Boston, 1916. Stiff boards. $175.

ALDINGTON, Richard. *Last Straws.* Hours Press. Paris, 1930. Green suede. One of 200 signed. $200.

ALDINGTON, Richard. *Stepping Heavenward.* Florence, Italy, 1931. One of 808 signed. In dustwrapper and slipcase. $200. London, 1931. $100.

ALDISS, Brian W. *The Brightfount Diaries.* London (1955). Author's first book. $100.

ALDISS, Brian W. *Greybeard.* New York (1964). $125. London (1964). $75.

ALDISS, Brian W. *Non-Stop.* London (1958). Red boards (Second printing in brown cloth). $250.

ALDISS, Brian W. *Starship.* New York (1959). First U.S. of *Non-Stop* with textual changes. $100.

ALDISS, Brian W. *Uncommon Danger.* London, 1937. $1,250.

ALDRICH, Thomas Bailey. See A., T. B.

ALDRICH, Thomas Bailey. *The Ballad of Babie Bell and Other Poems.* New York, 1859. First issue, with Broadway address for publisher (Johnson). BAL doesn't show two issues. $150.

ALDRICH, Thomas Bailey. *The Story of a Bad Boy.* Boston, 1870. First issue, with line 20 on page 14 reading "scattered" and line 10 on page 197 reading "abroad." $200. Second state, "scatter and aboard." $125. Boston, 1895. Illustrated by A. B. Frost. Decorated cloth. $75.

ALDRIDGE, Reginald. *Life on a Ranch.* New York, 1884. Frontispiece and 3 plates. Stiff wraps. $600.

ALDRIDGE, Reginald. *Ranch Notes in Kansas . . .* London, 1884. 4 plates. Pictorial cloth. First English edition of *Life on a Ranch.* $450.

ALEXANDER, E. P. *Military Memoirs of a Confederate.* New York, 1907. Maps, 3 plates. Cloth. $175.

ALEXANDER, Hartley B. (editor). *Sioux Indian Painting.* Nice, France (1938). 50 color plates. 2 vols., large folio, loose in pictorial cloth portfolios, with ties. One of 400, but many destroyed during war. $3,500.

ALEXANDER, John H. *Mosby's Men.* New York, 1907. $150.

ALEXANDER, William. *The Costumes of China.* London, 1805. With 50 color plates. $1,750.

ALEXANDER, William. *Picturesque Representations of the Dress and Manners of the Russians.* London (about 1823). 64 color plates. $750.

ALEXANDRE, Arsene. *The Decorative Art of Leon Bakst.* London, 1913. Notes on the Ballets by Jean Cocteau. Translated by Harry Melvill. Portrait. 77 plates, 50 in color. Folio, half vellum. $1,250. One of 80 with an original watercolor. $2,000.

ALGER, Horatio, Jr. See Starr, Julian. See also *Timothy Crump's Ward.*

ALGER, Horatio, Jr. *Abraham Lincoln, The Backwoods Boy.* New York, 1883. Illustrated. Pictorial cloth. With ads listing this book as no. 2 in "Boyhood and Manhood" series. $200.

ALGER, Horatio, Jr. *Bertha's Christmas Vision: An Autumn Sheaf.* Boston, 1856. Author's first book. Blind-stamped cloth. $1,500.

ALGER, Horatio, Jr. *Dan, the Detective.* New York, 1884. $750.

ALGER, Horatio, Jr. *The Five Hundred Dollar Check.* United States Book Co. New York (1891). First book edition, first issue, with "Porter & Coates" on spine. $1,250. Later issue, with "Lovell" on spine. $300.

ALGER, Horatio, Jr. *Grand'ther Baldwin's Thanksgiving.* Loring Publisher. Boston (1875). $300.

ALGER, Horatio, Jr. *Ragged Dick; or Street Life in New York with the Boot-Blacks.* Loring Publisher. Boston (1868). With *Fame and Fortune* listed in ads for publication in December and Dick standing alone on pictorial title page. $2,000.

ALGER, Horatio, Jr. *Robert Coverdale's Struggle.* Street & Smith. New York (1910). Pictorial colored wraps with New Medal Library No. 555/15 cents on cover. $750.

ALGER, Horatio, Jr. *The Western Boy.* (New York, 1878.) With G.W. Carleton ad at front of book and American News Company in gold at bottom of spine. $850.

ALGREN, Nelson. *The Man with the Golden Arm.* Garden City, 1949. First edition stated. Signed on tipped-in sheet. $200. Trade. $125. London, 1959. $75.

ALGREN, Nelson. *The Neon Wilderness.* Green cloth. Garden City, 1947. Advertisements for other books on back of dustwrapper. $125. With reviews of this book on back of dustwrapper. $100. London (1965). $50.

ALGREN, Nelson. *Never Come Morning.* New York (1942). Introduction by Richard Wright. $200. London (1958). $75.

ALGREN, Nelson. *Somebody in Boots.* New York (1935). Author's first book. $1,000. London (1937). $750.

ALHAMBRA (The). See Crayon, Geoffrey.

ALKEN, Henry. *The National Sports of Great Britain.* London, 1820 (–21). 50 colored plates. Folio. First issue, with engraved 1820 title page and with watermarks dated 1816 and 1818. $15,000. London, 1821. Second issue, without 1820 title page. $12,500. London, 1823. $7,500. London, 1825. First octavo edition. $2,000.

ALKEN, Henry. *Scraps from the Sketch-Books of Henry Alken.* London, 1821. 42 colored plates. $2,500. London, 1822. $1,250.

ALLAHAKBARRIE Book of Broadway Cricket for 1899. (London, 1899.) Parchment wraps (VAB). On Japanese vellum wraps. (By Sir James M. Barrie.) 520 numbered copies. $750.

ALLAN, J. T. (compiler). *Central and Western Nebraska, and the Experiences of Its Stock Growers.* (Cover title.) Omaha, 1883. 16 pp., pictorial wraps. (Note: A Union Pacific Land Department pamphlet.) $300.

ALLAN, J. T. (compiler). *Western Nebraska and the Experiences of Its Actual Settlers.* Omaha, 1882. 16 pp., wraps. $300.

ALLBEURY, Ted. *A Choice of Enemies.* New York, 1972. $100. London (1973). $100.

ALLEN, Miss A. J. (compiler). *Ten Years in Oregon.* Ithaca, N.Y., 1848. Portrait. Calf. $200. Second issue, same date, portrait omitted, pages added. Sheep. $200. Ithaca, 1850. $50.

ALLEN, Hervey, *Anthony Adverse.* New York, 1933. With publisher's monogram on copyright page and with numerous typographical errors, among them "Xaxier" for "Xavier" in line 6 of page 352, "ship" for "shop" in line 18 of page 1086, and the word "found" repeated in line 22 of page 397. $75. Deluxe issue: 3 vols., suede boards. One of 105 signed. $250. Limited Editions Club, New York, 1937. 3 vols., orange cloth. Slipcase. $75.

ALLEN, (William) Hervey. *Ballads of the Border.* (El Paso), 1916. Printed wraps. Author's name misspelled "Hervy" on copyright page. Author's first book. $600.

ALLEN, Hervey. *Israfel: The Life and Times of Edgar Allan Poe.* New York, 1926. 2 vols. First state, with wineglass on table in Longfellow portrait facing page 529. $150. Deluxe issue: three-quarters leather. One of 250. $300.

ALLEN, Hervey. *Wampum and Old Gold.* New Haven, 1921. Stiff wraps. One of 500. $75.

ALLEN, Hervey, and MABBOTT, Thomas O. (editors). *Poe's Brother.* New York (1926). One of 1,000. Slipcase. $125.

ALLEN, Ira. *A Concise Summary of the Second Volume of the Olive Branch.* Philadelphia, 1807. 24 pages. $125.

ALLEN, J. A. *Notes on the Natural History of Portions of Montana and Dakota.* Boston, 1874. 61 pp., wraps. $175.

ALLEN, James Lane. *Flute and Violin.* Cloth. New York, 1891. Sheets bulk 1 1/16 inches. Author's first book. $75.

ALLEN, John Fisk. *Victoria Regia; or the Great Water Lily of America.* Boston, 1854. 6 chromolithographed plates by William Sharp. Elephant folio $30,000.

ALLEN, Lewis M. *Printing with the Handpress.* Kentfield, 1969. Limited to 140 copies. $2,250.

ALLEN, Samuel. See Vesey, Paul.

ALLEN, William A. *Adventures with Indians and Game.* Chicago, 1903. 25 plates. Cloth, or half leather. $250.

ALLEN, Woody. *Don't Drink the Water.* French. New York, 1967. Author's first book. Wraps. $75. Random House. New York (1967). $250.

ALLEN, Woody. *Play It Again, Sam.* New York (1969). $200.

ALLIBONE, S. Austin. *A Critical Dictionary of English Literature, and British and American Authors . . .* Philadelphia, 1899. 5 vols. (including 2-vol. supplement). $225.

ALLIES' Fairy Book (The). 12 colored plates, other illustrations by Arthur Rackham. Buckram. London (1916). One of 525 signed by the artist. $1,000. Trade in blue cloth. First issue, with pictorial end papers. $150.

ALLINGHAM, Margery. *Black'er Chief Dick.* London, 1923. Author's first book. $250. Garden City, 1923. $200.

ALLINGHAM, William. *Poems.* London, 1850. Author's first book. $250.

ALLINGHAM, William. *Sixteen Poems.* Dundrum, Ireland, 1905. Selected by William Butler Yeats. Boards and linen. Dun Emer Press. One of 200. $275.

ALLISON, William. *The British Thoroughbred Horse.* London, 1901. $250. London, 1907. Second edition. $175.

ALNWICK Castle, with Other Poems. New York, 1827. (By FitzGreene Halleck.) Printed tan wraps bound in. $250.

ALPHA AND OMEGA. *Blight, the Tragedy of Dublin.* Dublin, 1917. (By Oliver St. John Gogarty, his first book written with Joseph O'Connor.) $250.

ALTER, J. Cecil. *James Bridger: Trapper, Frontiersman, Scout, and Guide.* Salt Lake City (1925). 18 plates. One of 1,000 signed. $250.

ALTOWAN; or Incidents of Life and Adventure in the Rocky Mountains. New York, 1846. By an Amateur Traveller. Edited by J. Watson Webb. 2 vols., cloth. (By Sir William Drummond Stewart.) (However, Howes states that this was "probably actually written by Webb.") $850.

ALTSHELER, Joseph Alexander. *The Sun of Saratoga.* New York, 1897. Author's first book. $200.

ALVAREZ, A. *(Poems).* Oxford, 1952. Author's first book. Wraps. Fantasy Poets no. 15. $100.

AMBLER, Eric. *Background to Danger.* New York, 1937. (First American edition of *Epitaph for a Spy.*) $500.

AMBLER, Eric. *Cause for Alarm.* London, 1938. $1,750.

AMBLER, Eric. *A Coffin for Dimitrios.* New York, 1939. $250.

AMBLER, Eric. *The Dark Frontier.* London, 1936. Author's first book. $1,500.

AMBLER, Eric. *Epitaph for a Spy.* London, 1938. $1,000.

AMBLER, Eric. *The Mask of Dimitrios.* London, 1937. $1,500.

AMBLER, Eric. *Uncommon Danger.* London, 1937. $1,750.

AMERICAN Arguments for British Rights. London, 1806. (By William Loughton Smith.) $150.

AMERICAN Caravan (The). New York, 1927. $200.

AMERICAN Caravan (The Second). New York, 1928. $125.

AMERICAN Chap-Book, The. Jersey City, 1904–5. 12 vols., bound in one with all covers preserved (Will Bradley). $850.

AMERICAN Shooter's Manual (The). Philadelphia, 1827. By a Gentleman of Philadelphia County (Jesse Y. Kester). Frontispiece, 2 plates, errata. With "ribbon" misspelled on page 235. $3,000. Second printing. $1,500.

AMERICANA-Beginnings: A Selection from the Library of Thomas W. Streeter. Morristown, N.J., 1952, 97 pp., wraps. One of 325. $200.

AMES, Joseph. *Catalogue of English Heads; or an Account of About Two Thousand Prints, Describing What Is Peculiar to Each . . .* London, 1748. $175.

AMIS, Kingsley. *Bright November.* London (1947). 32 pp., leatherette. Author's first book. $500.

AMIS, Kingsley. *Lucky Jim.* London, 1953. $650. Garden City, 1954. $200.

AMIS, Martin. *The Rachel Papers.* London, 1973. Author's first book. $350. New York, 1974. $125.

AMMONS, A. R. *Ommateum: With Doxology.* Philadelphia (1955—actually 1954). The poet's first book. 300 copies, 200 reportedly destroyed. $800.

AMSDEN, Charles A. *Navaho Weaving.* Santa Ana, 1934. 122 plates, many in color. $400. Albuquerque, 1948 (actually 1949). $100. Chicago (1964). $50.

AMUNDSEN, Roald. *"The Northwest Passage."* London, 1908. Illustrated, 2 folding maps in pocket. 2 vols., cloth. First edition in English. $150.

ANALYSIS of the Hunting Field (The). London, 1846. (By Robert Smith Surtees.) 7 colored plates by Henry Alken, 43 woodcuts. First issue, green cloth (some copies with preface dated 1846, some dated 1847—VAB). $1,000. Second issue, red cloth. $750.

ANCIENT and Modern Michilimackinac . . . (Cover title.) (St. James, Mich.), MDCCCLIV (1854). 48 pages. Wraps. (By James Jesse Strang.) First issue. $4,500. Another, dated 1854, obviously on later paper. $200.

ANDERSEN, Hans Christian. New York, 1949. *The Complete Andersen.* Translated by Jean Hersholt. Hand-colored illustrations by Fritz Kredel. 6 vols., buckram and boards. Limited Editions Club. Slipcase. $200.

ANDERSEN, Hans Christian. *Fairy Tales.* London (1932). 12 colored plates and numerous black-and white illustrations by Arthur Rackham. Vellum. $250. One of 525 signed by the artist. $1,000. Another edition: London (1924). 12 color plates by Kay Nielsen. Full vellum or morocco. One of 500 signed by Nielsen. $2,500. Trade. $600.

ANDERSEN, Hans Christian. *Stories from Hans Andersen.* London (1911). 28 color plates by Edmund Dulac. Vellum, silk ties. One of 750 signed by Dulac. $750. Pigskin. One of 100 on Japan paper. $1,250.

ANDERSON, David. *The Enchanted Galleon.* (San Francisco, 1930.) Signed frontispiece photo by Ansel Adams. One of 60. Slipcase. $600.

ANDERSON, Forrest. *Sea Pieces . . .* New York, 1935 (155 copies). Author's first book. $125.

ANDERSON, Frederick Irving. *Adventures of the Infallible Godahl.* New York (1914). Author's first book. $250.

ANDERSON, Maxwell. *Key Largo.* Washington, 1939. First edition stated. $125.

ANDERSON, Maxwell. *You Who Have Dreams.* New York, 1925. Author's first book, preceded by 4 collaborations in 1924/25. One of 975 numbered copies. $75. One of 25 signed and numbered copies. $300.

ANDERSON, Patrick. *A Tent for April.* Montreal, 1945. First regularly published book, preceded by two published items in his teens. Stiff wraps and dustwrapper. $150.

ANDERSON, Poul. *The Fox, The Dog and the Griffin . . .* Garden City (1966). $250.

ANDERSON, Poul. *Vault of the Ages.* Philadelphia (1952). Author's first book. $75.

ANDERSON, Robert L. *Thwarted Ambitions.* Marion, Va. (1935). Introduction by Sherwood Anderson. Wraps. $150. Marion (1935). Second edition. $50.

ANDERSON, Sherwood. *Alice and the Lost Novel.* London, 1929. One of 530 signed. $200.

ANDERSON, Sherwood. *Beyond Desire.* New York (1932). One of 165 signed. In slipcase. $300. Trade. $100.

ANDERSON, Sherwood. *Dark Laughter.* New York, 1925. One of 350 signed. Slipcase. $300. (There were also 20 copies lettered and signed by the author.) Trade. $175.

ANDERSON, Sherwood. *Death in the Woods and Other Stories.* New York (1933). $175.

ANDERSON, Sherwood. *Horses and Men.* New York, 1923. First issue, with top edges stained orange. $200.

ANDERSON, Sherwood. *Marching Men.* New York, 1917. Crimson cloth. In dustwrapper. $500; without dustwrapper $100.

ANDERSON, Sherwood. *Mid-American Chants.* New York, 1918. Yellow cloth. In dustwrapper $350; without dustwrapper $75.

ANDERSON, Sherwood. *The Modern Writer.* San Francisco, 1925. One of 950. In slipcase. $200. One of 50 on vellum, signed. $400.

ANDERSON, Sherwood. *Nearer the Grass Roots.* San Francisco, 1929. Half cloth. Grabhorn printing. One of 500 signed. $300.

ANDERSON, Sherwood. *A New Testament.* New York, 1927. One of 265 large paper copies, signed. In slipcase. $350. Trade. $150.

ANDERSON, Sherwood. *Puzzled America.* New York, 1935. $150.

ANDERSON, Sherwood. *Poor White.* New York, 1920. First issue with top edges stained blue (Johnson). Sheehy and Lohf don't consider this an issue point. $200. London (1921). $150.

ANDERSON, Sherwood. *Tar: A Midwest Childhood.* New York, 1926. $125. Another printing: New York (1926). Boards. One of 350 signed in glassine dustwrapper and slipcase. $300.

ANDERSON, Sherwood. *The Triumph of the Egg.* New York, 1921. First issue, with top edges stained yellow, in dustwrapper. $100.

ANDERSON, Sherwood. *Windy McPherson's Son.* New York, 1916. Author's first book. $300.

ANDERSON, Sherwood. *Winesburg, Ohio.* New York, 1919. Yellow cloth, paper label on spine. First issue, with top stained yellow, end paper map at front, line 5 of page 86 reading "lay," and with broken type in the word "the" in line 3 of page 251. In dustwrapper, $7,000 at auction in 1988; without dustwrapper $350. Second issue, top unstained. In dustwrapper $3,500; without dustwrapper $100. Limited Editions Club, New York, 1978. In slipcase. $100.

ANDRE, John. *Major Andre's Journal.* Boston, 1903. Edited by Henry Cabot Lodge. Facsimile maps, plans, and other illustrations. 2 vols., full vellum. One of 467. In slipcase. $650. One of 10 on Japan vellum. $1,000.

ANDREAS, A. T. *Atlas Map of Peoria County, Illinois.* Chicago, 1873. 25 maps in color. $350.

ANDREAS, A. T. *History of Chicago.* Chicago, 1884–86. Illustrated. 3 vols., morocco and cloth. $300. Full morocco. $450.

ANDREAS, A. T. *History of the State of Kansas.* Chicago, 1883. Morocco or pictorial boards. Folding map. $450.

ANDREAS, A. T. *Illustrated Historical Atlas of the State of Iowa.* Chicago, 1875. Colored maps and views. Three-quarters morocco. $750.

ANDREWS, Eliza Frances. *The War-Time Journal of a Georgia Girl, 1864–65.* New York, 1908. 16 plates. $125.

ANDREWS, Jane. *The Seven Little Sisters...* Boston, 1861. Author's first book. $125.

ANDREWS, Jane. *Ten Boys Who Lived on the Road from Long Ago to Now.* Boston, 1886. Illustrated by Charles Copeland. Pictorial cloth. $100.

ANDREWS, John. *History of the War with America, France, Spain, and Holland; Commencing in 1775 and Ending in 1783.* London, 1785–86. 4 vols. 24 plates, 6 folding maps and 1 single-page map (maps partially hand colored). $1,250.

ANDREWS, William Loring. *Among My Books.* New York, 1894. Limited to 50 numbered copies. 14 engravings and 13 other illustrations. $350.

ANDREWS, William Loring. *Bibliopegy in the United States and Kindred Subjects.* New York, 1902. Limited to 177 copies. $450.

ANDREWS, William Loring. *A Choice Collection of Books from the Aldine Presses.* New York, 1885. One of 50. Author's first book. Wraps. $500.

ANDREWS, William Loring. *An English XIX Century Sportsman, Bibliopole and Binder of Angling Books.* New York, 1906. Limited to 157 copies. $325.

ANDREWS, William Loring. *Gossip About Book Collecting.* New York, 1900. 2 vols. Limited to 157 copies for subscribers. 5 plates in first volume, 7 plates in second volume. $325.

ANDREWS, William Loring. *Jean Grolier, De Servier Viscount d'Aguisy . . .* New York, 1892. Limited to 140 copies on handmade paper and 10 on Japan. 14 colored plates. $350.

ANDREWS, William Loring. *The Old Booksellers of New York and Other Papers.* New York, 1895. 84 pages and 4 plates. Limited to 142 copies. $200.

ANDREWS, William Loring. *Sextodecimos Et Infra.* New York, 1899. Limited to 152 copies. Stiff wraps, dustwrapper and slipcase. $375.

ANDREWS, William Loring. *The Treatyse Of Fysshnyge Wyth An Angel . . .* (New York), 1903. Limited to 150 copies. $325.

ANGEL in the House (The). London, 1854. (By Coventry Patmore.) Cloth, paper label. $300. London, 1863. 2 vols. $200.

ANNEBERG, Maurice. *Type Foundries of America and Their Catalogs.* Baltimore, 1975. Limited to 500 copies. $325.

ANNUAL Review: History of St. Louis . . . St. Louis, 1854. Folding map. 47 pp., wraps. $350.

ANONYMOUS. (By Michael Fraenkel.) Paris (1930). Author's first book. Wraps. (First Carrefour Editions book, with Walter Lowenfels.) $200.

ANSTEY, Christopher. See *The New Bath Guide . . .*

ANTHOLOGY of Younger Poets (An). Philadelphia, 1932. Edited by Oliver Wells. Boards. One of 500. In dustwrapper. $175. (Contains 5 poems by William Faulkner.)

ANTHONY, Peter. *The Women in the Wardrobe.* London, 1951. (By Peter and Anthony Shaffer.) Author's first book. $125.

ANTIN, Mary. *From Plotzk to Boston.* Boston, 1899. Author's first book. Cloth. $250. Wraps. $150.

ANTIN, Mary. *The Promised Land.* Boston, 1912. "Published April 1912" on copyright page. $200. London, 1912. $150.

ANTI-TEXASS Legion (The): Protest of Some Free Men, States, and Presses Against the Texass Rebellion. New York, 1844. 72 pp., wraps. $500.

ANTONINUS, Brother. See Everson, William.

ANTONINUS, Brother. *A Canticle to the Waterbirds.* Berkeley, 1968. (By William Everson.) One of 200 signed. (Issued without dustwrapper.) $150. Trade in wraps (2,000 copies). $35.

ANTONINUS, Brother. *The Poet Is Dead: A Memorial for Robinson Jeffers.* San Francisco, 1964. Auerhahn Press. Boards and leather. (By William Everson.) One of 205 signed. In plain white dustwrapper. $150.

ANTONINUS, Brother. *Who Is She That Looketh Forth as the Morning.* Santa Barbara, 1972. (By William Everson.) One of 250 signed. In acetate dustwrapper. $175.

ANTRIM, Benajah J. *Pantography, Or Universal Drawings, In The Comparison Of Their Natural And Arbitrary Laws . . .* Philadelphia, 1843. $125.

APOCRYPHA (The). Cresset Press. London, 1929. Authorized version. Full-page woodcuts by Stephen Gooden, Eric Jones et al. Folio, black vellum. One of 30 on handmade paper with an extra set of illustrations signed by the artists. Slipcase. $1,000. Boards. One of 450. Slipcase. $350.

APOLLINAIRE, Guillaume. *The Poet Assassinated.* New York, 1923. Translated by Matthew Josephson. First American edition. $125.

APPEAL (An) to the Clergy of the Church of Scotland. Edinburgh, 1875. (By Robert Louis Stevenson.) 12 pp., stitched, without wraps. $6,000.

APPEL, Benjamin. *Brain Guy.* New York, 1934. Author's first book. $200.

APPERLEY, C. J. See Nimrod. See also *Memoirs of the Life of the Late John Mytton, Esq.*

APPLEGATE, Jesse. *A Day with the Cow Column in 1843.* Chicago, 1934. Caxton Club. Pictorial cloth. One of 300. $250. Another edition: (Portland), 1952. One of 225. $100.

APPLEGATE, Jesse. *Recollections of My Boyhood.* Roseburg, Ore., 1914. 99 pp., pictorial wraps. $500.

APPLEGATE, Rex. *Kill—Or Get Killed.* Harrisburg, Pa., 1932. First edition stated. $35.

ARAGON, Louis. *The Red Front.* Chapel Hill (1933). Translated by e. e. cummings. Stapled red wraps. First American edition. $300.

ARBER, Edward (editor). *A Transcript of the Registers of the Company of Stationers of London; 1554–1640 A.D.* (Gloucester, Mass. 1967), 5 vols., *1640–1708* (Gloucester, Mass., 1950), 3 vols. $275.

ARCHBOLD, Ann. *A Book for the Married and Single, the Grave and the Gay; and Especially Designed for Steamboat Passengers.* East Plainfield, Ohio, 1850. $750.

ARCHITEC-TONICS . . . New York, 1914. (First book illustrated by Rockwell Kent.) $100.

ARDIZZONE, Edward. *In a Glass Darkly.* London, 1929. (By J. Sheridan Le Fanu.) (First book illustrated by Ardizzone.) $150.

ARDY, Catherine. *The Color of Rain.* London, 1964. (By Emma Tennant, her first book.) $250.

ARISTOPHANES. *Lysistrata.* London, 1896. 8 plates by Aubrey Beardsley. Boards. One of 100. $1,250. London (1926). Translated by Jack Lindsay. Illustrated by Norman Lindsay. Half morocco. One of 725 signed by the artist. $750. Limited Editions Club, New York, 1934. Translated by Gilbert Seldes. Illustrated by Pablo Picasso. Boards. Slipcase. $3,000. (There also were 150 sets of 6 proofs, each signed by Picasso, issued in cloth portfolio and sold separately. $7,500.)

ARISTOTLE. *Politics and Poetics.* Limited Editions Club (New York), 1964. Illustrated by Leonard Baskin. Buckram. In slipcase. $200.

ARKWRIGHT, William. *The Pointer & His Predecessors.* London, 1906. Illustrated. Half or full morocco. Deluxe issue. One of 750. $500. Trade in cloth. $250.

ARLEN, Michael. *The Green Hat.* London (1924). $125. New York, 1925. (Acting version.) Boards. One of 175 signed. $150.

ARLEN, Michael. *The London Venture.* London, 1920. (Reportedly, the edition dated "1919" was actually printed later.) Author's first book. $150. New York (1920). $75.

ARLEN, Michael. *May Fair.* London (1925). $75.

ARMAGEDDON: A Fragment: Avalon. Charleston, S.C., 1923. Wraps. Contains poems by John Crowe Ransom and others. $250.

ARMES, George A. *Ups and Downs of an Army Officer.* Washington, 1900. Illustrated. Pictorial cloth. $250.

ARMITAGE, John. *The History of Brazil.* London, 1836. 2 portraits. 2 vols. London, 1836. $500.

ARMSMEAR: The Home, the Arm and the Armory of Col. Samuel Colt: A Memorial. New York, 1866. Plates. Cloth. Map inscribed by Mrs. Colt. $1,250. Full morocco. Presentation copy from Mrs. Colt. $1,750.

ARMSTRONG, A. N. *Oregon: A Brief History and Description of Oregon and Washington.* Chicago, 1857. $750.

ARMSTRONG, Elizabeth. *Robert Estienne, Royal Printer. An Historical Study of the Elder Stephanus.* Cambridge, 1954. $125.

ARMSTRONG, Moses K. *History and Resources of Dakota, Montana and Idaho.* Yankton, Dakota Territory, 1866. Map. Printed wraps. $3,500.

ARNETT, John Andrews. *Bibliopegia: Or, The Art of Bookbinding . . .* London, 1835. 9 plates. $500.

ARNETT, John. *An Inquiry into the Nature and Form of the Books of the Ancients . . .* London, 1837. 14 plates. $450.

ARNO, Peter. *Whoops, Dearie!* (New York, 1927.) Author's first book. $100.

ARNOLD, Elliot. *Blood Brother.* New York, 1936. $100.

ARNOLD, Henry V. *The Early History of the Devil's Lake Country,* Larimore, N. D., 1920. 105 pp., printed wraps. $125.

ARNOLD, Henry V. *The History of Old Pembina, 1780–1872.* Larimore, N.D., 1917. Wraps. $125.

ARNOLD, Matthew. See A. (pseudonym—first entry in list). See also *Alaric at Rome.*

ARNOLD, Matthew. *Cromwell: A Prize Poem.* Oxford, 1843. Wraps. $1,750.

ARNOLD, Matthew. *Culture and Anarchy.* London, 1869. $150.

ARNOLD, Matthew. *Essays in Criticism.* London, 1865. $150.

ARNOLD, Matthew. *God and the Bible.* London, 1875. $100.

ARNOLD, Matthew. *Last Essays on Church and Religion.* London, 1877. $150.

ARNOLD, Matthew. *Merope: A Tragedy.* London, 1858. $200.

ARNOLD, Matthew. *New Poems.* London, 1867. $150.

ARNOLD, Matthew. *Poems.* London, 1853. $300. London, 1855. (Second series.) $200. Boston, 1856. $100. 3 vols., London, 1895. $500.

ARNOLD, William Harris. *First Report of a Book-Collector; Comprising a Brief Answer to the Frequent Question "Why First Editions?"* New York, 1898. Second edition. Limited to 220 copies (first was only 85 copies). $200.

ARNOW, Harriette. See Simpson, Harriette

ARNOW, Harriette. *The Dollmaker.* New York, 1954. $150.

ARNOW, Harriette. *Hunter's Horn.* New York, 1949. Second book, first under real name. (First edition stated.) $100.

ARP, Jean. *Dreams and Projects.* New York (1952). 15 pages of text and 28 folded sheets with woodcuts by Arp, laid-in wrapper and blue board folder. One of 320 signed copies. $1,000.

AROUND the Horn in '49. See *Journal of the Hartford Union Mining and Trading Company.*

ARRANGEMENT of Places. Will Each Gentleman Kindly Take in to Dinner the Lady Seated on His Right? (New York), 1905. 12 pp., wraps. (Program of seventieth birthday dinner for Mark Twain at Delmonico's.) $250.

ARRINGTON, Alfred W. See Summerfield, Charles.

ART of Book Design, Works of Leningrad Artists, 1917–1964. Leningrad, 1966. $125.

ARTHUR Mervyn; or Memoirs of the Year 1793. Philadelphia, 1799–1800. (By the Author of *Wieland* [Charles Brockden Brown]). 2 vols. (For first English edition, see author entry.) $750.

ARTHUR, T. S. See *Insubordination . . .*

ARTHUR, T. S. *Ten Nights in a Bar-Room, and What I Saw There.* Philadelphia, 1854. First issue, with both Lippincott and Bradley named in imprint and woodcut frontispiece by Van Ingen (VAB). $200.

ASHBEE, C. R. *The Private Press: A Study in Idealism. To Which Is Added a Bibliography of the Essex House.* (London, 1909.) Limited to 127 numbered copies. $250.

ASHBEE, Henry Spencer. *An Iconography of Don Quixote, 1605–1895.* London, 1895. Half cloth. $200.

ASHBERY, John. *The New Spirit.* New York (1970). Pictorial wraps. One of 65 signed. $250. Also, 100 unsigned. $40.

ASHBERY, John. *Some Trees.* Foreword by W. H. Auden. New Haven, 1956. $200.

ASHBERY, John. *Sunrise in Suburbia.* New York, 1968. Wraps. One of 100 signed. $150. Also, 26 lettered and signed copies. $300.

ASHBERY, John. *Turandot and Other Poems.* New York, 1953. Illustrated. Wraps. One of 300. Author's first book. $850.

ASHDOWN, Clifford. *The Adventures of Romney Pringle.* London, 1902. (By R. Austin Freeman and J. J. Pitcairn.) $1,000.

ASHE, Thomas. *Travels in America.* London, 1808. 3 vols. $850. New York, 1808. First American edition in one volume, abridged. $300.

ASHLEY, Clifford W. *The Yankee Whaler.* Boston, 1926. Plates, some in color. Half cloth and boards. One of 156 signed, with an original drawing. Slipcase. $750. Trade. $250.

ASHLEY, William H. *The West of William H. Ashley.* Denver, 1964. Edited by Dale L. Morgan. Illustrated. Pictorial buckram. One of 750. $150. Deluxe issue: half calf. One of 250 signed in slipcase. $400.

ASHTON, Warren T. *Hatchie, the Guardian Slave.* Boston, 1853. (By William Taylor Adams.) Black cloth. Author's first book. $350.

ASIMOV, Isaac. *The End of Eternity.* Garden City, 1955. $250.

ASIMOV, Isaac. *Foundation.* New York (1951). First binding, in cloth with sheets bulking 1.9 cm. $450. Second binding in boards with sheets bulking 1.4 cm. $300.

ASIMOV, Isaac. *Foundation and Empire.* New York (1952). First binding in red boards with spine imprint 2.2 cm. across (2.8 cm. in second binding). First issue dustwrapper with 26 titles on back. $300.

ASIMOV, Isaac. *I, Robot.* New York (1950). Cloth. $500. Wraps. $150.

ASIMOV, Isaac. *Pebble in the Sky.* Garden City, 1950. Author's first book. $200.

ASIMOV, Isaac. *Second Foundation.* (New York, 1953.) First binding, blue boards. $300.

"ASK Mamma"; or, The Richest Commoner in England. London (1857) and 1858. (By Robert Smith Surtees.) 13 full-page color plates and 6 woodcuts by John Leech. 13 parts, red wraps. $1,250. London, 1858. Pictorial cloth. First book edition. $850.

ASQUITH, Cynthia. *The Ghost Book* . . . London, 1926. Author's first book. $400.

ASTLE, Thomas Astle. *The Origin and Progress of Writing, as Well Hieroglyphic* . . . London, 1784. 31 plates. $450.

ASTON, James. *First Lesson.* London (1932). (By T. H. White.) $350.

ASTON, James. *They Winter Abroad.* London, 1932. (By T. H. White). $350. New York, 1932. $250.

ATALANTIS. New York, 1832. (By William Gilmore Simms.) In original wraps. $750.

ATHELING, William. *The Issue at Hand.* Chicago, 1964 (By James Blish.) First edition stated. $75.

ATHERTON, Gertrude. See Lin, Frank.

ATHERTON, Gertrude. *Black Oxen.* New York (1923). One of 250 signed. $125.

ATHERTON, Gertrude. *The Conqueror.* New York, 1902. First state, with page ·numerals on page 546 in upper left corner. $125.

ATHERTON, Gertrude. *Hermia Suydam.* New York, 1889. Second book, first under her own name. Wraps. $150.

ATHERTON, Gertrude. *What Dreams May Come.* London, 1889. First English edition (of author's first book, which was issued in America under the pseudonym Frank Lin). $150.

ATHERTON, William. *Narrative of the Suffering & Defeat of the North-Western Army, Under General Winchester.* Frankfort, Ky., 1842. Leather-backed boards, printed paper label. $400.

ATKINS, Wm. (editor). *The Art and Practice of Printing.* London, no-date (circa 1920s). 6 vols. $150.

ATKINSON, George H. *Address* . . . *Upon The Possession, Settlement, Climate and Resources of Oregon and the Northwest Coast Including Some Remarks Upon Alaska.* New York, 1868. 17 pp. $150.

ATLEE, Philip. *The Inheritors.* New York, 1940. Author's first book. $125.

ATTACHÉ (The); or, Sam Slick in England. (Second series.) London, 1844. (By Thomas Chandler Haliburton.) 2 vols., ribbed plum-colored cloth. With 48 pages of ads at end of vol. 2 (VAB). $500.

ATTAWAY, William. *Blood on the Forge.* Garden City, 1941. $200.

ATTAWAY, William. *Let Me Breathe Thunder.* New York, 1939. Author's first book. $200.

ATTERLEY, Joseph. *A Voyage to the Moon.* New York, 1827. (By George Tucker.) $600.

ATWATER, Caleb. *A History of the State of Ohio.* Cincinnati (1838). $200.

ATWATER, Caleb. *Mysteries of Washington City.* Washington, 1844. Boards and leather. $200.

ATWATER, Caleb. *Remarks Made on a Tour to Prairie du Chien; Thence to Washington City.* Columbus, Ohio, 1831. $250.

ATWOOD, Margaret. *The Circle Game.* Contact Press. Toronto (1966). Stiff wraps. $500.

ATWOOD, Margaret. *Double Persephone.* Toronto, 1961. Author's first book. Wraps. $1500.

ATWOOD, Margaret. *The Edible Woman.* Toronto, 1969. $250. London, 1969. $150. Boston, 1969. $125.

ATWOOD, Margaret. *Snake Poems.* Toronto, 1983. 16 pages in accordion binding. One of 175 signed, numbered copies. $175.

ATWOOD, Margaret. *Unearthing Suite.* Toronto, 1983. 16 pages. Accordion binding. One of 175 signed, numbered copies. $175.

AUBREY-FLETCHER, Henry Lancelot. See Wade, Henry.

AUCHINCLOSS, Louis. See Lee, Andrew.

AUCHINCLOSS, Louis. *The Injustice Collectors.* Boston, 1950. Second book, first under own name. $150.

AUCHINCLOSS, Louis. *Sybil.* Boston, 1952. $125.

AUDEN, W. H. See Baudelaire, Charles; Rich, Adrienne Cecile.

AUDEN, W. H. *The Age of Anxiety.* New York (1947). $150. London (1948). $100.

AUDEN, W. H. *Another Time.* New York (1940). $300. London (1940). $200.

AUDEN, W. H. *The Collected Poetry.* New York (1945). $300.

AUDEN, W. H. *Collected Shorter Poems, 1930–1944.* London (1950). $200.

AUDEN, W. H. *Collected Shorter Poems, 1927–1957.* London (1966). $150.

AUDEN, W. H. *The Dance of Death.* London (1933). $300.

AUDEN, W. H. *The Double Man.* New York (1941). $250.

AUDEN, W. H. *The Enchafed Flood.* New York (1950). $125.

AUDEN, W. H. *Epithalamion.* Princeton, 1939. Single sheet, printed both sides, folded to make 4 pages. (About 100 printed.) $1,500.

AUDEN, W. H. *For the Time Being.* New York (1944). Boards and cloth. $250. London (1945). $125.

AUDEN, W. H. *Homage to Clio.* New York (1960). $150. London, 1960. $125.

AUDEN, W. H. *Look, Stranger!* London (1936). $350. (First American edition, of *On This Island.*)

AUDEN, W. H. *Louis MacNeice: A Memorial Address.* London, 1963. Printed wraps. $250.

AUDEN, W. H. *Marginalia.* (Cambridge, Mass., 1966). Engravings by Laurence Scott. Oblong, printed wraps. One of 150 signed by author and artist of which 45 copies were hors de commerce. $400.

AUDEN, W. H. *New Year Letter.* (London, 1941.) $250.

AUDEN, W. H. *On This Island.* New York (1937). Brown cloth. (The first was published in London, as *Look, Stranger!*) $300.

AUDEN, W. H. *The Orators: An English Study.* London (1932). $500 Revised edition. London (1934). $250.

AUDEN, W. H. *Our Hunting Fathers.* (Cambridge), 1935. Wraps. One of 22. $600. Also, one of 5 (from the 22) on Incudine paper and lettered A to E. $1,500.

AUDEN, W. H. *Poems.* (Hampstead, England), 1928. Wraps. 12 copies recorded. $15,000.

AUDEN, W. H. *Poems.* London (1930). Stiff wraps, dustwrapper. $500. Author's first regularly published book. New York (1934). Orange cloth. $200.

AUDEN, W. H. *Some Poems.* London (1940). $175.

AUDEN, W. H. *Sonnet.* (Cambridge) 1935. Wraps. One of 22. $750. One of 5 (of 22), Roman-numbered copies. $1,500.

AUDEN, W. H. *Three Songs for St. Cecilia's Day.* (New York) 1941. Wraps. One of 250. $750.

AUDEN, W. H. *Two Songs.* New York, 1968. Wraps. One of 26 signed and lettered copies. $500. One of 100 signed and numbered copies. $250.

AUDEN, W. H., and ISHERWOOD, Christopher. *The Ascent of F6.* London (1936). $300. New York (1937). Revised. $250. London (1937). Revised. $125.

AUDEN, W. H., and ISHERWOOD, Christopher. *The Dog Beneath the Skin, or, Where Is Francis?* London (1935). $300. New York, 1935. $200.

AUDEN, W. H., and ISHERWOOD, Christopher. *On the Frontier.* London (1938). $250. New York (1939). $200.

AUDSLEY, George Ashdown. *The Art of Organ-Building.* New York, 1905. Illustrated. 2 vols. $350.

AUDSLEY, George Ashdown. *The Ornamental Arts of Japan.* New York, 1882–84. 70 plates in gold and colors, 31 in monochrome, loose in 5 cloth portfolios. 2 vols., folio. Artist's proofs edition. One of 50 signed. $2,500. 2 vols., morocco. (Not signed.) $2,000.

AUDSLEY, George Ashdown, and BOWES, J. L. *The Keramic Art of Japan.* Liverpool, 1875. (80) 63 plates, 42 in gold and colors; 4 plates of potters' marks, other illustrations. Half morocco and cloth. $1,500. London, 1881. Cloth. $400.

AUDSLEY, William James. *Cottage, Lodge, and Villa Architecture.* London (circa 1870). Half leather and cloth. $400.

AUDUBON, John James. *The Birds of America from Original Drawings.* London, 1827–38. 435 double elephant folio hand-colored plates without text. 87 parts in wraps, or 4 leather-bound double elephant folio volumes. Rare in the original parts. $3,500,000. New York, 1840–44. 500 colored plates. 100 parts in wraps or 7 vols., full or half leather. First American and first octavo edition. $25,000. New York, 1937. Edited by William Vogt. 500 plates in color. One-volume edition. Buckram. One of 2,500 on all-rag paper. Slipcase. $300. Trade edition: buckram. In dustwrapper. $150. London, 1972–73. *(The Birds of America: A Selection of Plates.)* 2 vols., Ariel Press, folio, half cloth. One of 250. $2,000. One of 1,000. $750. Amsterdam, 1972–73. Facsimile edition. 435 color plates, 4 vols. in 6, folio, with a clothbound facsimile edition of Audubon's *Synopsis.* $17,500.

AUDUBON, John James. *Delineations of American Scenery and Character.* New York, 1926. One of 42 large paper copies. $500. Trade, same date. In dustwrapper. $75. (500 copies with London imprint.)

AUDUBON, John James. *Journal of John James Audubon, Made During His Trip to New Orleans in 1820–21* with *Journal of John James Audubon, Made While Obtaining Subscriptions to His "Birds of America," 1840–1843.* 2 vols. Boston, 1929. Edited by Howard Corning. 250 copies. Usually sold as a set. $375.

AUDUBON, John James. *The Original Water-Color Paintings by John James Audubon for the Birds of America.* New York, 1966. Edited by Marshall B. Davidson. 2 vols., brown cloth in slipcase. $200.

AUDUBON, John James. *Ornithological Biography; or, An Account of the Habits of the Birds of the United States of America.* Edinburgh, 1831–49 (actually 1839). 5 vols. The text volumes to accompany the double elephant folios of *The Birds of America.* $2,750.

AUDUBON, John James. *The Quadrupeds of North America.* See Audubon and Bachman, *The Viviparous Quadrupeds, etc.*

AUDUBON, John James. *A Synopsis of the Birds of America.* Edinburgh, 1839. Cloth, paper label. $1,250.

AUDUBON, John James, and BACHMAN, John. *The Viviparous Quadrupeds of North America.* New York, 1845–48. 150 colored plates without text. 30 parts in wraps, or 3 vols. (vol. 1, 1845; vol. 2, 1846; vol. 3, 1848). Folio set. $125,000 or more. Octavo in wraps. $9,000. Octavo (first) in binding. $5,000. Later octavo editions. $2,750.

AUDUBON, John Woodhouse. *Audubon's Western Journal, 1849–50.* Cleveland, 1906. Edited by Maria R. Audubon. Folding map, 6 plates. Reprint of Audubon's extremely rare and virtually unobtainable *Illustrated Notes of an Expedition Through Mexico and California.* $250.

AUDUBON, John Woodhouse. *The Drawings of John Woodhouse Audubon, Illustrating His Adventures Through Mexico and California.* San Francisco, 1957. Book Club of California. 34 full-page illustrations, including 2 in color. Folio, boards, and cloth. Grabhorn printing. One of 400. In plain dustwrapper. $350.

AUDUBON, Maria R. *Audubon and His Journals.* New York, 1897. Edited by Elliot Coues. Plates. 2 vols. cloth. $300. New York, 1900. 2 vols., cloth. $200.

AUER, Alois. *The Discovery of the Natural Printing Process.* Wien, 1854. 75 pages and 19 plates (one is double page) in folio. $2,000.

AUSCHER, Ernest Simon. *A History and Description of French Porcelain.* London, 1905. 24 plates in color. Morocco. $400.

AUSTEN, Jane. See *Elizabeth Bennet; Emma; Mansfield Park; Northanger Abbey; Pride and Prejudice; Sense and Sensibility.*

AUSTIN, Jane Goodwin. *Fairy Dreams . . .* Boston (1859). Author's first book. $75.

AUSTIN, Mary. *The Flock.* Boston, 1906. $200.

AUSTIN, Mary. *The Land of Little Rain.* Boston, 1903. Author's first book. $250. Boston, 1950. Illustrted by Ansel Adams. $100.

AUSTIN, Mary. *What the Mexican Conference Really Means.* New York (1915). Wraps. $100.

AUSTIN, Mary, and ADAMS, Ansel. *Taos Pueblo.* San Francisco, 1930. Photographs by Adams and text by Mrs. Austin. Folio, cloth, pigskin spine. Grabhorn printing. One of 107 (Johnson says 108) signed by author and illustrator. $15,000.

AUSTIN, Mary, and MARTIN, Ann. *Suffrage and Government.* New York, 1914. Printed wraps. $200.

AUSTIN, Stephen F. *Esposicion al Publico sobre los Asuntos de Tejas.* Mexico, 1835. 32 pp., stitched. With page 29 misnumbered 31. $17,500.

AUTHENTIC Narrative of the Seminole War (An), and of the Miraculous Escape of Mrs. Mary Godfrey, and Her Four Female Children. Providence, R.I., 1836. Folding frontispiece in color, 24 pp., plain wraps. $1,750. New York, 1836. $1,000.

AUTHORS Take Sides on the Spanish War. Left Review. London (1937). Wraps. $300.

AUTHORSHIP of the Imprecatory Psalms. Boston (1852). (By Thomas Bulfinch.) Author's first book. Wraps. $300.

AUTOBIOGRAPHY of an Ex-Colored Man. Boston, 1912. (By James W. Johnson.) Author's first book. $400.

AUTOCRAT of the Breakfast Table (The). Boston, 1858. (By Oliver Wendell Holmes.) With engraved half title, with period after word "Company" on title page, and with left endpaper at back headed "Poetry and the Drama" and right "School Books." $600. Boston, 1859. Illustrated. Large paper edition. $300. Limited Editions Club, New York, 1955. $60.

AVEDON, Richard (photographer). See Baldwin, James; Capote, Truman.

AVIRETT, James B. *The Memoirs of Gen. Turner Ashby and His Compeers.* Baltimore, 1867. Portrait. Cloth. $175.

AWAHSOOSE the Bear. (By Rowland Evans Robinson.) Forest and Stream Fables. New York (1886). Author's first book. Wraps. $200.

AXTON, David. *Prisoner of Ice.* Philadelphia, 1976. (By Dean Koontz.) $250.

AYESHA, The Maid of Mars. London, 1834. By the Author of "Zohrab" . . . (By James Morier.) 3 vols., in original boards. $400.

AYRTON, Michael. *Giles of Rais.* London (1945). (By Cecil Gray.) First book illustrated by Ayrton. Stiff wraps and dustwrapper. (200 signed, numbered copies.) $250.

B

B. E. B. *Sonnets.* England, 1847. By E.B.B. Reading (actually printed about 1883–90). (By Elizabeth Barrett Browning.) 47 pp., without wraps. Thomas J. Wise's forgery of "Sonnets from the Portuguese," which actually appeared first in the second edition of *Poems,* 1850. $3,500.

B., F. *The Kasidah of Haji Abdu El-Yezdi.* London (1880). Translated and annotated by his friend and pupil, F. B. (Sir Richard Burton). Yellow wraps. First issue, without Quaritch imprint. $1,000.

B., H. *The Bad Child's Book of Beasts.* Oxford (1896). (By Hilaire Belloc.) Pictorial boards. $400.

B., H. M. *Carmen Becceriense...* (Surrey, 1890.) (By Max Beerbohm.) 4 pages, Latin with notes in English. Author's first book. (2 known copies.) $5,000.

B., J. K. *The Lorgnette.* By J. K. B. New York (1886). (By John Kendrick Bangs.) Author's first book. $400.

BABBAGE, Charles. *On the Economy of Machinery and Manufactures.* London, 1832. $350.

BABBITT, E. D. *The Principles of Light and Color.* New York, 1878. $450.

BABBITT, E. L. *The Allegheny Pilot.* Freeport, Pa., 1855. 16 maps. 64 pp., wraps. $275.

BACHELLER, Irving. *The Master of Silence.* New York, 1892. Author's first book. $75.

BACKHOUSE, Janet. *John Scottowe's Alphabet Book.* (no place), 1974. $175.

BACON, Leonard. *The Ballad of Blonay...* Vevy, 1906. Author's first book. Wraps. $250.

BACON, Sir Francis. *The Twoo Bookes of Francis Bacon.* London, 1605. $2,000.

BADGER, Mrs. C. M. *Floral Bells From The Green-House & Garden.* New York, 1867. With 16 hand-colored lithographed plates. $1,650.

BADGER, Mrs. C. M. *Wild Flowers Drawn and Coloured From Nature.* New York and London, 1859. With 22 full-page color lithographs. $1,250.

BAER, Elizabeth. *Seventeenth Century Maryland, A Bibliography.* Baltimore, 1949. Limited to 300 copies. $300.

BAHR, Jerome. *All Good Americans.* New York, 1937. Preface by Ernest Hemingway. Blue cloth. $150. Reissued in yellow cloth, 1939 (with "A" on copyright page—an exception to the Scribner method of marking only first editions with an "A"). $50.

BAILEY, Washington. *A Trip to California in 1853.* (LeRoy, Ill.), 1915. Portrait. Printed wraps. $400.

BAILY, Francis. *Journal of a Tour in Unsettled Parts of North America in 1796 & 1797.* London, 1856. $400.

BAINBRIDGE, Beryl. *A Weekend with Claude.* (London) 1967. Author's first book. $250.

BAINBRIDGE, George C. *The Fly-Fisher's Guide.* Liverpool, 1816. 8 colored plates. $750.

BAIRD, Joseph A. *California's Pictorial Letter Sheets, 1849–1869.* San Francisco, 1967. Grabhorn printing. One of 475 signed. In plain dustwrapper. $275.

BAIRD, Spencer F., BREWER, T. M., and RIDGWAY, R. *The Water Birds of North America.* Boston, 1884. Hand-colored illustrations. 2 vols., cloth. $1,250.

BAKER, Carlos H. *Shadows in the Stone.* Hanover, N. H., 1930. 125 signed, numbered copies. Author's first book. Wraps. $150.

BAKER, Charles H. Collins. *Lely and the Stuart Portrait Painters.* London, 1912. 240 reproductions. 2 vols. One of 375. $500. Vellum. One of 30, with an extra set of plates. $1,250.

BAKER, D. W. C. (compiler). *A Texas Scrap-Book.* New York (1875). $450.

BAKER, David Erskine. *Biographia Dramatica, Or, A Companion to the Playhouse* . . . London, various publishers, 1812. 3 vols. Third edition. $200.

BAKER, Hozial H. *Overland Journey to Carson Valley, Utah.* Seneca Falls, N.Y., 1861. Woodcut frontispiece and other illustrations. 38 pp., yellow printed wraps. $6,000. San Francisco, 1973. Book Club of California. In plain dustwrapper. $100.

BALDWIN, James. *Giovanni's Room.* New York, 1956. $250.

BALDWIN, James. *Go Tell It on the Mountain.* New York, 1953. Author's first book. $500. London, 1954. $150.

BALDWIN, James. *If Beale Street Could Talk.* New York, 1974. Leatherette. One of 250 signed and numbered copies in slipcase. $150.

BALDWIN, James. *Nothing Personal.* New York, 1964. Illustrated by Richard Avedon. Boards. Issued without dustwrapper. In slipcase. $300.

BALDWIN, James. *A Story of the Golden Age.* New York, 1887. Illustrated by Howard Pyle. Decorated brown cloth. $100.

BALDWIN, James. *The Story of Siegfried.* New York, 1882. Illustrated by Howard Pyle. Pictorial cloth. $125.

BALDWIN, Joseph G. *The Flush Times of Alabama and Mississippi.* New York, 1853. $300.

BALDWIN, Joseph G. *Remarks of Mr. Baldwin* . . . (No city of publication on title page and not known. Montgomery, Alabama? 1843.) 16-page pamphlet. Author's first book. $600.

BALFOUR, James. *Reminiscences of Golf on St. Andrews Links.* Edinburgh, 1887. $1,250.

BALLANTYNE, Robert Michael. *Hudson's Bay . . .* Edinburgh, 1848. Author's first book. $1,000. Edinburgh/London, 1848. $350.

Ballantyne Press and Its Founders, The. Edinburgh, 1909. $125.

BALLARD, Ellis Ames. *Catalogue, Intimate and Descriptive of My Kipling Collection . . .* Philadelphia, 1935. 120 numbered copies. $165.

BALSTON, Thomas. *William Balston, Paper Maker, 1759–1849.* London, 1954. $125.

BALTES, F. W. *The Cost Of Printing, A System in Practical Operation . . .* Portland, 1894. $125.

BALWHIDDER, The Rev. Micah. *Annals of the Parish; or The Chronicle of Dalmailing.* Edinburgh, 1821. (By John Galt.) $200.

BANCROFT, George. *Poems.* Cambridge, Mass., 1823. $100.

BANCROFT, George. *Prospectus of a School . . .* (Cambridge, 1823. With J.C. Coggswell.) Author's first book. Wraps. $175.

BANCROFT, Hubert Howe. *The Works of Hubert Howe Bancroft.* San Francisco, 1883–90. Illustrated. 39 vols., cloth. $2,000. In morocco. $3,000.

BANDELIER, Adolph F. A. *The Gilded Man.* New York, 1893. $175.

BANDINI, Joseph. *A Description of California in 1828.* Berkeley, Calif., 1951. Illustrated. Boards and cloth. One of 400. $125.

BANGS, John Kendrick. See B., J. K.

BANGS, John Kendrick. *Bikey the Skicycle and Other Tales of Jimmie Boy.* New York, 1902. Illustrated by Peter Newell. Decorated cloth. $100.

BANGS, John Kendrick. *Mephistopheles: A Profanation.* New York, 1889. Red wraps. $125.

BANGS, John Kendrick. *Mr. Munchausen.* Boston, 1901. First state, with Small, Maynard copyright. (Not seen by BAL.) $150. Second state overstamped with "Noyes, Platt & Co." $75.

BANGS, John Kendrick. *Roger Camerden.* New York, 1887. Wraps. $175.

BANGS, John Kendrick. *Toppleton's Client.* London, 1893. Boards. $150. New York, 1893. $100.

BANKS, Ian. *The Wasp Factory.* London, 1984. Author's first book. $150.

BANNERMAN, Helen. *The Story of Little Black Sambo.* London, 1899. Colored plates. $1,500.

BANTA, William, and CALDWELL, J. W., Jr. *Twenty-seven Years on the Frontier, or Fifty Years in Texas.* Austin, 1893. Frontispiece. Wraps. $2,000.

BANTOCK, Miles. *On Many Greens.* Grossett & Dunlap, New York, 1901. $500.

BARBE-MARBOIS, François. *The History of Louisiana, Particularly the Cession of That Colony to the U.S.A.* Philadelphia, 1830. First edition in English. $750.

BARCLAY, E. J. *The Linotype Operator's Companion: A Treatise On How to Operate and Care for the Linotype Machine.* Cincinnati, 1898. $100.

BARHAM, Richard Harris. See Ingoldsby, Thomas.

BARING, Maurice. *Algae: An Anthology of Phrases.* London, 1928. Wraps, paper label. One of 100 signed. In dustwrapper and slipcase. $150.

BARKER, Eugene, C. *The Life of Stephen F. Austin.* Nashville, 1925. 2 maps, plan, 6 portraits. Boards and vellum. One of 250 signed. $450. Trade. $125.

BARKER, George. *Alanna Autumnal.* London, 1932. $125.

BARKER, George. *Poems.* London (1935). $100.

BARKER, George. *Thirty Preliminary Poems.* London, 1932. Author's first book. $150.

BARKER, Matthew Henry. *The Old Sailor's Jolly Boat.* London, 1844. 24 full-page engravings by George and Robert Cruikshank. $300.

BARLOW, Joel. *The Columbiad: A Poem.* Philadelphia, 1807. Portrait and 11 plates. (New edition of *The Vision of Columbus.* See below.) $200.

BARLOW, Joel. *Joel Barlow to His Fellow Citizens of the United States.* (Caption title.) (Philadelphia, 1801.) Wraps. First American edition. $250.

BARLOW, Joel. *The Vision of Columbus: A Poem in Nine Books.* Hartford, 1787. $200. (Reprinted as *The Columbiad.*)

BARNARD, George N. *Photographic Views of Sherman's Campaign.* New York (1866). 61 gold-toned albumen prints, mounted, with lithographic captions. Oblong folio, morocco. $25,000.

BARNES, Charles Merritt. *Combats and Conquest of Immortal Heroes.* San Antonio, 1910. Full morocco. $175.

BARNES, David M. *The Draft Riots in New York, July, 1863.* New York, 1863. 117 pp., wraps, or cloth. $175.

BARNES, Demas. *From the Atlantic to the Pacific, Overland, A series of Letters . . . Describing a Trip from New York, Via Chicago, Atchison . . .* New York, 1866. $150.

BARNES, Djuna. See *Ladies Almanack.*

BARNES, Djuna. *A Book.* New York (1923). 6 portraits, black boards, paper label. $400.

BARNES, Djuna. *The Book of Repulsive Women.* (New York, 1915.) Illustrated. Gold wraps. Author's first book. $400. Yonkers, 1948. Stiff wraps. One of 1,000. $100.

BARNES, Djuna. *A Night Among the Horses.* New York, 1929. $350.

BARNES, Djuna. *Nightwood.* London (1936). $350. New York (1937). Contains an introduction by T.S. Eliot. $100.

BARNES, Djuna. *Ryder.* New York, 1928. $250.

BARNES, Will C. *Apaches and Longhorns.* Los Angeles, 1941. Edited by Frank C. Lockwood. Illustrated. $150.

BARNES, William C. *Tales from the X-Bar Horse Camp.* Chicago, 1920. $125.

BARNES, William C., McCANN, Joseph W., and DUG, Alexander. *A Collation of Facts Relative to Fast Typesetting . . .* New York, 1887. $375.

BARNEY, James M. *Tales of Apache Warfare.* (Phoenix), 1933. 45 pp., wraps. $125.

BARNEY, Natalie C. See Tryphe.

BARNEY, Natalie C. *The One Who Is Legion.* London, 1930. $300.

BARNEY, Natalie C. *Poems & Poemes.* Paris & New York (1920). Wraps. Copies on blue paper. $300. white paper. $200.

BARNEY, Natalie C. *Quelques Portraits.* Paris, 1900. Author's first book. $300.

BARNUM, Phineas Taylor. *The Life of P. T. Barnum.* New York, 1855. Author's first book. $175.

BARR, Louise Farrow. *Presses of Northern California And Their Books, 1900–1933.* Berkeley, 1934. One of 400 numbered copies. $125.

BARR, Robert. *The Triumph of Eugene Valmont.* London, 1906. $400.

BARRETT, E. B. *The Battle of Marathon: A Poem.* London, 1820. (By Elizabeth Barrett Browning.) (50 copies.) $15,000.

BARRETT, Elizabeth Barrett. *Poems.* London, 1844. (By Elizabeth Barrett Browning.) 2 vols., dark green cloth, uncut. With ads in vol. 1 dated June 1. $1,000. No ads. $750. London, 1850. 2 vols. brown cloth. Second edition, first issue, with single address in imprint, called "New Edition." (First appearance of "Sonnets from the Portuguese" in a book.) $1,000.

BARRETT, Elizabeth B. *The Seraphim and Other Poems.* London, 1838. (By Elizabeth Barrett Browning.) $500.

BARRETT, Elizabeth, and BROWNING, Robert. *Two Poems.* London, 1854. (By Elizabeth Barrett Browning.) Printed wrappers. $400.

BARRETT, Ellen C. *Baja California, 1535–1956: A Bibliography.* Los Angeles, 1957. Blue cloth. One of 500. $150. Also, one of 50 signed. $300.

BARRETT, Timothy. *Nagashizuki, The Japanese Craft of Hand Papermaking.* North Hills, 1979. (Dard Hunter.) 300 numbered copies. $425.

BARRIE, Sir James M. See *The Allahakbarrie Book of Broadway Cricket for 1899.*

BARRIE, Sir James M. *The Admirable Crichton.* London (1914). Illustrated by Hugh Thomson. $175. One of 500 signed by Thomson. $500.

BARRIE, Sir James M. *Auld Licht Idylls.* London, 1888. First issue, with black endpapers (VAB). (Bibliographies call for green endpapers.) $150.

BARRIE, Sir James M. *Better Dead.* London, 1888 (actually 1887). Pictorial glazed yellow (or buff) wraps. Author's first book. $600.

BARRIE, Sir James M. *An Edinburgh Eleven.* London, 1889. ("Gavin Ogilvy" on front cover and "J.M. Barrie" on title page.) First issue in wraps. $300. Later issue same date: gray cloth. $200.

BARRIE, Sir James M. *The Little Minister.* London, 1891. 3 vols., brown cloth. With 16 pages of ads in vol. 1. $500.

BARRIE, Sir James M. *My Lady Nicotine.* London, 1890. First issue, with 6 pages of ads at back. $150.

BARRIE, Sir James M. *Peter Pan in Kensington Gardens.* London, 1906. Illustrated in color and black and white by Arthur Rackham. Vellum. One of 500 signed by Rackham. $2,500. Trade in cloth. $400. New York, 1906. $250.

BARRIE, Sir James M. *Quality Street.* (London, 1913.) Vellum with silk ties. One of 1,000 illustrated and signed by Hugh Thomson. $600. Trade in cloth. $200.

BARRIE, Sir James M. *A Window in Thrums.* London, 1889. With 6 pages of ads at back. $200.

BARROW, John. *A Chronological History of Voyages into the Arctic Regions.* London, 1818. Illustrated, folding map. $350.

BARROW, John. *A Voyage to Cochinchina, 1792–1793.* London, 1806. Double-page map, double-page chart, 26 colored aquatint plates. $1,250.

BARROWS, R. M. (compiler). *The Kitbook for Soldiers, Sailors, and Marines.* Chicago (1942). Pictorial boards. In pictorial mailing box. (Contains J.D. Salinger's story "The Hang of It," his first book appearance.) $150. Chicago, 1943. $75.

BARROWS, Willard. *Notes on Iowa Territory.* Cincinnati, 1845. Folding map. 46 pp., cloth, printed front cover label. $2,000.

BARRY, T. A., and PATTEN, B. A. *Men and Memories of San Francisco, in the "Spring of '50."* San Francisco, 1873. 2 plates. Flexible cloth. $150.

BARTH, John. *Chimera.* New York (1972). One of 300 signed in slipcase. $100.

BARTH, John. *The End of the Road.* Garden City, 1958. $250. London, 1962. $125.

BARTH, John. *The Floating Opera.* New York (1956). Author's first book. $300. London (1968). $50.

BARTH, John. *Giles Goat-Boy.* Garden City, 1966. 250 signed and numbered copies. Slipcase. $150. Trade. $50. London (1967). $60.

BARTH, John. *Lost in the Funhouse.* Garden City, 1968. 250 signed, numbered copies. Slipcase. $150. Trade. $50. London (1969). $75.

BARTH, John. *The Sot-Weed Factor.* Garden City, 1960. $300. London, 1961. $100.

BARTHELME, Donald. *Come Back, Dr. Caligari.* Boston (1964). Author's first book. $150. London, 1966. $75.

BARTHELME, Donald. *Snow White.* New York, 1967. $75. London, 1968. $60.

BARTLETT, Edward Everett. *The Typographic Treasures in Europe and a Study of Contemporaneous Book Production . . .* New York, 1925. $135.

BARTLETT, John. See *A Collection of Familiar Quotations.*

BARTLETT, John Russell. *Personal Narrative of Explorations and Incidents in Texas, New Mexico, California, . . .* New York, 1854. Folding map. 44 plates, 2 vols., pictorial cloth. $800. London, 1854. 2 vols. $750.

BARTON, James L. *Commerce of the Lakes.* Buffalo, 1847. Folding table. 80 pp., wraps. $450.

BARTON, William P. C. *A Flora of North America.* Philadelphia, 1821, 1822, 1823. 106 hand-colored plates. 3 vols. $7,500.

BARTON, William P. C. *The Vegetable Materia Medica of the U.S.; Or Medical Botany . . .* Philadelphia, 1817–18. 2 vols. 50 engraved colored plates. $3,000.

BARTRAM, William. *Travels Through North & South Carolina.* Philadelphia, 1791. Folding map, 8 plates, including frontispiece. Author's first book. $6,000. London, 1792. $1,500.

BASKIN, Leonard. *Ars Anatomica, A Medical Fantasia, Thirteen Drawings.* New York (1972). Contains 2 sets of 13 suites enclosed in portfolio. One of 300 lettered and signed sets. $450. One of 2,500. $250.

BASKIN, Leonard. *Figures of Dead Men.* (Boston), 1968. Preface by Archibald MacLeish. Illustrated. Boards and cloth. One of 100 signed by Baskin, with an original signed woodcut. $750.

BASKIN, Leonard. *To Colour Thought.* New Haven, 1967. One of 300 numbered copies. Slipcase. $350.

BASKIN, Leonard. *The Wood Engravings of Leonard Baskin, 1948–1959.* Northampton, 1961. 168 signed engravings. Folio, loose in half-morocco case. One of 24. $7,500.

BASS, W. W. (editor). *Adventures in the Canyons of the Colorado by Two of Its Earliest Explorers, James White and H.W. Hawkins.* Grand Canyon, 1920. Frontispiece, plate, facsimiles. 38 pp., wraps. $150.

BATES, Ed. F. *History . . . of Denton County Texas.* Denton, Tex. (1918). Plates. Cloth. $500.

BATES, H. E. *The Beauty of the Dead, and One Other Story.* Corvinus Press. London, 1941. One of 25. $500.

BATES, H. E. *Flowers and Faces.* Golden Cockerel Press. London, 1935. Engravings by John Nash. One of 325. $300.

BATES, H. E. *A German Idyll.* Golden Cockerel Press. Waltham Saint Lawrence, England, 1932. $350.

BATES, H. E. *The Last Bread: A Play in One Act.* London (1926). Wraps. Author's first book. $150.

BATES, H. E. *Sally Go Round the Moon.* London, 1932. White Owl Press. One of 21 signed. In slipcase. $500. Trade. $100.

BATES, H. E. *The Story Without an End.* White Owl Press. (London), 1932. One of 25 signed, with a leaf of manuscript. $400.

BATES, H. W. *The Naturalist on the River Amazon.* London, 1863. Illustrated, including folding map. 2 vols. $500.

BATES, J. H. *Notes of a Tour in Mexico and California.* New York, 1887. $100.

BATESON, F. W. (editor). *The Cambridge Bibliography of English Literature.* Cambridge, 1940. 5 vols. $275.

BATTERSHALL, Fletcher. *Bookbinding for Bibliophiles . . .* Greenwich, 1905. One of 350. $100.

BAUDELAIRE, Charles. *Intimate Journals.* London, 1930. Translated by Christopher Isherwood. Introduction by T.S. Eliot. One of 400 in slipcase. $350. One of 50 signed by Eliot. $1,250. New York, 1930. $175. Hollywood, 1947. Revised edition (with W.H. Auden introduction). $125.

BAUER, Max. *Precious Stones.* London, 1903. Translated from the German by L.J. Spencer. Plates. Half morocco. $750. London, 1904. $500.

BAUM, L. Frank. *American Fairy Tales.* Chicago, 1901. Illustrated. Pictorial cloth. $400.

BAUM, L. Frank. *The Army Alphabet.* Chicago, 1900. Illustrated by Harry Kennedy. Pictorial boards. $750.

BAUM, L. Frank. *The Book of Hamburgs.* Hartford, 1886. Author's first book. $1,500.

BAUM, L. Frank. *The Cowardly Lion and the Hungry Tiger.* Chicago (1913). Color plates. Boards. $350.

BAUM, L. Frank. *Dorothy and the Wizard of Oz.* Chicago (1908). Illustrated by John R. Neill. 16 full-color inserts. First issue, with "The Reilly & Britton Co." at bottom of spine versus "Reilly & Britton." $300. Second issue, $200.

BAUM, L. Frank. *The Enchanted Island of Yew.* Indianapolis (1903). Illustrated by Fanny Y. Cory. First state with Braunworth's imprint on copyright page, and illustration on page 238 incorrectly positioned over text. $500.

BAUM, L. Frank. *Father Goose's Year Book.* Chicago (1907). Illustrated. Pictorial paper over cloth. $300.

BAUM, L. Frank. *The Life and Adventures of Santa Claus.* Indianapolis, 1902. First state with headings "Book First," "Book Second," and "Book Third." $400 second state with headings "Youth," "Manhood," and "Old Age." $250.

BAUM, L. Frank. *The Marvelous Land of Oz.* Chicago, 1904. First issue, without "Published July, 1904" on copyright page. $750.

BAUM, L. Frank. *The Master Key.* Indianapolis (1901). Illustrated in color by Fanny Cory. Olive green cloth. First issue, with signatures of 8 pp. and with copyright line $1^{21}/_{32}$ inches wide. $400. Second issue, signatures of 16 pp. $300. Third issue, copyright line $1^{25}/_{32}$ inches wide. $200.

BAUM, L. Frank. *Mother Goose in Prose.* Chicago (1897). Illustrated by Maxfield Parrish. (His first book illustrations.) Way & Williams. Pictorial cloth. $6,000. Hill. Chicago (1901). 12 plates. Pictorial cloth. $1,000.

BAUM, L. Frank. *A New Wonderland.* New York, 1900. Illustrated by Frank Verbeck. $1,500. Secondary binding with blank endpapers. $1,000.

BAUM, L. Frank. *Ozma of Oz.* Chicago (1907). First issue, with illustration in color on page 221, and spine imprint "The Reilly & Britton Co." $300.

BAUM, L. Frank. *The Patchwork Girl of Oz.* Reilly & Britton. Chicago (1913). Light green pictorial cloth. First state, with the "C" in chapter 3 touching text. $200. Second state with correction, in light tan cloth. $100.

BAUM, L. Frank. *Queen Zixi of Ix.* New York, 1905. First state with terra-cotta and black text illustrations on pages 169–236. $500. Second state, with illustrations in turquoise and black on pages 169–84 and 221–36. $300.

BAUM, L. Frank. *The Road to Oz.* Reilly & Britton. Chicago (1909). First with text sheets on color-tinted paper and 2 pages of ads at end. $400. Later printings have an ad for *Rinkitink in Oz* (1916) on verso of ownership page.

BAUM, L. Frank. *The Sea Fairies.* Chicago (1911). First issue, with 3 heads on cover label. $400. Second issue has cover label showing girl on a sea horse. $150.

BAUM, L. Frank. *The Songs of Father Goose.* Chicago, 1900. Illustrated by W.W. Denslow. Colored pictorial boards. $750.

BAUM, L. Frank. *The Wonderful Wizard of Oz.* Chicago and New York, 1900. Illustrated by W.W. Denslow. Green cloth. First issue, with publisher's ads enclosed in box on page 2 and at end of book, and with an 11-line colophon. Publisher's imprint at base of spine stamped in green. $10,000. Second issue, with no box around ads, colophon in 13 lines, and imprint stamped in red. $3,000. (There are other points, and mixed states seem common.)

BAUM, L. Frank. *The Yellow Hen.* Chicago (1916). First state without ads for 6-volume series on verso of ownership leaf. $350. Second state, with ads. $200.

BAX, Clifford (editor). *Florence Farr, Bernard Shaw and W.B. Yeats.* Cuala Press. Dublin, 1941. Boards, linen spine, paper label. One of 500. In tissue dustwrapper. $150.

BAXLEY, H. Willis. *What I Saw on the West Coast of South and North America, and at the Hawaiian Islands.* New York, 1865. $400.

BAY, J. Christian. *A Handful of Western Books; A Second Handful of Western Books; A Third Handful of Western Books.* Cedar Rapids, Iowa, 1935–36–37. Illustrated. 3 vols., boards and cloth. Limited to 350, 400, and 400 copies, respectively. Issued in tissue dust wraps. Together, the three volumes. $200. Odd volumes. $50–$75 each.

BAY, J. Christian. *Three Handfuls of Western Books.* (Cedar Rapids) 1941. (Combined one-volume edition of preceding items.) Boards. One of 35. $175.

BAYDLON, Oliver. *The Paper Maker's Craft.* Leicester, 1965. Limited to "less than 400 copies." $200.

BAYLEY, Harold. *A New Light on the Renaissance, Displayed in Contemporary Emblems.* London (no-date). $125.

BAYLIES, Francis. *A Narrative of General Wool's Campaign in Mexico.* Albany, 1851. Frontispiece. 78 pp., printed yellow wraps. $350.

BEACH, Rex. *Pardners.* New York, 1905. Author's first book. $60. In dustwrapper. $300.

BEACH, Rex. *Spoilers.* New York, 1905. $30. In dustwrapper. $150.

BEADLE, Clayton. *Chapters on Papermaking.* London, 1908–9. 5 vols. $125.

BEAGLE, Peter S. *A Fine and Private Place.* New York, 1960. Author's first book. $75.

BEAGLE, Peter S. *The Last Unicorn.* New York (1968). Cloth. $100.

BEALE, Charles Willing. *The Secret of the Earth.* New York (1899). $400.

BEALE, Joseph Henry. *A Bibliography of Early English Law Books.* Cambridge (1926). $125.

BEALS, Carleton. *The Crime of Cuba.* Philadelphia (1933). 31 photographs by Walker Evans. His first book appearance. $175.

BEAN, Edwin F. (compiler). *Bean's History and Directory of Nevada County, California.* Nevada, Calif., 1867. Half leather and boards. $800.

BEARD, Charles A. *An Economic Interpretation of the Constitution of the United States.* New York, 1913. $250.

BEARD, Charles A. *The Office of the Justice . . .* New York, 1904. Author's first book. Wraps. $250.

BEARD, Charles R. *A Catalogue of the Collection of Martinware Formed by Frederick John Nettlefold.* (London), 1936. 31 color plates, 46 in black and white. Half brown morocco. $300.

BEARD, James. *Hors D'Oeuvres and Canapés.* New York (1940). Author's first book. $125.

BEARDSLEY, Aubrey. *A Book of Fifty Drawings.* London, 1897. $400. One of 50 on vellum. $1,000.

BEARDSLEY, Aubrey. *Fifty Drawings.* New York, 1920. One of 500. $400. (Beardsley experts doubt that these are Beardsley's drawings—VAB.)

BEARDSLEY, Aubrey. *Last Letters.* London, 1904. $150.

BEARDSLEY, Aubrey. *A Second Book of Fifty Drawings.* London, 1899. One of 1,000. $250. One of 50 on vellum. $750.

BEARDSLEY, Aubrey. *Six Drawings Illustrating Theophile Gautier's Romance, "Mademoiselle de Maupin."* London, 1898. 6 plates, loose in half-cloth portfolio, silk ties. One of 50. $750.

BEARDSLEY, Aubrey. *Under the Hill and Other Essays in Prose and Verse.* London, 1904. 16 illustrations by the author. One of 50 on Japan vellum. $850. Trade edition. $200.

BEASLEY, Gertrude. *My First Thirty Years . . .* (Paris, 1925.) Author's first book. Wraps. $450.

BEATON, Cecil. *The Book of Beauty.* London (1930). 27 photographic plates, 90 text drawings. Buckram. One of 110 signed. $600. Trade. $250.

BEATON, George. *Jack Robinson.* London (1933). (By Gerald Brenan.) $275.

BEATTIE, Ann. *Distortions.* Garden City, 1976. Author's first book. $100.

BEATTIE, Ann. *Chilly Scenes of Winter.* Garden City, 1976. (Issued simultaneously with *Distortions.*) $100.

BEATTIE, Ann. *Jacklighting.* Worcester, 1981. 26 signed, lettered copies. In dust-wrapper. $150. Wraps. $60.

BEATTIE, William. *Switzerland Illustrated.* London, 1836. With 2 engraved titles, folding map, and 106 plates by W.H. Bartlett. 2 vols. $1,250.

BEAUCHAMPE; or, the Kentucky Tragedy. Philadelphia, 1842. (By William Gilmore Simms.) 2 vols. $300.

BEAUMONT, Cyril W. *The History of Harlequin.* London, 1926. With a preface by Sacheverell Sitwell. 44 plates (5 colored), text decorations by Claudia Guercio. Decorated parchment boards, vellum spine. London, 1926. One of 325. $400.

BEAUMONT, Cyril W. *Puppets and the Puppet Stage.* London, 1938. 110 pp. of illustrations. $200.

BEAUMONT, Jean. *Jiu-Jitsu Partie Judo.* Paris, 1954. Limited to 1,250 copies. $150.

BEAUMONT, William. *Experiments and Observations on the Gastric Juice, and the Physiology of Digestion.* Plattsburg, N.Y., 1833. 3 engravings. $1,500. Boston, 1834. Second issue (first-edition sheets with Boston title page). $750. Edinburgh, 1838. First English edition. $500.

BEAUMONT, William. *The Physiology of Digestion.* Burlington, Vt., 1847. Edited by Samuel Beaumont. Cloth. Second edition of *Experiments and Observations on the Gastric Juice.* $500.

BECK, Lewis C. *A Gazetteer of the States of Illinois and Missouri.* Albany, 1823. Folding map, 5 plates. $1,500.

BECKER, Robert H. *Disenos of California Ranchos . . .* San Francisco, 1964. Grabhorn printing. One of 400. $600.

BECKER'S Ornamental Penmanship. Philadelphia (1876). Second edition, revised, with section at the end entitled "Designs in Flourishing." $200.

BECKETT, Samuel. See Crowder, Henry.

BECKETT, Samuel. *All Strange Away.* New York, 1976. Illustrated by Edward Gorey. One of 200 signed. In slipcase. $350. One of 26 lettered and signed. $600.

BECKETT, Samuel. *All That Fall: A Play.* New York (1957). One of 100 specially bound. $350. London, 1957. Wraps (issued as a holiday greeting by the publisher). $150.

BECKETT, Samuel. *Come and Go: Dramaticule.* London (1967). One of 100 signed. In slipcase. $300.

BECKETT, Samuel. *Echo's Bones and Other Precipitates.* Europa Press. Paris, 1935. 30 pp., printed wraps. One of 25 on Normandy vellum, signed. $1,000. One of 250 on Alfa paper, unsigned. $400.

BECKETT, Samuel. *Endgame.* London (1958). Translated by the author. Dark red cloth. First English edition. $200. New York (1958). Boards. First American edition. Limited issue. One of 100. Issued without dustwrapper. $200.

BECKETT, Samuel. *How It Is.* London (1964). (Series A and Series B.) Translated from the French by the author. 2 vols., vellum and morocco. Each, 100 signed. In tissue dustwrappers. In slipcase. $400 each.

BECKETT, Samuel. *The Lost Ones.* London, 1972. Half vellum (or half leather). One of 100 signed. In slipcase. $250.

BECKETT, Samuel. *Malone Dies.* New York (1956). Translated by the author. 120 pp., cream-colored canvas. One of 500. In transparent dustwrapper. $250. London, 1958. $150.

BECKETT, Samuel. *Molloy.* Paris, (1951). Printed wraps. First edition (in French). One of 500 on Alfa paper. $350. Olympia Press. Paris, (1955). Wraps. First edition in English. $250. New York (1955). $150.

BECKETT, Samuel. *More Pricks Than Kicks.* London, 1934. $3,000. London (1970). One of 100 signed. $350.

BECKETT, Samuel. *Murphy.* London (1938). First binding. Green cloth. $3,500. New York (1957). Boards and cloth. One of 100 signed. $600.

BECKETT, Samuel. *No's Knife: Collected Shorter Prose, 1945–1966.* London (1967). One of 100 signed. (Series A.) One of 100 signed. (Series B.) In slipcases. $300 each.

BECKETT, Samuel. *Poems in English.* London (1961). Mottled tan leatherlike cloth boards. One of 100 signed. $600. Cloth. One of 175 signed. In tissue dustwrapper. $300.

BECKETT, Samuel. *Proust.* Paris, 1931. Wraps. $300. London, 1931. $300. New York (1957). Limited first American edition. One of 250 signed. Issued without dustwrapper. $200. London, 1965. One of 100 signed. $350.

BECKETT, Samuel. *The Unnamable.* Grove Press. New York (1958). Translated by the author. One of 26 lettered copies, signed. $1,000. One of 100 numbered copies. $150. Another issue, wraps. $25.

BECKETT, Samuel. *Waiting for Godot.* New York, 1954. Translated by the author. $500. London (1956). $250.

BECKETT, Samuel. *Watt.* Collection Merlin: Olympia Press. Paris (1953). Printed wraps. One of 25, lettered A to Y, on fine paper and signed by Beckett. $1,500. First trade edition. Wraps. $200. New York (1959). $250.

BECKETT, Samuel. *Whoroscope.* Paris, 1930. Hours Press. Stapled wraps, with white (separate) band around the book. One of 100 signed and numbered (of a total edition of 300). $2,500. One of 200 unsigned. $1,250. Author's first separately published work.

BECKETT, Samuel, et al. *Our Exagmination Round His Factifaction for Incamination of Work in Progress.* Shakespeare and Company. Paris, 1929. Printed wraps. One of 96 (large paper) on verge d'Arches paper. $1,250. One of 200. $400.

BEDFORD, Hilory G. *Texas Indian Troubles.* Dallas, 1905. Decorated cloth. $350.

BEEBE, Henry. *The History of Peru.* Peru, Ill., 1858. Leather. $175.

BEEBE, Lucius. *François Villon . . .* Cambridge, 1921. Wraps. One of 50. $150.

BEEBE, William. *The Arcturus Adventure.* New York, 1926. One of 50 signed. Issued without dustwrapper. $400. First trade edition. $75.

BEEBE, William. *Galapagos: World's End.* New York, 1924. One of 100 signed. Issued without dustwrapper. $350. Trade. $100.

BEEBE, William. *A Monograph of the Pheasants.* London, 1918–22. 90 color plates, 20 maps, other illustrations. 4 vols., folio, cloth. One of 600. $4,000.

BEEBE, William. *Pheasants: Their Lives and Homes.* Garden City, 1926. 64 plates. 2 vols., vellum. One of 201 on large paper, signed. $1,000. Trade in 2 vols. $400. Garden City, 1931. 2 vols. $150. Garden City, 1936. 2 vols. in 1. $100.

BEEBE, William. *Two Bird-Lovers in Mexico.* Boston, 1905. Author's first book. First issue, Charles M. Beebe on cover, $1,500. Second issue, C. William Beebe on cover. $250. Third issue, gold sky background lacking, $125. Fourth issue, lacks pictorial design—just lettered, $60.

BEECHER, Edward. *Narrative of the Riots at Alton.* Alton, Ill., 1838. $150.

BEECHER, Harriet Elizabeth. *Primary Geography for Children . . .* Cincinnati, 1833. (Harriet Beecher Stowe's first book), with C. Beecher. $200.

BEECHER, Harriet Elizabeth. *Prize-Tale: A New England Sketch.* Lowell, Mass., 1834. In original plain wraps with cloth spine. First separate book by Harriet Beecher Stowe. $500.

BEECHER, Henry Ward. *Norwood, or Village Life in New England.* London, 1867. 3 vols., green cloth. $250. New York, 1868. $75.

BEECHEY, F. W. *An Account of a Visit to California.* (San Francisco, 1941). Grabhorn printing. Map, color plates. Half vellum. One of 350. $250.

BEECHEY, F. W. *Narrative of a Voyage to the Pacific and Beering's Strait.* London, 1831. 23 plates, 3 maps. 2 vols. Large paper "Admiralty" issue. $2,500. London, 1831. 2 vols. Second edition. $750. Philadelphia, 1832. $500.

BEECHEY, F. W. *A Voyage of Discovery Towards the North Pole.* London, 1843. Folding map, 6 plates. $500.

BEE-HUNTER (The); or, The Oak Openings. London, 1848. By the author of "The Pioneers" (James Fenimore Cooper). 3 vols., drab boards. First edition (of the novel published in America as *The Oak Openings*). $450.

BEER, Thomas. *The Mauve Decade.* New York, 1926. One of 165 signed. In slipcase. $100. One of 15 signed. $200.

BEERBOHM, Max. See H.M.B.

BEERBOHM, Max. *A Book of Caricatures.* London (1907). Frontispiece in color, 48 drawings. $200.

BEERBOHM, Max. *Caricatures of Twenty-Five Gentlemen.* London (1896). 25 plates. First issue with "Leonard/Smithers" on spine. $350. Second issue adds "& Co." $300.

BEERBOHM, Max. *Cartoons: "The Second Childhood of John Bull."* London (1901). 15 full-page tinted plates. $200. Second issue. Plates in cloth folder. $150.

BEERBOHM, Max. *The Happy Hypocrite: A Fairy Tale for Tired Men.* New York, 1897. Printed green wraps. Period on cover after Bodley Booklets No. 1, colophon dated December 1896. $300.

BEERBOHM, Max. *Rossetti and His Circle.* London (1922). 23 colored caricatures. One of 380 signed. In dustwrapper. $250. Trade. $100.

BEERBOHM, Max. *A Survey.* London, 1921. 52 plates, including colored frontispiece. Purple cloth. One of 275 signed. $300. Trade. $150. New York, 1921. $100.

BEERBOHM, Max. *Things New and Old.* London, 1921. Colored frontispiece, 49 other plates. White buckram. One of 380 signed and with extra signed plate. $300. Trade edition. $150.

BEERBOHM, Max. *The Works of Max Beerbohm.* New York, 1896. (1,000 copies—400 pulped.) $300. London, 1896. $150.

BEERBOHM, Max. *Zuleika Dobson.* London, 1911. Smooth brown cloth, or rough cloth. (No priority, but there were fewer copies bound in rough cloth.) $250. Limited Editions Club, New York, 1960. In slipcase. $60.

BEERS, F. W., and Co. *Atlas of the Counties of Lamoille and Orleans, Vermont.* New York, 1878. Maps in color. Half leather. $450.

BEETON, Mrs. Isabella. *The Book of Household Management.* London, 1861. Frontispiece and pictorial title in color, numerous other illustrations. 2 vols., cloth. First issue, with "18 Bouverie St." on woodcut title page. $600.

BEETON'S Christmas Annual. 28th Season. London, 1887. Illustrated. Wraps. (Contains first appearance of A. Conan Doyle's *A Study in Scarlet.*) $75,000 or more.

BEGBIE, Harold. *J. H. Taylor, or, The Inside of a Week.* London, 1925. $125.

BEHAN, Brendan. *The Hostage.* London, 1958. $100. New York (1958). First American edition. One of 26 signed. Issued without dustwrapper. $400. Trade. $60.

BEHAN, Brendan. *The Quare Fellow.* London (1956). Author's first book. $150. New York (1956). Cloth. One of 100. Issued without dustwrapper. $100. Wraps. $30.

BEHN, Mrs. Aphra. *LaMontre; or The Lover's Watch.* London, 1686. $200.

BEHN, Mrs. Aphra. *Poems Upon Several Occasions.* London, 1684. Author's first book. $600.

BEHRMAN, Samuel Nathaniel. *The Second Man.* New York, 1927. Author's first book, preceded by two collaborations. Stiff wraps in dustwrapper. $200. London, 1928. $100.

BELCAMP, Jeremy. *The History of New Hampshire.* Philadelphia, 1784; and Boston, 1791/92. 3 vols. $1,750.

BELCHER, Edward. *The Last of The Arctic Voyages; Being A Narrative Of The Expedition In H.M.S. Assistance . . . In Search Of Sir John Franklin, During The Years 1852–53–54. With Notes On The Natural History . . .* London, 1855. 2 vols. Volume I has 3 folding maps and 12 plates; volume II has 1 folding map and 22 plates; frontispiece in both volumes. $1,350.

BELCHER, Sir Edward. *Narrative of a Voyage Round the World . . . 1836–1842.* London, 1843. 19 plates, 3 maps in pocket. 2 vols. $1,000.

BELDAM, George W. *The World's Champion Golfers.* London (1924). 11 vols. Illustrated wraps. $400.

BELKNAP, Jeremy. See *The Foresters . . .*

BELL, Acton. *Agnes Grey.* London, 1947. (By Anne Brontë.) The third volume of *Wuthering Heights.* (1,000 copies.) $3,000.

BELL, Acton. *The Tenant of Wildfell Hall.* London, 1848. (By Ann Brontë, her only separate publication.) 3 vols. $35,000.

BELL, Clive. *Poems.* Hogarth Press. Richmond (London), 1921. Wraps. One of 350. $300.

BELL, Currer (editor). *Jane Eyre: An Autobiography.* London, 1847. (By Charlotte Brontë.) 3 vols. First issue, with 36-page catalogue at back of first volume, dated June and October, with half titles, and with a leaf advertising the *Calcutta Review* (VAB). (Not in Wise or Schwartz.) $18,000. London, 1848. Second edition. (Currer Bell as author instead of editor on title page.) $1,750.

BELL, Currer. *The Professor.* London, 1857. (By Charlotte Brontë.) 2 vols., plum-colored cloth. With 2 pages of ads at end of vol. 1 and 16 pages of ads at end of vol. 2, dated June 1857. $2,000. One-volume issue: London, 1857 (actually 1858). In a remainder binding, with 1858 ads, $1,000. New York, 1857. First American edition. $250.

BELL, Currer. *Shirley: A Tale.* London, 1849. (By Charlotte Brontë.) 3 vols., deep claret-colored cloth. With 16 pages of ads dated October 1849, at end of vol. 1. $3,000.

BELL, Currer. *Villette.* London, 1853. (By Charlotte Brontë.) 3 vols., olive-brown cloth. With 12 pages of ads dated January, 1853, in vol. 1 (VAB). $5,000.

BELL, Currer, Ellis, and Acton. *Poems.* London, 1846. (By Charlotte, Emily and Anne Brontë.) Dark green cloth. First issue, published by Aylott and Jones. $15,000. London, 1846 (actually 1848). Green cloth. Published by Smith, Elder & Co. Second issue, with 4-line errata slip. $1,500. Philadelphia, 1848. Boards. $600.

BELL, Ellis (and Acton). *Wuthering Heights.* London, 1847. 3 vols., claret-colored cloth (third volume titled *Agnes Grey*, by Acton Bell). (First two volumes by Emily Brontë, third by Anne Brontë.) (1,000 copies printed.) $75,000. New York, 1931. Illustrated by Clare Leighton. Cloth. One of 450 signed by the artist. $350.

BELL, Gertrude. *The Arab War.* Golden Cockerel Press. London, 1924. Half linen. One of 500. $350. One of 30. $500.

BELL, Horace. *Reminiscences of a Ranger.* Los Angeles, 1881. $300.

BELL, John. *Discourses on the Nature and Cure of Wounds.* Walpole, N.H., 1807. 2 plates. 2 vols. in 1. $200.

BELL, Solomon. *Tales of Travel West of the Mississippi.* Boston, 1830. (By William J. Snelling.) Map plates, boards and cloth, leather label. $600.

BELL, William A. *New Tracks in North America.* London, 1869. 2 vols. $750.

BELLAMY, Edward. See *Six to One: A Nantucket Idyl.*

BELLAMY, Edward. *Looking Backward, 2000–1887.* Boston, 1888. Pea green, orange-brown, or gray cloth. First issue, with printer's imprint of "J.J. Arakelyan" on copyright page. $350. Another (second) issue: gray wraps. $200. Limited Editions Club, New York, 1941. In slipcase. $125.

BELLOC, Hilaire. See B., H.

BELLOC, Hilaire. *Cautionary Tales for Children.* London (1908). Pictorial boards. $125.

BELLOC, Hilaire. *The Highway and Its Vehicles.* London, 1926. Illustrated. One of 1,250. $150.

BELLOC, Hilaire. *New Cautionary Tales.* London, 1930. One of 110 signed. $200.

BELLOC, Hilaire. *Verses and Sonnets.* London, 1896. Author's first book. $1,500.

BELLOW, Saul. *The Adventures of Augie March.* New York, 1953. First issue, with top edges orange. In first dustwrapper without reviews. $200. Second issue. $100.

BELLOW, Saul. *Dangling Man.* New York (1944). Author's first book. $600. London, 1946. $250.

BELLOW, Saul. *Henderson the Rain King.* New York, 1959. First issue, top edges yellow. $175. London (1959). $100.

BELLOW, Saul. *Herzog.* New York (1964). Stamped blue cloth. $75.

BELLOW, Saul. *The Victim.* New York (1947). $350. London (1948). First English edition. In dustwrapper. $150.

BELLOWS, George. *George W. Bellows: His Lithographs.* New York, 1927. In slipcase. $200.

BELOE, William. *Anecdotes of Literature and Scarce Books.* London, 1807–12. 6 vols. $250.

BELTRAMI, G. C. *A Pilgrimage in Europe and America.* London, 1928. 6 plates including folding map and plan, 2 vols. $600.

BEMELMANS, Ludwig. *Hansi.* New York, 1934. Author's first book. $350.

BEMELMANS, Ludwig. *Madeline.* New York, 1939. With 12 girls in illustration "They went home and broke their bread." $250. With 11 girls in illustration. $200.

BEMELMANS, Ludwig. *Small Beer.* New York, 1939. One of 75 with original colored illustrations in slipcase. $200.

BENAVIDES, Alonso de. *The Memorial of Fray Alonso de Benavides, 1630.* Chicago, 1916. Facsimile of Madrid edition of 1630. Boards. One of 300. $275.

BENCHLEY, Robert. *Of All Things.* New York, 1921. (Two states with and without ads at end, priority unknown.) Author's first book. $400. London, 1922. $250.

BENCHLEY, Robert. *20,000 Leagues Under the Sea, or David Copperfield.* New York (1928). $300.

BENDIRE, Charles. *Life Histories of North American Birds.* Washington, 1892–95. 19 color plates. 2 vols., folio, cloth. $300.

BENEDICT, Carl Peters. *A Tenderfoot Kid on Gyp Water.* Austin, 1943. Edited by J. Frank Dobie. One of 550. $250.

BENÉT, Stephen Vincent, and BENÉT, Rosemary. *A Book of Americans.* New York, 1933. One of 125 signed in slipcase. $125. Trade with publisher's monogram on copyright page. $40.

BENÉT, Stephen Vincent. *The Devil and Daniel Webster.* Weston, Vt. (1937). Illustrated by Harold Denison. One of 700 signed. In glassine dustwrapper and slipcase. $150. New York (1937). Trade. $50.

BENÉT, Stephen Vincent. *The Drug Shop; or Endymion in Edmonstoun.* (New Haven) 1917. Printed wraps. 100 copies only. $250.

BENÉT, Stephen Vincent. *Five Men and Pompey.* Boston, 1915. Wraps over boards. First state in purple wraps. $300. Second state, brown wraps. $75. (Note: Johnson says there were "a few copies" on handmade paper.) Author's first book.

BENÉT, Stephen Vincent. *John Brown's Body.* (Garden City, 1928.) One of 201 signed. In slipcase. $750. Trade: $100. Limited Editions Club, New York. 1948. John Steuart Curry illustrations. One of 1,500. In slipcase. $60.

BENÉT, Stephen Vincent, and BENET, Laura. *A Portrait and a Poem.* Paris, 1934. One of 50. $200.

BENÉT, William Rose. *Merchants from Cathay and Other Poems.* New York, 1913. Author's first book. $75.

BENJAMIN, Asher. *The American Builder's Companion . . .* Boston, 1827. Sixth edition. 67 plates. $1,250.

BENNETT, Arnold. See Bennett, E. A.

BENNETT, Arnold. *Anna of the Five Towns.* London, 1902. $125.

BENNETT, Arnold. *The Bright Island.* Golden Cockerel Press. London, 1924. Limp vellum. One of 200 signed. $150.

BENNETT, Arnold. *Elsie and the Child.* London, 1929. One of 100 signed. $600. One of 750. $250.

BENNETT, Arnold. *From the Log of the Velsa.* London, 1920. White cloth. One of 110 signed. $200.

BENNETT, Arnold. *Imperial Palace.* London (1930). 2 vols., vellum. One of 100 signed. $300. Trade. $75.

BENNETT, Arnold. *Journal 1929.* London, 1930. One of 75 signed. $300.

BENNETT, Arnold. *The Loot of Cities.* London (1904). Wraps. $400. Cloth. $300.

BENNETT, Arnold. *The Old Wives' Tale.* London, 1908. $400. London, 1927. 2 vols., parchment and cloth. Facsimile of the manuscript. One of 500 signed. $250. Limited Editions Club. New York, 1941. Illustrated by John Austen. 2 vols., in slipcase. $75.

BENNETT, E. A. *A Man from the North.* London, 1898. Red cloth, stamped in white. Arnold Bennett's first book. $300.

BENNETT, Emerson. *The Bandits of the Osage.* Cincinnati, 1847. Wraps. $600.

BENNETT, Emerson. *The Brigand* . . . New York, 1842. Author's first book. Wraps. $400.

BENNETT, Frederick D. *Narrative of a Whaling Voyage Around the World.* London, 1840. Frontispieces, folding map. 2 vols., cloth. $1,000.

BENNETT, George. *Gatherings of a Naturalist in Australasia.* London, 1860. 7 colored plates, one in sepia, numerous woodcuts. $500.

BENNETT, John. *Master Skylark: A Story of Shakespeare's Time.* New York, 1897. Illustrated by Reginald Birch, pictorial cloth. $125.

BENNETT, Melba Berry. *Robinson Jeffers and the Sea.* San Francisco, 1936. Grabhorn printing. Decorated boards, morocco spine. One of 300. $250.

BENSON, A. C. See Carr, Christopher.

BENSON, A. C. *William Laud, Archbishop of Canterbury.* London, 1887. (Second book, first under own name.) $125.

BENSON, Frank W. (illustrator). *Etchings and Drypoints.* Boston, 1919 (2), 1923 and 1929. 285 reproductions. Text by Adam E.M. Paff. 4 vols., each with frontispiece signed by Benson. In dustwrappers. $2,500.

BENSON, Henry C. *Life Among the Choctaw Indians.* Cincinnati, 1860. $300.

BENSON, John Howard. *The First Writing Book, An English Translation & Facsimile Text of Arrighi's Operina, The First Manual of the Chancery Hand.* New Haven, 1955. 300 copies signed by Benson. $125.

BENTLEY, E. C. See Clerihew, E.

BENTLEY, E. C. *Trent's Last Case.* London (1913). (*Woman In Black* in U.S.) $125.

BENTLEY, E. C. *The Woman in Black.* New York, 1913. (New title.) $100.

BENTLEY, Harry C., and LEONARD, Ruth S. *Bibliography of Works on Accounting by American Authors.* Boston, 1934–35. 2 vols. $225.

BENTON, Frank. *Cowboy Life on the Sidetrack.* Denver (1903). Illustrated. Pictorial cloth. $125.

BENTON, J.A. *California as She Was, as She Is, as She Is to Be.* Sacramento, 1850. 16 pp., wraps. $2,250.

BEPPO, A Venetian Story. London, 1818. (By George Gordon Noel, Lord Byron.) $300. Allen Press. (Kentfield) 1963. Oblong folio, loose as issued, with 35 plates. $650.

BERENSON, Bernard. *The Drawings of the Florentine Painters.* London, 1903. 180 full-page tinted plates. 2 vols., folio, half morocco. One of 355. $600. Chicago, 1938. 3 vols., small folio, boards, vellum spine. Amplified edition. $450.

BERENSON, Bernard. *A Sienese Painter of the Franciscan Legend.* London, 1909. 26 color illustrations. Boards and cloth. $250.

BERGER, Thomas. *Crazy in Berlin.* New York (1958). Author's first book. $175. London, 1963. $75.

BERGER. Thomas. *Little Big Man.* New York, 1964. $150. London, 1965. $100.

BERGMAN, Ray. *Trout.* Philadelphia, 1938. Flies in color. Full morocco. One of 149 signed. $1,250.

BERKELEY, Anthony. See *The Layton Court Mystery.*

BERLESE, Abbe. *Monography of the Genus Camellia, or an Essay on Its Culture, Description & Classification . . .* Boston, 1838. $250.

BERNARD. Auguste. *Geofroy Tory, Painter and Engraver.* (Cambridge, Mass.) 1909. Translated by George B. Ives. One of 370 designed by Bruce Rogers. $500.

BERNERS, Dame Juliana. *A Treatyse of Fysshynge with an Angle.* Ashendene Press. London (Chelsea), 1903. Woodcuts. Full green morocco. One of 25 on vellum. $3,500. Vellum. One of 150 on paper in slipcase. $600.

BERNSTEIN, Anne. *Three Blue Suits.* New York, 1933. One of 600 signed. In slip-case. Author's first book. $125.

BERQUIN-DUVALLON. See *Travels in Louisiana and the Floridas.*

BERRIGAN, Daniel. *Time Without Number.* New York, 1957. Author's first book. $40.

BERRY, W. Turner, and JOHNSON, A. F. *Catalogue of Specimens of Printing Types by English and Scottish Printers . . .* London, 1935. $250.

BERRY, Wendell. *Nathan Colter.* Boston, 1960. Author's first book. $250.

BERRY, Wendell. *November Twenty Six Nineteen Hundred Sixty Three.* New York (1964). Illustrated by Ben Shahn. Limited issue signed by Shahn and Berry. In slipcase. $200. Trade. $35.

BERRYMAN, John. *The Dispossessed.* New York (1948). $250.

BERRYMAN, John. *His Thought Made Pockets & The Plane Buckt.* Pawlet, Vt., 1958. Boards, leather spine. One of 26 lettered copies. $500. Wraps. One of 500 numbered copies. In printed envelope. $100.

BERRYMAN, John. *Homage to Mistress Bradstreet.* New York (1956). Illustrated by Ben Shahn. Boards. $150.

BERRYMAN, John. *Love and Fame.* New York, 1970. One of 250 signed. In slipcase. $250. Trade. $40.

BERRYMAN, John. *Poems.* Norfolk, Conn. (1942). New Directions. Printed blue wraps. Poet of the Month series. In dustwrapper. $100. Boards. One of 500 hardbound copies in dustwrapper. Author's first book. $300.

BERRYMAN, John. *Stephen Crane.* (New York, 1950.) $175.

BERT, Edmund. *Treatise of Hawks and Hawking.* London, 1891. Illustrated. Boards, leather spine. One of 100. $400.

BESSIE, Alvah C. *Dwell in the Wilderness.* New York (1935). Author's first book other than translations. $200.

BESTER, Alfred. *The Demolished Man.* Chicago (1953). Author's first book. Signed copies, $300. Unsigned copies, $200. London (1953). $75.

BETJEMAN, John. See O'Betjeman, Deirdre.

BETJEMAN, John. *Antiquarian Prejudice.* Hogarth Press. London, 1939. Wraps. $250.

BETJEMAN, John. *John Betjeman's Collected Poems.* London, 1958. Compiled by the Earl of Birkenhead. Scarlet leather. One of 100 signed. In slipcase. $350. Trade. $75.

BETJEMAN, John. *Continual Dew.* London (1937). $200.

BETJEMAN, John. *English Cities and Small Towns.* London, 1934. 8 color plates, 31 black-and-white illustrations. $250.

BETJEMAN, John. *A Few Late Chrysanthemums.* London, 1954. White buckram. One of 50 signed. $500. Trade. $100.

BETJEMAN, John. *Ghastly Good Taste.* London, 1933. Folding plate. Printed pink boards and cloth. First issue, with pages 119–20 not canceled. $300. London, 1970. Half leather. One of 200 signed in slipcase. $250.

BETJEMAN, John. *Mount Zion, or In Touch with the Infinite.* London (1931). Blue-and-gold pattern cover. $600. Striped paper cover. $500. Author's first book.

BETJEMAN, John. *New Bats in Old Belfries.* London, 1945. Red cloth, paper label. One of a few signed copies on special paper with colored title page. $500. Unsigned. $75.

BETJEMAN, John. *Old Lights for New Chancels.* London (1940). Portrait frontispiece. Wraps. In dustwrapper. $150.

BETJEMAN, John. *An Oxford University Chest.* London (1938). Photographs by Moholy-Nagy. Illustrations by Osbert Lancaster, etc. Marbled boards, cloth spine, gilt top. $250.

BETJEMAN, John. *Poems in the Porch.* Talbot Press. London, 1954. Pictorial wraps. $150.

BETJEMAN, John. *Selected Poems.* London, 1948. One of 18 signed. $600. Trade. $100.

BETJEMAN, John. *Summoned by Bells.* London, 1960. Illustrated. Full green leather, gilt top. One of 125 signed. $400. Trade. $50.

BETTS, Doris. *The Gentle Insurrection . . .* New York, 1954. Author's first book. $150.

BEVIER, Robert S. *History of the First and Second Missouri Confederate Brigades, 1861–1865.* St. Louis, 1879. $250.

BEWICK Gleanings. Newcastle, 1886. (By Thomas Bewick.) Edited by Julia Boyd. 53 plates. Green morocco. Large paper edition, signed. $500.

Bewick Memento With An Introduction By Robert Robinson . . . London (no-date, circa 1900). Includes 18 plates, 6 of which are first impressions from blocks by Bewick. $125.

BEWICK, Thomas. *A General History of Quadrupeds.* Newcastle, 1790. $750.

BEWICK, Thomas. *A History of British Birds.* Newcastle, 1797–1804. Woodcuts. 2 vols. $1,250.

BEY, Pilaff. *Venus in the Kitchen.* London (1952). Edited by Norman Douglas, with foreword by Graham Greene. Illustrated. $75.

BEYER, Edward. *Album of Virginia.* Richmond, 1856. 40 tinted lithograph views in folio plate volume and octavo text volume (seldom seen with text volume which adds little to the price). $7,500.

BEYNON, John. *The Secret People.* (By John Beynon Harris, his first book.) London (1935). $400.

BIANCO, Margery Williams. *Poor Cecco.* New York (or London) (1925). 7 mounted color plates by Arthur Rackham. First issue, with pictorial endpapers (VAB). In dustwrapper. Slipcase. $600. Second issue, plain end papers. $500. Deluxe signed issue: half-vellum and blue boards. One of 105 signed by the author. In dustwrapper. Slipcase. $6,000.

BIBLIOGRAPHICA, Papers on Books, Their History and Art. London, 1895–97. 12 parts bound in 3 volumes. $550.

BIBLIOGRAPHICAL and Retrospective Miscellany . . . , The. London, 1830. $225.

BIBLIOGRAPHY of Prohibited Books by Pisanus Fraxi. London and New York, 1962. 3 vols. Facsimile reprint of the 1877–85 first edition, limited to 1,000 copies of the Edition deLuxe. $125.

BIBLIOPHILE, The. A Magazine and Review for the Collector, Students and General Readers. London, 1809–1909. 3 vols. $225.

BIBLIOPHOBIA; Remarks on the Present Languid and Depressed State of Literature And The Book Trade . . . London, 1832. (Thomas Frognall Dibdin.) $225.

BIBLIOTHECA Americana, Catalogue of the John Carter Brown Library in Brown University ... Providence, various reprints. 7 volumes comprise a complete set. (An invaluable reference tool.) $450.

BICKHAM, George. *The Universal Penman; or, The Art of Writing Made Useful* ... London, 1743. Contains frontispiece and 212 engraved plates. $1,000.

BIDDLE, A. J. D. *Do or Die.* Washington, D.C., 1937. First edition stated. $50.

BIDDLE, Owen. *The Young Carpenter's Assistant.* Philadelphia, 1805. 46 plates. $400.

BIDWELL, George H. *The Printers' New Hand-Book. A Treatise On The Imposition Of Forms* ... New York (1875). $175.

BIDWELL, John. *A Journey to California* ... San Francisco, 1937. $150. (Note: Only one copy is known of the 1842 original of this narrative, and it is imperfect.)

BIERCE, Ambrose. See Bowers, Mrs. Dr. J. Milton; Grile, Dod; and Herman, William.

BIERCE, Ambrose. *Battle Sketches.* Shakespeare Head Press. London, 1930. Vellum. One of 350. In slipcase. $250.

BIERCE, Ambrose. *Black Beetles in Amber.* Western Authors Publishing Company. San Francisco, 1892. $400. Second issue. Printed gray wraps. Published by Johnson & Emigh. $200.

BIERCE, Ambrose. *Can Such Things Be?* New York (1893). Cloth. $200. Wraps. $500. Washington, 1903. New preface. $75.

BIERCE, Ambrose. *The Cynic's Word Book.* New York, 1906. Presumed first issue, without frontispiece (Johnson). $200. Frontispiece inserted. $175. (Reissued as *The Devil's Dictionary*.)

BIERCE, Ambrose. *Fantastic Fables.* New York, 1899. Tan-yellow cloth. With ads at back headed by "By Anna Fuller." $400.

BIERCE, Ambrose. *A Horseman in the Sky.* San Francisco, 1920. John Henry Nash printing. One of 400. $200.

BIERCE, Ambrose. *In the Midst of Life.* London, 1892. Blue Cloth (VAB). First English edition (of *Tales of Soldiers and Civilians*). $250. (Second issue in colored boards—VAB). New York, 1898. (Reprint of the *Tales* with 3 added stories.) $150.

BIERCE, Ambrose. *My Favorite Murder.* (New York, 1916.) Wraps. First separate edition. $150.

BIERCE, Ambrose. *The Shadow on the Dial and Other Essays.* San Francisco, 1909. Edited by S.O. Howes. Green buckram. $100.

BIERCE, Ambrose. *Shapes of Clay.* San Francisco, 1903. First issue, with transposed lines 5 and 6 on page 71. $400. Second issue, corrected. $250.

BIERCE, Ambrose. *Tales of Soldiers and Civilians.* E.L.G. Steele. San Francisco, 1891. $400. Some copies imprinted "Compliments of" on preliminary leaf and signed by Bierce—the so-called "limited" edition (Johnson). $1,000. Limited Editions Club, New York, 1943. Boards and leather. In slipcase. $125. (For first English edition see Bierce, *In the Midst of Life*.)

BIERCE, Ambrose. *Write It Right: A Little Blacklist of Literary Faults.* New York, 1909. First issue, 5¾ by 3 inches in size (VAB). (Johnson, 5½ inches tall.) (BAL, 6 by 3 7/8 inches.) $175. San Francisco, 1971. Grabhorn printing. One of 400. $125.

BIERCE, Ambrose, and DANZIGER, Gustav Adolph. (A pseudonym for Adolphe De Castro). *The Monk and the Hangman's Daughter.* Chicago, 1892. Illustrated by Theodore Hampe. Printed yellow wraps. $400. Gray cloth. $300. New York, 1907. New introduction by Bierce. $150. Limited Editions Club, New York, 1967. Slipcase. $60.

BIERSTADT, O. A. *The Library of Robert Hoe . . .* New York, 1805. 350 numbered copies. $300.

BIGELOW, Jacob. *American Medical Botany.* Boston, 1817–20. 60 color plates. Vols. 1–3 in 6 vols., or 6 parts. The first U.S. horticulture book printed in color. $3,000.

BIGELOW, Jacob. *A Discourse of Self-Limited Diseases.* Boston, 1835. Wraps. $500.

BIGGERS, Don H. *From Cattle Range to Cotton Patch.* Abilene, Tex. (1905). Illustrated. Stiff wraps. $4,500. Bandera, Tex., 1944. $125.

BIGGERS, Earl Derr. *Behind That Curtain.* Indianapolis (1928). With Bobbs-Merrill symbol on copyright page. $300.

BIGGERS, Earl Derr. *The Chinese Parrot.* Indianapolis (1926). $400.

BIGGERS, Earl Derr. *The House Without a Key.* Indianapolis (1925). First edition not stated, but bow and arrow monogram on copyright page. $500.

BIGGERS, Earl Derr. *Seven Keys to Baldpate.* Indianapolis (1913). Author's first book. $125.

BIGGS, William. *Narrative of William Biggs, While He Was a Prisoner with the Kickepoo Indians.* (No-place) June 1825. (Howes.) Copy in worn wraps at auction in 1988 for $6,000. Listed as (Edwardsville, Ill.), 1826.

Bindings of To-Morrow, A Record of the Work of the Guild of Women-Binders . . . London, 1902. $375.

BINYON, Laurence. *The Art of Botticelli.* London, 1913. Muirhead Bone etching, 23 color plates. Folio, cloth, vellum spine. One of 275. $250.

BINYON, Laurence. *The Court Painters of the Grand Moguls.* Oxford, 1921. 39 full-page plates, 9 colored. Cloth. $300.

BINYON, Laurence. *Dream-Come-True.* Eragny Press. London, 1905. Woodcut frontispiece. Boards. One of 175 on paper. $300. One of 10 on vellum. $1,250.

BINYON, Laurence. *The Engraved Designs of William Blake.* London, 1926. Plates. Half cloth and boards. One of 100 with an extra set of plates. $750. Without the extra plates. $350. Trade. $175.

BINYON, Laurence. *The Followers of William Blake.* London, 1925. 79 plates, 7 colored. Issued without dustwrapper. $200. One of 100. $500.

BINYON, Laurence. *Lyric Poems.* London, 1894. $250.

BINYON, Laurence. *Persephone.* London, 1890. Author's first book. (Newdigate Prize.) Wraps. $400.

BINYON, Laurence. *Poems.* Daniel Press. Oxford, 1895. Wraps. One of 200. $200.

BINYON, Laurence, and SEXTON, J. J. O'Brien. *Japanese Colour Prints.* London, 1923. 46 plates, some in color. $200. Pigskin. One of 100 signed, with an extra set of plates. $750.

BINYON, Laurence, WILKINSON, J.V.S., and GRAY, Basil. *Persian Miniature Painting.* London, 1923. Illustrated, including color plates. Folio, cloth. $750.

BIOGRAPHICAL Souvenir of the State of Texas. Chicago, 1889. Illustrated. Full leather. $650.

BIOGRAPHY of Joseph Lane. Washington, 1852. By Western. $1,000. Howes lists another copy same date but pseudonym "A Westerner" and notes authorship as being attributed to Robert Dale Owen.

BION and MOSCHOS. *Poems.* Bristol, 1794. (By Robert Lovell and Robert Southey, their first book.) $400.

BIRD, Bessie Calhoun. *Airs from the Wood Winds.* Philadelphia (1935). Author's only book. 25 signed, lettered copies, $200. 300 signed and numbered copies, $100.

BIRD, Robert Montgomery. See *The Adventures of Robin Day; Calavar; The Infidel; Nick-of-the-Woods; Peter Pilgrim; Sheppard Lee.*

Bird & Bull Commonplace Book, The. North Hills, 1971. 255 numbered copies. Envelope on inside rear cover with brass token inserted. Slipcase. $450.

Bird & Bull Number 13. North Hills, 1972. 140 numbered copies. First Bird & Bull publication to use paste paper for the cover. $475.

BIRKBECK, Morris. See *An Impartial Appeal.*

BIRKBECK, Morris. *An Appeal to the People of Illinois, on the Question of a Convention.* Shawneetown, 1823. 25 pp., wraps. (Howes B 465.) $1,250.

BIRKBECK, Morris. *Extracts from a Supplementary Letter from the Illinois.* New York, 1819. 29 pp., half leather. First edition. $1,250.

BIRKBECK, Morris. *Letters from Illinois.* Philadelphia, 1818. 2 folding maps. Boards and calf. $350.

BIRKBECK, Morris. *Notes on a Journey in America from the Coast of Virginia to the Territory of Illinois.* Philadelphia, 1817. $450. London, 1818. Map. $250.

BIRNEY, Earle. See Robertson, E.

BIRNEY, Earle. *David . . .* Toronto, 1942. (500 copies.) $200.

BISHOP, Elizabeth. *North & South.* Boston, 1946. Author's first book. $350.

BISHOP, J. Leander. *A History of American Manufactures from 1608 to 1860.* Philadelphia, 1864. 2 vols. $250.

BISHOP, John Peale. *Act of Darkness.* New York, 1935. Author's first and only novel. $150.

BISHOP, John Peale. *Green Fruit.* Boston, 1917. Boards and cloth. Author's first book. $200.

BISHOP, John Peale. *Minute Particulars.* New York, 1935. Wraps. One of 165 signed. In glassine dustwrapper. $350.

BISHOP, John Peale, and WILSON, Edmund. *The Undertaker's Garland.* New York, 1922. Wilson's first book and Bishop's second. In dustwrapper. $350. Boards. One of 50 for "bookseller friends." Issued without dustwrapper. $250.

BISHOP, Richard E. *Bishop's Birds: Etchings of Waterfowl and Upland Game Birds.* Philadelphia, 1936. 73 reproductions. One of 1,050. $250. One of 135 signed, with signed Bishop etching tipped in. $750.

BISHOP, Richard E. *Bishop's Wildfowl . . . Etchings and Oil Painting Reproductions.* (St. Paul) 1948. Text by E. Prestrud and R. Williams. Color plates. Full calf. $500.

BISHOP, Zealia. *The Curse of Yig.* Sauk City, Wis., 1953. Arkham House. $150.

Bishop's Specimens of Job Work for Printers, Being Suggestions for Setting Up . . . Oneonta, N.Y. (1890). $225.

BISLAND, Elizabeth (editor). *The Life and Letters of Lafcadio Hearn.* Boston, 1906. 2 vols. One of 200 with a page of an original manuscript by Hearn. $1,250. Trade. $100.

BITTING, Katherine. *Gastronomic Bibliography.* San Francisco, 1939. $225.

BLACK, E. L. *Why Do They Like it . . .* (Dijon, 1927.) Author's first book. Wraps. $250.

BLACKBIRD, Andrew J. *History of the Ottawa and Chippewa Indians of Michigan.* Ypsilanti, Mich., 1887. $250.

BLACKBURN, Henry. *Randolph Caldecott: A Personal Memoir of His Early Art Career.* London, 1886. $125.

BLACKBURN, Paul. *The Dissolving Fabric.* Divers Press. (Mallorca) 1955. Wraps. Author's first book. $225.

BLACKBURN, Paul. *Proensa.* (Majorca) 1953. Author's first book. (Translation.) $225.

BLACKER, William. *Art of Angling and Complete System of Fly-Making.* London, 1855. Illustrated, including frontispiece and 20 plates, usually hand colored. Not the first edition, but most common. $750.

BLACKMORE, Richard Doddridge. See Melanter.

BLACKMORE, Richard D. *Lorna Doone: A Romance of Exmoor.* London, 1869. 3 vols., blue cloth. $1,500.

BLACKMORE, William. *Colorado: Its Resources, Parks, and Prospects As a New Field for Emigration; With an Account of the Trenchara and Costilla Estates . . .* London, 1869. 3 folding maps and mounted frontispiece protrait of author. $650.

BLACKMUR, R. P. *Dirty Hands or The True Born Censor.* Cambridge, 1930. Wraps. $150.

BLACKMUR, R. P. *From Jordan's Delight.* New York, 1937. $100.

BLACKMUR, R. P. *The Good European & Other Poems.* Cummington, Mass., 1947. Cloth, paper label. Issued without dustwrapper. One of 40 signed. $250.

BLACKMUR, R. P. *T. S. Eliot.* (Cambridge, Mass.), 1928. Wraps. Off-print from *Hound & Horn.* Author's first book. $200.

BLACKSTONE, William. *Commentaries on the Laws of England.* Oxford, 1765–69. 4 vols., including 8-page "Supplement to First Edition." $15,000.

BLACKWELL, Elizabeth. *A Curious Herbal.* (No-place) 1739. 2 vols., containing 500 hand-colored engraved plates. $12,500.

BLACKWOOD, Algernon. *The Empty House and Other Ghost Stories.* London, 1906. Author's first book. $250. New York, 1917. $100.

BLACKWOOD, Algernon. *The Lost Valley.* New York, 1914. One of 500. $150.

BLADES, William. *The Enemies of Books.* London, 1880. Wraps. $100.

BLADES, William. *The Life and Typography of William Caxton...* London, 1861–63. 2 vols. $375.

BLAIR, Robert. *The Grave: A Poem.* London, 1808. Portrait and 12 etchings by Schiavonetti after designs by Blake. $1,000.

BLAKE, Alexander V. *The American Bookseller's Complete Reference Trade List, and Alphabetical Catalogue of Books Published in This Country . . .* Claremont, N.H., 1847. $450.

BLAKE, Nicholas. (C. Day-Lewis pseudonym.) *A Question of Proof.* London, 1935. (First book under this name.) $350.

BLAKE, W. O. *The History of Slavery and the Slave Trade.* Columbus, Ohio, 1857. $200.

BLAKE, William. *America, a Prophecy.* Lambeth, 1793. Rebound copy at auction in 1987. $160,000. Facsimile by William Muir. Edmonton, Canada, 1887. Wraps. One of 50. $750.

BLAKE, William. *Illustrations of the Book of Job.* London, 1825. Title page and 21 other plates engraved by Blake. Folio. With plate no. 1 misdated 1828. (In various bindings—cloth folders, wraps, morocco, etc.) $55,000 at auction in 1990 (a copy on India paper). Rebound. $17,500. London, 1902. Facsimile. Wraps. $350. New York, 1935. 6 parts, folio, wraps. One of 200. Slipcase. $1,500.

BLAKE, William. *The Note-Book of William Blake Called the Rossetti Manuscript.* London, 1935. Nonesuch Press. Edited by Geoffrey Keynes. 120 pp. in facsimile. Buckram. One of 650. In dustwrapper. $400.

BLAKE, William. *Pencil Drawings.* London, 1927. Nonesuch Press. Edited by Geoffrey Keynes. 82 facsimile plates. Half buckram. One of 1,550. In dustwrapper. $350. Second Series: London, 1956. One of 1,440. In dustwrapper. $250.

BLAKE, William. *Songs of Innocence.* London, 1789. Bound copy at auction in 1989. $300,000.

BLAKE, William. *Songs of Innocence and of Experience.* London, 1955. Trianon Press. Facsimile reproduction in collotype of the 54 plates from the 1794 original. Full morocco. One of 526 in slipcase. $750.

BLAKE, William. *The Writings of William Blake.* Nonesuch Press. London, 1925. Edited by Geoffrey Keynes. 3 vols., half-vellum and marbled boards. One of 1,500. In slipcase. $600. Thin paper issue: 3 vols. in 1, morocco or limp vellum. One of 75. $1,500.

BLAKEY, Dorothy. *Minerva Press, 1790–1820.* London, 1939. $150.

BLANCHARD, Rufus (publisher). *Citizen's Guide for the City of Chicago; Companion to Blanchard's Map of Chicago.* Chicago (1868). Printed stiff wraps, with the folding map bound in. $600.

BLANCK, Jacob. *Peter Parley to Penrod.* New York, 1938. One of 500. $150. New York, 1956. Second edition. Cambridge, Mass., 1961. $75.

BLAND, David. *A History of Book Illustration.* Cleveland (1958). Illustrated. $100.

BLEDSOE, A. J. *History of Del Norte County, California.* Eureka, Calif., 1881. Wraps. $2,500. (Howes notes that with one possible exception this is the rarest California local history.)

BLEDSOE, A. J. *Indian Wars of the Northwest.* San Francisco, 1885. Leather. $400. Cloth. $300.

BLEW, William C. A. *A History of Steeple-Chasing.* London, 1901. 28 illustrations, 12 hand-colored plates. $300.

BLIGH, William. *A Narrative of the Mutiny on Board His Majesty's Ship Bounty . . .* London, 1790. With 3 maps (2 folding), and a boat plan. $6,000.

BLIGH, William. *A Voyage to the South Sea . . .* London, 1792. With frontispiece and 6 maps/plans (4 folding), and 1 plate showing breadfruit. $3,000. Limited Editions Club. Adelaide, 1975. One of 2,000 copies. In slipcase. $150.

BLISS, Edward. *A Brief History of the New Gold Regions of Colorado Territory.* Map. New York, 1864. 30 pp., wraps. $2,500.

BLISS, William R. *Paradise in the Pacific; A Book of Travel, Adventure and Facts in the Sandwich Islands.* New York, 1873. Mounted photographic frontis. $500.

BLOCH, Robert. *The Eighth Stage of Fandom . . .* Chicago, 1962. First edition stated. One of 125 signed numbered copies. $400. One of 200 hardbound. $250. One of 400 in wraps. $50.

BLOCH, Robert. *The Opener of the Way.* Sauk City, Wis., 1945. $200.

BLOCH, Robert. *Psycho.* New York, 1959. $350.

BLOCH, Robert. *Sea Kissed.* (London, 1945.) Author's first book. Wraps. First issue, 39 pp., "Printed in Great Britain" on p. 39. $300. Second issue, 36 pp., "Printed in Eire" on p. 36. $250.

BLODGET, Lorin. *Climatology of the United States, and of the Temperate Latitudes of the North American Continent* . . . Philadelphia, 1857. Folding map. $150.

BLODGETT, Henry W. *Autobiography.* Waukegan, Ill., 1906. $125.

BLOME, Richard. *Hawking or Faulconry.* London, 1929. Cresset Press. One of 650. $300.

BLOWE, Daniel. *A Geographical, Commercial, and Agricultural View of the United States of America.* Liverpool (1820). Portrait, 2 maps, 4 plans. Calf. $300.

BLUE Grotto (The) and Its Literature. London, 1904. (By Norman Douglas.) 18 pp., printed red wraps. $200.

BLUNDELL, John W. F. *The Muscles and Their Story.* London, 1864. $100.

BLUNDEN, Edmund. *Dead Letters.* London, 1923. Decorated wraps, paper label. Pelican Press. One of 50. $150.

BLUNDEN, Edmund. *Japanese Garland.* Beaumont Press. London, 1928. 6 color plates. Boards and vellum. One of 80 signed. $250. Also, one of 310 signed. $125.

BLUNDEN, Edmund. *Masks of Time.* Beaumont Press. London, 1925. Illustrated by Randolph Schwabs. Boards and vellum. One of 80 on vellum, signed. $200. One of 310 on paper in plain dustwrapper. $100.

BLUNDEN, Edmund. *Pastorals: A Book of Verses.* London (1916). Wraps. $175.

BLUNDEN, E(dmund). C. *Poems 1913 and 1914.* (Horsham, 1914.) Author's first book. Wraps. (100 copies.) $1,200.

BLUNDEN, Edmund. *Poems, 1914–1930.* London, 1930. Buckram. Issued without dustwrapper. One of 200 signed. $175.

BLUNDEN, Edmund. *Retreat: New Sonnets and Poems.* (London, 1928.) One of 112 signed. $250. Garden City. $100.

BLUNDEN, Edmund. *Undertones of War.* London, 1928. $150.

BLUNT, Edmund M. *Traveller's Guide to and Through the State of Ohio, with Sailing Directions for Lake Erie.* New York, 1832. 16 pp. Leather. $1,000. New York, 1833. Folding map in color. 28 pp., leather. $600.

BLUNT, Wilfrid Scawen. See Proteus.

BLUNT, Wilfrid Scawen. *The Celebrated Romance of the Stealing of the Mare.* Gregynog Press. Newtown, Wales, 1930. Translated from the Arabic by Lady Anne Blunt and done into verse by W.S.B. Boards and leather. One of 275. $750. One of 25 (of this edition) especially bound in morocco. $2,000.

BLUNT, Wilfrid Scawen. *The Love-Lyrics and Songs of Proteus . . . with the Love-Sonnets.* Kelmscott Press. London, 1892. Woodcut borders and initials. Stiff vellum with ties. One of 300. $750.

BLY, Robert. *The Lion's Tail and Eyes.* Madison, 1962. (Author's first book with J. Wright and W. Duffy.) $125.

BLY, Robert. *The Silence in the Snowy Fields.* Middletown, 1962. Author's first solely authored book. Cloth. $150. Wraps. $50.

BOCCACCIO, Giovanni. *The Decameron.* London, 1620. 2 vols. $4,000. Ashendene Press. London, 1920. Folio, boards, and linen. One of 105 on paper. $2,000. One of 6 on vellum. $3,000. Limited Editions Club, New York, 1930. Translated by Frances Winwar. 2 vols. In slipcase. $125. Another Limited Editions Club, New York, 1940. Woodcuts by Fritz Kredel. One of 530. In slipcase. $250.

BOCCACCIO, Giovanni. *Life of Dante.* (Boston, 1904.) Translated by Philip Henry Wicksteed. Woodcut title portrait. Boards and vellum. One of 325 designed by Bruce Rogers in slipcase. $300.

BODE, Winston. *A Portrait of Pancho.* Austin, Tex., 1965. Illustrated. Full leather. One of 150 signed. In slipcase. $350. Trade. $50.

BODENHEIM, Maxwell. See Hecht, Ben, and Bodenheim, Maxwell.

BODENHEIM, Maxwell. *Minna and Myself.* New York, 1918. First issue, with "Master-Posner" for "Master-Poisoner" on page 67. Author's first book. $75.

BODENHEIM, Maxwell. *The Sardonic Arm.* Chicago, 1923. Issued without dust-wrapper. One of 575. $150.

BODKIN, M. McDonald. *Paul Beck: The Rule of Thumb Detective.* London, 1898. $500.

BODKIN, M. McDonald. *White Magic.* London, 1897. Author's first book. $150.

BOGAN, Louise. *Body of This Death: Poems.* New York, 1923. Author's first book. $600.

BOGAN, Louise. *Dark Summer.* New York, 1929. $350.

BOGAN, Louise. *The Sleeping Fury.* New York, 1937. $150.

BOGGS, Mae Helene Bacon (compiler). *My Playhouse Was a Concord Coach.* (Oakland, 1942.) Maps, illustrations. $350.

BOLDREWOOD [sic] Rolf (Bolderwood). *Robbery Under Arms: A Story of Life and Adventure in the Bush and in the Goldfields of Australia.* London, 1888. (By Thomas A. Browne.) Decorated green cloth. $1,750.

BOLLER, Henry A. *Among the Indians.* Philadelphia, 1868. Folding map, cloth, paper label. $1,000.

BOLTON, Arthur T. *The Architecture of Robert & James Adam.* London, 1922. 2 vols. $450.

BOLTON, George G. *A Specialist in Crime.* London, 1904. (Author's only book.) $150.

BOLTON, Herbert Eugene. *Anza's California Expeditions.* Berkeley, 1930. Folding map, illustrations. 5 vols. $500.

BOLTON, Herbert Eugene. *Athanase de Mezieres and the Louisiana-Texas Frontier.* Cleveland, 1914. Map, 2 facsimiles. 2 vols. $450.

BOLTON, Herbert Eugene. *The Rim of Christendom.* New York, 1936. 12 plates, 3 facsimiles. $150.

BOLTON, Herbert Eugene (translator). *Font's Complete Diary of the Second Anza Expedition.* Berkeley, 1931. Maps, plates, facsimiles. $150.

BOLTON, Theodore. *American Book Illustrators, Bibliographical Check Lists of 123 Artists.* New York, 1938. $250.

BOND, J. Wesley. *Minnesota and Its Resources.* Chicago, 1856. Folding map, 6 plates. Cloth. $100.

BOND, Nelson. *Exiles of Time.* Philadelphia, 1949. $75. One of 112 signed. In slipcase. $150.

BOND, Nelson. *Mr. Mergenthwirker's Lobblies and Other Fantastic Tales.* New York (1946). Author's first book. $75.

BOND, Nelson. *Nightmares and Daydreams.* Sauk City, Wis. (1968). $75.

BOND, Nelson. *The Thirty-first of February.* New York (1949). $100. One of 112 signed. In slipcase. $200.

BONFILS, Winifred B. *The Life and Personality of Phoebe Apperson Hearst.* San Francisco, 1928. John Henry Nash printing. Vellum. One of 1,000. In original tan flannel bag. $300.

BONNELL, George W. *Topographical Description of Texas.* Austin, 1840. Boards. $5,000.

BONNER, T. D. *The Life and Adventures of James P. Beckwourth, Mountaineer, Scout and Pioneer, . . .* New York, 1856. Frontispiece and plates. $350.

BONNEY, Edward. *Banditti of the Prairies; or, The Murderer's Doom!* Chicago, 1850. Pictorial wraps. With imprint "Chicago, W.W. Dannenhauer 1850" on front cover. $12,500. Philadelphia (1855). $400. Philadelphia, 1856. Third edition. $400. Chicago, 1856. $4,000. Chicago, 1858. 13 plates. Wraps. $2,500.

BONTEMPS, Arna. *God Sends Sunday.* New York, 1931. Author's first book. $250.

Book Collector, The. London, 1947–84. Complete run from vol. I, no.1 to volume 33, no.1 and *The Book Handbook,* 9 issues bound in 1 volume. Wraps. $1,250.

Book Collector's Packet, The. March 1932 through December 1939. 40 issues in 39 numbers. $200.

Book-Lore, A Magazine Devoted To Old Time Literature. London, 1885–87. 6 vols. $250.

BOOK of Commandments (A), for the Government of the Church of Christ. Zion (Independence, Mo.), 1833. Boards. (By Joseph Smith, Jr.) $30,000 and up.

BOOK of Common Prayer (The). Merrymount Press. New York (Boston), 1928. One of 500. $1,250.

BOOK of Job (The). Limited Editions Club, New York, 1946. Illustrated in color by Arthur Szyk. In slipcase. $300.

BOOK of Jonah (The). Waltham Saint Lawrence, 1926. Golden Cockerel Press. Illustrated by David Jones. Buckram. One of 175. In dustwrapper. $1,500.

BOOK of the Law of the Lord (The). Saint James, A.R.I. (Beaver Island, Lake Michigan, 1851). (By James Jesse Strang.) $25,000. (3 copies known.) (Beaver Island, 1856.) Second issue, original sheets, lacking title page (some supplied, and with preface, in modern type, circa 1920). $5,000. For a later edition, see James J. Strang entry.

BOOK of the Poets' Club (The). London, 1909. Orange wraps. (Includes first printings of four Ezra Pound poems.) $500.

BOOK of Princeton Verse 1916 (A). Princeton, 1916. Edited by Alfred Noyes. $75. (Includes poems by Edmund Wilson, John Peale Bishop, and others.)

BOOK of Princeton Verse II (A). Princeton (1919). (First book appearance of three poems by F. Scott Fitzgerald.) In dustwrapper. $400. Without dustwrapper. $100.

BOOK of Psalms (The). Limited Editions Club, New York, 1961. Illustrated by Valenti Angelo. One of 1,500 in slipcase. $150.

BOOK of Ruth (The). Nonesuch Press. London, 1923. One of 250. In slipcase. $350. Limited Editions Club, New York, 1947. Introduction by Mary Ellen Chase. Illustrated by Arthur Szyk. One of 1,950 in slipcase. $250.

BOOK of Vassar Verse (A). (Poughkeepsie, 1916.) (With 3 poems by Edna St. Vincent Millay.) $100.

BOOTH, Stephen. *The Book Called Holinshed's Chronicles.* San Francisco, 1968. Woodcut reproductions and original leaf from the 1587 edition. Decorated boards and cloth. One of 500. $200.

BORDEN, Gail, Jr. *Letters of. . . to Dr. Ashbel Smith.* Galveston, 1850. Wraps. $2,000.

BORDEN, Spencer. *The Arab Horse.* New York, 1906. $300.

BORDER Beagles: A Tale of Mississippi. Philadelphia, 1840. 2 vols., boards and cloth, paper labels. (By William Gilmore Simms.) $300.

BORGES, Jorge Luis. *The Congress.* London, 1974. Translated by Norman Thomas di Giovanni and Borges. Illustrated by Hugo Manning. Cloth. One of 50 signed. $300.

BORGES, Jorge Luis. *Deathwatch on the Southside.* Cambridge (1968). Wraps. One of 150 signed. $300.

BORNEMAN, Henry S. *Pennsylvania German Illuminated Manuscripts.* Norristown, Pa., 1937. 38 colored reproductions. Oblong folio, cloth. $250.

BORROW, George. See *Celebrated Trials.*

BORROW, George. *The Bible in Spain.* London, 1843. 3 vols., red cloth, paper labels. $350.

BORROW, George. *Faustus: His Life, Death and Descent Into Hell.* London, 1922. (Translated by Borrow.) $750.

BORROW, George. *Lavengro; the Scholar—the Gypsy—the Priest.* London, 1851. 3 vols., blue cloth, paper labels. $400. Limited Editions Club, New York, 1936. 2 vols., in slipcase. $100.

BORROW, George. *The Romany Rye.* London, 1875. 2 vols. $200.

BORROW, George. *Wild Wales: Its People, Language, and Scenery.* London, 1862. 3 vols., blue cloth, paper labels. $500.

BOSCANA, Father Geronimo. *Chinigchinich.* Santa Ana, 1933. Translated by Alfred Robinson. Color plates, maps. Folio, boards, and cloth. 1933. $300.

BOSQUI, Edward. *Memoirs.* Grabhorn Press. (Oakland), 1952. One of 350. $125.

BOSSCHERE, Jean de. *12 Occupations.* London, 1916. Decorated wraps. (Translated anonymously by Ezra Pound.) $750.

BOSSERT, Helmuth T. *Peasant Art in Europe.* London, 1927. 130 full-color plates and 32 plates in black and white. Folio, cloth. First English edition. (Originally Berlin, 1926.) $150. New York, 1927. $125.

BOSWELL, James. *An Account of Corsica* . . . Glasgow, 1768. Map. $3,000.

BOSWELL, James. *Boswell for the Defence.* London, 1960. Edited by W.K. Wimsatt and Frederick A. Pottle. Illustrated, folding maps. Blue buckram, gilt, calf spine, leather label. Yale deluxe edition. One of 350 in slipcase. $200.

BOSWELL, James. *Boswell in Holland, 1763-1764.* London, 1962. Edited by Frederick A. Pottle. Illustrated, folding map. Blue buckram and calf. Yale deluxe edition. One of 1,050 in slipcase. $150.

BOSWELL, James. *Boswell in Search of a Wife.* London, 1957. Edited by F. Brady and Frederick A. Pottle. Blue buckram and calf. Yale deluxe edition. One of 400 in slipcase. $150.

BOSWELL, James. *Boswell on the Grand Tour: Germany and Switzerland.* London, 1953. Edited by Frederick A. Pottle. Illustrated, folding map. Blue buckram and calf. London, 1953. Yale deluxe edition. One of 1,000. In slipcase. $125.

BOSWELL, James. *Boswell on the Grand Tour: Italy, Corsica, and France.* London, 1955. Edited by F. Brady and Frederick A. Pottle. Illustrated, folding maps. Blue buckram and calf. Yale deluxe edition. One of 400 in slipcase. $175.

BOSWELL, James. *Journal of a Tour to the Hebrides with Samuel Johnson, LL.D.* London, 1785. $1,000. New York, 1936. First complete edition. One of 816 in slipcase. $250.

BOSWELL, James. *The Life of Samuel Johnson.* London, 1791. 2 vols., with the "gve" reading on page 135 of vol. 1. $7,500. With "give" $2,500. Boston, 1807. First American edition. $750. Limited Editions Club, New York, 1938. 3 vols. in slipcase. $175.

BOSWORTH, Newton. *Hochelaga Depicta: The Early History and Present State of the City and Island of Montreal.* Montreal, 1839. Illustrated, including 2 folding maps. $400.

BOUCHER, Anthony. *The Case of the Seven of Calvary.* New York, 1937. Author's first book. $250.

BOUCHETTE, Joseph. *The British Dominions in North America; Or A Topographical and Statistical Description of the Provinces of Lower and Upper Canada, New Brunswich, Nova Scotia* . . . London, 1831 or 1832. 2 vol. 31 plates and maps. $1,250.

BOUCHETTE, Joseph. *A Topographical Description of the Province of Lower Canada, with Remarks Upon Upper Canada.* London, 1815. First English edition with 2 folding maps and 20(?) plates. $1,000. Much expanded second edition in 2 volumes. $1,000.

BOUGAINVILLE, Louis Antoine. *A Voyage Around the World, Performed by Order of His Most Christian Majesty, in the Years 1766, 1767, 1768, And 1769.* London, 1772. With 1 double-page plate and 5 folding maps. $3,750.

BOUGARD, R. *The Little Sea Torch.* London, 1801. First English edition, with 20 hand-colored plates and 24 hand-colored charts. $2,000.

BOULLE, Pierre. *The Bridge Over the River Kwai.* London, 1954. (First translation in English.) $150. New York, 1954. $75.

BOURDILLON, Francis W. *Among the Flowers, and Other Poems.* London, 1878. Decorated white cloth. Author's first book. $125.

BOURJAILY, Vance. *The End of My Life.* New York, 1947. Author's first book. $75.

BOURKE, John G. *An Apache Campaign in the Sierra Madre.* New York, 1886. Illustrated. Printed wraps or pictorial cloth. $500.

BOURKE, John G. *Mackenzie's Last Fight with the Cheyennes.* Governor's Island, N.Y., 1890. Portrait. 44 pp., printed wraps. $1,000.

BOURKE, John G. *On the Border with Crook.* New York, 1891. Frontispiece portrait, other plates. $300.

BOURKE, John G. *Scatologic Rites of All Nations.* Washington, 1891. $300.

BOURKE, John G. *The Snake-Dance of the Moquis of Arizona.* New York, 1884. 33 plates, some in color. Pictorial cloth. $350. London, 1884. Half calf. First English edition. $300.

BOURKE-WHITE, Margaret. *Eyes on Russia.* New York, 1931. Author's first book. $300.

BOURNE, Randolph. *The History of a Literary Radical.* New York, 1920. Edited by Van Wyck Brooks. In dustwrapper. $125.

BOURNE, Randolph. *Youth and Life.* Boston, 1913. Author's first book. $300.

BOVA, Ben. *Star Conquerors.* Philadelphia (1959). Author's first book. $175.

BOWDITCH, Nathaniel. *The New American Practical Navigator.* Newburyport, Mass., 1802. Folding frontispiece map, plates. $4,500.

BOWEN, Abel. *The Naval Monument.* Boston, 1816. 25 woodcuts. $250.

BOWEN, Elizabeth. *Ann Lee's and Other Stories.* London, 1926. $400. New York, 1927. $300.

BOWEN, Elizabeth. *The Death of the Heart.* London, 1938. $150.

BOWEN, Elizabeth. *Encounters.* London, 1923. Author's first book. In dustwrapper. $1,000.

BOWEN, Elizabeth. *Seven Winters.* Cuala Press. Dublin, 1942. Boards and linen. One of 450 in tissue dustwrapper. $200.

BOWER, B. M. *Chip of the Flying U.* New York: Street & Smith (1906). (By Bertha Muzzy Sinclair.) In dustwrapper. $250. Without dustwrapper. $50. (G. W. Dillingham Company edition is later.)

BOWER, B. M. *Happy Family.* New York (1910). (By Bertha Muzzy Sinclair.) In dustwrapper. $200. Without dustwrapper. $40.

BOWER, B. M. *Lure Of The Dim Trails.* New York (1907). (By Bertha Muzzy Sinclair). In dustwrapper. $200. Without dustwrapper. $40.

BOWERS, Mrs. Dr. J. Milton. *The Dance of Life: An Answer to the "Dance of Death."* San Francisco, 1877. Red or green cloth. (By Ambrose Bierce?) $150.

BOWLES, Jane. *In the Summer House.* New York (1954). $175.

BOWLES, Jane. *Plain Pleasures.* London (1966). $125.

BOWLES, Jane. *Two Serious Ladies.* New York, 1943. Author's first book. $600. London, 1965. $75.

BOWLES, Paul. *The Delicate Prey and Other Stories.* (New York, 1950.) $150.

BOWLES, Paul. *The Sheltering Sky.* London (1949). $350. New York (1949). $250.

BOWLES, Paul. *Two Poems.* (New York, 1934.) Wraps. Author's first book. $750.

BOWLES, Paul. *Yallah.* Zurich, 1956. Illustrated with photos. $250. New York, 1957. $175.

BOWYER, William. *The Origin of Printing in Two Essays . . .* London, 1776. $250.

BOX, Capt. Michael James. *Capt. James Box's Adventures and Explorations in New and Old Mexico.* New York, 1861. $1,250. New York, 1869. Second issue (original sheets with cancel title leaf). $600.

BOX, Edgar. *Death Before Bedtime.* New York, 1953. (By Gore Vidal.) $250.

BOX, Edgar. *Death in the Fifth Position.* New York, 1952. (By Gore Vidal.) $300.

BOX, Edgar. *Death Likes It Hot.* New York, 1954. (By Gore Vidal.) $250.

BOYD, James. *Bitter Creek.* New York, 1939. $75.

BOYD, James. *Drums.* New York-London, 1925. Author's first book. $250. New York (1928). Illustrated by N.C. Wyeth. One of 525 signed by author and artist. In slipcase. $500. Trade. $150.

BOYD, Nancy, *Distressing Dialogues.* New York (1924). (By Edna St. Vincent Millay.) First edition stated. $300.

BOYD, William. *A Good Man in Africa.* London, 1981. Author's first book. $175. New York, 1982. $60.

BOYLE, Jack. *Boston Blackie.* New York (1919). Author's first book. In dustwrapper. $750. Without dustwrapper. $125.

BOYLE, Kay. *The Crazy Hunter.* New York (1940). $125.

BOYLE, Kay. *The First Lover and Other Stories.* New York (1933). $175.

BOYLE, Kay. *Gentlemen, I Address You Privately.* New York, 1933. $150.

BOYLE, Kay. *Monday Night.* New York (1938). $125.

BOYLE, Kay. *Plagued by the Nightingale.* New York, 1931. Her first novel. $200. London, 1931. $125.

BOYLE, Kay. *A Statement.* (New York, 1932.) Drawing by Max Weber. Wraps. One of 175 signed. $250.

BOYLE, Kay. *Short Stories.* Black Sun Press. Paris, 1929. Printed wraps in gold or silver tied protective boards. One of 15 signed, numbered copies on Japan paper. $1,000. One of 150 on Van Gelder paper. In tissue dustwrapper. Slipcase. $350. One of 20 on Arches paper, for France. $1,000. Author's first book. (See following entry.)

BOYLE, Kay. *Wedding Day and Other Stories.* New York (1930). Decorated boards, cloth spine. (The author's first book, retitled as shown, also variant spine title, "Short/Stories.") Priority unknown. $150.

BOYLE, Kay. *The White Horses of Vienna.* New York (1936). $125.

BOYLE, T. Coraghessan. *Descent of Man.* Boston (1979). Author's first book. $125. London, 1980. $75.

BOYLES, Kate and Virgil. *Homesteaders.* Chicago, 1909. In dustwrapper. $250. Without dustwrapper. $50.

BOYLES, Kate and Virgil. *Lansford of the Three Bars.* Chicago, 1907. In dustwrapper. $250. Without dustwrapper. $50.

"BOZ." See Dickens, Charles. See also *Sketches by "Boz."*

"BOZ." *Master Humphrey's Clock.* London, 1840–41. (By Charles Dickens.) 88 weekly parts, white wraps. $2,000. Second edition: 20 monthly parts in 19, green wraps. $1,250. (For first book edition, see under Dickens's name.)

"BOZ." *Oliver Twist; or, The Parish Boy's Progress.* London, 1838. (By Charles Dickens.) Illustrated by George Cruikshank. 3 vols., in original reddish brown cloth. First issue, with "Rose Maylie and Oliver" plate in vol. 3 showing them at fireside. $4,500. Second issue showing them at church. $3,000. (For later editions see author entries under *Oliver Twist* and *The Adventures of Oliver Twist.*)

BRACKENRIDGE, H. H. See *A Poem On the Rising Glory . . .* and *Strictures on a Voyage to South America, etc.*

BRACKENRIDGE, H. M. *A Eulogy, on the Lives and Characters of John Adams & Thomas Jefferson.* Pensacola, Fla., 1826. 18 pp., plain wraps. (This is just an unusual imprint of an often-reprinted item.) $500.

BRACKENRIDGE, H. M. *Journal of a Voyage up the Missouri.* Baltimore, 1815. Printed boards. First edition (actually second appearance of the journal, which first appeared in author's *Views of Louisiana,* which see). $500. Baltimore, 1816 (cover date 1815). Boards. Second edition. $200.

BRACKENRIDGE, H. M. *Views of Louisiana; Together with a Journal of a Voyage up the Missouri River, in 1814.* Pittsburgh, 1814. $1,000. Baltimore, 1817. (Revised.) $300.

BRACKENRIDGE, Hugh Henry. *Gazette Publications.* Carlisle, Pa., 1806. Leather. $400.

BRADBURY, John. *Travels in the Interior of America.* Liverpool, 1817. With errata slip. $1,750. London, 1819. Folding map. Second edition. $1,250.

BRADBURY, Ray. *The Anthem Sprinters.* New York, 1963. $275.

BRADBURY, Ray. *Dandelion Wine.* Garden City, 1957. $175. London, 1957. $150.

BRADBURY, Ray. *Dark Carnival.* Sauk City, Wis., 1947. Author's first book. $750. London (1948). $300.

BRADBURY, Ray. *Fahrenheit 451.* New York (1953). (About 50 author's copies were bound in cloth.) $3,000. Asbestos boards. One of 200 signed. Issued without dustwrapper. $3,500. Trade. In cloth. $500. London, 1954. $250. Simultaneous issue by Ballantine in wraps. (Actually true first.) $40.

BRADBURY, Ray. *The Golden Apples of the Sun.* Garden City, 1953. $250. London, 1953. $175.

BRADBURY, Ray. *The Illustrated Man.* Garden City, 1951. $250. London, 1952. $200.

BRADBURY, Ray. *The Machineries of Joy.* New York, 1964. $125. London, 1964. $100.

BRADBURY, Ray. *The Martian Chronicles.* Garden City, 1950. First state in green binding. $600. Second state in blue binding. $500. New York, 1974. Limited Editions Club. 2,000 numbered copies signed by author and illustrator. $250.

BRADBURY, Ray. *A Medicine for Melancholy.* Garden City, 1959. $150.

BRADBURY, Ray. *The October Country.* New York (1955). 50 copies bound for author in full red cloth with gold stamping. $2,000. Trade. First state has Ballantine logo on spine inverted. $350. Second state with logo corrected. $350. London, 1956. $175.

BRADBURY, Ray. *The Silver Locusts.* London, 1951. First British edition (of *The Martian Chronicles*). $250.

BRADBURY, Ray. *Switch on the Night.* (New York, 1955.) $300. Later printings have pictorial covers without dustwrapper. (London) 1955. $200.

BRADBY, Anne. *Shakespeare Criticism 1919–1935.* London, 1936. Author's first book. $100.

BRADDON, Mary Elizabeth. *Garibaldi* . . . London, 1861. Author's first book. $400.

BRADDON, Mary Elizabeth. *Lady Audley's Secret.* London, 1862. (3 vols.) $400.

BRADFORD, Gamaliel. *Daughters of Eve.* Boston (1930). Illustrated. Cloth. One of 200 signed. $125.

BRADFORD, Gamaliel. *Types of American Character.* New York, 1895. Author's first book. $100.

BRADFORD, Roark. *Ol' Man Adam and His Chillun.* New York, 1928. Author's first book. $75.

BRADFORD, William. *The Arctic Regions.* (London, 1873.) 129 albumen prints. Folio, morocco. $10,000.

BRADLEY, David. *South Street.* New York, 1975. Author's first book. $150.

BRADLEY, Edward. *College Life.* Oxford, 1849–50. Author's first book. (6 parts in 5). $600.

BRADLEY, James. *The Confederate Mail Carrier.* Mexico, Mo., 1894. 15 plates. $350.

BRADLEY, Joshua. *Accounts of Religious Revivals in Many Parts of the United States From 1815 to 1818.* Albany, 1819. $125.

BRADLEY, Van Allen. *The Book Collector's Handbook Of Values.* New York (1982). The fourth, revised and enlarged edition. $100.

BRADLEY, William Aspenwall. *The Etching of Figures.* Marlborough-on-Hudson, N.Y., 1915. Half vellum. Dard Hunter paper and printing. One of 250. $950.

BRADSTREET, Anne. See *The Tenth Muse* . . .

BRADY, Cyrus Townsend. *Arizona.* New York, 1914. In dustwrapper. $150.

BRADY, William. *Glimpses of Texas.* Houston, 1871. Folding map in color. Stiff wraps, or cloth. $1,250.

BRAINE, John. *Room at the Top.* London, 1957. (Some with wraparound band.) Author's first book. $125. Boston, 1957. $40.

BRAITHWAITE, William S. *Lyrics of Life and Love.* Boston, 1904. Author's first book. $150.

BRAITHWAITE, William S. (editor). *Anthology of Magazine Verse for 1913.* Cambridge, Mass. (1913). Wraps or boards. (First of the Braithwaite anthologies.) $300.

BRAITHWAITE, William S. (editor). *Anthology of Magazine Verse for 1923.* Boston, 1923. Boards and cloth. Issued without dustwrapper. One of 245 signed by Braithwaite. $300. Trade in dustwrapper. $100.

BRAMAH, Ernest. *English Farming and Why I Turned it Up.* London, 1894. Issued without dustwrapper. Author's first book. $150.

BRAMAH, Ernest. *The Eyes of Max Corrados.* London, 1923. $1,000. New York (1924). $400.

BRAMAH, Ernest. *Kai Lung's Golden Hours.* London, 1924. One of 250 signed. $300. Trade. $200.

BRAMAH, Ernest. *Max Carrados.* London (1914). With ads dated "Autumn 1913." $600.

BRAMAH, Ernest. *The Transmutation of Ling.* London (1911). One of 500. $400.

BRAMAH, Ernest. *The Wallet of Kai Lung.* London (1900). Light green cloth. First issue, measuring 1½ inches thick. $350. London, 1923. Boards. One of 200 signed. $250.

BRAMAN, D. E. E. *Information About Texas.* Philadelphia, 1857. $600. Philadelphia, 1858. Second edition. $300.

BRAMMER, William. *The Gay Place.* Boston, 1961. Author's first book. First issue, rear dustwrapper flap has name of designer, $200. Second issue, rear dustwrapper flap has name of designer covered by design, $100. Third issue, rear dustwrapper flap has name of designer removed. $75.

BRAND, Max. *Calling Dr. Kildare.* New York, 1940. $200.

BRAND, Max. *Destry Rides Again.* New York, 1930. $300.

BRAND, Max. *The Untamed.* New York, 1919. Author's first book. Pseudonym of Frederick S. Faust. With dustwrapper. $400. Without dustwrapper. $150.

BRAND, Max. *Night Horseman.* New York, 1920. With dustwrapper. $250.

BRANDEIS, Louis D. *Other People's Money . . .* New York (1914). Author's first book. $250.

BRANDT, Herbert. *Arizona Bird Life.* Cleveland, 1951. Illustrated, including map and color plates. Green cloth. $200.

BRANGWYN, Frank. *The Etched Work of Frank Brangwyn.* London, 1908. One of 100. $200.

BRANGWYN, Frank. *The Historical Paintings in the Great Hall of the Worshipful Company of Skinners.* London, 1909. One of 525. $250. One of 25 on vellum. $750.

BRASHER, Rex. *Birds and Trees of North America.* (Kent, Conn., 1929–32). 867 hand-colored plates. 12 vols., oblong folio, half-leather folders. $7,500. New York, 1961–62. 4 vols. with 875 colored plates. $400.

BRASSINGTON, Salt. *A History of the Art of Bookbinding . . .* London, 1894. $450.

BRATT, John. *Trails of Yesterday.* Lincoln, Neb., 1921. Portrait frontispiece and plates. Pictorial cloth. $200.

BRAUTIGAN, Richard. *A Confederate General at Big Sur.* New York (1964). $200.

BRAUTIGAN, Richard. *The Galilee Hitch-Hiker.* San Francisco (1958). Wraps. $250.

BRAUTIGAN, Richard. *In Watermelon Sugar.* San Francisco (1968). One of 50 signed. $350.

BRAUTIGAN, Richard. *Lay the Marble Tea.* San Francisco (1959). Printed wraps. $300.

BRAUTIGAN, Richard. *The Octopus Frontier.* San Francisco (1960). Printed wraps. $250.

BRAUTIGAN, Richard. *The Pill Versus the Springhill Mine Disaster.* San Francisco (1968). Tan boards, brown cloth spine. One of 50 signed. $350.

BRAUTIGAN, Richard. *Please Plant This Book.* San Francisco (1968). Wraps, with eight seed packets enclosed. $175.

BRAUTIGAN, Richard. *The Return of the Rivers.* (San Francisco, 1958). Author's first book. Wraps. $1,000.

BRAVO (The): A Venetian Story. London, 1831. (By James Fenimore Cooper.) 3 vols. $300. Philadelphia, 1831. 2 vols. First American edition. $250.

BRAYTON, Matthew. *The Indian Captive.* Cleveland, 1860. 68 pp., printed green wraps. $2,500. Boards. $2,000. Fostoria, Ohio, 1896. Second edition. $250.

BRENNAN, Joseph Payne. *Heart of Earth.* Prairie City (1949). Author's first book. $250.

BRENNAN, Joseph Payne. *Nine Horrors and a Dream.* Sauk City, Wis. 1958. $125.

BRENNER, Anita. *The Wind That Swept Mexico.* New York (1943). Illustrated with photographs. $150.

BRETTON, James J. (editor). *Voices From The Press; A Collection of Sketches, Essays* . . . New York, 1850. $150.

BREVOORT, Elias. *New Mexico. Her Natural Resources* . . . Sante Fe, 1874. Wraps. $600.

BREWSTER, Sir David. *A Treatise on the Kaleidoscope.* Edinburgh, 1819. 7 plates. $250.

BRICE, Wallace. *A History of Fort Wayne.* Fort Wayne, Ind., 1868. 7 plates. Cloth. $150.

BRIDGENS, Richard. *Furniture, with Candelabra and Interior Decoration.* London, 1838. 60 full-page color plates. Folio, in original boards. $1,000.

BRIDGES, Robert. *Eros and Psyche, A Poem.* Gregynog Press. Newtown, Wales, 1935. Woodcuts from drawings by Edward Burne-Jones. White pigskin. One of 300. In buckram case. $1,000. One of 15 specially bound by George Fisher. $2,500.

BRIDGES, Robert, *Poems.* London, 1873. Author's first book (suppressed by him in 1878). $400.

BRIDGES, Robert. *Poems Written in the Year MCMXIII.* Ashendene Press. (London) 1914. Blue printed boards and cloth. One of 85 with initials in red or blue. In slipcase. $1,250. One of 6 on vellum. $2,500.

BRIDGES, Robert. *The Testament of Beauty.* Oxford, 1929. One of 50 signed. One of 200, unsigned. $125. Trade edition. $40. New York, 1929. One of 250. $100.

BRIDWELL, J. W. (compiler). *The Life and Adventures of Robert McKimie.* Hillsboro, Ohio, 1878. 56 pp., pictorial wraps. $1,500.

BRIEF Description of Western Texas (A). San Antonio, 1873. (By W.G. Kingsbury.) Pictorial wraps. $1,500.

BRIGGS, Charles Frederick. See *The Adventures of Harry Franco . . .*

BRIGGS, Clare. *Golf, The Book of a Thousand Chuckles.* Chicago (1916). $200.

BRIGGS, E. C., and ATTWOOD, R. M. *Address to the Saints in Utah and California, Polygamy Proven an Abomination by Holy Writ, Is Brigham Young President of the Church of Jesus Christ . . .* Plano, Ill., 1869. Wraps. Third edition (noted as "Revised by Joseph Smith and Wm. W. Blair.") $750.

BRIGGS, L. Vernon. *History of Shipbuilding on North River, Plymouth County, Massachusetts.* Boston, 1889. $200.

BRIGHAM, Clarence S. *Paul Revere's Engravings.* Worcester, Mass., 1954. 77 plates (some in color). $175.

BRILLAT-SAVARIN, J. A. *The Physiology of Taste.* Philadelphia, 1854. $1,250. London, 1925. Introduction by Arthur Machen. Portrait, other illustrations. Boards. One of 750. $200. Limited Editions Club, New York, 1949. Translated by M.F.K. Fisher. Half leather. 1,500 copies. In slipcase. $125.

BRINNIN, John Malcolm. *The Garden is Political.* New York, 1942. Author's first book. $50.

BRIQUET Album, A Miscellany On Watermarks . . . , The. Hilversum, 1952. 400 numbered copies. Volume two (one of the more difficult to find). $300.

BRISBANE, Albert. *Social Destiny of Man . . .* Philadelphia, 1840. Author's first book. $300.

BRISBIN, James S. *The Beef Bonanza.* Philadelphia, 1881. 8 plates. Pictorial cloth. $250.

BRITISH Librarian: Exhibiting A Compendious Review Or Abstract Of Our Most Scarce . . . London, 1738. 6 volumes bound in 1. $250.

BRITTON, Wiley. *Memoirs of the Rebellion on the Border, 1863.* Chicago, 1882. $100.

BRODIE, Walter. *Pitcairn's Island and The Islanders in 1850.* London, 1851. 4 plates. Cloth, paper label. $350. London, 1851. Second edition. $150.

BROMFIELD, Louis. *The Green Bay Tree.* New York, 1924. Author's first book. $300.

BRONK, William. *Light and Dark.* (Ashland, Mass.), 1956. Wraps. Author's first book. $150.

BRONSON, Edgar Beecher. *Red Blooded.* Chicago, 1910. With dustwrapper. $100. Without dustwrapper. $35.

BRONTË, Anne. See Bell, Acton; Bell, Currer.

BRONTË, Charlotte. See Bell, Currer.

BRONTË, Emily. See Bell, Ellis.

BROOKE, Arthur De Capell. *Travels Through Sweden, Norway, and Finmark, to the North Cape.* London, 1823. Map, 21 plates (2 colored). $400. London, 1831. Second edition. $200.

BROOKE, Arthur De Capell. *A Winter in Lapland and Sweden.* London, 1826. With frontispiece, 2 folding maps(?), and 27 plates. $350. London, 1827. Second edition. $200.

BROOKE, H. K. *Annals of the Revolution.* Philadelphia (1848). Boards. $150.

BROOKE, Jocelyn. *Six Poems.* Oxford, 1928. Author's first book. Wraps. $300.

BROOKE, Rupert. *The Bastille.* A. J. Lawrence, Rugby, 1905. Wraps. $4,000. George E. Over, Rugby, 1905 (1920). Wraps. $200.

BROOKE, Rupert. *Collected Poems.* New York, 1915. $300. (Of the first edition, 100 copies were especially bound for members of the Woodberry Society. $1,000.) London, 1919. Illustrated by Gwen Raverat. One of 1,000. $400. One of 13 on vellum. $2,500.

BROOKE, Rupert. *John Webster and the Elizabethan Drama.* New York, 1916. $250.

BROOKE, Rupert. *Lithuania: A Drama in One Act.* Chicago Little Theatre. Chicago, 1915. Pictorial brown wraps. $350.

BROOKE, Rupert. *1914 and Other Poems.* London, 1915. Portrait frontispiece. Dark blue cloth, paper label. $250. New York, 1915. American copyright edition: 87 copies, folded sheets. Bound in morocco or cloth and boards. $850.

BROOKE, Rupert, *"1914." Five Sonnets.* London, 1915. Printed wraps. In printed envelope. $300.

BROOKE, Rupert. *The Old Vicarage, Grantchester.* London, 1916. Gray wraps. $200.

BROOKE, Rupert. *Poems.* London, 1911. Dark blue cloth, paper label. Author's first book of verse and first commercial publication. (Issued without dustwrapper.) $450.

BROOKE, Rupert. *The Pyramids.* Rugby, 1904. Author's first book. Wraps. $6,000.

BROOKNER, Anita. *Watteau.* London, 1967. Author's first book. $150.

BROOKS, Bryant B. *Memoirs of Bryant B. Brooks.* Glendale, Calif., 1939. Plates. One of 150. $200.

BROOKS, Cleanth. *The Relations of the Alabama-Georgia Dialect . . .* Baton Rouge, 1935. Author's first book. $200.

BROOKS, Gwendolyn. *Annie Allen.* New York (1949). $200.

BROOKS, Gwendolyn. *The Bean Eaters.* New York (1960). $200.

BROOKS, Gwendolyn. *Bronzeville Boys and Girls.* New York (1956). First edition not stated. $150.

BROOKS, Gwendolyn. *Maud Martha.* New York (1953). $200.

BROOKS, Gwendolyn. *A Street in Bronzeville.* New York, 1945. Author's first regularly published book. $250.

BROSSARD, Chandler. *Who Walk in Darkness.* (New York, 1952) Author's first book. $100. London (1952). $75.

BROTHER Jonathan. Edinburgh, 1825. (By John Neal.) 3 vols. $250.

BROTHERHOOD, W. *Forty Years Among the Old Booksellers of Philadelphia, with Bibliographic Remarks.* Philadelphia, 1891. $100.

BROTHERS (The): A Tale of the Fronde. New York, 1835. 2 vols. (By Henry William Herbert.) First issue, in original brown cloth. Author's first book. $200.

BROUGHTON, James. *Songs for Certain Children.* San Francisco, 1947. Author's first book. $350.

BROUGHTON, William Robert. *A Voyage of Discovery to the North Pacific Ocean.* London, 1804. 9 plates and maps (7 folding). $5,000.

BROUILLET, J. B. A. *Authentic Account of the Murder of Dr. Whitman and Other Missionaries.* Portland, 1869. 108 pp., wraps. Second edition of *Protestantism in Oregon* (see item following). $1,500.

BROUILLET, J. B. A. *Protestantism in Oregon: Account of the Murder of Dr. Whitman, and the Ungrateful Calumnies of H.H. Spalding, Protestant Missionary.* New York, 1853. Wraps. $3,000.

BROWER, Jacob V. *Memoirs of Explorations in the Basin of the Mississippi.* Maps. St. Paul, Minn., 1898–1904. 8 vols., cloth. One of 300. $500.

BROWN, Benjamin. *Testimonies for the Truth: A Record of Manifestations of the Power of God . . . High Priest in the Church of Jesus Christ of Latter Day Saints.* Liverpool, 1853. $850.

BROWN, Bob. *Demonics.* Cagnes-sur-Mer, France, 1931. Wraps. $300.

BROWN, Bob. *Readies for Bob Brown's Machine.* Cagnes-sur-Mer, France, 1931. Wraps. $300.

BROWN, Bob. *The Remarkable Adventures of Christopher Poe.* Chicago, 1913. Author's first book. $300.

BROWN, Bob. *What Happened to Mary.* New York (1913). $150.

BROWN, Bob. *Words.* Hours Press. Paris, 1931. One of 150 signed. $300.

BROWN, Charles Brockden. See *Alcuin . . .*; and *Wieland . . .*

BROWN, Charles Brockden. *Arthur Mervyn: A Tale.* London, 1803. 3 vols. First English edition. $300. (The first edition was issued anonymously in America. See *Arthur Mervyn.*)

BROWN, Fredric. *The Dead Ringer.* New York, 1948. $300.

BROWN, Fredric. *The Fabulous Clipjoint.* New York, 1947. Author's first book. $350.

BROWN, Fredric. *Murder Can Be Fun.* New York, 1948. $250.

BROWN, Fredric. *What Mad Universe.* New York, 1949. $200.

BROWN, Henry. *History of Illinois.* New York, 1844. Map, cloth. $200.

BROWN, Henry. *A Narrative of the Anti-Masonick . . .* Batavia, 1829. $275.

BROWN, J. Cabell. *Calabazas, or Amusing Recollections of an Arizona "City."* San Francisco, 1892. Printed wraps. $250.

BROWN, J. Willard. *The Signal Corps, U.S.A., in the War of the Rebellion.* Boston, 1896. $150.

BROWN, James S. *California Gold: An Authentic History of the First Find.* Oakland, 1894. Portrait frontispiece. 20 pp., printed wraps. (55 copies printed.) $250.

BROWN, James S. *Life of a Pioneer.* Salt Lake City, 1900. Portrait. 2 plates. $125.

BROWN, Jesse, and WILLARD, A. M. *The Black Hills Trails.* Rapid City, S.D., 1924. Numerous illustrations. $125.

BROWN, John Arthur. *Short History of Pine Valley.* New Jersey, 1963. Privately printed. $100.

BROWN, John Henry. *History of Dallas County from 1837 to 1887.* Dallas, 1887. 114 pp., wraps. $200.

BROWN, John Henry, *History of Texas, 1685–1892.* St. Louis (1892–93). 25 plates. 2 vols., cloth. $350.

BROWN, John Henry. *Indian Wars and Pioneers of Texas.* Austin, Tex. (1896). Plates. $800.

BROWN, John Henry. *Political History of Oregon.* Portland, Ore., 1892. Vol. 1. (All published.) Illustrated, folding map. $400.

BROWN, John H(enry). *Reminiscences and Incidents, of "The Early Days" of San Francisco.* San Francisco (1886). Folding frontispiece plan. $600. San Francisco (1933). Grabhorn printing. Half cloth. One of 500. $100. One of 25 in morocco, with additional reproductions. $350.

BROWN, John Henry, and SPEER, W.S. *The Encyclopedia of the New West.* Marshall, Tex., 1881. In calf. $800.

BROWN, Joseph M. *Astyanax: An Epic Romance of Llion, Atlantis, and Amaraca.* New York, 1907. Illustrated. Cloth. $100.

BROWN, Paul. *Aintree.* Derrydale Press. New York, 1930. One of 850. $250. One of 50 large paper copies with an initialed drawing by Brown. $750.

BROWN, Samuel J. *In Captivity: The Experience, Privations and Dangers of Sam'l J. Brown . . .* Mankato, Minn. (1896). Full leather. $600.

BROWN, Samuel R. *The Western Gazetteer, or Emigrant's Directory.* Auburn, N.Y., 1817. First issue, with 3-line errata slip. $750. Second issue, with 4-line errata. $500. Third issue, with advertisements. $400.

BROWN, Sterling. *Southern Road.* New York, 1932. Author's first book. $1,000.

BROWN, William C. *The Sheepeater Campaign in Idaho.* Boise, 1926. Folding map. 32 pp., wraps. One of 50. $250.

BROWN, William H. *The Early History of the State of Illinois.* Chicago, 1840. 16 pp., printed wraps. $1,500.

BROWN, William Hill. See *The Power of Sympathy.*

BROWN, William Robinson. *The Horse of the Desert.* Derrydale Press. New York, 1929. Illustrated. Cloth. One of 750. In dustwrapper. $500. One of 75 signed. $3,000.

BROWN, William Wells. *Clotel: or, The President's Daughter.* London, 1853. $1,750.

BROWN, William Wells. *Clotelle: A Tale of the Southern States.* (New title.) Boston/New York (1864). Wraps. $1,500.

BROWN, William Wells. *The Narrative of . . . Fugitive Slave.* Boston, 1847. $1,000.

BROWNE, Francis F. *Volunteer Grain.* Way & Williams. Chicago, 1895. Green cloth. One of 160. (First book by the publisher.) $450.

BROWNE, J. Ross. *Adventures in the Apache Country.* New York, 1869. $250.

BROWNE, J. Ross. *Etchings of a Whaling Cruise.* New York, 1846. 13 plates. $750. New York, 1850. $400.

BROWNE, J. Ross. *Report of the Debates in the Convention of California on the Formation of the State Constitution.* Washington, 1850. $250.

BROWNE, Thomas A. See Boldrewood, Rolf.

BROWNE, Sir Thomas. *Religio Medici.* (London), 1643. First authorized edition. $3,000. Golden Cockerel Press. Waltham Saint Lawrence, 1923. One of 115. $500. Limited Editions Club, New York, 1939. John Henry Nash printing. In slipcase. $75.

BROWNING, Elizabeth Barrett. See B., E. B.; Barrett, E. B.; Barrett, Elizabeth B.; Barrett, Elizabeth Barrett. See also *An Essay on Mind; Prometheus Bound.*

BROWNING, Elizabeth Barrett. *Aurora Leigh.* London, 1857 (actually 1856). $250.

BROWNING, Elizabeth Barrett. *Casa Guidi Windows: A Poem.* London, 1851. $300.

BROWNING, Elizabeth Barrett, *Poems Before Congress.* London, 1860. Red cloth. With page 25, line 1 having single quote mark ' . . . different scarce." (Second impression, lines 1, 2, 3, and 5 reset and reads ". . . different scarce.") In some copies. 32-page publisher's catalogue dated February 1860 (no priority). $250.

BROWNING, Elizabeth Barrett. *Sonnets from the Portuguese.* The following are some separate editions. Copeland & Day. (Boston) 1896. Hand-colored illustrations. 750 copies. $500. London (1909). One of 500. $500. Montagnola, 1925. Morocco. One of 225. $750. San Francisco, 1925–27. 2 vols., half vellum (including facsimile volume). One of 250. $250. Limited Editions Club. New York, 1948. In slipcase. $100.

BROWNING, Robert. See Barrett, Elizabeth, and Browning, Robert. See also *Pauline: A Fragment of a Confession.*

BROWNING, Robert. *Bells and Pomegranates.* London, 1841–46. 8 parts, printed wraps. First edition, with half title for second part. $750. First book edition (parts bound in 1 volume, cloth, with the half title to the second part). $300.

BROWNING, Robert. *Dramatic Romances and Lyrics.* Ballantyne Press. London, 1899. Illustrated. Morocco. One of 10 on vellum. $1,000. Buckram. One of 210. $200.

BROWNING, Robert. *Dramatis Personae.* London, 1864. Red cloth. $125. Doves Press. (London, 1910.) Vellum. One of 250 on paper. $600. One of 15 on vellum. $6,000.

BROWNING, Robert. *Paracelsus.* London, 1835. In original drab boards, paper label. First issue, with 8 pages of ads at front dated Dec. 1, 1842. Author's first acknowledged book. $750.

BROWNING, Robert. *The Pied Piper of Hamelin.* London (1888). 35 colored illustrations by Kate Greenaway. Pictorial boards. $350. London, 1934. Illustrated by Arthur Rackham. Limp vellum. One of 410. In slipcase. $1,250. Trade. $250.

BROWNING, Robert. *The Ring and the Book.* London, 1868–69. 4 vols., dark green cloth. London, 1868–69. First edition, first binding, with spines of first 2 volumes in Arabic numerals and of next 2 in Roman numerals (VAB). All Roman numerals according to Schwartz who states later have Arabic on first two volumes. Wise just states second edition was in brown cloth. $400. Limited Editions Club. New York, 1949. 2 vols., boards and morocco in slipcase. $75.

BROWNING, Robert. *Sordello.* London, 1840. Boards, paper label. First issue, in boards. $400. Cloth. $150.

BROWNING, Robert H. K. *History of Golf.* London, 1955. $200. New York (1955). $150.

BROWNLOW, William. *A Political Register.* Jonesborough, Tenn., 1844. Boards. $225.

BROWNSON, Orestus Augustus. *An Address, On the Fifty-fifth . . .* Ithaca, 1831. Author's first book. Wraps. $300.

BROWNSTEIN, Michael. *Behind the Wheel.* (New York, 1967.) (200 copies.) Author's first book. Wraps. 6 signed, lettered copies, $200. 10 signed, numbered copies, $150. 184 unsigned copies, $50.

BRUFF, J. Goldsborough. *Gold Rush: The Journals, Drawings and Other Papers of J. Goldsborough Bruff.* New York, 1944. Edited by Georgia W. Read and Ruth Gaines. 21 plates, 2 vols., boards. $300.

BRUFFEY, George A. *Eighty-one Years in the West.* Butte, 1925. Portrait. Wraps. $125.

BRUNEFILLE, G.E. *Topo.* London, 1880. (By Gertrude Elizabeth Campbell.) Illustrated by Kate Greenaway. Cloth. $200.

BRUNSON, Alfred. *A Western Pioneer.* Cincinnati, 1872 and 1879. 2 vols., cloth. $125.

BRUNSON, Edward. *Profits in Sheep and Cattle in Central and Western Kansas.* Kansas City, 1883. 16 pp., wraps. $250.

BRUTUS. *The Crisis; or, Essays on the Usurpation of the Federal Government.* Charleston, 1827. (By Robert J. Turnbull.) Half morocco. $225.

BRYAN, Daniel. *The Mountain Muse.* Harrisonburg, 1813. $200.

BRYANT, Edwin. *What I Saw in California.* New York, 1848. $400. New York, 1848. Second edition. $200. Santa Ana, Calif., 1936. Half morocco. $200.

BRYANT, Gilbert Ernest. *The Chelsea Porcelain Toys.* London, 1925. 63 plates, 47 in color. One of 650 signed. $250.

BRYANT, William Cullen. *The Embargo: or, Sketches of the Times: A Satire.* (Cover title.) Boston, 1809. Second edition. $600. (For first edition, see title entry, *The Embargo.)*

BRYANT, William Cullen. *Hymns.* (New York, 1864). Brown-orange or blue cloth. First state, with reading "Dwells on Thy works in deep delight" in second line of fourth stanza on page 9. $250.

BRYANT, William Cullen. *Poems.* Cambridge, Mass., 1821. Boards or wraps bound in. $750. Not bound in. $300. New York, 1832. Second edition. $150. Limited Editions Club. New York, 1947. Illustrated by Thomas Nason. Leather. In slipcase. $75.

BRYANT, W. N. *Bryant's Texas Almanac and Railway Guide, 1881–1882.* (Cover title.) Dallas, 1881. Wraps. $375. Earlier: *Bryant's Texas Guide!* 2 folding maps. Wraps. Austin, 1875. $650.

BRYCE, James. *The American Commonwealth.* London, 1888. 3 vols. First printing with the chapter in vol. 3 on the Tweed Ring, later suppressed. $300. Second, with Tweed Ring matter omitted. $150.

BRYDGES, Sir Egerton. *Restituta; Or, Titles, Extracts, and Characters of Old Books in English Literature, Revived.* London, 1814–16. 28 numbers in 4 volumes. $150.

BRYHER. See Ellerman, Annie Winifred.

BRYHER, Winifred. *The Lament for Adonis.* London, 1918. Translated from the Greek. Wraps. Author's first book. $400. Also copies on handmade paper. $650.

BUCHAN, John. *The Pilgrim Fathers: The Newdigate Prize Poem, 1898.* Oxford, 1898. Wraps. $150.

BUCHAN, John. *Sir Quixote of the Moors.* London, 1895. Author's first book. First issue, with full title on spine. $300. New York, 1895. $150.

BUCHAN, John. *The Thirty-Nine Steps.* Edinburgh, 1915. $150.

BUCHANAN, Robert. *The Devil's Case.* London (1896). $150.

BUCHANAN, Robert. *The Fleshly School of Poetry.* London, 1872. Pink or violet pictorial wraps. $600.

BUCHANAN, Robertson. *Practical and Descriptive Essays on the Economy of Fuel, and Management of Heat.* Glasgow, 1810. 2 plates. $750.

BUCHANAN, Robertson. *A Practical Treatise on Propelling Vessels by Steam.* Glasgow, 1816. 17 plates, 1 folding. $500.

BUCK, Irving A. *Cleburne and His Command.* New York, 1908. Plates. $100.

BUCK, Pearl S. *East Wind: West Wind.* New York (1930). Author's first book. $350.

BUCK, Pearl S. *The Good Earth.* New York (1931). First issue, with "flees" for "fleas" in line 17 of page 100, with "John Day Publishing Company" on copyright page, and with top edges stained brown. $500. Later issue, green top edges. $400.

BUCK, Pearl S. *Sons.* New York (1932). One of 371 deluxe copies, signed in dustwrapper and slipcase. $200.

BUCKINGHAM, Nash. *De Shootinest Gent'man and Other Tales.* Edited by Col. Harold P. Sheldon. Derrydale Press. New York (1934). One of 950. $650.

BUCKINGHAM, Nash. *Mark Right!* Derrydale Press. New York (1936). One of 1,250. $400.

BUCKINGHAM, Nash. *Ole Miss.* Derrydale Press. New York (1937). Edited by Paul A. Curtis. One of 1,250. $500.

BUCKLEY, Francis. *English Baluster Stemmed Glasses of the 17th and 18th Centuries.* Edinburgh, 1912. 18 plates. Buckram. $300.

BUCKLEY, Francis. *Old London Drinking Glasses.* Edinburgh, 1913. 14 plates. Buckram. $200.

BUCKLEY, Wilfred. *Diamond Engraved Glasses of the 16th Century.* London, 1929. 33 plates. Boards. One of 250. $400.

BUCKLEY, William F., Jr. *God and Man at Yale.* Chicago, 1951. Author's first book. $125.

BUDGE, Sir E. A. Wallis. *Amulets and Superstitions.* London, 1930. 22 plates, 300 other illustrations. $250.

BUDGE, Sir E. A. Wallis. *The Gods of the Egyptians, or Studies in Egyptian Mythology.* London, 1904. 98 color plates. 2 vols., pictorial cloth. $300.

BUDGE, Jesse R. S. *The Life of William Budge By His Son.* Salt Lake City, 1915. $300.

BUECHNER, Frederick. *A Long Day's Dying.* New York, 1950. Author's first book. $75.

BUEL, J. W. *Life and Marvelous Adventures of Wild Bill, the Scout.* Chicago, 1880. Frontispiece and plate. 93 pp., pictorial wraps. Presumed first issue, with cover dated 1880. $1,500.

BUFFUM, E. Gould. *Six Months in the Gold Mines.* Philadelphia, 1850. Printed wraps, or cloth. Wraps. $450. Cloth. $300.

BUKOWSKI, Charles. *At Terror Street and Agony Way.* Black Sparrow Press. Los Angeles, 1968. One of 75 with an original illustration signed by the author, issued in glassine dustwrapper. $350.

BUKOWSKI, Charles. *Cold Dogs in the Courtyard.* (Chicago) 1965. Wraps. One of 500. $150.

BUKOWSKI, Charles. *Crucifix in a Deathhand.* Loujon Press. New Orleans (1965). Pictorial wraps. 3,100 signed copies. $250. (Some copies, with special inscriptions, at higher prices.)

BUKOWSKI, Charles. *The Curtains Are Waving, . . .* Black Sparrow Press. (Los Angeles) 1967. Printed wraps. One of 122 signed. $500.

BUKOWSKI, Charles. *The Days Run Away Like Wild Horses Over the Hills.* Los Angeles, 1969. One of 250 signed. In acetate dustwrapper. $250. One of 50 with a drawing by the author. $500.

BUKOWSKI, Charles. *Flower, Fist and Bestial Wail.* (Eureka, Calif., 1959). Author's first book. Wraps. (Two previous broadsides, 1950 and 1956.) $500.

BUKOWSKI, Charles. *Post Office.* Los Angeles, 1971. Boards. In acetate dustwrapper. One of 250 signed. $250. One of 50 signed, with an original drawing by the author. $500.

BUKOWSKI, Charles. *Run with the Hunted.* Chicago (1962). Pictorial wraps. $400.

BULFINCH, Thomas. See *Authorship.*

BULFINCH, Thomas. *The Age of Chivalry.* Boston, 1859. 6 illustrations. Brown cloth. $200.

BULFINCH, Thomas. *The Age of Fable.* Boston, 1855. First state, with names of both printer and stereotyper on copyright page. $250. Limited Editions Club, New York, 1958. Illustrated by Joe Mugnaini. In slipcase. $60.

BULKELEY, John, and CUMMINS, John. *A Voyage To The South Seas, In the Years 1740 . . .* Philadelphia, 1757. First American edition. $2,000.

BULLEN, Frank T. *The Cruise of the "Cachalot."* London, 1898. Folding map and plates. Author's first book. $200. New York, 1899. $75.

BULLEN, Henry Lewis. *Nicolas Jenson, Printer Of Venice . . .* San Francisco, 1926. Limited to 207 numbered copies with an original folio leaf from Plutarch's *Vitae Parallelae Illustrium Virorum* loosely inserted. $375.

BULLER, Sir Walter Lawry. *A History of the Birds of New Zealand.* London, 1873. 35 hand-colored plates. $3,500. London, 1887–88. 48 colored plates, 2 plain plates. 13 parts in 8, wraps. $3,000. London, 1888. 2 vols., half morocco. Second edition. $2,500.

BULLOCK, William. *Six Months Residence and Travels in Mexico.* London, 1824. Frontispiece, 15 plates (4 hand colored), a folding table, and 2 folding maps. $650.

BULL-US, Hector. *The Diverting History of John Bull . . .* New York, 1812. (By James K. Paulding, his first book.) $600.

BULWER-LYTTON, Edward. See Caxton, Pisistratus. See also *The Coming Race; Falkland; The Last Days of Pompeii; Pelham; Rienzi; Clytemnestra.*

BULWER-LYTTON, Edward. *Ismael; an Oriental Tale.* London, 1820. Boards. Author's first book. $300.

BUNIN, I. A. *The Gentleman from San Francisco and Other Stories.* Hogarth Press. (Richmond) 1922. Translated by Leonard Woolf. Boards. Issued without dustwrapper. With errata slip. $175.

BUNNER, H. C. *A Woman of Honor.* Boston, 1883. Author's first book. $100.

BUNTING, Basil. *Briggflatts.* London (1966). Wraps. One of 100 in black cloth and dustwrapper. $750. Leather. One of 26 signed and lettered copies. $2,500.

BUNTING, Basil. *First Book of Odes.* London (1965). One of 125, in green boards. Issued without dustwrapper. $250. Another issue, one of 50 copies in black boards and green dustwrapper. $300. Also, one of 26 signed and lettered in black leather and dustwrapper. $1,250.

BUNTING, Basil. *Loquitur.* London (1965). Full morocco. One of 26 signed. In dustwrapper. $1,250. One of 200 in cloth and dustwrapper. $250.

BUNTING, Basil. *Redimiculum Matellarum.* Milan, 1930. Wraps. Author's first book. $4,000.

BUNTING, Basil. *Two Poems.* Unicorn Press. No place, 1967. Wraps. One of 220. $75. One of 30 signed. $500.

BUNTING, Basil, and WILLIAMS, Jonathan. *Descant on Rawthey's Madrigal: Conversations with Basil Bunting.* Lexington, Ky. (1968). One of 25 signed by Bunting and Williams. In boards and dustwrapper. $750. One of 475 in white wraps, in light brown printed wrapper. $200.

BUNYAN, John. *The Pilgrim's Progress.* Chiswick Press. London, 1849. Portrait frontispiece. Full brown morocco, gilt. $300. London, 1928. Cresset Press. 10 wood engravings. 2 vols., folio, cloth. One of 195. $750. One of 10 on vellum with an extra suite of plates. $6,000. Limited Editions Club. New York, 1941. 29 William Blake illustrations in color. One of 1,500. In slipcase. $150.

BURCH, R. M. *Colour Printing and Colour Printers.* London, 1910. Second edition. $250.

BURDICK, William. *An Oration on the Nature and Effects of the Art of Printing.* Boston, 1802. The earliest book on printing history with a U.S. imprint. $1,250.

BURGESS, Anthony. See Kell, Joseph.

BURGESS, Anthony. *Beds in the East.* London (1959). $125.

BURGESS, Anthony. *A Clockwork Orange.* London (1962). In dustwrapper with price of 16 shillings. $650. New York (1963). $150.

BURGESS, Anthony. *The Doctor Is Sick.* London (1960). $125. New York (1960). $60.

BURGESS, Anthony. *The Enemy in the Blanket.* London (1958). $200.

BURGESS, Anthony. *Honey for the Bears.* London (1963). $125. New York (1964). $75.

BURGESS, Anthony. *The Right to An Answer.* London (1960). $150. New York (1961). $75.

BURGESS, Anthony. *Time for a Tiger.* London, 1956. Author's first book. $350.

BURGESS, Gelett. *The Nonsense Almanack for 1900.* New York (1899). Wraps. $150.

BURGESS, Gelett. *The Purple Cow!* (San Francisco, 1895.) Illustrated. 8 leaves. Author's first publication. First state of first printing (printed on both sides of leaf) on rough China paper. $250. Second state (printed on one side of leaf only). $100.

BURGESS, Gelett. *Vivette, or the Memoirs of the Romance Association.* Boston, 1897. Author's first book, aside from *The Purple Cow* leaflet. $150.

BURGESS, Thornton Waldo. *Old Mother West Wind.* Boston (1910). Pictorial tan cloth. Author's first book for children. $150.

BURKE, Henry Farnham. *Examples of Irish Bookplates from the Collections of Sir Bernard Burke . . .* Somerset Herald, 1894. $125.

BURKE, James Lee. *The Convict.* Baton Rouge, 1985. Cloth. $125. Wraps. $30.

BURKE, Kenneth. *The White Oxen and Other Stories.* New York, 1924. Author's first book. $400.

BURKE, Leda. *Dope-Darling.* London, 1919. (By David Garnett, his second book.) $150.

BURKE, Thomas. *Nights In Town.* London, 1915. $125.

BURKE, Thomas. *Verses.* (Guilford, 1906.) Author's first book. Wraps. (25 copies.) $1,000.

BURKE, W. S. (compiler). *Directory of the City of Council Bluffs and Emigrants' Guide to the Gold Regions of the West.* Council Bluffs, Iowa, 1866. Folding map. 32 pp., plus ads, patterned cloth. $2,500.

BURKE, William. See *Memoirs of William Burke . . .*

BURLEND, Rebecca. *A True Picture of Emigration.* London (1848). Wraps. $500.

BURNETT, Frances Hodgson. *The Drury Lane Boys' Club.* Washington, 1892. Blue wraps. $150.

BURNETT, Frances Hodgson. *Little Lord Fauntleroy.* New York, 1886. Illustrated by Reginald B. Birch. First issue, with De Vinne Press imprint at end. $200.

BURNETT, Frances Hodgson. *That Lass O'Lowrie's.* New York, 1877. Author's first book. First state, with illustrator's name on title page. $100. Without name, second state. $60.

BURNETT, Peter H. *Recollections and Opinions of an Old Pioneer.* New York, 1880. $200.

BURNETT, W. R. *Little Caesar.* New York, 1929. Author's first book. $500.

BURNETT, William R. *Saint Johnson.* New York, 1930. $100.

BURNEY, Fanny (Frances). *Evelina.* London, 1778. 3 vols. $3,500 at auction in 1987 for copy in contemporary calf.

BURNEY, James. *A Chronological History of the Discoveries in the South Sea or Pacific Ocean.* London, 1803–17. With 41 maps, charts, or plates. 5 vols. $12,500. (Auction price in 1988–89 from $1,000 to $16,000.)

BURNEY, James. *History of the Buccaneers of America.* London, 1816. 3 maps (2 folding). First separate edition. Large paper issue. $450. Trade. $300.

BURNHAM, Daniel H., and BENNETT, Edward H. *Plan of Chicago.* Chicago, 1909. Illustrated. Leather and/or cloth. One of 1,650 copies. $400. Full vellum. $600.

BURNS, John H. *Memoirs of a Cow Pony.* Boston (1906). Illustrated. Pictorial cloth. $500.

BURNS, John Horne. *The Gallery.* New York (1947). Author's first book. $100.

BURNS, Martin. *The Life Work of "Farmer Burns."* Omaha, 1911. $125.

BURNS, Robert. *Poems Ascribed to Robert Burns.* Glasgow, 1801. $500.

BURNS, Robert. *Poems, Chiefly In the Scottish Dialect.* Kilmarnock edition, 1786. Author's first book. $5,000. (Presentation copy brought $40,000 at auction in 1990.) Edinburgh, 1787. Second edition, first issue, with "skinking" on page 263. $750. Second issue, with "stinking" on page 263. $300.

BURNS, Robert. *Tam O'Shanter.* Essex House Press. London, 1902. Illustrated, colored by hand. Stiff vellum. One of 150 on vellum. $400.

BURNS, Tex. *Hopalong Cassidy & the Riders of High Rock.* New York, 1951. (By Louis L'Amour.) $125.

BURNS, Tex. *Hopalong Cassidy, Trouble Shooter.* New York, 1952. (By Louis L'Amour.) $125.

BURNSHAW, Stanley. *Poems.* Pittsburgh, 1927. Author's first book. $200.

BURPEE, Lawrence J. *The Search for the Western Sea.* London, 1908. 6 maps, 51 plates. $300. New York, 1908. $200. New York, 1936. Maps and plates. 2 vols. $100.

BURR, Aaron. *The Private Journal of Aaron Burr.* Rochester, 1903. Edited by W. K. Bixby. Portraits. 2 vols., half cloth. One of 250 signed by Bixby. $250.

BURR, Frederic M. *Life And Works of Alexander Anderson, M.D., The First American Wood Engraver.* New York. 1893. 725 numbered and signed copies. $150.

BURROUGHS, Edgar Rice. *At the Earth's Core.* Chicago, 1922. With "M.A. Donohue & Co." at bottom of copyright page. In dustwrapper. $2,000.

BURROUGHS, Edgar Rice. *Back to the Stone Age.* Tarzana, Calif. (1937). $500.

BURROUGHS, Edgar Rice. *Bandit of Hell's Bend.* Chicago, 1925. $850.

BURROUGHS. Edgar Rice. *The Beasts of Tarzan.* Chicago, 1916. With "W.F. Hall Printing Company, Chicago" at bottom of copyright page. In dustwrapper. $10,000. Without dustwrapper. $500.

BURROUGHS, Edgar Rice. *The Chessmen of Mars.* Chicago, 1922. $1,750.

BURROUGHS, Edgar Rice. *The Eternal Lover.* Chicago. 1925. With "M.A. Donohue . . ." on copyright page. $1,750.

BURROUGHS, Edgar Rice. *A Fighting Man of Mars.* New York (1931). With Metropolitan Books imprint. $500.

BURROUGHS, Edgar Rice. *The Girl from Hollywood.* New York (1923). Pebbled red cloth, lettered in green. $1,250. (Later in smooth red cloth.)

BURROUGHS, Edgar Rice. *Jungle Tales of Tarzan.* Chicago, 1919. In orange cloth with publisher's imprint on spine in three lines. In dustwrapper. $2,000. Without jacket. $300. Second issue, in two lines. $1,750. Without. $150. (Later in green cloth.)

BURROUGHS, Edgar Rice. *The Lad and the Lion.* Tarzana, Calif. (1938). $600.

BURROUGHS, Edgar Rice. *Lost On Venus.* Tarzana, Calif. (1935). $500.

BURROUGHS, Edgar Rice. *The Mucker.* Chicago, 1921. In dustwrapper. $2,000. Without dustwrapper. $250. Methuen. London (1921). In dustwrapper. $1,000. (Precedes American.)

BURROUGHS, Edgar Rice. *The Outlaw of Torn.* Chicago, 1927. First edition not stated. Publisher's Acorn on copyright page. $850.

BURROUGHS, Edgar Rice. *A Princess of Mars.* Chicago, 1917. With "W.F. Hall . . ." at bottom of copyright page. In dustwrapper. $5,000. Without dustwrapper. $400.

BURROUGHS, Edgar Rice. *The Return of Tarzan.* Chicago, 1915. With "W.F. Hall . . ." at bottom of copyright page. In dustwrapper. $6,000. Without dustwrapper. $500.

BURROUGHS, Edgar Rice. *The Son of Tarzan.* Chicago, 1917. With "W.F. Hall . . ." at bottom of copyright page and lacking dedication leaf (to Hubert Burroughs). In dustwrapper. $3,500. Lacking dustwrapper. $250.

BURROUGHS, Edgar Rice. *Tarzan and the Ant Men.* Chicago, 1924. With "A.C. McClurg/& Co." on spine. $1,500.

BURROUGHS, Edgar Rice. *Tarzan and the Golden Lion.* Chicago, 1933. With "M.A. Donohue . . ." at bottom of copyright page. $1,000.

BURROUGHS, Edgar Rice. *Tarzan and the Jewels of Opar.* Chicago, 1918. With "W.F. Hall . . ." at bottom of copyright page. In dustwrapper. $3,000. Without dustwrapper. $200.

BURROUGHS, Edgar Rice. *Tarzan and the Leopard Men.* Tarzana (1935). $500.

BURROUGHS, Edgar Rice. *Tarzan at the Earth's Core.* New York (1930). Metropolitan Books. Green cloth lettered in black. $850. Later with Grosset & Dunlap at foot of spine. In red cloth. $250.

BURROUGHS, Edgar Rice. *Tarzan, Lord of the Jungle.* Chicago, 1928. $1,500.

BURROUGHS, Edgar Rice. *Tarzan of the Apes.* Chicago, 1914. Frontispiece. Red cloth. First edition with printer's name on copyright page in Old English letters. In dustwrapper. $30,000. Without dustwrapper. $1,500. Author's first book. London (1917). Orange-colored cloth. With ads dated Autumn. $500.

BURROUGHS, Edgar Rice. *Tarzan Triumphant.* Tarzana (1932). Illustrated by Stanley Burroughs. First edition not stated. $450.

BURROUGHS, Edgar Rice. *Thuvia, Maid of Mars.* Chicago, 1920. With "M.A. Donohue . . ." at bottom of copyright page. In dustwrapper. $2,000.

BURROUGHS, Edgar Rice. *The War Chief.* Chicago, 1927. First edition not stated. Publisher's acorn on copyright page. $1,000.

BURROUGHS, Edgar Rice. *The Warlord of Mars.* Chicago, 1919. First issue, with "W.F. Hall" on copyright page. In dustwrapper. $1,250. Without dustwrapper. $150.

BURROUGHS, John. *Notes on Walt Whitman as Poet and Person.* New York, 1867. Blue wraps with leaves trimmed to 6⁹⁄16 inches high. $600. Later, 1867, cloth bound, leaves 7¼ inches high. $250.

BURROUGHS, John. *Wake-Robin.* New York, 1871. $350.

BURROUGHS, William. See Lee, William.

BURROUGHS, William S. *Ali's Smile.* (Brighton) 1971. Oblong, boards and cloth. One of 99 signed. (Issued with a Burroughs LP record.) $400.

BURROUGHS, William S. *The Last Words of Dutch Schultz.* London, 1970. One of 100 signed in tissue dustwrapper. $350.

BURROUGHS, William S. *The Naked Lunch.* Olympia Press. Paris (1959). Wraps. Green border on title page, "Francs 1500" on back cover. In dustwrapper. $350. New York (1962). $100.

BURROUGHS, William S. *The Soft Machine.* Olympia Press. Paris (1961). "Printed in France . . . June 1961" on p. 4. Wraps in dustwrapper. $250. New York (1966). New edition. Revised and augmented. $50. London (1968). Adds an appendix. Cloth. $50. Wraps. $25.

BURROUGHS, William S. *The Ticket That Exploded.* Olympia Press. Paris (1962). Wraps. In dustwrapper. $225.

BURROUGHS, William S. *Time.* New York, 1965. Illustrated by Brion Gysin. Wraps. One of 100 signed. $450. Trade. $75.

BURTON. Alfred. *The Adventures of Johnny Newcome in the Navy.* London, 1818. 16 colored plates by Rowlandson. (By John Mitford.) $750. (See John Mitford entry for second and third editions.)

BURTON, Harley True. *A History of the JA Ranch.* Austin, 1928. Portrait, map. $650.

BURTON, Sir Richard F. *The City of the Saints and Across the Rocky Mountains to California.* London, 1861. 8 plates, folding map, folding plan. $750.

BURTON, Sir Richard F. *Falconry in the Valley of the Indus.* London, 1852. Frontispiece, other plates. $1,000.

BURTON, Sir Richard F. *First Footsteps in East Africa; or, an Exploration of Harar.* London, 1856. With 2 maps and 4 colored plates. First issue, in dull violet cloth, with all edges uncut. $1,500. Second issue. Red cloth with bottom edge trimmed. $600.

BURTON, Sir Richard F. *Goa, and the Blue Mountains.* London, 1851. Folding map, plates. Author's first book. First issue, in fawn cloth, 5 by 8⅛ inches. $1,250. Second issue in light blue cloth, 4¾ by 8 inches. $500.

BURTON, Sir Richard F. *The Gold-Mines of Midian and the Ruined Midianite Cities.* London, 1878. Folding map. $600.

BURTON, Sir Richard F. *The Lake Regions of Central Africa.* London, 1860. Folding map. 12 colored plates. 2 vols. $850.

BURTON, Sir Richard F. *The Land of Midian (Revisited).* London, 1879. Folding map. 16 plates (6 colored). 2 vols. First issue, with ads dated "9.78" (VAB not in Penzer.) $750.

BURTON, Sir Richard F. *Letters from the Battlefields of Paraguay.* London, 1870. Engraved title, frontispiece, folding map. $600.

BURTON, Sir Richard F. *Personal Narrative of a Pilgrimage to El-Medinah and Meccah.* London, 1855–56. 16 plates (5 colored), 3 folding maps. 3 vols., cloth. $1,750.

BURTON, Sir Richard F. (translator). *The Book of the Thousand Nights and a Night.* (Arabian Nights). Limited Editions Club, New York, 1934. Illustrated by Valenti Angelo. 6 vols., boards, cowhide spines. In slipcase. $150. Another edition: New York, 1954. Illustrated in color by Arthur Szyk. 4 vols. In slipcase. $250.

BURTON, Robert. *The Anatomy of Melancholy.* London, 1621. $7,500. ("Superb" copy for $34,000 at auction in 1990.) Nonesuch Press. London, 1925–26. Illustrated by E. McKnight Kauffer. 2 vols., half vellum and boards. One of 750. $400. 2 vols. in one. One of 40 on vellum. $2,000.

BURTON, W. *Josiah Wedgwood and His Pottery.* London, 1922. 32 color plates, 84 in black and white. One of 1,500. In dustwrapper. $250.

BURY, Mrs. Edward. *A Selection Of Hexandrian Plants...* (London), 1831–34. Large folio. 51 hand-colored aquatints by Robert Havell. $50,000.

BUTCHER, S. D. *S. D. Butcher's Pioneer History of Custer Country.* Broken Bow, Neb., 1901. Cloth, or leather. $150.

BUTLER, Arthur G. *Foreign Finches in Captivity.* London, 1894. 60 hand-colored plates. $2,500. London, 1899. Second edition, illustrated with chromolithographs. $400.

BUTLER, Arthur G. *Lepidoptera Exotica.* London, 1874. Author's first book. $500.

BUTLER, Ellis Parker. See *Pigs Is Pigs.*

BUTLER, Ellis Parker. *Philo Gubb: Correspondence School Detective.* Boston, 1918. $100.

BUTLER, Mann. *A History of the Commonwealth of Kentucky.* Louisville, 1834. Portrait. $300.

BUTLER, Samuel. See *Erewhon.*

BUTLER, Samuel. *The Authoress of the Odyssey.* London, 1897. Maps and illustrations. $200.

BUTLER, Samuel. *A First Year in Canterbury Settlement.* London, 1863. Folding map. Red cloth. With 32 pages of ads and light brown endpapers. Author's first book. $400.

BUTLER, Samuel. *Seven Sonnets and A Psalm of Montreal.* Cambridge, 1904. Unbound, or printed wraps. $150.

BUTLER, Samuel. *The Way of All Flesh.* London, 1903. Red cloth, top edges gilt. $500. Limited Editions Club, New York, 1936. 2 vols., leather. In slipcase. $75.

BUTORINA, Evgenia. *The Lettering Art, Works By Moscow Book Designers, 1959–1974.* Kniga, 1977. Slipcase. $300.

BUTTERFIELD, C. W. *An Historical Account of the Expedition Against Sandusky.* Cincinnati, 1873. Portrait. $150.

BUTTERFIELD, C. W. *History of the Discovery of the Northwest.* Cincinnati, 1881. $175.

BUTTERFIELD, C. W. *History of the Girtys.* Cincinnati, 1890. $125.

BUTTERFIELD, C. W. *History of Seneca County, Ohio.* Sandusky, Ohio, 1848. $125.

BUTTERWORTH, Benjamin J. *The Growth of Industrial Art.* Washington, 1888. 200 full-page plates. Folio. $650. Washington, 1892. $500.

BUTTERWORTH, E. *Butterworth's Young Writer's Instructor. Designed for the Improvment of Youth.* (no-place), 1800. $225.

BUTTERWORTH, E. *Elegant Extracts for Butterworth & Son's Universal Penman* . . . (no-place) 1809. $225.

BUTTERWORTH, Hezekiah. *Zig-Zag Journeys in Europe.* Boston, 1880. $125.

BUTTS, Mary. *Armed with Madness.* London, 1928. Drawings by Jean Cocteau. One of 100. $350.

BUTTS, Mary. *The Crystal Cabinet.* London (1937). $175.

BUTTS, Mary. *Imaginary Letters.* Paris, 1928. Illustrated by Jean Cocteau. Cloth, paper label. Paris, 1928. One of 250. In glassine dustwrapper. $150.

BUTTS, Mary. *Scenes from the Life of Cleopatra.* London (1935). $175.

BUTTS, Mary. *Speed the Plow and Other Stories.* London, 1923. Yellow or red cloth. Author's first book. $500.

BYAM, Mrs. Lydia. *A Collection of Exotics from the Island of Antigua.* (London, 1797); *A Collection of Fruits from the West Indies.* London, 1800. 2 vols. in 1. $4,500.

BYERS, William N., and KELLOM, John H. *A Hand Book to the Gold Fields of Nebraska and Kansas.* Chicago, 1859. Map. Blue pictorial printed wraps. $8,500.

BYLES, Mather. *A Poem on the Death of His Late Majesty King George.* (Boston, 1727.) Author's first book. $1,000.

BYNNER, Witter. See Morgan, Emanuel, and Knish, Anne.

BYNNER, Witter. *An Ode to Harvard and Other Poems.* Boston, 1907. Cloth, or leather. Author's first book. $75.

BYNNER, Witter. *The Persistence of Poetry.* San Francisco, 1929. Book Club of California. Full red buckram. One of 325 signed in slipcase. $150.

BYRD, Richard E. *Little America.* New York, 1930. 74 maps and plates. Half vellum. One of 1,000 signed in slipcase. $200.

BYRD, Richard E. *Skyward.* New York, 1928. Boards. 58 maps and plates. One of 500 signed. In glassine dustwrapper. With extra set of plates. Boxed. $450. Trade. $75.

BYRD, William (of Westover). *The Writings of "Colonel William Byrd of Westover in Virginia, Esqr."* New York, 1901. Edited by John Spencer Bassett. Half vellum. One of 500. $125.

BYRNE, B. M. *Florida and Texas: A Series of Letters Comparing the Soil, Climate, and Productions of These States.* Ocala, Fla., 1866. 40 pp., wraps. Third edition (of *Letters on the Climate . . . ;* see below). $300.

BYRNE, B. M. *Letters on the Climate, Soils, and Productions of Florida.* Jacksonville, 1851. 28 pp., wraps. Second edition. $400. (The first edition was published in Ralston, Pa., according to Howes, who gives no date.)

BYRNE, Donn. *Brother Saul.* New York (1927). One of 500 signed. In slipcase. $75.

BYRNE, Donn. *The Foolish Matrons.* New York (1920). First edition, first issue with "I-U" on copyright page. In dustwrapper. $100.

BYRNE, Donn. *Hangman's House.* New York (1926). One of 350 signed. In slipcase. $100.

BYRNE, Donn. *Messer Marco Polo.* New York, 1921. Illustrated by C.B. Falls. Rust-colored cloth. With conjugate of pages 145–46 used as terminal lining paper and with perfect type in the word "of" in the last line of page 10 (Johnson, not in BAL). In dustwrapper. $125.

BYRNE, Donn. *Stories Without Women.* New York, 1915. Frontispiece. Red ribbed cloth. Author's first book. $125.

BYRNE, William S. *Directory of Grass Valley Township for 1865.* San Francisco, 1865. 144 pp., boards. $1,000.

BYRON, George Gordon Noel, Lord. See *The Age of Bronze; Beppo; English Bards and Scotch Reviewers; Ode to Napoleon Buonaparte; The Siege of Corinth.*

BYRON, George Gordon Noel, Lord. *The Bride of Abydos.* London, 1813. 72 pp. First issue, with errata slip and with only 20 lines on page 47. $300. Second issue, without errata slip and with 22 lines on page 47. $150.

BYRON, George Gordon Noel, Lord. *Childe Harold's Pilgrimage: Canto the Third.* London, 1816. First issue with "L" in "Lettre" under the word "La" in line above on title page; at the end of the first line of the second stanza on page 4 there is no exclamation mark. $300. Second issue, "L" under "U" in "CGLU"; and exclamation mark added. $150.

BYRON, George Gordon Noel, Lord. *Childe Harold's Pilgrimage: Canto the Fourth.* London, 1818. First issue, with page 155 ending with "the impressions of." $300.

BYRON, George Gordon Noel, Lord. *Childe Harold's Pilgrimage: A Romaunt.* (Containing cantos I and II.) London, 1812. First issue; with "Written beneath a Picture of J-V-D" on page 189 ("of J-V-D" omitted later). $500.

BYRON, George Gordon Noel, Lord. *Hebrew Melodies.* London, 1815. First issue, with ad for *Roger's Jacqueline.* $300. Second issue, without *Jacqueline* ad. $150.

BYRON, George Gordon Noel, Lord. *Hours of Idleness.* Newark, England, 1807. First issue, with line 2 of page 22 reading "Those tissues of fancy, . . ." $1,500. Second issue, reading "Those tissues of falsehood, . . ." $1,000.

BYRON, George Gordon Noel, Lord. *Manfred, a Dramatic Poem.* London, 1817. 80 pp. (originally in plain wraps). First issue, without quotation on title page and with printer's imprint in 2 lines on back of title page. $500. Second issue, with printer's imprint in one line. $300. Third issue, with *Hamlet* quotation on title page. $150.

BYRON, George Gordon Noel, Lord. *Mazeppa: A Poem.* London, 1819. (Originally in plain drab wraps.) First issue, with imprint on page 70. $350. Second issue, with imprint on back of page 71. $200.

BYRON, George Gordon Noel, Lord. *The Parliamentary Speeches of Lord Byron.* London, 1824. $750.

BYRON, George Gordon Noel, Lord. *The Prisoner of Chillon, and Other Poems.* London, 1816. (Originally in drab plain wraps.) First issue, with ads on back of last page. $300. Second issue with ads on front of last page. $150.

BYRON, George Gordon Noel, Lord. *Sardanapalus, The Two Foscari, Cain.* London, 1821. $300.

BYRON, George Gordon Noel, Lord. *Werner: A Tragedy.* London, 1823. First issue, with the words "The End" on page 188. $500. Second issue, without "The End" $150.

BYRON, Robert. *Europe in the Looking Glass . . .* London, 1926. Author's first book. $350.

C

C., C. *Poems for Harry Crosby.* Black Sun Press. Paris, 1931. (By Caresse Crosby.) Frontispiece. Boards. One of 22 on Van Gelder paper. $1,250. One of 500 on Lafuma paper. $600.

C.3.3. *The Ballad of Reading Gaol.* London (1898). (By Oscar Wilde.) Cinnamon-colored cloth, vellum spine. One of 30 on Japanese vellum. $6,000. Two-toned cloth. One of 800. $1,250. London, 1898. Second edition. $350. London, 1898. Third edition (bearing Wilde's name). One of 99 signed. $1,500. Limited Editions Club, New York, 1937. In slipcase. $100.

CABALLERIA Y COLLELL, Juan. *History of the City of Santa Barbara from Its Discovery to Our Own Days.* Santa Barbara, 1892. Translated by Edmund Burke. Plate, facsimile. 111 pp., wraps. $250.

CABELL, James Branch. *Branchiana.* Richmond, Va. (1907). (147 copies issued.) 10 copies in red cloth (Nelson Bond). $600. Green cloth. $400.

CABELL, James Branch. *Chivalry.* New York, 1909. Illustrated by Howard Pyle and others. Red cloth. In printed glassine dustwrapper. In slipcase. $125.

CABELL, James Branch. *The Cords of Vanity.* New York, 1909. First state, with "The" omitted on spine and cover. $100.

CABELL, James Branch. *The Eagle's Shadow.* New York, 1904. Author's first book. First state, with dedication "M.L.P.B." and frontispiece of seated figure. $100. Second state, dedicated to "Martha Louise Branch." $50.

CABELL, James Branch. *Gallantry.* New York, 1907. Illustrated in color by Howard Pyle. Decorated cloth, gilt top. First binding, silver-gray cloth, stamped with white, silver, and gold lettering. In printed glassine dustwrapper and slipcase. $200.

CABELL, James Branch. *Hamlet Had an Uncle.* New York (1940). One of 125 signed copies. In slipcase. $150.

CABELL, (James) Branch. *Jurgen.* New York, 1919. Reddish brown cloth. First state, with line rules on page 144 intact. $250. London, 1921. Illustrated by Frank C. Pape. First English edition. $175. Golden Cockerel Press. London, 1949. Half morocco. One of 500. $150. Full leather. With an extra engraving. In slipcase. $750.

CABELL, James Branch. *The Line of Love.* New York, 1905. Illustrated in color by Howard Pyle. Decorated green cloth, pictorial label. First state, binding stamped with white and gold lettering. In glassine dustwrapper. $200.

CABELL, James Branch. *The Majors and Their Marriages.* Richmond (1915). Wrappers or cloth. $500.

CABELL, James Branch. *Smith.* New York, 1935. $100. One of 153 signed in slipcase. $250.

CABELL, James Branch. *Taboo.* New York, 1921. One of 100 signed. In dustwrapper. $250. Also, 820 copies unsigned. In dustwrapper. $125.

CABEZA DE VACA, Alvar Nunez. *The Narrative of Alvar Nunez Cabeza de Vaca.* Washington, 1851. Translated by Buckingham Smith. 8 maps. One of 110. $1,250. New York 1871. Three-quarters morocco. One of 100. $500. (For another issue, under another title, see following entry.)

CABEZA DE VACA, Alvar Nunez. *Relation . . . of What Befel the Armament in the Indias Whither Pamphilo de Narvaez Went for Governor, etc.* San Francisco, 1929. Grabhorn printing. Hand decorations in color by Valenti Angelo. Boards. One of 300. In slipcase. $450.

CABINET of Natural History and American Rural Sports (The). Philadelphia, 1830–32–33. 3 vols., in original half calf. First book edition. Published by J. and T. Doughly; includes 29 monthly parts (dated 1830 to 1834). 57 plates, 54 colored. $6,000. In original parts. $12,500. Vols. I and II alone. $2,500.

CABLE, George W. *The Creoles of Louisiana.* New York, 1884. $200.

CABLE, George W. *Old Creole Days.* New York, 1879. First state, with no ads at back. $350. Second state with ads. $150. Author's first book. New York, 1897. Vellum. One of 204. $200. Limited Editions Club. New York, 1943. In slipcase. $100.

CABLE, George W. *The Southern Struggle for Pure Government.* Boston, 1890. Wrappers. $200.

CABLE, George W. *Strange True Stories of Louisiana.* New York, 1889. Illustrated. Pictorial cloth, paper label. $200. London, 1890. $125.

CAHAN, Abraham. *Yekl . . .* New York, 1896. Author's first book. $150.

CAHOON, Herbert. *The Overbrook Press Bibliography, 1934–1959.* Stamford (1963). Limited to only 150 copies. $450.

CAIN, James M. *Mildred Pierce.* New York, 1941. $200.

CAIN, James M. *Our Government.* New York, 1930. First solely authored book. $300.

CAIN, James M. *The Postman Always Rings Twice.* New York, 1934. $1,000.

CAIN, James M. *Serenade.* New York, 1937. $250.

CAIN, James M. *Three of a Kind.* New York, 1943. $250.

CAIN, Paul. *Fast One.* Garden City, 1933. Author's first book. $400.

CAIN, Paul. *Seven Slayers.* Hollywood (1946). Wraps. "First Book Publication" on copyright page. (By Peter Ruric). $200.

CALAVAR: or, The Knight of the Conquest. Philadelphia, 1834. (By Robert Montgomery Bird.) 2 vols., purple cloth, printed paper labels. $400. Author's first book. Philadelphia, 1847. 2 vols., printed wrappers. Revised edition. $200.

CALDER, Alexander. *Animal Sketching.* Pelham, N.Y. (1926). Author's first book. $350.

CALDWELL, Erskine. *American Earth.* New York, 1931. First edition, with code letter "A" on copyright page. $250.

CALDWELL, Erskine. *The Bastard.* New York (1929). Author's first book. One of 200 signed. In glassine dustwrapper. $650. One of 900 unsigned. $300.

CALDWELL, Erskine. *God's Little Acre.* New York, 1933. $1,000.

CALDWELL, Erskine. *Kneel to the Rising Sun and Other Stories.* New York, 1935. One of 300 signed, numbered copies. Issued without dustwrapper. In slipcase. $300. Trade edition. $150.

CALDWELL, Erskine. *Mama's Little Girl.* Mount Vernon, Me., 1932. 2 drawings by Alfred Morang. Printed wrappers. One of 75. $500.

CALDWELL, Erskine. *A Message for Genevieve.* Mount Vernon, 1933. Drawing by Alfred Morang. Printed wrappers. One of 100. $400.

CALDWELL, Erskine. *North of the Danube.* New York (1939). Photographs by Margaret Bourke-White. Linen. $250.

CALDWELL, Erskine. *Poor Fool.* New York, 1930. Illustrated. Blue buckram. Issued without dustwrapper. One of 1,000. $250.

CALDWELL, Erskine. *Tenant Farmer.* New York (1935). Green wrappers. $200.

CALDWELL, Erskine. *Tobacco Road.* New York, 1932. With code letter "A" on copyright page. $850.

CALDWELL, Erskine. *We Are the Living.* New York, 1933. One of 250 signed. In glassine dustwrapper and slipcase. $350. Trade. $175.

CALDWELL, Erskine, and BOURKE-WHITE, Margaret. *Say, Is This the U.S.A.* New York (1941). Illustrated. Pictorial boards. $250.

CALDWELL, J. A. *History of Belmont and Jefferson Counties. Ohio.* Wheeling, Ohio, 1880. Half leather. $200.

CALDWELL, J. F. J. *History of a Brigade of South Carolinians.* Philadelphia, 1866. Cloth. $250.

CALDWELL, Taylor. *Dynasty of Death.* New York, 1938. Author's first book. $50.

CALEF, Robert. *More Wonders of the Invisible World . . .* London, 1700. $5,000.

CALHOUN, James S. *Official Correspondence of James S. Calhoun While Indian Agent at Santa Fe.* Washington, 1915. Illustrated, 4 maps. Cloth. $200.

CALIFORNIA Gold Regions, with a Full Account of Their Mineral Resources . . . (New York, 1849.) $2,500.

CALIFORNIA Illustrated. New York, 1852. By a Returned Californian. (By J.M. Letts.) 48 plates. First issue, anonymous. $850. Later issue, same year, author named. $750. New edition. *Pictorial View of California,* 1853, with fewer plates. $350.

CALIFORNIA Sketches, with Recollections of the Gold Mines. Albany, 1850. Half leather. (By Leonard Kip.) $1,000.

CALISHER, Hortense. *In the Absence of Angels.* Boston, 1951. Author's first English publication. $125.

CALLAGHAN, Morley. *A Native Argosy.* New York, 1929. $250.

CALLAGHAN, Morley. *No Man's Meat.* Paris, 1931. Boards and cloth, paper label. One of 525 signed. In tissue dustwrapper and slipcase. $200.

CALLAGHAN, Morley. *Strange Fugitive.* New York, 1928. Author's first book. $350.

CALVERT, Frederick. *The Isle of Wight Illustrated.* London, 1846. Sepia lithograph frontispiece, colored map. 20 colored aquatint plates. $1,000.

CALVIN, Ross. *Sky Determines.* New York, 1934. Author's first book. $150.

CAMBERG, Muriel. *Out of a Book.* Leith, 1933? (By Muriel Spark, her first book.) $300.

CAMERON, Caddo. *Rangers Is Powerful Hard to Kill.* New York, 1936. $100.

CAMERON, Julia M. *Victorian Photographs of Famous Men and Fair Women.* London, 1926. (Contains an introduction by Virginia Woolf.) One of 450. Issued without dustwrapper. $850. New York, 1926. One of 250. Issued without dustwrapper. $750.

CAMP, Charles L. et al. *Essays For Henry R. Wagner.* San Francisco, 1947. Limited to 260 copies. $125.

CAMP, Walter, and BROOKS, Lillian. *Drives & Putts: A Book of Golf Stories.* Boston, 1899. $150.

CAMPBELL, Alexander, and OWEN, Robert. *Debate on the Evidence of Christianity.* Bethany, Va., 1829. 2 vols. in one, calf. $250.

CAMPBELL, Alexander, and RICE, N. L. *A Debate . . . on the Action, Subject, Design and Administration of Christian Baptism.* Lexington, Ky., 1844. $150.

CAMPBELL, Archibald. *A Voyage Round the World . . .* Edinburgh, 1816. Folding frontispiece map. $1,250. New York, 1817. Map. $750.

CAMPBELL, J. L. *Idaho and Montana Gold Regions.* Chicago, 1865. Map. Half morocco. Second edition. $3,000.

CAMPBELL, J. L. *The Great Agricultural & Mineral West.* Chicago, 1866. Folding ad leaf and map. Printed wraps. "Third Annual Edition." $1,250.

CAMPBELL, John W., Jr. *The Mightiest Machine.* Providence (1947). $75.

CAMPBELL, Patrick. *Travels in the Interior Inhabited Parts of North America.* Toronto, 1937. 3 plates. Cloth. First American edition. One of 550. $300.

CAMPBELL, Roy. *Adamastor: Poems.* London (1930). One of 90 signed. $250. Trade in first-issue dustwrapper with author's name twice on spine. $125. Second-issue jacket, corrected. $60. Cape Town, 1950. Half calf. Illustrated edition. $150.

CAMPBELL, Roy. *Broken Record.* London, 1934. $150. Vellum. One of 50 signed. $450. One of 8 signed. $600.

CAMPBELL, Roy. *Choosing a Mast.* London, 1931. Illustrated by Barnett Freedman. Boards. Issued without dustwrapper. One of 300 signed. $200.

CAMPBELL, Roy. *The Flaming Terrapin.* London, 1924. Boards, cloth spine, paper label. Author's first book. $200. New York, 1924. $150.

CAMPBELL, Roy. *Flowering Reeds: Poems.* London, 1933. One of 69 signed. Issued without dustwrapper. $275. One of 8 signed. $500. Trade in dustwrapper. $100.

CAMPBELL, Roy. *The Georgiad.* London, 1931. Boards and cloth. Issued without dustwrapper. One of 150 signed. $200. Vellum. One of 20 on goatskin parchment paper, signed. $500.

CAMPBELL, Roy. *Poems.* Hours Press. Paris, 1930. Decorated boards and morocco. One of 200 signed. $400.

CAMPBELL, Roy. *The Wayzgoose: A South African Satire.* London, 1928. $150.

CAMUS, Albert. *The Fall.* Allen Press. (Kentfield, Calif., 1966.) Folio, boards. One of 140. $400.

CAMUS, Albert. *The Outsider.* London (1946). (C. Connolly intro.) Author's first English publication. $200.

CAMUS, Albert. *September 15th, 1937.* Bronxville, 1963. Wrappers. One of 50 for presentation, privately printed by Valenti Angelo. $200.

CAMUS, Albert. *The Stranger.* (U.S. edition of *The Outsider.*) New York, 1946. (Does not include Connolly intro.) $100.

CANFIELD, Chauncey L. (editor). *The Diary of a Forty-Niner.* San Francisco, 1906. Colored map. Pictorial boards. $150.

CANNON, George Q. *Writings from the "Western Standard." Published in San Francisco.* Liverpool, 1864. Full morocco. $750.

CANNON, J. P. *Inside of Rebeldom: The Daily Life of a Private in the Confederate Army.* Washington, D.C., 1900. Cloth. $125.

CANOVA, Andrew P. *Life and Adventures in South Florida.* 4 plates. Palatka, Fla., 1885. Printed light green wrappers. $250.

CAPA, Robert. *Death in the Making.* New York (1938). Author's first book. $250.

CAPA, Robert. *Slightly Out of Focus.* New York, 1947. Photo illustrated. $175.

CAPE, Judith. *The Sun and the Moon.* Toronto, 1944. $175.

CAPEK, Karel. *Krakatit.* New York, 1925. $200.

CAPEK, Karl. *The Makropolous Affair.* London, 1922. (First English translation.) $200. Boston, 1925. $125.

CAPOTE, Truman. *Breakfast at Tiffany's.* New York (1958). $125. London (1958). $75.

CAPOTE, Truman. *A Christmas Memory.* New York (1966). One of 600 signed, numbered copies. Bright red slipcase. $350. Trade in beige boards with teal blue cloth spine, maroon slipcase (also noted in black cloth in bright red slipcase) $60. London, 1966? $50.

CAPOTE, Truman. *In Cold Blood.* New York (1965). One of 500 signed, numbered copies. Slipcase. $400. Signed extra leaf inserted. (Small number of copies issued.) $200. Trade. $40. London (1966). $50.

CAPOTE, Truman. *The Grass Harp.* (New York, 1951.) Rough beige cloth. $150. Second binding: smooth, fine-grained beige cloth. $125. London (1952). $100.

CAPOTE, Truman. *The Grass Harp: A Play.* New York (1952). (Reportedly only 500 copies.) $300.

CAPOTE, Truman. *Local Color.* New York (1950). $200. London (1950). 200 numbered copies in full leather. $500.

CAPOTE, Truman. *Observations.* New York (1959). Photographs by Richard Avedon. Slipcase. $275. London (1959). Slipcase. $250.

CAPOTE, Truman. *Other Voices, Other Rooms.* New York (1948). Author's first book. $225. London (1948). $100. Franklin Library, 1979. Signed "Limited Edition." $100.

CAPOTE, Truman. *The Thanksgiving Visitor.* New York (1968). One of 300 signed. Slipcase. (Note: published 11/21/68, last date copyright page is 1967.) $400. Trade in green or brown slipcase (priority unknown). $60. London (1969). $50.

CAPOTE, Truman. *A Tree of Night and Other Stories.* New York (1949). $150. London (1950). $100.

CAPRON, Elisha S. *History of California.* Boston, 1854. Colored map. $200.

CARELESS, John. *The Old English 'Squire: A Poem in Ten Cantos.* London, 1821. 24 colored plates. (By William A. Chatto.) $500.

CAREY, David. *Life in Paris.* London, 1822. Illustrated by George Cruikshank. $1,000. Large paper. $1,500.

CARLETON, James Henry. *The Battle Of Buena Vista, with the Operations of the "Army of Occupation" for One Month.* New York, 1848. 2 folding maps. Original wraps. $300.

CARLETON, William M. *Fax: A Campaign Poem.* Chicago, 1868. Illustrated. Printed wrappers. Author's first book. $750.

CARLTON, Robert. *The New Purchase: or, Seven and a Half Years in the Far West.* New York, 1843. 2 vols., boards. (By Baynard R. Hall.) $200.

CARLYLE, Thomas. See *Sartor Resartus.*

CARLYLE, Thomas. *The French Revolution.* London, 1837. 3 vols. in original boards and cloth. First issue, with 2 pages of ads at end of vol. 2. $750. London, 1839. 3 vols. Second edition. $300. London, 1910. Illustrated. 2 vols., half vellum. One of 150 on large paper. $200. Limited Editions Club. New York, 1956. In slipcase. $75.

CARLYLE, Thomas. *The Life of Friedrich Schiller.* London, 1825. Author's first book. $850.

CARLYLE, Thomas. *Occasional Discourse on the Nigger Question.* London, 1853. Wrappers. $600.

CARLYLE, Thomas. *Past and Present.* London, 1843. $150.

CARLYLE, Thomas. *Shooting Niagara: and After?* London, 1867. Printed green wrappers. $350.

CARMAN, Bliss. See Carmen [sic], Bliss.

CARMAN, Bliss. *The Gate of Peace: A Poem.* New York, 1907. Boards and cloth. One of 112 signed. $350. (Note: All except 24 destroyed by fire, says Johnson.)

CARMAN, Bliss. *Poems.* New York, 1904. 2 vols., half leather. One of 500 signed. $200. Boston, 1905. 2 vols., boards. One of 500 signed. $150.

CARMAN, Bliss. *The Princess of the Tower.* New York, 1906. Boards. One of 62 signed. $300.

CARMEN, Bliss. *Low Tide on Grand Pre.* Toronto (1889? 1890?). (By Bliss Carman.) 13 pp., wrappers. First edition (pirated), $3,000. Author's first book, with his name misspelled. New York, 1893. Lavender cloth. First American edition. $500. London, 1893. $250.

CARNEVALI, Emanuel. *A Hurried Man.* Contact Editions. Paris (1925). Wrappers. Author's first book. $175.

CARPENTER, Edward. *Narcissus* . . . London, 1873. Author's first book. $200.

CARR, Christopher. *Memoirs of Arthur Hamilton.* London, 1886. (By A.C. Benson, his first book.) $150.

CARR, Mrs. Comyns (Alice). *North Italian Folk: Sketches of Town and Country Life.* London, 1878. Hand-colored illustrations by Randolph Caldecott. Boards. One of 400. $300. (New York) 1878. First American edition. (250 copies.) $300.

CARR, John. *Early Times in Middle Tennessee.* Nashville, 1857. $200.

CARR, John. *Pioneer Days in California.* Eureka, Calif., 1891. $250.

CARR, John Dickson. *The Blind Barber.* New York, 1934. $1,500.

CARR, John Dickson. *Death Watch.* New York, 1935. $1,250.

CARR, John Dickson. *The Eight of Swords.* New York, 1934. $1,500.

CARR, John Dickson. *It Walks by Night.* New York, 1930. Author's first book. $2,500.

CARR, Spencer. *A Brief Sketch of La Crosse, Wisconsin.* La Crosse, 1854. 28 pp., sewn. $275.

CARRINGTON, Mrs. Henry B. See *Ab-Sa-Ra-Ka.*

CARRINGTON, John Bodman, and HUGHES, George Ravensworth. *The Plate of the Worshipful Company of Goldsmiths.* Oxford, 1926. Illustrated. Red cloth. $250.

CARROLL, H. Bailey. *The Texan Santa Fe Trail.* Canyon, Tex., 1951. Illustrated. In slipcase. $125.

CARROLL, Lewis. See Dodgson, Charles L.

CARROLL, Lewis. *Alice's Adventures in Wonderland.* London, 1865. (By Charles L. Dodgson.) 42 illustrations by John Tenniel. Red cloth. First edition (suppressed by the author). $75,000. New York, 1866. Red cloth. First American edition made up from the sheets of the English suppressed edition. $7,500. London, 1866. Red cloth. Second edition (and first published English edition). $3,000. Boston, 1869. Green cloth. First edition printed in America. $750. London, 1907. Illustrated by Arthur Rackham. Cloth. One of 1,130 signed by Rackham. $1,500. New York (1907). Half cloth. One of 550. $600. London, 1914. Tenniel illustrations. Vellum. One of 12 copies on vellum. $2,000. Ordinary issue. One of 1,000. $300. Limited Editions Club. New York, 1932. Signed by Alice Hargreaves, the original "Alice." $1,000. Unsigned $400. New York, 1969. Salvador Dali illustrations (13 plates), folio, loose signatures in folder and leather-backed case. Limited edition, signed by Dali. $2,500.

CARROLL, Lewis. *Alice's Adventures Under Ground.* London, 1886. (By Charles L. Dodgson.) 37 illustrations by the author. Red cloth, gilt edges. $1,000. (Note: This is a facsimile of the original manuscript from which *Alice's Adventures in Wonderland* was developed.)

CARROLL, Lewis. *Curiosa Mathematica.* London, 1888. (By Charles L. Dodgson.) Gray or tan cloth. $750.

CARROLL, Lewis. *Feeding the Mind.* London, 1907. (By Charles L. Dodgson.) Full flexible maroon morocco. $400. Boards or wraps. $250.

CARROLL, Lewis. *The Game of Logic.* London, 1886. (By Charles L. Dodgson.) With envelope containing 9 counters and board diagram. First (private) edition. $4,000. Only a few copies known. London, 1887. Second edition. $1,500.

CARROLL, Lewis. *The Hunting of the Snark.* London, 1876. (By Charles L. Dodgson.) Illustrated by Henry Holiday. Pictorial cloth, gilt edges. $500. New York, 1903. Illustrated by Peter Newell. $250.

CARROLL, Lewis. *Phantasmagoria and Other Poems.* London, 1869. (By Charles L. Dodgson.) $750.

CARROLL, Lewis. *Sylvie and Bruno.* London, 1889. (By Charles L. Dodgson.) Illustrated by Harry Furniss. $150.

CARROLL, Lewis. *Sylvie and Bruno Concluded.* London, 1893. (By Charles L. Dodgson.) Red cloth (white for presentation). Illustrated by Harry Furniss. First issue, with error in table of contents showing chapter 8 at page 110 (vs. 113). $125.

CARROLL, Lewis. *A Tangled Tale.* London, 1885. (By Charles L. Dodgson.) Illustrated by A. B. Frost. Pictorial cloth. $500.

CARROLL, Lewis. *Three Sunsets and Other Poems.* London, 1898. (By Charles L. Dodgson.) Frontispiece and other illustrations. $350.

CARROLL, Lewis. *Through the Looking Glass, and What Alice Found There.* London, 1872. (By Charles L. Dodgson.) 50 illustrations by John Tenniel. Red cloth. First issue, with "wade" on page 21. $1,000. Boston, 1872. First American edition. $250. Limited Editions Club. New York, 1935. Signed by Alice Hargreaves. In slipcase. $850. Unsigned. $300.

CARRUTHERS, George. *Paper-Making. Part I. First Hundred Years Of Paper-Making. Part II. First Century of Paper-Making in Canada.* Toronto, 1947. $125.

CARSON, Christopher. See Grant, Blanche C.

CARSON, James H. *Early Recollections of the Mines, and a Description of the Great Tulare Valley.* Stockton, Calif., 1852. Folding map. 64 pp. printed wrappers (with cover title reading "Second Edition. Life in California, etc."). First edition (in book form; earlier appearance in the San Joaquin *Republican*). $10,000.

CARSON, Rachel. *Silent Spring.* Boston, 1962. First edition stated. $100.

CARSTARPHEN, J. E. *My Trip to California in '49.* (Louisiana, Mo., 1914.) 8 pp., wrappers. Limited edition. $250.

CARTER, Angela. *Shadow Dance.* London, 1966. $150.

CARTER, Angela. *Unicorn.* Leeds, 1966. Author's first book. $250.

CARTER, E. S. *The Life and Adventures of E.S. Carter Including a Trip Across the Plains and Mountains in 1852* . . . St. Joseph, 1896. $1,250.

CARTER, Frederick. *D. H. Lawrence and the Body Mystical.* London, 1932. Frontispiece. One of 75 on vellum. In glassine dustwrapper. $150.

CARTER, Harry (editor). *Founier on Typefounding; the Text of the Manuel Typographique (1764–1766) Translated* . . . London, 1930. 16 double-page plates. One of 260 numbered copies. $250.

CARTER, John. *Binding Variants in English Publishing, 1820–1900.* London, 1932. Limited to 500 copies. $300.

CARTER, John (editor). *New Paths In Book Publishing, Essays By Various Hands.* London (1934). $75.

CARTER, John, and MUIR, Percy H. *Printing and the Mind of Man.* (London), 1967. $350.

CARTER, John, and POLLARD, Graham. *An Enquiry into the Nature of Certain 19th Century Pamphlets.* London, 1934. 4 plates. In dustwrapper. $250.

CARTER, Robert G. *Four Brothers in Blue.* Washington, 1913. Frontispiece. $650. Washington, 1913. Second edition (so-called "Imperfect Edition" made up of magazine installments bound with first-edition text). $1,250.

CARTER, Robert G. *Massacre of Salt Creek Prairie and the Cowboy's Verdict.* Washington, 1919. 48 pp., wrappers. $500.

CARTER, Robert G. *The Old Sergeant's Story: Winning the West from the Indians and Badmen in 1870 to 1876.* New York, 1926. Portrait, plates. $350.

CARTER, Robert G. *On the Border with Mackenzie.* Washington (1935). 3 portraits. Cloth. $1,500.

CARTER, Robert G. *On the Trail of Deserters.* Washington, 1920. Printed wrappers. One of 250. $500.

CARTER, Robert G. *Pursuit of Kicking Bird: A Campaign in the Texas "Bad Lands."* Washington, 1920. 44 pp., wrappers. (100 copies printed.) $500.

CARTER, Susannah. *The Frugal Housewife: or, Complete Woman Cook.* Philadelphia, 1802. Illustrated. Boards. $500.

CARTER, Thomas Francis. *The Invention of Printing in China and Its Spread Westward.* New York (1931). Revised with an introduction by Douglas McMurtrie on Carter. $100.

CARTER, W. A. *History of Fannin County, Texas.* Bonham, Tex., 1885. $1,000.

CARTIER-BRESSON, Henri. *The Decisive Moment.* New York (1955). Illustrated. Boards. In Matisse dustwrapper. With pamphlet of captions laid in. $650.

CARTIER-BRESSON, Henri. *The Europeans.* New York (1955). $500.

CARTIER-BRESSON, Henri. *The People of Moscow.* New York, 1955. Cloth. $300.

CARTLAND, Barbara. *Jig-Saw.* London (1925). Author's first book. $300.

CARUTHERS, W. A. See *The Kentuckian in New York.*

CARVER, Raymond. *Near Klamath.* Sacramento, 1968. Author's first book. Wraps. $1,500.

CARVER, Raymond. *Will You Please Be Quiet, Please?* New York, 1976. $350.

CARVER, Raymond. *Winter Insomnia.* (Santa Cruz, 1970.) Wraps. $125.

CARY, Arthur. *Verse.* Edinburgh, 1908. (Joyce Cary's first book.) $2,500.

CARY, Joyce. *Aissa Saved.* London, 1932. $400.

CARY, Joyce. *An American Visitor.* London, 1933. $300.

CASLER, John. *Four Years in the Stonewall Brigade.* Guthrie, Okla., 1893. Folding facsimile. $250.

CASLON'S Circular. Vol. I. (London) October 1875 to Spring 1896. 73 issues. $225.

CASPER, C. N. *Directory Of The Antiquarian Booksellers And Dealers In Second-Hand Books Of the United States . . .* Milwaukee, 1885. $100.

CASTANEDA, Carlos. *The Teachings of Don Juan: Yaqui Way of Knowledge.* Berkeley, 1968. Author's first book. $150.

CASTANEDA, Carlos E. *Our Catholic Heritage in Texas, 1519–1810.* Austin, 1936–42. 5 vols. $850.

CASTLE Dismal; or, the Bachelor's Christmas. New York, 1844. (By William Gilmore Simms.) Boards. $250.

CASTLE Rackment; An Hibernian Tale. London, 1800. (By Maria Edgeworth.) Boards. $200.

CASTLEMAN, Alfred L. *Army of the Potomac: Behind the Scenes.* Milwaukee, 1863. $100.

CASTLEMON, H. C. (Harry). *Frank on the Lower Mississippi.* Cincinnati, 1867. (By Charles Austin Fosdick.) $125.

CASTLEMON, H. C. *Frank the Young Naturalist.* Cincinnati, 1865. (By Charles Austin Fosdick, his first book.) $200.

CASTLEMON, Harry. *Guy Harris, the Runaway.* New York, 1887. (By Charles Austin Fosdick.) Printed wrappers. $125.

CASTLEMON, Harry. *The Sportsman's Club Among the Trappers.* Philadelphia, 1874. (By Charles Austin Fosdick.) Plates. $100.

CATALOG of the Avery Architectural Library, A Memorial Library of Architecture, Archaeology, and Decorative Art. New York, 1895. Limited to 1,000 copies. $300.

CATALOGUE of A Collection of Early German Books in the Library of C. Fairfax Murray. London, 1962. (Completed copies done up in 1981.) 2 vols. $225.

CATALOGUE of Books & Manuscripts in the Estelle Doheny Collection. Los Angeles, 1940–46–55. 3 vols. Each volume limited to 100 copies. $1,500.

CATALOGUE of First Editions of American Authors. New York, 1885. $100.

CATALOGUE of the Books Belonging to the Estate of the Late Mr. William Gowans, Bookseller of No. 115 Nassau Street . . . New York, 1871–72. 16 vols. $375.

CATALOGUE of the Collection of Joseph T. Tower, Jr. Class Of 1921 In The Institute Of Geographical Exploration . . . (No-place) privately printed, 1933. Limited to 110 copies. $150.

CATALOGUE of the Library Belonging To Mr. Thomas W. Field. New York, 1875. $135.

CATALOGUE of the Library of Robert Hoe of New York. New York, 1911–12. 8 vols. $350.

CATALOGUE of the Wheeler Gift of Books, Pamphlets and Periodicals in the Library of the American Institute of Electrical Engineers. New York, 1909. 2 vols. $300.

CATALOGUE of Valuable Printed Books and Fine Bindings from the Celebrated Collection . . . *J. R. Abbey.* London, 1965–78. 10 vols. $450.

CATES, Cliff D. *Pioneer History of Wise County, Texas.* Decatur, Tex., 1907. Illustrated. Stiff wrappers. $250.

CATESBY, Mark. *The Natural History of Carolina, Florida and the Bahama Islands* . . . London (1730–) 1731–1743 (–1747). 2 vols. 220 hand-colored engraved plates. $250,000.

CATHER, Willa. See McClure, S.S.; Milmine, Georgine. See also *The Sombrero.*

CATHER, Willa. *Alexander's Bridge.* Boston, 1912. Coarse blue or purple-mesh cloth. With "Willa S. Cather" on spine and half title before title page. $500. Second issue with half title after title page. $300. London, 1912. First English edition. $250.

CATHER, Willa. *April Twilights.* Boston, 1903. Brown boards, paper labels. Author's first book. Issued without dustwrapper. $1,250. New York, 1923. Boards and parchment. First revised edition. One of 450 signed in slipcase. $500. Trade. $125. London, 1924. $250.

CATHER, Willa. *Death Comes for the Archbishop.* New York, 1927. $450. Also boards and cloth. One of 175 signed. In dustwrapper and slipcase. $850. One of 50 on vellum, signed. In slipcase. $2,500. London, 1927. $250. New York, 1929. Illustrated by Harold von Schmidt. Vellum. One of 170 signed in slipcase. $500.

CATHER, Willa. *A Lost Lady.* New York, 1923. First issue, in green cloth with title at top of spine, and "of" correct in line 19 on page 174. $300. Second issue with Cather's name at top of spine. In green or tan cloth. $250. Boards and cloth. One of 20 lettered A to T, signed. In glassine dustwrapper and slipcase. $2,250. One of 200 numbered copies signed in slipcase. $600.

CATHER, Willa. *Lucy Gayheart.* New York, 1935. $125. Buckram. One of 749 signed. In dustwrapper and slipcase. $350.

CATHER, Willa. *My Antonia.* Boston, 1918. Illustrated by W. T. Benda. Brown cloth. First issue, with illustrations on glazed paper inserted. In dustwrapper. $2,000. Lacking dustwrapper. $400. London, 1919. $1,500. Lacking dustwrapper. $200.

CATHER, Willa. *My Mortal Enemy.* New York, 1926. In dustwrapper and slipcase. $200. Another issue, one of 220 signed in slipcase. $600.

CATHER, Willa. *Not Under Forty.* New York, 1936. $100. One of 333 large paper copies on vellum, signed. In dustwrapper and slipcase. $400.

CATHER, Willa. *The Novels and Stories of Willa Cather.* Boston, 1937–41. 13 vols., two-toned cloth. Autograph edition. One of 970 signed. In dustwrapper. $2,500.

CATHER, Willa. *O Pioneers!* Boston, 1913. Colored frontispiece by Clarence Underwood. First issue, either light yellow-brown or pale cream vertical ribbed cloth. With period after "Co." on spine touching "o," and with last page tipped in. $500. Second issue, in yellow-brown linen cloth, with period separated from "o." $300.

CATHER, Willa. *Obscure Destinies.* New York, 1932. $150. Vellum and boards. One of 260 on vellum, signed. In dustwrapper and slipcase. $500.

CATHER, Willa. *One of Ours.* New York, 1922. "Second printing, September 1922." $350. Boards. One of 35 on vellum, signed. In slipcase. $1,500. One of 310 on handmade paper, signed. In slipcase. $750.

CATHER, Willa. *The Professor's House.* New York, 1925. $400. Buckram and boards. One of 40 on vellum, signed. In slipcase. $1,500. One of 185, signed. In slipcase. $750.

CATHER, Willa. *Sapphira and the Slave Girl.* New York, 1940. $125. Half buckram. One of 520 signed. In dustwrapper and slipcase. $350.

CATHER, Willa. *Shadows on the Rock.* New York, 1931. First edition, advance issue, mislabeled "Second edition" on copyright page. $400. Regular trade edition ("First edition" on copyright page). $175. Marbled boards. Leather label. One of 619 signed. In dustwrapper and slipcase. $400. Full orange vellum. One of 199 on vellum, signed. In dustwrapper and slipcase. $850.

CATHER, Willa. *The Song of the Lark.* Boston, 1915. First issue, with boxed ads on copyright page and "moment" for "moments" in third line from bottom on page 8. $400. Second issue, the ads face half title and page 8 corrected. $175.

CATHER, Willa. *The Troll Garden.* New York, 1905. First issue, with "McClure Phillips & Co." at foot of spine. $800. Second issue has "Doubleday, Page & Co." $400.

CATHER, Willa. *Youth and the Bright Medusa.* New York, 1920. In dustwrapper. $500. One of 35 signed. $1,750.

CATHER, Willa, and CANFIELD, Dorothy. *The Fear That Walks by Noonday.* New York, 1931. Boards, paper label. One of 30. $2,500.

CATHERWOOD, Frederick. *Views of Ancient Monuments in Central America, Chiapas, and Yucatan.* London, 1844. Colored title page, engraved map, 25 lithographs. Folio, half morocco. Price depends on whether sets are fully colored. $40,000–$50,000. Or, only tinted. $20,000–$30,000. Book very susceptible to foxing and discoloration which badly affects many copies and greatly reduces value. Barre, Mass., 1965. One of 500 facsimile copies. $500.

CATHOLIC Anthology 1914–1915 (The). London, 1915. Edited by Ezra Pound. Gray boards. (Includes T.S. Eliot's "The Love Song of J. Alfred Prufrock" and 4 other poems.) $750.

CATICH, Edward M. *Eric Gill, His Social and Artistic Roots*. Iowa City, 1964. $100.

CATICH, Edward M. *Letters Redrawn from the Trajan Inscription in Rome*. Davenport, Iowa (1961). 2 parts (book and 93 plates) in case. $350.

CATICH, Edward M. *The Origin of the Serif; Brush Writing & Roman Letters*. Davenport, Iowa, 1968. $250.

CATICH, Edward M. *Reed, Pen, & Brush Alphabets For Writing And Lettering*. Davenport, (1972). 2 vols. 32 pages in book and 28 heavy leaves loosely inserted in portfolio. $375.

CATICH, Edward M. *The Trajan Inscription, an Essay by Edward M. Catich Together with an Original Rubbing from the Inscription*. Boston, 1973. Limited to 230 numbered copies signed by Catich. $250.

CATLIN, George. *Letters and Notes on the Manners, Customs, and Conditions of the North American Indians*. London, 1841. 2 maps (one folding), one chart, 309 illustrations. 2 vols., cloth, paper labels. $1,250. All early editions. $650–$850. New York. 1841. 2 vols., cloth. First American edition. $1,000.

CATLIN, George. *O-Kee-Pa, a Religious Ceremony*. London, 1867. 13 colored lithographs, with "folio reservatum" laid in. $5,000. Without "reservatum." $2,000. Philadelphia, 1867. Often subject to poor color, in which case price goes down drastically.

CATLIN, George. *North American Indian Portfolio*. London or New York, 1844. Either 25 or 31 plates mounted on cardboard. Text in cloth-backed wrappers. Large folio. With excellent color: $50,000–$60,000. Tinted: $15,000–$20,000. Often subject to poor color in which case price goes down drastically. New facsimile edition (1990). $1,250.

CATON, John Dean. *The Last of the Illinois, and a Sketch of the Pottawatomies*. Chicago, 1870. 36 pp., wrappers. $175.

CATTLE Raising in South Dakota. (Forest City, 1904.) 32 pp., wrappers. $200.

CAWEIN, Madison J. *Blooms of the Berry*. Louisville, 1887. Cloth. Author's first book. $75.

CAXTON, Pisistratus. *What Will He Do with It?* Edinburgh (1859). (By Edward Bulwer-Lytton.) 4 vols., cloth. $250.

CAXTON, William. *The History of Reynard the Foxe*. London, 1892. Kelmscott Press. Vellum. One of 300. $1,250.

CELEBRATED Collection of Americana Formed by the Late Thomas Winthrop Streeter (The). New York, 1966–69. 8 vols. $500.

CELEBRATED Trials and Remarkable Cases. (By George Borrow.) London, 1825. Author's first book. 6 vols. $500.

CELIZ, Fray Francisco. *Diary of the Alarcon Expedition into Texas, 1718–1719*. Los Angeles, 1935. Translated by Fritz L. Hoffman. 10 plates. One of 600. $300.

CELLINI, Benvenuto. *The Life of Benvenuto Cellini.* London, 1771. 2 vols. First edition in English. $250.

CENDRARS, Blaise. *Panama or the Adventures of My Seven Uncles.* New York, 1931. Translated from the French and illustrated by John Dos Passos. Stiff pictorial wrappers. New York, 1931. One of 300 signed by Cendrars and Dos Passos. In slipcase. $200.

CERVANTES, Miguel de. *The History of Don Quixote of the Mancha.* London, 1930. Nonesuch Press. P.A. Motteux's translation revised anew (1743). 21 illustrations by E. McKnight Kauffer. 2 vols., morocco. $450.

CERVANTES, Miguel de. *The History of the Valorous and Wittie Knight-Errant, Don Quixote of the Mancha.* London, 1927–28. Ashendene Press. Thomas Shelton translation. Woodcut initials and borders by Louise Powell. 2 vols., pigskin. One of 225 on paper. $3,000. One of 22 on vellum. $10,000.

CHABOT, Frederick Charles. *Pictorial Sketch of Mission San Jose de San Miguel de Aguayo on the San Antonio River.* San Antonio, 1935. Illustrated, including color plates and photographs. Full leatherette. One of 12. $1,250.

CHABOT, Frederick Charles. *With the Makers of San Antonio.* San Antonio, 1937. Illustrated. One of 25 copies (India proof issue) for presentation. $750.

CHADWICK, Henry. *The Game of Base Ball; How to Learn It, How to Play It, and How to Teach It.* New York (1868). First edition, with rules for 1868. $750.

CHAGALL, Marc (illustrator). *Drawings for the Bible.* (French issue: *Dessins pour la Bible.*) New York (and Paris), 1960. Text by Gaston Bachelard. Boards. (Constituting *Verve, No. 37/38.*) $4,000.

CHAGALL, Marc (illustrator). *Illustrations for the Bible.* New York (or Paris), 1956. Edited by Jean Wahl. Translated by Samuel Beckett from the Paris title of the same year *(Eaux-fortes pour la Bible).* 29 lithographs (17 in color), 105 plates. Pictorial boards in color. $5,000. (This is *Verve, No. 33/34,* issued in French and in English.)

CHAGALL, Marc (illustrator). *The Jerusalem Windows.* (French: *Vitraux pour Jerusalem.*) New York (or Monte Carlo), 1962. Text by Jean Leymarie. $1,250.

CHAGALL, Marc (illustrator). *The Lithographs of Chagall.* Monte Carlo and New York or Boston, 1960–74. Text by Fernand Mourlot. 27 original lithographs. 4 vols., quarto, cloth. $6,500.

CHAINBEARER (The), or, The Littlepage Manuscripts. London, 1845. (By James Fenimore Cooper.) 3 vols., tan boards. $350. New York, 1845. 2 vols., wrappers. $750. (Note: Name is misspelled "Fennimore" on front cover.)

CHALMERS, George. *The Life of Thomas Ruddimann, A.M., the Keeper, for Almost Fifty Years, of the Library . . .* London, 1794. $125.

CHAMBERS, Andrew Jackson. *Recollections.* No-place (1947). 40 pp., stapled. $175.

CHAMBERS, Charles E. S. *Golfing: A Handbook . . .* Edinburgh, 1887. $500.

CHAMBERS, Robert. *A Few Rambling Remarks on Golf . . .* Edinburgh, 1862. Illustrated wraps. $1,500.

CHAMBERS, Robert W. *In the Quarter.* Chicago, 1893. Author's first book. $150.

CHAMBERS, Robert W. *The King in Yellow.* Chicago, 1895. Green cloth with lizard design (preferred binding, perhaps earliest). $150. Second binding. $100.

CHAMBERS, Robert W. *The Read Republic: A Romance of the Commune.* New York, 1895. Pictorial cloth. $100.

CHAMISSO, Adelbert von. *A Sojourn at San Francisco Bay 1816.* San Francisco, 1936. Grabhorn printing. One of 250. $175.

CHAMPION, Joseph. *The Young Penman's Daily Practice . . .* (London) 1759. $225.

CHANDLER, Raymond. *The Big Sleep.* New York, 1939. Author's first book. $2,500.

CHANDLER, Raymond, *Farewell, My Lovely.* New York, 1940. $2,250.

CHANDLER, Raymond. *The Lady in the Lake.* New York, 1943. $1,500.

CHANDLER, Raymond. *The Little Sister.* London (1949). $300. Boston, 1949. $300.

CHANDLER, Raymond. *The Long Good-Bye.* London (1953). $300. Boston, 1954. $300.

CHANDLER, Raymond. *Playback.* London (1958). $200.

CHANDLER, Raymond. *The Smell of Fear.* London (1965). $150.

CHANDLESS, William. *A Visit to Salt Lake: Being a Journey Across the Plains and a Residence in the Mormon Settlements of Utah.* London, 1857. Folding map. $600.

CHANNING, William Ellery (1780–1842). *The Duties of Children.* Boston, 1807. With original wraps bound in. Author's first book. $300.

CHANNING, William Ellery (1780–1842). *A Sermon Delivered at the Ordination of the Rev. Jared Sparks . . .* Baltimore, 1819. $200.

CHANNING, William Ellery (1818–1901). *John Brown, and the Heroes of Harper's Ferry: A Poem.* Boston, 1886. Green cloth. $150.

CHANTICLEER: A Bibliography of The Golden Cockerel Press. Waltham Saint Lawrence, 1936. One of 300. $250.

CHANUTE, Octave. *Progress in Flying Machines.* New York (1894). 85 illustrations. $750.

CHAPELLE, Howard I. *The Baltimore Clipper.* Salem, Mass., 1930. Illustrated. Cloth (leatherette). $250. Marbled boards. One of 97. $400.

CHAPMAN, John Jay. See *The Two Philosophers.*

CHAPMAN, R. W. *Cancels.* London, 1930. Limited to 500 copies. $250.

CHAPPE D'AUTEROCHE, Jean. *A Voyage to California, to Observe the Transit of Venus . . .* London, 1778. Folding plan of Mexico City. First English translation from the French of 1772. $1,250.

CHAPPELL, Fred. *It Is Time, Lord.* New York, 1963. Author's first book. $125.

CHARLES Auchester. London, 1853. (By Elizabeth Sara Shepard.) Author's first book. 3 vols. $300.

CHARLEVOIX, Francis Xavier. *Histoire Et Description Générale De La Nouvelle France . . .* Paris, 1744. 3 vols. 28 maps, 96 plates on 22 sheets. $4,000.

CHARLEVOIX, Francis Xavier. *A Voyage to North America, Under The Command of the President King of France . . .* Dublin, 1766. 2 vols. 8 maps. 2 plates. $2,000.

CHARLEVOIX, Pierre F. X. *Journal of a Voyage to North America.* London, 1761. Folding map. 2 vols. $1,000.

CHARTERIS, Leslie. *X Esquire.* London, 1927. (By Charles Bowyer Lin, his first book.) $300.

CHASE, Charles M. *The Editor's Run in New Mexico and Colorado.* Lyndon, Vt., 1882. Illustrated. Pictorial wrappers. $250.

CHASE, Owen (and others). *Narratives of the Wreck of the Whale Ship "Essex."* Golden Cockerel Press. London, 1935. 12 wood engravings by Robert Gibbings. One of 275. Issued without dustwrapper. $850.

CHATEAUBRIAND, François A. *Travels In America And Italy . . .* London, 1828. 2 vols. $175.

CHATTERTON, E. Keble. *Ship-Models.* London, 1923. Edited by Geoffrey Holme. 142 plates, many in color. One of 1,000. $250.

CHATTERTON, E. Keble. *Steamship Models.* London, 1924. 128 plates, some in color. One of 1,000 signed. $300.

CHATTO, William A. See Careless, John.

CHATWIN, Bruce. *In Patagonia.* London, 1977. Author's first book. $300. New York (1978). $100.

CHAUCER, Geoffrey. *The Canterbury Tales.* London, 1913. Riccardi Press. Colored plates by W. Russell Flint. 3 vols., limp vellum, silk ties. One of 500. $750. Also, one of 12 on vellum, and with extra plates in cloth portfolio. $5,000 or more. New York, 1930. Illustrated by Rockwell Kent. 2 vols., pigskin. One of 75 signed. $1,500. Another issue. Cloth. One of 924 signed. $400. Golden Cockerel Press. Waltham Saint Lawrence, 1929–31. Eric Gill engravings. 4 vols., folio, boards, morocco spine. One of 485. $5,000. One of 15 on vellum. Slipcase. $10,000, or more. Limited Editions Club, New York. 1946. Illustrated by Arthur Szyk. Half pigskin. In slipcase. $250.

CHAUCER, Geoffrey. *Troilus and Criseyde.* Waltham Saint Lawrence, 1927. Golden Cockerel Press. 5 full-page illustrations, 5 half-page decorations, and engraved title page by Eric Gill. Folio, boards, and morocco. One of 219. $7,500.

CHEEVER, Henry T. *The Island World of the Pacific.* Glasgow (1850). Frontispiece. Calf. $300.

CHEEVER, John. *Atlantic Crossing.* (Cottondale, 1986). One of 90 numbered copies. Full leather in drop-tray box. $400.

CHEEVER, John. *The Enormous Radio and Other Stories.* New York, 1953. "I" on copyright page. $200. London, 1953. $125.

CHEEVER, John. *Homage to Shakespeare.* Stevenson (1968). One of 150 signed. In dustwrapper. $250.

CHEEVER, John. *The Housebreaker of Shady Hill and Other Stories.* New York, 1958. $75. London, 1958. $75.

CHEEVER, John. *The Leaves, the Lionfish and the Bear.* Los Angeles, 1980. 4 copies with printed name of recipient. $350. 26 signed and lettered copies. $200. 300 signed and numbered copies. $75.

CHEEVER, John. *Some People, Places and Things That Will Not Appear in My Next Novel.* New York (1961). $75. London, 1961. $60.

CHEEVER, John. *The Wapshot Chronicle.* New York (1957). $100. London, 1957. $75. Franklin Library, 1978. Signed "Limited Edition." $75.

CHEEVER, John. *The Way Some People Live.* New York (1943). Author's first book. $850.

CHENG, Man-ch'ing, and SMITH, Robert W. *T'ai-chi: The Supreme Exercise For Health, Sport, and Self-Defense.* Tokyo, 1967. First edition stated. $60.

CHERRY-GARRARD, Apsley. *The Worst Journey in the World: Antarctic, 1910–1913.* London, 1922. Maps and panoramas, color plates. 2 vols., boards, paper labels. $1,000.

CHESNUTT, Charles W. *The Colonel's Dream.* New York, 1905. Name spelled "Chestnutt" on spine and front. $250. Name spelled correctly. $175. London, 1905. $150.

CHESNUTT, Charles W. *The Conjure Woman.* Boston, 1899. Author's first book. 150 large paper copies. $1,000. Trade. $300. London, 1899. $200.

CHESNUTT, Charles W. *Frederick Douglass.* Boston, 1899. Limp leather. $300. London, 1899. $200.

CHESNUTT, Charles W. *The House Behind the Cedars.* Boston, 1900. $250.

CHESNUTT, Charles W. *The Wife of His Youth and Other Stories.* Boston, $250.

CHESTER, Alfred. *Here Be Dragons.* Paris, 1955. Author's first book. Wraps. 125 deluxe copies, $125. One of 1,000. $75.

CHESTERTON, G. K. *Charles Dickens Fifty Years After.* No-place, 1920. Wrappers. One of 25. $200.

CHESTERTON, G. K. *Collected Poems.* London, 1927. Boards and parchment. One of 350 signed. $150.

CHESTERTON, G. K. *The Coloured Lands.* London, 1938. Illustrated by the author. Boards. In dustwrapper. $100.

CHESTERTON, G. K. *Graybeards at Play: Rhymes and Sketches.* London, 1900. Boards and buckram. Author's first book. $750.

CHESTERTON, G. K. *The Incredulity of Father Brown.* London (1926). $350. New York, 1926. $200.

CHESTERTON, G. K. *The Innocence of Father Brown.* London, 1911. Illustrated by S.S. Lucas. Red cloth. $200. New York, 1911. $75.

CHESTERTON, G. K. *London.* London, 1914. 10 tipped-in photogravure plates by Alvin Langdon Coburn. $350.

CHESTERTON, G. K. *The Scandal of Father Brown.* London (1935). $250. New York, 1935. $150.

CHESTERTON, G. K. *The Secret of Father Brown.* London (1927). $300. New York, 1927. $150.

CHESTERTON, G. K. *The Wisdom of Father Brown.* London, 1914. $200. New York, 1915. $75.

CHEW, Beverly. *Essays & Verses About Books.* New York, privately printed, 1926. Limited to 275 copies. (Printed by D.B. Updike at Merrymount Press.) $100.

CHICAGO Illustrated. (Cover title.) (Chicago, 1866–67.) 52 tinted lithograph views. Text by James W. Sheahan. Oblong folio, morocco. Jevne and Almini, publishers. First edition, second issue $8,000–$10,000. (The original issue was in 13 parts and is now very rare. Probable value: $17,500 or more.) New York, 1952. 12 plates. Portfolio. Reprint edition. $200.

CHIDSEY, Donald Barr. *John the Great: The Times and Life of a Remarkable American, John L. Sullivan.* Garden City, 1942. $40.

CHILD, Andrew. *Overland Route to California.* Milwaukee, 1852. Full leather. $6,000.

CHILD, John, Major. *New-England's Jonas Cast Up at London . . .* London, 1647. $8,500.

CHILD, Lydia Maria. See *Emily Parker; Evenings in New England; The First Settlers in New England; The Frugal Housewife; Hobomok.*

CHILDRESS, Alice. *Like One of the Family.* Brooklyn (1956). Author's first book. $125.

CHILDS, C. G. (engraver). *Views in Philadelphia and Its Vicinity.* Philadelphia, 1827–(30). Engraved title page, plan, 24 engraved views. Cloth or boards. $3,000.

CHINESE Poems. London, 1916. (By Arthur Waley.) Author's first book. Wraps. (About 50 copies.) $1,500.

CHITTENDEN, Hiram M. *The American Fur Trade of the Far West.* New York, 1902. Folding map, plan, 3 facsimiles, 6 plates. 3 vols., green cloth. $750. New York, 1935. Plates. 2 vols. In slipcase. $250.

CHITTENDEN, Hiram M. *History of Early Steamboat Navigation on the Missouri River.* New York, 1903. 16 plates. 2 vols. One of 950. $400.

CHIVERS, Thomas Holley. *The Lost Pleiad and Other Poems.* New York, 1845. Printed tan wrappers. $400.

CHIVERS, Thomas Holley. *Memoralia.* Philadelphia, 1853. Boards. $250.

CHIVERS, Thomas Holley. *Nacoochee: or, The Beautiful Star.* New York, 1837. In original cloth. $600.

CHIVERS, Thomas Holley. *The Path of Sorrow.* Franklin, T(enn.), 1832. In original blue boards, purple cloth, paper label. Author's first book. $850.

CHRISTIANISM: Or Belief and Unbelief Reconciled. (London, 1832.) (By Leigh Hunt.) 59 pp., in original cloth, paper label. (75 printed.) $750.

CHRISTIE, Agatha. *Hercule Poirot's Christmas.* London (1939). $600.

CHRISTIE, Agatha. *The Hound of Death and Other Stories.* London (1933). $600.

CHRISTIE, Agatha. *The Man in the Brown Suit.* London, 1924. $2,500. New York, 1924. $1,000.

CHRISTIE, Agatha. *Murder for Christmas: A Poirot Story.* New York, 1939. U.S. title for *Hercule Poirot's Christmas.* $300.

CHRISTIE, Agatha. *Murder in the Calais Coach.* New York, 1934. (U.S. title for *Murder on the Orient Express.*) $750.

CHRISTIE, Agatha. *Murder in Mesopotamia.* London (1936). $400. New York, 1936. $250.

CHRISTIE, Agatha. *Murder on the Orient Express.* London (1934). $2,000. New York, 1934. Unspecified number of copies for publisher's presentation. $800.

CHRISTIE, Agatha. *The Mysterious Affair at Styles.* New York, 1920. Author's first book. In dustwrapper. $6,000. London, 1921. $6,000.

CHRISTIE, Agatha. *Sad Cypress.* London (1940). $350. New York, 1940. $200.

CHRISTIE, Richard Copley. *Etienne Dolet, The Martyr of the Renaissance, A Biography.* London, 1899. Second edition, revised and corrected. $125.

CHRONICLES of the City of Gotham. New York, 1830. (By James Kirke Paulding.) $200.

CHUBB, Ralph. *Manhood.* Curridge, 1924. Author's first book. (200 copies.) Wraps. $250.

CHURCHILL, Sir Winston S. *Addresses Delivered in the Year 1940 to the People of Great Britain.* San Francisco, 1940. 250 copies. $350.

CHURCHILL, Sir Winston S. *Amid These Storms.* New York, 1932. U.S. title of *Thoughts and Adventures.* $300.

CHURCHILL, Sir Winston S. *Arms and the Covenant: Speeches.* London, 1938. Dark blue cloth, top edge stained blue. $600. First issue sheets used in a "cheap" edition. $400.

CHURCHILL, Sir Winston S. *Beating the Invader.* (London, 1941.) Single leaf, printed on both sides. (There is a later issue, overprinted in red in the top left-hand corner, regarding the evacuation of invaded areas. Both issues dated 5/41.) $250.

CHURCHILL, Sir Winston S. *Great Contemporaries.* London (1937). Dark blue buckram, top edge stained blue. $400. London (1938). "Revised Edition 1938." $300. London, 1943. $200.

CHURCHILL, Sir Winston S. *Ian Hamilton's March.* London, 1900. Dark red cloth, black endpapers. Folding map tipped in preceding 4 pages advertisements, then 32-page catalog on thinner paper. $600. New York, 1900. $500.

CHURCHILL, Sir Winston S. *India: Speeches.* London (1931). Orange cloth. $850. Orange wraps with price of 1/-net (second printing in green wraps. No other difference). $450.

CHURCHILL, Sir Winston S. *Liberalism and the Social Problem.* London, 1909. Plum buckram. $500. New York, 1910. $400.

CHURCHILL, Sir Winston S. *London to Ladysmith via Pretoria.* London, 1900. Maps and plans. Fawn-colored cloth. $750. "New Impression" added to title page. $300. New York, 1900. $500. Toronto (1900). Smooth light brown cloth. $200.

CHURCHILL, Sir Winston S. *Lord Randolph Churchill.* London, 1906. 2 vols. $600. New York, 1906. 2 vols. $450.

CHURCHILL, Sir Winston S. *Marlborough: His Life and Times.* London (1933–38). 4 vols. Vol. one is signed. 155 copies issued of each volume. In slipcases (label on slipcase of vol. one has number of set). The set. $3,500. Trade edition. 4 vols. The set. $800. New York, 1933–38. 6 vols. $600.

CHURCHILL, Sir Winston S. *My African Journey.* London, 1908. Pictorial red cloth. $750. New York, 1909. $450.

CHURCHILL, Sir Winston S. *My Early Life.* London, 1930. With boxed list of 11 of Churchill's works on verso of half title. $1,250. Second issue adds 12th title, *The World Crisis.* $1,000.

CHURCHILL, Sir Winston S. *The People's Rights.* London (1910). Cherry red cloth. Index at rear. $750. Wraps. Published simultaneously. $500. Second issue with index deleted and a second appendix added. $300.

CHURCHILL, Sir Winston S. *The River War.* London, 1899. 2 vols. $3,000. New York, 1899. $1,500. London, 1902. "New and Revised Edition." 1 vol. 40-page catalog at rear. $500.

CHURCHILL, Sir Winston S. *A Roving Commission.* New York, 1930. U.S. title for *My Early Life.* $300.

CHURCHILL, Sir Winston S. *Savrola.* New York, 1900. Dark blue cloth. $750. London, 1900. First state: without copyright notice. $750. Second state: copyright notice. $600. Colonial edition. $600. Strand, W.C. (1908). First illustrated edition. Wraps. $300.

CHURCHILL, Sir Winston S. *Step by Step, 1936–1939.* London, 1939. Green cloth. $500. New York, 1939. $250.

CHURCHILL, Sir Winston S. *The Story of the Malakand Field Force.* London, 1898. $3,500. Second state: errata slip tipped in immediately preceding first folding map. $2,500. Colonial Library edition. $1,500.

CHURCHILL, Sir Winston S. *Thoughts and Adventures.* London (1932). Sandy brown cloth. $600.

CHURCHILL, Sir Winston S. *While England Slept.* New York, 1938. U.S. title for *Arms And The Covenant.* $250.

CHURCHILL, Sir Winston S. *The World Crisis.* London, 1923–31. 6 vols. $2,250. New York, 1923–31. 6 vols. $1,800.

CHURCHILL, Sir Winston S., and MARTINDALE, C. C., S. J. *Charles IXth, Duke of Marlborough, K.G.* London (1934). Wraps. $250.

CHURTON, Henry. *Toinette.* New York, 1874. (By Albion W. Tourgee, his first novel.) $100.

CINCINNATUS. *Travels on the Western Slope of the Mexican Cordillera.* San Francisco, 1857. Engraved title page. Cloth. (By Marvin T. Wheat.) $400.

CINDERELLA. Retold by C. S. Evans. London, 1919. Frontispiece in color and numerous silhouette illustrations by Arthur Rackham. Half cloth. In dustwrapper. $600. Half vellum: one of 325 on vellum, signed by Rackham, with an extra plate. $1,250.

CLANCY, Tom. *The Hunt for Red October.* Annapolis (1984). Author's first book. No statement of edition, no series or numbers on copyright page, and no price on dustwrapper. $650.

CLAPCOTT, C. B. *Rules of the Ten Oldest Golf Clubs.* Edinburgh, 1935. Limited to 500 copies. Wraps. $600.

CLAPPE, Louise A. K. S. *California in 1851 (in 1852): The Dame Shirley Letters.* San Francisco, 1933. Grabhorn printing. 2 vols. One of 500. $250.

CLAPPERTON, R. H. *Paper, An Historical Account of Its Making by Hand from the Earliest Times Down to the Present Day.* Oxford, 1934. Limited to 250 numbered copies. $1,250.

CLAPPERTON, R. H. *The Paper-Making Machine, Its Invention, Evolution and Development.* Oxford (1967). 18 foldout plates. $275.

CLARK, Charles E. *Prince and Boatswain: Sea Tales from the Recollection of Rear-Admiral Charles E. Clark.* Greenfield, Mass. (1915). Blue cloth. (Edited by John P. Marquand and James M. Morgan.) Marquand's first book. $175.

CLARK, Charles M. *A Trip to Pike's Peak and Notes by the Way.* Chicago, 1861. Frontispiece, 18 woodcuts. $850.

CLARK, Daniel. *Proofs of the Corruption of Gen. James Wilkinson, and of His Connexion with Aaron Burr.* Philadelphia, 1809. $750.

CLARK, Daniel M. *The Southern Calculator, or Compendious Arithmetic.* Lagrange, Ga., 1844. Boards. $175.

CLARK, John Willis. *The Care of Books; An Essay on the Development of Libraries and Their Fittings* . . . Cambridge, 1909. Second edition. $125.

CLARK, Robert. *Golf: A Royal & Ancient Game.* Edinburgh, 1875. Signed, limited edition. $2,000. Trade edition. $1,250. Large paper. Second edition, Edinburgh, 1893. $750.

CLARK, Roland. *Gunner's Dawn.* Derrydale Press. New York, 1937. Signed frontispiece. Leatherette. One of 950. In slipcase. $750. One of 50 signed with 8 signed engravings. $2,500.

CLARK, Roland. *Pot Luck.* West Hartford, Vt. (1945). Illustrated, including signed frontispiece etching. Half leather. One of 150. $800. Another issue, one of 460 signed. In slipcase. $300. Trade edition. $50.

CLARK, Roland. *Roland Clark's Etchings.* Derrydale Press. New York (1938). Illustrated, with a signed frontispiece etching. Folio, cloth. One of 800. Slipcase. $1,000. Half morocco. One of 50 (presentation) with 2 signed etchings. $3,500.

CLARK, Stanley. *The Life and Adventures of the American Cowboy.* (Providence) 1897. Illustrated. Pictorial wrappers. $300. Another edition, title changed to *True Life in the Far West by the American Cowboy.* Wrappers with author's photo. (Providence, about 1898?) $200.

CLARK, Thomas D. *Travels in the Old South, A Bibliography.* Norman (1969). 3 vols. In slipcase. Reprint. $150.

CLARK, Tom. *Airplanes.* (Essex, England), 1966. Wraps. 4 signed and numbered copies. $300. Trade. $75.

CLARK, Tom. *To Give a Painless Light.* No-place. 1963. Author's first book. Typescript carbon (3 copies). $750.

CLARK, Tom. *The Sand Burg.* London (1966). Wraps. 4 signed and numbered copies. $300. Trade. $75.

CLARK, Walter (editor). *Histories of the Several Regiments and Battalions from North Carolina in the Great War, 1861–1865.* Raleigh, 1901. Plates. 5 vols. $750.

CLARK, Walter Van Tilburg. *Christmas Comes to Hjalsen.* Reno, 1930. Pictorial wrappers. In original mailing envelope. Author's first book. $400.

CLARK, Walter Van Tilburg. *The Ox-Bow Incident.* New York (1940). $200.

CLARK, Walter Van Tilburg. *Ten Women in Gale's House.* Boston (1932). First edition not stated. $300.

CLARKE, A. B. *Travels in Mexico and California.* Boston, 1852. Printed wraps. $1,500. Cloth. $1,250.

CLARKE, Arthur C. *Earthlight.* New York (1955). Cloth. $500. Wraps. $30.

CLARKE, Arthur C. *A Fall of Moondust.* New York (1961). $175.

CLARKE, Arthur C. *Interplanetary Flight.* London (1950). Author's first book. $125.

CLARKE, Austin. *The Vengeance of Fiona.* Dublin, 1917. Author's first book. $200.

CLARKE, Lewis. *Narrative of the Sufferings of Lewis Clarke During a Captivity of More Than Twenty-five Years.* Boston, 1845. Portrait. Wrappers. $150.

CLARKSON, Thomas. *The History of the Rise, Progress, and Accomplishment of the Abolition of the African Slave-Trade . . .* London, 1808. 2 vols. Large folding plate. $500.

CLASS Poem. (Cambridge, Mass.) 1938. Printed wrappers. (By James Russell Lowell.) Author's first published work. $600.

CLASS Poem. 1915. (New Haven) 1915. (By Archibald MacLeish.) 4 pp. Author's first separately published work. $2,500.

CLAVELL, James. *King Rat.* Boston (1962). Author's first book. $250. London (1963). $125.

CLAVELL, James. *Noble House.* New York (1980). 500 signed, numbered copies. In slipcase. $100. Trade edition. $25. London, 1981. $25.

CLAVELL, James. *Tai-Pan: A Novel of Hong Kong.* New York, 1966. $100. London, 1966. $75.

CLAY, John. *My Life on the Range.* Chicago (1924). $350.

CLAYTON, W(illiam). *The Latter-Day Saints' Emigrants' Guide.* St. Louis, 1848. 24 pp., plain wrappers. $6,000.

CLEMENS, Samuel Langhorne. See Twain, Mark. See also *Date 1601; What Is Man?*

CLEMENT, Hal. *Needle.* Garden City, 1950. Author's first book. $100.

CLERIHEW, E. *Biography for Beginners.* London (1905). (By E.C. Bentley, his first book.) Illustrated by G. K. Chesterton. Wraps. $300.

CLEVELAND, H.W.S. *Landscape Architecture . . .* Chicago, 1873. $350.

CLEVELAND, Richard J. *A Narrative of Voyages and Commercial Enterprises.* Cambridge, Mass., 1842. 2 vols. $650.

CLOCKMAKER (The); or the Sayings and Doings of Samuel Slick of Slickville. Halifax, 1836. (By Thomas Chandler Haliburton.) Cloth, paper label. $750. Philadelphia, 1836. Boards. First United States edition. $350. Boston, 1838. $150.

CLOUGH, A. H. *A Consideration of Objects . . .* Oxford, 1847. Author's first book. $500.

CLUM, Woodworth. *Apache Agent: The Story of John P. Clum.* Boston, 1936. Illustrated, including frontispiece in color of Geronimo. $100.

CLUTTERBUCK, Captain. *The Monastery.* Edinburgh, 1820. (By Sir Walter Scott.) 3 vols. $250.

CLYMER, W. B., and GREEN, Charles R. *Robert Frost, A Bibliography.* Amherst, 1937. Limited to 650 copies. $125.

CLYTEMNESTRA . . . (By Edward Robert Bulwer-Lytton.) London, 1855. Author's first book. $350.

COATES, Robert M. *The Eater of Darkness.* Contact Editions. (Paris, 1926.) Author's first book. Wrappers, paper labels. $400. New York, 1929. $300.

COATES, Robert M. *The Outlaw Years.* Macaulay, New York (1930). $150.

COATES, Robert M. *Yesterday's Burdens.* New York (1933). $150.

COBB, Humphrey. *Paths of Glory.* New York, 1935. $75. London (1935). $50. His only book.

COBB, Irvin S. *Back Home.* New York (1912). First printing with "Plimpton Press" slug on copyright page, and first binding, with publisher's name in 3 lines on spine. Author's first book. $60.

COBBETT, Thomas B. *Colorado Mining Directory.* Denver, 1879. $750.

COBBETT, William. *Rural Rides.* London, 1830. Woodcut map. $400.

COBDEN-SANDERSON, T. J. *Amantium Irae: Letters to Two Friends, 1864–1867.* Hammersmith (London), 1914. Doves Press. Frontispiece portrait. Limp vellum. One of 150. $750. In a Doves binding of morocco. $2,000.

COBDEN-SANDERSON, T. J. *Credo.* London, 1908. Doves Press. One of 250. $500.

COBDEN-SANDERSON, T. J. *The Ideal Book or Book Beautiful.* London, 1900. Doves Press. Vellum. One of 300. $650. One of 12 on vellum. $3,000.

COBURN, Alvin Langdon. *London.* New York (1909). Introduction by Hilaire Belloc. 20 tipped-in Coburn photogravures. Folio, boards. $2,500.

COBURN, Alvin Langdon. *Men of Mark.* London, 1913. With 33 tipped-in photogravures. $1,500.

COBURN, Alvin Langdon. *More Men of Mark.* New York, 1922. With 33 mounted collotype portraits. $500.

COBURN, Wallace D. *Rhymes from the Round-up Camp.* (Great Falls, Mont.), 1899. 8 Charles M. Russell drawings. Limp pictorial morocco. First issue, with "the" instead of "a" in title. $500. Second issue, with "a." $350. Second edition. $250.

COCKERELL, S. C. (editor). *Laudes Beatae Mariae Virginis.* Kelmscott Press. London, 1896. Printed in red, black, and blue. Boards and linen. One of 250. $600. One of 10 on vellum. $3,000.

COCKERELL, S. C. (editor). *Some German Woodcuts of the 15th Century.* Kelmscott Press. London, 1897. 35 reproductions. Boards and linen. One of 225. $750. One of 8 on vellum. $3,500.

COCTEAU, Jean. *Orphee.* London, 1933. Translated by Carl Wildman. Frontispiece by Pablo Picasso. Boards. First edition in English. One of 100 signed by Cocteau and Picasso. $1,500.

COESTER, A. See Costler, Dr. A.

COETZEE, J. M. *Dusklands.* Johannesburg, 1974. Author's first book. $250.

COFFEY, Brian. *Blood Risk.* Indianapolis, 1973. (By Dean Koontz.) $250.

COFFIN, Joshua. *A Sketch of the History of Newbury, Newburyport, and West Newbury.* Boston, 1845. Map, tables. $175.

COFFINBERRY, Andrew. *Forest Rangers.* Columbus, 1842. $250.

COGSWELL, Joseph Green. *Life of Joseph Green Cogswell as Sketched in His Letters.* New York, 1874. Tipped-in photograph frontispiece. Limited to 322 copies. $150.

COHEN, Leonard. *Let Us Compare Mythologies.* Montreal (1956). Author's first book. $750.

COHN, Albert M. *A Bibliographical Catalogue Of The Printed Works Illustrated By George Cruikshank.* London, 1914. $225.

COHN, Albert M. *George Cruikshank: A Catalogue Raisonne.* London, 1924. Limited to 500 copies. $450.

COHN, David L. *New Orleans and Its Living Past.* Boston, 1941. One of 1,000 signed. $300.

COHN, Louis Henry. *A Bibliography of the Works of Ernest Hemingway.* New York, 1931. One of 500. $150.

COKE, Henry J. *A Ride Over the Rocky Mountains to Oregon and California.* London, 1852. $350.

COLBERT, E. *Chicago: Historical and Statistical Sketch of the Garden City.* Chicago, 1868. 120 pp., wrappers. $150.

COLE, G.D.H. *The Brooklyn Murders.* London, 1923. Author's first book. $350.

COLE, George Watson. *Catalogue of Books Relating to the Discovery and Early History of North and South America . . .* New York, 1951. 5 vols. Reprint of the scarce 1907 first edition, which was limited to only 150 copies. $225.

COLERIDGE, Samuel T. See *Lyrical Ballads.*

COLERIDGE, Samuel T. *Biographia Literaria.* London, 1817. 2 vols. $750.

COLERIDGE, Samuel T. *Christabel: Kubla Khan, A Vision: The Pains of Sleep.* London, 1816. First issue, with 4 pages of February ads at back, and with a half title. $1,000. With March ads. $500. London, 1904. Eragny Press. Colored frontispiece. Boards. One of 226 on paper. $600. One of 10 on vellum. $3,000 or more.

COLERIDGE, Samuel T. *The Fall of Robespierre.* London, 1794. Author's first book. $3,500.

COLERIDGE, Samuel T. *Notes, Theological, Political, and Miscellaneous.* London, 1853. $250.

COLERIDGE, Samuel T. *Osorio: A Tragedy.* London, 1873. $150.

COLERIDGE, Samuel T. *Poems Chosen Out of the Works of Samuel Taylor Coleridge.* Kelmscott Press. London, 1896. Woodcut borders and initial letters. Vellum. One of 300. $850. One of 8 on vellum. $4,000 or more.

COLERIDGE, Samuel Taylor. *Remorse: A Tragedy in Five Acts.* London, 1813. $750.

COLERIDGE, Samuel T. *The Rime of the Ancient Mariner.* New York, 1877. Illustrated by Gustave Doré. $600. London, 1899. Vale Press. Illustrated by Charles Ricketts. Boards. One of 210. $350. London, 1903. Essex House, Frontispiece. Vellum. One of 150 on vellum. $850. London (1910). Illustrated by Willy Pogany. Calf. One of 525 signed by Pogany. $750. Cloth bound: $350. Bristol, England, 1929. 10 engravings by David Jones. Canvas. One of 60 with extra set of engravings, signed by the artist. $4,000. Boards and cloth. One of 400 signed by Jones. $1,000. London, 1944. Corvinus Press. Half buckram. (21 copies.) $750.

COLERIDGE, Samuel T. *Sibylline Leaves: A Collection of Poems.* London, 1817. With errata leaf. $750.

COLERIDGE, Samuel T. *Specimens of the Table Talk of the Late Samuel Taylor Coleridge.* London, 1835. Frontispiece. 2 vols., in original boards and paper label. $750.

COLERIDGE, Samuel T. *Zapolya.* London, 1817. $600.

COLES, Manning. *Drink to Yesterday.* London (1940). (By Cyril Henry Coles and Adelaide Manning, their first book.) $600.

COLETTE. *The Vagrant.* London, 1912. Author's first book. $250.

COLLECTED Catalogues of Dr. A.S.W. Rosenbach, 1904–1951 (The). New York (1967). 10 vols. $500.

COLLECTION of Book Plate Designs by Louis Rhead. Boston, 1907. Limited to 150 copies. $225.

COLLECTION of Familiar Quotations (A). Cambridge, Mass., 1855. (By John Bartlett.) Brown cloth. $300. Blue cloth. $150.

COLLECTION of Receipts . . . (A). Philadelphia, 1958. First book of Henry Morris (Bird & Bull Press.) $1,250.

COLLES, Christopher. *A Survey of the Roads of the United States of America.* (New York), 1789. Engraved title and 83 map-sheets in portfolio. $20,000.

COLLIER, John. *Green Thoughts.* London, 1932. One of 550 signed. With errata slip. $150.

COLLIER, John. *His Monkey Wife.* London, 1930. Author's first book. $350. New York, 1935. $200.

COLLIER, John. *Pictures in the Fire.* London, 1958. $100.

COLLIER, John. *Tom's A-Cold.* London, 1933. $250.

COLLIER, John. *Witch's Money.* New York, 1948. One of 350 signed in glassine dustwrapper. $250.

COLLINS, Charles. *Collins' History and Directory of the Black Hills.* Central City, Dakota Territory, 1878. 91 pp., printed yellow wrappers. $2,500.

COLLINS, Charles (compiler). *Collins' Omaha Directory.* (Omaha, 1866.) Printed boards. $1,250.

COLLINS, David. *An Account of the English Colony in New South Wales.* London, 1798–1802. 2 vols., 3 maps. 23 plates. $5,000.

COLLINS, Dennis. *The Indians' Last Fight; or, the Dull Knife Raid.* (Girard, Kan., about 1915.) 8 plates. Cloth. $200.

COLLINS, John S. *Across the Plains in '64.* Omaha, 1904. Pictorial cloth. $150.

COLLINS, Mrs. Nat. *The Cattle Queen of Montana.* St. James, Minn., 1894. Compiled by Charles Wallace. Illustrated. Stiff wrappers. $3,500. Spokane (about 1898–1902). Plates. Pictorial wrappers. $600.

COLLINS, Wilkie. *After Dark.* London, 1856. 2 vols. $500.

COLLINS, Wilkie. *Antonina.* London, 1850. 3 vols., cloth. Author's first novel. $750.

COLLINS, Wilkie. *The Dead Secret.* London, 1857. 2 vols. $750.

COLLINS, Wilkie. *The Evil Genius.* London, 1886. 3 vols. First English edition. $600.

COLLINS, Wilkie. *The Law and the Lady.* London, 1875. 3 vols. $600. New York, 1875. Illustrated. Wrappers. First American edition. $250.

COLLINS, Wilkie. *Memoirs of the Life of William Collins, R.A.* London, 1848. 2 vols., cloth. Author's first book. $450.

COLLINS, Wilkie. *Mr. Wray's Cash-Box.* London, 1852. Frontispiece. $250.

COLLINS, Wilkie. *The Moonstone: A Romance.* London, 1868. 3 vols., purple cloth. First issue, with half titles, with misprint "treachesrouly" on page 129 of vol. 2, and with ads in vols. 2 and 3. $6,000.

COLLINS, Wilkie. *No Name.* London, 1862. 3 vols., red cloth. $600.

COLLINS, Wilkie. *The Queen of Hearts.* London, 1859. 3 vols. $2,500.

COLLINS, Wilkie. *The Woman in White.* New York, 1860. Illustrated by John McLenan. Brown cloth. First issue, with the woman on spine in white. $600. London, 1860. 3 vols., cloth. First English edition (published a month after the first American edition), first issue, with ads at end of vol. 3 dated August 1, 1860. $6,000.

COLMAN, George, the Younger. See Mathers, John.

COLOPHON (The): A Book Collector's Quarterly. New York, 1930–50. 48 vols., boards, including clothbound indexes and *The Annual of Bookmaking.* Complete set. $1,000.

COLT, Harry S., and ALLISON, C. H. *Some Essays on Golf Course Architecture.* London, 1920. $800.

COLT, Miriam Davis. *Went to Kansas.* Watertown, N.Y., 1862. $500.

COLTON, Calvin. *Tour of the American Lakes.* London, 1853. 2 vols., boards. $200.

COLTON, J. H. (publisher). See *The State of Indiana Delineated.*

COLTON, J. H. (publisher). *Particulars of Routes, Distances, Fares . . .* New York, 1849. 12 pp. (11 of text.) (Caption title.) With Colton's Map of the United States . . . and a Plan of the Gold Region. Map folded into brown cloth covers, with printed paper label; text attached to inside of front cover. First issue, with "longitude West from Greenwich" at top of map. $2,000.

COLTON, Walter. *Three Years in California.* New York, 1850. Map, 6 portraits, 6 plates, folding facsimile. Black cloth. $400.

COULTANT, C. G. *The History of Wyoming from The Earliest Known Discoveries . . . Volume I* (all published). Laramie, 1899. $250.

COLUMBUS, Christopher. *The Voyages of Christopher Columbus; Being the Journals, . . .* Argonaut Press. London, 1930. Translated by Cecil Jane. 5 maps. One of 1,050. $150.

COMBE, William. See: *Doctor Syntax.* See also *The English Dance of Death; The Dance of Life; The Tour of Doctor Prosody; A History of Madeira; Journal of Sentimental Travels, etc.; The History of Johnny Quae Genus.*

COMBS, Leslie. *Narrative of the Life of Gen. Leslie Combs.* (Cover title.) (New York, 1852.) 23 pp., plus errata leaf, wrappers. $500. (Washington) 1852. 20 pp., printed wrappers. $500.

COMFORT, Will L. *Apache.* New York, 1930. $200.

COMFORT, Will L. *Routledge Rides Alone.* Philadelphia, 1910. In dustwrapper. $250. Without dustwrapper. $50.

COMING Race (The). Edinburgh (1871). (By Edward Bulwer-Lytton.) Scarlet-orange cloth, blocked in black and gold. $250.

COMMERCIAL Tourist (The); or, Gentleman Traveller; A Satirical Poem. London, 1822. (By Charles William Hempel.) 5 colored plates by Cruikshank. $300.

COMPLETE Art of Boxing According to the Modern Method . . . (The). London, 1788. By an Amateur of Eminence. $1,500.

COMPOSITOR'S Handbook: Designed as a Guide in the Composing Room. With The practice as to Book, Job . . . London, 1854. $225.

COMPTON-BURNETT, Ivy. *Dolores.* Edinburgh, 1911. Author's first book (suppressed by her). $450.

COMPTON-BURNETT, Ivy. *Pastors and Masters.* London, 1925. $300.

CONARD, Howard Louis. *"Uncle Dick" Wootton, the Pioneer Frontiersman of the Rocky Mountain Region.* Chicago, 1890. Portrait, 31 plates. Decorated cloth, or leather and cloth. $450.

CONCISE History of the Origin and Progress of Printing with Practical Instructions to the Trade in General. London, 1770. $350.

CONCLIN, George. *Conclin's New River Guide, or a Gazeteer of All the Towns on the Western Waters.* Cincinnati, 1850. 44 full-page route maps. 128 pp., wrappers. $350.

CONDON, Richard. *The Manchurian Candidate.* New York (1959). $125.

CONEY, John. *Engravings of Ancient Cathedrals . . .* London, 1842. Folio. $300.

CONFEDERATE Receipt Book. Richmond, 1863. Wrappers. $750.

CONFESSIONS of an English Opium-Eater. London, 1822. (By Thomas De Quincey.) First issue, with ad leaf at end. $1,000. Second issue, lacking ad leaf. $750. Philadelphia, 1823. First American edition. $450. Limited Editions Club. New York, 1930. Boards. In slipcase. $100.

CONFESSIONS of Harry Lorrequer (The). Dublin, 1839. (By Charles Lever.) Author's first book. Illustrated by "Phiz." 11 parts, pictorial pink wrappers. $400. First edition in book form. In original boards. $250. Cloth. $150.

CONFESSIONS of J. Lackington, Late Bookseller, at the Temple of the Muses, in a Series of Letters To A Friend . . . London, 1804. $150.

CONGREVE, William. *The Way of the World.* London, 1700. $2,000.

CONJECTURAL Observations On the Origin and Progress of Alphabetic Writing. London, 1772. 3 foldout plates. $400.

CONKLIN, E. *Picturesque Arizona.* New York, 1878. Illustrated. Green cloth. $175.

CONNELL, Evan S., Jr. *The Anatomy Lesson.* New York, 1957. Author's first book. $100.

CONNELL, Evan S., Jr. *Mrs. Bridge.* New York, 1959. $150.

CONNELLEY, William E. *Quantrill and the Border Wars.* Cedar Rapids, Iowa, 1910. $100.

CONNELLEY, William E. *The War with Mexico, 1846–47; Doniphan's Expedition.* Topeka, 1907. 2 maps, illustrations. $150.

CONNELLEY, William E. *Wild Bill and His Era.* New York, 1933. 12 plates. $150.

CONNELLY, Marc. *Dulcy.* New York, 1921. Author's first book, written with G.S. Kaufman. $300.

CONNELLY, Marc. *The Green Pastures.* New York, 1930. Illustrated in color by Robert Edmond Jones. Green boards. One of 550 signed. In slipcase. $300. Some signed copies issued in morocco. $400. Trade. $100.

CONNETT, Eugene V. *Magic Hours.* Derrydale Press. New York, 1927. 2 mounted plates by the author. 20 pp., gray boards, paper label. One of 100. (First Derrydale Press book.) $10,000.

CONNETT, Eugene V. (editor). *American Big Game Fishing.* Derrydale Press. New York (1935). Illustrated, including color plates. In dustwrapper. Slipcase. $500.

CONNETT, Eugene V. (editor). *Upland Game Bird Shooting in America.* Derrydale Press. New York, 1930. Illustrated, including color plates. Pictorial cloth. One of 850. $600. Brown morocco. One of 75 with 6 original signed etchings. $3,000.

CONNICK, Charles J. *Adventures in Light and Color.* New York (1937). Color plates and collotype plates. Buckram. Deluxe issue, one of 300 with 42 plates in color, 48 in collotype. $400. Trade edition: 36 colored plates. $200. London, 1937. 36 color plates, 48 in collotype. $200.

CONNOLLY, A. P. *A Thrilling Narrative of the Minnesota Massacre and the Sioux War of 1862–1863.* Chicago (1896). Illustrated. $200.

CONNOLLY, Cyril. See Palinurus.

CONNOLLY. Cyril. *The Rock Pool.* Obelisk Press. Paris (1936). Wrappers. Author's first book. $400. New York, 1936. $200. London, 1947. $75.

CONOVER, George W. *Sixty Years in Southwest Oklahoma.* Andarko, 1927. Illustrated. Issued without dustwrapper. $100.

CONQUEST (The) . . . By a Negro Pioneer (Oscar Micheaux). Lincoln, Nebr., 1913. Author's first book. $250.

CONRAD Memorial Library (A), The Collection of George T. Keating. Garden City, 1929. (Joseph Conrad.) Limited to 501 numbered copies. $275.

CONRAD, Joseph. See *The Nigger of the "Narcissus," Preface.* (Under *N.*)

CONRAD, Joseph. *"Admiralty Paper."* (New York, 1925.) Facsimile plate. Blue wrappers. One of 93. $450.

CONRAD, Joseph. *Almayer's Folly: A Story of an Eastern River.* London, 1895. Author's first book. Dark green cloth. First issue, with first "e" missing in "generosity" in the second line from last on page 110. $1,250. New York, 1895. $600.

CONRAD, Joseph. *The Arrow of Gold: A Story Between Two Notes.* Garden City, 1919. Dark blue cloth. First issue, with the reading "credentials and apparently" in line 16 of page 5. In dustwrapper. $400. Second issue ("credentials and who") in dustwrapper. $250. London (1919). Dark green cloth. First English edition, first state, with running head intact on page 67 (including "A"). In dustwrapper. $600. Without dustwrapper. $125.

CONRAD, Joseph. *Chance: A Tale in Two Parts.* London (1913). Sage green cloth. First issue, with "First published in 1913" on verso of integral title page. $3,000. Second issue with "First published in 1914" on tipped-in page. $350. Third issue with "First published in 1914" on integral page. $200. Garden City, 1913. Dark blue cloth. First American edition. One of 150 issued for copyright purposes. $500. New York, 1914. $200.

CONRAD, Joseph. *The Children of the Sea.* New York, 1897. Mottled blue-gray cloth. First edition of the book published in England in 1898 as *The Nigger of the "Narcissus."* $400.

CONRAD, Joseph. *Joseph Conrad's Letters to His Wife.* London, 1927. Limp imitation leather. Issued without dustwrapper. One of 220 signed by Jessie Conrad. $250.

CONRAD, Joseph. *Laughing Anne: A Play.* London, 1923. Full vellum, gilt top, uncut. One of 200 signed in slipcase. $500.

CONRAD, Joseph. *Lord Jim.* Edinburgh and London, 1900. Gray-green cloth. $350. New York, 1900. $200.

CONRAD, Joseph. *The Mirror of the Sea; Memories and Impressions.* London (1906). Light green cloth. First edition, with 40 pages of ads dated August 1906. $400. New York, 1906. Blue cloth. $200.

CONRAD, Joseph. *The Nigger of the "Narcissus."* London, 1898. First published English edition of *The Children of the Sea.* With "H" in "Heinemann" on spine the same size as rest of letters and 16 pages of ads. $400. Limited Editions Club, New York, 1965. In slipcase. $75. (See also title entry, anonymous.)

CONRAD, Joseph. *Nostromo: A Tale of the Seaboard.* London, 1904. Bright blue cloth. $350. New York, 1904. $200. Limited Editions Club, New York, 1961. Slipcase. $100.

CONRAD, Joseph. *Notes by Joseph Conrad in a Set of His First Editions in the Possession of Richard Curle.* London, 1925. Buckram, paper label. One of 100 signed by Curle. $150.

CONRAD, Joseph. *Notes on Life and Letters.* Dent, London, 1921. Green cloth. Advance printing with "Privately printed" on copyright page. $2,000. London,

1921. First issue of trade edition with "S" and "A" missing from the word "Sea" in "Tales of the Sea" in eighth line of table of contents. $250. Third issue, with corrected page on canceled leaf. $150.

CONRAD, Joseph. *Notes on My Books.* London, 1921. Boards, parchment spine, paper labels. First English edition. One of 250 signed. In dustwrapper. $500.

CONRAD, Joseph. *One Day More: A Play in One Act.* London, 1917. Blue wrappers. One of 25 signed by Clement Shorter, who had it printed privately. $1,000. Beaumont Press. London (1919). Boards. First published edition. One of 24 on vellum. $2,500 or more. One of 250. $500. Garden City, 1910. One of 250 signed in dustwrapper. $400.

CONRAD, Joseph. *An Outcast of the Islands.* London, 1896. $500. New York, 1896. First American edition. Wrappers. $400. Green cloth. $250. Deluxe edition in ¾ roan and marbled boards. $450.

CONRAD, Joseph. *The Point of Honor: A Military Tale.* New York, 1908. Illustrated by Dan Sayre Groesbeck. Decorated cloth. With "McClure" at base of spine. $250. With "Doubleday/Page & Co." at base of spine. $150.

CONRAD, Joseph. *The Rescue: A Romance of the Shallows.* Garden City, 1920. Dark blue cloth. In dustwrapper. Priced "Net $1.90." $350. In dustwrapper. With "Net $2.00." $200. London, 1920. Flexible red wraps (text differing from other editions). First English edition. One of 40 privately printed advance copies. $1,750. London, 1920. Green cloth. First published English edition. In dustwrapper. $250.

CONRAD, Joseph. *The Rover.* London (1923). Green cloth. $250. Garden City, 1923. Boards. First American edition. One of 377 signed. In dustwrapper and slipcase. $400. Trade. $175.

CONRAD, Joseph. *The Secret Agent: A Drama in Three Acts.* London, 1923. Portrait frontispiece. Boards and parchment. One of 1,000 signed in dustwrapper. $500.

CONRAD, Joseph. *The Secret Agent: A Simple Tale.* London (1907). Red cloth. First edition, with 40 pages of September ads at end. $350.

CONRAD, Joseph. *A Set of Six.* London (1908). First issue, with ads dated February 1908 and with the list of Conrad's works including "The Secret Agent (with Ford M. Hueffer)." $750. Second issue, with ads dated February 1908, with Hueffer's name between "The Secret Agent" and "The Inheritors." $250. Third issue with ads dated June 1908. $150.

CONRAD, Joseph. *The Shadow-Line: A Confession.* London (1917). "First issue of this edition: Marois 1917" on copyright page and pale green cloth. With 18 pages of ads at end. In dustwrapper. $400. Without dustwrapper. $100.

CONRAD, Joseph. *Some Reminiscences.* Paul R. Reynolds. New York, 1908. Yellow wrappers (advance issue for copyright purposes). One of about 6 copies. $3,000 or more. London, 1912. Dark blue cloth. First published edition. First edition not stated. $150.

CONRAD, Joseph. *Suspense.* Garden City, 1925. One of 377. In tissue and paper dustwrapper and slipcase. $350. Trade. $150. London, 1925. Dark red cloth. $200.

CONRAD, Joseph. *Tales of Unrest.* New York, 1898. Brown cloth. $300. London, 1898. Dark green cloth. First English edition, first issue, with all edges untrimmed. $300. Edges cut and gilted. $250.

CONRAD, Joseph. *'Twixt Land and Sea Tales.* London, 1912. Olive green cloth. First issue, with "Secret" instead of "Seven" on front cover. $1,500. Second issue, with "Seven" stamped over erased word "Secret." $300. Third issue with cover corrected. $150. New York, 1912. "Deep Sea" binding (remainder sheets from 1912 edition). First edition not stated (nor is Doran colophon present on copyright page). $300.

CONRAD, Joseph. *Typhoon.* New York, 1902. First issue in dark-green cloth with 4 pages of ads. $300. Second issue in maroon cloth. $250. London, 1903. Dark gray cloth. First English edition, first issue, with windmill device and without "Reserved for the Colonies only" on verso of half title. $300. Second issue. $250.

CONRAD, Joseph. *Victory: An Island Tale.* Garden City, 1915. Dark blue cloth. $75. London (1915). Red cloth, with 35 pages of ads at back dated Autumn and "Author's Note," which is not in the American edition. $75.

CONRAD, Joseph. *Within the Tides: Tales.* London, 1915. Sage green cloth. $100.

CONRAD, Joseph. *Youth: A Narrative and Two Other Stories.* Edinburgh, 1902. Light green cloth. With ads dated "10/02" at end. $500.

CONRAD, Joseph, and HUEFFER, Ford M. *The Inheritors: An Extravagant Story.* New York, 1901. Advance copies in beige pictorial cloth with sky in gold and with the dedication leaf reading "To Boys and Christina." Only a few copies known. $2,000 or more. First published edition, with a corrected dedication, on a stub: "To Borys and Christina" and sky in gold. $500. Second issue with sky in cover-cloth color. $300. London, 1901. Yellow cloth. First issue, without dedication leaf (most copies). With 32 pages of ads and publisher's device on spine with initials. $400. Without catalogue. $300. Without initials in publisher's device. $250. Also, remaindered in smooth yellow nonpictorial cloth. $150.

CONRAD, Joseph, and HUEFFER, Ford M. *Romance: A Novel.* London, 1903. Bright blue cloth. With 8 pages of ads at end. $350. New York, 1904. $250.

CONROY, Jack. *The Disinherited.* (New York, 1933.) Author's first book. Pictorial dustwrapper. $175. Printed dustwrapper. $125. Both dustwrappers. $300.

CONROY, Pat. *The Boo.* Verona (1970). Author's first book. First edition stated. $1,000. New York, 1981. Wraps. $50.

CONROY, Pat. *The Water Is Wide.* Boston, 1972. $250.

CONSIDERANT, Victor. *European Colonization in Texas.* New York, 1855. First edition in English. 38 pp., wrappers. $600.

CONSTABLE, Henry. *Poems and Sonnets.* London, 1897. Woodcut border, ornamental woodcut initials. White pigskin. One of 210. $400.

CONSTANTINE, K. C. (pseudonym). *The Blank Page.* (New York), 1974. $125.

CONSTANTINE, K. C. (pseudonym). *The Rocksburg Railroad Murders.* New York, 1972. Author's first book. First issue, no reviews on back of dustwrapper. $250. Second issue, reviews on back of dustwrapper. $175.

CONSTITUTION and Laws of the Cherokee Nation. St. Louis, 1875. Leather. $400.

CONSTITUTION and Laws of the Muskogee Nation. St. Louis, 1880. Sheep. $250.

CONSTITUTION and Playing Rules of the International Baseball Association . . . and Championship Record for 1877. Jamaica Plain, Mass., 1878. 77 pp., wrappers. $450.

CONSTITUTION of the Republic of Mexico and the State of Coahuila and Texas (The). New York, 1832. Half calf. $1,250.

CONSTITUTION of the State of Sequoyah. (Muscogee, Indian Territory, 1905.) Folding map in color. 67 pp., self-wrappers. First edition, with last page numbered. $2,500. Second edition, same date, no page number on last page. $1,000.

CONSTITUTION of the State of West Texas. (Cover title.) Austin (1868). 35 pp., wrappers. $600.

CONSTITUTION of the U.S.A. . . . Also, an Act to Establish a Territorial Government for Utah. Salt Lake City, 1852. 48 pp., sewn. $600.

CONTACT Collection of Contemporary Writers. Contact Editions. (Paris, 1925.) Edited by Robert McAlmon. Wrappers. One of 300. $750. (Contains work by Ernest Hemingway, James Joyce, Ezra Pound, Gertrude Stein, William Carlos Williams, and others.)

COOK, D.J. *Hands Up, or 20 Years of Detective Life in the Mountains and on the Plains.* Denver, 1882. 32 plates. Wrappers. $500. Cloth, same date, later issue. $350. Denver, 1897. Second edition, enlarged, with *20 Years* changed to *35 Years* in title. $150.

COOK, Frederick A. *Through the First Antarctic Night 1898–1899.* London, 1900. Map, 4 colored and 72 monochrome illustrations. $500.

COOK, James H. *Fifty Years on the Old Frontier.* New Haven, 1923. Plates. $250.

COOK, John R. *The Border and the Buffalo.* Topeka, 1907. Plates. $150.

COOKE, John Esten. See Effingham, C. See also *Leather Stocking and Silk; The Life of Stonewall Jackson.*

COOKE, John Esten. *The Last of the Foresters . . .* New York, 1856. $300.

COOKE, John Esten. *A Life of General Robert E. Lee.* New York, 1871. $150.

COOKE, John Esten. *Surry of Eagle's Nest.* New York, 1866. Illustrated by Winslow Homer. With Bruce and Huntington imprint. $250.

COOKE, Philip St. George. *The Conquest of New Mexico and California.* New York, 1878. Folding map. $250.

COOKE, Philip St. George. *Scenes and Adventures in the Army.* Philadelphia, 1857. $400.

COOKSON, Mrs. James. *Flowers Drawn And Painted In India.* London (1835). 31 hand-colored lithographs. $10,000.

COOLIDGE, Calvin. *Address Delivered By . . .* Boston, 1916. $300.

COOLIDGE, Dane. *The Fighting Fool.* New York, 1918. In dustwrapper. $125.

COOLIDGE, Dane. *Hidden Water.* Chicago, 1910. Author's first book. In dustwrapper. $200. Without dustwrapper. $40.

COOLIDGE, Dane. *The Texican.* Chicago, 1911. In dustwrapper. $150. Without dustwrapper. $30.

COON, James Churchill. *Log of the Cruise of 1889 D.T.S.C., New Smyrna to Lake Worth, East Coast of Florida.* Lake Helen, Fla., 1889. Wraps. $150.

COOPER, J. W. *Game Fowls, Their Origin and History.* West Chester, Pa. (1869). Colored lithographs. Pictorial green cloth, gilt. $250.

COOPER, James Fenimore. See *The Bee-Hunter; The Bravo; The Chainbearer; The Deerslayer; The Headsman; The Last of the Mohicans; The Monikins; The Pathfinder; The Pilot; The Prairie; Precaution; Ravensnest; The Redskins; Satanstoe; The Spy; The Two Admirals; The Water Witch; The Wept of Wish Ton-Wish; The Wing-and-Wing; Wyandotte.*

COOPER, James Fenimore. *The American Democrat.* Cooperstown, 1839. In original green cloth. $350.

COOPER, James Fenimore. *The Battle of Lake Erie.* Cooperstown, N.Y., 1843. Printed wrappers. $600.

COOPER, James Fenimore. *The History of the Navy of the United States of America.* Philadelphia, 1839. Maps. 2 vols., in original cloth. $400. London, 1839. 2 vols., in original cloth. First English edition. $350.

COOPER, James Fenimore. *The Jack O'Lantern.* London, 1842. 3 vols., drab brown boards, purple cloth, paper spine labels. First edition (of the novel issued anonymously in America as *The Wing-and-Wing,* which see as title entry). $500.

COOPER, James Fenimore. *Lives of Distinguished American Naval Officers.* Philadelphia, 1846. 2 vols. Cloth. $400. Wrappers. $600.

COOPER, James Fenimore. *Notions of the Americans.* London, 1828. 2 vols. $350. Philadelphia, 1828. 2 vols. $250.

COOVER, Robert. *The Origin of the Brunists.* New York (1966). Author's first book. $150. London, 1967. $75.

COOVER, Robert. *A Theological Position.* New York, 1972. $100.

COOVER, Robert. *The Universal Baseball Association, J. Henry Waugh, Proprietor.* New York (1968). $100. London (1970). $60.

COPPARD, A. E. *Adam and Eve and Pinch Me.* Golden Cockerel Press. Waltham Saint Lawrence, 1921. White buckram. One of 160 (from an edition of 500). $300. Orange boards. One of 340. $150. New York, 1922. Boards and cloth. $100.

COPPARD, A. E. *Pink Furniture.* London, 1930. Illustrated. Vellum. One of 260 signed. In dustwrapper. $175. Trade. $75.

COPPARD, A. E. *Silver Circus.* (London, 1928.) Full vellum. Issued without dustwrapper. One of 125 signed. $200. Trade. $125.

CORBETT, James J. *The Roar of the Crowd: The True Tale of the Rise and Fall of a Champion.* New York, 1925. $100.

CORELLI, Marie. *Barabbas.* London (1893). 3 vols. $400.

CORLE, Edwin. *Fig Tree John.* New York, 1935. $150.

CORLE, Edwin. *Mojave.* New York, 1934. Author's first book. $175.

CORLE, Edwin. *People of The Earth.* New York, 1939. $100.

CORNER, William. *San Antonio de Bexar.* San Antonio, 1890. Map, 16 plates. $100.

CORNFORD, Frances. See F.C.D.

CORNFORD, Frances. *Autumn Midnight.* London, 1923. Woodcuts by Eric Gill. Wrappers. $150.

CORNFORD, Frances. *Poems.* Hampstead (1910). Author's first book. $200.

CORNISH, Geoffrey S., and WHITTEN, Ronald W. *The Golf Course.* London, 1984. Limited edition of 200. Signed by Cornish. Leather slipcase. $150.

CORNWALL, Bruce. *Life Sketch of Pierre Barlow Cornwall.* San Francisco, 1906. 6 portraits. $175.

CORRILL, John. *A Brief History of the Church of Christ of Latter Day Saints.* St. Louis, 1839. Sewn, as originally issued. $5,000.

CORSO, Gregory. *Ankh.* New York, 1971. Oblong, magenta wrappers. One of 100 signed. $125. Another, one of 26 signed. $250.

CORSO, Gregory. *Gasoline.* City Lights Books. San Francisco (1958). Wrappers. $75.

CORSO, Gregory. *The Vestal Lady on Brattle and Other Poems.* Cambridge, Mass., 1955. Printed wrappers. Author's first book. $250.

CORVO, Baron (Frederick William Rolfe). See Rolfe, Fr. See also *Tarcissus.*

CORVO, Baron. *Chronicles of the House of Borgia.* London, 1901. (By Frederick William Rolfe.) 10 plates. Pictorial red buckram. $400. New York, 1901. Dark red or black cloth. First American edition. $300.

CORVO, Baron. *The Desire and Pursuit of the Whole.* London (1934). (By Frederick William Rolfe.) First binding in veridian (dark green) cloth. $250. Remainder binding in light green. Issued without dustwrapper. $75. London (1953). Cloth. In dustwrapper. $25.

CORVO, Baron. *In His Own Image.* London, 1901. (By Frederick William Rolfe.) With 1 ad leaf at end. $500.

CORVO, Baron. *Letters to Grant Richards.* (Hurst, England, 1952.) (By Frederick William Rolfe.) Peacocks Press. Boards. Issued without dustwrapper. One of 200. $250.

CORVO, Baron. *Stories Toto Told Me.* London, 1898. (By Frederick William Rolfe.) Printed green wrappers. No. 6 of the Bodley Booklets. $500.

COSTANSO, Miguel. *The Spanish Occupation of California.* San Francisco, 1934. Portraits, folding maps. Boards. One of 550. In slipcase. $250.

COSTLER, Dr. A. *Encyclopedia of Sexual Knowledge.* London (1934). (By Arthur Koestler, his first book.) $300.

COSTLER, Dr. A. *The Practice of Sex.* London (1936). (By Arthur Koestler.) ("Co-ester" on title page.) $250.

COTTEN, Bruce. *Housed on the Third Floor, Being a Collection of North Carolinians.* Baltimore, 1941. 100 facsimiles of title pages. $275.

COTTON, John. *God's Promise . . .* London, 1630. Author's first book. $750.

COTTON, Rev. Henry. *A Typographical Gazetteer.* Oxford, 1831. Second edition, corrected and much enlarged. $150.

COUES, Elliott (editor). *New Light on the Early History of the Greater Northwest.* New York, 1897. Frontispiece, facsimile, 3 maps in pocket of vol. 3. 3 vols., cloth. One of 1,000. $400. Half vellum. One of 100 on large paper. $600.

COUES, Elliott (editor). *On the Trail of a Spanish Pioneer: The Diary and Itinerary of Francisco Garces . . .* New York, 1900. 2 vols. Limited to 950 copies. $300.

COURTAULD, George. *Address to Those Who May Be Disposed to Remove to the United States of America.* Sudbury, 1820. 40 pp., wrappers. $1,000.

COUTS, Cave J. *From San Diego to the Colorado in 1849.* Los Angeles, 1932. 3 maps on 2 sheets. $125.

COUTS, Joseph. *A Practical Guide for the Tailor's Cutting Room.* London (1848). 27 plates, 13 colored and 18 diagrammatic plates. Half morocco. $750.

COWAN, Robert E. *A Bibliography of the History of California and the Pacific West, 1510–1906.* San Francisco, 1914. One of 250. In slipcase. $400. San Francisco, 1933. 3 vols., boards and cloth. $350.

COWARD, Noël. *"I'll Leave It to You."* London, 1920. Wrappers. Author's first book. $350.

COWLEY, Malcolm. *Blue Juniata: Poems.* New York (1929). Cloth. $400.

COWLEY, Malcolm. *Exile's Return.* New York (1934). $300.

COWLEY, Malcolm. *Racine.* Paris, 1923. Wrappers. Author's first book. $2,000.

COWLEY, Malcolm, and MANNIX, Daniel P. *Black Cargo . . .* New York (1962). $200.

COWTAN, Robert. *Memories Of The British Museum.* London, 1872. $100.

COX, A.B. See *The Layton Court Mystery.*

COX, Edward Godfrey. *A Reference Guide to the Literature of Travel . . .* Seattle, 1948–50. 3 vols. Reprint of the first edition. $350.

COX, Isaac. *The Annals of Trinity County.* San Francisco, 1940. John Henry Nash printing. One of 350 in slipcase. $125.

COX, James. *Historical and Biographical Record of the Cattle Industry and the Cattlemen of Texas and Adjacent Territory.* St. Louis, 1895. Colored frontispiece, other illustrations. Decorated leather. $5,000. New York, 1959. 2 vols., half leather. In slipcase. One of 500. $250.

COX, Palmer. *The Brownies Around the World.* New York (1894). $200.

COX, Palmer. *The Brownies at Home.* New York (1893). Pictorial boards. $250.

COX, Palmer. *The Brownies: Their Book.* New York (1887). Green glazed pictorial boards. First issue, with DeVinne Press seal immediately below copyright notice. $750. Second issue, with seal about 2½ inches from bottom of page. $500.

COX, Palmer. *Queer People with Wings and Stings and Their Kweer Kapers.* Philadelphia (1888). Pictorial boards. $175.

COX, Palmer. *Squibs of California.* Hartford, 1874. $200.

COX, Ross. *Adventures on the Columbia River.* London, 1831. 2 vols. $1,000. New York, 1832. Cloth or boards. $500.

COX, Sandford C. *Recollections of the Early Settlement of the Wabash Valley.* Lafayette, Ind., 1860. $125.

COX, William D. *Boxing in Art and Literature.* New York, 1935. $50.

COXE, George Harmon. *Murder With Pictures.* New York, 1935. Author's first hardcover book. $250.

COXE, John Redman. *The American Dispensatory* . . . Philadelphia, 1806. $225.

COXE, Louis O. *The Sea Faring and Other Poems.* New York (1947). Author's first book. $60.

COXE, Louis O. *Uniform of Flesh.* Princeton, 1947. Author's first book (written with R.H. Chapman). Mimeographed sheets in stiff wraps. $150.

COXE, William. *A View of the Cultivation of Fruit Trees* . . . Philadelphia, 1817. $375.

COY, Owen C. *Pictorial History of California.* Berkeley (1915). 261 photographs. $150.

COYLE, Kathleen. *Picadilly.* London, 1923. Author's first book. $300.

COYNER, David H. *The Lost Trappers.* Cincinnati, 1847. $600. Cincinnati, 1850. Second edition. $250.

COZZENS, Frederick S. See Haywarde, Richard.

COZZENS, Frederick S. *Acadia.* New York, 1859. 2 plates. $150.

COZZENS, James Gould. *Cock Pit.* New York, 1928. $300.

COZZENS, James Gould. *Confusion.* Boston, 1924. Author's first book. $600.

COZZENS, James Gould. *Michael Scarlett.* New York, 1925. $300.

CRABBE, George. *Tales of the Hall.* London, 1819. 2 vols. $200.

CRACKANTHORPE, Hubert. *Wreckage.* London, 1893. With 16 pages of ads dated October 1892. Author's first book. $150.

CRAIG, Edward Gordon. *Ellen Terry and Her Secret Self.* London, 1931. White cloth. One of 256 signed in slipcase. $400.

CRAIG, Edward Gordon. *Nothing or the Bookplate.* London (1931). Reissue of 1925 edition. $100.

CRAIG, John R. *Ranching with Lords and Commons.* Toronto (1903). 17 plates. Pictorial cloth. $400.

CRAIG, Maurice. *Irish Bookbindings, 1600–1800.* London, 1954. 58 plates, full-color frontispiece. $350.

CRAIK, Dinah M. See *The Adventures of a Brownie; The Fairy Book; John Halifax, Gentleman; The Ogilvies.*

CRAKES, Sylvester. *Five Years a Captive Among the Black-Feet Indians.* Columbus, Ohio, 1858. 6 plates. $1,250.

CRAM, Ralph Adams. *Ruined Abbeys of Great Britain.* Boston, 1927. Full calf. One of 350 signed. $200.

CRANCH, Christopher Pearse. *A Poem Delivered in the First Congregation Church* . . . Boston, 1840. Author's first book. Wraps. $200.

CRANCH, Christopher Pearse. *Giant Hunting: or, Little Jacket's Adventures.* Boston, 1860. Illustrated. Pictorial cloth. $150.

CRANCH, Christopher Pearse. *The Last of the Huggermuggers.* Boston, 1856. $200.

CRANE, Hart. See *The Pagan Anthology.*

CRANE, Hart. *The Bridge.* Black Sun Press. Paris, 1930. 3 photographs by Walker Evans. Stiff printed wrappers. One of 200 (weighing 19¼ ounces). In glassine dustwrapper and silver slipcase. $2,000. Also, 25 advance copies not for sale, on thin paper and weighing 15¼ ounces. $3,500. One of 50 on Japan vellum; signed. In glassine dustwrapper and slipcase. $10,000. Also, 8 lettered copies on vellum, signed by the poet. $15,000. New York (1930). First American edition. $500.

CRANE, Hart. *The Collected Poems of Hart Crane.* Liveright Publishers, Inc. New York (1933). Edited by Waldo Frank. Portrait frontispiece. Red cloth. $300. Second printing with imprint of "Liveright Publishing Corporation." $125. Brown cloth. One of 50 "for presentation to the friends . . ." $600.

CRANE, Hart. *Two Letters.* Brooklyn Heights, 1934. Leaflet, 4 pp. One of 50. $600.

CRANE, Hart. *Voyages.* New York, 1957. Illustrated by Leonard Baskin. Oblong, wrappers in board folder. One of 975. $400.

CRANE, Hart. *White Buildings.* (New York) 1926. Foreword by Allen Tate. Author's first book. First issue, with Tate's first name misspelled "Allan." $2,750. Second issue, with tipped-in title page, Tate's name spelled correctly. $1,500.

CRANE, Stephen. See Smith, Johnston. See also *The Lanthorn Book; Pike County Puzzle.*

CRANE, Stephen. *Active Service.* New York (1899). $200. London, 1899. $125.

CRANE, Stephen. *The Black Riders and Other Lines.* Boston, 1895. Yellow cloth or gray decorated boards. (500 copies.) $600. Plain boards, paper label. One of 50 printed in green ink on vellum. $3,000. 3 copies bound in vellum. $5,000.

CRANE, Stephen. *George's Mother.* New York, 1896. $200. London, 1896. $125.

CRANE, Stephen. *Great Battles of the World.* Philadelphia, 1901. Illustrated by John Sloan. $200. London, 1901. $125.

CRANE, Stephen. *Last Words.* London, 1902. Maroon cloth stamped in gold and blind stamped. $300. Red or brown cloth stamped in black, presumed remainder bindings. $200.

CRANE, Stephen. *The Little Regiment and Other Episodes of the American Civil War.* New York, 1896. First printing, with ads at back, headed "Gilbert Parker's Best Books." $200. London, 1897. $125.

CRANE, Stephen. *Maggie: A Girl of the Streets.* New York, 1896. Cream yellow buckram. Second (revised) edition, first state, with title page printed in capital and lower-case letters. $400. Second state, capital letters only. $200. London, 1896. First English (revised) edition. $300. (For first edition, see Johnston Smith, *Maggie: A Girl of the Streets.*)

CRANE, Stephen. *The Monster and Other Stories.* New York, 1899. $300. London, 1901. Revised edition, with 4 stories added. $200. (No American edition of this revision recorded.)

CRANE, Stephen. *The Open Boat and Other Tales of Adventure.* New York, 1898. Dark-green pictorial cloth. $250. London, 1898. First English edition, with 9 added stories. $250.

CRANE, Stephen. *The Red Badge of Courage.* New York, 1895. "Gilbert Parker's Best Books . . ." in ads at back with perfect type in the last line on page 225. $750. (Second printing includes this title in ads.) New York, 1896. $150. New York, 1944. Limited Editions Club. Illustrated. Embossed morocco. In slipcase. $200.

CRANE, Stephen. *The Third Violet.* New York, 1897. $175. London, 1897. $125.

CRANE, Stephen. *War Is Kind.* New York, 1899. Illustrated by Will Bradley. Pictorial gray boards. $1,000.

CRANE, Stephen. *Whilomville Stories.* New York, 1900. $150. London, 1900. $100.

CRANE, Stephen. *Wounds in the Rain.* London, 1900. With catalog dated "August 1900." Second binding has "October, 1908." Printed from American plates, but preceded that edition by three days. $150. New York (1900). $150.

CRANE, Stephen, and BARR, Robert. *The O'Ruddy.* New York (1903). $150.

CRANE, Walter. *The Bases of Design.* London, 1898. Blue-gray cloth. $200.

CRANE, Walter. *Flora's Feast.* London, 1889. Illustrated by the author. $150.

CRANE, Walter. *Of the Decorative Illustration of Books Old and New.* London, 1896. Illustrated. Cloth. One of 130. $200.

CRANE, Walter. *Slate and Pencil-Vania.* London, 1885. Illustrated. Pictorial half cloth. $250.

CRANE, Walter. *Triplets.* London, 1899. Designs in color by Crane. Half vellum. One of 750. $600.

CRANFORD. London, 1853. By the author of "Mary Barton," "Ruth," etc. (By Elizabeth C. Gaskell.) Green cloth. $750.

CRAPSEY, Adelaide. *Verse.* Rochester, 1915. Author's first book. $75.

CRARY, Mary. *The Daughters of the Stars.* London, 1939. Illustrated by Edmund Dulac. Half vellum. One of 500 signed by the author and the artist. In dustwrapper. $750.

CRAWFORD, F. Marion. *Katharine Lauderdale.* London, 1894. 3 vols. $150.

CRAWFORD, F. Marion. *Our Silver. . .* New York, 1881. Author's first book. Wraps. $300.

CRAWFORD, Lewis F. *Rekindling Camp Fires.* Bismarck, N.D. (1926). One of 100 signed. In slipcase. $400. Trade edition. Cloth. In dustwrapper. $150.

CRAWFORD, Lucy. *The History of the White Mountains.* Portland, Me., 1846. $125.

CRAWSHAY, Richard. *The Birds of Tierra del Fuego.* London, 1907. 21 color plates by J.G. Keulemans, 23 photographic views, map. Half morocco. One of 300. $1,250.

CRAYON, Geoffrey. *The Alhambra.* London, 1832. (By Washington Irving.) 2 vols. $200. Philadelphia, 1832. Anonymously published ("By the Author of 'The Sketch-Book.'") 2 vols. $250.

CRAYON, Geoffrey. *Bracebridge Hall, or The Humourists.* New York, 1822. (By Washington Irving.) 2 vols. $350. London, 1822. Text ending on page 403, vol. 2. $250. New York, 1896. Surrey edition. Arthur Rackham illustrations. 2 vols., pictorial cloth. $300.

CRAYON, Geoffrey. *The Sketch Book of Geoffrey Crayon, Gent.* New York, 1819–20. 7 parts, wrappers. (By Washington Irving.) Parts 1 through 5 dated 1819, parts 6 and 7 dated 1820. $2,500. Rebound in book form. $350. (Note: Second editions so identified on wrappers. Also see BAL.)

CREASEY, John. *Seven Times Seven.* London, 1932. Author's first book. $350.

CREELEY, Robert. *All That Is Lovely in Men.* Asheville, 1955. Drawings by Dan Rice. Pictorial wrappers. Jargon No. 10. One of 200 signed by Creeley and Rice. In dustwrapper. $350.

CREELEY, Robert. *The Charm.* Perishable Press. (Mt. Horeb, Wis.) 1967. Leather-backed cloth. One of 250 signed. Issued without dustwrapper. $250. San Francisco, 1969. Wrappers. One of 100 signed. $150.

CREELEY, Robert. *Divisions and Other Early Poems.* (Mt. Horeb), 1968. Wrappers. One of 110. $300.

CREELEY, Robert. *For Love, Poems 1950–1960.* New York (1962). Cloth. $150. Wraps. $40.

CREELEY, Robert. *The Gold Diggers.* Divers Press. (Mallorca) 1954. Wrappers. $175. New York (1965). Cloth. $50. Wraps. $25.

CREELEY, Robert. *The Immoral Proposition.* (Baden, Germany, 1953.) Wrappers. (200 copies.) $400.

CREELEY, Robert. *Le Fou.* Columbus, Ohio, 1952. Frontispiece. Decorated wrappers. Author's first book. $600.

CREELEY, Robert. *Poems, 1950–1965.* London (1966). Vellum and boards. One of 100 signed in slipcase. $500.

CREELEY, Robert. *The Whip.* (Worcester, England) 1957. Cloth. One of 100. $300. Wrappers. One of 500. $150.

CREMONY, John C. *Life Among the Apaches.* San Francisco, 1868. $350.

CREUZBAUR, Robert (compiler). *Route from the Gulf of Mexico and the Lower Mississippi Valley to California and the Pacific Ocean.* New York, 1849. 5 maps in pocket. $7,500.

CREVÈCOEUR, Michel-Guillaume-Jean de. See *Letters.*

CREVEL, Rene. *Mr. Knife, Miss Fork.* Black Sun Press, Paris, 1931. With 19 photograms. Translated by Kay Boyle. Illustrated by Max Ernst. One of 200. $4,500. One of 50 specially bound, signed by Crevel and Ernst. $7,500.

CREWS, Harry. *The Gospel Singer.* New York, 1968. Author's first book. $600.

CREWS, Harry. *Naked In Garden Hills.* New York, 1969. Without two dots at bottom of copyright page and in dustwrapper without reviews for this title on back. $150. London, 1973. Wraps. $50.

CREYTON, Paul. *Paul Creyton's Great Romance!!!! Kate the Accomplice; or, the Preacher and the Burglar.* Boston (1849). Pictorial pink wrappers. (By John Townsend Trowbridge.) With 1849 cover date. Author's first book. $1,500.

CRISPIN, Edmund. *The Case of the Gilded Fly.* London, 1944. Author's first book. $150.

CROAKER, Croaker & Co., and CROAKER, Jun. *Poems.* New York, 1819. 36 pp., printed tan wrappers. (By Joseph Rodman Drake and Fitz-Greene Halleck.) First book by each author. $750.

CROCKET, George L. *Two Centuries in East Texas.* Dallas (circa 1932). $200.

CROCKETT, David. *An Account of Col. Crockett's Tour to the North and Down East.* Philadelphia, 1835. $200.

CROCKETT, David. *A Narrative of the Life of Col. David Crockett.* Philadelphia, 1834. Written by Himself. With 22 pages of ads at end. $250.

CROFTS, Freeman Wills. *The Cask.* London, 1920. Author's first book. In dustwrapper. $1,500.

CROFTS, Freeman Wills. *The Groote Park Murder.* London (1923). $500.

CROFTS, Freeman Wills. *The Pit-Prop Syndicate.* London (1922). $600.

CROMBIE, Charles. *Rules of Golf Illustrated.* (California, 1905.) $1,250.

CROMWELL: An Historical Novel. New York, 1838. (By Henry William Herbert.) 2 vols., in original brown cloth, paper labels. First issue, with 12 pages of ads. $200.

CRONIN, A. J. *Dust Inhalation by Hematite Miners.* (London) 1926. Author's first book. Wraps. Offprint. $300.

CRONIN, A. J. *Hatter's Castle.* London, 1931. $150.

CRONIN, A. J. *Investigations In First-Aid Organization* . . . London, 1927. Wraps. $250.

CROSBY, Caresse. See C.,C.

CROSBY, Caresse. *Crosses of Gold: A Book of Verse.* Paris, 1925. Hand-colored illustrations. Green parchment. Author's first book. One of 100. $1,000. Exeter (England), 1925. Wraps. $200.

CROSBY, Caresse. *Graven Images.* Boston, 1926. $400.

CROSBY, Caresse. *Painted Shores.* Paris, 1927. Illustrated with 3 watercolors. Wrappers. One of 222 on Arches paper. In tissue dustwrapper. $500.

CROSBY, Everett. *Susan's Teeth and Much About Scrimshaw.* (Nantucket, 1955.) Cloth and boards in glassine dustwrapper. $1,200.

CROSBY, Harry. *Chariot of the Sun.* Black Sun Press. Paris, 1931. Introduction by D.H. Lawrence. Wrappers. One of 500. $600.

CROSBY, Harry. *Mad Queen: Tirades.* Black Sun Press. Paris, 1929. Drawing by Caresse Crosby. Stiff wrappers. One of 20 signed. $2,000. One of 100. $1,000.

CROSBY, Harry. *Shadows of the Sun.* Black Sun Press. Paris, 1929. Printed wrappers. One of 44. In glassine jacket. $1,750.

CROSBY, Harry. *Sleeping Together: A Book of Dreams.* Black Sun Press. Paris, 1931. Wrappers. One of 500. $650.

CROSBY, Harry. *Torchbearer.* Black Sun Press. Paris, 1931. Notes by Ezra Pound. Wrappers. One of 500. $600.

CROSBY, Henry Grew. *Anthology.* (Paris, 1924.) Author's first book. Wraps. $1,750.

CROSBY, Sylvester S. *The Early Coins of America.* Boston, 1875. With 2 folding facsimiles and 10 plates. $600.

CROTCHET Castle. London, 1831. By the author of *Headlong Hall.* (Thomas Love Peacock.) In original boards, paper label. $850.

CROTHERS, Samuel McCord. *Miss Muffet's Christmas Party.* St. Paul (1892). Pictorial vellum wrappers. Author's first book. $250.

CROTTY, D. G. *Four Years Campaigning in the Army of the Potomac.* Grand Rapids, 1894. $100.

CROWDER, Henry, BECKETT, Samuel, ALDINGTON, Richard, et al. *Henry-Music.* Hours Press. Paris, 1930. Pictorial boards. One of 100 signed by Crowder. (Includes poems by the authors set to music by Crowder, a black musician.) $3,500.

CROWLEY, Aleister. See *Therion, The Master.* See also *Aceldama.*

CROWLEY, Aleister. *Ahab and Other Poems.* London, 1903. Wrappers. $300. Vellum. Printed on vellum. $750.

CROWLEY, Aleister. *Magick in Theory and Practice.* London, 1929. In dustwrapper. $500.

CROWLEY, Aleister. *Moonchild: A Prologue.* London, 1929. $300.

CROWLEY, Aleister. *Olla: An Anthology of Sixty Years of Song.* London (1946). One of 500. $250. One of 20 on handmade paper. $1,000.

CROWLEY, Aleister. *Songs of the Spirit.* London, 1898. One of 50. $750.

CROWLEY, Aleister. *The Soul of Osiris.* London, 1901. Boards, cloth spine, paper label. $350.

CRUIKSHANK, George. See *The Humourist.*

CRUIKSHANK, George. *George's Table Book.* London, 1845. $250.

CRUIKSHANK, George. *Illustrations of Time.* London, 1827. 6 leaves of illustrations. Oblong, wrappers. $500.

CRUMLEY, James. *The Muddy Fork: A Work in Progress.* Northridge, 1984. 50 signed, numbered copies. $200. 200 signed, numbered copies. $100.

CRUMLEY, James. *One to Count Cadence.* New York, 1969. Author's first book. $300.

CRUMLEY, James. *The Pigeon Shoot.* Santa Barbara, 1987. 26 signed and lettered copies. In slipcase. $300. 350 signed and numbered copies. $75.

CRUMLEY, James. *The Wrong Case.* New York, 1975. $300. London, 1976. $125.

CRYSTAL Age (A). London, 1887. (By W.H. Hudson.) Black or red cloth. First edition, with 32 pages of ads at end. $500.

CUFFE, Paul. *Narrative of the Life and Adventures of Paul Cuffe, a Pequot Indian.* New York, 1839. Wraps. $350.

CUISINE Creole (La). New York (1885). (Compiled by Lafcadio Hearn.) Pictorial cloth. $1,000. New Orleans, 1922. Second edition. $150.

CULLEN, Countee. *The Ballad of the Brown Girl.* New York, 1927. 500 numbered copies. Slipcase. $175. Trade edition in slipcase. $125.

CULLEN, Countee. *The Black Christ and Other Poems.* New York, 1929. 128 signed, numbered copies. Slipcase. $300. Trade. $150.

CULLEN, Countee. *Color.* New York, 1925. Author's first book. $300.

CULLEN, Countee. *Copper Sun.* New York, 1927. 100 signed and numbered copies. In slipcase. $350. 500 copies. $150. Trade. $125.

CULLEN, Countee (editor). *Caroling Dusk.* New York, 1927. $125.

CUMING, F(ortescue). *Sketches of a Tour to the Western Country.* Pittsburgh, 1810. $750.

CUMINGS, Samuel. *The Western Pilot.* Cincinnati, 1825. $1,000. (Note: issued annually. Earlier more valuable ranging from $1,000 down to $250.)

CUMMING, Alexander. *The Elements of Clock and Watch Work.* London, 1766. $3,500.

CUMMINGS, E. E. See *Eight Harvard Poets.* See also Aragon, Louis.

CUMMINGS, E. E. *&* New York, 1925. Green gold-flecked boards. One of 111 on Vidalon paper, signed. Slipcase. $500. One of 222 on rag paper, signed. Slipcase. $400.

CUMMINGS, E. E. *Anthropos: The Future of Art.* (New York, 1944.) Half cloth. One of 222. In cloth dustwrapper. Slipcase. $275.

CUMMINGS, E. E. *Christmas Tree.* New York, 1928. Green decorated boards. In glassine dustwrapper. $400.

CUMMINGS, E. E. *CIOPW.* New York, 1931. Cloth. Issued without dustwrapper. One of 391 signed. $1,000.

CUMMINGS, E. E. *Eimi.* (New York, 1933.) Yellow cloth. One of 1,381 signed. In dustwrapper. $600. New York, (1958). Boards and cloth. Third edition. One of 26 lettered and signed. In glassine jacket. $400.

CUMMINGS, E. E. *The Enormous Room.* New York (1922). With word ("shit") in last line on page 219. $750. Word inked out. $500. London, 1928. Includes Robert Graves's introduction. $350.

CUMMINGS, E. E. *50 Poems.* New York (1940). Cloth. One of 150 signed. In glassine dustwrapper. Slipcase. $400.

CUMMINGS, E. E. *Him.* New York, 1927. Decorated boards, vellum spine and corners. One of 160 signed in slipcase. $450. Trade. $200.

CUMMINGS, E. E. *is 5.* New York, 1926. Gold-flecked orange boards, cloth spine. $300. Black boards. One of 77 signed in slipcase. $750.

CUMMINGS, E. E. *95 Poems.* New York (1958). One of 300 signed in glassine dustwrapper and slipcase. $250.

CUMMINGS, E. E. *No Thanks.* (New York, 1935.) One of 90 on handmade paper, signed. In glassine dustwrapper. $400. Morocco. One of 9 on Japan vellum, signed. With a manuscript page. $2,000. Trade. One of 900 on Riccardi Japan paper. In dustwrapper. $175.

CUMMINGS, E. E. *Poems 1905–1962.* London, 1963. Edited by George J. Firmage. Half calf. One of 225. With errata slip. In acetate dustwrapper. $350.

CUMMINGS, E. E. *Santa Claus.* New York (1946). Frontispiece. One of 250 signed. In glassine jacket. $300. Trade. $125.

CUMMINGS, E. E. *Tulips and Chimneys.* New York, 1923. $400. Mount Vernon, N.Y., 1937. Boards, vellum spine. One of 481. In dustwrapper. $300. (Of this edition, there were supposed to have been 629 signed by the author, but 148 sets of sheets were lost between printer and binder.)

CUMMINGS, E. E. *W [Viva: Seventy New Poems].* New York, 1931. Folio, buckram and boards. One of 95 signed. In glassine dustwrapper. $750. Trade. $250.

CUMMINGS, E. E. *XLI Poems.* New York, 1925. $300.

CUMMINGS, Marcus. *Architecture: Designs for Street Fronts . . .* Troy, 1865. $600.

CUMMINGS, Ray. *The Girl in the Golden Atom.* London (1922). Author's first book. $500. New York, 1923. In light yellow-brown cloth with "I-X" on copyright page. $400.

CUMMINS, Ebenezer H. *A Summary Geography of Alabama.* Philadelphia, 1819. $2,000.

CUMMINS, Ella Sterling. *The Story of the Files: A Review of California Writers and Literature.* (San Francisco) 1893. Illustrated. Decorated boards or cloth. $200.

CUMMINS, Jim. *Jim Cummins' Book.* Denver, 1903. $850.

CUMMINS, Mrs. Sarah J. W. *Autobiography and Reminiscences.* (La Grande, Ore., 1914.) Portrait. Wraps. $125.

CUNARD, Nancy. *Black Man and White Ladyship: An Anniversary.* (Toulon) 1931. 10 pp., red wrappers. $400.

CUNARD, Nancy. *Outlaws.* London, 1921. Author's first book. Assumed issued without dustwrapper. $200.

CUNARD, Nancy (editor). *Negro: Anthology.* London, 1934. Illustrated, including colored folding map. Brown buckram. Issued without dustwrapper. $3,000.

CUNARD, Nancy. *Parallax.* Hogarth Press. London, 1925. Pictorial boards. Issued without dustwrapper. $600.

CUNDALL, H. M. *Birket Foster, R.W.S.* London, 1906. One of 500 numbered copies signed by the publisher and containing an original etching. $250.

CUNDALL, Joseph. See also Percy, Stephen.

CUNDALL, Joseph. *On Bookbindings, Ancient and Modern.* London, 1881. $100.

CUNNINGHAM, A. B. *Murder at Deer Lick.* New York, 1939. $300.

CUNNINGHAM, A. B. *Singing Mountains.* New York, 1919. Author's first book. $300.

CUNNINGHAM, Eugene. *Diamond River Man.* Boston, 1934. $100.

CUNNINGHAM, Eugene. *Famous in the West.* El Paso, 1926. Illustrated. Printed wraps. $200.

CUNNINGHAM, Eugene. *The Ranger Way.* Boston, 1937. $100.

CUNNINGHAM, Eugene. *Spiderweb Trail.* Boston, 1934. $100.

CUNNINGHAM, Eugene. *Texas Sheriff.* Boston, 1925. $200.

CUNNINGHAM, Eugene. *Triggernometry: A Gallery of Gunfighters.* New York, 1934. 21 plates. Pictorial cloth. $250.

CUNNINGHAM, J. V. *The Helmsman.* San Francisco, 1942. Author's first book. (300 copies in total.) Cloth. $600. Wraps. $250.

CUNNINGHAME GRAHAM, R. B. See Graham.

CURIE, Marie. *Pierre Curie.* New York, 1923. One of 100 signed. $1,250.

CURLEY, Edwin A. *Nebraska: Its Advantages, Resources and Drawbacks.* London, 1875. Illustrated. $150.

CURRIE, Barton. *Fishers of Books.* Boston, 1931. 2 vols. Limited to 365 numbered and signed copies. $100.

CURTIS, Edward S. *The North American Indian.* Cambridge, Mass., 1907–30. Preface by Theodore Roosevelt. More than 1,500 plates. 20 quarto vols., half morocco, and 20 half morocco portfolios of plates. One of 500 sets (about half this number actually issued). Signed by Curtis and Roosevelt (some by Curtis only). $100,000 or more.

CURTIS, George William. See *Nile Notes of a Howadji.*

CURTIS, W. and others. *The Botanical Magazine.* London, 1787–1982. A complete run. Vols. 1–184, plus 5 vols of index, etc. Nearly 10,000 hand-colored plates and over 500 printed in color. $20,000. Individual volumes $100 to $500.

CURTISS, Daniel S. *Western Portraiture, and Emigrants' Guide.* New York, 1852. Illustrated, folding map. $300.

CURTISS, Frederick, and HEARD, John. *The Country Club 1882–1932.* Brookline, 1932. $250.

CURWEN, Henry. *A History of Booksellers, The Old and the New.* London (1873). $100.

CURWOOD, James Oliver. *Danger Trail.* Indiana, 1910. In dustwrapper. $150. Without dustwrapper. $30.

CURWOOD, James Oliver. *Gold Hunters.* Indiana, 1909. In dustwrapper. $150. Without dustwrapper. $30.

CURWOOD, James. *Wolf Hunters.* Indiana, 1908. In dustwrapper. $150. Without dustwrapper. $30.

CUSHING, Frank Hamilton. *My Adventures in Zuni.* Santa Fe (1941). One of 400. $450.

CUSHING, Luther S. *Manual of Parliamentary Practice.* Boston, 1845. Leather. $350.

CUSHMAN, H. B. *A History of the Choctaw, Chickasaw and Natchez Indians.* Greenville, Tex., 1899. $300.

CUSTER, Elizabeth B. *"Boots and Saddles," or Life in Dakota with General Custer.* New York, 1885. $125. Later printing: same date but adds portrait and map (Howes). $75.

CUSTER, Elizabeth B. *Tenting on the Plains.* New York, 1887. Frontispiece. Gray cloth. $75. In three-quarter morocco. $250.

CUSTER, George A. *My Life on the Plains.* New York, 1874. 8 illustrations. $175.

CUTBUSH, James. *The American Artist's Manual.* Philadelphia, 1814. 39 plates. 2 vols., $250.

CUTTS, James M. *The Conquest of California and New Mexico.* Philadelphia, 1847. Map, 3 plans. $300.

CYNWAL, Wiliam (*sic*). In Defence of Woman. Golden Cockerel Press. London, (1956). 10 colored engravings. Full blue morocco. One of 100 with an extra engraving. $300. Another, one of 500. $100.

D

D., F. C. *The Holtbury Idyll.* No-place (ca. 1908). (By Francis Crofts Darwin Cornford, her first book.) $1,250.

D., H. *Choruses from Iphigeneia in Aulis.* Cleveland, 1916. Translated from the Greek of Euripides. (By Hilda Doolittle.) Wraps. 40 numbered copies. $1,250. London, 1916. Stiff wraps. $250.

D., H. *Collected Poems.* New York, 1925. (By Hilda Doolittle.) $300.

D., H. *Hedylus.* Stratford-on-Avon (Oxford), 1928. Decorated boards and cloth. (By Hilda Doolittle.) One of 775. $250.

D., H. *Hymen.* New York, 1921. Pale green wraps. (By Hilda Doolittle.) $400. London, 1921. Boards. $300.

D., H. *Kora and Ka.* (Dijon, 1934.) Printed wraps. (By Hilda Doolittle.) One of 100. $500.

D., H. *Palimpsest.* Contact Editions. (Paris) 1926. Wraps. (By Hilda Doolittle.) $250. Boston, 1926. Decorated boards and cloth. One of 700. $250.

D., H. *Sea Garden: Imagist Poems.* London, 1916. Stiff printed wraps. (By Hilda Doolittle.) Except for a translation, her first book. $300. Boston, 1917. Green wraps. $200.

D., H. *Selected Poems.* New York (1957). One of 50 signed. $250. (Issued without dustwrapper.)

DACUS, J. A. *Life and Adventures of Frank and Jesse James.* St. Louis, 1880. $350.

DAHL, Roald. *The Gremlins.* New York (1943). Author's first book. $500. London (1944). $350.

DAHL, Roald. *Over to You . . .* New York (1946). $250. London, 1946. $200.

DAHL, Roald. *Some Time Never.* New York, 1948. $150.

DAHL, Roald. *Someone Like You.* New York, 1953. $125.

DAHLBERG, Edward. *Bottom Dogs.* London (1929). Introduction by D.H. Lawrence. Author's first book. One of 520. $250. Trade. $100. New York, 1930. $150.

DAHLBERG, Edward. *The Confessions of Edward Dahlberg.* New York (1971). One of 200 signed. In slipcase. $150.

DAHLBERG, Edward. *Do These Bones Live?* New York (1941). $100.

DAHLBERG, Edward. *The Flea of Sodom.* London (1950). $100.

DAHLBERG, Edward. *From Flushing to Calvary.* New York (1932). $200.

DAHLBERG, Edward. *Kentucky Blue Grass Henry Smith.* Cleveland, 1932. Drawings by Augustus Peck. One of 10 signed. In dustwrapper. $750. One of 85 numbered copies (not signed). In dustwrapper. $300.

DAHLBERG, Edward. *The Sorrows of Priapus.* Thistle Press. (New York, 1957.) Illustrated by Ben Shahn. Printed white boards. One of 150 signed by author and artist. Extra signed lithograph laid in. In glassine dustwrapper. In slipcase. $600.

DALE, Edward Everett. *The Range Cattle Industry.* Norman, Okla., 1930. Plates. $200.

DALE, Harrison Clifford (editor). *The Ashley-Smith Explorations.* Cleveland, 1918. 2 maps, 3 plates. One of 750. $200. Glendale, Calif., 1941. Revised edition. One of 750. $200. (This edition is the most desirable text.)

DALI, Salvador. *Hidden Faces.* New York, 1944. $100. London, 1973. Half vellum. One of 100 signed by Dali. With limited pamphlet *Postface to Hidden Faces.* In slipcase. $750.

DALI, Salvador. *The Secret Life of Salvador Dali.* New York, 1942. Illustrated. Cloth, pictorial labels. One of 119 copies with an original Dali drawing. In dustwrapper and slipcase. $1,500. Trade edition. $200.

DALTON Brothers and Their Astounding Career of Crime (The). Chicago, 1892. By an Eye Witness. Pictorial wraps. $250.

DALTON, Emmett. *When the Daltons Rode.* Garden City, 1931. Portrait and plates. Pictorial cloth. $150.

DAMON, S. Foster. *William Blake: His Philosophy and Symbols.* Boston, 1924. Boards. First American edition. $50.

DAMON, Samuel C. *A Journey to Lower Oregon and Upper California, 1848–49.* Honolulu, 1849. Sheets from the periodical *The Friend,* with title page added. $850. San Francisco, 1927. Grabhorn printing. One of 250. $150.

DAMPIER, William. *A New Voyage Round the World.* London, 1927. 4 maps, portrait. Half vellum. One of 975 on vellum. $300.

DANA, Edmund. *Geographical Sketches on the Western Country, Designed for Emigrants and Settlers.* Cincinnati, 1819. Boards. $900.

DANA, J. G., and THOMAS, R. S. *A Report of the Trial of Jereboam O. Beauchamp.* Frankfort, Ky. (1826). 153 pp., wraps. $500.

DANA, Richard Henry, Jr. See *Two Years Before the Mast.*

DANA, Richard Henry, Jr. *To Cuba and Back: A Vacation Voyage.* Boston, 1859. $125.

DANCE *of Life (The).* London, 1817. (By William Combe.) Frontispiece. Engraved title, 26 plates by Thomas Rowlandson. $1,000.

DANIEL, John W. *Character of Stonewall Jackson.* Lynchburg, Va., 1868. $125.

DANIELS, Jonathan. *Devil Trends.* Chapel Hill, 1922. Author's first book. $100.

DANIELS, William M. *A Correct Account of the Murder of Generals Joseph and Hyrum Smith, at Carthage, on the 27th Day of June, 1844.* Nauvoo, Ill., 1845. 24 pp., wraps. First edition, first issue, without plates. $4,500. Second issue, with 2 woodcut engravings added. $4,500. Rebound (both issues) with paper covers bound in. $1,100.

DANISH *Eighteenth Century Bindings, 1730–1780.* Copenhagen, 1930. 102 plates. $350.

DANNAY, Frederic. See Queen, Ellery.

DARBY, William. *The Emigrant's Guide to the Western and Southwestern States and Territories.* New York, 1818. 3 maps, 2 tables. $400.

DARBY, William. *A Geographical Description of the State of Louisana.* Philadelphia, 1816. Map. $350. New York, 1817. Second edition, with 2 maps and large folding map. $750.

DARBY, William. *A Tour from the City of New York, to Detroit, in the Michigan Territory.* New York, 1819. 3 folding maps (1 in some copies). $400.

DARLINGTON, Mary Carson (editor). *Fort Pitt and Letters from the Frontier.* Pittsburgh, 1892. 3 maps, 3 plates. One of 100 large paper copies. $300. Ordinary issue, one of 200. $200.

DARLOW, T. H., and MOULE, H. F. *Historical Catalogue of the Printed Editions of Holy Scripture in the Library . . .* New York, 1963. Reprint of the 1903 first edition. $300.

DARROW, Clarence. *A Persian Pearl.* Chicago, 1899. Author's first book. (Edited by.) $200.

DARROW, Clarence. *Resist Not Evil.* Chicago, 1903. $250.

DARWIN, Bernard. *Golf Courses of the British Isles.* London, 1910. $1,000. New York, 1911. $750.

DARWIN, Bernard. *Green Memories.* London (1928). $750.

DARWIN, Bernard and others. *History of Golf in Britain.* London, 1952. $250.

DARWIN, Bernard. *John Gully and His Times.* London, 1935. $35.

DARWIN, Bernard. *Tee Shots and Others.* London, 1911. $400.

DARWIN, Charles. *The Descent of Man.* London, 1871. Illustrated. 2 vols., green cloth. First issue, with errata on back of title page in vol. 2 and with ads in each volume dated January. $1,000. Second issue. $600. New York, 1871. 2 vols. $350.

DARWIN, Charles. *The Expression of the Emotions in Man and Animals.* London, 1872. Plates. $750. London, 1890. $200.

DARWIN, Charles. *Extracts from Letters Addressed to Prof Henslow* . . . Cambridge (1835?). Author's first book. In original wraps. $10,000.

DARWIN, Charles. *Journal of Researches*. . . London, 1839. $1,750. New York, 1846. 2 vols. $600.

DARWIN, Charles. *On the Origin of Species by Means of Natural Selection.* London, 1859. Green cloth. Two quotations on page (ii) and with ads at end dated June. $10,000. London, 1860. Folding diagram. Second edition with 3 quotations on page (ii) and no ads. $4,000. (Second issue of this edition had "Fifth Thousand" on title page.) New York, 1860. Folding diagram. First American edition with 2 quotations facing title page. $1,000. New York, 1963. Limited Editions Club. Leather. In slipcase. $175.

DARWIN, Charles. *The Voyage of H.M.S. Beagle.* Limited Editions Club. New York, 1956. Illustrated by Robert Gibbings. Folio, decorated sailcloth. One of 1,500. In slipcase. $125.

DATE 1601. Conversation, as It Was by the Social Fireside, in the Times of the Tudors. (West Point, N.Y., 1882.) First authorized edition. 7 single leaves, with title on front of first leaf, unbound. (By Samuel Langhorne Clemens.) $1,000. There have been numerous printings of this item. The first 2 in 1880 by Alexander Gunn in Cleveland, Ohio, were 8 ⁹⁄16 by 7 on wove paper in self-wrapper (first printing). $2,500. Second printing 8 ⁷⁄16 by 7 ¹⁄16 on laid paper in self-wraps. $1,750.

DAUBENY, Charles. *Journal of a Tour Through the United States and Canada . . . 1837–1838.* Oxford, 1843. Folding map. $1,000.

DAVENPORT, Cyril. *Cameo Book-Stamps Figured and Described.* London, 1911. $200.

DAVENPORT, Cyril. *English Embroidered Bookbindings.* London, 1899. $200. Another issue. One of 50. $450.

DAVENPORT, Cyril. *English Heraldic Book-Stamps, Figured and Described.* London, 1909. $250.

DAVENPORT, Cyril. *Roger Payne: English Bookbinder of the Eighteenth Century.* Caxton Club. Chicago, 1929. One of 250. $500.

DAVENPORT, Cyril. *Royal English Bookbindings.* London, 1896. Frontispiece, 7 other color plates, 27 other illustrations. $125.

DAVENPORT, Cyril. *Samuel Mearne, Binder to King Charles II.* Chicago, 1906. Limited to 252 copies. $500.

DAVENPORT, Cyril. *Thomas Berthelet, Royal Printer and Bookbinder to Henry VIII . . .* Chicago, 1901. Limited to 252 copies. $375.

DAVENPORT, Homer. *My Quest of the Arab Horse.* Cloth. New York, 1909. $250.

DAVIDSON, Donald. *Lee in the Mountains and Other Poems.* Boston, 1938. $250.

DAVIDSON, Donald. *An Outland Piper.* Boston, 1924. Boards. Author's first book. $250.

DAVIDSON, Donald. *The Tall Men.* Boston, 1927. $250.

DAVIDSON, Donald. *The Tennessee.* New York, 1946–48. 2 vols. $175.

DAVIDSON, Gordon Charles. *The North West Company.* Berkeley, 1918. 5 folding maps. $125.

DAVIDSON, James Wood. *The Living Writers of the South.* New York, 1869. (Contains first book appearance of Joel Chandler Harris.) $250.

DAVIDSON, John. *Diabolus Amans.* Glasgow, 1885. Author's first book. $750.

DAVIDSON, John. *Plays.* London, 1894. Aubrey Beardsley frontispiece. Pictorial cloth. One of 500. $350.

DAVIE, Donald. *(Poems) Fantasy Poets.* (Oxford, 1954.) Cloth. $450. Wraps. $250.

DAVIES, Hugh W. *Catalogue of a Collection of Early French Books in The Library of C. Fairfax Murray.* London, 1961. Reprint of the very scarce first edition. $175.

DAVIES, Henry, Gen. *Ten Days on the Plains.* New York (no-date). Without photographs. $1,750.

DAVIES, Rhys. *The Song of Songs and Other Stories.* London (1927). Author's first book. Wraps. One of 100 signed. $150. 900 unsigned copies. $40.

DAVIES, Robertson. *At My Heart's Core.* Toronto, 1950. Cloth. $175. Wraps. $40.

DAVIES, Robertson. *Eros at Breakfast . . .* Toronto, 1949. $200.

DAVIES, Robertson. *Shakespeare's Boy Actor.* London (1939). Author's first book. $750.

DAVIES, Robertson. *Shakespeare for Young Players . . .* Toronto, 1942. $400.

DAVIES, W. H. *The Autobiography of a Super-Tramp.* London, 1908. Preface by Bernard Shaw. $150.

DAVIES, W. H. *The Soul's Destroyer, and Other Poems.* (London, 1905.) Buff printed wraps. Author's first book. $500.

DAVIOT, Gordon. *The Man in the Queue.* London, 1929. Author's first mystery. $200.

DAVIS, C. H. (editor.) *Narrative of the North Polar Expedition.* Washington, 1876. $500.

DAVIS, Charles Thomas. *The Manufacture of Leather, Being a Description . . .* Philadelphia, 1885. Includes 12 tipped-in samples of dyed leathers. $300.

DAVIS, Charles Thomas. *The Manufacture of Paper; Being a Description* . . . Philadelphia, 1886. $175.

DAVIS, Duke. *Flashlights from Mountain and Plain.* Bound Brook, N.J., 1911. Illustrated by Charles M. Russell. $125.

DAVIS, Edmund. W. *Salmon-Fishing on the Grand Cascapedia.* (New York) 1904. Half vellum. One of 100. $1,250.

DAVIS, H. L. *Honey in the Horn.* New York, 1935. $100.

DAVIS, Hubert. *The Symbolic Drawings* . . . *for "An American Tragedy."* (New York, 1930.) Foreword by Theodore Dreiser. 20 drawings. Folio, gold and silver boards, cloth spine. One of 525 signed by Dreiser and Davis. $250.

DAVIS, Paris M. *An Authentick History of the Late War Between the United States and Great Britain.* Ithaca, 1829. $200.

DAVIS, Rebecca Harding. *Margaret Howth: A Story of To-Day.* Boston, 1862. Author's first book. $60.

DAVIS, Richard Harding. *The Adventures of My Freshman.* (Bethlehem, Pa., 1883.) Wraps. Author's first book. (About 10 copies known to exist.) $1,500.

DAVIS, Richard Harding. *Cuba in War Time.* New York, 1897. Illustrated by Frederic Remington. Boards. $175.

DAVIS, Richard Harding. *Dr. Jameson's Raiders vs. the Johannesburg Reformers.* New York, 1897. Wraps. $300.

DAVIS, Richard Harding. *Gallegher and Other Stories.* New York, 1891. First issue in yellow wraps. $400. Later, cloth. $200.

DAVIS, William Heath. *Sixty Years in California.* San Francisco, 1889. $300. San Francisco, 1929. 44 maps and plates. Half morocco. Second edition. One of 2,000 (with title changed to *Seventy-five Years in California*). $200.

DAVIS, William J. (editor.) *The Partisan Rangers of the Confederate States Army.* Louisville, 1904. 65 plates. (By Adam R. Johnson.) $150.

DAVIS, William W. H. *El Gringo; or New Mexico and Her People.* New York, 1857. Frontispiece. $250.

DAVIS, William W. H. *The Fries Rebellion.* Doylestown, Pa., 1899. 10 plates. $150.

DAVIS, William W. H. *The Spanish Conquest of New Mexico: 1527-1703.* Doylestown, 1869. Folding map, plate. $350.

DAVISON, Lawrence H. *Movements in European History.* London, 1921. (By D.H. Lawrence.) First binding in brown cloth. Issued without dustwrapper. $350. Second binding, light blue cloth. $250.

DAVY, Sir Humphrey. *On the Safety Lamp for Coal Miners.* London, 1818. Folding plate. $750.

DAVY Crockett's Almanac, of Wild Sports in the West. Nashville (1834 to 1841). Pictorial wraps. Depending on condition, the Nashville almanacs for these years are worth individually from $750 to $1,250 each, possibly more. Other Crockett Almanacs with Boston and Philadelphia imprints through the 1830s and into the 1850s retail at $100 to $500.

DAWSON, Fielding. *A Simple Wish for a Sincere . . .* Black Mountain (1949). Author's first book. Wraps. $250.

DAWSON, Fielding. *6 Stories of the Love of Life.* Black Mountain (1949). Wraps. $225.

DAWSON, Lionel. *Sport in War.* London, 1936. Illustrated by Lionel Edwards. Half leather. One of 75 signed. $500.

DAWSON, Moses. *A Historical Narrative of the Civil and Military Services of Maj.-Gen. William Henry Harrison.* Cincinnati, 1824. First issue, with 15-line errata slip. $500. Later issue, with 24-line errata slip: $350.

DAWSON, Nicholas. *California in '41. Texas in '51. Memoirs.* (Austin, Tex., about 1910.) Frontispiece. $750.

DAWSON, Peter. *Crimson Horseshoe.* (By Jonathan H. Glidden.) New York, 1914. In dustwrapper. $100.

DAWSON, Simon J. *Report on the Exploration of the Country Between Lake Superior and the Red River Settlement and the Assiniboine and Saskatchewan.* Toronto, 1859. Illustrated, folding maps. $400.

DAWSON, Thomas F., and SKIFF., F. J. V. *The Ute War: A History of the White River Massacre, etc.* Denver, 1879. 184 pp. $1,250.

DAWSON, William Leon. *The Birds of California.* San Diego, 1923. Illustrated. 4 vols., folio cloth. $500. Half leather. One of 350. $750. One of 100 signed. $750.

DAWSON, William Leon. *The Birds of Ohio.* Columbus, Ohio, 1903. Illustrated. 2 vols. $150.

DAWSON, William Leon, and BOWLES, John H. *The Birds of Washington.* Seattle, 1909. 2 vols., boards. One of 200 signed. $250. "Edition De Luxe." One of 85. $350.

DAY, Sherman. *Report of the Committee on Internal Improvements, on the Use of the Camels on the Plains, May 30, 1885.* (Sacramento), 1885. 11 pp. $125.

DAY-LEWIS. See Blake, Nicholas.

DAY-LEWIS, Cecil. *Beechen Vigil & Other Poems.* London (1925). Green wraps (although at least one copy in cloth). Author's first book. $500.

DAY-LEWIS, Cecil. *Country Comets.* London, 1928. Boards. Slipcase. $150.

DAY-LEWIS, Cecil. *The Magnetic Mountain.* London, 1933. Hogarth Press. Boards. One of 100 signed. Issued without dustwrapper. $250. Trade, issued without dustwrapper. $100.

DAY-LEWIS, Cecil. *Noah and the Waters.* London, 1936. Hogarth Press. One of 100 signed. In dustwrapper. $250. Trade in dustwrapper. $100.

DAY-LEWIS, Cecil (translator). *The Graveyard by the Sea.* London (1945—actually 1947). (With title page for Paul Valéry's *Le Cimetière Marin* as right-hand page beside the title page for Day-Lewis's translation.) Marbled wraps. One of 500. In fawn envelope. $350.

DEAN, Bashford. *A Bibliography of Fishes.* New York, 1916–23. 3 vols. in leather. $350.

DEAN, Henry. *Dean's Recently Improved Analytical Guide to the Art of Penmanship* . . . New York (1808). Second edition. $300.

DEARBORN, Henry. *The Revolutionary War Journals of Henry Dearborn, 1775–1783.* Chicago, 1939. Caxton Club. 6 plates. One of 350. Slipcase. $200.

DEARDEN, Robert R., Jr., and WATSON, Douglas S. *An Original Leaf from the Bible of the Revolution and an Essay Concerning It.* San Francisco, 1930. Grabhorn printing. One of 515 with leaf from 1782 Bible. $300. One of 50 with 2 leaves. $600. One of 15 with 2 leaves plus a leaf from the Benjamin Franklin printing of the "Confession of Faith." $750.

DEBAR, J. H. *The West Virginia Handbook and Immigrant's Guide.* Parkersburg, W.VA., 1870. Folding map. $150.

DE BARTHE, Joe. *The Life and Adventures of Frank Grouard, Chief of Scouts.* St. Joseph., Mo. (1894). Frontispiece, 67 plates. Pictorial cloth. $350.

DEBURY, Richard. *Philobiblon, A Treatise on the Love of Books.* London, 1832. First translation into English. $500. Albany, 1861. Limited to 230 copies. $225.

DEBURY, Richard. *The Philobiblon of Richard DeBury, Edited from* . . . New York, 1889. 3 vols. Limited to 300 copies. $265.

DEBURY, Richard. *Philobiblon of Richard DeBury, Bishop of Durham.* (San Francisco, 1925.) Limited to 250 copies. $225.

DEBURY, Richard. *Philobiblon, Richard DeBury, The Text and Translation of E.C. Thomas* . . . Oxford (1960). One of 500 numbered copies. $135.

DE CAMP, L. Sprague. *Demons and Dinosaurs.* Sauk City, Wis., 1970. $175.

DE CAMP, L. Sprague. *A Gun for Dinosaur* . . . Garden City, 1963. $200.

DE CAMP, L. Sprague, and PRATT, Fletcher. *Land of Unreason.* New York (1942). Cloth. $200.

DE CHAIR, Somerset. *The Golden Carpet.* Golden Cockerel Press. London, 1943. Frontispiece. Half morocco. One of 470. $175. One of 30 specially bound and inscribed. $400.

DECKER, Peter. *A Descriptive Check List Together with Short Title Index . . . 7500 Items of Western Americana* . . . New York, 1960. Limited to 550 numbered copies. $100.

DECLARATION *of the Immediate Cause Which Induce and Justify the Secession of South Carolina from the Federal Union, and the Ordinance of Secession.* Charleston, 1860. Wraps. First issue, with misprinted "Cause" for "Causes." $450.

DE CORDOVA, J. *Texas: Her Resources and Her Public Men.* Philadelphia, 1858. Tables. First issue, without index. $250.

DE CORDOVA, J. *The Texas Immigrant and Traveller's Guide Book.* Austin, 1856. $1,750.

DEERSLAYER (The): or, The First War-Path. Philadelphia, 1841. By the author of *The Last of the Mohicans.* (James Fenimore Cooper.) 2 vols., purple cloth, paper labels on spine. $1,500. London, 1841. 3 vols. $1,000.

DEFOE, Daniel. *The Life and Strange Surprising Adventures of Robinson Crusoe.* London, 1719. $6,000.

DE FOREST, John W. *History of the Indians of Connecticut . . .* Hartford, 1851. Author's first book. First issue, page vii misnumbered iiv. $150.

DE FOREST, John W. *Miss Ravenel's Conversion from Secession to Loyalty.* New York, 1867. Cloth. $100.

DE GIVRY, G. *Witchcraft, Magic and Alchemy.* London (1931). Translated by J.C. Locke. 366 illustrations, 10 color plates. In dustwrapper. $200.

DE GOURMONT, Remy. *The Natural Philosophy of Love.* New York (1922). Translated by Ezra Pound. Boards. $300. London, 1926. $150.

DE GOUY, L.P. *The Derrydale Cook Book of Fish and Game.* New York (1937). 2 vols., buckram. One of 1,250 in slipcase. $400.

DE HASS, Wills. *History of the Early Settlement and Indian Wars of Western Virginia.* Wheeling, W. Va., 1851. 4 plates, folding facsimile. Decorated cloth. $250.

DEIGHTON, Len. *The Ipcress File.* London (1962). Author's first book. First issue, no reviews on front dustwrapper flap. $500. New York, 1963. $150.

DELAFIELD, John, Jr. *An Inquiry into the Origin of the Antiquities of America.* New York, 1839. 11 plates, including 18-foot-long folding tissue-paper plate. $400.

DE LA MARE, Walter. See Ramal, Walter.

DE LA MARE, Walter. *Broomsticks and Other Tales.* London, 1925. Wood engravings. Half cloth, leather label on spine. One of 278 signed. $125.

DE LA MARE, Walter. *Desert Islands and Robinson Crusoe.* London, 1930. Engravings by Rex Whistler. One of 650 signed. $150. Trade edition. $100.

DE LA MARE, Walter. *Down-Adown-Derry.* London, 1922. Illustrated by Dorothy P. Lathrop. Blue cloth. In dustwrapper. $150.

DE LA MARE, Walter. *Henry Brocken.* London, 1904. First issue, without gilt on top edges. $75.

DE LA MARE, Walter. *Lispet, Lispett and Vaine.* London, 1923. Woodcut decorations. Limp vellum. One of 200 signed in slipcase. $150.

DE LA MARE, Walter. *The Lord Fish.* London (1933). Illustrated by Rex Whistler. Parchment. One of 60 signed. In dustwrapper and slipcase. $250.

DE LA MARE, Walter. *Songs of Childhood.* London, 1923. Colored plates. Vellum and boards. One of 310 signed. In dustwrapper. $200. (Published earlier under his pen name, Walter Ramal.)

DE LA MARE, Walter. *The Three Mulla-Mulgars.* London, 1910. First issue, with errata slip. In dustwrapper. $350. Without dustwrapper. $100. London (1925). Illustrated by J.B. Shepherd. Boards. One of 250 signed. $150.

DELAND, Margaret. *The Old Garden and Other Verses.* Boston, 1886. Author's first book. White cloth and flowered cloth. $100. Boston, 1894. Illustrated by Walter Crane. $200.

DELANO, Alonzo. See *Pen-Knife Sketches.*

DELANO, Alonzo. *Life on the Plains and Among the Diggings.* Auburn, N.Y., 1854. Frontispiece and 3 plates. First issue, with page 219 misnumbered 119 and with no mention of number of thousands printed. $600.

DELANO, Alonzo. *A Narrative of Voyages and Travels, in the Northern and Southern Hemispheres.* Boston, 1817. 2 portraits, folding map, errata leaf. $850.

DELANO, Judah. *Washington (D.C.) Directory.* Washington, 1822. Calf. $700.

DELANO, Reuben. *Wanderings and Adventures of Reuben Delano.* Worcester, Mass., 1846. 3 plates. 102 pp., wraps. $250.

DELAVAN, James. See *Notes on California and the Placers.*

DELAY, Peter J. *History of Yuba and Sutter Counties, California.* Los Angeles, 1924. Illustrated. Three-quarters leather. $150.

DELILLO, Don. *Americana.* Boston, 1971. Author's first book. $125.

DELL, Floyd. *Runaway.* New York (1925). One of 250 signed. In slipcase. $150.

DELL, Floyd. *Women as World Builders.* Chicago, 1913. Author's first book. $150.

DEMIJOHN, Thom. *Black-Alice.* Garden City, 1968. (By Thomas K. Disch and John T. Sladek.) $175.

DEMOCRACY: An American Novel. New York, 1880. (By Henry Adams.) No. 112 in "Leisure Hour Series." Presumed first issue in white cloth, and printed red endpapers, with March 31, 1880, in last line on front pastedown. $500.

DEMOS: A Story of English Socialism. London, 1886. (By George Gissing.) 3 vols., brown cloth. $500.

DEMPSEY, Jack. *Round-By-Round: An Autobiography.* New York, 1940. $90.

DENBY, Edwin. *In Public, in Private: Poems.* Prairie City, Ill. (1948). Illustrated. Blue cloth. $150. Gray cloth. $125.

DENBY, Edwin. *Second Hurricane.* Boston (1938). Author's first book. Wraps. $200.

DENTON, Sherman F. *As Nature Shows Them: Moths and Butterflies of the United States East of the Rocky Mountains.* Boston (1898–1900). 56 colored plates. 2 vols., half leather. One of 500. $1,500. Boston (1900). 3 vols. $500.

DEPONS, François. *Travels in Parts of South America, During the Years 1801–1804.* London, 1806. Folding map and plan. $250. London, 1807. 2 vols. $300.

DEPONS, François. *A Voyage to the Eastern Part of Terra Firma.* New York, 1806. Translated by an American Gentleman. Map. 3 vols. (Translated by Washington Irving, Peter Irving, and George Caines.) First edition in English. Washington Irving's first book. $400.

DEPREDATIONS and Massacre by the Snake River Indians. (Washington) 1861. 16 pp., sewn. $125.

DE QUILLE, Dan. *History of the Big Bonanza.* Hartford, 1876. Illustrated. Decorated cloth. (By William Wright.) First issue, without plate no. 44. $125.

DE QUILLE, Dan. *A History of the Comstock Silver Lode and Mines.* Virginia City, Nev. (1889). Printed wraps. (By William Wright.) $200.

DE QUINCEY, Thomas. See *Confessions of an English Opium Eater; Klosterhiem, or, The Masque.*

DE QUINCEY, Thomas. *The Logic of Political Economy.* Edinburgh, 1844. $750.

DE RICCI, Seymour. *A Census of Caxtons.* Oxford, 1909. Wraps. $175.

DE RICCI, Seymour. *French Signed Bindings In The Mortimer L. Schiff Collection.* New York, 1935. 3 vols. and *British and Miscellaneous Signed Bindings In The Mortimer L. Schiff Collection.* New York, 1935. 1 vol. The 4 vols: $2,250.

DERLETH, August. *In Re: Sherlock Holmes.* Sauk City, Wis., 1945. $150.

DERLETH, August. *The Memoirs of Solar Pons.* Sauk City, Wis., 1951. Foreword by Ellery Queen. $125.

DERLETH, August. *Murder Stalks the Wakely Family.* New York, 1934. $400.

DERLETH, August. *Not Long for This World.* Sauk City, Wis., 1978. $150.

DERLETH, August. *Place of Hawks.* New York (1935). $125.

DERLETH, August. *The Reminiscences of Solar Pons.* Sauk City, Wis., 1961. $100.

DERLETH, August. *The Return of Solar Pons.* Sauk City, Wis., 1958. $100.

DERLETH, August. *Someone in the Dark.* (Sauk City, Wis.) 1941. Arkham House. First issue, 17.6 cm. tall. $500. Later: Falsely issued "first edition," a facsimile, bound with a headband (not on the first binding) and 18.35 cm. tall. $250.

DERLETH, August. *Something Near.* Sauk City, Wis., 1945. $150.

DERLETH, August. *To Remember.* Vermont, 1931. Author's first book. Wraps. (29-page pamphlet.) $400.

DERLETH, August, and LOVECRAFT, H. P. *The Lurker at the Threshold.* Sauk City, Wis., 1945. $150.

DE ROOS, Fred F. *Personal Narrative of Travels in the United States and Canada in 1826.* London, 1827. 14 plates and plans. $400. Second edition, same date. 14 lithographs, 2 maps. $300.

DERRY, Derry Down. *A Book of Nonsense.* London (1846). Illustrated. Oblong, printed wraps. (By Edward Lear.) One of 175. Author's first book for children. (For second edition, see Lear listing.) $7,500.

DESCENDANT (The). New York, 1897. (By Ellen Glasgow.) First printing, with single imprint on title page, and first binding, with author's name omitted from spine. Author's first book. $125.

DESCRIPTION of Central Iowa (A), with Especial Reference to Polk County and DesMoines, the State Capital. Des Moines, 1858. 32 pp., stitched. $500.

DESCRIPTIVE Account of the City of Peoria (A). Peoria, 1859. 32 pp., wraps. $275.

DESCRIPTIVE Bibliography of the Books Printed at the Ashendene Press, 1895–1935. Chelsea, 1935. 15 collotype plates, 10 of bindings; 2 photogravures, and numerous specimen pages, initial letters, woodcuts, etc. Cowhide. One of 390. Slipcase. $2,000.

DESCRIPTIVE, Historical, Commercial, Agricultural, and Other Important Information Relative to the City of San Diego, California. (San Diego) 1874. 22 photographs. 51 pp., wraps. $1,750.

DE SHIELDS, J. T. *Border Wars of Texas*. Tioga, Tex., 1912. $275.

DE SHIELDS, J. T. *Cynthia Ann Parker*. St. Louis, 1886. Frontispiece, 3 portraits. $275.

DES IMAGISTES: An Anthology. New York, 1914. (Edited by Ezra Pound including poems by Pound and James Joyce.) $300. London, 1914. First English issue (American sheets). $200.

DE SMET, Pierre-Jean. *Letters and Sketches . . .* Philadelphia, 1843. With folded allegorical leaf and 12 plates. First with 252 (later 244) pages. $750.

DE SMET, Pierre-Jean. *Life, Letters and Travels of Father Jean-Pierre de Smet*. New York, 1905. Edited by Hiram M. Chittenden. Map, 3 plates, 3 facsimiles. 4 vols. $600.

DE SMET, Pierre-Jean. *Oregon Missions and Travels over the Rocky Mountains . . .* New York, 1847. Folding map, 12 plates. $400.

DESPERATE Remedies: A Novel. London, 1871. 3 vols., red cloth. (By Thomas Hardy.) Author's first book (500 printed). $3,500. New York, 1874. Yellow cloth. With "Author's Edition" on copyright page. $300.

DESTINY; or The Chiefs Daughter. Edinburgh, 1831. 3 vols. (By Susan Edmonstone Ferrier.) $250.

DEUTSCH, Babette. *Banners*. New York (1919). Boards, paper label. Author's first book. In dustwrapper. $300. Without dustwrapper. $60.

DEUTSCH, Babette. *A Brittle Heaven*. New York (1926). $200.

DEUTSCH, Babette. *Fire for the Light*. New York (1930). $150.

DEVINNE, Theodore L. *The Invention of Printing*. New York, 1876. Half morocco. $250. New York, 1878. Second edition. $200.

DEVINNE, Theodore L. *The Printers' Price List, A Manual . . .* New York, 1871. Second edition. $350.

DEVINNE, Theodore L. *Title Pages as Seen by a Printer*. New York, 1901. Limited to 325 copies. $275.

DEVOTO, Bernard. *Across the Wide Missouri.* Boston, 1947. 81 plates, some in color. One of 265. In slipcase. $150. Trade in cloth. $50.

DEVOTO, Bernard. *The Crooked Mile.* New York, 1924. Author's first book. $125.

DEVRIES, Hugo. *The Mutation Theory.* Chicago, 1909–10. 12 color plates, text illustrations. 2 vols. $250.

DEVRIES, Peter. *Angels Can't Do Better.* New York (1944). $300.

DEVRIES, Peter. *But Who Wakes the Bugler?* Boston, 1940. Illustrated by Charles Addams. Cloth. Author's first book. $300.

DEVRIES, Peter. *The Handsome Heart.* New York (1943). $275.

DEWEY, John. *Psychology.* New York, 1887. Author's first book. $350.

DE WITT, David Miller. *The Judicial Murder of Mary E. Surratt.* Baltimore, 1895. $125.

DE WOLFF, J. H. *Pawnee Bill (Maj. Gordon W. Lillie): His Experience and Adventures on the Western Plains.* No-place, 1902. Illustrated. Pictorial boards. $200.

DEXTER, A. Hersey. *Early Days in California.* (Denver) 1886. Pictorial cloth. $250.

DIARY of Isaiah Thomas, 1805–1828 (The). Worcester, 1909. 2 vols. $200.

DIAZ DEL CASTILLO, Bernal. *The Discovery and Conquest of Mexico, 1517–1521.* Limited Editions Club, New York, 1942. Translated by A. P. Maudslay. Illustrated by Miguel Covarrubias. Leather. In slipcase. $250.

DIAZ DEL CASTILLO, Bernal. *The True History of the Conquest of Mexico.* London, 1800. Translated by Maurice Keatinge. Map, errata leaf. First edition in English. $600.

DIBDIN, Thomas Frognall. *A Bibliographical, Antiquarian and Picturesque Tour in the Northern Counties of England and in Scotland.* London, 1838. 2 vols. $250.

DIBDIN, Thomas Frognall. *A Bibliographical, Antiquarian and Picturesque Tour in France and Germany.* London, 1829. 3 vols. Second edition. $125.

DIBDIN, Thomas Frognall. *The Bibliographical Decameron.* London, 1817. 3 vols. $700.

DIBDIN, Thomas Frognall. *Bibliomania; Or Book Madness . . .* London, 1809. $300. London, 1811. Second edition. $275. London, 1842. (Includes a reprint of the 1809 edition.) $150. London, 1876. Revision of the 1842 edition. $200. Boston, 1903. 4 vols. Reprint of the 1842 edition. Limited to 489 copies. $400.

DIBDIN, Thomas Frognall. *Bibliosophia; Or Book-Wisdom, Containing Some Account . . .* London, 1810. $225.

DIBDIN, Thomas Frognall. *Bibliotheca Spenceriana.* 7 vols. composed of the following: London, 1814–15. 4 vols. London, 1822. 2 vols. London, 1923. The set. $750.

DIBDIN, Thomas Frognall. *An Introduction to the Knowledge of Greek And Latin Classics . . .* London, 1827. 2 vols. Fourth (and best) edition. $275.

DIBDIN, Thomas Frognall. *The Library Companion; Or, The Young Man's Guide, And the Old Man's Comfort* . . . London, 1824. 2,000 copies of small paper edition printed. $150. London, 1825. Second edition. 2 vols. bound in one. $175.

DIBDIN, Thomas Frognall. *Poems.* London, 1797. Author's first book. (500 copies.) $600.

DIBDIN, Thomas Frognall. *Reminiscences of a Literary Life.* London, 1836. 2 vols. $350.

DIBDIN, Thomas Frognall. *Typographical Antiquities; Or The History of Printing in England, Scotland and Ireland* . . . London, 1810,–12,–16,–19. 4 vols. $800.

DICK, Philip K. *Confessions of a Crap Artist* . . . New York, 1975. Issued without dustwrapper. One of 90 signed. $250. One of 410. $150. Wraps. (500 copies.) $40.

DICK, Philip K. *Do Androids Dream of Electric Sheep?* Garden City, 1968. $350.

DICK, Philip K. *A Handful of Darkness.* London (1955). First issue, blue boards, lettered in silver, $750. Second issue, orange boards, lettered in black. $500. (Later dustwrapper has *World of Change* on rear panel.) Also variant in blue boards with black lettering. $500.

DICK, Philip K. *The Man in the High Castle.* New York (1962). $450.

DICK, Philip K. *A Maze of Death.* Garden City, 1970. $500.

DICK, Philip. K. *The Three Stigmata of Palmer Eldritch.* Garden City, 1965. $850.

DICK, Philip K. *Time Out of Joint.* Philadelphia (1959). $300.

DICK, R. A. *The Ghost and Mrs. Muir.* Chicago/New York (1945). $125.

DICKENS, Charles. See "Boz." Also see *Sketches by "Boz."*

DICKENS, Charles. Note: The "Parts" price estimates below assume that the "points" are correct, but not necessarily all of the ad placements called for by Hatton & Cleaver may be exact.

DICKENS, Charles. *The Adventures of Oliver Twist.* London, 1846. 24 illustrations by George Cruikshank. 10 monthly parts, green wraps. "New edition." (Actually third edition, as stated in preliminary pages, and sometimes called first octavo edition; for earlier editions see *Oliver Twist* under "Boz" and Dickens.) $3,000. London, 1846. Slate-colored cloth. $1,000.

DICKENS, Charles. *American Notes for General Circulation.* London, 1842. 2 vols., horizontally ribbed or vertically ribbed (variant), brown cloth. First state, with initial pages misnumbered "x–xvi." $1,000. Second state corrected. $600.

DICKENS, Charles. *The Battle of Life: A Love Story.* London, 1846. Engraved title page and frontispiece by Maclise. First-issue imprint on engraved title page in 3 lines, with "A Love Story" printed. $600. Second issue, with imprint in 3 lines and "A Love Story" engraved on a scroll. $400. Other variants have imprint on one line and Cupid carrying the scroll. $300.

DICKENS, Charles. *Bleak House.* London, 1852–53. Illustrated by H. K. Browne. 20 parts in 19, blue pictorial wraps. $1,500. London, 1853. Green cloth. First book edition. $1,000.

DICKENS, Charles. *A Child's History of England.* London, 1852–53–54. Frontispiece. 3 vols., reddish cloth. First state of vol. I with ad page (212) listing 4 books plus the 5 Christmas books, and ad page (324) in vol. III has "Collected and Revised" for this title. $1,250. Second state, vol. I ad begins with this title plus 7 works and the Christmas books. Vol. III states "Corrected and Revised." $1,000.

DICKENS, Charles. *The Chimes.* London, 1845. 13 illustrations. Engraved title page. Red cloth. First issue, with imprint as part of engraved title. $600. Second issue, publisher's name printed below engraving. $350. Limited Editions Club, New York, 1931. Illustrated by Arthur Rackham. In slipcase. $600.

DICKENS, Charles. *A Christmas Carol.* London, 1843. 4 colored plates and 4 wood-cuts by John Leech. Brown cloth. There doesn't seem to be a final agreement on the first issue and would suggest some detailed research on any copy in original cloth with 1843 or 1844 on title page. But most seem to go along with "Stave I" (not "Stave One") on first text page, and with red-and-blue lettered title page and yellow endpapers. $3,500. Second issue, with "Stave I," $3,000. Third issue, with "Stave One," $3,000. Philadelphia, 1844. Yellow cloth. First American edition. $1,000. London (1915). Illustrated in color by Arthur Rackham. Pictorial vellum. Large paper edition. One of 525. $1,500. Limited Editions Club, Boston, 1934. In slipcase. $125.

DICKENS, Charles. *The Complete Works of Charles Dickens.* Nonesuch Press. London, 1937–38. Edited by Arthur Waugh, Hugh Walpole, Walter Dexter, and Thomas Halton. Illustrated. 23 vols., buckram (each volume a different color), leather labels, gilt, with an original engraved steel plate. One of 877 sets. $4,000.

DICKENS, Charles. *The Cricket on the Hearth.* London, 1846. Crimson cloth. First state, with ad page (175) without heading "New Edition of Oliver Twist." $350. Second state. $250. Limited Editions Club, New York, 1933. In slipcase. $150.

DICKENS, Charles. *Dombey and Son.* London, 1846–47–48. Illustrated by H.K. Browne. 20 parts in 19, green pictorial wraps. With 12-line errata slip in part V. $1,250. New York, 1846–48. 20 parts in 19, wraps. First American edition. $2,500. London, 1848. Dark green cloth. (Also noted in blue cloth.) First book edition. $750. Limited Editions Club, New York, 1957. 2 vols. In slipcase. $75.

DICKENS, Charles. *Great Expectations.* London, 1861. 3 vols., violet (or yellowish green variant) cloth. First issue, with 32 pages of ads dated May 1861 in 3 places. (Later issues/editions had the edition on the title page and later ad dates.) $2,000. Limited Editions Club, New York, 1937. In slipcase. $150.

DICKENS, Charles. *Hard Times, for These Times.* Bradbury & Evans. London, 1854. Olive green cloth. $600. Limited Editions Club, New York, 1966. In slipcase. $75.

DICKENS, Charles. *The Life and Adventures of Martin Chuzzlewit.* London, 1844. Illustrated by "Phiz," 20 parts in 19, green wraps. (There is no priority assigned to copies with English pound sign after "100" in reward notice on engraved title page.) $1,500. London, 1844. Blue cloth (later, brown). First book edition. $750.

DICKENS, Charles. *The Life and Adventures of Nicholas Nickleby.* London, 1838–39. Frontispiece portrait by Maclise, illustrations by Phiz. 20 parts in 19, green pictorial wraps. First issue, with "vister" for "sister" in line 17, page 123, part IV and "Chapman and Hall" on frontispiece and first four plates. $2,000. London, 1839. In original olive green cloth. First book edition. 1 vol. $600. 2 vols. $750.

DICKENS, Charles. *Little Dorrit.* London, 1855–57. Illustrated by H.K. Browne. 20 parts in 19, blue wraps. First issue, with errata slip in part XVI ("Rigaud" should have been "Blandois"), and uncorrected errors in part XV. $1,250. London, 1857. Olive green cloth. First book edition. $750.

DICKENS, Charles. *Master Humphrey's Clock.* London, 1840–41. Illustrated by George Cattermole and H.K. Browne, 3 vols., brown cloth. With clock on front pointing to volume number. (No hands on clock on variant binding.) First book edition. $850. (See entry under "Boz" for editions in parts.)

DICKENS, Charles. *The Mystery of Edwin Drood.* London, 1870. 12 illustrations by S.L. Fildes. 6 parts, green pictorial wraps. $750. London, 1870. Green cloth with sawtooth border around front cover. First book edition. $350.

DICKENS, Charles. *Oliver Twist.* London, 1839. 3 vols., in original brown cloth. Second edition (or third issue of the 1838 original, see "Boz" entry). With Dickens on title page instead of "Boz." $500. (For third, or first octavo, edition see Dickens, *The Adventures of Oliver Twist.*)

DICKENS, Charles. *Our Mutual Friend.* London, 1864–65. Illustrations by Marcus Stone. 20 parts in 19, green pictorial wraps. $1,750. London, 1865. 2 vols., reddish brown cloth. First book edition. $1,250.

DICKENS, Charles. *The Personal History of David Copperfield.* London, 1849–50. Illustrated by H.K. Browne. 20 parts in 19, green pictorial wraps. $6,000. London, 1850. Dark green cloth. First book edition, first state, with engraved title page dated 1850. $1,000.

DICKENS, Charles. *Pictures from Italy.* London, 1846. Illustrations on wood by Samuel Palmer. Blue cloth. $500.

DICKENS, Charles. *The Posthumous Papers of the Pickwick Club.* London, 1836. Illustrated by R. Seymour and Phiz. 20 parts in 19, green wraps. With "Tony Veller" on signboard on engraved title, and others. $5,000. London, 1837. In original slate or purplish black cloth. First book edition, first issue, with the name "Tony Veller" on the signboard. "S. Veller" on page 342, line 5; "this friends" for "his friends" on page 400, line 21 and "f" in "of" imperfect in the headline on page 432. $3,000. Philadelphia, 1836–37. 5 vols., in original boards. First American edition. $2,000. Limited Editions Club, New York. 1933. 2 vols., cloth. In slipcase. $150.

DICKENS, Charles. *A Tale of Two Cities.* London, 1859. Illustrated by H.K. Browne, 8 parts in 7, blue wraps. First state, with page 213 misnumbered "113." $6,000. London, 1859. Red cloth. First book edition, first state. $2,500. Second issue, page 213 correctly numbered. In red or green cloth. $1,500.

DICKENS, Charles. *The Uncommercial Traveller.* London, 1861. Reddish purple cloth. With ads dated December 1860. $600.

DICKENS, Charles. *The Village Coquettes: A Comic Opera.* London, 1836. Gray boards, or unstitched, unopened sheets. Original boards. $1,000. In sheets. $750.

DICKENSON, Luelia. *Reminiscences of a Trip Across the Plains in 1846.* San Francisco, 1904. Pictorial cloth. $500.

DICKERSON, Philip J. *History of the Osage Nation.* (Cover title.) (Pawhuska, Oklahoma Indian Territory, 1906.) Illustrations and map. 144 pp., wraps. $250.

DICKEY, James. *Buckdancer's Choice.* Middletown, Conn., (1965). $125.

DICKEY, James. *Drowning With Others.* Middletown, Conn. 1962. Author's first book. Cloth. $200. Wraps. $125.

DICKEY, James. *The Eye-Beaters, Blood, Victory, Madness, Buckhead and Mercy.* Garden City, 1970. One of 250 signed. In slipcase. $200. Trade. $75.

DICKEY, James. *Helmets.* Middletown (1964). Cloth. $125. Wraps. $35.

DICKEY, James. *Two Poems of the Air.* Portland, Ore. (1964). Calligraphic text. Decorated boards. Oblong, decorated boards. One of 300 signed by the poet and the calligrapher, Monica Moseley Pincus. In slipcase. $250.

DICKINSON, Emily. See *A Masque of Poets.*

DICKINSON, Emily. *Letters of Emily Dickinson.* Boston, 1894. Edited by Mabel Loomis Todd. 2 vols., medium yellowish green buckram. With Roberts Brothers imprint on spine. First printing and first issue of second printing the same. $400. (Later in brown cloth and still later by Little Brown.)

DICKINSON, Emily. *Poems.* Boston, 1890. Edited by Mabel Loomis Todd and T.W. Higginson. Author's first book. White and gray cloth. $3,000. (In tissue dustwrapper and slipcase, $5,000 or more.) London, 1891. First English edition. $600. Limited Editions Club. New York, 1952. Morocco. In slipcase. $75.

DICKINSON, Emily. *Poems: Second Series.* Boston, 1891. Edited by T.W. Higginson and Mabel Loomis Todd. $750. Some special copies issued in decorated boards, calf spine. $1,000.

DICKINSON, Emily. *Poems: Third Series.* Roberts Brothers. Boston, 1896. Edited by Mabel Loomis Todd. ("Second edition" so stated.) $450.

DICKINSON, Emily. *The Single Hound: Poems of a Lifetime.* Boston, 1914. $450. Boston, 1915. $150.

DICKINSON, Emily. *Unpublished Poems.* Boston, 1935. Edited by Martha Dickinson Biachi and Alfred Leete Hampson. One of 525 deluxe copies. In slipcase. $500. Boston, 1936. $125.

DIDIMUS, H. *New Orleans as I Found It.* New York, 1845. Double columns, 125 pp., wraps. (By Edward H. Durrell.) $350.

DIDION, Joan. *Run River.* New York (1963). Author's first book. $100. London (1964). $100.

DIDION, Joan. *Slouching Towards Bethlehem.* New York (1968). $75. London, 1969. $75.

DI DONATO, Pietro. *Christ in Concrete.* Esquire Publishers. Chicago (1937). In glassine jacket. Author's first book. $75.

DIEHL, Edith. *Bookbinding: Its Background and Technique.* New York, 1946. 2 vols. $250.

DIENST, Alex. *The Navy of the Republic of Texas, 1835–1845.* Temple, Tex. (1909). Blue leather (presentation binding). $750. Cloth. $300.

DIETZ, August. *The Postal Service of the Confederate States of America.* Richmond, 1929. 2 color plates. Half leather. $150.

DILLARD, Annie. *Tickets for a Prayer Wheel.* Columbia, Mo. (1974). Author's first book. $200.

DILLON, George. *The Flowering Stone.* New York, 1931. $60.

DIMSDALE, Thomas J. *The Vigilantes of Montana.* Virginia City, Mont., 1866. 228 pp., printed wraps. $2,500. Rebound in half calf, $1,750. Virginia City, 1882. 241 pp., printed wraps. Second edition. $250. Cloth. $150.

DINESEN, Isak. *Out of Africa.* New York (1938). $150.

DINESEN, Isak. *Seven Gothic Tales.* New York, 1934. One of 1,010 copies in slipcase. In leather. $350. In black cloth. $250. Trade. $150. London, 1934. In Rex Whistler dustwrapper. $150.

DIOMEDI, Alexander. *Sketches of Modern Indian Life.* (Woodstock, Md., 1894?) 79 pp., wraps. $150.

DI PRIMA, Diane. *New Mexico Poems.* (New York, 1968.) Wraps. One of 50 signed. $150.

DI PRIMA, Diane. *This Kind of Bird Flies Backward.* (New York, 1958). Wraps. Author's first book. $40.

DIRECTORY of the City of Mineral Point for the Year 1859. Mineral Point, Wis., 1859. Map. 64 pp., sewed. $250.

DIRECTORY of Newark for 1835–6. Newark, N.J., 1835. Half leather. $500 and up.

DIRINGER, David. *The Alphabet, A Key to the History of Mankind.* London (1968). 2 vols. Third edition, completely revised. $250.

DISCH, Thomas M. See Demijohn, Thom.

DISCH, Thomas M. *Camp Concentration.* London, 1968. $250. Garden City, 1969. $100.

DISCH, Thomas M. *Under Compulsion.* London, 1968. $300.

DISCOURSE on the Aborigines of the Valley of the Ohio (A). Cincinnati, 1838. (By William Henry Harrison.) Folding map, 51 pp., wraps. $600. Some copies with corrections in Harrison's hand. $1,000.

DISNEY, Walt (or Disney Studios). *The Adventures of Mickey Mouse: Book I.* Philadelphia (1931). Illustrated. Pictorial boards. Issued without dustwrapper. $1,000. London, 1931. $750.

DISNEY, Walt. *Little Red Riding Hood and the Big Bad Wolf.* Philadelphia (1934). Illustrated. Boards. Issued without dustwrapper. $400.

DISNEY, Walt. *Mickey Mouse.* Racine, Wis. (1933). Illustrated. Pictorial wraps. $350.

DISNEY, Walt. *The Pop-Up Minnie Mouse.* New York (1933). Illustrated with 3 double-page pop-up cutouts. Pictorial boards. Issued without dustwrapper. $750.

DISNEY, Walt. *Stories from Walt Disney's Fantasia.* New York (1940). Illustrated. Boards. In dustwrapper. $500.

DISRAELI, Benjamin. See *Henrietta Temple; The Letters of Runnymede; The Tragedy of Count Alarcos; Vivian Grey; The Young Duke.*

DISRAELI, Benjamin. *Coningsby; or, The New Generation.* London (1844). Boards. $200.

DISRAELI, Benjamin. *Sybil, or The Two Nations.* London (1845). 3 vols., half cloth. $150.

DISSERTATION on the History . . . of the Bible . . . (A). (By Timothy Dwight.) New Haven, 1772. Author's first book. Wraps. $250.

DISTURNELL, John. *The Influence of Climate in North and South America.* New York, 1867. $125.

DISTURNELL, John (publisher). *Disturnell's Guide Through the Middle, Northern, and Eastern States.* New York, June, 1847. Map of New York City, folding map. Cloth. $125.

DISTURNELL, John (publisher). *The Emigrant's Guide to New Mexico, California, and Oregon.* New York, 1849. Cloth. Folding map, 46 pp. First issue, with map published by Colton. $2,000. Second issue, wraps with map by Disturnell. $2,000. New York, 1850. Cloth. $1,250.

DISTURNELL, John (publisher). *The Great Lakes or Inland Seas of America.* New York, 1868. Cloth. $200.

DISTURNELL, John (publisher). *The Upper Lakes of North America: A Guide.* New York, 1857. Cloth. $150.

DIX, John Ross. See Jones, J. Wesley.

DIXON, Richard W. *Odes and Eclogues.* Oxford, 1884. Daniel Press. Wraps. One of 100. $250.

DIXON, Sam Houston. *The Heroes of San Jacinto.* Houston, 1932. $125.

DIXON, Sam Houston. *The Poets and Poetry of Texas.* Austin, 1885. Illustrated. $250.

DIXON, Thomas, Jr. *The Clansman.* New York, 1905. $75.

DOBIE, J. Frank. *Apache Gold and Yaqui Silver.* Boston, 1939. Illustrated by Tom Lea. First (Sierra Madre) edition. One of 265 signed by author and artist in slipcase. $1,000. Trade. $175.

DOBIE, J. Frank. *Bigfoot Wallace and the Hickory Nuts.* Austin, 1936. 7 pp., wraps. One of 300 signed. $400.

DOBIE, J. Frank. *Carl Sandburg and Saint Peter at the Gate.* Austin, 1966. Illustrated. Boards. One of 750 in slipcase. $200.

DOBIE, J. Frank. *Coronado's Children,* Dallas (1930). Maps, illustrated. First issue, without the word "clean" in dedication. $350.

DOBIE, J. Frank. *The First Cattle in Texas and the Southwest.* Austin, 1939. 29 pages, stapled. First separate edition. $150.

DOBIE, J. Frank. *The Flavor of Texas.* Dallas, 1936. $300.

DOBIE, J. Frank. *John C. Duval, First Texas Man of Letters.* Dallas, 1939. Illustrated. One of 1,000. In dustwrapper. $300.

DOBIE, J. Frank. *The Longhorns.* Boston, 1941. 16 plates by Tom Lea. Rawhide. One of 265 signed. Slipcase. $1,500. Trade in pictorial cloth. $60.

DOBIE, J. Frank. *The Mustangs.* Boston (1952). Illustrated. Leather. One of 100 with original drawing. Slipcase. $2,500. Trade. $75.

DOBIE, J. Frank. *On the Open Range.* Dallas (1931). One of 750. Issued without dustwrapper. $500.

DOBIE, J. Frank. *Tales of the Mustang.* Dallas, 1936. Boards. One of 300 for the Book Club of Texas. Slipcase. $1,250.

DOBIE, J. Frank. *A Vaquero of the Brush Country.* Dallas, 1929. First issue, with "Rio Grande River" (in error) on end-sheet maps. Author's first commercially published (trade) book. $400.

DOBIE, J. Frank, and others (editors). *Mustangs and Cow Horses.* Austin, 1940. $275.

DOBSON, Austin. *Horace Walpole, A Memoir.* New York, 1890. Illustrated by Percy and Leon Moran. Boards. One of 50 on Japan paper. $150. Limited to 484 numbered copies. $125.

DOBSON, Austin. *Vignettes in Rhyme.* London, 1873. Author's first book. $200.

DOCTOROW, E. L. *Big as Life.* New York (1966). $175.

DOCTOROW, E. L. *The Book of Daniel.* New York (1971). $75.

DOCTOROW, E. L. *Loon Lake.* New York (1980). One of 350 signed, issued without dustwrapper in slipcase. $100. Signed tipped-in page. $60. Trade. $25.

DOCTOROW, E. L. *Ragtime.* New York (1975). One of 150 signed, issued without dustwrapper, in slipcase. $150. Unspecified number in brown cloth with signed tipped-in sheet. $75. Trade edition. $40. London (1975?). $35.

DOCTOROW, E. L. *Welcome to Hard Times.* New York, 1960. Author's first book. $300.

DODDRIDGE, Joseph. *Notes, on the Settlement and Indian Wars, of the Western Parts of Virginia and Pennsylvania . . .* Wellsburgh, Va., 1924. Calf. $400.

DODGE, Grenville M. *Biographical Sketch of James Bridger, Mountaineer, Trapper and Guide.* Kansas City (1905). 2 plates. 10 leaves, wraps. First edition, without preface. $150. New York, 1905. 3 plates, one folding. 27 pp. Wraps. $100.

DODGE, Grenville M. *How We Built the Union Pacific Railway.* Council Bluffs, Iowa. (1908.) 30 plates. Printed wraps. First edition, first issue, without printer's name on page before title page. $150. Second issue. $100.

DODGE, Grenville M. *Union Pacific Railroad, Report of G.M. Dodge, Chief Engineer, to the Board of Directors on a Branch Line from the Union Pacific Railroad to Idaho, Montana, Oregon, and Puget's Sound.* Washington, 1868. Large folding map. 13 pp., wraps. $300. Second edition, same date. $225.

DODGE, J. R. *Red Men of the Ohio Valley.* Springfield, Ohio, 1859. Illustrated. $100. Springfield, 1860. Second edition. $75.

DODGE, M. E. *Hans Brinker; or, The Silver Skates.* New York, 1866. Frontispiece with either one or two leaves of ads (no priority). 3 plates by Thomas Nast. (By Mary Mapes Dodge.) $500.

DODGE, M. E. *The Irvington Stories.* New York, 1865. (By Mary Mapes Dodge.) Frontispiece, 4 plates. Author's first book. $125.

DODGE, Mary Mapes. See Dodge, M. E.

DODGE, Orvil. *Pioneer History of Coos and Curry Counties, Oregon.* Salem, Ore., 1898. Illustrated. $200.

DODGE, Richard Irving. See *A Living Issue.*

DODGE, Richard Irving. *The Black Hills.* New York, 1876. 14 tinted plates, folding map. $125.

DODGE, Richard Irving. *Our Wild Indians.* Hartford, 1882. Illustrated. Cloth. $125.

DODGE, Richard Irving. *The Plains of the Great West and Their Inhabitants.* New York, 1877. Illustrated, folding map. $125.

DODGE, Theodore A. *Riders of Many Lands.* New York, 1894. 19 illustrations by Frederick Remington. $125.

DODGSON, Campbell (editor). *An Iconography of the Engravings of Stephen Gooden.* London, 1944. Illustrated. Buckram. One of 500. $200. Buckram vellum spine, with original proof frontispiece (etching) signed by Gooden. One of 160. Slipcase. $450.

DODGSON, Charles L. See Carroll, Lewis.

DODGSON, Charles L. *Curiosa Mathematica.* London, 1888. $1,000.

DODGSON, Charles L. *Lawn Tennis Tournaments.* London, 1883. 10 pp., sewn, without wraps. $750.

DODSON, Owen. *Powerful Long Ladder.* New York, 1946. Author's first book. $100.

DODSON, W.C. (editor). *Campaigns of Wheeler and His Cavalry, 1862–1865.* Atlanta, 1899. $150.

DOMENECH, Emmanuel. *Seven Years' Residence in the Great Deserts of North America.* London, 1860. Folding map, 5 tinted plates. 2 vols. $750.

DOMESTIC Manners of the Americans. London, 1832. 24 plates, 2 vols. (By Frances Trollope.) $400. New York, 1832. First American edition. $250.

DONAN, P. *Gold Fields of Baker County, Eastern Oregon.* Portland (1898). Folding map, 36 pp., wraps. $200.

DONLEAVY, J. P. *The Ginger Man.* Paris (1955). Green wraps. With "1500 francs" on rear cover. Author's first book. Olympia Press. $500. London, 1956. $125. Paris, 1958. Original dustwrapper flaps. $250. New dustwrapper flaps glued on. $100. New York (1958). $75.

DONNE, John. *The Holy Sonnets of John Donne.* London (1938). Limited to 550 copies signed by Eric Gill. $135.

DONNE, John. *Juvenilia* . . . London, 1633. $1,250.

DONNE, John. *Poems* . . . *With Elegies on the Author's Death.* London, 1633. $5,000.

DONNE, John. *Pseudo-Martyr* . . . London, 1610. Author's first book. $6,000.

DONOHO, M. H. *Circle-Dot, a True Story of Cowboy Life 40 Years Ago.* Topeka, 1907. Frontispiece. $100.

DONOVAN, Dick. *The Man Hunter.* London, 1888. (By Joyce E. Muddock, her first book.) $350.

DOOLITTLE, Hilda. See D.,H.; Helforth, John.

DORING, Ernest N. *The Guadagnini Family of Violin Makers.* Chicago, 1949. Illustrated. $600.

DORN, Edward. *The Shoshoneans.* New York, 1966. Photographs. Oblong, cloth. In dustwrapper. $200.

DORN, Edward. *What I See in the Maximus Poems.* (Ventura, Calif.) 1960. Wraps. Author's first book. $175.

DOS PASSOS, John. See Cendrars, Blaise.

DOS PASSOS, John. *Airways, Inc.* New York (1928). $250.

DOS PASSOS, John. *Facing the Chair: Story of the Americanization of Two Foreign-born Workmen.* Boston, 1927. Stiff olive-drab wraps. $150.

DOS PASSOS, John. *Henry and William Ford and Hearst* . . . San Francisco, 1940. 35 copies. Wraps. $400.

DOS PASSOS, John. *The 42nd Parallel.* New York, 1930. Decorated orange boards. Code "A-E" on copyright page. $250. London (1930). $200.

DOS PASSOS, John. *1919.* New York (1932). $200. London (1932). $150.

DOS PASSOS, John. *One Man's Initiation—1917.* London (1920). Pale blue mesh cloth. First state has a broken "d" and the word "flat" obliterated on page 35, line 32. $750. Second state: perfect "d" and "flat." $500. New York, 1922. Title page is a cancel on a stub, verso of title page blank. Shiny smooth maroon cloth, cream-colored paper label on spine, top-edge trimmed and stained maroon. First state with broken "d" and obliterated "flat" on page 35, line 32. $600. Second state with perfect "d" and "flat" on page 35, line 32. $500.

DOS PASSOS, John. *Orient Express.* New York (1927). Code "M-A" on copyright page. Lavender boards and lavender paper label on shiny blue cloth spine, top edge trimmed and stained wine-colored maroon. $250. Second-state binding: blue cloth with paper label on spine. $150. London (1928). States "First issued in Traveler's Library." $150.

DOS PASSOS, John. *A Pushcart at the Curb.* New York (1922). Colored pictorial boards, cream-colored paper label on black cloth spine. $300.

DOS PASSOS, John. *Rosinante to the Road Again.* New York (1922). Yellow boards. $300.

DOS PASSOS, John. *Three Soldiers.* New York (1921). Publisher's colophon not found in any state of first printing. 3 blank integral leaves at front, none at back, endpapers front and back. "Signing" for "singing" on page 231, line 13. First-state dustwrapper has publisher's blurb on front, spine, and back. $500. Second state: 2 blank integral leaves in front, none in back, endpapers front and back, pages 9–10 tipped onto pages 11–12, "signing" for "singing" page 213, line 31. Dustwrapper has a quotation from the *Brooklyn Daily Eagle* as last item on front panel. $400. Third state: like first, has 3 blank integral leaves in front and none in back, endpapers front and back, "signing" has been corrected to "singing." Dustwrapper same as second state except the quote from the *Brooklyn Daily Eagle* has been replaced by one from *Stars and Stripes.* $300. Fourth state: 2 integral blank leaves at front and 3 at back, no endpapers (the first and last leaves being pastedowns); "singing" at page 213, line 31. Dustwrapper as in third state but with price on spine blacked over. $250. Fifth state: 3 blank integral leaves in front and 4 in back, endpapers in front and back. $250. (Note: priority of third, fourth, and fifth states presumed.) London (1922). page 383 "Printed by Anchor Press Ltd . . ." $400.

DOS PASSOS, John. *U.S.A. (The 42nd Parallel, 1919, The Big Money).* New York, (1938). 1-vol. trilogy. First appearance of short sketch by Dos Passos. Last copyright date 1937, but not published until January 1938. $100. London (1938). $75. Boston, 1946. Illustrated by Reginald Marsh, 3 vols. Limited to 365 numbered copies, signed by Dos Passos and Marsh. Slipcase. $450. Trade edition. 3 vols. Slipcase. $200.

DOSTOEVSKY, F. *The Grand Inquisitor.* (London) 1930. Translated by S.S. Koteliansky. Introduction by D.H. Lawrence. One of 300. In slipcase. $250.

DOSTOEVSKY, F. *Poor Folk.* London, 1894. (Beardsley cover.) First English publication. $150.

DOUGHTY, Charles M. *Travels in Arabia Deserta.* Cambridge, 1888. Illustrated, folding map in pocket. 2 vols. $1,500. New York, 1923. Introduction by T.E. Lawrence. 2 vols. $300. Limited Editions Club, New York, 1953. $125.

DOUGLAS, Lord Alfred. *The City of the Soul.* London, 1899. Vellum boards. $125.

DOUGLAS, Lord Alfred. *My Friendship with Oscar Wilde.* New York, 1932. $150.

DOUGLAS, Lord Alfred. *Poems.* Paris, 1896. Author's first book. Text in English and French. Portrait frontispiece. Wraps. One of 20 on Hollande paper. (Usually inscribed.) $450. Ordinary issue. $150.

DOUGLAS, C. L. *Cattle Kings of Texas.* Dallas (1939). Illustrated. $125. Second edition, same date. Rawhide. Limited. $400.

DOUGLAS, C. L. *Famous Texas Feuds.* Dallas (1936). Illustrated. Decorated cloth and leather. In dustwrapper. $125.

DOUGLAS, C. L. *The Gentlemen in White Hats.* Dallas (1934). $125.

DOUGLAS, David. *Journal Kept by David Douglas During His Travels in North America, 1823–27.* London, 1914. Portrait. Cloth. One of 500. $250.

DOUGLAS, Ellen. *A Family Affair.* Boston, 1962. Author's first book. $100.

DOUGLAS, James. *The Gold Fields of Canada.* Quebec, 1863. 18 pp., wraps. $500.

DOUGLAS, Norman. See Bey, Pilaff; Douglass, G. Norman; Normyx. See also *The Blue Grotto and Its Literature; Some Antiquarian Notes; Three Monographs.*

DOUGLAS, Norman. *The Angel of Manfredonia.* San Francisco, 1929. One of 225 signed. Issued without dustwrapper. $150.

DOUGLAS, Norman. *Birds and Beasts of the Greek Anthology.* (Florence, Italy) 1927. Frontispiece. Blue boards, paper label. One of 500 signed. Issued without dustwrapper. $150.

DOUGLAS, Norman. *Capri: Materials for a Description of the Island.* Florence, 1930. Illustrated. Boards and cloth, leather label. One of 500 signed. $150. Blue cloth. Deluxe issue. One of 103 signed. $500.

DOUGLAS, Norman. *Experiments.* (Florence) 1925. Boards, paper label. One of 300 signed. In dustwrapper. $125. London, 1925. One of 300 signed. $125.

DOUGLAS, Norman. *How About Europe?* Decorated boards. (Florence) 1929. One of 550 signed. $150. London, 1930. Orange cloth. In dustwrapper. $60.

DOUGLAS, Norman. *In the Beginning.* (Florence) 1927. Printed boards, leather label. One of 700 signed. $150. New York (1928). Boards. First American edition. $75. London, 1928. $100.

DOUGLAS, Norman. *London Street Games.* London (1916). St. Catherine Press. Buckram. One of 500. $150. London (1931). Boards and cloth. Second edition. One of 110 signed. $150. Trade. $50.

DOUGLAS, Norman. *Looking Back: An Autobiographical Excursion.* London, 1933. 2 vols., boards and buckram. One of 535 signed. $150. New York, 1933. $50.

DOUGLAS, Norman. *One Day.* Hours Press. Chapelle-Reanville, France, 1929. Portraits. Full scarlet leather. One of 200 on Rives paper, signed. $250. Boards. One of 300. $100.

DOUGLAS, Norman. *Paneros.* Florence (1930). Gold cloth and boards, leather label. One of 250 signed. In dustwrapper. Slipcase. $150. London, 1931. Boards and cloth. First English edition. One of 650. $100. New York, 1932. Illustrated. Vellum. First American edition. One of 750. Slipcase. $100.

DOUGLAS, Norman. *Some Limericks.* (Florence), 1928. Gold-colored linen. One of 110 signed. $350. (New York) 1928. Cloth. First American edition. $125. (Florence) 1929. Wraps. $100. Buckram. $75.

DOUGLAS, Norman. *South Wind.* London (1917). $150. London (1922). One of 150 on blue paper, signed. $250. New York, 1928. Illustrated by Valenti Angelo. One of 250 signed by Douglas. In slipcase. $250. 2 vols. in 1, half morocco. One of 40 signed. $300. Limited Editions Club, New York, 1932. In slipcase. $75.

DOUGLASS, G. Norman. *On the Herpetology of the Grand Duchy of Baden.* London, 1894. 64 pp., pale gray-blue wraps. (By Norman Douglas.) $1,250.

DOUGLASS, G. Norman. *Report on the Pumice Stone Industry of the Lipari Islands.* 8 pp., London, 1895. (By Norman Douglas.) One of 125. $1,000.

DOVE, Rita. *Ten Poems.* Lisbon, 1977. $100.

DOW, Goerge Francis. *The Arts and Crafts In New England.* Topsfield, 1927. $200.

DOW, George Francis. *The Sailing Ships of New England: Series I–III.* Salem, 1922,–24,–28. 3 vols. written with John Robinson. $350.

DOW, George Francis. *Slave Ships and Slaving.* Salem, 1923. Illustrated. Buckram. Issued without dustwrapper. $200. Half cloth. Large paper. One of 97. $400.

DOW, George Francis. *Whale Ships and Whaling.* Salem, 1925. Illustrated. Buckram. Issued without dustwrapper. One of 950. $300. Half cloth. Large paper. One of 97. Issued without dustwrapper. $500.

DOW, Lorenzo. *The Life and Travels of Lorenzo Dow.* Hartford, 1804. Half calf. $300.

DOWDEN, Edward. *Mr. Tennyson and Mr. Browning.* (London) 1863. Author's first book. $250.

DOWDEN, Edward. *A Woman's Reliquary.* Cuala Press. Dundrum, Ireland, 1913. One of 300. $100.

DOWNEY, Fairfax. *Indian-Fighting Army.* New York, 1941. $200.

DOWNIE, William. *Hunting for Gold: Personal Experiences in the Early Days on the Pacific Coast.* San Francisco, 1893. Frontispiece. Half morocco or cloth. $200.

DOWNING, A. J. *Cottage Residences . . .* New York, 1842. $400.

DOWNING, Andrew Jackson. *The Architecture of Country Houses.* New York, 1850. Illustrated. Pictorial cloth. $400.

DOWNING, Andrew Jackson. *The Fruits and Fruit Trees of America.* London, 1845. $1,000. 68 hand-colored plates. Half morocco. New York, 1850. $1,000.

DOWSON, Ernest. *Decorations: In Verse and Prose.* London, 1899. $750.

DOWSON, Ernest. *The Pierrot of the Minute.* London, 1897. Illustrated by Aubrey Beardsley. One of 300 on handmade paper. $500. One of 30 on Japanese vellum. $7,000 at auction in 1990. New York, 1923. Grolier Club. One of 300 designed by Bruce Rogers. In slipcase. $250.

DOWSON, Ernest. *The Poems of Ernest Dowson.* London, 1905. Illustrated by Aubrey Beardsley. $400.

DOWSON, Ernest. *Verses.* London, 1896. Cover decorations by Aubrey Beardsley. Vellum. One of 30 on Japan paper. $2,000. One of 300 on handmade paper. $500.

DOYLE, A. Conan. See *Beeton's Christmas Annual; Dreamland and Ghostland.*

DOYLE, A. Conan. *The Adventures of Sherlock Holmes.* London, 1892. Illustrated by Sidney Paget. Light blue cloth. $2,000. New York, 1892. First issue, with "if had" on page 65, line 4. $2,000. Second issue, with "if he had," $600.

DOYLE, A. Conan. *The Case-Book of Sherlock Holmes.* London (1927). Pink cloth, lettered in gilt. $4,000. Colonial issue in light gray cloth, lettered in black. $2,000. New York, 1927. $1,000.

DOYLE, A. Conan. *The Doings of Raffles Haw.* London, 1892. Dark blue cloth. First edition not stated. $200.

DOYLE, A. Conan. *The Firm of Girdlestone.* London, 1890. $500.

DOYLE, A. Conan. *The Great Shadow.* Bristol, England, 1892. Pictorial wraps. $250.
Later printing in cloth. $150.

DOYLE, A. Conan. *His Last Bow.* John Murray. London, 1917. In dustwrapper.
$5,000. Without dustwrapper. $300. Colonial issue, G. Bell. London, 1917. In
dustwrapper. $2,000. Without dustwrapper. $150. New York (1917). Orange cloth.
First edition not stated. $150. Later in dark red cloth. $75.

DOYLE, A. Conan. *The History of Spiritualism.* London (1926). 2 vols. $400.

DOYLE, A. Conan. *The Hound of the Baskervilles.* George Newnes, Ltd. London,
1902. Illustrated by Sidney Paget. Decorated red cloth. $2,000. Colonial issue,
Longman's Green. London, 1902. $600. New York (1902). First issue, without the
"Published 1902" line on copyright page. $650. Second issue. $200. Third issue with
tipped-in title page, with "illustrated." $150. Fourth state same as third, but title
page integral. $100.

DOYLE, A. Conan. *The Land of Mist.* London (1926). In dustwrapper. $125. green
cloth. $750. New York (1926). $300.

DOYLE, A. Conan. *The Memoirs of Sherlock Holmes.* London, 1894. Illustrated by
Sidney Paget. Blue cloth, gold letters. $1,500. New York, 1894. Blue cloth. First
American edition. Including 1 story not in English edition or later American
editions. $750.

DOYLE, A. Conan. *My Friend the Murderer.* New York (1893). Blue cloth. $250.

DOYLE, A. Conan. *The Refugees: A Tale of Two Continents.* London, 1893. 3 vols.,
green cloth. $2,000. New York, 1893. $125.

DOYLE, A. Conan. *The Return of Sherlock Holmes.* McClure, Phillips & Co., 1905.
(Preceding English edition by a month.) Black or blue (variant) cloth. ·$1,000.
George Newnes, Ltd., London, 1905. $2,000. Remainder sheets issued by Smith,
Elder & Co. London, 1907. $200.

DOYLE, A. Conan. *The Sign of Four.* London, 1890. Frontispiece. Dark-red cloth.
First issue, with "Spencer Blackett's Standard Library" on spine. Probable early
issue with "8" missing on page "138." $7,500. Remainder sheets issued by Griffin
Farran & Co. (on spine), with same title page as first. $2,500.

DOYLE, A. Conan. *The Speckled Band.* Samuel French, Ltd., London, 1912. Stage
diagrams. Printed light green wraps. $2,000. Second printing with dark green
wraps. $300. (Later in brown wraps). Collier. New York, 1891. Wraps. $1,500.

DOYLE, A. Conan. *A Study in Scarlet.* London, 1888. Illustrated. White wraps. First
edition in book form, first issue, with "younger" correctly spelled in the preface.
$40,000. With "youuger." $25,000. Philadelphia, 1890. Wraps. $6,000. Cloth.
$4,000. London, 1891. Second edition. $350.

DOYLE, A. Conan. *The Valley of Fear.* New York (1914). Illustrated by Arthur I.
Keller. Red cloth. $350. Smith, Elder & Co. London, 1915. First English edition.
$350.

DOYLE, A. Conan. *The White Company.* London, 1891. 3 vols., dark red cloth.
$2,500. John Lovell Co. New York (1891). Wraps. $300. Lovell, Coryell & Co.
(1892). Wraps. $200.

DOYLE, A. Conan, and BARRIE, James M. *Jane Annie: Or the Good Conduct Prize.* London, 1893. Wraps. $300.

DRABBLE, Margaret. *A Summer Bird-Cage.* London, 1963. Author's first book. $150.

DRABBLE, Margaret. *Virginia Woolf: A Personal Debt.* New York, 1973. Wraps. One of 110 signed. $200.

DRAEGER, Donn F., and SMITH, Robert W. *Asian Fighting Arts.* Tokyo, 1969. First edition stated. $50.

DRAGO, Harry Sinclair. *Outlaws on Horseback.* New York, 1964. Illustrated, map. One of 150 signed. In slipcase. $175.

DRAGO, Harry Sinclair. *Wild, Woolly & Wicked.* New York, 1960. Illustrated by Nick Eggenhofer. One of 250 signed. $150. Trade. $35.

DRAGOON Campaigns to the Rocky Mountains. New York, 1836. By a Dragoon. Blue cloth. (By James Hildreth.) $500.

DRAKE, Benjamin. *The Life and Adventures of Black Hawk.* Cincinnati, 1838. Portrait and plates. $250.

DRAKE, Benjamin. *Life of Tecumseh, and His Brother the Prophet.* Cincinnati, 1841. $125.

DRAKE, Benjamin. *Tales and Sketches of the Queen City.* Cincinnati, 1838. $125.

DRAKE, Benjamin, and MANSFIELD, E. D. *Cincinnati in 1826.* Cincinnati, 1827. 2 plates. In original morocco. $600.

DRAKE, Daniel. *An Account of Epidemic Cholera, as It Appeared in Cincinnati.* Cincinnati, 1832. 46 pp., in original wraps. $350.

DRAKE, Daniel. *Natural and Statistical View, or Picture of Cincinnati and the Miami Country.* Cincinnati, 1815. 2 folding maps. $750.

DRAKE, Daniel. *Pioneer Life in Kentucky: A Series of Reminiscential Letters from Daniel Drake, M.D., of Cincinnati to His Children.* Cincinnati, 1870. Portrait. Cloth. $300.

DRAKE, Daniel. *A Practical Treatise on the History, Prevention, and Treatment of Epidemic Cholera.* Cincinnati, 1832. In original cloth, paper spine label. $650.

DRAKE, Daniel. *A Systematic Treatise: Historical, Etiological, and Practical, on the Principal Diseases of the Interior Valley of North America.* (First series.) Cincinnati, 1850. Maps and plates. Full leather. $1,000. Philadelphia, 1854. (Second series.) $400.

DRAKE, Joseph Rodman. See Croaker.

DRAKE, Joseph Rodman. *The Culprit Fay and Other Poems.* New York, 1835. Frontispiece, vignette title page. Blue or purple cloth. $75. Also bound in leather. $150. New York, 1923. Grolier Club. One of 300. $75.

DRAKE, Leah Bodine. *A Hornbook for Witches.* Sauk City, Wis., 1950. $1,250.

DRAKE, Morgan. *Lake Superior Railroad: Letter to the Hon. Lewis Cass.* Pontiac, 1853. 24 pp., wraps. $300.

DRANNAN, Capt. William F. *Thirty-one Years on the Plains and in the Mountains.* Chicago, 1899. Illustrated. $175.

DRAPER, John William. *Human Physiology.* New York. 1856. $150.

DRAYSON, Capt. Alfred W. *Sporting Scenes Amongst the Kaffirs of South Africa.* London, 1858. 8 colored plates by Harrison Weir. $750.

DRAYTON, John. *Memoirs of the American Revolution.* Charleston, 1821. Portrait, 2 maps. 2 vols. $1,500.

DRAYTON, John. *A View of South-Carolina.* Charleston, 1802. 2 maps, 2 tables, 3 plates. $2,000.

DRAYTON, Michael. *The Battle of Agincourt . . .* London, 1627. $1,000.

DREAM Drops, or Stories from Fairy Land. Boston (1887). By a Dreamer. (Amy Lowell, her first book.) Wraps (151 copies). $1,750. Cloth (99 copies). $2,500.

DREAM of Gerontius (The). London, 1866. (By John Henry, Cardinal Newman.) Wraps. First edition, printed dedication "J.H.N." $2,000.

DREAMLAND and Ghostland: An Original Collection of Tales and Warnings. London (1887). 3 vols., pictorial red cloth. First edition, first binding (red cloth). (Contains 6 stories by A. Conan Doyle.) $850.

DREISER, Theodore. See Davis, Hubert.

DREISER, Theodore. *An American Tragedy.* New York, 1925. 2 vols., black cloth, white endpapers. First issue, with Boni & Liveright imprint. In slipcase. $300. Another (later) issue. 2 vols., blue boards and cloth. First limited edition. One of 795 signed. In slipcase. $400. London, 1926. $150. Limited Editions Club, New York, 1954. In slipcase. $125.

DREISER, Theodore. *Chains: Lesser Novels and Stories.* New York, 1927. Decorated boards and cloth. One of 440 signed in slipcase. $350. Trade. $75.

DREISER, Theodore. *The Color of a Great City.* New York (1923). $300.

DREISER, Theodore. *Dawn: A History of Myself.* New York (1931). One of 275 signed. In slipcase. $450. Trade. $125.

DREISER, Theodore. *Dreiser Looks at Russia.* New York, 1928. $200.

DREISER, Theodore. *The Financier.* New York, 1912. With "Published October, 1912" and "K-M" on copyright page. $100.

DREISER, Theodore. *Free, and Other Stories.* New York, 1918. In dustwrapper. $600. Without dustwrapper. $150.

DREISER, Theodore. *A Gallery of Women.* New York, 1929. 2 vols., boards and vellum. One of 560 signed in slipcase. $400. Trade. 2 vols. In slipcase. $200. (Precedes limited.)

DREISER, Theodore. *The "Genius."* New York, 1915. First issue, 1¾ inches thick, and with page 497 so numbered. $175. Second issue, 1½ inches thick, no number on page 497. $125.

DREISER, Theodore. *The Hand of the Potter.* New York, 1918. First issue, in light green boards with natural linen spine, with front cover lettered in dark green. $150. Second issue. With blue cloth spine. $100.

DREISER, Theodore. *Hey, Rub-A-Dub-Dub!* New York, 1920. In dustwrapper. $400.

DREISER, Theodore. *Jennie Gerhardt.* New York, 1911. Frontispiece. Mottled light blue cloth. First issue, with "is" for "it" on line 30 of page 22. $250. Second issue, text corrected. $125. (There are two bindings, either "Dreiser" or "Theodore Dreiser," the latter is agreed to be first, but the former is much scarcer.)

DREISER, Theodore. *My City.* New York (1929). Colored etchings by Max Pollack. Folio, boards, and cloth. Issued without dustwrapper, in slipcase. One of 275 signed. $350.

DREISER, Theodore. *The Seven Arts: Life, Art and America.* New York, 1917. 28 pp., cream wraps. $200.

DREISER, Theodore. *Sister Carrie.* New York, 1900. Dark red cloth. Author's first book. $1,500. London, 1901. $350. New York, 1907. Colored frontispiece. First illustrated edition. $200. Limited Editions Club, New York, 1939. In slipcase. $175.

DREISER, Theodore. *A Traveler at Forty.* New York, 1913. Illustrated by W. Glackens. Red cloth. $150.

DREYFUS, John *The Survival of Baskerville's Punches.* Cambridge, 1949. Limited to 250 copies. $125.

DREYFUS, John (editor). *Typographical Partnership* . . . New York, 1971. Limited to 350 copies. $100.

DREYFUS, John. *The Work of Jan Van Krimpen* . . . London, 1952. $100.

DRIFTWOOD Flames. Nashville (1923). (Includes 5 poems by Robert Penn Warren, his first book appearance.) $500.

DRINKWATER, John. *Loyalties.* Beaumont Press. (London) 1918. Illustrated. Vellum and boards. One of 30 on Japan vellum, signed. $1,000. Boards and cloth. One of 120. $300. One of 50 with hand-colored illustrations. $750.

DRINKWATER, John. *Poems.* Birmingham, England, 1903. Author's first book. $250.

DRINKWATER, John. *Tides: A Book of Poems.* Beaumont Press. (London) 1917. One of 250. $200. Full vellum. One of 20 on vellum, signed. $1,500.

DRINKWATER, John, and RUTHERSTON, Albert. *Claud Lovat Fraser: A Story of His Life.* London, 1923. Portrait frontispiece by Rutherston, 39 Fraser illustrations, 20 in color. One of 450 signed. $200.

DRIPS, Joseph H. *Three Years Among the Indians in Dakota.* Kimball, S.D., 1894. 139 pp., wraps. $1,000.

DRUMHELLER, "Uncle Dan." *"Uncle Dan" Drumheller Tells Thrills of Western Trails in 1854.* Spokane, 1925. Portraits. $125.

DRURY, Dru. *Illustrations of Exotic Entomology.* London, 1837. Edited by J.O. Westwood. 150 hand-colored plates. 3 vols. $2,000.

DRURY, The Rev. P. Sheldon (editor). *The Startling and Thrilling Narrative of the Dark and Terrible Deeds of Henry Madison, and His Associate and Accomplice Miss Ellen Stevens, Who Was Executed by the Vigilance Committee of San Francisco, on the 20th September Last.* Cincinnati (1857). Illustrated. 36 pp., pictorial wraps. $300. Philadelphia, 1865. $150.

DRYDEN, John. *Alexander's Feast.* London, 1697. $750. Essex House. London, 1904. Vellum. One of 140 on vellum. $400.

DRYDEN, John. *All for Love.* San Francisco, 1929. 2 vols., folio, half vellum. John Henry Nash printing. One of 250. $200.

DRYDEN, John. *Dramatic Works.* Nonesuch Press. London, 1931–32. Edited by Montague Summers. 6 vols., buckram and marbled boards. $400. One of 50 sets on Van Gelder paper. $600.

DRYDEN, John. *Of Dramatick Poesie.* London, 1668. $1,250. Another edition: London, 1928. Preceded by a *Dialogue on Poetic Drama by T.S. Eliot.* Marbled boards, cloth spine. One of 580. In dustwrapper and slipcase. $500. Boards and vellum. One of 55 signed by Eliot. In dustwrapper and slipcase. $1,250.

DU BOIS, John. *Campaigns in the West, 1856–61: The Journal and Letters of Col. John Du Bois with Pencil Sketches by Joseph Heger.* Tucson, 1949. Plates, folding map. Boards and leather. Grabhorn Printing. One of 300 signed by George P. Hammond as editor. $300.

DU BOIS, John Witherspoon. *Life and Times of William Lowndes Yancey.* Birmingham, Ala., 1892. 9 plates. $150.

DU BOIS, W. E. Burghardt. *The Gift of Black Folk in the Making of America.* Boston, 1924. $750.

DU BOIS, W. E. Burghardt. *The Souls of Black Folk.* Chicago, 1903. $400.

DU BOIS, W. E. Burghardt. *Suppression of the American Slave Trade.* New York, 1896. Author's first book. $750.

DUBUS, André. *The Lieutenant.* New York, 1967. Author's first book. $100.

DU CHAILLU, Paul. *Stories of the Gorilla Country.* New York, 1868. Woodcuts. Pictorial cloth. $150.

DUDLEY-SMITH, T. See Smith, T. Dudley.

DUFF, E. Gordon. *Early English Printing.* London, 1896. Illustrated. Folio, half morocco. One of 300. $200.

DUFF, E. Gordon. *William Caxton.* Chicago, 1905. Caxton Club. Boards and cloth. One of 145 with an original leaf from Chaucer's *Canterbury Tales* of 1478. $2,000. One of 107 without the leaf. $300.

DUFLOT DE MOFRAS, Eugene. *Exploration du Territoire de l'Oregon.* Paris, 1844. Illustrated. 2 vols., leather; plus atlas, folio, cloth. $5,000.

DUFLOT DE MOFRAS, Eugene. *Travels on the Pacific Coast.* Santa Ana, 1937. Translated by Marguerite E. Wilbur. 2 folding maps, 8 plates. 2 vols., half leather. $175.

DULAC, Edmund. *Edmund Dulac's Fairy Book.* New York or London (1916). 15 color plates. Ivory cloth. One of 350 signed. $500.

DULAC, Edmund. *Sinbad the Sailor and Other Stories from the Arabian Nights.* London (1911). Illustrated by Dulac. Vellum. One of 500 signed. $750.

DU MAURIER, Daphne. *I'll Never Be Young Again.* London, 1932. $125.

DU MAURIER, Daphne. *The Loving Spirit.* London, 1931. Author's first book. $250.

DU MAURIER, Daphne. *Rebecca.* London, 1938. $600.

DU MAURIER, George. *Sir Gawaine Hys Penance: A Legend of Camelot.* (London) 1866. Author's first book. Wraps. $1,000.

DU MAURIER, George. *Trilby.* London, 1894. 3 vols. $500. London, 1895. Illustrated. Half vellum. One of 250 signed. $1,000. New York, 1895. Vellum. One of 250 signed. $750.

DUNBAR, James. *The Practical Papermaker; A Complete Guide to the Manufacture of Paper.* Leith, Scotland, 1881. Second edition. $125.

DUNBAR, Paul Laurence. *Howdy, Honey, Howdy.* New York, 1905. $150.

DUNBAR, Paul Laurence. *Joggin' Erlong.* New York, 1906. Illustrated. $150.

DUNBAR, Paul Laurence. *L'il Gal.* New York, 1904. Photographs by Leigh Richmond Miner. Pictorial green cloth. $200.

DUNBAR, Paul Laurence. *Lyrics of Lowly Life.* New York, 1908. $125.

DUNBAR, Paul Lawrence. *Majors and Minors: Poems.* (Toledo, 1895.) Frontispiece portrait. (By Paul Laurence Dunbar.) $600.

DUNBAR, Paul (Laurence). *Oak and Ivy.* Dayton, Ohio, 1893. Blue cloth. Author's first book. $750.

DUNBAR, Paul Laurence. *Poems of Cabin and Field.* New York, 1899. Illustrated. Pictorial cloth. $250.

DUNBAR, Paul Laurence. *The Strength of Gideon and Other Stories.* New York, 1900. Illustrated by E.W. Kemble. $200.

DUNBAR, Paul Laurence. *The Uncalled.* New York, 1898. $300.

DUNCAN, Isadora. *Art of the Dance.* New York, 1928. $500.

DUNCAN, Isadora. *My Life.* New York, 1927. One of 650. $400.

DUNCAN, John M. *Travels Through Part of the United States and Canada in 1818 and 1819.* Glasgow, 1823. 14 maps and plates. 2 vols. $400. New York, 1823. 2 vols. $200.

DUNCAN, L. Wallace. *History of Montgomery County, Kansas.* Iola, Kan., 1903. Half leather. $150.

DUNCAN, L. Wallace. *History of Wilson and Neosho Counties, Kansas.* Fort Scott, Kan., 1902. $150.

DUNCAN, Robert. *A Book of Resemblances.* New Haven, 1966. Illustrated by Jess (Collins). Cloth. One of 203 signed. In tissue dustwrapper. $200.

DUNCAN, Robert. *Caesar's Gate: Poems, 1949–1950.* Divers Press. (Mallorca) 1955. Illustrated by Jess (Collins). Wraps. One of 200. $350. One of 13 signed. $1,000.

DUNCAN, Robert. *Derivations.* London (1968). Fulcrum Press. One of 162 signed. $300. Trade edition. $75.

DUNCAN, Robert. *The First Decade.* Fulcrum Press. (London, 1968.) Cloth. One of 150 signed. In dustwrapper. $250. Trade. $40.

DUNCAN, Robert. *Heavenly City, Earthly City.* (Berkeley) 1947. Author's first book. Illustrated by Mary Fabilli. White boards. $850. (One of 100 specially signed green cloth presentation copies. $1,750.)

DUNCAN, Robert. *Letters.* (Highlands, N.C. 1958.) Decorated wraps. One of 450. $150. Boards and calf. One of 60 signed, with an original drawing by Duncan on endpapers. $250.

DUNCAN, Robert. *Medieval Scenes.* San Francisco (1950). Wraps. One of 250 signed. $350.

DUNCAN, Robert. *A Selection of 65 Drawings.* Los Angeles, 1970. One of 300 signed in cloth portfolio. $175. One of 26 lettered copies, signed, with an original drawing. $450.

DUNDASS, Samuel. *Journal of Samuel Rutherford Dundass.* Steubenville, Ohio, 1857. 60 pp., wraps. $4,000.

DUNIWAY, Mrs. Abigail J. *Captain Gray's Company; or, Crossing the Plains and Living in Oregon.* Portland, 1859. $2,000.

DUNLAP, William. *Diary: Memoirs of a Dramatist.* New York, 1931. 3 vols., buckram. One of 100. Issued without dustwrapper. $200.

DUNLAP, William. *The Life of Charles Brockden Brown.* Philadelphia, 1815. Frontispiece. 2 vols. (Note: Contains first printing of "Memoirs of Carwin" and other Brown items.) $250.

DUNLAP, William. *A History of the American Theatre.* New York, 1832. $100. London, 1833. 2 vols. First English edition. $100.

DUNLAP, William. *A History of the New Netherlands.* New York, 1839–40. 2 folding maps. 2 vols. In original boards or cloth. With errata leaf. $250.

DUNLAP, William. *History of the Rise and Progress of the Arts of Design in the United States.* New York, 1834. 2 vols. $250. Boston, 1918. Plates. 3 vols. $250.

DUNLAP, William. *Memoirs of the Life of George Frederick Cooke.* New York, 1813. Frontispieces. 2 vols. $400.

DUNLAP, William. *A Narrative of the Events Which Followed Bonapart's Campaign,* . . . Hartford, 1814. Frontispiece. 5 plates. Leather. $400.

DUNN, Jacob Piatt. *Massacres of the Mountains.* New York, 1886. Folding map and illustrations. Pictorial cloth. $350.

DUNN, John. *History of the Oregon Territory and British North-American Fur Trade.* London, 1844. Folding map. Cloth. $1,250.

DUNN, John. *The Oregon Territory and the British North American Fur Trade.* Philadelphia, 1845. Wraps. First American edition (of *History of the Oregon Territory, etc.*). $750.

DUNNE, Finley Peter. See *Mr. Dooley in Peace and in War.*

DUNNE, Finley Peter. *Mr. Dooley at His Best.* New York, 1938. One of 520, with a page of the original manuscript. $200.

DUNNE, John Gregory. *Delano: The Story of the California Grape Strike.* New York, 1967. Author's first book. $75.

DUNNING, Ralph Cheever. *Rococo.* Black Manikin Press. Paris, 1926. Author's first book. $200. (First book of this press).

DUNSANY, Lord. *The Book of Wonder.* London, 1912. Illustrated by Sidney H. Sime. $150.

DUNSANY, Lord. *The Chronicles of Rodriquez.* London/New York, 1922. Frontispiece. Light brown cloth, vellum spine, leather label. One of 500 signed. $400.

DUNSANY, Lord. *The Gods of Pegana.* London, 1905. Author's first book. Drummer blind-stamped on front cover. $250. Without drummer. $200.

DUNSANY, Lord. *The King of Elfland's Daughter.* London (1924). Frontispiece. Orange cloth, vellum spine, leather label. One of 250 signed. In dustwrapper. $450.

DUNSANY, Lord. *The Old Folks of the Centuries: A Play.* London, 1930. One of 100 signed. $600.

DUNSANY, Lord. *Selections from the Writings of Lord Dunsany.* Cuala Press. Churchtown, Dundrum, Ireland, 1912. Edited and with introduction by William Butler Yeats. Boards and linen. One of 250. $250.

DUNSANY, Lord. *The Sword of Welleran and Other Stories.* London, 1908. Illustrated by Sidney Sime. $150.

DUNSANY, Lord. *Time and the Gods.* London, 1906. Illustrated by Sidney Sime. In brown boards with green cloth spine. $200. Second binding in green boards. London (1922). Illustrated. Orange cloth, vellum spine, leather label. One of 250 signed in dustwrapper. $450.

DUNSANY, Lord. *Tales of War.* Dublin (1918). $100. Boston, 1918. $75.

DUNTHORNE, Gordon. *Flower and Fruit Prints of the 18th and Early 19th Centuries.* Washington, 1938. Illustrated. Folio, cloth. One of 750, with folding plate listing subscribers. In slipcase. $750.

DUNTON, John. *The Life And Errors of John Dunton, Citizen of London* . . . London, 1818. 2 vols. bound in one. Contains much of the 1705 edition with the edition of a memoir and a few omissions. $275.

DU PONT, S. F. *Extracts from Private Journal-Letters of Capt. S.F. Du Pont During the War with Mexico.* Wilmington, 1885. Boards. $2,000.

DU PONT, Samuel F. *Official Dispatches and Letters of Rear Admiral DuPont, 1846–48; and 1861–63.* Wilmington, 1883. Half leather. $2,000.

DURRELL, Lawrence. See Norden, Charles; Peeslake, Gaffer; Royidis, Emmanuel.

DURRELL, Lawrence. *The Alexandria Quartet.* London (1962). Buckram. First collected edition of *Justine, Balthazar, Mountolive,* and *Clea.* One of 500 signed. In slipcase. $400. New York (1962). Marbled boards. First American edition. One of 199 signed. In slipcase. $500.

DURRELL, Lawrence. *Balthazar.* London, 1958. $250.

DURRELL, Lawrence. *Beccafico Le Becfigue.* Montpellier, 1963. Translated and edited by F. J. Temple. Wraps. One of 150 signed. $300.

DURRELL, Lawrence. *Bitter Lemons.* London, 1957. Illustrated. $150.

DURRELL, Lawrence. *The Black Book.* Obelisk Press. Paris (1938). Wraps. $750. Paris (1959). Wraps and dustwrapper. $60. New York, 1960. First American edition. In dustwrapper. $50.

DURRELL, Lawrence. *Clea.* London (1960). $200.

DURRELL, Lawrence. *Deus Loci.* Ischia, Italy, 1950. Printed blue-gray wraps. One of 200 signed. $350.

DURRELL, Lawrence. *In Arcadia.* Turret Books. London, 1968. Music by Wallace Southam. Wraps. One of 100 signed. $30.

DURRELL, Lawrence. *Justine.* London, 1957. $400.

DURRELL, Lawrence. *Mountolive.* London (1958). $300.

DURRELL, Lawrence. *Nothing Is Lost, Sweet Self.* Turret Books. (London, 1967.) Music by Wallace Southam. Pictorial wraps. One of 100 signed. $250.

DURRELL, Lawrence. *Pied Piper of Lovers.* London, 1935. Author's first novel. $3,000.

DURRELL, Lawrence. *A Private Country: Poems.* London (1943). Gray cloth. $350.

DURRELL, Lawrence. *Private Drafts.* Proodos Press. (Nicosia, Cyprus) 1955. Illustrated. Very small, pictorial wraps. One of 100 signed. $600.

DURRELL, Lawrence. *Quaint Fragment.* Cecil Press. (London) 1931. Portrait. Blue wraps, or rose-red boards and cloth. Author's first book. $36,000 at auction in 1990.

DURRELL, Lawrence. *Six Poems, from the Greek of Sekillianos and Seferis.* Rhodes, 1946. Pictorial wraps. $600.

DURRELL, Lawrence. *Ten Poems*. Caduceus Press. London, 1932. One of 12 signed copies. In buckram. $15,000. Wraps. $2,000.

DURRELL, Lawrence. *Transition: Poems*. London, 1934. $3,000.

DURRELL, Lawrence. *Zero and Asylum in the Snow*. Rhodes, 1946. Wraps. $300.

DUSTIN, Fred. *The Custer Tragedy*. Ann Arbor, 1939. 3 folding maps in pocket. Blue cloth. One of 200. $400.

DUVAL, John C. *The Adventures of Big-Foot Wallace*. Philadelphia, 1871. 8 plates. Green cloth. $600.

DUVAL, John C. *Early Times in Texas*. Austin, 1892. $275.

DUVAL, K. D., and SMITH, Sydney Goodsir (editors). *Hugh MacDiarmid: a Festschrift*. Edinburgh (1962). Cloth. One of 50 with holograph poem signed by MacDiarmid tipped in. In dustwrapper. $250.

DWIGGINS, W. A. *Towards a Reform of the Paper Currency*. Limited Editions Club. New York, 1932. One of 452 signed. In dustwrapper and slipcase. $350.

DWIGHT, Theodore. *An Oration, Spoken Before the Society of the Cincinnati*. New Haven, 1792. Author's first book. $200.

DWIGHT, Timothy. *Travels in New-England and New York*. New Haven, 1821–22. 3 maps. 4 vols. With errata slip in last volume. $450.

DWINELLE, John W. *The Colonial History of the City of San Francisco*. San Francisco, 1863. Map. Printed wraps. $750. San Francisco, 1866. 3 maps (one folding), 3 plates, errata and addenda slips. $1,250.

DWYER, K. R. *Chase*. New York, 1972. (By Dean Koontz.) $300.

DYER, Mrs. D. B. *"Fort Reno," or Picturesque "Cheyenne and Arrapahoe Army Life,"* *Before the Opening of Oklahoma*. New York, 1896. 10 plates. $225.

DYES, Eva Emery. *The Conquest*. Chicago, 1902. In dustwrapper. $250.

DYKES, W. R. *The Genus Iris*. Cambridge, 1913. 48 colored plates. Folio, cloth. $1,000. Half morocco. $1,500.

E

E., A. *The Dublin Strike*. (Caption title.) (London, 1913.) 8 pp., self-wraps. (By George W. Russell.) $175.

E., A. *Gods of War, with Other Poems*. Dublin, 1915. (By George W. Russell.) Brown wraps. $150.

E., A. *Homeward Songs by the Way*. Dublin, 1894. (By George W. Russell.) Wraps. Author's first book. $250.

E., A. *Midsummer Eve.* New York, 1928. (By George W. Russell.) Boards. One of 450 signed. $200.

E., A. *Salutation: A Poem on the Irish Rebellion of 1916.* London 1917. (By George W. Russell.) Wraps. One of 25 signed. $400.

EARHART, Amelia. *The Fun of It: Random Records of My Own Flying and Of Women in Aviation.* New York, 1932. With broadcast record in pocket at back. $750.

EARHART, John F. *The Color Printer, A Treatise on the Use of Colors in Typographic Printing.* Cincinnati, 1892. 92 full-color plates. $650.

EARHART, John F. *The Harmonizer.* Cincinnati, 1897. $225.

EARLE, Ferdinand (editor). *The Lyric Year.* New York, 1912. First state, with "careful gentlemen" for "polite gentleman" in line 13 of page 25. (Contains first appearance of Edna St. Vincent Millay's "Renascence.") $125.

EARLE, Thomas (compiler). *The Life, Travels and Opinions of Benjamin Lundy.* Philadelphia, 1847. Colored folding map. $750.

EARLY, Gen. Jubal A. *Autobiographical Sketch and Narrative of the War Between the States.* Philadelphia, 1912. $200.

EARLY, Gen. Jubal A. *A Memoir of the Last Year of the War for Independence in the Confederate States of America.* Toronto, 1866. $250. Lynchburg, 1867. First United States edition. $250.

EASTLAKE, William. *Go in Beauty.* New York (1956). Author's first book. $200. London, 1957. $75.

EASTMAN, Mary H. *The American Aboriginal Portfolio.* Philadelphia (1853). Engraved title page; 26 plates. $600.

EATON, Daniel Cady. *The Ferns of North America.* Salem, Mass., 1879, and Boston, 1880. 2 vols. $400.

EBERHART, Mignon G. *The Patient in Room 18.* Garden City, 1929. Author's first book. $250.

EBERHART, Richard. *A Bravery of Earth.* London (1930). Author's first book. $300. New York (1930). $200.

EBERHART, Richard. *Brotherhood of Men.* Banyan Press. (Pawlet, Vt. 1949.) Wraps. One of 200 signed. $200. One of 26 signed. $400.

EBERHART, Richard. *Collected Verse Plays.* Chapel Hill (1962). Boards and cloth. One of 100 signed. In glassine dustwrapper. $200.

EBERHART, Richard. *Reading the Spirit.* London, 1936. $175. New York, 1937. $150.

EBERHART, Richard. *Thirty-one Sonnets.* New York (1967). One of 99 signed. In slipcase. $175. Trade. $40.

ECHOES. By Two Writers. (Lahore, India, 1884.) Printed wraps. Light brown wraps. (By Rudyard Kipling, with eight poems credited to his sister Beatrice.) First edition, printed at the Civil and Military Gazette Press. $750.

ECKEL, John C. *The First Editions of the Writings of Charles Dickens.* London/New York, 1932. Revised and enlarged edition. Limited to 750 numbered copies. $225.

EDDINGTON, Arthur Stanley. *Stellar Movements and the Structure of the Universe.* London, 1914. Author's first book. $150.

EDDISON, E. R. *A Fish Dinner in Memison.* New York, 1941. One of 998 numbered copies. $200.

EDDISON, E. R. *Poems, Letters and Memories of Philip Sidney Nairn.* London, 1916. Author's first book. (109-page introduction by Eddison.) Issued without dustwrapper. $200.

EDDISON, E. R. *The Worm Ouroboros.* London (1922). First issue, no blind-stamped windmill on rear cover. $450. Second issue, with windmill. $350. New York, 1926. $150.

EDDY, Mary Baker. See Glover, Mary Baker.

EDE, Charles (editor). *The Art of the Book.* London (1951). In slipcase. $125.

EDE, Harold Stanley. *A Life of Gaudier-Brzeska.* London, 1930. Numerous plates (some colored), other illustrations. One of 350. In dustwrapper and slipcase. $600.

EDELMAN, George W. *Guide to the Value of California Gold.* Philadelphia, 1850. Unbound. $1,750.

EDGAR, Patrick Nisbett. *The American Race-Turf Register. Vol. 1.* (All published.) New York, 1833. $750.

EDGERTON, Clyde. *Raney.* Chapel Hill, 1985. $100.

EDGEWORTH, Maria. See *Castle Rackment; The Modern Griselda*

EDMONDS, Walter D. *Drums Along the Mohawk.* Boston, 1936. $150.

EDMONDS, Walter D. *Rome Haul.* Boston, 1929. Author's first book. With "Published February, 1929" on copyright page. (Presentation) edition one of 1,001. $450. Trade. $350.

EDWARD, David B. *The History of Texas.* Cincinnati, 1836. Folding map in color. $750.

EDWARDS, Billy. *Gladiators of the Prize Ring, or Pugilists of America.* Chicago (1895). Illustrated. Folio, red cloth. $250.

EDWARDS, Bryan. *The History, Civil and Commercial, of the British Colonies in the West Indies . . .* London, 1793. 2 vols. 2 folding maps, 5 folding tables. $1,250.

EDWARDS Chicago Directory (The). Chicago, 1871. 40 pp., boards. "Fire edition." $400.

EDWARDS, E. I. *Desert Voices: A Descriptive Bibliography.* Los Angeles, 1958. Illustrated. Tan buckram. One of 500. In dustwrapper. $125.

EDWARDS, E. I. *The Valley Whose Name Is Death.* Pasadena, 1940. Map. One of 1,000. Issued without dustwrapper. $125.

EDWARDS, Edward. *Free Town Libraries, Their Formation, Management, And History . . .* London, 1869. $100.

EDWARDS, Frank S. *A Campaign in New Mexico with Col. Doniphan.* Philadelphia, 1847. Folding map. $750. Philadelphia, 1848. (Cover date.) Wraps. $850.

EDWARDS, John. *A Select Collection of One Hundred Plates, Consisting of the Most Beautiful and Exotic British Flowers Which Grow in Our English Gardens.* (Noplace) 1775. First edition, second issue. 100 engraved plates, colored by hand. $40,000.

EDWARDS, John N. *Shelby and His Men, or The War in the West.* Cincinnati, 1867. Portrait, folding map. $300.

EDWARDS, John N. *Shelby's Expedition to Mexico.* Kansas City, 1872. $250.

EDWARDS, Philip Leget. *California in 1837.* Sacramento, 1890. Wraps. $300.

EDWARDS, Philip Leget. *The Diary of Philip Leget Edwards: The Great Cattle Drive from California to Oregon in 1837.* Grabhorn Press. San Francisco, 1932. Boards. One of 500. (This reprints *California in 1837.*) $150.

EDWARDS, Samuel E. *The Ohio Hunter.* Battle Creek, 1866. $750.

EDWARDS, Sydenham Teast, et al. *The Botanical Register.* 1815–47. 33 vols. 2,719 hand-colored and engraved plates. $35,000.

EDWARDS, W. F. (publisher). *W.F. Edwards' Tourists' Guide and Directory of the Truckee Basin.* Truckee, Calif., 1883. Illustrated. Cloth. $750.

EFFINGHAM, C. *The Virginia Comedians.* New York, 1854. 2 vols., wraps, or cloth. (By John Esten Cooke.) Wraps (cover date 1855—VAB). Not seen (BAL). $300. Cloth. $200.

EGAN, Pierce. *Anecdotes of the Turf . . .* London, 1827. With 13 hand-colored plates. $600.

EGAN, Pierce. *Boxiana: Or Sketches of Ancient and Modern Pugilism.* London, 1812. $2,500.

EGGLESTON, Edward. *The Book of Queer Stories, and Stories Told on a Cellar Door.* Chicago, 1871. $150.

EGGLESTON, Edward. *The Hoosier School-Boy.* New York, 1883. Illustrated by George D. Bush. Pictorial cloth. First edition, first issue, with "Cousin Sukey" frontispiece and first chapter ending on page 16. $250.

EGGLESTON, Edward. *The Manual: A Practical Guide to the Sunday-School Work.* Chicago, 1869. First issue, with A. Zeese imprint. Author's first book (except for 1865 pamphlet). $150.

EGGLESTON, Edward. *Mr. Blake's Walking-Stick.* Chicago, 1870. Frontispiece and one plate. Light gray wraps. $200.

EGGLESTON, Edward. *To the Friends of the Sanitary Commission in Minnesota.* 1865? Author's first book. 4-page appeal for funds. $500.

EGLE, William H. *History of the Counties of Dauphine and Lebanon (Pennsylvania).* Philadelphia, 1883. $125.

EGLINTON, John. *Irish Literary Portraits.* London, 1935. (By William C. Magee.) $125.

EGLINTON, John. *Some Essays and Passages.* Cuala Press. Dundrum, Ireland, 1905. Selected by William Butler Yeats. Boards, linen spine. (By William C. Magee.) One of 200. $200.

EIGHT Harvard Poets. New York, 1917. Boards. (Contains poems by e.e. cummings, John Dos Passos, and others.) $100.

EIGNER, Larry. *From the Sustaining Air.* (Mallorca) 1953. (250 copies.) Wraps. $300.

EIGNER, Larry. *Poems.* Canton, Mass., 1941. Author's first book. Wraps. (25 copies.) $2,000.

EISENHOWER, Dwight D. *The White House Years: Mandate for Change, 1953–1956.* Garden City, 1963. Cloth. One of 1,434 signed in slipcase. $600.

EISENHOWER, Dwight D. *The White House Years: Waging Peace, 1956–1961.* Garden City, 1965. One of 1,434 signed in slipcase. $600.

EL GABILAN. Salinas, Calif., 1919. Pictorial cloth. Salinas High School Year Book, with 3 contributions by John Steinbeck, his first appearance in print. $1,000.

ELIOT, George. See Strauss, Dr. David Friedrich, and Evans, Marian.

ELIOT, George. *Adam Bede.* Edinburgh, 1859. 3 vols., orange-brown cloth. (By Mary Ann Evans.) $2,250.

ELIOT, George. *Daniel Deronda.* Edinburgh, 1876. (By Mary Ann Evans.) 8 parts, wraps. With erratum slip in part 3. $1,000. First book edition, 4 vols., maroon cloth. Without inserted "contents" leaves. $1,000.

ELIOT, George. *Felix Holt, the Radical.* Edinburgh, 1866. 3 vols., red-brown–colored cloth. (By Mary Ann Evans.) $600.

ELIOT, George. *Middlemarch: A Study of Provincial Life.* Edinburgh, 1871. 8 parts, pictorial wraps. (By Mary Ann Evans.) $3,500. Edinburgh, 1871–72. 4 vols., blue cloth. First book edition. $3,000.

ELIOT, George. *The Mill on the Floss.* Edinburgh, 1860. 3 vols., orange-brown–colored cloth. (By Mary Ann Evans.) $1,000.

ELIOT, George. *Romola.* London, 1863. 3 vols., green cloth. (By Mary Ann Evans.) First issue, with 2 pages of ads at end of vol. 2. $1,500.

ELIOT, George. *Scenes of Clerical Life.* Edinburgh, 1858. 2 vols., maroon cloth. (By Mary Ann Evans.) Author's first book. (Preceded by 2 translations). $2,500.

ELIOT, George. *Silas Marner: The Weaver of Raveloe.* Edinburgh, 1861. Orange-brown cloth. (By Mary Ann Evans.) $600.

ELIOT, T. S. See Ridler, Anne; Perse, St. John; Dryden, John. See also *The Catholic Anthology; Ezra Pound: His Metric and Poetry; Harvard Class Day 1910.*

ELIOT, T. S. *After Strange Gods: A Primer of Modern Heresy.* London (1934). $200. New York, 1933. $175.

ELIOT, T. S. *Animula.* (London, 1929.) Wraps. (Note: unsold copies reissued in 1938 in green paper envelopes printed in brown "The Original First . . .") $75. London, 1929. Yellow boards. 400 signed and numbered copies. $400.

ELIOT, T. S. *Ara Vus Prec.* (London, 1920.) 30 signed, numbered copies (numbered 5–34). Spine label reads *Ara Vos Prec* (which is the correct spelling) title page reads *Ara Vus Prec.* $3,500. 220 numbered (but not signed) copies. Error remains on title page. $2,500. 10 copies not numbered. (There appear to have been more.) $1,500. (Note: There were also 4 presentation copies printed on Japan vellum.)

ELIOT, T. S. *Ash-Wednesday.* New York/London, 1930. 600 signed, numbered copies. In cellophane dustwrapper with white paper flaps and in plain brown cardboard box (200 copies in English edition/400 copies American). $600. London, 1930. $300. New York, 1930. $150.

ELIOT, T. S. *The Cocktail Party.* London (1950). 19,950 copies printed. Gallup notes "about half" of the copies have misprint "here" for "her" page 29, line 1. $100. Misprint corrected. $75. New York (1950). Approximately 10 copies with pages 35–36 printed on uncanceled leaf. $500. Pages 35–36 printed on cancel leaf. $75. (Later printings have code letters/numbers below copyright notice.)

ELIOT, T. S. *Dante.* London (1929). In gray dustwrapper. Earliest state of dustwrapper has no review excerpts on front flap and back. $250. 125 signed and numbered copies. $850.

ELIOT, T. S. *East Coker: A Poem.* London, 1940. Wire stitched. Reprint from the Easter number of *The New English Weekly.* 500 copies printed. $400. London (1940). Yellow wraps. $100.

ELIOT, T. S. *Elizabethan Essays.* London (1934). First issue, with misprint on half title, "No. 21" for "No. 24." $300. Second issue corrects error. Spine stamped in gold. $200. Third state copies measure 18 cm in height, half title correctly reprinted. Spine stamped in silver. $100.

ELIOT, T. S. *For Lancelot Andrewes.* London (1928). $300. Garden City, 1929. $200.

ELIOT, T. S. *Four Quartets.* New York (1943). States "First American edition" on copyright page. $1,000. Second impression does not state "First." Dustwrapper has flap price of $2.00, and the dustwrapper has three states: lighter type with *Essays Ancient & Modern* as one of the 6 titles and publisher's address as "NY." $350. Heavy block letters with *Family Reunion* as 1 of the 6 titles and address as "NY 17." $200. Heavy block letters with 9 titles listed on back through *Possum . . .* (also $2.00 and NY). $175. London (1944). $150. London (1960). 290 signed, numbered copies in marbled paper cardboard box. $2,250.

ELIOT, T. S. *Homage to John Dryden.* London, 1924. Wraps. $200. (New York, 1964). Wraps. Off-print with no indication of publisher, place, or date. $60.

ELIOT, T. S. *Journey of the Magi.* (London, 1927.) Wraps (note: unsold copies were reissued in 1938 in mauve paper envelopes printed in black "The Original First . . ."). $75. (London, 1927.) 350 numbered copies (not signed). $200. New

York, 1927. 27 numbered copies (12 were for sale). $1,000. Iowa City, 1953. 260 copies. Wraps. Mailed in blue paper envelope. $100.

ELIOT, T. S. *John Dryden: The Poet, The Dramatist, the Critic.* New York, 1932. One of 110 copies, of which 100 are signed and numbered. $1,000. New York, 1932. $250.

ELIOT, T. S. *Marina.* (London, 1930.) Wraps. $100. 400 signed and numbered copies $400.

ELIOT, T. S. *Murder in the Cathedral.* (No-place) 1935. Gray wraps. $400. White wraps. $600. London (1935). $200. New York (1935). $200.

ELIOT, T. S. *Old Possum's Book of Practical Cats.* London (1939). $450. New York (1939). $275. London (1940). First illustrated edition. $150.

ELIOT, T. S. *Poems.* Hogarth Press. Richmond, England, 1919. Wraps of various colors and textures and white printed label. First issue: page 13, line 6, "aestival" for "estivale" and page 13, line 12, "capitaux" for "chapitaux." $3,000. In marbled wraps, most with black printed label. Misprints corrected. $2,250.

ELIOT, T. S. *Poems, 1909–1925.* London, 1925. $500. 85 signed, numbered copies. $2,250. New York/Chicago (1932). Laid paper watermarked with a crown and "Antique De Luxe BCMSH" and cream dustwrapper printed in blue without price at bottom on back flap. $250.

ELIOT, T. S. *A Practical Possum.* Cambridge, Mass., 1947. Wraps. 60 numbered copies (states 80 copies but actually only 60 were printed). $1,750.

ELIOT, T. S. *Prufrock and Other Observations.* London, 1917. Author's first book. Wraps. $2,750.

ELIOT, T. S. *Religious Drama: Medieval and Modern.* New York, 1954. 26 signed, lettered copies. Limitation page inserted. $1,250. 300 signed and numbered copies. Limitation page inserted. $500.

ELIOT, T. S. *The Rock.* London (1934). Wraps. Note on Iconoclasm scene laid-in some copies. Priced at 1 shilling. Wraps have flaps folded over endpaper. $150. Boards in dustwrapper. $200. New York, 1934. $150.

ELIOT, T. S. *The Sacred Wood.* London (1920). First state with "Methuen" at foot of spine in letters approximately 3 mm. and in dustwrapper without subtitle on front. $850. Second state with letters 3.5 mm, dustwrapper includes subtitle and adds "Books by A. Clutton-Brock" on back. $600. Third state adds 8 pages of publisher's advertisements inserted after page 156. $400. New York, 1921. (No dustwrapper mentioned in Gallup but copy in dustwrapper auctioned in 1982.) In dustwrapper. $750.

ELIOT, T. S. *Selected Essays, 1917–1932.* London (1932). One of 115 signed. $1,250. Trade edition. $200. New York (1932). $150.

ELIOT, T. S. *Shakespeare and the Stoicism of Seneca.* London, 1927. Wraps $250.

ELIOT, T. S. *Thoughts After Lambeth.* London (1931). $250. Wraps. $75.

ELIOT, T. S. *Triumphal March.* (London, 1931). Wraps. $100. London, 1931. 300 signed, numbered copies. Issued without dustwrapper. $450.

ELIOT, T. S. *Two Poems.* (Cambridge, 1935.) Wraps. 22 copies, 5 on Arches (numbered 1–5); 5 on Normandie (numbered I–V); 5 on Bremen (lettered a–e); 5 on Brussels (lettered A–E); 2 on Brussels (lettered x and xx). $2,500.

ELIOT, T. S. *The Use of Poetry and the Use of Criticism.* London (1933). Top page edge stained blue. $250. Cambridge, 1933. $250.

ELIOT, T. S. *The Waste Land.* New York, 1922. 1,000 numbered copies in total. Approximately 500 copies in first state. Flexible cloth boards and "mountain" correctly spelled on page 41, number on colophon 5 mm high. $3,500. Approximately 500 copies in second state. Stiff cloth boards and "mount in" for "mountain" on page 41. Number on colophon 2 mm high. $2,750. New York (1923). 1,000 numbered copies. Misprint "mount in" remains. "Second Edition." $750. Richmond, 1923. 3 states of label exist and apparently issued simultaneously. $2,000. London (1962). 300 signed, numbered copies. $2,250. London (1971). In slipcase without dustwrapper. $250. Trade. $60. New York (1971). 250 numbered copies. $250. Trade. $40.

ELIOT, T. S. *What Is a Classic?* London (1945). Wraps. Contains statements on the aims of the Virgil Society by Eliot and others. $250. Cloth. Statements not included. $100.

ELIOT, T. S. *Words for Music.* Bryn Mawr (1935). Wraps. 20 copies. 2 copies lettered "A" and "B." $3,000. 6 copies lettered "a–f." $2,750. 6 copies numbered "1–6." $2,750. 6 copies numbered "I–VI." $2,750. Note: there are indications that the total edition exceeds the above 20 copies.

ELIZABETH Bennet; or, Pride and Prejudice: A Novel. Philadelphia, 1832. (By Jane Austen.) 2 vols., in original boards and linen, paper label. First American edition of *Pride and Prejudice.* $1,500.

ELKIN, Stanley. *Boswell.* New York (1964). Cloth. Author's first book. $100.

ELKIN, Stanley. *The Making of Ashenden.* London, 1972. Wraps. One of 100 signed. $125. Trade. $35.

ELKUS, Richard J. *Alamos.* Grabhorn Press. San Francisco, 1965. Foreword by Barnaby Conrad. Half suede and cloth. One of 487. $150.

ELLERMAN, Annie Winifred. *Region of Lutany* . . . London, 1914. Author's first book. Wraps. $750.

ELLERMAN, Sir John. See Black, E. L.

ELLICOTT, Andrew. *The Journal of Andrew Ellicott.* Philadelphia, 1803. 14 maps and plates. With errata leaf. $2,000. Philadelphia, 1814. Second edition. $1,500.

ELLIOTT, D. G. *A Monograph of the Felidae, or Family of Cats.* London, 1883. 43 hand-colored lithographs. Folio, full morocco. $20,000.

ELLIOTT, D. G. *A Monograph of the Bucerodtidae* . . . London, 1877–82. 3 plain and 57 hand-colored plates. Half leather. $10,000.

ELLIOTT, D. G. *The New and Heretofore Unfigured Species of the Birds of North America.* New York (1866–69). 72 hand-colored plates. 2 vols., half morocco. $10,000.

ELLIOTT, W. J. *The Spurs.* (Spur, Tex., 1939.) Plates and map. Cloth. Issued without dustwrapper. $250.

ELLIOTT, David Stewart. *Last Raid of the Daltons.* Coffeyville, Kan., 1892. Illustrated. 72 pp., wraps. $500.

ELLIS, Edward S. See *On the Plains.*

ELLIS, Edward S. *The Life and Adventures of Col. David Crockett.* New York, 1861. Half leather. $150.

ELLIS, Edward S. *The Life and Times of Christopher Carson.* New York (1861). Wraps. $150.

ELLIS, Frederick S. (editor). *Psalmi Penitentiales.* Kelmscott Press. London, 1894. Woodcut designs and initials. Boards and linen. One of 300. $600. One of 12 on vellum. $3,500.

ELLIS, Frederick S. (editor). *The Romance of Syr Ysambrace.* Kelmscott Press. London, 1897. Printed in black and red. Woodcut borders and designs by E. Burne-Jones. Boards and linen. One of 350. $500. One of 8 on vellum. $4,000.

ELLIS, Havelock. *The New Spirit.* London, 1890. Author's first book. $150.

ELLIS, John B. *Free Love and Its Votaries; or, American Socialism Unmasked.* New York (1870). Illustrated. $300.

ELLIS, Martha and Ted. *Alphabet of New York Bookshops.* Buffalo, 1940. Limited to 40 numbered copies and initialed by the author. $100.

ELLIS, William. *The American Mission in the Sandwich Islands.* Honolulu, 1866. Boards. $400.

ELLIS, William. *Polynesian Researches, During a Residence of Nearly Six Years in the South Sea Islands.* London, 1829. 10 plates and maps, 16 woodcuts, 2 vols. $750.

ELLISON, Harlan. *The Deadly Streets.* New York (1958). Author's first book. Wraps. $60.

ELLISON, Harlan. *Love Ain't Nothing but Sex Misspelled.* New York (1968). $150.

ELLISON, Harlan. *Rumble.* New York (1958). Pictorial wraps. $75.

ELLISON, Ralph. *Invisible Man.* New York (1952). Author's first book. $350.

ELLISON, Ralph. *Shadow and Act.* New York (1964). $100.

ELLSWORTH, Henry W. *Valley of the Upper Wabash, Indiana . . .* New York. Folding map, folding plan, and 2 folding lithographs. $350.

ELWES, Henry John. *A Monograph of the Genus Lilium . . .* [with] *Supplement . . .* 1880, 1933–62. 2 vols. in 4. Includes 78 hand-colored lithographed plates and 10 chromolithographed plates, 1 photograph and 1 colored map. $12,500.

ELY, William. *The Big Sandy Valley. A History of the People and Country from the Earliest Settlement to the Present Time.* Catlettsburg, Ky., 1887. $225.

EMBARGO (The), or Sketches of the Times; A Satire. By a Youth of Thirteen. (Cover title.) Boston, 1808. 12 pp., self-wraps (stitched). (By William Cullen Bryant.) $5,000. (For second edition, see author and title.)

EMERSON, Charles L. *Rise and Progress of Minnesota Territory.* St. Paul, 1855. 64 pp., pictorial printed wraps. $750.

EMERSON, Lucy. *The New-England Cookery.* Montpelier, Vt., 1808. $350.

EMERSON, Peter Henry. *Marsh Leaves.* (London, 1895.) 16 photogravures. One of 300. $2,500. One of 100. $5,000.

EMERSON, Ralph Waldo. See *Nature.*

EMERSON, Ralph Waldo. *An Address Delivered Before the Senior Class in Divinity College. Cambridge . . . 15 July, 1838.* Boston, 1838. 31 pp., in original blue wraps. $400.

EMERSON, Ralph Waldo. *An Address Delivered in the Court-House in Concord, Massachusetts, on 1st August, 1844, on the Anniversary of the Emancipation of the Negroes in the British West Indies.* Boston, 1844. 34 pp., tan wraps. $300.

EMERSON, Ralph Waldo. *The American Scholar.* ("An Oration Delivered Before the Phi Beta Kappa Society.") Boston, 1837. 26 pp. Original wraps. $750. Unlettered cloth. $350.

EMERSON, Ralph Waldo. *The Conduct of Life.* Boston, 1860. First issue, with ads for this title as "Nearly Ready." $350.

EMERSON, Ralph Waldo. *English Traits.* Boston, 1856. $175.

EMERSON, Ralph Waldo. *Essays.* Boston, 1841. (6 bindings, no priority, but without "First Series" on spine.) $1,000. London, 1906. Vellum. Doves Press. One of 300 on paper. $600. One of 25 printed on vellum. $3,500. Limited Editions Club, New York, 1934. (First and second series.) In slipcase. $125.

EMERSON, Ralph Waldo. *Essays: Second Series.* Boston, 1844. First binding, with "2D Series" on spine. $350. Second binding with "Second Series" on spine, in brown or purple cloth. $250.

EMERSON, Ralph Waldo. *Letters and Social Aims.* Boston, 1876. $200.

EMERSON, Ralph Waldo. *May-Day and Other Pieces.* Boston, 1867. Various cloth colors. $200. White cloth may have been a special binding. $300.

EMERSON, Ralph Waldo. *The Method of Nature.* Boston, 1841. 30 pp., printed tan wraps. $400.

EMERSON, Ralph Waldo. *An Oration Delivered Before the Literary Societies of Dartmouth College, July 24, 1838.* Boston, 1838. Wraps. $300.

EMERSON, Ralph Waldo. *Poems.* London, 1847. First issue, with "Chapman Brothers" on foot of spine and ads dated Nov. 16, 1846. $600. Boston, 1847. Glazed boards or black cloth. First issue, with 8 pages preceding title page, including 4 pages of ads dated Jan. 1, 1847. $1,000. Limited Editions Club, New York, 1945. Full leather. In slipcase. $75.

EMERSON, Ralph Waldo. *Representative Men.* Boston, 1850. Black or brown cloth. With or without hourglass design on front and back covers. (No priority—Myerson.) First printing sheets bulk. ⁵⁄₆ inches versus ⁷⁄₈ inches in second printing—BAL. $250. London, 1850. Brown or green cloth. First English edition (possibly issued simultaneously). $200.

EMERSON, Ralph Waldo. *Society and Solitude.* Boston, 1870. $150.

EMILY Parker, or Impulse, Not Principle. Boston, 1827. Frontispiece. Buff boards. (By Lydia Maria Child.) $200.

EMMA. By the author of "Pride and Prejudice," . . . London, 1816. (By Jane Austen.) 3 vols. $5,000. Limited Editions Club, New York, 1964. Illustrated in color by Fritz Kredel. Buckram. Slipcase. $75.

EMMETT, Chris. *Shanghai Pierce, a Fair Likeness.* Norman (1953). Illustrated, map. $150.

EMMONS, Richard. *The Fredoniad.* Boston, 1827. Author's first book. 4 vols. $200.

EMMONS, Samuel Franklin. *Geology and Mining Industry of Leadville, Colorado.* Washington, 1883. 2 vols., half leather, including atlas with colored maps. $500.

EMORY, William H. *Notes of a Military Reconnaissance.* Washington, 1848. 68 plates, 6 maps and plans. Cloth. House or Senate version. $750.

EMPSON, William. *Letter IV.* London, 1929. Author's first book. $250.

EMPSON, William. *Poems.* London, 1935. $175.

ENGELS, Frederick. *Socialism, Utopian, and Scientific.* London, 1892. First edition in English. $400.

ENGLE, Paul. *Worn Earth.* New Haven, 1932. Boards. Author's first book. $125.

ENGLEHARDT, Zephyrin. *The Franciscans in Arizona.* Harbor Springs, Mich., 1899. Map, plates. 236 pp., wraps. $250.

ENGLEHARDT, Zephyrin. *The Franciscans in California.* Harbor Springs, 1897. Illustrated. Wraps. $250.

ENGLISH Bards and Scotch Reviewers. London (1809). 54 pp. (By George Gordon Noel, Lord Byron.) First issue, without preface. $1,500. Later issue, with preface. $400.

ENGLISH Dance of Death (The). London, 1814–16. (By William Combe.) Frontispiece, engraved title, and 74 color plates by Thomas Rowlandson. 24 parts, wraps. $750. London, 1815–16. 2 vols. $1,000.

ENGRAVED In the Wood, A Collection of Wood Engravings by George Mackley. London, 1889. Limited to 600 numbered copies signed by Mackley. Stiff wraps. $300.

ENSLIN, Theodore. *The Work Proposed.* (Ashland, Mass.) 1958. Author's first book. (Limited to 250 copies.) Stiff wraps. $175.

EPIPSYCHIDION: Verses, . . . London, 1821. (By Percy Bysshe Shelley.) $3,500. Montagnola, Italy, 1923. Vellum. One of 222. $1,250.

EPISTLES And Gospels for All Sundays and Holidays Throughout the Year. New Edition . . . Detroit, 1812. "Reprinted from the 6th Edition of Dublin 1794 . . ." $1,850.

EPITOME of Electricity and Galvanism (An). Philadelphia, 1809. By Two Gentlemen of Philadelphia. (By Jacob Green and Ebenezer Hazard.) $250.

EPSTEIN, Jacob. *Epstein: An Autobiography.* London, 1955. Illustrated. Leatherette. One of 195 signed. Issued without dustwrapper. $350.

EPSTEIN, Jacob. *Let There Be Sculpture: An Autobiography.* (London, 1940.) Vellum. One of 100 signed. $400.

EPSTEIN, Jacob. *Seventy-Five Drawings.* London, 1929. Oblong, vellum. One of 220 signed. Issued without dustwrapper. $450.

ERDRICH, Louise. *Jacklight.* New York (1984). Author's first book. Wraps. $150.

EREWHON, or Over the Range. London, 1872. Brown cloth. (By Samuel Butler.) $250. Newton, Wales, 1932. Gregynog Press. Illustrated. Sheep. One of 275 on Japan vellum. $400. One of 25 specially bound in morocco by George Fisher. $1,000. Limited Editions Club, New York, 1934. Introduction by Aldous Huxley. Illustrated by Rockwell Kent. Slipcase. $150.

ERMAN, Adolph. *Travels In Siberia; Including Excursions Northwards, Down the Obi, to the Polar Circle, and Southwards, to the Chinese Frontier.* London, 1848. 2 vols. Folding frontispiece map. $450.

ESHLEMAN, Clayton. *Mexico & North.* (New York/San Francisco, 1961.) (New York/San Francisco imprint but actually printed in Tokyo.) Author's first book. Wraps. (26 lettered copies.) $200. Regular edition. $60.

ESPEJO, Antonio de. *New Mexico: Otherwise the Voiage of Anthony Espeio, Who in the Yeare 1583, with His Company, Discovered a Lande of 15 Provinces, etc.* (Lancaster, 1928.) Boards. One of 200. $300.

ESSAY on Mind (An), with Other Poems. London, 1826. (By Elizabeth Barrett Browning.) First issue, with the reading "found" in line 15, page 75. $750.

ESSAYS from Poor Robert the Scribe. Doylestown, Pa., 1815. (By Charles Miner.) $200.

ESSAYS honoring Lawrence C. Wroth. Portland, 1951. Limited to 360 copies (stated in prospectus). $100.

ESSE, James. *Hunger: A Dublin Story.* Dublin, 1918. Printed wraps. (By James Stephens.) $150.

ESTIENNE, Henri. *The Frankfort Book Fair.* Chicago, 1911. Caxton Club. One of 300. $250.

EUPHRANOR: A Dialogue on Youth. London, 1851. Green cloth. (By Edward Fitz-Gerald.) $300. London, 1885. Green cloth, or stitched, without ads at end. Second edition. $100.

EVANS, Jr., Charles. *Chick Evans' Golf Book.* Chicago, 1921. Signed limited edition. $500. Trade edition (1925). $125.

EVANS, Elwood. *Puget Sound: Its Past, Present and Future.* Olympia, Wash., 1869. 16 pp., wraps. $250.

EVANS, Elwood. *Washington Territory.* Olympia, 1877. 51 pp., wraps. $250.

EVANS, Estwick. *A Pedestrious Tour, of 4,000 Miles, Through the Western States and Territories.* Concord, N.H., 1819. Portrait. Boards. $1,000.

EVANS, Evan. *Montana Rides Again.* New York, 1934. (By Frederick Faust.) $250.

EVANS, Marian. *The Essence of Christianity.* London, 1854. Author's first book. First issue, black cloth with "Marian Evans" on spine, $1,000. Second issue, purple cloth with "George Eliot" on spine, $750. (Evans's translation of Ludwig Feverbach's book. The only use of her real name.)

EVANS, Walker. *The Crime of Cuba.* Philadelphia (1933). Book by Carleton Beals. First book appearance of Evans's photos. $175.

EVARTS, Hal. *Painted Stallion.* Boston, 1926. $100.

EVELYN, John. *Memoirs, Illustrative of the Life and Writings of John Evelyn, Esq., F.R.S.* London (Bath), 1818. Edited by William Bray. Folding pedigree, 8 plates. 2 vols. $500.

EVELYN, John. *Sculptura; Or, the History and Art of Chalcography, and Engraving in Copper . . .* London, 1769. "Second Edition," but actually later printing of the second edition of 1755. Contains 3 engraved plates. $375.

EVENINGS in New England. Boston, 1824. By an American Lady. (By Lydia Maria Child.) $150.

EVENTS in Indian History, Beginning with an Account of the Origin of the American Indians . . . Lancaster, Pa., 1841. (By James Wimer.) 8 plates. Sheepskin. $200.

EVERARD, Edward. *A Bristol Printing House.* London, no date in book (1903). Cloth folder with loosely inserted cord-tied book. $150.

EVERARD, Harry S.C. *History of the Royal and Ancient Golf Club, St. Andrews From 1754–1900.* 1907. $1,250.

EVERETT, Edward. *A Defence of Christianity.* Boston, 1814. Boards, paper label. Author's first book. $100.

EVERETT, Edward. *An Oration Delivered on the Battlefield of Gettysburg . . .* New York, 1863. 48 pp., cloth wraps. Includes one of the early book appearances of Abraham Lincoln's Gettysburg Address. (See also Lincoln, Abraham.) $2,500.

EVERETT, Horace. *Regulating the Indian Department.* (Washington, 1834.) Folding map. $300.

EVERSON, William. See Antoninus, Brother.

EVERSON, Bill (William). *These Are the Ravens.* (Cover title.) San Leandro, Calif., 1935. 11 pp., stapled self-wraps. Author's first book. $500.

EVERSON, William. *Blame It on the Jet Stream.* Santa Cruz, 1978. Illustrated. Oblong, boards. One of 150 signed, issued without dustwrapper. $250.

EVERSON, William. *The Blowing of the Seed.* New Haven, 1966. Green or brown flowered boards, leather spine. One of 203 signed. $250. Also, 15 numbered. $500.

EVERSON, William. *In the Fictive Wish.* (Berkeley, 1967.) Oyez Press. One of 200 signed. In plain white dustwrapper. $200.

EVERSON, William. *The Masculine Dead Poems, 1938–1940.* Prairie City, Ill. (1942). With tipped-in errata sheet. $900. Without errata. $750.

EVERSON, William. *Poems: MCMXLII.* (Waldport, Ore., 1945.) Self-wraps. One of 500. $250.

EVERSON, William. *A Privacy of Speech.* Berkeley, 1949. Illustrated. Boards. One of 100. $2,500.

EVERSON, William. *The Residual Years.* (Waldport, 1944.) Illustrated by the author. Wraps. One of 330 signed. $300. New Directions. (New York, 1948.) Boards. One of 1,000. (A collection of 4 prior works.) $150.

EVERSON, William. *San Joaquin.* Lost Angeles, 1939. One of 100, issued without dustwrapper. $1,250.

EVERSON, William. *Triptych for the Living.* (Oakland, 1951.) Illustrated. Limp vellum. One of 200 (actually fewer than 100). $1,250.

EVERSON, William. *War Elegies.* Waldport, 1944. Wraps. Expanded edition of *X War Elegies.* One of 975. $250. One of 30 in full calf, signed. (Bound and signed in 1970s.) $1,000.

EVERSON, William. *X War Elegies.* Waldport, 1943. Wraps. First state, wraps lettered in black and yellow. $350.

EVERSON, William. *The Year's Declension.* Berkeley, 1961. One of 100 signed. $400.

EVERTS, Truman C. *Thirty-Seven Days of Peril.* San Francisco, 1923. Grabhorn printing. One of 375. $100.

EVERTS and KIRK. *The Official State Atlas of Nebraska.* Philadelphia, 1885. Plates, 207 colored maps. Half calf. $500.

EVERY Man His Own Printer; or, Lithography Made Easy. London, 1854. $350.

EVERYTHING for the Printer. New York, 1902. Wraps. Includes 49 pages of single color samples. $125.

EVIDENCE Concerning Projected Railways Across the Sierra Nevada Mountains. Carson City, Nev., 1865. Calf. $1,000.

EVIL of Intoxicating Liquor (The) and the Remedy. Park Hill, Okla., 1844. 24 pp., sewed. $400.

EWELL, Thomas T. *A History of Hood County, Texas.* Granbury, Tex., 1895. Cloth. $600.

EXAMPLES of Modern Book Binding, Designed and Executed by Robt. Riviere & Son. London, 1919. 69 full-page plates and 8 in full color. Limited to 200 copies. $450.

EXLEY, Frederick. *A Fan's Notes.* New York (1968). Author's first book. $100.

EYE Witness (An). *Satan in Search of a Wife.* London, 1831. 4 full-page woodcuts and 2 vignettes by George Cruikshank. (By Charles Lamb.) $500.

EZRA Pound: His Metric and Poetry. New York, 1917. (By T. S. Eliot.) Portrait frontispiece by Gaudier-Brzeska. Rose paper boards, lettered in gold on front cover. In plain buff dustwrapper. $500. Lacking dustwrapper. $450.

F

F., M. T. *My Chinese Marriage.* New York, 1921. Katherine Anne Porter's first book. Green boards and cloth. (By Mai Taim Franking, ghosted by Porter.) With dustwrapper. $1,250. Without dustwrapper $75.

FACSIMILES of Royal, Historical, Literary, and Other Autographs in the Department of MSS., British Museum. London, 1899. Edited by George F. Warner, 150 plates. 5 parts, folio, sewn. $300.

FACTS Concerning the City of San Diego, the Great Southwestern Seaport of the United States, with a Map Showing the City and Its Surroundings. San Diego (1888). 14 pp., wraps. $400.

FACTS Respecting Indian Administration in the Northwest (The). (Victoria?, 1886.) 74 pp., wraps. $250.

FAHEY, Herbert. *Early Printing in California.* San Francisco, 1956. Grabhorn Press. Illustrated. One of 400. $300.

FAIR Death (A). London 1881 (By Sir Henry Newbolt.) Author's first book. Wraps. $125.

FAIR, James R. *Give Him to the Angels: The Story Of Harry Greb.* New York, 1946. $60.

FAIRBAIRN, W. E. *Defendu, Scientific Self-Defense.* Shanghai, 1925. $75.

FAIRBAIRN, W. E. *Scientific Self Defense.* Shanghai, 1931. $75.

FAIRBANKS, George R. *Early History of Florida.* St. Augustine, 1857. 82 pp., sewn. $250.

FAIRBANKS, George R. *The Spaniards in Florida.* Jacksonville, 1868. 120 pp., wraps. $250.

FAIRCHILD, T. B. *A History of the Town of Cuyahoga Falls, Summit County.* Cleveland, 1876. 39 pp. $250.

FAIRFIELD, Asa Merrill. *Fairfield's Pioneer History of Lassen County, California.* San Francisco (1916). 4 plates, folding map. Pictorial cloth. $200.

FAIRMAN, Henry Clay. *The Third World* . . . Atlanta, 1895. Author's first book. $350. New York, 1896. $125.

FAIRY Book (The). New York, 1837. Frontispiece and 81 woodcuts by Joseph A. Adams. In original brown cloth. (By Dinah M. Craik.) $300.

FAIRY Garland (A). London (1928). 12 colored illustrations by Edmund Dulac. Half vellum. One of 1,000 signed by the artist. $500.

FALCONER, Thomas. *Letters and Notes on the Texan Santa Fe Expedition, 1841–42.* New York, 1930. Edited by F.W. Hodge. Portrait. Half cloth. Issued without dustwrapper. $150.

FALCONER, Thomas. *On the Discovery of the Mississippi, and On the South-Western, Oregon, and Northwestern Boundary of the United States.* London, 1844. Folding map, errata leaf. Cloth. First issue, with the map (later absent). $1,000.

FALCONER, William. *A Universal Dictionary of the Marine.* London, 1769. With 12 folding plates. $1,000.

FALKLAND. London, 1827. (By Edward Bulwer-Lytton.) Author's first novel. $750.

FALKNER: A Novel. London, 1837. 3 vols., in original cloth, paper labels. (By Mary Wollstonecraft Shelley.) $1,000.

FALKNER, J. Meade. *The Lost Stradivarius.* London, 1895. Author's first book. $500.

FAMILY Robinson Crusoe (The). London, 1814. Translated from the German of M. Wiss (Johann David Wyss.) 2 vols. First edition in English. $1,500. See also *The Swiss Family Robinson.*

FANNY. New York, 1819. 49 pp., with printed gray wraps bound in. (By Fitz-Greene Halleck.) Author's first separate book. (Note: There also exists a pirated 1819 edition, 67 pp.) $400.

FANSHAWE; A Tale. Boston, 1828. (By Nathaniel Hawthorne.) Brown or buff boards, purple cloth spine, paper labels. Author's first book. $15,000.

FANTE, John. *Ask the Dust.* New York, 1939. Cloth. $100.

FANTE, John. *Wait Until Spring, Bandini.* New York (1938). Author's first book. $200.

FARMER, Philip José. *The Fabulous Riverboat.* New York (1971). $200.

FARMER, Philip José. *Flesh.* (New York, 1960). Wraps. $40. Garden City, 1968. Revised, first hardcover. First edition stated. $250.

FARMER, Philip José. *The Green Odyssey.* New York, 1957. Author's first book. Cloth. $1,000. Wraps. $30.

FARNHAM, S. B. *The New York and Idaho Gold Mining Co.* New York, 1864. Folding map. 23 pp., wraps. $500.

FARNHAM, Thomas J. *History of Oregon Territory.* New York, 1844. Frontispiece map. Wraps. $500.

FARNHAM, Thomas J. *Travels in the Californias.* New York, 1844. Map and plates. First edition, second (or clothbound) issue. $1,750.

FARNHAM, Thomas J. *Travels in the Great Western Prairies.* Poughkeepsie, 1841. Cloth, leather label. $750. Poughkeepsie, 1843. Tan boards, lavender cloth. $1,000 and up. London, 1843. $350.

FARNIE, H. B. *The Golfers Manual.* Scotland, 1857. (Pseudonym is A Keen Hand.) $2,500. London, 1947. Limited to 750 copies. $400.

FARQUHARSON, Martha. *Elsie Dinsmore.* New York, 1867. (By Martha Finley.) Red cloth. $2,000.

FARRELL, J.G. *A Man from Elsewhere.* London, 1963. Author's first book. $125.

FARRELL, James T. *Calico Shoes and Other Stories.* New York (1934). $250.

FARRELL, James T. *Gas-House McGinty.* New York, 1933. $300.

FARRELL, James T. *Guillotine Party.* New York (1935). $200.

FARRELL, James T. *Judgment Day.* New York, 1935. With "thay" for "they" in third line of page 218 (VAB). $300.

FARRELL, James T. *A Misunderstanding.* New York, 1949. One of 300 signed. In tissue jacket. $150.

FARRELL, James T. *$1,000 a Week and Other Stories.* New York (1942). $175.

FARRELL, James T. *Tommy Gallagher's Crusade.* New York (1939). $200.

FARRELL, James T. *Young Lonigan: A Boyhood in Chicago Streets.* New York, 1932. Author's first book. $400. Reissued in 1935 with new introduction by F. Thrasher inserted, title page still dated 1932. $200.

FARRELL, James T. *The Young Manhood of Studs Lonigan.* New York (1934). Brown cloth. First edition, with errata slip listing 8 typographical errors, among them "Connolly" for "Connell" in line 18 of page 88. (VAB.) $350.

FAST, Howard. *Two Valleys.* New York, 1933. Author's first book. $350.

FAULKNER, J. P. *Eighteen Months on a Greenland Whaler.* New York, 1878. Portrait. Cloth. $300.

FAULKNER, William. See Petersen, Carl.

FAULKNER, William. *Absalom, Absalom!* New York, 1936. 300 signed, numbered copies. Issued without dustwrapper in slipcase. $2,000. Trade. $500. London (1937). Cream cloth stamped in red and black, top edge red. In glassine dustwrapper with glued-on printed flaps. $450. Franklin Library, Franklin Center, 1978. $60.

FAULKNER, William. *As I Lay Dying.* New York (1930). Initial capital "I" on page 11, line 1 not aligned (dropped so that the top of the letter is almost at the bottom of the first line of text). Preferred state of binding has lettering complete and undamaged. $2,500. Initial capital "I" on page 11, line 1 correctly aligned. $1,750. London, 1935. Blue cloth stamped in white, top edge blue. $750.

FAULKNER, William. *Collected Stories of William Faulkner.* New York (1950). Title page printed in blue and black, top edge stained blue. $275.

FAULKNER, William. *Doctor Martino and Other Stories.* New York, 1934. 360 signed numbered copies. $1,000. Trade. $500. London, 1934. $600.

FAULKNER, William. *A Fable.* (New York, 1954). 1,000 signed and numbered copies in slipcase. $500. Trade. Maroon cloth, top edge gray. $100. London, 1955. $60.

FAULKNER, William. *Go Down, Moses and Other Stories.* New York (1942). 100 signed and numbered copies. $6,000. Trade. Black cloth, top edge stained red. $400. Various colors of cloth with top unstained. $300. London, 1942. $300.

FAULKNER, William. *A Green Bough.* New York, 1933. 360 signed and numbered copies. Issued with dustwrapper. $850. Trade. $300.

FAULKNER, William. *The Hamlet.* New York, 1940. 250 signed and numbered copies. In slipcase. $2,000. Trade. Back of dustwrapper has ads for other books. $450. Back of dustwrapper has reviews of this book. $350. London, 1940. $350.

FAULKNER, William. *Idyll in the Desert.* New York, 1931. 400 signed and numbered copies. $750. (No trade edition.)

FAULKNER, William. *Intruder in the Dust.* New York (1948). $200. London, 1949. $150.

FAULKNER, William. *Jealousy and Episode.* Minneapolis, 1955. 500 numbered copies. $350. (No trade edition.)

FAULKNER, William. *Knight's Gambit.* New York (1949). $175. London, 1951. $150.

FAULKNER, William. *Light in August.* (New York, 1932.) Issued with a glassine wrapper over dustwrapper. $750. London, 1933. $500.

FAULKNER, William. *The Mansion.* New York (1959). 500 signed, numbered copies. in acetate dustwrapper without slipcase. $600. Trade. $75.

FAULKNER, William. *The Marble Faun.* Boston (1924). Author's first book. $20,-000.

FAULKNER, William. *The Marionettes.* (Charlottesville, 1975.) One of 26 lettered copies. Unbound gatherings on Arches paper in box. $450. 100 numbered copies. Unbound in slipcase. $350. Trade. $25.

FAULKNER, William. *The Marionettes: A Play in One Act.* Oxford, 1975. 10 lettered copies. Facsimile edition in boards with monograph by Ben Wasson *A Memory of Marionettes,* a pamphlet. Laid into box. $500. 500 numbered copies. $200.

FAULKNER, William. *Mirrors of Chartres Street.* (Minneapolis, 1953.) One of 1,000 numbered copies. $250.

FAULKNER, William. *Miss Zilphia Gant.* Book Club of Texas. (Dallas), 1932. One of 300 numbered copies. $1,500.

FAULKNER, William. *Mosquitoes.* New York, 1927. In red-on-green dustwrapper with mosquito. $2,000. In dustwrapper with card players on yacht and Boni & Liveright (original publisher) on spine. $5,000.

FAULKNER, William. *New Orleans Sketches.* Tokyo, 1955. Dark blue and medium blue cloth bindings. $300. Wraps. $150.

FAULKNER, William. *Notes on a Horsethief.* Greenville, Miss., 1950. One of 975 signed and numbered copies. Issued in tissue dustwrapper without slipcase. $600.

FAULKNER, William. *Pylon.* New York, 1935. One of 310 signed and numbered copies issued without dustwrapper in slipcase. $1,000. Trade. $500. (Later-printing dustwrapper is blank on back.) London, 1935. Rose-brown binding, top edge stained rose; bottom edge untrimmed, two leaves of ads at end. $350. Bright red binding, top edge unstained, bottom edge trimmed, no ads. $200.

FAULKNER, William. *The Reivers: A Reminiscence.* New York (1962). One of 500 signed and numbered copies. In acetate dustwrapper without slipcase. $750. Trade. Red cloth, top edges stained red and without Book of Month Club blind stamp on back cover. $75. London, 1962. $50.

FAULKNER, William. *Requiem for a Nun.* New York (1951). One of 750 signed and numbered copies. Issued without dustwrapper or slipcase. $750. Trade. With top edge stained gray (presumed first issue). $125. London, 1953. $90.

FAULKNER, William. *A Rose for Emily and Other Stories.* New York (1945). Wraps. $150. Tokyo, 1956. Wraps. $75.

FAULKNER, William. *Salmagundi.* Milwaukee, 1932. One of 525 numbered copies in box. (First 26 copies have bottom edge untrimmed and top edge even with top of cover.) $1,250. One of 499. $600.

FAULKNER, William. *Sanctuary.* New York (1931). $2,000. London, 1931. Wine-red cloth stamped in gold; four pages of ads. $600. Bright red cloth stamped in black. No ads. $500.

FAULKNER, William. *Sartoris.* New York (1929). $3,000. London, 1932. Blue cloth, top edge stained blue. $750. Tan cloth, top edge unstained. $350.

FAULKNER, William (editor). *Sherwood Anderson & Other Famous Creoles.* New Orleans, 1926. One of 50 numbered copies signed by William Spratling (the caricaturist). Bound in decorative boards with frontispiece and illustrations hand tinted by Spratling. $8,500. One of 200 numbered copies (limitation notice indicates 250 numbered copies). Green boards. $3,000. Label is pasted over original limitation statement stating "Second Issue 150 copies January 1927." $2,000.

FAULKNER, William. *Soldiers' Pay.* New York, 1926. $8,500. London, 1930. $750.

FAULKNER, William. *The Sound and the Fury.* New York (1929). Ad on rear dustwrapper panel has *Humanity Uprooted* priced at $3.00. $7,500. Ad priced $3.50. $5,000. London, 1931. Bound in black cloth, top edge stained red. $750. Mustard cloth stamped in red. Top edge unstained without publisher's imprint on spine. $600.

FAULKNER, William. *These 13.* New York (1931). One of 299 signed and numbered copies. Large paper edition issued in tissue wrapper. $1,750. Trade. $750. London, 1933. Blue cloth stamped in gold, top edge green. $600.

FAULKNER, William. *This Earth.* New York, 1932. Stiff tan wraps in plain white envelope. $250.

FAULKNER, William. *The Town.* New York (1957). One of 450 signed and numbered copies in acetate dustwrapper without slipcase. $750. Trade. Red cloth, top edge stained gray. Dustwrapper has "5/57" on front flap. Threaded gray endpapers. $100. Various cloths, plain endpapers, various top edge colors. Without dustwrapper point. $40. London, 1958. $60.

FAULKNER, William. *The Unvanquished.* New York (1938). One of 250 signed and numbered copies issued without dustwrapper or slipcase. $1,250. Trade. $400. London, 1938. Dustwrapper assumed (not seen). $750. Without dustwrapper. $150.

FAULKNER, William. *The Wild Palms.* New York (1939). One of 250 signed and numbered copies. Issued in glassine wrapper without slipcase. $1,250. Trade. Tan cloth, stamped in gold and green on spine. $300. Tan cloth, stamped in brown and green on spine. $250. London, 1939. $250.

FAUST, Frederick. *Dionysus in Hades.* Oxford, 1931. Boards. One of 500. (The real Max Brand.) $125.

FAUX, William. *Memorable Days in America.* London, 1823. $500.

FAY, Bernard. *Notes on the American Press at the End of the Eighteenth Century.* New York, 1927. Limited to 325 copies. $125. In slipcase.

FEARING, Kenneth. *Angel Arms.* New York, 1929. Author's first book. $200.

FEARING, Kenneth. *The Big Clock.* New York (1946). $125.

FEARING, Kenneth. *Dead Reckoning.* New York (1938). $250.

FEAST of the Poets (The). London, 1814. By the Editor of the Examiner. (By Leigh Hunt.) $300.

FEATHERSTONHAUGH, George W. *A Canoe Voyage Up the Minnay Sotor.* London 1847. 2 folding maps, 2 plates, 2 vols. $600.

THE Federalist: A Collection of Essays . . . New York, 1788. 2 vols. (By Hamilton, Madison, and Jay.) $7,500.

FEIBLEMAN, James K. *Death of the God in Mexico.* New York (1931). Author's first book. $150.

FEIKEMA, Feike. *The Golden Bowl.* St. Paul, 1944. (By Frederick Manfred, his first book.) $125.

FELDENKRAIS, M. *Higher Judo: Ground Work.* London, 1952. $60.

FELDENKRAIS, M. *Judo.* London, 1944. $75.

FELDENKRAIS, M. *Practical Unarmed Combat.* London, 1942. $75.

FELLOWS-JOHNSTON, Annie. *The Little Colonel.* Boston, 1896. $125.

FENOLLOSA, Ernest F. *Certain Noble Plays of Japan.* Cuala Press. Churchtown, Dundrum, Ireland, 1916. From manuscripts of Fenollosa, chosen and finished by Ezra Pound. Introduction by W.B. Yeats. Boards, linen spine. One of 350. $250.

FENOLLOSA, Ernest F. *The Chinese Written Character as a Medium for Poetry.* London (1936). Foreword by Ezra Pound. Black cloth, parchment spine. $300. New York (1936). Green boards. $200.

FENTON, James. *Our Western Furniture.* Oxford (1968). Author's first book. 12 signed and numbered copies. $500. Wraps. (200 copies.) $250.

FERBER, Edna. *Dawn O'Hara: The Girl Who Laughed.* New York (1911). Colored frontispiece. Author's first book. $100.

FERBER, Edna. *A Peculiar Treasure.* New York, 1939. One of 351 signed in slipcase. $125.

FERBER, Edna. *Show Boat.* Garden City, 1926. Green boards, white vellum spine. One of 201 signed in slipcase. $250. Trade. $75.

FERGUSON, Charles D. *The Experiences of a Forty-Niner During Thirty-Four Years' Residence in California and Australia.* Cleveland, 1888. $200.

FERGUSON, Helen. *A Charmed Circle.* London (1929). Author's first book. $350.

FERGUSON, John. *Bibliotheca Chemica; A Bibliography of Books on Alchemy, Chemistry and Pharmaceutics.* London (1954). 2 vols. Second edition. Adds a new introduction. $175.

FERGUSSON, Harvey. *Blood of the Conquerors.* New York, 1921. $250.

FERGUSSON, Harvey. *Wolf Song.* New York, 1927. $150. Also one of 100 signed. $450.

FERGUSSON, Harvey. *Grant of Kingdom.* New York, 1950. $75.

FERLINGHETTI, Lawrence. *Pictures of the Gone World.* San Francisco (1955). Author's first book and first City Lights book. Stiff black printed wraps (priced at $.65). With wraparound label (500 copies). $300. Boards. One of 25 signed. $600.

FERLINGHETTI, Lawrence. *The Secret Meaning of Things.* (New York, 1968.) One of 150 signed. In slipcase. $175. Trade. $40.

FERRIAR, John. *The Bibliomania, An Epistle, To Richard Heber, Esq . . .* London, 1809. $225.

FERRIER, Susan Edmonstone. See *Destiny, or, The Chief's Daughter; Marriage.*

FERRINI, Vincent. *No Smoke.* Portland, Me., 1941. Author's first book. $60.

FERRIS, Benjamin G. *Utah and the Mormons, The History, Government . . .* New York, 1854. $150.

FEUCHTWANGER, Dr. Lewis. *A Popular Treatise on Gems.* New York, 1859. With frontispiece and 17 plates. $750.

FEUCHTWANGER, Dr. Lewis. *A Treatise on Gems.* New York, 1838. In original cloth. $1,250.

FICKE, Arthur Davison. See Morgan, Emanuel, and Knish, Anne.

FICKE, Arthur Davison (and Thomas Newell Metcalf). *Their Book.* (Chicago, 1901.) Author's first book. (50 numbered copies.) $250.

FICKE, Arthur Davison. *From the Isles.* (Surrey) 1907. Wraps. $100.

FIELD, Eugene. *A Little Book of Western Verse.* Chicago, 1889. Blue-gray boards and cloth. One of 250 large paper copies. $200. New York, 1890. Trade in cloth. $75.

FIELD, Eugene. *The Love Affairs of a Bibliomaniac.* New York, 1896. Frontispiece. Blue cloth. First issue, with 8 titles listed. $100. Half vellum. One of 150 on Holland paper. $200.

FIELD, Eugene. *Love-Songs of Childhood.* New York, 1894. One of 106 on Van Gelder paper. $150. One of 15 on Japan vellum. $300. Trade. Blue cloth. $40.

FIELD, Eugene. *Poems of Childhood.* New York, 1904. Frontispiece and 8 color plates by Maxfield Parrish. $250.

FIELD, Eugene. *Tribune Primer.* (Denver, 1881.) Gray-blue wraps. Author's first book. $6,000. Brooklyn, 1882. $500.

FIELD, Joseph E. *Three Years in Texas.* Greenfield, Mass., 1836. In original wraps. $3,500.

FIELD, Peter. *Dry Gulch Adams.* New York, 1934. (By Laura and Thayer Hobson.) $250.

FIELD, Peter. *Outlaws Three.* New York, 1934. (By Laura and Thayer Hobson, their first book.) $250.

FIELD, Rachel. *Hitty: Her First Hundred Years.* New York, 1929. Illustrated by Dorothy P. Lathrop. Decorated cloth, paper label. $150.

FIELD, Rachel. *Rise Up, Jennie Smith.* New York (1918). Author's first book. Wraps. $175.

FIELD, Stephen J. *Personal Reminiscences of Early Days in California.* (San Francisco, 1880?) $250. Second edition (Washington, 1893). Half morocco. $150.

FIELD, Thomas W. *An Essay Towards an Indian Bibliography Being a Catalogue of Books Relating to the History . . .* Columbus, 1951. Reprint of the very scarce 1873 first edition. $125.

FIELDING, Henry. *Amelia.* London, 1752. 4 vols. $800.

FIELDING, Henry. *The History of Tom Jones . . .* London, 1746. 6 vols. $3,500.

FIELDING, Sarah. *The Adventures of David Simple.* London, 1744. $1,000.

FIELDING, T. H. *A Picturesque Description of the River Wye.* London, 1841. 12 colored aquatint plates. In original cloth. $1,500.

FIELDING, T. H., and WALTON, J. *A Picturesque Tour of the English Lakes.* London, 1821. Color vignette and 48 colored aquatint plates. $1,500. Large paper issue. $2,000.

FIFTY Years' Recollections of an Old Bookseller. London, 1837. Second edition with 11 full-page plates. (Bookseller William West.) $150.

FIGUEROA, José. *The Manifesto.* San Francisco, 1855. (Translated from the original as published in Monterey in 1835.) Printed wraps. First edition in English. $1,250.

FILISOLA, Gen. Vicente. *Evacuation of Texas.* Columbia, Tex., 1837. 68 pp., half leather. First edition in English. $5,000, possibly more. (Sometimes called "the first real book published in Texas.")

FILLEY, William. *Life and Adventures of William Filley.* Chicago, 1867. 7 plates and half-page cut, 96 pp., wraps. Printed by Fergus. $1,500. Another edition, same place and date: 112 pp., wraps. Printed by Filley & Ballard. Second edition. $600.

FINCHAM, Henry W. *Artists and Engravers of British and American Bookplates* . . . New York, 1897. One of 40 numbered copies signed by E.P. Bartlett. $150.

FINLAY, Ian H. *The Sea-Bed* . . . Edinburgh (1958). Author's first book. Wraps. In dustwrapper. $200.

FINLEY, Ernest L. (editor). *History of Sonoma County.* (California.) Santa Rosa, 1937. Morocco. $100.

FINLEY, James B. *History of the Wyandott Mission at Upper Sandusky, Ohio.* Cincinnati, 1840. Calf. $250.

FINLEY, Martha. See Farquharson, Martha.

FINNEY, Charles G. *The Circus of Doctor Lao.* New York, 1935. Illustrated. Author's first book. $175. Limited Editions Club, Lunenberg, 1982. In slipcase. $100.

FINNEY, Jack. *Time And Again.* New York (1970). (By Walter Braden Finney.) $125.

FINNY, Sterling. *Less Than Nothing* . . . New York (1927). (By E.B. White, his first book.) Issued without dustwrapper. $250.

FIRBANK, Arthur Ronald. *Odette D'Antrevernes.* London, 1905. Author's first book. Pink or blue-gray wraps. $400. Also, large paper signed copies on vellum. $1,500.

FIRBANK, Ronald. *The Flower Beneath the Foot.* London, 1923. $300. New York, 1924. $200.

FIRBANK, Ronald. *Odette: A Fairy Tale for Weary People.* London, 1916. Illustrated. Wraps. First separate edition. $200.

FIRBANK, Ronald. *Prancing Nigger.* Introduction by Carl Van Vechten. New York (1924). $200.

FIRBANK, Ronald. *The Princess Zoubaroff.* London, 1920. In dustwrapper. $300.

FIRBANK, Ronald. *Santal.* London, 1921. Wraps. $250.

FIRBANK, Ronald. *Sorrow in Sunlight.* London, 1925. First English edition (of *Prancing Nigger).* One of 1,000. $200.

FIRBANK, Ronald. *A Study in Temperament.* London, 1905. Wraps. $350. Also, one of 10 on vellum signed. $1,250.

FIRST Lessons in Grammar . . . (By Elizabeth Peabody.) Boston, 1830. Author's first book. $150.

FIRST Settlers of New England (The), or, Conquest of the Pequods, Narragansets and Pokanokets. Boston (1829). By a Lady of Massachusetts (Lydia Maria Child). First issue, with undated title page. $250. Second issue with tipped-in dated title page. $150.

FISH, Daniel. *Lincoln Bibliography.* New York (1906). Red cloth. One of 75 signed. In slipcase. $200.

FISH, H. C. *The Voice of Our Brother's Blood: Its Source and Its Summons.* Newark, 1856. 16 pp., sewn. $125.

FISHER, Harry C. *The Mutt and Jeff Cartoons.* Boston, 1910. Oblong folio, pictorial boards and cloth. First Mutt and Jeff book. $175.

FISHER, M. F. K. *Serve It Forth.* New York, 1937. Author's first book. $300.

FISHER, Richard S. *Indiana: Its Geography, Statistics, County Topography.* New York, 1852. Large folding map in color. $250.

FISHER, Vardis. See *Idaho: A Guide in Word and Picture.*

FISHER, Vardis. *Children of God, an American Epic.* Caldwell, 1939. Leather. One of 100 signed. $300. New York, 1939. $100.

FISHER, Vardis. *City of Illusion.* New York (1941). $75. Caldwell, 1941. One of 1,000. $100. Morocco. One of 100 signed. $300.

FISHER, Vardis. *Dark Bidwell.* Boston, 1931. $150.

FISHER, Vardis. *Forgive Us Our Virtues.* Caldwell, 1938. One of 75 signed. In morocco. $350. Trade. $100.

FISHER, Vardis. *In Tragic Life.* Caldwell, 1932. $150. Leather. One of 25 signed. $450. Garden City, 1932. $100.

FISHER, Vardis. *The Neurotic Nightingale.* (Milwaukee, 1935.) One of 300 signed. $200.

FISHER, Vardis. *No Villain Need Be.* Caldwell, 1936. $150. One of 75 in full leather, signed. $300. Garden City, 1936. $100.

FISHER, Vardis. *Sonnets to an Imaginary Madonna.* New York, 1927. Author's first book. $250.

FISHER, Vardis. *Toilers of the Hills.* Boston, 1928. $150.

FISHER, Vardis. *We Are Betrayed.* Caldwell (1935). First edition stated. $150. Morocco. One of 75 signed. $350. Garden City, 1935. $100.

FISKE, John. *Tobacco and Alcohol.* New York, 1869. Author's first book. $300.

FITCH, Clyde. *The Knighting of the Twins and Ten Other Tales.* Boston (1891). Decorated cloth. Author's first book. $150.

FITCH, Ensign Clarke. *Saved by the Enemy.* New York, 1898. (By Upton Sinclair, his first book.) $200.

FITE, Emerson D., and FREEMAN, Archibald (editors). *A Book of Old Maps Delineating American History.* Cambridge, Mass., 1926. 74 maps in facsimile, colored frontispiece. Folio, cloth. $250.

FITTS, Dudley. *Two Poems.* No-place (1932). Wraps. One of 100 signed. Author's first book. $150.

FITZGERALD, Edward. See Aeschylus. See also *Euphranor; Polonius; Rubaiyat of Omar Khayyam; Salaman and Absal.*

FITZGERALD, Edward. *Letters and Literary Remains of Edward FitzGerald.* London, 1889. Edited by William Aldis Wright. Frontispiece plates. 3 vols. $350. London, 1902–3. 7 vols. One of 775. $500.

FITZGERALD, F. Scott. See *A Book of Princeton Verse II.*

FITZGERALD, F. Scott. *All the Sad Young Men.* New York, 1926. Dark green cloth. Publisher's seal on copyright page. Earliest state of dustwrapper has woman's lips on front unbattered. (They become progressively more battered on later printings.) $1,000.

FITZGERALD, F. Scott. *The Beautiful and Damned.* New York, 1922. "Published March, 1922" on copyright page. Scribners' seal not on copyright page. First printing of dustwrapper has book title on front in white outlined in black. $850. In second printing dustwrapper with front title letters in black. $300. London (1922). Blue cloth. $750.

FITZGERALD, F. Scott. *The Crack-up.* (no-place, 1945.) Title page printed in red-brown and black. (Later printings have title page printed in black only and no colophon on page 348.) $150. (no-place or date.) First English issue has paper label pasted on page 2. "This is a New Directions Book distributed through the British Empire . . ." $100.

FITZGERALD, F. Scott., et al. *The Evil Eye: A Musical Comedy in Two Acts.* (Cincinnati/New York/London on cover), 1915. $1,500.

FITZGERALD, F. Scott. *FIE! FIE! FI-FI!* (Cincinnati/New York/London on cover) 1914. $1,500.

FITZGERALD, F. Scott. *Flappers and Philosophers.* New York, 1920. "Published September, 1920" and publisher's seal on copyright page. In dustwrapper. $2,000. London (1922). $1,000.

FITZGERALD, F. Scott. *The Great Gatsby.* New York, 1925. First state includes the following differences: on page 60, line 16 "chatter" vs. "echolalia," page 119, line 22 "northern" vs. "southern," page 205, lines 9–10 "sick in tired" vs. "sickantired," page 211, lines 7–8 "Union Street Station" vs. "Union Station." Scribners' seal on copyright page. First state of dustwrapper: on back blurb line 14 has lowercase *j* in "jay Gatsby" which is hand-corrected in ink in most copies. $5,000. Second state of dustwrapper has back blurb line 14 corrected to uppercase *J* in "Jay Gatsby." $1,750. London (1926) "Published 1926" on copyright page. $1,500. Limited Editions Club. New York (1980). One of 2,000 numbered copies signed by Fred Meyer, the illustrator. Slipcase. $150.

FITZGERALD, F. Scott. *The Mystery of the Raymond Mortgage.* New York, 1960. 750 copies. Wraps. $250.

FITZGERALD, F. Scott. *Safety First.* Cincinnati/New York/London (1916). $1,500.

FITZGERALD, F. Scott. *Tales of the Jazz Age.* New York, 1922 "Published September, 1922" and Scribners' seal on copyright page. $1,250. London/Glasgow . . . (1923). $1,000.

FITZGERALD, F. Scott. *Taps at Reveille.* New York, 1935. Price rubber-stamped on front flap of some copies in two sizes: 3/16 inch and 1/8 inch high. First state with pages 349–52 not canceled and page 351, lines 29–30 reading "Oh, catch it—oh, catch it . . ." $1,500. Dustwrapper price printed. Second state with pages 349–52 canceled; page 351, lines 29–30 reading "Oh, things like that happen . . ." $750.

FITZGERALD, F. Scott. *Tender Is the Night.* New York, 1934. Dustwrapper (front flap) has blurbs by Eliot, Mencken, and Rosenfeld. $1,250. London, 1934. $750. New York, 1951. First state has following errors: page xi, line 18 "xett' "; page xiv, line 19 "tsandards"; page xviii, line 23 "b each"; page xviii, line 24 "accompanied." (A publisher errata sheet was enclosed in review copies.) $200. Errors in text corrected on 3 cancel leaves. $150. Limited Editions Club, New York, 1983. 2,000 copies signed by Fred Meyer, the illustrator. Slipcase. $150.

FITZGERALD, F. Scott. *This Side of Paradise.* New York, 1920. Author's first book (three previous music scores). "Published April, 1920" on copyright page. Dustwrapper priced either "$1.75" or "$1.75 net," priority undetermined. $4,000. Signed "Author's Apology" tipped-in third printing. $1,250. London (1921). $1,500.

FITZGERALD, F. Scott. *The Vegetable.* New York, 1923. "Published April, 1923" on copyright page. $650.

FITZGERALD, Robert. *Poems.* New York, 1935. Author's first book. $125.

FITZGERALD, Zelda. *Save Me the Waltz.* New York, 1932. Green cloth. Author's first book. $1,000.

FITZSIMMONS, Robert. *Physical Culture and Self Defense.* Philadelphia, 1903. $100.

FIVE Cummington Poets. Cummington, Mass., 1939. Wraps. One of 300. $250.

FIVE on Paper, A Collection of Five Essays on Papermaking . . . Bird & Bull Press, 1963. Limited to 169 numbered copies. (The paper in this edition has some acidity problem.) $750.

FIVE Young American Poets. New Directions. Norfolk, Conn., 1940, 1941, and 1944. 3 vols. $200, $150, and $125, respectively.

FLADER, Louis (editor). *Achievement in Photo-Engraving and Letterpress Printing.* Chicago (1927). $125.

FLANIGAN, J.H. *Mormonism Triumphant! Truth Vindicated, Lies Refuted, the Devil Mad, And Priestcraft in Danger!!! . . .* Liverpool, 1849. Printed self-wrapper. $225.

FLANNER, Janet. *An American In Paris . . .* New York (1940). First edition not stated. $250.

FLANNER, Janet. *The Cubical City.* New York, 1926. Author's first book. $400.

FLAUBERT, Gustave. *Salambo.* London, 1886. First edition in English. $100. Another one of 200. $200. London, 1931. Golden Cockerel Press. One of 500. $175.

FLAUBERT, Gustave. *A Sentimental Education.* London 1898. Illustrated. 2 vols., blue cloth. First English edition. $200.

FLECKER, James. *The Best Man* . . . Oxford, 1906. Author's first book. Wraps. $300.

FLECKER, James. *The Bridge of Fire: Poems.* London, 1907. Wraps. First issue, no quote from Sunday Times. $125.

FLECKER, James. *God Save the King.* (London, 1915.) Wraps. One of 20. $250.

FLEISCHER, Nat. *From Milo to London.* New York, 1936. $100.

FLEISCHER, Nat. *Jack Dempsey the Idol of Fistiana.* New York, 1924. Limited to 250 copies signed by author and subject. $200.

FLEMING, Alexander. *Penicillin.* London, 1946. $350. Philadelphia, $200.

FLEMING, Ian. *Casino Royale.* London (1953). Author's first book. Bottom front flap of dustwrapper blank except for price. $1,500. New York, 1954. $400.

FLEMING, Ian. *Diamonds Are Forever.* London (1956). $500. New York, 1956. $150.

FLEMING, Ian. *Dr. No.* London (1958). Front cover stamped with woman's figure or blank, no clear priority. $250. New York, 1958. $100.

FLEMING, Ian. *Diamonds Are Forever.* London (1956). $500. New York, 1956. $150.

FLEMING, Ian. *Live and Let Die.* London (1954). $850. New York, 1955. $200.

FLEMING, Ian. *Moonraker.* London (1955). $850. New York, 1955. $250.

FLEMING, Ian. *On Her Majesty's Secret Service.* London (1963). One of 220 signed and numbered copies. In plain plastic/acetate dustwrapper without slipcase. $1,750. Trade edition. $75. (New York, 1963.) $60.

FLEMING, Sanford. *Memorial of the People of Red River to the British and Canadian Governments.* Quebec, 1863. 7 pp., printed front paper cover. $600.

FLEMING, Walter L. *Documentary History of Reconstruction.* Cleveland, 1906–7. 9 facsimiles. 2 vols., half calf. $150.

FLETCHER, John Gould. *Fire and Wine.* London (May, 1913.) Author's first or second book. (There were 5 published in 1913.) $125.

FLETCHER, John Gould. *Japanese Prints.* Boston, 1918. Four Seas Press. $150. Full leather. One of 25 on vellum with a signed manuscript poem by Fletcher. $500.

FLETCHER, William Younger. *English Bookbindings in the British Museum.* London, 1895. Limited to 500 numbered copies. 63 plates. $400.

FLETCHER, William Younger. *Foreign Bookbindings in the British Museum.* London, 1896. Limited to 500 numbered copies. 63 plates. $400.

FLINDERS, Matthew. *A Voyage to Terra Australis* . . . London, 1814. 2 vols., plus atlas. $12,000.

FLINDERS, Matthew. *Narrative of His Voyage in the Schooner Francis.* Golden Cockerel Press. Waltham Saint Lawrence, 1946. Engravings by John Buckland Wright. One of 750. $850. One of 100. $1,000.

FLINT, Timothy. *A Condensed Geography and History of the Western States, or the Mississippi Valley.* Cincinnati, 1828. 2 vols. $400.

FLINT, Timothy. *Indian Wars of the West.* Cincinnati, 1833. $150.

FLINT, Timothy. *Recollections of the Last Ten Years.* Boston, 1826. $300.

FLINT, Timothy. *A Sermon, Preached* . . . Newburyport, 1808. Author's first book. $200.

FLINT, W. Russell. *Breakfast in Perigord.* London, 1968. Illustrated. Half morocco. One of 525 signed by Flint. In slipcase. $600.

FLINT, W. Russell. *Drawings.* London, 1950. 134 plates. Half morocco. One of 125 signed by Flint, with an original drawing in folder at end. Slipcase. $1,000. One of 500. $750. Trade in cloth. In dustwrapper. $300.

FLOWER, Richard. *Letters from Illinois, 1820–1821.* London, 1822. 76 pp., original wraps. $1,000. Rebound. $750.

FOLEY, Edwin. *The Book of Decorative Furniture.* London (1910–11). 2 vols. 100 mounted color plates. $250.

FOOL'S Errand (A). By One of the Fools. New York, 1879. (By Albion W. Tourgee.) $125.

FOOTE, Henry Stuart. *Texas and the Texans.* Philadelphia, 1841. 2 vols. $850.

FOOTE, Shelby. *The Merchant of Bristol.* (Greenville, 1947.) Author's first book. Wraps. (260 signed, numbered copies.) $350.

FOOTE, Shelby. *Tournament.* New York, 1949. $125.

FORBES, Alexander. *California: A History.* London, 1839. Folding map and lithographed plates. $1,250. San Francisco, 1919. Map, 10 plates. One of 250 signed by the publisher. $350. San Francisco, 1937. John Henry Nash printing. Marbled boards. One of 650 in dustwrapper. $150.

FORBES, Edwin. *Life Studies of the Great Army.* New York (1876). 40 plates. $1,500.

FORBES, Edwin. *Thirty Years After: An Artist's Story of the Great War.* New York (1890). 80 full-page plates, 20 portraits. 4 vols., folio. $250. 2-vol. edition $150.

FORBES, Sir James. *Oriental Memoirs.* London, 1813. 93 plates (28 hand colored), 4 vols. $2,500. London, 1834–35. 3 vols. (including atlas). $1,250.

FORBES, James Grant. *Sketches, Historical and Topographical, of the Floridas.* New York, 1821. With the map. $600. Without map. $350.

FORBUSH, Edward Howe. *Birds of Massachusetts and other New England States.* (Boston), 1925–27–29. Color illustrations by L.A. Fuertes. 3 vols. $400.

FORD, Charles Henri. *A B C's.* Prairie City, Ill. (1940). $300.

FORD, Charles Henri. *The Garden of Disorder and Other Poems.* London (1938). Boards and cloth. One of 30 signed. (Issued without dustwrapper.) $250. 460 unsigned copies. $100. Also, Norfolk (1938). (English edition in New Directions dustwrapper.) $100.

FORD, Charles Henri. *A Pamphlet of Sonnets.* Majorca, 1936. Drawing by Pavel Tchelitchew. Printed wraps. One of 50 signed by Ford and Tchelitchew. $400.

FORD, Charles Henri, and TYLER, Parker. *The Young and Evil.* Paris (1933). Wraps. The first book for both authors. 50 numbered copies. $500. Trade. $300.

FORD, Ford Madox. See Conrad, Joseph, and Hueffer, Ford Madox. (Note: Ford changed his name from Hueffer to Ford in 1919.) See also *The Imagist Anthology.*

FORD, Ford Madox. *The Good Soldier.* London, 1915. $400.

FORD, Ford Madox. *The Great Trade Route.* New York, 1937. First issue, without illustrator's name on title page or dustwrapper. $200.

FORD, Ford Madox. *It Was the Nightingale.* London (1934). $200.

FORD, Ford Madox. *Joseph Conrad: A Personal Remembrance.* London, 1924. Frontispiece, 2 other plates. $300.

FORD, Ford Madox. *Last Post.* London (1928). $150.

FORD, Ford Madox. *Mister Bosphorus and the Muses.* London (1923). Illustrated by Paul Nash. Half cloth. One of 70 signed by the artist. In dustwrapper. $500. Trade edition in dustwrapper. $300.

FORD, Ford Madox. *New Poems.* New York, 1927. One of 325 signed in glassine dustwrapper. $300.

FORD, Ford Madox. *New York Is Not America.* London, 1927. $250. (New York, 1927.) $175.

FORD, Ford Madox. *No More Parades.* London (1925). $250.

FORD, Ford Madox. *The Wicked Man.* New York (1931). $250.

FORD, Ford Madox. *Women & Men.* Three Mountains Press. Paris, 1923. Wraps. One of 300. $500.

FORD, Henry Chapman. *Etchings of the Franciscan Missions of California.* New York, 1883. 24 matted plates, unbound, 28 pp. of text, stitched, in half-morocco portfolio. Imperial edition. One of 50 signed by the artist. $2,000 and up.

FORD, Paul Leicester. See Gaine, Hugh.

FORD, Paul Leicester. *Franklin Bibliography.* Brooklyn, 1889. Half leather. Limited to 500 copies. $135.

FORD, Paul Leicester (editor). *Webster Genealogy . . . . By Noah Webster.* Brooklyn, 1876. 16 pp., oversize wraps. (250 copies.) Ford's first book, printed by him on his own press at age 11. $200.

FORD, Richard. *A Piece of My Heart.* New York, 1976. Author's first book. $150.

FORD, Richard. *The Ultimate Good Luck.* Boston, 1981. $100.

FORD, Thomas. *A History of Illinois . . .* Chicago, 1854. First issue, with "1814" (instead of "1818") in the extended title (VAB). $300.

FORD, Thomas. *Message of the Governor . . . the Disturbances in Hancock County.* Springfield, Ill., 1844. 21 pp., unbound. $1,500.

FORD, Webster. *Songs & Sonnets.* Chicago, 1910. (By Edgar Lee Masters.) $125.

FORDHAM, Mary Weston. *Magnolia Leaves.* Tuskegee (1897). Author's first book. Introduction by Booker T. Washington. $150.

FOREMAN, Grant. *Advancing the Frontier.* Norman, Okla., 1933. Maps. $100.

FOREMAN, Grant. *Indian Removal.* Norman, 1932. $150.

FOREMAN, Grant. *Pioneer Days in the Early Southwest.* Cleveland, 1926. Illustrated. $150.

FORESTER, C. S. *The African Queen.* London (1935). $1,250. Boston, 1935. $600.

FORESTER, C. S. *Brown on Resolution.* London (1929). $850.

FORESTER, C. S. *Josephine, Napoleon's Empress.* London (1925). "Published 1925" on copyright page. $750. London (1925). Ads dated June 1928. $600. New York, 1925. $400.

FORESTER, C. S. *Loves Lies Dreaming.* Indianapolis (1927). $600. Indianapolis (1927). First issue has "C.E. Forester" vs. "C.S. Forester" on cover. $400.

FORESTER, C. S. *Marionettes at Home.* London (1936). $750. Orange cloth. "3/6 net" on spine of dustwrapper. $600.

FORESTER, C. S. *Napoleon and His Court.* London (1924). "Published 1924" on copyright page. First issue is in blue cloth. $1,000. New York, 1924. $600.

FORESTER, C. S. *The Paid Piper.* London (1924). $2,500. London (1924). Ads dated May 1925. $2,000. Toronto (1924). $1,500.

FORESTER, C. S. *A Pawn Among Kings.* London (1924). Author's first book. $2,000. Toronto (1924). $1,200.

FORESTER, C. S. *Plain Murder.* London (1930). $500.

FORESTER, C. S. *The Shadow of the Hawk.* London (1928). $1,200.

FORESTER, C. S. *Single-Handed.* New York, 1929. First American edition of *Brown on Resolution.* $400.

FORESTER, Frank. See Forrester, Frank; Herbert, Henry William.

FORESTER, Frank. *American Game in Its Seasons.* New York, 1853. (By Henry William Herbert.) Illustrated by the author. $250.

FORESTER, Frank. *The Complete Manual for Young Sportsmen.* New York, 1856. (By Henry William Herbert.) Illustrated by the author. $350.

FORESTER, Frank. *Field Sports in the United States, and the British Provinces of America.* London 1848. (By Henry William Herbert.) 2 vols., green cloth. First issue, with "Provinces of America" on title page (changed later to "Provinces of North America"). (VAB) $300. New York, 1849. 2 vols., green cloth. First American edition, first issue, with "Rutted Grouse" frontispiece. "Burgess Stringer" on spine (later "Stringer"). (Issued as *Frank Forester's Field Sports of the United States, . . .).* $300.

FORESTER, Frank. *Frank Forester and His Friends.* London, 1849. (By Henry William Herbert.) 3 vols., salmon cloth. $300.

FORESTER, Frank. *Frank Forester's Fish and Fishing of the United States and British Provinces of North America.* London, 1849. (By Henry William Herbert.) Illustrated by the author. Blue cloth. $250. New York, 1850. $200.

FORESTER, Frank. *Frank Forester's Fugitive Sporting Sketches.* Westfield, Wis., 1879. (By Henry William Herbert.) Edited by Will Wildwood (Fred E. Pond.) Wraps. $250. Cloth. $150.

FORESTER, Frank. *Frank Forester's Horse and Horsemanship of the United States and British Provinces of North America.* New York, 1857. (By Henry William Herbert.) Plates, pedigree tables. 2 vols., purple cloth. $350.

FORESTER, Frank. *Hints to Horse-Keepers.* New York, 1859. Frontispiece, 23 plates. (By Henry William Herbert.) $250.

FORESTER, Frank. *Trouting Along the Catasauqua.* Derrydale Press. New York, 1927. (By Henry William Herbert.) One of 423. In dustwrapper. $400.

FORESTERS. An American Tale (The). (By Jeremy Belknap.) Boston, 1792. 3 variants, no priority. $600.

FORNEY, Col. John W. *What I Saw in Texas.* (Cover title.) Philadelphia (1872). Map and plates. 92 pp., pictorial wraps. $400. Second edition. $300.

FORREST, Lieut. Col. Charles R. *A Picturesque Tour Along the Rivers Ganges and Jumna, in India.* London, 1824. With hand-colored title and 24 colored plates. $2,500.

FORREST, Earle R. *Missions and Pueblos of the Old Southwest.* Cleveland, 1929. $200.

FORREST, John. *Explorations in Australia.* London, 1875. With 4 folding maps, and 7 portraits and plates. $1,500.

FORSTER, E. M. *Abinger Harvest.* London (1936). First issue, including "A Flood in the Office" (pages 278–81). $500. Second issue, without "A Flood in the Office," and pages 277–82 canceled. $250.

FORSTER, E. M. *Alexandria: A History and a Guide.* Alexandria, Egypt, 1922. Folding map in pocket at rear. Boards. Issued without dustwrapper. $400. Alexandria, 1938. Boards. Second edition. One of 250 signed. Issued without dustwrapper. $600.

FORSTER, E. M. *Anonymity: An Enquiry.* Hogarth Press. London, 1925. Illustrated boards. $250.

FORSTER, E. M. *Desmond McCarthy.* Millhouse Press. No-place, 1952. One of 72. Gray wraps. $175.

FORSTER, E. M. *The Eternal Moment and Other Stories.* London, 1928. First binding in maroon cloth with gold stamping. In dustwrapper priced 5 s(hillings). $400. Second binding, stamped in black. $250.

FORSTER, E. M. *The Government of Egypt.* London (1920). Wraps, paper label. (Official recommendations of a Labour committee, 1919.) $400.

FORSTER, E. M. *Howard's End.* London, 1910. $200.

FORSTER, E. M. *The Longest Journey.* London, 1907. $300.

FORSTER, E. M. *A Passage to India.* London, 1924. Red cloth. $750. Boards and cloth. One of 200 signed, issued without dustwrapper. In slipcase. $1,000.

FORSTER, E. M. *Pharos and Pharillon.* Hogarth Press. Richmond, 1923. Blue boards with cloth spine. Issued without dustwrapper. $600. New York, 1923. Orange cloth. First American edition. $250.

FORSTER, E. M. *A Room with a View.* London, 1908. $500.

FORSTER, E. M. *The Story of the Siren.* Hogarth Press. Richmond, 1920. Wraps. (500 copies printed.) First state with front label reading "The Story/of the Siren." (The other two states have title as single line or "The Story of the/Siren.") $750. Later states. $450.

FORSTER, E. M. *Where Angels Fear to Tread.* Edinburgh, 1905. Author's first book. First issue, with this title not mentioned in ads at back. $600. With title in ads. $350. New York, 1920. Black cloth. First American edition in dustwrapper. $500.

FORSTER, John Reinold. *Observations Made During a Voyage Round the World* . . . London, 1778. 2 folding tables. Folding map. Appended to the text an errata leaf and list of subscribers. $3,500.

FORSYTH, Frederick. *The Biafra Story.* (Middlesex, 1969.) Author's first book. Wraps. $125.

FORSYTH, Frederick. *The Day of the Jackal.* London (1971). $150.

FORSYTH, James W., and GRANT, F. D. *Report of an Expedition up the Yellowstone River, Made in 1875.* Washington, 1875. Folding map. 17 pp., wraps. $250.

FORT, Charles. *The Book of the Damned.* New York, 1919. In dustwrapper. $350. Without dustwrapper. $75.

FORT, Charles. *The Outcast Manufacturers.* New York, 1909. Author's first book. Blue ribbed cloth lettered in gold. $150. Blue mesh cloth lettered in red. $125.

FORTRESS of Sorrento (The). (By Mordecai M. Noah). New York, 1808. Author's first book. Wraps. $750.

FORTUNES of Colonel Torlogh O'Brien (The). Dublin, 1847. (By Joseph Sheridan le Fanu.) 10 monthly parts, wraps. $1,500. First book edition. Illustrated. $650.

FORTUNES of Perkin Warbeck (The). London, 1830. (By Mary Wollstonecraft Shelley.) 3 vols., in original boards, cloth spine, printed labels. $1,000.

FOSTER, B. F. *Foster's System of Penmanship; Or, The Art of Rapid Writing* . . . Boston, 1835. 15 plates. $175.

FOSTER, Charles. *The Gold Placers of California.* Akron, Ohio, 1849. Map. Printed wraps. $5,000 and up.

FOSTER, George G. (editor). *The Gold Regions of California.* New York, 1848. Frontispiece map. Printed wraps. $1,000. London (1849). $750.

FOSTER, George G. *New York by Gas-Light.* New York, 1850. Wraps. $500.

FOSTER, Isaac. *The Foster Family, California Pioneers.* (Santa Barbara, 1925.) $150.

FOSTER, James S. *Advantages of Dakota Territory.* Yankton, 1873. 51 pp., wraps. $1,500.

FOSTER, James S. *Outlines of History of the Territory of Dakota and Emigrant's Guide to the Free Lands of the Northwest.* Yankton, 1870. Folding map. 127 pp., wraps. $2,500 and up.

FOSTER, Myles Birket. *A Day in a Child's Life.* (London, 1881.) Illustrated by Kate Greenaway. Glazed boards and cloth. $200.

FOUNTAIN, Albert J. *Bureau of Immigration of the Territory of New Mexico: Report of Dona Ana County.* Santa Fe, 1882. 34 pp., wraps. $400.

FOUQUE, F. H. K. de La Motte. *Undine.* London, 1909. Illustrated in color by Arthur Rackham. Vellum with ties. One of 1,000 signed by Rackham. $1,250. Trade. $250. Limited Editions Club, New York, 1930. In slipcase. $75.

FOUR Gospels of the Lord Jesus Christ (The). Golden Cockerel Press. Waltham Saint Lawrence, 1931. Decorations by Eric Gill. Half pigskin. One of 488. In slipcase. $6,000. One of 12 on vellum. $30,000.

FOUREGEAUD, Victor H. *The First Californiac.* Allen Press. San Francisco, 1942. Illustrated. Blue boards and calf. One of 225. $600.

FOWLER, Jacob. *The Journal of Jacob Fowler.* New York, 1898. One of 950. $200.

FOWLER, Laurence Hall, and BAER, Elizabeth. *The Fowler Architectural Collection of the Johns Hopkins University.* Baltimore, 1961. One of 250, first issue (10 or 12 copies) with "Lawrence" on title page. $1,000. Corrected ("Laurence"). $800.

FOWLES, John. *The Aristos.* Boston (1964). $200. London, 1964. $150.

FOWLES, John. *The Collector.* London, 1963. Author's first book. In first dustwrapper, without publisher's blurbs. $650. Boston (1963). $100.

FOWLES, John. *The Ebony Tower.* London (1974). $200. Boston (1974). $50.

FOWLES, John. *The French Lieutenant's Woman.* London (1969). $200. Boston (1969). $75.

FOWLES, John. *The Magus.* London (1966). $250. Boston, 1966. $100.

FOX, John, Jr. *A Cumberland Vendetta and Other Stories.* New York, 1896. Author's first book with final entry in contents as "Hell Fer Sartain." $100. With "On Hell-Fer-Sartain Creek." $75.

FOX, John, Jr. *The Little Shepherd of Kingdom Come.* New York, 1903. Illustrated by F.C. Yohn. Smooth red cloth, paper label. One of 100 (signed by Fox and Yohn—VAB). $250. Trade edition. Red cloth with only Scribners' device on copyright page and no ads for other Fox books on verso or half title. $150. New York, 1931. Illustrated by N.C. Wyeth. Half vellum. One of 512 signed by Wyeth. $750.

FOX, Lady Mary. *Account of an Expedition to the Interior of New Holland.* London, 1837. $300.

FRAENKEL, Michael. See *The Need for Anonymity; Anonymous* and *Werther's.*

FRAENKEL, Michael. *Bastard Death.* Paris (1936). Wraps. $125.

FRAENKEL, Michael. *Werther's Younger Brother.* New York (1931). Wraps. Author's first book (aside from a pamphlet collaboration). One of 400. $150.

FRAME, Janet. *The Lagoon.* Christchurch, 1951. Author's first book. $350.

FRANCHERE, Gabriel. *Narrative of a Voyage to the Northwest Coast of America,* . . . New York, 1854. 3 plates. First edition in English. $450.

FRANCIS, Dick. *Dead Cert.* London, 1962. Author's first mystery. $1,000. New York, 1962. $350.

FRANCIS, Dick. *For Kicks.* London (1965). $300. New York (1965). $175.

FRANCIS, Dick. *Nerve.* London (1964). $600. New York (1964). $250.

FRANCIS, Dick. *Sport of Queens.* London, 1957. Author's first book. $250. New York, 1969. $150.

FRANCIS, Grant R. *Old English Drinking Glasses.* London, 1926. 72 plates. Buckram. $300.

FRANK, Anne. The Diary of a Young Girl. Garden City, 1952. $100.

FRANK Fairleigh; or Scenes from the Life of a Private Pupil. London, 1850. (By Frank E. Smedley.) Illustrated by George Cruikshank. 15 parts, blue-green wraps. First issue, with dated title page (VAB). $750. Second issue in cloth. $200.

FRANK, Robert. *The Americans.* New York (1959). Introduction by Jack Kerouac. 83 plates. Oblong. $400. New York, 1969. Revised and enlarged. $150.

FRANK, Waldo. *The Dark Mother.* New York (1920). In dustwrapper. $150.

FRANK, Waldo. *The Unwelcome Man.* Boston, 1917. Author's first book. $125.

FRANKENSTEIN; or The Modern Prometheus. London, 1818. 3 vols., in original boards, paper labels. (By Mary Wollstonecraft Shelley.) $75,000 or more. Rebound copies. $15,000. London, 1831. Third edition. With a new preface by the author. In original cloth. $750. New York, 1833. First American edition. 2 vols. $2,000. Limited Editions Club, New York, 1934. In slipcase. $150.

FRANKLIN, Benjamin. *Autobiography.* London, 1793. First edition in English. $400.

FRANKLIN, Colin. *Emery Walker, Some Light on His Theories of Printing . . .* Cambridge, 1973. Limited to 500 copies. $225.

FRANKLIN, Colin. *Themes in Aquatint.* San Francisco, 1978. Limited to 500 copies. 16 full-color plates. $250.

FRANKS, David. *The New-York Directory.* New York, 1786. 82 pp. $4,000. New York, 1909. Folding map. Printed wraps. Reprint. $150.

FRAZER, Sir James George. *Totemism.* Edinburgh, 1887. Author's first book. $300.

FREDERIC, Harold. *In the Valley.* New York, 1890. 16 plates by Howard Pyle. Cloth. $125.

FREDERIC, Harold. *Seth's Brother's Wife.* New York, 1887. First issue, with 1886 copyright and no ads. Author's first book. $175.

FREDERICK, J. V. *Ben Holladay, the Stagecoach King.* Glendale, Calif., 1940. Folding map. Issued without dustwrapper. $150.

FREDERICK, John. *Riders of the Silences.* New York, 1920. (By Frederick Faust.) In dustwrapper. $200.

FREE-and-Easy Songbook (The). Philadelphia, 1834. Plates. Davy Crockett portrait on title page. $300.

FREEDLEY, Edwin T. (editor). *Leading Pursuits and Leading Men.* Philadelphia (1854). $125.

FREEMAN, Douglas Southall. *R.E. Lee: A Biography.* New York, 1934–35. 4 vols. $300.

FREEMAN, James W. See *Prose and Poetry of the Live Stock Industry.*

FREEMAN, R. Austin. See Ashdown, Clifford.

FREEMAN, R. Austin. *The Cat's Eye.* London (1923). $750. New York, 1927. First American edition. $350.

FREEMAN, R. Austin. *Felo de Se?* London (1937). $250.

FREEMAN, R. Austin. *John Thorndyke's Cases.* London, 1909. $600.

FREEMAN, R. Austin. *A Journey to Bontuku.* (London, 1893). Author's first book. Wraps. (Off-print.) $1,000.

FREEMAN, R. Austin. *Mr. Polton Explains.* London, 1940. $250. New York, 1940. Red cloth. First American edition. $150.

FREEMAN, R. Austin. *The Red Thumb Mark.* London, 1907. Cloth. $750. Wraps. $600.

FREEMAN, R. Austin. *Travels and Life in Ashanti and Japan.* London, 1898. $850.

FREMAUX, Leon J. *New Orleans Characters.* (New Orleans) 1876. Litho title with border, hand-colored oval portrait, and 16 color plates. Folio, cloth, and morocco. $2,000.

FREMONT, John Charles. *Geographical Memoir Upon Upper California.* Senate Misc. Doc. No. 148. Washington, 1848. 67 pp., wraps. With folding map. $750. Without map. $400.

FREMONT, John Charles. *Narrative of the Exploring Expedition to the Rocky Mountains, in the year 1842, etc.* Syracuse, 1847. Folding map by Rufus B. Sage, 2 plates. Cloth. (First publication of the famous Sage map.) $1,250.

FREMONT, John Charles. *Oregon and California: The Exploring Expedition to the Rocky Mountains, Oregon and California.* Buffalo, 1849. 2 portraits; 2 plates. Cloth. $75. (One of several reprints of *Report of the Exploring Expedition.*)

FREMONT, John Charles. *Report of the Exploring Expedition to the Rocky Mountains in the Year 1842.* Washington, 1845. 22 plates., 5 maps, 2 folding. House or Senate editions. $800.

FREMONT, John Charles. *Report on an Exploration of the Country Lying Between the Missouri River and the Rocky Rocky Mountains, . . .* Senate Doc. 243. Washington, 1843. 6 plates, folding map. Wraps. $400.

FRENCH, Capt. W. J. *Wild Jim, the Texas Cowboy and Saddle King.* Antioch, Ill., 1890. Portrait. 76 pp., wraps. $1,250.

FRENCH, William. *Some Recollections of a Western Ranchman.* London (1927). Gray cloth. $500. New York (1928). $400.

FRENEAU, Philip. See *A Poem, On the Rising Glory . . .*

FRENEAU, Philip. *The American Village.* New York, 1772. $350.

FRESHFIELD, Douglas W. *The Exploration of the Caucasus.* London, 1896. 2 vols. $850.

FREUD, Sigmund. *The Interpretation of Dreams.* London, 1913. Author's first book. $600.

FREUD, Sigmund. *Totem and Taboo.* New York, 1918. $300.

FRIDGE, Ike. *History of the Chisum War . . . Cowboy Life on the Frontier.* Electra, Tex. (1927). Stiff wraps. $400.

FRIEDMAN, Bruce Jay. *Far from the City of Class.* New York, 1963. $125.

FRIEDMAN, Bruce Jay. *Stern.* New York, 1962. Author's first book. $75.

FRIEDMAN, I. K. *The Lucky Number.* Chicago, 1896. Author's first book. $75.

FRIES, Waldemar H. *The Double Elephant Folio, The Story of Audubon's Birds of America.* Chicago, 1973. $150.

FRINK, F. W. *A Record of Rice County, Minnesota, in 1868.* Faribault, Minn., 1868. 24 pp., wraps. $200. Faribault, 1871. Second edition. $75.

FRINK, Margaret A. *Journal of the Adventures of a Party of California Gold-Seekers.* (Oakland, 1897.) 2 frontispieces. $1,250.

FROST, A. B. *A Book of Drawings.* New York, 1904. Illustrated. Folio, boards. $200.

FROST, A. B. *Sports and Games in the Open.* New York, 1899. 53 color plates. Folio, pictorial cloth portfolio. $350.

FROST, John. *History of the State of California.* Auburn, Calif., 1850. Contemporary morocco. $275.

FROST, John. *The Mexican War and Its Warriors.* New Haven, 1849. Colored frontispiece, other plates, map. $225.

FROST, Robert. See Robinson, Edwin Arlington.

FROST, Robert. *A Boy's Will.* London, 1913. Author's first regularly published book. Binding A: bronzed brown pebbled cloth, gilt stamped. $3,000. Binding B: cream vellum-paper boards stamped in red (including border rule). $1,500. Binding C: cream linen-paper wraps, stamped in black without a border rule. 8-petaled flowers. $750. Binding D: cream linen-paper wraps, stamped in black. 4-petaled flowers $650. 135 signed and numbered copies in wraps. $1,000. New York, 1915. Fine linen cloth and white endpapers. "Aind" for "And" on last line of page 14. $400.

FROST, Robert. *Collected Poems.* Random House. New York, 1930. 1,000 signed and numbered copies. $350. New York (1930). States "First trade edition." $250. London, 1930. $250.

FROST, Robert. *Complete Poems.* New York, 1949. One of 500 signed and numbered copies. Issued without dustwrapper. In slipcase. $400. New York (1949). $125. Limited Editions Club, New York, 1950. 1,500 signed and numbered copies. 2 vols. in slipcase. $450. London (1951). $125.

FROST, Robert. *A Considerable Speck.* No-place (1939). Fewer than 100 copies printed. Single sheet folded to 4 pages. $600.

FROST, Robert. *The Cow's in the Corn.* Gaylordsville, 1929. One of 91 signed and numbered copies. Issued with dustwrapper. $750.

FROST, Robert. *A Further Range.* New York (1936). One of 803 signed and numbered copies issued without dustwrapper. In slipcase. $300. Trade. $100. London (1937). $100.

FROST, Robert. *The Gold Hesperidee.* (Cortland, 1935.) 8 pp., tan wraps. Colophon page has "Cortland NY/A." Page 7, second line from bottom "Twas Sunday and Square Hale was dressed for meeting." Unnumbered on limitation page. Leaves measure 162 by 114 mm. $600. One of 200 numbered copies. Colophon page has "Cortland NY/B." Yellow wraps. Line noted above has been reset so that "for meeting" is on separate line. Leaves measure 183 by 127 mm. $400. Reported 67 copies issued in pale yellow wraps with the word "English" stamped under "copy number" on page 2. $500.

FROST, Robert. *Hard Not to Be King.* New York, 1951. One of 300 signed and numbered copies. $500.

FROST, Robert. *In the Clearing.* New York (1962). One of 1,500 signed and numbered copies. In slipcase. $175. Trade. $50. London (1962). Introduction by Robert Graves not in U.S. edition. $60.

FROST, Robert. *The Lone Striker.* (New York, 1933.) Wraps. Issued in envelope. (Some used as a Christmas card by Frost.) $100.

FROST, Robert. *A Masque of Reason.* New York (1945). One of 800 signed and numbered copies issued without dustwrapper in slipcase. $250. Trade. $60.

FROST, Robert. *Mountain Interval.* New York (1916). First state: page 88, lines 6 and 7 repeated lines; " 'Come' " for " 'Gone,' " page 63 line 6 from bottom. Photo of plaster bust of Frost facing title page. $150. Second state: errors corrected. Plaster bust photo present. $100.

FROST, Robert. *New Hampshire.* New York, 1923. One of 350 signed and numbered copies. In white slipcase. $500. Trade. $350. London, 1924. $400. Hanover, 1955.

750 signed and numbered copies. In semi-transparent rough white Japanese paper dustwrapper. $250.

FROST, Robert. *North of Boston.* London (1914). First issue, binding A: coarse green cloth. $2,000. New York, 1914 (Binding B). U.K. sheets with Holt title page. $1,250. London (1914). First issue, binding C: fine green cloth. $1,000. Binding D: blue cloth. $750. Binding E: coarse green cloth, measuring 200 by 145 mm, all edges trimmed, rubber-stamped on page iv. $650. Binding F: coarse green cloth, measuring 195 by 150, top edge trimmed, others rough cut, rubber-stamped on page iv. $600.

FROST, Robert. *Selected Poems.* New York, 1923. "March, 1923" on copyright page. $500. London (1923). $400.

FROST, Robert. *Steeple Bush.* New York, 1947. One of 751 signed and numbered copies issued without dustwrapper in slipcase. $250. Trade. $75.

FROST, Robert. *Three Poems.* Hanover, N.H. (1935). Wraps. One of 125 numbered copies. $600.

FROST, Robert. *To a Young Wretch.* (New York, 1937.) Wraps. (Christmas poem. Seven imprints with quantities varying from 25 to 275 copies.) $150 to $250.

FROST, Robert. *A Way Out.* Harbor Press. New York, 1929. One of 485 signed and numbered copies issued without dustwrapper. $400.

FROST, Robert. *West-Running Brook.* New York (1928). Lacks "First Edition" statement. $175. States "First Edition." $125. One of 1,000 numbered copies signed by Frost and frontis and three plates pencil signed by artist J.J. Lankes. Slipcase. $450.

FRUGAL Housewife (The). By the Author of *Hobomok.* Boston, 1829. (By Lydia Maria Child.) $250.

FRY, Christopher. *The Boy with a Cart.* London, 1939. Wraps. Author's first book. $150.

FRY, Edmund. *Pantographia; Containing Accurate Copies of All the Known Alphabets* . . . London, 1799. $450.

FRY, Frederick. *Fry's Traveler's Guide, and Descriptive Journal of the Great North Western Territories.* Cincinnati, 1865. $750.

FRY, James B. *Army Sacrifices of . . .* New York, 1879. $400.

FRY, Roger. *Giovanni Bellini.* London, 1899. Illustrated. Boards and cloth. Author's first book. $150.

FUCHS, Daniel. *Summer in Williamsburg.* New York (1934). Author's first book. $300.

FUGARD, Athol. *The Blood Knot.* Johannesburg, 1963. Author's first book. (Issued without dustwrapper.) $200.

FUGITIVES, An Anthology of Verse. New York (1928). Decorated paper boards, cloth back. Issued in dustwrapper. $1,750. Without dustwrapper. $200.

FULKERSON, H. S. *Random Recollections of Early Days in Mississippi.* Vicksburg, 1885. Wraps. $600. Cloth. $400.

FULLER, C. L. *Pocket Map and Descriptive Outline History of the Black Hills of Dakota and Wyoming.* Rapid City, 1887. Folding map. 56 pp., stiff wraps. $850.

FULLER, Emeline. *Left by the Indians, or Rapine, Massacre and Cannibalism on the Overland Trail in 1860.* (Cover title.) (Mt. Vernon, Iowa, 1892.) Portrait. 41 pp., printed wraps. First edition $300. New York, 1936. Facsimile reprint. One of 200. $75.

FULLER, Henry Blake. See Page, Stanton.

FULLER, Henry Blake. *The Cliff-Dwellers.* New York, 1893. First issue, with author's name on front cover as "Henry Fuller." $150.

FULLER, R. Buckminister. *Nine Chains to the Moon.* Philadelphia (1938). Author's first book. $150.

FULLER, Roy. *Poems.* London (1940). Author's first book other than a privately printed book. $150.

FULLER, Sarah Margaret. *Conversations with Goethe.* Boston, 1839. Author's first book. (Translated by Fuller.) $500.

FULLER, Sarah Margaret. *Guenderode.* Boston, 1842. $400.

FULLER, Sarah Margaret. *Summer on the Lakes . . .* Boston/New York, 1844. $300. New York, 1845. Wraps. $100.

FULLER, Sarah Margaret. *Woman in the 19th Century.* New York, 1845. Wraps. $400. Cloth. $250.

FULLMER, John S. *Assassination of Joseph and Hyrum Smith, the Prophet and the Patriarch of the Church of Jesus Christ of Latter-Day Saints.* Liverpool, 1855. 40 pp., half leather. $750.

FULTON, A. R. *The Red Men of Iowa.* Des Moines. 1882. 26 plates. $200.

FULTON, Robert. *Torpedo War, and Submarine Explosions.* New York, 1810. 5 plates. $1,500 or more.

FURBER, George C. *The Twelve Months Volunteer.* Cincinnati, 1848. $200.

FURST, Herbert (editor). *The Woodcut, An Annual.* London, 1927–30. 4 vols. Limited to 750 copies except for vol. 4, which was limited to 700 copies. Contains examples of woodcuts by leading wood engravers. $650.

G

GADDIS, William. *The Recognitions.* New York (1955). Cloth. Author's first book. $250. London (1962). Dark blue cloth. States "First published in . . ." $125.

GAG, Wanda. *Millions of Cats.* New York, 1928. $200. Another issue. One of 250 signed and with a signed engraving. $1,000.

GAINE, Hugh. *The Journals of Hugh Gaine, Printer.* New York, 1902. Edited by Paul Leicester Ford. Plates. 2 vols., boards. One of 350. $150. Cloth. One of 30 printed on Japan paper. $300.

GAINES, Ernest J. *Catherine Carmier.* New York, 1964. Author's first book. $150. London, 1966. $100.

GALE, George. *Upper Mississippi.* Chicago, 1867. Frontispiece, maps, plates. $150.

GALL, James. *A Historical Sketch of the Origin and Progress of Literature for the Blind* . . . Edinburgh, 1834. Frontispiece printed in raised letters. $275.

GALLAGHER, Tess. *Stepping Outside.* Lisbon, Iowa (1974). Author's first book. Wraps. $250.

GALLAHER, James. *The Western Sketch-Book.* Boston, 1850. Plates. $250.

GALLATIN, A. E., and OLIVER, L. M. *A Bibliography of the Works of Max Beerbohm.* Cambridge, 1952. $135.

GALLATIN, Albert. *Considerations on the Currency and Banking System of the United States.* Philadelphia, 1831. $200.

GALLATIN, Albert. *Letters of Albert Gallatin on the Oregon Question.* Washington, 1846. Stitched pamphlet. $100.

GALLATIN, Albert Eugene. *Art and the Great War.* New York, 1919. Illustrated. Folio, full morocco. One of 100 signed. Boxed. $400. Trade. $125.

GALLICO, Paul. *Farewell to Sport.* New York, 1938. Author's first book. $200.

GALLICO, Paul. *The Snow Goose.* London, 1946. Illustrated by Peter Scott, including 4 color plates. Morocco. One of 750 signed. $300. Trade. $60.

GALSWORTHY, John. See Sinjohn, John.

GALSWORTHY, John. *The Forsyte Saga.* London, 1922. First issue, with genealogical table pulling out to the right. Green cloth. In dustwrapper. $250. Red leather in dustwrapper. $350. Green leather. One of 275 signed. $500.

GALSWORTHY, John. *The Island Pharisees.* London, 1904. First (unpublished) issue, with "Wold" for "Dolf" as author of *Uriah the Hittite* in list of novels. $1,000. First published edition. $150.

GALSWORTHY, John. *The Man of Property.* London, 1906. First issue, with broken bar of music on page 200. $150.

GALT, John. See Balwhidder, The Rev. Micah. See also *The Provost; Ringan Gilhaize; The Steam-Boat.*

GALT, John. *The Bachelor's Wife.* Edinburgh, 1824. $150.

GALT, John. *Lawrie Todd.* London 1830. 3 vols., in original cloth. $450. New York, 1830. 2 vols. in one, in original boards. First American edition. $200.

GALTON, Francis. *Finger Prints.* London, 1892. 16 plates. $500.

GALTON, Francis. *Hereditary Genius.* London, 1869. Folding table. $600. New York, 1870. $400.

GAMESKEEPER at Home (The). London, 1878. (By Richard Jefferies.) $250.

GANCONAGH. *John Sherman and Dhoya.* London (1891). (By William Butler Yeats.) Gray cloth, lettered in blue; also in yellow wraps, lettered in black. Cloth. $1,250. Wraps. $750. (Note: The cloth issue is scarcer than the one in wraps.)

GANNET(T), William, C. *The House Beautiful.* River Forest, Ill., Winter, 1896–97. (Auvergne Press.) With designs by Frank Lloyd Wright. Folio, half leather. One of 90 signed by Wright and William Winslow, the publisher. $3,000.

GARCES, Francisco. *On the Trail of the Spanish Pioneer.* New York, 1900. Translated by Elliott Coues. Illustrated. 2 vols. One of 950. $500.

GARCIA LORCA, Federico. *Bitter Oleander.* London, 1935. Author's first book. $300.

GARCIA MARQUEZ, Gabriel. See Marquez, Gabriel Garcia.

GARD, Wayne. *Sam Bass.* Boston, 1936. Illustrated. $125.

GARDEN, Alexander. *Anecdotes of the Revolutionary War in America.* Charleston, 1822. First series. Boards. $400. Charleston, 1828. Boards. Second series. $200.

GARDINER, E. Norman. *Athletics of the Ancient World.* Oxford, 1930. $75.

GARDINER, John, and HEPBURN, David. *The American Gardener.* Georgetown, D.C., 1818. New enlarged edition (first issued in 1804) making it the second U.S. garden book. $475.

GARDNER, Alexander. See *Photographic Sketch Book of the War.*

GARDNER, Erle Stanley. *The Case of the Lucky Legs.* New York, 1934. $600.

GARDNER, Erle Stanley. *The Case of the Sulky Girl.* New York, 1933. $750.

GARDNER, Erle Stanley. *The Case of the Velvet Claws.* New York, 1932. Author's first book. $1,000.

GARDNER, John. *The Complete Works of the Gawain Poet.* Chicago (1965). Translated by Gardner. $200.

GARDNER, John. *The Forms of Fiction.* New York, 1962. (Author's first book [with Lennis Dunlap] preceded by Ph.D. dissertation.) Issued without dustwrapper. $100.

GARDNER, John. *Grendel.* New York, 1971. Illustrated. $175. (London, 1972.) $75.

GARDNER, John. *The Resurrection.* (New York, 1966.) Author's first novel. $500.

GARDNER, John. *The Wreckage of Agathon.* New York (1970). $150.

GARLAND, Hamlin. *The Book of the American Indian.* New York 1923. Colored frontispiece and 34 plates by Frederic Remington. Folio, boards, and cloth. In dustwrapper and slipcase. $300.

GARLAND, Hamlin. *Cavanagh, Forest Ranger.* New York, 1910. $100.

GARLAND, Hamlin. *Main-Travelled Roads.* Boston, 1891. Gray printed wraps. First issue with "First Thousand" at bottom of front cover. $250. Blue or gray cloth with sheets bulking ⁹/₁₆ inches versus ⅞ inches (later). $150.

GARLAND, Hamlin. *Under the Wheel: A Modern Play in Six Scenes.* Boston, 1890. Wraps. Author's first book. $400.

GARNEAU, Joseph, Jr. *Nebraska: Her Resources, Advantages and Development.* (Cover title.) Omaha, 1893. 24 pp., printed wraps. $125.

GARNER, James W. *Reconstruction in Mississippi.* New York, 1901. Cloth. $100.

GARNETT, David. See Burke, Leda.

GARNETT, David. *The Grasshoppers Come.* London, 1931. Illustrated. Yellow buckram. One of 200 signed. $175. Trade $75.

GARNETT, David. *The Kitchen Garden . . .* London (1909). (Translated and adapted by Garnett from French work of Prof. Gressent.) Wraps. $200.

GARNETT, Richard. See *Primula.*

GARNETT, Richard. *The Twilight of the Gods and Other Tales.* London, 1888. $150.

GARRARD, Lewis H. *Wah-To-Yah, and the Taos Trail.* Cincinnati, 1850. First issue, with page 269 misnumbered 26. $1,000. Grabhorn Press. San Francisco, 1936. Boards. One of 550. $250.

GARRETT, Edmund H. (editor). *Victorian Songs.* Boston, 1895. Illustrated by Garrett. Vellum, gilt. One of 225. $200.

GARRETT, Julia Kathryn. *Green Flag over Texas.* New York, 1939. Maps. $125.

GARRETT, Pat F. *The Authentic Life of Billy, The Kid.* Santa Fe, 1882. Frontispiece and 5 plates. 137 pp., pictorial blue wraps. First edition, with ad inside back wrapper, misnumbered pages at the back, and one errata slip. $4,000 or more.

GARRUD, W. H. *The Complete Jujitsuan.* New York, 1914. $60.

GARTH, Will. (House pseudonym attributed to Henry Kuttner.) *Dr. Cyclops.* New York, 1940. $125.

GARVIE, James. *Abraham Lincoln toni kin, qa Aesop tawoyake kin.* (Life of Abraham Lincoln and Aesop's Fables.) Santee [Indian] Agency, Neb., 1893. 17 pp., printed wraps. $250.

GASCOYNE, David. *Opening Day.* London (1932). $350.

GASCOYNE, David. *Poems, 1937–1942.* (London, 1943.) Color illustrations. Pictorial boards. $200.

GASCOYNE, David. *Roman Balcony . . .* London, 1932. Author's first book. $1,000.

GASKELL, Elizabeth C. See *Cranford; Mary Barton; North and South.*

GASKELL, Elizabeth C. *The Life of Charlotte Brontë.* London, 1857. 2 vols. $600.

GASKELL, Elizabeth C. *Sylvia's Lovers.* London, 1893. 3 vols., cloth. $750.

GASKELL, Jane. *The Serpent.* (London, 1963.) $125.

GASKELL, Philip. *John Baskerville, A Bibliography.* Chicheley, 1973. 17 plates and a facsimile of a type specimen in a pocket at the back. Reprinted with additions from the 1959 edition. $100.

GASS, Patrick. *Gass's Journal of the Lewis and Clark Expedition.* Chicago, 1904. Edited by James K. Hosmer. Illustrated. $200. One of 75 on large paper. $350.

GASS, Patrick. *A Journal of the Voyages and Travels of a Corps of Discovery, Under the Command of Capt. Lewis and Capt. Clark...* Pittsburgh, 1807. $1,000. London, 1808. First English edition. $750. Philadelphia, 1810. Second edition (without plates). $350. Philadelphia, 1810. 6 plates added. $300.

GASS, William H. *Omensetter's Luck.* (New York, 1966.) Author's first book. $200. London, 1967. $75.

GASS, William H. *The First Winter of My Married Life.* Northridge, 1979. 26 signed, and lettered copies. $125. 275 signed and numbered copies. Issued without dustwrapper or slipcase. $60.

GASS, William H. *Willie Masters' Lonesome Wife.* (Evanston, 1968.) 100 signed and numbered copies. Issued without dustwrapper. $200. 300 copies (not signed or numbered). Issued without dustwrapper. $75. Also in wraps. $35. Another edition. New York, 1971. $35.

GAUGUIN, Paul. *Intimate Journals.* New York, 1921. Translated by Van Wyck Brooks. 27 illustrations by Gauguin. First edition in English issued without dustwrapper. One of 530. $400.

GAUTIER, Theophile. *One of Cleopatra's Nights.* New York, 1882. Translated by Lafcadio Hearn. First issue with publisher's name in capital letters on spine. $250.

GAY, Frederick A. *For Gratuitous Distribution: Sketches of California.* (Cover title.) (New York, 1848.) 16 pp., printed wraps. $750.

GEE, Ernest R. *Early American Sporting Books, 1734 to 1846.* Derrydale Press. New York, 1928. One of 500. $250.

GEM of the Rockies! (The): Manitou Springs. Manitou Springs. Colo. (about 1885). Plates and tables, 23 pp., printed wraps. $100.

GENERAL and Statistical Description of Pierce County (Wisconsin). (Prescott, Wis., 1854.) 9 pp., sewn. $200.

GENERAL Instructions to Deputy Surveyors. Little Rock, 1837. Folding diagram. 25 pp., sewn. $150.

GENET, Jean. *Our Lady of the Flowers.* Paris (19.9). Author's first English publication. (475 copies.) Imitation red morocco, issued without dustwrapper. $200.

GENET, Edmond Charles. *Memorial on the Upward Forces of Fluids.* Albany, 1825. Folding table, 6 plates. $1,250.

GENIUS of Oblivion (The), and Other Poems. Concord, N.H., 1823. By a Lady of New-Hampshire. (By Sarah Josepha Hale). Author's first book. $125.

GENT, Thomas. *The Life of Mr. Thomas Gent, Printer, of York* . . . London, 1832. $250.

GENTHE, Arnold. *As I Remember.* New, York, 1936. 112 photographic illustrations. Half leather. One of 250 signed. $750. Trade. $150.

GENTHE, Arnold. *Impressions of Old New Orleans: A Book of Pictures.* New York (1926). Foreword by Grace King with 101 plates. Green boards and cloth. $300. Also one of 200. $600.

GENTHE, Arnold. *Pictures of Old Chinatown.* New York, 1908. Author's first book, with text by Will Irwin. $125.

GEORGE, Henry. *Our Land and Land Policy, National and State.* San Francisco, 1871. Folding map in black and red. 48 pp., printed wraps. Author's first book. $600.

GEORGE, Henry. *Progress and Poverty.* San Francisco, 1879. Green or blue cloth. "Author's Edition." First issue, with the slip asking that no reviews be printed (VAB). $1,000. Second issue, without the slip referring to reviews. $400.

GEORGE, Mason. *The Young Backwoodsman.* Boston, 1829. (By Timothy Flint.) $150.

GEORGIA Scenes, Characters, Incidents, etc., in the First Half Century of the Republic. Augusta, Ga., 1835. By a Native Georgian. In original brown boards with cloth back and paper labels. (By Augustus Baldwin Longstreet.) Author's first book. $3,000. New York, 1840. Illustrated. Second edition. $300.

GERHARD, Fred. *Illinois as It Is.* Chicago, 1857. Map. Frontispiece, 3 folding maps. $250.

GERHARDI, William. *Futility.* London (1922). Author's first book. $200.

GERNSBACK, Hugo. *Ralph 124C41: A Romance of the Year 2660.* Boston, 1925. Illustrated. Blue cloth. Author's first book. $600.

GERRING, Charles. *Notes on Printers and Booksellers With A Chapter On Chap Books.* London, 1900. $100.

GERSHWIN, George. *George Gershwin's Song-Book.* New York, 1932. Illustrated by Alajolov. Portrait, song reproductions. Full blue morocco. One of 300 signed by Gershwin and Alajolov. $2,500. Trade. $400.

GERSHWIN, George. *Porgy and Bess.* New York, 1935. Frontispiece in color. Morocco. One of 250 signed by Gershwin, DuBose Heyward, and others. In slipcase. $4,000.

GERSTAECKER, Friedrich. *Scenes of Life in California.* Grabhorn Press. San Francisco, 1942. One of 500. $125.

GESNER, Abraham. *Remarks on the Geology and Minerology of Nova Scotia.* Halifax, 1836. In original cloth with folding frontispiece, folding hand-colored map and plate. $300.

GHIRARDELLI, Ynez. *The Artist H. Daumier.* Grabhorn Press. San Francisco, 1940. One of 250. $175.

GHOST in the Bank Of England (The). London, *1888*. (By Eden Philpotts, his first book.) $500.

GIBBINGS, Robert. *Iorana! A Tahitian Journal.* Boston, 1932. Author's first book. One of 385 signed and numbered copies. $350. Trade edition in slipcase. $175.

GIBBINGS, Robert. *The Wood Engravings of Robert Gibbings.* London (1959). Illustrated. Boards. In acetate dustwrapper. $250.

GIBBONS, Floyd. *The Red Napoleon.* New York (1929). $200.

GIBRAN, Kahlil. *The Madman: His Parables and Poems.* New York, 1918. Author's first book. $100.

GIBRAN, Kahlil. *Sand and Foam.* New York, 1926. Illustrated by the author. Boards. One of 95 signed. Issued without dustwrapper. $350.

GIBRAN, Kahlil. *Twenty Drawings.* New York, 1919. $300.

GIBSON, Charles Dana. *Americans.* New York, 1900. Illustrated. Oblong folio, cloth. One of 200 signed. $300. Trade. $125.

GIBSON, Charles Dana. *Drawings.* New York, 1897. Oblong folio, boards and cloth. Author's first book. $200.

GIBSON, Charles Dana. *Eighty Drawings, Including the Weaker Sex.* New York, 1903. Oblong folio, cloth. One of 250 signed. $300.

GIBSON, Charles Dana. *London, As Seen by Gibson.* New York, 1897. Illustrated. Oblong folio, cloth. One of 250. $250.

GIBSON, Wilfrid Wilson. *Urlyn the Harper.* London 1902. Wraps. Author's first book. $150.

GILBERT, Michael. *Close Quarters.* London, 1947. Author's first book. $150.

GILBERT, Paul T., and BRYSON, Charles L. *Chicago and Its Makers.* Chicago, 1929. $150. Full morocco. One of 2,000. $500.

GILBERT, W. S. *The "Bab" Ballads: Much Sound and Little Sense.* London, 1869. Illustrated by the author. Green cloth. First issue, with Hotten imprint on title page. $400.

GILBERT, W. S. *The Mikado.* London, 1928. $250.

GILBERT, W. S. *A New and Original Extravaganza Entitled Dulcamara; or, The Little Duck and the Great Quack.* London, 1866. Illustration. Orange wraps. Author's first published work. $750.

GILBERT, William. *On the Magnet, Magnetick Bodies . . .* London, 1900. Woodcuts. Folio, limp vellum, silk ties. One of 250. $400.

GILBEY, John F. *Secret Fighting Arts of the World.* Tokyo, 1963. (By Robert W. Smith.) First edition stated. $50.

GILCHRIST, Alexander. *Life of William Blake.* London, 1863. 2 vols. $400. London, 1880. 2 vols. Second edition. $300.

GILCHRIST, Ellen. *In the Land of Dreamy Dreams.* Fayetteville, 1981. Cloth. $300. Wraps. (1,000 copies.) $100.

GILCHRIST, Ellen. *The Land Surveyor's Daughter.* (Fayetteville) 1979. Author's first book. Wraps. $200.

GILDER, Richard Watson. *The New Day.* New York, 1876. Author's first book. $60.

GILHAM, William B. *Manual of Instruction for the Volunteers and Militia of the Confederate States.* Richmond, 1862. Folding charts. $400.

GILHESPY, F. Brayshaw. *Crown Derby Porcelain.* Leigh-on-Sea (1951). One of 600. In dustwrapper. $750.

GILL, Brendan. *Death in April and Other Poems.* Windham, 1935. Author's first book. $200.

GILL, Eric. *Art-Nonsense and Other Essays.* London, 1929. One of 100 signed in half calf. $600. Trade. $200.

GILL, Eric. *Clothes.* London, 1931. 10 wood engravings by the author. Boards, leather spine. One of 160 signed. $450.

GILL, Eric. *Clothing Without Cloth: An Essay on the Nude.* Golden Cockerel Press. London, 1931. 4 wood engravings by the author. One of 500. $450.

GILL, Eric. *Drawings from Life.* London (1940). 36 plates. $125.

GILL, Eric. *The Engravings of Eric Gill.* Wellingborough, 1983. 2 vols. One of 85. $1,250. Another one of 1,350. $300.

GILL, Eric. *An Essay on Typography.* (London, 1931.) Illustrated. Cloth. One of 500 signed. In dustwrapper. $350.

GILL, Eric. *From the Jerusalem Diary.* (London) 1953. Illustrated. Half cloth. One of 300. $250.

GILL, Eric. *Serving at Mass.* Sussex, 1916. Author's first book. Wraps. $1,200.

GILL, Eric (illustrator). See *The Four Gospels of the Lord Jesus Christ.*

GILL, Tom. *Red Earth.* New York, 1937. $100.

GILLELAND, J. C. *The Ohio and Mississippi Pilot.* Pittsburgh, 1820. 16 maps. $1,250.

GILLELEN, F. M. L. *The Oil Regions of Pennsylvania.* Pittsburgh (1865?). 17 maps (one folding), frontispiece, 3 other plates. 67 pp., wraps. $1,000.

GILLETT, James B. *Six Years with the Texas Rangers.* Austin (1921). 8 plates. Without dustwrapper. $150.

GILLIAM, Albert M. *Travels Over the Table Lands and Cordilleras of Mexico . . .* Philadelphia, 1846. 3 folding maps and 10 plates. $750.

GILPIN, William. *The Central Gold Region. The Grain, Pastoral, and Gold Regions of North America . . .* Philadelphia, 1860. 6 maps. $400.

GILPIN, William. *Mission of the North American People, Geographical, Social, and Political* . . . Philadelphia, 1873. 6 folding maps. Reprint with additions (second edition) of Gilpin's *The Central Gold Region* (1860). $150.

GINSBERG, Allen. *Ankor Wat.* London (1969). Fulcrum Press. 10 photographs by Alexandra Lawrence. One of 100 signed. $350.

GINSBERG, Allen. *Careless Love.* Madison, Wis. (1978). Wraps. One of 280 signed. $150.

GINSBERG, Allen. *Howl for Carl Solomon.* San Francisco, 1955. Wraps. (50 mimeographed copies.) Author's first book. $6,000.

GINSBERG, Allen. *Howl and Other Poems.* San Francisco (1956). Introduction by William Carlos Williams. Printed wraps. Cover price 75 cents. $500. (Note: *Howl* appeared originally as *Howl for Carl Solomon.*) San Francisco, 1971. Pictorial cloth. Issued without dustwrapper. One of 275 signed. $250.

GINSBERG, Allen. *The Moments Return.* San Francisco, 1970. Illustrated. Half cloth. One of 200. Issued without dustwrapper. $250. Half leather. One of 14 in a special binding. $750.

GINSBERG, Allen. *Planet News: 1961–1967.* San Francisco, 1968. One of 500 signed. In slipcase. $175.

GINSBERG, Allen. *Siesta in Xbalba and Return to the States.* Near Icy Cape, Alaska, July, 1956. Self-wraps, stapled. One of about 56 copies mimeographed. $4,000.

GINSBERG, Allen. *T. V. Baby Poems.* (London, 1967.) Cape Goliard Press. One of 100 signed. In dustwrapper. $300. Trade in wraps. $75. New York, 1968. Wraps. $40.

GINX'S Baby: His Birth and Other Misfortunes. London, 1870. (By John Edward Jenkins.) Author's first book. $250.

GISSING, George. See *Demos: A Story of English Socialism.*

GISSING, George. *Born in Exile.* London, 1892. 3 vols., slate gray cloth. $500.

GISSING, George. *By the Ionian Sea: Notes of a Ramble in Southern Italy.* London, 1901. Illustrated in color and black and white. White cloth. $150.

GISSING, George. *Charles Dickens: A Critical Study.* London, 1898. $200.

GISSING, George. *The Emancipated.* London, 1890. 3 vols., boards and cloth. $600.

GISSING, George. *New Grub Street.* London, 1891. 3 vols., dark green cloth. $1,250.

GISSING, George. *The Private Papers of Henry Ryecroft.* Westminster, England, 1903. With 3 ad leaves. $175. New York, 1903. $125.

GISSING, George. *Workers in the Dawn.* London, 1880. 3 vols., light brown cloth. First edition, with black endpapers. Author's first book. $4,000.

GLADSTONE, William. *The State in Its Relations with the Church.* London, 1838. Author's first book. $300.

GLASGOW, Ellen. See *The Descendant.*

GLASGOW, Ellen. *The Freeman and Other Poems.* New York, 1902. $250.

GLASGOW, Ellen. *Phases of an Inferior Planet.* New York, 1898. With erratum slip. $250.

GLEANINGS from the Inside History of the Bonanzas. (San Francisco, 1878.) 40 pp., printed wraps. $125.

GLEESON, William. *History of the Catholic Church in California.* San Francisco, 1871–72. 4 maps and plans, 9 plates. 2 vols., cloth. $350. San Francisco, 1872. 2 vols. in one. Second edition. $200.

GLENN, Allen. *History of Cass County (Missouri).* Topeka, 1917. $150.

GLISAN, R. *Journal of Army Life.* San Francisco, 1874. Folding table, 21 plates. $200.

GLOVER, Mary Baker. *Science and Health, with Key to the Scriptures.* Boston, 1875. Black or purple cloth. (By Mary Baker Eddy.) First issue, with errata slip and without index. $2,500. Lynn, Mass., 1878. Second edition. $600. Lynn, 1881. 2 vols., cloth. Third edition. $300.

GODDARD, R. H. *A Method of Reading Extreme Altitudes.* Washington, 1919. 10 plates. Wraps. $1,750.

GODWIN, Gail. *The Perfectionists.* New York (1970). Author's first book. $100.

GODWIN, William. *Essay on Sepulchres.* London, 1809. Engraved frontispiece. $300.

GODWIN, William. *Fleetwood: or, The New Man of Feeling.* London, 1805. 3 vols. $450.

GODWIN, William. *Life of Geoffrey Chaucer.* London, 1803. 2 vols. $250.

GODWIN, William. *Mandeville: A Tale of the 17th Century in England.* London, 1817. 3 vols. $500.

GODWIN, William. *Of Population . . . An Answer to Mr. Malthus' Essay.* London, 1820. $1,000.

GOFF, Frederick R. *Incunabula in American Libraries . . .* New York, 1964, with first supplement. New York, 1972. 2 vols. 1972. First edition of third census. $250.

GOGARTY, Oliver St. John. See *Alpha and Omega.*

GOGARTY, Oliver St. John. *Elbow Room.* Cuala Press. Dublin, 1939. Boards, linen spine. One of 450 in glassine dustwrapper. $150.

GOGARTY, Oliver St. John. *An Offering of Swans.* Cuala Press. Dublin, 1923. Introduction by William Butler Yeats. Boards and cloth, paper label. One of 300 in dustwrapper. $300.

GOGARTY, Oliver St. John. *Wild Apples.* Cuala Press. Dublin, 1930. Preface by William Butler Yeats. Boards and linen. One of 250 in dustwrapper. $200.

GOGOL, Nikolai. See *Homelife in Russia.*

GOLD-HUNTER'S ADVENTURE . . . (The). (By William Henry Thomes.) Boston, 1864. Author's first book. $250.

GOLD, Michael. *Jews Without Money.* New York (1930). $100.

GOLD, Silver, Lead, and Copper Mines of Arizona. (Philadelphia, 1867.) 40 pp., printed wraps. $500.

GOLDER, Frank Alfred et al. *The March of the Mormon Battalion from Council Bluffs to California . . .* New York (1928). $150.

GOLDING, W. G. (William). *Poems.* London, 1934. Wraps. Author's first book. $2,500.

GOLDING, William. *Free Fall.* London (1959). $200.

GOLDING, William. *The Inheritors.* London (1959). $300.

GOLDING, William. *Lord of the Flies.* London (1954). Red cloth. Author's first book. $1,750. New York (1954). $300.

GOLDING, William. *Pincher Martin.* London (1956). $250.

GOLDSCHMIDT, E. P. *Gothic & Renaissance Bookbindings Exemplified . . .* London/ New York, 1928. Limited to 750 copies. $500.

GOLDSCHMIDT, E. P. *The Printed Book of the Renaissance.* Cambridge, 1930. 7 plates. One of 750. $250.

GOLDSMID, Edmund. *A Bibliographical Sketch of the Aldine Press At Venice . . .* Edinburgh, 1887. Revised and corrected by Goldsmid from Renouard's *Annales De L'Imprimerie Des Aldes.* $125.

GOLDSMITH, Oliver. See Willington, James.

GOLDSMITH, Oliver. *Overland in Forty-Nine.* Detroit, 1896. 148 pp., pictorial boards. $850.

GOLDSMITH, Oliver. *She Stoops to Conquer.* London, 1773. $3,000.

GOLDSMITH, Oliver. *The Vicar of Wakefield.* Salisbury, 1766. 2 vols. $3,500. London (1929). 12 color illustrations and some in black and white by Arthur Rackham. Parchment. One of 575 signed by the artist. In slipcase. $1,000.

GOLDSTONE, Adrian H., and PAYNE, John. *John Steinbeck, A Bibliographical . . .* Austin (1974). Limited to 1,200 copies. $100.

GOLFIANA, Or a Day at Gullane. No-place. 1869. Wraps. $1,500.

GOLL, Claire. *The Diary of a Horse.* New York, 1946. 4 illustrations by Chagall. One of 320. $300.

GOLL, Yvan. *Jean Sans Terre (Landless John).* Grabhorn Press. San Francisco, 1944. Preface by Allen Tate. Translated by William Carlos Williams and others. Illustrated. Folio, boards. One of 175. $350.

GOOD, P. P. *A Materia Medica Animalia.* Cambridge, Mass., 1853. 24 color plates. $400.

GOODHUE, Bertram Grosvenor. *Book Decorations.* New York, 1931. Limited to 400 copies. $150.

GOODMAN, Mitchell. *Light from Under a Bushel.* Perishable Press. Madison, 1968. Wraps. One of 100. $200.

GOODMAN, Paul. *The Break-Up of Our Camp and Other Stories.* (Norfolk, 1949.) $100.

GOODMAN, Paul. *The Copernican Revolution.* Saugatuck, Conn. (1946). Wraps. $150.

GOODMAN, Paul. *The Drama of Awareness.* No-place, no date (late 1940s). Wraps. $150.

GOODMAN, Paul. *The Facts of Life.* New York (1945). $125.

GOODMAN, Paul. *The State of Nature.* New York (1946). $175.

GOODMAN, Paul. *Stop-light: 5 Dance Poems.* Harrington Park, N.J., 1941. In first dustwrapper (red and black without "Vinco" on the spine). $200. In later jacket. $100.

GOODMAN, Paul. *Ten Lyric Poems.* (New York, 1934.) 8 leaves, self-wraps. Author's first book. $250.

GOODNER, Ross. *The 75-Year History of Shinnecock Hills Golf Club.* Southhampton (1966). Limited to 500 copies. $100.

GOODNIGHT, Charles, III. *The Loving Brand Book.* Austin, 1965. Illustrated. Leather. One of 119. Slipcase. $400.

GOODRICH, Samuel G. See Parley, Peter.

GOODSPEED, Charles E. *Angling in America.* Boston, 1939. One of 755 signed. $500.

GOODSPEED, Charles E. *Yankee Bookseller, Being the Reminiscences of Charles E. Goodspeed.* Boston, 1937. 310 numbered and signed copies. Slipcase. $125.

GOODWIN, H. C. *Pioneer History; or Cortland County and the Border Wars of New York.* New York, 1859. 3 portraits. $100.

GOODWIN, Mrs. L. S. *The Gambler's Fate: A Story of California.* Boston, 1864. Woodcuts. 50 pp., pictorial wraps. $100.

GOODYEAR, W. A. *The Coal Mines of the Western Coast of the United States.* San Francisco, 1877. $150.

GORDIMER, Nadine. *Face to Face.* Johannesburg (1949). Author's first book. $500.

GORDIMER, Nadine. *Six Feet of Country.* London, 1956. $125. New York, 1956. $60.

GORDIMER, Nadine. *The Soft Voice of the Serpent.* New York, 1952. $100. London (1953). $150.

GORDON, Caroline. *Aleck Maury, Sportsman.* New York, 1934. First binding in green cloth. $300. Second binding in blue cloth. $200.

GORDON, Caroline. *The Forest of the South.* New York, 1945. $200.

GORDON, Caroline. *The Garden of Adonis.* New York, 1937. $300.

GORDON, Caroline. *Green Centuries.* New York, 1941. $150.

GORDON, Caroline. *None Shall Look Back.* New York, 1937. $150.

GORDON, Caroline. *Penhally.* New York, 1931. Author's first book. $1,000.

GORDON, J. E. H. *A Practical Treatise on Electric Lighting.* London, 1884. 23 plates, other illustrations. $300.

GORES, Joe. *Marine Salvage.* Garden City, 1971. $100.

GORES, Joe. *A Time of Predators.* New York, 1969. Author's first book. $125.

GOREY, Edward. See: Weary, Ogdred.

GOREY, Edward. *Amphigorey.* New York, 1972. One of 50 signed. In slipcase. With original watercolor. $750. Trade in dustwrapper. $100.

GOREY, Edward. *The Doubtful Guest.* Garden City, 1957. $100.

GOREY, Edward, *The Iron Tonic.* Albondocani Press. New York, 1969. Decorated wraps. One of 200 signed. $200.

GOREY, Edward. *The Listing Attic.* New York, 1954. $150.

GOREY, Edward. *The Object Lesson.* Garden City, 1958. $125.

GOREY, Edward. *The Sopping Thursday.* New York, 1970. Cloth. One of 26 signed and lettered copies in slipcase, with original unpublished drawing. $750. Wraps. One of 300 signed. $100.

GOREY, Edward. *The Unstrung Harp.* New York (1953). Illustrated by the author. Decorated boards. Author's first book. $150.

GOREY, Edward. *The Willowdale Handcar.* Indianapolis (1962). Illustrated. Pictorial wraps. $75.

GOREY, Edward. *The Wuggly Ump.* Philadelphia (1963). Illustrated. Oblong, pictorial boards in dustwrapper. $100.

GORHAM Golf Book. New York, 1903. $600.

GORMAN, Herbert. *James Joyce.* New York, 1924. (Note: Contains new material by Joyce.) $200.

GOSNELL, Harpur Allen (editor). *Before the Mast in the Clippers.* Derrydale Press. New York, 1937. Composed of the Diaries of Charles A. Abbey. Illustrated. Boards. One of 950. $150.

GOSSE, Philip H. *The Birds of Jamaica.* London, 1847–49. 2 vols., with 52 hand-colored plates. $10,000.

GOSSE, Philip H. *Letters from Alabama.* London, 1855. $800.

GOTHEIN, M. L. *A History of Garden Art.* London or New York (1928). Illustrated, 2 vols. $500.

GOTHEIN, Marie Luise. *A History of Garden Art.* London, 1928. 2 vols. $500.

GOTO, Seikichiro. *Japanese Paper and Papermaking.* (No-place), Bijutsushuppansha (1958). 2 vols. Cord-tied decorated stiff paper wraps contained in cloth folder. Includes 170 tipped-in woodcuts and 59 specimens of Japanese paper. $2,500.

GOTTSCHALK, Laura Riding. *The Close Chaplet.* London, 1926. Author's first book. $600. New York (1926). Tissue dustwrapper. $450. See also Riding, Laura.

GOUDY, Frederic W. *Typologia: Studies in Type Design and Type-Making.* Berkeley, 1940. Half morocco. One of 300 signed in slipcase. $250. Trade. $100.

GOUGE, William M. *The Fiscal History of Texas.* Philadelphia, 1852. $225.

GOULD, E.W. *Fifty Years on the Mississippi.* St. Louis, 1889. Frontispiece. Pictorial cloth. $300.

GOULD, John. *The Birds of Asia.* London, 1850–83. Edited by R.B. Sharpe. 530 hand-colored lithographed plates. 7 vols., folio, half (or full) morocco. $150,000.

GOULD, John. *The Birds of Australia.* London, 1837–38. 2 vols., with 20 hand-colored plates. $75,000. London, 1840–69. 8 vols. 681 hand-colored lithographed plates. Folio morocco (including 41 parts and supplement volume). $250,000.

GOULD, John. *The Birds of Great Britain.* London, 1862–73. 367 hand-colored lithographed plates. 5 vols., half morocco. $60,000.

GOULD, John. *Birds of New Guinea and the Adjacent Papuan Islands.* London, 1875–88. 320 hand-colored plates. 5 vols., folio half morocco. $90,000.

GOULD, Joseph. *The Letter-Press Printer . . .* London, 1876. $125.

GOULD, Stephen. *The Alamo City Guide.* (San Antonio), 1882. Illustrated. Pictorial wraps. $750.

GOVE, Capt. Jesse A. *The Utah Expedition, 1857–58.* Concord, N.H., 1928. 5 plates. $125. One of 50 on large paper. $300.

GOYEN, William. *The House of Breath.* New York (1950). Author's first book. $100. London, 1951. $75.

GOYEN, William. *New York* and *Work in Progress.* (Winston-Salem, 1983.) 40 signed and numbered copies. Issued without dustwrapper. $100. 160 signed copies (not numbered). $40.

GRABHORN, Edwin. *Figure Prints of Old Japan.* Book Club of California. San Francisco, 1959. 52 reproductions. Boards. Grabhorn printing. One of 400 in dustwrapper. $500.

GRABHORN, Edwin. *Landscape Prints of Old Japan.* Book Club of California. San Francisco, 1960. 52 full-color plates. Boards. Grabhorn printing. One of 450. $500.

GRABHORN, Robert. *A Short Account of the Life and Work of Wynkyn de Worde.* Grabhorn Press. San Francisco, 1949. One of 375. $500.

GRACE Darling. Carlisle, England (1843). (By William Wordsworth.) 4 pp. (foolscap folded to form pamphlet). $1,000. (Note: An unauthorized, undated reprint bearing a Newcastle imprint also exists.)

GRAFFIS, Herb. *The P.G.A.: The Official History of the Professional Golfers Association of* . . . New York (1975). $100.

GRAFTON, Sue. *"A" Is for Alibi.* New York (1982). $350.

GRAFTON, Sue. *"B" Is for Burglar.* New York (1985). $150.

GRAFTON, Sue. *Keziah Dane.* New York (1967). Author's first book. $300.

GRAHAM, Maria. *Journal of a Residence in Chile During the Year 1822 and a Voyage from Chile to Brazil in 1823.* London, 1824. With hand-colored frontispiece and 15 colored plates. $500.

GRAHAM, R. B. Cunninghame. *The District of Menteith.* Stirling (Scotland), 1930. Illustrated, including an original etching by Sir D. Y. Cameron. Folio, half calf. One of 250 signed. In dustwrapper and slipcase. $400.

GRAHAM, R. B. Cunninghame. *Notes on the District of Menteith.* London, 1895. Printed gray wraps. $150.

GRAHAM, Tom. *Hike and the Aeroplane.* New York (1912). Colored illustrations by Arthur Hutchins. Decorated cloth. (By Sinclair Lewis, his first book.) First issue, with "August, 1912" on copyright page. $1,250.

GRAHAM, W. A. *Major Reno Vindicated.* Hollywood, 1935. 30 pp., wraps. $100. One of 100 signed. Full leather. $400.

GRAHAM, W. A. (editor). *The Official Record of a Court of Inquiry Convened . . . By Request of Major Marcus A. Reno to Investigate His Conduct at the Battle of the Little Big Horn, etc.* Pacific Palisades, Calif., 1951. Multigraphed, 2 vols., folio, cloth. One of 125. $750.

GRAHAME, Kenneth. *Dream Days.* New York, 1899 (actually 1898). First issue, with 15 pages of ads at end dated 1898. $150. London and New York (1902). Illustrated by Maxfield Parrish. $150. London (1930). Illustrated by Ernest H. Shepard. Boards and vellum. One of 275 signed in slipcase. $300.

GRAHAME, Kenneth. *The Golden Age.* London, 1895. $150. London, 1900 (actually 1899). With 16 pages of ads dated 1895. Illustrated by Maxfield Parrish. $125. London, (1928). Illustrated by Ernest H. Shepard. Boards and vellum. One of 275 signed. $400. Trade. $75.

GRAHAME, Kenneth. *Pagan Papers.* London, 1894. Title page designed by Aubrey Beardsley. Author's first book. One of 450. $200.

GRAHAME, Kenneth. *The Wind in the Willows.* London (1908). Frontispiece by Graham Robertson. Pictorial cloth. $2,000. New York, 1908. $350. London (1931). Illustrated by Ernest H. Shepard. Map. Gray boards and cloth. One of 200 signed. In dustwrapper and slipcase. $1,500. Limited Editions Club, New York, 1940. Edited by A. A. Milne. Illustrated by Arthur Rackham. Boards and cloth in slipcase. $750. London, 1951. Illustrated by Rackham. Full white calf. One of 500 in slipcase. $750.

GRAINGER, M. *Grainger's New Copy-Book or, The Running Hand Made Easy.* London (no-date, circa 1730). Engraved title page, 31 engraved plates numbered 2–32. $575.

GRANT, Blanche C. (editor). *Kit Carson's Olsen Story.* Taos, 1926. Plates. 138 pp., wraps. $85.

GRANT, Maxwell. *The Living Shadow.* New York (1933). (By Walter B. Gibson.) Pictorial boards. First hardbound of *Shadow.* Issued without dustwrapper. $100.

GRANT, U. S. *Personal Memoirs.* New York, 1885–86. 2 vols., full leather. $300. Trade, cloth. $100. Half leather. $150.

GRAU, Shirley Ann. *The Black Prince and Other Stories.* New York, 1955. Author's first book. Dustwrapper without reviews. $75. With reviews. $60.

GRAVES, John. *Goodbye to a River.* New York, 1960. $100.

GRAVES, John. *Home Place.* Ft. Worth, 1958. Author's first book. Wraps. (200 copies.) $400.

GRAVES, Richard S. *Oklahoma Outlaws.* (Oklahoma City, 1915.) Illustrated. 131 pp., pictorial red wraps. $200.

GRAVES, Robert. See Riding, Laura (and Graves).

GRAVES, Robert. *Adam's Rib.* Trianon Press. (London, 1955.) 26 signed and lettered copies. In slipcase. $400. 250 signed and numbered copies. In slipcase. $250. Trade. $125. New York (1958). 100 signed and numbered copies. $200. Trade. $50.

GRAVES, Robert. *Beyond Giving: Poems.* (London) 1969. One of 536 signed copies. In dustwrapper. $125.

GRAVES, Robert. *But It Still Goes On.* London (1930). Refers to "the child she bare" first paragraph on page 157. Dustwrapper is green printed in blue and black. $300. "child she bare" deleted on page 157, which is on a stub. $200. Page 157 is not on a stub. $125. New York (1931). Dark green cloth with top edge stained black. $200.

GRAVES, Robert. *Colophon to Love Respelt.* (London) 1967. 386 signed copies. $150.

GRAVES, Robert. *Country Sentiment.* London (1920). In dustwrapper. $300. New York, 1920. Higginson called for blue boards, but we have noted two variants in dark blue pebbled cloth and in a maroon cloth. $300.

GRAVES, Robert. *The English Ballad.* London, 1927. Presumed first issue bound in bright red cloth, top edge only trimmed; height is 19.5 cm; dustwrapper height is 19.8 cm. $350. Presumed later issue bound in dull red cloth having a faded appearance; all edges trimmed; height is 19.0 cm; dustwrapper height is 19.0 cm. $300. Note: Higginson describes a book "bound in red cloth," "top edges only trimmed"; height "18.8" cm, which doesn't sound like either of above?

GRAVES, Robert. *Fairies and Fusiliers.* London (1917). Orange-red cloth stamped in gilt, publisher's imprint on spine ⅝ inch across. Secondary binding in red cloth stamped in green, publisher's imprint ¾ inch across. $750. New York, 1918. $600.

GRAVES, Robert. *The Feather Bed.* Richmond (England), 1923. 250 signed. $500.

GRAVES, Robert. *Goliath and David.* (London, 1916.) Wraps. (200 copies printed.) $2,250.

GRAVES, Robert. *Good-bye to All That.* London (1929). Contains Sassoon poem on pages 341/342/343. $1,000. Asterisks in shape of *v* mark deletions on pages 290/

341/342 and 343. $400. London (1930). Type reset to eliminate deletions. $150. New York (1930). Dustwrapper has price, this book in ads on back cover and ad for book on back flap has price. Publisher's logo stamped in middle of front cover and double-ruled lines run diagonally on both front and back covers. $250.

GRAVES, Robert. *I Claudius.* London, 1934. $750. New York, 1934. $350.

GRAVES, Robert. *Impenetrability or the Proper Habit of English.* London, 1926. $250.

GRAVES, Robert. *John Kemp's Wager: A Ballad Opera.* Oxford, 1925. Wraps. $300. One of 100 signed. $850.

GRAVES, Robert. *Lars Porsena, or The Future of Swearing and Improper Language.* London (1927). $250. New York (1927). Higginson calls for blue cloth, but seen in variant bindings. $250. London, 1972. One of 100 signed and numbered copies. In glassine dustwrapper and slipcase. $150.

GRAVES, Robert. *Lawrence and the Arabs.* London (1927). Mustard-colored (dark orange-brown color) cloth. $350. Garden City, 1928. (Later printings lack "First Edition" statement.) $200.

GRAVES, Robert. *Mock Beggar Hall.* Hogarth Press. London, 1924. $400.

GRAVES, Robert. *My Head! My Head!* London, 1925. $400. New York, 1925. $400.

GRAVES, Robert. *Over the Brazier.* London, 1916. Wraps. Author's first book. $1,250.

GRAVES, Robert. *The Pier-Glass.* London (1921). $600. New York, 1921. Bound in green cloth. $400. Orange paper-covered boards. $350.

GRAVES, Robert. *Poems 1953.* London (1953). One of 250 signed and numbered copies. Issued in transparent parchment wrapper. $300. Trade. $60.

GRAVES, Robert. *Poems (1914–1926).* London, 1927. $300. New York, 1929. $300.

GRAVES, Robert. *Poems (1914–1927).* London, 1927. One of 115 signed and numbered copies. Issued with dustwrapper in plain white slipcase. $1,000.

GRAVES, Robert. *The Real David Copperfield.* London (1933). Higginson states spine stamped in gold, Elsworth Mason states gold was trial state. $400. Spine stamped in black. $250.

GRAVES, Robert. *The Shout.* London, 1929. One of 530 signed and numbered copies. $250.

GRAVES, Robert. *Treasure Box.* (London, 1919). Plain blue wraps. $2,000.

GRAVES, Robert. *Welchman's Hose.* London, 1925. In transparent parchment dustwrapper. $400.

GRAVES, Robert. *Whipperginny.* London (1923). $350. New York, 1923. $500.

GRAVES, W. W. *Annals of Osage Mission.* St. Paul, Kan., 1935. Illustrated. $200.

GRAY, A. B. *Charter of the Texas Western Railroad Company . . .* Cincinnati, 1855. $1,750.

GRAY, Asa. *Elements of Botany.* New York, 1836. $300.

GRAY, Asa. *A Manual of the Botany of the Northern United States.* Boston, 1848. $300.

GRAY, David. *The Sporting Works of David Gray.* Derrydale Press. New York, 1929. Illustrated. 3 vols. One of 750. In slipcase. $200.

GRAY, Henry. *Anatomy, Descriptive and Surgical.* London, 1858. $1,000. Philadelphia, 1859. Illustrated. Calf. $500.

GRAY, John. *Silver Points.* London, 1893. Author's first book. (250 copies.) $650.

GRAYDON, Alexander. *Memoirs of a Life, Chiefly Passed in Pennsylvania, Within the Last 60 Years.* Harrisburg, 1811. $125. Edinburgh, 1822. $100.

GREAT Eastern Gold Mining Co. (The). New York, 1880. Map. 7 pp., wraps. $200.

GREAT Steam-Duck (The) . . . An Invention of Aerial Navigation. Louisville, 1841. By a Member of the LLBB. 32 pp. $2,500.

GREAT Trans-Continental Railroad Guide. Chicago, 1869. Wraps. $500.

GREAVES, Richard. *Brewster's Millions.* Chicago, 1903. (By George Barr McCutcheon.) $100.

GRECE, Charles F. *Facts and Observations Respecting Canada, and the United States of America.* London, 1819. $400.

GREELEY, Horace. *An Overland Journey from New York to San Francisco.* New York, 1860. $250.

GREEN, Anna Katharine. *The Circular Study.* New York, 1900. $125.

GREEN, Anna Katharine. *Hand and Ring.* New York, 1883. Wraps. $500. Cloth. $300.

GREEN, Anna Katharine. *The Leavenworth Case: A Lawyer's Story.* New York, 1878. "F" missing from "fresh," last line on page 215. Author's first book. $2,500.

GREEN, Ben K. *Back to Back.* Boards. Austin, 1970. One of 850 signed. Slipcase. $200.

GREEN, Ben K. *The Color of Horses.* Flagstaff, Ariz. (1974). Illustrated in color. Half cloth. One of 150 signed. In slipcase. $200. Trade. $60.

GREEN, Ben K. *Horse Conformation . . .* (Ft. Worth, 1963.) Author's first book. $125.

GREEN, Ben K. *The Last Trail Drive Through Downtown Dallas.* Flagstaff (1971). Illustrated. Half leather. One of 100 signed and with a Joe Beeler drawing in ink and watercolor. In slipcase. $750. Trade. $75.

GREEN, Ben K. *The Shield Mares.* Austin, 1967. One of 750 signed. In slipcase. $300.

GREEN, Ben K. *A Thousand Miles of Mustangin'.* Flagstaff (1972). One of 150 signed. Boxed. $250. Trade. $75.

GREEN, Ben K. *Wild Cow Tales.* New York, 1969. In dustwrapper. $100. One of 300 signed. $300.

GREEN, Henry. *Back.* London, 1950. $150.

GREEN, Henry. *Blindness.* London, 1926. Author's first book. $1,500. New York (1926). $300.

GREEN, Henry. *Concluding.* London, 1948. $200.

GREEN, Henry. *Nothing.* London, 1950. $150.

GREEN, Henry. *Party Going.* London, 1939. $500.

GREEN, Jonathan S. *Journal of a Tour on the Northwest Coast of America in the Year 1829.* New York, 1915. Edited by Edward Eberstadt. Boards, paper label. One of 150. $200. (Note: There were also 10 copies on Japan vellum worth more.)

GREEN Mountain Boys (The). Montpelier, Vt., 1839. (By Daniel Pierce Thompson.) 2 vols. In original boards with paper labels. Presumed first issue, with publisher's name misspelled "Waltton" in copyright notice in vol. 2. $750.

GREEN, Mowbray A. *The Eighteenth Century Architecture of Bath.* Bath, England, 1904. Plates and plans. Buckram. One of 500. $300.

GREEN, Thomas. *The Universal Herbal, or Botanical, Medical and Agricultural Dictionary.* Liverpool (1816–20). Colored plates. 2 vols., contemporary half calf, gilt paneled spines. $1,000. London, 1824. 2 vols., with frontispiece, plates, and 101 plain and 4 hand-colored plates. $500.

GREEN, Thomas J. *Journal of the Texian Expedition Against Mier.* New York, 1845. 11 plates, 2 plans. $600.

GREEN, Thomas M. *The Spanish Conspiracy.* Cincinnati, 1891. $250.

GREENAN, Edith. *Of Una Jeffers.* Los Angeles, 1939. 5 photographic illustrations. One of 250. In dustwrapper. $200.

GREENAWAY, Kate. See Harte, Bret; Mavor, William; Taylor, Jane and Ann.

GREENAWAY, Kate. *A Apple Pie.* Routledge. London (1886). Colored illustrations. Oblong, half cloth. $400.

GREENAWAY, Kate. *Almanacks.* London (1883–95 and 1897). Illustrated in color by the author. Pictorial boards, wraps, or cloth. (With no *Almanack* issued in 1896). $3,500.

GREENAWAY, Kate. *Kate Greenaway's Book of Games.* London (1889). 24 plates. Pictorial boards. $400.

GREENAWAY Kate. *Marigold Garden.* (London, 1885.) Illustrated in color by the author. Pictorial boards and cloth. $200.

GREENAWAY, Kate. *Under the Window: Pictures and Rhymes for Children.* London (1878). Colored illustrations. Pictorial boards. First issue, with printer's imprint on back of title page and "End of Contents" at foot of page 14. $250.

GREENAWAY, Kate (illustrator). *Language of Flowers.* London (1884). Colored illustrations. Boards. $250.

GREENAWAY, Kate (illustrator). *Mother Goose or The Old Nursery Rhymes.* London (1881). Illustrated in color by Kate Greenaway. Various colors of cloth, or wraps. $200.

GREENAWAY, Kate, and CRANE, Walter. *The Quiver of Love.* Marcus Ward & Co. (London, 1876.) Colored illustrations. Cloth. $600.

GREENE, Graham. See Bey, Pilaff.

GREENE, Graham. *Babbling April: Collected Poems.* Oxford, 1925. Author's first book. $3,000.

GREENE, Graham. *The Bear Fell Free.* London, 1935. One of 250 signed and numbered copies (out of 285 in total). (Dark green cloth, although the British Library copy of the unnumbered edition is black.) $1,250.

GREENE, Graham. *Brighton Rock.* New York, 1938. "Published in June 1938." Also noted with wraparound band. $500. London (1938). "Published July 1938." $2,500. (Perfect copy has sold for considerably more.)

GREENE, Graham. *Confidential Agent.* London/Toronto (1939). $750. New York, 1939. $350.

GREENE, Graham. *A Gun for Sale.* Garden City, 1936. $750. London (1936). Published one month after American edition. $1,750.

GREENE, Graham. *The Heart of the Matter.* London/Toronto (1948). $150. New York, 1948. "For the friends of Viking Press." $200. Trade. Boards covered in maroon embossed paper with spine in ivory cloth. $75.

GREENE, Graham. *It's a Battlefield.* London (1934). $1,000. Garden City, 1934. $400.

GREENE, Graham. *The Lawless Roads.* London/New York/Toronto (1939). Red cloth with letters in gold. All but 1 photograph by Greene per acknowledgment on page 8. (Photos vary in later printings.) $1,500. Second binding in red cloth with blue letters. $1,000.

GREENE, Graham. *The Man Within.* London (1929). $1,500. Garden City, 1929. Wobbe calls for a white dustwrapper printed in blue with "Advertisements for other books published by Heinemann." We believe this may have been the description of the U.K. edition (Wobbe A2) as there is no dustwrapper description under A2. The only dustwrapper we have seen on the U.S. edition is primarily green with spine blocks in light green. $600.

GREENE, Graham. *May We Borrow Your Husband?* London (1967). One of 500 signed. Issued in a clear acetate dustwrapper and slipcase. $300. Trade. $50. New York (1967). $35.

GREENE, Graham. *The Name of Action.* London (1930). Wobbe calls for price of 7s6d and dustwrapper with reviews of *The Man Within* on back cover. $3,000. With 3s6d on spine and reviews on dustwrapper flap. $1,200. Garden City, 1931. $1,500.

GREENE, Graham. *Our Man in Havana.* London (1958). $75. New York (1958). $50.

GREENE, Graham. *The Power and the Glory.* London (1940). $3,000.

GREENE, Graham. *The Quiet American.* London (1955). $100. New York, 1956. $50.

GREENE, Max. *The Kanzas Region.* New York, 1856. 2 maps. Wraps. $750. Cloth. $500.

GREENEWALT, Crawford H. *Hummingbirds.* Garden City (1960). With 69 mounted color plates. Morocco. One of 500 signed in slipcase. $600. Trade in cloth. In dustwrapper. $300.

GREENHOW, Robert. *The Geography of Oregon and California.* Boston, 1845. Folding map. Wraps. Later edition of his *Memoir.* $500.

GREENHOW, Robert. *The History of Oregon and California.* Boston, 1844. Map. Calf. Enlarged edition of his *Memoir.* $400. Boston, 1845. Wraps. "Second edition." $300.

GREENHOW, Robert. *Memoir, Historical and Political on the Northwest Coast . . .* Washington, 1840. Folding map. Sewn. (Senate Document 174.) $500.

GREER, James K. *Bois d'Arc to Barb'd Wire.* Dallas, 1936. Plates, maps. Pictorial cloth. $150.

GREER, James K. *Colonel Jack Hays: Texas Frontier Leader and California Builder.* New York, 1952. Illustrated. $125.

GREER, James K. (editor). *A Texas Ranger and Frontiersman.* Dallas, 1932. $125.

GREGG, Alexander. *History of the Old Cherraws.* New York, 1867. 4 maps. $400.

GREGG, Asa. *Personal Recollections of the Early Settlement of Wapsinonoc Township and the Murder of Atwood by the Indians.* West Liberty, Iowa (about 1875–80). Tables. Dark purple wraps. $750.

GREGG, Josiah. *Commerce of the Prairies.* New York, 1844. 2 vols, 2 folding maps, 6 plates. Brown pictorial cloth. First issue, with only New York in imprint. $1,750. Second issue, with imprint "New York and London." $1,000. New York, 1845. 2 vols. Cloth. Second edition. $750.

GREGOIRE, H. *An Enquiry Concerning the Intellectual and Moral Faculties, and Literature of Negroes.* Brooklyn, 1810. Translated by D.B. Warden. $500.

GREGORY, Horace. *Chelsea Rooming House.* New York (1930). Author's first book. $100.

GREGORY, Isabella Augusta Persse, Lady. *Coole.* Cuala Press. Dublin, 1931. Boards and linen. One of 250. In tissue dustwrapper. $150.

GREGORY, Isabella Augusta Persse, Lady. *The Kiltartan Poetry Book.* Cuala Press. Dundrum, Ireland, 1918. Boards and linen. One of 400. $150.

GREGORY, Joseph W. *Gregory's Guide for California Travellers via the Isthmus of Panama.* New York, 1850. 46 pp., wraps. $1,500.

GREGORY, Thomas Jefferson, and others. *History of Solano and Napa Counties, California.* Los Angeles, 1912. Illustrated. Maps. Three-quarters leather. $125.

GRESSENT, Professor. See Garnett, David.

GRESWELL, William Parr. *Annals of Parisian Typography* . . . London, 1818. $150.

GREVILLE, Fulke, Lord Brooke. *Caelica.* Gregynog Press. Newtown, Wales, 1936. Edited by Una Ellis-Fermor. Boards and leather. One of 225. $500. Blue morocco, specially decorated by the Gregynog bindery. $1,500.

GREY, Zane. *American Anglers in Australia.* London (1937). Code letters "B–M" on copyright page. $650.

GREY, Zane. *Betty Zane.* New York (1903). No mention of edition on the title page. Author's first book. Issued without dustwrapper. $1,200. States "Second Edition" in small letters near the center of the title page. Issued without dustwrapper. $750.

GREY, Zane. *The Day of the Beast.* New York (1922). Code letters "G–W" on copyright page and states "First Edition." $500.

GREY, Zane. *The Heritage of the Desert.* New York, 1910. No code letters on copyright page. In dustwrapper. $1,000. Without dustwrapper. $200.

GREY, Zane. *The Last of the Plainsmen.* New York, 1908. $1,250. Without dustwrapper. $250.

GREY, Zane. *Riders of the Purple Sage.* New York, 1912. In dustwrapper. $1,000. Without dustwrapper. $300. New York (1921). Code letters "K–V" on copyright page. $500.

GREY, Zane. *Tales of Fishes.* New York (1919). Code letters "F–T" on copyright page. $100.

GREY, Zane. *Tappan's Burro.* New York (1923). States first and contains code letters "I–X" on copyright page. $300.

GREYSLAER: A Romance of the Mohawk. London, 1840. (By Charles Fenno Hoffman.) 3 vols., in original boards with paper labels. $500. New York, 1840. 2 vols., in original cloth, and paper labels on spines. New York, 1840. $300.

GREYVENSTEIN, Chris. *The Fighters: A Pictorial History of South African Boxing From 1881.* Cape Town, 1981. Stated first. $50.

GRIEVE, C. M. See MacDiarmid, Hugh.

GRIEVE, C. M. *Annals of Five Senses.* Montrose (Scotland), 1923. Author's first book. $350.

GRIEVE, Maud. *A Modern Herbal.* London (1931). 96 plates. 2 vols. $600. New York, 1931. 2 vols. $500.

GRIFFIN, John H. *The Devil Rides Outside.* Fort Worth, 1952. Author's first book. $75.

GRIFFIN, Marcus. *Fall Guys: The Barnums of Bounce.* Chicago, 1937. $60.

GRIFFITH, D. W. *The Rise and Fall of Free Speech in America.* Los Angeles, 1916. Author's first book. $300.

GRIFFITH, George. *A Honeymoon in Space.* London, 1901. Pictorial cloth. $100.

GRIFFITH, Thomas W. *Sketches of the Early History of Maryland.* Baltimore, 1821. Frontispiece. $200.

GRIFFITHS, A. F. *Bibliotheca Angelo-Poetica; Or, A Descriptive Catalogue* . . . London, 1815. $175.

GRIFFITHS, D., Jr. *Two Years' Residence in the New Settlements of Ohio.* London, 1835. Frontispiece. $750.

GRILE, Dod. *Cobwebs: Being the Fables of Zambri, the Parsee.* (London, about 1884.) Heavy pictorial printed wraps, or boards. "Fun" Office. (By Ambrose Bierce.) Reprint edition of *Cobwebs from an Empty Skull.* $300.

GRILE, Dod. *Cobwebs from an Empty Skull.* London, 1874. Illustrated. Blue, brown, or green cloth. (By Ambrose Bierce.) $450.

GRILE, Dod. *The Fiend's Delight.* London (1872). (By Ambrose Bierce.) Author's first book. $600. New York (1873). Brown or purple-brown cloth. First American edition, without publisher's ads. $400.

GRILE, Dod. *Nuggets and Dust Panned Out in California.* London (1873). Yellow pictorial wraps. (By Ambrose Bierce.) $1,000.

GRIMES, Martha. *The Man With A Load of Mischief.* Boston (1981). Author's first book. $125.

GRIMKE, A. E. *Appeal to the Christian Women of the South.* (New York, 1836). Author's first book. In original wraps. $250.

GRIMM, Jacob L. K. and W. K. *The Fairy Tales of the Brothers Grimm.* London, 1909. Translated by Mrs. Edgar Lucas. Illustrated with color plates by Arthur Rackham. Vellum. One of 750 signed by Rackham. $2,000. Trade. $300.

GRIMM, Jacob L. K. and W. K. *Hansel and Gretel and Other Stories.* London, 1920. First separate edition. Without dustwrapper. $100. Illustrated by Kay Nielsen. Boards. London (1925). One of 600 signed by Nielsen. $4,000. New York, 1925. Red cloth. Issued without dustwrapper. $1,250.

GRIMM, Jacob L. K. and W. K. *Little Brother and Little Sister.* London (1917). Color plates by Arthur Rackham. One of 525 signed by Rackham, with an extra plate. $1,500. Lacking extra plate. $750. Trade. $250.

GRIMM, M. M. *German Popular Stories.* London, 1823 and 1826. Author's first book. 2 vols. First edition in English. First issue without umlaut over "a" in "marchen" on title page. $5,000.

GRIMSLEY, Will. *Golf: Its History, People, and Events.* Englewood Cliffs (1966). $60.

GRINNELL, George Bird. *The Cheyenne Indians: Their History and Way of Life.* New Haven, 1923. Illustrated. 2 vols., with a folding map and 48 plates. Without dustwrapper. $250.

GRINNELL, George Bird. *Pawnee Hero* . . . New York, 1889. Author's first book. $200.

GRINNELL, Joseph, and STORER, Tracy I. *Animal Life in the Yosemite.* Berkeley, 1924. Illustrations (some in color). Without dustwrapper. $300.

GRINNELL, Joseph et al. *The Game Birds of California.* Berkeley, 1918. 16 color plates, other illustrations. $200.

GRISWOLD, David D. *Statistics of Chicago, Ills., Together with a Business Advertiser, and Mercantile Directory for July, 1843.* (Chicago) 1843. 24 pp., printed wraps. $1,000.

GRISWOLD, Rufus W. *The Republican Court.* New York, 1856. Morocco. $175.

GRISWOLD, Wayne. *Kansas Her Resources and Developments.* Cincinnati, 1871. Illustrated. Printed wraps. $100.

GROMBACH, John V. *The Saga of Sock.* New York, 1949. $40.

GRONOW, Rees Howell. *The Reminiscences and Recollections of Captain Gronow.* London, 1889. 2 vols. One of 875. $350.

GROPIUS, Walter. *The New Architecture and the Bauhaus.* (London, 1935.) First English translation of the author's work. $350.

GROSSMITH, George. *The Diary of a Nobody.* Bristol, England (1892). Illustrated by Weedon Grossmith. Light brown cloth. $450.

GROSZ, George. *Ecce Homo.* New York, 1965. $150.

GROSZ, George. *George Grosz: Twelve Reproductions from His Original Lithographs.* Chicago, 1921. Wraps. Author's first book. $350.

GROUPED Thoughts and Scattered Fancies. Richmond, Va., 1845. (By William Gilmore Simms.) Wraps. $350.

GROVER, La Fayette (editor). *The Oregon Archives.* Salem, 1853 (actually 1854). Printed yellow wraps. $1,250.

GROWOLL, A. *Three Centuries Of English Booktrade Bibliography* . . . New York, 1903. One of 550 numbered copies. $100.

GRUBB, Davis. *The Night of the Hunter.* (New York, 1953.) Author's first book. 1,000 signed. $125. Regular trade. $75. London (1954). $50.

GRUBB, Davis. *Twelve Tales of Suspense and the Supernatural.* New York (1964). $100.

GRUBER, Frank. *Peace Marshall.* New York, 1939. Author's first book. $150.

GRUMBACH, Doris. *The Short Throat, The Tender Mouth.* Garden City, 1964. $150.

GRUMBACH, Doris. *The Spoil of the Flowers.* Garden City, 1962. Author's first book. $150.

GUERIN, Maurice de. *The Centaur.* (Montague, Mass.) 1915. Translated by George B. Ives. Boards. One of 135. Bruce Rogers typography. $1,250.

GUIDE, Gazetteer and Directory of Nebraska Railroads. Omaha, 1872. Folding map, 6 plates. 210 pp., wraps. (By J. M. Wolfe.) $400.

GUIDE for Emigrants to Minnesota (A). By a Tourist. St. Paul, 1857. Map. 16 pp., printed blue wraps. $250.

GUILD, Jo. C. *Old Times in Tennessee.* Nashville, 1878. Green cloth. $200.

GUINEY, Louise Imogen. *"Monsieur Henri." A Footnote to French History.* New York, 1892. One of 50 signed. $250.

GUINEY, Louise Imogen. *Songs at the Start.* Boston, 1884. Author's first book. Half morocco. $150. Cloth. $100.

GUNN, Otis B. *New Map and Hand-Book of Kansas and the Gold-Mines.* Pittsburgh, 1859. Large map in color, folding into black cloth covers, and accompanied by text pamphlet *(Gunn's Map and Hand-Book . . .),* bound in salmon-colored printed wraps. $3,500. Lacking the text pamphlet, $2,500.

GUNN, Thom. *Fighting Terms.* (Oxford, 1954.) First issue, final *t* in "thought" omitted on first line on page 38. Yellow cloth issued without dustwrapper. $400. Second issue, corrected. $250. Wraps. $175.

GUNN, Thom. *A Geography.* Iowa City, 1966. Wraps. One of 220 signed. $300.

GUNN, Thom. *Mandrakes.* London (1973). Illustrated by Leonard Baskin. Half vellum. One of 150 signed. In slipcase. $600.

GUNN, Thom. *(Poems.)* Fantasy Press. Oxford, 1953. Author's first book. Wraps. $850.

GUNNISON, John W. *The Mormons; or, Latter-Day Saints, in the Valley of the Great Salt Lake.* Philadelphia, 1852. Frontispiece. Dark blue cloth. $350.

GUNSAULUS, Helen C. *The Clarence Buckingham Collection of Japanese Prints: The Primitives.* Chicago (1955). Plates. Folio, cloth. One of 500. $1,500.

GUTENBERG Bible. New York, 1968. 3-vol. facsimile. Slipcase. $225.

GUTHRIE, A. B., Jr. *The Big Sky.* New York, 1947. One of 500 signed. In dustwrapper. $150. Trade. $100.

GUTHRIE, A. B., Jr. *Murders at Moon Dance.* New York, 1943. Author's first book. $450.

GUTHRIE, A. B., Jr. *The Way West.* New York, 1949. $150.

GUTHRIE, Ramon. *Trobar Clus.* Northampton, 1923. Author's first book. One of 250 signed. In dustwrapper. $150. Lacking jacket. $75.

GUTHRIE, Woody. *Bound For Glory.* New York, 1945. Author's first book. $150.

GUY Rivers: A Tale of Georgia. New York, 1834. (By William Gilmore Simms.) 2 vols. $150.

H

H., H. (translator). *Bathmendi: A Persian Tale.* Boston, 1867. Translated from the French of Florian. Printed wraps. (Translated by Helen Hunt Jackson), her first publication. $200.

H., H. *Verses.* Boston, 1870. (By Helen Hunt Jackson.) Author's first book. $250.

HABBERTON, John. *Helen's Babies.* Boston, 1876. Author's first book. Wraps. First issue measures $1^3/_{16}$ inches thick. $250.

HABERLY, Loyd. *Anne Boleyn, and Other Poems.* Gregynog Press. Newtown, Wales, 1934. Printed in red and black on handmade paper. Niger morocco. One of 300. $500. One of 15 (from the edition) elaborately bound. $1,250.

HABERLY, Loyd. *Artemis: A Forest Tale.* Mound City Press. (St. Louis, 1942.) Illustrated in color by Haberly. Full green morocco. One of 240. $200.

HABERLY, Loyd. *The Crowning Years and Other Poems.* Stoney Down (England), 1937. Half morocco. (150 copies.) $300.

HABERLY, Loyd. *Medieval English Pavingtiles.* Oxford, 1937. Half morocco. One of 425. $600.

HABERLY, Loyd. *Poems.* Seven Acres Press. Long Crendon, 1930. Dark blue morocco. One of 120. $400.

HACKENSCHMIDT, George. *Complete Science of Wrestling.* London (no-date). $50.

HACKETT, James. *Narrative of the Expedition Which Sailed from England in 1817, to Join the South American Patriots.* London, 1818. $300.

HAEBLER, Konrad. *The Early Printers of Spain and Portugal.* London, 1897 (1896). 33 plates reproducing title pages. $150.

HAFEN, LeRoy R. (editor). *The Mountain Men and the Fur Trade of the Far West.* Glendale, Calif., 1965-72. 10 vols. In plain dustwrappers. $750.

HAFEN, LeRoy R. *The Overland Mail, 1849-1869.* Cleveland, 1926. Map, 7 plates. Issued without dustwrapper. $200.

HAFEN, LeRoy R. *Overland Routes to the Gold Fields.* Glendale, 1942. 7 plates, folding map. Cloth. Issued without dustwrapper. $100.

HAFEN, LeRoy R. and Ann W. (editors). *The Far West and the Rockies, 1820-75.* Glendale, 1954-61. 15 vols. $1,250.

HAFEN, LeRoy R., and GHENT, W. J. *Broken Hand: The Life Story of Thomas Fitzpatrick, Chief of the Mountain Men.* Denver, 1931. Map, 8 plates. Cloth-backed boards. One of 100 large paper copies, signed. $300. Cloth. One of 500. In dustwrapper. $150.

HAFEN, LeRoy R., and YOUNG, Francis Marion. *Fort Laramie and the Pageant of the West, 1834–1890.* Glendale, 1938. $125.

HAFEN, Mary Ann. *Recollections of a Handcart Pioneer of 1860.* Denver, 1938. Plates. Cloth. Issued without dustwrapper. $200.

HAGEDORN, Herman, Jr. *The Silver Blade.* Berlin, 1907. Author's first book. Wraps. $100.

HAGEN, Walter. *Walter Hagen Story.* New York, 1956. $100.

HAGGARD, H. Rider. *Allan Quatermain.* London, 1887. With 20 full-page illustrations. Blue cloth. With no footnote on the frontispiece. $750. Brown pebbled cloth. One of 112 on large paper. $1,500. New York, 1887. Wraps. $300.

HAGGARD, H. Rider. *Allan's Wife and Other Tales.* London, 1889. One of 100 on large paper. In red cloth. $350. Trade in brown pebbled cloth. $200.

HAGGARD, H. Rider. *Black Heart and White Heart and Other Stories.* London, 1900. $200.

HAGGARD, H. Rider. *Cetywayo and His White Neighbours.* London, 1882. Author's first book. (750 copies.) $600.

HAGGARD, H. Rider. *Cleopatra.* London, 1889. Morocco spine and brown cloth. One of 57 on large paper. $450. Trade in blue cloth. $150.

HAGGARD, H. Rider. *Colonel Quaritch, V.C.: A Tale of Country Life.* London, 1888. 3 vols., red cloth. $500. London, 1889. 1 vol. $150.

HAGGARD, H. Rider. *Dawn.* London, 1884. 3 vols., olive-green cloth. Author's first novel. $9,500 at auction in 1990. London, 1887. 1 vol. $150.

HAGGARD, H. Rider. *Heart of the World.* New York, 1895. Green cloth. $150. London, 1896. Blue cloth. $100.

HAGGARD, H. Rider. *Jess.* London, 1887. Red cloth. $300.

HAGGARD, H. Rider. *King Solomon's Mines.* London, 1885. Folding colored frontispiece, map. Bright red cloth. First issue, with the ads dated "5G.8.85." $7,500. Second issue, with ads dated "5G.10.85." $1,500.

HAGGARD, H. Rider. *Mr. Meeson's Will.* London, 1888. Red cloth. With "Johnson" for "Johnston" in line 1 of page 284. $150. New York, 1888. Wraps. (May have preceded English.) $150.

HAGGARD, H. Rider. *Montezuma's Daughter.* London, 1893. Blue cloth. $125.

HAGGARD, H. Rider. *She: A History of Adventure.* New York, 1886. Printed wraps. $500. London, 1887. Illustrated. Blue cloth. First English edition, first issue, with "Godness me" in line 38, page 269. $250.

HAGGARD, H. Rider. *The Witch's Head.* London, 1885. 3 vols., gray cloth. $8,800 at auction in 1990.

HAINES, Elijah M. *The American Indian.* Chicago, 1888. Half morocco. $100.

HAINES, Elijah M. *Historical and Statistical Sketches of Lake County, State of Illinois.* Waukegan, Ill., 1852. Folding frontispiece. 112 pages, printed wraps. $300.

HAKEWILL, James. *A Picturesque Tour of the Island of Jamaica.* London, 1825. 21 colored aquatint plates. $3,500.

HAKEWILL, James. *A Picturesque Tour of Italy.* London, 1820. With engraved title and 63 plates. Folio. $750.

HALDANE, Charlotte. *Man's World.* London, 1926. Author's first book. $150.

HALE, Edward Everett. See *The Man Without a Country; Margaret Percival In America.*

HALE, Edward Everett. *Kanzas and Nebraska.* Boston, 1854. Folding map. $150.

HALE, Edward Everett. *A Tract for the Day: How to Conquer Texas Before Texas Conquers Us.* Boston, 1845. 16 pp., self-wraps. $150.

HALE, John. *California as It Is.* Grabhorn Press. San Francisco, 1954. One of 150. $175.

HALE, Lucretia P. *The Peterkin Papers.* Boston, 1880. Illustrated by F.G. Attwood. $250.

HALE, Sarah Josepha. See *The Genius of Oblivion.*

HALE, Sarah Josepha. *Northwood: A Tale of New England.* Boston, 1827. 2 vols. $150.

HALE, Sarah Josepha (editor). *The Good Little Boy's Book.* New York (about 1848). Printed flexible boards. $125.

HALE, Will. *Twenty-four Years a Cowboy and Ranchman in Southern Texas and Old Mexico.* Hedrick (Headrick), Oklahoma Territory (1905). 268 pp., stiff purplish blue wraps. (By William Hale Stone.) $5,000.

HALEY, Alex. *Roots.* Garden City, 1976. In full leather. Author's first book. One of 500 signed. In slipcase. $200. Trade. $40.

HALEY, J. Evetts. *Charles Goodnight, Cowman and Plainsman.* Boston, 1936. Illustrated by Harold Bugbee. $150.

HALEY, J. Evetts. *Charles Schriener, General Merchandise: The Story of a Country Store.* Austin, 1944. Illustrated by Harold Bugbee. $175.

HALEY, J. Evetts. *Fort Concho on the Texas Frontier.* San Angelo, 1952. Illustrated by Harold Bugbee. One of 185 signed. In dustwrapper and slipcase. $600. Trade edition. $200.

HALEY, J. Evetts. *The Heraldry of the Range.* Canyon, Tex., 1949. Illustrated by Harold Bugbee. $500.

HALEY, J. Evetts. *Life on the Texas Range.* Austin, 1952. Photographs by Erwin E. Smith. Pictorial cloth. In slipcase. $150.

HALEY, J. Evetts. *The XIT Ranch of Texas.* Chicago, 1929. 2 maps, 30 plates. Author's first book. $400.

HALFORD, Frederic M. *Dry Fly Entomology.* London, 1897. With 18 plain and 28 hand-colored plates, and 100 artificial flies in sunken mounts. 2 vols., morocco. One of 100 copies, signed. $3,500.

HALFORD, Frederic M. *The Dry-Fly Man's Handbook.* London, 1913. Illustrated. Leather and cloth. One of 100 signed. $1,000.

HALFORD, Frederic M. *Modern Development of the Dry Fly.* London (1910). With 43 plates, and 33 mounted flies, 9 in sunken mounts. 2 vols., leather and cloth. One of 75 signed. In slipcase. $4,000.

HALIBURTON, Thomas Chandler. See *The Clockmaker.*

HALKETT, John. *Statement Respecting the Earl of Selkirk's Settlement of Kildonan . . .* London (1817). Folding map. First issue without a printer or date on title. $1,000.

HALKETT, Samuel, and LAING, John. *Dictionary of Anonymous and Pseudonymous English Literature.* Edinburgh, 1926–1962. New and revised edition by Dr. James Kennedy et al. 9 vols. Complete with index and second supplement volume and other supplements to 1960. $750.

HALL, Arthur Vine. *Table Mountain . . .* Capetown (1896). Author's first book. $175.

HALL, Basil. *The Great Polyglot Bibles.* Book Club of California. San Francisco, 1966. Folio, loose in wraps. One of 400. In slipcase. $600.

HALL, Capt. Basil. *Forty Etchings, from Sketches made with the Camera Lucida, in North America, in 1827 and 1828.* Edinburgh, 1829. Folding map, 40 etchings on 20 plates. $400.

HALL, Capt. Basil. *Travels in North America.* Edinburgh, 1829. Colored folding map, folding table, 3 vols. $300. Philadelphia, 1829. Illustrated. 2 vols. $200.

HALL, Carroll D. (editor). *Donner Miscellany.* Book Club of California. San Francisco, 1947. (Printed by the Allen Press.) One of 350. $250.

HALL, Donald. *Exile.* Swinford (1952). Wraps. $200.

HALL, Donald. *Exiles and Marriages.* New York, 1955. $75.

HALL, Donald. *(Poems.)* Fantasy Poets No. 4. Oxford (1952). Wraps. $200.

HALL, Edward H. *The Great West . . .* New York, 1864. Map. 89 pp. with folding map, printed wraps. $600.

HALL, Francis. *Travels in Canada and the United States in 1816 and 1817.* London, 1818. Folding map. $300. Boston, 1818. First American edition. $200.

HALL, Frederic. *The History of San Jose and Surroundings.* San Francisco, 1871. With folding map and 4 plates. $300.

HALL, George Eli. *A Balloon Ascension at Midnight.* San Francisco, 1902. Illustrated by Gordon Ross. One of 30 on vellum, signed. $750. One of 1,175. $150.

HALL, Halworthy. *Dormie One.* New York, 1917. $250. Limited edition. 1944. $150.

HALL, Henry (editor). *The Tribune Book of Open-Air Sports.* New York, 1887. (This is the first book printed without using movable type.) $250.

HALL, James. *Letters from the West.* London, 1828. $500.

HALL, James. *Notes on the Western States.* Philadelphia, 1838. In original cloth. (Later edition of *Statistics of the West.*) $250.

HALL, James. *Sketches of History, Life, and Manners in the West. Vol. 1.* (All published.) Cincinnati, 1834. $350. Philadelphia, 1835. Frontispiece. 2 vols. First complete edition. $400.

HALL, James. *Statistics of the West.* Cincinnati, 1836. Purple cloth. $150.

HALL, James Norman. See Nordhoff, Charles B. (For *Mutiny on the Bounty.*)

HALL, James Norman. *Kitchener's Mob.* Boston, 1916. Author's first book. In dustwrapper. $350. Without dustwrapper. $60.

HALL, James Norman, and NORDHOFF, Charles B. (editors). *The Lafayette Flying Corps.* Boston, 1920. Illustrated, including colored plates. 2 vols., blue cloth. In dustwrapper. $750.

HALL, Manly P. *An Encyclopedic Outline of Masonic, Cabbalistic and Rosicrucian Symbolical Philosophy.* San Francisco, 1928. Colored plates, text illustrations. Folio boards and vellum. John Henry Nash printing. One of 550 signed. In slipcase. $500.

HALL, Marguerite Radclyffe. *The Forgotten Island.* London, 1915. $100.

HALL, (Marguerite) Radclyffe. *The Master of the House.* London (1932). Buckram, vellum spine. One of 172 signed. $350. Trade. $125. New York (1932). $100.

HALL, Marguerite Radclyffe. *Poems of the Past and Present.* London, 1910. $200.

HALL, Marguerite Radclyffe. *A Sheaf of Verses.* London, 1908. $200.

HALL, Marguerite Radclyffe. *'Twixt Earth and Stars.* London, 1906. Author's first book. $200.

HALL, (Marguerite) Radclyffe. *The Well of Loneliness.* London (1928). First state, with "whip" for "whips" on page 50, line 3. In dustwrapper. $300. New York, 1928. Boards and cloth. One of 500. In slipcase. Issued simultaneously. $150. New York, 1929. 2 vols., half cloth. One of 225 signed. In slipcase. $350.

HALL, Marshall. *New Memoir on the Nervous System.* London, 1843. 5 plates. $200.

HALL, Marshall. *Principles of the Theory and Practice of Medicine.* Boston, 1839. $150. (Contains new material by Oliver Wendell Holmes.)

HALL, Samuel R. *Lectures to Female Teachers on School-Keeping.* Boston, 1832. $150.

HALL, Samuel R. *Lectures on School-Keeping.* Boston, 1829. $150.

HALLECK, Fitz-Greene. See Croaker. See also *Alnwick Castle; Fanny.*

HALLENBECK, Cleve. *The Journal of Fray Marcos de Niza.* Dallas, 1949. $150.

HALPER, Albert. *Chicago Side-Show.* New York, 1932. Author's first book. (110 copies.) Wraps. $250.

HALSEY, R. T. H. *Pictures of Early New York on Dark Blue Staffordshire Pottery* . . . New York, 1899. 155 illustrations, mostly in color. One of 268 on hand-made paper. $350. One of 30 on vellum. $750.

HALSTEAD, Murat. *The Caucuses of 1860.* Columbus, Ohio, 1860. $125.

HAMADY, Walter. *The Disillusioned Solipsist.* Mt. Horeb, 1954. Author's first book. (60 copies.) (Also first Pershable Press.) $2,000.

HAMADY, Walter. *Hand Papermaking.* Perry, 1982. Limited to 200 numbered copies and signed by the author beneath the plate on page 19. 9 leaves of paper samples. $450.

HAMBLETON, Chalkley J. *A Gold Hunter's Experience.* Chicago, 1898. Green cloth. $500.

HAMERTON, Philip G. *Etching and Etchers.* London, 1868. Illustrated. Half morocco. $1,250. London, 1880. Third edition. (With a Whistler etching.) $750.

HAMILTON, Dr. Alexander (1712–56). *Hamilton's Itinerarium.* St. Louis, 1907. Map. Half leather. One of 487. In slipcase. $150.

HAMILTON, Clive. *Spirits in Bondage.* London, 1919. Author's first book. $300.

HAMILTON, Edmond. *The Horror on the Asteroid.* London, 1936. Author's first book. $600.

HAMILTON, Edmond. *The Metal Giants.* Swanson Book Co., Washborn, North Dakota (1932). 40 mimeographed pages issued as science fiction reprints no. 1, but no other printing known. His first book. $350.

HAMILTON, Gail. *Country Living and Country Thinking.* Boston, 1862. By Mary Abigail Dodge, her first book. $150.

HAMILTON, Gail. *Gala-Days.* Boston, 1863. (By Mary Abigail Dodge.) $125.

HAMILTON, Gail. *A Woman's Wrongs: A Counter-Irritant.* Boston, 1868. (By Mary Abigail Dodge.) $150.

HAMILTON, Gerald. See Weston, Patrick.

HAMILTON, H. W. *Rural Sketches of Minnesota.* Milan, Ohio, 1850. 40 pp., printed wraps. $750.

HAMILTON, John P. *Travels Through the Interior Provinces of Colombia.* London, 1827. Map, 7 plates. 2 vols. $400.

HAMILTON, Patrick. *The Resources of Arizona.* Prescott, 1881. 120 pp., gray wraps. Second edition. $200. San Francisco, 1884. Folding map. Cloth. Third edition. $200. (For first edition, see title entry under "R.")

HAMILTON, Sinclair. *Early American Book Illustrators and Wood Engravers 1679–1870.* Princeton (1970), 1968. 2 vols. Third and first printings, respectively. $375.

HAMILTON, W. T. *My Sixty Years on the Plains.* New York, 1905. Edited by E. T. Sieber. 8 plates (6 by Charles M. Russell). $200.

HAMILTON, Walter. *Dated Book-Plates (Ex Libris) with a Treatise on Their Origin and Development.* London, 1895. $100.

HAMILTON, The Rev. William, and IRVIN, the Reverend S. M. *An Ioway Grammar.* Iowa and Sac Mission Press. (Wolf Creek, Neb.), 1848. Wraps. $1,500.

HAMMER, William J. *Radium, and Other Radio-Active Substances.* New York, 1903. $200.

HAMMETT, Dashiell. *The Dain Curse.* New York, 1929. With "dopped in" for "dropped in" in line 19 of page 260. (May be in all copies of the first edition.) $2,750. London, 1930. "First published 1930 . . ." Richard Layman calls for a skull and crossbones on front upper right-hand corner but also noted without this. $1,250.

HAMMETT, Dashiell. *The Glass Key.* London/New York, 1931. (Published January 20.) $1,000. New York/London, 1931. (Published April 24.) $1,750.

HAMMETT, Dashiell. *The Maltese Falcon.* New York/London, 1930. $3,250. London/New York, 1930. $1,000.

HAMMETT, Dashiell. *Red Harvest.* New York, 1929. Author's first book. $2,500.

HAMMETT, Dashiell. *Secret Agent X-9.* (Book One.) Philadelphia (1934). Issued without dustwrapper. $500.

HAMMETT, Dashiell. *Secret Agent X-9.* (Book Two.) Philadelphia (1934). Issued without dustwrapper. $400.

HAMMETT, Dashiell. *The Thin Man.* New York, 1934. No priority on dustwrapper color. $1,500. London, 1934. $600.

HAMMETT, Dashiell, and COLODNY, Robert. *The Battle of the Aleutians.* (San Francisco, 1944.) Blue wraps. $300.

HAMMOND, John Martin. *Colonial Mansions of Maryland and Delaware.* Philadelphia, 1914. 65 plates. $250.

HANCOCK, H. Irving, and HIGASHI, K. *The Complete Kano Jiu Jitsu.* New York, 1926. $100.

HANCOCK, R. R. *Hancock's Diary: or, a History of the 2d Tennessee Confederate Cavalry.* Nashville, 1887. 2 plates. $150.

HAND Book of Monterey and Vicinity (The). Monterey, 1875. 152 pp., printed wraps. $150.

HAND-BOOK of Ness County, the Banner County of Western Kansas. Chicago, 1887. 36 pp., wraps. $250.

HANDLEY Cross: or, Mr. Jorrock's Hunt. London, 1853–54. (By Robert Smith Surtees.) 17 color plates and numerous woodcuts by John Leech. 17 parts in pictorial wraps. First illustrated edition. With all the ads and slips and with the words "with the aid of the illustrious Leech" in the preface. $2,000. London, 1854. Cloth. First illustrated hardbound edition. $500.

HANDLEY Cross: or, The Spa Hunt. London, 1843. 3 vols., boards and cloth. (By Robert Smith Surtees.) $400.

HANDMADE Papers of the World. Tokyo, 1979. Large folio box containing 6 books and cases. One of 1,100 numbered copies. $1,750.

HANDY, W. C. *Blues: An Anthology.* New York, 1926. Author's first book. Edited by Handy. $300.

HANLEY, James. *Boy.* London, 1931. $150. One of 145. $250. One of 15 signed. $450.

HANLEY, James. *Captain Bottell.* London, 1933. One of 99 signed. In dustwrapper. $300.

HANLEY, James. *Drift.* London, 1930. Author's first book. (10 signed copies.) $1,000. Trade (490 copies). $150.

HANLEY, James. *Men in Darkness.* London (1931). Preface by John Cowper Powys. One of 105 signed. $300.

HANNA, Charles A. *The Wilderness Trail* . . . New York, 1911. Maps and illustrations. 2 vols. One of 1,000. $300.

HANNAH, Barry. *Geronimo Rex.* New York (1972). Author's first book. $125.

HANNOVER, Emil. *Pottery and Porcelain: A Handbook for Collectors.* London, 1925. 3 vols., cloth. Issued without dustwrappers. $400.

HANSARD, T. C. *Treatises on Printing and Type-Founding.* Edinburgh, 1841. 3 fold-out plates. $175.

HANSARD, Thomas C. *Typographia: An Historical Sketch of the Art of Printing* . . . London, 1825. $350.

HARDIE, Martin. *English Coloured Books.* London (1906). $125.

HARDIN, John Wesley. *The Life of John Wesley Hardin.* Seguin, Tex., 1896. Portrait, other illustrations. 144 pp., printed wraps. First issue, with portrait of Hardin's brother mislabeled "John." $250. Second issue, with the Hardin portrait tipped in. $150.

HARDIN, Mrs. Philomelia Ann Maria Antoinette. *Everybody's Cook and Receipt Book.* (Cleveland, 1842.) In original printed boards. $500.

HARDING, George L. *Don Augustin V. Zamorano: Statesman, Soldier, Craftsman, and California's First Printer.* Los Angeles, 1934. $250.

HARDWICK, Elizabeth. *The Ghostly Loves.* New York, 1945. Author's first book. $250.

HARDY, John. *A Collection of Sacred Hymns, Adapted to the Faith and Views of the Church of Jesus Christ of Latter Day Saints.* Boston, 1843. 160 pp., full calf. $2,500.

HARDY, Joseph. *A Picturesque and Descriptive Tour in the Mountains of the High Pyrenees.* London, 1825. Map, 24 hand-colored plates. $500.

HARDY, Thomas. See *Desperate Remedies; Under the Greenwood Tree.*

HARDY, Thomas. *A Changed Man.* London, 1913. Frontispiece and map. Green cloth. $250. New York, 1913. Blue cloth. $100.

HARDY, Thomas. *The Dynasts: A Drama of the Napoleonic Wars.* London, 1903–6–8. 3 vols., green cloth. First issue, with 1903 on title page of vol. 1. $1,500. London, 1927. Portrait etching, signed by Francis Dodd, 3 vols., half vellum. One of 525 signed by Hardy. In clear dustwrappers. $750.

HARDY, Thomas. *Far from the Madding Crowd.* London, 1874. 12 illustrations by H. Patterson. 2 vols., pictorial green cloth. $3,500. Limited Editions Club, New York, 1958. Half leather. In slipcase. $125.

HARDY, Thomas. *The Hand of Ethelberta.* London, 1876. 11 illustrations by George Du Maurier. 2 vols., terra-cotta cloth. First issue, with "two or three individuals" instead of "five or six individuals" in caption facing page 146 in vol. 1 (VAB). $1,000.

HARDY, Thomas. *Human Shows: Far Phantasies; Songs and Trifles.* London, 1925. $175.

HARDY, Thomas. *Jude the Obscure.* (London, 1896.) Map, etching by H. Macbeth-Raeburn. Green cloth. First issue, with Osgood's name on title page and spine (VAB). $350. New York, 1896. $100. Limited Editions Club, New York, 1969. In slipcase. $75.

HARDY, Thomas. *A Laodicean; or, The Castle of the De Stancys.* London, 1881. 3 vols., slate-colored cloth. First issue, without the word "or" on half title of vol. 1. $1,250. Second issue, with the word "or" on half title of vol. 1. $750.

HARDY, Thomas. *Late Lyrics and Earlier.* London, 1922. In dustwrapper. $200.

HARDY, Thomas. *Life's Little Ironies.* London (1894). $200. New York, 1894. $125.

HARDY, Thomas. *The Mayor of Casterbridge.* London, 1886. 2 vols., blue cloth. $3,500. New York, 1886. Wraps. First American edition. $400. Limited Editions Club, New York, 1964. Half morocco. In slipcase. $100.

HARDY, Thomas. *Moments of Vision and Miscellaneous Verses.* London, 1917. $250.

HARDY, Thomas. *A Pair of Blue Eyes.* London, 1873. 3 vols. First issue, in green cloth, with "c" dropped or missing from the word "clouds" in last line on page 5 of vol. 2. $5,000. Second issue, in blue cloth. $1,500.

HARDY, Thomas. *Poems of the Past and the Present.* (London, 1902.) White (cream) or dark green cloth. $400.

HARDY, Thomas. *The Return of the Native.* London, 1878. Frontispiece map. 3 vols., brown cloth. First binding, with double blind rule on back cover (VAB). First issue lacking single quote mark after "A Pair of Blue Eyes" on title page (Cutler & Stiles). First binding with triple blind frame on back. (Second had double) (Sadleir). $6,000. Second binding. $5,000. New York, 1878. Cream-colored cloth. $500. London, 1929. Illustrated by Clare Leighton. Batik boards, vellum spine. One of 500 signed by the artist. In slipcase. $300. American issue: Buckram. One of 1,000 signed. $200.

HARDY, Thomas. *Tess of the D'Urbervilles.* (London, 1891.) 3 vols., brownish yellow cloth with gilt design on cover. With "Chapter XXV" for "Chapter XXXV" and with "road" for "load" on page 198, vol. 3 (VAB). $6,000. (London, 1892.) Second issue, with corrections and dated 1892. $1,500. New York, 1892. $400. London, 1926. 41 wood engravings by Vivien Gribble, folding map. Marbled boards, vellum spine. One of 325 signed. In dustwrapper. $600.

HARDY, Thomas. *The Trumpet-Major.* London, 1880. 3 vols., decorated red cloth. $15,000 at auction in 1990. New York, 1880. $250.

HARDY, Thomas. *Two on a Tower: A Romance.* London, 1882. 3 vols., green cloth. $7,500. New York, 1882. Decorated yellow cloth. $300.

HARDY, Thomas. *Wessex Tales, Strange, Lively and Commonplace.* London, 1888. 2 vols., green cloth. $1,500.

HARDY, Thomas. *The Woodlanders.* London, 1887. 3 vols. First binding in smooth dark green cloth. First issue, with ad leaf at end of vol. 1 (VAB). $1,750. Second binding, pebbled dark green cloth. $1,000.

HARFORD, Henry. *Fan: The Story of a Young Girl's Life.* London, 1892. (By W. H. Hudson.) 3 vols., sage green cloth. $7,500.

HARGRAVE, Catherine Perry. *A History of Playing Cards . . .* Boston (1930). $350.

HARLAN, Jacob Wright. *California, '46 to '88.* San Francisco, 1888. Portrait frontispiece. $150.

HARLAN, Robert D. (editor). *Bibliography of the Grabhorn Press . . .* San Francisco, 1972. Full calf with raised design and leather onlay. The third and final volume of the Grabhorn bibliography. $850.

HARLAND, John Whitfield. *The Printing Arts, An Epitome of the Theory . . .* London, 1892. 12 plates. $150.

HARLAND, Marion. *Alone.* Richmond, 1854. Author's first book. $350.

HARLOW, Alvin F. *Old Towpaths.* New York, 1926. Illustrated. $125.

HARLOW, Neal. *The Maps of San Francisco Bay.* Grabhorn Press. San Francisco, 1950. Folio, half leather. One of 375. In dustwrapper. $600.

HARMAN, S. W. *Hell on the Border.* Fort Smith, Ark. (1898). Portrait, map. Stiff printed green wraps. $500.

HARMON, Daniel Williams. *A Journal of Voyages and Travels in the Interiour* [*sic*] *of North America.* Andover, Mass., 1820. Portrait, folding map. First issue, with map placed opposite title page and with no errata slip. $500.

HAROLD the Dauntless. Edinburgh, 1817. Boards. (By Sir Walter Scott.) $250.

HARPEL, Oscar H. *Harpel's Typography or Book of Specimens . . .* Cincinnati, 1870. $1,200.

HARPER, Frances E. W. *Iola Leroy, or Shadows Uplifted.* Philadelphia, 1892. Author's first book. $300.

HARRIS, Frank. *Elder Conklin and Other Stories.* New York, 1894. Author's first book. $75. London, 1895. $50.

HARRIS, Frank. *The Man Shakespeare and His Tragic Life Story.* London, 1909. Boards and vellum. One of 150 on large paper, signed. $125. Trade in green cloth. $50.

HARRIS, Frank. *Oscar Wilde: His Life and Confessions.* New York, 1916. 2 vols. Japan paper issue. In half morocco and slipcase. $175.

HARRIS, Henry. *California's Medical Story.* Grabhorn Press. San Francisco, 1932. Half morocco. One of 200. $125.

HARRIS, Joel Chandler. See Davidson, James Wood.

HARRIS, Joel Chandler. *Daddy Jake the Runaway.* New York (1889). Pictorial cream-colored glazed boards. $450. London, 1890 (actually 1889). $250.

HARRIS, Joel Chandler. *Free Joe and Other Georgian Sketches.* New York, 1887. Pictorial red cloth. $250.

HARRIS, Joel Chandler. *Nights with Uncle Remus.* Boston, 1883. Pictorial gray cloth. $350.

HARRIS, Joel Chandler. *On the Plantation.* New York, 1892. Pictorial cloth. $150.

HARRIS, Joel Chandler. *Tales of the Home Folks in Peace and War.* Boston, 1898. $150.

HARRIS, Joel Chandler. *The Tar-Baby and Other Rhymes of Uncle Remus.* New York, 1904. $250.

HARRIS, Joel Chandler. *Uncle Remus and Brer Rabbit.* New York (1906). Oblong, pictorial boards. $350.

HARRIS, Joel Chandler. *Uncle Remus and His Legends of the Old Plantation.* London, 1881. Olive green cloth. First English edition of *Uncle Remus: His Songs and His Sayings.* $400.

HARRIS, Joel Chandler. *Uncle Remus: His Songs and His Sayings.* New York, 1881. Illustrated by Frederick S. Church and James S. Moser. Pictorial blue cloth. First issue, with "presumptive" for "presumptuous" in last line, page 9, and with no mention of this book in ads at back. Author's first book. $1,500. Second issue, with "presumptuous" in last line, page 9. $300. (For first English edition, see preceding entry.) New York, 1895. Illustrated by A. B. Frost. Vellum. One of 250 signed. $750. Trade. Red buckram. $100. Limited Editions Club, New York, 1957. Illustrated. Pictorial cloth in slipcase. $100.

HARRIS, Joel Chandler. *Uncle Remus Returns.* Boston, 1918. In dustwrapper. $500. Without dustwrapper. $100.

HARRIS, Mark. *The Southpaw.* Indianapolis/New York (1953). First edition stated. $125.

HARRIS, Mark. *Trumpet to the World.* New York (1946). Author's first book. $60.

HARRIS, Robert. *Sixty Years of Golf.* London, 1953. $120.

HARRIS, Sarah Hollister. *An Unwritten Chapter of Salt Lake, 1851–1901.* New York, 1901. $300.

HARRIS, Thaddeus Mason. *The Journal of a Tour into the Territory Northwest of the Allegheny Mountains.* Boston, 1805. 4 maps (3 folding) and a folding plate. $600.

HARRIS, Thomas M. *Assassination of Lincoln.* Boston (1892). Illustrated. Pictorial cloth. $200.

HARRIS, William Charles. *The Fishes of North America That Are Captured on Hook and Line.* New York, 1898. vol. 1. (All published.) Illustrated. Folio, half leather. $750.

HARRIS, William R. *The Catholic Church in Utah.* Salt Lake City (1909). Map, 25 plates. Cloth. Also issued in 2 vols. $150.

HARRISON, Bill. *The Galactic Hero.* Garden City, 1965. $150.

HARRISON, E.J. *The Fighting Spirit of Japan.* New York, 1912. $100. London, 1913. Gilt mounted samurai on front. $100.

HARRISON, E. J. *The Thrilling, Startling and Wonderful Narrative of Lieutenant Harrison.* Cincinnati, 1848. Illustration in text. 30 pp., printed buff wraps. $2,500 or more.

HARRISON, Fairfax. *The Belair Stud 1747–1761.* Richmond, 1929. $250.

HARRISON, Jim. *Outlyer and Ghazals.* New York (1971). $250. Wraps. $35.

HARRISON, Jim. *Plain Song.* New York (1965). Author's first book. $150.

HARRISON, Jim. *Walking.* Cambridge, 1967. 26 signed and lettered copies. $400. 100 signed and numbered copies. $175.

HARRISSE, Henry. *Bibliotheca Americana Vetustissima . . .* New York, 1866. Limited to 400 copies. $225.

HART, George. *The Violin: Its Famous Makers and Their Imitators.* London, 1875. $200. Boston, 1884. $150.

HART, Joseph C. See *Miriam Coffin . . .*

HART, Joseph C. *The Romance of Yachting.* New York, 1848. $200.

HARTE, Bret. See *Outcroppings.*

HARTE, Bret. *Condensed Novels and Other Papers.* New York, 1867. Illustrated by Frank Bellew. Violet cloth. Author's first book. $250.

HARTE, Bret. *"Excelsior."* (Cover title.) Five Points, N.Y. (1877). 16 pp., oblong, blue wraps. First edition, first issue, with Donaldson imprint. $150. Later issue, without Donaldson imprint. $100. Also issued in cloth. $100.

HARTE, Bret. *Gabriel Conroy.* Hartford, 1876. First binding in mauve cloth. $200. London (1876). Warne & Co. 3 vols. $600.

HARTE, Bret. *The Heathen Chinee.* Chicago, 1870. 9 lithographed cards in envelope. First separate edition. $600.

HARTE, Bret. *The Lost Galleon and Other Tales.* San Francisco, 1867. $300.

HARTE, Bret. *The Luck of Roaring Camp and Other Sketches.* Boston, 1870. Without the story "Brown of Calaveras." $750. Boston, 1870. Second edition, with "Brown of Calaveras." $250. San Francisco, 1916. John Henry Nash printing. Half cloth. One of 260. $200. San Francisco, 1948. Grabhorn Press. Folio, half cloth. One of 300. $150.

HARTE, Bret. *Mliss: An Idyl of Red Mountain.* New York (1873). Printed wraps. (Pirated edition of the story, which originally appeared in *The Luck of Roaring Camp.* Contains 50 additional chapters by R.G. Densmore.) First issue, with Harte's name on the title page and front cover. $750. Second issue, with Harte's name removed and with page 34 a cancel leaf. $350. San Francisco, 1948. Grabhorn Press. Half cloth. One of 300. $125.

HARTE, Bret. *Poems.* Boston, 1871. With Fields, Osgood monogram on title page and "S.T.K." for "T.S.K." on page 136. $200.

HARTE, Bret. *The Queen of the Pirate Isle.* London (1886). 28 color illustrations by Kate Greenaway. Decorated cloth. First issue, bound in unbleached linen, with green endpapers, gilt edges. $300. Boston, 1887. $200.

HARTE, Bret. *San Francisco in 1866.* Grabhorn Press. San Francisco, 1951. One of 400. Issued without dustwrapper. $250.

HARTE, Bret. *Tales of the Gold Rush.* Limited Editions Club, New York, 1944. In slipcase. $75.

HARTE, Bret. *The Wild West.* Harrison of Paris. Paris (1930). Hand-colored illustrations. Burlap. One of 36 on vellum. In slipcase. $750. One of 840. In slipcase. $150.

HARTE, Bret, and TWAIN, Mark. *Sketches of the Sixties.* San Francisco, 1926. One of 250. $250. Trade. $100.

HARTLEY. L. P. *Night Fears* . . . London, 1924. Author's first book. $300.

HARTLEY, L. P. *The Traveling Grave and Other Stories.* Sauk City, Wis., 1948. $125.

HARTLEY, Marsden. *Adventures in the Arts.* New York (1921). Author's first book. $300.

HARTLEY, Marsden. *Twenty-five Poems.* (Paris, 1923.) Wraps. $400.

HARTSHORNE, Albert. *Old English Glasses.* London, 1897. Color frontispiece, plates, numerous drawings. Folio, vellum, and cloth. $200.

HARTZENBUSCH, Juan Eugenio. *The Lovers of Teruel.* Gregynog Press. Newtown, Wales, 1938. Translated by Henry Thomas. Morocco. One of 175. $600. One of 20 specially bound in morocco by George Fisher. $1,200.

HARVARD Class Day 1910. (Cover title.) (Cambridge, Mass.) 1910. Illustrated. 17 leaves, stiff cream wraps, red cord ties. (Includes a class ode by T. S. Eliot, his first contribution to a book.) $1,000.

HARVARD Lyrics. Boston, 1899. (Includes "Vita Mea," the first published work of Wallace Stevens.) $250.

HARVEY, Henry. *History of the Shawnee Indians.* Cincinnati, 1855. First issue, without portrait and preface dated "Sept. 21." $350. With portrait and preface dated "Ninth month." $250.

HARVEY, William. *The Anatomical Exercises . . .* London, 1653. First edition in English. $2,000. Nonesuch Press. London (1928). Edited by Geoffrey Keynes. Drawing by Stephen Gooden. Full morocco. One of 1,450. $250.

HASHEESH Eater (The). New York, 1857. (By Fitz-Hugh Ludlow, his first book.) $250.

HASKINS, C. W. *The Argonauts of California.* New York, 1890. $400.

HASTAIN, E. *Township Plats of the Creek Nation.* Muskogee, Okla., 1910. Full limp morocco. $400.

HASTINGS, Frank S. *A Ranchman's Recollections.* Chicago, 1921. In dustwrapper. $300. Without dustwrapper. $150.

HASTINGS, Lansford W. *The Emigrant's Guide to Oregon and California.* Cincinnati, 1845. 152 pp., in original wraps, or printed boards. $15,000.

HASTINGS, Lansford W. *A New History of Oregon and California.* Cincinnati, 1849. Frontispiece. Half cloth. $1,000.

HASTINGS, Sally. *Poems, on Different Subjects. To Which Is Added a Descriptive Account of a Family Tour to the West, in the Year 1800.* Lancaster, Pa., 1808. $250.

HASWELL, Anthony (editor). *Memoirs and Adventures of Capt. Matthew Phelps.* Bennington, Vt., 1802. Leather. $850.

HATCH, Benton L. *A Check List of the Publications of Thomas Bird Mosher of Portland, Maine.* Gehenna Press, 1966. One of 500 numbered copies in slipcase. $250.

HATFIELD, Edwin F. *History of Elizabeth, New Jersey.* New York, 1868. 8 plates. Morocco. $150.

HATTERAS, Owen. *Pistols for Two.* New York, 1917. Pink wraps. (By H. L. Mencken and George Jean Nathan.) $250.

HATTON, Thomas, and CLEAVER, Arthur H. *A Bibliography of the Periodical Works of Charles Dickens . . .* London, 1933. 250 large paper copies. $350.

HAULTAIN, Theodore Arnold. *Mystery of Golf.* Boston, 1908. Limited to 440 copies. Slipcase. $400. London, 1910. $120.

HAVEN, Charles T., and BELDEN, Frank A. *History of the Colt Revolver.* New York, 1940. In slipcase. $300. Morocco. Signed. In slipcase. $600.

HAWBUCK Grange; or, The Sporting Adventures of Thomas Scott, Esq. London, 1847. (By Robert Smith Surtees.) 8 illustrations by "Phiz." Blind-stamped pictorial red cloth. With April ads. $450.

HAWES, William Post. *Sporting Scenes and Sundry Sketches.* New York, 1842. Edited by Frank Forester. Illustrated. 2 vols., cloth. $200.

HAWKER, Peter. *Instructions to Young Sportsmen.* London, 1814. $750. London, 1816. Second edition. $450. London, 1824. Third edition. $400. Philadelphia, 1846. First American edition. $250.

HAWKER, The Reverend Robert S. *The Cornish Ballads and Other Poems.* London, 1869. Green cloth. $125.

HAWKER, The Reverend Robert S. *The Quest of the Sangraal: Chant the First.* Exeter, England, 1864. Cloth. Printed on vellum. $500.

HAWKES, J. C. B., Jr. *Fiasco Hall.* Cambridge, Mass., 1943. (By John Hawkes.) Author's first book. Wraps. $750.

HAWKES, John. *The Beetle Leg.* (New York, 1951.) First edition not stated. First issue in orange cloth. $200. Second issue in red cloth. $150.

HAWKES, John. *The Cannibal.* New Directions. (Norfolk, Conn., 1949.) First edition not stated, first binding in gray cloth. (Second printing in rust cloth.) $225.

HAWKES, John. *Lunar Landscapes.* New Directions. (New York, 1969.) First edition not stated. One of 150 signed. Issued without dustwrapper in slipcase. $175. Trade. $40.

HAWKES, John. *Second Skin.* New Directions. (New York, 1964.) First edition not stated. One of 100 signed in slipcase. $250. Trade. $75.

HAWKINS, Alfred. *Hawkins's Picture of Quebec; with Historical Recollections.* Quebec, 1834. 14 plates. $300.

HAWKINS, Rush C. *Titles of the First Books from the Earliest Presses . . .* New York, 1884. Limited to 300 numbered copies. Two frontispieces and 25 plates. $150.

HAWKS of Hawk-Hollow (The). Philadelphia, 1835. (By Robert Montgomery Bird.) 2 vols., in original purple cloth, paper labels. $400.

HAWLEY, Walter A. *Oriental Rugs: Antique and Modern.* New York, 1913. Plates. Half morocco. $250. New York, 1922. $150.

HAWLEY, Zerah. *A Journal of a Tour Through Connecticut, Massachusetts, New York, etc.* New Haven, 1822. $400.

HAWTHORNE, Nathaniel. See *Fanshawe; Peter Parley's Universal History; The Sister Years.*

HAWTHORNE, Nathaniel. *Biographical Stories for Children.* Boston, 1842. $750.

HAWTHORNE, Nathaniel. *The Blithedale Romance.* London, 1852. 2 vols. $600. Boston, 1852. Tan cloth. First American edition, with 4 pages of ads at end. $200.

HAWTHORNE, Nathaniel. *The Celestial Rail-Road.* Boston, 1843. 32 pp., buff wraps. Wilder & Co. or James F. Fish. First edition and first separate printing. $5,000. (No priority established for two publishers.)

HAWTHORNE, Nathaniel. *Doctor Grimshawe's Secret.* Boston, 1883. Edited by Julian Hawthorne. Pictorial cloth. $250. Large paper issue. One of 250 numbered copies; some signed by the editor. $600.

HAWTHORNE, Nathaniel. *Famous Old People, Being the Second Epoch of Grandfather's Chair.* Boston, 1841. In original cloth, paper label. $750.

HAWTHORNE, Nathaniel. *The Gentle Boy: A Thrice-Told Tale.* Boston, 1839. Engraved frontispiece. In original wraps. $2,500.

HAWTHORNE, Nathaniel. *Grandfather's Chair: A History.* Boston, 1841. In original cloth, paper label. $750.

HAWTHORNE, Nathaniel. *The House of the Seven Gables.* Boston, 1851. Brown cloth. With the last letters, *(T* and *H)* of the last words in lines 1 and 2 on page 149 battered and not complete. $1,500. (Exceptionally fine copy for $4,000 at auction in 1990.) Second through fifth printing, also dated 1851, but type fixed. $150. Limited Editions Club, New York, 1935. In slipcase. $100.

HAWTHORNE, Nathaniel. *Liberty Tree, with the Last Word of Grandfather's Chair.* Boston, 1841. Cloth, paper label. With second line of page 24 ending "Meet in A Con-." $600. (Second printing had "Meet in Con-.")

HAWTHORNE, Nathaniel. *Life of Franklin Pierce.* Boston, 1852. Frontispiece. Printed wraps, cloth. $400.

HAWTHORNE, Nathaniel. *The Marble Faun; or The Romance of Monte Beni.* Boston, 1860. 2 vols., brown cloth. With "Preface" preceding "Contents" and "for" versus "on" on page 225, line 22, in vol. 1. $400.

HAWTHORNE, Nathaniel. *Mosses from an Old Manse.* New York, 1846. With "T.B. Smith . . . and R. Craighead's . . ." on copyright page. 2 vols. Wraps. $4,000. 1 vol. issue in cloth. $750.

HAWTHORNE, Nathaniel. *Passages from the American Note-Books.* Boston, 1868. 2 vols., green cloth. With spine reading "Ticknor & Co." (Later, "Fields, Osgood & Co.") $500. London, 1870. 2 vols. First English edition. $150.

HAWTHORNE, Nathaniel. *The Scarlet Letter.* Boston, 1850. Brown cloth. With "reduplicate" in line 20 of page 21; instead of "repudiate" and no preface. $2,500. (Fine copy for $4,500 at auction in 1990.) Boston, 1850. Second edition with preface. $400. Third edition with "Hobart and Robbins" on copyright page instead of "Metcalf and Co." $200. New York (1915). Illustrated by Hugh Thomson. $250. New York, 1928. Grabhorn Press. Colored woodblocks by Valenti Angelo. Half morocco. One of 980. In dustwrapper. $250. Limited Editions Club, New York, 1941. Illustrated by Henry Varnum Poor. Leather. In slipcase. $100.

HAWTHORNE, Nathaniel. *The Snow-Image and Other Twice-Told Tales.* Boston, 1852. Brown cloth. $350. London, 1851. First English edition. (Issued simultaneously with American first edition, BAL suggests.) Titled *The Snow-Image, and Other Tales.)* $200.

HAWTHORNE, Nathaniel. *Tanglewood Tales, for Girls and Boys.* Boston, 1853. Decorated cloth. Without "George C. Rand" imprint on copyright page. $1,000.

London, 1853. Green cloth. First edition (preceding the American edition by a few days.) $350. London (1918). Illustrated by Edmund Dulac. Half vellum. One of 500 signed by Dulac. $1,000. Trade in cloth. $200.

HAWTHORNE, Nathaniel. *Transformation.* London, 1860. 3 vols., old rose cloth. First English edition of *The Marble Faun.* Published one week earlier. $1,250.

HAWTHORNE, Nathaniel. *Twice-Told Tales.* Boston, 1837. Brownish cloth. $4,500. ($7,000 at auction in 1990.) Limited Editions Club, New York, 1966. Colored illustrations by Valenti Angelo. Blue cloth. In slipcase. $60.

HAWTHORNE, Nathaniel. *A Wonder-Book for Girls and Boys.* Boston, 1852. With "lifed" in line 3 of page 2, instead of "lifted." $2,000. (An excellent copy for $4,500 at auction in 1990.) London, 1852. 8 engravings. Decorated blue cloth. First English edition. $600. London, 1893. Illustrated by Walter Crane. Decorated cloth. $150. Cambridge, Mass., 1893. Crane illustrations. Vellum. One of 250. $1,250. Ordinary issue, cloth. $250. London (1922). Illustrated by Arthur Rackham. White buckram. One of 600 signed by the artist. In slipcase. $1,250.

HAY, John. *Jim Bludso of the Prairie Bell, and Little Breeches.* Boston, 1871. Illustrated by S. Eytinge, Jr. 23 pp., printed orange wraps. Author's first book. $100.

HAY, John. *Letters of John Hay and Extracts from His Diary.* Washington, 1908. 3 vols., cloth, paper labels. $350.

HAYAKAWA, S. J. *Language in Thought and Action.* Madison, 1939. Author's first book. Wraps. $150.

HAYCOX, Ernest. *Brand Fires on the Ridge.* New York, 1929. $150.

HAYCOX, Ernest. *Free Grass.* New York, 1929. Author's first book. $175.

HAYCOX, Ernest. *Night Raid.* New York, 1929. $150.

HAYDEN, Ferdinand V. *Geological and Geographical Atlas of Colorado.* (Washington) 1877. 20 double-page maps, mostly colored. Three-quarters morocco. $850.

HAYDEN, Ferdinand V. *Sun Pictures of Rocky Mountain Scenery.* New York, 1870. 30 mounted photographs. Half morocco. $2,500.

HAYDEN, Ferdinand V. *The Yellowstone National Park.* Boston, 1876. 2 maps. Illustrated in color by Thomas Moran. Folio, half morocco portfolio. $10,000 or more.

HAYMOND, Creed. *The Central Pacific Railroad.* San Francisco, 1888. $200.

HAYMOND, Henry. *History of Harrison County, West Virginia.* Morgantown, W. Va. (1910). $125.

HAYWARD, John (compiler). *English Poetry: An Illustrated Catalogue of First and Early Editions . . .* Cambridge, 1950. Limited to 550 copies. In dustwrapper. $150.

HAYWARDE, Richard. *Prismatics.* New York, 1853. (By Frederick Swartwout Cozzens, his first book.) $250.

HAYWOOD, John. *The Civil and Political History of the State of Tennessee.* Knoxville, 1823. First edition, with tipped-in copyright slip and inserted printed slip. $1,500.

HAYWOOD, John. *The Natural and Aboriginal History of Tennessee.* Nashville, 1823. Leather. First edition, with errata leaf. $2,000.

HAZARD, Ebenezer. *Historical Collections . . .* Philadelphia, 1792/94. 2 vols. $600.

HAZEN, Gen. W. B. *A Narrative of Military Service.* Boston, 1885. Map, illustrations. $250.

HAZEN, Gen. W. B. *Our Barren Lands.* Cincinnati, 1875. 53 pp., printed blue wraps. $600.

HAZEN, Gen. W. B. *Some Corrections of "Life on the Plains."* (Cover title.) St. Paul, 1875. 18 pp., wraps. $750.

HAZLITT, William. *Characters of Shakespear's* [sic] *Plays.* London, 1817. $250.

HAZLITT, William. *The Fight.* Woodstock, N.Y. Limited to 1,000 copies. Signed by Marjorie Barlow. $50.

HAZLITT. William. *Lectures on the English Poets.* London, 1818. First edition, with 4 pages of ads at end dated May 1, 1818 (VAB). $200.

HAZLITT, William. *Political Essays, with Sketches of Public Characters.* London, 1819. $300.

HEADLONG Hall. London, 1816. (By Thomas Love Peacock.) $400.

HEADSMAN (The). London, 1833. (By James Fenimore Cooper.) 3 vols., in original tan boards, or rose-colored cloth. $600. Philadelphia, 1833. 2 vols., in original blue boards. First American edition. $750.

HEAL, Ambrose. *The Signboards of Old London Shops.* London, 1947. One of 250 large paper copies. $300.

HEANEY, Seamus. *Death of a Naturalist.* London (1966). $350. New York, 1966. (English sheets.) $250.

HEANEY, Seamus. *Eleven Poems.* Belfast (1965). Author's first book. First issue: laid paper, wraps, red-violet sun, $750. Second issue: wove paper, dark maroon sun, $400. Third issue: gray paper in stiff green wraps, $150.

HEAP, Gwinn Harris. *Central Route to the Pacific.* Philadelphia, 1854. Folding map (not in all copies), 13 tinted plates. First edition, first issue, with plate IV lacking a plate or page number. $1,500. Another issue, without map. $500.

HEARN, Lafcadio. See Bisland, Elizabeth; Gautier, Theophile. See also *La Cuisine Creole; Historical Sketch-Book and Guide to New Orleans.*

HEARN, Lafcadio. *Chita: A Memory of Last Island.* New York, 1889. Salmon-colored cloth. $350.

HEARN, Lafcadio. *Editorials from the Kobe Chronicle.* (Cover title.) (New York, 1913.) Printed white wraps. One of 100, with an addenda slip tipped in. $750.

HEARN, Lafcadio. *Gleanings in Buddha-Fields.* Boston, 1897. $300.

HEARN, Lafcadio. *Glimpses of Unfamiliar Japan.* Boston, 1894. 2 vols., black or olive cloth. $400.

HEARN, Lafcadio. *"Gombo Zhebes." Little Dictionary of Creole Proverbs.* New York, 1885. $350.

HEARN, Lafcadio. *In Ghostly Japan.* Boston, 1899. Illustrated. Pictorial blue cloth. $200.

HEARN, Lafcadio. *Japan: An Attempt at Interpretation.* New York 1904. Colored frontispiece. Tan cloth. $400.

HEARN, Lafcadio. *Japanese Fairy Tales.* Tokyo (1898–1903). 5 vols., wraps. *(The Boy Who Drew Cats, The Goblin Spider, The Old Woman Who Lost Her Dumpling, The Fountain of Youth, Chin Chin Kobakama.)* $1,250 for complete sets. It would be best to look these up in BAL to ascertain first or early printings. Macrae-Smith Co. Philadelphia, 1931. 5 vols. $500.

HEARN, Lafcadio. *A Japanese Miscellany.* Boston, 1901. Pictorial green cloth. Without "October 1901" on copyright page is the first (Perkins). $250. Although BAL states that the sequence is not determined. With "October 1901." $200.

HEARN, Lafcadio. *Kokoro.* Boston, 1896. $250.

HEARN, Lafcadio. *Kotto.* New York, 1902. Illustrated. Pictorial olive cloth. First state, with background of title page upside down, artist's monogram in upper right corner. $300. Second state. $200.

HEARN, Lafcadio. *Kwaidan.* Boston, 1904. Blue-green pictorial cloth. (Second printing in tan.) $250. Limited Editions Club, New York, 1932. Color plates. Printed silk binding. In silk wraparound case. $150.

HEARN, Lafcadio. *The Romance of the Milky Way.* Boston, 1905. With "Published October 1905" on copyright page. Gray cloth. $275.

HEARN, Lafcadio. *Shadowings.* Boston, 1900. Pictorial blue cloth. $250.

HEARN, Lafcadio. *Some Chinese Ghosts.* Boston, 1887. Red cloth. $500. Various other colored cloths. $400.

HEARN, Lafcadio. *Stray Leaves from Strange Literature.* Boston, 1884. Author's first book. $350.

HEARN, Lafcadio. *Two Years in the French West Indies.* New York, 1890. $300.

HEARON, Shelby. *At Home After 1840 . . .* Austin, 1966. Author's first book. 100 signed and numbered copies. $150. (Text by Hearon, drawings by Peggy Goldstein.) Trade, one of 1,000. $60.

HEART, Capt. Jonathan. *Journal.* Albany, N.Y., 1885. Edited by C. W. Butterfield. 94 pp., tan printed wraps. One of 150. $175.

HEARTMAN, Charles F. *The New-England Primer.* New York, 1915. Facsimiles. Boards. One of 265. $150. New York, 1934. Cloth. One of 300. $75.

HEARTMAN, Charles F., and CANNY, James R. *A Bibliography of the First Printings of Edgar Allan Poe.* Hattiesburg, Miss., 1940. $150.

HEBARD, Grace R. *Sacajawea.* Glendale, 1933. One of 750 copies. $150.

HEBARD, Grace R. *Washakie.* Cleveland, 1930. 7 maps, 16 plates. $175.

HEBARD, Grace R., and BRININSTOOL, E. A. *The Bozeman Trail.* Cleveland, 1922. Plates, 2 folding maps. 2 vols. Without dustwrapper. $250. Glendale, Calif., 1960. 2 vols. in one. Issued without dustwrapper. $75.

HEBISON, W. C. *Early Days in Texas and Rains County.* Emory, Tex., 1917. 50 pp., wraps. $250.

HECHT, Anthony. *A Summoning of Stones.* New York (1954). Author's first book. $125.

HECHT, Ben. *Erik Dorn.* New York, 1921. First issue, yellow lettering on cover. $500.

HECHT. Ben. *The Bewitched Tailor.* New York, 1941. Drawing by George Grosz. 8 pp., printed wraps. One of 875 signed by author and artist. $750.

HECHT, Ben. *Fantazius Mallare.* Chicago, 1922. Illustrated by Wallace Smith. One of 2,000. $150.

HECHT, Ben. *The Hero of Santa Maria.* New York (1920). Author's first book (with Kenneth Goodman). Wraps. $200.

HECHT, Ben. *A Jew in Love.* New York (1931). Cloth. One of 150 signed. In slipcase. $350. Trade: first issue, with exactly 34 lines on page 306, as in the signed edition (VAB). $150. Later issue, 32 lines. $100.

HECHT, Ben. *The Kingdom of Evil.* Chicago, 1924. One of 2,000. $125.

HECHT, Ben. *A Thousand and One Afternoons in Chicago.* Chicago (1922). Illustrated. $200.

HECHT, Ben, and BODENHEIM, Maxwell. *Cutie, a Warm Mama.* Chicago, 1924. Orange cloth or orange boards and cloth. (By Ben Hecht alone.) One of 200(?). $150.

HECHT, Ben, and FOWLER, Gene. *The Great Magoo.* New York (1933). $125.

HECHT, Ben, and MACARTHUR, Charles. *The Front Page.* New York, 1928. $300.

HECKENDORN & WILSON. *Miners' and Business Men's Directory.* (For Tuolumne, Calif.) Columbia, Calif., 1856. 104 pp., printed wraps. $2,500.

HECKETHORN, Charles William. *The Printers of Basle in the XV and XVI Centuries . . .* London, 1897. $275.

HECKEWELDER, John. *An Account of the History, Manners, and Customs of the Indian Nations.* Philadelphia, 1818. Calf. $250. Philadelphia, 1819. Second edition. $150.

HECKEWELDER, John. *A Narrative of the Mission of the United Brethren Among the Delaware and Mohegan Indians.* Philadelphia, 1820. Portrait and errata slip. $250. Cleveland, 1907. 3 maps, 5 plates. Three-quarters leather. One of 160 on large paper. $300.

HEGAN, Alice Caldwell. *Mrs. Wiggs of the Cabbage Patch.* New York, 1901. First issue, with gold sky on cover. Author's first book. $75.

HEINLEIN, Robert A. *Assignment in Eternity.* Reading, Pa. (1953). 500 numbered copies signed on tipped-in page. $650. Trade. First binding: brick red cloth, gilt lettering. "Heinlein" 3 mm high on spine. $250. Second binding: green boards, spine lettered in black. $150. Third binding: red cloth. "Heinlein" 2 mm high on spine. $100. London (1955). $150.

HEINLEIN, Robert A. *Beyond This Horizon.* Reading, Pa., 1948. One of 500 signed and numbered copies. Brick red cloth. $750. Trade. Brick red cloth or medium blue cloth. Priority unknown. Variant blue dustwrapper is a proof dustwrapper. $300.

HEINLEIN, Robert A. *The Discovery of the Future.* (Cover title.) (Los Angeles, 1941.) Wraps. "Limited First Edition (200)" on front wrapper. Printed in green ink. $1,500. Adds "Reprint (100)" under original limitation. Peach-colored front cover. 18 pages including covers. $600.

HEINLEIN, Robert A. *Double Star.* Garden City, 1956. Published at $2.95. $750. London (1958). $300.

HEINLEIN, Robert A. *The Green Hills of Earth.* Chicago (1951). Signed on tipped-in page. $500. Trade. $200. London, 1954. $100.

HEINLEIN, Robert A. *The Man Who Sold the Moon.* Chicago (1950). Signed on tipped-in page. $500. Trade. $200. London (1953). $75.

HEINLEIN, Robert A. *Revolt in 2100.* Chicago (1953). Signed on tipped-in page. $500. Trade. $200. London (1964). $75.

HEINLEIN, Robert A. *Rocket Ship Galileo.* New York (1947). Publisher's seal on copyright page. Published at $2.00. $400. London, 1971. $40.

HEINLEIN, Robert A. *Starman Jones.* New York (1953). Publisher's seal on copyright page. Published at $2.50. $250. London (1954). $100.

HEINLEIN, Robert A. *Starship Troopers.* New York (1959). $750. (London, 1961). $100.

HEINLEIN, Robert A. *Stranger in a Strange Land.* New York (1961). "C22" on page 408. Dustwrapper priced $4.50. $1,000. London, 1965. $250.

HEINS, Henry Hardy. *A Golden Anniversary Bibliography of Edgar Rice Burroughs.* West Kingston, R.I., 1964. Complete edition, revised. $300.

HELFORTH, John. *Nights.* (Dijon, France, 1955.) Printed wraps. (By Hilda Doolittle.) One of 100. $500.

HELLER, Elinor, and MAGEE, David. *Bibliography of the Grabhorn Press, 1915–1940.* San Francisco, 1940. Illustrated. Full leather. One of 210 specially bound. $600. Trade in boards. $300. See also Dorothy and David Magee entry for a related work.

HELLER, Joseph. *Catch-22.* New York, 1961. Author's first book. $500. London, 1962. $200.

HELLMAN, Lillian. *The Children's Hour.* New York, 1934. Author's first book. $750.

HELM, Mary S. *Scraps of Early Texas History.* Austin, 1884. $600.

HELPER, Hinton R. *The Land of Gold.* Baltimore, 1855. $300.

HEMANS, Felicia. *Poems.* Liverpool, 1808. Author's first book. $200.

HEMENWAY, Charles. *Memoirs of My Day in and out of Mormondom.* Salt Lake City, 1887. $150.

HEMINGWAY, Ernest. See Bahr, Jerome; Cohn, Louis Henry; Faulkner, William, *Salmagundi;* North, Joseph; Paul, Elliot. See also *Kiki's Memoirs; Somebody Had to Do Something; Senior Tabula.*

HEMINGWAY, Ernest. *Across the River and into the Trees.* London (1950). Precedes American edition by 3 days. $250. New York, 1950. First issue of dustwrapper with yellow lettering on spine. $125. Second issue of dustwrapper with orange lettering on spine. $75.

HEMINGWAY, Ernest. *Death in the Afternoon.* New York, 1932. $1,250. London (1932). $750.

HEMINGWAY, Ernest. *A Farewell to Arms.* New York, 1929. 510 signed numbered copies. Slipcase. $5,000. Trade. Contains publisher's seal on copyright page. No disclaimer on page [x] ("None of these characters . . ."). $1,000. Second printing with disclaimer. $300. London (1929). Page 66, line 28 "seriosu." $500.

HEMINGWAY, Ernest. *The Fifth Column and the First Forty-nine Stories.* New York, 1938. $1,000. London (1939). $600.

HEMINGWAY, Ernest. *For Whom the Bell Tolls.* New York, 1940. Photographer's name missing from back panel of dustwrapper. $500. Photographer's name on back panel. $200. London (1941). $400. Limited Editions Club, Princeton, 1942. 15 copies for presentation by the author. $3,500. 1,500 copies signed by Lynd Ward, the illustrator. Slipcase. $200.

HEMINGWAY, Ernest. *God Rest You Merry Gentlemen.* New York, 1933. 300 numbered copies. $1,000.

HEMINGWAY, Ernest. *Green Hills of Africa.* New York, 1935. (Price assumes book is without usual fading/discoloration of spine.) $1,000. London (1936). $750.

HEMINGWAY, Ernest. *In Our Time.* Three Mountains Press. Paris, 1924. 170 numbered copies. $15,000. New York, 1925. $2,500.

HEMINGWAY, Ernest. *Introduction to Kiki of Montparnasse.* (Cover title.) New York, 1929. Wraps. With wraparound band. $300.

HEMINGWAY, Ernest. *The Old Man and the Sea.* New York, 1952. 30 sets of sheets bound for presentation in black buckram. $5,000. Trade. Deep blue ink in Hemingway photograph changed to olive in later states of the dustwrapper. $350. London (1952). First dustwrapper not printed on both sides. $75. Limited Editions Club. 425 numbered copies signed by Alfred Eisenstaedt. Slipcase. $1,000.

HEMINGWAY, Ernest. *The Spanish Earth.* Cleveland, 1938. Pictorial endpapers showing F.A.I. banner. $1,250. Plain endpapers. $500.

HEMINGWAY, Ernest. *The Sun Also Rises.* New York, 1926. Publisher's seal on copyright page. page 181, line 26 "stoppped" vs. "stopped." Dustwrapper error: "In Our Times" vs. "Time." $12,000. Errors corrected. $1,500.

HEMINGWAY, Ernest. *Three Stories & Ten Poems.* (Paris, 1923.) Wraps. Author's first book. $12,000.

HEMINGWAY, Ernest. *The Torrents of Spring.* New York, 1926. $2,500. Paris, 1932. Large paper edition (7½ by 5⅝ inches and priced at 125 francs). Wraps. $500. Small paper edition (6¹⁄₁₆ by 4¾ inches and priced 10 francs). $250. London (1933). $750.

HENDERSON, Elliot Blaine. *Plantation Echoes.* Columbia, S.C., 1904. Author's first book. $150.

HENDERSON, Ian, and STIRPIK, David I. *Golf in the Making.* England, 1979. Limited to 300 signed copies. $200. Trade. $120.

HENDERSON, Robert W. *Early American Sport: A Chronological Check-List.* New York, 1937. Limited to 400 copies. $150.

HENDRYX, James B. *Connie Morgan in Alaska.* New York, 1916. In dustwrapper. $250.

HENDRYX, James B. *Gun Brand.* New York, 1917. In dustwrapper. $200.

HENDRYX, James B. *Promise.* New York, 1915. In dustwrapper. $250.

HENDRYX, James B. *Texan.* New York, 1918. In dustwrapper. $200.

HENLEY, William Ernest. *A Book of Verses.* London, 1888. Stiff printed wraps. Author's first book. One of 75 large paper copies. $600. Regular edition in stiff wraps. $150.

HENLEY, William Ernest. *London Types.* London, 1898. 12 colored illustrations by William Nicholson. Vellum. $500. Cloth. $300.

HENNEPIN, Father Louis. *A Description of Louisiana.* New York, 1880. Translated by John G. Shea. One of 250. $300.

HENRIETTA Temple: A Love Story. London, 1837. (By Benjamin Disraeli.) 3 vols., in original cloth. $300.

HENRY, Alexander. *Travels and Adventures in Canada and the Indian Territories.* New York, 1809. First issue, without the portrait by Maverick. $500. Second issue, with portrait. $1,000. Boston, 1901. Cloth. One of 700. $250.

HENRY, Edward Richard. *Classification and Use of Fingerprints.* London, 1900. 11 plates, 3 folding. $200.

HENRY, John Joseph. *An Accurate and Interesting Account of the Hardships and Sufferings of That Band of Heroes, Who Traversed the Wilderness in the Campaign Against Quebec in 1775.* Lancaster, Pa., 1812. $300.

HENRY, John Joseph. *Campaign Against Quebec.* Watertown, N.Y., 1844. Sheep. Revised edition of *An Accurate and Interesting Account . . .* $150.

HENRY, O. *Cabbages and Kings.* New York, 1904. Pictorial cloth. (By William Sidney Porter.) First issue, with "McClure, Phillips & Co." on spine. Author's first book. $200.

HENRY, O. *The Four Million.* New York, 1906. (By William Sidney Porter.) $150.

HENRY, O. *The Gentle Grafter.* New York, 1908. (By William Sidney Porter.) $150.

HENRY, O. *Heart of the West.* New York, 1907. (By William Sidney Porter.) $100.

HENRY, O. *The Hiding of Black Bill.* New York (about 1913?). (By William Sidney Porter.) Pictorial wraps. $250.

HENRY, O. *Roads of Destiny.* New York, 1909. (By William Sidney Porter.) First state, with "h" missing in line 6 on page 9. $100.

HENRY, O. *Rolling Stones.* Cloth. Garden City, 1912. (By William Sidney Porter.) $125.

HENRY, O. *Sixes and Sevens.* Garden City, 1911. (By William Sidney Porter.) $125.

HENRY, O. *The Voice of the City.* New York, 1908. (By William Sidney Porter.) First binding, with McClure imprint on spine. $125. Limited Editions Club, New York, 1935. Buckram. In slipcase. $125.

HENRY, O. *Waifs and Strays: 12 Stories.* Garden City, 1917. (By William Sidney Porter.) One of 200. $350.

HENRY, Samuel. *A New and Complete American Medical Family Herbal.* New York, 1814. $850.

HENRY, Samuel J. *Foxhunting Is Different.* Derrydale Press. New York (1938). Pictorial cloth. One of 950. $150.

HENRY, Will. *No Survivors.* New York, 1950. (By Henry Allen, his first book). $100.

HENTY, G. A. *All But Lost.* London, 1869. 3 vols. $1,500.

HENTY, G. A. *A March on London.* London, 1898 (1897). 8 plates. $500.

HENTY, G. A. *The March to Coomassie.* London, 1874. $750.

HENTY, G. A. *The March to Magdala.* London, 1868. $1,500.

HENTY, G. A. *The Queen's Cup.* London, 1897. 3 vols. With ads dated November 1896. $1,750.

HENTY, G. A. *Search for a Secret.* London, 1867. 3 vols. Author's first book. $3,000.

HENTY, G. A. *The Tiger of Mysore.* London, 1896 (actually 1895). Map, 12 plates. $400.

HENTY, G. A. et al. *Brains and Bravery.* London, 1903. 8 plates by Arthur Rackham. $400.

HERBERT, Sir A. P. *Poor Poems and Rotten Rhymes.* Winchester, England. 1910. Author's first book. Wraps. $175.

HERBERT, Edward, Lord. *The Autobiography of Edward, Lord Herbert of Cherbury.* Gregynog Press. Newtown, Wales, 1928. Wood engravings by H. W. Bray. Folio, buckram. One of 300. $400. One of 25 specially bound in morocco. $1,500.

HERBERT, Frank. *The Dragon in the Sea.* Garden City, 1956. $350.

HERBERT, Frank. *Dune.* Philadelphia (1965). $750. First edition stated but also states that the book is published in Canada by Ambassador (later Thomas Nelson) and does not have an ISBN number (added later).

HERBERT, Frank. *Survival and the Atom.* (Santa Rosa, 1950). Author's first book. Wraps. An off-print. $400.

HERBERT, George. *Poems.* Gregynog Press. Newtown, Wales, 1923. Illustrated. Marbled boards and cloth. One of 300. $600. One of 43 specially bound in morocco. $1,500.

HERBERT, Henry William. See Forester, Frank; Forrester, Frank; Hawes, William Post. See also *The Brothers; Cromwell.*

HERBERT, Henry William. *The Quorndon Hounds.* Philadelphia, 1852. Frontispiece, 3 plates. $500.

HERBERT, Henry William. *The Warwick Woodlands.* Philadelphia, 1845. Wraps. $2,000 at auction in 1990.

HERBERT, J. A. *Illuminated Manuscripts.* London, 1911. Color frontispiece, 50 other plates. $250.

HERBST, Josephine. *Nothing Is Sacred.* New York, 1928. Author's first book. $125.

HERD, Alexander (Sandy). *My Golfing Life.* London, 1923. $250. New York, 1923. $150.

HERFORD, Oliver. *Artful Anticks.* New York, 1888. Author's first book. $125.

HERGESHEIMER, Joseph. *Berlin.* New York, 1932. One of 125 signed. In slipcase. $150.

HERGESHEIMER, Joseph. *Java Head.* New York, 1919. One of 100. $100.

HERGESHEIMER, Joseph. *The Lay Anthony.* New York, 1914. Author's first book. $75.

HERGESHEIMER, Joseph. *The Limestone Tree.* New York, 1931. One of 225 signed. In dustwrapper and slipcase. $100.

HERMAN, William. *The Dance of Death: Author's Copy.* (San Francisco, 1877.) Brown or green cloth. (By Ambrose Bierce and Thomas A. Harcourt.) $400. San Francisco, 1877. Red or blue cloth. Second edition, with dated title page. $150.

HERNDON, William H., and WEIK, Jesse W. *Herndon's Lincoln: The True Story of a Great Life.* Chicago (1889). 3 vols., 63 plates, blue cloth. $400. Chicago, 1890. 3 vols. Second edition. $175.

HERRICK, Robert. *One Hundred and Eleven Poems.* Golden Cockerel Press. London, 1955. Illustrated by W. Russell Flint. Sheepskin. One of 105 copies issued with 8 extra plates signed by Flint. In slipcase, $2,000. Cloth, parchment spine. One of 450. In slipcase. $600.

HERRICK, Robert. *Poems.* Kelmscott Press. (London, 1895.) Woodcut title page. Vellum. One of 250. $1,500. One of 8 on vellum. $5,000.

HERRICK, Robert. *Selections from the Poetry of Robert Herrick.* Boston, 1882. Illustrated. $150.

HERRING, Richard. *Paper & Paper Making, Ancient and Modern.* London, 1856. 30 specimens of paper. 24 pages of publisher's ads. $400.

HERRING, Richard. *A Practical Guide to the Varieties and Relative Values of Paper* . . . London, 1860. 230 specimens of paper bound in at end. $1,250.

HERSEY, John. *Men on Bataan.* New York, 1942. Author's first book. $175.

HESSE, Herman. *Demian.* New York, 1923. $300.

HESSE, Herman. *In Sight of Chaos.* Zurich, 1923. Issued without dustwrapper. $200.

HESSE, Herman. *Steppenwolf.* London (1929). First English edition. $600.

HEWITSON, William. *Illustrations of New Species of Exotic Butterflies.* London (1856)–76. 300 plates. 5 vols., half morocco. $2,750.

HEWITT, Edward R. *Secrets of the Salmon.* New York, 1922. One of 780. Issued without dustwrapper. $400.

HEWITT, Graily. *Lettering for Students and Craftsmen.* London, 1930. Illustrated. White buckram. One of 380 signed. Issued without dustwrapper. $350.

HEWITT, Graily. *The Pen & Type-Design.* London, 1928. One of 250. $200.

HEWITT, Randall H. *Across the Plains and Over the Divide.* New York (1906). Folding map, portrait, 58 plates. Pictorial cloth. $300.

HEWITT, Randall H. *Notes by the Way: Memoranda of a Journey Across the Plains, from Dundee, Ill., to Olympia, W. T. May 7 to November 3, 1862.* Olympia, Wash., 1863. 58 pages, printed wraps. $3,000 and up.

HEWLETT, Maurice. *The Song of the Plow.* London (1916). One of 100 signed in dustwrapper and slipcase. $100.

HEYER, Georgette. *The Black Moth.* Boston, 1921. Author's first book. $150.

HEYWARD, Du Bose. See Gershwin, George.

HEYWARD, Du Bose. *Brass Ankle.* New York (1931). One of 100 signed in slipcase. $150. Trade. $60.

HEYWARD, Du Bose. *The Half Pint Flask.* New York, 1929. One of 175 signed. In dustwrapper. $100.

HEYWARD, Du Bose. *Porgy.* New York (1925). First issue, in gold-stamped binding. $400. Black-stamped binding. $300.

HEYWARD, Du Bose and Dorothy. *Porgy A Play in Four Acts.* Garden City, 1927. $200.

HEYWARD, Du Bose. *Skylines and Horizons.* New York, 1924. Author's first book. $125.

HIBBERT, Thomas, and BUIST, Robert. *The American Flower Garden Directory.* Philadelphia, 1832. Color frontispiece. $225.

HICKMAN, William. *Brigham's Destroying Angel* . . . New York, 1872. Pictorial cloth. $125.

HIGBEE, Elias, and THOMPSON, R. B. *The Petition of the Latter-Day Saints.* Washington, 1840. 13 pages, sewn. $500.

HIGGINS, F. R. *Arable Holdings: Poems.* Cuala Press. Dublin, 1933. Boards and linen. One of 300. In tissue dustwrapper. $125.

HIGGINS, Godfrey. *Anacalypsis, an Attempt to Draw Aside the Veil of the Saitic Isis.* London, 1836. 6 engraved plates. 2 vols. With errata slip. $250.

HIGHSMITH, Patricia. *The Blunderer.* New York, 1954. $300. London, 1956. $200.

HIGHSMITH, Patricia. *Strangers on a Train.* New York, 1950. Author's first book. $400. London, 1950. $400.

HIGHSMITH, Patricia. *The Talented Mr. Ripley.* New York, 1955. $250. London, 1957. $200.

HILDRETH, Richard. *The History of Banks.* Boston, 1837. $150.

HILDRETH, Samuel P. *Biographical and Historical Memoirs of the Early Pioneer Settlers of Ohio.* Cincinnati, 1852. 6 plates. $150.

HILDRETH, Samuel P. *Genealogical and Biographical Sketches of the Hildreth Family.* Marietta, Ohio, 1840. $150.

HILDRETH, Samuel P. *Memoirs of the Early Pioneer Settlers of Ohio.* Cincinnati, 1854. Leather. Later reprint of *Biographical and Historical Memoirs.* $125.

HILDRETH, Samuel P. *Pioneer History.* Cincinnati, 1848. Folding map, 8 plates. Half leather. $200.

HILL, W. H., A. F., and A. E. *Antonio Stradivari, His Life and Work.* London, 1902. Morocco. One of 100. $1,500. Half vellum. $750. London, 1909. Second edition. $300.

HILL, W. H., A. F., and A. E. *The Violin-Makers of the Guarnieri Family.* London, 1931. Plates. Half vellum. One of 200. Issued without dustwrapper. $1,000.

HILLERMAN, Tony. *The Blessing Way.* New York, 1970. Author's first book. $350.

HILLERMAN, Tony. *The Dance of the Dead.* New York, 1973. $250.

HILLERMAN, Tony. *The Fly on the Wall.* New York, 1971. $300.

HILLERMAN, Tony. *The Great Taos Bank Robbery.* Albuquerque, 1973. $250.

HILLS, Sir John. *Points of a Racehorse.* London, 1903. Illustrated. Folio. $400.

HILLS, John Waller. *A History of Fly-Fishing for Trout.* London, 1921. One of 50. Issued without dustwrapper. $250.

HILLS, John Waller. *A Summer on the Test.* London (1924). 12 plates by N. Wilkinson. One of 300 signed. Issued without dustwrapper. $750. One of 25, with plates signed by the artist. $1,500.

HILLYER, Robert. *Sonnets and Other Lyrics.* Cambridge, Mass., 1917. Author's first book. $60.

HILTON, Harold H. *My Golfing Reminiscences.* London, 1907. $350.

HILTON, Harold H., and SMITH, Garden C. *Royal and Ancient Game of Golf.* London, 1912. Limited deluxe edition, 100 copies. $2,000. Limited to 900 copies. $1,000.

HILTON, James. *Catherine Herself.* London (1920). Author's first book. $400.

HILTON, James. *Good-bye, Mr. Chips.* Boston, 1934. $250.

HIMES, Chester B. *If He Hollers Let Him Go.* New York, 1947. Author's first book. $225. London, 1947. $125.

HIMES, Chester. *Pinktoes.* Olympia Press. Paris (1961). Wraps. "Printed in July 1961" on back page. $150. New York (1965). $60. London, 1965. $50.

HIMSELF. See *Sheppard Lee.*

HIND, Arthur M. *Giovanni Battista Piranesi . . .* London, 1922. 74 plates. Limited to 500 copies. $150.

HIND, Arthur M. *An Introduction to a History of Woodcut . . .* London, 1935. 2 vols. $175.

HIND, Henry Youle. *Narrative of the Canadian Red River Exploring Expedition of 1857 . . .* London, 1860. Plates, 8 maps (2 folding), 1 folding plan. 2 vols., brown cloth. $1,500.

HIND, Henry Youle. *North-West Territory.* Toronto, 1859. 8 folding maps and plans, and 3 plates. $750.

HIND, Henry Youle. *A Sketch of an Overland Route to British Columbia.* Toronto, 1862. Folding map. Dark green flexible cloth, paper label on front cover. First edition, with errata slip. $1,500.

HINDLEY, Charles. *The History of the Catnach Press . . .* London, 1886. One of 250 numbered large paper copies signed by the author. $150.

HINE, Daryl. *Five Poems.* Toronto (1954). Author's first book. Wraps. $250.

HINKLE, James F. *Early Days of a Cowboy on the Pecos.* Roswell, N.M., 1937. Illustrated. 35 pages, pictorial wraps. One of 35 copies. $750.

HINTON, Richard J. *The Hand-Book of Arizona.* San Francisco, 1878. 4 maps, 16 plates. $200.

HINTS Towards Forming the Character of a Young Princess. London, 1805. 2 vols. (By Hannah More.) $350.

HIPKINS, A. J., and GIBB, William. *Musical Instruments: Historic, Rare, and Unique.* London, 1888. 50 color plates. Half leather. One of 1,040. $750.

HIRSCHMAN, Jack. *Fragments.* (New York, 1952). Author's first book. (Privately published.) Wraps. $250.

HIRSHBERG, Dr. L. K. *What You Ought to Know About Your Baby.* New York, 1910. (Written in collaboration with H. L. Mencken.) $1,000.

HISTORICAL Account of the Rise and Progress of the Colonies of South Carolina and Georgia . . . London, 1779. 2 vols. $3,000.

HISTORICAL and Descriptive Review of the Industries of Tacoma, 1887. Los Angeles, 1887. 108 pp., unbound. $150.

HISTORICAL and Descriptive Review of the Industries of Walla Walla. No-place, 1891. 112 pp., wraps. $150.

HISTORICAL and Scientific Sketches of Michigan. Detroit, 1834. $200.

HISTORICAL Sketch Book and Guide to New Orleans and Environs. New York, 1885. Plates, folding map. (By Lafcadio Hearn, George W. Cable et al.) First issue, with spelling "Bizoin" (instead of "Bisoin") at head of title page. In reddish brown stiff wraps, with map laid in. $1,000. Later issues in wraps or cloth with map. $750. Without map. $500.

HISTORICAL War Map (The). Indianapolis, 1862. Folding maps, plus maps in text. 56 pages, printed boards. Asher & Co. $400.

HISTORY OF Alameda County, California. Oakland, 1883. Portraits. (By J. P. Munro-Fraser.) $300.

HISTORY of Amador County, California. Oakland, 1881. Full leather. $300.

HISTORY Of Arizona Territory Showing Its Resources and Advantages . . . San Francisco, 1884. 60 lithographed plates (2 double page). Folding map. $2,000.

HISTORY of the Arkansas Valley, Colorado. Chicago, 1881. Illustrated. Half leather. $300.

HISTORY of the City of Denver, Arapahoe County, and Colorado. Chicago, 1880. Illustrated. Half morocco. $400.

HISTORY of the Counties of Woodbury and Plymouth, Iowa. Chicago, 1890–91. Half leather. $150.

HISTORY of Crawford and Richland Counties, Wisconsin. Springfield, Ill., 1884. Cloth. (By C. W. Butterfield and George A. Ogle.) $125.

HISTORY of the Detection and Trial of John A. Murel, the Great Western Land Pirate. (Lexington, Ky., 1835.) Wraps. (By Augustus Q. J. Walton.) $900.

HISTORY of Franklin, Jefferson, Washington, Crawford and Gasconade Counties, Missouri. Chicago, 1888. Illustrated. Half leather. $150.

HISTORY of the Great Lakes. Chicago, 1899. Plates, 5 double-page maps. 2 vols., cloth. (Edited by John B. Mansfield.) $150.

HISTORY of Henry Esmond (The). London, 1852. 3 vols., brown cloth, paper labels. (By William Makepeace Thackeray.) First edition, with 16 pages of ads dated September (VAB). Dated October (Van Duzer). $750.

HISTORY of Idaho Territory. San Francisco, 1884. 2 maps, 69 plates, 2 facsimiles. Half morocco. $500.

HISTORY of the Indian Wars with the First White Settlers of the United States (A). Montpelier, Vt., 1812. Leather. (By Daniel C. Sanders.) $1,750. Rochester, 1828. Boards. Second edition. (Chapter 27 omitted.) $250.

HISTORY of Ink. New York (circa 1860). 16 plates (with full-color title page and 1 plate in color). 7 pages of notices from the press. $150.

HISTORY of Johnny Quae Genus (The). London, 1822. (By William Combe.) 24 colored plates by Thomas Rowlandson. 8 parts, in original wraps. $1,250. London, 1822. Boards. First book edition. $500.

HISTORY of the Late Expedition to Cuba . . . New Orleans. 1850. Second issue with appendix not contained in the first issue. $1,250.

HISTORY of the Late War in the Western Country. Lexington, Ky., 1816. Boards or leather. (By Robert B. McAfee.) First edition, with the "extra" printed leaf (of Gen. Winchester's criticism) at end. $850. Bowling Green, Ohio (1919). Cloth. One of 300. $150.

HISTORY of Los Angeles County, California. Oakland, 1880. Colored folding map, 113 lithographs. Morocco and cloth. $600.

HISTORY of Madeira (A). London, 1821. (By William Combe.) 27 colored plates. $750.

HISTORY of Marin County, California. San Francisco, 1880. Frontispiece, 35 portraits. Full sheep. (By J. P. Munro-Fraser.) $600.

HISTORY of Mendocino County, California. San Francisco, 1880. Portraits. Sheep. $600.

HISTORY of Montana, 1739–1885. Chicago, 1885. Folding map, plates. Half morocco. (Edited by Michael A. Leeson.) $750.

HISTORY of Napa and Lake Counties, California. San Francisco, 1881. Illustrated. Full sheep. $400.

HISTORY of Nevada. Oakland, 1881. 116 plates. Half morocco. (Edited by Myron Angel.) $600.

HISTORY of Pike County, Missouri. Des Moines, 1883. Half leather. $150.

HISTORY of the Regulators of Northern Indiana. Indianapolis, 1859. 67 pages in printed yellow wraps. $1,000.

HISTORY of Sangamon County, Illinois. Chicago, 1881. Illustrated. Half leather. $125.

HISTORY of San Joaquin County, California. Oakland, 1879. Illustrated. Oblong folio, leather. (By Frank T. Gilbert.) $500.

HISTORY of San Luis Obispo County, California. Oakland, 1883. Portraits and scenes. Half leather. (By Myron Angel.) $450.

HISTORY of Santa Barbara and Ventura Counties, California. Oakland, 1883. Half leather. (By Jesse D. Mason.) $200.

HISTORY of a Six Weeks' Tour Through a Part of France, Switzerland, Germany, and Holland. London, 1817. In original boards, green cloth spine, paper label. (By Percy Bysshe Shelley.) $2,500 or more. Rebound. $1,000.

HISTORY of Sonoma County, California. San Francisco, 1880. Illustrated. Three-quarters leather. $200.

HISTORY of Texas (A), or The Emigrant's Guide to the New Republic, by a Resident Emigrant. New York, 1844. Frontispiece colored. $600. Not colored. $400.

HISTORY of Waukesha County, Wisconsin. Chicago, 1880. Illustrated. Half leather. $125.

HISTORY of Wayne County, New York. Philadelphia, 1877. Illustrated. Half leather. $100.

HITTELL, John S. *The Commerce and Industries of the Pacific Coast of North America.* San Francisco, 1882. Folding colored map, plates. $150.

HITTELL, John S. *A History of the City of San Francisco.* San Francisco, 1878. Cloth. $200.

HITTELL, John S. *The Resources of Vallejo.* (Vallejo, Calif., 1869.) Folding map. Printed wraps. $500.

HITTELL, John S. *Yosemite: Its Wonders and Its Beauties.* San Francisco, 1868. 20 mounted photographic views by "Helios." Green cloth. $2,000.

HITTELL, Theodore H. (editor). *Adventures of James Capen Adams, Mountaineer and Grizzly Bear Hunter, of California.* San Francisco, 1860. 12 wood engravings. $300. Boston, 1860. 12 plates. $200.

HOAG, Jonathan E. *The Poetical Works of Jonathan E. Hoag.* New York, 1923. Preface by H. P. Lovecraft and contains 6 of his poems. $1,250.

HOBAN, Russell. *Riddley Walker.* London (1980). $125.

HOBBS, James. *Wild Life in the Far West.* Hartford, 1872. 20 plates, colored frontispiece. $350. Hartford, 1873. Second edition. $150.

HOBOMOK, a Tale of Early Times. Boston, 1824. (By Lydia Maria Child, her first book). $400.

HOBSON, G. D. *Bindings in Cambridge Libraries . . .* Cambridge, 1929. Limited to 230 copies. 72 full-page plates. $1,800.

HOBSON, G. D. *English Binding Before 1500.* Cambridge, 1929. 55 full-page plates. $650.

HOBSON, G. D. *Thirty Bindings.* First Edition Club. London, 1926. 30 plates. Limited to 600 copies. $250.

HOBSON, Laura Z. See Field, Peter.

HOBSON, Laura Z. *A Dog Of His Own.* New York, 1941. $200.

HOBSON, R. L. *A Catalogue of Chinese Pottery and Porcelain in the Collection of Sir Percival David.* London, 1934. 180 plates, mostly in color. Folio, linen. In portfolio box. $1,500. Silk boards. One of 30 on vellum, signed by Hobson. Slipcase. $4,000.

HOBSON, R. L. *Chinese Art.* London, 1927. 100 color plates. $200. New York, 1927. $200.

HODGE, Frederick W. *Handbook of American Indians North of Mexico.* Map. Washington, 1907–10. 2 vols. $300. Washington, 1912. 2 vols. $200.

HODGE, Hiram C. *Arizona as It Is.* New York, 1877. Frontispiece, 2 plates and double-page map. $400.

HODGSON, Adam. *Letters from North America.* London, 1824. Map, plate. 2 vols. (First English edition of *Remarks During a Journey . . .*) With 2 errata slips. $400.

HODGSON, Adam. *Remarks During a Journey Through North America in the Years 1819–21 . . .* New York, 1823. First (pirated) edition. $500.

HODGSON, J. E. *The History of Aeronautics in Great Britain.* Oxford, 1924. Colored frontispiece, 150 plates, some colored. Buckram. Issued without dustwrapper. One of 1,000. $750.

HODGSON, Joseph. *The Alabama Manual and Statistical Register for 1869.* Montgomery, 1869. Printed boards. $300.

HODGSON, Joseph. *The Cradle of the Confederacy.* Mobile, 1876. Cloth. $175.

HODGSON, Ralph. *The Last Blackbird and Other Lines.* London, 1907. Author's first book. First issue, edges uncut. $75.

HODGSON, William Hope. *The Boats of the 'Glen Carrig.'* London, 1907. Author's first book. $1,000.

HODGSON, William Hope. *The Calling of the Sea.* London (1920). In dustwrapper. $500.

HODGSON, William Hope. *Captain Gault.* New York, 1918. $350.

HODGSON, William Hope. *The House on the Borderland and Other Novels.* London, 1908. $600. Sauk City, Wis., 1946. $300.

HODGSON, William Hope. *The Night Land.* London, 1912. $750.

HODNETT, Edward. *English Woodcuts, 1480–1535.* London, 1935. $100.

HOE, Robert. *A Lecture on Bookbinding as a Fine Art.* New York, 1886. 63 full-page plates. Limited to 200 copies. $325.

HOFFMAN, Charles Fenno. See *Greyslaer; A Winter in the West.*

HOFFMAN, Charles Fenno. *The Pioneers of New York.* New York, 1848. 55 pages, printed tan wraps. With seal on front cover 1⅜ inches wide. (In later reprint seal was 1⅛ inches.) $250.

HOFFMAN, Charles Fenno. *Wild Scenes in the Forest and Prairie.* London, 1839. 2 vols., in original boards, paper label on spine. $250. New York, 1843. 2 vols., boards. First American edition. $200.

HOFFMANN, Carl. *A Practical Treatise on the Manufacture of Paper in All Its Branches.* Philadelphia, 1873. 129 wood engravings and 5 large folding plates. $450.

HOGG, James. *Scottish Pastorals . . .* Edinburgh, 1801. Author's first book. $500.

HOGG, Robert, and BULL, H. G. (editors). *The Herefordshire Pomona, Containing Original Figures and Descriptions of the Most Esteemed Kinds of Apples and Pears.* London, 1876–85. 77 colored plates, 3 plain plates. 2 vols., wraps or leather. $6,000.

HOLBROOK, John Edwards. *Ichthyology of South Carolina.* Vol. I (all published). Charleston, 1855–(57). 28 colored plates. Three-quarters morocco. $12,500. Charleston, 1860. Second edition. $8,500.

HOLDEN, W. C. *Rollie Burns; or, An Account of the Ranching Industry on the South Plains.* Dallas (1932). Maps, illustrations. Tan cloth. $200. Green cloth, without frontispiece. $150.

HOLDEN, W. C. *The Spur Ranch.* Boston (1934). $200.

HOLDER, Charles F. *All About Pasadena and Its Vicinity.* Boston, 1889. Wraps. $150.

HOLLADAY, Benjamin. *Table of Distances of the Overland Daily Stage Line from Atchinson . . .* New York, 1863. Leaflet. $3,000.

HOLLEY, Mary Austin. *Texas: Observations, Historical, Geographical and Descriptive.* Baltimore, 1833. Folding map. $5,000. Lexington, Ky., 1836. Map in color. Gray cloth. Second edition (but essentially different) $3,000. Austin, 1981. One of 350. In dustwrapper. $300.

HOLLIDAY, George H. *On the Plains in '65.* No-place, 1883. 97 pages, printed wraps. $1,500.

HOLLINGSWORTH, John McHenry. *Journal.* San Francisco, 1923. Frontispiece in color. Half buckram. One of 300. $175. One of 50 large paper copies. Half vellum. $250.

HOLLISTER, Ovando J. *History of the First Regiment of Colorado Volunteers.* Denver, 1863. 178 pages, printed wraps. $3,500 and up. *(See The March of the First.)*

HOLLISTER, Ovando J. *The Mines of Colorado.* Springfield, Mass., 1867. Enlarged edition of *The Silver Mines. . . .* $250.

HOLLISTER, Ovando J. *The Silver Mines of Colorado.* Central City, 1867. 87 pp., printed wraps. $1,000.

HOLLISTER, Uriah S. *The Navajo and His Blanket.* Denver, 1903. 10 color plates, other illustrations. $300.

HOLLO, Anselm. *Text and Fin Poems.* Birmingham (England), 1961. Wraps. (300 copies.) $150.

HOLLO, Anselm. *Sateiden Valilla.* Helsinki, 1956. Author's first book. $150.

HOLMAN, Louis A. *The Graphic Processes . . .* Boston, 1926. 24 loose fascicules in a cloth-covered case. $475.

HOLMAN, William R. *Library Publications.* San Francisco (1965). Limited to 350 copies. 16 tipped-in examples in text and 16 additional examples in rear pocket of book. $375.

HOLMES, John Clellon. *Go.* New York, 1952. Author's first book. $400.

HOLMES, Oliver Wendell. See Hall, Marshall. See also *The Autocrat of the Breakfast-Table; The Poet at the Breakfast-Table.*

HOLMES, Oliver Wendell. *The Benefactors of the Medical School of Harvard University.* Boston, 1850. Tan wraps. $250.

HOLMES, Oliver Wendell. *Border Lines of Knowledge in Some Provinces of Medical Science.* Boston, 1862. First edition, with Ticknor & Co. imprint on spine. $200.

HOLMES, Oliver Wendell. *The Claims of Dentistry.* Boston, 1872. Tan wraps. $250.

HOLMES, Oliver Wendell. *The Contagiousness of Puerperal Fever.* (Caption title.) (Boston, 1843.) 28 pp., printed buff wraps. $7,500 at auction in 1988.

HOLMES, Oliver Wendell. *Currents and Counter-Currents in Medical Science: An Address . . . Before the Massachusetts Medical Society.* Boston, 1860. Printed salmon-colored wraps. $400.

HOLMES, Oliver Wendell. *Elsie Venner: A Romance of Destiny.* Boston, 1861. 2 vols., brown cloth. "Probable" first printing, with ads dated January 1861. $200.

HOLMES, Oliver Wendell. *Homoeopathy, and Its Kindred Delusions.* Boston, 1842. Tan boards, paper label. $350.

HOLMES, Oliver Wendell. *Humorous Poems.* Boston, 1865. Portrait frontispiece. Printed wraps. $200. Cloth. $150.

HOLMES, Oliver Wendell. *Poems.* Boston, 1836. In original decorated cloth, paper label. With Boston imprint only. Author's first book. $350. Later 1836 issue. Boston and New York imprint. $150.

HOLMES, Oliver Wendell. *The Position and Prospects of the Medical Student.* Boston, 1844. Printed tan wraps. $500.

HOLMES, Oliver Wendell. *The Professor at the Breakfast-Table.* Boston, 1860. Cloth. $150. Beveled cloth, edges gilt. Large paper. $250.

HOLMES, Justice Oliver Wendell. *The Common Law.* Boston, 1881. Author's first book. Leather. $1,000. Cloth. $750.

HOLMES, Roberta E. *The Southern Mines of California.* San Francisco, 1930. Grabhorn Press. Plates and maps. Boards. One of 250. $175.

HOMAGE to a Bookman, Essays on Manuscripts . . . Berlin, 1967. $125.

HOME Life in Russia. London, 1854. (By Nikolai Gogol.) Author's first book. 2 vols. $750.

HOMER. *The Odyssey of Homer.* (London) 1932. Translated by T. E. Shaw (T. E. Lawrence). With 25 large rondels in gold and black. Small folio, black morocco. One of 530 designed by Bruce Rogers. In slipcase. $2,000. Note: A few copies were signed by Lawrence, "T. E. Shaw," and Rogers. $5,000. New York, 1932. Morocco (11 copies) ($9,000 at auction in 1990.) Calf (about 23 copies). First American edition (for copyright purposes). $3,000. Boston, 1929. Translated by George H. Palmer. Illustrated by N. C. Wyeth. $200. One of 550 signed. With an extra set of color plates. $1,250.

HOMES in Texas on the Line of the International and Great Northern Railroad. Chicago, 1879. 79 pages, wraps. (By N. W. Hunter.) $350.

HONCE, Charles. Books and Ghosts... Mount Vernon, N.Y., 1948. One of 111 copies. $150.

HONCE, Charles. For Loving a Book... Mount Vernon, N.Y., 1945. One of 111. $200.

HONCE, Charles. Notes from a Bookman's Cuff... New York, 1949. One of 111. $125.

HONCE, Charles. The Public Papers of a Bibliomaniac... Mount Vernon, N.Y., 1942. One of 100. $325.

HONCE, Charles. A Vincent Starrett Library... Mount Vernon, N.Y., 1941. Limited to 100 copies. $225.

HOOD, Thomas. Humorous Poems. London, 1893. One of 250 on large paper. $250.

HOOKER, Joseph Dalton. Exotic Flora. Edinburgh, 1823–27. 3 vols. 233 hand-colored plates, some folding. $4,000.

HOOKER, Joseph Dalton. Illustrations of Himalayan Plants. (London, 1855.) Lithographed title within hand-colored border, 24 hand-colored plates. $12,500.

HOOKER, Joseph Dalton. The Rhododendrons of Sikkim-Himalaya. 1849–51. 3 parts. Vignette title, 30 hand-colored lithographed plates. $10,000.

HOOVER, Herbert C. Fishing for Fun. New York (1963). One of 200 signed. In slipcase. $500.

HOOVER, Herbert C. A Remedy for Disappearing Game Fish. New York, 1930. Woodcuts. Marbled boards and cloth. One of 990. In slipcase. $250.

HOOVER, Herbert C. The Principles of Mining. New York, 1909. Author's first book (with Lou Henry Hoover). $350.

HOOVER, Herbert C., and HOOVER, Lou Henry (translators). De Re Metallica. London, 1912. From the Latin of Georgius Agricola. Illustrated. Parchment boards. First English edition. $750.

HOPE, Anthony. The Dolly Dialogues. London, 1894. (By A. H. Hawkins.) 4 plates by Arthur Rackham. Tan wraps. First issue, with "Dolly" as running headband on left-hand pages (VAB). $750. Blue cloth. $350.

HOPE, Anthony. The Prisoner of Zenda. London (1894). (By A. H. Hawkins.) Dark red cloth. First issue, with list of 17 (not 18) titles on page 311 (VAB). $300.

HOPKINS, Gerard Manley. Poems. London (1918). Edited by Robert Bridges. 2 portraits, 2 double-page facsimiles. Blue-gray boards and linen. Author's first book. In dustwrapper. $2,000. Without dustwrapper. $750.

HOPKINS, Gerard Manley. *Selected Poems.* London, 1954. Nonesuch Press. One of 1,100. $175.

HOPKINS, Gerard T. *A Mission to the Indians, from the Indian Committee of Baltimore Yearly Meeting, to Fort Wayne in 1804.* Philadelphia, 1862. Edited by Martha E. Tyson, 198 pp., wraps. $300.

HOPKINS, Harry C. *History of San Diego: Its Pueblo Lands and Water.* San Diego (1929). Issued without dustwrapper. $100.

HOPKINSON, Cecil. *Collecting Golf Books 1743–1938.* London, 1938. $750.

HOPPE, E. O. (photographer). See King, Richard.

HOPPE, E. O. *Studies From the Russian Ballet.* London (1911). Folio. $750.

HOPWOOD, Avery. See Rinehart, Mary Roberts.

HORBLIT, Harrison D. *One Hundred Books Famous in Science.* New York, 1964. Limited to 1,000 copies. $500.

HORGAN, Paul. *The Fault of Angels.* New York (1933). $150.

HORGAN, Paul. *Great River: The Rio Grande in American History.* New York, 1954. Illustrated, including color plates. 2 vols., tan cloth. One of 1,000 signed. Slipcase. $250. Trade. 2 vols., black cloth. Slipcase. $75.

HORGAN, Paul. *The Habit of Empire.* New Mexico, 1938. $250.

HORGAN, Paul. *Lamb of God.* Roswell, 1927. Wraps. (60 copies.) $1,500.

HORGAN, Paul. *Men of Arms.* Philadelphia (1931). (Juvenile.) (500 copies.) $600.

HORGAN, Paul. *Villanelle of Evening.* No-place, 1926. Author's first book. Wraps. (200 copies.) $1,250.

HORN, Hosea B. *Horn's Overland Guide . . .* New York, 1852. Folding map. First issue, 78 pages. $1,750. Second issue, same date, 83 pages. $1,350.

HORNBY, C. H. St. J. *A Descriptive Bibliography of the Books Printed at the Ashendene Press, MDCCCXV–MCMXXXV.* Chelsea, 1935. 390 numbered and signed copies. Last book of the press. In slipcase. $1,850.

HORNE, Bernard S. *The Compleat Angler, 1653–1967.* Pittsburgh, 1970. Limited to 300 numbered copies bound in cloth (out of 500 total). $175.

HORNE, Thomas Hartwell. *An Introduction to the Study of Bibliography. . .* London, 1814. 2 vols. 11 plates. $175.

HORNUNG, E. W. *Mr. Justice Raffles.* London, 1909. $100.

HORSE-SHOE Robinson. Philadelphia, 1835. (By John Pendleton Kennedy.) 2 vols., in original purple cloth, paper labels on spines. $500.

HOSACK, David. *Essays on Various Subjects of Medical Science.* New York, 1824–30. 3 vols. $300.

HOSMER, Hezekiah L. *Early History of the Maumee Valley.* Toledo, Ohio, 1858. 70 pages, printed wraps. $450.

HOSMER, Hezekiah L. *Montana: An Address . . . Before the Travellers' Club, New York City, January, 1866.* (Cover title.) New York, 1866. 23 pages, printed wraps. $600.

HOSMER, John Allen. *A Trip to the States, by the Way of the Yellowstone and Missouri.* Virginia City, Mont., 1867. Cloth, or tan printed boards. $3,500.

HOUDINI, Harry. *A Magician Among the Spirits.* New York, 1924 (By Ehrich Weiss.) Issued without dustwrapper. $300.

HOUDINI, Harry. *The Right Way to Do Wrong: An Exposé of Successful Criminals.* Boston, 1906. (By Ehrich Weiss.) Author's first book. Wraps. $200.

HOUGH, Emerson. *54–40 Or Fight.* Indianapolis, 1909. In dustwrapper. $150.

HOUGH, Emerson. *Heart's Desire.* New York, 1905. In dustwrapper. $200.

HOUGH, Emerson. *Magnificent Adventure.* New York, 1916. In dustwrapper. $125.

HOUGH, Emerson. *The Singing Mouse Stories.* New York, 1895. Author's first book. $150.

HOUGH, Emerson. *The Story of the Cowboy.* New York, 1897. Decorated cloth. $200.

HOUGH, Emerson. *The Story of the Outlaw.* New York, 1907. With printer's rule in heading at top of page v. $150.

HOUGH, Emerson. *The Way to the West.* Indianapolis (1903). With "October" on copyright page. $150.

HOUGH, Franklin B. *History of Jefferson County, New York.* Albany, 1854. Half leather. $150.

HOUGH, Franklin B. *History of St. Lawrence and Franklin Counties, New York.* Albany, 1853. With 3 folding maps. Half leather. $250.

HOUGH, Franklin B. *Washingtonia.* Roxbury, Mass., 1865. Plates, folding map. 2 vols., half morocco. One of 91. $350. Wraps. One of 200 on large paper. $300.

HOUGHTON Library 1942–1967 (The). Cambridge, 1967. 10 full-color plates. $100.

HOUGHTON, Jacob. *The Mineral Region of Lake Superior.* Buffalo, 1846. 2 maps on one folding sheet. $150.

HOUGHTON, T. S. *The Printers' Practical Every-Day-Book.* London, 1841. $400.

HOUGHTON, W. *British Fresh-Water Fishes.* London (1879). Illustrated. With 41 color plates, 2 vols. $1,000.

HOUSE, Homer D. *Wild Flowers of New York.* Albany, 1918. Illustrated in color. 2 vols. $150.

HOUSEHOLD, Geoffrey. *The Terror of Villedonga.* London (1936). Author's first book. $150.

HOUSEHOLD, Geoffrey. *The Third Hour.* London, 1937. $75.

HOUSMAN, A. E. *Fragment of a Greek Tragedy.* Cambridge, 1921. Printed wraps. $300.

HOUSMAN, A. E. *Last Poems.* London, 1922. First issue, with comma and semicolon missing after "love" and "rain," respectively, on page 52. In dustwrapper. $150.

HOUSMAN, A. E. *More Poems.* London (1936). Portrait. Morocco and cloth. One of 379. In dustwrapper. $250. Trade edition in cloth. $125. New York, 1936. First American edition. $100.

HOUSMAN, A. E. *A Shropshire Lad.* London, 1896. Gray-blue boards, vellum spine, paper label. Author's first book. First state, with the word "Shropshire" on the label exactly 33 mm wide. $1,500. Second state, measuring 37 mm. $750. New York, 1897. Boards, vellum spine. $850. (Note: The entire first edition was 500 copies, 350 for England and 150 for America, with a substitute New York title page.)

HOUSMAN, Clemence. *The Were-Wolf.* London, 1896. $200.

HOUSMAN, Laurence. *False Premises.* Oxford, 1922. One of 150 signed. Issued without dustwrapper. $150.

HOUSMAN, Laurence. *A Farm in Fairyland.* London, 1894. Author's first book. $250.

HOUSMAN, Laurence. *Followers of St. Francis.* London, 1923. $150.

HOUSMAN, Laurence. *Stories from the Arabian Nights.* London (1907). Mounted color plates by Edmund Dulac. $250. Vellum with silk ties. One of 350 signed. $1,250.

HOUSTOUN, Mrs. Matilda C. *Texas and the Gulf of Mexico.* London, 1844. 10 plates. 2 vols., cloth. $750. Philadelphia, 1845. Frontispiece of Santa Anna. Wraps. $300.

HOVEY, Richard. *Poems.* Washington, 1880. Author's first book. Cloth. $500. Wraps. $250.

HOW the Buffalo Lost His Crown. (New York, 1894.) (By John H. Beacom.) Illustrated by Charles M. Russell. 44 pp., oblong, brown cloth. $1,500. Half decorated calf. Presentation copy signed by Beacom. $2,000.

HOW to Win in Wall Street. New York, 1881. By a Successful Operator. (Joaquin Miller.) $300.

HOW, George E., and HOWE, Jane P. *English and Scottish Silver Spoons*... London, 1952–57. Photographs. 3 vols. One of 550. In dustwrappers. $1,000. Without dustwrapper. $750. One of 50 specially bound. Issued without dustwrapper. $1,500.

HOWARD, Benjamin C. *A Report of the Decisions of the Supreme Court*... *in the Case of Dred Scott vs. John F. A. Sandford.* New York, 1857. (The Dred Scott Decision.) $2,500.

HOWARD, Brian. *God Save the King.* Hours Press. Paris (1930). Author's first book. (150 copies.) $300.

HOWARD, H. R. See *The Life and Adventures of Joseph T. Hare.*

HOWARD, H. R. (editor). *The History of Virgil A. Stewart, and His Adventures in Capturing and Exposing the "Great Western Land Pirate" (John A. Murrell) and His Gang.* New York, 1836. Howard's first book. $250.

HOWARD, Jas. H. W. *Bond and Free.* Harrisburg, 1886. Frontispiece portrait. Author's first book. First issue, with portrait opposite title page. $300.

HOWARD, Joseph Jackson. *Baronets, The Wardour Press Series of Armorial Book-plates.* London, 1895. Limited to 200 copies. Signed by the compiler, Mitchell L. Hughes. $175.

HOWARD, McHenry. *Recollections of a Maryland Confederate Soldier.* Baltimore, 1914. Folding map and 24 plates. $300.

HOWARD, Oliver Otis. *Account of Gen. Howard's Mission to the Apaches and Navajos.* No-place, no-date. 12 pages, wraps. $150.

HOWARD, Oliver Otis. *My Life and Experiences Among Our Hostile Indians.* Hartford, (1907). $250.

HOWARD, Oliver Otis. *Nez Percé Joseph.* Boston, 1881. 2 portraits and 2 maps. $200.

HOWARD, Robert E. *Always Comes Evening.* Sauk City, Wis., 1957. $450.

HOWARD, Robert E. *The Coming of Conan.* New York (1953). $150.

HOWARD, Robert E. *Conan the Barbarian.* New York (1954). $200.

HOWARD, Robert E. *Conan the Conqueror.* New York (1950). $150.

HOWARD, Robert E. *The Dark Man and Others.* Sauk City, Wis., 1963. $200.

HOWARD, Robert E. *Etchings in Ivory.* Pasadena, Tex., 1968. On laid paper, watermarked "Tweedweave." (268 copies.) Wraps. $250.

HOWARD, Robert E. *A Gent from Bear Creek.* London (1937). Author's first book. With "First printed . . . 1937" on copyright page. $4,000. West Kingston, R.I., 1965. First American edition. $125.

HOWARD, Robert E. *King Conan.* New York (1953). $150.

HOWARD, Robert E. *The Pride of Bear Creek.* West Kingston, R.I., 1966. $150.

HOWARD, Robert E. *Skull-Face and Others.* Sauk City, Wis., 1946. $600.

HOWARD, Robert E. *The Sword of Conan.* New York (1952). $150.

HOWBERT, Irving. *The Indians of the Pike's Peak Region.* New York, 1914. 4 plates. $75.

HOWE, E. D. *History of Mormonism.* Painesville, Ohio, 1840. Frontispiece. Second edition of *Mormonism Unvailed.* $1,250.

HOWE, E. D. *Mormonism Unveiled.* Painesville, 1834. Frontispiece. In original cloth. $3,000.

HOWE, E. W. *The Story of a Country Town.* Atchison, Kan., 1883. Illustrated by W. L. Wells. Green decorated cloth. First issue, with "D. Caldwell, Manufacturer,

Atchison, Kan." rubber-stamped inside front cover and no lettering at foot of spine. Author's first book. $100. (Later in reddish brown or blue cloth; or green cloth with paper label "McPike & Fox" on pastedown.)

HOWE, Henry. *Historical Collections of the Great West.* Cincinnati, 1850. 2 vols. in one, cloth. $100. Cincinnati, 1852. $75.

HOWE, Henry. *Historical Collections of Ohio.* Cincinnati, 1847. Map, woodcuts. $125. Cincinnati, 1848. $125. Cincinnati, 1875. $100.

HOWE, Henry. *Historical Collections of Virginia.* Charleston, S.C., 1845. Map, illustrations, engraved title page. $150.

HOWE, John. *A Journal Kept by Mr. John Howe, While He Was Employed as a British Spy, During the Revolutionary War.* Concord, N.H., 1827. 44 pages. $400.

HOWE, Julia Ward. See *Passion-Flowers.*

HOWE, Julia Ward. *Later Lyrics.* Boston, 1866. Green or purple cloth. (Contains first book appearance of "Battle Hymn of the Republic.") $200.

HOWE, Mark A. De Wolfe. *Rari Nantes: Being Verses and a Song.* Boston, 1893. Wraps. One of 80. Author's first book. $175.

HOWE, Octavius T. *The Argonauts of '49.* Cambridge, Mass., 1923. Illustrated. Half cloth. In dustwrapper. $200.

HOWE, Octavius T., and MATTHEWS, Frederick C. *American Clipper Ships, 1833–58.* Salem, 1926–27. 2 vols. 114 plates. Vol. 1, marbled boards; vol. 2, cloth. In dustwrapper. $400.

HOWELL, James. *Instructions for Forreine Travell.* London, 1642. $850.

HOWELLS, William Dean. See *Poems of Two Friends.*

HOWELLS, William Dean. *Between the Dark and the Daylight.* New York, 1907. $150.

HOWELLS, William Dean. *A Hazard of New Fortunes.* New York, 1890. Illustrated. Wraps. With the cloth edition of this title listed as "in-press" on inside of front wrapper. $600. With title listed at "$2.00." $300. Cloth, 2 vols. $250.

HOWELLS, William Dean. *My Mark Twain.* New York, 1910. Sage-colored cloth. $125.

HOWELLS, William Dean. *The Rise of Silas Lapham.* Boston, 1885. Blue or brown cloth. With "Mr. Howells's Latest Works" (later "Novels"), ad facing title page and with unbroken type in the word "sojourner" at bottom of page 176. $125. Limited Editions Club, New York, 1961. Illustrated. Buckram. In slipcase. $60.

HOWELLS, William Dean. *Suburban Sketches.* Boston, 1871. Illustrated by A. Hoppin. Author's first book of fiction. $250. Boston, 1872. Revised and enlarged edition. $75.

HOWELLS, William Dean. *Venetian Life. . .* London (1866). $500. New York, 1866. $400. Cambridge, Mass., 1892. 18 aquatints. 2 vols., vellum. One of 250 on vellum. $250. Cambridge, 1907. 2 vols., boards. One of 550 signed. $350.

HOWELLS, William Dean, and HAYES, J. L. *Lives and Speeches of Abraham Lincoln and Hannibal Hamlin.* Columbus, Ohio, 1860. 96 pages, printed buff wraps. First issue, with pages 95–96 blank. $300. Second issue, engraving of Republican Wigwam, Chicago, on page 96. $200.

HOWELLS, William Dean, TWAIN, Mark, et al. *The Niagara Book.* Buffalo, 1893. Cloth, or printed wraps. With no ads at end, page 226 blank, and copyright notice in 3 lines. $250.

HOWISON, John. *Sketches of Upper Canada* . . . Edinburgh, 1821. $250.

HOWITT, Samuel. *The British Sportsman.* London, 1812. (A reprint.) Frontispiece, 71 plates. $2,000.

HOWLAND, S. A. *Steamboat Disasters and Railroad Accidents in the United States* . . . Worcester, Mass., 1840. Calf. $350.

HOWLEY, James P. *The Beothucks or Red Indians of Newfoundland.* Cambridge, Mass., 1915. Plates. $350.

HOYEM, Andrew. *The Wake.* San Francisco, 1963. Author's first book. 35 deluxe copies. $250. Wraps. (750 copies.) $40.

HOYNINGEN-HUENE, George. *African Mirage.* New York, 1938. Author's first book. $175.

HRDLICKA, Ales. *The Anthropology of Florida.* DeLand, 1922. Issued without dustwrapper. $150.

HUBBARD, Elbert. *A Message to Garcia.* East Aurora, N.Y., 1899. Suede. One of 450. $100.

HUBBARD, Gurdon Saltonstall. *Incidents in the Life of Gurdon Saltonstall Hubbard.* (Chicago) 1888. Edited by Henry E. Hamilton. Frontispiece. $200.

HUBBARD, John Niles. *Sketches of Border Adventures, in the Life and Times of Maj. Moses Van Campen.* Dansville, N.Y., 1841. Leather. $300. Bath, N.Y., 1841. Leather. $200.

HUBBARD, L. Ron. *Buckskin Brigades.* New York, 1937. Author's first book. $3,000.

HUBBARD, L. Ron. *Dianetics.* New York (1950). $400.

HUBBARD, L. Ron. *Final Blackout.* Providence (1948). $250.

HUBBARD, L. Ron. *Slaves of Sleep.* Chicago, 1948. $250.

HUBBARD, L. Ron. *Typewriter in the Sky* . . . New York (1951). $250.

HUBBARD, Robert. *Historical Sketches of Roswell Franklin and Family.* Dansville, N.Y., 1839. In original half leather. $350.

HUDSON, Derek. *Arthur Rackham: His Life and Work.* London, 1960. Color plates. $250. New York (1960). $200.

HUDSON River Portfolio. See Wall, W. G.

HUDSON, Stephen. *Celeste and Other Sketches.* (London) 1930. (By Sydney Schiff.) Wood engravings. Decorated cloth. One of 50 on Japan vellum, signed, with an extra set of engravings. Slipcase. $750.

HUDSON, W. H. See Harford, Henry; Sclater, P. L.; and Hudson, W. H. See also *A Crystal Age.*

HUDSON, W. H. *Birds in a Village.* London, 1893. Chocolate-colored buckram. $150.

HUDSON, W. H. *British Birds.* London, 1895. With 8 plain and 8 color plates. Green cloth. $200.

HUDSON, W. H. *Far Away and Long Ago.* London, 1918. In dustwrapper. $250. London, 1931. Illustrated. Vellum. One of 110. $500. Limited Editions Club, New York, 1943. Illustrated. Half leather. In slipcase. $150.

HUDSON, W. H. *Green Mansions.* London, 1904. Light green cloth. First binding, without publisher's design on back cover. $350. Second issue. $250. London, 1926. Illustrated. One of 165. $250. Limited Editions Club, New York, 1935. In slipcase. $75.

HUDSON, W. H. *Idle Days in Patagonia.* London, 1893. Crimson buckram. With 2 ad leaves at end and publisher's device on back cover. One of 1,750. $250. Variants without ads or device. $150.

HUDSON, W. H. *Lost British Birds.* (London, 1894.) 32 pp., light green wraps. Priced at seven pence. $600. (Reprint dated 1894 on the cover.)

HUDSON, W. H. *The Purple Land That England Lost.* London, 1885. 2 vols., light blue cloth. Author's first book. First issue, with October ads in second volume. $1,500. Later issue in purple cloth. $750.

HUEFFER, Ford Madox. See Conrad, Joseph, and Hueffer, Ford Madox. See also Ford, Ford Madox (for books published after 1919, when he changed his name).

HUEFFER, Ford Madox. *The Brown Owl.* London, 1892 (actually 1891). (By Ford Madox Ford.) Author's first book. $600.

HUEFFER, Ford Madox. *Between St. Dennis and St. George.* London, 1915. (By Ford Madox Ford.) $600.

HUEFFER, Ford Madox. *The Feather.* London, 1892. (By Ford Madox Ford.) $400.

HUEFFER, Ford Madox. *The Fifth Queen.* London, 1906. (By Ford Madox Ford.) $250.

HUEFFER, Ford Madox. *From Inland and Other Poems.* London, 1907. (By Ford Madox Ford.) Wraps. $250.

HUEFFER, Ford Madox. *The Queen Who Flew.* London, 1894. (By Ford Madox Ford.) Illustrated. Vellum. One of 25 signed. $1,250. Trade in decorated cloth. $300.

HUGHES, Dorothy B. *The So Blue Marble.* New York (1940). Author's first book. $175.

HUGHES, John T. *California: Its History, Population, Climate, Soil, Productions, and Harbors.* Cincinnati, 1848. 105 pp., printed wraps. $850.

HUGHES, John T. *Doniphan's Expedition. Containing an Account of the Conquest of New Mexico.* Cincinnati, 1847. 144 pages. Wraps. First issue does not state "Cheap Edition" on front wrap. $2,500. Cincinnati, 1848. Wraps. $300. Cloth. With portrait of Doniphan and map. (Best edition according to Howes.) $500. Second issue adding portrait of Price and list of illustrations. $400.

HUGHES, Langston. *Dear Lovely Death.* Amenia, N.Y., 1931. 100 signed copies. $1,000.

HUGHES, Langston. *Fine Clothes to the Jew.* New York, 1927. $750.

HUGHES, Langston. *Scottsboro Limited: Four Poems and a Play in Verse.* New York, 1932. 30 copies signed by Hughes and Prentiss Taylor, the illustrator. $1,250. Trade. Wraps. $300.

HUGHES, Langston. *Shakespeare in Harlem.* New York, 1942. $200.

HUGHES, Langston. *The Weary Blues.* New York, 1926. First issue dustwrapper without blurb for *Fine Clothes to the Jew.* Author's first book. $1,250.

HUGHES, Richard. *Gipsy-Night and Other Poems.* London (1922). Portrait. Author's first book. Golden Cockerel Press. One of 750. $150. Chicago, 1922. Portrait. Boards and cloth. One of 63 signed, with a special proof of portrait. $200.

HUGHES, Richard. *A High Wind in Jamaica.* London, 1929. First complete English edition. One of 150 signed. $350. Trade. $150. (The first edition was published in New York as *The Innocent Voyage.*)

HUGHES, Richard. *The Innocent Voyage.* New York, 1929. Decorated blue boards and blue linen. $250. Limited Editions Club, New York, 1944. Leather. In slipcase. $75. (Published in England as *A High Wind in Jamaica.*)

HUGHES, Richard. *The Sisters' Tragedy.* Oxford, 1922. Wraps. $125.

HUGHES, Sukey. *Washi, The World of Japanese Paper.* Tokyo (1978). Limited to 1,000 copies. 102 actual specimens of paper. $450.

HUGHES, Ted. *Animal Poems.* London (1967). Wraps. One of 100 signed. $500.

HUGHES, Ted. *The Burning of the Brothel.* Turret Books. (London, 1966.) Woodcuts in color. Printed wraps. One of 300. $200. One of 75 signed by Hughes. $600.

HUGHES, Ted. *Crow.* London, 1970. $100. London (1973). 12 drawings by Leonard Baskin. One of 400 signed. In slipcase. $400.

HUGHES, Ted. *Crow Wakes.* Essex, 1971. One of 200. $200.

HUGHES, Ted. *Eat Crow.* London, 1971. Illustrated by Leonard Baskin. Black leather. One of 150 signed in slipcase. $500.

HUGHES, Ted. *Eclipse.* Knotting, 1976. Wraps. One of 50 signed. $400.

HUGHES, Ted. *The Hawk in the Rain.* London (1957). Author's first book. $200. New York (1957). $150.

HUGHES, Ted. *Prometheus on His Crag.* London, 1973. Illustrated. Purple morocco. One of 160 signed, with a signed Leonard Baskin drawing. In slipcase. $600.

HUGHES, Ted. *Spring Summer Autumn Winter.* London, 1973. One of 140 signed. In glassine jacket and slipcase. $300.

HUGHES, Thomas. See *Tom Brown at Oxford; Tom Brown's School Days.*

HUGO, Richard F. *Poems.* (Portland, 1959.) Author's first book. Wraps. $150.

HUGO, Richard F. *A Run of Jacks.* Minnesota (1961). $150.

HUGO, Victor. *Les Miserables.* London, 1862. 3 vols., cloth. First edition in English. $850.

HUGO, Victor. *Toilers of the Sea.* London, 1866. 3 vols., pebbled green cloth. First edition in English. $400. Limited Editions Club, New York, 1960. In slipcase. $125.

HUIE, William Bradford. *The Revolt of Mamie Stover.* New York (1951). $75.

HULME, T. E. *An Introduction to Metaphysics.* New York (1912). Translation and introduction by Hulme (his first book) of Henri Bergson's work. $150. London, 1913. $125.

HULME, Wyndham E. et al. *Leather for Libraries.* London, 1905. $150.

HULTON, Paul, and QUINN, David Beers. *The American Drawings of John White, 1577–1590.* London, 1964. Frontispiece, 160 plates, 76 in color. 2 vols., folio, red buckram. $750.

HUMANITAS (pseudonym). *Hints for the Consideration of the Friends of Slavery* . . . Lexington, Ky., 1805. 32 pp. $2,000.

HUMASON, W. L. *From the Atlantic Surf to the Golden Gate.* Hartford, 1869. $250.

HUME, Fergus. *The Mystery of the Hansom Cab.* Melbourne, 1886. Author's first book. (4 known copies.) $2,000. London, 1887. Wraps. $600.

HUME, Hamilton. *A Brief Statement of Facts in Connection with an Overland Expedition from Lake George to Port Phillip in 1824.* Sydney, 1855. $7,500.

HUMOURIST (The). London, 1819–20. (By George Cruikshank.) 40 colored etchings, including vignette title pages by George Cruikshank. 4 vols. First issue, without "Vol. 1" on title page and with all plates dated 1819. $3,000. Second issue, dated 1819–22: 4 vols. $2,750. London, 1892. 4 vols., half morocco. One of 70 on large paper. $1,000. One of 260. $500.

HUMPHREY, William. *The Last Husband and Other Stories.* New York, 1953. Author's first book. $150.

HUMPHREYS, Arthur L. *Old Decorative Maps and Charts.* London, 1926. One of 1,500. In dustwrapper. $350. Half vellum. Deluxe edition. One of 100 with separate mounted plates. $600.

HUMPHREYS, David. *An Historical Account of the Incorporated Society for the Propagation of the Gospel in Foreign Parts* . . . London, 1730. Two folding maps. $1,000.

HUMPHREYS, H. Noel. *A History of the Art of Printing from Its Invention to* . . . London, 1868. Second issue with the section on references at the end of the book in the first issue suppressed because of errors. 100 facsimiles in photolithography. $150.

HUMPHREYS, Henry Noel. *The Illuminated Books of the Middle Ages.* London, 1844–49. 39 colored plates, one plain plate. Folio, half calf. $1,500. Small paper edition. $500.

HUMPHREYS, Henry Noel. *Masterpieces of the Early Printers and Engravers . . .* London, 1870. 81 full-page illustrations. $300.

HUMPHREYS, Henry Noel. *The Origin and Progress of the Art of Writing . . .* London, 1855. Second edition. First was 1852. $500.

HUMPHRIES, Sydney. *Oriental Carpets, Runners and Rugs.* London, 1910. Illustrated. Folio, cloth. $350.

HUNEKER, James. *Mezzotints in Modern Music.* New York, 1899. Author's first book. $125.

HUNEKER, James. *Painted Veils.* New York (1920). Blue boards, vellum spine. First edition, on watermarked paper. One of 1,200 signed. $200. New York, 1929. 12 color plates by Majeska. One of 1,250. $100.

HUNT. J. H. L. *Juvenilia; or, A Collection of Poems.* London, 1801. Frontispiece. Leigh Hunt's first book. $400.

HUNT, James H. *A History of the Mormon War.* St. Louis, 1844. $1,000.

HUNT, James H. *Mormonism: Embracing the Origin, Rise and Progress of the Sect.* St. Louis, 1844. Expanded edition of the foregoing title. With errata leaf. $1,250.

HUNT, John. *Gazetteer of the Border and Southern States.* Pittsburgh, 1863. Folding map in color. $300.

HUNT, Leigh. See Hunt, J. H. L. See also *Christianism; The Feast of the Poets; Sir Ralph Esher.*

HUNT, Leigh. *The Autobiography of Leigh Hunt.* London, 1850. Portraits. 3 vols. $750.

HUNT, Leigh. *The Correspondence of Leigh Hunt.* London, 1862. Edited by his eldest son. Portrait. 2 vols., tan cloth. $350.

HUNT, Leigh. *A Jar of Honey from Mount Hybla.* London, 1848. Engraved title page. First binding in glazed boards. $500. Later issue is plain cloth. $200.

HUNT, Leigh. *Men, Women and Books.* Portrait. London, 1847. 2 vols., orange cloth. $300. New York, 1847. 2 vols. $200.

HUNT, Leigh. *The Palfrey.* London, 1842. 6 woodcuts. $600.

HUNT, *Leigh. Stories from the Italian Poets . . .* London, 1846. 2 vols., dark blue cloth. With December ads (VAB). $250.

HUNT, Leigh. *The Story of Rimini: A Poem.* London, 1816. With half title. $250.

HUNT, Leigh. *Ultra-Crepidarius: A Satire on William Gifford.* London, 1823. Wraps bound in. $400.

HUNT, Lynn Bogue. *An Artist's Game Bag.* Derrydale Press. New York, 1936. 4 color plates, other illustrations. Full leatherette. One of 1,250. $450. Trade in cloth. $125.

HUNT, Richard S., and RANDEL, Jesse F. *Guide to the Republic of Texas.* New York, 1839. Folding map, 63 pages in original cloth. $2,500.

HUNT, Richard S., and RANDEL, Jesse F. *A New Guide to Texas.* New York, 1845. Folding map, 62 pages, cloth. Second edition of preceding title. $2,000. New York, 1846 *(sic)*. With map dated 1848. $1,750.

HUNT, T. Dwight. *The Past and Present of the Sandwich Islands.* San Francisco, 1853. $400.

HUNT, Thomas Frederick. *Designs for Parsonage Houses . . .* London, 1827. $400.

HUNT, Violet. *The Maiden's Progress.* London, 1894. Author's first book. $250. New York, 1894. $200.

HUNTER, Alexander. *Johnny Reb and Billy Yank.* New York, 1905. Illustrated. $350.

HUNTER, Dard. *Before Life Began, 1883–1923.* Cleveland, Rowfant Club. Slipcase. Limited to 219 numbered copies signed by Bruce Rogers. $400.

HUNTER, Dard. *The Literature of Papermaking, 1390–1800.* (Chillicothe, 1925.) Signatures loosely inserted in a three-quarter cloth portfolio with cloth ties. Limited to 190 numbered and signed copies. $2,500.

HUNTER, Dard. *Massachusetts Institute of Technology: Dard Hunter Paper Museum.* (Cambridge, Mass., 1939.) Frontispiece photograph. Printed wraps with woodcut on front. $250.

HUNTER, Dard. *My Life with Paper.* New York, 1958. Two specimens of paper tipped in. $125.

HUNTER, Dard. *Old Papermaking.* Chillicothe, 1923. One of 200 numbered and signed copies. Nine leaves mounted with paper samples. Author's first book on papermaking. $2,500.

HUNTER, Dard. *Papermaking: The History and Technique of an Ancient Craft.* New York, 1943. Second edition, revised and enlarged. Foldout map. $150.

HUNTER, Dard. *Papermaking by Hand in America.* Chillicothe, 1950. Limited to 210 numbered copies signed by both Hunter and Dard Hunter, Jr. Hand-colored frontispiece. 96 facsimiles tipped in, 27 reproductions of watermarks and 42 full-size reproductions of old paper labels. In drop-leaf slipcase. $8,000.

HUNTER, Dard. *Papermaking by Hand in India.* New York, 1939. Limited to 370 numbered copies, signed by Hunter and Elmer Adler. 27 paper specimens. Boxed. $1,750.

HUNTER, Dard. *Paper-Making in the Classroom.* Peoria (1931). $375.

HUNTER, Dard. *Papermaking in Indo-China.* (Chillicothe) 1947. One of 182 signed by Hunter. In slipcase with leather tips on openings. Many reproductions and two actual specimens tipped in. $1,500.

HUNTER, Dard. *Papermaking in Pioneer America.* Philadelphia, 1952. $100.

HUNTER, Dard. *A Papermaking Pilgrimage to Japan, Korea and China.* New York, 1936. Limited to 370 numbered copies signed by Hunter and Elmer Adler. 50 tipped-in paper specimens. 68 photogravure illustrations. Slipcase. $1,850.

HUNTER, Dard. *Papermaking Through Eighteen Centuries.* New York, 1930. In dustwrapper. $250.

HUNTER, Dard. *Primitive Papermaking.* Chillicothe, 1937. Signatures loosely inserted in portfolio with cloth ties, in slipcase. One of 200 signed and numbered copies. $3,500.

HUNTER, Dard. *Romance of Watermarks* . . . Cincinnati (no-date, circa 1940). Limited to 210 copies. Slipcase. $300.

HUNTER, George. *Reminiscences of an Old Timer* . . . San Francisco, 1887. 16 plates. Pictorial cloth. $350.

HUNTER, J. Marvin (compiler). *The Trail Drivers of Texas* . . . (San Antonio, 1920–23.) Illustrated. 2 vols., with an additional revised vol. one. The set of three (usually sold this way). $800. Nashville, 1925. 2 vols. in one, one of 100. $1,250. Trade. $200. New York, 1963. 2 vols., half morocco. Slipcase. $200.

HUNTER, J. Marvin, and ROSE, Noah H. *The Album of Gun-Fighters.* (Banders, Tex., 1951.) Pictorial cloth. $150. Limited edition, with signed slip. $250.

HUNTER, Capt. John. *An Historical Journal of the Transactions at Port Jackson and Norfolk Island* . . . London, 1793. With portrait, 13 plates, and 2 folding maps. $4,000.

HUNTER, John D. *Manners and Customs of Several Indian Tribes Located West of the Mississippi.* Philadelphia, 1823. $500.

HUNTER, John D. *Memoirs of a Captivity Among the Indians of North America.* London, 1823. First English edition of *Manners and Customs.* $300.

HUNTER, Robert. *The Links.* New York, 1926. $300.

HUNTER, William S., Jr. *Hunter's Ottawa Scenery.* Ottawa, 1855. Engraved title page, folding map, and 13 plates. Folio, cloth. $1,250.

HUNTER, William S., Jr. *Hunter's Panoramic Guide from Niagara Falls to Quebec.* Boston, 1857. Engraved title, folding panoramic chart. Pictorial cloth. $250. Montreal, 1860. $200.

HUNTINGTON, D. B. *Vocabulary of the Utah and Sho-Sho-Ne, or Snake Dialect, with Indian Legends and Traditions.* Salt Lake City, 1872. 32 pages, stitched. $300.

HURSTON, Zora Neale. *Jonah's Gourd Vine.* Philadelphia, 1934. Author's first book. $1,000. London, 1934. $750.

HURSTON, Zora Neale. *Mules and Men.* Philadelphia, 1935. $600. London, 1936. $400.

HURSTON, Zora Neale. *Seraph on the Suwanee.* New York, 1948. $200.

HURSTON, Zora Neale. *Tell My Horse.* Philadelphia (1938). $350.

HUSTON, John. *Frankie and Johnny.* New York, 1930. Illustrated by Miguel Covarrubias. $150.

HUTCHINGS, James M. *Scenes of Wonder and Curiosity in California.* San Francisco (1860). Cloth. $250. Sheep. $600. San Francisco, 1861. Second edition (or issue). $150.

HUTCHINS, Thomas. *An Historical Narrative and Topographical Description of Louisiana and West Florida . . .* Philadelphia, 1784. Stitched wraps, uncut and untrimmed. $2,500.

HUTCHINSON, Horace. *British Golf Links.* 1897. Large paper edition (250 copies). Wraps. $1,750. Trade. $1,000.

HUTCHINSON, Horace. *50 Years of Golf.* London, 1919. $350.

HUTCHINSON, Horace. *Golf: Badminton Library.* 1890. Limited edition on large paper. $750. Trade. $300.

HUTCHINSON, Horace. *A Golfing Pilgrim on Many Links.* London, 1898. $400. New York, 1898. $400.

HUTCHINSON, Horace (edited by). With LANG, Andrew, et al. *Famous Golf Links.* London, 1891. $750.

HUTTON, William. *The Life of William Hutton . . .* London, 1817. Second edition, with additions. $350.

HUXLEY, Aldous. See *Jonah.*

HUXLEY, Aldous. *After Many a Summer.* London, 1939. $250.

HUXLEY, Aldous. *Along the Road.* London, 1925. Top edge green. $175. New York (1925). Boards. One of 250 signed. In dustwrapper and slipcase. $300.

HUXLEY, Aldous. *Antic Hay.* London, 1923. Top edge yellow. $400.

HUXLEY, Aldous. *Apennine.* Gaylordsville, N.Y., 1930. Boards and cloth, paper label. One of 91 signed. Issued without dustwrapper. In slipcase. $400.

HUXLEY, Aldous. *Arabia Infelix and Other Poems.* Fountain Press. New York, 1929. Boards and cloth. One of 692 signed. $150.

HUXLEY, Aldous. *Brave New World.* London, 1932. Buckram, leather label. One of 324 signed. In acetate dustwrapper. $2,000. Trade. $750. Garden City, 1932. First American edition. One of 250 signed. $1,250. Trade. $250. Limited Editions Club. New York, 1974. In slipcase. $100.

HUXLEY, Aldous. *Brief Candles.* New York, 1930. Fountain Press. First American edition. One of 842 signed. $150. Trade. $75. London, 1930. Red cloth. $100.

HUXLEY, Aldous. *The Burning Wheel.* Oxford, 1916. Woodcut decorations. Yellow wraps, paper label. Author's first book. $800.

HUXLEY, Aldous. *The Cicadas and Other Poems.* London, 1931. Boards and cloth. One of 160 signed. In dustwrapper (VAB). $300. Trade. $150.

HUXLEY, Aldous. *Crome Yellow.* London, 1921. Yellow cloth, top stained green. In dustwrapper. $300.

HUXLEY, Aldous. *The Defeat of Youth and Other Poems.* (Oxford, 1918.) Without title page. Decorated stiff wraps. $300.

HUXLEY, Aldous. *Do What You Will.* London, 1929. One of 260 signed. In glassine jacket without slipcase. $250. Trade. $150.

HUXLEY, Aldous. *Essays New and Old.* London, 1926. Florence Press. One of 650 signed. In dustwrapper. (No trade edition.) $300.

HUXLEY, Aldous. *Eyeless in Gaza.* London, 1936. Decorated boards and brown buckram. One of 200 signed. Issued without dustwrapper or slipcase. $500. Trade. $300.

HUXLEY, Aldous. *Holy Face and Other Essays.* London, 1929. Colored illustrations. Buckram. One of 300. Issued without dustwrapper in slipcase. $250.

HUXLEY, Aldous. *Leda.* London, 1920. One of 160 signed. $300. Trade in dustwrapper. $250. Garden City, 1929. One of 361 signed. Issued without dustwrapper in slipcase. $200.

HUXLEY, Aldous. *Little Mexican and Other Stories.* London, 1924. Top edge crimson. (Issued in U.S. as *Young Archimedes . . .*) $250.

HUXLEY, Aldous. *Mortal Coils.* London, 1922. Top stained blue. $200.

HUXLEY, Aldous. *Music at Night and Other Essays.* New York, 1931. Fountain Press. One of 842 signed. Issued without dustwrapper in slipcase. $250. Trade. $75. London, 1931. $125.

HUXLEY, Aldous. *On the Margin.* London, 1923. Green cloth, top stained blue. First edition, with page "vi" numbered "v" in error (Cutler & Stiles) "vii" (Casanova). $200. Second issue corrected and top green edge. $150.

HUXLEY, Aldous. *Point Counter Point.* London, 1928. One of 256 signed. $400. Trade in orange cloth. $300.

HUXLEY, Aldous. *Selected Poems.* Oxford, 1925. Decorated boards. Issued without dustwrapper. $100. One of 100 signed with vellum spine. $300.

HUXLEY, Aldous. *Vulgarity in Literature.* London, 1930. One of 260 signed. $250. (A few copies were bound in leather [VAB].) Trade in decorated boards. $125.

HUXLEY, Aldous. *Words and Their Meanings.* Los Angeles (1940). One of 100 signed. In dustwrapper. $250.

HUXLEY, Aldous. *The World of Light.* London, 1931. One of 160 signed. In glassine jacket without slipcase. $250. Trade. $125.

HUXLEY, Aldous. *Young Archimedes and Other Sketches.* New York, 1924. $250.

HUXLEY, T. H. *Evidence as to Man's Place in Nature.* London, 1863. $350.

HYDE, George E. *The Early Blackfeet and Their Neighbors.* Denver, 1933. 45 pages, wraps. One of 75. $200.

HYDE, George E. *The Pawnee Indians.* Denver, 1934. 2 vols., printed wraps. One of 100. $200.

HYDE, George E. *Rangers and Regulars.* Denver, 1933. 47 pages, wraps. One of 50. $150.

HYDE, S. C. *Historical Sketch of Lyon County, Iowa.* Le Mars, Iowa, 1872. Map. 40 pages, wraps. $150.

HYNE, C. J. Cutliffe. *The Lost Continent.* London, 1900. $100.

HYPERION: A Romance. New York, 1839. By the author of "Outre-Mer." 2 vols. (Henry Wadsworth Longfellow.) $350.

I

IBÁÑEZ, Vicente Blasco. *The Four Horsemen of the Apocalypse.* New York, 1918. First American edition. In dustwrapper. $350. Without jacket, $75.

IBSEN, Henrik. *Peer Gynt: A Dramatic Poem.* London (1936). Illustrated in color by Arthur Rackham. Full white vellum. One of 460 signed by Rackham. In slipcase. $1,250. Trade edition. $300. Philadelphia (1936). $250. New York, 1955. Limited Editions Club. Illustrated. Pictorial boards. In slipcase. $50.

IDAHO: A Guide in Word and Picture. Caldwell, Idaho, 1937. Illustrated. Pictorial cloth. (Edited by Vardis Fisher.) $300. First Work Projects Administration (WPA) State Guide.

IDE, Simeon. *The Conquest of California: A Biography of William B. Ide.* Grabhorn Press. Oakland, 1944. Illustrations, map. Boards and cloth. One of 500. $150.

IDE, William Brown. *A Biographical Sketch of the Life of William B. Ide . . . And . . . Account of the Virtual Conquest of California . . .* (Claremont, N.H., 1880.) (By Simeon Ide.) Half leather and cloth. (80 copies issued.) $1,000. Another edition: printed wraps. (Claremont, 1885?) $600.

IDE, William Brown. *Who Conquered California?* Claremont, N.H. (1880? 1885?) (By Simeon Ide.) Printed boards and cloth. $450.

IDEAL Husband (An). London, 1899. By the Author of *Lady Windermere's Fan.* (By Oscar Wilde.) Lavender cloth. Large paper issue: one of 100. $1,500. One of 12 signed on vellum. $6,000. Trade. One of 1,000. Light brownish red linen. $450.

IGNATOW, David. *Poems.* Prairie City (1948). Author's first book. $350.

I KUNSTITUSHUN i Micha i nan vlhpisa Chickasha, Okla i nan apesa yvt apesa tokmak oke. ("Chickasaw People, Their Constitution and Their Law 1857–59. 1867–68. 1870–72.") Translated from English to Chickasaw by Allen Wright. Chickasha, Okla., 1872. $450.

ILLUSTRATED Atlas and History of Yolo County, California (The). San Francisco, 1879. 50 plates, map in color. Atlas folio, cloth. $650.

ILLUSTRATED History of Los Angeles County (An). Chicago, 1889. Illustrated. Full morocco. $650.

ILLUSTRATED History of San Joaquin County (An). Chicago, 1890. Full leather. $500.

IMAGINARY Conversations of Literary Men and Statesmen. London, 1824. (By Walter Savage Landor.) 2 vols. $150. (Note: Three other volumes of the *Conversations* subsequently appeared.) Limited Editions Club, New York, 1936. Linen. In slipcase. Signed by Mardersteig. $150.

IMAGIST Anthology (The). New York (1930). Edited by Ford Madox Ford and Glenn Hughes. One of 1,000. $300. London, 1930. Yellow cloth. First English edition. $200.

IMBERDIS, J. *Papyrius; Or, the Craft of Paper.* Bird & Bull Press (North Hills), 1961. One of 113. $650.

IMPARTIAL Appeal (An) to the Reason, Interest, and Patriotism of the People of Illinois, on the Injurious Effects of Slave Labour. (Philadelphia?) 1824. (By Morris Birkbeck.) 16 pages, unbound. $2,000 and up. (Note: Only 4 copies known.)

IMPORTANCE of Being Earnest (The). By the Author of *Lady Windermere's Fan.* London, 1899. (By Oscar Wilde.) Reddish brown linen. $350. One of 100 on large paper, signed. $3,500. Vellum. One of 12 on Japan paper, signed. $5,000. New York, 1956. 2 vols., decorated boards. One of 500. In slipcase. $300.

IMPRINT (The). London, 1913. Complete set of 9 vols., all published. Stiff paper wraps. $300.

INCIDENTAL Numbers. London, 1912. Boards. (By Elinor Wylie. Her first book.) One of 65. $5,000.

INDIAN Council in the Valley of the Walla-Walla, 1855 (The). San Francisco, 1855. (By Lawrence Kipp.) 2 pages, pale blue printed wraps. $1,000. Eugene, Ore., 1897. $100.

INDIAN Treaties Printed by Benjamin Franklin, 1736–1762. Philadelphia, 1938. Folio, with leather spine label. Top stained red. Slipcase. One of 500 numbered copies. $350.

INDIAN Missions (The), in the United States of America, etc. Philadelphia, 1941. 34 pages, plain blue wraps. (This Jesuit report includes two letters of Pierre Jean De Smet.) $1,500 or more.

INEZ: A Tale of the Alamo. New York, 1855. (By Augusta Jane Evans Wilson.) Author's first book. $250.

INFIDEL (The); or The Fall of Mexico. Philadelphia, 1835. (By Robert Montgomery Bird.) 2 vols., in original purple cloth, paper labels. $350.

INGE, William. *Bus Stop.* New York (1955). $125.

INGE, William. *Come Back, Little Sheba.* New York (1950). Author's first book. $125.

INGE, William. *Picnic.* New York (1953). $125.

INGELOW, Jean. *Poems.* London, 1867. $250.

INGERSOLL, Luther A. *Century Annals of San Bernardino County.* (1769 to 1904.) Los Angeles, 1904. Portraits and views. Full morocco. $125.

INGERSOLL, Robert G. *An Oration Delivered . . . at Rouse's Hall, Peoria, Ill., at the Unveiling of a Statue of Humboldt, September 14th, 1869.* Peoria, 1869. Wraps. Author's first published work. $150.

INGOLDSBY, Thomas. *The Ingoldsby Legends, or Mirth and Marvels.* London, 1840–42–47. (By Richard Harris Barham.) Etchings by George Cruikshank and John Leech. 3 vols., brown cloth. with misprint "topot" on page 350 of vol. 3 and blank page 236 in vol. 1 (VAB). $1,000. London, 1898. Illustrated by Arthur Rackham. Green cloth. $350. London, 1907. Illustrated by Rackham. White vellum. One of 560 signed by Rackham. $1,000. Trade in cloth. $300.

INGRAHAM, Joseph Holt. See *The South-West.*

INGRAHAM, Joseph Holt. *Pierce Tenning, or, The Lugger's Chase.* Boston, 1846. Illustrated. 95 pp., stitched. Wraps. $300.

IN MEMORIAM. London, 1850. (By Alfred, Lord Tennyson.) Dark purple cloth. First issue, with "baseness" for "bareness" in line 3, page 198. $750. London, 1933. Nonesuch Press. Limp vellum. $500. Boards. One of 2,000. $150.

INMAN, Col. Henry. *The Old Santa Fe Trail.* New York, 1897. Frontispiece, 8 plates by Frederic Remington, folding map. $200.

INMAN, Col. Henry. *Stories of the Old Santa Fe Trail.* Kansas City, 1881. Pictorial cloth. Author's first book. $250.

INMAN, Col. Henry (editor). *Buffalo Jones' 40 Years of Adventure.* Topeka, 1899. 43 plates. Pictorial cloth. $200.

INMAN, Col. Henry, and CODY, William F. *The Great Salt Lake Trail.* New York, 1898. Map, 8 plates. Pictorial buckram. First binding, blue (later brown). $175.

INNES, Michael. *Death at the President's Lodging.* London, 1936. Author's first book. $500.

INNES, Michael. *Seven Suspects.* (New title.) New York, 1936. $250.

INSTRUCTION for Heavy Artillery . . . for the Use of the Army of the United States. Charleston, 1862. 39 plates, tables, charts. $600.

INSUBORDINATION . . . New York, 1841. (By T. S. Arthur. His first book.) $300.

INVINCIBLE, Ned. *The Rose That Bloometh in My Heart.* (Louisville?, 1908.) Author's first book. $200.

IRON, Ralph. *The Story of an African Farm.* London, 1883. (By Olive Schreiner.) 2 vols. Author's first book. $1,500. Limited Editions Club, Uganda (New York), 1961. Illustrated by Paul Hogarth. In slipcase. $100.

IRVING, John. *Setting Free the Bears.* New York (1968). Author's first book. $350.

IRVING, John. *The Water Method Man.* New York (1972). $125. London, 1980. Wraps (assumed). $25.

IRVING, John. *The Hotel New Hampshire.* New York (1981). One of 550 signed. Full leather, in slipcase. $125. Trade. $30. London (1981). $40.

IRVING, John Treat, Jr. *The Hawk Chief: A Tale of the Indian Country.* Philadelphia, 1837. 2 vols., in original cloth. $350.

IRVING, John Treat, Jr. *The Hunters of the Prairie, or the Hawk Chief.* London, 1837. 2 vols., in original boards and cloth. First English edition of *The Hawk Chief.* $250.

IRVING, John Treat, Jr. *Indian Sketches, Taken During an Expedition to the Pawnee Tribes.* Philadelphia, 1835. 2 vols. $150. London, 1835. 2 vols. First English edition. $150.

IRVING, Washington. See Crayon, Geoffrey; Depons, François; Knickerbocker, Diedrich; Langstaff, Launcelot; Oldstyle, Jonathan. See also *Abbotsford; Legends of the Conquest of Spain; A Tour on the Prairies.*

IRVING, Washington. *Chronicles of Wolfert's Roost.* Edinburgh (London), 1855. Tan cloth. First issue, with *Constable's Miscellany* listed as "In the Press . . . Volume V" (later reading, "Volume VII"). $300.

IRVING, Washington. *A History of the Life and Voyages of Christopher Columbus.* London, 1828. 2 folding maps, 4 vols., boards, paper labels. $500. New York, 1828. Folding map. 3 vols. First American edition. $300.

IRVING, Washington. *The Legend of Sleepy Hollow.* New York (1897). Designs by Will Bradley. Pictorial boards. $300. London (1928). Cloth. Illustrated by Arthur Rackham. $400. One of 250 signed by Rackham. $1,500. Philadelphia (1928). $400.

IRVING, Washington. *The Life of George Washington.* New York, 1855–59. 5 vols., cloth. With dates as follows: vols. I and 2, 1855; 3, 1856; 4, 1857, and 5, 1859. $300. Large paper edition (vol. 2 dated 1856). One of 110 copies. $500.

IRVING, Washington. *The Rocky Mountains.* Philadelphia, 1837. "Digested from the Journal of Captain B. L. E. Bonneville . . . by Washington Irving." 2 folding maps. 2 vols. in original blue cloth, printed labels. First issue, with no ads and 2 blank fly leaves at each end. $400.

IRVING, Washington. *Voyages and Discoveries of the Companions of Columbus.* London, 1831. $250. Philadelphia, 1831. $200.

IRWIN, Margaret. *Madame Fears the Dark . . .* London, 1935. $200.

ISELIN, Isaac. *Journal of a Trading Voyage Around the World, 1805–1808.* (New York, about 1897.) (100 copies printed.) $400.

ISHERWOOD, Christopher. See Auden, W. H., and Isherwood, Christopher; Baudelaire, Charles.

ISHERWOOD, Christopher. *All the Conspirators.* London, 1928. Author's first novel. $1,250.

ISHERWOOD, Christopher. *The Berlin Stories: The Last of Mr. Norris, Goodbye to Berlin.* New Directions. (Norfolk, Conn.) 1945. $125.

ISHERWOOD, Christopher. *Goodbye to Berlin.* Hogarth Press. London, 1939. $1,000.

ISHERWOOD, Christopher. *The Last of Mr. Norris.* New York, 1935. $500.

ISHERWOOD, Christopher. *Lions and Shadows: An Education in the Twenties.* London, 1938. Portrait frontispiece. In first binding or blue cloth lettered in black. $600.

Later (most) lettered in gilt. $500. (Both states have turned up in the "Hogarth Crown Library No. 4." Dustwrapper. Issued in 1943.) New Directions. Norfolk (1947). $150.

ISHERWOOD, Christopher. *The Memorial: Portrait of a Family.* Hogarth Press. London, 1932. First binding in pale pink, lettered in blue. $500. Later binding in blue or ochre. $400. New Directions. Norfolk (about 1946). $100.

ISHERWOOD, Christopher. *Mr. Norris Changes Trains.* Hogarth Press. London, 1935. $600.

ISHERWOOD, Christopher. *Prater Violet.* New York (1945). Gray cloth. $125. London (1946). $125.

ISHERWOOD, Christopher. *Sally Bowles.* Hogarth Press. London, 1937. $500.

ISHIKAWA, T., and DRAEGER, D.F. *Judo Training Methods: A Sourcebook.* Tokyo, 1962. Stated first. $50.

IVANHOE: A Romance. Edinburgh, 1820. (By Sir Walter Scott.) 3 vols. $750. New York. 1951. Limited Editions Club. Illustrated. 2 vols., pictorial cloth. In slipcase. $75.

IVES, Charles. *Essays Before a Sonata.* New York, 1920. Author's first book. Issued without dustwrapper? $350.

IVES, Joseph C. *Report Upon the Colorado River of the West.* Washington, 1861. 4 folding maps, 32 plates. Senate issue. $650.

IVINS, Virginia W. *Pen Pictures of Early Western Days.* (Keokuk, Iowa), 1905. Plates. $350. Second edition. (Keokuk) 1908. $175.

J

JACKSON, A. P., and COLE, E. C. *Oklahoma! Politically and Topographically Described.* Kansas City (1885). Map (not in all copies). Pictorial wraps in color. $500.

JACKSON, A. W. *Barbariana: or Scenery, Climate, Soils and Social Conditions of Santa Barbara City and County.* San Francisco, 1889. 48 pages, printed wraps. $125.

JACKSON, Andrew. *Message from the President of the United States, in Compliance with a Resolution of the Senate Concerning the Fur Trade and Inland Trade to Mexico.* (Washington, 1832.) 86 pp., unbound. Senate Doc. 90. $300.

JACKSON, Benjamin Daydon. *Guide to the Literature of Botany.* London, 1881. $125.

JACKSON, Benjamin Daydon. *Vegetable Technology: A Contribution Towards a Bibliography* ... London, 1882. This is vol. XI of the Publications of the Index Society. $125.

JACKSON, Charles. *The Lost Weekend.* New York (1944). Author's first book. $100.

JACKSON, Charles James. *An Illustrated History of English Plate . . .* London, 1911. Colored frontispiece. 76 photogravure plates, 2 vols., half morocco. $500.

JACKSON, Mrs. F. Nevill. *Toys of Other Days.* London, 1908. 9 color plates, 273 plain illustrations. Full vellum. One of 50. $350. Morocco. One of 150. $200. Trade in cloth. $100.

JACKSON, George. *Sixty Years in Texas.* (Dallas, 1908.) Plates. Cloth. First edition, first issue, with 322 pages. $200.

JACKSON, Helen Hunt. See H. H.

JACKSON, Helen Hunt. *The Procession of Flowers in Colorado.* Boston, 1886. One of 100. $200.

JACKSON, Helen Hunt. *Ramona.* Boston, 1884. Decorated cloth. $600. Limited Editions Club, Los Angeles, 1959. Introduction by J. Frank Dobie. Cloth. In slipcase. $50.

JACKSON, Holbrook. *The Anatomy of Bibliomania.* London, 1930. 2 vols. Limited to 1,048 numbered copies. $250. Morocco. One of 48 signed. $400. New York, 1931. 2 vols. $150.

JACKSON, Holbrook. *The Fear of Books.* London, 1932. Full black morocco. One of 40 (of an edition of 2,048), signed. $400. Trade in buckram (2,008 copies). $75.

JACKSON, John. *The Practical Fly-Fisher.* London, 1854. 10 hand-colored plates. $1,000.

JACKSON, Shirley. *The Bird's Nest.* New York (1954). $100.

JACKSON, Shirley. *Hangsaman.* New York (1951). $125.

JACKSON, Shirley. *The Lottery.* New York, 1949. With publisher's initials on copyright page. $350.

JACKSON, Shirley. *The Road Through the Wall.* New York (1948). Author's first book. $200.

JACKSON, William A. *An Annotated List of the Publications of the Rev. Thomas Frognall Dibdin . . .* Cambridge, 1965. Limited to 500 copies. $175.

JACOB, J. G. *The Life and Times of Patrick Gass.* Wellsburg, Va., 1859. 4 plates. Cloth. $650.

JACOBS, Thomas Jefferson. *Scenes, Incidents and Adventures in the Pacific Ocean . . .* New York, 1844. Folding plate, numerous other illustrations. $350.

JACOBS, W. W. *Many Cargoes.* London, 1896. Author's first book. 52 pages of ads dated autumn, 1896. With portrait and 6 hand-colored plates. $125.

JACOBSEN, Josephine. *Let Each Man Remember.* Dallas (1940). $300.

JACOBSEN, Josephine. *The Marbled Satyr . . .* New York (1928). Author's first book. $250.

JAEGER, Benedict, and PRESTON, H. C. *The Life of North American Insects.* Providence, 1854. With portrait and 6 hand-colored plates. $250.

JAMES, Edwin (editor). *Account of an Expedition from Pittsburgh to the Rocky Mountains.* Philadelphia, 1822–23. 2 maps, 8 plates. 3 vols. (including atlas). $3,500. London, 1823. 3 vols. First English edition. $1,750.

JAMES, Edwin (editor). *A Narrative of the Captivity and Adventures of John Tanner.* New York, 1830. Frontispiece portrait. $600.

JAMES, Fred. *The Klondike Goldfields and How to Get There.* London, 1897. Map. 68 pages, tan wraps. $450.

JAMES, Henry. See Besant, Walter.

JAMES, Henry. *The Ambassadors.* London, 1903. Crimson cloth. (Second printing in blue cloth.) $200. New York, 1903. Blue boards. "Published November, 1903" on copyright page. In blue linen dustwrapper. $750. Without dustwrapper. $175. Limited Editions Club, New York, 1963. Illustrated. Boards. In slipcase. $60.

JAMES, Henry: *The American.* Boston, 1877. With Osgood imprint on spine. $350.

JAMES, Henry. *The American Scene.* London, 1907. Maroon buckram. $150. New York, 1907. $100.

JAMES, Henry. *The Aspern Papers: Louisa Pallant: The Modern Warning.* London, 1888. 2 vols., blue cloth. $300. London, 1888. First American edition. $125.

JAMES, Henry. *The Awkward Age.* New York, 1899. Brown cloth. The volume bulking 1⅝ inches thick (1⅜ inches later—Edel & Laurence, although BAL doesn't agree). $200. London, 1899. Light blue cloth. (Issued simultaneously.) $250.

JAMES, Henry. *The Beast in the Jungle.* Kentfield, Calif., 1963. Allen Press. Illustrated. Boards. One of 130. $600.

JAMES, Henry. *The Better Sort.* New York, 1903. Rose-colored cloth. With "Published, February, 1903" on copyright page. $125. London, 1903. Red cloth. First English edition (simultaneous). $150.

JAMES, Henry. *The Bostonians.* London, 1886. 3 vols., blue cloth. $12,000 at auction in 1990. London, 1886. First 1-vol. edition. $300. New York, 1886. Orange cloth with maroon spine. Probable first binding. $250. Blue-black cloth. $150.

JAMES, Henry. *A Bundle of Letters.* Boston (1880). Stiff printed wraps. First edition, Blanck's state A (no priority) is considered primary by Edel & Laurence, with comma after "Jr." on front cover. $400.

JAMES, Henry. *Confidence.* London, 1880. 2 vols. $1,000. Boston, 1880. Brick-colored cloth (1 vol.). First issue, with Houghton, Osgood imprint on spine. $400. Second issue, Houghton, Mifflin. $250.

JAMES, Henry. *Daisy Miller: A Comedy.* (London) 1882. Wraps. (18 privately printed copies.) $3,000. Boston, 1883. First published edition. $1,000.

JAMES, Henry. *Daisy Miller: A Study.* New York, 1879. Printed tan or gray wraps, or green cloth. First issue with 79 titles in Harper's Half Hour Series at front. Wraps. $7,500. Cloth: $2,500. Limited Editions Club, New York, 1969. In slipcase. $100.

JAMES, Henry. *Daisy Miller and an International Episode.* New York, 1892. Vellum. One of 250. $450. Trade in cloth. $150.

JAMES, Henry. *The Diary of a Man of Fifty, and A Bundle of Letters.* New York, 1880. Tan wraps. $300. Green cloth. $200.

JAMES, Henry. *Embarrassments.* London, 1896. Blue cloth. With 4 irises on front of binding. (Second had 9 irises.) $200. New York, 1896. $450.

JAMES, Henry. *English Hours.* London, 1905. Illustrated by Joseph Pennell. Gray cloth. $150. Second binding, with dark green buckram spine and green boards. $100. Boston, 1905. Cloth, or half morocco. First American trade. $100. Boards. One of 421 ("400 copies printed") on large paper. $300.

JAMES, Henry. *The Europeans: A Sketch.* London, 1878. 2 vols., blue cloth. $1,000. Boston, 1879. First American edition in 1 vol. $250.

JAMES, Henry. *An International Episode.* New York, 1879. Gray wraps, or flexible green cloth. First state, with last line on page 44 repeated as the first line of page 45. Wraps. $500. Cloth. $300.

JAMES, Henry. *Letters of Henry James to Walter Berry.* Black Sun Press. Paris, 1928. Printed vellum wraps. One of 16 on Japan vellum, each with an original letter. $2,500. One of 100 on Van Gelder paper. $500.

JAMES, Henry. *A Little Tour in France.* Boston, 1885 (actually 1884). Light brown cloth. First binding with James R. Osgood imprint. $350. Second issue had Houghton Mifflin. $200.

JAMES, Henry. *The Madonna of the Future and Other Tales.* London, 1879. 2 vols., blue cloth. $1,250.

JAMES, Henry. *The Other House.* London, 1896. 2 vols., blue cloth. $1,000. (Note: Second edition so stated, but first one-volume in 1897 states "First edition, 2 vols., October, 1896.") New York, 1896. First American edition in 1 vol. (published simultaneously or earlier than the London edition?). $200.

JAMES, Henry. *A Passionate Pilgrim, and Other Tales.* Boston, 1875. Author's first book. First binding, with "J. R. Osgood & Co." on spine. $850. Second issue, "Houghton Osgood & Co." $400. Third issue, "Houghton, Mifflin & Co." $300.

JAMES, Henry. *The Portrait of a Lady.* London, 1881. 3 vols., blue or dark green cloth. With or without ads. (Edel and Laurence believe December 1881 ads are first, but only 750 copies in total.) $2,000. Boston, 1882. 1 vol. in light tan or forest green cloth with period after "Copyright, 1881." $500. Limited Editions Club, New York. 1967. Colored plates. Marbled boards and cloth. In slipcase. $60.

JAMES, Henry. *The Princess Casamassima.* London, 1886. 3 vols., blue cloth. $2,500. London, 1886. (In 1 vol.) $300.

JAMES, Henry. *The Reverberator.* London, 1888. 2 vols., blue or green cloth. $850. London/New York, 1888. Blue cloth. First American edition. $250.

JAMES, Henry. *Roderick Hudson.* Boston, 1876. Author's first novel. First binding, with J. R. Osgood imprint on spine. $400. Later binding. Houghton Mifflin imprint on spine. $250.

JAMES, Henry. *The Siege of London.* Boston, 1883. Cloth. First issue with Osgood imprint on spine. $350. Second issue with Houghton Mifflin. $200.

JAMES, Henry. *The Spoils of Poynton.* London, 1897. Blue cloth. $300. Boston, 1897. (May have been simultaneous.) $200.

JAMES, Henry. *Stories Revived.* London, 1885. 3 vols. Primary binding, blue cloth with brown endpapers. $2,000. Variant binding in blue-green cloth with blue on white patterned endpapers. $1,750.

JAMES, Henry. *Transatlantic Sketches.* Boston, 1875. First binding, with Osgood imprint on spine. $750. Later binding with Houghton Mifflin. $600.

JAMES, Henry. *Washington Square.* New York, 1881. Dark olive-green cloth. $350. Limited Editions Club, New York, 1971. In slipcase. $60.

JAMES, Henry. *Washington Square: The Pension Beaurepas: A Bundle of Letters.* London, 1881. 2 vols. With last page numbered "371" and "H. James Jr." on spine. $1,500. Second printing (only 250 copies), with last page "271" and "Henry/James Jr." on spine. $1,000.

JAMES, Henry. *Watch and Ward.* Boston, 1878. With blank leaf after page 219. $600. Without last leaf. $400.

JAMES, Jason W. *Memorable Events in the Life of Capt. Jason W. James.* No-place (about 1911). Frontispiece. $500.

JAMES, Jason W. *Memories and Viewpoints.* Roswell, N.M., 1928. Issued without dustwrapper. $400.

JAMES, Jesse, Jr. *Jesse James, My Father.* Kansas City, Mo., 1899. (Ghostwritten by A. B. Macdonald?) 4 portraits. White printed wraps. $200.

JAMES, M. R. *Ghost Stories of an Antiquary.* London, 1904. Author's first book. $250.

JAMES, M. R. *Wailing Well.* Stanford, Dingley, 1928. One of 150. Issued without dustwrapper. $600.

JAMES, Norah C. *Sleeveless Errand.* Paris, 1929. First Continental edition of the author's first book. First book published by J. Kahane. One of 50 signed copies. $400. One of 450 unsigned copies. $125.

JAMES, P. D. *A Mind to Murder.* London, 1963. $300. New York, 1967. $125.

JAMES, P. D. *Cover Her Face.* London, 1962. Author's first book. $400. New York, 1962. $125.

JAMES, Philip. *Children's Books of Yesterday.* London, 1933. Edited by G. Geoffrey Holme. Cloth. $150.

JAMES, Thomas. *Three Years Among the Indians and Mexicans.* Waterloo, Ill., 1846. 130 pages, plain wraps. $15,000 or more. St. Louis, 1916. 12 plates. Half cloth. Second edition. One of 365. $300.

JAMES, Will. *All in the Day's Riding.* New York, 1933. $150.

JAMES, Will. *Cow Country.* New York, 1927. $250.

JAMES, Will. *Cowboys North and South.* New York, 1924. Author's first book. $400.

JAMES, Will. *Drifting Cowboy.* New York, 1925. $300.

JAMES, Will. *Lone Cowboy: My Life Story.* New York, 1930. One of 250. $750. Trade. $125.

JAMES, Will. *Smoky the Cowhorse.* New York, 1926. $300.

JAMES, William. *A Full and Correct Account of the Military . . . War Between Great Britain and the United States . . .* London, 1818. 2 vols. 4 folding maps. $1,000.

JAMES, William. *The Principles of Psychology.* New York, 1890. 2 vols. Author's first book. $750. London (1890). First English edition. $400.

JAMESON, Anna Brownell. *The Beauties of the Court of King Charles II.* London, 1833. 21 hand-colored engraved portraits on India paper. In original calf. $600.

JANSON, Charles William. *The Stranger in America.* London, 1807. Engraved title page, plan of Philadelphia, 9 (sometimes 10) aquatint plates. $750. Philadelphia, 1807. $400.

JANVIER, Thomas A. *The Aztec Treasure-House.* New York, 1890. Illustrated by Fréderic Remington. Decorated cloth. $150.

JANVIER, Thomas A. *Color Studies.* New York, 1885. Author's first book. (1,000 copies.) $150.

JARRELL, Randall. *Blood for a Stranger.* New York (1942). Author's first book. $350.

JARRELL, Randall. *Little Friend, Little Friend.* New York, 1945. First edition, not stated. $300.

JARRELL, Randall. *Losses.* New York (1948). First edition, stated. $350.

JARRELL, Randall. *Pictures from an Institution.* New York, 1954. $100.

JARRELL, Randall. *The Seven-League Crutches.* New York (1951). $200.

JEFFERIES, Richard. See *The Gamekeeper at Home.*

JEFFERIES, Richard. *Bevis: The Story of a Boy.* London, 1882. 3 vols., green cloth. $600.

JEFFERIES, Richard. *Greene Ferne Farm.* London, 1880. $250.

JEFFERIES, Richard. *Hodge and His Masters.* London, 1880. 2 vols. $300.

JEFFERIES, Richard. *Jack Brass, Emperor of England.* London, 1873. 12 pages, tan wraps. $600.

JEFFERIES, Richard. *The Open Air.* London, 1885. Printed cloth. $250.

JEFFERIES, Richard. *Restless Human Hearts.* London, 1875. 3 vols. $750.

JEFFERIES, Richard. *Wood Magic: A Fable.* London, 1881. 2 vols. $300.

JEFFERS, Robinson. See Powell, Lawrence Clark; Sterling, George; *Continent's End.*

JEFFERS, Robinson. *An Artist.* Frontispiece. (Austin, 1928.) 16 pages, wraps. One of 96 (Alberts states records show 200 copies). (Printed by John S. Mayfield.) $750.

JEFFERS, Robinson. *Be Angry at the Sun.* New York (1941). Marbled boards and cloth. One of 100 signed. In glassine dustwrapper. Slipcase. $750. Trade. $100.

JEFFERS, Robinson. *The Beaks of Eagles.* San Francisco, 1936. Grabhorn Press. Folio, 3 leaves, printed yellow wraps. $500.

JEFFERS, Robinson. *Californians.* New York, 1916. Blue cloth. In dustwrapper. $750. Lacking dustwrapper. $175. "Advance Copy, For Review Only" (perforation on title page). $850. Lacking dustwrapper. $200. Author's first commercially published book. No-place, 1971. Boards and cloth. Introduction by William Everson. One of 50 (of an edition of 500) signed by Everson. Issued without dustwrapper. $225. Trade. $60.

JEFFERS, Robinson. *Cawdor and Other Poems.* New York, 1928. Buckram. One of 375 on large paper, signed. In dustwrapper and slipcase. $350. Trade. $175. London, 1929. Hogarth Press. Boards. First English edition. $300.

JEFFERS, Robinson. *Dear Judas and Other Poems.* New York, 1929. Boards and cloth. First edition (preceding the limited edition). $150. Also, one of 375 signed. In glassine dustwrapper. Slipcase $350. Also, one of 25 lettered copies. $1,000. London, 1930. Hogarth Press. Boards. Issued without dustwrapper. $350.

JEFFERS, Robinson. *Descent to the Dead.* New York (1931). Boards and vellum. One of 500 signed. Issued without dustwrapper. In unmarked slipcase. $450. (No trade editions issued.) Also 50 copies marked "Review," signed. $600.

JEFFERS, Robinson. *Flagons and Apples.* Los Angeles, 1912. (By John Robinson Jeffers). Author's first book. $1,000.

JEFFERS, Robinson. *Give Your Heart to the Hawks.* New York, 1933. One of 200 signed. 1–185 for sale. In slipcase. $450. Trade edition. $125.

JEFFERS, Robinson. *The Loving Shepherdess.* New York, 1956. One of 115 copies signed by Robinson and Jean Kellogg. Boxed. $1,200. (Some with extra suite of plates may be priced higher.)

JEFFERS, Robinson. *Medea.* New York (1946). First issue with pages 99–100 integral, word "least" lacking at page 99 line 21. $125. Word "least" present page 99, line 21. $100. First English issue with labels on title page and dustwrapper flap. $100.

JEFFERS, Robinson. *Poems.* San Francisco, 1928. Approximately 10 signed copies. Specially bound in half (red) morocco in slipcase. $2,000. One of 310 signed and numbered copies. Issued in unmarked slipcase. $1,200. (Note: copies also signed by Ansel Adams would be priced higher.)

JEFFERS, Robinson. *Poetry, Gongorism and a Thousand Years.* (Los Angeles) 1949. 200 copies. Boards without dustwrapper. $350.

JEFFERS, Robinson. *Return: An Unpublished Poem.* San Francisco, 1934. 3 copies on vellum specially bound in morocco. $1,500. 250 numbered copies. Issued in flexible wraps. $300.

JEFFERS, Robinson. *Roan Stallion, Tamar, and Other Poems.* New York, 1925. $300. (Note: dustwrappers of later printings are marked with the number of printing.) One of 12 signed and numbered copies in blue or red binding. $1,200. London, 1928. $400.

JEFFERS, Robinson. *Rock and Hawk.* (No-place) 1934. 20 copies in wraps. Reportedly more than 20 were actually printed. Printed by Frederic Prokosch. $400.

JEFFERS, Robinson. *Solstice and Other Poems.* New York, 1935. 320 signed copies. In unprinted gray dustwrapper. $450. Trade. $125.

JEFFERS, Robinson. *Stars.* (Pasadena) 1930. 72 copies. Reportedly all but 6 were destroyed. Black boards without dustwrapper. $1,250. Second edition in blue wraps. 110 copies. $750.

JEFFERS, Robinson. *Such Counsels You Gave to Me.* New York (1937). One of 300 signed and numbered copies. Issued in dustwrapper and slipcase. $450. Trade. $125.

JEFFERS, Robinson. *Tamar and Other Poems.* New York (1924). Gray unmarked dustwrapper. $500.

JEFFERS, Robinson. *Themes in My Poems.* San Francisco, 1956. Plain brown dustwrapper. (350 copies.) $350.

JEFFERS, Robinson. *Thurso's Landing and Other Poems.* New York (1932). One of 200 signed. 1–185 for sale. There were also 6 out-of-series copies. Issued in cellophane dustwrapper and slipcase. $450. Trade. $150.

JEFFERS, Una. *Visits to Ireland: Travel Diaries of Una Jeffers.* Los Angeles, 1954. Foreword by Robinson Jeffers. Boards and cloth. Ward Ritchie Press. One of 300. Slipcase. $250.

JEFFERSON, Thomas. See *A Native . . .*

JEFFERSON, Thomas. *An Appendix to the Notes on Virginia Relative to the Murder of Logan's Family.* Philadelphia, 1800. 58 pages, sewn. $450.

JEFFERSON, Thomas. *A Manual of Parliamentary Practice for the Use of the Senate of the United States.* Washington, 1801. Calf. $850.

JEFFERSON, Thomas. *Message from the President of the United States, Communicating Discoveries Made in Exploring the Missouri, Red River, and Washita by Capts. Lewis and Clark, Dr. Sibley, and Mr. Dunbar . . .* Washington, 1806. 2 folding tables, map (in some copies). 171 pages, unbound. "Printed by Order of the Senate." With map. $10,000. Without map. $2,500.

JEFFERSON, Thomas. *Notes on . . . Virginia.* (Paris), 1782. (Printed 1785.) Folding table. Pages 51–54, 167–68, 181–82, and 183–84 in uncanceled state. 200 copies printed and given away. ($150,000 at auction in 1989 for a presentation copy.) [First published edition: see next entry.] London, 1787. Map. Table. $5,000. Philadelphia, 1788. Folding sheet. $1,000.

JEFFERSON, Thomas. *Observations sur la Virginie.* Paris, 1786. Two errata lists (Howes: one on 1/4 page, the other 2½ pages). Folding map. The first published edition of his famous work on his native state, issued the year after the private issue for presentation. $6,000. Lacking map. $2,000.

JEFFREY, J. K. See *The Territory of Wyoming.*

JEFFREYS, Thomas. *The Natural and Civil History of the French Dominions in North America* . . . London, 1760. 2 vols. in 1. 18 large folding engraved maps and plans. $7,500.

JENKINS, John. *The Art of Writing, Reduced to a Plain and Easy System* . . . Cambridge (1813). Revised, enlarged, and improved. Book I. 10 unnumbered engraved plates. $550.

JENKINS, John H. *Cracker Barrel Chronicles: A Bibliography of Texas Town and Country Histories.* Austin, 1965. Full tan leather. $150.

JENKS, Ira C. *Trial of David F. Mayberry, for the Murder of Andrew Alger.* (Cover title.) Janesville, Wis., 1855. 48 pages, wraps. $300.

JENNINGS, N. A. *A Texas Ranger.* New York, 1899. Tan pictorial cloth. $300.

JENNINGS, Oscar. *Early Woodcut Initials* . . . London (1908). $150.

JEREMIAH. See *The Lamentations of Jeremiah.*

JEROME, Chauncey. *History of the American Clock Business for the Past 60 Years.* New Haven, 1860. $300.

JEROME, Jerome K. *The Idle Thoughts of an Idle Fellow.* London, 1886. $150.

JEROME, Jerome K. *On Stage and Off.* London, 1885. Author's first book. $200.

JEROME, Jerome K. *Three Men in a Boat.* Bristol, England, 1889. Illustrated. Light blue cloth. First issue, with title page reading as follows: "Bristol/J. W. Arrowsmith, Quay Street/London/Simpkin, Marshall & Co., 4 Stationer's Hall Court/ (rule) 1889/All rights reserved/" (VAB). $200. New York, 1890. $100.

JEROME, Jerome K. *Told After Supper.* London, 1891. Illustrated. Pictorial red cloth. $150.

JERROLD, Douglas. *A Man Made of Money.* London, 1849. 12 plates by John Leech. 6 parts, pictorial wraps, and cloth. In parts. $750. Cloth. $400.

JEWETT, Sarah Orne. *Betty Leicester.* Boston, 1890. Decorated cloth. With this book last in ad opposite title page. With 10 titles (11 titles later). $125.

JEWETT, Sarah Orne. *Betty Leicester's English Christmas.* Boston, 1894. White cloth. $400.

JEWETT, Sarah Orne. *A Country Doctor.* Boston, 1884. $300.

JEWETT, Sarah Orne. *The Country of the Pointed Firs.* Boston, 1896. Without blank leaf following ads at end. $200. Second printing with extra leaf. $100.

JEWETT, Sarah Orne. *Deephaven.* Boston, 1877. Cloth. With the reading "was" versus "so" in line 16, page 65. Author's first book. $450. Later printing with "so." $100.

JEWITT, John R. *A Journal, Kept at Nootka Sound.* Boston, 1807. 48 pages. $5,000.

JEWITT, John R. *Narrative of the Adventures and Sufferings of John R. Jewitt.* Middletown, 1815. Edited by Richard Alsop. 2 plates. First issue, with Loomis & Richards imprint. $1,000. Second issue, Seth Richards imprint. $750. New York (about 1815). $400.

JHABVALA, R. Prawer. *Amrita.* New York, 1956. (New title.) First American edition of first book. $125.

JHABVALA, R. Prawer. *To Whom She Will.* London (1955). Author's first book. $150.

JOAQUIN (The Claude Duval of California); or The Marauder of the Mines. New York (1865—actually later, in the 1870s). (By Henry L. Williams.) 160 pages, pictorial wraps. $200. New York, 1888. Decorated cloth. Second edition. $125.

JOCKNICK, Sidney. *Early Days on the Western Slope of Colorado.* Denver, 1913. 25 plates. $200.

JOHANNSEN, Albert. *The House of Beadle and Adams and its Dime Novels.* Norman, Okla. (1950). 2 vols. and *Volume III: Supplement* . . . 1962. $125.

JOHN Cheney and His Descendants, Printers In Banbury Since 1767. Banbury, 1936. 70 full-page plates, 2 large foldout plates. $125.

JOHN Halifax, Gentleman. London, 1856. (By Dinah M. Craik.) 3 vols., brown cloth. First issue with 3 pages of ads at end of vol. 1, one page at end of vol. 2, and 2 pages at end of vol. 3 (VAB). $600.

JOHN Marr and Other Sailors. New York, 1888. (By Herman Melville.) 103 pp., printed yellow wraps. One of 25. $25,000. Princeton, 1922. Half cloth. One of 175. $250.

JOHN, W. D. *Swansea Porcelain.* London, 1958. 20 color illustrations, others in black and white. Buckram. Issued without dustwrapper. $250.

JOHN Woodvil: A Tragedy. London, 1802. (By Charles Lamb.) $250.

JOHNSON, A. F. *Decorative Initial Letters.* London, 1931. 500 numbered copies. 122 plates of examples. $175.

JOHNSON, B. S. *Traveling People.* London (1963). $150.

JOHNSON, Benj. F. (of Boone). *"The Old Swimmin'-Hole" and 'Leven More Poems.* Indianapolis, 1883. Wraps. (By James Whitcomb Riley.) Author's first book. $750. (Note: There exists a 1909 facsimile, which lacks the "W" in "William" on page 41. Value: about $35.)

JOHNSON, Crisfield (compiler). *The History of Cuyahoga County, Ohio.* Cleveland, 1879. Double-column pages. Half morocco. $125.

JOHNSON, Don Carlos. *A Brief History of Springville, Utah.* Springville, 1900. Illustrated. Wraps. First edition, with errata slip. $250.

JOHNSON, Dorothy. *Beulah Bunny Tells All.* New York, 1942. Author's first book. $100.

JOHNSON, Dorothy. *Indian Country.* New York, 1953. $75.

JOHNSON, Edmund C. *Tangible Typography: Or, How the Blind Read.* London, 1853. 10 plates of raised letters. $250.

JOHNSON, Edwin F. *Railroad to the Pacific, Northern Route.* New York, 1854. 3 maps, 8 plates. Boards and calf. Second (actually first) edition. $350.

JOHNSON, Frank M. *Forest, Lake and River* . . . Boston, 1902. Portrait and colored frontispiece. 2 vols., bound in suede. One of 350. $400.

JOHNSON, Harrison. *Johnson's History of Nebraska.* Omaha, 1880. Frontispiece, other illustrations; folding map in color. Blue cloth. $175.

JOHNSON, Henry L. *Gutenberg and the Book* . . . New York, 1932. One of 750. With facsimile page from the Gutenberg Bible. In folding case. $125.

JOHNSON, Henry L. *An Introduction to Logography* . . . London, 1783. $1,500.

JOHNSON, Jack. *Jack Johnson in the Ring and Out.* Chicago, 1927. Stated first. $75.

JOHNSON, James Weldon. See *The Autobiography* . . .

JOHNSON, James Weldon. *Along This Way.* New York, 1933. $350.

JOHNSON, James Weldon. *Fifty Years and Other Poems.* Boston (1917). Half cloth. One of 110 on Japan vellum, signed. $1,000.

JOHNSON, James Weldon. *God's Trombones.* New York, 1927. $300.

JOHNSON, James Weldon. *Saint Peter Relates an Incident of the Resurrection Day.* New York, 1940. Folio, black boards, gilt. One of 200 signed in slipcase. $750.

JOHNSON, John. *Typographia, Or The Printer's Instructor* . . . London, 1824. 2 vols. $150.

JOHNSON, Lionel. *The Art of Thomas Hardy.* London, 1894. Portrait. Boards. One of 150. $650. Trade in cloth. $200.

JOHNSON, Lionel. *Poems.* London, 1895. One of 750. $350. One of 25 signed. $3,500.

JOHNSON, Lionel. *Sir Walter Raleigh in the Tower.* (Chester) 1885. Author's first book. Wraps. $6,000.

JOHNSON, Lionel. *Twenty-one Poems.* Dun Emer Press. Dundrum, Ireland, 1904. Selected by William Butler Yeats. Boards and linen. One of 220. $350.

JOHNSON, Merle. *American First Editions, Revised and Enlarged by Jacob Blanck.* New York (1942). Fourth and best edition. $150.

JOHNSON, Merle. *A Bibliography of Mark Twain.* New York, 1910. Author's first book. (500 copies.) $150. New York, 1935. Second edition, revised and enlarged. $150.

JOHNSON, Overton, and WINTER, William H. *Route Across the Rocky Mountains* . . . Lafayette, Ind., 1846. Cloth-backed boards. $3,500.

JOHNSON, Ronald. *A Line of Poetry, A Row of Trees.* Highlands, 1964. Author's first book. One of 50 signed and numbered copies. $200. Stiff wraps. (500 copies.) $75.

JOHNSON, Samuel. *An Account of the Life of Mr. Richard Savage.* London, 1744. $1,500.

JOHNSON, Samuel. *A Diary of a Journey into North Wales.* London, 1816. Edited by R. Duppa. Plates. $300.

JOHNSON, Samuel. *A Dictionary of the English Language* . . . London, 1755. 2 vols. In contemporary binding. $10,000 ($27,500 in original boards at auction in 1990.) In later bindings. $7,500.

JOHNSON, Samuel. *A Journey to the Western Islands of Scotland.* London, 1775. $600. Baltimore, 1810. First American edition. $250.

JOHNSON, Samuel. *London: A Poem, and the Vanity of Human Wishes.* London, 1930. Introduction by T.S. Eliot. One of 150 signed by Eliot. $850.

JOHNSON, Sid S. *Some Biographies of Old Settlers.* (Only vol. I published.) Tyler, Tex., 1900. $200.

JOHNSON, Sidney S. *Texans Who Wore the Gray.* Tyler (about 1907). Illustrated. $350.

JOHNSON, Mrs. Susannah. *A Narrative of the Captivity of Mrs. Johnson.* Windsor, Vt., 1807. Second edition. $275.

JOHNSON, Theodore T. *Sights in the Gold Region, and Scenes by the Way.* New York, 1849. $400. New York, 1850. Second edition. Folding map, 7 plates (2 colored). $200.

JOHNSTON, Charles. *A Narrative of the Incidents Attending the Capture, Detention, and Ransom of* . . . New York, 1827. Boards. $350.

JOHNSTON, Lieut. Col. J. E. et al. *Reports of the Secretary of War, with Reconnaisances of Routes from San Antonio to El Paso* . . . Washington, 1850. 2 folding maps, 72 plates. $800.

JOHNSTON, William G. *Experiences of a Forty-niner.* Pittsburgh, 1892. Portrait and 13 plates. (With later, separately issued, folding blueprint map and an extra portrait.) $850.

JOHONNOT, Jackson. *The Remarkable Adventures of Jackson Johonnot.* Boston, 1793. $750. Many reprints in Howes, with the last being Greenfield, Mass., 1816. 24 pages. $400. (First appeared in Beer's almanac, Hartford [1792]).

JOINVILLE, John, Lord of. *The History of Saint Louis, King Louis of France.* Gregynog Press. Newtown, Wales, 1937. Illustrated. Dark maroon morocco. One of 200. In slipcase. $1,250.

JOKL, Ernst, M.D. *The Medical Aspect of Boxing.* Pretoria, 1941. $75.

JOLAS, Eugene. See *Transition Stories.*

JOLAS, Eugene. *Cinema: Poems.* New York, 1926. Author's first book. $250.

JOLAS, Eugene. *Secession in Astropolis.* Black Sun Press. Paris, 1929. Wraps. One of 100. In slipcase. $200.

JONAH: Christmas, 1917. Holywell Press. Oxford, 1917. Wraps. (By Aldous Huxley.) One of 50. $3,500.

JONES, A. D. *Illinois and the West.* Boston, 1838. Folding map. In original cloth. $150.

JONES, Anson B. *Memoranda and Official Correspondence Relating to the Republic of Texas, Its History and Annexation.* New York, 1859. Portrait. $400. Chicago (1966). Map, facsimile letter. Leather. One of 150. Slipcase. $100.

JONES, Charles Colcock. *Religious Instruction of the Negroes in the United States.* Savannah, 1842. $750.

JONES, Charles C., Jr. *Antiquities of the Southern Indians.* New York, 1873. 30 plates. $300.

JONES, Charles C., Jr. *The Dead Towns of Georgia.* Savannah, 1878. Maps. $200.

JONES, Charles C., Jr. *Historical Sketch of the Chatham Artillery.* Albany, 1867. 3 maps. $200.

JONES, Charles C., Jr. *The History of Georgia.* Boston, 1883. 19 maps and plates. 2 vols., cloth. $350.

JONES, Charles C., Jr. *The History of Savannah, Georgia.* Syracuse, 1890. 21 portraits. Half leather. $300.

JONES, Charles C., Jr. *The Siege of Savannah in December, 1864.* Albany, Ga., 1874. 184 pages, wraps. $200. One of 10 on large paper. $300.

JONES, Charles C., Jr. (editor). *The Siege of Savannah in 1779.* Albany, 1874. Map, index (not in all copies). Wraps. One of 100. With the index. $200. Without index. $100.

JONES, Charles Jess (Buffalo). See Inman, Col. Henry.

JONES, D. W. *Forty Years Among the Indians.* Salt Lake City, 1890. With portrait (not in all copies). $150.

JONES, David. *A Journal of Two Visits Made to Some Nations of Indians on the West Side of the River Ohio, in the Years 1772 and 1773.* Burlington, N.J., 1774. $10,000. New York, 1865. Wraps. Second edition. One of 200. $200. One of 50 on large paper. $350.

JONES, David. *The Anathemata.* London (1952). $250.

JONES, David. *In Parentheses.* London, 1937. Illustrated by the author. Author's first book. $850. London (1961). Introduction by T. S. Eliot. Blue cloth. One of 70 signed by Jones and Eliot in plastic dustwrapper. $1,250. New York (1962). Tan cloth. First American edition. With Eliot introduction not listed on contents page. $75. With introduction listed. $40.

JONES, David. *The Tribune's Visitation.* (London, 1969.) One of 150 signed. $350. Trade. $75.

JONES, E. Alfred. *The Old Silver of American Churches.* Letchworth, England, 1913. 145 plates. Folio, buckram. One of 500. $850. One of 6 on handmade paper. $1,500.

JONES, Edith Newbold. *Verses.* Newport, R.I., 1878. Author's first book. Wraps. $25,000.

JONES, Edward Smyth. See Invincible Ned.

JONES, Edward Smyth. *Souvenir Poem.* (Louisville?, 1908.) $150.

JONES, Gwyn. *The Green Island.* Golden Cockerel Press. London, 1946. Woodcuts by John Petts. Green and gray morocco. One of 100. $200. Also one of 400. $75.

JONES, Herschel V. *Adventures in Americana.* New York, 1928. 300 plates. 2 vols., black cloth. One of 200. $250. With third volume of collection by W. Eames Publisher. New York, 1938. $350.

JONES, James. *From Here to Eternity.* New York, 1951. Author's first book. Presentation edition, with signed and numbered tipped-in page (no total limitation, but about 1,500 copies). $300. Without signed page. $150.

JONES, James. *The Thin Red Line.* New York (1962). $100.

JONES, James Athearn. See Murgatroyd, Matthew.

JONES, Jonathan H. *A Condensed History of the Apache and Comanche Indian Tribes.* San Antonio, 1899. Illustrated. (Note: Better known by its cover title, *Indianology.*) $950.

JONES, J. Wesley. *Amusing and Thrilling Adventures of a California Artist, while Daguerreotyping a Continent . . .* Boston, 1854. (Written by John Ross Dicks.) Illustrated, including 4 woodcuts in text. 92 pages, pictorial wraps. (By George Spencer Phillips.) $2,750.

JONES, LeRoi. *Cuba Libre.* (Cover title.) New York (1961). Wraps. $250.

JONES, Leroi. *Spring and So Forth.* New Haven, 1960. Author's first book. $300.

JONES, Owen. *The Grammar of Ornament.* London, 1856. 100 colored lithographs, engraved title page (illuminated), woodcuts. Large folio. $450. London (1856). Quarto. With an additional 12 plates. $375.

JONES, Adj. Gen. R. *General Orders, No. 16, Reporting General Court Martial Convened at Fort Kearney, Oregon Route, for Offense Committed There.* Washington, 1851. 11 pages, sewn. $200.

JONES, Robert Tyre, Jr., and KEELER, O.B. *Down the Fairway.* New York, 1927. Signed limited edition in slipcase. $500. Trade. $120.

JONES, Thomas A. *J. Wilkes Booth.* Chicago, 1893. Illustrated. Cloth. $125.

JONES, William Carey. *Land Titles in California.* San Francisco, 1852. 55 pages, wraps. $750.

JONSON, Ben. *A Croppe of Kisses: Selected Lyrics.* Golden Cockerel Press. London, 1937. Edited by John Wallis. Folio, morocco and buckram. One of 250. $300. One of 50 specially bound in morocco. $850.

JONSON, Ben. *Every Man Out of His Humour.* London, 1600. Author's first book. $2,500.

JONSON, Ben. *The Masque of Queenes.* London, 1930. Illustrated by Inigo Jones. Folio, red vellum. One of 350. In slipcase. $200.

JONSON, Ben. *Volpone: or The Foxe.* New York, 1898. Illustrated by Aubrey Beardsley. One of 100 on vellum. $750. Decorated cloth. One of 1,000. $400. Limited Editions Club, New York, 1952. In slipcase. $75.

JORDAN, Thomas, and PRYOR, J. P. *The Campaigns of Lieut. Gen. N. B. Forrest.*
New Orleans, 1868. 6 maps, 6 plates. $175.

JORROCK'S Jaunts and Jollities. London, 1838. (By Robert Smith Surtees.) 12 illustrations by Phiz. In original decorated cloth. $500. Philadelphia, 1838. 2 vols., in
original half cloth. First American edition. $400. London, 1843. 15 color plates by
Henry Aiken. Green cloth. Second edition, first state, with 8 pages of ads and
printer's imprint at end. $1,250. Second edition, late state, with ads announcing a
new edition of *The Life of John Mytton.* $750. London, 1869. 16 colored Aiken
plates. Third edition. $500. Limited Editions Club, New York, 1932. Slipcase. $100.

JOSEPHSON, Matthew. *Galimathias.* New York (1923). Author's first book. Stiff
wraps. (250 numbered copies). $150.

JOSSELYN, John. *An Account of Two Voyages to New-England.* London, 1674.
Printer's dragon device on the recto of the preliminary license leaf. Errata. List of
printer's advertisements. $6,500.

JOSSELYN, John. *New-England Rarities Discovered: In Birds, Beasts, Fishes, Serpents*
. . . London, 1672. Folding plate woodcut and 11 text woodcuts. $7,500.

*JOURNAL of the Convention to Form a Constitution for the State of Wisconsin: Begun
and Held at Madison on the 5th Day of October, 1846.* Madison, 1847. Boards and
calf. $275.

*JOURNAL of the Expedition of Dragoons Under the Command of Col. Henry Dodge
to the Rocky Mountains During the Summer of 1835.* (Washington, 1836.) (By Lt.
G. P. Kingsbury.) 2 folding maps. Wraps. $350. Cloth. $200.

JOURNAL of the Hartford Union Mining and Trading Company. On board the Henry
Lee, 1849. 88 pages, wraps. (By George G. Webster, or John Linville Hall, who
printed it?) $5,000 or more. Second edition (with title revised to *Around the Horn
in '49—Journal...*). (Wethersfield, Conn., or Hartford, 1898.) $150. San Francisco,
1928. Book Club of California. Half cloth. One of 250 printed by the Grabhorns.
$100.

*JOURNAL of the First Session of the Senate of the United States . . . March 4th,
1789 . . .* New York, 1789. (Contains the Bill of Rights as originally proposed.)
$12,500.

JOURNAL of Sentimental Travels in the Southern Provinces of France. London, 1821.
(By William Combe.) 18 colored plates by Thomas Rowlandson. $1,000.

JOURNAL of a Tour Around Hawaii, the Largest of the Sandwich Islands. Boston,
1825. (By William Ellis.) 5 plates, folding map. $850.

JOURNEY to California with Observations About the Country... San Francisco, 1937.
(By John Bidwell.) (First of a series of three works republished by John Henry
Nash.) $125.

JOYCE, James. See Gorman, Herbert; Jolas, Maria; Skeffington, F. J. C.; and Joyce,
James A. See also *Des Imagistes; The Dublin Book of Irish Verse; The Venture.*

JOYCE, James. *Anna Livia Plurabelle.* New York, 1928. Edited by Padraic Colum.
One of 800 signed. $1,500. One of 50 on green paper not signed. $3,500. London
(1930). Wraps. First English edition. $150.

JOYCE, James. *Chamber Music.* London, 1907. First issue (16.2 by 11 cm) with thick laid endpapers, horizontal chain lines and poems, and signature "c" well centered. $6,000. Second issue (15.8 by 11 cm) with thick wove endpapers and signature "c" poorly centered. $1,500. Third variant (15.9 by 10.9 cm) with thin wove transparent endpapers. $1,500. (No priority on variants.)

JOYCE, James. *Collected Poems.* Black Sun Press. New York, 1936. Frontispiece portrait. Decorated boards. One of 750. In glassine dustwrapper. $750. One of 50 on vellum, signed. In tissue dustwrapper and slipcase. $4,000. One of 3 lettered and signed copies, $12,500. New York, 1937. Trade in dustwrapper. $750.

JOYCE, James. *Dubliners.* London, 1914. Red cloth. $1,750. New York, 1916. Cloth. First American issue (from the English sheets). $1,250. New York, 1917. First edition from American sheets. Second printing stated. $300.

JOYCE, James. *Exiles.* London, 1918. Green boards and cloth. $600. New York, 1918. Boards and buckram. $350. New York, 1951. Half cloth. One of 1,900. In dustwrapper. $200.

JOYCE, James. *Finnegan's Wake.* London, 1939. Buckram. One of 425 on large paper, signed. In slipcase. $4,500. London (1939). $1,500. New York, 1939. $500.

JOYCE, James. *Haveth Childers Everywhere: Fragment from Work in Progress.* Paris, 1930. Stiff printed wraps. One of 500 on Vidalon paper. In glassine dustwrapper and slipcase. $850. Also 75 "Writer's Copies." $1,250. One of 100 on Japanese vellum, signed. In slipcase. $3,500. One of 10 on vellum, signed. In glassine dustwrapper and slipcase. $7,500.

JOYCE, James. *The Holy Office.* (Pola, Austria-Hungary, 1904 or 1905?) Broadside. (Fewer than 100 printed. The author's first separately published work. Preceded by *Two Essays.*) $8,500.

JOYCE, James. *Ibsen's New Drama.* London (1930). Foolscap, boards, paper label. One of 40. Issued without dustwrapper. $2,000.

JOYCE, James. *James Clarence Mangan.* London (1930). Foolscap, boards, paper label. One of 40. $2,000.

JOYCE, James. *The Mime of Mick, Nick, and the Maggies.* The Hague, Netherlands, 1934. Designs in color by Lucia Joyce. Stiff white wraps. In slipcase. One of 1,000. $600. Also, 29 copies signed by Joyce and his daughter. $6,000.

JOYCE, James. *Pomes Penyeach.* Paris, 1927. With errata slip. $400. One of 13 on handmade paper. $3,500. Paris and London, 1932. Oblong folio sheets on Japan paper, illuminated by Lucia Joyce. Green silk folder. One of 25 signed. $25,000. Paris and London, 1932. $300. Faber & Faber. London (1933.) Wraps. First edition printed in England. $200.

JOYCE, James. *A Portrait of the Artist as a Young Man.* New York, 1916. Blue cloth. $1,000. London (1917). Green cloth. First English issue (from American sheets). $600. London, 1924. Revised edition. $600. Limited Editions Club, New York, 1968. In slipcase. $75.

JOYCE, James. *Stephen Hero.* London, 1944. $350. New York (1944). $150.

JOYCE, James. *Storiella as She Is Syung.* Corvinus Press. (London, 1937.) Flexible orange vellum. One of 176. In slipcase. $2,000. One of 25 (of the 176) signed by Joyce. In slipcase. $6,000.

JOYCE, James. *Tales Told of Shem and Shaun: Three Fragments from Work in Progress.* Black Sun Press. Paris, 1929. Portrait by Brancusi. Wraps. One of 500 on Van Gelder paper. In glassine dustwrapper and slipcase. $1,000. One of 100 on vellum, signed (plus 50 not-for-sale copies). In slipcase. $3,000. London (1932). Boards. First English edition (retitled *Two Tales of Shem and Shaun*). In dustwrapper. $250.

JOYCE, James. *Two Essays.* See Skeffington, F.J.C.

JOYCE, James. *Ulysses.* Paris, 1922. Printed blue wraps. One of 100 on Dutch handmade paper, signed. $40,000. One of 150 on Verge d'Arches paper. $15,000. One of 740 on handmade paper. $10,000. (Various later printings of the Paris edition appeared through the 1920s.) London, 1922. Egoist Press. Blue wraps. First English edition (printed in France), with errata slip and 4-page leaflet of press notices. One of 2,000. $3,000. London, 1923. Second English edition (printed in France). Most confiscated by British customs agents. $6,000. Paris, 1928. Eighth printing, type entirely reset. $750. Paris, 1927. Blue wraps. First American edition, unauthorized Samuel Roth piracy. $500. Hamburg (1932). Odyssey Press. 2 vols., printed wraps. First Odyssey Press edition. (One of 25 signed?) $2,000. Trade edition. $300. (New York, 1934.) First authorized American edition. Cream-colored cloth. In dustwrapper. $350. Limited Editions Club, New York, 1935. Illustrated by Henri Matisse. Pictorial buckram. One of 250 signed by Joyce and Matisse. $6,000. One of 1,250 signed only by Matisse. $3,000. (There were also 6 signed proofs of the Matisse etchings for this book issued in an edition of 150 in canvas portfolios.) London, 1936. Green buckram. First English edition to be printed in England. One of 900. In dustwrapper. $850. Vellum. One of 100 signed. In slipcase. $6,000.

JUDD, A. N. *Campaigning Against the Sioux.* (Watsonville, Calif., 1906.) Plate, other illustrations. 45 pages, pictorial wraps. $1,000. Watsonville, 1909. Wraps. Second edition. $400.

JUDD, Silas. *A Sketch of the Life and Voyages of Capt. Alvah Judd Dewey . . .* Chittenango, N.Y., 1838. In original boards and cloth. $750.

JUGAKU, Bunsho. *Paper-Making by Hand in Japan.* Tokyo, 1959. 24 specimens of handmade paper. $550.

JUSTICE and Expediency; or Slavery Considered with a View to Its Rightful and Effectual Remedy, Abolition. Haverhill, Mass. 1833. Stitched without covers, as issued. (By John Greenleaf Whittier.) $650.

JUSTICE, Donald. *The Old Bachelor . . .* Miami, 1951. Author's first book. Wraps. (240 copies.) $600.

JUSTICE, Donald. *The Summer Anniversaries.* Middletown, Conn. (1960). Cloth. $60. Wraps. $25.

K

K., R. A. *Signa Severa.* Eton College, 1906. Author's first book. Wraps. $350.

KABOTIE, Red. *Designs from the Ancient Mimbrenos, with Hopi Interpretation.* Grabhorn Press. San Francisco, 1949. Half cloth. One of 250. $250.

KAFKA, Franz. *America.* London (1938). Translated by Edwin and Willa Muir. Cloth. $250.

KAFKA, Franz. *The Castle.* London, 1930. Author's first book to be translated into English. $400. New York, 1930. $250.

KAFKA, Franz. *The Great Wall of China and Other Pieces.* London, 1933. Translated by Edwin and Willa Muir. $300.

KAHN, Roger. *Inside Big League Baseball.* New York, 1962. Author's first separate book. $100.

KAIN, Saul. *The Daffodil Murderer.* (London) 1913. (By Siegfried Sassoon.) Yellow (orange) wraps printed in red. $250.

KALTENBORN, H. V. *Kaltenborn Edits the News.* New York (1937). Ghostwritten by Mary McCarthy, her first book. Cloth. $150. Wraps in dustwrapper. $75.

KANE, Elisha Kent. *Arctic Explorations.* Philadelphia, 1856. 22 plates and 3 maps (2 folding). 2 vols., pictorial cloth. $400.

KANE, Elisha Kent. *The U.S. Grinnel Expedition in Search . . .* New York, 1854. $350.

KANE, Paul. *Wanderings of an Artist Among the Indians of North America.* London, 1859. Folding map, 8 colored plates, woodcuts. $1,750.

KANE, Thomas Leiper. *The Mormons.* Philadelphia, 1850. 84 pages. Printed wraps. $400.

KANO, Jigoro. *Judo.* Tokyo, 1937. Wraps. $40.

KANO, Jigoro. *Ju Jutsu and Judo: What Are They?* Tokyo (no-date). Wraps. $50.

KANT, Immanuel. *Critick of Pure Reason.* London, 1838. In original green cloth and paper label. First edition in English. $1,500.

KANTOR, MacKinlay. *Andersonville.* Cleveland (1955). $40. Limited, signed edition. In slipcase. $150.

KANTOR, MacKinlay. *Diversey.* New York, 1928. Author's first book. In dustwrapper without reviews. $150. (Also first book published by Coward-McCann.)

KARPINSKI, Louis C. *Bibliography of Mathematical Works Printed in America Through 1850.* Ann Arbor, 1940. $200.

KATHERINE Walton; or, The Rebel of Dorchester. Philadelphia, 1851. (By William Gilmore Simms.) $400.

KAUFMAN, George. *Dulcy.* New York (1921). Author's first book (with Marc Connelly). $300.

KAVANAGH, Patrick. *D'Olier Music Co's Famous Songs.* Dublin, 1930. Author's first book. Wraps. $750.

KAVANAGH, Patrick. *The Great Hunger.* Cuala Press. Dublin, 1942. Boards and linen. One of 250. In dustwrapper. $200.

KAVANAGH, Patrick. *Ploughman* . . . London, 1936. Wraps. $1,000.

KAYE-SMITH, Sheila. *The Tramping Methodist.* London, 1908. Author's first book. $100.

KAZANTZAKIS, Nikos. *Christopher Columbus.* Allen Press. Kentfield, Calif., 1972. 22 folded sheets in gold wraps. One of 140. In slipcase. $500.

KAZANTZAKIS, Nikos. *Zorba the Greek.* London (1952). Author's first book. (First English translation.) $150.

KEATING, William H. (compiler). *Narrative of an Expedition to the Source of St. Peter's River, Lake Winnepeek* . . . Philadelphia, 1824. Folding map, 15 plates. 2 vols. $1,750. London, 1825. Maps, plates, tables. 2 vols. First English edition. $650.

KEATS, John. *Endymion: A Poetic Romance.* London, 1818. First issue, with one line of errata (not 5) and 2 (not 5) ad leaves at end. $3,000. Second issue, with 5-line errata. $2,500. New York, 1902. Elston Press. Blue cloth. $250. Golden Cockerel-Press. London (1947). Wood engravings. Buckram and vellum. One of 400. $600. Vellum. One of 100 specially bound. $2,000.

KEATS, John. *The Eve of St. Agnes.* Auvergne Press. (River Forest, Ill.), 1896. Title page design by Frank Lloyd Wright. Cloth. One of 65. $1,250. Essex House. London, 1900. Boards. One of 125 on vellum. $600.

KEATS, John. *Lamia, Isabella, The Eve of St. Agnes, and Other Poems.* London, 1820. With half title and 8 pages of ads at end. In original boards. $10,000. Rebound. $1,500. Golden Cockerel Press. Waltham Saint Lawrence, England, 1928. Wood-cuts by Robert Gibbings. Sharkskin and cloth. One of 500. $500. One of 15 on vellum. In sharkskin binding by Sangorski & Sutcliffe. $3,500.

KEATS, John. *Letters of John Keats to Fanny Brawne, Written in the Years 1819 and 1820.* London, 1878. Edited by Harry Buxton Forman. Etched frontispiece and facsimile. One of 50. $500. Trade. $100.

KEATS, John. *Life, Letters, and Literary Remains of John Keats.* London, 1848. Edited by Richard Monckton Milnes. Engraved portrait and facsimile. 2 vols., cloth. $750. New York, 1848. $250.

KEATS, John. *Poems.* London, 1817. Woodcut vignette of Spenser on title page. In original boards. Paper label on spine. $15,000. Rebound. $5,000.

KEATS, John. *Poetical Works.* London, 1840. Printed in double columns within ruled borders. In original yellow wraps. First complete collected edition. $750.

KEEN HAND, A. See Farnie, H.B.

KEEP Cool. Baltimore, 1817. (By John Neal.) 2 vols. Author's first book. $300.

KEES, Weldon. *Collected Poems.* Stone Wall Press. Iowa City, 1960. Boards and leather. One of 200. $250.

KEES, Weldon. *The Last Man.* San Francisco, 1943. One of 300. (Issued without dustwrapper.) Author's first book. $250.

KEITH, G. M. *A Voyage to South America and the Cape of Good Hope.* London, 1810. First issue, printed by Phillips. $1,500. London, 1819. Revised edition, printed by Vogel. With list of subscribers. $1,500.

KELEHER, William A. *The Fabulous Frontier.* Santa Fe (1945). 11 plates. Cloth. One of 500. In dustwrapper. $125.

KELEHER, William A. *The Maxwell Land Grant.* Santa Fe (1942). Illustrated. Pictorial cloth. In dustwrapper. $200.

KELL, Joseph. *One Hand Clapping.* London (1961). (By Anthony Burgess.) $250.

KELLER, David H. *The Lady Decides.* Philadelphia, 1950. One of 400 signed. Issued without dustwrapper. In slipcase. $150.

KELLER, David H. *The Sign of the Burning Hart.* No-place, 1938. One of 100. $250. No-place (1948). First American edition. One of 250 signed. In dustwrapper. $100.

KELLER, George. *A Trip Across the Plains.* (Massilon, Ohio, 1851.) 58 pages, printed wraps. $5,000.

KELLEY, Edith Summers. *Weeds.* New York (1923). Author's first book. $150.

KELLEY, Emma Dunham. *Megda.* Boston, 1891. Author's first book. $600.

KELLEY, Hall J. *General Circular to All Persons of Good Character Who Wish to Emigrate to the Oregon Territory.* Charlestown, Mass. 1831. 28 pages, wraps bound in. $2,000.

KELLEY, Hall J. *History of Colonization of the Oregon Territory.* Worcester, Mass., 1850. 12 pages, sewn. $5,000.

KELLEY, Hall J. *A History of the Settlement of Oregon and the Interior of Upper California.* Springfield, Mass., 1868. 128 pages, printed wraps. $5,000.

KELLEY, Hall J. *A Narrative of Events and Difficulties in the Colonization of Oregon and the Settlement of California.* Boston, 1852. 92 pages, printed wraps. $5,000.

KELLEY, William Melvin. *A Different Drummer.* Garden City, 1962. Author's first book. $75.

KELLEY-HAWKINS, Emma D. *Four Girls at Cottage City.* Boston, 1898. $400.

KELLOGG, Jay C. *The Broncho Buster Busted and Other Messages.* (Tacoma, 1932.) Wraps. $200.

KELLY, Charles. *Old Greenwood: The Story of Caleb Greenwood, Trapper, Pathfinder and Early Pioneer of the West.* Salt Lake City, 1936. One of 350. In dustwrapper. $300.

KELLY, Charles. *The Outlaw Trail: A History of Butch Cassidy and His Wild Bunch.* Salt Lake City, 1938. Illustrated. Pictorial cloth (leatherette). One of 1,000. In dustwrapper. $300.

KELLY, Charles. *Salt Desert Trails.* Salt Lake City, 1930. Illustrated. Cloth (leatherette). $300.

KELLY, Charles (editor). See Lee, John D.

KELLY, Charles, and HOWE, Maurice L. *Miles Goodyear, First Citizen of Utah*. Salt Lake City, 1937. 350 numbered copies. $150.

KELLY, L. V. *The Range Men: The Story of the Ranchers and Indians of Alberta*. Toronto, 1913. Illustrated. Pictorial cloth. $750.

KELLY, Robert. *Armed Descent*. Hawk's Well Press. (New York, 1961.) Wraps. Author's first book. $100.

KELLY, Robert. *Her Body Against Time*. Mexico City, 1963. Cloth (about 50 copies.) $250. Wraps. $50.

KELLY, William. *An Excursion to California over the Prairie, Rocky Mountains, and Great Sierra Nevada*. London, 1851. 2 vols. $650.

KEMPTON-Wace Letters (The). New York, 1903. Green decorated cloth. (By Jack London and Anna Strunsky.) $500.

KENDAL and Windermere Railway. Two Letters Reprinted from the Morning Post. London (1844). (By William Wordsworth.) Sewn. First edition, with Whittaker imprint (VAB). $400. Kendal, England (1845). 24 pages, single sheet folded. Revised edition, with Branthwaite imprint. $200. Second issue has "four pence" added to title page. $100.

KENDALL, George W., and NEBEL, Carl. *The War Between the United States and Mexico*... New York/Philadelphia, 1851. Map and 12 hand-finished colored plates (which are susceptible to foxing, affecting price). Large folio laid in a folding cloth portfolio. $6,000.

KENDALL, George Wilkins. *Narrative of the Texan Santa Fe Expedition*... New York, 1844. 5 plates, folding map. 2 vols. $750. London, 1844. Map, 5 plates. 2 vols. First English edition. $750. New York, 1856. 2 vols. Seventh edition, with two extra chapters and part of Falconer's diary. $2,500.

KENDERDINE, T. S. *A California Tramp and Later Footprints*. Newtown, Pa., 1888. 39 views. Pictorial cloth. $250.

KENEALLY, Thomas. *The Place at Whitton*. London (1964). Author's first book. $150.

KENILWORTH. Edinburgh, 1821. 3 vols. (By Sir Walter Scott.) $400.

KENNEDY, Edward G. *The Etched Work of Whistler*... Grolier Club. New York, 1910. 6 vols. (Text vol. and half cloth plate folders.) One of 402. $2,000.

KENNEDY, John F. *Inaugural Address*. Los Angeles, 1965. Portrait. Vellum. One of 1,000. $350.

KENNEDY, John F. *Profiles in Courage*. New York (1956). $300. New York, 1961. "Inaugural Edition." $60.

KENNEDY, John F. *Why England Slept*. New York, 1940. Author's first book. $500. London (1940). Red cloth. With ads dated 1940. $150.

KENNEDY, John F. (editor). *As We Remember Joe*. (Cambridge, Mass., 1945.) Portrait frontispiece, photographs. Red cloth. $2,000. (Reprinted with title page in black only.)

KENNEDY, John P., and BLISS, Alexander (editors). *Autograph Leaves of Our Country's Authors.* Baltimore, 1864. $125.

KENNEDY, John Pendleton. See Secondthoughts, Solomon. See also *Horse-Shoe Robinson; Rob of the Bowl; Swallow Barn.*

KENNEDY, John Pendleton. *Memoirs of the Life of William Wirt.* Philadelphia, 1849. Portrait and folding facsimile. 2 vols., black cloth. $600.

KENNEDY, William. *The Ink Truck.* New York, 1969. Author's first book. $300. London (1970). Black cloth stamped in silver on spine only. $150.

KENNEDY, William. *Legs.* New York (1975) $150. London, 1976. $75.

KENNEDY, William. *Texas: Its Geography, Natural History, and Topography.* New York, 1844. 118 pages, wraps. (Reprint in part of *Texas. The Rise, Progress . . .*) $500.

KENNEDY, William. *Texas: The Rise, Progress and Prospects of the Republic of Texas.* London, 1841. Maps, charts. 2 vols. $5,000. 2 vols. in one, cloth. $1,000. Second edition, same date. $750.

KENNER, Hugh. *Paradox in Chesterton.* London, 1948. Author's first book. $125.

KENT, Henry W. (compiler). *Bibliographical Notes on One Hundred Books Famous in English Literature.* Grolier Club. New York, 1903. Half vellum. One of 305. $300. (Issued as a supplement to the Grolier Club title of 1902, *One Hundred Books Famous in English Literature,* which was also limited to 305 copies.) $200. Together, the two books. $500.

KENT, Rockwell. See *Architectonics.*

KENT, Rockwell. *A Birthday Book.* New York, 1931. Illustrated by the author. Pictorial cloth (silk). One of 1,850 signed. Issued without dustwrapper. $350.

KENT, Rockwell. *The Bookplates and Marks of Rockwell Kent.* New York, 1929. 85 plates. Decorated cloth. One of 1,250 signed. In dustwrapper. $250.

KENT, Rockwell. *Forty Drawings . . . to Illustrate the Works of William Shakespeare.* (Garden City, 1936.) Portfolio of drawings. One of 1,000. In slipcase. $250.

KENT, Rockwell. *Greenland Journal.* New York (1962). With a set of 6 lithographs, one signed. In slipcase. $350.

KENT, Rockwell. *Later Bookplates & Marks of Rockwell Kent.* New York, 1937. Illustrated. One of 1,250 signed. Issued without dustwrapper in slipcase. $250.

KENT, Rockwell. *N. by E.* New York, 1930. Illustrated. Pictorial silvered blue buckram. One of 900 signed. $250. Linen, with an extra page, for presentation. One of 100. In slipcase. $400. Trade. $100.

KENT, Rockwell. *The Seven Ages of Man.* New York, 1918. First collection of his illustrations. $200.

KENT, Rockwell. *Voyaging Southward from the Strait of Magellan.* New York, 1924. Tan buckram. In dustwrapper. $350. Blue boards. One of 110 signed, with an extra signed woodcut. $600.

KENT, Rockwell. *Wilderness: A Journal of Quiet Adventure in Alaska.* New York, 1920. 69 illustrations. Author's first book. First binding. Gray linen. In dustwrapper. $350. Second binding, tan pictorial boards. In dustwrapper. $250.

KENTUCKIAN in New-York (The). By a Virginian. New York, 1834. 2 vols. (By W. A. Caruthers.) $300.

KENYON, Frederic G. *Ancient Books and Modern Discoveries.* Chicago, 1927. One of 350. 20 plates. In dustwrapper and slipcase. $375.

KENYON, William Asbury. *Miscellaneous Poems.* Chicago, 1845. $350.

KER, Henry. *Travels Through the Western Interior of the United States.* Elizabethtown, N.J., 1816. $600.

KERCHEVAL, Samuel. *A History of the Valley of Virginia.* Winchester, Va., 1833. $750.

KEROUAC, Jack. *Big Sur.* New York (1962). $150. (London, 1963.) Bound in blue or black cloth. $100.

KEROUAC, Jack. *The Dharma Bums.* New York, 1958. $200. (London, 1959.) First printing incorrectly states "First Published 1950." Red, blue, or black binding, priority unknown. $150.

KEROUAC, Jack. *Doctor Sax.* New York (1959). Four signed and numbered copies. Numbered 1–4. $2,000. One of 26 signed and lettered copies. $1,750. Trade. $600.

KEROUAC, Jack. *Excerpts from Visions of Cody.* (New York, 1959.) One of 750 signed. (There are an additional 55 out-of-series copies.) $650.

KEROUAC, Jack. *Mexico City Blues.* New York (1959). 4 signed copies. $2,000. One of 26 signed and lettered copies. $1,500. Trade. $750. Wraps. Evergreen Original E-184. $50.

KEROUAC, Jack. *On the Road.* New York, 1957. Review copies issued with additional white dustwrapper with printed blurb, "This is a copy of the first edition." $1,250. Trade. $600. (London, 1958.) Author's photo on dustwrapper rear flap. $300.

KEROUAC, Jack. *The Subterraneans.* New York (1958). 100 copies bound in half cloth. $600. Trade. $300. Wraps. Printed in black and green. $40.

KEROUAC, John (Jack). *The Town and the City.* New York (1950). Author's first book. $500. London (1951). Author's name given as John Kerouac. $250. New York (1960). Wraps. Author's name given as Jack Kerouac. $25.

KERR, Hugh. *A Poetical Description of Texas, etc.* New York, 1838. In original cloth. $1,250.

KERR, John. *The Golf Book of East Lothian.* Edinburgh, 1896. Limited signed edition. $1,500.

KERSH, Gerald. *Jews Without Jehovah.* London, 1934. Author's first book. $150.

KESEY, Ken. *One Flew Over the Cuckoo's Nest.* New York (1962). Author's first book. $500. London (1962, actually 1963). $125.

KESEY, Ken. *Sometimes a Great Notion.* New York (1964). First issue has publisher's logo (Viking ship) on half title. $200. London, 1966. $100.

KETTELL, Samuel. *Specimens of American Poetry, with Critical and Biographical Notices.* Boston, 1829. 3 vols. $200.

KEYES, Daniel. *Flowers for Algernon.* New York (1966). Author's first book. $500.

KEYNES, Geoffrey. *A Bibliography of Dr. Robert Hooke.* Oxford, 1960. $75.

KEYNES, Geoffrey. *Bibliotheca Bibliographici, A Catalogue of the Library Formed by Geoffrey Keynes.* 45 plates. One of 500 copies. $175.

KEYNES, Geoffrey. *Blake Studies, Notes on His Life and Works in Seventeen Chapters.* London, 1949. 48 full-page plates. $125.

KEYNES, Geoffrey. *Engravings by William Blake; The Separate Plates, A Catalogue Raisonnee.* Dublin, 1956. 45 plates. One of 500 copies. $225.

KEYNES, Geoffrey. *A Study of the Illuminated Books of William Blake, Poet, Printer, Prophet.* London (1964). 32 color plates. One of 525 signed and numbered copies. $275.

KEYNES, Geoffrey, and WOLF, Edwin 2nd. *William Blake's Illuminated Books, A Census.* New York, 1953. One of 400 copies. $175.

KEYNES, John Maynard. *The Economic Consequences of the Peace.* London, 1919. In dustwrapper. $750. Without dustwrapper. $200.

KEYNES, John Maynard. *The General Theory of Employment, Interest, and Money.* London, 1936. $500. New York, 1936. Cloth. $250.

KEYNES, John Maynard. *Indian Currency and Finance.* London, 1913. $750.

KHERDIAN, David. *Homage to Adana.* Mt. Horeb, Wis. (1970). One of 120. $125.

KHERDIAN, David. *On the Death of My Father and Other Poems.* Fresno (1970). Introduction by William Saroyan. One of 26 signed by the poet and Saroyan. $250.

KIDD, J. H. *Personal Recollections of a Cavalryman with Custer's Michigan Cavalry Brigade in the Civil War.* Ionia, Mich., 1908. $250.

KIKI'S Memoirs. Paris, 1930. Translated by Samuel Putnam. Introduction by Ernest Hemingway. Illustrated. Wraps. With glassine wrapper and imprinted band around book. $300.

KILBOURN, John. *Columbian Geography.* Chillicothe, Ohio, 1815. $300.

KILBOURN, John. *The Ohio Gazeteer, or Topographical Dictionary.* Columbus, 1816. $400.

KILBOURNE, E. W. *Strictures on Dr. I. Garland's Pamphlet, Entitled "Villainy Esposed," with Some Account of His Transactions in Lands of the Sac and Fox Reservation, etc., in Lee County, Iowa.* Fort Madison, Iowa, 1850. 24 pages, sewn. $250.

KILGOUR Collection of Russian Literature, 1750–1920 . . . Cambridge, 1959. $100.

KILMER, Joyce. *Summer of Love.* New York, 1911. Gilt top. First issue, with the Baker & Taylor imprint at foot of spine (later Doubleday, Page & Co.). Author's first book. $250.

KILMER, Joyce. *Trees and Other Poems.* New York (1914). First few printings were in tan-gray boards, top edge gilt and without "Printed in U.S.A." on copyright page. $125.

KIMBALL, Fiske. *The Domestic Architecture of the American Colonies and of the Early Republic.* New York, 1922. In dustwrapper. $250.

KIMBALL, Fiske. *Mr. Samuel McIntire, Carver, the Architect of Salem.* Portland, Me., 1940. Illustrated. One of 675. In slipcase. $200.

KIMBALL, Fiske. *Thomas Jefferson, Architect.* Boston, 1916. Illustrated. Cloth. One of 350. In dustwrapper. $300.

KIMBALL, Heber C. *The Journal of Heber C. Kimball.* Nauvoo, Ill., 1840. Edited by R. B. Thompson. 60 pages, printed wraps. $1,250.

KINDER, Louis H. *Formulas for Bookbinders.* East Aurora, 1905. One of 490 signed and numbered copies. Two full-page plates. $500.

KING and Queen of Hearts (The). London, 1805. (By Charles Lamb.) Approximately 5¼ by 4 inches with 15 plain or colored illustrations. Early (earliest?) printing, undated cover, name of "Hodgkins" misspelled on cover (VAB). $1,500. Various cover dates have been noted: 1806, 1808, 1809, etc. $750.

KING, Alexander. *Gospel of the Goat.* Chicago, 1928. 30 plates. Folio, boards and morocco. One of 100. Issued without dustwrapper. $250.

KING, C. W. *Antique Gems and Rings.* London, 1872. Illustrated. 2 vols. Leather. $300. Cloth. $300.

KING, C. W. *The Natural History of Gems or Decorative Stones.* London, 1867. $250.

KING, Charles. *The Fifth Cavalry in the Sioux War to 1876: Campaigning with Crook.* Milwaukee, 1880. 134 pages, printed wraps. $2,500. Second edition, 1890. $100.

KING, Frank M. *Longhorn Trail Drivers.* (Los Angeles, 1940.) Illustrated. One of 400 signed. Issued without dustwrapper. $150.

KING, Frank M. *Wranglin' the Past.* (Los Angeles, 1935.) Portrait. Leatherette. One of 300 signed. Issued without dustwrapper. $250.

KING, Jeff, and CAMPBELL, Joseph. *Where the Two Came to Their Father: A Navaho War Ceremonial.* New York (1943). 18 silk-screen prints. 2 vols., quarto, wraps, in large cloth portfolio. $750.

KING, Martin Luther, Jr. *Stride Toward Freedom.* New York, 1958. Author's first book. $175.

KING, Richard, and HOPPE, E. O. *The Book of Fair Women.* London, 1922. Text by King, photographs by Hoppe. In dustwrapper. $750.

KING, W. Ross. *The Sportsman and Naturalist in Canada.* London, 1866. 6 color plates, other illustrations. $350.

KING, Stephen. *Carrie.* Garden City, 1974. $450. (London, 1974.) $650.

KING, Stephen. *Cujo.* Viking, New York (1981). $35. Mysterious Press, New York (1981). 26 signed and lettered copies. "Not For Sale" in acetate dustwrapper and slipcase. $1,250. 750 signed and numbered copies without dustwrapper in slipcase. $350. London (1982). $40.

KING, Stephen. *The Dark Tower: The Gunslinger.* West Kingston, R.I. (1982). 26 signed and lettered copies. Issued in dustwrapper and slipcase. $2,500. 500 signed and numbered copies in dustwrapper and slipcase. $1,250. Trade. Dustwrapper also lists limited-edition price. $450. Second printing indicated. Dustwrapper does not list limited edition. $150. New York, 1988. Wraps. $10.

KING, Stephen. *The Dark Tower II: The Drawing of the Three.* (West Kingston, R.I., 1987.) 850 signed and numbered copies in dustwrapper and slipcase. $450. Trade. $100.

KING, Stephen. *Firestarter.* Huntington Woods, 1980. One of 725 signed and numbered copies. $500. 26 signed and lettered copies. Issued without dustwrapper or slipcase. $2,500. Trade. $50. London (1980). $125.

KING, Stephen. *Night Shift.* Garden City, 1978. Dustwrapper price: $8.95. $650. (London, 1978.) $350.

KING, Stephen. *Salem's Lot.* Garden City, 1975. First-issue dustwrapper priced at $8.95, refers to "Father Cody" in dustwrapper write-up. $1,000. Second issue: dustwrapper price clipped and $7.95 added. "Father Copy" in dustwrapper write-up. $750. Third issue: Dustwrapper priced at $7.95 and "Cody" changed to "Callahan" on dustwrapper write-up. $500. (London, 1976.) $400.

KING, Stephen. *The Stand.* Garden City, 1978. Dustwrapper price $12.95. $175. (London, 1979.) $200.

KING, Stephen. *The Stand/The Complete and Uncut Edition.* (New York, 1990.) One of 52 signed and lettered copies. $1,250. One of 1,250 signed and numbered copies by King and Bernie Wrightson. In ebony box. $650. Trade. $25. (London, 1990.) $30.

KING, William. *Chelsea Porcelain . . .* London, 1922. 171 illustrations (7 colored). Buckram. $175. Pigskin. One of 75 signed. $275. One of 13 on vellum. Issued without dustwrapper. $500.

KINGLAKE, A. W. *Eothen, or Traces of Travel Brought Home from the East.* London, 1844. Frontispiece in color, colored plate. Boards and cloth. $450.

KINGMAN, John. *Letters, Written by John Kingman, While on a Tour to Illinois and Wisconsin, in the Summer of 1838.* Hingham, Mass., 1842. 48 pages, printed wraps. $1,000.

KINGSLEY, Charles. *At Last: A Christmas in the West Indies.* London, 1871. 2 vols., cloth. $250. New York, 1871. 1 vol. $150.

KINGSLEY, Charles. *The Heroes; or, Greek Fairy Tales for My Children.* Cambridge, 1856. 8 illustrations by the author. Pink decorated cloth. $400. London, 1912.

Riccardi Press. Illustrated by W. Russell Flint. Vellum. One of 500. In dustwrapper. $600. One of 12 on vellum, with a duplicate set of plates. $3,000.

KINGSLEY, Charles. *The Saint's Tragedy* . . . London, 1848. Author's first book. $300.

KINGSLEY, Charles. *The Water-Babies.* London, 1863. First issue, with "L'Envoi" leaf. $750. Without the leaf. $500. London, 1909. 42 colored plates by Warwick Goble. Vellum. One of 260. $400.

KINGSLEY, Charles. *Westward Ho!* Cambridge, 1855. 3 vols., blue cloth. With 16 pages of ads at end of vol. 3 dated February 1855. $500. Boston, 1855. $200. Limited Editions Club, New York, 1947. Illustrated. 2 vols., boards. In slipcase. $75.

KINGSLEY, Henry. *The Recollections of Geoffrey Hamlyn.* Cambridge, 1859. 3 vols., blue cloth. Author's first book. $300.

KINNELL, Galway. *What a Kingdom It Was.* Boston, 1960. Boards. Author's first book. $125.

KINNELL, Galway (translator). *Bitter Victory.* By Rene Hardy. Garden City, 1956. Kinnell's first book appearance. $150.

KINSELLA, Thomas. *Nightwalker.* Dublin, 1967. Wraps. $100.

KINSELLA, Thomas. *The Starlit Eye.* Dublin, 1952. One of 175. $600.

KINSELLA, W. P. *Dance Me Outside.* (Ottawa) 1977. Author's first book. Cloth. $250. Wraps. $40.

KINSELLA, W. P. *Scars: Stories.* (Ottawa) 1978. Cloth. $200. Wraps. $40.

KINSELLA, W. P. *Shoeless Joe.* Boston, 1982. $100.

KINZIE, Mrs. Juliette A. See *Narrative of the Massacre at Chicago.*

KINZIE, Mrs. Juliette A. *Wau-Bun, the "Early Day" in the North-West.* New York, 1856. 6 plates. Pictorial cloth. $300. London, 1856. First English edition. $225.

KIP, Lawrence. See *The Indian Council in the Valley of the Walla Walla.*

KIP, Lawrence. *Army Life on the Pacific.* New York, 1859. $350.

KIPLING, Rudyard. See *Echoes; Quariette.*

KIPLING, Rudyard. *An Almanac of Twelve Sports* . . . London, 1898. 12 color plates by William Nicholson. Pictorial boards. $400.

KIPLING, Rudyard. *Barrack-Room Ballads and Other Verses.* London, 1892. $200. One of 225 on large paper. $350. Half vellum and buckram. One of 30 on vellum. $1,500. (For first American edition, see Kipling, *Departmental Ditties.)*

KIPLING, Rudyard. *"Captains Courageous": A Story of the Grand Banks.* London, 1897. 22 illustrations. Blue cloth, gilt edges. $300.

KIPLING, Rudyard. *The City of Dreadful Night and Other Places.* Allahabad (India), 1891. Gray-green pictorial wraps. No. 14 of Wheeler's Indian Library. First published (and second Indian) edition. $1,500. Allahabad and London (1891). Wraps. First English edition. $500. Grosset & Co. New York, 1899. $200.

KIPLING, Rudyard. *Collected Verse.* New York, 1907. Red cloth. Without index (VAB) not mentioned in Livingston. $100. New York, 1910. Color illustrations. Half vellum. First illustrated edition. One of 125 signed. $750. London, 1912. Limp vellum. One of 100 signed. $750. One of 500. $200.

KIPLING, Rudyard. *Departmental Ditties and Other Verses.* Lahore, India, 1886. Pictorial tan wraps. (Issued in the form of a government envelope with flap tied with red tape.) $2,500. Calcutta, India, 1886. Printed boards. Second edition. $1,000. London, 1897. Illustrated. Vellum and cloth. First English (and first illustrated) edition. One of 150 on large paper. $750.

KIPLING, Rudyard. *The Five Nations.* London, 1903. Limp vellum. One of 30 on vellum. $1,250. Boards. One of 200 large paper copies. $350. Trade edition. $100.

KIPLING, Rudyard. *In Black and White.* Allahabad (India, 1888). Gray-green pictorial wraps. No. 3 of the Indian Railway Library. $400. Allahabad and London (1890). Gray-green wraps. First English edition. $250.

KIPLING, Rudyard. *The Jungle Book.* London, 1894. Blue pictorial boards. $350. New York, 1894. $150. Limited Editions Club. New York, 1968. *(The Jungle Books.)* In slipcase. $125.

KIPLING, Rudyard. *Just So Stories for Little Children.* London, 1902. Illustrated by the author. Decorated red cloth. $750.

KIPLING, Rudyard. *Kim.* New York, 1901. Green cloth. First issue, without chapter headings except chapters 8 and 13. $125. London, 1901. $300. Limited Editions Club. New York, 1962. Cloth. In slipcase. $50.

KIPLING, Rudyard. *The Light That Failed.* London, 1891. Blue cloth. $250.

KIPLING, Rudyard. *The Phantom 'Rickshaw and Other Tales.* Allahabad (India), 1889. Gray-green pictorial wraps. No. 5 of the Indian Railway Library. First binding, without periods after A H in "A H Wheeler" on front cover. $750. Second issue, with periods. $600. London (1890). First English edition. $300.

KIPLING, Rudyard. *Poems, 1886–1929.* London, 1929. 3 vols., red morocco. One of 525 signed. In dustwrapper. $1,250. Garden City, 1930. 3 vols., vellum boards. One of 537 signed. $1,000.

KIPLING, Rudyard. *Puck of Pook's Hill.* London, 1906. $250. New York, 1906. 4 color plates by Arthur Rackham. Pictorial cloth. First illustrated edition. $150.

KIPLING, Rudyard. *Schoolboy Lyrics.* Lahore (India), 1881. Brown printed or plain white wraps. Plain white wraps presumed to precede. Author's first book. $12,000.

KIPLING, Rudyard. *Sea and Sussex from Rudyard Kipling's Verse.* London, 1926. 24 color plates by Donald Maxwell. Boards and vellum. One of 500 signed in dustwrapper and slipcase. $750. Garden City, 1926. One of 150 signed. $1,000.

KIPLING, Rudyard. *The Second Jungle Book.* London, 1895. $200. New York, 1895. $75.

KIPLING, Rudyard. *Soldier Tales.* London, 1896. Illustrated. Blue cloth. $300.

KIPLING, Rudyard. *Soldiers Three.* Allahabad (India), 1888. Pictorial wraps. First state, without cross-hatching on barrack doors on the cover. $1,000. Second issue, with the cross-hatching and without period after "No" in "No 1." $750.

KIPLING, Rudyard. *Songs of the Sea.* London, 1927. Vellum and boards. One of 500 large paper copies, signed. In dustwrapper. $750.

KIPLING, Rudyard. *The Story of the Gadsbys.* Allahabad (India), 1888. Gray-green pictorial wraps. No. 2 of the Indian Railway Library. $750.

KIPLING, Rudyard. *Under the Deodars.* Allahabad (India), 1888. Wraps. No. 4 of the Indian Railway Library. First state of wraps, without shading around "No. 4" and "One Rupee." $750. Later, with shading on wraps. $500. London (1890). Wraps. First English edition. $350.

KIPLING, Rudyard. *Wee Willie Winkle and Other Child Stories.* Allahabad (India), 1888. Gray-green pictorial wraps. No. 6 of the Indian Railway Library. First issue, with periods after "A" and "H" on cover. $1,500. (Livingston notes the covers were retouched or reëngraved at least five times.) Allahabad, 1889. Wraps. Second edition. $750. London (1890). Wraps. $750.

KIPLING, Rudyard. *The White Man's Burden.* London, 1899. Lilac-colored printed wraps. First English edition (a Thomas J. Wise forgery). $600. (Note: There also exists a true first edition, for copyright, issued in 10 copies, gray wraps, in New York in 1899. $750.)

KIPLING, Rudyard. *With the Night Mail.* New York, 1909. Color plates. $250.

KIRKALDY, Andrew. *Fifty Years of Golf: My Memories.* London, 1921. $300. New York, 1921. $300. (Note: Second edition leaves out "My" in title.)

KIZER, Carolyn. *Poems.* (Portland, Oregon, 1959). Author's first book. Wraps. $125.

KIZER, Carolyn. *The Ungrateful Garden.* Bloomington (1961). Cloth. $75. Wraps. $25.

KLINE, Otis Adelbert. *Maza of the Moon.* Chicago, 1930. First edition not stated. $600.

KLONDYKE Mines and the Golden Valley of the Yukon (The). No-place, 1897. 24 pages, self-wraps. $150.

KLOSTERHEIM: or the Masque. By the English Opium Eater. Edinburgh, 1832. (By Thomas De Quincey.) In original boards, paper label. $750.

KNEEDLER, H. S. *The Coast Country of Texas.* Cincinnati, 1896. 76 pages, wraps. $250.

KNEEDLER, H. S. *Through Storyland to Sunset Seas.* Cincinnati, 1896. Wraps. $150.

KNEELAND, Samuel. *The Wonders of the Yosemite Valley and California.* Boston, 1872. With 10 mounted albumen photographs by John Soule. $650.

KNIBBS, Henry Hubert. *Overland Red.* Boston, 1914. In dustwrapper. $150.

KNIBBS, Henry Hubert. *The Ridin' Kid From Powder River.* Boston, 1919. In dustwrapper. $100.

KNIBBS, Henry Hubert. *Sundown Slim.* Boston, 1915. In dustwrapper. $150.

KNIBBS, Henry Hubert. *Tang of Life.* Boston, 1918. In dustwrapper. $125.

KNICKERBOCKER, Diedrich. *A History of New York, from the Beginning of the World to the End of the Dutch Dynasty.* New York, 1809. Engraved plate. 2 vols. (By Washington Irving.) First state, with 268 pp. in vol. 1. $1,000. London, 1839. Illustrated by George Cruikshank. $300. New York, 1867. 2 vols., full morocco. Author's revised edition. $500. New York, 1900. Illustrated by Maxfield Parrish. $200.

KNIGHT, Dr. (John), and SLOVER, John. *Indian Atrocities.* Nashville, 1843. 96 pages, plain yellow boards, cloth spine. $3,000 or more. Cincinnati, 1867. Printed wraps. One of 500. $150.

KNISH, Anne. See Morgan, Emanuel, and Knish, Anne.

KNOBLOCK, Byron W. *Bannerstones of the North American Indian.* La Grange, Ill., 1939. Frontispiece in color, 270 plates. Half leather. One of 50 signed. $250.

KNOWLES John. *A Separate Peace.* London (1959). Author's first book. $600. New York, 1960. In pictorial dustwrapper. $300. In printed dustwrapper. $125.

KNOX, Dudley W. *Naval Sketches of the War in California.* New York, 1939. 28 colored drawings by William H. Meyers. Introduction by Franklin D. Roosevelt. Boards, white leather spine. Grabhorn printing. One of 1,000. $300.

KOCH, Frederick H. (editor). *Carolina Folk-Plays, Second Series.* New York, 1924. (Contains "The Return of Buck Gavin," Thomas Wolfe's first appearance in a book.) $250.

KOCH, Kenneth. *Poems.* (With Nell Blain *Prints.*) New York, 1953. Author's first book. Stiff wraps. $500.

KODOKAN, The. *Illustrated Kodokan Judo.* Tokyo, 1955. First edition stated. $40.

KOESTLER, Arthur. See Costler, A.

KOESTLER, Arthur. *Spanish Testament.* London, 1937. Cloth. $250. Wraps. (Left Book Club.) $75.

KOHL, J. G. *Kitchi-Gami: Wanderings Round Lake Superior.* London, 1860. Illustrated. Half calf. First edition in English. $450.

KONINGSMARKE, the Long Finne: A Story of the New World. New York, 1823. 2 vols. (By James Kirke Paulding.) $300.

KOONTZ, Dean. See Axton, David; Coffey, Brian; Dwyer, K.R.; North, Anthony.

KOONTZ, Dean. *Night Chills.* New York, 1976. $200.

KOOP, Albert J. *Early Chinese Bronzes.* London, 1924. 110 plates (3 colored). $300. Calf. One of 40 on China paper, signed. $500. New York, 1924. $300.

KOOPS, Matthias. *Historical Account of the Substances Which Have Been Used to Describe Events . . . from the Earliest Date to the Invention of Paper.* London, 1800. Printed on paper made of straw alone. $1,350.

KORNBLUTH, C. M. *Not This August.* Garden City, 1955. $150.

KOSEWITZ, W. F. von. *Eccentric Tales, from the German.* London, 1827. 20 hand-colored etched plates by George Cruikshank from sketches by Alfred Crowquill. $1,000.

KOSINSKI, Jerzy. See Novak, Joseph.

KOSINSKI, Jerzy. *Notes of the Author on The Painted Bird.* New York, 1965. Wraps. $75.

KOSINSKI, Jerzy. *The Painted Bird.* Boston (1965). First book under his name. Extraneous line top of page 270. $200.

KOTZEBUE, Otto von. *A New Voyage Round the World, 1823–26.* London, 1830. 3 maps and 2 plates. 2 vols. First edition in English. $1,500.

KOTZEBUE, Otto von. *A Voyage of Discovery, Into the South Sea and Beering's Straits.* London, 1821. Colored plates, engraved folding charts. 3 vols. First edition in English. $2,500.

KRAKEL, Dean F. *The Saga of Tom Horn.* (Laramie, 1954.) First edition (suppressed). In dustwrapper. $350. Second edition, with text on pages 13 and 54 revised. $200.

KRAMER, Sidney. *A History of Stone & Kimball and Herter S. Stone & Co. With a Bibliography* . . . Chicago, 1940. One of 500 copies. $125.

KREYMBORG, Alfred. *Love, Life, and Other Studies.* New York (1908). One of 500. $100.

KREYMBORG, Alfred (editor). *Others for 1919: An Anthology of the New Verse.* New York, 1917. Boards. In dustwrapper. $300.

KROEBER, Alfred L. *Handbook of the Indians of California.* Washington, 1925. Folding map, 10 other maps, 73 plates on 38 sheets. Cloth. Issued without dustwrapper. $175.

KRUSENSTERN, A. J. von. *Voyage Round the World in the Years 1803, 1804, 1805, and 1806.* London, 1813. 2 color plates, folding map. 2 vols. First edition in English. $4,000.

KRUTCH, Joseph Wood. *Comedy and Conscience*. . . New York, 1924. Author's first book. Wraps. $150.

KUNDERA, Milan. *The Joke.* New York, 1969. Author's first book. $100.

KUNITZ, Stanley J. *Intellectual Things.* Garden City, 1930. Author's first book. $125.

KUNZ, George Frederick. *The Book of the Pearl.* New York, 1908. Illustrated, including color plates. Pale blue cloth. $750. London, 1908. White buckram. First English edition. $500.

KUNZ, George Frederick. *The Curious Lore of Precious Stones.* Philadelphia (1913). 86 illustrations (6 in color). Pictorial cloth. $250.

KUNZ, George Frederick. *Gems and Precious Stones of North America*. . . New York, 1890. 8 colored plates, other illustrations. With errata slip. $750.

KUNZ, George Frederick. *Ivory and the Elephant in Art, in Archaeology, and in Science.* Garden City, 1916. Illustrated. $250.

KUNZ, George Frederick. *Rings for the Finger.* Philadelphia, 1917. $200.

KUTTNER, Henry, and MOORE, C. L. *No Boundaries.* New York (1955). $300.

KUWASHIMA, T. S., and WELCH, A. R. *Judo: Forty-one Lessons in the Modern Science of Jiu Jitsu.* New York, 1938. $50.

KUYKENDALL, Ivan Lee. *Ghost Riders of the Mogollon.* San Antonio (1954). Boards. In dustwrapper. (Suppressed.) $600.

KUYKENDALL, Judge W. L. *Frontier Days.* (Denver) 1917. Portrait. $200.

L

L., E. V. *Sparks from a Flint: Odd Rhymes for Odd Times.* London, 1890. (By E. V. Lucas.) His first book. $100.

LA BREE, Ben (editor). *The Confederate Soldier in the Civil War, 1861–1865.* Louisville, 1895. Illustrated. Folio, cloth. $175.

LACKINGTON, James. *Memoirs of the First Forty-five Years of the Life of James Lackington . . .* London (1791). $100.

LACROIX, Paul. *Science and Literature in the Middle Ages . . .* New York, 1878. First English translation of the 1868 first edition which was published in France, with an American title page. $135.

LA CUISINE Creole. New York (1885). (By Lafcadio Hearn). With introduction on two pages. $2,000. (Other early editions also valuable.)

LADA-MOCARSKI, Valerian. *Bibliography of Books on Alaska Published Before 1868.* New Haven, 1969. $300.

LADIES Almanack . . . Written and Illustrated by a Lady of Fashion. Paris, 1928. (By Djuna Barnes.) Pictorial wraps. One of 1,000. $350. Vellum. One of 40 with hand-colored plates. $1,000.

LADY Audley's Secret. London, 1862. (By Mary E. Braddon.) 3 vols., blue cloth. $400.

LA FARGE, Oliver. *Laughing Boy.* Boston, 1929. Author's first book. (Previous collaboration.) $150.

LAFITTE: The Pirate, of the Gulf. New York, 1836. (By Joseph Holt Ingraham.) 2 vols. $200.

LA FONTAINE, Jean de. *The Fables of Jean de la Fontaine.* London, 1931. Translated into English verse by Edward Marsh. 26 engravings on copper by Stephen Gooden. 2 vols., vellum. One of 525 signed by the translator and artist. $600.

LA FRENTZ, F. W. *Cowboy Stuff.* New York, 1927. Illustrated by Henry Ziegler. Boards. Issued without dustwrapper. First issue, with 49 plates. One of 500. $500.

LAHONTAN, Louis Armand, Baron de. *New Voyages to North-America . . .* London, 1703. 2 vols. 4 maps and 20 plates. Without the frontispiece in vol. II (which is not usually present). $3,500.

LAKESIDE Classics. Chicago, 1903–90. 87 vols. Complete set. $1,750. Individual volumes range from $10 to $100 or so.

LAMANTIA, Philip. *Erotic Poems.* (Berkeley) 1946. Author's first book. Issued without dustwrapper. $300.

LAMAR, Mirabeu B. *Verse Memorials.* New York, 1857. Author's first book. $1,500.

LAMB, Charles. See An Eye Witness. See also *The Adventures of Ulysses; The King and Queen of Hearts; The Last Essays of Elia; The New Year's Feast on His Coming of Age, Poetry for Children.*

LAMB, Charles. *Album Verses, with a Few Others.* London, 1830. In original cloth-backed boards, paper label. $350.

LAMB, Charles. *The Letters of Charles Lamb, to Which Are Added Those of His Sister Mary Lamb.* (London, 1935.) Edited by E. V. Lucas. 3 vols., cloth. $250.

LAMB, Charles. *A Masque of Days.* London, 1901. Illustrated by Walter Crane. Half cloth. $200.

LAMB, Charles. *Specimens of English Dramatic Poets, Who Lived About the Time of Shakespeare: with Notes.* London, 1808. $350.

LAMB, Charles. *Tales from Shakespeare.* London, 1807. 20 plates by William Mulready. 2 vols. First issue, with imprint on back of page 235 (VAB). $1,500. Second issue, back of page 235 blank (VAB). (Thomsen thought the blank page was first issue.) $1,250. London, 1909. Arthur Rackham color plates. Buckram with ties. One of 750 large paper copies, signed by Rackham. $1,250. Trade edition, in cloth. $300. (Note: Mary Lamb collaborated in writing this book.)

LAMB, Charles. *The Works of Charles Lamb.* London, 1818. 2 vols. First issue, with ads at end dated "June, 1818." $200. London, 1903. Edited by William Macdonald. 12 vols. In half vellum. $600.

LAMB, M.C. *Leather Dressing Including Dyeing, Staining & Finishing.* London, 1925. Third edition and completely rewritten. $200.

LAMBERT, Aylmer Bourke. *A Description of the Genus Pinus.* 1803–7. 47 engraved plates, all but 3 colored by hand (Nissen 1123 states that there are 25 colored copies in all, with coloring by William Hooker). $35,000. 1832. 2 vols. Engraved portrait and 75 engraved or lithographed plates colored by hand. (The publisher was erratic in terms of how many plates were included but usually had at least 72.) $4,500.

LAMBOURNE, Alfred. *An Old Sketch-Book Dedicated to the Memory of My Father.* Boston (1892). 18 plates. 53 pages, plates. 78 pages, atlas folio, half morocco and tan cloth. $500.

LAMBOURNE, Alfred. *Scenic Utah: Pen and Pencil.* New York, 1891. 20 plates. "Edition Deluxe" on printed label, numbered and signed. $500.

LAMENTATIONS of Jeremiah (The). Gregynog Press. Newtown, Wales, 1933. Folio, morocco. Issued without dustwrapper or slipcase. One of 250. $1,500.

LAMON, Ward H. *The Life of Abraham Lincoln.* Boston, 1872. Plates and facsimiles. Green or rust-colored cloth. $200.

L'AMOUR, Louis. *Guns of the Timberlands.* New York, 1955. $300.

L'AMOUR, Louis. *Silver Canyon.* New York, 1956. $300.

L'AMOUR, Louis. *Smoke From This Altar.* Oklahoma City (1939). Author's first book. $750.

L'AMOUR, Louis. *Sitka.* New York, 1957. $300.

LAMPMAN, Archibald. *Among the Millet...* Ottawa, 1888. Author's first book. First issue, double rule above and below title on spine. $175.

LAMSON, David R. *Two Years' Experience Among the Shakers.* West Boylston, Mass., 1848. Illustrated. $175.

LANDAUER, Bella C. *Early American Trade Cards from the Collection of Bella C. Landauer.* New York, 1927. 44 plates. Limited to 550 copies. $150.

LANDE, Lawrence. *The Lawrence Lande Collection of Canadiana in the Redpath Library . . .* Montreal, 1965. 113 pages of plates. With *Rare and Unusual Canadiana; First Supplement to the Lande Bibliography.* First volume is signed and limited to 950 copies. Second volume is signed and limited to 500 copies. The pair. $325.

LANDOR, A. Henry Savage. *Across Wildwest Africa.* London, 1907. 2 vols., folding map. $250.

LANDOR, Walter Savage. See *Count Julian: A Tragedy; The Dun Cow; Imaginary Conversations; Pericles and Aspasia; Popery, British and Foreign; Simonidea.*

LANDOR, Walter Savage. *Gebir, Count Julian and Other Poems.* London, 1831. In original boards, cloth spine, label. $400.

LANDOR, Walter Savage. *Imaginary Conversations of Literary Men and Statesman.* London, 1826–28. 3 vols. $400. Limited Editions Club, Verona, 1936. In slipcase. $150.

LANDOR, Walter Savage. *The Last Fruit Off an Old Tree.* London, 1853. Purple cloth. First edition, with 8 pages of ads. $150.

LANE, Walter P. *Adventures and Recollections of Gen. Walter P. Lane.* Marshall, Tex., 1887. Portrait. 114 pages, wraps. $1,000.

LANG, Andrew. *Ballads and Lyrics of Old France, with Other Poems.* London, 1872. White cloth. Author's first book. $175.

LANG, Andrew. *The Blue Fairy Book.* London, 1889. Illustrated. Boards. One of 113. $500. Trade. $200. New York (about 1897). McLaughlin. Pictorial boards. $150.

LANG, Andrew. *The Green Fairy Book.* London, 1892. One of 150. $400. Trade in green cloth. $200.

LANG, Andrew. *Prince Charles Edward.* London, 1900. Illustrated. Half morocco. One of 350. $400. One of 1,500 in wraps. $300.

LANG, Andrew. *The Princess Nobody.* London (1884). Illustrated. Half cloth. $350.

LANG, Andrew. *The Red Fairy Book.* London, 1890. Illustrated. Gray-and-white boards. One of 113 on large paper. $500. Trade. $200.

LANG, Andrew. *XXII Ballades in Blue China.* London, 1880. Full vellum. $350. Another copy, morocco. $450.

LANG, Andrew et al. *Batch of Golfing Papers.* London, 1892. $250. New York, 1897. $150.

LANG, Andrew (translator). *The Miracles of Madame Saint Katherine of Fierbois.* Chicago: Way & Williams, 1897. Red vellum. First American edition. One of 50 on vellum. $350.

LANGFORD, Nathaniel Pitt. *Vigilante Days and Ways.* Boston, 1890. 15 plates. 2 vols., pictorial cloth. $350. New York, 1893. $200.

LANGLEY, Henry G. *The San Francisco Directory for the Year 1858.* San Francisco, 1858. $750.

LANGSDORFF, George H. von. *Narrative of the Rezanov Voyage to Nueva California, 1806.* San Francisco, 1927. Map, plates. Half cloth. In dustwrapper. One of 260. $250.

LANGSDORFF, George H. von. *Voyages and Travels in Various Parts of the World During 1803–7.* London, 1813–14. Folding map and 20 plates. 2 vols. First English edition. $3,000. Carlisle, Pa., 1817. Folding plate. 2 vols. in one. First American edition (abridged). $1,000.

LANGSTAFF, Launcelot, et al. *Salmagundi; or, The Whim-Whams and Opinions of Launcelot Langstaff, Esq., and Others.* New York, 1807–8. 2 vols., wraps. $750. 20 parts, wraps. $2,500. (By Washington Irving, William Irving, and James Kirke Paulding.) Difficult to identify, see BAL.

LANGSTON, Mrs. George. *History of Eastland County, Texas.* Dallas, 1904. $300.

LANGWORTHY, Franklin. *Scenery of the Plains, Mountains and Mines.* Ogdensburgh, N.Y., 1855. $500.

LANGWORTHY, Lucius H. *Dubuque: Its History, Mines, Indian Legends.* Dubuque, Iowa (1855). 82 pages, printed green wraps. $250.

LANHAM, Edwin. *Sailors Don't Care.* Paris, 1929. Author's first book. One of 10 signed and numbered copies. $650. Wraps. $400. New York, 1930. $150.

LANIER, Sidney. *The Boy's Mabinogion.* New York, 1881. Illustrated by Alfred Fredericks. Decorated cloth. $200.

LANIER, Sidney. *Florida: Its Scenery, Climate, and History.* Philadelphia, 1876. Illustrated. $350.

LANIER, Sidney. *Tiger-Lilies.* New York, 1867. First state, with title page on a stub. Author's first book. $300.

LANMAN, Charles. *Adventures in the Wilds of the United States and British American Provinces.* Philadelphia, 1856. Illustrated. 2 vols. First American edition. $500.

LANMAN, Charles. *Adventures of an Angler in Canada . . .* London, 1848. Frontispiece. Half leather. $600.

LANMAN, Charles. *A Summer in the Wilderness.* New York, 1847. $300.

LANMAN, Charles. *A Tour to the River Saguenay . . .* Philadelphia, 1848. $350.

LANMAN, James H. *History of Michigan.* New York, 1839. Folding map. $200.

LANTHORN Book (The). New York (1898). Half brown leather and green cloth. (By Stephen Crane and others.) One of 125 signed by Crane and the other contributors. $3,000. Some not signed by Crane. $400.

LAPHAM, I. A. *A Geographical and Topographical Description of Wisconsin.* Milwaukee, 1844. Folding map (with 1844 copyright). (First bound book printed in Wisconsin.) $650.

LAPHAM, I. A. *A Wisconsin . . .* Milwaukee, 1946. Colored map (dated 1845). Second edition (of *A Geographical and Topographical Description of Wisconsin*). $350.

LARCOM, Lucy. *Similitudes.* Boston, 1854. Author's first book. $75.

LARDNER, Ring W. *Bib Ballads.* Chicago (1915). Illustrated by Fontaine Fox. Decorated brown cloth. Author's first book (500 printed). First edition not stated. Issued without dustwrapper in box. $750. Without box. $350.

LARDNER, Ring W. *The Big Town.* Indianapolis (1921). Illustrated. In dustwrapper. $650. Without dustwrapper. $150.

LARDNER, Ring W. *Gullible's Travels.* Indianapolis (1917). First edition, not stated. In dustwrapper. $600. Without dustwrapper. $125.

LARDNER, Ring W. *How to Write Short Stories (with Samples).* New York, 1924. $400.

LARDNER, Ring. *Lose with a Smile.* New York, 1933. $500.

LARDNER, Ring W. *The Love Nest and Other Stories.* New York, 1925. $350.

LARDNER, Ring W. *March 6th the Homecoming.* (Chicago, 1914). First edition not stated. Issued without dustwrapper. $5,000.

LARDNER, Ring W. *My 4 Weeks in France.* Indianapolis (1918). First edition not stated. In dustwrapper. $350. Without dustwrapper. $75.

LARDNER, Ring W. *Regular Fellows I Have Met.* Chicago, 1919. First edition not stated. Green flexible suede. Issued without dustwrapper. $500.

LARDNER, Ring W. *Stop Me If You've Heard This One.* New York, 1929. Boards. Issued without dustwrapper as a promotional item. First edition not stated. $350.

LARDNER, Ring W. *You Know Me Al.* New York (1916). Brown cloth. First edition not stated and no Doran colophon. In dustwrapper. $750. Without dustwrapper. $150.

LARDNER, Ring W., Jr. *The Young Immigrunts.* Indianapolis (1920). (With a preface by the father.) Portraits by Gaar Williams. Pictorial boards. First edition not stated. In dustwrapper. $200.

LARDNER, Ring W., Jr. *Zanzibar Place.* Michigan (1903). Author's first book. Wraps. $6,000.

LARDNER, Ring W., and KAUFMAN, George S. *June Moon.* New York, 1930. Mauve cloth. With "A" on copyright page. $200.

LARIMER, Mrs. Sarah L. *The Capture and Escape; or, Life Among the Sioux.* Philadelphia, 1870. 5 plates. $150.

LARIMER, William. *Reminiscences of Gen. William Larimer and of His Son William H. H. Larimer.* Lancaster, Pa., 1918. Plates, portraits, folding chart. Morocco. $750.

LARKIN, Philip. *Jill.* London (1946). $500.

LARKIN, Philip. *The North Ship.* London (1945). Author's first book. $1,000.

LARKIN, Philip. *XX Poems.* Belfast, 1951. One of 100. $1,500.

LAROQUE, Francois A. *Journal of François A. Laroque from the Assiniboine to the Yellowstone, 1805.* Ottawa, 1910. 82 pages, printed wraps. $175.

LARPENTEUR, Charles. *Forty Years a Fur Trader of the Upper Mississippi.* New York, 1898. 18 maps and plans. 2 vols., blue cloth. One of 950. $400.

LA SALLE, Charles E. *Colonel Crocket, the Texas Trailer.* New York, no-date (1871). 84 pages, pictorial wraps. $150.

LA SALLE, Rene Robert Cavelier. *Relation of the Discoveries and Voyages of Cavelier de La Salle.* Caxton Club. Chicago, 1901. English and French texts. Half vellum. One of 227. $300.

LAST Days of Pompeii (The). London, 1834. (By Edward Bulwer-Lytton.) 3 vols. With errata slips in each volume. $600. New York, 1834. 2 vols. First American edition. $300. Limited Editions Club, New York, 1956. Illustrated. In slipcase. $75.

LAST Man (The). London, 1826. 3 vols., boards. (By Mary Wollstonecraft Shelley.) With ad leaf at end of vol. 1. $1,500.

LAST of the Mohicans (The). Philadelphia, 1826. By the Author of "The Pioneers," (James Fenimore Cooper.) 2 vols., in original tan boards, paper labels. BAL notes various differences, but no clear priorities. $7,500. Rebound. $1,250. London, 1826, 3 vols., in original boards. First English edition. $2,500. Rebound. $750. Limited Editions Club, New York, 1932. Illustrated. Half buckram. Slipcase. $100.

LATHAM, H. *Trans-Missouri Stock Raising . . .* Omaha, 1871. Map. 88 pages, wraps. $6,000. Denver, 1962. Illustrated. Pictorial cloth. One of 999. In dustwrapper. $60.

LATHEN, Emma. *Banking on Death.* New York, 1961. Author's first book. $200.

LATIMER, Jonathan. *Murder in the Madhouse.* Garden City, 1935. Author's first book. $350.

LATIMORE, Sarah Briggs, and HASKELL, Grace Clark. *Arthur Rackham, A Bibliography.* Los Angeles, 1936. One of 550 numbered copies. Slipcase. $425.

LATOUR, A. Lacarriere. *Historical Memoir of the War in West Florida and Louisiana in 1814–15.* Philadelphia, 1816. With an atlas. 2 vols. $1,750.

LATROBE, Charles Joseph. *The Rambler in Mexico.* London, 1836. Folding map. $250.

LATTER Struggles in the Journey of Life . . . Edinburgh, 1833. $125.

LAUFER, Berthold. *Paper and Printing in Ancient China.* Chicago, 1931. One of 250. $125.

LAUGHTON, L. G. Carr. *Old Ship Figure-Heads and Sterns.* London, 1925. 8 colored plates, 48 in monochrome. With 2 portfolios of plates. Three-quarters pigskin. One of 100. $500. Trade in cloth and dustwrapper. $350.

LAURENCE, Margaret. *A Tree for Poverty.* Nairobi, 1954. Author's first book. (Somali anthology edited by Laurence.) $1,250.

LAURENCE, Margaret. *This Side of Jordan.* Toronto, 1960. $200.

LAVIN, Mary. *Tales from Bective Bridge.* Boston, 1942. Author's first book. (999 copies.) $150. London (1943). $150.

LAW of Descent and Distribution Governing Lands of the Creek Nation, as Held by C. W. Raymond, Judge of the U.S. Court for the Indian Territory. No-place, 1903. 14 pages, printed wraps. Democrat Printing Co. $250.

LAWS of Jamaica, Passed by the Assembly . . . 1684 . . . London, 1684. Folding map. (First collected laws of the island.) $2,000.

LAWRENCE, Ada, and GELDER, Stuart. *Young Lorenzo: Early Life of D.H. Lawrence.* Florence (1932). Illustrated. Vellum. One of 740 (or 750). In dustwrapper. $250.

LAWRENCE, D. H. See Davison, Lawrence H.; Verga, Giovanni.

LAWRENCE, D. H. *Apocalypse.* Florence, Italy, 1931. Photographic frontispiece. Boards, leather label. One of 750. $250. London (1932). Frontispiece. First English edition. $200.

LAWRENCE, D. H. *Collected Poems.* London, 1928. 2 vols., boards, parchment spines. One of 100 signed. $1,000. Trade edition: 2 vols., brown cloth. $250. New York (1929). 2 vols., brown cloth. First American edition. In dustwrapper and slipcase. $200.

LAWRENCE, D. H. *The Escaped Cock.* Black Sun Press. Paris, 1929. Color frontispiece by Lawrence. White wraps. One of 450 on Van Gelder paper. In glassine dustwrapper and slipcase. $500. One of 50 on vellum, signed. $1,750. (Published later in England as *The Man Who Died.*)

LAWRENCE, D. H. *Fantasia of the Unconscious.* New York, 1922. Blue ribbed cloth. $350. London, 1923. $300.

LAWRENCE, D. H. *Kangaroo.* London (1923). Brown cloth. $300. New York, 1923. Blue cloth. $200.

LAWRENCE, D. H. *Lady Chatterley's Lover.* (Florence, Italy) 1928. Mulberry boards, paper spine label. One of 1,000 signed. In plain dustwrapper. $3,000.

LAWRENCE, D. H. *The Ladybird . . .* London (1923). (Published in America as *The Captain's Doll.*) $350.

LAWRENCE, D. H. *Last Poems.* Florence, 1932. Edited by Richard Aldington and G. Orioli. Frontispiece in color. Boards, paper label. One of 750 in dustwrapper and slipcase. $450. London, 1933. $150. New York, 1933. $125.

LAWRENCE, D. H. *The Lost Girl.* Brown cloth. London (1920). First issue, with page 256, line 15 reading ". . . she was taken to her room . . ." and with page 268 reading "whether she noticed anything in the bedrooms, in the beds." In dustwrapper. $600. Second issue, page 256 reads ". . . she let be." and 268 deletes the last six words of first issue. Both pages are tipped in. In dustwrapper. $400. (There is also a third issue, changed on integral pages.) New York, 1921. $300.

LAWRENCE, D. H. *The Man Who Died.* London, 1931. Buckram. Issued without dustwrapper. (First English edition of *The Escaped Cock*). $150.

LAWRENCE, D. H. *Mornings in Mexico.* London, 1927. $500. New York, 1927. $300.

LAWRENCE, D. H. *The Paintings of D. H. Lawrence.* Mandrake Press. London (1929). 26 colored plates. Folio, half morocco and green cloth. One of 500. $1,000. One of 10 on Japan paper. $6,000.

LAWRENCE, D. H. *Pansies.* London (1929). $300. Limited issue: one of 250 signed. In dustwrapper. $750. Another (later) edition, same place and date. White wraps. "Definitive and Complete Edition." Portrait frontispiece. One of 500 signed. In glassine dustwrapper and slipcase. $500. Limp leather. One of 50. $750. Pink wraps. (Not signed.) $150. New York, 1929. First American edition. In dustwrapper. $150.

LAWRENCE, D. H. *The Prussian Officer and Other Stories.* London (1914). In blue cloth stamped in gold and with 20 pages of ads at back. $300. Second issue, in light blue cloth stamped in dark blue and with 16 pages of ads. $200. New York, 1914. $150.

LAWRENCE, D. H. *Psychoanalysis and the Unconscious.* New York, 1921. Gray boards. In dustwrapper. $400. London, 1923. First English edition. In dustwrapper. $300.

LAWRENCE, D. H. *The Rainbow.* London (1915). Blue-green cloth. With ads dated "Autumn, 1914" (VAB). $850. Variant issue in red or brown cloth or wraps. $400. New York, 1916. $200.

LAWRENCE, D. H. *Rawdon's Roof.* London, 1928. Decorated boards. One of 530 signed. $600.

LAWRENCE, D. H. *St. Mawr.* (With "The Princess.") London (1925). Brown cloth with "Contents" showing text beginning on page 9. $250. Second issue corrected to show page 7. New York, 1925. First separate edition (without "The Princess"). $175.

LAWRENCE, D. H. *Sea and Sardinia.* New York, 1921. 8 colored plates. Boards and cloth. $400. London, 1923. $350.

LAWRENCE, D. H. *Sons and Lovers.* London (1913). Dark blue cloth. Presumed first state(s), without date on title page (Schwartz) or with dated title page tipped in

(Roberts). $300. (Dated page integral is agreed to be later.) New York, 1913. Purple cloth. $200.

LAWRENCE, D. H. *Studies in Classic American Literature.* New York, 1923. $350.

LAWRENCE, D. H. *Sun.* Black Sun Press. Paris, 1928. Marbled wraps. London, 1926. One of 100. $850. Wraps. First unexpurgated edition. One of 150 tied in a gold folder. $1,500. One of 15 on vellum, signed. In glassine dustwrapper and gold folder slipcase. $5,000.

LAWRENCE, D. H. *Tortoises.* New York, 1921. Pictorial boards. In dustwrapper. $400. Without dustwrapper. $100.

LAWRENCE, D. H. *Touch and Go.* London, 1920. Flexible orange boards, paper labels. In dustwrapper. $400. New York, 1920. Orange boards. First American edition. In dustwrapper. $300.

LAWRENCE, D. H. *The Trespasser.* London, 1912. Presumed first issue in dark blue cloth. $750. Second(?), Colonial(?), Trial(?) issue in green cloth. $650. New York, 1912. $400.

LAWRENCE, D. H. *Twilight in Italy.* London (1916). Dark blue cloth. $500. (Variant noted in light blue cloth.)

LAWRENCE, D. H. *The Virgin and the Gipsy.* Florence, 1930. White boards, paper label. One of 810. In dustwrapper and slipcase. $350. London (1930). $250.

LAWRENCE, D. H. *The White Peacock.* New York, 1911. Blue cloth. Author's first book. First issue, with integral title page and 1910 copyright date. $3,500. Second issue, with a tipped-in title page and 1911 copyright date. $2,000. London, 1911. Dark blue-green cloth. First issue, with publisher's windmill device on back cover and with pages 227–28 and 229–30 tipped in. $750. With leaves integral. $400.

LAWRENCE, D. H. *Women in Love.* New York, 1920. Dark blue cloth. One of about 16 or 18 copies signed and numbered by Lawrence. Without dustwrapper. $2,000. Unsigned copies. $300. New York, 1920 (actually 1922). First English edition. One of 50 signed. (American sheets.) Without dustwrapper. $2,500. London (1921). First English published edition. In brown boards. $300.

LAWRENCE, D. H. (translator). *The Story of Dr. Manente.* Florence (1929). By A. F. Grazzini. Frontispiece, 2 plates. Parchment boards. One of 200 signed by Lawrence. In tissue jacket. $750. One of 1,000. In dustwrapper. $125.

LAWRENCE, Frieda. *"Not I, But the Wind."* Santa Fe, N.M., 1934. One of 1,000 signed. $300. London, 1935. $125.

LAWRENCE, Richard Hoe (compiler). *History of the Society of Iconophiles of the City of New York.* New York, 1930. Reproductions of 119 plates. Boards and morocco issued without dustwrapper. One of 186. $250.

LAWRENCE, T. E. See Graves, Robert; Homer; Shaw, T. E. See also *The Seven Pillars of Wisdom.*

LAWRENCE, T. E. *Carchemish.* London, 1914. Author's first book with C. L. Woolley. $2,000.

LAWRENCE, T. E. *Crusader Castles.* Golden Cockerel Press. London, 1936. Portraits and facsimiles, 2 maps in envelope. 2 vols., half red morocco. One of 1,000 issued without dustwrapper or slipcase. $1,500.

LAWRENCE, T. E. *The Diary of T. E. Lawrence.* Corvinus Press. London, 1937. Illustrated. Boards and morocco. One of 203. $3,000. Morocco. One of 30 on Canute paper in slipcase. $6,000. Another: limp vellum. One of 40 on Medway paper in slipcase. $5,000.

LAWRENCE, T. E. *An Essay on Flecker.* Corvinus Press. London, 1937. Buckram. One of 30. $4,500. New York, 1937. Printed wraps. First American edition. One of 56 for copyright purposes. $2,000.

LAWRENCE, T. E. *Letters.* London, 1938. Edited by David Garnett. Maps and plates. Buckram. $150.

LAWRENCE, T. E. *Men in Print.* Golden Cockerel Press. (London, 1940.) Half morocco. One of 500. $750. Morocco. One of 30 specially bound with extra facsimile. Slipcase. $2,000.

LAWRENCE, T. E. *Minorities.* London, 1971. Edited by J. M. Wilson. Preface by C. Day-Lewis. Frontispiece portrait. Half calf, leather label. One of 125 signed by Day-Lewis. In glassine dustwrapper. $750.

LAWRENCE, T. E. *The Mint: A Day-book of the R.A.F. Depot Between August and December, 1922.* London (1955). Leather and blue cloth. First published edition. One of 2,000 issued without dustwrapper in slipcase. $250. Garden City, 1955. One of 1,000 issued without dustwrapper in slipcase. $125.

LAWRENCE, T. E. *Revolt in the Desert.* London, 1927. Frontispiece, map, and portraits. Buckram. In dustwrapper. $500. Half morocco. One of 315 on large paper. $750. New York, 1927. $150. Buckram. One of 250. $600.

LAWRENCE, T. E. *Secret Dispatches from Arabia.* Golden Cockerel Press. London (1939). Portrait frontispiece. Morocco and cloth. One of 970. $650. White pigskin. One of 30 with part of the manuscript of *The Seven Pillars of Wisdom.* $2,500.

LAWRENCE, T. E. *Seven Pillars of Wisdom (The).* (London) 1926. 66 plates, other illustrations, 4 folding maps. Full leather. One of 170 copies inscribed "Complete" and signed "T.E.S." (for T. E. Shaw, Lawrence's adopted name). $35,000. (For first American copyright edition, with no author named, see title entry.) London (1935). Buckram and leather. First published edition. One of 750. In dustwrapper and slipcase. $1,000. Trade in buckram and dustwrapper. $300. Garden City, 1935. Buckram and leather. First published American edition. One of 750 in dustwrapper and slipcase. $750. Trade. $200.

LAWRENCE, T. E. *Shaw-Ede: T. E. Lawrence's Letters to H. S. Ede.* Golden Cockerel Press. London, 1942. 7 pages of facsimiles. Morocco. One of 470. Issued without dustwrapper or slipcase. $600. One of 30 specially bound. $2,000.

LAWRENCE, T. E. *The Wilderness of Zin.* (London, 1915.) (With C.L. Woolley.) $750.

LAWRENCE, W. J. *The Elizabethan Playhouse and Other Studies.* Shakespeare Head Press. Stratford-on-Avon, England, 1912–13. 30 plates. 2 vols., boards and cloth. One of 760. $200.

LAWS and Decrees of the State of Coahuila and Texas, in Spanish and English. Houston, 1839. In original calf. $1,000.

LAWS and Regulations of Union District, Clear Creek County, C.T. Central, C.T. (Colorado Territory), 1864. 19 pages, printed wraps. $1,250.

LAWS for the Better Government of California. San Francisco, 1848. 68 pages. Only 2 copies known of this first English book printed in California. $5,000 or more.

LAWS of the Cherokee Nation. Tahlequah, Indian Territory, 1852. Half leather. English language edition. $1,250.

LAWS of the Choctaw Nation, Made and Enacted by the General Council from 1886 to 1890. (In English and Choctaw.) Atoka, Indian Territory, 1890. One of 250. $300.

LAWS of Gregory District, February 18 & 20, 1860. (Cover title.) Denver, 1860. 12 pages, printed wraps. $2,000 or more.

LAWS of the Territory of Louisiana (The). St. Louis, 1808 (actually 1809). $10,000 or more.

LAWS of the Territory of New Mexico. Santa Fe, N.M., 1862. 71 pages, wraps. $500.

LAWS of the Town of San Francisco (The). San Francisco, 1847. 8 pages, wraps. $3,000 or more.

LAWYERS and Legislators, or Notes on the American Mining Companies. London, 1825. (By Benjamin Disraeli.) $350.

LAY, William, and HUSSEY, Cyrus M. *A Narrative of the Mutiny on Board the Ship Globe of Nantucket.* New-London, Conn., 1828. $400.

LAYARD, Georges. *George Cruikshank's Portraits of Himself.* London, 1897. Illustrated. Vellum and cloth. One of 250 large paper copies signed by Layard. $300.

LAYNE, J. Gregg. *Annals of Los Angeles.* San Francisco, 1935. Plates. One of 200. $175.

LAYTON Court Mystery (The). London, 1925. By "?" (Anthony Berkeley, pseudonym of A.B. Cox.) Author's first book. $400.

LAYTON, Irving. *Here and Now.* Montreal, 1945. Author's first book. Wraps. $750.

LAZARUS, Emma. *Poems and Translations.* New York, 1867. Author's first book. $150.

LAZARUS, Emma. *Songs of a Semite.* New York, 1882. $100.

LEA, Albert M. *Notes on the Wisconsin Territory.* Philadelphia, 1836. Folding map. 53 pages, in original printed boards. $1,000.

LEA, Homer. *The Vermilion Pencil.* New York, 1908. $75.

LEA, Pryor. *An Outline of the Central Transit, in a Series of Six Letters to Hon. John Hemphill.* Galveston, 1859. 32 pages, printed wraps. $125.

LEA, Tom. *Calendar of the Twelve Travelers Through the Pass of the North.* El Paso, Tex., 1946. Illustrated. Folio, cloth. Carl Hertzog printing. One of 365 signed. In dustwrapper. $1,000.

LEA, Tom. *Hands of Cantu.* Boston, 1964. Specially signed on tipped-in sheet. $150. Also, one of 100 signed, in full morocco in slipcase. $2,500.

LEA, Tom. *The King Ranch.* Boston (1957). Illustrated by the author. 2 vols., buckram. Issued without dustwrapper in slipcase. $250. Limited "Private Edition," printed on paper watermarked with running "W" brand. 2 vols., decorated linen. In slipcase. $1,500.

LEA, Tom. *Peleliu Landing.* El Paso, 1945. Illustrated. Green cloth. Carl Hertzog printing. One of 500 signed. In glassine dustwrapper. $1,250.

LEA, Tom. *Randado.* (El Paso, 1941.) Carl Hertzog printing. Stiff wraps. One of 100 signed. $3,500.

LEA, Tom. *The Wonderful Country.* Boston, 1952. $75.

LEACH, A. J. *Early Day Stories: The Overland Trail* . . . (Norfolk, Neb., 1916.) 7 plates. $125.

LEACOCK, Stephen. *Canada: The Foundations of Its Future.* Montreal, 1941. 31 full-page illustrations. Issued without dustwrapper in slipcase. $125. Also issued in morocco. $300.

LEACOCK, Stephen. *Elements of Political Science.* Boston, 1906. Author's first book. $125.

LEACOCK, Stephen. *Literary Lapses: A Book of Sketches.* Montreal, 1910. Author's first book of humor. $125.

LEACOCK, Stephen. *Nonsense Novels.* London, 1911. $150. New York, 1911. $125. Montreal, 1911. Green cloth. First Canadian edition. $150. London, 1921. Illustrated by John Kettlewell, including 8 color plates. First illustrated edition in dustwrapper. $250.

LEADBEATER, Mary. *Cottage Dialogues Among the Irish Peasantry.* London, 1811, and Dublin, 1813. Edited by Maria Edgeworth. Illustrated. 2 vols. $250.

LEADVILLE Chronicle Annual. Leadville, Colo., 1881. 40 pages, wraps. $250.

LEADVILLE, Colorado: The Most Wonderful Mining Camp in the World. Colorado Springs, 1879. 44 pages, printed wraps. (By John L. Loomis.) $350.

LEAF, Munro. *The Story of Ferdinand.* New York, 1936. Illustrated by Robert Lawson. Pink decorated boards, cloth spine. In dustwrapper. $300.

LEAF, Munro. *Wee Gillis.* New York, 1938. Illustrated by Robert Lawson. Burlap, paper labels. One of 525 signed. In slipcase. $300. Trade in boards and dustwrapper. $125.

LEAR, Edward. See Derry, Derry Down.

LEAR, Edward. *A Book of Nonsense.* London, 1855. Illustrated. Oblong, stiff wraps with 72 plates. Second (and enlarged) edition. $4,000. (For first edition see Derry Down Derry.)

LEAR, Edward. *Illustrated Excursions in Italy.* London, 1846. Map, 30 plates. 2 vols., folio, cloth. $2,000.

LEAR, Edward. *Illustrations of the Family Psittacidae, or Parrots.* London, 1830–32. 42 hand-colored plates. $25,000.

LEAR, Edward. *Journal of a Landscape Painter in Corsica . . .* London, 1870. Frontispiece and 39 plates. $600.

LEAR, Edward. *Journals of a Landscape Painter in Albania.* London, 1851. Map and 20 plates. $1,250.

LEAR, Edward. *Journals of a Landscape Painter in Southern Calabria.* London, 1852. 2 maps and 20 plates. $1,250.

LEAR, Edward. *Laughable Lyrics.* London, 1877. $500.

LEAR, Edward. *Nonsense Songs, Stories, Botany, and Alphabets.* London, 1871. $650. Boston, 1871. $500.

LEAR, Edward. *Views in Rome and Its Environs.* London, 1841. Engraved title and 25 plates. Folio, half morocco. Plates hand colored would be more with litho title and 20 plates. Author's first book. $3,000.

LEAR, Edward. *Views in the Seven Ionian Islands.* London, 1863. Illustrated. Folio. $3,500.

LEATHER Stocking and Silk. New York, 1854. (By John Esten Cooke.) Author's first book. $200.

LEAVES of Grass. Brooklyn, 1855. (By Walt Whitman.) Portrait frontispiece on plain paper. Dark green cloth, gilt and blind-stamped, marbled endpapers. First issue, without ads or reviews; first binding, gilt lettering and borders on both covers. $15,000. Second issue, plain yellow endpapers, no gold on back cover or borders. $4,000. Third issue, same as second but with ads or press notices bound in. $2,500. (Johnson differentiates between the second and third, while Wells and Goldsmith only mention that ads were inserted in front or back in the second issue.) Brooklyn, 1856. Second edition, with 20 additional poems. $1,750. Boston, "Year '85 of the States (1860–61)." Third edition, first issue, with "George C. Rand & Avery" on copyright page, portrait on tinted paper, orange-colored (or brick red) cloth. $500. Later issues, without "Rand & Avery." Same date, with portrait on white paper. $450. New York, 1867. 338 pages with title poem only. $300. Later issues/editions added other poems. $150. Washington, 1871. Wraps. Title poem only. Fifth edition. $1,000. Camden, 1876. Half cream-colored calf and marbled boards. Sixth edition. "Author's edition," signed on title page. $1,250. Boston, 1881–82. Yellow cloth. Seventh edition, first issue (very rare), with "Third edition" on title page. $1,000. Second issue, without "Third Edition" on title page. $250. Camden, 1882. Dark green cloth. "Author's Edition," signed. $1,500. Philadelphia, 1882. Yellow cloth. "First Philadelphia edition," published by Rees, Welsh and Company. $200. Philadelphia, 1889. Limp black morocco. One of 300 signed. 70th Birthday Edition. $1,500. Philadelphia, 1891–92. First issue, brown wraps with yellow paper label on backstrip. $1,500. Later issue: dark green cloth or gray wraps. $750. New York, 1930. Grabhorn printing. 37 woodcuts. Leather-backed mahogany boards. One of 400. $1,750. Limited Editions Club, New York, 1942. Edward Weston photographs. 2 vols., boards. In slipcase. $750.

LEAVES of Grass Imprints: American and European Criticisms of "Leaves of Grass." Boston, 1860. 64 pages, printed brown wraps. $1,250.

LE CARRÉ, John. *Call for the Dead.* London, 1960. Author's first book. $1,750. New York, 1962. In white dustwrapper. $450.

LE CARRÉ, John. *A Murder of Quality.* London, 1962. $1,250. New York, 1963. $350.

LE CARRÉ, John. *A Small Town in Germany.* London (1968). $100. New York (1968). One of 500 signed and numbered copies. In tissue dustwrapper. $300. Trade. $60.

LE CARRÉ, John. *The Spy Who Came in from the Cold.* London, 1963. $400. New York (1964). $100.

LE CONTE, Joseph. *A Journal of Ramblings Through the High Sierras of California.* San Francisco, 1875. 9 mounted photos. Blue cloth. $2,500.

LE DUC, W. G. *Minnesota Year Book and Traveller's Guide for 1851.* St. Paul (1851). Folding map. Boards, leather spine. First year of issue. $250. Other issues: For 1852, with frontispiece plate. $100. For 1853, folding map. $75.

LEDYARD, John. *A Journal of Captain Cook's Last Voyage to the Pacific Ocean . . .* Hartford, 1783. Without the rare map (which Howes states is "usually missing.") $7,500.

LEDYARD, John. See *The Adventures of a Yankee.*

LEE, Andrew. *The Indifferent Children.* New York (1947). (By Louis Auchincloss.) Author's first book. $150.

LEE, Daniel, and FROST, Joseph H. *Ten Years in Oregon.* New York, 1844. Folding frontispiece map. $275.

LEE, Dennis. *The Kingdom of Absence.* Toronto (1967). Author's first book. 300 numbered copies. Wraps. $125.

LEE, Harper. *To Kill a Mockingbird.* Philadelphia (1960). Author's only book. With dustwrapper photo of author by Truman Capote. First edition stated. $1,000. London (1960). $125.

LEE, Maj. Henry, Jr. *The Campaign of 1781 in the Carolinas.* Philadelphia, 1824. $200.

LEE, James P. *Golf in America.* New York, 1895. First golf book published in U.S. $750.

LEE, John D. *The Journals of John D. Lee, 1846–47 and 1859.* Salt Lake City, 1938. Edited by Charles Kelly. One of 250. In dustwrapper. $300.

LEE, L. P. (editor). *History of the Spirit Lake Massacre!* (Cover title.) New Britain, Conn. Illustrated. 48 pages, pictorial wraps. 1857. $200.

LEE, Manfred Bennington. See Ellery Queen.

LEE, Nelson. *Three Years Among the Comanches.* Albany, N.Y., 1859. 2 plates (including portrait title page). Wraps, or cloth. $2,000.

LEE, William, *Junkie.* (and) HELBRANT, Maurice, *Narcotic Agent.* New York (1953). Back-to-back in pictorial wraps. Ace Books (015). (*Junkie* is by William Burroughs, his first book.) $250.

LEE Trial (The)! An Exposé of the Mountain Meadows Massacre. Salt Lake City, 1875. 64 pages, printed wraps. $1,250.

LEECH, John. *Follies of the Year.* London (1864). 21 hand-colored plates. Oblong, leather-backed cloth. First collected edition. $500.

LEECH, John. *Hunting: Incidents of the Noble Science.* London, 1865. 13 color plates. Oblong, half cloth portfolio. $1,000 and up.

LEECH, John. *Portraits of Children of the Nobility.* London, 1841. Frontispiece and 7 plates. $600.

LEEPER, David Rohrer. *The Argonauts of Forty-nine.* South Bend, 1894. Illustrated. Cloth. $150.

LEESE, Jacob P. *Historical Outline of Lower California.* New York, 1865. 46 pages, printed wraps. $175.

LE FANU, Joseph Sheridan. See *The Fortunes of Colonel Torlogh O'Brien.*

LE FANU, Joseph Sheridan. *All in the Dark.* London, 1866. 2 vols., in claret cloth. $1,000. In white (presentation) cloth. $1,500.

LE FANU, Joseph Sheridan. *Checkmate.* London, 1871. 3 vols. $6,000.

LE FANU, Joseph Sheridan. *Chronicles of Golden Friars.* London, 1871. 3 vols., in violet cloth. $4,000.

LE FANU, Joseph Sheridan. *The Cock and the Anchor.* Dublin, 1845. Author's first book. In dark green linen. $2,000.

LE FANU, Joseph Sheridan. *The Evil Guest.* London (1895). Illustrated. Dark green cloth with March ads. $600.

LE FANU, Joseph Sheridan. *Ghost Stories and Tales of Mystery.* Dublin, 1851. Illustrated by "Phiz." Red pictorial cloth. $1,250. Violet cloth blocked in gold on front and spine. $850. Red cloth blocked on spine only. $600.

LE FANU, Joseph Sheridan. *Green Tea and Other Ghost Stories.* Sauk City, Wis., 1945. $150.

LE FANU, Joseph Sheridan. *Guy Deverell.* London, 1865. 3 vols., cloth. $3,000.

LE FANU, Joseph Sheridan. *The House by the Churchyard.* London, 1863. 3 vols., royal blue cloth. $5,000. 3 vols., grass green cloth. $5,000.

LE FANU, Joseph Sheridan. *In a Glass Darkly.* London, 1872. 3 vols. $3,000. London, 1929. Illustrated by Edward Ardizzone, his first book of illustrations. $250.

LE FANU, Joseph Sheridan. *Madame Crowl's Ghost and Other Tales of Mystery.* London, 1923. $400.

LE FANU, Joseph Sheridan. *The Rose and the Key.* London, 1871. 3 vols., brown cloth. $2,500.

LE FANU, Joseph Sheridan. *The Wyvern Mystery.* London, 1869. 3 vols., dark maroon cloth. $3,000.

LE GALLIENNE, Richard. *My Ladies' Sonnets.* (Liverpool) 1887. Author's first regularly published book. Boards. One of 50 signed. $500. Trade. $250.

LE GALLIENNE, Richard. *Robert Louis Stevenson: An Elegy and Other Poems, Mostly Personal.* London, 1895. One of 500. $125. One of 75 on large paper. $150. Boston, 1895. One of 500. $100.

LE GALLIENNE, Richard. *The Romance of Perfume.* London, 1928. Illustrated by Georges Barbier. Boards. Issued without dustwrapper. $300.

LE GALLIENNE, Richard. *Volumes In Folio.* London, 1889. 50 large paper copies. $300. 250 regular copies. $150. (Also first book published by Elkin Mathews.)

LEGENDS of the Conquest of Spain. Philadelphia, 1835. By the Author of *The Sketch-Book,* (Washington Irving.) In original green cloth, paper label. $500.

LEGION Book (The). London, 1929. Edited by H. Cotton Minchin. Stephen Gooden copperplate of "Mounted Soldier" (self-portrait) on title page, numerous other illustrations, including 9 color plates. Full white pigskin, gilt and blind stamped. One of 100 signed by authors and artists, by Edward, Prince of Wales, and by 5 prime ministers. (Gift book published for the Prince of Wales.) $1,000.

LEGMAN, Gershon. *Love & Death . . .* (New York, 1949.) Cloth. $200. Wraps. $75.

LE GRAND, Mr. *A Voyage to Abyssinia by Father Jerome Lobo.* London, 1735. (Translated by Samuel Johnson, his first book.) $1,000.

LEGROS, Lucient Alphonse and GRANT, John Cameron. *Typographical Printing-Surfaces . . .* London, 1916. $375.

LE GUIN, Ursula. *The Farthest Shore.* New York, 1972. $150.

LE GUIN, Ursula. *From Elfland to Poughkeepsie.* Portland, Ore., 1973. Wraps. One of 100 signed. $125. One of 26 hardbound copies signed, issued without dustwrapper. $350. Also, one of 100 signed and numbered in wraps. $150. Trade in wraps, one of 650 numbered copies. $40.

LE GUIN, Ursula. *The Lathe of Heaven.* New York (1971). $300.

LE GUIN, Ursula. *The Left Hand of Darkness.* Ace, New York (1969). Wraps, first edition not stated and no mention of Hugo and Nebula awards. $40. Also Walker, New York (1969). "Published in . . . 1969 . . ." First hardcover. $350.

LE GUIN, Ursula. *A Wizard of Earthsea.* Berkeley (1968). No statement of edition. With vertical line or smudge on title page in either library or trade bindings which are embossed on covers. Dustwrapper priced $3.95. $500. (Later printings have no smudge, covers printed without embossment [stamping] and dustwrapper unpriced.)

LEHMANN, John. *A Garden Revisited and Other Poems.* Hogarth Press. London, 1931. $125.

LEHMUSTO, Heikki. *Painin Historia.* (History of wrestling.) Helsinki, 1939. $350.

LEIBER, Fritz, Jr. *Night's Black Agents.* Sauk City, Wis., 1947. Arkham House. Author's first book. $150.

LEIDERMAN, E. E. *The Science of Wrestling and the Art of Jiu Jitsu.* New York, 1923. Issued without dustwrapper. $40.

LEIGH, William R. *The Western Pony.* New York (1933). 6 color plates. Cloth. (100 copies.) In dustwrapper. $500. With an extra signed plate laid in. $750.

LEIGHTON, John. *Suggestions in Design . . .* London, no-date (circa 1880). 101 plates. $300.

LEINSTER, Murray. *Sidewise in Time.* Chicago, 1950. (By Will F. Jenkins.) $150.

LELAND, Charles Godfrey. *Maister Karl's Sketch-Book.* Philadelphia, 1855. Author's first book. $200.

LELAND, Charles Godfrey. *The Union Pacific Railway.* Philadelphia, 1867. 95 pages, printed wraps. $300.

LEMAY, Alan. *Gunsight Trail.* New York, 1931. $100.

LEMAY, Alan. *Painted Ponies.* New York (1927). Author's first book. $150.

LEMAY, Alan. *The Searchers.* New York, 1954. One of 800 signed. $125. Trade. $50.

LEMOINE, Henry. *Typographical Antiquities.* London, 1797. $350.

LENGEL, Frances. *The Carnal Days of Helen Seferis.* Paris, 1954. (By Alexander Trocchi, his first book.) Wraps. $175.

LEONARD, Elmore. *The Bounty Hunters.* Author's first book. Houghton-Mifflin. Boston, 1954. $1,000. Ballantine, New York, 1954. Wraps. $100. London, 1956. $500.

LEONARD, Elmore. *Escape from Five Shadows.* Boston, 1956. $750. London, 1957. $300.

LEONARD, Elmore. *Glitz.* New York (1965). One of 26 signed and lettered copies. Issued without dustwrapper in slipcase. $200. One of 500 signed and numbered copies. Issued without dustwrapper in slipcase. $75. Trade. $25. (London/Harmondsworth, 1985). $30.

LEONARD, Elmore. *The Law at Randado.* Boston, 1955. $850. London, 1957. $400.

LEONARD, Elmore. *Unknown Man: No. 89.* New York, 1977. $250. London (1977). $100.

LEONARD, H. L. W. *Oregon Territory.* Cleveland, 1846. 88 pages, printed blue or buff wraps. $3,000 or more.

LEONARD, Hugh E. *Handbook of Wrestling.* New York, 1897. Limited to 300 copies. $125.

LEONARD, William Ellery. *Byron and Byronism in America.* Boston, 1905. Author's first book. $150.

LEONARD, William Ellery. *A Son of Earth: Collected Poems.* New York, 1928. Portrait frontispiece. Cream boards, paper label. One of 35 lettered copies, signed. $150.

LEONARD, William Ellery. *Two Lives.* New York, 1925. Cloth. First published edition. One of 150 signed. $100.

LEONARD, William Ellery (translator). *The Tale of Beowulf.* New York, 1932. Illustrated by Rockwell Kent. Folio. One of 950. Issued without dustwrapper. $250.

LEONARD, Zenas. *Narrative of the Adventures of Zenas Leonard.* Clearfield, Pa., 1839. 87 pages. $20,000. Cleveland, 1904. Illustrated. One of 520. $300.

LEROUX, Gaston. *The Phantom of the Opera.* Indianapolis, 1911. Illustrated in color. $150.

LEROUX DE LINCY, A. J. V. *Researches Concerning Jean Grolier, His Life and His Library.* Grolier Club. New York, 1907. Color plates. Full leather. One of 300. $600.

LESLIE, Shane. *The Cantab.* London, 1925. (Suppressed.) Cloth. $125.

LESLIE, Shane. *Songs of Oriel.* Dublin, 1908. Author's first book. $100.

LESSING, Doris. *African Stories.* London (1964). $125.

LESSING, Doris. *The Golden Notebook.* London (1962). $125.

LESSING, Doris. *The Grass Is Singing.* London (1950). Author's first book. $175. New York, 1950. $100.

LESSING, Doris. *The Habit of Being.* London, 1957. Cloth. $100.

LESSING, Doris. *Martha Quest.* London (1952). $150.

LESTER, C. Edwards. *Sam Houston and His Republic.* New York, 1846. Portrait (not in all copies), maps. Half calf. $350.

LESTER, John C., and WILSON, D. L. *Ku Klux Klan: Its Origin, Growth and Disbandment.* Nashville, 1884. 117 pages, wraps. $750.

LETTER of Amerigo Vespucci (The), Describing His Four Voyages to the New World. Grabhorn Press. San Francisco, 1926. Hand-colored map and illustrations by Valenti Angelo. Vellum. One of 250. In slipcase. $500.

LETTERS from An American Farmer. (By Michael Crevecoeur). London, 1782. Author's first book. Wraps. $1,000.

LETTERS of Runnymede (The). London, 1836. (By Benjamin Disraeli.) In original cloth. $250.

LETTS, J. M. See *California Illustrated; A Pictorial View of California.*

LEVER, Charles. See Lorrequer, Harry. See also *The Confessions of Harry Lorrequer.*

LEVER, Charles. *Davenport Dunn.* London, 1857–59. Illustrated by H. K. Browne ("Phiz"). 20 parts, wraps. $750.

LEVER, Charles. *The Knight of Gwynne: A Tale of the Time of the Union.* London, 1846–47. Frontispiece, title page, and 38 plates by "Phiz." 20 parts in 19, wraps. $250.

LEVER, Charles. *Luttrell of Aran.* London, 1863–65. Illustrated. 16 parts in 15, pictorial wraps. $500.

LEVER, Charles. *The O'Donoghue: A Tale of Ireland.* Dublin, 1845. 13 parts in 11, wraps. Dublin, 1845. $500. First binding in red cloth. $200.

LEVER, Charles. *Roland Cashel.* London, 1848–49. 20 parts in 19, wraps. $400. London, 1850. First book edition. $200.

LEVERTOFF (LEVERTOV), Denise. *The Double Image.* Cresset Press. London, 1946. Author's first book. $200.

LEVERTOV, Denise. *The Cold Spring and Other Poems.* New Directions. (New York) 1968. One of 100 signed. $400.

LEVERTOV, Denise. *In the Night: A Story.* Albondocani Press. New York, 1968. Wraps. One of 150 signed. $100.

LEVERTOV, Denise. *Three Poems.* Perishable Press. Mt. Horeb, Wis., 1968. Stiff wraps. One of 250. In dustwrapper. $125.

LEVINE, Philip. *The Names of the Lost: Poems.* (Iowa City) 1976. One of 200 signed. Issued without dustwrapper. $125.

LEVINE, Philip. *On the Edge.* Stone Wall Press. Iowa City (1963). One of 225 signed. Issued without dustwrapper. Author's first book. $250.

LEVY, Julien. *Surrealism.* Black Sun Press. New York, 1936. 64 illustrations. Pictorial boards. In dustwrapper. $450.

LEWIS, Alfred Henry. *Black Lion Inn.* New York, 1903. $200.

LEWIS, Alfred Henry. *Wolfville.* New York (1897). First issue, with "Moore" in perfect type on page 19, line 18. Author's first book. In dustwrapper. $500. Without dustwrapper. $175.

LEWIS, Alfred Henry. *Wolfville Days.* New York (1902). Red cloth. $125.

LEWIS, Alfred Henry. *Wolfville Folks.* New York, 1908. $300.

LEWIS, C. S. See Hamilton, Clive.

LEWIS, Cecil Day. See Day-Lewis, Cecil.

LEWIS, C. T. *George Baxter (Colour Printer) . . .* London, 1908. $125.

LEWIS, C. T. Courtney. *The Picture Printer of the Nineteenth Century, George Baxter.* London, 1911. 21 illustrations in full color. $125.

LEWIS, C. T. Courtney. *The Story of Picture Printing In England During the Nineteenth Century.* London (1928). 61 plates. $300.

LEWIS, Elisha J. *The American Sportsman.* Philadelphia, 1855. Illustrated. $200.

LEWIS, Elisha J. *Hints to Sportsmen.* Philadelphia, 1851. Cloth. $150.

LEWIS, J. O. *The Aboriginal Port Folio.* Philadelphia, 1836 (actually 1835). 72 colored portraits. (Sometimes more, but frequently fewer, which would affect the price.) 3

advertisement leaves (constituting, with title leaf, all the text). 10 parts, wraps. $20,000. Bound set: Philadelphia, 1835–36. 72 plates. Folio, cloth. $12,500.

LEWIS, Janet. *The Friendly Adventures of Ollie Ostrich.* Garden City, 1923. $300.

LEWIS, Janet. *The Indians in the Woods.* (Bonn, Germany, 1922.) Author's first book. Wraps. $400.

LEWIS, John Frederick. *Illustrations of Constantinople*... London (1838). Folio, litho title, and 25 plates. $4,000.

LEWIS, John Frederick. *Sketches of Spain and Spanish Character.* London (1836). Lithograph title page and 25 tinted plates. Folio, in original half morocco. $2,000.

LEWIS, Matthew Gregory. See *Tales of Terror.*

LEWIS, Matthew Gregory. *Journal of a West India Proprietor in the Island of Jamaica.* London, 1834. $250.

LEWIS, Matthew Gregory. *The Life and Correspondence of Matthew Gregory Lewis.* London, 1839. Illustrated. 2 vols., boards. Issued without dustwrapper. $250.

LEWIS, Matthew Gregory. *The Monk.* London, 1796. Author's first book. $3,000.

LEWIS, Matthew Gregory. *Poems.* London, 1812. $400.

LEWIS, Matthew Gregory. *Romantic Tales.* London, 1808. 4 vols. $600.

LEWIS, Matthew Gregory. *Tales of Wonder.* London, 1801. 2 vols. $600. 2 vols. on large paper. $750. Dublin, 1801. 2 vols. $400.

LEWIS, Meriwether, and CLARK, William. *History of the Expedition Under the Command of Captains Lewis and Clark*... Philadelphia, 1814. Prepared for the press by Paul Allen (actually by Nicholas Biddle). Folding map and 5 charts. 2 vols. $12,500. New York, 1842. Folding map. 2 vols., calf. Abridged edition. $500. New York, 1893. Edited by E. Coues. Map. 4 vols., boards and cloth. $350. Chicago, 1902. Edited by James K. Hosmer. 2 vols., cloth. $125.

LEWIS, Meriwether, and CLARK, William. *Original Journals of the Lewis and Clark Expedition, 1804–1806.* New York, 1904–5. Edited by Reuben Gold Thwaites. 2 vols., cloth, including atlas of maps and plates. One of 790. $1,250. 7 vols. in 14, plus atlas, boards. One of 50 sets on Japan paper. $5,500. One of 200 sets on Van Gelder paper. $3,500. New York, 1959–60. 8 vols., cloth. Facsimile of 1904–5 edition. $450.

LEWIS, Meriwether, and CLARK, William. *Journals of the Lewis and Clark Expedition.* Limited Editions Club, Hartford, 1962. 2 vols. In slipcase. $200.

LEWIS, Meriwether, and CLARK, William. *Travels to the Source of the Missouri River and Across the American Continent to the Pacific Ocean.* London, 1814. Edited by Thomas Rees. Folding map and 5 charts. First English edition of *History of the Expedition,* ... $5,000. London, 1815. 6 maps. 3 vols. Second English edition. $1,250.

LEWIS, Oscar. *Hearn and His Biographers.* Westgate Press (Grabhorn printing). San Francisco, 1930. Facsimiles. Boards and cloth in portfolio. One of 350. $350.

LEWIS, Oscar. *The Origin of the Celebrated Jumping Frog of Calaveras County.* Grabhorn Press. San Francisco, 1931. Decorated by Valenti Angelo. Boards. One of 250. $200.

LEWIS, Sinclair. See Graham, Tom.

LEWIS, Sinclair. *Arrowsmith.* New York (1925). Blue boards and buckram. One of 500 signed. In glassine dustwrapper and slipcase. $400. First trade with "second printing" on copyright page. $200.

LEWIS, Sinclair. *Babbitt.* New York (1922). Blue cloth. First state, with "Purdy" for "Lyte" in line 4, page 49. $600.

LEWIS, Sinclair. *Cheap and Contented Labor.* (New York) 1929. Illustrated. 32 pages, pictorial blue wraps. First state, without quotation marks in front of "Dodsworth" on title page. $150. Later, error corrected. $75.

LEWIS, Sinclair. *Dodsworth.* New York (1929). With "Published, March, 1929" on copyright page. $200.

LEWIS, Sinclair. *Elmer Gantry.* New York (1927). Blue cloth. First binding with "G" on spine resembling "C" (reading "Elmer Cantry"). $350. Later binding, corrected. $250.

LEWIS, Sinclair. *Free Air.* New York, 1919. Decorated blue cloth. $450. Without dustwrapper. $100.

LEWIS, Sinclair. *The Innocents.* New York (1917). With "Published October, 1917/ F-R" on copyright page. In dustwrapper. $600. Without dustwrapper. $150.

LEWIS, Sinclair. *The Job.* New York (1917). Green cloth. With "Published February, 1917/B-R" on copyright page. In dustwrapper. $600. Without dustwrapper. $150. (Remaindered copies have tipped-in leaf advertising *Main Street* and others.)

LEWIS, Sinclair. *Keep Out of the Kitchen.* (New York, 1929.) Printed boards. First edition not stated. (Advertising promotion piece for the story in *Cosmopolitan* magazine.) $500.

LEWIS, Sinclair. *Main Street.* New York, 1920. Dark blue cloth. First issue, with perfect folio on page 54. In dustwrapper. $1,000. Without dustwrapper. $200. Limited Editions Club, New York, 1937. Grant Wood illustrations. In slipcase. $500.

LEWIS, Sinclair. *Our Mr. Wrenn.* New York, 1914. With "M–N" on copyright page. Author's second book and the first under his own name. (For first book, see entry under Graham, Tom.) $75.

LEWIS, W. S., and PHILLIPS, P. C. (editors). *The Journal of John Work.* Cleveland, 1923. Map. Illustrations. Issued without dustwrapper. $250.

LEWIS, Wyndham. *The Apes of God.* London (1931). Illustrated by the author. Light tan cloth. One of 750 signed in dustwrapper. $750. Trade. $300. New York, 1932. $250.

LEWIS, Wyndham. *The Art of Being Ruled.* London, 1926. $600.

LEWIS, Wyndham. *Blasting and Bombardiering: Autobiography 1914–1926.* London, 1937. $250.

LEWIS, Wyndham. *The Caliph's Design.* London, 1919. The Egoist, Ltd. Boards. No statement of edition. Issued without dustwrapper. $500.

LEWIS, Wyndham. *The Childermass: Section I.* (All published.) London, 1928. Yellow buckram. One of 225 signed. In dustwrapper. $750. Trade edition. $350. New York, 1928. $250.

LEWIS, Wyndham. *Count Your Dead: They Are Alive!* London (1937). Yellow cloth. First edition stated. $750.

LEWIS, Wyndham. *The Diabolical Principle and the Dithyrambic Spectator.* London, 1931. First binding in gold-stamped cloth. $450.

LEWIS, Wyndham. *Doom of Youth.* London, 1932. First English edition (withdrawn). $850. New York, 1932. $350.

LEWIS, Wyndham. *Hitler.* London, 1931. $400.

LEWIS, Wyndham. *The Ideal Giant.* London (1917). Boards and cloth. (About 200.) Author's first written work, a collection of stories. $1,000.

LEWIS, Wyndham. *Left Wings Over Europe, or, How to Make a War About Nothing.* London (1936). Cloth. $300.

LEWIS, Wyndham. *Tarr.* New York, 1918. Red cloth. $300. Blue cloth. $200. London, 1918. $200.

LEWIS, Wyndham. *Thirty Personalities and a Self-Portrait.* London (1932). 31 plates, loose in buckram and board portfolio. One of 200 signed. $1,000.

LEWIS, Wyndham. *Timon/Athens/Timon/Shakespeare/Timon* (upside down). (Cover title.) (London, 1913.) 16 illustrations for Shakespeare's *Timon of Athens,* without a title page. Limited edition, plates laid loose in a folder. Author's first "book." $2,000.

LEWIS, Wyndham. *The Wild Body: A Soldier of Humour and Other Stories.* London, 1927. Decorated boards, cloth spine. One of 79 signed (of 85 total). In dustwrapper. $1,000. Trade in orange or red cloth. In cream-colored dustwrapper. $350.

LHOMOND, M. *Elements of French Grammar.* Portland (Brunswick), Me., 1830. (Translated anonymously by Henry Wadsworth Longfellow, his first book.) Paper label. $250.

LHOMOND, M. *French Exercises.* Portland (Brunswick), Me., 1830. Purple cloth, paper label. (Translated anonymously by Henry Wadsworth Longfellow.) $250. This book and Lhomond's *Elements of French Grammar* were bound as one volume later in 1830, and this combined book edition was "the first book to bear Longfellow's name on the title page." $350.

LIBER Amoris: or, The New Pygmalion. London, 1823. (By William Hazlitt.) $250. London, 1894. Illustrated. Buckram. One of 500. $125.

LIBER Scriptorum: The First Book of the Authors' Club. New York, 1893. Full morocco. One of 251 signed by contributors. $1,500. *Liber Scriptorum: The Second Book, etc.* New York, 1921. Morocco. One of 251. $300.

LIEBLING, A. J. *Back Where I Came From.* New York (1938). Orange-tan cloth. $350.

LIEBLING, A. J. *Chicago: The Second City.* New York, 1952. Illustrated by Steinberg. Pictorial boards. $75.

LIEBLING, A. J. *Mink and Red Herring.* Garden City, 1949. $175.

LIEBLING, A. J. *The Telephone Booth Indian.* Garden City, 1942. Gray cloth. $150.

LIEBLING, A. J. *They All Sang . . .* New York, 1934. Author's first book. $200.

LIFE and Adventures of Broncho John: His Second Trip up the Trail, by Himself. (Valparaiso, Ind., 1908.) (Cover title.) Illustrated. 32 pages. pictorial wraps. (By John H. Sullivan.) $300.

LIFE and Adventures of Calamity Jane. By Herself. Livingston, Mont. (1896). Portrait. 8 pages, wraps. $350.

LIFE and Adventures (The) of Joseph T. Hare, the Bold Robber and Highwayman. New York, 1847. 16 engravings. Pictorial wraps. (By H. R. Howard.) $250.

LIFE and Adventures of Robert Voorhis, the Hermit of Massachusetts. Providence, 1829. Portrait. Wraps. First edition, first issue, with "Voorhis" in the title. $200. Later: *Life and Adventures of Robert.* $100.

LIFE and Travels of Josiah Mooso (The). Winfield, Kan., 1888. Portrait. $500.

LIFE and Writings of Maj. Jack Downing of Downingville (The), Away Down East in the State of Maine. Boston, 1833. (By Seba Smith.) In original boards. $200.

LIFE in California During a Residence of Several Years . . . By an American (Alfred Robinson). New York, 1846. 9 plates. $500.

LIFE of Col. Edwards. No-place, no-date (1842). 8 engravings. 31 pages, folded sheets, uncut and unsewn. First edition (?). $1,500.

LIFE of Joaquin Murieta the Brigand Chief of California (The). San Francisco, 1859. (By John R. Ridge.) 7 full-page plates. Pictorial wraps (dated 1861). Second ("spurious") edition. $2,500. (See also *Yellow Bird*).

LIFE of MA-KA-TAI-ME-SHE-KIA-KIAK or Black Hawk. Cincinnati, 1833. Tan boards and cloth. (J. B. Patterson, editor.) $400. Boston, 1834. Pale green boards. $200.

LIFE of Stonewall Jackson (The). By a Virginian. Richmond, 1863. Printed wraps. (By John Esten Cooke.) First edition, with Ayres & Wade imprint. $250.

LILLIBRIDGE, Will. *Ben Blair.* Chicago, 1905. In dustwrapper. $150.

LILLIBRIDGE, Will. *Where the Trail Divides.* New York, 1907. In dustwrapper. $125.

LIN, Frank. *What Dreams May Come.* Chicago (1888). Author's first book. (By Gertrude Atherton.) (For first English edition, see author listing.) Wraps. $300. Cloth. $150.

LINCOLN, Abraham. *The Life and Public Services of General Zachary Taylor.* Boston, 1922. Marbled boards. One of 435. In slipcase. $250.

LINCOLN, Abraham, and DOUGLAS, Stephen A. *Political Debates.* Columbus, Ohio, 1860. Brown rippled, or tan cloth. First issue, with no ads, no rule on copyright page, and with a "2" at foot of page 17. $600.

LINCOLN, Abraham, and EVERETT, Edward. *The Gettysburg Solemnities: Dedication of the National Cemetery at Gettysburg, Pennsylvania, November 19, 1863* . . . (Cover title.) Washington (1863). 16 pages, printed pamphlet. First known printing in pamphlet form of the Gettysburg Address. $25,000. See also, Everett, Edward.

LINCOLN, Mrs. D. A. *Frozen Dainties.* Nashua, N. H., 1889. 32 pages, wraps. $350.

LINCOLN, Mrs. D. A. *Mrs. Lincoln's Boston Cook Book.* Boston, 1884. Marbled boards, cloth spine and corners. $1,250.

LINCOLN, Joe. *Cape Cod Ballads and Other Verse.* Trenton, N.J., 1902. (By Joseph C. Lincoln.) Drawings by E. W. Kemble. Decorated yellow cloth. Author's first book. $125.

LINDBERGH, Charles A. *The Spirit of St. Louis.* New York, 1953. Limited and signed "Presentation Edition" in dustwrapper. $750. Trade. $125.

LINDBERGH, Charles A. *"We": The Famous Flier's Own Story of His Life and His Trans-Atlantic Flight.* New York, 1927. Illustrated. Half vellum. One of 1,000 signed. Slipcase. $1,000. Trade in blue or red cloth. $125.

LINDERMAN, Frank Bird. *Beyond the Law.* New York, 1933. $125.

LINDERMAN, Frank Bird. *Lige Mount Free Trapper.* New York, 1922. $175.

LINDLEY, John. *Pomologia Britannica; or Figures and Descriptions of the Most Important Varieties of Fruit Cultivated in Great Britain.* London, 1841. 152 colored plates. 3 vols., half brown morocco. $6,000.

LINDSAY, David. *Devil's Tor.* London (1932). $450.

LINDSAY, David. *Journal of the Elder Scientific Exploring Expedition 1891–92.* Adelaide, 1893. Wraps, with a folder of maps. $1,500.

LINDSAY, David. *A Voyage to Arcturus.* London (1920). Author's first book. (Red cloth, 8 page catalog at rear.) $1,000.

LINDSAY, Jack. See Graves, Robert.

LINDSAY, Jack. *Fauns and Ladies.* Sydney, 1923. Author's first book. $600.

LINDSAY, Jack. *Storm at Sea.* London, 1935. Illustrated. Half morocco. One of 250 signed. $350.

LINDSAY, Norman. *The Etchings of Norman Lindsay.* London, 1927. Cloth folio. One of 129. $1,500. Buckram, vellum spine. One of 31 signed, with a signed etching by Lindsay. $3,000.

LINDSAY, Norman. *A Homage to Sappho.* Fanfrolico Press. London, 1928. Illustrated by Jack Lindsay. Vellum. One of 70 signed. $3,000.

LINDSAY, Norman. *Norman Lindsay's Book.* Sydney, 1912. Author's first book, preceded by illustrated book. (Also noted as *Norman Lindsay's Book Vol 1 & 2.* Sydney, 1912–15.) $750.

LINDSAY, Norman. *Selected Pen Drawings.* Sydney, 1968. $250.

LINDSAY, Vachel. *The Candle in the Cabin.* New York, 1926. $150.

LINDSAY, Vachel. *Collected Poems.* New York, 1923. Half cloth. One of 400 signed. $300. Trade. $150. New York, 1925. Illustrated by Lindsay. Pictorial boards. First illustrated edition. One of 350 signed. In slipcase. $200. Trade. $75.

LINDSAY, Vachel. *General William Booth Enters into Heaven and Other Poems.* New York, 1913. Red cloth. Author's first book. $100.

LINDSAY, Vachel. *The Golden Book of Springfield.* New York, 1920. Boards. In dustwrapper. $300.

LINDSAY, Vachel. *A Handy Guide for Beggars.* New York, 1916. $250.

LINDSAY, Vachel. *A Memorial of Lincoln Called The Heroes of Time.* (Springfield, Ill., 1908/1909). 12 pages, stitched wraps. $650.

LINDSAY, Vachel. *Rhymes to Be Traded for Bread.* (Springfield, 1912.) 12 pages, self-wraps. $500.

LINDSAY, Vachel. *The Soul of the City Receives the Gift of the Holy Spirit.* (Springfield, 1913.) Illustrated by the author. Wraps. $400.

LINDSAY, Vachel. *The Tramp's Excuse and Other Poems.* (Cover title.) (Springfield, Ill., 1909.) Decorations by the author. Printed wraps with cord tie. $1,500.

LINDSAY, Vachel. *The Tree of Laughing Bells.* (New York, 1905.) Author's first book. Wraps. $2,500.

LINDSAY, William S. *History of Merchant Shipping and Ancient Commerce.* London, 1874–76. 3 maps, 3 plates, numerous other illustrations. 4 vols., cloth. $400.

LINDSEY, Charles. *The Prairies of the Western States.* Toronto, 1860. 100 pages, wraps. $250.

LINDSLEY, John Berrien. *The Military Annals of Tennessee.* Nashville, 1886. 2 plates. $175.

LINES on Leaving the Bedford St. Schoolhouse. (Boston, 1880.) (By George Santayana.) 4 pages, plain wraps. Author's first published work. $750.

LINFORTH, James (editor). *Route from Liverpool to Great Salt Valley.* Liverpool, July 1854 to September 1855. Folding map and 30 full-page plates. 120 pages, plus "Notice to Subscribers." 15 paperbound parts (bound). $7,500. Liverpool, 1855. Boards. First book edition with a map partly colored by hand. $4,500.

LINGUAL Exercises for Advanced Vocabularians. By the author of *Recreations* (Siegfried Sassoon.) Cambridge, 1925. One of 90. $400.

LINN, John J. *Reminiscences of Fifty Years in Texas.* New York, 1883. Illustrated. With errata slip. $200.

LINSLEY, Daniel C. *Morgan Horses.* New York, 1857. Illustrated. $175.

LINTON, W.J. *The History of Wood-Engraving in America.* Boston, 1882. 1,000 signed and numbered copies. 20 full-page plates. $225.

LINTON, William James. *The Masters of Wood-Engraving.* London, 1889. 196 plates (165 mounted), colored frontispiece. One of 600 signed and numbered copies. $650.

LIPSCOMB, George. *The History and Antiquities of the County of Buckingham.* London, 1831. Numerous maps, plates, and woodcuts. 4 vols., half leather. $750. London, 1847. 4 vols. $750.

LIST of Catalogues of English Book Sales, 1676–1900 Now in the British Museum. (London) 1915. $250.

LITERARY Antiquary (A), Memoir of William Oldys, Esq. London, 1862. $250.

LITTELL, William. *Festoons of Fancy.* Louisville, Ky., 1814. $4,000.

LITTLE, James A. *From Kirtland to Salt Lake City.* Salt Lake City, 1890. $250.

LITTLE, James A. *Jacob Hamblin, A Narrative of His Personal Experience . . .* Salt Lake City, 1881. $150.

LITTLE, James A. *What I Saw on the Old Santa Fe Trail.* Plainfield, Ind. (1904). Frontispiece. 127 pages, printed wraps. $150.

LITTLEFIELD, George Emery. *The Early Massachusetts Press, 1638–1711.* Boston, 1907. 2 vols. 175 numbered copies. $125.

LIVING Issue (A). Washington, 1882. (By Richard Irving Dodge.) 37 pages, wraps. (Suppressed portion of Dodge's *Our Wild Indians.*) $300.

LIVINGSTON, Luther S. *Auction Prices of Books . . .* New York, 1905. 4 vols. Limited to 750 sets. $175.

LIVINGSTON, Luther S. *Franklin and His Press at Passy.* Grolier Club. New York, 1914. Illustrated. Boards and cloth. One of 300. $250.

LIZARS, John. *A System of Anatomical Plates of the Body, with Descriptions and Observations.* Edinburgh (1822–26). Text volume, plus folio atlas of 101 colored plates. $1,250.

LLEWELLYN, Richard. *How Green Was My Valley.* London (1939). Yellow buckram, leather label. Author's first book. One of 200 signed. In slipcase. $250. Trade in dustwrapper. $100. New York, 1940. $75.

LLEWELLYN, Richard. *None But the Lonely Heart.* London, 1943. One of 250 signed. $175. Trade. $75.

LOBO, Father Jerome. See Le Grand, Mr.

LOCKE, David Ross. See Nasby, Petroleum V.

LOCKER, Frederick. *London Lyrics.* London, 1857. Author's first book. $250.

LOCKINGTON, John. *Bowle's New and Complete Book of Cyphers.* London, no-date (circa 1785). 24 numbered engraved plates and an additional engraved plate showing coronets and helmets of the nobility. $350.

LOCKRIDGE, Richard. *Mr. and Mrs. North.* New York, 1936. Author's first book. $125.

LOCKRIDGE, Richard and Frances. *The Norths Meet Murder.* New York, 1940. $150.

LOCKRIDGE, Ross, Jr. *Raintree County.* Boston, 1948. Author's first (and only) book. $75.

LOCKWOOD, Frank C. *Arizona Characters.* Los Angeles, 1928. Illustrated. Pictorial cloth. $125.

LOCKWOOD, Frank C. *Pioneer Days in Arizona.* New York, 1932. Illustrated. $100.

LOCKWOOD, Luke Vincent. *The Pendleton Collection.* Providence, 1904. 102 full-page plates. Morocco. One of 150 on Japan vellum, signed. $1,500.

LOCKYER, Joseph N., and RUTHERFORD, W. *Rules of Golf.* London, 1896. $300. New York, 1896. $300.

LODGE, David. *The Picturegoers.* London, 1960. Author's first book. $275.

LOFTING, Hugh. *Doctor Dolittle's Post Office.* New York (1923). $250.

LOFTING, Hugh. *The Story of Doctor Dolittle.* New York, 1920. Illustrated by the author. Decorated orange-colored cloth, pictorial paper label. In dustwrapper. $350.

LOGUE, Christopher. *The Girls.* London, 1969. Half leather. One of 26 signed. $300.

LOGUE, Christopher. *A Song for Kathleen.* London, 1958. Self-wraps. One of 100. $125.

LOGUE, Christopher. *Wand and Quadrant.* Paris, 1953. Author's first book. Wraps. 300 numbered copies. $125. 300 unnumbered copies. $75.

LOMAX, John A. *Cowboy Songs.* New York, 1910. Pictorial cloth. $150.

LONDON, Charmian. *The Book of Jack London.* London, 1921. Illustrated. 2 vols., blue cloth. In dustwrapper. $350. New York, 1921. 2 vols. First American edition in dustwrapper. $350.

LONDON, Jack. See *The Kempton-Wace Letters.*

LONDON, Jack. *The Abysmal Brute.* New York, 1913. "Published May, 1913" on copyright page. Smooth olive green cloth stamped in black. $150. Variant binding in rough green cloth stamped in black and green. $125.

LONDON, Jack. *The Acorn Planter.* New York, 1916. "Published February, 1916" on copyright page. Three forms of binding, no known priority. $1,000. London (1916). $200.

LONDON, Jack. *Adventure.* London/Edinburgh . . . (1911). "First published in 1911" on copyright page (actually published in February). $250. New York, 1911. "Published March 1911." Blue cloth stamped in white and blue. $250.

LONDON, Jack. *Burning Daylight.* New York, 1910. First printing: "Published October 1910" on copyright page. One blank leaf follows page (374). At foot of spine

"Macmillan" or "The/Macmillan/Company"—no clear priority. $200. Second printing: As above but 3 blank leaves follow page (374). $100. London, 1911. $75. (Chicago, 1911.) Wraps. $100.

LONDON, Jack. *The Call of the Wild.* New York/London, 1903. "Set Up, Electrotyped and Published July 1903" on copyright page. $600. London, 1903. $350. Morang, Toronto, 1903. Blue-green cloth. $300. Limited Editions Club, New York, 1960. Slipcase. $150.

LONDON, Jack. *Children of the Frost.* New York/London, 1902. "Set Up and Electrotyped September, 1902" on copyright page. $500. London, 1902. $250.

LONDON, Jack. *The Cruise of the Dazzler.* New York, 1902. "Published October, 1902" on copyright page. $600. London, 1906. $300.

LONDON, Jack. *The Cruise of the Snark.* New York, 1911. "Published June 1911" on copyright page. $400. London, 1913. $150.

LONDON, Jack. *A Daughter of the Snows.* Philadelphia, 1902. "Published October, 1902" on copyright page. (Note: Second editions are exactly the same except "Second Edition" added on first half title. $400. London, 1904. $150.

LONDON, Jack. *Dutch Courage and Other Stories.* New York, 1922. "Published September 1922" on copyright page. $1,500. London (1923). $500.

LONDON, Jack. *The God of His Fathers and Other Stories.* New York, 1901. $450. London, 1902. $250.

LONDON, Jack. *Hearts of Three.* London (no-date). Published 1918. (Note: in later printings *Island Tales* is listed under "Books by Jack London" on p. [iv]). $200. New York, 1920. "Published, September, 1920" on copyright page. $350.

LONDON, Jack. *The Human Drift.* New York, 1917. "Published, February, 1917" on copyright page. $400. London (1919). $100.

LONDON, Jack. *The Iron Heel.* New York, 1908. "Published February, 1908" on copyright page. $200. London, 1908. $100.

LONDON, Jack. *The Jacket.* London (1915). "Published 1915." $350. (First U.K. edition of *The Star Rover.*) $350.

LONDON, Jack. *The Little Lady of the Big House.* New York, 1916. "Published April, 1916" on copyright page. (Variant: Copyright notices read "Copyright 1915 / by Jack London / copyright, 1916 / by Jack London." BAL also notes a "variant" with 1915 on title page. This would seem to us to be an advance copy and would be worth considerably more than the 1916.) $175. London (1916). $75.

LONDON, Jack. *Lost Face.* New York, 1910. "Published March, 1910" on copyright page. $200. London (no-date) (1915). $75.

LONDON, Jack. *Love of Life.* New York/London, 1907. "Published September, 1907" on copyright page. $350. London, 1908. $125.

LONDON, Jack. *Martin Eden.* Macmillan, New York, 1908. Wraps. Printed for copyright purposes only. "Published (blank), 1908" on copyright page. Tan paper dustwrapper. $1,000. New York, 1909. "Published September 1909" on copyright page. $250. Donohue, Chicago, 1908. $300. London, 1910. $125.

LONDON, Jack. *Michael, Brother of Jerry.* New York, 1917. "Published, November, 1917" on copyright page. $150.

LONDON, Jack. *The Mutiny of the Elsinore.* New York, 1914. "Published September 1914" on copyright page. $250. London (1915). $100.

LONDON, Jack. *On the Makaloa Mat.* New York, 1919. "Published, September 1919" on copyright page. $200. London (1920). $75.

LONDON, Jack. *The People of the Abyss.* New York, 1903. "Published October, 1903" on copyright page. $450. London, 1903. $150.

LONDON, Jack. *Revolution.* Chicago (1909). Wraps. Ads on page (32) headed: "A Socialist Success." Publisher's address: 118 Kinzie Street. Terminal ads. $300. Ads on page (32) headed: "Pocket Library of Socialism." Publisher's address in terminal ads: 118 W. Kinzie Street. $300. Ads on page (32) headed "Socialist Periodicals." Address is "118 West Kinzie." $200. Ads on page (32) headed: "Study Socialism." $150. Ads on page 32 headed: "Socialist Literature." $100.

LONDON, Jack. *Revolution and Other Essays.* New York, 1910. "Published March, 1910" on copyright page. Maroon stamped in gold and blind stamped, on spine "The Macmillan Company." Terminal ads (priority listed as probable in BAL). $400. Variant: brown cloth, stamped in black, on spine: "Macmillan." No ads. $300. London, 1920. $100.

LONDON, Jack. *The Road.* New York, 1907. "Published November, 1907" on copyright page. Gray cloth stamped in gold and black. $450. Variant binding (possible remainder) stamped in black only, top edges not gilt. $350. London, 1914. $150.

LONDON, Jack. *The Scarlet Plague.* New York, 1912. Printed blue wraps. Presumably printed for copyright purposes. $1,000. New York, 1915. "Published May 1915" on copyright page. $350. London, 1915. $100.

LONDON, Jack. *Scorn of Women.* New York/London, 1906. "Published November, 1906" on copyright page. Top edges gilt. On spine "The Macmillan Company." $1,500. Variant binding with top edges not gilt. "Macmillan" on spine. $1,250. London, 1907. $350.

LONDON, Jack. *The Sea-Wolf.* New York, 1904. Title page not a cancel. Copyright notices dated 1904 only. $3,000. Title page is a cancel. Copyright notices dated 1903 and 1904. "Published October, 1904." Some copies stamped in gold on spine (not white) but, no known priority. $200. London, 1904. $100. Limited Editions Club, Hartford, 1961. $100.

LONDON, Jack. *The Son of the Sun.* Garden City, 1912. $200. London, 1913. $75.

LONDON, Jack. *The Son of the Wolf.* Boston/New York, 1900. Author's first book. Three trial bindings (no priority). Rough grass green V cloth, stamped in silver; greenish black V cloth, stamped in silver; white buckram stamped in red only. $2,000. First printing: gray cloth stamped in silver. Pagination (i–viii); no blank leaf following page (252); collation: (4), 2–22(6). $750. Second printing: gray cloth stamped in silver. Pagination: (i–vi) blank leaf following page (252). $500. Third printing: Same as second except collation differs: 1–21(6), 22(4). $300. London, 1900. Cancel title page of first printing. $1,500. London, 1902. Copyright page blank. Red cloth stamped in gold on front and spine, spine imprint "Pitman," gold-stamped design on spine, blind-stamp design on front. Collation: (i–viii), (1)–251, (251–253). Ads including *God of His Father* and Gorky's *Three Men.* $600.

LONDON, Jack. *The Star Rover.* New York, 1915. "Published October, 1915." $300. (For first U.K. edition, see *The Jacket.*)

LONDON, Jack. *White Fang.* New York, 1906. "Published October, 1906" on copyright page. Presumed earliest state with title leaf integral. $200. Presumed later state with title leaf tipped in. $100. London, 1907. $100. Limited Editions Club, Lutenburg, Vt., 1973. $75.

LONG, Frank Belknap. *The Hounds of Tindalos.* Sauk City, Wis., 1946. Black cloth. $150.

LONG, Frank Belknap, Jr. *A Man from Genoa and Other Poems.* Athol, Mass., 1926. Author's first book. $750.

LONG, Haniel. *Poems.* New York, 1920. Author's first book. $300.

LONG, Huey P. *My First Days in the White House.* Harrisburg, 1935. Illustrated. Boards. $200.

LONG Island Atlas. New York, 1873. Published by Beers, Comstock & Cline. $350.

LONG, Stephen H. *Voyage in a Six-Oared Skiff to the Falls of St. Anthony in 1817.* Philadelphia, 1860. Wraps. $250.

LONGFELLOW, Henry Wadsworth. See M. Lhomond's *Elements of French Grammar* (Longfellow's first book) and *French Exercises.* See also *Hyperion; Outre-Mer.*

LONGFELLOW, Henry Wadsworth. *The Courtship of Miles Standish.* London, 1858. 135 pages, drab printed wraps, imprinted "Author's Protected" Edition." $600. Cloth. Second printing. $350. Boston, 1858. Brown cloth. First printing, with "treacherous" for "ruddy" in third line of page 124 and "October, 1858" ads. $250. Also, purple blue, or salmon cloths with extra gilt. $400.

LONGFELLOW, Henry Wadsworth. *Evangeline: A Tale of Acadie.* Boston, 1847. Brown or yellow boards, paper label. With line 1, page 61, reading "Long . . ." (for "Lo . . ."). $400. Reading "Lo." $250.

LONGFELLOW, Henry Wadsworth. *The Golden Legend.* Boston, 1851. $200.

LONGFELLOW, Henry Wadsworth. *Poems on Slavery.* Cambridge, 1842. 31 pages, printed yellow wrapper. $600.

LONGFELLOW, Henry Wadsworth. *The Song of Hiawatha.* London, 1855. With March ads. Wraps. $1,000. Cloth. $300. Boston, 1855. Brown cloth with panels blind stamped. First printing, with October or November ads and "dove" for "dived" in line 7 of page 96. $300. Gray-green, or red with panel stamped in gilt. $500. Boston, 1891. Illustrated by Frederic Remington. Vellum. One of 250. $600. Cloth or half leather. $300.

LONGFELLOW, Henry Wadsworth. *Voices of the Night.* Cambridge, 1839. In original tan or drab boards with paper label. First state, with line 10 on page 78 reading "His, Hector's arm" instead of "The arm of Hector." $750. Second state. $300. Author's first book of poetry. (There are other points worth checking as BAL states. No copy examined had all the original readings.)

LONGMAN, W. *Tokens of the Eighteenth Century Connected With Booksellers . . .* London, 1916. Three plates. $125.

LONGSTREET, Augustus Baldwin. See *Georgia Scenes, Characters, Incidents, etc.*

LONGSTREET, Augustus Baldwin. *An Oration . . .* (Augusta, 1831.) Wraps. $3,500.

LONGSTREET, James. *From Manassas to Appomattox.* Philadelphia, 1896. 44 maps and plates, 2 leaves of facsimiles. Cloth. $350.

LOOMIS, Augustus. *Scenes in the Indian Country.* Philadelphia, 1859. $275.

LOOMIS, Chester A. *A Journey on Horseback Through the Great West, in 1825.* Bath, N.Y. (1820s). 27 pages. $350.

LOOS, Anita. *"Gentlemen Prefer Blondes."* New York, 1925. Illustrated. First issue, with "Divine" for "Devine" on contents page. $350.

LOOS, Anita. *How to Write Photoplays.* New York, 1920. Author's first book (with W. J. Emerson). $200.

LOOS, Anita. *Breaking Into the Movies.* New York (1921). (With John J. Emerson.) $200.

LORCA, Federico Garcia. *Bitter Oleander.* London, 1935. Author's first English publication. $300.

LORIMER, George Horace. *Letters from a Self-Made Merchant to His Son.* Philadelphia, 1901. 36 pages, wraps. $150. Boston, 1902. Cloth. First (complete) edition. $100.

LORING, Rosamond B. *Decorated Book Papers . . .* Cambridge, 1942. 250 numbered copies. $600.

LORREQUER, Harry (pseudonym for Charles Lever). See *The Confessions of Harry Lorrequer.*

LORREQUER, Harry. *Charles O'Malley, the Irish Dragoon.* Dublin, 1841. (By Charles Lever.) Illustrated by H. K. Browne ("Phiz"). 22 parts in 21, printed pink pictorial wraps. $850. Dublin, 1841. 2 vols., boards. First edition in book form. $300. London, 1897. 16 plates by Arthur Rackham. $200.

LOSSING, Benson J. *A Memorial of Alexander Anderson, M.D., The First Engraver on Wood in America.* New York, 1872. 38 plates. $175.

LOSKIEL, George Henry. *History of the Mission of the United Brethren Among the Indians in North America.* In three parts. London, 1794. Folding frontispiece map. First English edition. $750.

LOTHROP, Harriet M. S. See Sidney, Margaret.

LOUDON, Archibald. *A Selection of Some of the Most Interesting Narratives, of Outrages, Committed by the Indians, in Their Wars, with the White People.* Carlisle, Pa., 1808–11. 2 vols. $5,000 or more.

LOUDON, J. C. *The Suburban Gardener and Villa Companion . . .* London, 1838. In original cloth. $400.

LOUDON, Mrs. Jane. *British Wild Flowers.* London, 1846. 60 hand-colored plates. Cloth. $2,500. London (1849). Second edition. $2,000. Later editions, 1855, 1859, etc., are worth almost as much.

LOUGHBOROUGH, John. *The Pacific Telegraph and Railway* . . . St. Louis, 1849. Two folding maps. $2,500.

LOUGHEED, Victor. *Vehicles of the Air.* Chicago (1909). $200.

LOVE Epistles of Aristaenetus (The). London, 1771. (By Richard Sheridan. His first book.) $1,250.

LOVE, Robertus. *The Rise and Fall of Jesse James.* New York, 1926. Frontispiece. Issued without dustwrapper. $150.

LOVECRAFT, H. P. *Beyond the Wall of Sleep.* Sauk City, Wis., 1943. $1,000.

LOVECRAFT, H. P. *The Cats of Ulthar.* (Cassia, Fla.) 1935. 16 pages, wraps. One of 40 on ordinary paper. $2,500. Also 2 copies on red lion text. $3,500.

LOVECRAFT, H. P. *The Haunter of the Dark.* London, 1951. Introduction by August Derleth. Cloth. $150.

LOVECRAFT, H. P. *Marginalia.* Sauk City, Wis., 1944. $250.

LOVECRAFT, H. P. *The Outsider and Others.* Sauk City, Wis., 1939. (First book published by August Derleth's Arkham House.) $1,250.

LOVECRAFT, H. P. *The Shadow Over Innsmouth.* Everett, Pa., 1936. Illustrated. In dustwrapper. $4,000. Author's first published book. (Earliest copies—about 10— were issued without errata sheet. The dustwrappers [two types: one printed in yellow and one with an illustration in green] were a later addition, according to Currey.)

LOVECRAFT, H. P. *The Shunned House.* Athol, Mass., 1928. Author's first book, other than four pamphlets/offprints. Bound by Paul Cook. $4,000. Unbound, folded. signatures sold by Derleth (about 50). $1,750. Various bindings between 1928–63. $1,750. Arkham House. Sauk City, Wis., 1963. 100 copies in plain brown dustwrapper. $1,250.

LOVECRAFT, H. P. *Something About Cats and Other Pieces.* Sauk City, Wis., 1949. Edited by August Derleth. Cloth. $150.

LOVECRAFT, H. P., and DERLETH, August. *The Lurker at the Threshold.* Sauk City, Wis., 1945. $150.

LOVELL, Robert. See Bion and Moschus; Southey, Robert.

LOVER, Samuel. *Handy Andy: A Tale of Irish Life.* London, January–December, 1842. Illustrated by the author. 12 parts, printed wraps. $500. London, 1842. Green cloth. First edition in book form. $250.

LOVESEY, Peter. *Wobble to Death.* London, 1970. Author's first book. $100.

LOW, John L. *F. G. Tait: A Record.* London, 1900. $150.

LOWE, Percival. *Five Years a Dragoon '49 to '54.* Kansas City, 1906. $125.

LOWELL, Amy. See *Dream Drops.*

LOWELL, Amy. *A Dome of Many-Colored Glass.* Boston, 1912. Boards, cloth spine, paper labels. Author's first book aside from *Dream Drops.* $300.

LOWELL, Amy. *The Madonna of Carthagena.* No-place, 1927. Wraps. One of 50. $150.

LOWELL, Amy. *What's O'Clock.* Boston, 1925. Gray-blue boards and cloth. $150.

LOWELL, James Russell. See Wilbur, Homer. See also *Class Poem.*

LOWELL, James Russell. *Heartsease and Rue.* Boston, 1888. $125.

LOWELL, James Russell. *Ode Recited at the Commemoration of the Living and Dead Soldiers of Harvard University, July 21, 1865.* Cambridge, 1865. Gray boards, paper label. One of 50. $750.

LOWELL, James Russell. *Poems.* Cambridge, 1844. Boards, paper label. $250.

LOWELL, James Russell. *Poems.* Boston, 1849. 2 vols., boards or cloth. $200.

LOWELL, James Russell. *Under the Willows and Other Poems.* Boston, 1869. Cloth. First issue, with errata slip at page 286 and page 97 signed "7." (Later corrected to "5".) $125.

LOWELL, James Russell. *A Year's Life.* Boston, 1841. Boards, paper label. First edition, with errata slip. Author's first book (preceded by *Class Poem* pamphlet). $400.

LOWELL, Maria. *Poems.* Cambridge, Mass., 1855. 68 pages, half leather. $300.

LOWELL, Robert. *4 by Robert Lowell.* (Cambridge, Mass., 1969.) Illustrated by Robert Scott. Decorated wraps, stitched. One of 126 copies, signed by Lowell. (4 broadsides, 1 for each poem.) $600.

LOWELL, Robert. *Land of Unlikeness.* Cummington, Mass., 1944. Author's first book. Printed boards. One of 224 copies. In tissue jacket. $3,000. One of 26 signed and numbered copies. $7,500.

LOWELL, Robert. *Life Studies.* London (1959). $350. New York, 1959. $150.

LOWELL, Robert. *Lord Weary's Castle.* New York (1946). $300.

LOWELL, Robert. *The Mills of the Kavanaughs.* New York (1951). $275.

LOWELL, Robert. *Poems, 1938–1949.* London (1950). $350.

LOWES, John Livingston. *The Road to Xanadu.* Boston, 1927. One of 300. Slipcase. $200.

LOWMAN, Al (compiler). *This Bitterly Beautiful Land: A Texas Commonplace Book.* (Austin, 1972.) Woodcuts. Folio, cloth. One of 275 signed. $750.

LOWNDES, Mrs. Belloc. *The Lodger.* London (1913). $125.

LOWNDES, William Thomas. *The Bibliographer's Manual of English Literature.* London, 1890. 6 vols. Reprint of the 1864 edition, the best edition. $250.

LOWRY, Malcolm. *Hear Us O Lord from Heaven Thy Dwelling Place.* Philadelphia (1961). $125.

LOWRY, Malcolm. *Lunar Caustic.* London (1968). First edition in English. Cloth. $250. Wraps, in dustwrapper. $125. (Published in Paris, in French, in 1963.)

LOWRY, Malcolm. *Ultramarine.* London (1933). Author's first book. $5,000. Philadelphia, 1962. First American edition, revised. $125. Toronto (1963) or London (1963). $100.

LOWRY, Malcolm. *Under the Volcano.* New York (1947). Gray cloth. First edition not stated. $750. London (1947). $600.

LOWRY, Robert. *Hutton Street.* Cincinnati, 1940. Illustrated. Pictorial wraps. Author's first book? $150.

LOWRY, Robert. *The Journey Out.* (Bari, Italy, 1945.) Boards. 250 signed copies. $150. 100 unsigned copies. $100.

LOY, Mina. *Lunar Baedeker.* (Paris, 1923.) Printed wraps. $750.

LOY, Mina. *Lunar Baedeker & Time Tables.* Highlands, N.C., 1958. Cloth. Jargon 23. One of 50 signed "author's copies." In acetate dustwrapper. (Contains an introduction by William Carlos Williams and others.) $500.

LOY, Mina. *Songs to Joannes.* New York, 1917. Author's first book. (April issue of *Others* magazine.) Wraps. $300.

LUBBOCK, Basil. *Adventures by Sea from the Art of Old Time.* London, 1925. 115 plates, including 22 in color. Buckram. One of 1,750. Issued without dustwrapper. $350.

LUBBOCK, Basil. *The Last of the Windjammers.* Boston, 1927. Illustrated. 2 vols., cloth in dust wrappers. $750.

LUBBOCK, Basil, and SPURTING, John. *Sail: The Romance of the Clipper Ship.* London, 1927–30–36. 78 full-page color plates. 3 vols. One of 1,000 in dustwrapper. $1,500.

LUCAS, E. V. See L., E. V.

LUCAS, E. V. *Edwin Austin Abbey Royal Academician, The Record of His Life and Work.* New York, 1921. 2 vols. $125.

LUCAS, E.V. *Playtime and Company.* London (1925). Illustrated by Ernest H. Shepard. Vellum. One of 15 on vellum, signed by author and artist. $1,250. Boards and cloth. One of 100 signed. In dustwrapper. $300.

LUCAS, Thomas J. *Camp Life and Sport in South Africa.* London, 1878. Frontispiece and 3 plates. $600.

LUCAS, Thomas J. *Pen and Pencil Reminiscences of a Campaign in South Africa.* London (1861). 21 colored plates. $1,000.

LUCAS, Victoria. *The Bell Jar.* London (1963.) (By Sylvia Plath.) $1,000. New York, 1971. $125.

LUCE, Edward S. *Keoghe, Comanche and Custer.* (St. Louis) 1939. Illustrated. Cloth. Limited, signed edition. In dustwrapper. $350.

LUDLOW, Fitz-Hugh. See *The Hasheesh Eater.*

LUDLOW, N. M. *Dramatic Life as I Found It.* St. Louis, 1880. $150.

LUDLUM, Robert. *The Scarlatti Inheritance.* New York (1971). Author's first book. In printed acetate dustwrapper (Note: there is also a Book-of-the-Month Club edition which states "First . . ." It does have a blind stamp on bottom right corner of back cover, but it is easy to overlook). $150. London (1971). $75.

LUDLUM, Robert. *The Osterman Weekend.* New York (1972). Printed acetate dustwrapper. Priced $6.95 with "A 3918" on bottom right corner of back (dustwrapper) panel. Also noted: "First Printing" copies with "7452" where price should be and same number (A 3918) on back; and "First Printing" copies with no price and "7452" at bottom right corner of back dustwrapper panel. The latter two editions do not have Book-of-the-Month dots, but the covers (book) are smoother and lighter blue than the true first. $125. London, 1972. $75.

LUHAN, Mabel Dodge. *Lorenzo in Taos.* New York, 1932. Illustrated. Author's first book. $250.

LUHAN, Mabel Dodge. *Taos and Its Artists.* New York, 1947. Illustrated. Red cloth. $250.

LUMPKIN, Wilson. *The Removal of the Cherokee Indians from Georgia.* Wormsloe, Ga., 1907. 2 portraits. 2 vols., cloth. One of 500. $300.

LURIE, Alison. *V. R. Lang.* Munich (1959). Author's first book. (300 copies.) Wraps. (Edward Gorey cover.) $200.

LUTTIG, John C. *Journal of a Fur-Trading Expedition on the Upper Missouri.* St. Louis, 1920. Folding map, 4 plates. Boards and cloth. One of 365. Issued without dustwrapper. $300.

LYELL, Charles. *Principles of Geology.* London, 1930–32–33. Maps and plates. 3 vols., leather. $1,250.

LYELL, Charles. *Travels in North America.* London, 1845. Map, 6 plates. 2 vols. $600.

LYELL, James P. R. *Early Book Illustration in Spain.* London, 1926. Colored frontispiece, 247 other illustrations. One of 500. Issued without dustwrapper. $250.

LYMAN, Albert. *Journal of a Voyage to California, and Life in the Gold Diggings.* Hartford, 1852. Illustrated. Wraps. $1,000. Cloth. $750.

LYMAN, George D. *John Marsh, Pioneer.* New York, 1930. One of 150 signed. Issued without dustwrapper. $200.

LYMINGTON, Lord. *Spring Song of Iscariot.* Black Sun Press. Paris, 1929. Wraps. One of 125 on Van Gelder paper. $400. One of 25 on Japan paper. $750.

LYNCH, Bohun. *The Prize Ring.* London, 1925. One of 1,000. Issued without dustwrapper. $200. Trade. $50.

LYNCH, Thomas. *The Printer's Manual, A Practical Guide for Compositors and Pressmen.* Cincinnati, 1872. Second edition. First appeared in 1859. $200.

LYON, G.F. *A Brief Narrative of an Unsuccessful Attempt to Reach Repulse Bay . . .* London, 1825. Folding map, 7 plates and 1 table. $425.

LYON, G. F. *The Private Journal of Capt. G. F. Lyon, of H.M. Hecla.* London, 1824. $500. Boston, 1824. First American edition with frontispiece, folding map, and 6 plates. $400.

LYON, Harris Merton. *Sardonics: Sixteen Sketches.* New York, 1909. Author's first book. $125.

LYON, John. *The Harp of Zion, A Collection of Poems.* Liverpool, 1853. Errata slip. $250.

LYONS, Arthur. *The Second Coming: Satanism in America . . .* New York (1970). Author's first book. $175.

LYRE, Pinchbeck. *Poems.* (London, 1931.) (By Siegfried Sassoon.) In glassine dust-wrapper. $100.

LYRICAL Ballads with Other Poems. Bristol, 1798. (By William Wordsworth and Samuel Taylor Coleridge.) $15,000. London, 1798. $7,500. London, 1800. 2 vols., in original drab boards. Second edition (so designated on the first volume alone). $10,000. London, 1802. 2 vols., boards. Third edition. $1,500.

LYTLE, Andrew. *At the Moon's Inn.* Indianapolis/New York (1941). First edition stated. $300.

LYTLE, Andrew. *Bedford Forrest and His Critter Company.* New York, 1931. Author's first book. Illustrated. Pictorial black cloth, paper labels. First issue by Minton, Balch. $400. Putnam, New York (1931). $150.

LYTLE, Andrew. *The Long Night.* Indianapolis (1936). $300.

LYTLE, Andrew. *A Name For Evil.* Indianapolis (1947). $200.

LYTTON, Lord (Edward Bulwer). See Bulwer-Lytton, Edward.

LYTTON, Lord Edward Bulwer. *Ismael: An Oriental Tale.* London, 1820. $350.

LYTTON, Edward Robert. See *Clytemnestra.*

M

M'CLUNG, John A. *Sketches of Western Adventure.* Maysville, Ky., 1832. In original boards, linen spine. $2,500. Philadelphia, 1832. Second edition. $600.

M'DONELL, Alexander. *A Narrative of Transactions in the Red River Country.* London, 1819. Folding map. Boards. $1,000.

MACARIA: or, Altars of Sacrifice. Richmond, 1864. 183 pages, wraps. (By Augusta Jane Evans Wilson.) $300.

MacARTHUR, Douglas. *Military Demolitions.* (Fort Leavenworth, Kan., 1909.) Printed wraps. $500.

MacARTHUR, James. *New South Wales: Its Present State and Future Prospects.* London, 1837. Colored map. (Written by Edward Edwards from MacArthur's notes.) $850.

MACAULAY, Rose. *Catchwords and Claptrap.* Hogarth Press. London, 1926. Printed boards. Issued without dustwrapper. $150.

MACAULAY, Thomas Babington. *Evening: A Poem.* Cambridge, 1821. Wraps bound in. $400.

MACAULAY, Thomas Babington. *Lays of Ancient Rome.* London, 1842. Brown cloth. $300.

MACAULAY, Thomas Babington. *Pompeii.* (Cambridge, 1819.) Author's first book. $250.

MACAULEY, Rose. *Abbots Verney.* London, 1906. Author's first book. $100.

MacBETH, George. *A Form of Words.* Oxford, 1954. Author's first book. One of 150. $125.

MacCABE, Julius P. Bolivar. *A Directory of Cleveland and the Cities of Ohio for the Years 1837–1838.* Cleveland, 1837. In original printed boards. $1,000.

MacCABE, Julius P. Bolivar. *Directory of the City of Detroit.* Detroit, 1837. In original printed boards. $1,000.

MacCABE, Julius P. Bolivar. *Directory of the City of Milwaukee.* Milwaukee, 1847. Full leather. $650.

MacCARTHY, Desmond. *The Court Theatre 1904–1907.* London, 1907. Author's first book. $125.

MacDIARMID, Hugh. See Duval, K. D.; Grieve, C. M. (Note: The following listings under MacDiarmid's name include books with title pages reading "M'Diarmid" and "Mc'Diarmid.")

MacDIARMID, Hugh. *A Drunk Man Looks at the Thistle.* Edinburgh, 1926. (By C. M. Grieve.) $250.

MacDIARMID, Hugh. *Direadh I, II, III.* Frenich, Foss, England, 1974. (By C. M. Grieve.) Boards and leather. One of 200 signed. In slipcase. $200.

MacDIARMID, Hugh. *Penny Wheep.* (Edinburgh) 1926. (By C. M. Grieve.) Blue cloth. $250. Second binding in boards. $175.

MacDIARMID, Hugh. *Sangschaw.* (Edinburgh) 1925. (By C. M. Grieve.) Poet's first book of verse. $600.

MacDIARMID, Hugh. *Stony Limits and Other Poems.* London, 1934. (By C. M. Grieve.) $200.

MacDIARMID, Hugh. *The Kind of Poetry I Want.* Edinburgh, 1961. (By C. M. Grieve.) Boards and vellum. One of 300 signed. In slipcase. $600. One of 500. In slipcase. $150.

MacDIARMID, Hugh. *To Circumjack Cencrastus, or the Curly Snake.* Edinburgh, 1930. (By C. M. Grieve.) Wraps. $200. Cloth. $175.

MacDONAGH, Donagh. *Twenty Poems.* Dublin, 1934. Author's first book (with Niall Sheridan). Wraps. $150.

MacDONAGH, Donagh. *Veterans and Other Poems.* Dublin, 1941. Cuala Press. Boards and linen. One of 270. $250.

MacDONALD, George. *At the Back of the North Wind.* London, 1871. Illustrated by Arthur Hughes. In bright blue pictorial (gold-stamped) cloth. $1,500. Second binding omits gold framing. $1,000. New York, 1871. $1,000. Philadelphia, 1919. Illustrated by J. W. Smith. $150.

MacDONALD, George. *Dealings with the Fairies.* London, 1867. Illustrated by Arthur Hughes. Blue cloth. $1,250. In green cloth. $750.

MacDONALD, George. *Malcolm.* London, 1875. 3 vols. $600.

MacDONALD, George. *Phantasies.* London, 1858. With 16 pages of ads at end (VAB). 24 pages of ads dated July 1859 (Sadleir). $750.

MacDONALD, George. *The Princess and the Goblin.* London, 1897. Illustrated by Arthur Hughes. $1,500.

MacDONALD, George. *Within and Without: A Dramatic Poem.* London, 1855. Author's first book. $1,500.

MacDONALD, James, and SINCLAIR, James. *History of Hereford Cattle.* London, 1886. Illustrated. $150.

MacDONALD, James. *Food from the Far West.* London, 1878. Decorated cloth. $250. New York (1878). Cloth. First American edition. $250.

MacDONALD, John D. *Nightmare in Pink.* New York (1964). Wraps. $50. London (1966). Cloth. $100. New York (1976). Cloth. $150.

MacDONALD, John D. *The Brass Cupcake.* New York, 1950. Author's first book. Wraps. $50.

MacDONALD, John D. *The Deep Blue Goodbye.* New York (1964). Wraps. $60. London (1965). Cloth. $100. New York (1975). Cloth. $200.

MacDONALD, John D. *Wine of the Dreamer.* New York (1951). First hardback. $150.

MacDONALD, John Ross. *The Drowning Pool.* New York, 1950. (By Kenneth Millar.) $300.

MacDONALD, Ross. See Millar, Kenneth.

MacDONALD, Ross. *The Chill.* New York, 1964. (By Kenneth Millar.) $125.

MacDONALD, Ross. *The Galton Case.* New York, 1959. (By Kenneth Millar.) $250.

MacDONALD, Ross. *The Zebra-Striped Hearse.* New York, 1962. $200.

MacDONALD, William Colt. *Law of the Forty Fives.* New York (1933). $75.

MacDONALD, William Colt. *Restless Guns.* New York, 1929. Author's first book. $150.

MacDOUGALL, William. *The Red River Rebellion.* Toronto, 1870. 68 pages, wraps. $150.

MacFALL, Haldane. *Aubrey Beardsley: The Clown, the Harlequin, the Pierrot of His Age.* New York, 1927. Illustrated. Cloth. Issued without dustwrapper. $150.

MacFALL, Haldane. *Aubrey Beardsley, the Man and His Work.* London, 1928. Portrait and 10 plates. Half cloth. In dustwrapper. $300. Cloth. One of 100 on handmade paper, with 6 extra illustrations. $500.

MacFALL, Haldane. *The Book of Lovat.* London, 1923. Half cloth. One of 150 signed. In dustwrapper. $500. Trade in dustwrapper. $125.

MacFALL, Haldane. *The Wooings of Jezebel Pettyfer.* London, 1898. Pictorial cloth. Author's first book. First issue, with portrait of Jezebel on front cover. (Most copies reportedly destroyed by fire.) $200.

MACHEN, Arthur. See Siluriensis, Leolinus.

MACHEN, Arthur. *Bridles and Spurs.* Cleveland, 1951. Green boards and cloth. Grabhorn printing for the Rowfant Club. One of 178. In slipcase. $200.

MACHEN, Arthur. *Dog and Duck.* London, 1924. Illustrated. Batik boards and cloth. One of 150 (of an edition of 900) signed. In dustwrapper. $250.

MACHEN, Arthur. *Eleusinia.* Hereford, 1881. Author's first book. Wraps. (2 known copies). $10,000 or more.

MACHEN, Arthur. *Notes and Queries.* London, 1926. Green buckram, paper label. One of 265 signed. In dustwrapper. $150. Trade. $60.

MACHEN, Arthur. *The Canning Wonder.* London, 1925. Boards and vellum. One of 130 signed. In dustwrapper. $150. Trade. $60.

MACHEN, Arthur. *The Green Round.* London (1933). $100. Sauk City, Wis., 1968. $60.

MACHEN, Arthur. *The Hill of Dreams.* London, 1907. Frontispiece. Dark red buckram. First edition, with "E. Grant Richards" at bottom of spine. $200. London (1922). One of 150 signed in dustwrapper. $300.

MACHEN, Arthur. *The Shining Pyramid.* Chicago, 1923. Edited by Vincent Starrett. Illustrated. Black cloth. One of 875. In dustwrapper. $125. London, 1925. Blue cloth. First English edition. One of 250 signed in dustwrapper. $175. Trade. $50.

MACHEN, Arthur. *The Three Impostors.* London, 1895. Blue cloth. $150.

MACK, Solomon. *A Narraitive [sic] of the Life of Solomon Mack.* Windsor, Vt., (1811?). 48 pages $1,250.

MacKAIL, J. W. *The Life of William Morris.* London, 1899. 22 illustrations. 2 vols. $150.

MacKAY, Charles. *Memoirs of Extraordinary Popular Delusions and the Madness of Crowds.* London, 1841. 5 portraits. 3 vols., gray cloth. $350.

MacKAY, Charles. *The Mormons: Their Progress and Present Condition.* London, 1851. 10 parts, wraps. $500. London, 1851. Cloth. First book edition. $175.

MacKAY, Malcolm S. *Cow-Range and Hunting Trail.* New York, 1925. 38 illustrations. $250.

MacKAYE, Percy. *Johnny Crimson.* Boston, 1895. Author's first book. Wraps. $350.

MacKAYE, Percy. *The Mystery of Hamlet, King of Denmark.* New York, 1950. Folio, cloth. One of 357 signed copies. Issued without dustwrapper. $300.

MacKENNA, F. Severne. *Worcester Porcelain.* Leigh-on-Sea, 1950. Frontispiece in color, 80 plates. Buckram. One of 500 signed. In dustwrapper. $400.

MacKENZIE, Alexander. *Voyages from Montreal, on the River St. Lawrence, Through the Continent of North America.* London, 1801. Frontispiece, 3 folding maps. $2,750. London, 1802. Second edition, 2 vols. $1,500. New York, 1802. Folding map. $1,000. Philadelphia, 1802. 2 vols. $750.

MacKENZIE, Alister. *Golf Architecture: Economy in Course Construction.* London, 1920. $800.

MacKENZIE, Alister. *Dr. MacKenzie's Golf Architecture.* Worcester, 1982. Limited to 700 copies. $100.

MacKENZIE, Compton. *Extraordinary Women.* London, 1928. One of 100 signed. $250.

MacKENZIE, Compton. *Poems.* Oxford, 1907. Gray wraps. Author's first book. $200.

MACKERN, Louie (Mrs.), and BOYS, M. *Our Lady of the Green.* London, 1899. $250.

MacLAVERTY, Bernard. *Secrets and Other Stories.* Belfast, 1977. Author's first book. $125.

MacLEAN, Norman. *A River Runs Through It.* (Chicago, 1976). First edition not stated. $150.

MacLEISH, Archibald. *American Letters for Gerald Murphy.* Arroyo Grande, 1935. Half leather and cloth. One of 150 issued without dustwrapper. $200.

MacLEISH, Archibald. *Einstein.* Black Sun Press. Paris, 1929. Printed wraps. One of 100 on Van Gelder paper. In slipcase. $300. One of 50 on vellum, signed. In slipcase. $1,500.

MacLEISH, Archibald. *New Found Land.* Black Sun Press. Paris, 1930. Wraps. One of 100 numbered copies. Slipcase. $250. One of 35 on vellum, signed. Slipcase. $1,000. One of 10 of the vellum copies initialed by Harry Crosby. $1,500. Boston, 1930. (Printed in Paris.) Blue boards. In slipcase. $125.

MacLEISH, Archibald. *Nobodaddy.* Cambridge, Mass., 1926. Black cloth. One of 700. Issued without dustwrapper. $100. One of 50 on large paper. $125.

MacLEISH, Archibald. *Public Speech; Poems.* New York (1936). Full calf. One of 275 signed. In glassine dustwrapper and slipcase. $200.

MacLEISH, Archibald. See *Class Poem,* 1915.

MacLEISH, Archibald. *Songs for a Summer Day.* (New Haven) 1913. Wraps. Author's first regularly published book. $500.

MacLEISH, Archibald. *The Happy Marriage and Other Poems.* Boston, 1924. Boards, paper label. $150.

MacLEISH, Archibald. *The Pot of Earth.* Cambridge, 1925. Gold decorated boards. One of 100 on handmade paper. In dustwrapper and slipcase. $250. Boston, 1925. $125.

MacLEISH, Archibald. *Tower of Ivory.* New Haven, 1917. Boards, paper labels. $150.

MacLEOD, Fiona. *Pharais.* Derby, 1894. Author's first book. 75 signed and numbered copies. $200.

MacNEICE, Louis. *Autumn Journal.* London, 1939. $150.

MacNEICE, Louis. *Blind Fireworks.* London, 1929. Author's first book. $750.

MacNEICE, Louis. *I Crossed the Minch.* London (1938). Illustrated. $175.

MacNEICE, Louis. *The Earth Compels.* London, 1939. $150.

MacNEICE, Louis. *The Last Ditch.* Dublin, 1940. Cuala Press. Boards, linen spine, paper label. One of 450. In tissue dustwrapper. $200. One of 25 signed. $350.

MacNEICE, Louis. *Poems.* London, 1935. $200.

MacNEICE, Louis. *Poems.* New York (1937). (Same title as the 1935 book but not the same content.) $200.

MACOMB, David B. *Answer to Enquiries Relative to Middle Florida.* Tallahassee, 1827. 5 unnumbered leaves. $1,500.

MacQUOID, Percy, and EDWARDS, Ralph. *The Dictionary of English Furniture.* London, 1924–27. 3 vols., with 52 color plates. In dustwrapper. $750.

MacQUOID, Percy. *The History of English Furniture.* London, 1904–8. Illustrated, including color plates. 4 vols., buckram. $750.

MADAN, Falconer. *The Early Oxford Press, A Bibliography of Printing and Publishing At Oxford.* Oxford, 1895. One of 700 copies issued with the 3 actual specimen leaves. $275.

MADARIAGA, Salvador de. *Don Quixote: An Introductory Essay in Psychology.* Gregynog Press. Newton, Wales, 1934. Boards and linen. One of 250. $400.

MADDEN, Frederic W. *Coins of the Jews.* London, 1881. Illustrated. Folio, half leather. $250.

MADDEN, R. R. *The Island of Cuba.* London, 1849. $200.

MADISON, James. *Message from the President of the United States, Recommending an Immediate Declaration of War Against Great Britain.* Washington, 1812. 12 pages. sewn. $225.

MAGEE, David. *The Hundredth Book: A Bibliography of . . . The Book Club of California.* San Francisco, 1958. 18 reproductions, many in color. Folio, half cloth. Grabhorn printing. One of 400. In dustwrapper. $400.

MAGEE, Dorothy, and MAGEE, David. *Bibliography of the Grabhorn Press, 1940–1956.* San Francisco, 1957. Illustrated. Folio, half morocco. One of 225. $850. (See Heller entry for related work.)

MAGOFFIN, Susan Shelby. *Down the Santa Fe Trail and into Mexico.* New Haven, 1926. Edited by Stella M. Drumm. Map, plates. In dustwrapper. $150.

MAGOUN, F. Alexander. *The Frigate Constitution and Other Historic Ships.* Salem, 1928. Illustrated, including 16 folding plates. Buckram. One of 97 large paper copies. Issued without dustwrapper. $500. Trade issued without dustwrapper. $125.

MAGRUDER, Allan B. *Political, Commercial and Moral Reflections, on the Late Cession of Louisiana, to the United States.* Lexington, Ky., 1803. $3,000.

MAGUIRE, H. N. *The Coming Empire: A Complete and Reliable Treatise on the Black Hills, Yellowstone and Big Horn Regions.* Sioux City, Iowa, 1878. 7 plates, folding map. $500.

MAGUIRE, H. N. *The Lakeside Library: The People's Edition of the Black Hills and American Wonderland.* (Caption title.) Chicago, 1877. Illustrations and map. 36 pages, stitched. $450.

MAHAN, A. T. *The Influence of Sea Power upon History.* Boston, 1890. $400.

MAHAN, A. T. *The Navy in the Civil War.* New York, 1883. Illustrated. Cloth. Author's first book. $250.

MAID Marian. London, 1822. (By Thomas Love Peacock.) $250.

MAILER, Norman. *Barbary Shore.* New York (1951). Black boards with white lettering. 2 dustwrappers on first edition apparently issued simultaneously: red and black; red and green. Proof copies with both variants of dustwrapper also noted. $200. London (1952). $75.

MAILER, Norman. *Deaths for the Ladies and Other Disasters.* New York (1962). Black and white cloth, with white lettering, in black-and-white dustwrapper. $200. Simultaneously published in wraps. $40. (London, 1962.) $125.

MAILER, Norman. *Gargoyle, Guignol, False Closet.* Dublin, 1964. 2 pages. One of 100. $250.

MAILER, Norman. *Marilyn.* Grosset & Dunlap (New York, 1973.) Limited signed edition in clam-shell case. $200. (Grosset & Dunlap, New York, 1973.) $50. (London, 1973.) $50.

MAILER, Norman. *The Naked and the Dead.* New York (1948). First regularly published book. $300. London, 1949. 253 copies, 240 numbered. In full leather. $500. Trade. $150. Franklin Library, 1979. Signed by Mailer. $100.

MAILER, Norman. *Of a Small and Modest Malignancy Wicked and Bristling with Dots.* Northridge, 1980. 100 signed and numbered copies. In leather without dustwrapper in slipcase. $250. 300 signed and numbered copies. In cloth in slipcase. $150.

MAILLARD, N. Doran. *The History of the Republic of Texas, from the Discovery of the Country to the Present Time.* London, 1842. Folding map. Dark blue cloth. $2,500.

MAITLAND, Margaret. *Passages in the Life of...* London, 1849. Author's first book. 3 vols. $350.

MAJORS, Alexander. *Seventy Years on the Frontier.* Chicago, 1893. Frontispiece and plates. (Without illustrations.) Blue pictorial cloth or wraps. $200.

MALAMUD, Bernard. *The Assistant.* New York, 1957. Reviews of *The Natural* on back panel of dustwrapper. $125. Reviews of this title on back panel. $75. London, 1959. $60.

MALAMUD, Bernard. *The Natural.* New York (1952). Red, blue, or gray cloth. Author's first book. (Priority unknown.) $350. London, 1963. $150.

MALAMUD, Bernard. *The Tenants.* New York (1971). 250 copies with signed tipped-in sheet. $100. First binding in orange cloth. $40. London (1972). $30.

MALET, Capt. H. E. *Annals of the Road.* London, 1876. 10 colored plates, woodcuts. $300.

MALKIN, B. H. *A Father's Memoirs of His Child.* London, 1806. Folding map, 3 plates. $200.

MALORY, Sir Thomas. *Le Morte D'Arthur.* London (1893–94). Illustrated by Aubrey Beardsley. 12 parts printed wraps. One of 300 on Dutch handmade paper. $6,000. 3 vols., pictorial cloth. One of 300. $3,500. 2 vols., cloth. One of 1,500. $2,000. London. 1909. Cloth. Second Beardsley edition. $500. London, 1910–11. Riccardi Press. Illustrated in color by W. Russell Flint. 4 vols., limp vellum or boards. One of 500. In dustwrappers and slipcases. $1,000. Also, one of 12 on vellum in a Riviere binding. $9,000. London, 1917. Illustrated by Arthur Rackham. Vellum. One of 500 signed by Rackham. $1,250. New York, 1917. Full leather. American Rackham edition. One of 250. In slipcase. $1,000. London or New York, 1917. Clothbound Rackham issues. $300. London, 1927. Illustrated by Beardsley. One of 1,600. $750. London, 1933. Shakespeare Head Press. Illustrated. 2 vols., morocco. One of 370. $750. Limited Editions Club, New York, 1936. Illustrated by Robert Gibbings. 2 vols., boards. In slipcase. $275.

MALRAUX, André. *The Conquerors.* London, 1929. Author's first book. (First English translation.) $150.

MALRAUX, André. *The Metamorphosis of the Gods.* Garden City, 1960. Illustrated. Red morocco. First American edition. One of 50 signed. In slipcase. $600. Trade. $100.

MALRAUX, André. *The Psychology of Art.* (New York, 1949–50.) Illustrated. 3 vols., cloth. In dustwrapper and slipcase. $300.

MALRAUX, André. *The Voices of Silence.* Garden City, 1953. Illustrated. Cloth. First American edition. In dustwrapper and slipcase. $150. Full leather. One of 160 signed in slipcase. $500.

MALTHUS, Thomas Robert. *Definitions in Political Economy...* London, 1827. $400.

MALTHUS, Thomas Robert. *An Essay on the Principle of Population.* London, 1803. Second edition. $1,500. (Note: The anonymous first edition, London, 1798, $4,500.) Washington, 1809. 2 vols. First American edition. $1,000.

MALTHUS, Thomas Robert. *Principles of Political Economy . . .* London, 1820. $1,500. Boston, 1821. First American edition. $750.

MALTZ, Albert. *Black Pit.* New York (1935). Author's first book. $150.

MAN Without a Country (The). Boston, 1865. (By Edward Everett Hale.) 23 pages, terra-cotta wraps. First issue, without the publisher's printed yellow "Announcement" slip tipped in. $1,000. Second issue, with the "Announcement" slip tipped in. $600. Limited Editions Club, New York, 1936. In slipcase. $60.

MANGAM, William D. *The Clarks of Montana.* (New York, Silver Bow Press) 1939. Illustrated, including folding facsimile. Stiff brown wraps. $300. Second edition (rewritten and retitled *The Clarks: An American Phenomenon*). New York, 1941. Blue cloth. $250.

MANLY, William Lewis. *Death Valley in '49.* San Jose, 1894. 4 plates. $300.

MANN, E.B. *Blue-Eyed Kid.* New York, 1932. $125.

MANN, E.B. *Gamblin' Man.* New York, 1934. $100.

MANN, E.B. *The Man from Texas.* New York, 1931. Author's first book. $150.

MANN, Horace. *Lectures on Education.* Boston, 1845. Author's first book preceded by a number of pamphlets. $300.

MANN, Thomas. *The Beloved Returns.* New York, 1940. First American edition. One of 395 signed. In dustwrapper and slipcase. $400. Trade. $75.

MANN, Thomas. *Buddenbrooks.* London, 1924. Author's first book. Translated by H. T. Lowe-Porter. 2 vols. First edition in English. $300.

MANN, Thomas. *Doctor Faustus.* New York, 1948. Green cloth. First edition in English. $125.

MANN, Thomas. *The Magic Mountain.* New York, 1927. 2 vols., half vellum. One of 200 signed. $1,000. Limited Editions Club, New York, 1962. Illustrated. Half cloth. In slipcase. $150.

MANN, Thomas. *Nocturnes.* New York, 1934. Lithographs by Lynd Ward. Pictorial cloth. One of 1,000 signed. In slipcase. $400.

MANN, Thomas. *Sleep, Sweet Sleep.* (New York) 1934. Boards. In glassine dustwrapper. $200.

MANSFIELD, Edward D. *Exposition of the Natural Position of Mackinaw City, and the Climate, Soil, and Commercial Elements of the Surrounding Country.* Cincinnati, 1857. 2 maps. 47 pages, printed wraps. $300.

MANSFIELD, Katherine. *The Aloe.* London, 1930. Buckram. One of 750. $600. New York, 1930. First American edition. One of 975. In dustwrapper and slipcase. $400.

MANSFIELD, Katherine. *Bliss and Other Stories.* London (1920). Brick red cloth. With page 13 numbered 3. In white dustwrapper with author's portrait. $850. New York, 1921. Cloth, paper label. First American edition. In dustwrapper. $600.

MANSFIELD, Katherine. *The Doves' Nest and Other Stories.* London (1923). Blue-gray cloth, blue spine lettering. First issue, with verso of title page blank. One of 25. $1,500. Second issue, with "First published June, 1923" on verso of title page. $500.

MANSFIELD, Katherine. *The Garden Party and Other Stories.* London (1922). With "sposition" for "position" in last line on page 103. Light blue cloth, lettered in blue. In strawberry-colored dustwrapper with blue lettering. One of 25. $2,000. Later binding state, orange (ochre) lettering. $1,000. New York, 1922. One of 50 "for booksellers." $500. London (1939). Verona Press. 16 color lithographs by Marie Laurencin. Decorated cloth. One of 1,170. In dustwrapper and slipcase. $4,000. Full morocco. One of 30. In slipcase. $4,000.

MANSFIELD, Katherine. *In a German Pension.* London (1911). Green cloth. Author's first book. In orange (ochre) dustwrapper. $3,000. Without dustwrapper. $600.

MANSFIELD, Katherine. *The Little Girl and Other Stories.* New York, 1924. First American edition (of *Something Childish and Other Stories.*) $450.

MANSFIELD, Katherine. *Prelude.* Hogarth Press. Richmond, England (1918). Blue pictorial wraps. With design on front cover by J. D. Fergusson. $1,500. Without design. $1,250. (Also noted with design on both covers—at auction in 1990.) $2,000.

MANSFIELD, Katherine. *Something Childish and Other Stories.* London (1924). Gray buckram. First issue, without "First published 1924" on verso of title page. $1,500. Second issue. $600.

MANSFIELD Park: A Novel. London, 1814. By the Author of *Sense and Sensibility and Pride and Prejudice* (Jane Austen.) 3 vols., blue boards, white paper labels. First edition, with vols. I and III bearing Sidney imprint on back of half titles (Schwartz) and vol. II the Roworth imprint. $3,500. Keynes has the reverse (I and III by Roworth and II by Sidney). But at least they both agree that Sidney wasn't involved in the second edition. London, 1816. 3 vols. $1,000.

MANTAGUE, William K. *Golf of Our Fathers.* Duluth, Minn. 1952. Limited edition (no limitation cited). $150.

MANUAL of Military Surgery. Prepared for the Use of the Confederate States Army . . . Richmond, 1862. 30 lithographic plates. $2,250. Richmond, 1863. $1,500. (By John J. Chisholm.)

MARCH of the First (The). (First Regiment of Colorado Volunteers.) Denver, 1863. 36 pages, stitched, plus 4 pages of ads. $4,000 or more. (See Hollister, Ovando J.)

MARCH, William. *Company K.* New York, 1933. Author's first book. Issued in clear dustwrapper with printed paper flaps. $300.

MARCLIFFE, Theophilus. *The Looking Glass: A True History of the Early Years of an Artist.* London, 1805. (By William Godwin.) $600.

MARCY, Randolph B. *Exploration of the Red River of Louisiana* . . . (Senate Exec. Doc. 54.) Washington, 1853. 65 plates. 2 maps. 2 vols., brown cloth and green cloth (atlas case). $500. Washington, 1854. Second edition, printed by Tucker. $400. Washington, 1854. House version, printed by Nicholson. $400.

MARCY, Randolph B. *The Prairie Traveler: A Hand-Book for Overland Expeditions.* New York, 1859. Map, frontispiece. 10 plates. $500.

MARDERSTEIG, Hans. *Pastonchi: A Specimen of a New Letter for Use on the "Monotype."* (London, 1928.) Illustrated with plates and booklet inserts. Marbled boards and vellum. One of 200 on Fabriano paper, printed by Mardersteig. $500.

MARGARET Percival in America. Boston, 1850. (By Edward Everett Hale, his first book.) $125.

MARK Twain's Sketches. See Twain, Mark.

MARKET Harborough; or, How Mr. Sawyer Went to the Shires. London, 1861. (By George John Whyte-Melville.) $300.

MARKHAM, Edwin. *The Man with the Hoe.* San Francisco, 1899. 4 pages, printed wraps. First book edition. $500. (Earlier, Jan. 15, 1899 as a special supplement to San Francisco *Sunday Examiner,* containing first separate printing of the poem, 44 pages $250.) New York, 1899. Green cloth. Second edition, first issue, with "fruitless" for "milkless" in line 5, page 35. $75.

MARKHAM, Edwin. *New Poems: Eighty Songs at Eighty.* Garden City, 1932. Portrait. Boards and leather. One of 100 signed. In slipcase. $200. Trade. $50.

MARLOWE, Christopher. *Edward the Second.* Aquila Press. London, 1929. Hand-colored illustrations. Folio, vellum. One of 40. $600. One of 500. $200.

MARQUAND, John P. See Clark, Charles E.

MARQUAND, John P. *The Late George Apley.* Boston, 1937. First issue, with "Pretty Pearl" in first line of page 19. $250.

MARQUAND, John P. *Ming Yellow.* Boston, 1935. $300.

MARQUAND, John P. *No Hero.* Boston, 1935. $250.

MARQUAND, John P. *Thank You, Mr. Moto.* Boston, 1936. $250.

MARQUAND, John P. *The Unspeakable Gentleman.* New York, 1922. Author's first novel. With Scribners seal on copyright page. $150. Boards and cloth. Limited, signed, for booksellers. $250.

MARQUEZ, Gabriel Garcia. *No One Writes the Colonel.* New York (1968). $200.

MARQUEZ, Gabriel Garcia. *One Hundred Years of Solitude.* New York (1970). Without series of numbers on last leaf of book. (All printings have "First edition" on copyright page.) First issue dustwrapper has period at end of first paragraph on front flap. Changed to exclamation point. $500. (Limited Editions Club, New York, 1982). Leather spine in slipcase. $250.

MARQUIS, Don. *Archy and Mehitabel.* Garden City, 1927. $125.

MARQUIS, Don. *Danny's Own Story.* Garden City, 1912. Illustrated by E. W. Kemble. Green cloth. Author's first book. $75.

MARQUIS, Don. *How Hank Signed the Pledge in a Cistern.* New York (about 1912). Wraps. $150.

MARQUIS, Thomas B. *A Warrior Who Fought Custer.* Minneapolis, 1931. First binding, with "Midwest" on spine. $125.

MARRIAGE: A Novel. Edinburgh, 1818. 3 vols., boards. (By Susan Edmonstone Ferrier, her first book.) $300.

MARROT, H.V. *William Bulmer—Thomas Bensley, A Study in Transition.* London, 1930. 300 numbered copies. $125.

MARRYAT, Frank. *Mountains and Molehills . . .* London, 1855. (By Francis S. Marryat.) 18 woodcuts, 8 color plates. Salmon-colored cloth. $500. New York, 1855. Frontispiece. Pictorial cloth. $200.

MARRYAT, Frederick. See *Mr. Midshipman Easy; Olla Podrida; Percival Keene; Snarleyyow.*

MARRYAT, Frederick. *A Code of Signals for Use of Vessels . . .* London, 1818. Author's first book. $250.

MARRYAT, Frederick. *A Diary in America.* London, 1839. 6 vols. (Parts I and II, each 3 vols.), in original boards. $450. Philadelphia, 1839–40. 3 vols., in original half cloth (2 vols., 1839, and 2d series, 1 vol., 1840). First American edition. $300.

MARRYAT, Frederick. *Masterman Ready.* London, 1841–42–43. Illustrated. 3 vols., cloth. $350.

MARRYAT, Frederick. *The Mission.* London, 1845. Map, frontispiece. 2 vols., cloth. First edition, with 32 pages of ads in vol. 1. $250.

MARRYAT, Frederick. *Narrative of the Travels and Adventures of Monsieur Violet, in California, Sonora and Western Texas.* London, 1843. Map. 3 vols., cloth. $500. Second edition: London, 1843. 3 vols., cloth. With map. Retitled: *The Travels and Romantic Adventures of Monsieur Violet . . .* $400.

MARSH, James B. *Four Years in the Rockies.* New Castle, Pa., 1884. Portrait. $600.

MARSH, Ngaio. *A Man Lay Dead.* London, 1934. Author's first book. $350.

MARSH, Ngaio. *The Nursing Home Murder.* London, 1935. $600.

MARSH, W. Lockwood. *Aeronautical Prints and Drawings.* London, 1924. Illustrated, including color plates. In dustwrapper. $350. Pigskin. One of 100. $600.

MARSHALL, Humphrey. *Arbustrum Americanum.* Philadelphia, 1785. $1,250.

MARSHALL, Humphrey. *The History of Kentucky.* Frankfort, 1812. $1,250. Frankfort, 1824. 2 vols. Second edition. $300.

MARSHALL, John. *Opinion of the Supreme Court . . . , in the Case of Samuel Worcester Versus the State of Georgia.* Washington, 1832. 39 pages. $200. Second edition, same date. 20 pages. $150.

MARSHALL, John. *The Life of George Washington . . .* Philadelphia, 1804–47. 5 vols. plus atlas containing 10 maps. $1,250.

MARSHALL, L. G. *The Arabian Art of Taming and Training Wild and Vicious Horses.* (Circleville, Ohio) 1857. 36 pages, wraps. $300.

MARSHALL, Paule. *Brown Girl, Brownstones.* New York, 1959. Author's first book. $250. London, 1960. $125.

MARSHALL, William I. *Acquisition of Oregon, and the Long Suppressed Evidence About Marcus Whitman.* (Seattle) 1911. Portrait. 2 vols., green cloth. $250.

MARTIAL Achievements of Great Britain and Her Allies from 1799 to 1815 (The). London (1814–15). 52 colored plates. $3,000. London (about 1835). 51 color plates. $1,750.

MARTIN, Aaron. *An Attempt to Show the Inconsistency of Slave-Holding, with the Religion of the Gospel.* Lexington, Ky., 1807. 16 pages. $2,500.

MARTIN, H.B. *Fifty Years of American Golf.* New York, 1936. Signed limited edition. $500. Trade. $300.

MARTIN, H.B. *Garden City Golf Club 1899–1949.* Garden City, 1949. Limited to 600 copies. $150.

MARTIN, H.B., and HALLIDAY, A.B. *St. Andrews* [New York] *Golf Club 1888–1938.* Hastings-on-Hudson, N.Y., 1938. One of 500 signed copies. $200.

MARTIN Faber, the Story of a Criminal. New York, 1838. 2 vols., in original cloth. (By William Gilmore Simms.) $400.

MARTIN, John Stuart. *The Curious History of the Golf Ball.* New York, 1968. 500 signed copies. $200.

MARTINEAU, Harriet. *The English Lakes.* Windermere, 1858. With folding map and plates. $400.

MARTINEAU, Harriet. *Retrospect of Western Travel.* London, 1838. 3 vols., in original cloth. $350. New York, 1838. 2 vols., in original half linen. $250.

MARTINEAU, Harriet. *Society in America.* London, 1837. 3 vols., in original cloth. $350. New York, 1837. 2 vols., in original cloth. $250.

MARVEL, Ik. *Fresh Gleanings.* New York, 1847. (By Donald G. Mitchell.) 2 vols., printed wraps. $125. Or 1 volume in cloth. $75.

MARVIN, Frederic R. *Yukon Overland: The Gold-Digger's Handbook.* Cincinnati, 1898. Folding map, 18 plates. Printed orange wraps. $250.

MARX, Groucho. *Beds.* New York, 1930. With publisher's colophon on copyright page. $250.

MARX, Karl. *Capital.* Humboldt Publishing Co. New York (1886). First edition in English. $1,250. London, 1887. 2 vols., red cloth. $1,250. New York, 1889. $500.

MARY BARTON; A Tale of Manchester Life. London, 1848. (By Elizabeth C. Gaskell.) 2 vols., mulberry cloth. Author's first book. $500.

MASEFIELD, John. *Ballads.* London. 1903. Printed wraps. No. 13 of "The Vigo Cabinet Series." $150.

MASEFIELD, John. *The Coming of Christ.* London, 1928. Boards and vellum. One of 275 signed. In dustwrapper. $200.

MASEFIELD, John. *John M. Synge: A Few Personal Recollections.* Cuala Press. Dundrum, Ireland, 1915. Boards and linen. One of 350. $150. Signed by W. B. Yeats on colophon page. $350.

MASEFIELD, John. *Salt Water Ballads.* London, 1902. Author's first book. Blue buckram. First issue, with Grant Richards imprint on title page. $500. Second issue with "Elkin Mathews" (much less common). $350.

MASEFIELD, John. *Some Memories of W. B. Yeats.* Cuala Press. Dublin, 1940. Boards and linen. One of 370. In tissue dustwrapper. $250.

MASON, Bobbie Ann. *Nabokov's Garden.* Ann Arbor (1974). Author's first book, (precedes *The Girl Sleuth*). Cloth. $175. Wraps. $40.

MASON, George Henry. *The Costume of China.* London, 1800. Folio with 60 hand-colored plates. $2,000. London, 1804. $1,500. London, 1806. $1,000.

MASON, John. *More Papers Hand Made by John Mason.* Leicester, 1967. Numbered and signed. $450.

MASON, Richard Lee. *Narrative of Richard Lee Mason in the Pioneer West.* New York (1915). Half leather. One of 160. $100. One of 10 on vellum. $200.

MASON, Van Wyck. *The Vesper Service Murders.* New York, 1931. Author's first book. $150.

MASON, Otis T. *Aboriginal American Basketry . . .* Washington, 1902, 248 plates, 2 vols. $400.

MASON, Otis T. *Indian Basketry.* New York, 1904. Illustrated, including color plates. 2 vols., pictorial buckram. $500.

MASON, Z. H. *A General Description of Orange County, Florida.* Orlando (1881). Map. 56 pages, wraps. $300.

MASQUE of Poets (A). Boston, 1878. Black or red cloth. With Emily Dickinson's poem "Success," her only book appearance in her lifetime. $300.

MASSEY, W. *The Origin and Progress of Letters.* London, 1763. Five foldout plates in first section and one foldout plate at the end of the second section. $750.

MASSON, L. F. R. *Les Bourgeois de la Compagnie du Nord-Ouest.* Quebec, 1889–90. Folding map. 2 vols., green-and-orange wraps. $750.

MASTERS, Edgar Lee. See Ford, Webster; Wallace, Dexter.

MASTERS, Edgar Lee. *A Book of Verses.* Chicago, 1898. Gray boards. Author's first book. $450.

MASTERS, Edgar Lee. *Gettysburg, Manila, Acoma.* New York, 1930. Cloth. One of 375 signed. In dustwrapper and slipcase. $200.

MASTERS, Edgar Lee. *The Leaves of the Tree.* Chicago, 1909. Printed wraps. $100.

MASTERS, Edgar Lee. *Lee: A Dramatic Poem.* New York, 1926. One of 250 signed. Issued without dustwrapper. $250. Trade edition in dustwrapper. $100.

MASTERS, Edgar Lee. *Lincoln: The Man.* New York, 1931. Illustrated. Half vellum and cloth. One of 150 signed. In glassine dustwrapper. $300.

MASTERS, Edgar Lee. *The New Spoon River.* New York, 1924. Vellum and boards. One of 360 signed. $200.

MASTERS, Edgar Lee. *Spoon River Anthology.* New York, 1915. Blue cloth. First issue, measuring exactly ⅞ inch across top of book. $400. Limited Editions Club, New York, 1942. Illustrated. Buckram. In slipcase. $175.

MASTERS, John. *The Compleat Indian Angler.* London, 1938. Author's first book. $150.

MATHER, E. Powys. *Procreant Hymn.* Golden Cockerel Press. Waltham St. Lawrence, England, 1916. Engravings by Eric Gill. Buckram. One of 200. $1,000.

MATHER, Increase. *The Mystery of Israel's Salvation.* (London) 1669. Author's first book. $3,500.

MATHERS, John, and A Solid Gentleman. *The History of Mr. John Decastro . . .* London, 1815. (By George Colman, the younger.) 4 vols. $200.

MATHESON, Richard. *Born of Man and Woman.* Philadelphia, 1954. Author's first book. $300.

MATHESON, Richard. *Hell House.* New York (1971). $150.

MATHESON, Richard. *A Stir of Echoes.* Philadelphia (1958). $150.

MATHEWS, A. E. *Canyon City, Colorado, and Its Surroundings.* New York, 1870. Map. 5 plates. $4,000.

MATHEWS, A. E. *Pencil Sketches of Colorado.* (New York) 1866. 23 plates in color. $7,500. Facsimile reprint. (Denver, 1961.) Oblong folio, cloth. $150.

MATHEWS, A. E. *Pencil Sketches of Montana.* New York, 1868. 31 plates (4 folding). $7,500.

MATHEWS, Alfred E. *Gems of Rocky Mountain Scenery.* New York, 1869. 20 plates. $3,000.

MATHEWS, Alfred E. *Interesting Narrative; Being a Journal of the Flight of Alfred E. Mathews, of Stark Co., Ohio, from the State of Texas, etc.* (New Philadelphia, Ohio), 1861. 34 pages, sewn. $1,750.

MATHEWS, Edward J. *Crossing the Plains . . . in '59.* No-place, 1930. Issued without dustwrapper. $600.

MATHEWS, Mrs. M. M. *Ten Years in Nevada.* Buffalo, N.Y., 1880. Illustrated. Leather, or cloth. $500.

MATHISON, Thomas. *The Goff: A Heroi-Comical Poem in Three Cantos.* Edinburgh, 1743. Wraps. $15,000.

MATSELL, George W. *Vocabulum; or, the Rogue's Lexicon.* New York (1859). Cloth. $300.

MATSON, N. *French and Indians of the Illinois River.* Princeton, Ill., 1874. Frontispiece (an original signed photograph). Green cloth. $300.

MATSON, N. *Memories of Shaubena.* Chicago, 1878. Illustrated. $200.

MATTHEWS, Sallie Reynolds. *Interwoven, a Pioneer Chronicle . . .* Houston, 1936. Portrait. Orange suede. First binding. $400.

MATTHEWS, William. *Modern Bookbinding Practically Considered* . . . New York, 1889. 8 full-page plates. One of 300 copies. $225.

MATTHIESSEN, Peter. *At Play in the Fields of the Lord.* New York (1965). $100.

MATTHIESSEN, Peter. *In the Spirit of Crazy Horse.* New York (1983). (This book was recalled by the publisher.) $150.

MATTHIESSEN, Peter. *Race Rock.* New York (1954). Author's first book. $175.

MATTHIESSEN, Peter. *Wildlife in America.* New York, 1959. $150.

MATURIN, Charles Robert. See *Melmoth the Wanderer.*

MATURIN, Charles Robert. *Women; Or, Pour et Contre: A Tale.* Edinburgh, 1818. 3 vols. $600.

MAUGHAM, Robin. *The 1946 Ms.* London, 1943. Author's first book. $150.

MAUGHAM, W. Somerset. *Ah King: Six Stories.* London (1933). Blue cloth. $125. Buckram. One of 175 signed. In slipcase. $300. Garden City, 1933. $100.

MAUGHAM, W. Somerset. *Ashenden, or The British Agent.* London, 1928. Blue-gray cloth. $1,250. Garden City, 1928. $400.

MAUGHAM, W. Somerset. *Cakes and Ale.* London (1930). Blue cloth. Presumed first state with "won" instead of "won't" in line 14 of page 147. $200. Second issue, corrected. $150. Garden City, 1930. $100. London (1954). Decorations by Graham Sutherland. Boards and leather. One of 1,000 signed. In slipcase. $500.

MAUGHAM, W. Somerset. *The Explorer.* London, 1908 (actually 1907). $250. New York, 1909. $175.

MAUGHAM, W. Somerset. *The Gentleman in the Parlour.* London (1930). $250.

MAUGHAM, W. Somerset. *The Hero.* London, 1901. Red cloth. $350.

MAUGHAM, W. Somerset. *The Land of the Blessed Virgin.* London, 1905. $400.

MAUGHAM, W. Somerset. *Liza of Lambeth.* London, 1897. Decorated green cloth. Author's first book. $750. London, 1947. Vellum and boards. Jubilee edition. One of 1,000 signed. In dustwrapper. $300.

MAUGHAM, W. Somerset. *The Magician.* London, 1908. $250. New York, 1909. $200.

MAUGHAM, W. Somerset. *The Making of a Saint.* Boston, 1898. First issue, with "In Press" under this title in ads and in pictorial cloth with spine lettering in gold. $350. Second issue without "In Press" and spine in gold and black or black only. $250.

MAUGHAM, W. Somerset. *A Man of Honour.* London, 1903. Printed wraps. Chapman & Hall. $400. With "Literary Supplement" on cover. $750.

MAUGHAM, W. Somerset. *Mrs. Craddock.* London, 1902. $300.

MAUGHAM, W. Somerset. *The Moon and Sixpence.* London (1919). Sage green cloth. No statement of edition, first issue, with 4 pages of ads, including a list of 6 (not

7) novels by Eden Phillpotts. In dustwrapper. $1,000. Without dustwrapper. $200. New York (1919). Green cloth, with "Maugham" on cover ("Maughan" spelling a variant per Stott), In dustwrapper. $850. Without dustwrapper. $150.

MAUGHAM, W. Somerset. *My South Sea Island.* Chicago, 1936. Wraps. First issue, with "Sommerset" on title page. $850. Second issue, error corrected. One of 50. $350.

MAUGHAM, W. Somerset. *Of Human Bondage.* Doran, New York (1915). Green cloth. First issue, without Doran monogram on copyright page, weighing 33½ ounces and misprint in line 4 of page 257. $600. Second issue corrects page 257 and weighs 30 ounces. $300. London (1915). Blue cloth. First English edition. $500. Garden City, 1936. Illustrated by Schwabs. Buckram. First illustrated edition. One of 751 signed. In dustwrapper and slipcase. $450. Limited Editions Club, New York, 1938. Edited by Theodore Dreiser. Illustrated by John Sloan. 2 vols. In slipcase. $600.

MAUGHAM, W. Somerset. *Of Human Bondage; With a Digression on the Art of Fiction.* (Washington) 1946. Printed boards. One of 500 signed. Issued without dustwrapper. $200.

MAUGHAM, W. Somerset. *The Painted Veil.* New York (1925). $200. Boards. One of 250 signed. In dustwrapper. $350. London (1925). Blue cloth. First English edition, first issue, 8 books listed on verso of half title. $250. With 26 titles listed on verso of half title. $150.

MAUGHAM, W. Somerset. *The Razor's Edge.* Garden City, 1944. Buckram. One of 750 signed. Issued without dustwrapper. In slipcase. $300. Trade edition. $150. London (1944). $200.

MAUGHAM, W. Somerset. *The Summing Up.* London (1938). $150. Garden City, 1938. $100. New York, 1954. Buckram. One of 391 signed. In slipcase. $250.

MAUGHAM, W. Somerset. *A Writer's Notebook.* London (1949). Blue buckram, vellum spine. One of 1,000 signed. In slipcase. $350. Trade edition in first issue dustwrapper listing "Maughamiana" on back flap. $75. Garden City, 1949. One of 1,000 signed. In slipcase. $175. Trade. $60.

MAULDIN, Bill. *Mud, Mules and Mountains.* (Italy), 1944. Introduction by Ernie Pyle. 48 pages, wraps. $150.

MAULDIN, William Henry (Bill). *Star Spangled Banter.* San Antonio, 1941. Pictorial wraps. The cartoonist's first book. $200.

MAUND, Benjamin. *The Botanic Garden.* 1825 (–1850). 18 vols. in 16 including supplements. 312 hand-colored plates. $12,000.

MAURELLE, Don Antonio. *Abstract of a Narrative of an Interesting Voyage from Manilla to San Blas . . .* Boston, 1801. $450.

MAUROIS, André. *Ariel: A Shelley Romance.* (London), 1935. Penguin Books. Wraps. First edition of the first Penguin paperback. In dustwrapper. $150.

MAUROIS, André. *The Silence of Colonel Bramble.* London, 1919. Author's first English publication. In dustwrapper. $200. New York, 1920. $150.

MAURY, M. F. *The Physical Geography of the Sea.* New York, 1855. 12 plates. $600.

MAVOR, William. *The English Spelling-Book.* London, 1885. Illustrated by Kate Greenaway. Pictorial boards. First Greenaway edition. $200.

MAW, George. *A Monograph of the Genus Crocus . . .* London, 1886. Cloth, with a colored double-page map, 2 double-page tables, and 81 hand-colored plates. $4,000.

MAW, Henry Lister. *Journal of a Passage from the Pacific to the Atlantic . . .* London, 1829. Folding map. $750.

MAWE, John. *Travels in the Interior of Brazil.* London, 1812. Map, 8 plates. $750. Philadelphia, 1816. Illustrated. $400. London, 1821. Map, 5 color plates. Second edition. $500.

MAXIMILIAN, Prince of Wied. *Travels in Brazil . . .* London, 1820. Portrait, folding map, and 9 plates. First English edition. $1,000.

MAXIMILIAN, Prince of Wied. *Travels in the Interior of North America.* London, 1843–44. Translated by H. E. Lloyd. Folding map, 81 colored vignettes and plates. 2 vols. (text plus atlas folio volume). $150,000 or more. (Copy in contemporary calf for 110,000 pounds at Auction in 1988.)

MAXWELL, William. *Bright Center of Heaven.* New York, 1934. Author's first book. $350. Toronto, 1934. $150.

MAXWELL, William. *They Came Like Swallows.* New York, 1937. First edition stated. $150. Toronto, 1937. $75.

MAXWELL, William Henry. *Life and Times of the Right Honourable William Henry Smith, M.P . . .* Edinburgh/London, 1893. 2 vols. 25 illustrations. $150.

MAY, Robert L. *Rudolph the Red-Nosed Reindeer.* (Chicago) 1939. Illustrated in color by Denver Gillen. Pictorial orange wraps. (Christmas giveaway for Montgomery Ward.) $300.

MAYER, Alfred M. (editor). *Sport with Gun and Rod . . . in American Woods and Waters.* Edinburgh, 1884. Illustrated. 2 vols., half leather. $400.

MAYER, Luigi. *Views in the Ottoman Dominions . . .* London, 1810. 71 colored plates. 2 or 3 vols., folio. $6,000.

MAYHEW, Augustus. *Paved with Gold, or The Romance and Reality of London Streets.* London (1857–58). Illustrated by Hablot K. Browne. 13 parts, wraps. $600. London, 1858. Cloth. First book edition. $200.

MAYHEW, Experience. *Indian Narratives.* Boston (1829). Frontispiece. Half leather and boards. Issued without dustwrapper. First American edition. $200.

MAYHEW, Henry. *London Labour and the London Poor with Those That Will Not Work.* London, 1862. 4 vols. $750.

MAYNARD, Charles J. *An Atlas of Plates from the Directory to the Birds of Eastern North America.* West Newton, Mass., 1905. Wraps. $600.

MAYNARD, Charles J. *The Butterflies of New England.* Boston, 1886. 8 hand-colored lithographs. Half morocco. $350.

MAYO, Robert. *Political Sketches of Eight Years in Washington.* Baltimore, 1839. Cloth. Issued without dustwrapper. $275.

McADAM, R. W. *Chickasaws and Choctaws.* Comprising the Treaties of 1855 and 1866. Ardmore, Okla., 1891. 67 pages, wraps. $375.

McAFEE, Robert B. See *History of the Late War in the Western Country.*

McALMON, Robert. *Being Geniuses Together.* London (1938). Blue cloth. First edition not stated. $1,250.

McALMON, Robert. *A Companion Volume.* Contact Editions. (Paris, 1923.) Gray wraps. $600.

McALMON, Robert. *Distinguished Air (Grim Fairy Tales).* Contact Editions. Paris, 1925. Half leather. One of 103 on paper. $1,000. One of 12 on vellum. $2,500.

McALMON, Robert. *Explorations.* Egoist Press. London, 1921. Author's first book. Issued without dustwrapper. $750.

McALMON, Robert. *A Hasty Bunch.* Contact Editions. (Paris, 1922.) Wraps. $600.

McALMON, Robert. *Not Alone Lost.* New Directions. Norfolk, Conn. (1937). $250.

McALMON, Robert. *Post-Adolescence.* Contact Editions. (Paris, 1923.) Wraps. First edition not stated. In glassine dustwrapper. $500.

McALMON. Robert. *The Portrait of a Generation.* Contact Editions. Paris (1926). Stiff wraps. One of 200. $850. Vellum. One of 10 signed. $2,000.

McCAFFREY, Anne. *Restoree.* New York (1967). "First Printing: September 1967." Wraps. Author's first book. $40. London (1968). First hardcover. $200.

McCAIN, Charles W. *History of the S.S. "Beaver."* Vancouver, 1804. Illustrated. Blue cloth. $175.

McCALL, Ansel J. *Pick and Pan: Trip to the Diggins in 1849.* Bath, N.Y., 1889. Printed wraps. $650.

McCALL, George A. *Letters from the Frontiers.* Philadelphia, 1868. $400.

McCALL, Hugh. *The History of Georgia.* Savannah, 1811–16. 2 vols. $1,000.

McCALLA, William L. *Adventures in Texas.* Philadelphia, 1841. Black cloth. $1,250.

McCARTER, Margaret H. *Price of the Prairie.* Chicago, 1910. In dustwrapper. $150.

McCARTER, Margaret H. *Winning the Wilderness.* New York, 1914. In dustwrapper. $125.

McCARTHY, Mary. See Kaltenborn, H. V.

McCARTHY, Mary. *The Company She Keeps.* (New York), 1942. Author's first book under her own name. $150.

McCARTHY, Mary. *Venice Observed.* Paris/New York (1956). Illustrated. $100.

McCAULEY, J. E. *A Stove-Up Cowboy's Story.* Dallas, 1943. One of 700 copies. $375.

McCLELLAN, Henry B. *The Life and Campaigns of Maj. Gen. J.E.B. Stuart.* Boston, 1885. Portrait and 7 folding maps. $250.

McCLELLAND, Nancy. *Duncan Phyfe . . .* New York (1939). One of 350 signed. In slipcase. $250.

McCLELLAND, Nancy. *Historic Wallpapers . . .* Philadelphia, 1924. Illustrated, including color plates. Half cloth. Limited edition. $450. Trade. $300.

McCLINTOCK, John S. *Pioneer Days in the Black Hills.* Deadwood (1939). Edited by Edward Senn. Illustrated. Cloth. Issued without dustwrapper. $200.

McCLINTOCK, Walter. *Old Indian Trails.* Boston, 1923. 28 plates, including 4 in color. Pictorial cloth. Issued without dustwrapper. $175.

McCLINTOCK, Walter. *The Old North Trail.* London, 1910. Folding map, 9 color plates. $100.

McCLURE, Michael. *The Cherub.* Black Sparrow Press. Los Angeles, 1970. Full leather. One of 26 signed, with a drawing by the author. $250. Boards. One of 250 signed. $100.

McCLURE, Michael. *Hail Thee Who Play.* Black Sparrow Press. Los Angeles, 1968. Printed yellow boards and cloth. One of 75 signed, with a drawing by the author. $150. Printed wraps. One of 250 signed. $60.

McCLURE, Michael. *Passage.* Big Sur, Calif., 1956. Stiff wraps. Author's first book. Published as *Jargon 20.* One of 200. $450.

McCLURE, Michael. *The Sermons of Jean Harlow & The Curses of Billy the Kid.* San Francisco, 1968. Wraps. $50. Later, boards. One of 50 signed. $200.

McCLURE, S. S. *My Autobiography.* New York (1914). (Ghost-written by Willa Cather.) First issue, with "Sept, 1914" on copyright page and an extraneous line 13 on page 239. "H.H. Rogers . . ." $300. Second issue corrects page 239 with cancel page. $250. (Second printing had "May 1914" on copyright page.)

McCOLLUM, William. *California As I Saw It.* Buffalo, 1850. 72 pages, wraps. $7,500.

McCONKEY, Mrs. Harriet E. (Bishop). *Dakota War Whoop; or, Indian Massacres and War in Minnesota.* St. Paul, 1863. 6 portraits. Cloth. $350.

McCONNELL, H. H. *Five Years a Cavalryman.* Jacksboro, Tex., 1889. Text on pink paper. $200.

McCONNELL, Joseph Carroll. *The West Texas Frontier.* Jacksboro, Tex. 1933. $150.

McCOOK, Henry C. *American Spiders and Their Spinningwork.* London, 1889–93. Portrait, 35 hand-colored plates. 3 vols. "Author's Edition." One of 250. $1,250. Philadelphia, 1889–93. 3 vols. One of 750. $750.

McCORKLE, John, and BARTON, O. S. *Three Years with Quantrell.* Armstrong, Mo. (1914). 11 plates. Stiff maroon wraps. $350.

McCORMICK, Richard C. *Arizona: Its Resources and Prospects.* New York, 1865. Folding map. 22 pages, buff printed wraps. $200.

McCORMICK, S. J. *Almanac for the Year 1864; Containing Useful Information Relative to the Population, Progress and Resources of Oregon, Washington and Idaho.* Portland (1863). 56 pages, wraps. $500.

McCOY, Horace. *They Shoot Horses, Don't They?* New York, 1935. Author's first book. Tan cloth. $350. London, 1935. $250.

McCOY, Isaac. *History of Baptist Indian Missions . . .* Washington, 1840. In original cloth. $500.

McCOY, Isaac. *Remarks on the Practicability of Indian Reform.* Boston, 1827. 47 pages, wraps. $400. Half leather. $350. New York, 1829. Half leather. Second edition. $300.

McCOY, Isaac. *Remove Indians Westward.* (Caption title.) (Washington), 1829. 48 pages $150.

McCOY, James C. *Jesuit Relations of Canada, 1632–1673, A Bibliography.* Paris, 1937. 350 numbered copies. $250.

McCOY, Joseph G. *Historic Sketches of the Cattle Trade of the West and Southwest.* Kansas City, 1874. Portraits and plates. Pictorial cloth. $1,500.

McCRACKEN, Harold. *The American Cowboy.* Garden City, 1973. Illustrated, including color plates. Cloth. One of 300 signed. In slipcase. $250. Trade. $50.

McCRACKEN, Harold. *The Charles M. Russell Book.* Garden City, 1957. Illustrated, including color plates. One of 250 signed. Leather. $750. Trade in buckram. $100.

McCRACKEN, Harold. *The Frank Tenney Johnson Book.* Garden City, 1974. Illustrated, including color plates, by Johnson. One of 350 signed, with an extra color plate. In slipcase. $500.

McCRACKEN, Harold. *The Frederic Remington Book.* Garden City, 1966. Illustrated. Leather. One of 500 signed. In slipcase. $600.

McCRACKEN, Harold. *Frederic Remington's Own West.* New York, 1960. Illustrated. Calf. One of 167 signed. In slipcase. $500.

McCRACKEN, Harold. *George Catlin and the Old Frontier.* New York, 1959. Illustrated, including colored plates. Decorated leather. One of 250, with extra color plate tipped in at front. In slipcase. $500. Trade. $75.

McCREERY, John. *The Press, A Poem.* Liverpool, 1803. $350.

McCULLERS, Carson. *The Ballad of the Sad Cafe.* Boston, 1951. $150.

McCULLERS, Carson. *The Heart Is a Lonely Hunter.* Boston, 1940. Cloth. Author's first book. $400.

McCULLERS, Carson. *The Member of the Wedding.* Boston, 1946. Cloth. $150.

McCULLERS, Carson. *Reflections in a Golden Eye.* (Boston) 1941. First issue with clear cellophane window on front panel of dustwrapper. $350. Second issue, printed dustwrapper. $150.

McCULLEY, Johnson. *Mark of Zorro.* New York, 1924. $125.

McCULLEY, Johnson. *John Standon of Texas.* New York, 1924. $100.

McCULLOUGH, Colleen. *Tim.* New York (1974). Author's first book. $75.

McCUTCHEON, George Barr. See Greaves, Richard.

McCUTCHEON, George Barr. *A Fool and His Money.* New York, 1913. One of 50 signed. $150.

McCUTCHEON, George Barr. *Graustark.* Chicago, 1901. Pictorial cloth. Author's first book. First issue, with "Noble" instead of "Lorry" in line 6 of page 150. $100.

McCUTCHEON, George Barr. *The Prince of Graustark.* New York, 1914. Color illustrations by A. I. Keller. Boards. One of 40 signed. $200. Trade. $75.

McCUTCHEON, John T. *Bird Center.* Chicago, 1904. Illustrated. Pictorial boards and cloth. $100.

McDANIELD, H. F., and TAYLOR, N. A. *The Coming Empire: or, 2,000 miles in Texas on Horseback.* New York (1877). $150.

McDONALD, Charles B. *Scotland's Gift, Golf: Reminiscenses.* New York, 1928. Limited signed edition in slipcase. $1,000. Trade. $500.

McDONALD, Frank V. (editor). *Notes Preparatory to a Biography of Richard Hayes McDonald. Vol. 1.* (All published.) Cambridge, Mass., 1881. Illustrated. Brown cloth. One of 150. $750.

McDONALD, John. *Biographical Sketches of Gen. Nathaniel Massie, Gen. Duncan McArthur, Capt. William Wells, and Gen. Simon Kenton.* Cincinnati, 1838. In original calf. $500.

McELROY, Joseph. *Ship Rock. A Place.* Concord, N.H. (1980). 13 copies specially bound for presentation, quarter leather and boards. $250. 26 signed and lettered copies. $150. 200 signed and numbered copies. $75.

McELROY, Joseph. *A Smuggler's Bible.* New York (1966). Author's first book. $200. Toronto, 1966. $100. London (1968). $100.

McEWAN, Ian. *First Love, Last Rites.* London, 1975. Author's first book. $75.

McFEE, William. *Casuals of the Sea.* London, 1916. Frontispiece in color. $125.

McFEE, William. *The Harbourmaster.* Garden City, 1931. Boards and cloth. One of 377 signed. In slipcase. $175. Garden City, 1932. $75.

McFEE, William. *Iron Men and Wooden Ships.* New York, 1924. Woodcuts by Edward A. Wilson. Folio, boards. One of 200 signed. In slipcase. $200.

McFEE, William. *Letters from an Ocean Tramp.* London, 1908. Colored frontispiece. Blue cloth. Author's first book. First state, with "Cassell & Co." at foot of spine. $125.

McGAW, James F. *Philip Seymour, or, Pioneer Life in Richland County, Ohio.* Mansfield, Ohio, 1858. 2 plates. $200.

McGEE, I., and Maria. *The Mormon Endowment: A Secret Drama, or Conspiracy in the Nauvoo Temple in 1846.* Syracuse, 1847. Illustrated. 24 pages, pictorial wraps. (2 known copies.) $3,500 or more.

McGEE, Joseph H. *Story of the Grand River Country, 1821–1905.* (Gallatin, Mo., 1909.) Portrait. Brown printed wraps. $125.

McGINLEY, Phyllis. *On the Contrary.* Garden City, 1934. Author's first book. $150.

McGLASHAN, C. F. *History of the Donner Party: A Tragedy of the Sierras.* Truckee, Calif. (1879). $750. San Francisco, 1880. Illustrated. Second edition. $350.

McGOVAN, James. *Brought to Bay.* Edinburgh, 1878. Author's first book. $200.

McGOWAN, Edward. *Narrative of Edward McGowan.* San Francisco, 1857. Illustrated. Pictorial wraps. $1,000. San Francisco, 1917. (As *Narrative of Ned McGowan.*) One of 200. $200.

McGREEVY, Thomas. *Introduction To . . . Da Vinci.* London, 1929. Author's first book, 875 numbered copies. (McGreevy's translation of Valéry's work.) $100.

McGUANE, Thomas. *The Bushwhacked Piano.* New York (1971). $100.

McGUANE, Thomas. *In The Crazies.* Seattle, 1984. 185 signed copies with large portfolio of 10 various-sized plates signed and numbered by artist Russell Chatham. Book signed by both McGuane and Chatham. $1,500.

McGUANE, Thomas. *The Sporting Club.* New York (1968). Author's first book. $125.

McILVAINE, William, Jr. *Sketches of Scenery and Notes of Personal Adventure, in California and Mexico.* Philadelphia, 1850. 16 plates, including engraved title page. Purplish cloth. $2,500. San Francisco, 1951. Grabhorn printing. Folio, half cloth. One of 400. $200.

McINTIRE, Jim. *Early Days in Texas: A Trip to Hell and Heaven.* Kansas City, Mo. (1902). 16 plates, pictorial cloth. $300.

McKAY, Claude. *Banjo.* New York, 1929. Decorated boards and cloth. $300.

McKAY, Claude. *Gingertown.* New York, 1932. $400.

McKAY, Claude. *Harlem Shadows: The Poems of Claude McKay.* New York (1922). Boards and cloth, paper label. $600.

McKAY, Claude. *A Long Way from Home.* New York (1937). Green cloth. $250.

McKAY, Claude. *Songs of Jamaica.* Kingston, 1912. Wraps over boards. Author's first book. $2,500.

McKAY, Claude. *Spring in New Hampshire and Other Poems.* London, 1920. Wraps. $500.

McKAY, George L. *American Book Auction Catalogues 1713–1934, A Union List.* New York, 1937. $225.

McKAY, George L. *A Stevenson Library Catalogue . . . Volumes One and Two.* New Haven, 1951, 1952. 2 vols. One of 500 copies. $300.

McKAY, William, and ROBERTS, W. *John Hoppner, R.A.* London, 1909. $300. London, 1909–14. 2 vols., buckram (including supplement). $400.

McKEE, James Cooper. *Narrative of the Surrender of a Command of U.S. Forces at Fort Fillmore, N.M., in July A.D. 1861.* (Cover title.) New York, 1881. 30 pages, printed self-wraps. Second edition. $500. (The rare first edition appeared in Prescott, Arizona Territory, in 1878. Estimated value: $2,000 or more.)

McKEE, Dr. W. H. *The Territory of New Mexico and Its Resources.* New York, 1866. Map. 12 pages, printed wraps. $1,250.

McKENNEY, Thomas L. *Sketches of a Tour to the Lakes.* Baltimore, 1827. 29 full-page engravings, some in color. $400.

McKENNEY, Thomas L., and HALL, James. *History of the Indian Tribes of North America.* Biddle, Philadelphia, 1836–38–44. Map, 120 colored plates and list of subscribers. 3 vols., folio, cloth, or half leather. $20,000. Many early editions are still prized for the quality of the Indian portraits, and prices for these editions have ranged in recent years from $7,500 to $15,000 at auction. A modern version, in small quarto format: Edinburgh, 1933–34. 3 vols., blue cloth. In dustwrappers. Slipcase. $450.

McKIM, Randolph H. *A Soldier's Recollections: Leaves from the Diary of a Young Confederate.* New York, 1911. $150.

McKNIGHT, George S. *California 49er: Travels from Perrysburg to California.* (Cover title.) Perrysburg, Ohio, 1903. 27 pages, printed red wraps. $350.

McKUEN, Rod. *And Autumn Came.* New York (1954). Author's first book. $100.

McLEOD, Donald. *A Brief Review of the Settlement of Upper Canada.* Cleveland, 1841. Cloth, paper label. $800.

McLEOD, Donald. *History of Wiskonsan, from Its First Discovery to the Present Period.* Buffalo, 1846. 4 plates, folding map. $500. (Howes notes some copies have plates and no map and others map and no plates.) Without map. $250.

McLUHAN, Herbert Marshall. *The Mechanical Bride.* New York (1951). Cloth. Author's first book. $150. Reprinted in "Ltd. Edition" (dustwrapper flap). Priced at $12.50 versus $4.50 for original. White endpapers and white lettering on cover versus yellow endpaper and gold lettering on reprint. Copyright pages the same.

McMASTER, S. W. *Sixty Years on the Upper Mississippi . . .* Rock Island, Ill., 1893 (printer's foreword dated Galena, Ill., 1895). 300 pages, flexible wraps. $300.

McMURTRIE, Douglas C. *Early Printing in New Orleans, 1764–1810.* New Orleans, 1929. Illustrated. Half cloth. One of 410. Issued without dustwrapper. $175.

McMURTRIE, Douglas C. *The Golden Book.* Chicago, 1927. Illustrated. Half morocco. One of 220 signed. $125. Trade in cloth. In dustwrapper. $60.

McMURTRY, Larry. See Ray, Ophelia.

McMURTRY, Larry. *Horseman, Pass By.* New York (1961). Author's first book. $750.

McMURTRY, Larry. *In a Narrow Grave.* Austin, 1968. First edition not stated. First printing with "skycrapers" vs. "skyscrapers" on page 105, line 12, and many other errors. All but 15 reportedly destroyed but seems more common. $1,000. 250 signed and numbered copies. Slipcase. $750. Second printing (edition not stated). $250. Third printing with "B" on copyright page. $100.

McMURTRY, Larry. *It's Always We Rambled: An Essay on Rodeo.* New York, 1974. 300 signed and numbered copies. Issued without dustwrapper. $250.

McMURTRY, Larry. *The Last Picture Show.* New York, 1966. $200.

McMURTRY, Larry. *Leaving Cheyenne.* New York (1963). $750.

McMURTRY, Larry. *Lonesome Dove.* New York (1985). $175.

McNEIL, Samuel. *McNeils [sic] Travels in 1849, to, Through and from the Gold Regions.* Columbus, Ohio, 1850. 40 pages, plain wraps. $7,500 or more.

McPHEE, John. *Alaska—Images of the Country.* San Francisco (1981). 500 signed and numbered copies. Issued without dustwrapper in slipcase. $200. Trade. $60.

McPHEE, John. *A Sense of Where You Are.* New York (1965). Author's first book. $200.

McPHEE, John. *The Headmaster.* New York (1966). $100.

McSHEEHY, H. J. *A Hunt in the Rockies.* Logansport, Ind., 1893. Frontispiece and photographs. 135 pages, printed red wraps. $600.

McWILLIAMS, John. *Recollections . . .* Princeton (about 1920). Portrait. Cloth. $150.

MEAD, Peter B. *An Elementary Treatise on American Grape Culture and Wine Making.* (New York) 1867. $250.

MEADE, L. T. *The Medicine Lady.* London, 1892. Author's first book. $200.

MEANS, James. *Manflight.* Boston, 1891. 29 pages, printed wraps. $250.

MEANS, James. *The Problem of Manflight.* Boston, 1894. Diagrams. 20 pages, pictorial wraps. $250.

MEARES, John. *Voyages Made in the Years 1788 and 1789, From China . . .* London, 1790. 10 maps and plans, 17 illustrations, including frontispiece portrait of Meares. $3,000.

MEEKER, Ezra. *Washington Territory West of the Cascade Mountains.* Olympia, Wash., 1870. 52 pages, printed wraps. $1,000.

MEIKLE, James. *Famous Clyde Yachts, 1880–87.* Glasgow, 1888. 31 colored aquatints, mounted as drawings, with tissue guards. Atlas folio, cloth. $400.

MELANTER. *Poems.* London, 1854. (By R. D. Blackmore, his first book.) $600.

MELINCOURT. London, 1817. By the Author of *Headlong Hall.* (Thomas Love Peacock.) 3 vols. $300.

MELINE, James F. *Two Thousand Miles on Horseback.* New York, 1867. Map. $250.

MELISH, John. *A Geographical Description of the United States . . .* Philadelphia, 1815. 3 maps. $600. Philadelphia, 1816. 5 maps. Second edition. $500. Philadelphia, 1818. 4 maps. Third edition. $500. Philadelphia, 1822. 12 maps. $500.

MELISH, John. *A Military and Topographical Atlas of the United States.* Philadelphia, 1813. 8 maps and plans, 5 folding. $1,250. Philadelphia, 1815. 12 maps and plans, 9 folding and colored in outline. Half leather. $1,250.

MELLICHAMPE: A Legend of the Santee. New York, 1836. (By William Gilmore Simms.) 2 vols., in original cloth, paper labels. $600.

MELMOTH the Wanderer. Edinburgh, 1820. (By Charles Robert Maturin.) 4 vols. $750. Edinburgh, 1821. 4 vols. Second edition. $400.

MELTZER, David. *Round the Poem Box.* Los Angeles, 1969. Leather. One of 26 signed, with an original illustration by the author. $150. One of 125 signed. Issued without dustwrapper. $50.

MELTZER, David, and SCHENKER, Donald. *Poems.* (San Francisco, 1957.) First book for both poets. Glazed white wraps, taped spine (as issued). One of 470. $75. Hardbound. One of 25 signed. $250. 5 signed in blood. $400.

MELVILLE, Herman. See *John Marr and Other Sailors; Timoleon.*

MELVILLE, Herman. *The Apple Tree and Other Sketches.* Princeton, 1922. Boards. One of 175 on handmade paper. In slipcase. $250. Trade without dustwrapper. $75.

MELVILLE, Herman. *Battle-Pieces and Aspects of the War.* New York, 1866. $1,000. (There was no English edition.)

MELVILLE, Herman. *Billy Budd* [and] *Benito Cereno.* Limited Editions Club, New York, 1965. Illustrated. White sailcloth. In slipcase. $75.

MELVILLE, Herman. *Clarel: A Poem and Pilgrimage in the Holy Land.* New York, 1876. 2 vols. $2,000.

MELVILLE, Herman. *The Confidence-Man.* New York, 1857. With Miller and Holman on copyright page. $2,500. London, 1857. Yellow-brown cloth. First English edition, first issue, without "Roberts" in publisher's name below ads on recto of front free endpaper (VAB). $2,000.

MELVILLE, Herman. *Israel Potter.* New York, 1855. Purple-brown or green cloth, yellow endpapers. With spine initials F.Y. & E ornamented with pendants and heading on page 141 "Chapter XVI." (Corrected to "XIV" in second printing.) $2,500. London, 1855. $850.

MELVILLE, Herman. *Mardi: and A Voyage Thither.* London, 1849. 3 vols., pale green cloth, white endpapers with blue designs. $1,250. New York, 1849. 2 vols. First American edition. $1,500.

MELVILLE, Herman. *Moby-Dick; or, The Whale.* New York, 1851. Slate blue, black, brown, or scarlet cloth, orange or marbled endpapers. First American edition, with publisher's circular device blind stamped at center of sides. $15,000 or more. (For first edition, see *The Whale.*) Chicago, 1930. Lakeside Press. Illustrated by Rockwell Kent, 3 vols., silver-decorated cloth. One of 1,000. In aluminum slipcase. $2,500. Trade edition: one volume in dustwrapper. $250. Limited Editions Club, New York, 1943. Illustrated by Boardman Robinson. 2 vols., full morocco. In slipcase. $250. San Francisco, 1979. Illustrated by Barry Moser. Full morocco. One of 250. In slipcase. $3,000.

MELVILLE, Herman. *Narrative of a Four Months' Residence Among the Natives of a Valley of the Marquesas Islands; or, A Peep at Polynesian Life.* London, 1846.

Author's first book. Map. 2 parts, wraps, or cloth (2 parts bound as one). (Published later that year in New York as *Typee*), first issue, with the reading "Pomarea" on page 19, line 1. Wraps. $15,000. Red cloth. $5,000. Second issue: "Pomare." $2,500. London, 1847. Cloth. $750.

MELVILLE, Herman. *Omoo: A Narrative of Adventures in the South Seas.* London, 1847. Map. 2 parts printed gray or brown wraps, or cloth (in one volume). Wraps. $10,000. Red cloth. $2,000. New York, 1847. Frontispiece map, 1 illustration. 2 parts, cream-white wraps, or pictorial cloth (1 vol.). First American edition. Wraps. $5,000. Cloth. $2,000. Limited Editions Club, New York, 1961. Illustrated. White linen. In slipcase. $125.

MELVILLE, Herman. *The Piazza Tales.* New York, 1856. Pale blue cloth. (Schwartz noted that the first copies off the press had yellow endpapers, not mentioned in BAL.) $2,000. London, 1856. First English edition. American sheets with tipped-in title page. $1,000.

MELVILLE, Herman. *Pierre; or, The Ambiguities.* New York, 1852. Cloth. $1,000. Wraps. $2,500. London, 1852. Blue embossed cloth, yellow endpapers. American sheets with tipped-in title page. $600.

MELVILLE, Herman. *Redburn: His First Voyage.* London, 1849. 2 vols., dark blue cloth, white endpapers with the blue pattern (Schwartz). Yellow or white—no priority (BAL). $3,000. New York, 1849. With ads ending on page 10 (BAL). Cloth. $2,000. Wraps. $3,000. (Schwartz had 14-page catalog dated October 1849 as first issue, BAL would seem to call this the second printing.)

MELVILLE, Herman. *Typee: A Peep at Polynesian Life.* New York, 1846. Map frontispiece. 2 parts, thick fawn-colored printed wraps. First American edition of the author's first book *(Narrative of a Four Months' Residence Among the Natives of a Valley of the Marquesas).* $5,000. Cloth (blue or brown), in one volume. First American book edition. $2,000. New York, 1847. Cloth. Revised edition, with 8 pages of ads. $1,000. Limited Editions Club, New York, 1935. Illustrated. Printed boards. In slipcase. $125.

MELVILLE, Herman. *The Whale.* London, 1851. 3 vols., bright-blue and off-white cloth, cream-colored endpapers. (Published later that year in New York as *Moby-Dick.*) $75,000 or more.

MELVILLE, Herman. *White-Jacket; or, the World in a Man-of-War.* London, 1850. 2 vols., light blue cloth. $1,000. New York, 1850. 2 parts, yellow wraps. $7,500. Cloth with "Harper and Brothers" in ornate frame on sides, 6 pages of ads at end and signature mark "T" not on page 433. 1 vol. $1,500. London, 1853. 2 vols. in one, cloth. First English 1-vol. edition. $750.

MEMOIRS of a Fox-Hunting Man. London (1928). (By Siegfried Sassoon.) Blue cloth. First issue, with rough trimmed fore edges. $200. One of 260 signed. $400. London (1929). Illustrated by William Nicholson. Vellum. One of 300 signed. In dustwrapper and slipcase. $750.

MEMOIRS of an Infantry Officer. London (1930). (By Siegfried Sassoon.) Blue cloth. First issue, with untrimmed edges. In dustwrapper. $300. Blue cloth. One of 750 signed. Issued without dustwrapper. $500. London, 1931. Illustrated by Barnett Freedman. Parchment (or vellum) boards. One of 320 signed. In dustwrapper and slipcase. $500. Trade. $125.

MEMOIRS of the Life of the Late John Mytton, Esq. London, 1835. (By C. J. Apperley.) 12 plates in color by John Alken. In original cloth. $1,500. London, 1837. 18

plates. In original cloth. Second edition. $750. London, 1851. 18 plates. Third edition. $600.

MEMOIRS of William Burke, A Soldier of the Revolution, Reformed from Intemperance . . . Hartford, 1837. (By William Burke.) $250.

MEMORANDA: Democratic Vistas. Washington, 1871. (By Walt Whitman.) Light green wraps. $850. (For later printing, see Whitman entry under this title.)

MEMORIAL and Biographical History of Johnson and Hill Counties, Texas. Chicago, 1892. Illustrated. Leather. $450.

MEMORIAL and Biographical History of McLennan, Falls, Bell and Coryell Counties, Texas. Chicago, 1893. Half leather. $450.

MEMORIAL to the President and Congress for the Admission of Wyoming Territory to the Union. Cheyenne, 1889. 75 pages, wraps. $150.

MENCKEN, H. L. See Hatteras, Owen; Hirshberg, Dr. L. K.

MENCKEN, H. L. The American Language. New York, 1919. Black cloth. One of 1,500. In dustwrapper. $400. One of 25 signed. In dustwrapper. $1,500.

MENCKEN, H. L. The Artist. Boston, 1912. Pictorial boards. $250. (Facsimile in 1923 in plain boards [almost cardboard] and dustwrapper, no indication of later printing. $25.)

MENCKEN, H. L. Damn! A Book of Calumny. New York, 1918. In dustwrapper. $600. Without dustwrapper. $150.

MENCKEN, H. L. George Bernard Shaw: His Plays. Boston, 1905. $200.

MENCKEN, H. L. In Defense of Women. New York, 1918. Philip Goodman on title page. No statement of edition, first issue, with publisher's name misspelled "Ppilip." In dustwrapper. $750. Second printing, with name corrected. In dustwrapper. $450.

MENCKEN, H. L. A Little Book in C Major. New York, 1916. $300.

MENCKEN, H. L. Notes on Democracy. New York (1926). $150. One of 200 signed. $400. Vellum. One of 35 on vellum, signed. $1,750.

MENCKEN, H. L. The Philosophy of Friedrich Nietzsche. Boston, 1908. Red cloth. With "Friedrich" omitted on spine. $200.

MENCKEN, H. L. Prejudices: First Series. New York (1919). In dustwrapper. $500. Without dustwrapper. $100. One of 50 signed. In slipcase. $1,000.

MENCKEN, H. L. Prejudices: Second Series. New York (1920). In dustwrapper. $350. Without dustwrapper. $75. One of a few large paper copies, signed. $1,000.

MENCKEN, H. L. Prejudices: Third Series. New York (1922). $300. One of 110 signed. In slipcase. $750.

MENCKEN, H. L. Prejudices: Fourth Series. New York (1924). $250. One of 200 signed. In slipcase. $600.

MENCKEN, H. L. Prejudices: Fifth Series. New York (1926). $250. One of 200 signed. In slipcase. $500.

MENCKEN, H. L. *Prejudices: Sixth Series.* New York (1927). $200. One of 50 on vellum, signed. $1,000. One of 140 on rag paper, signed. $600.

MENCKEN, H. L. *Ventures into Verse.* Baltimore, 1903. Author's first book. Illustrated. Boards, paper label, or brown wraps. Wraps. $5,000. Boards. $7,500. (About 100 copies believed printed in all; 45 noted are in boards, and presumably the rest were in wraps.) Baltimore (1960). Second edition (facsimile of the first edition). One of 250. $60.

MENCKEN, H. L., NATHAN, George Jean, and WRIGHT, Willard Huntington. *Europe After 8:15.* New York, 1914. 7 plates by Thomas Hart Benton. First binding, decorated yellow cloth with blue stamping. $150. Second binding, stamped in gold. $100.

MENDOZA, Daniel. *The Art of Boxing.* London, 1789. $2,500.

MERA, H. P. *The Rain Bird: A Study in Pueblo Design.* Santa Fe, 1937. Illustrated by Tom Lea. Wraps. In dustwrapper. $150.

MERCEDES of Castile: Or, the Voyage to Cathay. Philadelphia, 1840. By the Author of *The Bravo.* 2 vols., in original cloth, paper labels. (By James Fenimore Cooper.) $450.

MERCER, A.S. *The Banditti of the Plains.* (Cheyenne, 1894.) Illustrated. Map. Cloth. $3,000. Grabhorn Press. San Francisco, 1935. Illustrated. Half cloth. One of 1,000. $150.

MERCER, A.S. *Washington Territory: The Great North-West.* Utica, 1865. 38 pages, printed wraps. $1,000.

MEREDITH, George. *Diana of the Crossways.* London, 1885. 3 vols. First complete book edition. $400.

MEREDITH, George. *The Egoist.* London, 1879. 3 vols. $750.

MEREDITH, George. *Farina.* London, 1857. $400.

MEREDITH, George. *Modern Love and Poems of the English Roadside.* London, 1862. Green cloth. $300. Portland, Me., 1891. Heavy printed wraps. First American edition. $125.

MEREDITH, George. *The Ordeal of Richard Feverel.* London, 1859. 3 vols., brown cloth. $850.

MEREDITH, George. *Poems.* London (1851). Author's first book. With half title and with errata slip at end. Purple cloth. $1,000. Green cloth. $750.

MEREDITH, George. *Rhoda Fleming: A Story.* London, 1865. 3 vols., cloth. $600.

MEREDITH, George. *The Shaving of Shagpat.* London, 1856. Brown cloth. $250. Limited Editions Club, New York, 1955. Illustrated. Boards and leather. In slipcase. $50.

MEREDITH, William. *Love Letter from an Impossible Land.* New Haven, 1944. Author's first book. Boards. $125.

MERRICK, George B. *Old Times on the Upper Mississippi.* Cleveland, 1909. Illustrated. Blue cloth. $150.

MERRILL, James. *The Black Swan and Other Poems.* Athens, 1946. Wraps. One of 100. $2,000.

MERRILL, James. *First Poems.* New York, 1951. Author's first commercially published book. One of 990. $200.

MERRILL, James. *Jim's Book: A Collection of Poems and Short Stories.* New York, 1942. Maroon buckram and gray boards. In glassine dustwrapper. $4,000.

MERRIMAN, Henry Seton. *From One Generation to Another.* London, 1892. (By Hugh Stowell Scott.) 2 vols., pea green cloth. $300.

MERRITT, Abraham. *Dwellers in the Mirage.* New York (1932). $200.

MERRITT, Abraham. *The Face in the Abyss.* New York (1931). $225.

MERRITT, Abraham. *The Moon Pool.* New York, 1919. Author's first book. First printing, without ad on page (434). Sheets bulk 3.2 cm. Spine imprint "Putnam" in upper and lower case. $750. Without dustwrapper. $100.

MERRITT, Abraham. *The Ship of Ishtar.* New York, 1926. $250.

MERRYMOUNT; a Romance of the Massachusetts Colony. Boston, 1849. 2 vols. (By John Lathrop Motley.) $250.

MERTON, Thomas. *Elected Silence.* (London, 1949). First U.K. edition of *The Seven-Storey Mountain.* $175.

MERTON, Thomas. *Encounter—Thomas Merton & D.T. Suzuki.* (Monterey, Ky.) 1988. 60 numbered copies. Issued without dustwrapper. $250.

MERTON, Thomas. *Hagia Sophia.* Lexington, 1962. 69 numbered copies. Number of copies signed undetermined. Signed. $850. Unsigned. $500.

MERTON, Thomas. *Original Child Bomb.* New Directions. (New York, 1961.) 500 signed and numbered copies. Issued in plain cellophane wrapper. $350. Trade. Issued without dustwrapper. $40.

MERTON, Thomas. *Prometheus/A Meditation.* (King Library, Lexington, Ky.) 1958. 150 copies. Issued without dustwrapper. $300.

MERTON, Thomas. *Seeds of Contemplation.* (Mt. Vernon, N.Y., 1949.) 100 signed and numbered copies. Issued in brown slipcase. $1,000. Trade. $100.

MERTON, Thomas. *The Seven-Storey Mountain.* New York (1948). Off-white cloth with black lettering in first-state dustwrapper with caption on one of the pictures on back "Author second from the left." $1,000. Assumed second issue in black cloth. In first-state dustwrapper. $500. In second-issue dustwrapper with caption "Author on the left." $400. (Note: last paragraph on back dustwrapper flap of both states mentions Catholic Press Association Award for 1948, which is not on later-printing dustwrappers.) See *Elected Silence* for first U.K. edition.

MERTON, Thomas. *Thirty Poems.* Norfolk (1944). Author's first book. $250. Wraps in dustwrapper. $100.

MERTON, Thomas. *The Tower of Babel.* (*Jubilee,* New York, no-date, 1955?) An offprint. 16 pages in pictorial cover, priced 25 cents on back. $300. (New Directions, Norfolk, 1957). 250 signed and numbered copies. Issued in slipcase. $1,200.

MERWIN, W. S. *The Dancing Bears.* New Haven, 1954. $200.

MERWIN, W. S. *A Mask for Janus.* New Haven, 1952. Foreword by W. H. Auden. Author's first book. Blue boards. $300.

MERYMAN, Richard. *Andrew Wyeth.* Boston, 1968. Color plates. Oblong, two-tone buckram. $350. (Note: There was also a deluxe edition, suede and buckram, 300 signed copies, published at $2,500.)

MESSAGE of the President to Both Houses of Congress. . . . First Session of the 18th Congress. Washington. Giles & Seaton, 1823. (By James Monroe.) 8 leaves. Washington, 1823. Broadside. $4,000 or more. (3 known copies.) Senate issue (simultaneous with House issue). $500. (The Monroe Doctrine.)

METCALF, Samuel L. *A Collection of Some of the Most Interesting Narratives of Indian Warfare in the West.* Lexington, 1821. Portrait. $1,000.

METCALFE, John. *The Feasting Dead.* Sauk City, Wis., 1954. $125.

METCALFE, John. *The Smoking Leg.* London, 1925. Author's first book. $125.

METZDORF, Robert F. *The Tinker Library, A Bibliographical . . .* New Haven (1959). One of 500 copies. $150.

MEW, Charlotte. *The Farmer's Bride.* London, 1916. Author's first book. Wraps. $150.

MEXICO in 1842 . . . to Which Is Added, an Account of Texas and Yucatan, and of the Santa Fe Expedition. New York, 1842. (By George F. Folsom.) Folding map. $750.

MEYER, George. *Autobiography of George Meyer: Across the Plains with an Ox Team in 1849.* Shenandoah, Iowa, 1908. 2 portraits. Printed tan wraps. $350.

MEYERS, John C. *Wrestling from Antiquity to Date.* St. Louis, 1931. Gilt wrestler on cover. No dustwrapper issued. $75.

MEYERS, William H. *Journal of a Cruise to California and the Sandwich Islands.* Grabhorn Press. San Francisco, 1955. Frontispiece, 10 color plates. Folio, half leather. One of 400 for the Book Club of California. In dustwrapper. $400.

MEYERS, William H. *Sketches of California and Hawaii.* Book Club of California. (San Francisco) 1970. Folio, cloth, paper label. One of 450. Issued without dustwrapper. $250.

MEYNELL, Alice. See Thompson, A.C.

MEYNELL, Alice. *Poems.* London, 1893. Brown cloth. First edition (under this title). One of 50 signed. $200. (For first edition, see Thompson, A.C., *Preludes.*) London, 1913. Portrait. Blue boards and cloth. One of 250 signed. $125. Trade in blue buckram. $50.

MEYNELL, Alice. *Ten Poems, 1913–1915.* Westminster (London), 1915. Limp vellum. One of 50. $250.

MEYNELL, Francis. *Typography.* Pelican Press. London, 1923. Illustrated, including color. Buckram. Issued without dustwrapper. $200.

MEYRICK, Samuel R. *A Critical Inquiry into Antient Armour . . .* London, 1824. Illustrated, including hand-colored plates. 3 vols., folio. $1,000.

MEYRICK, Samuel R., and SKELTON, J. *Engraved Illustrations of Antient Arms and Armour, from the Collection of Llewelyn Meyrick.* London, 1830. 2 frontispieces, 2 engraved titles, 2 vignettes, and 151 engraved plates. 2 vols. $500.

MICHAUX, André. *Histoire Des Chênes De L'Amérique.* Paris, 1801. 36 full-page engravings and 7 plates. $2,750.

MICHAUX, François-André. *The North America Sylva.* Paris, 1819. 3 vols. First English edition. 156 stipple-engraved plates printed in colors and finished by hand. $12,000.

MICHAUX, F. A. *Travels to the Westward of the Allegheny Mountains.* London, 1805. Translated by B. Lambert. (Printed by Mawman.) Folding map. First English edition. $600. London, 1805. (Printed by Crosby.) Boards. Second English edition. $400. London, 1805. (Printed by Phillips.) Another translation. Third English edition. $300.

MICHEAUX, Oscar. See *The Conquest.*

MICHENER, James. *Tales of the South Pacific.* New York, 1947. $350. New York, 1950. 1,500 signed copies. Special ABA edition without dustwrapper. $150.

MICHENER, James. *The Unit in the Social Studies.* Cambridge (1940). Author's first book, with Harold M. Long. Wraps. $500.

MIDDLETON, Christopher. *Poems.* London (1944). Author's first book. $75.

MILES, Henry D. *Pugilistica: Being One Hundred and Forty-four Years in the History of British Boxing.* London, 1880. 3 vols. Stated first. $1,000.

MILES, Gen. Nelson A. *Personal Recollections and Observations . . .* Chicago, 1896. Illustrated by Frederic Remington and others. Pictorial cloth, leather, or half leather. First issue, with caption under frontispiece reading "General Miles." $250. Second issue, with rank under portrait as "Maj. Gen." $200.

MILES, William. *Journal of the Sufferings and Hardships of Capt. Parker H. French's Overland Expedition to California.* Chambersburg, Pa., 1851. 24 pages, printed wraps. $3,500.

MILL, John Stuart. *Autobiography.* London, 1873. Green cloth. First issue, without errata. $300. With errata. $250.

MILL, John Stuart. *On Liberty.* London, 1859. $1,000.

MILL, John Stuart. *Principles of Political Economy.* London, 1848. 2 vols. $2,500. London, 1849. 2 vols., cloth. Second edition. $750.

MILL, John Stuart. *The Subjection of Women.* London, 1869. $1,000.

MILLAR, Kenneth. See Macdonald, John Ross, and Macdonald, Ross, pseudonyms.

MILLAR, Kenneth. *Blue City.* New York, 1947. $300.

MILLAR, Kenneth. *The Dark Tunnel.* New York, 1944. Author's first book. $2,500.

MILLAR, Kenneth. *Trouble Follows Me.* New York, 1946. $750.

MILLAR, Margaret. *The Invisible Worm.* Garden City, 1941. Author's first book. $250.

MILLAY, Edna St. Vincent. See Boyd, Nancy; Earle, Ferdinand.

MILLAY, Edna St. Vincent. *The Ballad of the Harp-Weaver.* New York, 1922. Illustrated. Pictorial wraps. One of 500. First edition stated. $200. One of 5 on Japan vellum. $1,500.

MILLAY, Edna St. Vincent. *The Buck in the Snow and Other Poems.* New York, 1928. $100. One of 479 signed. In glassine dustwrapper and slipcase. $200. Boards and vellum. One of 36 on vellum, signed. In glassine dustwrapper and slipcase. $1,250. London, 1928. $100.

MILLAY, Edna St. Vincent. *The Harp-Weaver and Other Poems.* New York, 1923. $150.

MILLAY, Edna St. Vincent. *The King's Henchman.* New York, 1927. Boards and cloth. $100. One of 158 signed. In glassine dustwrapper and slipcase. $300. One of 31 on vellum, signed. $750. "Artist's Edition." One of 500 signed. $150.

MILLAY, Edna St. Vincent. *Poems.* London, 1923. $200.

MILLAY, Edna St. Vincent. *Renascence and Other Poems.* New York, 1917. Author's first book. Black cloth. First issue, on Glaslan watermarked paper. In dustwrapper. $750. Without dustwrapper. $125. White vellum paper boards. One of 15 (actually 17) on Japan vellum, signed. $6,000.

MILLER, Arthur. *All My Sons.* New York (1947). $150.

MILLER, Arthur. *Death of a Salesman.* New York, 1949. Pictorial orange cloth. $200. London, 1949. $75.

MILLER, Arthur. *Situation Normal.* New York (1944). Author's first book. $200.

MILLER, Benjamin S. *Ranch Life in Southern Kansas and the Indian Territory.* New York, 1896. Frontispiece. 163 pages, printed wraps. $400.

MILLER, Francis Trevelyan. *The World in the Air.* New York, 1930. 1,200 illustrations, 2 vols. Issued without dustwrapper. $450. One of 500 signed. $850.

MILLER, Henry. *Account of a Tour of the California Missions, 1856.* Grabhorn Press. San Francisco, 1952. Pencil drawings by Miller. 59 pages, boards. One of 375. In slipcase. $125.

MILLER, Henry. *The Air-Conditioned Nightmare.* New Directions. (New York, 1945.) Tan cloth with photos tipped in. $150. (Second printing, 1948, in gray cloth with photos printed.)

MILLER, Henry. *Aller Retour New York.* Paris (1935). Wraps. One of 150 signed. $1,500. (New York) 1945. Cloth. (Issued without dustwrapper.) One of 500. $50.

MILLER, Henry. *Black Spring.* Obelisk Press. Paris (1936). Pictorial wraps. $750. Paris (1938). Wraps. Second edition. $150. New York (1963). $40. (Somewhat more with yellow paper censorship band, "Cannot be bought in England and U.S.A.")

MILLER, Henry. *The Books in My Life.* (Norfolk, Conn., 1952.) (Printed in Ireland.) First issue with four tipped-in photographs. $150.

MILLER, Henry. *The Colossus of Maroussi.* Colt Press. San Francisco (1941). Boards and cloth. One of 100 signed. Issued without dustwrapper. $750. In dustwrapper. $300. London, 1942. $150.

MILLER, Henry. *The Cosmological Eye.* New Directions. Norfolk (1939). His first U.S. publication. Tan cloth, with brown lettering and photograph of an eye inset on front cover. In first-state dustwrapper, spine lettered in white. Priced at $2.50. $250. (Second was in 1944, without eye and priced at $3.00.) London (1945). $100.

MILLER, Henry. *Into the Night Life.* (Berkeley, 1947.) Illustrated by Bezalel Schatz. Folio, cloth. One of 800 signed by the author and the artist. Without dustwrapper in slipcase. $850. (300 reportedly destroyed.) One of 14 signed, numbered copies without illustrations. $1,000.

MILLER, Henry. *Maurizius Forever.* Colt Press. San Francisco, 1946. Colored drawings by Miller. Green boards. One of 500. Printed at the Grabhorn Press. In plain brown dustwrapper. $200.

MILLER, Henry. *Money and How It Gets That Way.* Paris (1938). Wraps. Booster Broadside No. 1. With copyright notice written in by Miller. $1,000. The other copies. $350. Berkeley, 1946. Wraps. $75.

MILLER, Henry. *Quiet Days in Clichy.* Olympia Press. Paris, 1956. Photographs by Brassai. Printed wraps. $450.

MILLER, Henry. *Scenario (A Film with Sound.).* Paris, 1937. Double-page frontispiece by Abraham Rattner. Wraps, unbound. One of 200 signed. $1,000.

MILLER, Henry. *The Smile at the Foot of the Ladder.* New York (1948). Pictorial boards and cloth. $200.

MILLER, Henry. *Tropic of Cancer.* Obelisk Press. Paris (1934). Preface by Anaïs Nin. Author's first book. Decorated wraps. With "First published September 1934" on copyright page and with wraparound band. $6,500. New York, 1940. First (printed) American edition. Issued without dustwrapper. $175. Also, wraps. $150. New York (1961). Grove Press. Introduction by Karl Shapiro. Preface by Anaïs Nin. Patterned boards and cloth. One of 100 signed. First authorized American edition. (Issued without dustwrapper.) $400. Trade in boards and dustwrapper. $50.

MILLER, Henry. *Tropic of Capricorn.* Obelisk Press. Paris (1939). Decorated wraps. "First published Feb., 1939" with price on spine and with errata slip. $1,000.

MILLER, Henry. *Watercolors, Drawings and His Essay "The Angel Is My Watermark!"* London, 1962. Illustrated. Small folio, cloth. With each of the 12 reproductions signed by Miller. $1,250. New York (1962). In acetate dustwrapper. $200.

MILLER, Henry. *What Are You Going to Do About Alf?* Paris (1935). Printed wraps. $2,500. Paris (1938). Wraps. Second edition with two-page foreword not in first edition. $200. Berkeley (1944). Printed self-wraps. $75. (London, 1971.) First English edition. One of 100 signed. In dustwrapper. $250. Unsigned copies (250). $100.

MILLER, Henry. *The World of Sex.* (Chicago, 1940.) One of 250. In dustwrapper. $400. Later edition in blue cloth. (New York, no date.) "One of 1,000." Issued without dustwrapper. $60. Paris (1957). 125 pages in wraps. Revised edition. $100.

MILLER, Henry, HILER, Hilaire, and SAROYAN, William. *Why Abstract?* New Directions. (New York, 1945.) $200. Falcon Press. London (1948). First English edition. $150.

MILLER, Cincinnatus H. *Joaquin, et al.* Portland, Ore., 1869. (By Joaquin Miller.) $750.

MILLER, Joaquin. See Miller, Cincinnatus H. See also *How to Win in Wall Street; Specimens.*

MILLER, Joaquin. *'49, The Gold-Seeker of the Sierras.* New York, 1884. Printed wraps. $300. Also issued in cloth, and in boards and cloth. $200.

MILLER, Joaquin. *An Illustrated History of Montana.* Chicago, 1894. Illustrated. 2 vols., morocco. $300.

MILLER, Joaquin. *Life Amongst the Modocs: Unwritten History.* London, 1873. $250.

MILLER, Joaquin. *Overland in a Covered Wagon.* New York, 1930. Edited by Sidney A. Firman. Illustrated. $200.

MILLER, Joaquin. *Pacific Poems.* London, 1871. Green cloth, gilt. $1,250.

MILLER, Joaquin. *Songs of the Mexican Seas.* Boston, 1877. $150.

MILLER, Joaquin. *Songs of the Sierras.* London, 1871. $200. Boston, 1871. Probable first binding, with "R.B." at foot of spine and "Thoughts about Art" on page (i) not (iv). $300.

MILLER, Joaquin. *Unwritten History: Life Among the Modocs.* Hartford, 1874. First American edition (of *Life Amongst the Modocs*). $300.

MILLER, Lewis B. *A Crooked Trail.* Pittsburgh (1908). Wraps, cloth spine. $150.

MILLER, Lewis B. *Saddles and Lariats.* Boston, 1912. Illustrated. Pictorial cloth. $125.

MILLER, Patrick. *The Green Ship.* Golden Cockerel Press. London, 1936. 8 wood engravings by Eric Gill, with an extra set of the plates on Japan vellum. Full morocco. One of 62. $1,000. Half morocco and boards. One of 134. $500.

MILLER, Patrick. *The Natural Man.* London, 1924. Author's first book. $125.

MILLER, Patrick. *Woman in Detail.* Golden Cockerel Press. London, 1947. 5 illustrations by Mark Severin, with a duplicate set of the 5 plates and with 3 additional ones in a pocket at the end. Half morocco and boards. One of 100 signed. $300. One of 430. $100.

MILLER, T. L. *History of Hereford Cattle.* Chillicothe, Mo., 1902. Illustrated. Pictorial cloth. $100.

MILLER, Thomas. *Common Wayside Flowers.* London, 1860. Illustrated by Birket Foster. Decorated brown cloth. $300.

MILLER, Walter M., Jr. *A Canticle for Leibowitz.* Philadelphia/New York, 1960. $750. London (1960). $250.

MILLS, Anson. *Big Horn Expedition.* No-place, no-date (1874?). Folding map. 15 pages, tan printed wraps. $600.

MILLS, Robert. *Atlas of the State of South Carolina.* Baltimore (about 1826). 29 double-page maps, colored by hand. Folio, half leather. (Issued to accompany Mills's *Statistics.* See item following.) $3,500.

MILLS, Robert. *Statistics of South Carolina.* Charleston, 1826. Map (not in all copies). $250.

MILLS, Samuel J., and SMITH, Daniel. *Report of a Missionary Tour . . . West of the Allegheny Mountains.* Andover, 1815. Original wraps, bound in. $500.

MILLS, William W. *Forty Years at El Paso, 1858–1898.* (Chicago, 1901.) Frontispiece. Cloth. (Printed at El Paso, Tex.) $250. El Paso, 1962. Mesquite Edition. $200.

MILMINE, Georgine. *The Life of Mary Baker G. Eddy and the History of Christian Science.* New York, 1909. Edited by Willa S. Cather. (Largely written by Cather.) $500. London, 1909. $350.

MILNE, A. A. *The Christopher Robin Story Book.* London (1926). Illustrated by Ernest H. Shepard. Pictorial cloth. $300. New York (1929). Pictorial boards and cloth. One of 350 signed. $1,000.

MILNE, A. A. *The House at Pooh Corner.* London (1928). Decorations by Ernest H. Shepard. Boards and buckram. One of 350, signed. In dustwrapper. $1,500. Vellum. One of 20 on Japan paper, signed. $3,000. Trade in pink cloth. $400. New York (1928). Illustrated. Cloth. First American edition. One of 250 signed. $1,000. Trade. $200.

MILNE, A. A. *Lovers in London.* London, 1905. Author's first book. $125.

MILNE, A. A. *Now We Are Six.* London (1927). Illustrated by Ernest H. Shepard. Boards and cloth. One of 200 signed. In dustwrapper. $1,500. Vellum. One of 20 on Japan paper, signed. $3,000. Trade in pictorial maroon cloth. $350.

MILNE, A. A. *The Red House Mystery.* London (1922). $350.

MILNE, A. A. *Toad of Toad Hall: A Play from Kenneth Grahame's Book "The Wind in the Willows."* London (1929). Board and buckram. One of 200 signed by Milne and Grahame. In dustwrapper. $1,250. Trade. $300.

MILNE, A. A. *When We Were Very Young.* London (1924). Illustrated by Ernest H. Shepard. Boards and cloth. One of 100 signed. In dustwrapper. $5,000. Trade, first issue in pictorial blue cloth, plain end papers, page ix not numbered. In dustwrapper. $2,000. Later copies. $1,750. New York (1924). Pictorial boards and cloth. First American edition. One of 100 signed. In dustwrapper. $3,500.

MILNE, A. A. *Winnie-the-Pooh.* London (1926). Illustrated by Ernest H. Shepard. Boards and buckram. One of 350 signed. In dustwrapper. $5,000. Vellum. One of 20 on vellum, signed. $8,500. Trade edition in pictorial green cloth. $1,000. New York (1926). Pictorial boards and cloth. First American edition. One of 200 signed. In dustwrapper. $3,000.

MILNS, William. *The Penman's Repository* . . . Clerkenwell, 1787. First edition title page states that 20 alphabets are included. $450.

MILTON, John. *Four Poems: L'Allegro, Il Penseroso, Arcades, Lycidas.* Gregynog Press. Newtown, 1933. Wood engravings by Blair Hughes-Stanton. Red morocco. One of 250 on Japan vellum. $1,000.

MILTON, John. *Paradise Lost.* Golden Cockerel Press. London, 1937. Woodcuts by Mary Groom. Half pigskin. One of 200. $1,500. One of 4 on vellum. $10,000.

MILTON, John. *Paradise Lost* [and] *Paradise Regained.* Doves Press. London, 1902–5. Printed in red and black. 2 vols., vellum. One of 300. $3,000. 2 vols., vellum. One of 25 on vellum. $10,000.

MILTON, John. *Paradise Lost* [and] *Paradise Regained.* Cresset Press. London, 1931. Illustrated by D. Galanis. 2 vols., folio, pigskin. One of 195. In slipcase. $750. 2 vols., sharkskin. One of 10 on vellum. In slipcase. $4,000.

MILTON, John. *Poems in English.* Nonesuch Press. London, 1926. 53 plates by William Blake. 2 vols., half vellum and brown boards. One of 1,450 on Van Gelder paper. $400. 2 vols. in one, vellum. One of 90 on India paper. $1,500.

MILTON, John. *Three Poems of John Milton.* Ashendene Press. London, 1896. One of 50. $1,500.

MINER, Dorothy (editor). *Studies in Art and Literature for Belle Da Costa Greene.* Princeton, 1954. $225.

MIRIAM Coffin, or, The Whale Fisherman: A Tale. New York/Philadelphia, 1834. (By Joseph C. Hart, his first book.) 2 vols. in original cloth. $1,250.

MIRRLEES, Hope. *Paris: A Poem.* Hogarth Press. Richmond, England, 1919. Wraps, paper label. $600.

MIRROR of Olden Time Border Life. Abingdon, Va., 1849. (By Joseph Pritts.) 13 plates (17 in some). Leather. $350.

MISFORTUNES of Elphin (The). London, 1829. (By Thomas Love Peacock.) $400. Newtown, Wales, 1928. Gregynog Press. Woodcuts. Buckram-backed cloth. One of 250. $300. Morocco. One of 25 bound by George Fisher. $2,000.

MR. DOOLEY in Peace and in War. Boston, 1898. (By Finley Peter Dunne.) Green cloth. Author's first book. $60.

MR. FACEY Romford's Hounds. London, 1864–65. (By Robert Smith Surtees.) 24 color plates by John Leech and "Phiz" (H. K. Browne). 12 parts, pictorial wraps. First edition, with first-state wraps of part I reading "Mr. Facey Romford's Hounds" (second state and all subsequent parts read "Mr. Romford's Hounds"). $1,250. London, 1865. Pictorial cloth. First book edition. $350.

MR. MIDSHIPMAN Easy. London, 1836. (By Frederick Marryat.) 3 vols., in original boards. $400.

MR. SPONGE'S Sporting Tour. London, 1852–53. (By Robert Smith Surtees.) 13 color plates and 84 woodcuts by John Leech. 13 parts in 12, pictorial wraps. First edition, first issue, with the dedication to Lord Elcho (second issue reading "Earl Elcho"). $1,000. Second issue. $750. London, 1853. First book edition in pictorial cloth. $350.

MITCHEL, Martin. *History of the County of Fond du Lac Wisconsin.* Fond du Lac, 1854. 96 pages, printed yellow wraps. $200.

MITCHELL, Dewey. *Skilled Defense.* Cleveland, 1936. Embossed cover, gilt figures. (9½ by 12 inches.) $75.

MITCHELL, Donald G. See Marvel, Ik.

MITCHELL, Donald G. *The Dignity of Learning: A Valedictory Oration.* New Haven, 1841. Printed wraps. $200.

MITCHELL, Isaac. *The Asylum; or, Alonzo and Melissa.* Poughkeepsie, 1811. Frontispiece. 2 vols., calf. Author's first (and only) book. (Note: Many later editions appeared with Daniel Jackson, Jr., as the author.) $500.

MITCHELL, Joseph. *The Missionary Pioneer.* New York, 1827. $300.

MITCHELL, Margaret. *Gone with the Wind.* New York, 1936. Gray cloth. First printing, with "Published May, 1936" on copyright page and no note of other printings. In first-issue dustwrapper, with *Gone with the Wind* listed in the second column of Macmillan book list on back panel. $3,000. In second-issue jacket, with the novel listed at top of list in first column. $850. Without jacket. $300.

MITCHELL, S. Augustus. See *Illinois in 1837.*

MITCHELL, S. Augustus (publisher). *A New Map of Texas . . . and an Accompaniment to Mitchell's New Map of Texas, Oregon and California, with the Regions Adjoining.* Philadelphia, 1846. Cloth and 46 pages, text and large colored map, folding into leather covers. $2,000.

MITCHELL, S. Augustus (publisher). *Description of Oregon and California, Embracing an Account of the Gold Regions.* Philadelphia, 1849. Folding map in color. Gold-stamped cloth. $1,500.

MITCHELL, S. Augustus. *Traveller's Guide Through the United States.* Philadelphia (1836). Folding map. 74 pages, in original leather. First edition under this title. $600. Philadelphia, 1839. In original half leather. $400.

MITCHELL, S. Weir. See S., E. W., and M., S. W. See also *The Wonderful Stories of Fuz-Buz the Fly.*

MITCHELL, S. Weir. *Hugh Wynne, Free Quaker.* New York, 1897. Illustrated by Howard Pyle. 2 vols. First issue, in tan cloth with tipped-in title page and with last word on page 54, vol. 1, being "in" (later "her") and line 16 on page 260, vol. 2, reading "between" (later "lines of in-"). $200. Later issue, text corrected. 2 vols., gray boards, white cloth spines, paper labels. One of 60 large paper copies, signed, with separate plates by Howard Pyle laid in. $750. (Note: A few copies of the first issue exist with an 1896 title page, as publication was delayed).

MITCHELL, S. Weir. *Researches upon the Venom of the Rattlesnake.* Washington, 1861. Folio, wraps. $750.

MITCHELL, S. Weir, et al. *Gunshot Wounds and Other Injuries of Nerves.* Philadelphia, 1864. Wraps. $1,000.

MITCHELL, W. H. *Geographical and Statistical Sketch of the Past and Present of Goodhue County.* Minneapolis, 1869. 191 pages, wraps. $125.

MITFORD, John. *The Adventures of Johnny Newcome in the Navy.* London, 1819. Color plates. Second edition. $300. London, 1823. Third edition with 20 colored plates. $325. (See Alfred Burton entry for first edition.)

MITFORD, Mary Russell. *Our Village.* London, 1824. $250. London, 1893. Illustrated by Hugh Thompson. Cloth. One of 470. $400. London, 1910. Thompson illustrations. Half leather. $200.

MITFORD, Mary Russell. *Poems.* London, 1810. Author's first book. With leaf of "Alterations." $400.

MIVART, St. George. *Dogs, Jackals, Wolves, and Foxes . . .* London, 1890. With 45 color plates. $1,250.

MIVART, St. George. *A Monograph of the Lories, or Brush-Tongued Parrots.* London, 1896. 61 colored plates and 4 colored maps. $4,500.

MIYAKE, T., and TANI, Y. *The Game of Ju Jitsu.* London, 1906. $200.

MODERN Griselda (The). London, 1805. (By Maria Edgeworth.) $200.

M'MAHON, Bernard. *The American Gardener's Calendar.* Philadelphia, 1806. Folding table. $375.

MOELLHAUSEN, Baldwin. *Diary of a Journey from the Mississippi to the Coasts of the Pacific with a United States Government Expedition.* London, 1858. Translated by Mrs. Percy Sinnett. Illustrations, including color plates. Folding map. 2 vols. First edition in English. $1,500.

MOFFETTE, Joseph F. *The Territories of Kansas and Nebraska.* New York, 1855. 2 folding maps. $1,250. New York, 1856. Second edition. $600.

MOKLER, A. J. *History of Natrona County, Wyoming.* Chicago, 1923. Illustrated. Buckram. $250.

MOLL Pitcher, a Poem. Boston, 1832. (By John Greenleaf Whittier.) $750. (Copy in original wraps at Doheny sale for $7,500.) Philadelphia, 1840. *(Moll Pitcher, and the Minstrel Girl: Poems.)* Wraps. $500.

MOMADAY, N. Scott. *House Made of Dawn.* New York (1968). $75.

MOMADAY, N. Scott. *The Journey of Tai-Me.* Santa Barbara (1968). (100 copies.) Slipcase. $500.

MONASTERY (The). Edinburgh, 1820. (By Sir Walter Scott.) 3 vols. $300.

MONETTE, John W. *History of the Discovery and Settlement of the Valley of the Mississippi.* New York, 1846. 3 maps, 4 plans, 2 plates. $500.

MONIKINS (The): A Tale. By the author of *The Spy.* London, 1835. (By James Fenimore Cooper.) 3 vols., in original drab tan boards. $500. Philadelphia, 1835. 2 vols., in original boards. First American edition. $400.

MONK, Maria. *Awful Disclosures.* New York, 1836. Author's first book. $400.

MONKS, William. *History of Southern Missouri and Northern Arkansas.* West Plains, Mo., 1907. $125.

MONROE Doctrine (The). See *Message of the President . . .* (1823).

MONROE, Harriet. *Valeria and Other Poems.* Chicago, 1891. Vellum and cloth. Subscriber's edition, 300 copies. Author's first book. $200. Chicago, 1892. Cloth. First published edition. $75.

MONROE, James. *The Memoir of James Monroe, Esq., Relating to His Unsettled Claims Upon the People and Government of the U.S.* Charlottesville, Va., 1828. 60 pages, sewn. $200.

MONT Saint Michel and Chartres. Washington, 1904. (By Henry Adams.) Blue cloth, leather label on spine. Privately printed. $2,000. Washington, 1912. Second (first revised and enlarged) edition. (500 copies.) $1,000. Boston, 1913. Half brown cloth and tan boards. First published edition. $125. Limited Editions Club, New York, 1957. Cloth and leather. In slipcase. $100.

MONTAGUE, C. E. *A Hind Let Loose.* London (1910). Author's first book. One of 150 copies. $150. Regular edition. $75.

MONTAIGNE, Michel de. *Essays.* London, 1603. Translated by John Florio. 3 parts in 1, folio. $2,500. Boston, 1902–3–4. 3 vols., folio, half cloth. One of 265 designed by Bruce Rogers. In folding cases. $1,000. London, 1931. Nonesuch Press. 2 vols., full morocco. In slipcase. $200. Limited Editions Club. New York, 1946. 4 vols. In slipcase. $75.

MONTANA, Its Climate, Industries and Resources. Helena, Mont., 1884. Illustrated. 74 pages, wraps. $300.

MONTANA Territory, History and Business Directory 1879. Helena (1879). (By F. W. Warner.) Map. 5 plates. Printed boards and leather. $600.

MONTGOMERY, L. M. *Anne of Green Gables.* New York, 1908. Author's first book. $300.

MONTULE, Eduard. *A Voyage to North America, and the West Indies, in 1821.* London, 1821. Folding and full-page plates. Original wraps bound in. First edition in English. $400.

MOODIE, Susanna. *Roughing It in the Bush; Or, Life in Canada.* New York, 1852. 2 vols. Wraps. $750.

MOODY, William Vaughn. *The Masque of Judgment.* Boston, 1900. Author's first book. $60. Boards. One of 150. $150.

MOODY, William Vaughn. *Poems.* Boston, 1901. Boards. One of 150 on large paper. $125.

MOORCOCK, Michael. *The Stealer of Souls.* London, 1963. In orange boards. Author's first book. $100. Later binding in green. $75.

MOORCOCK, Michael. *Stormbringer.* London (1965). $100.

MOORE, Sir Alan Hilary. *Sailing Ships of War, 1800–1860.* London, 1926. 90 full-page plates, 12 in color. One of 1,500. Issued without dustwrapper. $350. Half leather. One of 100. Issued without dustwrapper. $600.

MOORE, Brian. *Judith Hearne.* London, 1955. (First hardback.) $300.

MOORE, Brian. *The Lonely Passion of Judith Hearn.* Boston (1955). $125.

MOORE, Brian. *Wreath for a Redhead.* Winnipeg, 1951. Author's first book. Wraps. $200.

MOORE, C. L. *Doomsday Morning.* Garden City, 1957. $125.

MOORE, C. L. *Shambleau and Others.* New York (1953). $200.

MOORE, Clement C. See *A New Translation, . . .; The New York Book of Poetry; Observations upon Certain Passages in Mr. Jefferson's "Notes on Virginia."*

MOORE, Clement C. *The Night Before Christmas.* New York, 1902. Color plates by W. W. Denslow. Pictorial boards. $500. Philadelphia (1931). 4 color plates and text drawings by Arthur Rackham. Cloth. In dustwrapper. $400. London (1931). Wraps. In dustwrapper. $400. London or Philadelphia (1931). Vellum. One of 550. In slipcase. $1,250.

MOORE, Clement C. *Poems.* New York, 1844. Brown boards. $400.

MOORE, Clement C. *A Visit from St. Nicholas.* New York, 1862. Illustrated by F.O.C. Darley. Pictorial wraps. $750.

MOORE, Edward. *We Moderns: Enigmas and Guesses.* London (1918). (By Edwin Muir, his first book). Blue pebble-grained cloth, with spine label lettered in red. In dustwrapper. $750. Without dustwrapper. $200.

MOORE, Edward A. *The Story of a Cannoneer Under Stonewall Jackson.* New York, 1907. $200.

MOORE, George. *Flowers of Passion.* London, 1878. Black cloth. Author's first book. With 1877 copyright and errata slip. $300.

MOORE, George. *Literature at Nurse, or, Circulating Morals.* London, 1885. Self-wraps, sewn. $450.

MOORE, George. *A Modern Lover.* London, 1883. 3 vols., blue cloth. $450.

MOORE, George. *Peronnik the Fool.* New York, 1926. Boards. Issued without dustwrapper. Bruce Rogers printing. $100. Chapelle-Reanville, France, 1928. Hours Press. Revised edition. One of 200 signed. Issued without dustwrapper. $200. London, 1933. Engravings by Stephen Gooden. Full vellum. Issued without dustwrapper. One of 525 signed by author and artist. $250.

MOORE, H. Judge. *Scott's Campaign in Mexico.* Charleston, 1849. $500.

MOORE, Henry. *Heads, Figures and Ideas.* London, 1958. $300. One of 150 with a signed Moore lithograph in color. $750.

MOORE, Marianne. *The Absentee: A Comedy in Four Acts.* New York, 1962. Blue cloth. One of 326 signed. In tissue dustwrapper. $200.

MOORE, Marianne. *Complete Poems.* New York (1967). Half buckram. $100.

MOORE, Marianne. *Eight Poems.* New York (1963). 10 hand-colored drawings. Half cloth. One of 195 signed. In slipcase. $1,000.

MOORE, Marianne. *Nevertheless.* New York (1944). $200.

MOORE, Marianne. *Observations.* New York, 1924. $750.

MOORE, Marianne. *The Pangolin and Other Verse.* (London) 1936. Drawings by George Plank. Decorated boards, paper label. One of 120. $1,250.

MOORE, Marianne. *Poems.* Egoist Press. London, 1921. Decorated wraps, paper label. Author's first book. $600.

MOORE, Marianne (translator). *The Fables of La Fontaine.* New York, 1954. One of 400 signed. In glassine jacket and slipcase. $300. Trade. $100. New York (1965). Revised edition. $50.

MOORE, Marianne. *What Are Years.* New York, 1941. $250.

MOORE, Marinda B. (Mrs. M. B.) *The Geographical Reader for the Dixie Children.* Raleigh, 1863. 48 pages, boards. $750.

MOORE, S. S., and JONES, T. W. *The Traveller's Directory.* Philadelphia, 1802 38 maps on 22 leaves. 52 pages. $2,500. Philadelphia, 1804. $1,250.

MOORE, Thomas. *The Epicurean: A Tale.* London, 1827. $150.

MOORE, Thomas. *Lalla Rookh, an Oriental Romance.* London, 1817. $300.

MOORE, Thomas. *Lyrics and Satires.* Cuala Press. Dublin, 1929. Selected by Sean O'Faolain. 5 designs by Hilda Roberts. Boards and cloth. One of 130. In dustwrapper. $125.

MOORE, Thomas. *Paradise and the Peri.* (London, 1860.) Illuminated borders. Folio, leather, or cloth. $300.

MOORE, Thomas. *Tom Crib's Memorial to Congress.* London, 1819. $1,500.

MOORE, Thomas (translator). *The Odes of Anacreon.* London, 1800. Author's first book. $250.

MOORE, T. Sturge. *A Brief Account of the Origin of the Eragny Press.* London, 1903. Eragny Press. Illustrated. Boards. One of 235. $1,000. One of 6 on vellum. $6,000.

MOORE, T. Sturge. *The Little School: A Posy of Rhymes.* Eragny Press. London, 1905. Woodcuts. Boards. One of 185. In dustwrapper. $750. Morocco. One of 10 on vellum. $4,000.

MOORE, T. Sturge. *The Vinedresser and Other Poems.* Unicorn Press. London, 1899. Cloth. $100.

MOORE, T. Sturge. *Two Poems.* London, 1893. Author's first book. $250.

MORE, Hannah. See *Hints Towards Forming the Character of a Young Princess.*

MORE, Hannah. *Sacred Dramas, Chiefly Intended for Young Persons.* London, 1782. $300.

MORE, Hannah. *Slavery: A Poem.* London, 1788. $600.

MORE, Hannah. *Strictures on the Modern System of Female Education.* London, 1799. 2 vols. $1,000.

MORE, Sir Thomas. *Utopia.* Kelmscott Press. London, 1893. Woodcut borders and initials, printed in black and red. Vellum with ties. $1,500. One of 6 on vellum. $7,500. Golden Cockerel Press. Waltham Saint Lawrence, England, 1929. Decorations by Eric Gill. Buckram. $300. Limited Editions Club, New York, 1934. Woodcuts by Bruce Rogers. Vellum and boards. In slipcase. $150.

MORECAMP, Arthur. *The Live Boys; or, Charlie and Nasho in Texas.* Boston (1878). (By Thomas Pilgrim, his first book.) Pictorial cloth. $300.

MORES, Edward Rowe. *A Dissertation Upon English Typographical Founders and Founderies . . .* New York, 1924. Limited to 250 copies. $125.

MORFI, Juan Agustin. *History of Texas, 1673–1779.* Albuquerque, 1935. Map, 4 plates. 2 vols., boards and cloth. One of 500. $250. New York, 1967. Facsimile edition. $75.

MORGAN, Charles. *The Gunroom.* London, 1919. Author's first novel. $75.

MORGAN, Dale L. See Ashley, William H.

MORGAN, Dale L. *Jedediah Smith and the Opening of the West.* Indianapolis (1953). 20 plates. Cloth. In dustwrapper. $150.

MORGAN, Dale L., and WHEAT, Carl I. *Jedediah Smith and His Maps of the American West.* San Francisco, 1954. 7 folding maps. One of 530. Issued without dustwrapper. $850.

MORGAN, Dick T. *Morgan's Manual of the U.S. Homestead and Townsite Laws.* Gutfirie, Okla., 1893. Buff printed wraps. $300.

MORGAN, Emanuel. *Pins for Wings.* (New York, 1920.) (By Witter Bynner.) Illustrated by William Sophier. Boards. Issued without dustwrapper. $150.

MORGAN, Emanuel, and KNISH, Anne. *Spectra: A Book of Poetic Experiments.* New York, 1916. (By Witter Bynner [Morgan] and Arthur Davison Ficke [Knish].) (Issued without dustwrapper.) $200.

MORGAN, Jane. *Tales for Fifteen.* New York, 1823. (By James Fenimore Cooper.) Printed tan boards. $1,000.

MORGAN, John Hill, and FIELDING, Mantle. *The Life Portraits of Washington and Their Replicas.* Philadelphia (1931). Illustrated. Folio, cloth. One of 1,000. $100. Full morocco. Limited, signed by the authors. In dustwrapper and slipcase. $300.

MORGAN, Lewis H. *The American Beaver and His Works.* Philadelphia, 1868. Map, 23 plates. $250.

MORGAN, Lewis H. *The League of the Ho-De'-No-Sau-Nee, or Iroquois.* Rochester, N.Y., 1851. 21 plates, map, table. $350. Maps and plates colored by hand. $600.

MORGAN, Martha M. (editor). *A Trip Across the Plains in the Year 1849.* San Francisco, 1864. 31 pages, printed wraps. $6,000.

MORGAN, Thomas J. *A Glance at Texas.* Columbus, 1844. 16 pages, three-quarters morocco. $1,500.

MORIER, James. See *Ayesha.*

MORING, Thomas. *50 Book Plates Engraved on Copper.* London, 1901. 50 full-page plates. $175.

MORISON, Samuel Eliot. *Harrison Gray Otis.* Boston, 1913. Author's first book. $200.

MORISON, Stanley. *The Art of the Printer.* London, 1925. $250. New York, 1926. $125.

MORISON, Stanley. *The English Newspaper.* Cambridge, 1932. Illustrated. Folio, cloth. $350.

MORISON, Stanley. *Four Centuries of Fine Printing.* London (1924). 390 numbered copies. Issued without dustwrapper. $450. Morocco. One of 13 signed. $750. London (1949). 272 facsimile title pages. Calf. Second edition, revised. One of 200. $250.

MORISON, Stanley. *John Bell, 1745–1831, Bookseller, Printer, Publisher, Type-founder . . .* Cambridge, 1930. Limited to 300 copies. $275.

MORISON, Stanley. *John Fell, The University Press and the "Fell" Types . . .* Oxford, 1967. One of 1,000 copies. $375.

MORISON, Stanley. *Modern Fine Printing.* London, 1925. Facsimiles. Folio, cloth. One of 650 in English. Issued without dustwrapper. $350.

MORISON, Stanley. *Splendour of Ornament . . .* London, 1968. One of 400 copies. $200.

MORISON, Stanley. *On Type Faces, Examples of the Use of Type for the Printing of Books.* London, 1923. One of 750 copies. $150.

MORISON, Stanley. *The Typographic Book 1450–1935.* Chicago, 1963. $175.

MORISON, Stanley. *Typographic Design in Relation to Photographic Composition.* San Francisco, 1959. One of 400 copies. $150.

MORLEY, C. D. *The Eighth Sin.* Oxford, 1912. (By Christopher Morley.) Printed pale blue-gray wraps. Author's first book. One of 250. $1,250.

MORLEY, Christopher. *The Haunted Bookshop.* New York, 1919. First edition not stated. The first-state points have been disputed for years. Both Johnson and Casanova state: "First state has number 76 at bottom of proper page, type above it, 'Burroughs,' is unbroken; page 100, line 1, reads 'Sty' vs. 'Styx.' " Lee (no. 5) remained uncertain. In dustwrapper. $500. Without dustwrapper. $100.

MORLEY, Christopher. *Parnassus on Wheels.* Garden City, 1917. First edition not stated. With space between the "Y" and "e" in "Years" on page 4, line 8, and missing an "l" from "goldenrod" on page 169, line 11. In first-state dustwrapper with "vibrating" instead of "beating" on front cover. $600. Without dustwrapper. $150.

MORLEY, Christopher. *Songs for a Little House.* New York (1917). Boards. First edition without publisher's monogram, first state, has quotation from Southwell facing title page. In dustwrapper. $500. Without dustwrapper. $100.

MORLEY, Christopher. *Where the Blue Begins.* Garden City, 1922. Pictorial cream-and-blue marbled boards, blue cloth spine. $150. London (1925). Illustrated by Arthur Rackham, including 4 color plates. Half black cloth and white boards. First deluxe illustrated edition. One of 175 signed by Rackham. In slipcase. $1,500. London and New York (1925). Rackham illustrations. Half black cloth and green-and-blue boards. First American deluxe edition. One of 100 signed by Morley and Rackham. In tissue dustwrapper and slipcase. $2,000. London (1925). Rackham illustrations. Blue cloth. First Rackham trade edition. In dustwrapper. $250.

MORPHIS, J. M. *History of Texas.* New York, 1874. Plates, folding map in color. $200.

MORRELL, Benjamin. *Narrative of Four Voyages to the South Seas, North and South Pacific Ocean.* New York, 1832. Portrait. $600.

MORRELL, Z. N. *Flowers and Fruits in the Wilderness; or 36 Years in Texas.* Boston, 1872. $400.

MORRIS, Eastin. *The Tennessee Gazetteer.* Nashville, 1834. In original printed boards, leather spine. $1,500.

MORRIS, Henry. *Guilford & Green.* (North Hills, 1970.) With pocket containing a specimen of the paper that was to be used for the cover of the book. 210 numbered copies. $500.

MORRIS, Henry. *Japonica . . .* North Hills, 1981. One of 250 in half morocco. $400.

MORRIS, Henry. *No. V-109, The Bibliography of a Printing Press.* No-place, 1978. Miniature book (6.1 by 4.7 cm). 150 numbered copies. $450.

MORRIS, Henry. *Omnibus, Instructions for Amateur Papermakers . . .* (North Hills) 1967. 500 numbered copies. $350.

MORRIS, Henry. *The Paper Maker, A Survey of Lesser-Known Hand Paper Mills in Europe and North America . . .* North Hills, 1974. 175 numbered copies. $600.

MORRIS, Henry. *Pepperpot: Ingredients . . .* North Hills, 1977. "Approximately 250 copies." $275.

MORRIS, Henry. *Roller-Printed Paste Papers for Bookbinding.* North Hills, 1975. 215 numbered copies. $350.

MORRIS, Joseph. *The "Spirit Prevails." Containing the Revelations, Articles and Letters Written by . . .* San Francisco, 1886. $1,750.

MORRIS, William. *Child Christopher and Goldilind the Fair.* Kelmscott Press. London, 1895. Woodcuts. 2 vols., decorated boards and cloth. One of 600. $500. One of 12 on vellum. $3,000.

MORRIS, William. *The Defence of Guenevere, and Other Poems.* London, 1858. Author's first book. $600. Kelmscott Press. London, 1892. Printed in black and red. Woodcut borders. Vellum with ties. One of 300. $1,000. One of 10 on vellum. $5,000.

MORRIS, William. *A Dream of John Ball and a King's Lesson.* Kelmscott Press. London, 1892. Woodcut borders and designs by Morris and E. Burne-Jones. Vellum with ties. One of 300. $750. Another issue: one of 11 on vellum. $5,000.

MORRIS, William. *The Earthly Paradise.* Kelmscott Press. London, 1896–97. Woodcut title. 8 vols., vellum with ties. One of 225. $2,000. One of 6 on vellum. $8,000.

MORRIS, William. *News from Nowhere.* Kelmscott Press. London, 1892. Woodcut frontispiece, borders, and initials. Vellum with ties. One of 300. $1,250. One of 10 on vellum. $7,500.

MORRIS, William. *Poems by the Way.* Kelmscott Press. London, 1891. Vellum. One of 300 on paper. $750. One of 13 on vellum. $5,000.

MORRIS, William. *Printing: An Essay.* Park Ridge, Ill., 1903. Boards. $300.

MORRIS, William. *The Story of the Glittering Plain.* Kelmscott Press. London, 1891. Woodcut title and borders. Illustrations by Walter Crane. Vellum with ties. One of 200. In slipcase. $1,500. London, 1894. Vellum. One of 250. In slipcase. $1,250. One of 7 on vellum. $6,000.

MORRIS, William. *The Sundering Flood.* Kelmscott Press. London, 1897. Woodcuts. Boards and cloth. One of 300. $600.

MORRIS, William. *The Water of the Wondrous Isles.* Kelmscott Press. London, 1897. Woodcut borders and initials. Vellum with ties. One of 250. $1,250. One of 6 on vellum. $7,500.

MORRIS, William. *The Wood Beyond the World.* Kelmscott Press. London, 1894. Woodcut frontispiece, other illustrations. Vellum with ties. One of 350. $1,000. One of 8 on vellum. $6,000.

MORRIS, Wright. *The Home Place.* New York, 1948. Illustrated. $175.

MORRIS, Wright. *The Inhabitants.* New York, 1946. Illustrated with author's photographs. $150.

MORRIS, Wright. *Man and Boy.* New York, 1951. $150.

MORRIS, Wright. *The Man Who Was There.* New York, 1945. $300.

MORRIS, Wright. *My Uncle Dudley.* New York (1942). Author's first book. $850.

MORRIS, Wright. *The World in the Attic.* New York, 1949. $250.

MORRISON, Arthur. *The Dorrington Deed-Box.* London (1896). Illustrated. Red cloth. $600.

MORRISON, Arthur. *The Painters of Japan.* London, 1911. 2 vols. $300.

MORRISON, Arthur. *Martin Hewitt, Investigator.* London, 1894. $1,000.

MORRISON, Arthur. *The Shadows Around Us . . .* London, 1891. Author's first book. $250.

MORRISON, Arthur. *Tales of Mean Streets.* London, 1894. Green cloth. With October ads (VAB). $200.

MORRISON, James. *The Journal of the Boatswain's Mate of the Bounty.* Golden Cockerel Press. (London) 1935. Buckram. One of 325. $750.

MORRISON, James Douglas. *The Lords.* Los Angeles, 1969. Author's first book. (100 copies.) $225.

MORRISON, James Douglas. *The New Creatures.* Los Angeles, 1969. (100 copies.) $200.

MORRISON, James Douglas. *The Lords and the New Creatures.* New York, 1970. $125.

MORRISON, Toni. *The Bluest Eye.* New York (1970). Author's first book. $400. London, 1979. $75.

MORRISON, Toni. *Sula.* New York, 1974. $175. London, 1974. $50.

MORROW, William C. *Blood-Money.* San Francisco, 1882. Cloth. $225.

MORSE, A. Reynolds. *Salvador Dali: A Study of His Life and Work.* Greenwich, Conn. (1958). Illustrated. Oblong folio, cloth. First American edition. In acetate dustwrapper. $150.

MORSE, Jedidiah. *A Report to the Secretary of War . . . on Indian Affairs.* New Haven, 1822. Folding colored map. With errata leaf. $650.

MORSE, John F., and COLVILLE, Samuel. *Illustrated Historical Sketches of California.* Sacramento, 1854. No. 1 (all published). Frontispiece. Pictorial wraps. $750.

MORSE, Samuel French. *Time of Year.* (Cumington), 1943. One of 275. $150.

MORSE, Samuel French. *The Yellow Lilies.* Hanover, 1935. Author's first book. One of 85 signed. $200.

MORSE, S., and BRINCKLE, Gertrude. *Howard Pyle, A Record of His Illustrations and Writings.* Wilmington, 1921. 500 numbered copies. $200.

MORTIMER, Ruth. *Catalogue of Books and Manuscripts.* Cambridge, 1964. Part I. 2 vols. $300.

MORTIMER, Ruth. *Catalogue of Books and Manuscripts.* Cambridge, 1974. Part II. 2 vols. $250.

MORTON of Morton's Hope . . . (By John Lothrop Motley.) London, 1839. Author's first book. 3 vols. $350.

MORTON'S Hope . . . (By John Lothrop Motley.) New York, 1839. 2 vols. $300.

MOSKOWITZ, Sam. *The Immortal Storm: A History of Science-Fiction Fandom.* Atlanta, 1951. Spiral-bound wraps. One of 150. $150.

MOSS, Howard. *The Wound and the Weather.* New York (1946). Author's first book. $100.

MOTLEY, John Lothrop. See *Morton . . .* and *Morton's Hope.*

MOTLEY, Willard. *Knock on Any Door.* New York (1947). Gray cloth. Author's first book. $100.

MOTT, Mrs. Mentor. *The Stones of Palestine.* London, 1865. 12 mounted photographs by Francis Bedford. $750.

MOULTRIE, William. *Memoirs of the American Revolution.* New York, 1802. 2 vols. $1,000.

MOUNSEER Nontongpaw: A New Version. (By Mary W. Shelley.) London, 1808. Author's first book. Wraps. $5,000.

MOWRY, Sylvester. *Memoir of the Proposed Territory of Arizona.* Washington, 1857. Map (not in all copies). 30 pages, printed wraps. $1,750.

MOXON, Joseph. *Mechanick Exercise on the Whole Art of Printing (1683–4).* London, 1962. 2 foldout plates. Second edition. Contains a bibliography of Moxon's work. $150.

MOXON, Joseph. *Moxon's Mechanick Exercises or the Doctrine of Handy Works Applied to the Art of Printing.* New York, 1896. A reprint of the first edition of 1683. 2 vols. 450 numbered copies. $375.

MUELLER, Hans Alexander. *Woodcuts & Wood Engravings: How I Make Them.* New York, 1939. Loose signatures inserted in a clamshell box. One of 250 copies. $225.

MUIR, Edwin. See Moore, Edward.

MUIR, Edwin. *Chorus of the Newly Dead.* Hogarth Press. Richmond, England, 1926. Wraps, paper label. $250.

MUIR, Edwin. *First Poems.* Hogarth Press. London, 1925. Boards, printed label. Issued without dustwrapper. $300.

MUIR, Edwin. *Latitudes.* New York, 1924. $200. London, 1926. $150.

MUIR, John. *The Mountains of California.* New York, 1894. Illustrated. Tan cloth. Author's first book. First edition, first issue, with folio 1 on first text page. $500. Without folio 1. $400.

MUIR, John (editor). *Picturesque California.* San Francisco (1888). 130 full-page plates, other illustrations. 2 vols., folio, calf. $1,000.

MUIR, Percy. *Catnachery.* San Francisco, 1955. Five foldout plates. One of 325 copies. $100.

MUIR, Percy H. *English Children's Books, 1600–1900.* London, 1954. Illustrated, including color plates. $125. New York, 1954. Illustrated. Blue cloth. First American edition. $125.

MUIR, Percy H. (editor). *A. F. Johnson: Selected Essays on Books and Printing.* Amsterdam, 1970. Two folding maps. $125.

MUIR, Percy H. *Points, Second Series, 1866–1934.* London, 1934. One of 750 copies. Issued without dustwrapper. $100.

MUIR, Percy H. *Points, 1874–1930, Being Extracts from a Bibliographer's Note-Book.* London, 1931. One of 500 copies. Issued without dustwrapper. $125.

MUJUMDAR, D. C. *Encyclopedia of Indian Physical Culture.* Baroda (India), 1950. First edition stated. $50.

MUJUMDAR, S. *Strongmen Over the Years.* Lucknow (India), 1942. $100.

MULFORD, Clarence E. *Bar-20.* New York, 1907. First issue with "Blazed star" in list of illustrations. Author's first book. In dustwrapper. $600. Without dustwrapper. $150. Second issue, in dustwrapper. $500. Without dustwrapper. $100.

MULFORD, Clarence E. *Hopalong Cassidy.* Chicago, 1910. In dustwrapper. $350.

MULFORD, Clarence E. *Orphan.* In dustwrapper. $400.

MULLAN, John. *Miners' and Travelers' Guide to Oregon,* . . . New York, 1865. Folding colored map. $750.

MULLAN, John. *Report on the Construction of a Military Road from Fort Walla Walla to Fort Benton.* Washington, 1863. 4 folding maps, 10 plates. $450.

MULOCK, Dinah Maria (Mrs. Craik). See *The Adventures of a Brownie; The Fairy Book; John Halifax, Gentlemen; The Ogilvies.*

MUMEY, Nolie. *Calamity Jane.* Denver, 1950. Folding map, illustrations, 2 pamphlets in envelope at end. Boards, pictorial label. One of 200 signed. $175.

MUMEY, Nolie. *John Williams Gunnison.* Denver, 1955. Colored portrait, plates, folding map. Boards. One of 500 signed. Issued without dustwrapper. $125.

MUMEY, Nolie. *The Life of Jim Baker.* Denver, 1931. Frontispieces, other illustrations, map. Boards. One of 250 signed. Issued without dustwrapper. $250.

MUMEY, Nolie. *March of the First Dragoons to the Rocky Mountains in 1835.* Denver, 1957. Errata slip, plates, folding map. Boards. One of 350 signed. $150.

MUMEY, Nolie. *A Study of Rare Books.* Denver, 1930. Illustrated. Half cloth and boards. 1,000 signed, numbered copies. Author's first book. Issued without dustwrapper. $200.

MUMFORD, Lewis. *The Story of Utopias.* New York (1922). Author's first book. $300.

MUNBY, A. M. L. *Phillipps Studies.* Cambridge, 1951–1960. 5 vols. (complete set). $250.

MUNDY, Talbot. *The Ivory Trail.* Indianapolis (1919). Cloth. In dustwrapper. $400. Without dustwrapper. $100.

MUNDY, Talbot. *Queen Cleopatra.* Indianapolis (1929). One of 265 signed. $500.

MUNDY, Talbot. *Rung Ho!* New York, 1914. Author's first book. $150.

MUNDY, Talbot. *Tros of Samothrace.* New York, 1934. $300.

MUNRO, Alice. *Dance of the Happy Shades.* (Toronto, 1968.) Author's first book. $250.

MUNRO, H. H. See Saki.

MUNRO, H. H. *The Rise of the Russian Empire.* London, 1900. Author's first book. $250.

MUNRO, Robert. *A Description of the Genessee Country, in the State of New-York.* New York, 1804. (By Charles Williamson.) Map, 16 pages. $350.

MUNSELL, Charles. *Collection of Songs of the American Press* . . . Albany, 1868. $100.

MUNSELL, J. *A Chronology of Paper and Paper-Making.* Albany, 1857. Second edition, revised and enlarged. $175.

MUNSON, Gorham. *Waldo Frank: A Study.* New York (1923). Original photographic frontispiece portrait by Alfred Stieglitz. Boards. One of 500. $350.

MUNSON, Laura Gordon. *Flowers from My Garden.* New York, 1864. Frontispiece and 17 hand-colored reproductions. $950.

MURDOCH, Iris. *Sartre: Romantic Rationalist.* London, 1953. Author's first book. $175.

MURDOCK, Joseph S. F. *The Library of Gold 1743–1966.* Detroit, 1968. Slipcase. $300.

MURGATROYD, Captain Matthew. *The Refugee.* New York, 1825. (By James Athearn Jones, his first book.) 2 vols. $400.

MURRAY, Charles A. *Travels in North America.* London, 1839. 2 plates. 2 vols., in original cloth. $400. New York, 1839. 2 vols., in original cloth. First American edition. $350.

MURRAY, David. *Robert & Andrew Foulis and The Glasgow Press . . .* Glasgow, 1913. $125.

MURRAY, Hugh. *Historical Account of Discoveries and Travels In North America . . .* London, 1829. 2 vols. bound in 1, plus folding map. $400.

MURRAY, Lois L. *Incidents of Frontier Life.* Goshen, Ind., 1880. 2 portraits. $200.

MURRAY, Pauli. *Proud Shoes.* New York (1956). Author's first book. $125.

MURRELL, William. *A History of American Graphic Humor.* New York, 1933, 1938. 2 vols. $125.

MYERS, J. C. *Sketches on a Tour Through the Northern and Eastern States.* Harrisonburg, Va., 1849. Leather. $250.

MYRICK, Herbert. *Cache la Poudre: The Romance of a Tenderfoot in the Days of Custer.* New York, 1904. $150. Buckskin. One of 500 signed. $350.

MYSTERIES and Miseries of San Francisco (The). New York (1853). By a Californian. $1,500.

MYSTERIES of Mormonism (The): A Full Exposure of Its Secret Practices and Hidden Crimes. By an apostle's wife. New York (1882). Wraps. $250.

MYSTERIOUS Marksman (The): Or The Outlaws of New York. Cincinnati (about 1855). (By Emerson Bennett.) Wraps. $400.

N

NABOKOFF, Vladimir. *Laughter in the Dark.* Indianapolis (1938). (By Vladimir Nabokov.) Author's first book to be issued in the United States. (Published in England as *Camera Obscura.*) First issue in green cloth. $500. Variants. $350. London (1961). $125.

NABOKOFF-SIRIN, Vladimir. *Camera Obscura.* London (1936). Translated by Winifred Roy. (By Vladimir Nabokov.) First novel by the author to be published in English. (See *Laughter in the Dark,* above.) $3,000.

NABOKOFF-SIRIN, Vladimir. *Despair.* London (1937). (By Vladimir Nabokov.) $3,500.

NABOKOV, Vladimir. *Bend Sinister.* New York (1947). $200. London (1960). $150.

NABOKOV, Vladimir. *Conclusive Evidence: A Memoir.* New York (1951). Also has "A-A" on copyright page. $225.

NABOKOV, Vladimir. *The Eye.* New York, 1965. Publisher's address on copyright page. Dustwrapper printed on white laid uncoated paper with Trident Press mentioned at bottom of back flap. $60. London (1966). $40.

NABOKOV, Vladimir. *Invitation to a Beheading.* New York (1959). $75. London (1960). $75.

NABOKOV, Vladimir. *Lolita.* Olympia Press. Paris (1955). 2 vols. Printed price "Francs : 900" on back cover. $600. New York (1958). 1 vol. (Note: Book club copies have "Book Club Edition" on the corner of front flap [without dustwrapper cannot be distinguished from the trade edition].) $125. London (1959). $75.

NABOKOV, Vladimir. *Nikolai Gogol.* Norfolk, Conn. (1944). Tan cloth with brown lettering, 5 titles listed on verso of half title. Dustwrapper priced "$1.50." $150. Tan cloth with blue stamping and 14 titles listed on verso of half title. Dustwrapper price "$2.00" and 14 titles listed on back flap. $100. London (1947). $100.

NABOKOV, Vladimir. *Nine Stories.* (New York, 1947.) Published as *Direction Two.* This issue was devoted entirely to Nabokov. (Probably a few copies in cloth, perhaps black, would be worth quite a bit more.) $200.

NABOKOV, Vladimir. *Pale Fire.* New York (1962). Red endpapers. $150. London (1962). $75.

NABOKOV, Vladimir. *Poems.* Garden City, 1959. The Library of Congress deposit copy has "A25" on lower-right corner of page 44. $150. "A26" on lower-right corner of page 44. (Priority unknown, but we assume this might be a later issue.) $125. London (1961). $100.

NABOKOV, Vladimir. *The Real Life of Sebastian Knight.* Norfolk, Conn. (1941). First-issue binding: woven red burlap. $600. Bound in smooth red cloth. There were two variant dustwrappers with author's name spelled "Nabokov" or "Nabokoff," but priority unknown. $250. London (1945). $125.

NABOKOV, Vladimir. *Speak, Memory.* London, 1951. First issue in blue-green cloth with black stamping on dustwrapper without *Daily Mail* device on spine and at bottom of front flap. $225. Second issue in blue cloth and gilt stamping in dustwrapper with Daily Mail device on spine and at bottom of front flap. $175.

NABOKOV, Vladimir (translator). *Three Russian Poets: Selections from Pushkin, Lermontov, and Tyutchev.* Norfolk (1944). Stiff wraps. Variant (a): plain gray paper boards. Dustwrapper gray with brown lettering and "$1.,00" on upper corner of front flap. $200. Variant (b): Tan stapled pamphlet. Dustwrapper bluish gray with brown lettering and "$0.50" in lower-right corner of front flap. $125. London, 1947. $125.

NAIPAUL, V. S. *The Mystic Masseur.* London, 1957. Author's first book. $300. New York (1959). $100.

NANSEN, Fridtjof. *Farthest North.* London, 1897. 127 maps and 16 colored plates, 2 vols., pictorial cloth. $275. New York, 1897. 2 vols. $200.

NAPTON, William B. *Over the Santa Fe Trail,* 1857. Kansas City, 1905. Illustrated. 99 pages, pictorial wraps. $250.

NARRATIVE and Report of the Causes and Circumstances of the Deplorable Conflagration at Richmond. (Richmond, Va.?) 1812. $200.

NARRATIVE of the Adventures and Sufferings of Capt. Daniel D. Heustis (A). Boston, 1847. Frontispiece, 168 pages, printed wraps. $1,250.

NARRATIVE of Arthur Gordon Pym (The). New York, 1838. (By Edgar Allan Poe.) In original blue or gray cloth, paper label on spine. $4,000. London, 1838. Cloth. First English edition. $3,000. Limited Editions Club, New York, 1930. Boards. In slipcase. $125.

NARRATIVE of Captivity Among the Indians of North America . . . Chicago (1912). 2 vols. Stiff paper wraps. $125.

NARRATIVE of the Captivity and Providential Escape of Mrs. Jane Lewis. (Cover title.) (New York), 1833. (By William P. Edwards?) Woodcut plate. 24 pages. $350.

NARRATIVE of the Captivity and Sufferings of Ebenezer Fletcher of New-Ipswich (A). Windsor, Vt., 1813. 22 pages, stitched. Second edition. $300. New-Ipswich, N.H., 1827. Fourth edition (so stated; it is actually the third edition). $150 and up. New-Ipswich (about 1828). $75. (Note: There are only 3 known copies of the first edition, published in Amherst in 1798.)

NARRATIVE of the Captivity and Sufferings of Mrs. Hannah Lewis. Boston, 1811. (By William P. Edwards.) 24 pages, including folding woodcut plate. $600. Second edition, same date. $450.

NARRATIVE of the Capture and Burning of Fort Massachusetts. Albany, 1870. (By the Reverend John Norton.) Boards. One of 100. $100. (Note: The first edition, Boston, 1748, is very rare.)

NARRATIVE of the Capture and Providential Escape of Misses Frances and Almira Hall, etc. (St. Louis?) 1832. (By William P. Edwards?) Plate. 24 pages. $400. Later: 26 pages. (1833). Second edition. $300.

NARRATIVE of Dr. Livingston's Discoveries in Central Africa, from 1849 to 1856. London, 1857. Folding woodcut map. Illustrated boards. With David Livingstone's name spelled "Livingston." $500.

NARRATIVE of the Extraordinary Life of John Conrad Shafford. New York, 1840. Frontispiece, 25 pages, wraps. $300. New York, 1841. $150.

NARRATIVE of the Facts and Circumstances Relating to the Kidnapping and Presumed Murder of William Morgan (A). Batavia, N.Y., 1827. 36 pages. $250.

NARRATIVE of the Massacre at Chicago, August 15, 1812, and of Some Preceding Events. Chicago, 1844. (By Mrs. Juliette A. Kinzie.) Frontispiece map. 34 pages, printed wraps. $3,500.

NARRATIVE of Occurrences (A), in the Indian Countries of North America. London, 1807. (By Samuel Hull Wilcocke?) $750.

NARRATIVE of the Sufferings and Adventures of Capt. Charles H. Barnard (A). New York, 1829. Folding map, 6 plates. $250.

NARRATIVE of the Sufferings of Massy Harbison. Pittsburgh, 1825. 66 pages. $600. Pittsburgh, 1828. 98 pages. Second edition. $350. Beaver, Pa., 1836. Fourth edition. $150.

NARRATIVE of the Suppression by Col. Burr (A), of the "History of the Administration of John Adams." New York, 1802. (By James Cheetham.) $150.

NARRATIVE of the Tragical Death of Mr. Darius Barber and His Seven Children (A). Boston (about 1818). Frontispiece. 24 pages. $1,500.

NASBY, Petroleum V. *The Nasby Papers.* Indianapolis, 1864. (By David Ross Locke.) 64 pages, printed wraps. Author's first book. First binding, with "Indianaolis" on front cover. $200. Second binding, spelled correctly. $150.

NASH, Ogden. *Free Wheeling.* New York, 1931. $250.

NASH, Ogden. *Happy Days.* New York, 1933. $175.

NASH, Ogden. *Hard Lines.* New York, 1931. Illustrated by O. Soglow. Tan cloth. $250.

NATHAN, George Jean. See Hatteras, Owen; Mencken, H. L., and Nathan, George Jean.

NATHAN, Robert. *Autumn.* New York, 1921. $300.

NATHAN, Robert. *Peter Kindred.* New York, 1919. Author's first book. In dustwrapper. $500. Without dustwrapper. $100.

NATIVE (A). (By Thomas Jefferson.) *A Summary View of the Rights of British America . . .* Williamsburg (1774). Author's first book. $25,000. Philadelphia, 1774. $10,000.

NATURE. Boston, 1836. (By Ralph Waldo Emerson.) Emerson's first published book. First state, with page 94 misnumbered 92. $850. Correctly numbered. $450.

NAVAL Achievements of Great Britain and Her Allies from 1793 to 1817 (The). London (1817). Engraved title and 55 hand-colored plates. $6,000. (Almost as much with plates watermarked in the 1820s.)

NAVAL Monument (The) . . . Boston, 1816. (By Abel Bowen.) 26 plates. Calf. $400.

NAVIGATOR (The). Pittsburgh, 1804. (By Zadok Cramer.) Fourth edition (of *The Ohio and Mississippi Navigator,* which see) and first edition with this title. $2,500. Pittsburgh, 1806. 14 charts. 94 pages. Fifth edition. $2,000. Also, Pittsburgh, 1808. $1,000. Pittsburgh, 1811. $750. Pittsburgh, 1814. $500.

NAYLOR, Gloria. *The Women of Brewster Place.* New York, 1982. Author's first book. $300.

NEAGOE, Peter (editor). *Americans Abroad.* The Hague, Netherlands, 1932. Illustrated. First binding in gray cloth. $350. Second binding in yellow cloth, tan cloth spine. $300. (Contains Henry Miller's first book appearance, as well as new material by William Carlos Williams and others.)

NEAGOE, Peter. *Storm.* New Review. Paris, 1932. Author's first book (preceded by Obelisk edition). Wraps. $150. (One copy noted in cloth.)

NEAL, John. See Adams, Will. See also *Authorship: A Tale; Brother Jonathan; Keep Cool; Seventy-Six.*

NEAL, John. *The Moose-Hunter; or, Life in the Maine Woods.* New York (1864). Wraps. First issue, with no. 73 announced on the inside of the front cover. $450.

NEAL, John. *Rachel Dyer: A North American Story.* Portland, Me., 1828. $200.

NEED for Anonymity (The). Paris (1930). (By Michael Fraenkel and Walter Loewenfels.) Wraps. Fraenkel's first book. $175.

NEESE, George M. *Three Years in the Confederate Horse Artillery.* New York, 1911. $250.

NEGRO Pioneer, A. See *The Conquest.*

NEIHARDT, John G. *Black Elk Speaks.* New York, 1932. Illustrated, including color plates. Decorated cloth. $200.

NEIHARDT, John G. *A Bundle of Myrrh.* (New York, 1903.) Limp leather. One of 5. $1,000. New York, 1907. Boards and cloth. Revised edition. $150.

NEIHARDT, John G. *Collected Poems.* New York, 1926. 2 vols. One of 250 signed. $250.

NEIHARDT, John G. *The Divine Enchantment: A Mystical Poem.* New York, 1900. Cloth. Author's first book. $750.

NEIHARDT, John G. *The Song of the Indian Wars.* New York, 1925. One of 500 signed. $350. Trade. $150.

NEIL, John B. *Biennial Message of the Governor of Idaho to the 11th Session of the Legislature of Idaho Territory.* Boise City, Idaho, 1880. 19 pages, wraps. $150.

NEILSON, Shaw. *Heart of Spring.* Sydney, 1919. Author's first book. $350.

NEMEROV, Howard. *The Image and the Law.* (New York, 1947.) Cloth. Author's first book. $100.

NEMEROV, Howard. *The Painter Dreaming in the Scholar's House.* New York, 1968. Oblong, stiff wraps. One of 100 signed. In dustwrapper. $125. One of 26 signed. $200.

NEPHITE Records (The). (Independence, Mo.), 1899. (First printing of *The Book of Mormon* under this title.) $350.

NERUDA, Pablo. *Bestiary/Bestiario.* New York (1965). Woodcuts by Antonio Frasconi. Folio, boards, and cloth. One of 300 signed, with a signed frontispiece woodcut. In slipcase. $250.

NERUDA, Pablo. *Heights of Macchu Picchu.* London (1966). First English edition. $125.

NERUDA, Pablo. *We Are Many.* London (1967). Translated by Alastair Reid. Boards. First edition in English. One of 100 signed. In dustwrapper. $175.

NESBIT, Edith. *Ballads and Lyrics of Socialism, 1883–1908.* London, 1908. $100.

NESBIT, Edith. *Lays and Legends.* London, 1886. Author's first book. $200.

NESBIT, Edith. *The Railway Children.* London (1906). 20 plates. $150.

NETTLE, George. *A Practical Guide for Emigrants to North America.* London, 1850. Folding map in color. Printed yellow wraps. $250.

NEVILL, Ralph. *British Military Prints.* London, 1909. Plates, including color. $150.

NEVILL, Ralph. *Old English Sporting Books.* London, 1924. Plates, including color. Buckram. One of 1,500. Issued without dustwrapper. $300.

NEVILL, Ralph. *Old English Sporting Prints and Their History.* London, 1923. 103 full-page plates, 47 in color. Buckram. One of 1,500. Issued without dustwrapper. $300.

NEW-Englands Plantation. London, 1630. 11 leaves. First issue without the author's name (Francis Higginson) on title. $8,500.

NEW Bath Guide, or, Memoirs . . . (The). (By Christopher Anstey). London, 1766. Author's first book. $200.

NEW ENGLAND Primer Improved . . . Paisley, 1776. Original wraps, bound in. $2,000.

NEW SPAIN and the Anglo-American West: Contributions Presented to Herbert E. Bolton. (Los Angeles, 1932.) Portrait. 2 vols., cloth. One of 500. Slipcase. $250.

NEW TESTAMENT of Our Lord and Saviour Jesus Christ. New York, 1848. Translated into the Choctaw Language. Leather. $500. New York, 1854. Second edition. $100.

NEW Texas Spelling Book (The). Houston, 1863. (By E. H. Cushing.) Pictorial boards. $1,250.

NEW Topographical Atlas of St. Lawrence County, New York. Philadelphia, 1865. Colored maps and plans. $250.

NEW Translation with Notes (A), of the Third Satire of Juvenal. New York, 1806. (By Clement C. Moore and John Duer.) With "Additional Errata" leaf. Moore's first book appearance. $400.

NEW Year's Feast on His Coming of Age (The). London, 1824. (By Charles Lamb.) Hand-colored woodcuts. $350.

NEW YORK Book of Poetry (The). New York, 1837. (Edited anonymously by Charles Fenno Hoffman.) Engraved half title. In original cloth. (Contains first book appearance of Clement C. Moore's "A Visit from St. Nicholas.") $450.

NEW ZEALAND, Graphic and Descriptive. London, 1877. Edited by W.T.L. Travers and C. D. Barraud. Map, 25 colored lithographic views, 19 other views on 6 plates, woodcuts in text. Folio, half cloth. $250.

NEWBERRY, J. S. *Report on the Properties of the Ramshorn Consolidated Silver Mining Company at Bay Horse, Idaho.* New York (1881). 16 pages, wraps. $150.

NEWBOLT, Sir Henry. See *A Fair Death.*

NEWELL, Rev. Chester. *History of the Revolution in Texas.* New York, 1838. Folding map. In original cloth. $2,500.

NEWELL, Peter. See *Topsys & Turveys.*

NEWELL, Peter. *The Hole Book.* New York (1908). Illustrated in color by the author. Stapled blue cloth, pictorial cover label. With "Published October 1908" below copyright notice. $250.

NEWELL, Peter. *A Shadow Show.* New York, 1896. 36 color plates. Pictorial boards. $400.

NEWHALL, J. B. *The British Emigrants' "Hand Book."* (Cover title.) London, 1844. 99 pages, printed yellow wraps. $850.

NEWHALL, John B. *Sketches of Iowa.* New York, 1841. Map in color. Cloth. $1,250.

NEWLOVE, John. *Grave Sirs.* Vancouver, 1962. Author's first book. Stiff wraps. $200.

NEWMAN, Frances. *The Hard-Boiled Virgin.* New York, 1926. $200.

NEWMAN, John Henry, Cardinal. See *The Dream of Gerontius; Verses on Various Occasions.*

NEWMAN, John Henry, Cardinal. *Apologia Pro Vita Sua.* London, 1864. 8 parts, printed wraps. $1,250. London, 1864. First book edition. $500.

NEWMAN, John Henry, Cardinal, et al (editors). *Lyra Apostolics.* Derby, England, 1836. Purple cloth. $500.

NEWMARK, Harris. *Sixty Years in Southern California. 1853–1913.* New York, 1916. 33 plates. $150. Boston, 1930. Edited by M. H. and M. R. Newmark. 43 plates. Cloth. Issued without dustwrapper. $125.

NEWTON, A. Edward. *The Amenities of Book Collecting and Kindred Affections.* Boston, 1918. Author's first book. First issue, without index and page 268, line 3 "piccadilly." First-state dustwrapper has no printing on the covers except the spine. $225. With index. Second-state dustwrapper with printing on the front panel. $100.

NEWTON, A. Edward. *A Magnificent Farce and Other Diversions of a Book Collector.* Boston (1921). One of 265 signed. Slipcase. $100. Trade. $50.

NEWTON, A. Edward. *Mr. Strahan's Dinner Party.* San Francisco, 1930. One of 350 signed. $150.

NEWTON, A. Edward. *On Books and Business.* (New York) 1930. Boards. One of 325 signed. $150.

NEWTON, A. Edward. *Rare Books, etc.* (Sale catalogue.) New York, 1941. Illustrated. 3 vols., printed gray boards. In dustwrapper. $125.

NEWTON, Sir Isaac. *The Mathematical Principles of Natural Philosophy.* London, 1729. 2 vols. $3,500.

NEWTON, Sir Isaac. *Opticks* . . . London, 1704. With 19(?) folding plates. $7,500.

NEWTON, J. H. (editor). *History of the Pan-handle* . . . *West Virginia.* Wheeling, W. Va., 1879. Maps and plates. $200.

NEWTON, J. H. (editor). *History of* . . . *Venango County, Pennsylvania.* Columbus, Ohio, 1879. 47 plates. Half leather. $300.

NEWTON, James. *A Complete Herbal.* London, 1752. With portrait and 175 plates. $1,000.

NICHOLS, Beach. *Atlas of Schuyler County, New York.* Philadelphia, 1874. Folio, 21 maps in color, 31 leaves. $350.

NICHOLS, John. *The Milagro Beanfield War.* New York, 1974. $150.

NICHOLS, John. *The Sterile Cuckoo.* New York, 1965. Author's first book. $100.

NICHOLSON, James B. *A Manual of the Art of Bookbinding* . . . Philadelphia, 1856. 12 plates of bindings and 7 samples of marbled paper. $750.

NICHOLSON, William. *An Alphabet.* London, 1898. 14 leaves. $275.

NICK of the Woods, or The Jibbenainosay. Philadelphia, 1837. 2 vols., in original purple cloth, paper label. (By Robert Montgomery Bird.) $350.

NICOLLETT, Joseph Nicolas. *Report Intended to Illustrate a Map of the Hydrographical Basin of the Upper Missouri River.* Senate Doc. 237, 26th Congress, 2d session. Washington, 1843. Folding map, 170 pages, wraps or cloth. $350. Washington, 1845. House Doc. 52. Smaller map. Sewn. $150.

NICOLSON, Harold. *Paul Verlaine.* London (1921 on spine). Author's first book. $300.

NICOLSON, Harold. *Sweet Waters.* London, 1921. $300.

NICOLSON, Marjorie Hope. *Voyages to the Moon.* New York, 1948. $75.

NIEDECKER, Lorine. *New Goose.* Prairie City (1946). Author's first book. $1,250.

NIELSEN, Kay (illustrator). *East of the Sun and West of the Moon.* London (1914). (By Peter Christen Asbjornsen and Jorgen I. Moe.) 25 color plates. Cloth. $1,250. Vellum. One of 500 signed. $3,500.

NIGGER of the "Narcissus" (The). Preface. (Caption title only.) (Hythe, England, 1902.) (By Joseph Conrad.) Wire-stitched sheets. One of 100. Privately printed for Conrad, who had suppressed this preface in the first edition of his 1898 novel. (About 40 copies were accidentally destroyed.) $2,500.

NIGHTINGALE, Florence. *Notes on Nursing.* London (1859). Flexible cloth. $500. Later ads dated 1860. $300. New York, 1860. $200.

NIGHTMARE Abbey. London, 1818. (By Thomas Love Peacock.) $600.

NILE Notes of a Howadji. New York, 1851. (By George William Curtis.) Author's first book. Tan wraps. $200. Cloth: $100.

NIMMO, Joseph, Jr. *Range and Ranch Cattle Traffic.* (Caption title.) (Washington, 1884.) 4 folding maps, 200 pages, wraps. $2,000.

NIMROD. *The Life of a Sportsman.* London, 1842. (By C.J. Apperley.) 36 colored plates by Alken. First issue, in blue cloth. $1,500. Second issue, red cloth. $1,250. London, 1901. 2 vols., boards, folio. One of 60 large paper copies. $600. Trade edition. $250.

NIMROD'S Hunting Tours . . . London, 1903. (By C. J. Apperley.) 18 hand-colored plates. One of 500. $500.

NIN, Anaïs. *Children of the Albatross.* New York, 1947. $150.

NIN, Anaïs. *D. H. Lawrence: An Unprofessional Study.* Paris, 1932. Facsimiles. Black cloth. Author's first book. One of 550. $300.

NIN, Anaïs. *The House of Incest.* Paris (1936). Wraps. One of 249 signed. $500. (New York, 1947.) Gemor Press. Illustrated by Ian Hugo. Pictorial orange cloth. Issued without dustwrapper. $125. One of 50 signed. $250.

NIN, Anaïs. *Ladders to Fire.* New York, 1946. $150.

NIN, Anaïs. *This Hunger.* Gemor Press. (New York, 1945.) 5 hand-colored woodcuts by Ian Hugo. Decorated boards. One of 50 signed. Issued without dustwrapper. $400. Trade edition: one of 1,000. Issued without dustwrapper. $175.

NIN, Anaïs. *Under a Glass Bell and Other Stories.* New York (1944). (300 copies.) In dustwrapper. $350.

NIN, Anaïs. *Winter of Artifice.* Obelisk Press. Paris (1939). Wraps. $200. (New York, 1942.) Copper engravings by Ian Hugo. Pictorial boards. Issued without dustwrapper. (500 printed.) $250.

NINA Balatka. Edinburgh, 1867. (By Anthony Trollope.) 2 vols. First issue, with ad leaf inset in vol. 1. $750.

NINETY-FIRST Psalm (The). Golden Cockerel Press. (London, 1944.) 4 leaves. Wood engravings. In slipcase. $300. One of 50 specially bound. $750.

NISHIYAMA, H., and BROWN, Richard. *Karate, the Art of "Empty Hand" Fighting.* Tokyo, 1960. First edition stated. $50.

NIXON, Howard M. *Sixteenth-Century Gold-Tooled Bookbindings in the Pierpont Morgan Library.* New York, 1971. $200.

NOAH, Mordecai Manuel. See *The Fortress.*

NOBLE Fragment (A), Being a Leaf of the Gutenberg Bible 1450–1455 . . . New York, 1921. Title page, 4-page introduction by Newton and original leaf from the Gutenberg Bible. Slipcase. $15,000.

NOBLE Heritage (A), Two Conjugate Leaves From the First Edition of the Bishops' Bible . . . No-place (1973). Stiff wraps, slipcase. 220 numbered copies. $100.

NOGUCHI, Yone. *Hiroshige.* New York, 1921. Wraps. One of 750 with color frontispiece and 19 collotype plates. $400.

NOGUCHI, Yone. *Seen & Unseen.* San Francisco, 1896. Author's first book. $200.

NONESUCH Century (The): An Appraisal, a Personal Note and a Bibliography of the First Hundred Books Issued by the Press, 1923–1934. London, 1936. Illustrated. Buckram. One of 750. In dustwrapper. $600.

NORDEN, Charles. Panic Spring. New York (1937). (By Lawrence Durrell.) $1,000.

NORDHOFF, Charles. California for Health, Pleasure and Residence . . . New York, 1872. Illustrated, map. $200.

NORDHOFF, Charles B. See Hall, James Norman (for The Lafayette Flying Corps).

NORDHOFF, Charles B., and HALL, James Norman. Mutiny on the Bounty. Boston, 1932. First issue, with plain endpapers. $300. With pictorial endpapers. $150. Limited Editions Club, New York, 1947. In slipcase. $250.

NORMAN, Don Cleveland. The 500th Anniversary, Pictorial Census of the Gutenberg Bible. Chicago, 1961. Illustrated. Full leatherette. One of 985. In slipcase. $600.

NORMYX. Unprofessional Tales. London, 1901. (By Norman Douglas and Elsa Fitzgibbon.) Pictorial white cloth. One of 750 copies. Norman Douglas's first book, written in collaboration with his wife. $750.

NORRIS, Frank. McTeague: A Story of San Francisco. New York, 1899. Red cloth. With "moment" as last word on page 106. $600. San Francisco, 1941. Colt Press. Illustrated. Buckram and boards. One of 500. Issued without dustwrapper. $175.

NORRIS, Frank. Moran of the Lady Letty. New York, 1898. Green cloth. $150.

NORRIS, Frank. The Octopus. New York, 1901. Red cloth. With "J. J. Little" device on copyright page. (Later printings have "Manhattan Press.") $350.

NORRIS, Frank. The Responsibilities of the Novelist and Other Literary Essays. New York, 1903. In green cloth stamped in gold. (Also, a variant stamped in white with spine label.) $200.

NORRIS, Frank. Yvernelle: A Legend of Feudal France. Philadelphia, 1892 (actually 1891). Illustrations, some in color. Author's first book. Cloth. $1,000. Leather. $1,500.

NORRIS, J. W. A Business Advertiser and General Directory of the City of Chicago for the Year 1845–6. Chicago, 1845. Folding plate. 156 pages, wraps. $1,750.

NORRIS, J. W. General Directory and Business Advertiser of the City of Chicago for the Year 1844. Chicago, 1844. 116 pages, printed wraps. First printing. $2,250. Cloth, with binder's slip bound in. $2,000. (Note: This is the first Chicago city directory.)

NORTH-American and the West-Indian Gazetteer. London, 1776. Two folding maps. $1,000.

NORTH and South. London, 1855. 2 vols. (By Elizabeth C. Gaskell.) $750.

NORTH, Andrew. Plague Ship. New York (1956). (By Alice Mary Norton, whose main pseudonym is André Norton.) Probable first issue in tan boards. (Tan and red cloth believed later). $200.

NORTH, Anthony. Strike Deep. New York, 1974. (By Dean Koontz.) $250.

NORTH, Joseph. *Men in the Ranks: The Story of 12 Americans in Spain.* New York, 1939. Foreword by Ernest Hemingway. Wraps. $250.

NORTH, Thomas. *Five Years in Texas; or, What You Did Not Hear During the War.* Cincinnati, 1870. $400.

NORTHANGER Abbey; and Persuasion. London, 1818. By the Author of *Pride and Prejudice . . .* Jane Austen. 4 vols. $3,000.

NORTHERN Route to Idaho (The). St. Paul (1864). (By D. D. Merrill.) Large folding map, 8 pages of text. $1,750.

NORTON, André. See North, Andrew.

NORTON, André. *The Beast Master.* New York (1959). (By Alice Mary Norton.) $150.

NORTON, André. *The Prince Commands . . .* New York, 1934. (By Alice Mary Norton, her first book.) $750.

NORTON, André. *Shadow Hawk.* New York (1960). (By Alice Mary Norton.) $125.

NORTON, André. *Star Man's Son, 2250 A.D.* New York (1952). (By Alice Mary Norton, her first science-fiction novel.) $300.

NORTON, F. J. *A Descriptive Catalogue of Printing in Spain and Portugal, 1501–1520.* Cambridge (1978). $225.

NOTES on California and the Placers. New York, 1850. (By James Delavan.) 2 plates (not in all copies). 128 pages, printed wraps. $2,500 or more.

NOTORIOUS Outlaw (The), Jessie James. New York (1883?). 13 pages, pictorial wraps. First (?) edition. $600.

NOTT, Kathleen. *Mile End.* Hogarth Press. London, 1938. Author's first book. $125.

NOTT, Stanley Charles. *Chinese Jade Throughout the Ages.* London, 1936. 39 color illustrations, 182 in black and white. In dustwrapper. $200.

NOVAK, Joseph. *The Future Is Ours, Comrade.* Garden City, 1960. (By Jerzy Kosinski, his first book.) $250.

NOVAK, Joseph. *No Third Path.* Garden City, 1962. (By Jerzy Kosinski.) $125.

NOWLIN, William. *The Bark Covered House.* Detroit, 1876. 6 plates. $1,500.

NOYES, Al J. *In the Land of Chinook: or, The Story of Blaine County.* Helena, Mont. (1917). 24 plates. $250.

NOYES, Alva J. *The Story of Ajax: Life in the Big Horn Basin.* Helena, Mont., 1914. Frontispiece, 12 plates. $350.

NOYES, John Humphrey. *History of American Socialisms.* Philadelphia, 1870. $150.

NUTT, Frederic. *The Complete Confectioner.* New York, 1807. Frontispiece. First American edition. $250.

NUTTALL, Thomas. *The Genera of North American Plants.* Philadelphia, 1818. 2 vols. $300.

NUTTALL, Thomas. *Journal of Travels into the Arkansa Territory, During the Year 1819* . . . Philadelphia, 1821. Folding map, 5 plates. Boards. $1,000.

NUTTING, Wallace. *The Clock Book.* Framingham, Mass., 1924. In dustwrapper. $150.

NYE, Nelson C. *Pistols for Hire.* New York, 1941. $100.

NYE, Nelson C. *Two-Fisted Cowboy.* New York, 1936. Author's first book. $100.

NYE-STARR, Kate. *A Self-Sustaining Woman; or, The Experience of Seventy-Two Years.* Chicago, 1888. Portrait. Red cloth. $3,000.

O

OAK Openings (The); or, The Bee-Hunter. New York, 1848. By the Author of *The Pioneers,* James Fenimore Cooper. 2 vols., printed tan wraps. First American edition. $600.

OAKES, William. *Scenery of the White Mountains.* Cambridge, 1848. 16 colored plates (relatively common in tinted copies, but seldom found with the plates colored). $2,750.

OATES, Joyce Carol. *By the North Gate.* New York (1963). Author's first book. $150.

OATES, Joyce Carol. *Upon the Sweeping Flood and Other Stories.* New York (1966). $150.

OATES, Joyce Carol. *With Shuddering Fall.* New York (1964). $200.

OATES, Joyce Carol. *Women in Love and Other Poems.* New York, 1968. Decorated wraps. One of 150 signed. $250.

O'BETJEMAN, Deirdre. *Some Immortal Hours: A Rhapsody of the Celtic Twilight.* London, 1962. (By John Betjeman.) 7 leaves, folio. A facsimile printing of the author's holograph manuscript, hand colored and signed by Betjeman. $1,000.

O'BRIEN, Fitz-James. *Poems and Stories.* Boston, 1881. Author's first book. $250.

O'BRIEN, Fitz-James. *What Was It?* New York, 1974. Drawings by Leonard Baskin. Wraps. One of 200 signed by Baskin. $250.

O'BRIEN, Flann. *At Swim-Two-Birds.* London (1939). Black cloth. Author's first book. $2,000. Gray-green cloth. Issued in 1941 or 1942. $800. New York (1951). ("First published 1939" stated). $100.

O'BRIEN, Kate. *Distinguished Villa.* London, 1926. Author's first book. $175.

O'BRIEN, Tim. *If I Die in a Combat Zone.* New York (1973). Author's first book. $400. London (1973). $50.

O'BRIEN, Tim. *Northern Lights.* (New York, 1975.) $125. London (1976). $75.

O'BRYAN, William. *A Narrative of Travels in the United States . . . and Advice to Emigrants and Travellers Going to That Interesting Country.* London, 1836. Portrait. Dark blue cloth. $350.

OBSERVATIONS on the Wisconsin Territory. Philadelphia, 1835. Folding map. Cloth. (By William Rudolph Smith.) $650.

OBSERVATIONS upon Certain Passages in Mr. Jefferson's "Notes on Virginia." New York, 1804. 32 pages, plain blue-gray wraps, bound in. (Attributed to Clement C. Moore, his first if he wrote it.) $500.

O'CASEY, Sean. See O'Cathasaigh, P.

O'CASEY, Sean. *The Plough and the Stars.* London, 1926. Portrait. Boards and cloth. $150. New York, 1926. $100.

O'CASEY, Sean. *Two Plays.* London, 1926. $200.

O'CATHASAIGH, P. *The Story of the Irish Citizen Army.* Dublin, 1919. (By Sean O'Casey, his first book.) Gray wraps. $200. Second issue in tan wraps. $100.

O'CONNOR, Flannery. *The Artificial Nigger and Other Tales.* London (1957). The first U.K. edition of *A Good Man Is Hard to Find.* $300.

O'CONNOR, Flannery. *A Good Man Is Hard to Find.* New York (1955). (Dustwrapper spine is usually faded. The estimated price would be for unfaded one.) $500.

O'CONNOR, Flannery. *The Violent Bear It Away.* New York (1960). $250. London (1960). $150.

O'CONNOR, Flannery. *Wise Blood.* New York (1952). Author's first book. $850. London (1955). $300.

O'CONNOR, Frank. *A Lament for Art O'Leary.* Cuala Press. Dublin, 1940. Boards. One of 130. In dustwrapper. $600.

O'CONNOR, Frank. *Guests of the Nation.* London, 1931. Author's first book. $400.

O'CONNOR, Frank. *A Picture Book.* Cuala Press. Dublin, 1943. Illustrated by Elizabeth Rivers. Boards, linen spine. One of 480. In dustwrapper. $250.

O'CONNOR, Frank. *The Saint and Mary Kate.* London, 1932. $250.

O'CONNOR, Frank. *Three Old Brothers and Other Poems.* London (1936). $250.

O'CONNOR, Frank. *Three Tales.* Cuala Press. Dublin, 1941. Boards, linen spine. One of 250. In dustwrapper. $350.

O'CONNOR, Frank. *The Wild Bird's Nest.* Cuala Press. Dublin, 1932. Boards and cloth. One of 250. $250.

O'CONNOR, Jack. *Boom Town.* New York, 1938. $200.

O'CONNOR, Jack. *Conquest.* New York, 1930. Author's first book. $250.

OCULUS. *The Home of the Badgers.* Milwaukie [*sic*], 1845. (By Josiah B. Grinnell.) 36 pages, tan printed wraps. $1,500. (For second edition, see *Sketches of the West.*)

O'DAY, Nell. *A Catalogue of Books Printed by John Henry Nash . . .* San Francisco, 1937. One of 500 copies. $100.

ODE Performed in the Senate-House, Cambridge, on the Sixth of July, MDCCCXLVII at the First Commencement After the Installation of His Royal Highness the Prince Albert, Chancellor of the University. Cambridge, 1847. (By William Wordsworth.) 8 pages, printed wraps. $1,250.

ODE to Napoleon Buonaparte. London, 1814. 16 pages, wraps bound in. (By George Gordon Noel, Lord Byron.) $1,000.

ODES. (London, 1868.) (By Coventry Patmore.) Gray wraps. $300.

ODETS, Clifford. *Golden Boy.* New York (1937). $150.

ODETS, Clifford. *Three Plays.* New York (1935). Author's first book. $150.

OEHLER, Andrew. *The Life, Adventures, and Unparalleled Sufferings of Andrew Oehler.* (Trenton, N.J.) 1811. $500.

O'FAOLAIN, Sean. *Midsummer Night Madness & Other Stories.* London (1932). Preface by Edward Garnett. Author's first book. $250. New York, 1932. $125.

O'FAOLAIN, Sean. *A Nest of Simple Folk.* London (1933). $200.

O'FAOLAIN, Sean. *There's a Birdie in the Cage.* London, 1935. First separate edition. One of 285 signed. In dustwrapper. $150.

OFFICIAL Historical Atlas of Alameda County. Oakland, 1878. Folding maps, full-page views. Atlas folio, half leather. $650.

OFFICIAL State Brand Book of Colorado (The). Denver, 1894. Illustrated. $750.

OFFICINA Bodoni (The), The Operation of A Hand-Press During the First Six Years of Its Work. Paris/New York, 1929. One of 500 copies. $650.

O'FLAHERTY, Liam. *The Assassin.* London (1928). One of 150 signed. Issued without dustwrapper. $250.

O'FLAHERTY, Liam. *The Black Soul.* London (1924). $150.

O'FLAHERTY, Liam. *The Child of God.* London, 1926. Wraps. One of 100 signed. $250. One of 25 signed. $400.

O'FLAHERTY, Liam. *Civil War.* London, 1925. Wraps. One of 100 signed. $250.

O'FLAHERTY, Liam. *The Hollywood Cemetery.* London, 1935. $350.

O'FLAHERTY, Liam. *The Informer.* London (1925). $350.

O'FLAHERTY, Liam. *Return of the Brute.* London, 1929. $200. New York, 1930. $125.

O'FLAHERTY, Liam. *Thy Neighbor's Wife.* London (1923). Black cloth. Author's first book. $200.

OGDEN, George W. *Letters from the West.* New Bedford, Mass., 1823. $600.

OGILVIES (The). London, 1849. (By Dinah Maria Mulock.) 3 vols., cloth. Author's first novel. $300.

O'HARA, Frank. *A City Winter and Other Poems.* New York, 1951. Illustrated by Larry Rivers. Decorated wraps. One of 130. $500. Boards and cloth. One of 20 with an original drawing by Rivers. $1,500.

O'HARA, Frank. *The Collected Poems of Frank O'Hara.* New York, 1971. In suppressed dustwrapper with a photograph of Larry Rivers's drawing of a nude O'Hara. $175. In later jacket. $50.

O'HARA, Frank. *In Memory of My Feelings.* New York (1967). Illustrated. Folio, printed sheets in folder and slipcase. One of 2,500. $200.

O'HARA, Frank. *Robert Motherwell with Selections from the Artist's Writings.* New York (1965). Cloth. $250. Wraps. $50.

O'HARA, John. *Appointment in Samarra.* New York (1934). Author's first book. Black cloth. Errata slip laid in. In dustwrapper with "Recent Fiction" on back panel. $1,000.

O'HARA, John. *Butterfield 8.* New York (1935). $250.

O'HARA, John. *The Doctor's Son.* New York (1935). $1,250.

O'HARA, John. *Hope of Heaven.* New York (1938). $300.

O'HARA, John. *Pal Joey.* New York (1940). $250.

O'HARA, John. *Ten North Frederick.* New York (1955). $125.

OHASHI, M. *Scientific Jiu-Jitsu.* New York, 1912. Wraps. $50.

OLD, R. O. *Colorado: United States, of America. Its History, Geography, and Mining.* London, 1869. 64 pages, printed tan wraps. $600.

OLDER, (Mr. and Mrs.) Fremont. *The Life of George Hearst, California Pioneer.* San Francisco, 1933. Illustrated. Vellum. John Henry Nash printing. $400.

OLDHAM, J. Basil. *Blind Panels of English Binders.* Cambridge, 1958. 67 plates. $250.

OLDHAM, J. Basil. *English Blind-Stamped Bindings.* Cambridge, 1952. 61 plates. One of 750 copies. $250.

OLDHAM, J. Basil. *Shrewsbury School Library Binding, Catalogue Raisonne.* Oxford, 1943. Frontispiece and 62 plates. 200 numbered copies. $1,000.

OLDHAM, Williamson S., and WHITE, George W. *Digest of the General Statute Laws of the State of Texas.* Austin, 1859. $350.

OLDSTYLE, Jonathan. *Letters of Jonathan Oldstyle, Gent.* New York, 1824. By the Author of *The Sketch-Book,* Washington Irving. $300.

OLIPHANT, Laurence. *Minnesota and the Far West.* Edinburgh, 1855. Folding map and 7 plates. Half leather. $250.

OLIVER, Frederick S. See *Phylos the Tibetan.*

OLIVER, John W. (publisher). *Guide to the New Gold Region of Western Kansas and Nebraska.* New York, 1859. Folding map. 32 pages, printed wraps. $6,000.

OLLA Podrida. London, 1840. (By Frederick Marryat.) 3 vols., in original boards and cloth, or cloth. $300.

OLLIVANT, Alfred. *Bob: Son of Battle.* New York, 1898. Green decorated cloth. Author's first book. $150.

OLMAN, Morton and John. *The Encyclopedia of Golf Collectibles.* Florence, Ala. (1985). Limited edition. $125.

OLMSTED, Frederick Law. *A Journey Through Texas . . .* New York, 1857. Frontispiece and folding map. $300.

OLSEN, Tillie. *Tell Me a Riddle.* Philadelphia, 1961. Author's first book. Cloth. $250. Wraps. $40. London (1964). First English edition. $100.

OLSON, Charles. *Call Me Ishmael.* Grove Press. New York (1947). Yellow cloth. First edition not stated. Author's first book. $250. New York (1958). Cloth. Issued without dustwrapper. One of 100. $200. (No limitation.) $100. Wraps. $25.

OLSON, Charles. *Human Universe and Other Essays.* San Francisco, 1965. Edited by Donald Allen. Woodcut by Robert LaVigne, photography by Kenneth Irby. Decorated boards, vellum spine. One of 250. In plain dustwrapper. $300.

OLSON, Charles. *Letter for Melville 1951.* (Black Mountain, N.C., 1951.) Wraps. One of about 40. $750. One of 10 with watercolor design by Charles Oscar. $1,500.

OLSON, Charles. *The Maximus Poems.* New York, 1960. Boards. First complete edition. One of 26 lettered and signed. $1,000. One of 75 signed. $750. (Issued without dustwrapper.) Trade in wraps. (First printing has $1.95 on back cover.) $50.

OLSON, Charles. *Y & X.* Black Sun Press. (Washington) 1948. Illustrated by Corrado Cagli. Printed gray wraps. First edition not stated. One of at least 118 in slipcase. $500. White wraps. One of 400 in envelope. $300. (Offset reprint in 1950 without date on title page).

OMAR Khayyam. See *The Rose Garden of Omar Khayyam; Rubaiyat of Omar Khayyam.*

ON English Prose Fiction as Rational Amusement. (Caption title.) (London, 1869?) (By Anthony Trollope.) 44 pages, sewn. $1,000.

ON the Plains; or, The Race for Life. New York (1863). 62 pages, pictorial yellow wraps. (By Edward S. Ellis.) $400.

ON the "White Pass" Pay-Roll. Chicago, 1908. By the President of the White Pass & Yukon Route (S. H. Graves). 15 plates. Dark blue cloth. $350.

ONDAATJE, Michael. *The Dainty Monsters.* Toronto, 1967. Author's first book. 500 numbered copies. $200.

ONDERDONK, James L. *Idaho: Facts and Statistics.* San Francisco, 1885. Wraps. $300.

ONE and Twenty: Duke Narrative and Verse, 1924–1945. (Contains two short stories by William Styron, his first book appearance.) $125.

ONE Hundred and Seventy-six Historic and Artistic Book-Bindings Dating from the Fifteenth Century to the Present Time. New York, 1895. 2 vols. One of 200 copies on Imperial Japanese Paper. $800.

ONE Hundred Books Famous in English Literature. See Kent, Henry W.

ONE Hundred Influential American Books Printed Before 1900. New York, 1947. One of 600 copies. $275.

O'NEILL, Eugene. See Sanborn, Ralph; Shay, Frank. See also *George Pierce Baker, a Memorial.*

O'NEILL, Eugene. *Ah. Wilderness!* New York, 1933. $125. Blue calf. One of 325 signed. In slipcase. $400.

O'NEILL, Eugene. *All God's Chillun Got Wings, and Welded.* New York (1924). Buff boards and cloth. $350.

O'NEILL, Eugene. *Anna Christie.* London (1923). First separate edition. Yellow boards in dustwrapper. $300. Wraps. $250. New York, 1930. 12 illustrations by Alexander King. Purple and red boards, black cloth spine. First illustrated (and first American) edition. One of 775. In dustwrapper and slipcase. $400. One of 12 in morocco, signed and with an original lithograph. $1,000.

O'NEILL, Eugene. *Before Breakfast.* New York, 1916. Light blue-green wraps. First separate edition. $400.

O'NEILL, Eugene. *Beyond the Horizon.* New York (1920). Brown boards and cloth. Probable first state, with small letters on front cover ¼ inch high. In dustwrapper. $350. Second state with letters ⅛ inch high. (Atkinson considers them variants.) $300.

O'NEILL, Eugene. *Desire Under the Elms.* New York, 1925. Pictorial black cloth. First separate edition. $450.

O'NEILL, Eugene. *Dynamo.* New York, 1929. $150. Purple vellum. One of 775 signed. In slipcase. $300.

O'NEILL, Eugene. *The Emperor Jones; Diff'rent; The Straw.* New York (1921). Buff boards and cloth. First issue (VAB) with plain (not mottled) boards. In dustwrapper. $300. (Atkinson identifies 2 variants both in tan boards. One has "Eugene G. O'Neill" and the other lacks the "G.") Cincinnati (1921). White wraps. $250. New York, 1928. 8 illustrations in color by Alexander King. Boards and cloth. One of 775 signed. In dustwrapper and slipcase. $500.

O'NEILL, Eugene. *Gold.* New York, with 1920 copyright but published in (1921). Blue-green boards and cloth. In dustwrapper. $400.

O'NEILL, Eugene. *The Great God Brown: The Fountain; The Moon of the Caribbees and Other Plays.* New York, 1926. Green cloth. $250. London (1926). *(The Great God Brown.)* Bright blue cloth. First English edition. $200.

O'NEILL, Eugene. *The Hairy Ape; Anna Christie; The First Man.* New York (1922). Buff boards and cloth. In dustwrapper. $300. London (1923). *(The Hairy Ape and Other Plays.)* Bright blue cloth. First English edition. In dustwrapper. $150. New York (1929). 9 illustrations in color by Alexander King. Boards. First separate and illustrated edition. One of 775 signed. In dustwrapper and slipcase. $350.

O'NEILL, Eugene. *Long Day's Journey into Night.* New Haven, 1956. Black-and-gray cloth. First edition stated. $125.

O'NEILL, Eugene. *Marco Millions.* New York, 1927. $150. Vellum and boards. One of 450 signed. In slipcase. $350.

O'NEILL, Eugene. *The Moon of the Caribbees and Six Other Plays of the Sea.* New York, 1919. Brown boards and cloth. First state, ⅞ inch thick (Johnson). In dustwrapper. $500. Second state, 1³⁄₁₆ inches thick. In dustwrapper. $450. (Atkinson calls these variants, not states.)

O'NEILL, Eugene. *Mourning Becomes Electra.* New York, 1931. Cloth. $150. Japan vellum. One of 550 signed. In slipcase. $400.

O'NEILL, Eugene. *Strange Interlude.* New York, 1928. $150. Another (later) issue: vellum. One of 775 signed. In slipcase. $350.

O'NEILL, Eugene. *Thirst and Other One Act Plays.* Boston (1914). Dark gray boards, tan cloth spine, paper labels. Author's first book. $400.

ONGANIA, Ferd. *Early Venetian Printing Illustrated.* Venice/New York, 1895. $100.

ONIONS, Oliver. *The Compleat Bachelor.* London, 1900. Author's first book. $60.

ONKEN, Otto. See Wells, William.

OPPEN, George. *Discreet Series.* New York, 1934. Preface by Ezra Pound. Author's first book. $500.

OPPENHEIMER, Joel. *Four Poems to Spring.* (Black Mountain, 1951.) Author's first book. Wraps. $250.

OPPENHEIMER, Joel. *The Dancer.* Highlands, N.C., 1952. *(Jargon 2.)* $500.

OPTIC, Oliver. See Ashton, Warren T.

OPTIC, Oliver. *The Boat Club; or, The Bunkers of Rippleton.* Boston, 1855. (By William Taylor Adams.) Frontispiece, 3 plates. Slate-purple pictorial cloth. $200. Pictorial presentation binding. $300. First Oliver Optic book.

ORCUTT, William Dana. *The Book in Italy.* New York, 1928. Plates, including color. Folio, boards. One of 750. In dustwrapper. $100. London, 1928. One of 12 lettered copies (reserved for the author). $125.

ORCUTT, William Dana. *In Quest of the Perfect Book.* Boston, 1926. Plates, including color. Half vellum. One of 365. In dustwrapper. $125. Trade. $40.

ORCZY, Baroness. *The Emperor's Candlesticks.* London, 1899. Author's first book. $175.

OREGON: Agricultural, Stock Raising, Mineral Resources, Climate . . . (Published by U.P.R.R.) Council Bluffs, Iowa, 1888. 68 pages, wraps. $200.

O'REILLY, Bernard. *Greenland, the Adjacent Seas, and the North-West Passage* . . . London, 1818. 3 folding charts, 18 plates. $750.

O'REILLY, Harrington. *Fifty Years on the Trail.* London, 1889. Illustrated by Paul Frenzeny. Pictorial cloth. $200. London, 1890. Wraps. Second edition. $150. New York, 1889. First American edition. $125.

ORIGINAL Leaf from Francisco Paolou's Life of the Venerable Father Junipero Serro, 1787. . . (San Francisco) 1958. One of 177 copies. Contains an original leaf. Stiff paper wraps. $150.

ORIGINAL Leaf from the Polycronicon Printed by William Caxton at Westminster in the year 1482 . . . with an Appreciation . . . by Edwin Grabhorn. San Francisco, 1938. 297 copies with an original leaf from the *Polycronicon* mounted. $900.

ORIGO, Iris. *Allegra.* Hogarth Press. London, 1935. In dustwrapper with wraparound band. $100.

ORIOLI, G. *Adventures of a Bookseller.* Florence, Italy (no-date). Stiff paper wraps. One of 300 signed and numbered copies. $150.

ORME, Edward. *Collection of British Field Sports* . . . London, 1807–8. Colored title page and 20 colored plates after Howitt. Oblong folio. $45,000. Guildford, England, 1955. 29 color plates. Facsimile. Folio, full crimson morocco. One of 20 with an original plate included. $1,500. Trade edition in half morocco. $400.

ORR, George. *The Possession of Louisiana by the French.* London, 1803. 44 pages. $400.

ORR, N. M. (compiler). *The City of Stockton.* Stockton, Calif., 1874. 64 pages, printed wraps. $200.

ORR and Ruggles. *San Joaquin County.* Stockton, 1887. Map, plates. 130 pages, wraps. $200.

ORTON, Richard H. *Records of California Men in the War of the Rebellion, 1861–1867.* Sacramento, 1890. $100.

ORVIS, Charles F., and CHENY, A. Nelson (compilers). *Fishing with the Fly* . . . Manchester, Vt., 1883. Frontispiece map and 15 color plates. $300.

ORWELL, George. *Animal Farm: A Fairy Story.* London, 1945. $1,250. New York (1946). Black cloth. $125.

ORWELL, George. *Burmese Days.* New York, 1934. $900. London, 1935. $1,250.

ORWELL, George. *A Clergyman's Daughter.* London, 1935. $1,500. New York, 1936. $850.

ORWELL, George. *Down and Out in Paris and London.* London, 1933. First printing. $3,000. Second printing. $400. Third printing. $175. New York, 1933. $1,000.

ORWELL, George. *Homage to Catalonia.* London, 1938. $1,500. New York (1952). $60.

ORWELL, George. *Inside the Whale.* London, 1940. $1,200.

ORWELL, George. *Keep the Aspidistra Flying.* London, 1936. $1,500. New York (1956). $100.

ORWELL, George. *The Lion and the Unicorn.* New York, 1941. $200.

ORWELL, George. *Nineteen Eighty-four.* London, 1949. Red dustwrapper seems to be preferred (priority uncertain), both noted in Book Society wraparound bands. $1,000. Green dustwrapper. $750. New York (1949). Red dustwrapper also preferred on U.S. edition (Book-of-the-Month Club edition was blue and perhaps that is why blue is considered later). $200. Blue dustwrapper. $150.

ORWELL, George. *The Road to Wigan Pier.* London, 1937. Cloth and dustwrapper. $1,000. Left Book Club edition. Limp oilcloth covers. $100. First half of text as supplementary offering for May 1937. 32 plates, chapters 1 to 7 only. Limp oilcloth covers. $750. New York (1958). $75.

ORWELL, George. *Shooting an Elephant and Other Essays.* London, 1950. $125. New York (1950). $100.

OSBORNE, Eric. *Victorian Detective Fiction.* London, 1966. Introduction by John Carter. One of 500 signed by Carter and by Dorothy Glover and Graham Greene, whose collection is catalogued in the book. In dustwrapper. $500.

OSBORNE, John. *Look Back in Anger.* Evans Brothers. London, 1957. His first published play. Wraps. $150. Faber. London, 1957. Cloth. $100. New York, 1957. $50.

OSBORNE, John, and CREIGHTON, Anthony. *Epitaph for George Dillon.* London (1958). $125.

OSCEOLA; or, Fact and Fiction: A Tale of the Seminole War. New York, 1838. By a Southerner (James Birchett Ransom). $250.

OSGOOD, Ernest Staples. *The Day of the Cattleman.* Minneapolis, 1929. 14 plates and maps. In dustwrapper. $250.

OSGOOD, Frances S. *The Floral Offering . . . of Poetry.* New York, 1847. With 10 hand-colored plates. $650.

O'SHAUGHNESSY, Arthur W. E. *An Epic of Women and Other Poems.* London, 1870. Pictorial title page, 2 plates, precedes title page. Purple cloth. Author's first book. $200.

O'SHAUGHNESSY, Arthur W. E. *Songs of a Worker.* London, 1881. $150.

OSLER, Sir William. *An Alabama Student and Other Biographical Essays.* Oxford, England, 1908. $150. New York, 1908. $125.

OSLER, Sir William (editor). *Bibliotheca Osleriana: A Catalogue of Books Illustrating the History of Medicine and Science.* Oxford, 1929. $600.

OSLER, Sir William. *The Cerebral Palsies of Children.* Philadelphia, 1889. $200.

OSLER, Sir William. *The Evolution of Modern Medicine.* New Haven, 1921. $250.

OSLER, Sir William. *Incunabula Medica: A Study of the Earliest Printed Medical Books, 1467–1480.* London, 1923. Illustrated. Boards and cloth. Issued without dustwrapper. $600.

OSLER, Sir William. *The Principles and Practice of Medicine.* New York, 1892. With "Georgias" on leaf preceding table of contents, and last set of ads dated March 1892. In sheep. $1,500. Cloth. $1,000. Edinburgh, 1894. Second state reading "Gorgias" with later dated ads. $500. First English edition. $750.

OTIS, James. *Toby Tyler or Ten Weeks with a Circus.* New York, 1881. (By James Otis Kaler.) Illustrated by W. A. Rogers. Light brown, green, or orange cloth. $400.

OTTLEY, William Young. *An Inquiry Concerning the Invention of Printing . . .* London, 1862. 37 full-page plates. $250.

OUIDA. *Syrlin.* London, 1880 vols., cloth. (By Marie Louise de la Ramee.) $350.

OUIDA. *Under Two Flags.* London, 1867. 3 vols. (By Marie Louise de la Ramee.) $500.

OUIMET, Francis. *A Game of Golf: A Book of Reminiscenses.* Boston, 1932. Signed limited edition in slipcase. $450.

OURSLER, Fulton. See Abbot, Anthony.

OUTCROPPINGS: Being Selections of California Verse. San Francisco, 1866. (Edited anonymously by Bret Harte.) Probable first issue, with "Staining" spelled "Braining" on page 70 and with no ornament on page 102. $300.

OUTRE-MER: A Pilgrimage Beyond the Sea. Nos. I and II. Boston, 1833 and 1834. (By Henry Wadsworth Longfellow.) In original marbled wraps and blue wraps or boards. $1,500. (See BAL.) Also issued clothbound as 2 vols. in one. $500.

OVID. The Amores of P. Ovidius Naso. Golden Cockerel Press. Waltham Saint Lawrence, England, 1932. Translated by E. Powys Mathers. 5 engravings on copper by T. E. Laboureur. Half morocco issued without dustwrapper. One of 350. $350.

OWEN, John Pickard. *The Fair Haven.* London, 1873. By the late John Pickard Owen. Edited by William Bickersteth Owen. (By Samuel Butler.) $125.

OWEN, Richard E., and COX, E. T. *Report on the Mines of New Mexico.* (Cover title.) Washington, 1865. 59 pages, printed wraps. $600.

OWEN, Robert. See Campbell, Alexander.

OWEN, Robert. *A New View of Society.* London, 1813–14. 4 parts in 1, boards. $1,500. London, 1816. Boards. Second edition. $300.

OWEN, Wilfred. *Poems.* London, 1920. Author's first book. Cloth, paper label. In dustwrapper. $1,500. New York (1921). In dustwrapper. $600. London, 1931. First complete edition. $250.

OWEN, Wilfred. *Thirteen Poems.* Gehenna Press. Northampton, Mass., 1956. Drawings by Ben Shahn and Leonard Baskin. Folio, half morocco. One of 400 signed by Baskin. Issued without dustwrapper. $350. One of 35 specially bound and with a proof of portrait signed by both artists. $1,250.

OWENS, Rochelle. *Not Be Essence That Cannot Be.* New York (1961). Stiff printed wraps. Author's first book. $60.

OWL Creek Letters (The). (By William C. Prime.) New York, 1848. Author's first book. $150.

OZICK, Cynthia. *Trust.* New York (1966). Author's first book. $200. London (1966). $75.

P

P., E. *Hugh Selwyn Mauberley.* Ovid Press. (London) 1920. (By Ezra Pound.) One of 165 from an edition of 200. $3,500. Cloth. One of 20 signed. $4,000. Parchment boards. One of 15 on vellum. $4,500.

PACKARD, Wellman, and LARISON, G. *Early Emigration to California.* Bloomington, Ill., 1928. 2 portraits, 23 pages, printed wraps. One of 30. $600.

PADGETT, Lewis. *The Brass Ring.* New York (1946). First edition stated. $300.

PADGETT, Lewis. *A Gnome There Was and Other Tales of Science Fiction and Fantasy.* New York, 1950. First edition not stated. $150.

PAGAN Anthology (The). New York (1918). Boards, paper label. (Contains 2 poems by Hart Crane, constituting his first book appearance.) $350.

PAGE, Stanton. *The Chevalier of Pensieri-Vani.* Boston (1890). Cloth, or wraps. (By Henry Blake Fuller, his first book.) Wraps. $500. Cloth. $150.

PAGE, Thomas Nelson. *In Old Virginia.* New York, 1887. Pictorial cloth. Author's first book. First issue, with advertisement headed "Popular Books . . . Old Creole Days . . ." $100.

PAGE, Thomas Nelson. *Two Little Confederates.* New York, 1888. Illustrated. Blue cloth. With 10 ad pages at back. (Second had 8 pages.) $125.

PAGES, Pierre Marie. *Travels Round the World in the Years 1767 . . .* London, 1791. 2 vols. First English edition, after the first, in French, in 1782. $1,750.

PAINE, Albert Bigelow. See White, W. A. *Rhymes . . .*

PAINE, Albert Bigelow. *Captain Bill McDonald, Texas Ranger.* New York, 1909. Illustrated. $200. Morocco. $300.

PAINE, Albert Bigelow. *Gabriel a Poem.* (Fort Scott, Kan., 1899.) Author's first book. Wraps. $300.

PAINE, Albert Bigelow. *Thomas Nast: His Period and His Pictures.* New York, 1904. Illustrated. $150.

PALEY, Grace. *The Little Disturbances of Man.* Garden City, 1959. Author's first book. $125. London, 1960. $75.

PALGRAVE, Francis Turner. *The Golden Treasury of the Best Songs and Lyrical Poems of the English Language.* Cambridge, 1861. One of 500. $1,750.

PALINURUS. *The Unquiet Grave: A Word Cycle.* London, 1944. (By Cyril Connolly.) Curwen Press. Frontispiece and 3 collotype plates. Cloth. $350. Gray wraps. One of 1,000. $150.

PALLADINO, Lawrence B. *Indian and White in the Northwest.* Baltimore, 1894. Illustrated. Cloth, or half leather. $150.

PALLAS, P. S. *Travels Through the Southern Provinces of the Russian Empire . . .* London, 1802–3. 4 folding maps and 51 plates (42 folding). 2 vols. First English edition. $1,250. (The more hand-colored plates the better.)

PALLISER, John. *Exploration—British North America.* London, 1859–65. 4 parts bound in 1. 16 maps. $8,500.

PALMER, H. E. *The Powder River Indian Expedition, 1865.* Omaha, 1887. 59 pages, printed gray wraps. $350.

PALMER, Harry. *Base Ball: The National Game of the Americans.* Chicago, 1888. 69 pages, wraps. $600.

PALMER, Joel. *Journal of Travels over the Rocky Mountains, to the Mouth of the Columbia River, etc.* Cincinnati, 1847. Brown printed wraps. First issue, with date 1847 on paper cover not overprinted or changed, and with errata slip tipped in. $3,000. Cincinnati, 1852. Half leather. Second edition. $750.

PALMER, S. *The General History of Printing, from Its First Invention in the City of Maintz . . .* London, 1732. $550.

PALMER, Stuart. *The Ace of Jades.* New York, 1931. Author's first book. $300.

PALMER, Stuart. *The Penguin Pool Murders.* New York, 1931. $250.

PALMER, William J. *Report of Surveys Across the Continent.* Philadelphia, 1869. 3 maps and profile, 20 photographic plates. Wraps. $850. Later issue, cloth. $600.

PALTSITS. Victor Hugo. *Washington's Farewell Address, in Facsimile . . .* New York, 1935. One of 500 copies. $200.

PAPWORTH, John B. *Hints on Ornamental Gardening.* London, 1823. 28 hand-colored plates, sepia plate, woodcut plans. $1,250.

PAPWORTH, John B. *Rural Residences . . .* London, 1818. 27 full-page hand-colored aquatint plates. Boards. $1,000.

PAPWORTH, John B. *Select Views of London.* London, 1816. 76 colored aquatint plates, 5 folding. First book edition. $2,500.

PARK, Munro. *Travels in the Interior Districts of Africa.* London, 1799. With 3 folding maps, 6 plates, and 2 leaves of music. $600.

PARK, William J. *Art of Putting.* Edinburgh, 1920. $300.

PARK, William Jr. *Game of Golf.* London, 1896. $150.

PARKER, A. A. *A Trip to the West and Texas.* Concord, N.H., 1835. 2 plates. Map. $400. Concord, 1836. Colored folding map and 3 plates. Second edition. $400. (Note: Howes reports 2 plates in the first edition, VAB's copy came with 3. Howes says not all copies of the second edition included the map; in such cases the value would be less.)

PARKER, Aaron. *Forgotten Tragedies of Indian Warfare in Idaho.* Grangeville, Idaho, 1925. 10 pages, double column, wraps. $150.

PARKER, Dorothy. *After Such Pleasures.* New York, 1933. One of 250 signed. In slipcase. $200. Trade edition. $100.

PARKER, Dorothy. *Death and Taxes.* New York, 1931. One of 250 signed. In slipcase. $250. Trade states, "Second printing before publication." $125.

PARKER, Dorothy. *Men I'm Not Married To.* Garden City, 1922. First edition stated. Author's first separate book, preceded by some collaborations. (Bound dos-a-dos with *Women I'm Not Married To,* by Franklin P. Adams.) In dustwrapper. $400.

PARKER, Dorothy. *Sunset Gun.* New York, 1928. Boards and cloth. One of 275 signed. In slipcase. $250. Trade. $150.

PARKER, Frank J. (editor). *Washington Territory! The Present and Prospective Future of the Upper Columbia Country.* Walla Walla, Wash., 1881. 17 pages, printed wraps. $1,000.

PARKER, J. M. *An Aged Wanderer: A Life Sketch of . . . a Cowboy, on the Western Plains in Early Days.* San Angelo, Tex., no-date. 32 pages, wraps. $850.

PARKER, John R. *The United States Telegraph Vocabulary.* Boston, 1832. 3 plates, one in color. $200.

PARKER, Robert B. *The Godwulf Manuscript.* Boston, 1974. Author's first Spenser mystery. $275. (London, 1974.) $150.

PARKER, Robert B. *God Save the Child.* Boston, 1974. $275. (London, 1975.) $125.

PARKER, Robert B. *Mortal Stakes.* Boston, 1975. $200. (London, 1976.) Issued without front endpaper. $100.

PARKER, Samuel. *Journal of an Exploring Tour Beyond the Rocky Mountains.* Ithaca, N.Y., 1838. Folding map, plate. In original cloth. $500.

PARKER, Solomon. *Parker's American Citizen's Sure Guide.* Sag Harbor, N.Y., 1808. $150.

PARKER, W. B. *Notes Taken During the Expedition Commanded by Capt. R. B. Marcy . . .* Philadelphia, 1856. $750.

PARKER & HUYETT. *The Illustrated Miners' Hand-Book and Guide to Pike's Peak.* St. Louis, 1859. (By Nathan H. Parker and D. H. Huyett.) 6 plates, 2 folding maps. Cloth. $5,000.

PARKINSON, C. Northcote. *Edward Pellew . . .* London (1934). Author's first book. $125.

PARKMAN, Francis. *The California and Oregon Trail.* New York, 1849. 2 vols., printed wraps. $12,500. Or clothbound in one volume with frontispiece and engraved title page, and terminal catalog inserted, not integral. $1,500.

PARKMAN, Francis. *History of the Conspiracy of Pontiac and the War of the North American Tribes* . . . Boston, 1851. 4 maps. $200.

PARKMAN, Francis. *The Oregon Trail.* Boston, 1892. Illustrated by Frederic Remington. Leather. $600. Pictorial tan cloth. $400. Boston, 1925. Illustrated by Remington and N. C. Wyeth. Half cloth. One of 875. $250. New York, 1943. Limited Editions Club. In slipcase. $150.

PARLEY, Peter. *Peter Parley's Universal History, on the Basis of Geography.* Boston, 1837. (By Nathaniel Hawthorne and his sister Elizabeth.) 2 vols., in original cloth. $4,000 at auction in 1990.

PARLEY, Peter. *The Tales of Peter Parley About America.* Boston, 1827. (By Samuel G. Goodrich.) 32 (30?) engravings. In original blue boards, red leather spine. Author's first book. $3,500.

PARMLY, Levi Spear. *A Practical Guide to the Management of the Teeth.* Philadelphia, 1819. $500.

PARNELL, Thomas. *Poems.* Cuala Press. Dublin, 1927. Selected by Lennox Robinson. Boards and linen. One of 200. In dustwrapper. $125.

PARRISH, Anne. *A Pocketful of Poses.* New York (1923). Author's first book. $100.

PARRISH, Maxfield. See Baum, L. Frank.

PARRISH, M. L. *Charles Kingsley and Thomas Hughes, First Editions* . . . London, 1936. One of 150 copies. $350.

PARRISH, M. L. *Victorian Lady Novelists* . . . London, 1933. 150 numbered copies. $350.

PARRISH, M. L. *Wilkie Collins and Charles Reade* . . . London, 1940. 150 numbered copies. $350.

PARRY, William Edward. *Journal of a Second Voyage for the Discovery of a North-West Passage* . . . London, 1824–25. 39 plates, maps, and charts. 2 vols. $750.

PARRY, William Edward. *Journal of a Voyage for the Discovery of a North-West Passage* . . . *in the Years, 1819–20.* London, 1821. 20 plates and maps. $650. Philadelphia, 1821. $600.

PARSONS, Edward Alexander. *The Wonder and the Glory* . . . New York, 1962. $125.

PARTINGTON, C. F. *The Printer's Complete Guide.* London, 1825. $125.

PARTISAN (The): A Tale of the Revolution. New York, 1835. (By William Gilmore Simms.) 2 vols., in original cloth, paper labels. $600.

PARTRIDGE, C. S. *Stereotyping, The Papier-Mâché Process.* Chicago, 1892. $175.

PASADENA as It Is Today from a Business Standpoint. (Cover title.) (Pasadena, 1886.) 32 pages, printed wraps. $200.

PASADENA, California, Illustrated. Pasadena, 1886. Plates. 45 pages, pictorial wraps. $125.

PASADENA, Los Angeles County, Southern California. Los Angeles, 1898. 36 pages, wraps. $125.

PASSAGES from the Diary of a Late Physician. New York, 1831. (By Samuel Warren.) Author's first book. (Pirated.) $350. London, 1832. 2 vols. $150.

PASSION-Flowers. Boston, 1854. (By Julia Ward Howe.) Author's first book. $175.

PASTERNAK, Boris. *Doctor Zhivago.* London, 1958. First edition in English. $250. New York, 1958. $100.

PASTERNAK, Boris. *Selected Poems.* London, 1946. $150.

PATCHEN, Kenneth. *Before the Brave.* New York (1936). Red cloth. Author's first book. $300.

PATCHEN, Kenneth. *The Dark Kingdom.* New York (1942). Wraps, painted by the author. One of 75 signed. In slipcase with an original watercolor on cover. $650. Trade. $150.

PATCHEN, Kenneth. *The Famous Boating Party.* (New York, 1954.) Boards and cloth. One of 50 with covers hand painted by Patchen and signed. $500. Trade in dustwrapper. $125.

PATCHEN, Kenneth. *First Will and Testament.* New Directions. Norfolk (1939). Red buckram. One of 800. $200. Padell. New York (1948). Second edition. With poem added. $60.

PATCHEN, Kenneth. *Hurrah for Anything.* Highlands, N.C., 1957. Illustrated. Gray self wraps. One of 100 "Prepared and painted by . . .". $750. Trade. $150.

PATCHEN, Kenneth. *The Journal of Albion Moonlight.* (Mount Vernon, N.Y., 1941.) ¾ leather and buckram. One of 50 signed. In slipcase. $600. Second issue: one of 295 signed. In dustwrapper. $300. First trade edition: United Book Guild. New York, 1944. $125. (Reprinted later by both Papell and New Directions.)

PATCHEN, Kenneth. *Orchards, Thrones and Caravans.* San Francisco (1952). Boards. "Vellum edition." One of 120 signed. $500. Boards. One of 90. "Engraver's edition," with cover engraving by David Ruff, signed by Patchen and Ruff. $600.

PATCHEN, Kenneth. *Panels for the Walls of Heaven.* (Berkeley) 1946. Boards and dustwrapper. $250. Also, 150 copies with cover painted by Patchen and numbered and signed on back. In acetate dustwrapper. $750.

PATCHEN, Kenneth. *Red Wine and Yellow Hair.* New York (1949). Boards and cloth. One of 108 with covers hand painted by author and with limitation notice in Patchen's hand, signed. Issued without dustwrapper. $650. Trade edition in dustwrapper. $125.

PATCHEN, Kenneth. *Sleepers Awake.* (New York, 1946.) Red cloth. First (black paper) edition. One of 148 signed. In dustwrapper. $350. White cloth, with original decoration on cover by the author. One of 75 signed. In dustwrapper. $500. Trade edition. $125.

PATER, Walter. *An Imaginary Portrait.* Daniel Press. London, 1894. Wraps. One of 250. $150.

PATER, Walter. *Imaginary Portraits.* London, 1887. $150.

PATER, Walter. *Plato and Platonism: A Series of Lectures.* New York, 1893. One of 100. $200.

PATER, Walter. *Sebastian Van Storck.* London, 1927. 8 colored plates. One of 1,050. With one plate signed by the artist. First English edition. $300.

PATER, Walter. *Studies in the History of the Renaissance.* London, 1873. Dark green cloth. Author's first book. $150.

PATHFINDER *(The); or, The Inland Sea.* By the author of *The Pioneers.* London, 1840. (By James Fenimore Cooper.) 3 vols., in original boards and cloth, paper labels. $1,000. Philadelphia, 1840. 2 vols., green or purple cloth, paper labels. First American edition, first issue, without copyright notice in vol. I and with printer's imprint at about center of page 2. $1,500. Limited Editions Club, New York, 1965. Buckram. In slipcase. $60.

PATMORE, Coventry. See *The Angel in the House: Odes.*

PATMORE, Coventry. *Faithful For Ever.* London, 1860. $200.

PATMORE, Coventry. *Poems.* London, 1844. Author's first book. $600.

PATMORE, Henry John. *Poems.* Daniel Press. Oxford, 1884. Vellum. One of 125. $350.

PATON, Alan. *Cry, the Beloved Country.* London, 1948. $150. New York, 1948. $75.

PATON, Alan. *Meditation for a Young Boy Confirmed.* London, 1944. Author's first book. Wraps. $250.

PATON, Lucy Allen. *Selected Bindings from the Gennadius Library.* Cambridge, 1924. 300 numbered copies. 38 plates in color. $650.

PATON, Walter. *Paton's Flowers of Penmanship.* London, 1840. 2 engraved title pages and 12 engraved plates. $125.

PATTERSON, A. W. *History of the Backwoods; or, The Region of the Ohio.* Pittsburgh, 1843. Folding map. $450.

PATTERSON, Lawson B. *Twelve Years in the Mines of California.* Cambridge, Mass., 1862. $250.

PATTERSON, Mark. *The Estiennes, A Biographical Essay . . .* San Francisco, 1949. One of 390 copies. Contains leaves printed by Henri Estienne in 1510, Robert Estienne in 1544, and Henri II in 1592. $250.

PATTERSON, Samuel. *Narrative of the Adventures and Sufferings of Samuel Patterson.* Palmer, Mass., 1817. $500. (Ghostwritten by Ezekiel Terry. Wright Howes cites an 1817 Rhode Island printing as the first edition, and lists this Palmer edition as a "second issue.")

PATTIE, James O. *The Personal Narrative of James O. Pattie, of Kentucky . . .* Cincinnati, 1831. Edited by Timothy Flint. 5 plates. Mottled calf. Published by John H. Wood. $12,500. Cincinnati, 1833. Second issue (reissue of the 1831 sheets with new title page). $2,500.

PATTON, The Reverend W. W., and ISHAM, R. N. *U.S. Sanitary Commission, No. 38: Report on the Condition of Camps and Hospitals at Cairo . . . Paducah and St. Louis.* Chicago, 1861. 12 pages, stitched. $250.

PAUL, Elliot. *Imperturbe A Novel of Peace Without Victory.* New York, 1924. "Published, April 1924" on copyright page. $300.

PAUL, Elliot. *Impromptu A Novel in Four Movements.* New York, 1923. "Published, March 1923." on copyright page. $300.

PAUL, Elliot. *Indelible, A Story of Love . . .* Boston, 1922. Author's first book. $400.

PAUL, Elliot, and ALLEN, Jay. *All the Brave.* New York (1939). Illustrated by Luis Quintinalla. Preface by Ernest Hemingway. Pictorial wraps. $75.

PAUL, William. *The Rose Garden.* London, 1848. 15 color plates. $750.

PAULDING, Hiram. *Journal of a Cruise of the United States Schooner Dolphin.* New York, 1831. Folding map. $1,250.

PAULDING, James Kirke. See Langstaff, Launcelot. See also *Chronicles of the City of Gotham; Koningsmarke; A Sketch of Old England; Westward Ho!*

PAULDING, James Kirke. *The Backwoodsman: A Poem.* Philadelphia, 1818. With pages (177–80) present. $300. (Second state has pages 177–80 excised.)

PAULDING, James Kirke. *Slavery in the United States.* New York, 1836. In original cloth. $500.

PAULINE: A Fragment of a Confession. London, 1833. (By Robert Browning.) Gray or brown boards, paper label. Author's first book. $25,000. London, 1886. Edited by Thomas J. Wise. Boards. One of 400. $200. One of 25 on large paper. $400.

PAULISON, C. M. K. *Arizona: The Wonderful Country . . .* Tucson, 1881. 31 pages, printed wraps. $2,500.

PAYNE, John Howard. *Clari; or, The Maid of Milan; An Opera, in Three Acts.* London, 1823. (Contains the first printing of "Home! Sweet Home!") $300.

PAYNE, John Howard. *Indian Justice: A Cherokee Murder Trial at Tahlequah in 1840.* Oklahoma City, 1934. Edited by Grant Foreman. Illustrated. $150.

PAYNE, John Howard, and BISHOP, Henry R. *Home! Sweet Home! Sung by Miss M. Tree, in Clari.* London (1823). 4 pages, folio, sheet music. First separate edition. $750.

PEACOCK, Francis. *Sketches Relative to the History and Theory, but More Especially to the Practice of Dancing.* Aberdeen, Scotland, 1805. $300.

PEACOCK, Thomas Love. See *Crotchet Castle; Headlong Hall; Maid Marian; Melincourt; The Misfortunes of Elphin; Nightmare Abbey; Rhododaphne.*

PEACOCK, Thomas Love. *The Genius of the Thames.* London, 1810. $350.

PEACOCK, Thomas Love. *Palmyra and Other Poems.* London, 1806. Frontispiece. $500.

PEAKE, Mervyn. *Captain Slaughterboard Drops Anchor.* (London, 1939.) Illustrated. 48 pages, boards and cloth. Author's first book. Reportedly most destroyed, assume it was issued without dustwrapper. $2,500. London, 1945. Color illustrations. Second edition. $250.

PEAKE, Mervyn. *Gormenghast.* London, 1950. $150.

PEAKE, Mervyn. *Letter from a Lost Uncle.* London, 1948. $300.

PEAKE, Mervyn. *Mr. Pye.* London, 1953. $250.

PEAKE, Mervyn. *Titus Groan.* (London) 1946. $250.

PEALE, Rembrandt. *Graphics; A Manual of Drawing and Writing...* New York, 1835. Errata slip. $250.

PEARSE, James. *A Narrative of the Life of James Pearse.* Rutland, Vt., 1825. $350.

PEARSON, Edwin. *Banbury Chap Books and Nursery Toy Book Literature...* London, 1809. One of 550 copies. $100.

PEARY, Robert E. *Nearest the Pole...* London, 1907. With color frontispiece, 2 folding maps, and 95 photogravures. $250.

PEARY, Robert E. *The North Pole.* London, 1910. $150. New York, 1910. One of 500 signed. $500.

PEATTIE, Donald Culross. *An Almanac for Moderns.* New York (1935). Lynd Ward illustrations. $75. Limited Editions Club, New York, 1938. In slipcase. $60.

PEATTIE, Donald Culross. *Audubon's America.* Boston, 1940. Color plates and other illustrations. $60. Limited edition, with an extra set of color plates. $175.

PEATTTIE, Donald Culross. *Blown Leaves.* (Chicago) 1916. Author's first book. Wraps. $1,000.

PECK, George. *Adventures of One Terrence McGrant...* New York, 1871. Author's first book. $150.

PECK, George. *Peck's Bad Boy and His Pa.* Chicago, 1883. First issue, with the text ending on page 196, the last word in perfect type, and with the printer's rules on the copyright page ⅞ inch apart (VAB). Wraps. $500. Cloth. $400.

PECK, John M. *A Gazetteer of Illinois.* Jacksonville, Ill., 1834. $250. Philadelphia, 1837. Second edition. $150.

PECK, John M. *A Guide for Emigrants, Containing Sketches of Illinois, Missouri, and the Adjacent Parts.* Boston, 1831. Map in color. $200. Enlarged edition: Boston, 1836. (Retitled *A New Guide for Emigrants to the West.*) $200.

PEEK, Peter V. *Inklings of Adventure in the Campaigns of the Florida Indian War.* (Cover title.) Schenectady, 1846. 72 pages, double columns, printed yellow wraps. $5,000 or more. Schenectady, 1860. Pictorial wraps. $350.

PEESLAKE, Gaffer. *Bromo Bombastes: A Fragment from a Laconic Drama.* Caduceus Press. London, 1933. (By Lawrence Durrell.) Black boards, paper label. One of 100. $2,000 or more.

PEIRCE, A. C. *A Man from Corpus Christi.* New York, 1894. $250.

PELAYO: A Story of the Goth. New York, 1838. (By William Gilmore Simms.) 2 vols., in original cloth, paper labels. $600.

PEMBERTON, Sir Max. *Diary of A Scoundrel.* London, 1891. Author's first book. $200.

PEMBERTON, Sir Max. *Jewel Mysteries I Have Known* . . . London, 1894. $150.

PEN Knife Sketches; Or, Chips off the Old Block. Sacramento, 1853. (By Alonzo Delano.) 24 full-page illustrations. Wraps. $600. Second edition, same year: $400. (For a modern reprint, see entry under author's name.)

PENDENNIS, Arthur (editor). *The Newcomes.* London, 1853–55. (By William Makepeace Thackeray.) Illustrated by Richard Doyle. 24 parts in 23, yellow wraps. $1,000. London, 1854–55. 2 vols., cloth. First book edition. $400.

PENDLETON, Nathaniel Green. *Military Posts—Council Bluffs to the Pacific Ocean.* (Caption title.) (Washington, 1843.) Folding map. Sewn. $300.

PENNELL, Elizabeth R., and PENNELL, Joseph. *The Glory of New York.* New York, 1926. 24 color reproductions. Folio, cloth. One of 350. In dustwrapper and slipcase. $250.

PENNELL, Elizabeth R., and PENNELL, Joseph. *Our Philadelphia.* Philadelphia, 1914. Boards. One of 289 signed. With 10 extra lithographs. $350. Trade. $100.

PENNELL, Joseph. *The Adventures of an Illustrator* . . . Boston, 1925. Illustrated. Half leather. Limited edition, signed. Issued without dustwrapper. $300. Trade in cloth. In dustwrapper. $150.

PENTLAND Rising (The). Edinburgh, 1866. (By Robert Louis Stevenson.) His first book. Green wraps. $3,500.

PEPYS, Samuel. *Memoirs* . . . *Comprising His Diary from 1659 to 1669.* London, 1825. Edited by Richard, Lord Braybrooke. Portraits, views, and facsimiles. 2 vols. $1,250. London, 1828. 5 vols., boards. Second (and first octavo) edition. $500. Limited Editions Club, New York, 1942. Illustrated. 10 vols., pictorial boards and buckram. $150.

PERCIVAL Keene. London, 1842. (By Frederick Marryat.) 3 vols. $200.

PERCY, Stephen. *Robin Hood and His Merry Foresters.* New York, 1855. (By Joseph Cundall.) 8 full-page hand-colored illustrations. $450.

PERCY, Walker. *Bourbon.* Winston-Salem (1979). One of 30 signed and numbered (Roman numerals) copies. Marbled wraps and dustwrapper. $350. One of 200 signed and numbered copies. $175. (Reissued in 1981. Adds Percy's favorite drink.)

PERCY, Walker. *The Last Gentleman.* New York (1966). $125. London (1967). $100.

PERCY, Walker. *The Moviegoer.* New York, 1961. Author's first book, preceded by a number of off-prints. $1,000. London, 1963. $300.

PERCY, Walker. *Questions They Never Asked Me.* Northridge, 1979. One of 50 signed and numbered copies. Bound in full blue leather. $250. One of 300 signed and numbered copies in patterned paper-covered boards and cloth spine. $125.

PERCY, Walker. *Symbol as Need.* (New York) 1954. Author's first work. Offprint from *Thought.* Stapled printed wraps with title page as cover. $500.

PERELMAN, S. J. *Dawn Ginsbergh's Revenge.* New York (1929). Apple green "plush" binding. Author's first book. $1,000. Second silver binding. $750.

PEREZ DE LUXAN, Diego. *Expedition into New Mexico Made by Antonio de Espejo,* 1582–1583 . . . Los Angeles, 1929. Translated by George Peter Hammond and Agapito Rey. Half vellum in dustwrapper. One of 500 copies. $300.

PERICLES and Aspasia. London, 1836. (By Walter Savage Landor.) 2 vols., in original drab boards, blue-green cloth, paper labels. $250. Philadelphia, 1839. 2 vols., in original cloth. First American edition. $200.

PERKINS, Charles Elliott. *The Pinto Horse.* Santa Barbara, 1927. Illustrated by Edward Borein. Pictorial boards. $200.

PERLES, Alfred. *Reunion in Big Sur.* London, 1959. Wraps. One of 25 signed. $125. Trade. $40.

PERRY, Oliver Hazard. *Hunting Expeditions of Oliver Hazard Perry.* Cleveland, 1899. 3 plates. Cloth. One of 100. $750.

PERRY, T. *An Easy Grammar of Writing; Or, Penmanship Analysed.* London, 1817. Third edition. (First issued in 1810.) $150.

PERRY, Thomas. *The Butcher's Boy.* New York, 1982. Author's first book. $100.

PERSE, St. J. *Anabasis.* London, 1930. (By Alexis St. Leger Leger.) French and English texts. Translated by T. S. Eliot. Blue-green cloth. First edition in English. $250. Green cloth. One of 350 signed by Eliot. In cellophane dustwrapper and slipcase. $600. Second trade edition: London, 1930 (actually 1937). Green cloth. In green dustwrapper. $150. New York (1938). Black cloth. First American edition (second edition, revised). $150.

PETER Pilgrim; or a Rambler's Recollections. Philadelphia, 1838. (By Robert Montgomery Bird.) 2 vols., in original green or purple muslin, paper labels. $400.

PETERKIN, Julia. *Black April.* Indianapolis (1927). First edition not stated. First issue with "wood ducks quacked" on page 17, lines 32–33 and dust wrapper without Crawford blurb on front. $125. Second issue with "ducks piped" and Crawford blurb. $75.

PETERKIN, Julia. *Green Thursday.* New York, 1924. Author's first book. (2,000 numbered copies). $100.

PETERKIN, Julia. *Roll Jordon Roll.* New York, 1933. One of 375 copies signed by Peterkin and the photographer, Doris Ullman. In slipcase. $3,000. Trade in dustwrapper. $300.

PETERS, Curtis Arnoux. See Arno, Peter.

PETERS, DeWitt C. *Kit Carson's Life.* Hartford, 1874. Illustrated. $125. Hartford, 1875. $100. London (about 1875). $100. (Note: This is an enlarged version of the title following.)

PETERS, DeWitt C. *The Life and Adventures of Kit Carson, the Nestor of the Rocky-Mountains.* New York, 1859. 10 plates. $400. New York, 1859. $300.

PETERS, Fred J. *Railroad, Indian and Pioneer Prints by N. Currier and Currier and Ives.* New York, 1930. Illustrated. One of 750. In dustwrapper and slipcase. $250.

PETERS, Fred J. *Sporting Prints By N. Currier . . .* New York, 1930. One of 750. In dustwrapper and slipcase. $250.

PETERS, Harry T. *America on Stone: A Chronicle of American Lithography.* Garden City, 1931. 154 plates, 18 in color. One of 751 copies. Issued in dustwrapper and slipcase. $600.

PETERS, Harry T. *California on Stone.* Garden City, 1935. 112 plates. One of 501 copies. In dustwrapper and slipcase. $600.

PETERS, Harry T. *Currier and Ives, Printmakers to the American People.* Garden City, 1929–31. 300 reproductions (including color). 2 vols. One of 510. In dustwrapper. $750. Garden City, 1942. Cloth. Special edition in one volume. In dustwrapper. $125.

PETERSEN, Carl. *Each in Its Ordered Place: A Faulkner Collector's Notebook.* Ann Arbor (1975). First printing in green morocco-grained cloth. (1,000 copies.) In dustwrapper (VAB). $175. Second printing (identified on copyright page as "first printing"). Orange cloth. (400 printed.) Issued without dustwrapper. $125.

PETRY, Ann. *Country Place.* Boston, 1947. $125.

PETRY, Ann. *The Drugstore Cat.* New York (1949). $150.

PETRY, Ann. *The Street.* Boston, 1946. Author's first book. $150.

PETTER, Rodolphe. *English-Cheyenne Dictionary.* Kettle Falls, Wash., 1913–15. Folio, full black calf. One of 100. $200.

PHAIR, Charles. *Atlantic Salmon Fishing.* Derrydale Press. New York (1937). Edited by Richard C. Hunt. Illustrated. Folio, cloth. One of 950. In dustwrapper. $600. 2 vols., half morocco. One of 40 signed, with portfolio of mounted flies. $7,500.

PHELPS'S Traveller's Guide Through the United States. New York, 1838. (By Humphrey Phelps.) Folding map in original leather. $750.

PHILBY, H. St. J. B. *A Pilgrim in Arabia.* Golden Cockerel Press. London, 1943. Portrait. Buckram, leather spine. One of 350. $600. One of 30 signed with cellotype supplement. $1,250.

PHILIP Dru, Administrator. New York, 1912. (By Col. E. M. House.) $200.

PHILLIPS, D. L. *Letters from California.* Springfield, Ill., 1877. $250.

PHILLIPS, Jayne Anne. *Sweethearts.* Carrboro, 1976. Author's first book, preceded by two related broadsides. 10 copies hand bound in boards and signed. $600. (400 copies.) Wraps. $175. St. Paul, 1978. (600 copies.) Wraps. $75.

PHILLIPS, John C. *A Bibliography of American Sporting Books.* Boston (1930). $250.

PHILLIPS, Philip A. S. *Paul de Lamerie, Citizen and Goldsmith of London.* London, 1935. Illustrated. Folio, cloth. One of 250. $500.

PHILLIPS, Philip Lee. *A List of Geographical Atlases in the Library of Congress with Bibliographical Notes.* Washington, 1909, 1909, 1914, 1920. 4 vols. $500.

PHILLIPS, Sir Richard. *Modern London . . .* London, 1804. Folding frontispiece, folding map, 31 colored plates. $2,000. London, 1805. With engraved frontispiece, folding map, and 52 plates (31 hand colored). $1,250.

PHILLPOTTS, Eden. See *The Ghost in the Bank of England.*

PHILLPOTTS, Eden. *A Dish of Apples.* London (1921). Illustrations, including color, by Arthur Rackham. White cloth. One of 500 signed. $1,250. One of 55 on Batchelor's Kelmscott paper. $1,750. Trade in cloth, without dustwrapper. $250.

PHILLPOTTS, Eden. *The Girl and the Faun.* London, 1916. Illustrated by Frank Brangwyn. Half vellum. One of 350 signed. $300. Trade. $75.

PHILLPOTTS, Eden. *My Adventure in the Flying Scotsman.* London, 1888. Colored cloth. $1,000. Wraps. $1,250.

PHILOBIBLION (The), *A Monthly Bibliographical Journal.* New York, 1861–63. 2 vols. complete in XXIV numbers. Complete set of this periodical. $250.

PHOTOGRAPHIC *Sketch Book of the War.* Washington (1865–66). (By Alexander Gardner.) 100 gold-toned albumen prints, with leaf of text for each. 2 vols., oblong folio, morocco. $17,500.

PIATT, John J. See *Poems of Two Friends.*

PICHON, Baron Jerome. *The Life of Charles Henry Count Hoym . . .* New York, 1899. (Binding executed by the Club Bindery of New York.) Limited to 303 copies. $100.

PICHON, Leon. *The New Book-Illustration in France.* London, 1924. Translated by Herbert B. Grimsditch. $100.

PICKETT, Albert James. *History of Alabama, and Incidentally of Georgia and Mississippi.* Charleston, 1851. Map, 3 plans, 8 plates. 2 vols. $300. Second edition, same place and date. $200.

PICKETT, Albert James. *Invasion of the Territory of Alabama, by 1,000 Spaniards, Under Ferdinand de Soto, in 1540.* Montgomery, 1849. 41 pages, wraps. $500.

PICKTHALL, Marmaduke. *Said the Fisherman.* London, 1903. Author's first book. $75.

PICTORIAL *View of California (A).* New York, 1853. By a Returned Californian. (By J. M. Letts.) 48 plates. Later edition of *California Illustrated.* $400.

PIGMAN, Walter Griffith. *Journal.* Mexico, Mo., 1942. Edited by Ulla Staley Fawkes. Boards. $100.

PIGS Is Pigs. Chicago, 1905. Railways Appliances Company. (By Ellis Parker Butler.) Decorated oyster white wraps. (Note: Author's name appears only in decoration on first text page.) $200.

PIKE, Albert. *Prose Sketches and Poems, Written in the Western Country.* Boston, 1834. Brown cloth, leather label. Author's first book. $2,000.

PIKE, Corp. (James). *The Scout and Ranger.* Cincinnati, 1865. Portrait, 24 plates. Black cloth. First issue, with errata leaf and uncorrected errors. $850. Second issue, without errata leaf. $600.

PIKE County Puzzle, Vol. 1. No. 1. (Burlesque of country newspaper.) Camp Interlaken, Pa., 1894. (By Stephen Crane.) 4 pages $750.

PIKE, Z. M. *An Account of Expeditions to the Sources of the Mississippi* . . . Philadelphia, 1810. Portrait, 4 maps, 2 charts, 3 tables. 2 vols. $4,250. Maps in separate cloth atlas-folder. $2,500.

PIKE, Z. M. *An Account of a Voyage up the Mississippi River.* (Washington, 1807?) Map. 68 pages $5,000.

PIKE, Z. M. *Exploratory Travels Through the Western Territories of North America.* London, 1811. 2 maps. First English edition (of *An Account of Expeditions to the Sources of the Mississippi*). $2,000.

PILCHER, Joshua. *Report on the Fur Trade and Inland Trade to Mexico.* Washington, 1832. $275.

PILGRIM, Thomas. See Morecamp, Arthur.

PILOT (The): A Tale of the Sea. New York, 1823. By the Author of *The Pioneers,* James Fenimore Cooper. 2 vols. $250. London, 1824. 3 vols. First English edition. $300. Limited Editions Club, New York, 1968. In slipcase. $50.

PIM, Herbert Moore. *The Pessimist.* Dublin, 1914. Author's first book. $125.

PINCKNEY, Josephine. *Sea-Drinking Cities.* New York, 1927. Author's first book. One of 225 signed and numbered copies. $250. Trade. $125.

PINKERTON, A. F. *Jim Cummins: or, The Great Adams Express Robbery.* Chicago, 1887. Illustrated. Pictorial cloth. $150.

PINKERTON, Allan. *The Expressman and the Detective.* Chicago, 1874. $175.

PINKERTON, Allan. *Tests on Passenger Conductors.* Chicago, 1867. 35 pages, wraps. Author's first book. $250.

PINKERTON, Allan. *Thirty Years a Detective.* Hartford, 1884. Illustrated. $250.

PINTER, Harold. *The Birthday Party: A Play in Three Acts.* (Encore Publishers.) London (1959). Pictorial wraps. Author's first book. $200.

PINTER, Harold. *The Birthday Party and Other Plays.* London (1960). $150.

PINTER, Harold. *The Caretaker.* London (1960). Wraps. $150.

PINTER, Harold. *Monologue.* (London, 1973.) Full leather. One of 100 signed. In slipcase. $250. Trade, in boards with oversize dustwrapper. $50.

PINTER, Harold. *No Man's Land.* London (1975). One of 150 signed. In acetate jacket. $125.

PINTER, Harold. *Old Times.* London, 1971. One of 150 signed. In acetate jacket. $200.

PIPER, Watty. *The Little Engine That Could.* New York (1930). Illustrated in color by Lois Lenski. $250.

PITMAN, Benn (reporter). *The Assassination of President Lincoln and the Trial of the Conspirators.* Cincinnati, 1865. Illustrated. $400.

"PLAIN or Ringlets?" London, 1859–60. (By Robert Smith Surtees.) 13 colored plates. Other illustrations by John Leech. 13 parts in 12, wraps. $750. London, 1860. Pictorial cloth. First book edition. $350.

PLAIN Speaker (The): Opinions on Books, Men, and Things. London, 1826. (By William Hazlitt.) 2 vols. First collected edition. $300.

PLANTE, David. *The Ghost of Henry James.* London (1970). Author's first book. No errata slip. $125. Errata slip tipped in correcting errors on pages 8, 113, and 133. $100. Boston, 1970. $75.

PLATH, Sylvia. See Lucas, Victoria. See also *A Winter Ship.*

PLATH, Sylvia. *Ariel.* London (1965). $200. New York (1966). $100.

PLATH, Sylvia. *The Colossus.* London (1960). Author's first regularly published book. $850. New York, 1962. $150.

PLATH Sylvia. *Crystal Gazer and Other Poems.* Rainbow Press. London, 1971. Vellum, leather, or half buckram. One of 400. In slipcase. $200.

PLATH, Sylvia. *Lyonnesse.* Rainbow Press. London, 1971. Vellum, leather, or half leather. One of 300. Issued without dustwrapper. In slipcase. $200. One of 100 with special manuscript reproductions on endpapers. In slipcase. $300.

PLATH, Sylvia. *Pursuit.* Rainbow Press. (London) 1973. Drawings and an etching by Leonard Baskin. Morocco. One of 100 with signed frontispiece by Baskin. In slipcase. $750.

PLATH, Sylvia. *Uncollected Poems.* Turret Books. (London, 1965.) Facsimile. Wraps. In dustwrapper. One of 150. $400.

PLATO. *The Phaedo of Plato.* Golden Cockerel Press. Waltham Saint Lawrence, England, 1930. Translated by William Jowett. Title and initials in red buckram. With letter laid in calling attention to error of translator's name as William instead of Benjamin. $250.

PLATT, P. L., and SLATER, N. *The Travelers' Guide Across the Plains, upon the Overland Route to California.* Chicago, 1852. Folding map. 64 pages, printed yellow wraps. $7,500 or more. San Francisco, 1963. Edited by Dale Morgan. Illustrated. Black boards, orange cloth spine. Second edition. In acetate dustwrapper. $125.

PLEASANTS, J. Hall, and SILL, Howard. *Maryland Silversmiths, 1715–1830.* Baltimore, 1930. Illustrated. Half cloth. One of 300. Issued without dustwrapper. $400.

PLEASANTS, W. J. *Twice Across the Plains, 1849–1856.* San Francisco, 1906. 10 plates, 2 portraits. Pictorial green cloth. $500.

PLIMPTON, George. *Letters In Training.* No-place, 1946. Author's first book. $300.

PLIMPTON, George. *The Rabbit's Umbrella.* New York, 1955. $125.

PLOMER, Henry R. *English Printers' Ornaments.* London, 1924. One of 500 copies. $100.

PLOMER, Henry R. *Wynkyn De Worde & His Contemporaries from the Death of Caxton to 1535.* London, 1925. $100.

PLOMER, William. *Address Given at the Memorial Service for Ian Fleming.* (London) 1962. $150.

PLOMER, William. *The Case Is Altered.* Hogarth Press. London, 1932. $200.

PLOMER, William. *Notes for Poems.* Hogarth Press. London, 1927 (actually 1928). Cloth. In tissue jacket. $250.

PLOMER, William. *Sado.* London, 1931. $175.

PLOMER, William. *Turbott Wolfe.* London, 1925. Author's first book. $250.

PLUMBE, John, Jr. *Sketches of Iowa and Wisconsin . . .* St. Louis, 1839. Folding map on thin paper. 103 pages, in original printed wraps. $3,000.

PLUNKETT, Joseph Mary. *The Circle and the Sword.* Dublin, 1911. Author's first book. Wraps. $200.

POE, Edgar Allan. See *The Narrative of Arthur Gordon Pym; Tamerlane and Other Poems.*

POE, Edgar Allan. *Al Aaraaf, Tamerlane, and Minor Poems.* Baltimore, 1829. In original blue or reddish tan boards, ivory paper spine. (Some copies misdated 1820 on title page; a few also stitched, without covers.) $75,000.

POE, Edgar Allan. *The Bells and Other Poems.* London (about 1912). 28 color plates by Edmund Dulac. Folio, decorated vellum with silk ties. One of 750 large paper copies, signed by Dulac. $1,000. Issued without dustwrapper. $300.

POE, Edgar Allan. *The Conchologist's First Book.* Philadelphia, 1839. Illustrated. In original printed pictorial boards and leather spine. First state, with snail plates in color. $1,000. Plates uncolored. $750. Philadelphia, 1840. Boards. Second edition. $350.

POE, Edgar Allan. *Eureka: A Prose Poem.* New York, 1848. Black cloth. With 12 or 16 pages of ads at end. $1,200. New York (about 1928). Facsimile edition of a copy with Poe's own handwritten revisions. One of 50. $300.

POE, Edgar Allan. *The Fall of the House of Usher.* Black Sun Press, Paris, 1928. Illustrated by Alastair. Printed wraps. One of 300. $600. Limited Editions Club, New York, 1985. In box. $400.

POE, Edgar Allan. *Mesmerism: "In Articulo Mortis . . ."* London, 1846. 16 pages, stitched, without covers. $1,250.

POE, Edgar Allan. *Murders in the Rue Morgue.* Philadelphia (1895). Facsimile of Drexel Institute manuscript. 2 watercolors. Folio, half morocco. $250. Allen Press. Antibes (1958). Boards. One of 150. $600.

POE, Edgar Allan. *Poems.* New York, 1831. In original pale green cloth. Second edition (so identified on title page, but actually the first edition). $30,000 or more. London, 1900. Illustrated by W. Heath Robinson. $300. Limited Editions Club, New York, 1943. Slipcase. $150.

POE, Edgar Allan. *The Prose Romances of Edgar A. Poe, etc. Uniform Serial Edition . . . No. 1. Containing the Murders in the Rue Morgue, and The Man That Was Used Up.* Philadelphia, 1843. 40 pages Rebound at auction in 1990 for $60,000. Also, see Poe, *Murders in the Rue Morgue.*

POE, Edgar Allan. *The Raven and Other Poems.* New York, 1845. Printed wraps, or cloth. First issue, with "T. B. Smith, Stereotyper" on copyright page. $52,000 for a very good copy in wraps at auction in 1990. London, 1846. First English edition with new title page tipped in over sheets of the American first. $2,500.

POE, Edgar Allan. *The Raven and Other Poems. (&) Tales.* New York, 1845. 2 vols. in one, dark blue cloth. First edition of each work in the one-volume format; first issue of *The Raven* (see preceding entry) and third issue of *Tales* (see entry following), without stereotyper's slug. $6,000. (East Hampton, 1980.) Title poem only. Illustrated by Alan James Robinson, his first book. Folio, one of 100 signed in box. $2,000.

POE, Edgar Allan. *Tales.* New York, 1845. First state, with T. B. Smith and H. Ludwig slugs on copyright page, 12 pages of ads at back. Printed buff wraps. $50,000 at auction in 1990. Cloth. $25,000 or more.

POE, Edgar Allan. *Tales of the Grotesque and Arabesque.* Philadelphia, 1840. 2 vols., in original purplish cloth, paper labels. First state with page 213 in vol. 2 wrongly numbered 231. $15,000. Second state, page 213 correctly numbered. $12,500. 2 vols. in one. Page 213 correctly numbered, 4 pages of ads bound in at end. $7,500. (Only 750 copies in total, and the sheets were issued up to 1849 with new title pages per Robertson.) Chicago, 1930. Lakeside Press. Full morocco. One of 1,000. $300.

POE, Edgar Allan. *Tales of Mystery and Imagination.* London, 1919. Illustrated by Harry Clarke. Pictorial vellum. One of 170 signed by Clarke. $2,500. London, (1935). Illustrated by Arthur Rackham. Full pictorial vellum. One of 460 signed by Rackham. $2,500. First trade edition. Cloth. In dustwrapper. $750. Limited Editions Club, New York, 1941. In slipcase. $125.

POEM on the Rising Glory of America. Philadelphia, 1772. (By Hugh Henry Brackenridge and Philip Freneau.) Both authors' first book. $500.

POEMS. Chiswick Press. (London, 1906.) (By Siegfried Sassoon.) Wraps. Author's first book. $5,000. London (1911). Wraps. One of 35 signed. $750.

POEMS by Two Brothers. London (1827). (By Alfred, Charles, and Frederick Tennyson.) Alfred Tennyson's first book. Large paper copies. $1,750. Small paper copies. $1,000.

POEMS of Two Friends. Columbus, Ohio, 1860. (By William Dean Howells and John J. Piatt.) Brown cloth. Howells's first book. $600.

POET at the Breakfast-Table (The). Boston, 1872. (By Oliver Wendell Holmes.) First state, with "Talle" for "Table" in the running head on page 9. $250.

POETRY for Children, Entirely Original. London, 1809. (By Charles and Mary Lamb.) Illustrated. 2 vols. $1,000. Boston, 1812. Boards. First American edition. $600.

POHL, Frederik. *Alternating Currents.* New York, 1956. Author's first separate book. Cloth. $500. Wraps. $35.

POIKILOGRAPHIA, Or Various Specimens of Ornamental Penmanship . . . London (no-date.) (circa 1830s.) 23 engraved plates. $225.

POLK, James K. *The Diary of James K. Polk.* Chicago, 1910. 4 vols. $250.

POLLARD, Alfred W. *An Essay on Colophons . . .* Chicago, 1905. One of 255 copies. $250.

POLLARD, Alfred W. *Shakespeare Folios and Quartos.* London, 1909. Illustrated. Boards. $300.

POLLARD, Edward A. *The First Year of the War.* Richmond, 1862. 374 pages, printed wraps. $400.

POLLARD, Edward A. *Observations in the North.* Richmond, 1865. 142 pages, wraps. $500.

POLLARD, Edward A. *The Seven Days' Battles in Front of Richmond.* Richmond, 1862. 45 pages, printed wraps. $600.

POLLARD, Edward A. *The Southern Spy.* Richmond, 1861. 103 pages, wraps. $600.

POLLARD, Hugh B. C. *A History of Firearms.* London, 1926. Illustrated. Cloth. Issued without dustwrapper. $200. London, 1930. $150.

POLLARD, Hugh B. C., and BARCLAY-SMITH, Phyllis. *British and American Game-Birds.* Derrydale Press. New York, 1939. Illustrated. Half leather. One of 125. $650. London, 1945. Half leather. Issued without dustwrapper. $350.

POLLEY, J. B. *Hood's Texas Brigade.* New York, 1910. 25 plates. $500.

POLLEY, J. B. *A Soldier's Letters to Charming Nellie.* New York, 1908. 16 plates. $350.

POLLOCK, J. M. *The Unvarnished West: Ranching as I Found It.* London (1911). Illustrated. Pictorial cloth. $350.

POLONIUS: A Collection of Wise Saws and Modern Instances. London, 1852. (By Edward FitzGerald.) Green cloth. $150.

POOLE, Ernest. *Katharine Breshovsky: For Russia's Freedom.* Chicago, 1905. Pictorial wraps. Author's first book. $250.

POOR, M. C. *Denver, South Park and Pacific.* Denver, 1949. Illustrated, with map in pocket. Cloth. One of 1,000 signed. In dustwrapper. $350.

POOR Sarah. (Park Hill, Indian Territory, Oklahoma) 1943. Park Hill Mission Press. 18 pages, sewn. $250. (Note: Originally this story of "a pious Indian woman" was a publication of the American Tract Society of New York.)

POORE, Ben Perley. *A Descriptive Catalogue of the Government Publications of the United States . . .* Washington, 1885. Cloth. $150. New York, 1962. 2 vols., cloth. $125.

POORTENAAR, Jan. *The Art of the Book and Its Illustration.* London (1935). $125.

POPE, Alexander. *The Rape of the Lock.* London, 1714. First separate edition with frontispiece and 5 plates. $1,250. ($10,000 in original wraps at auction in 1990.) London, 1896. Illustrated by Aubrey Beardsley. $500.

POPERY, British and Foreign. London, 1851. (By Walter Savage Landor.) Printed wraps. $200.

PORCHER, Francis P. *Resources of the Southern Fields and Forests, Medical, Economical, and Agricultural, Being Also a Medical Botany of the Confederate States.* Charleston, 1863. Half leather. $1,350.

PORTALIS, Baron Roger (editor). *Researches Concerning Jean Grolier, His Life and His Library.* New York, 1907. One of 300 copies. 13 chromolithographed plates. $550.

PORTEAUX, A. *Practical Guide for the Manufacture of Paper and Boards.* Philadelphia, 1866. Translated from the French by Horatio Paine. $250.

PORTER, Edwin H. *The Fall River Tragedy*... Fall River, Mass., 1893. Plates. $500.

PORTER, Eleanor H. *Pollyanna.* Boston, 1913. Illustrated. Pink silk cloth. $300. London, 1913. Blue cloth, pictorial cover label. First English edition. $125.

PORTER, Gene Stratton. *Friends in Feathers.* Garden City, 1917. Pictorial cloth. $150.

PORTER, Gene Stratton. *The Keeper of the Bees.* Garden City, 1925. Pictorial cloth. $150.

PORTER, Gene Stratton. *Laddie: A True-Blue Story.* New York, 1913. 4 color plates. $250.

PORTER, Gene Stratton. *The Song of the Cardinal.* Indianapolis (1903). Illustrated by the author's camera studies. Buckram. Author's first book. $150.

PORTER, Jane. *The Scottish Chiefs: A Romance.* London, 1810. 5 vols. With errata leaf at end of vol. 1. $400.

PORTER, Katherine Anne. See F., M. T.

PORTER, Katherine Anne. *A Christmas Story.* New York (1967). Illustrated by Ben Shahn. Oblong cloth. One of 500 signed by both author and artist. In slipcase. $200.

PORTER, Katherine Anne. *Flowering Judas.* New York (1930). Boards and cloth. One of 600. In glassine dustwrapper. $250. New York (1935). Cloth. First augmented edition. $250.

PORTER, Katherine Anne. *French Song Book.* (Paris) 1933. Blue boards and cloth. One of 595 signed. In dustwrapper. $400. One of 15 on Spanish paper specially bound, signed. $2,500.

PORTER, Katherine Anne. *Hacienda.* (New York, 1934.) One of 895. With errata slip and page 52 uncorrected. In slipcase. $300. With page 52 corrected and tipped in. $125.

PORTER, Katherine Anne. *The Leaning Tower and Other Stories.* New York (1944). $125.

PORTER, Katherine Anne. *Noon Wine.* Detroit, 1937. Decorated boards, paper label. One of 250 signed. In slipcase. $500.

PORTER, Katherine Anne. *Outline of Mexican Popular Arts and Crafts.* (Los Angeles), 1922. Pictorial wraps. $3,500.

PORTER, Katherine Anne. *Pale Horse, Pale Rider.* New York (1939). $250.

PORTER, William Sidney (or, later, Sydney). See Henry, O.

PORTFOLIO (A) Honoring Harold Hugo for His Contribution to Scholarly Printing. (No-place) 1978. 38 separate folders loosely inserted in a cloth case. $200.

PORTRAIT and Biographical Record of Denver and Vicinity. Chicago, 1898. Leather. $350.

POSNER, David. *And Touch.* Trenton, 1940. Author's first book. $100.

POSNER, David. *Love as Image.* London, 1952. Wraps. One of 150. $125.

POSNER, David. *A Rake's Progress.* London (1967). 17 plates. Black cloth with black plastic spine. Issued without dustwrapper. With errata leaf. $200.

POSNER, David. *S'un Casto Amor.* Oxford, 1953. Wraps. One of 30. $150.

POST, Melville Davisson. *The Corrector of Destinies.* New York (1908). $500.

POST, Melville Davisson. *The Strange Schemes of Randolph Mason.* New York, 1896. Author's first book. Wraps. $350. Cloth. $300.

POST, Melville Davisson. *Uncle Abner.* New York, 1918. Blue cloth. $150.

POSTON, Charles D. *Apache Land.* San Francisco, 1878. Portrait and views. $250.

POSTON, Charles D. *Speech of the Hon. Charles D. Poston, of Arizona, on Indian Affairs.* New York, 1865. 20 pages, printed wraps. $750.

Statement Respecting the Earl of Selkirk's Settlement Upon the Red River, in North America. London, 1817. (By John Halkett.) $850.

POTT, J. S. *A Plain Statement of Fact, etc.* (Claims of Florida inhabitants against British forces.) London, 1838. 16 pages, half morocco. $400.

POTTER, Ambrose George. *A Bibliography of the Rubaiyat of Omar Khayyam . . .* London, 1929. 300 numbered copies. $175.

POTTER, Beatrix. *Ginger and Pickles.* London, 1909. Illustrated by the author. Pictorial boards. In dustwrapper. For $2,100 at auction in 1990. New York, 1909. $450.

POTTER, Beatrix. *The Pie and the Patty-Pan.* London, 1905. Illustrated in color by the author. Pictorial cloth. $600. New York, 1905. $350.

POTTER, Beatrix. *The Roly-Poly Pudding.* London, 1908. Illustrated in color by the author. With "All rights reserved" at bottom of title page. $400.

POTTER, Beatrix. *The Story of a Fierce Bad Rabbit.* London, 1906. Illustrated by the author. Panoramic wallet-style cloth binding. $450.

POTTER, Beatrix. *The Tailor of Gloucester.* London, 1903. $1,250. Another edition, privately printed: (London, 1903 or 1904). Limited to 500. $3,500.

POTTER, Beatrix. *The Tale of Mrs. Tiggy-Winkle.* London, 1905. Frontispiece and 26 colored illustrations by the author. Boards. $500.

POTTER, Beatrix. *The Tale of Mrs. Tittlemouse.* London, 1910. Color plates. Boards. $450.

POTTER, Beatrix. *The Tale of Peter Rabbit.* London (1901). Colored frontispiece, 41 illustrations in black and white by the author. Boards, flat spine. December, 1901 (privately printed). One of 250. $50,000 at auction in 1990. (London) 1902. Boards, rounded spine. Second issue, February, 1902 (also privately printed). One of 200. $3,000. London, 1902. First published edition (trade edition) with Holly Lear endpapers; and "wept" for "shed" on page 51. $1,000.

POTTER, Beatrix. *Wag-by-Wall.* London, 1944. Illustrated. Cloth. One of 100. In dustwrapper. $600.

POTTER, Jack. *Lead Steer and Other Tales.* Clayton, N.M., 1939. Illustrated. Pictorial wraps. $200.

POTTLE, Frederick A. *Boswell and the Girl from Botany Bay.* New York, 1937. Boards and cloth. One of 500. $75.

POTTLE, Frederick A. *The Literary Career of James Boswell.* Oxford, 1929. $125.

POUND, Ezra. See P. E.; Bosschere, Jean de; Fenollosa, Ernest. See also *The Book of the Poets' Club; The Catholic Anthology; Des Imagistes.*

POUND, Ezra. *A Lume Spento.* (Venice) 1908. Green wraps. Author's first book. $50,000. Milan (1958). Stiff gray wraps. One of 2,000. In dustwrapper. $125. (New York, 1965.) First American edition. In acetate dustwrapper. $60.

POUND, Ezra. *ABC of Reading.* London, 1934. Red cloth. $300. New Haven, 1934. $200.

POUND, Ezra. *Antheil and the Treatise on Harmony.* Paris, 1924. Three Mountains Press. Red wraps. One of 40 on Arches paper. $1,250. Trade. One of 560. $600. Unsold copies later issued with buff label pasted on title page "Contact Editions . . ." $400. Chicago, 1927. Brown cloth. First American edition. $400.

POUND, Ezra. *Canto CX.* (Cambridge, 1965.) Frontispiece drawing of Pound. Wraps. One of 80. $600.

POUND, Ezra. *Cantos LII–LXXI.* London (1940). $250. Norfolk (1940). First American edition. One of 500 with envelope and pamphlet, *Notes on Ezra Pound's Cantos, Structure and Rhetoric.* $200. One of 500 without the envelope. $125.

POUND, Ezra. *Canzoni.* London, 1911. First binding in gray cloth with Pound's name on cover. $600. Second binding in brown boards without author's name. $400.

POUND, Ezra. *Cathay.* London, 1915. (Translated by Pound.) Printed wraps. $600.

POUND, Ezra. *Diptych Rome-London.* New Directions. (Norfolk, 1958.) Folio, boards. One of 125 signed. In slipcase. $1,000. (London, 1958.) Faber & Faber. One of 50 signed. In slipcase. $1,250. Milan (1958). One of 25 signed. In slipcase. $1,500. (These books were issued simultaneously as part of a total edition of 200 produced at the Officina Bodoni in Verona, Italy.)

POUND, Ezra. *A Draft of the Cantos 17–27.* London, 1928. Initials by Gladys Hynes. Folio, red vellum boards. Issued without dustwrapper. One of 70 on Roma paper. $1,750. Also 24 lettered copies: 4 on vellum signed by the author and the artist. $6,000; 5 on Japan paper, signed by Pound. $5,000; 15 unsigned on Whatman paper. $3,500.

POUND, Ezra. *A Draft of XXX Cantos.* Paris, 1930. Hours Press. Beige linen. One of 200. $1,500. Red-orange leather. One of 10 on Texas Mountain paper, signed. $5,000. (Note: There were also 2 on vellum for Pound.) New York (1933). First American edition. $350. London (1933). Black cloth. First English edition. In dustwrapper. $250.

POUND, Ezra. *Drafts and Fragments of Cantos CX–CXVII.* New Directions and Stone Wall Press. New York (1968). Folio, red cloth, paper labels. With errata slip. One of 310 signed (in total for the three publishers). In slipcase. $750. New York, 1968. Trade edition. $100. Faber & Faber. London (1970). $75.

POUND, Ezra. *Exultations.* London, 1909. Dark red boards. Probable first issue with "Exultations/of/Ezra Pound" on front cover. $500. Second deletes "of." $350.

POUND, Ezra. *Gaudier-Brzeska: A Memoir.* London, 1916. Illustrated. Gray-green cloth. $300. American issue: Olive green cloth. $350. London (1939). Green cloth. In dustwrapper. $600. New Directions. New York (1961). ". . . this edition first published 1960." $400.

POUND, Ezra. *Imaginary Letters.* Black Sun Press. Paris, 1930. Stiff printed white wraps. One of 300. In glassine dustwrapper and slipcase. $850. One of 50 on vellum, signed. In slipcase. $2,000. (There were also 25 copies not for sale.)

POUND, Ezra. *Indiscretions; or Une Revue de Deux Mondes.* Three Mountains Press. Paris, 1923. Gray boards and yellow cloth. Issued without dustwrapper. $1,000.

POUND, Ezra. *Instigations.* New York (1920). In dustwrapper. $1,000.

POUND, Ezra. *Pavannes and Divisions.* New York, 1918. Frontispiece. First binding in blue boards. $250. Later bindings, blue or gray cloth, or gray boards. $150.

POUND, Ezra. *Personae.* London, 1909. Drab boards. $500. New York, 1926. Dark blue cloth. $350.

POUND, Ezra. *The Pisan Cantos.* (New York, 1948.) Black cloth. No statement of edition. $250. London (1949). Black cloth. First English edition with a number of omissions and expurgations. $150.

POUND, Ezra. *Poems 1918–1921, Including Three Portraits and Four Cantos.* New York (1921). Boards and vellum. In dustwrapper. $650.

POUND, Ezra. *Provenca: Poems Selected from "Personae" "Exultations" and "Canzoniere."* Boston (1910). With tan boards stamped in dark brown measuring 1.5 cm. across the top. Later (1917?) in tan boards stamped in green measuring 1.4 cm. across. $150. Boston (1917). The first of his books to be published in America. $150.

POUND, Ezra. *Quia Pauper Amavi.* London (1919). Egoist, Ltd. Boards and cloth, paper label. One of 110 on handmade paper, signed. (Issued without dustwrapper.) $1,750. Trade, issued without dustwrapper. $400.

POUND, Ezra. *A Quinzaine for This Yule.* (London, 1908.) Wrapper. First issue, with "Weston St. Llewmy" for "Weston St. Llewmys" in line 6 on page 21. $17,500. Second issue, corrected. $12,500.

POUND, Ezra. *Selected Poems.* London (1928). Introduction by T. S. Eliot. Gray boards. One of 100 signed. Issued without dustwrapper. $1,500. Trade in green cloth. In dustwrapper. $350.

POUND, Ezra. *The Sonnets and Ballate of Guido Cavalcanti.* Boston (1912). (Translated by Pound.) Boards, vellum paper spine. $300. London, 1912. Gray cloth. First English edition, with ads at back. $250.

POUND, Ezra. *Umbra.* London, 1920. Gray boards and cloth. In dustwrapper. $600. Boards, parchment. One of 100 signed. $1,500.

POUND, Ezra (editor). *Active Anthology.* London (1933). $400.

POWELL, Anthony. *Afternoon Men.* London, 1931. Author's first novel. $1,500. New York (1932). $600.

POWELL, Anthony. *Agents and Patients.* London, 1936. $1,750.

POWELL, Anthony. *Barnard Letters.* London, 1928. Author's first book. (Edited and introduction.) $1,000.

POWELL, Anthony *Caledonia: A Fragment.* London (1934). $750.

POWELL, Anthony. *From a View to a Death.* London, 1933. $750.

POWELL, Anthony. *Venusberg.* London, 1932. $850.

POWELL, C. Frank. *Life of Gen. Zachary Taylor.* New York, 1846. 96 pages, wraps. $200.

POWELL, H. M. T. *The Santa Fe Trail to California, 1849–1852.* Grabhorn Press. San Francisco (1931). Edited by Douglas S. Watson. Maps and other illustrations. Half morocco. One of 300. $1,500.

POWELL, J. W. *Canyons of the Colorado.* Meadville, Pa., 1895. Illustrated, including 10 folding plates. Cloth. $1,250.

POWELL, Lawrence Clark. *An Introduction to Robinson Jeffers.* (Dijon, France, 1932.) Author's first book. 225 copies, 85 for presentation. $300.

POWELL, Lawrence Clark. *Robinson Jeffers, the Man and His Work.* Los Angeles, 1934. Foreword by Robinson Jeffers. Decorations by Rockwell Kent. One of 750. $200.

POWELL, Willis J. *Tachyhippodamia, or, Art of Quieting Wild Horses in a Few Hours.* New Orleans, 1838. $1,000.

POWER, Tyrone. *Impressions of America.* London, 1836. 2 plates. 2 vols. $500. Philadelphia, 1836. 2 vols. $300.

POWERS, J. F. *Prince of Darkness and Other Stories.* Garden City, 1947. Author's first book. $125.

POWERS, Stephen. *Afoot and Alone: A Walk from Sea to Sea by the Southern Route.* Hartford, 1872. 12 plates. Cloth. $200.

POW-KEY, Sohn. *Early Korean Typography.* (No-place) 1982. Revised edition. $275.

POWYS, John Cowper. *Corinth.* (Oxford, 1891). Author's first book. Wraps. Cover states "English Verse." Powys's name appears at the end of text. $750.

POWYS, John Cowper. *A Glastonbury Romance.* New York, 1932. One of 204 signed. Issued without dustwrapper. $300.

POWYS, John Cowper. *In Defense of Sensuality.* New York, 1930. $150. London, 1930. First English edition. $125.

POWYS, John Cowper. *Lucifer, a Poem.* London, 1956. Half morocco. Issued without dustwrapper. One of 560 signed. $250.

POWYS, John Cowper. *Odes and Other Poems.* London, 1896. $600.

POWYS, John Cowper. *The Owl, the Duck and—Miss Rowe! Miss Rowe!* Black Archer Press. Chicago, 1930. Boards. One of 250 signed. In slipcase. $275.

POWYS, John Cowper. *Poems.* London, 1899. Boards. $400.

POWYS, John Cowper. *Rodmoor: A Romance.* New York, 1916. $200.

POWYS, John Cowper, and POWYS, Llewellyn. *Confessions of Two Brothers.* Rochester, 1916. In dustwrapper. $300. Without dustwrapper. $60.

POWYS, Llewellyn. *The Book of Days.* Golden Cockerel Press. London, 1937. 12 etchings. Half green morocco. One of 55 signed, with an extra set of plates. $600. Ordinary copies (245 of 300). $350.

POWYS, Llewellyn. *Glory of Life.* Golden Cockerel Press. (London, 1934.) Woodcuts by Robert Gabbings. Vellum and cloth. One of 275. $500. One of 2 on vellum. $3,000.

POWYS, Llewellyn. *The Twelve Months.* Oxford, 1936. Illustrated by Robert Gibbings. Morocco. Issued without dustwrapper. One of 100 signed. $300.

POWYS, T. F. *An Interpretation of Genesis.* London, 1907. $400. London, 1929. One of 490 signed. In slipcase. $250. New York, 1929. White boards. First American edition. One of 260 signed. In glassine dustwrapper and slipcase. $250.

POWYS, T. F. *The Key of the Field.* London, 1930. Woodcut frontispiece. Buckram. One of 550 signed. In dustwrapper. $175.

POWYS, T. F. *Mr. Weston's Good Wine.* London, 1927. Illustrated. One of 650 signed. $200.

POWYS, T. F. *Soliloquies of a Hermit.* London, 1918. First English edition (of *The Soliloquy of a Hermit*). Light blue boards. In dustwrapper. $275. Without dustwrapper. $60. Dark blue boards, a little less.

POWYS, T. F. *The Soliloquy of a Hermit.* New York, 1916. Author's first book. In dustwrapper. $350. Without dustwrapper. $60.

POWYS, T. F. *Two Stories.* Hastings, England, 1967. Illustrated with wood engravings. Half leather. One of 25 signed by the illustrator Reynolds Stone. In slipcase. $600. One of 525. $150.

POWYS, T. F. *Uncle Dottery.* Bristol, England, 1930. Illustrated by Eric Gill. Half vellum and green linen. One of 300 signed. In dustwrapper. $250. Same issue: one of 50, with an extra set of engravings. $650.

POWYS, T. F. *When Thou Wast Naked.* Golden Cockerel Press. London, 1931. One of 500 signed. $250.

PRACTICAL Guide for Emigrants to North America (A). London, 1850. (By George Nettle.) Folding map in color. 57 pages, printed wraps. $250.

PRAIRIE (The): A Tale. By the Author of *The Spy.* London, 1827. (By James Fenimore Cooper.) 3 vols. $500. Philadelphia, 1827. 2 vols. First American edition, with copyright notices corrected by slip pasted in. $500. Limited Editions Club, New York, 1940. In slipcase. $75.

PRAIRIEDOM: Rambles and Scrambles in Texas. New York, 1845. By A. Suthron, Frederick Benjamin Page. Map. $1,000. New York, 1846. Second edition. $350.

PRATT, E. J. See *Rachel . . .*

PRATT, Orson. *A Series of Pamphlets . . . to Which is Appended a Discussion Held in Bolton . . . Also a Discussion Held in France . . .* Liverpool, 1851. Folding plate. Primary variant of this omnibus issue with "R. James" listed as the publisher on the general title. $1,000. Variant (later) printing of the general title-leaf, with Richards listed as the publisher. $750.

PRATT, Orson. *A Series of Pamphlets on the Doctrines of the Gospel . . .* Salt Lake City, 1884. First American edition. $125.

PRATT, Parley Parker. *History of the Late Persecution Inflicted by the State of Missouri Upon the Mormons . . .* Detroit, 1839. Three known copies. Only one has all the original pages. The other two have a few facsimile pages. An imperfect copy. $5,000.

PRATT, Parley Parker. *Key to the Science of Theology . . .* Liverpool/London, 1855. $1,250.

PRATT, Parley Parker. *A Voice of Warning and Instruction to All People . . .* New York, 1837. $1,750.

PRECAUTION: A Novel. New York, 1820. (By James Fenimore Cooper, his first book.) 2 vols. First issue, with errata leaf. $2,000. London, 1821. 3 vols. $1,500.

PRESCOTT, George Bartlett. *The Speaking Telephone . . .* New York, 1878. Illustrated. $250.

PRESCOTT, William H. *The History of the Conquest of Mexico.* London, 1947. Maps, other illustrations. 3 vols., cloth. $600. New York, 1843. 3 vols., with "track" on page 5, sixth line up. (Second printing had Tracy.") $500.

PRESCOTT, William H. *The History of the Conquest of Peru.* London, 1847. Illustrated. 2 vols., cloth. $500. New York, 1847. 2 vols. First issue, with no period after "integrity," line 20, page 467 in vol. II (VAB), not mentioned by BAL. $400. Mexico City, 1957. Limited Editions Club. Leather. In slipcase. $125.

PRICE, Reynolds. *Late Warning.* New York, 1968. Wraps. One of 26 signed and lettered copies. $250. One of 150 signed and numbered copies. Wraps. $150.

PRICE, Reynolds. *A Long and Happy Life.* New York, 1962. Author's first book, preceded by an off-print. First-state dustwrapper: rear panel prints names in pale green. $125. Second-state dustwrapper: names in dark green. $75. London, 1962. $75.

PRICE, Reynolds. *The Names and Faces of Heroes.* New York, 1963. $100. London, 1963. $125.

PRICHARD, James C. *A Treatise on Diseases of the Nervous System.* Part I (all published.) London, 1822. $750.

PRICHARD, James C. *A Treatise on Insanity* . . . London, 1835. $750. Philadelphia, 1837. $300.

PRIDE and Prejudice. London, 1813. By the Author of *Sense and Sensibility* (Jane Austen.) 3 vols., blue boards, paper labels. With November ads (VAB, but published January 1813?) and with ruled lines in half title of vol. 3 1²∕₅ inches (1 inch in second edition [Schwartz]). $45,000 at auction in 1988. Rebound. $6,000. Limited Editions Club, New York, 1940. In slipcase. $100.

PRIDEAUX, Sara T. *Bookbinders and Their Craft.* New York, 1903. 500 numbered copies. $225.

PRIDEAUX, S. T. *An Historical Sketch of Bookbinding.* London, 1893. $100.

PRIEST, Josiah. *Stories of the Revolution* . . . Albany, 1836. Folding plate. 32 pages, in original wraps. $250.

PRIEST, Josiah. *A True Narrative of the Capture of David Ogden.* (Cover title.) Lansingburgh, 1840. Woodcut. Self-wraps. $250.

PRIESTLEY, J. B. *Brief Diversions.* Cambridge, 1922. $150.

PRIESTLEY, J. B. *The Chapman of Rhymes.* London, 1918. Wraps. Author's first book. $400.

PRIESTLEY, J. B. *The Town Major of Miraucourt.* London, 1930. Vellum. Issued without dustwrapper. One of 525 signed. $250.

PRIME, William Cowper. See *The Owl Creek Letters* . . .

PRIMULA . . . (By Richard Garnett, his first book.) London, 1858. $250.

PRINCE, William Robert, and PRINCE, William. *A Treatise on the Vine.* New York, 1830. $600.

PRINTED Pages from English Literature. New York (1925). Clamshell box with title page and 20 folders, each containing a leaf from a book important in the history of English literature. 200 numbered copies. $500.

PRINTED Pages from European Literature. New York, 1925. Drop-back box containing explanatory leaf and 20 folders, each containing a leaf from a book famous in European literature. 200 numbered copies. $500.

PRITCHETT, R. T. *Smokiana, Ye Pipes of All Nations.* London, 1890. $1,000.

PRITCHETT, V. S. *Marching Spain.* London (1928). Author's first book. Cloth. $250. Wraps. (Left Book Club.) $75.

PRITTS, Joseph. *Mirror of Olden Time Border Life.* Abingdon, Va., 1849. 13 plates (17 in a few copies). $300.

PROCEEDINGS of Congress, in 1796, on the Admission of Tennessee as a State, into the Union. Detroit, 1835. 15 pages $400.

PROCEEDINGS of a Convention to Consider the Opening of the Indian Territory, Held at Kansas City, Mo., Feb, 8, 1888. Kansas City, 1888. 80 pages, wraps. $450.

PROCEEDINGS of the First Annual Session of the Territorial Grange of Montana. Diamond City, 1875. $350.

PROCEEDINGS of a General Meeting Held at Chester Courthouse, July 5th, 1831. Columbia, S.C., 1832. 16 pages $200.

PROCEEDINGS of the Harbor and River Convention. Held in Chicago, July 5th, 1847. Chicago, 1847. 79 pages, wraps. $300.

PROCEEDINGS of a Meeting, and Report of a Committee of Citizens in Relation to Steamboat Disasters in the Western Lakes. Cleveland, 1850. 22 pages, sewn. $200.

PROCEEDINGS of the National Ship Canal Convention. Chicago, 1863. Wraps. $200.

PROCEEDINGS of the Republican National Convention, Held at Chicago, May 16, 17 and 18, 1860. Albany, 1860. 153 pages, wraps. $450. Chicago, 1860. 44 pages, sewn. $250.

PROCEEDINGS of the St. Louis Chamber of Commerce, in Relation to the Improvement of the Navigation of the Mississippi River. St. Louis, 1842. 44 pages, sewn. $250.

PROCEEDINGS of Sundry Citizens of Baltimore, Convened for the Purpose of Devising the Most Efficient Means of Improving the Intercourse Between That City and the Western States. Baltimore, 1827. 38 pages $250.

PROCEEDINGS of the Virginia Assembly, on the Answers of Sundry States to Their Resolutions . . . December, 1798. Philadelphia, 1800. $1,000.

PROCTOR, Robert. *The Printing of Greek in the Fifteenth Century.* Oxford, 1900. $225.

PROGRESSIVE Men of Southern Idaho. Chicago, 1904. Frontispiece by Charles M. Russell, other illustrations. Leather. $350.

PROKOSCH, Frederic. *Age of Thunder.* New York (1945). One of 30 signed, sheet of original manuscript bound in. Issued without dustwrapper in slipcase. $250. Trade. $60.

PROKOSCH, Frederic. *Death at Sea: Poems.* New York, 1940. Cloth. One of 55 signed, sheet of original manuscript bound in. Issued without dustwrapper in slipcase. $250.

PROKOSCH, Frederic. *Three Songs—Three Images.* New Haven, 1932. 2 vols., wraps. One of 10 large paper copies. $300.

PROMETHEUS Bound. London, 1833. Translated from the Greek of Aeschylus. And *Miscellaneous Poems by the Translator.* (By Elizabeth Barrett Browning.) In original dark blue cloth, paper label on spine. $400.

PROPERT, W. A. *The Russian Ballet in Western Europe, 1909–1920 . . .* London or New York, 1921. Illustrated, including color plates. Issued without dustwrapper. One of 500. $600.

PROSCH, T. W. *McCarver and Tacoma.* Seattle (1906). 2 plates. $125.

PROSE and Poetry of the Live Stock Industry of the United States. Vol. 1. (All published.) Denver and Kansas City (1905). Leather. (Edited by James W. Freeman.) $5,000. New York, 1959. Half leather. In slipcase. $150.

PROSPECTUS of the Leadville & Ten Mile Narrow Gauge Railway Company of Leadville, Col. (Cover title.) Leadville, 1880. 20 pages, printed wraps. $350.

PROSPERO and CALIBAN. *The Weird of the Wanderer.* London, 1912. (By Baron Corvo [Frederick William Rolfe] and Charles Harry Pirie-Gordon.) $300.

PROTEUS. *Sonnets and Songs.* London, 1875. (By Wilfrid Scawen Blunt, his first book.) $200.

PROUD, Robert. *The History of Pennsylvania, In North America . . .* Philadelphia, 1797–98. 2 vols. Folding map. Frontispiece portrait. $600.

PROUST, Marcel. *47 Unpublished Letters from Marcel Proust to Walter Berry.* Paris, 1930. Black Sun Press. White wraps. One of 200 on Arches paper. In slipcase. $400. Also an issue of 15, including an original autograph letter. $2,500.

PROUST, Marcel. *Swann's Way.* Limited Editions Club. New York, 1954. In slipcase. $150.

PROVOST (The). Edinburgh, 1822. (By John Galt.) $250.

PSALMAU Dafydd. Gregynog Press. (Newtown, Wales, 1929.) Decorated paper covers, morocco spine. One of 200. $400. (Note: *The Psalms of David* in Welsh.) Also, one of 25 bound in morocco. $10,000.

PUBLIC Libraries in the United States . . . Washington, 1876. $100.

PUGET SOUND Business Directory and Guide to Washington Territory, 1872. Olympia (1872). 3 colored plates of ads. Boards and leather. $750.

PUGET SOUND Directory, 1887. No-place, 1887. (By R. L. Polk.) Illustrated. Boards. $500.

PULITZER, Ralph. See Burke, John.

PURDY, Al. *The Enchanted Echo.* Vancouver, 1944. Author's first book. $600.

PURDY, James. *Don't Call Me by My Right Name and Other Stories.* New York, 1956. Blue-gray or white (variant) printed wraps. Author's first book. $175.

PURDY, James. *An Oyster Is a Wealthy Beast.* (San Francisco, 1967.) Oblong boards. One of 50 signed, with an original drawing. $300. Also, 200 signed copies in wraps. $150.

PURDY, James. *63: Dream Palace.* New York, 1956. Printed wraps. $150.

PUSHKIN, Alexander. *The Golden Cockerel.* Limited Editions Club, New York (1949). Illustrated and signed by Edmund Dulac. Cloth. In slipcase. $175.

PUSS in Boots. New York (1880s). Illustrated in color. 10 pages, pictorial boards. McLaughlin book with overlays on center spread. $250.

PUTNAM, Samuel. *Evaporation . . .* Winchester, 1923. (Author's first book, with Mark Turbyfill.) $150.

PUZO, Mario. *The Dark Arena.* New York (1955). Author's first book. $75.

PUZO, Mario. *The Godfather.* New York (1969). $125.

PYLE, Howard. *Howard Pyle's Book of the American Spirit.* 1923. Edited by Merle Johnson and Francis J. O'Dowd. Illustrated, including color plates, by Pyle. With "B-X" on copyright page. In dustwrapper. $450. One of 50 signed by the editors. In dustwrapper. $850. Also, one of 6 signed copies, with an original Pyle drawing for the book. $1,250.

PYLE, Howard. *Howard Pyle's Book of Pirates.* New York, 1921. Edited by Merle Johnson. Illustrated, including color plates, by Pyle. Boards and cloth. With "D-V" on copyright page. In dustwrapper. $400. One of 50 on vellum, signed by Johnson. In dustwrapper and slipcase. $1,250.

PYLE, Howard. *The Merry Adventures of Robin Hood.* New York, 1883. Illustrated, including color plates, by Pyle. Full leather. $750. Cloth. $400. London, 1883. $300. New York, 1933. Illustrated by N. C. Wyeth and with 2 drawings by Andrew Wyeth. Cloth. Brandywine Edition. $300.

PYLE, Howard. *Otto of the Silver Hand.* New York, 1888. Illustrated by the author. Half calf and cloth. $400.

PYLE, Howard. *Pepper and Salt.* New York, 1886. Illustrated by the author. Pictorial buckram. $350.

PYLE, Howard. *The Ruby of Kishmoor.* New York, 1908. Illustrated by author. $300.

PYLE, Howard. *The Story of the Champions of the Round Table.* New York, 1905. $300.

PYLE, Howard. *The Story of the Grail and the Passing of Arthur.* New York, 1910. Illustrated by the author. $250.

PYLE, Howard. *The Story of King Arthur and His Knights.* New York, 1903. Illustrated by the author. Cloth. $250.

PYLE, Howard. *The Wonder Clock.* New York, 1888. Illustrated by the author. Half leather. $400.

PYLE, Howard. *Yankee Doodle.* New York, 1881. Pictorial boards. First book illustrated by Pyle. $500.

PYM, Barbara. *Some Tame Gazelle.* London, 1950. Author's first book. $200.

PYNCHON, Thomas. *The Crying of Lot 49.* Philadelphia (1966). $250. London (1967). $150.

PYNCHON, Thomas. *Gravity's Rainbow.* New York (1973). $350. Wraps. Simultaneous paperback issue. $60. London (1973). $200.

PYNCHON, Thomas. *V.* Philadelphia (1963). Author's first book. $500. London, 1963. $250.

PYNE, W. H. *The Costume of Great Britain.* London, 1804 (actually after 1817). 60 hand-colored plates. $2,000.

PYNE, W. H. *The History of the Royal Residences of Windsor Castle, St. James's Palace, Carlton House, Kensington Palace, Hampton Court, Buckingham House, and Frogmore.* London, 1819. 100 colored engravings. 3 vols. With 100 hand-colored plates. $6,000. Large paper. $7,500. Plates not colored. $2,500.

Q

QUARTETTE. By Four Anglo-Indian Writers. Lahore, India, 1885. (By Rudyard Kipling and his sister, mother, and father.) Wraps. $2,000 or more.

QUARTO-Millenary, The First 250 Publications and First 25 years... Limited Editions Club... New York, 1959. 2,250 numbered copies. In slipcase. $275.

QUEEN, Ellery. *The Chinese Orange Mystery.* New York, 1934. (By Frederic Dannay and Manfred B. Lee.) $650.

QUEEN, Ellery. *The Dutch Shoe Mystery.* New York, 1931. (By Frederic Dannay and Manfred B. Lee.) $1,000.

QUEEN, Ellery. *The Egyptian Cross Mystery.* New York, 1932. (By Frederic Dannay and Manfred B. Lee.) $750.

QUEEN, Ellery. *The French Powder Mystery.* New York, 1930. $1,000.

QUEEN, Ellery. *Roman Hat Mystery.* New York, 1929. (By Frederic Dannay and Manfred B. Lee, their first book.) $3,000.

QUEEN, Ellery. *The Spanish Cape Mystery.* New York, 1935. (By Frederic Dannay and Manfred B. Lee.) $600.

QUEEN, Ellery (editor). *The Misadventures of Sherlock Holmes.* Boston, 1944. Frontispiece by F. D. Steele. (Edited by Frederic Dannay and Manfred B. Lee.) $400.

QUEENY, Edgar M. *Cheechako.* New York, 1941. Illustrated. One of 1,200. $150.

QUEENY, Edgar M. *Prairie Wings: Pen and Camera Flight Studies.* New York, 1946. Illustrated. $400. Morocco. One of 225 signed. $1,000. Philadelphia, 1947. Cloth. Second edition. $250.

QUENNELL, Peter. *Masques and Poems.* Berkshire (1922). Author's first book. $175.

QUILLER-COUCH, Sir Arthur. See Rackham, Arthur, *Arthur Rackham's Book of Pictures.*

QUILLER-COUCH, Sir Arthur. *Dead Man's Rock.* London, 1887. Author's first book. $300.

QUILLER-COUCH, Sir Arthur. *In Powder and Crinoline.* London (1913). Illustrated by Kay Nielsen, including 26 color plates. Boards, buckram spine. $750. Vellum. One of 500 signed. $3,500.

QUILLER-COUCH, Sir Arthur. *The Sleeping Beauty and Other Fairy Tales.* London (about 1910). 30 colored plates by Edmund Dulac. $300. Morocco. One of 1,000. $600.

QUILLER-COUCH, Sir Arthur. *The Twelve Dancing Princesses and Other Fairy Tales.* New York (about 1920). Illustrated by Kay Nielsen. Pictorial cloth. In dustwrapper. $500.

QUINBY, Jane. *Beatrix Potter, A Bibliographical Check List.* New York, 1954. Cloth with stiff paper wraps bound in. Limited to 250 copies. $200.

QUINN, Seabury. *Roads.* (New York, 1938). Wraps. Reprinted from "Weird Tales." $1,000. Sauk City, Wis., 1948. $100.

R

R. B. Adam Library Relating to Dr. Samuel Johnson and His Era (The). London/New York, 1929, 1930. 4 vols. (the fourth was issued separately in 1930 without dustwrapper). The first 3 volumes were limited to 500 copies, the fourth volume was limited to 225 copies. The 4 together. $800.

R., J. *Poems.* (London) 1850. (By John Ruskin.) $1,000.

RACHEL: A Sea-Story of Newfoundland. New York, 1917. (By E. J. Pratt.) Author's first book. Wraps. $3,000.

RACKHAM, Arthur. *The Arthur Rackham Fairy Book.* London (1933). Illustrated, including color. Full vellum. One of 460 signed. In slipcase. $1,250.

RACKHAM, Arthur. *Arthur Rackham's Book of Pictures.* London, 1913. Edited by Sir Arthur Quiller-Couch. Illustrated, including color. $300. One of 1,030 signed by Rackham. $750. Another: one of 30, inscribed and with an original drawing. $2,000. New York (1914). $250. London (1927). In dustwrapper. $300.

RACKHAM, Bernard. *The Ancient Glass of Canterbury Cathedral.* London, 1949. 21 plates in color and 80 in monochrome. Buckram. Issued without dustwrapper. $300.

RACKHAM, Bernard, and READ, Herbert. *English Pottery . . .* London, 1924. $150. Pigskin. One of 75 signed. $300.

RADCLIFFE, Ann. *The Mysteries of Udolpho.* London, 1794. 4 vols. $750.

RADCLIFFE, James. *The British Youth's Instructor.* With *New British Penman.* With *Beauties of Writing.* London (no-date) (circa 1794). 3 vols. 12 plates, 12 plates, 23 plates, respectively. $500.

RADER, J. L. *South of Forty* . . . Norman, Okla., 1947. $150.

RADIGUET, Raymond. *The Count's Ball.* New York (1929). First edition in English. $200.

RADIGUET, Raymond. *The Devil in the Flesh.* New York, 1932. First American edition. $250.

RAFINESQUE, C. S. *Medical Flora; Or, Manual of the Medical Botany* . . . Philadelphia, 1828–30. 2 vols. 100 plates printed in colored ink. $1,250.

RAFINESQUE-SCHMALTZ, C. S. *The American Nations* . . . Philadelphia, 1836. $1,250.

RAINE, Kathleen. *Six Dreams and Other Poems.* London, 1968. One of 100 signed. $175.

RAINE, Kathleen. *Stone and Flower.* London (1943). Illustrated. Author's first book. $125.

RAINE, William MacLeod. *Brand Blotters.* New York (1912). In dustwrapper. $200.

RAINE, William MacLeod. *Bucky O'Connor.* New York (1910). In dustwrapper. $250.

RAINE, William MacLeod. *Cattle Brands: A Sketch of Bygone Days in the Cow-Country.* Boston (1920). 8 pages, wraps. $250.

RAINE, William MacLeod. *A Daughter of Raasay.* New York (1902). Author's first book. In dustwrapper. $750. Lacking dustwrapper. $150.

RAINE, William MacLeod. *Mavericks.* New York (1912). In dustwrapper. $200.

RAINE, William MacLeod. *Texas Ranger.* New York (1911). In dustwrapper. $250.

RAINE, William MacLeod. *Wyoming.* New York (1908). In dustwrapper. $300.

RAINES, C. W. *A Bibliography of Texas.* Austin, Tex., 1896. $400. Facsimile reprint. Houston, 1955. One of 500. In slipcase. $75.

RAITT, W. *The Digestion of Grasses and Bamboo for Paper-Making.* London, 1931. 20 plates and a tipped-in specimen of paper produced from bamboo. $175.

RAKOSI, Carl. *Two Poems.* New York (1932). Pictorial wraps. Author's first book. $200.

RALFE, J. *The Naval Chronology of Great Britain.* London, 1820. 60 colored plates. 3 vols., half morocco. $6,000.

RALPH, Julian. *On Canada's Frontier.* New York, 1892. Illustrated. By Frederic Remington. $300.

RAMAL, Walter. *Songs of Childhood.* London, 1902. Frontispiece. Decorated blue cloth and vellum. (By Walter De La Mare, his first book.) $750.

RAMSAY, David. *The History of South Carolina.* Charleston, 1809. 2 folding maps. 2 vols. $850.

RAMSAY, David. *Military Memoirs of Great Britain* . . . Edinburgh, 1779. 12 portraits. $650.

RAMSEY, J. G. M. *The Annals of Tennessee.* Charleston, 1853. Folding map and plan. Leather, or cloth. $350. Philadelphia, 1853. Second edition. $250.

RAND, Ayn. *Atlas Shrugged.* New York (1957). "10/57" bottom of front dustwrapper flap and publisher's name and address bottom of back flap. $250. New York (1967). One of 2,000 signed and numbered copies. Acetate dustwrapper in slipcase. $600.

RAND, Ayn. *The Fountainhead.* Indianapolis (1943). First edition stated. Red cloth, dustwrapper priced at $3.00 with Bobbs-Merrill titles on back. $1,500. Green cloth, dustwrapper priced at $3.00 with photograph of author on back with three reviews. $500. London, 1947. $750.

RAND, Ayn. *The Night of January 16th.* New York (1936). Issued in blue wraps with several different addresses. Priority of addresses unknown, but First Edition stated. $400. New York/Cleveland (1968). "First Printing 1968." $60.

RAND, Ayn. *We the Living.* New York, 1936. Author's first book. "Published April, 1936." $2,000. London (1936). $1,250.

RANKIN, Melinda. *Texas in 1850.* Boston, 1850. $300.

RANSOM, John Crowe. See *Armageddon* . . .

RANSOM, John Crowe. *Chills and Fever.* New York, 1924. $500.

RANSOM, John Crowe. *Grace After Meat.* London, 1924. Boards, paper label. Issued without dustwrapper. $450.

RANSOM, John Crowe. *Poems About God.* New York, 1919. Brown boards, paper label. Author's first book. $600.

RANSOM, John Crowe. *Two Gentlemen in Bonds.* New York, 1927. $750.

RANSOM, Will. *Private Presses and Their Books.* New York, 1929. One of 1,200. $200.

RANSOM, Will. *Selective Check Lists of Press Books* . . . New York, 1945–50. 12 parts bound in 1. Original paper wrappers bound in. $250.

RANSOME, Arthur. *Oscar Wilde: A Critical Study.* London, 1912. $75.

RANSOME, Arthur. *The Souls of the Street* . . . London, 1904. Author's first book. $75.

RAREY, J. S. *The Modern Art of Taming Wild Horses.* Columbus, Ohio, 1856. Wraps. $500. Austin, 1856. 62 pages, wraps. Third edition, revised and corrected. $300.

RATHBONE, Frederick. *Old Wedgwood.* London, 1898. Illustrated, including color plates. 8 parts in 1 volume, folio. Half morocco. One of 200. $1,000.

RAVENSCROFT, Edward James. *The Pinetum Britannicum.* Edinburgh/London, [1863–] 1884. 3 vols. 48 hand-colored plates, 4 mounted albumen prints, 1 engraved plate of maps. $6,000.

RAVENSNEST: or, The Redskins. London, 1846. (By James Fenimore Cooper.) 3 vols., in original boards, green or blue cloth spine. First English edition of *The Redskins.* $600.

RAWLINGS, Marjorie Kinnan. *Cross Creek Cookery.* New York, 1942. First issue in pictorial cloth and endpapers. $125. Second issue in tan cloth with white endpapers. $75.

RAWLINGS, Marjorie Kinnan. *Golden Apples.* New York, 1935. $175.

RAWLINGS, Marjorie Kinnan. *South Moon Under.* New York, 1933. Author's first book. $200.

RAWLINGS, Marjorie Kinnan. *When the Whippoorwill,* New York, 1940. $150. Scribners' "A" not on copyright page.

RAWLINGS, Marjorie Kinnan. *The Yearling.* New York, 1938. $100. New York, 1939. Signed by author and illustrator, N. C. Wyeth. One of 770. In dustwrapper and slipcase. $750.

RAWSON, Clayton. *Death from a Top Hat.* New York, 1938. Author's first book. $350.

RAWSTORNE, Lawrence. *Gamonia: or the Art of Preserving Game.* London, 1837. 15 hand-colored plates. In original green morocco. With errata slip at end (VAB). $2,000.

RAY, Gordon N. *The Art of the French Illustrated Book, 1700–1914.* New York (1982). 2 vols. $175.

RAY, Ophelia. *Daughter of the Tejas.* New York (1965). (By Larry McMurtry, as ghostwriter.) In gray dustwrapper. $100. In white jacket. $75.

REACH, Angus B. *Clement Lorimer . . .* London (1849). Author's first book. $400.

READ, C. Rudston. *What I Heard, Saw and Did at the Australian Gold Fields.* London, 1853. Large folding map, tinted lithograph plates. $450.

READ, Herbert. See Rackham, Bernard.

READ, Herbert. *English Stained Glass.* London, 1926. Colored frontispiece, 70 full-page plates. Issued without dustwrapper. $250.

READ, Herbert. *The Green Child.* London (1935). $300.

READ, Herbert. *Mutations of the Phoenix.* Hogarth Press. London, 1923. Issued without dustwrapper. $350.

READ, Herbert. *Naked Warriors.* London, 1919. (First commercial.) $250.

READ, Herbert. *Songs of Chaos.* London (1915). Author's first book. $350.

READ, Herbert, et al. *Surrealism.* London, 1936. Plates. Cloth. Issued without dustwrapper. $250.

READ, Thomas Buchanan. *Paul Redding . . .* Boston, 1845. Author's first book. $150.

READE, Charles. *The Cloister and the Hearth.* London, 1861. 4 vols. First issue, without ads and with words transposed on page 372 of vol. 2. $1,500. New York, 1861. $300. Limited Editions Club, New York, 1932. In slipcase. $100.

READE, Charles. *"It Is Never Too Late to Mend."* London, 1856. 3 vols. $400.

READE, Charles. *Peg Woffington.* London, 1853. Author's first book. $200.

READING and Collecting, A Monthly Review of Rare and Recent Books. Chicago, 1936–38. Complete run (vol. one, no. 1 to vol. two, no. 3). Bound in 2 vols. $125.

REAGAN, John H. *Memoirs, with Special Reference to Secession and the Civil War.* New York, 1906. 4 plates. $200.

REANEY, James. *The Red Heart.* Toronto, 1949. Author's first book. $350.

REAVEY, George. *Faust's Metamorphoses . . .* Seine (1932). Author's first book. Wraps. $250.

REDPATH, James, and HINTON, Richard J. *Hand-book to Kansas Territory and the Rocky Mountains' Gold Region.* New York, 1859. 3 maps in color on 2 large folding sheets. $850.

REDSKINS (The). New York, 1846. By the author of *The Pathfinder* (James Fenimore Cooper). 2 vols., in original printed brown wraps. $1,250. (For first English edition, see *Ravensnest.*)

REED, Andrew, and MATHESON, James. *A Narrative of the Visit to the Americas Churches by the Deputation from the Congregational Union of England and Wales.* London, 1835. 4 plates, folding map. 2 vols., in original leather. $250.

REED, Ishmael. *The Free-Lance Pallbearers.* Garden City, 1967. Author's first book. $100.

REED, J. W. *Map of and Guide to the Kansas Gold Region.* New York, 1859. Map. 24 pages, printed wraps. $4,500.

REED, John. *The Day in Bohemia.* New York, 1913. Stiff printed wraps. One of 500. In slipcase. $200.

REED, John. *Insurgent Mexico.* New York, 1914. $150.

REED, John. *Sangar: To Lincoln Steffens.* Boards. Riverside, Conn., 1913. Stiff wraps. 500 copies. In slipcase. $200.

REED, John. *Ten Days That Shook the World.* Illustrated. New York, 1919. In dustwrapper. $1,000. Lacking dustwrapper. $350.

REED, Nathaniel. *The Life of Texas Jack.* (Tulsa, 1936.) Illustrated. Pictorial wraps. $500.

REED, Ronald. *The Nature and Making of Parchment.* (Leeds) 1975. 450 numbered copies. $250.

REED, S. G. *A History of the Texas Railroads.* Houston (1941). Blue cloth. Limited, signed edition. Issued without dustwrapper. $300.

REED, Silas. *Report of. . . Surveyor General of Wyoming Territory, for the Year 1871.* Washington, 1871. Tables. 46 pages, wraps. $300.

REED, Talbot Baines. *A History of the Old English Letter Foundries. . .* London, 1887. Half leather. $300. London (1952). Revised and enlarged. $125.

REES, William. *Description of the City of Keokuk.* Keokuk, Iowa, 1854. 24 pages, printed self-wraps. $300. Keokuk, 1855. 22 pages, with wrapper title. Second edition. $200.

REES, William. *The Mississippi Bridge Cities: Davenport, Rock Island and Moline.* (Rock Island, Ill.), 1854. Woodcut frontispiece. 32 pages, sewn. $200.

REESE, Lizette Woodworth. *A Branch of May: Poems.* Baltimore, 1887. Gray cloth. Author's first book. $250.

REEVE, Arthur B. *The Silent Bullet.* New York, 1912. Author's first book. $100.

REEVE, Arthur B. *The Black Hand.* London, 1912. $100.

REID, Forrest. *Apostate.* London (1926). One of 50 signed. $300.

REID, Forrest. *Illustrators of the Sixties.* London (1928). $100.

REID, Forrest. *The Kingdom of Twilight.* London, 1904. Author's first book. $150.

REID, John C. *Reid's Tramp, or A Journal of the Incidents of Ten Months' Travel Through Texas, New Mexico, Arizona, Sonora, and California.* Selma, Ala., 1858. $10,000.

REID, Mayne. *The Headless Horseman.* London (1866). 20 plates. 2 vols. (By Thomas M. Reid.) $400.

REID, Mayne. *No Quarter!* London, 1888. 3 vols., cloth. (By Thomas M. Reid.) $350.

REID, Mayne. *The Quadroon; or, A Lover's Adventures in Louisiana.* London, 1856. 3 vols., orange or gray cloth. (By Thomas M. Reid.) $600.

REID, Mayne. *The White Chief: A Legend of Northern Mexico.* London, 1855. 3 vols. (By Thomas M. Reid.) Author's first book. $600.

REID, Mayne. *The Wood-Rangers.* London, 1860. 3 vols. (By Thomas M. Reid.) $500.

REID, Samuel C., Jr. *The Scouting Expeditions of McCulloch's Texas Rangers.* Philadelphia, 1847. 12 plates and double-page map. $750. Philadelphia, 1848. $750.

REID, Thomas M. See Reid, Mayne.

REIGN of Terror in Kansas (The). Boston, 1856. (By Charles W. Briggs.) 34 pages, wraps. $850.

REISER, Anton. *Albert Einstein: A Biographical Portrait.* New York, 1931. Author's first book (translated anonymously by Louis Zukofsky). $500. London (1931). $400.

RELIEF Business Directory, Names and New Locations in San Francisco, Oakland, Berkeley and Alameda of 4,000 San Francisco Firms and Business Men. Berkeley, May 1906. 64 pages, wraps. (Issued after the great earthquake and fire of 1906.) $250.

RELIGIO Bibliopolae, in Imitation of Dr. Browns Religio Medici . . . London, 1691. (John Dunton.) $600.

REMARQUE, Erich Maria. *All Quiet on the Western Front.* London (1929). Buckram. First edition in English. $200. Boston, 1929. Gray cloth. $100. Limited Editions Club, New York, 1969. In slipcase. $100.

REMARQUE, Erich Maria. *The Road Back.* London (1931). First edition in English. $100. Boston, 1931. $75.

REMINGTON, Frederic. *Crooked Trails.* New York, 1898. 49 plates. Pictorial tan cloth. $250.

REMINGTON, Frederic. *Done in the Open.* New York, 1902. Introduction by Owen Wister. Illustrations by Remington. 90 pages, folio, cream-colored pictorial boards. First issue, with Russell imprint and with "Frederick" instead of "Frederic" on front cover. $1,000. Suede leather. One of 250 signed. $1,500.

REMINGTON, Frederic. *Drawings.* New York, 1897. 61 plates. Oblong folio, pictorial boards and cloth. $750. Suede leather. One of 250 signed. $1,500. New York, 1898. $500.

REMINGTON, Frederic. *Frontier Sketches.* Chicago (1898). Illustrated by the author. Oblong, pictorial boards. $500.

REMINGTON, Frederic. *John Ermine of the Yellowstone.* New York, 1902. Illustrated by the author. Brown cloth. In dustwrapper. $500. Without dustwrapper. $150. (First editions and reprints, misspell "Remington" on spine.)

REMINGTON, Frederic. *Men with the Bark On.* New York, 1900. Illustrated by the author. Pictorial orange-tan cloth. First issue, ⅞ inch thick. $250. Second issue, 1⅛ inches. $175.

REMINGTON, Frederic. *Pony Tracks.* New York, 1895. Author's first book. Illustrated by the author. Brown decorated cloth. $400. Suede. $1,000.

REMINGTON, Frederic. *A Rogers Ranger in the French and Indian War.* (New York) 1897. Printed wraps. $300.

REMINGTON, Frederic. *Sundown Leflare.* New York, 1899. Illustrated by the author. Brown pictorial cloth. $150.

REMINGTON, Frederic. *Way of an Indian.* New York, 1906. In dustwrapper. $400.

REMINISCENCES of a Campaign in Mexico. Nashville, 1849. (By John B. Robertson.) Map, frontispiece. $600.

REMSBURG, John E., and REMSBURG, George J. *Charley Reynolds, Soldier, Hunter, Scout and Guide.* Kansas City, 1931. Portrait. First book edition. One of 175. $200.

REMY, Jules, and BRENCHLEY, Julius L. *A Journey to Great Salt Lake City.* London, 1861. Map, 10 plates. 2 vols., cloth. First edition in English. $850.

RENAULT, Mary. *Purposes of Love.* London, 1939. Author's first book. $250.

RENAULT, Mary. *Promise of Love.* New York, 1940. (New title.) $125.

RENDELL, Ruth. *From Doon with Death.* London, 1964. Author's first book. $125.

RENDELL, Ruth. *A New Lease of Death.* London, 1967. $150. New York, 1967. $75.

RENDELL, Ruth. *To Fear a Painted Devil.* London, 1965. $125. New York, 1965. $100.

RENNER, Frederic G. *Charles M. Russell: Paintings, Drawings, and Sculpture in the Amon G. Carter Collection. A Descriptive Catalogue.* Austin (1966). Illustrated, including color. Decorated cloth. One of 250 signed, and with an extra color plate and a portfolio of color plates laid in. Slipcase. $300.

REPLY to the Essay on Population, by the Rev. T. R. Malthus (A). London, 1807. (By William Hazlitt.) $1,000.

REPORT from a Select Committee of the House of Representatives, on the Overland Emigration Route from Minnesota to British Oregon. St. Paul, Minn., 1858. Printed wraps, marbled spine. $650.

REPORT from the Select Committee on the Hudson's Bay Company. London, 1857. 3 elephant folio colored folding maps by Arrowsmith. Half morocco. $1,350. There was also an advance issue in wraps, 2 parts, same date would be same value.

REPORT of the Proceedings Connected with the Disputes Between the Earl of Selkirk and the North-West Company. London, 1819. (Samuel Hull Wilcocke, editor.) $850. Montreal, 1819. $1,350.

REPORT on the Governor's Message Relating to the "Political Situation" "Polygamy," and "Governmental Action." Salt Lake, 1882. 13 pages, wraps. $150.

REPORT on the Typography of the Cambridge University Press . . . (No-place) 1950. One of 500 copies as one of the Cambridge Christmas books. $100.

REPORTS of the Committee of Investigation Sent in 1873, by the Mexican Government, to the Frontier of Texas. New York, 1875. 3 folding maps. Boards and leather. $600.

REPPLIER, Agnes. *Books and Men.* Boston, 1882. Author's first book. $75.

REPTON, Humphry. *Observations on the Theory and Practice of Landscape Gardening.* London, 1803. Portrait frontispiece and 27 plates, 10 in full color. $5,000. London, 1805. $4,000.

REVELL, Alexander H. *Pro and Con of Golf.* Chicago (1915). $150.

REVERE, Joseph W. *A Tour of Duty in California.* New York, 1849. 6 plates, folding map. $500.

REXROTH, Kenneth. *The Art of Worldly Wisdom.* Decker Press. Prairie City, Ill., 1949. $350. Sausalito, Calif. (1953). Second edition. In dustwrapper. $125.

REXROTH, Kenneth. *In What Hour.* New York, 1940. Author's first book. $200.

REXROTH, Kenneth. *The Phoenix and the Tortoise.* New York, 1944. $200.

REXROTH, Kenneth. *The Signature of All Things.* (New York, 1950.) $150.

REYNARDSON, C. T. S. Birch. *'Down the Road' or Reminiscences of a Gentleman Coachman.* London, 1875. Colored lithographs. $250. Second edition, same date. $150.

REYNOLDS, J. N. *Voyage of the United States Frigate Potomac.* New York, 1835. Illustrated. In original half leather. $400.

REYNOLDS, John. *My Olden Times.* (Belleville) 1855. Portrait. $750.

REYNOLDS, John. *The Pioneer History of Illinois.* Belleville, 1852. $400.

REYNOLDS, John. *Sketches of the Country on the Northern Route from Belleville, Ill., to the City of New York, and Back by the Ohio Valley.* Belleville, 1854. $500.

REZNIKOFF, Charles. *Five Groups of Verse.* New York (1927). One of 375. In dustwrapper. $300.

REZNIKOFF, Charles. *Going To and Fro and Walking Up and Down.* New York (1941). $250.

REZNIKOFF, Charles. *Jerusalem the Golden.* New York (1934). $250.

REZNIKOFF, Charles. *Nine Plays.* New York (1927). One of 400. In dustwrapper. $300.

REZNIKOFF, Charles. *Rhythms.* Brooklyn (1918). Wraps. Author's first book. $1,000.

RHEES, William J. *Manual of Public Libraries* . . . Philadelphia, 1859. $275.

RHODE, John. *A.S.F. The Story of a Great Conspiracy.* London (1924). Author's first book. $200.

RHODES, Eugene Manlove. *Bransford in Arcadia.* New York, 1914. In dustwrapper. $300. Without dustwrapper. $60.

RHODES, Eugene Manlove. *The Desire of the Moth.* New York, 1916. In dustwrapper. $250. Without dustwrapper. $50.

RHODES, Eugene Manlove. *Good Men and True.* New York, 1910. Author's first book. In dustwrapper. $500. Without dustwrapper. $150.

RHODES, Eugene Manlove. *Once in the Saddle and Paso Por Aqui.* Boston, 1927. $200.

RHODES, Eugene Manlove. *The Proud Sheriff.* Boston, 1935. $200.

RHODES, Eugene Manlove. *Stepsons of Light.* Boston (1921). $200.

RHODES, Eugene Manlove. *West Is West.* New York, 1917. In dustwrapper. $250. Without dustwrapper. $50.

RHODES, W. H. *Caxton's Book.* San Francisco, 1876. Author's first book. $250.

RHODODAPHNE: or The Thessalian Spell: A Poem. London, 1818. (By Thomas Love Peacock.) $250.

RHYS, Jean. *Left Bank* . . . New York (1927). Author's first book. $600.

RICARDO, David. *On the Principles of Political Economy, and Taxation.* London, 1817. $7,500.

RICE, Anne. *Interview with the Vampire.* New York, 1976. Author's first book. $400.

RICE, Craig. *8 Faces at 3.* New York, 1939. Author's first book. $150.

RICH, Adrienne Cecile. *Ariadne: A Play in Three Acts and Poems.* (Baltimore) 1939. (The poet's first published work.) 59 pages, blue wraps. In tissue dustwrapper. $1,500.

RICH, Adrienne Cecile. *A Change of World.* New Haven, 1951. Foreword by W. H. Auden. Author's first book as an adult. $400.

RICH, Adrienne Cecile. *The Diamond Cutters and Other Poems.* New York (1955). $100.

RICH, Adrienne Cecile. *Not I, But Death.* Baltimore, 1941. Wraps. $1,500.

RICHARD Hurdis; or, the Avenger of Blood. Philadelphia, 1838. (By William Gilmore Simms.) 2 vols., in original cloth, paper labels. $500.

RICHARDS, Franklin D. (editor). *A Compendium of the Faith and Doctrines of the Church of Jesus Christ of the Latter-Day Saints . . .* Liverpool, 1857. $250. Salt Lake City, 1882. Second edition, expanded. Errata slip. $150.

RICHARDS, Laura E. *Five Mice in a Mouse-Trap.* Boston, 1881. $175.

RICHARDS, Thomas Addison. *American Scenery Illustrated.* New York (1854). Morocco. $175.

RICHARDS, Thomas Addison. *Georgia Illustrated.* Penfield, Ga., 1842. Plates. 44 pages, leather. $400.

RICHARDS, Thomas Addison. *The Romance of American Landscape.* New York (1854). 16 engravings. Morocco. $250.

RICHARDSON, Dorothy. *Dawn's Left Hand.* London (1931). $175.

RICHARDSON, Dorothy. *Gleanings from the Work of George Fox.* London, 1914. $200.

RICHARDSON, Dorothy. *Interim.* London (1919). In dustwrapper. $300.

RICHARDSON, Dorothy. *Pointed Roofs.* London, 1915. $150.

RICHARDSON, Dorothy. *The Quakers Past and Present.* London, 1914. Author's first book. $250.

RICHARDSON, Rupert N. *The Comanche Barrier to South Plains Settlement.* Glendale, Calif., 1933. Cloth. Issued without dustwrapper. $300.

RICHARDSON, William H. *The Journal of William H. Richardson: A Private Soldier in Col. Doniphan's Command.* Baltimore, 1847. 84 pages, wraps. $4,000. Baltimore, 1848. Illustrated. Half leather. Second edition. $1,000. New York, 1848. Third edition. $750.

RICHLER, Mordecai. *The Acrobats.* London, 1954. Author's first book. $250.

RICHMOND, C. W., and VALLETTE, H. F. *A History of Du Page County, Illinois.* Chicago, 1857. $275.

RICHMOND During the War; Four Years of Personal Observation. New York, 1867. (By Sally A. Brock.) $200.

RICHTER, Conrad. *Brothers of No Kin and Other Stories.* New York (about 1924). Red cloth. Author's first book. In white (first) dustwrapper. $600. In later (orange) jacket. $400.

RICHTER, Conrad. *Human Vibrations, The Mechanics of Life and Mind.* Harrisburg (1925). First edition not stated. $350.

RICHTER, Conrad. *Sea of Grass.* New York, 1937. $125.

RICHTER, Conrad. *Tracy Cromwell.* New York, 1942. $100.

RICHTER, Conrad. *The Trees.* New York, 1940. One of 255 copies. In Slipcase. $175. Trade. $125.

RICHTHOFEN, Walter, Baron von. *Cattle-Raising on the Plains of North America.* New York, 1885. $500.

RIDGE, John R. See Yellow Bird.

RIDGE, John R. *Poems.* San Francisco, 1868. Original photograph as frontispiece. $250.

RIDGE, Lola. *Firehead.* New York, 1929. Half morocco. One of 30 signed. $200. Trade. $75.

RIDGE, Lola. *The Ghetto . . .* New York, 1918. Author's first book. In dustwrapper. $250.

RIDING, Laura. See Gottschalk, Laura Riding.

RIDING, Laura. *Americans.* Primavera Press. (Los Angeles) 1934. 200 numbered copies. Issued without dustwrapper. $400.

RIDING, Laura. *Collected Poems.* London (1938). Green cloth over boards, buff dustwrapper printed in black and orange. $250. New York (1938). Royal blue cloth over boards, buff dustwrapper printed in dark blue and black. $250.

RIDING, Laura. *Experts Are Puzzled.* London (1930). Beige cloth over boards, cream dustwrapper printed in black. $250.

RIDING, Laura. *Four Unposted Letters to Catherine.* Paris (1930). One of 200 signed and numbered copies. Issued in tissue dustwrapper. $450.

RIDING, Laura. *Laura and Francesca.* Deya, Majorca, 1931. One of 200 signed and numbered copies. Issued in tissue dustwrapper. $350.

RIDING, Laura. *The Life of the Dead.* London (1933). One of 200 signed and numbered copies. Wraps. Signed by both Riding and the illustrator, John Aldridge. $450.

RIDING, Laura. *Lives of Wives.* London (1939). Green cloth, buff dustwrapper, printed in black and sienna. $200. New York (1939). Brown cloth, buff dustwrapper printed in black and yellow. $250.

RIDING, Laura. *Love as Love, Death as Death.* London, 1928. 175 signed and numbered copies. Beige cloth over boards. Issued in tissue dustwrapper. $600.

RIDING, Laura. *No Decency Left.* London (1932). Written with Robert Graves under the pseudonym Barbara Rich. $1,750.

RIDING, Laura. *A Trojan Ending.* Majorca/London (1937). Folding map in rear. $300. New York (1937). Gray cloth over boards. $150. Variant binding in red cloth, front design in black, spine omits design. $125.

RIDING, Laura. *Twenty Poems Less.* Paris, 1930. One of 200 signed and numbered copies. Issued in tissue dustwrapper. $400.

RIDINGS, Sam P. *The Chisholm Trail.* Guthrie, Okla. (1936). Folding map, frontispiece, and text illustrations. $300.

RIDLER, Anne. See Bradby, Anne.

RIDLER, Anne (editor). *The Little Book of Modern Verse.* London, 1941. Preface by T. S. Eliot. $100.

RIDLER, Anne. *Poems.* London, 1939. Author's first book. (Most destroyed in the Blitz.) $150.

RILEY, James Whitcomb. See Johnson, Benj. F. (of Boone).

RILEY, James Whitcomb. *The Flying Islands of the Night.* Indianapolis, 1892. Cloth. In vellum dustwrapper. $200. Another issue (actually 1891): white flexible boards. In dustwrapper. $250.

RILKE, Rainer Maria. *Poems.* New York, 1918. The author's first English translation. In dustwrapper. $400.

RIMBAUD, Arthur. See Schwartz, Delmore.

RINEHART, Mary Roberts. *The Man in Lower Ten.* Indianapolis (1909). Illustrated by Howard Chandler Christy. $100.

RINGAN Gilhaize or The Covenanters. Edinburgh, 1823. (By John Galt.) 3 vols. $350.

RINGWALT, John Luther (editor). *American Encyclopedia of Printing.* Philadelphia, 1871. 20 plates including a full-color frontispiece. $250.

RIPLEY, R. S. *The War with Mexico.* New York, 1849. 2 vols. $175.

RISTER, Carl Coke. *The Southwestern Frontier, 1865–1881.* Cleveland, 1928. Maps. $150.

RITCHIE, Ward. *Job Printing in California.* Los Angeles, 1955. One of 200 copies. $225.

RIVERS, Elizabeth. *Stranger in Aran.* Cuala Press. Dublin, 1946. Illustrations (4 in color) by author. Boards, linen spine. One of 280. In dustwrapper. $200.

RIVES, Reginald. *The Coaching Club, Its History, Records, and Activities.* Derrydale Press. New York, 1935. Illustrated. One of 300. $600. One of 30. $2,000.

ROB of the Bowl. Philadelphia, 1838. 2 vols., in original cloth, paper labels on spines. (By John Pendleton Kennedy.) $400.

ROB Roy. Edinburgh, 1818. (By Sir Walter Scott.) 3 vols. $250.

ROBBINS, Aurelia. *A True and Authentic Account of the Indian War, etc.* New York, 1836. 28 pages, in original wraps. $500.

ROBBINS, Tom. *Another Roadside Attraction.* Garden City, 1971. Author's first book. $300.

ROBBINS, Tom. *Even Cowgirls Get the Blues.* Boston, 1976. $175.

ROBERTS, B. H. *The Life of John Taylor.* Salt Lake, 1892. Author's first book. $175.

ROBERTS, David. *The Holy Land.* London 1842–43–49. 3 vols. $15,000.

ROBERTS, Elizabeth Madox. *In the Great Steep's Garden.* (Cover title.) (Colorado Springs, 1915.) Wraps. Author's first book. $4,000.

ROBERTS, Elizabeth Madox. *Under the Tree.* New York, 1922. $350.

ROBERTS, Kenneth. *Europe's Morning After.* New York (about 1921). First issue, with "B-V" on copyright page. Author's first book. $500.

ROBERTS, Kenneth. *Lydia Bailey.* Garden City, 1947. Gray buckram. One of 1,050 signed, with a page of the manuscript, with corrections in Roberts's hand, laid in. In dustwrapper and slipcase. $200. Trade edition. $60.

ROBERTS, Kenneth. *Northwest Passage.* Garden City, 1937. $75. 2 vols., cloth. One of 1,050 signed. In dustwrappers and slipcases. $250.

ROBERTS, Kenneth. *Rabble in Arms.* Garden City, 1933. $150.

ROBERTS, Kenneth. *Sun Hunting.* Indianapolis (1922). $400.

ROBERTS, Kenneth. *Trending into Maine.* Boston, 1938. Illustrated by N. C. Wyeth. $100. One of 1,075 signed by Roberts and Wyeth. In slipcase. $600. With an extra set of the Wyeth plates in envelope. $750.

ROBERTS, Kenneth. *Why Europe Leaves Home.* (Indianapolis, 1922.) $400.

ROBERTS, Oran M. *A Description of Texas.* St. Louis, 1881. 8 colored plates, 5 double-page maps. $450.

ROBERTS, W. H. *Northwestern Washington.* Port Townsend, Wash., 1880. Folding map. 52 pages, wraps. $450.

ROBERTSON, E. *Conversations With Trotsky.* London, 1936. Author's first book. $1,500.

ROBERTSON, John W. *Francis Drake and Other Early Explorers Along the Pacific Coast.* 28 maps. Grabhorn Press. San Francisco, 1927. Illustrations by Valenti Angelo. Vellum and boards. One of 1,000. $350.

ROBERTSON, Wyndham, Jr. *Oregon, Our Right and Title* . . . Washington, 1846. Folding map. Boards and cloth, or printed wraps. $2,000.

ROBESON, Paul. *Here I Stand.* New York (1958). Author's first book. Cloth. $300. Wraps. $125.

ROBIDOUX, Mrs. Orral M. *Memorial to the Robidoux Brothers.* Kansas City, 1924. Map. 16 plates. Cloth. Issued without dustwrapper. $100.

ROBINSON, Charles. N. *Old Naval Prints, Their Artists and Engravers.* London, 1924. Illustrated, including 24 plates in color. $300.

ROBINSON, Edwin Arlington. *Cavender's House.* New York, 1929. One of 500 signed. In slipcase. $175. Trade edition. $60.

ROBINSON, Edwin Arlington. *The Children of the Night.* Muslin. Boston, 1897. One of 50 on Japan vellum. $1,500. Cloth. One of 500 on Batchworth laid paper. $450.

ROBINSON, Edwin Arlington. *The Glory of the Nightingales.* New York, 1930. One of 500 signed. In slipcase. $200. Trade edition. $75.

ROBINSON, Edwin Arlington. *King Jasper.* New York, 1935. Introduction by Robert Frost. One of 250 large paper copies. $175. Trade edition. $100.

ROBINSON, Edwin Arlington. *The Man Who Died Twice.* New York, 1924. One of 500 signed. In slipcase. $300. Trade edition. $150.

ROBINSON, Edwin Arlington. *The Torrent and the Night Before.* (Gardiner, Maine) 1896. Blue wraps. Author's first book. $2,000. New York, 1928. One of 110 signed. $400.

ROBINSON, Jacob. *Sketches of the Great West.* Portsmouth, N.H., 1848. 71 pages, wraps. $4,500.

ROBINSON, John, and DOW, George F. *The Sailing Ships of New England, 1607–1907.* Salem, 1922–24–28. 3 vols., cloth. Series I, II, and III. $500.

ROBINSON, Lennox (editor). *A Little Anthology of Modern Irish Verse.* Cuala Press. Dublin, 1928. Blue boards, linen back, paper label. One of 300. In plain dustwrapper. $150.

ROBINSON, Rowland Evans. See *Forest and Stream Fables; Awahsoose the Bear.*

ROBINSON, Rowland Evans. *Uncle 'Lisha's Shop.* New York, 1887. $125.

ROBINSON, W. Heath. *Bill the Minder.* London, 1912. Illustrated by the author, including 16 color plates. Vellum. One of 380 signed. $2,000.

ROBINSON, William Davis. *Memoirs of the Mexican Revolution.* Philadelphia, 1820. $350. London, 1821. 2 vols. $300.

ROCHESTER, John Wilmot, Earl of. *Collected Works.* Nonesuch Press. London, 1926. Edited by John Hayward. Boards and buckram. $250. Boards and vellum. One of 75. $400.

ROCK, Marion Tuttle. *Illustrated History of Oklahoma.* Topeka, 1890. 90 plates. $275.

ROCKY Mountain Directory and Colorado Gazettier for 1871. Denver (1870). Illustrated. $750.

RODD, Rennell. *Songs to the South.* London, 1881. Author's first book. (Previously 1880 Newdigate prize poem). $175.

RODENBOUGH, Theodore F. *From Everglade to Canon with the Second Dragoons.* New York, 1875. 2 folding maps. $1,250.

RODITI, Edouard. *Poems for F.* Paris (1935). Author's first book. Wraps. $300.

RODITI, Edouard. *Prison Within Prison.* Prairie City, Ill. (1941). Wraps. $200.

RODKER, John. *Poems.* London (1914). Wraps. Author's first book. 50 signed and numbered copies. $600. Trade. $200.

ROETHKE, Theodore. *The Lost Son and Other Poems.* Garden City, 1948. First edition stated. $300. London (1948). $125.

ROETHKE, Theodore. *Open House.* New York, 1941. Author's first book. One of 1,000. $600.

ROETHKE, Theodore. *Praise to the End!* Garden City, 1951. $350.

ROETHKE, Theodore. *Sequence, Sometimes Metaphysical.* Iowa City (1963). Illustrated. Boards. One of 270. In slipcase. $250. One of 60 signed. In slipcase. $600.

ROETHKE, Theodore. *The Waking: Poems 1933–1953.* Garden City, 1953. First edition stated. $150.

ROETHKE, Theodore. *Words for the Wind.* London, 1957. $150. Garden City, 1958. $100.

ROGERS, A. N. *Communication Relative to the Location of the U.P.R.R. Across the Rocky Mountains Through Colorado Territory.* Central City, Colo., 1867. Wraps. $600.

ROGERS, Bruce. *Paragraphs on Printing.* New York, 1943. $125.

ROGERS, Robert. *Journals of Maj. Robert Rogers.* London, 1765. $1,000.

ROGERS, Will. *The Illiterate Digest.* New York, 1924. One of 250 signed. In dustwrapper. $750.

ROGET, Peter Mark. *Thesaurus of English Words.* Boston, 1854. First American edition. $150.

ROHMER, Sax. *Daughter of Fu-Manchu.* Garden City, 1931. $300.

ROHMER, Sax. *The Insidious Dr. Fu-Manchu.* New York, 1913. (New title for *Mystery of . . .*). $125.

ROHMER, Sax. *Pause!* London, 1910. Author's first book. $300.

ROHMER, Sax. *Mystery of Dr. Fu-Manchu.* London (1913). $250.

ROHMER, Sax. *She Who Sleeps.* Garden City, 1928. $350.

ROLFE, Frederick William. See Corvo, Baron; Corvo, Frederick Baron; *Prospero and Caliban.*

ROLFE, Fr. *Don Tarquinio.* London, 1905. First binding in violet cloth. $600. Later, red cloth. $300.

ROLFE, Fr. *Hadrian the Seventh.* London, 1904. First issue, purple cloth; title and drawing stamped in white. $1,000. Second issue, title and drawing blind stamped. $600.

ROLLINSON, John K. *History of the Migration of Oregon-Raised Herds to Mid-Western Markets: Wyoming Cattle Trails.* Caldwell, Idaho, 1948. Plates, maps, colored frontispiece by Frederic Remington. One of 1,000 signed. Issued without dustwrapper. $125.

ROLVAAG, O. E. *Giants in the Earth.* New York, 1929. $125.

ROOSEVELT, Eleanor. *This I Remember.* New York (1949). Frontispiece and plates. Buckram. One of 1,000 on large paper, signed. In slipcase. $200. Trade edition. $40.

ROOSEVELT, Eleanor. *This is My Story.* New York, 1937. One of 258 signed. $300.

ROOSEVELT, Franklin D. *The Democratic Book, 1936.* (Philadelphia) 1936. Illustrated. Folio, wraps. Limited edition, signed by F.D.R. $750.

ROOSEVELT, Franklin D. *The Happy Warrior: Alfred E. Smith.* Boston, 1928. $350.

ROOSEVELT, Franklin D. *Whither Bound?* Boston, 1926. Author's first book. $500.

ROOSEVELT, Theodore. *Big Game Hunting in the Rockies and on the Great Plains.* New York, 1899. 55 etchings. Full tan buckram. One of 1,000 signed. $1,000.

ROOSEVELT, Theodore. *Hunting Trips of a Ranchman.* New York, 1885. 20 plates. Buckram. Limited Medora Edition of 500. $1,250. Various deluxe publisher bindings. $1,500. New York 1886. $350. London, 1886. Illustrated. First English (and second) edition. $250.

ROOSEVELT, Theodore. *Naval War of 1812.* New York, 1882. Author's first separate book. $450.

ROOSEVELT, Theodore. *Outdoor Pastimes of an American Hunter.* New York, 1905. 49 plates. Half calf and boards. One of 260 signed. $1,500. Trade edition. $150.

ROOSEVELT, Theodore. *Ranch Life and the Hunting Trail.* New York (1888). Illustrated by Frederic Remington. All edges gilt, light-colored, coarse weave, tan buckram, cover design in green and gold. $750.

ROOSEVELT, Theodore. *The Rough Riders.* New York, 1899. $250.

ROOSEVELT, Theodore. *Some American Game.* New York, 1897. Wraps. $850.

ROOSEVELT, Theodore. *The Summer Birds of the Adirondacks.* (Salem, 1877.) Author's first book with H. D. Minot. Wraps. $1,750.

ROOSEVELT, Theodore. *The Wilderness Hunter.* New York (1893). Tan or brown cloth. First edition, with chapter headings in brown (VAB). $600. Buckram. One of 200 signed. $1,500.

ROOSEVELT, Theodore. *The Winning of the West.* New York, 1889–96. 4 vols. (Vol. 1: 1889; vol. 2: 1889; vol. 3: 1894; vol. 4: 1896.) First issue, with "diame-" as last word on page 160 and "ter" as first word on page 161. $750. New York, 1900. 4 vols. $250. Half morocco. One of 200 with a page of manuscript. $2,000.

ROOT, Frank A., and CONNELLEY, William E. *The Overland Stage to California.* Topeka, 1901. Map. Pictorial cloth. $350.

ROOT, Riley. *Journal of Travels from St. Josephs . . . to Oregon . . .* Galesburg, Ill., 1850. 143 pages, printed wraps and cloth spine. $4,000.

ROS, Amanda. *Irene Iddesleigh.* Belfast, 1897. Author's first book. With slip of "Printer's Errors." (A novel often called the foremost example in the English language of bad writing—VAB.) $100.

ROSE, Victor M. *Ross' Texas Brigade.* Louisville, 1881. Illustrated. $1,500.

ROSEN, Peter. *Pa-Ha-Sa-Pah, or The Black Hills of South Dakota.* St. Louis, 1895. 27 plates. Pictorial cloth. $400.

ROSENBACH, A. S. W. *A Book Hunter's Holiday, Adventures with Books and Manuscripts.* Boston, 1936. 760 signed and numbered copies. Slipcase. $150.

ROSENBACH, A. S. W. *Books and Bidders, The Adventures of a Bibliophile.* Boston, 1927. 785 signed and numbered large paper copies. $135.

ROSENBACH, A. S. W. *Early American Children's Books.* Portland, Me., 1933. One of 585 signed, numbered copies. Slipcase. $400.

ROSENBERG, Isaac. *Night and Day.* (London, 1912.) Author's first book. Wraps. $7,500.

ROSENBERG, Isaac. *Poems.* London, 1922. Portrait. $600.

ROSENBERG, Isaac. *Youth.* London, 1915. Wraps. $750.

ROSENTHAL, Leonard. *The Kingdom of the Pearl.* New York or London (1920). Illustrated in color by Edmund Dulac. Boards and vellum. One of 100 signed by Dulac. In dustwrapper. $1,000. Boards and cloth. In dustwrapper. One of 675. $500.

ROSENWALD, Lessing. *Recollections of a Collector.* Jenkintown, 1976. One of 250 copies. Slipcase. $300.

ROSS, Alexander. *Adventures of the First Settlers on the Oregon or Columbia River.* London, 1849. Frontispiece (in some copies), folding map. $1,000.

ROSS, Alexander. *The Fur Hunters of the Far West.* London, 1855. 2 vols. Map, 2 plates. $1,250.

ROSS, Alexander. *The Red River Settlement.* London, 1856. Frontispiece. $400.

ROSS, James, and GARY, George. *From Wisconsin to California, and Return . . .* Madison, 1869. Rebound with original wraps bound in. $750.

ROSS, John. *Narrative of a Second Voyage in Search of a North-West Passage . . .* London, 1835. Charts, folding map, plans, 25 plates (9 in color). $1,000. Also issued in 2 vols. $500.

ROSS, John. *A Voyage of Discovery . . . for the Purpose of Exploring Baffin's Bay* . . . London, 1819. Folding maps, tables, plates (15 in color). $1,500.

ROSS, Mrs. William P. *The Life and Times of Honorable William P. Ross.* Fort Smith, 1893. Portrait. $150.

ROSSETTI, Christina. *Goblin Market.* London, 1862. With 16-page catalog at rear. $750. London, 1893. Illustrated by Laurence Housman. $350. London (1933). Illustrated by Arthur Rackham, including 4 color plates. Pictorial wraps. First Rackham edition. In dustwrapper. $500. First deluxe Rackham edition. Limp vellum. One of 410 signed by Rackham. In slipcase. $1,500. Philadelphia (1933). First American edition. $450.

ROSSETTI, Christina. *Poems.* Gregynog Press. Newtown, Wales, 1930. Chosen by Walter de la Mare. Wood-engraving portrait by R. A. Maynard. Printed on Japanese vellum. Red morocco, by the Gregynog bindery. One of 25 specially bound. In slipcase. $2,000. One of 300. Boards and calf. $500.

ROSSETTI, Christina. *Speaking Likenesses.* London, 1874. Blue cloth. First binding. $600.

ROSSETTI, Christina. *Verses.* London, 1847. Author's first book. $4,000. Eragny Press. Hammersmith (London), 1906. One of 175 on paper. $400. One of 10 on vellum. $2,000.

ROSSETTI, Dante Gabriel. *Ballads and Narrative Poems.* Kelmscott Press. London, 1893. Woodcut title and initials. Limp vellum with ties. One of 310. $1,250. One of 6 on vellum. $7,500.

ROSSETTI, Dante Gabriel. *Hand and Soul.* London, 1869. Wraps. First separate edition. $500. Kelmscott Press (for Way & Williams, Chicago). London, 1895. Woodcut title and borders. Vellum. One of 525 (300 for America and 225 for England). $1,000. One of 21 on vellum (10 for England and 11 for America). $5,000. London, 1899. Vale Press. Morocco. One of 210. In dustwrapper. $600.

ROSSETTI, Dante Gabriel. *Poems.* (London, 1869.) Printed wraps. First edition privately printed. $1,500. London, 1870. Cloth. First published edition. $350.

ROSSETTI, Dante Gabriel. *Sir Hugo the Heron.* London, 1843. Author's first book. $1,750.

ROSSETTI, Dante Gabriel. *Sonnets and Lyrical Poems.* Kelmscott Press. London, 1894. Woodcut title and borders by William Morris. Printed in black and red. Vellum with ties. One of 310. $600. One of 6 on vellum. $4,000.

ROSSETTI, William Michael. *The Comedy of Dante Allighieri.* London, 1865. Translated by Rossetti, his first book. $250.

ROSSETTI, William Michael. *Swinburne's Poems and Ballads.* London, 1866. $200.

ROSSI, Mario M. *Pilgrimage in the West.* Cuala Press. Dublin, 1933. Boards and linen. One of 300. $125.

ROTH, Henry. *Call It Sleep.* New York, 1934. Author's first book. $1,500. London, 1963. $60.

ROTH, Philip. *Goodbye, Columbus.* Boston, 1959. Black cloth. Author's first book. $250. London, 1959. (Title story only.) $125.

ROTHSCHILD, Lord. *The History of Tom Jones, A Changeling.* Cambridge, 1951. One of 150 copies. $350.

ROWLANDSON, Mary. *A True History of the Captivity & Restoration of Mrs. Mary Rowlandson* . . . London, 1682. $12,500.

ROYALL, Anne. See *Sketches of History, Life, and Manners, in the United States.*

ROYIDIS, Emmanuel. *Pope Joan.* London (1954). Translated by Lawrence Durrell. $100.

RUBAIYAT of Omar Khayyam, The Astronomer-Poet of Persia. London, 1859. Translated into English verse. Brown wraps. (Translated by Edward FitzGerald.) First edition (250 printed). $15,000. London, 1868. Wraps. Second English edition. $2,000. London, 1872. Half leather and dark red cloth. Third English edition. $350. London, 1896. Ashendene Press. Gray wraps. One of 50. $2,750. Boston, 1898. First American edition. $400. London, 1909. Illustrated by Edmund Dulac. Vellum. One of 750 signed by Dulac. In slipcase. $1,000. London, 1913. Riccardi Press. One of 12 on vellum. $1,500. London, 1938. Golden Cockerel Press. Illustrated. Vellum. One of 270. $500. Morocco. One of 30 with extra engravings. $2,500. New York, 1940. Heritage Press. Color plates by Arthur Szyk. Pictorial padded calf and marbled boards. $175. Limited Editions Club (Westport), 1935. In slipcase. $150.

RUDO Ensayo. See Smith, Buckingham.

RUKEYSER, Muriel. *Elegies.* No-place (1949). Boards. One of 300 signed. In slipcase. $125.

RUKEYSER, Muriel. *Theory of Flight.* New Haven, 1935. Author's first book. $250.

RULES and Orders of the House of Representatives of the Territory of Washington, 1864–5. Olympia, Washington Territory, 1864. 32 pages $200.

RULES and Regulations of the Utah and Northern Railway, for the Government of Employees. Salt Lake City, 1879. Calf. $150.

RULES, Regulations, and By-Laws of the Board of Commissioners to Manage the Yosemite Valley and Mariposa Big Tree Grove. Sacramento, 1885. 23 pages, wraps. $200.

RUNYON, Damon. *The Tents of Trouble.* New York (about 1911). Flexible cloth. Author's first book. $150.

RUPP, I. Daniel. *History of Lancaster County, Pennsylvania.* Lancaster, 1844. Illustrated. Sheep. $150.

RUPPANEER, Antoine. *Hypodermic Injections in the Treatment of Neuralgia, Rheumatism, Gout, and Other Diseases.* Boston, 1865. $850.

RUSHDIE, Salman. *Grimus.* London, 1975. Author's first book. $250. New York (1979). $75.

RUSHDIE, Salman. *Midnight's Children.* New York, 1981. $200.

RUSHDIE, Salman. *The Satanic Verses.* (London, 1988). In blue binding. (Also variant in green library binding?) $300. (New York, 1989). $75.

RUSKIN, John. See R., J.

RUSKIN, John. *The King of the Golden River.* London, 1851. Illustrated by Richard Doyle. $600. New York, 1930. Illustrated. Black calf. One of 50, each with a holograph letter, signed by Ruskin, tipped in. In slipcase. $600. London (1932). Illustrated by Arthur Rackham. Vellum. One of 570 signed by Rackham. In slipcase. $750. Trade. $200.

RUSKIN, John. *The Harbours of England.* London, 1856. 12 mezzotint plates by J. M. W. Turner. Folio, decorated blue cloth. $500.

RUSKIN, John. *Lectures on Landscape.* Orpington, 1897. 25 plates. Folio, cloth. $500.

RUSKIN, John. *The Nature of Gothic: A Chapter of the Stones of Venice.* Kelmscott Press. London, 1892. Preface by William Morris. Illustrated. Vellum with ties. One of 500. $750.

RUSKIN, John. *Praeterita: Outlines of Scenes and Thoughts Perhaps Worthy of Memory in My Life Past.* Sunnyside, Orpington, Kent, 1885–89. 28 original parts, printed wraps. $750. One of 600 large paper copies. $350.

RUSKIN, John. *Salsette and Elephanta . . .* Oxford, 1839. Author's first book. Wraps. $1,000.

RUSKIN, John. *The Seven Lamps of Architecture.* London, 1849. 14 plates. $250.

RUSKIN, John. *The Stones of Venice.* London, 1851–53. Illustrated, 3 vols. $1,750.

RUSSELL, Alex J. *The Red River Country, Hudson's Bay and Northwest Territories, etc..* Ottawa, 1869. Folding map. Wraps. $250. Montreal, 1879. Folding map, 8 folding plates. Wraps. Third edition. $250.

RUSSELL, Bertrand. See Whitehead, Alfred North.

RUSSELL, Bertrand. *German Social Democracy.* London, 1896. Author's first book. $1,500.

RUSSELL, Charles M. (illustrator). See *How the Buffalo Lost His Crown.*

RUSSELL, Charles M. *Back-trailing on the Old Frontiers.* Great Falls, Mont., 1922. 16 full-page drawings by the author. 56 pages, pictorial wraps. $1,250.

RUSSELL, Charles M. *Good Medicine.* New York, 1930. Introduction by Will Rogers, Illustrated by the author. In dustwrapper. $300. (With title page dated 1929). Half buckram. One of 134 on large paper. $2,000. From the same issue: Blue buckram. One of 59 copies for presentation. $3,000.

RUSSELL, Charles M. *More Rawhides.* Great Falls, 1925. Illustrated by the author. 60 pages, pictorial wraps. $300.

RUSSELL, Charles M. *Pen and Ink Drawings.* Pasadena (1946). 2 vols., oblong boards and cloth. $400.

RUSSELL, Charles M. *Pen Sketches.* (Great Falls, 1899.) 12 plates. Oblong, in cloth. No title page. Title and author are on front cover "Indian head" plate. $1,500. Second, in black morocco with titles printed on each plate and "skull" is on front cover. $1,250. Third lacks titles on plates. $1,000. Fourth has "Published by W. T. Ridgley Printing Company . . ." stamped in lower left-hand corner. $850. Others in portfolios, bound in blue boards, etc. $850.

RUSSELL, Charles M. *Rawhide Rawlins Stories.* Great Falls, 1921. Author's first book. Illustrated by the author. Pictorial wraps. $400. Full limp leather. Presentation copy. $750.

RUSSELL, Charles M. *Studies of Western Life.* Cascade, Montana (1890). $6,000. New York, 1890. First issue, no text on "War." $2,000. Second issue, text on "War." $1,750.

RUSSELL, Charles M. *Trails Plowed Under.* New York, 1927. $250.

RUSSELL, Eric Frank. *Sinister Barrier.* Surrey (1943). Author's first book. $400. Reading, 1948. (500 signed and numbered copies.) $125. Trade. $75.

RUSSELL, George W. See E., A.

RUSSELL, Osborne. *Journal of a Trapper, or Nine Years in the Rocky Mountains* ... (Boise, 1914.) Blue cloth. (100 printed.) $750. Boise (1921). Second edition. (100 copies.) $200.

RUSSELL, W. Clark. *Fra Angelo.* London, 1865. Author's first book. Wraps. $2,500.

RUSSELL, W. Clark. *The Hunchback's Charge.* London, 1867. 3 vols. $2,000.

RUSSELL, W. Clark. *The Tale of the Ten.* London, 1896. 3 vols. $600.

RUSSELL, W. Clark. *The Wreck of the "Grosvenor."* London, 1877. 3 vols. $1,750.

RUSSELL, William. See Waters.

RUST, Margaret. *The Queen of the Fishes.* Eragny Press. Epping, England, 1894. 16 woodcuts, 4 colored, by Lucien Pissarro. One of 130 on vellum. (The first book produced by this press.) $2,500.

RUTHERFORD, Ernest. *Radio-Activity.* Cambridge, 1904. $400.

RUXTON, George F. *Life in the Far West.* Edinburgh, 1849. $250. New York, 1849. $200.

RUZICKA, Rudolph. *Studies in Type Design. Alphabets with Random Quotations.* Hanover (1968). Slipcase containing 11 folders and 10 plates. $125.

RYAN, Abram Joseph. *Father Ryan's Poems.* Mobile, 1879. Portrait and one illustration. Author's first book. $150. Large paper edition (retitled *Poems: Patriotic, Religious, Miscellaneous*). Baltimore, 1880. $100.

RYAN, William R. *Personal Adventures in Upper and Lower California in 1848–49.* London, 1850. 23 plates. $750.

S

S., E. W., and M., S. W. *The Children's Hour.* Philadelphia, 1864. (By Elizabeth W. Sherman and S. Weir Mitchell.) $350.

S., I. *Doctor Transit.* New York, 1925. (By Isidor Schneider, his first book.) $125.

S., P. B. *Zastrozzi: A Romance.* London, 1810. (By Percy Bysshe Shelley.) $750. Golden Cockerel Press. London, 1955. Plates. Morocco. One of 60 on vellum with duplicate set of 8 plates. In slipcase. $600. Boards. One of 200. In slipcase. $175.

S., S. *Vigils.* (Bristol) 1934. Frontispiece by Stephen Gooden. Full morocco. (By Siegfried Sassoon.) One of 23 signed by the author and the artist. $1,500. One of 272 signed by Sassoon. $450.

S., S. H. *Nine Experiments.* Hempstead, England, 1928. (By Stephen Spender.) Author's first book. Green wraps. One of about 18 copies issued. $6,000.

SABATINI, Rafael. *The Tavern Knight.* London, 1914. Author's first book. $100.

SABIN, Edwin L. *Building the Pacific Railway.* Philadelphia, 1919. $100.

SABIN, Edwin L. *Kit Carson Days (1809–1868).* Chicago, 1914. Maps, plates. Brown cloth. $150. New York, 1935. 2 vols., cloth. Revised edition. One of 1,000. In slipcase. $200. One of 200 signed. $400.

SABIN, Edwin L. *Magic Mashie and Other Golf Stories.* New York, 1902. Decorative cloth. $150.

SACK and Destruction of the City of Columbia, S.C. Columbia, 1865. Wraps. (By William Gilmore Simms.) $300.

SACKVILLE-WEST, Victoria. *All Passion Spent.* London, 1931. $175. New York, 1931. $75.

SACKVILLE-WEST, Victoria. *Chatterton.* Seven Oaks, 1909. Author's first book. Printed wraps. $4,000. Sevenoaks, 1909. Dark blue boards with gilt lettering (2 known copies.) No known dustwrapper. $5,500.

SACKVILLE-WEST, Victoria. *Constantinople.* London, 1915. Wraps. $600.

SACKVILLE-WEST, Victoria. *The Edwardians.* (London) 1930. One of 125 signed and numbered copies. Issued without dustwrapper. $400. Trade. With dustwrapper. $175. Garden City, 1930. $75.

SACKVILLE-WEST, Victoria. *The Garden.* London, 1946. One of 750 signed and numbered copies. Issued in plain paper dustwrapper. $250. Trade. Red boards with silver lettering on spine in decorated red dustwrapper lettered in black. $75. New York, 1946. Light green boards printed in dark green. In yellow and green dustwrapper lettered in green and white. $50.

SACKVILLE-WEST, Victoria. *Heritage.* London (1919). Red cloth blind stamped on front. Spine printed in black. Dustwrapper gray printed in red. $750. New York (1919). Light brown cloth printed on front and spine or with just a paper label on front. Priority unknown. $350.

SACKVILLE-WEST, Victoria. *Knole and the Sackvilles.* London, 1922. White boards and light tan dustwrapper, both illustrated by William Nicholson. $400. New York (no-date, 1924?). Verso states "Printed in England." Tipped-in title page. Doran imprint at foot of spine. No colophon on copyright page. $250.

SACKVILLE-WEST, Victoria. *Orchard and Vineyard.* London, 1921. "To-" on verso of title. Light blue boards with paper labels and cloth spine. Light blue dustwrapper lettered in black. $250.

SACKVILLE-WEST, Victoria. *Nursery Rhymes.* London, 1947. One of 25 signed and numbered copies. Numbered 1 to 25. Orange-red cloth with vellum parchment corners and spine. In white dustwrapper with gilt decoration (as on book), lettered in black on spine. $1,250. One of 525 numbered copies. $250. London (1950). Trade. Yellow boards lettered in red. In white dustwrapper lettered and decorated in blue, red, and black. $50.

SACKVILLE-WEST, Victoria. *Sissinghurst.* London, 1931. One of 500 signed and numbered copies. Issued without dustwrapper. $500. Warlingham. One of 500 signed and numbered copies. "Second Edition." Flexible beige cloth without dustwrapper. $200.

SACKVILLE-WEST, Victoria. *Twelve Days.* London, 1928. $250. New York, 1928. $250.

SADLEIR, Michael. *The Evolution of Publishers' Binding Styles, 1770–1900.* London, 1930. One of 500 copies. $350.

SADLEIR, Michael. *Fanny by Gaslight.* London, 1940. $150.

SADLEIR, Michael. *Hyssop.* London (1915). Author's first novel. $75.

SADLEIR, Michael. *XIX Century Fiction: A Bibliographical Record.* London (1951). Illustrated. 2 vols., cloth. One of 1,025. $500. New York, 1969. Reprint. $350.

SAGE, Rufus B. *Scenes in the Rocky Mountains . . .* Philadelphia, 1847. Half calf. Second edition. $500. (For first edition, see title entry.)

SAGE, Rufus B. *Wild Scenes in Kansas and Nebraska, the Rocky Mountains . . .* Philadelphia, 1855. Half leather. Third ("revised") edition (of *Scenes in the Rocky Mountains,* which see under title entry.) $200.

ST. CLAIR, Maj. Gen. (Arthur). *A Narrative of the Manner in Which the Campaign Against the Indians, in the Year 1791, Was Conducted.* Philadelphia, 1812. First edition, with errata. $500.

ST. IRVYNE; or, The Rosicrucian: A Romance. London, 1811. By a Gentleman of the University of Oxford. (Percy Bysshe Shelley.) $1,500.

ST. RONAN'S Well. Edinburgh, 1824. (By Sir Walter Scott.) 3 vols., in original boards. $750.

SAINT Bride Foundation Catalogue of the Technical Reference Library of Works on Printing . . . London, 1919. $250.

SAINT-EXUPÉRY, Antoine de. *Flight to Arras.* New York (1942). Translated by Bernard Lamotte. First American edition. $100. Also one of 500 signed. In slipcase. $400.

SAINT-EXUPÉRY, Antoine de. *The Little Prince.* Reynal & Hitchcock. New York (1943). Translated from the French by Katherine Woods. Illustrated in color by the author. First American edition. One of 525. Signed. In dustwrapper. $1,250. Trade. $300.

SAINT-EXUPÉRY, Antoine de. *Night-Flight.* Paris, 1932. Translated by Stuart Gilbert. Wraps. In cellophane dustwrapper. $200. New York, 1932. First American edition. $100.

SAINT-EXUPÉRY, Antoine de. *Wind, Sand and Stars.* New York (1939). Translated by Lewis Galentiere. First American edition. One of 500 signed. In slipcase. $300. Trade. $75.

SAISSY, Jean-Antoine. *An Essay on the Diseases of the Internal Ear.* Baltimore, 1829. Frontispiece sheep. First American edition. $500.

SAKI. *Beasts and Super-Beasts.* London, 1914 (By H. H. Munro.) $125.

SAKI. *Reginald.* London (1904). (By H. H. Munro.) Red cloth. $200.

SAKI. *The Westminster Alice.* London, 1902. (By H. H. Munro.) Pictorial cloth. $300. Green wraps. $250.

SALAMAN and Absal: An Allegory. London, 1856. Translated from the Persian of Jami by Edward FitzGerald. Frontispiece. Blue cloth. $175.

SALE, Edith Tunis. *Manors of Virginia in Colonial Times.* Philadelphia, 1909. 49 plates. $200.

SALINGER, J. D. See Barrows, R. M. *The Kit Book for Soldiers, Sailors and Marines.*

SALINGER, J. D. *The Catcher in the Rye.* Boston, 1951. Author's first book. First edition so stated. Bixby states the first issue dustwrapper has a photograph of Salinger on the back panel which was dropped on later printings, but we have seen later printings with the photo in a priced dustwrapper which was slightly taller than the first printing. Presumed earliest form of dustwrapper omits Book-of-the-Month Club slug. We have never seen a copy without slug at the bottom of rear flap and assume this would be the place it is omitted. $1,500. London (1951). $300.

SALINGER, J. D. *For Esme—With Love and Squalor . . .* London (1953). $200. First U.K. edition of *Nine Stories.*

SALINGER, J. D. *Nine Stories.* Boston (1953). $1,000.

SALINGER, J. D. *Raise High the Roof Beam, Carpenters, and Seymour: An Introduction.* Boston (1963). Copyright dates are 1955 and 1959 but published in 1963. First issue contains no dedication page. $350. Second issue has dedication page before half title (in front of title page). $125. Third issue has dedication tipped in after title page. $50. London (1963) $60.

SALMON, Richard. *Trout Flies.* New York, 1975. Fly-tying material tipped in. Full maroon leather. First edition, deluxe issue. One of 29 signed, with an original drawing by the author. In dustwrapper and slipcase. $1,500. Green cloth. One of 560 signed. In slipcase. $500.

SALPOINTE, John B. *A Brief Sketch of the Mission of San Xavier del Bac with a Description of Its Church.* San Francisco, 1880. 20 pages, wraps. $300.

SALPOINTE, John B. *Soldiers of the Cross.* Banning, Calif., 1898. Portrait. 45 plates. $300.

SALT Lake City Directory and Business Guide (The). Salt Lake City, 1869. Folding map, folding view. 53–219 pages, as issued, boards. (By Edward L. Sloan.) $1,000.

SALTEN, Felix. *Bambi, A Life in the Woods.* New York, 1928. First edition in English. Illustrated by Kurt Wiese. Pictorial boards. $300.

SALTER, James. *The Hunters.* New York (1956). Author's first novel. $200.

SALTUS, Edgar. *Balzac.* Boston, 1884. Author's first book. $60.

SALZMANN, C. G. *Gymnastics for Youth.* London, 1800. 9 plates. First English edition. $500. Philadelphia, 1802. $350.

SAMPSON, Henry. *A History of Advertising from the Earliest Times.* London, 1875. $175.

SAN BERNARDINO County, California, Illustrated Description of. San Bernardino, 1881. 34 pages, printed wraps. $250.

SAN FRANCISCO Bay and California in 1776. Providence, 1911. Maps and facsimiles. 7 pages, boards. (By Pedro Font.) One of 125. $250.

SAN FRANCISCO Board of Engineers: Report upon the City Grades. San Francisco, 1854. 27 pages, wraps. $150.

SAN FRANCISCO Directory for the Year 1852–53. San Francisco, 1852. Frontispiece, double-page map. Half leather. $850.

SANBORN, Franklin Benjamin. *Emancipation In the West Indies.* Concord, 1862. Author's first book. Wraps. $200.

SANDBURG, Carl. See Sandburg, Charles A.

SANDBURG, Carl. *Abraham Lincoln: The Prairie Years.* New York (1926). 2 vols., blue cloth. In dustwrapper and slipcase. $200. Large paper issue: 2 vols., boards and cloth. First state, with line 9 on page 175 of vol. I reading "ears" instead of "eyes." One of 260 signed. In dustwrapper. $500. Second state. $400.

SANDBURG, Carl. *Abraham Lincoln: The War Years.* New York (1939–41). 4 vols., blue cloth. In dustwrapper and slipcase. $250. Large paper issue: Brown buckram. One of 525 sets on all rag paper, numbered and signed. In dustwrapper and slipcase. $450.

SANDBURG, Carl. *The American Songbag.* New York (1927). $200.

SANDBURG, Carl. *Chicago Poems.* New York, 1916. With ads at back dated "3'16." The poet's first book, aside from the pamphlet *In Reckless Ecstasy.* In dustwrapper. $850. Without dustwrapper. $150.

SANDBURG, Carl. *The Chicago Race Riots.* New York, 1919. Printed wraps. $300.

SANDBURG, Carl. *Cornhuskers.* New York, 1918. First state with page 3 so numbered at foot of page. In dustwrapper. $300. Without dustwrapper. $60.

SANDBURG, Carl. *Early Moon.* New York (1930). $175.

SANDBURG, Carl. *Good Morning, America.* New York, 1928. $100. Limited issue. One of 811 signed. Issued without dustwrapper. $150.

SANDBURG, Carl. *Incidentals.* Galesburg (1907). Wraps. $2,500.

SANDBURG, Carl. *A Lincoln and Whitman Miscellany.* Chicago, 1938. One of 250. $200.

SANDBURG, Carl. *Mary Lincoln, Wife and Widow.* New York (1932). $100. Large paper issue. One of 260 signed. Issued without dustwrapper. $175.

SANDBURG, Carl. *Potato Face.* New York (1930). $150.

SANDBURG, Carl. *Remembrance Rock.* New York (1948). $60. 2 vols., Buckram. One of 1,000 signed. In glassine dustwrapper and slipcase. $175.

SANDBURG, Carl. *Rootabaga Pigeons.* New York (1923). Illustrated. Pictorial cloth. $250.

SANDBURG, Carl. *Rootabaga Stories.* New York (1922). Illustrated by Maud and Miska Petersham. Pictorial cloth. $250.

SANDBURG, Carl. *Smoke and Steel.* New York, 1920. Green boards. In dustwrapper. $250. Without dustwrapper. $50.

SANDBURG, Carl. *Steichen the Photographer.* New York (1929). One of 925 signed by author and artist. Issued without dustwrapper. $1,000.

SANDBURG, Charles A. *In Reckless Ecstasy.* Galesburg, Ill., 1904. Wraps. (By Carl Sandburg.) Author's first book. $12,500.

SANDERS, Daniel C. *A History of the Indian Wars with the First Settlers of the United States.* Montpelier, Vt., 1812. $1,500.

SANDERS, Capt. John. *Memoir on the Military Resources of the Valley of the Ohio.* Pittsburgh, 1845. 19 pages, unbound. $200. Washington, 1845. 24 pages, unbound. $100.

SANDOZ, Mari. *The Beaver Men.* New York (1964). Illustrated. Half leather. One of 185 signed. $300. Trade. $100.

SANDOZ, Mari. *The Cattlemen.* New York (1958). $75. Advance presentation copy, signed. $150. Half cloth. One of 199 signed. In slipcase. $250.

SANDOZ, Mari. *Crazy Horse.* New York, 1942. $125.

SANDOZ, Mari. *Old Jules.* Boston, 1935. Author's first book. $125.

SANDOZ, Mari. *Old Jules Country.* New York, 1965. Folding map. Illustrated by Bryan Forsyth. Half leather. One of 250 signed and specially bound. $250. Trade. $60.

SANDOZ, Maurice. *On the Verge.* Garden City (1959). Illustrated in color by Salvador Dali. $100.

SANDS, Frank. *A Pastoral Prince: The History and Reminiscences of Joseph Wright Cooper.* Santa Barbara, 1893. Illustrated. Pictorial cloth. $200.

SANFORD, John. See Shapiro, Julian L.

SANFORD, John. *The Old Man's Place.* New York, 1935. 25 (recently) signed and numbered copies. $125. Unsigned. $75.

SANSOM, Joseph. *Sketches of Lower Canada, Historical and Descriptive.* New York, 1817. Frontispiece view of Quebec. $200.

SANSOM, William. *Fireman Flower.* London, 1944. $150.

SANTAYANA, George. See *Lines on Leaving the Bedford St. Schoolhouse.*

SANTAYANA, George. *Poems.* London (1922). One of 100 signed. $200.

SANTAYANA, George. *Sonnets and Other Verses.* Cambridge, Mass., 1894. Author's first book. One of 450. $150. Limp vellum. One of 50 on vellum. $500.

SANTEE, Ross. *Babbling Springs.* New York, 1949. $100.

SANTEE, Ross. *Cowboy.* New York, 1928. $150.

SANTEE, Ross. *Hardrock & Silver Stage.* New York, 1949. $100.

SANTEE, Ross. *Men and Horses.* New York (1926). Author's first book. $200.

SANTLEBEN, August. *A Texas Pioneer.* New York, 1910. $400.

SAPPINGTON, John. *The Theory and Treatment of Fevers.* Arrow Rock, Mo., 1844. $150.

SARGEANT, J. A. *Sumo the Sport and the Tradition.* Tokyo, 1959. Stated first. $40.

SARGENT, Charles Sprague. *The Silva of North America.* Boston, 1890–1902. 14 vols., printed boards. $2,000.

SARGENT, George B. *Notes on Iowa.* Map. New York, 1848. 74 pages $1,000.

SAROYAN, William. *A Christmas Psalm.* Grabhorn Press. San Francisco (1935). In brown boards. (Also variant in rose boards, white cloth spine). With greeting card and envelope, as issued, laid in. One of 200 signed. $400.

SAROYAN, William. *The Daring Young Man on the Flying Trapeze.* New York, 1934. Author's first book. Gray cloth, paper label. $250. London (1935). First English edition. $200.

SAROYAN, William. *The Fiscal Hoboes.* New York, 1949. One of 250 signed. In green boards. Issued without dustwrapper. $250. Wraps. Also 250 copies, but assume not signed. $100.

SAROYAN, William. *Fragment.* (San Francisco, 1938.) Folio, wraps. One of 150 signed. $300.

SAROYAN, William. *Harlem as Seen by Hirschfeld.* New York (1941). 24 mounted plates, some in color. Folio. One of 1,000. In slipcase. Slipcase. $1,500.

SAROYAN, William. *Little Children.* New York (1937). $200.

SAROYAN, William. *My Name Is Aram.* New York (1940). $175.

SAROYAN, William. *A Native American.* San Francisco, 1938. One of 450 signed. Issued without dustwrapper. $200.

SAROYAN, William. *Those Who Write Them and Those Who Collect Them.* Black Archer Press. Chicago, 1936. In pale green calendared wraps with drawing of author on front. One of 50. $250. (Later reissued with same limitation statement, but in rough rose-colored wraps.)

SAROYAN, William. *Three Times Three.* Los Angeles (1936). One of 250 signed. $250.

SARRE, F. *Islamic Bookbindings.* London (no-date) (circa 1923). 550 numbered copies. 38 tipped-in plates. $500.

SARTON, George. *Introduction to the History of Science.* (no-place), 1927, 1931, 1931. 3 vols. $150.

SARTON, May. *Encounter in April.* Boston, 1938. Author's first book. $350.

SARTOR Resartus. (London) 1834. (By Thomas Carlyle.) (Reprinted from *Fraser's Magazine.*) One of about 50 privately printed for the author's friends. In full morocco, $1,500. London, 1838. In original boards and calf. First published English edition. $250. Doves Press. London, 1907. Vellum. One of 300. $400. One of 15 on vellum. $2,500.

SASSOON, Siegfried. See Kain, Saul; Lyre, Pinchbeck; S., S. See also *Lingual Exercises for Advanced Vocabularians; Memoirs of a Fox-Hunting Man; Memoirs of an Infantry Officer; Poems.*

SASSOON, Siegfried. *Counter-Attack and Other Poems.* London, 1918. Wraps. $200. New York (1918). First American edition. In dustwrapper. $200.

SASSOON, Siegfried. *Emblems of Experience.* Cambridge, 1951. Wraps. One of 75 signed. $250.

SASSOON, Siegfried. *The Heart's Journey.* New York/London, 1927. Boards and parchment. One of 500 signed. $350. One of 9 on green paper. $850. London, 1928. Trade. $150. New York, 1929. First edition not stated. $125.

SASSOON, Siegfried. *The Old Huntsman and Other Poems.* London, 1917. With errata slip. In dustwrapper. $250. Without dustwrapper. $75.

SASSOON, Siegfried. *Picture Show.* (Cambridge) 1919. Boards. One of 200. In plain dustwrapper. $450. Without dustwrapper. $300.

SASSOON, Siegfried. *The Redeemer.* Cambridge, 1916. One of about 250. Unnumbered leaves, an off-print from *Cambridge* magazine. $250.

SASSOON, Siegfried. *Satirical Poems.* London, 1926. $300. New York, 1926. $300.

SASSOON, Siegfried. *Sherston's Progress.* London, 1936. Buckram. One of 300 signed. $300. Trade. $150. Garden City, 1936. First American edition. $100.

SASSOON, Siegfried. *To the Red Rose.* London, 1931. One of 400 signed. In green boards. Issued without dustwrapper. $200. Wraps. $60.

SASSOON, Siegfried. *War Poems.* London, 1919. In dustwrapper. $400.

SATANSTOE; or, The Littlepage Manuscripts. New York, 1845. By the Author of *Miles Wallingford.* 2 vols., printed yellow wraps. (By James Fenimore Cooper.)

First American edition. $1,000. London, 1845. 3 vols., boards, paper label. $750. (Cooper's name appeared on the title page of this edition.)

SATTERLEE, M. P. *A Detailed Account of the Massacre by the Dakota Indians of Minnesota in 1862.* Minneapolis, 1923. Wraps. $150.

SAUER, Martin. *An Account of a Geographical and Astronomical Expedition to the Northern Parts of Russia . . .* London, 1802. Folding map, 14 plates. $1,000.

SAUNDERS, Frederic. *The Author's Printing and Publishing Assistant . . .* New York, 1839. $175.

SAUNDERS, James E. *Early Settlers of Alabama.* Part 1. (All published.) New Orleans, 1899. $175.

SAUNDERS, Louise. *The Knave of Hearts.* New York, 1925. Illustrated in color by Maxfield Parrish. Pictorial cloth. In plain buff dustwrapper. $1,250.

SAUNDERS, Marshall. *Beautiful Joe: An Autobiography.* Philadelphia, 1894. Mottled olive cloth. First issue, with American Baptist Publication Society imprint. $125.

SAUVAN, Jean-Baptiste-Balthazar. *Picturesque Tour of the Seine, from Paris to the Sea.* London, 1821. Map, colored vignette title and tailpiece, 24 colored aquatint plates. In original half morocco. $5,000. One of 50 on large paper. $6,000.

SAVAGE, Timothy. *The Amazonian Republic, Recently Discovered in the Interior of Peru.* New York, 1842. In original boards, paper label. $250.

SAVAGE, William. *A Dictionary of the Art of Printing.* London, 1841. $225.

SAVAGE, William. *Practical Hints on Decorative Printing.* London, 1822. 60 plates and engravings. $5,500.

SAVOY (The): An Illustrated Quarterly. London, 1896. Illustrations by Aubrey Beardsley. 8 parts. (All published.) Decorated boards and wraps. $1,750.

SAWYER, Charles J., and DARTON, F. J. Harvey. *English Books, 1475–1900, A Signpost for Collectors.* Westminster, 1927. 2 vols. One of 2,000 copies. $175.

SAWYER, Lorenzo. *Way Sketches.* New York, 1926. One of 385. $125. Large paper issue. Boards, parchment spine. One of 35. In glassine dustwrapper. $150.

SAXTON, Charles. *The Oregonian; or History of the Oregon Territory.* Oregon City, 1846. No. 1 (all published). 48 pages, printed wraps. $1,750.

SAYERS, Dorothy L. *Catholic Tales and Christian Songs.* (Oxford, 1918.) $300.

SAYERS, Dorothy L. *Clouds of Witness.* London, 1926. $1,250. New York, 1927. $1,000.

SAYERS, Dorothy L. *Gaudy Night.* London, 1935. $850.

SAYERS, Dorothy L. *Op. 1.* Oxford, 1916. Wraps. Author's first book. $600.

SAYERS, Dorothy L. *Unnatural Death.* London, 1927. $1,250.

SAYERS, Dorothy L. *The Unpleasantness at the Bellona Club.* London, 1928. $1,000. New York, 1928. $850.

SAYERS, Dorothy L. *Whose Body?* New York (1923). First issue, without "Inc." after Boni & Liveright on title. $2,000. London (1923). $1,250.

SAYERS, Dorothy L., and BYRNE, M. St. Clare. *Busman's Honeymoon: A Detective Comedy.* London, 1937. $750.

SAYERS, E. *A Treatise on the Culture of the Dahlia and Cactus.* Boston, 1839. $375.

SAYLES, John. *Pride of the Bimbos.* Boston, 1975. Author's first book. $100.

SCAMMON, Charles M. *The Marine Mammals of the North-Western Coast of North America* . . . San Francisco, 1874. 27 plates. $1,000.

SCARBOROUGH, Dorothy. *The Wind.* New York, 1925. $150.

SCENES in the Rocky Mountains, Oregon, California, New Mexico, Texas and Grand Prairies. Philadelphia, 1846. By a New Englander (Rufus B. Sage). Folding map. Printed wraps, or cloth. Either binding. $1,500. (For later editions, see author.)

SCHAEFER, Jack. *Monte Walsh.* Boston, 1963. $200.

SCHAEFER, Jack. *Shane.* Boston, 1949. Author's first book. $1,000.

SCHAEFFER, L. M. *Sketches of Travels in South America, Mexico and California.* New York, 1860. $200.

SCHALDACH, William J. (artist). *Fish by Schaldach.* 60 full-page plates, 8 in color. Pictorial parchment. Philadelphia, 1937. One of 157 signed. $1,750. One of 1,560. Issued without dustwrapper. $300.

SCHARF, John Thomas. *History of the Confederate States Navy* . . . New York, 1887. 42 plates. $250. Albany, 1894. Second edition. $125.

SCHARF, John Thomas. *History of Delaware.* Philadelphia, 1888. 2 vols., half morocco. $750.

SCHARF, John Thomas. *History of Maryland* . . . Baltimore, 1879. Folding charts and maps. Illustrated. 3 vols., half leather. $350.

SCHARF, John Thomas. *History of Westchester County, New York.* Philadelphia, 1886. Illustrated, 2 vols. $250.

SCHARF, John Thomas. *History of Western Maryland.* Philadelphia, 1882. Map, 109 plates, table. 2 vols., cloth. $250.

SCHARMANN, H. B. *Overland Journey to California* . . . (New York, 1918.) Portrait. First edition in English. $250.

SCHATZ, A. H. *Opening a Cow Country.* Ann Arbor, 1939. Plates, maps. Wraps. $125.

SCHLEY, Frank. *American Partridge and Pheasant Shooting.* Frederick, Md., 1877. $175.

SCHLOSSER, Leonard B., and MORRIS, Henry. *A Pair on Paper, Two Essays on Paper History and Related Matters.* North Hills, 1976. One of 220 numbered copies. $300.

SCHNEIDER, Isidor. See S., I.

SCHOBERL, Frederick. *Picturesque Tour from Geneva to Milan by Way of the Simplon.* London, 1820. Plan and 36 color plates. $2,000.

SCHOEPF, Johann David. *Travels in the Confederation.* Philadelphia, 1911. Translated and edited by Alfred J. Morrison. Portrait, 2 facsimiles. 2 vols. First edition in English. $150.

SCHOMBURGK, Robert H. *The History of Barbados...* London, 1848. Map, 8 plates. Half calf. $1,000.

SCHOOLCRAFT, Henry R. *Algic Researches.* New York, 1839. 2 vols., in original cloth. $450.

SCHOOLCRAFT, Henry R. *Historical and Statistical Information Respecting the ... Indian Tribes ...* Philadelphia, 1851–57. Numerous maps, plates, and tables. 6 vols., cloth. $4,000. (For reprint, see Schoolcraft, *Information Respecting the History, etc.*)

SCHOOLCRAFT, Henry R. *The Indian Tribes of the United States.* Philadelphia, 1884. Edited by Francis S. Drake. 100 plates. 2 vols., buckram. $850. London, 1885. 2 vols., cloth. $600. (A condensation from Schoolcraft.)

SCHOOLCRAFT, Henry R. *Information Respecting the History, Condition, and Prospects of the Indian Tribes of the United States.* Philadelphia, 1853–57. Illustrated. 6 vols., cloth. Reprint of *Historical and Statistical Information* in a smaller format. $1,750.

SCHOOLCRAFT, Henry R. *Inquiries Respecting the History ... of the Indian Tribes of the United States.* (Caption title.) (Washington, about 1847–50). Printed wraps. $400.

SCHOOLCRAFT, Henry R. *Journal of a Tour into the Interior of Missouri and Arkansaw.* London, 1821. Folding map. $400.

SCHOOLCRAFT, Henry R. *The Myth of Hiawatha, and Other Oral Legends.* Philadelphia, 1856. $125.

SCHOOLCRAFT, Henry R. *Narrative of an Expedition Through the Upper Mississippi to Itasca Lake ...* New York, 1834. 5 maps (2 folding). $400.

SCHOOLCRAFT, Henry R. *Narrative Journal of Travels Through the Northwestern Regions of the U.S. ...* Albany, 1821. Engraved title page, folding map, 7 plates. $400.

SCHOOLCRAFT, Henry R. *Notes on the Iroquois.* Albany, 1847. $450.

SCHOOLCRAFT, Henry R. *Personal Memoirs of a Residence of 30 Years with the Indian Tribes.* Philadelphia, 1851. Portrait (not in all copies). $300.

SCHOOLCRAFT, Henry R. *Travels in the Central Portions of the Mississippi Valley.* New York, 1825. 5 maps and plates. $500.

SCHOOLCRAFT, Henry R. *A View of the Lead Mines of Missouri.* New York, 1819. 3 plates. Author's first book. $600.

SCHOOLCRAFT, Henry R., and ALLEN, James. *Expedition to North-West Indians.* (Caption title.) (Washington, 1834.) Map. 68 pages. $250.

SCHREINER, Olive. See Iron, Ralph.

SCHREYVOGEL, Charles. *My Bunkie and Other Pictures of Western Frontier Life.* New York, 1909. 36 plates. Oblong pictorial boards. $1,000.

SCHULBERG, Budd. *What Makes Sammy Run?* New York (1941). Author's first book. $500.

SCHULTZ, Christian. *Travels on an Inland Voyage . . .* New York, 1810. Portrait, 2 plates, and 5 folding maps. 2 vols. bound in 1. $1,000.

SCHULTZ, James Willard. *Red Crow's Brother.* Boston, 1927. $150.

SCHULTZ, James Willard. *Sinopah the Indian Boy.* Boston, 1913. In dustwrapper. $250.

SCHULTZ, James Willard. *Skull Head the Terrible.* Boston, 1929. $150.

SCHUYLER, James. *Salute.* New York (1960). Original silk-screen prints by Grace Hartigan. Folio, boards. Author's first book. One of 200 signed. In glassine dustwrapper. $400.

SCHWARTZ, Delmore. *Genesis: Book One.* New Directions. (New York, 1943.) First edition not stated. $200.

SCHWARTZ, Delmore. *In Dreams Begin Responsibilities.* Norfolk, Conn. (1938). Author's first book. $250.

SCHWARTZ, Delmore. *Shenandoah.* Norfolk (1941). Boards. $200. Wraps. $100.

SCHWARTZ, Delmore. *The World Is a Wedding.* (Norfolk, 1948.) $125.

SCHWATKA, Frederick. *Four Summers in Alaska.* St. Louis, 1892. $175.

SCHWATKA, Frederick. *Report of a Military Reconnaissance in Alaska Made in 1883.* Washington, 1885. $250.

SCHWERDT, C. F. G. R. *Hunting, Hawking, Shooting . . .* London, 1928–37. 382 plates, including many in color. 4 vols., folio, in original full or half morocco. One of 300 signed. $5,000.

SCLATER, P. L., and HUDSON, W. H. *Argentine Ornithology.* London, 1888–89. 20 hand-colored plates. 2 vols., blue-gray boards. One of 200 signed. $2,500. Trade. $1,500.

SCORESBY, William, Jr. *Journal of a Voyage to the Northern Whale-Fishery.* Edinburgh, 1823. 8 maps and plates. $500.

SCOT, Reginald. *The Discoverie of Witchcraft.* (London) 1930. Edited by Montague Summers. Cloth, or morocco and buckram. One of 1,275. In dustwrapper. $250.

SCOTT, Evelyn. *On William Faulkner's "The Sound and the Fury."* (New York, 1929). Wraps. $250.

SCOTT, Evelyn. *Precipitations.* New York, 1920. Author's first book. First issue, blue-green cloth with labels. $200. Second issue, red cloth (priority assumed). $150.

SCOTT, J. E. *A Bibliography of the Works of Sir Henry Rider Haggard.* Bishop's Stortford, 1947. 500 numbered copies. $125.

SCOTT, James L. *A Journal of a Missionary Tour Through Pennsylvania . . .* Providence, 1843. $450.

SCOTT, Michael. See *Tom Cringle's Log.*

SCOTT, Paul. *"I Gerontius."* London (1941?). Author's first book. Wraps. $500.

SCOTT, Paul. *Johnnie Sahib.* London, 1952. $250.

SCOTT, Peter. *Morning Flight.* London, 1935. 16 color plates. One of 750 signed. In dustwrapper. $500.

SCOTT, Peter. *Wild Chorus.* London (1938). Illustrated by the author, including mounted color plates. Blue cloth. One of 1,250 signed. In dustwrapper and slipcase. $400.

SCOTT, R. F. *Scott's Last Expedition.* London, 1913. Illustrated, including folding maps and color plates. 2 vols. $300.

SCOTT, Sir Walter. See Clutterbuck, Captain. See also *Harold the Dauntless; Ivanhoe; Kenilworth; The Monastery; Rob Roy; Saint Ronan's Well; Waverley.*

SCOTT, Sir Walter. *The Lady of the Lake.* London, 1810. Portrait. $300. Large paper issue. $400.

SCOTT, Winfield. *Elegy for Robinson.* New York (1936). Author's first book. Wraps. $200.

SCOTT, Winfield. *Memoirs of Lieut. Gen. Scott.* New York, 1864. Portraits. 2 vols. $125.

SCRIPPS, J. L. *The Undeveloped Northern Portion of the American Continent.* Chicago, 1856. 20 pages, printed wraps. $350.

SCROPE, William. *The Art of Deer-Stalking.* London, 1838. 12 plates. In original wraps. $500.

SCROPE, William. *Days and Nights of Salmon Fishing in the Tweed.* London, 1843. 13 plates. Wraps. $750.

SEALSFIELD, Charles. *The Cabin Book; or, Sketches of Life in Texas.* New York, 1844. (By Karl Posti.) 3 parts, printed wraps. First American edition. $1,500. London, 1852. First English edition. $450.

SEARLE, Ronald. *Co-Operation in a University Town.* London (1939). (By W. Henry Brown.) Searle's first book illustrations. $125.

SEARLE, Ronald. *Forty Drawings.* Cambridge, 1946. $250.

SEAVER, James E. *A Narrative of the Life of Mrs. Mary Jemison, Who Was Taken by the Indians in the Year 1755 . . .* Canandaigua, N.Y., 1824. $1,250. Howden, 1826. First U.K. edition. $1,000.

SECONDTHOUGHTS, Solomon. *Quodlibet.* Philadelphia, 1840. (By John Pendleton Kennedy.) In original cloth. $250.

SEDGWICK, Catharine M. *The Linwoods; or "Sixty Years Since" in America.* New York, 1835. 2 vols., in original cloth, paper labels. $125.

SEDGWICK, John. *Correspondence of John Sedgwick.* (New York), 1902–3. 2 vols. One of 300. $250.

SEEGER, Alan. *Poems.* New York, 1916. Author's first book. In dustwrapper. $350. Without dustwrapper. $50.

SELKIRK (Thomas Douglas), Earl of. *A Sketch of the British Fur Trade in North America.* London, 1816. $1,250.

SELTZER, Charles Alden. *The Range Rider.* New York, 1911. In dustwrapper. $150.

SELTZER, Charles Alden. *The Two-Gun Man.* New York, 1911. In dustwrapper. $150.

SENDAK, Maurice. *Atomics for the Millions.* New York (1947). By Edinoff & Ruchlis. (First book illustrated by Sendak.) (Statement on paper quality on copyright page omitted in later printings.) In dustwrapper. $600.

SENIOR Tabula. Oak Park, Ill., June, 1917. (Includes "Class Prophecy," by Ernest Hemingway.) Printed wraps. $1,250.

SENSE and Sensibility. London, 1811. By a Lady (Jane Austen). 3 vols. First issue, with no printer's imprint on half titles, with ruled lines on half title in vol. I measuring $\frac{4}{5}$ inch ($1\frac{1}{7}$ inches in second), and with ruled lines in vol. II $\frac{4}{5}$ inch ($1\frac{3}{10}$ inches in second). $13,000. For rebound copy at auction in 1990. Second, $4,000.

SERVICE, Robert W. *Rhymes of a Red Cross Man.* Toronto, 1916. $150. New York, 1916. Pictorial red cloth. $100.

SERVICE, Robert W. *Roughneck.* New York, 1913. $150.

SERVICE, Robert W. *Song of a Sourdough.* Toronto, 1907. "Author's Edition." $175.

SERVISS, Garrett P. *A Columbus of Space.* Illustrated. New York, 1911. $100.

SERVISS, Garrett P. *The Moon Metal.* New York, 1900. Author's first book. $150.

SETON, Ernest Thompson. *Animal Heroes.* New York, 1905. $200.

SETON, Ernest Thompson. *How to Play Indian.* Philadelphia, 1903. $600. This book was reissued under many titles and eventually became *The Boy Scouts of America* . . . in 1910.

SETON, Ernest Thompson. *Life Histories of Northern Animals.* New York, 1909. 2 vols. $400. London, 1910. 2 vols. $300.

SETON, Ernest Thompson. *A List of the Mammals of Manitoba.* Toronto (1886). Author's first book. Wraps. $1,500.

SETON, Ernest Thompson. *Studies in the Art Anatomy of Animals.* London, 1896. $750.

SETON, Ernest Thompson. *Wild Animals I Have Known.* New York, 1898. 20 drawings by author. Pictorial cloth. First issue, without the words "The Angel whispered don't go" in the last paragraph on page 265. $350. London (1898). First English edition. $250.

SETON-THOMPSON, Ernest. *The Birch-Bark Roll of the Woodcraft Indians.* New York, 1906. Illustrated. 71 pages, birchbark wraps. First separate edition (part of *How to Play Indian*). $300.

SETON-THOMPSON, Ernest. *Boy Scouts of America: A Handbook of Woodcraft, Scouting, and Life-craft.* New York, 1910. Pictorial wraps. "Probable earlier state," with printer's slug on copyright page (VAB). $400.

SETTLE, Mary Lee. *The Love Eaters.* London (1954). Author's first book. $250. New York (1954). (First edition not stated.) $175.

SETTLE, Mary Lee. *The Kiss of Kin.* London (1955). $200. New York (1955). Code on copyright page "G-E." First edition not stated. $150.

SEUSS, Dr. *And to Think I Saw It on Mulberry Street.* New York, 1937. Illustrated in color by the author. Pictorial boards. (By Theodore Geisel.) Author's first nonsense book for children. $350.

SEUSS, Dr. *The Seven Lady Godivas.* New York (1939). Color illustrations. Pictorial cloth. (By Theodore Geisel.) $300.

SEVEN Little Sisters Who Live on the Round Ball That Floats in the Air (The). Boston, 1861. Decorated cloth. (By Jane Andrews.) Author's first book. $150.

SEVEN Pillars of Wisdom (The). George H. Doran. New York, 1926. (By T. E. Lawrence.) Specimen sheets. Half red buckram, vellum spine. First American (copyright) edition, with author's name accidentally omitted from title page. One of 24 (stated 22), of which 10 were offered for sale. $7,500. (For first edition, see Lawrence.)

1796–1896, One Hundred Years, MacKellar, Smiths and Jordan Foundry. Philadelphia (1896). $200.

SEVENTY-SIX . . . (A Novel). Baltimore, 1823. 2 vols. (By John Neal.) $200.

SEWARD, W. H. *Communication upon the Subject of an Intercontinental Telegraph . . .* Washington, 1864. Folding map. 52 pages, wraps. $1,000.

SEWELL, Anna. *Black Beauty.* London (1877). Blue, red, or green cloth. With horse's head looking right, but see Carter's *More Binding Variants* for more details. $1,250. Boston (1890). First American edition. Orange printed wraps. $600. Or buff boards. $300. London, 1915. Illustrated in color by Lucy Kemp-Welch. Cloth. One of 600 signed. $750.

SEXAGENARIAN (The); Or, The Recollections of a Literary Life. London, 1817. 2 vols. $275.

SEXTON, Anne. *All My Pretty Ones.* Boston, 1962. $100.

SEXTON, Anne. *To Bedlam and Part Way Back.* Boston, 1960. Author's first book. $125.

SEYD, Ernest. *California and Its Resources . . .* London, 1858. 18 plates (some tinted), 2 folding maps. $750.

SEYMOUR, E. S. *Emigrant's Guide to the Gold Mines of Upper California.* Chicago, 1849. Folding map. 104 pages, wraps. $3,500.

SEYMOUR, E. S. *Sketches of Minnesota.* New York, 1850. Printed wraps, or cloth. Wraps. $300. Cloth. $250.

SEYMOUR, Silas. *A Reminiscence of the Union Pacific Railroad.* Quebec. 1873. Plates. Printed wraps. $350.

SEYMOUR, W. D. *The Isthmian Routes.* New York, 1863. 27 pages, sewn. $200.

SEYMOUR, William N. *Madison Directory and Business Advertiser.* Madison, Wis., 1855. Map. Leather. $300.

SHAARA, Michael. *The Killer Angels.* New York, 1974. $100.

SHACKLETON, E. H. *The Heart of the Antarctic.* London, 1909. Illustrated, including color plates and folding maps. 3 vols. $500. Limited issue. 3 vols. signed by all in the Shore party. One of 300. $2,000. Philadelphia, 1909. 2 vols. $250.

SHAFFER, Ellen. *The Garden of Health* . . . Book Club of California. (San Francisco, 1957.) Folio, boards and linen. One of 300, with a leaf from the 1499 *Hortus Sanitates.* In dustwrapper. $250.

SHAFFER, Ellen. *The Nuremberg Chronicle* . . . *A Monograph.* Plantin Press. Los Angeles, 1950. Illustrated. 61 pages, pictorial cloth. One of 300, with an original leaf from *The Chronicle* (1497). $350.

SHAHN, Ben (illustrator). *The Alphabet of Creation* . . . New York (1954). Signed frontispiece, other illustrations. One of 50 signed. In slipcase. $1,750.

SHAHN, Ben. *Love and Joy About Letters.* New York, 1963. Slipcase. $125.

SHAKESPEARE, William. *Comedies, Histories and Tragedies.* Oxford, 1901 (1902). Introduction by Sidney Lee. Facsimile from the first folio edition. Folio, cloth. One of 1,000 signed. $350. Limited Editions Club, New York, 1939–40. 37 vols. $1,250.

SHAKESPEARE, William. *Julius Caesar.* London, 1913. Doves Press. Vellum. One of 200. $750. One of 15 on vellum. $3,000. Grabhorn Press. San Francisco, 1954. Illustrated by Mary Grabhorn. Folio, half leather. One of 180. $300.

SHAKESPEARE, William. *Macbeth.* Grabhorn Press. (San Francisco, 1952.) Illustrations in color by Mary Grabhorn. Boards, leather spine. One of 180. In slipcase. $300.

SHAKESPEARE, William. *The Merry Wives of Windsor.* London, 1910. Illustrated by Hugh Thomson. Pictorial vellum, silk ties. One of 350 signed by the artist. $500.

SHAKESPEARE, William. *A Midsummer Night's Dream.* London, 1908. Iliustrated by Arthur Rackham. Full white vellum with ties. One of 1,000 signed by Rackham. $1,250. Trade. Gold-stamped cloth. $350. Grabhorn Press. San Francisco, 1955. Illustrated in color by Mary Grabhorn. Parchment. One of 180. In slipcase. $300.

SHAKESPEARE, William. *Othello.* Grabhorn Press. San Francisco, 1956. Portraits in color by Mary Grabhorn. Boards, leather spine. One of 185. $300.

SHAKESPEARE, William. *The Poems of William Shakespeare.* Boston, 1807. $200. Kelmscott Press. London, 1893. Edited by F. S. Ellis. Limp vellum with ties. One of 500. $1,250. One of 10 on vellum. $6,000.

SHAKESPEARE, William. *Poems and Sonnets.* Golden Cockerel Press. London, 1960. Morocco. One of 100. $750. Buckram. One of 470. $200. Limited Editions Club, New York, 1941. 2 vols. In slipcase. $250.

SHAKESPEARE, William. *Sonnets.* London, 1909. Doves Press. Vellum. One of 250. $800.

SHAKESPEARE, William. *The Tempest.* London, 1908. 40 color plates by Edmund Dulac. Vellum with ties. One of 500 signed by Dulac. $850. Cloth. $200. Montagnola, Italy, 1923 (actually 1924). Green vellum. One of 230. $1,200. London (1926). Vellum. 21 color plates by Rackham. One of 520 signed by Rackham. In dustwrapper. $1,200. Trade. Cloth. In dustwrapper. $500. San Francisco, 1951. Grabhorn Press. Illustrated by Mary Grabhorn. Half cloth. One of 160. $400.

SHAKESPEARE, William. *Venus and Adonis.* Doves Press. London, 1912. Vellum. One of 200. $850.

SHANGE, Ntozake. *For Colored Girls Who Have Considered Suicide...* (San Lorenzo, 1975.) Author's first book. Wraps. First issue, name spelled Ntosake; $.95 cover price. $125.

SHAPIRO, Julian L. *The Water Wheel.* Ithaca (1933). Author's first book. $400.

SHAPIRO, Karl. *Poems.* Baltimore, 1935. Cloth. Author's first book. One of 200 signed. $1,000.

SHAPIRO, Karl. *Trial of a Poet.* New York (1947). One of 250 signed. In tissue dustwrapper and slipcase. $125. Trade. $40.

SHAPIRO, Karl. *V-letter and Other Poems.* New York (1944). $100.

SHARP, William. See MacLeod, Fiona.

SHARPE, Tom. *Riotus Assembly.* London (1971). Author's first book. $200.

SHAW, Edward. *The Modern Architect.* Boston, 1855. 65 plates. $450.

SHAW, George Bernard. See *This Is the Preachment on Going to Church.*

SHAW, George Bernard. *Androcles and the Lion.* London, 1913. Printed wraps. First edition, with title page reading: "Rough Proof—Unpublished." One of 50 privately printed. $650. London, 1916. Cloth. (With *Overruled and Pygmalion* added to title.) $100.

SHAW, George Bernard. *Back to Methuselah: A Metabiological Pentateuch.* London, 1921. Light gray-green cloth. $400. Limited Editions Club, New York, 1939. In slipcase. $60.

SHAW, George Bernard. *Cashel Byron's Profession.* (London), 1886. Printed blue wraps. $1,250. Chicago, 1901. Pictorial cloth. First American edition. $100.

SHAW, George Bernard. *How to Settle the Irish Question.* Dublin (1917). Blue printed wraps. $150. Second issue. Green wraps. $100.

SHAW, George Bernard. *The Intelligent Woman's Guide to Socialism and Capitalism.* London, 1928. Green cloth. $200. New York, 1928. $125.

SHAW, George Bernard. *Love Among the Artists.* Chicago, 1900. Green cloth. First authorized edition. $150.

SHAW, George Bernard. *Man and Superman.* Westminster (London), 1903. $200. Limited Editions Club, New York, 1962. Pictorial cloth and wraps. 2 vols. In slipcase. $125.

SHAW, George Bernard. *Nine Answers.* No-place (1923). Green boards. One of 62 privately printed by Jerome Kern. $300. One of 150. $125.

SHAW, George Bernard. *Passion, Poison and Petrifaction.* New York (1907). Printed wraps. $200.

SHAW, George Bernard. *The Perfect Wagnerite.* London, 1898. $175.

SHAW, George Bernard. *Plays: Pleasant and Unpleasant.* London, 1898. Portrait. 2 vols., green cloth. $250. Chicago, 1898. 2 vols. First American edition. $150.

SHAW, George Bernard. *Pygmalion: A Romance in Five Acts.* London, 1912. Printed wraps. First issue, with title page reading: "Rough Proof, Unpublished." $1,000. Three other "proofs" in 1913 and 1914. $500. New York (1914). Extract from *Everybody's Magazine.* In cloth. $150.

SHAW, George Bernard. *Saint Joan: A Chronicle Play.* London, 1924. First published edition. $350. London (1924). Illustrated by Charles Ricketts. Folio, boards and cloth. First illustrated edition. One of 750. In dustwrapper. $600.

SHAW, George Bernard. *Shaw Gives Himself Away: An Autobiographical Miscellany.* Gregynog Press. Newtown, Wales, 1939. Frontispiece woodcut portrait. Dark green morocco, inlaid with red leather. With original crayon caricature of Shaw by Paul Nash. One of 275. $1,750.

SHAW, George Bernard. *An Unsocial Socialist.* London, 1887. Scarlet cloth. First edition, first state, with title of Shaw's first novel incorrectly given on title page and with publisher's name spelled wrong on spine. $1,250. Second state, with novel's title corrected and with publisher's name on spine stamped over. $500.

SHAW, George Bernard. *War Issues for Irishmen: An Open Letter to Col. Arthur Lynch from Bernard Shaw.* Dublin, 1918. Gray wraps. (Suppressed.) $1,250.

SHAW, Henry. *The Decorative Arts, Ecclesiastical and Civil, of the Middle Ages.* London, 1851. 41 engravings, 18 in color. Half leather. $500.

SHAW, Henry. *Dresses and Decorations of the Middle Ages.* London, 1843. Handcolored plates and other illustrations. 2 vols., folio, boards. $600.

SHAW, Henry. *Examples of Ornamental Metal Work.* London, 1836. 50 plates. $150.

SHAW, Irwin. *Bury the Dead.* New York (1936). Author's first book. $150.

SHAW, Irwin. *Sailor Off the Bremen.* New York, 1939. $150.

SHAW, Irwin. *The Young Lions.* New York (1948). $100. Also special numbered copies for booksellers issued in acetate dustwrapper. $100.

SHAW, R. C. *Across the Plains in Forty-nine.* Farmland, Ind., 1896. $175.

SHAW, T. E. (adopted name). See Homer; Lawrence, T. E.

SHAY, Frank (editor). *Iron Men and Wooden Ships.* Garden City, 1924. Introduction by William McFee. Illustrated by Edward A. Wilson. One of 200 with a lithograph signed by Wilson. $250.

SHEA, John Gilmary. *Discovery and Exploration of the Mississippi Valley . . .* Clinton Hall, 1852. Folding map. $200.

SHEA, John Gilmary. *Early Voyages Up and Down the Mississippi . . .* Albany, N.Y., 1861. $125. Large paper issue. $200.

SHEA, John Gilmary. *A History of the Catholic Church Within . . . the United States.* New York, 1886–92. Illustrated. 4 vols. $200.

SHELLEY, Donald A. *The Fraktur-Writings of Illuminated Manuscripts of the Pennsylvania Germans.* (Allentown, 1961.) $125.

SHELLEY, Mary W. See *Falkner; The Fortunes of Perkin Warbeck; Frankenstein; History of a Six Weeks Tour . . . ; The Last Man; Mounseer Nontongpaw . . . ; Valperga.*

SHELLEY, Percy Bysshe. See *S., P. B.* See also *History of a Six Weeks' Tour, etc . . . ; St. Irvyne; Epipsychidion.*

SHELLEY, Percy Bysshe. *Adonais: An Elegy on the Death of John Keats.* Pisa, Italy, 1821. 25 pages, in original blue ornamental wraps. $46,000 at auction in 1990. Rebound copies. $2,500. Cambridge (London), 1829. In original green wraps. Second (first English) edition. $2,000.

SHELLEY, Percy Bysshe. *Alastor: or, The Spirit of Solitude: and Other Poems.* London, 1816. $2,000.

SHELLEY, Percy Bysshe. *The Cenci.* (Leghorn) Italy, 1819. (250 copies.) $3,000. London, 1821. First English edition. $600.

SHELLEY, Percy Bysshe. *The Complete Works of Percy Bysshe Shelley.* London, 1926–27. 10 vols., cloth, vellum spines. One of 780. In slipcase. $1,000.

SHELLEY, Percy Bysshe. *Hellas: A Lyrical Drama.* London, 1822. $1,500.

SHELLEY, Percy Bysshe. *Laon and Cythna.* London, 1818. First issue, with 4 line quotation from Pindar on half title. $5,000. Second issue, same date, without Pindar lines. $3,500.

SHELLEY, Percy Bysshe. *Letters of Percy Bysshe Shelley.* London, 1852. With an Introductory Essay by Robert Browning. Dark red cloth. (Suppressed as forgeries.) $450.

SHELLEY, Percy Bysshe. *The Masque of Anarchy: A Poem.* London, 1832. Preface by Leigh Hunt. In original gray-blue boards. With white spine label lettered vertically "Shelley's Masque." $1,250.

SHELLEY, Percy Bysshe. *Miscellaneous Poems.* London, 1826. $400.

SHELLEY, Percy Bysshe. *Poems. (Poetical Works.)* Kelmscott Press. (Hammersmith, 1894–95). 3 vols., vellum. (250 copies.) $1,500. One of 6 on vellum. $7,500. (London, 1901–2.) Vale Press. Decorations by Charles Ricketts. 3 vols., white buckram. $600. London, 1914. Doves Press. Limp vellum. One of 200. $850. One of 12 on vellum. $6,000. Limited Editions Club, New York, 1971. In slipcase. $100.

SHELLEY, Percy Bysshe. *Posthumous Poems.* London (1824). First issue, without errata leaf. $4,000.

SHELLEY, Percy Bysshe. *Prometheus Unbound.* London, 1820. First issue, with "Miscellaneous" misprinted "Misellaneous" in table of contents. $1,500. Second issue, with misprint corrected. $750. Essex House Press, London, 1904. Morocco. One of 20 on vellum. $1,500. Limp vellum. One of 200 on paper. $300.

SHELLEY, Percy Bysshe. *Queen Mab: A Philosophical Poem.* London, 1813. First (privately printed) edition. Shelley removed the title, dedication, and imprint from many copies. Unmutilated copy. $15,000. Mutilated copy. $1,000. London, 1821. Second (first published) edition. $300.

SHELLEY, Percy Bysshe. *Rosalind and Helen.* London, 1819. With 2 ad leaves at end. $1,250.

SHEPARD, Odell. *A Lonely Flute.* Boston, 1917. Author's first book. In dustwrapper. $250. Without dustwrapper. $50.

SHEPPARD, Elizabeth Sara. See *Charles Auchester.*

SHEPPARD Lee. New York, 1836. Written by Himself. (By Robert Montgomery Bird.) 2 vols., in original floral cloth. $400.

SHERIDAN, Philip H. *Outline Descriptions of the Posts in the Military Division of the Missouri, etc.* Chicago, 1872. Maps, including a folding map. $1,750.

SHERIDAN, Philip H. *Record of Engagements with Hostile Indians Within the Military Division . . .* Chicago, 1882. $600.

SHERIDAN, Richard Brinsley. See *The Love Epistles . . .*

SHERIDAN, Richard Brinsley. *The Critic . . .* London, 1781. $600.

SHERIDAN, Richard Brinsley. *Pizarro.* London, 1799. $450.

SHERMAN, Elizabeth Ware. See S., E. W., and M., S. W.

SHERWOOD, J. Ely. *California: Her Wealth and Resources . . .* New York, 1848. 40 pages, wraps. $4,000.

SHIEL, M. P. *Children of the Wind.* London, 1923. $300.

SHIEL, M. P. *The Dragon.* London (1913). $200.

SHIEL, M. P. *The Last Miracle.* London, 1906. Pictorial black cloth. $125.

SHIEL, M. P. *Prince Zaleski.* London, 1895. Author's first book. Decorated purple cloth. First, with 2 ad catalogues at back. $250. Boston, 1895. $100.

SHIEL, M. P. *The Purple Cloud.* London, 1929. One of 105 signed. Issued without dustwrapper. $400.

SHIEL, M. P. *Shapes in the Fire.* London, 1896. $200.

SHIELDS, G. O. *The Battle of the Big Hole.* New York, 1889. 8 plates. $250.

SHIELDS, G. O. *Cruising in the Cascades.* Chicago, 1889. $350.

SHILLIBEER, Lieut. J. *A Narrative of the Briton's Voyage to Pitcairn's Island* . . . Taunton, 1817. 12 plates. With errata leaf and instructions to the binder. $1,750. London, 1817. 11 plates. Second edition. $1,000. London, 1818. 12 plates. Half calf. Third edition. $600.

SHINN, Charles Howard. *Graphic Description of Pacific Coast Outlaws.* (Caption title.) (San Francisco, about 1890–95.) Portrait. 32 pages, wraps. $450.

SHINN, Charles Howard. *Mining Camps.* New York, 1885. $250.

SHINN, Charles Howard. *Pacific Rural Handbook.* San Francisco, 1879. $175.

SHINTON, William Edward. *Lectures on an Improved System of Teaching the Art of Writing.* London, 1823. 13 engraved plates. $350.

SHIPLEY, Conway. *Sketches in the Pacific.* London, 1851. 26 tinted plates. Folio, cloth. $6,000.

SHIPMAN, Mrs. O. L. *Taming the Big Bend.* (Marfa, Tex., 1926.) Folding map, 4 plates. $250.

SHORT (A) Account of the Life and Work of Wynkyn de Worde . . . San Francisco, 1949. One of 375 copies. Includes an original leaf from *The Golden Legend.* $450.

SHORT, Luke. *Ambush.* Boston, 1950. (Pseudonym of Frederick D. Glidden). $100.

SHORT, Luke. *Hard Money.* New York, 1940. (Pseudonym of Frederick D. Glidden). $125.

SHORTER, Alfred H. *Paper Mills and Paper Makers in England, 1495–1800.* Hilversum, 1957. One of 600 copies. $450.

SHORTHOUSE, J. Henry. *John Inglesant.* Birmingham (England), 1880. Author's first book. 3 vols. $350. Also 1 vol. $200.

SHUTE, Henry A. *The Real Diary of a Real Boy.* Boston, 1902. $150.

SHUTE, Nevil. *Marazan.* London, 1926. Author's first book. $300.

SIDNEY Lawton Smith, Designer, Etcher, Engraver . . . Boston, 1931. One of 200 copies. $150.

SIDNEY, Margaret. *Five Little Peppers and How They Grew.* Boston (1880). Green, blue, or brown pictorial cloth. (By Harriet M. S. Lathrop, her first book). First state, with 1880 copyright and with caption on page 231 reading " . . . said Polly." $350.

SIEBERT, Wilbur Henry. *Loyalists in East Florida.* DeLand, Fla., 1929. 6 maps and plates. 2 vols., buckram. Issued without dustwrapper. One of 355. $250.

SIEGE of Corinth (The). London, 1816. (By George Gordon Noel, Lord Byron.) $400.

SILKIN, Jon. *The Portrait* . . . Ilfracombe (1950). Author's first book. Wraps. $150.

SILL, Edward Rowland. See *Poem and Valedictory Oration* . . .

SILL, Edward Rowland. *The Hermitage* . . . New York, 1868. $125.

SILLIMAN, Benjamin. *A Description of the Recently Discovered Petroleum Region in California.* (Cover title.) New York, 1864. Printed wraps. $650.

SILLIMAN, Benjamin. *Report upon the Oil Property of the Philadelphia and California Petroleum Co.* Philadelphia, 1865. 2 maps. 36 pages, wraps. $500, possibly more.

SILLITOE, Alan. *The Loneliness of the Long Distance Runner.* London (1959). $150.

SILLITOE, Alan. *Without Beer or Bread.* Dulwich Village, 1957. Author's first book, other than a translation. Wraps. $400.

SILURIENSIS, Leolinus. *The Anatomy of Tobacco.* London (1884). White parchment boards. (By Arthur Machen.) Author's first book (aside from the anonymous privately printed pamphlet *Eleusinia.*) $250.

SILVER Mines of Virginia and Austin, Nevada. Boston, 1865. 19 pages, wraps. $350.

SIMAK, Clifford D. *All Flesh Is Grass.* Garden City, 1965. $125.

SIMAK, Clifford D. *City.* (New York, 1952.) $300.

SIMAK, Clifford D. *The Creator.* (Los Angeles, 1946.) Wraps. No statement of edition. Author's first book. $125.

SIMAK, Clifford D. *Time and Again.* New York, 1951. $125.

SIMAK, Clifford D. *Way Station.* Garden City, 1963. $350.

SIMENON, Georges. *The Crime of Inspector Maigret.* New York, 1932. Author's first book. First English translation. $250.

SIMMONS, Albert Dixon. *Wing Shots: A Series of Camera Studies of* . . . *Birds* . . . *on the Wing.* Derrydale Press, New York (1936). $150.

SIMMS, Jeptha R. *The American Spy, or Freedom's Early Sacrifice.* Albany, 1846. 63 pages, wraps. $150.

SIMMS, Jeptha R. *Trappers of New York.* Albany, 1850. 4 plates. $150. Albany, 1860. $100.

SIMMS, William Gilmore. See *Beauchampe; Border Beagles; Grouped Thoughts and Scattered Fancies; Guy Rivers; Martin Faber; Mellichampe; The Partisan; Pelayo; Richard Hurdis; Sack and Destruction of Columbia, S.C.; The Wigwam and the Cabin; The Yemassee.*

SIMMS, William Gilmore. *Areytos; or, Songs of the South.* Charleston, 1846. Wraps. $650.

SIMMS, William Gilmore. *The Cassique of Accabee.* Charleston, 1849. Wraps. $500.

SIMMS, William Gilmore. *The Forayers; or, The Raid of the Dog-Days.* New York, 1855. $300.

SIMMS, William Gilmore. *Helen Halsey; or, The Swamp State of Conelachita.* New York, 1845. Wraps. $400.

SIMMS, William Gilmore. *Lyrical and Other Poems.* Charleston, 1827. Author's first book. $500.

SIMMS, William Gilmore. *Poems: Descriptive, Dramatic, Legendary and Contemplative.* New York, 1853. 2 vols. $350. Charleston, 1853. 2 vols. $300.

SIMMS, William Gilmore. *Southward Ho! A Spell of Sunshine.* New York, 1854. $300.

SIMON, André L. *Bibliotheca Vinaria* . . . (London, 1979). 600 numbered copies. Facsimile reprint of the 1913 edition. $125.

SIMON, Neil. *Heidi.* New York, 1959. Author's first book with William Friedberg. Wraps. $125.

SIMON, Neil. *Come Blow Your Horn.* New York, 1963. (With Danny Simon.) $125.

SIMON, Oliver (editor). *The Curwen Press Miscellany.* London, 1931. 275 numbered copies. Slipcase. $850.

SIMPSON, George. *Narrative of a Journey Round the World, During the Years 1841 and 1842.* London, 1847. Portrait, folding map. 2 vols. $850. Philadelphia, 1847. 2 vols. in 1. First American edition. $300.

SIMPSON, Harriette. *Mountain Path.* New York (1936). See also Arnow, Harriette.

SIMPSON, Henry I. *The Emigrant's Guide to the Gold Mines.* New York, 1848. Folding map. 30 pages, wraps. $3,000. Without map. $1,000.

SIMPSON, Capt. James H. *Report of Explorations Across the Great Basin of the Territory of Utah* . . . Washington, 1876. Folding map, plates, errata leaf. $400.

SIMPSON, James H. *Journal of a Military Reconnaissance from Santa Fe, N.M., to the Navajo Country.* Philadelphia, 1852. Folding map, 72 plates, including color. First separate printing. $750.

SIMPSON, James H. *Report from the Secretary of War . . . and Map of the Route from Fort Smith, Ark., to Santa Fe, N.M.* (Caption title.) (Washington, 1850.) 4 folding maps. Stitched. Senate issue. $500. House issue. 1 folding map. 2 plates. $350.

SIMPSON, James H. *Report of the Secretary of War . . . and Map of Wagon Roads in Utah.* (Caption title.) (Washington, 1859.) Large folding map. $300.

SIMPSON, James H. *Report of . . . on the Union Pacific Railroad and Branches* . . . Washington, 1866. 4 folding maps. Wraps. $450.

SIMPSON, Louis. *The Arrivistes: Poems, 1940–1949.* New York (1949). Wraps. Author's first book. $200. Paris (1950). $175.

SIMPSON, Thomas. *Narrative of the Discoveries on the Northwest Coast of America.* London, 1843. 2 maps in front pocket. $650.

SIMPSON, Walter G. *Art of Golf.* Edinburgh, 1887. $750. New York, 1892. $700.

SINCLAIR, Upton. See Fitch, Ensign Clarke.

SINCLAIR, Upton. *The Jungle.* Jungle Publishing Co., New York, 1906. First state, with unbroken type on copyright page and with "Sustainers' Edition" label on front pastedown. $300. New York, 1906. Green cloth. First issue, with Doubleday imprint and with the "I" in date on copyright page in perfect type. $200. Jungle Publishing. Without label. $150.

SINCLAIR, Upton. *King Midas.* New York, 1901. $100.

SINCLAIR, Upton. *Springtime and Harvest.* New York, 1910. $250.

SINGER, Isaac Bashevis. *The Family Moskat.* New York, 1950. Author's first English publication. $150.

SINGLETON, Arthur. *Letters from the South and West.* Boston, 1824. (By Henry Cogswell Knight.) $250.

SINISTRARI, Ludovico. *Demoniality.* London, 1927. Translated into English by Montague Summers. Vellum. Issued without dustwrapper. One of 90 (of an edition of 1,290) on handmade paper, signed by Summers. $350. One of 1,200. $150.

SINJOHN, John. *From the Four Winds.* London, 1897. (By John Galsworthy, his first book.) Olive green cloth. One of 500. $500.

SINJOHN, John. *Jocelyn.* London, 1898. (By John Galsworthy.) First issue, with "you" for "my" on page 257, third line from bottom. $400.

SINJOHN, John. *A Man of Devon.* Edinburgh and London, 1901. (By John Galsworthy.) Blue cloth. With ads dated "4/01." $350.

SINJOHN, John. *Villa Rubein.* London, 1900. (By John Galsworthy.) Cherry red cloth. $350.

SIR John Chiverton. London, 1826. (By William H. Ainsworth and John P. Aston.) Ainsworth's first book. $300.

SIRINGO, Charles A. *A Cowboy Detective.* Chicago, 1912. Pictorial cloth. First issue, published by Conkey. $300. Another binding: special first issue presentation copies, in pebble-grained leather (unrecorded in bibliographies—VAB), inscribed by Siringo. $600. Second issue, same date. 2 vols., wraps. $200. New York, 1912. Pictorial wraps. $200.

SIRINGO, Charles A. *History of "Billy the Kid."* (Santa Fe, 1920.) 142 pages, stiff pictorial wraps. $750.

SIRINGO, Charles A. *A Lone Star Cowboy.* Santa Fe, 1919. Pictorial cloth. $300.

SIRINGO, Charles A. *Riata and Spurs* . . . Boston, 1927. 16 plates. Pictorial cloth. $500. Boston (1927). Pictorial cloth. Second printing, with many changes. $150.

SIRINGO, Charles A. *The Song Companion of a Lone Star Cowboy.* Santa Fe (1919). Pictorial wraps. $750.

SIRINGO, Charles A. *A Texas Cowboy, or, Fifteen Years on the Hurricane Deck of a Spanish Pony.* Chicago, 1885. Illustrated, including chromolithographic frontispiece in color. Wraps. $10,000. Black pictorial cloth. $7,500. Chicago, 1886. Siringo & Dobson. 8 plates, 347 pages. Second edition. $1,000. Another issue, same collation, same place and date. Rand McNally, wraps. $750. New York (1886). Wraps. $300. New York (1950). Illustrated by Tom Lea. Cloth. $125.

SIR Ralph Esher; or, Adventures of a Gentleman of the Court of Charles II. London, 1832. 3 vols., in original boards. (By Leigh Hunt.) $600.

SISTER Years (The); Being the Carrier's Address, to the Patrons of the Salem Gazette, for the First of January, 1839. (Cover title.) Salem, Mass., 1839. 8 pages, in original printed self-wraps. (By Nathaniel Hawthorne.) $1,500.

SITGREAVES, Lorenzo. *Report of an Expedition down the Zuni and Colorado Rivers.* Washington, 1853. 79 plates, some tinted; folding map. $650. Washington, 1854. $500.

SITWELL, Edith. See Sitwell, Osbert.

SITWELL, Edith. *Alexander Pope.* London (1930). Illustrated. Yellow buckram. One of 220 signed. In dustwrapper and slipcase. $200.

SITWELL, Edith. *Collected Poems.* London, 1930. One of 320 signed. In dustwrapper. $200. Trade. $100.

SITWELL, Edith. *Facade.* London, 1920. Colored frontispiece. One of 150 signed. Issued without dustwrapper. $300.

SITWELL, Edith. *Five Poems.* London, 1928. One of 275 signed. $200.

SITWELL, Edith. *The Mother and Other Poems.* Oxford, 1915. Wraps. Author's first book. (500 copies, 200 pulped.) $1,250.

SITWELL, Edith. *The Pleasures of Poetry.* First, second, and third series. London, 1930–31–32. 3 vols. $300.

SITWELL, Edith. *Popular Song.* London, 1928. One of 500 signed. Issued without dustwrapper. $150.

SITWELL, Edith. *The Wooden Pegasus.* Oxford, 1920. In dustwrapper. $175.

SITWELL, Osbert. *At the House of Mrs. Kinfoot.* London, 1921. Wraps. One of 101 signed. Issued without dustwrapper. $250.

SITWELL, Osbert. *The Collected Satires and Poems of Osbert Sitwell.* (London) 1931. Portrait frontispiece. Cloth. Issued without dustwrapper. Limited and signed. $200.

SITWELL, Osbert. *England Reclaimed.* London, 1927. One of 165 signed. In dustwrapper. $200.

SITWELL, Osbert. *Twentieth Century Harliquinade . . .* Oxford, 1916. (Author's first book with Edith Sitwell.) (500 copies.) Wraps. $200.

SITWELL, Osbert. *Who Killed Cock-Robin?* London, 1921. In yellow paper wrapper pasted to spine (8⅕ inches high). $250. Later with wrapper pasted to boards. (7⅜ inches high.) $200.

SITWELL, Osbert. *The Winstonburg Line: 3 Satires.* London, 1919. Pictorial wraps. Author's first separate book. $200.

SITWELL, Sacheverell. *The Cyder Feast and Other Poems.* (London) 1927. Yellow buckram. One of 165 signed. Issued without dustwrapper. $250.

SITWELL, Sacheverell. *The People's Palace*. Oxford, 1918. Author's first book. Frontispiece. Wraps. (400 copies.) $250.

SITWELL, Sacheverell. *Two Poems, Ten Songs*. London, 1929. Decorated boards. One of 275 signed. $200.

SITWELL, Sacheverell, and LAMBERT, Constant. *The Rio Grande*. London, 1929. One of 75 signed. $350. Unsigned (but numbered). $200.

SITWELL, Sacheverell, BLUNT, Wilfred, and SYNGE, Patrick M. *Great Flower Books, 1700–1900*. London, 1956. 36 plates, 20 in color. Folio, half morocco. One of 295 signed by the authors. In slipcase. $1,250. Half cloth. One of 1,750. In dustwrapper. $850.

SITWELL, Sacheverell, BUCHANAN, Handasyde, and FISHER, James. *Fine Bird Books, 1700–1900*. London, 1953. 38 plates in color, 36 in black and white. Folio, half morocco. One of 295 signed by the three authors. $1,250. Buckram and boards. One of 2,000. In dustwrapper. $750.

SIX to One; A Nantucket Idyl. New York, 1878. Tan or gray cloth. (By Edward Bellamy, his first book.) Cloth. $400. Later state, printed wraps. $300.

SIXTY Years of the Life of Jeremy Levis. New York, 1831. 2 vols., boards, cloth spines, paper labels. (By Laughton Osborn.) $125.

SKEEN, William. *Early Typography*. Colombo, 1872. Revised edition. $125.

SKEFFINGTON, F. J. C., and JOYCE, James A. *Two Essays*. Dublin (1901). 4 leaves, pink printed wraps. Joyce's first published book, containing his essay "The Day of the Rabblement." $7,000.

SKETCH of the Geographical Rout [sic] of a Great Railway . . . Between the Atlantic States and the Great Valley of the Mississippi. New York, 1829. (By William C. Redfield.) Folding map. 16 pages. $400. New York, 1830. Second edition. $250.

SKETCH of Old England (A). New York, 1822. By a New England Man. 2 vols. (By James Kirke Paulding.) $200.

SKETCH of St. Anthony and Minneapolis. St. Anthony, 1857. Frontispiece, 4 plates, map. 32 pages, wraps. With errata slip. $300.

SKETCH of the Seminole War, and Sketches During the Campaign. Charleston, 1836. Leather. $450.

SKETCHES by "Boz." London, 1836–37. Illustrated by George Cruikshank. 3 vols. (First series, 1836, 2 vols., dark green cloth; second series, 1837, pink cloth.) (By Charles Dickens, his first book.) $5,000. London, 1837–39. 20 parts, pictorial pink wraps. (Complete sets with all ads and wraps in the first state are rare.) $25,000.

SKETCHES of History, Life and Manners in the United States. New Haven, 1826. (By a Traveller, Anne Royall, her first book.) Woodcut frontispiece view. $250.

SKETCHES of the West, or the Home of the Badgers. Milwaukee, 1847. Folding map. 48 pages, wraps. (By Josiah B. Grinnell.) Second edition (of *The Home of the Badgers*, which see under Grinnell's pseudonym, Oculus). $1,000.

SKINNER, J. S. *The Dog and the Sportsman*. New York, 1845. Illustrated, including engraved title page. $350.

SLAUGHTER, Mrs. Linda W. *The New Northwest.* Bismarck, 1874. 24 pages, wraps. $1,500.

SLAVE (The); or, The Memoirs of Archy Moore. (By Richard Hildreth, his first book.) Boston, 1836. 2 vols. $300.

SLICK, Jonathan. *High Life in New York.* (New York, 1843.) Author's first book. Wraps. $150.

SLOAN, Edward L. See *Salt Lake City . . .*

SLOAN, Sir Hans. *A Voyage to the Islands Madera.* London, 1707–25. 2 vols., folio, with 240 plates. $8,500.

SLOAN, Robert. W. *Utah Gazetteer and Directory of Logan, Ogden, Provo and Salt Lake Cities.* Salt Lake City, 1884. $300.

SLOCUM, John J., and CAHOON, Herbert. *A Bibliography of James Joyce, 1882– 1941.* London, 1953. $150.

SLOCUM, Joshua. *Sailing Alone Around the World.* New York, 1900. $175.

SLOCUM, Joshua. *Voyage of the Destroyer from New York to Brazil.* Boston, 1894. 47 pages, wraps. $200.

SMART, Stephen F. *Leadville, Ten Mile . . . and All Other Noted Colorado Mining Camps.* Kansas City, 1879. 2 folding maps, 56 pages, printed wraps. $650.

SMEDLEY, Frank E. See *Frank Fairleigh.*

SMEDLEY, William. *Across the Plains in '62.* (Denver, 1916.) Map and portrait. 56 pages, boards. $350.

SMITH, A.J.M. *Poetry of Robert Bridges.* Montreal, no date on title page and not known. (Early 1930s.) Author's first book. Wraps. $1,200.

SMITH, A.J.M. *News of the Phoenix . . .* Toronto, 1943. $125.

SMITH, Adam. *The Theory of Moral Sentiments.* London, 1759. Author's first book. $4,000.

SMITH, Alexander. *Dreamthorp.* London, 1863. $150. Boston, 1864. $100.

SMITH, Alexander. *Poems.* London, 1853. Author's first book. With inserted ads dated November 1852. $75.

SMITH, Alice R. H., and SMITH, D. E. H. *The Dwelling Houses of Charleston.* Philadelphia, 1917. $150.

SMITH, Captain Allan C., U.S.A. *The Secrets of JuJitsu: A Complete Course in Self Defense.* Columbus, 1920. 7 vols. Wraps. $75.

SMITH, Ashbel. *Reminiscences of the Texas Republic.* Galveston, 1876. Wraps. One of 100. $750.

SMITH, Buckingham (translator). *The Discovery of Florida.* Grabhorn printing for the Book Club of California. (San Francisco, 1946.) Decorations by Mallette Dean.

Folio, gold boards and cloth. One of 280. $450. (For an earlier printing, see next entry.)

SMITH, Buckingham (translator). *Narratives of the Career of Hernando de Soto in the Conquest of Florida.* New York, 1866. Folding map. Boards. One of 75. $850.

SMITH, Buckingham (translator). *Rudo Ensayo, Tentativae de una Provencional Descripcion Geographica de la Provincia de Sonora.* San Agustin (St. Augustine, Fla., actually Albany, N.Y.), 1863. (By Juan Nentuig?) 208 pages, printed gray wraps. One of 10 large paper copies. $1,000. One of 160. $600.

SMITH, Charles Hamilton. *Selections of the Ancient Costume of Great Britain & Ireland . . .* London, 1814. 60 full-page color plates. $1,500. London, 1815. $1,250.

SMITH, Clark Ashton. *The Abominations of Yondo.* Sauk City, Wis., 1960. $150.

SMITH, Clark Ashton. *The Dark Chateau and Other Poems.* Sauk City, Wis., 1951. $650.

SMITH, Clark Ashton. *The Double Shadow and Other Fantasies.* (Cover title.) (Auburn, Calif., 1933.) 30 pages, wraps. $350.

SMITH, Clark Ashton. *Genius Loci and Other Tales.* Sauk City, Wis., 1948. $200.

SMITH, Clark Ashton. *Lost Worlds.* Sauk City, Wis., 1944. $350.

SMITH, Clark Ashton. *Odes and Sonnets.* San Francisco, 1918. Preface by George Sterling. Decorations by Florence Lundborg. Blue boards, tan cloth spine, paper label. One of 300. $300.

SMITH, Clark Ashton. *Out of Space and Time.* Sauk City, Wis., 1942. $500.

SMITH, Clark Ashton. *Spells and Philtres.* Sauk City, Wis., 1958. $400.

SMITH, Clark Ashton. *The Star-Treader and Other Poems.* San Francisco, 1912. Buff pictorial boards. Author's first collection of verse. In dustwrapper. $300. Without dustwrapper. $100.

SMITH, David Eugene. *Rara Arithmetica . . .* Boston, 1908. $125.

SMITH, Edward E. *The Skylark of Space.* (Buffalo Book Co. Providence, 1946). (Author's first book with Mrs. Lee Hawkins Garby.) $300. Hadley Co. Providence (1947). $60.

SMITH, Edward E. *The Spacehounds of IPC . . .* Reading, 1947. First edition stated. In dustwrapper listing 4 titles on rear panel. $125. One of 300 signed. $250. In second issue, dustwrapper with 11 titles on back. $75. (The first Fantasy Press book.)

SMITH, Edward E. *Triplanetary.* Reading, Pa., 1948. $150. Also one of 500 signed. $250.

SMITH, Emma (editor). *A Collection of Sacred Hymns for the Church of the Latter Day Saints.* Kirtland, Ohio, 1835. In original marbled boards and cloth. $7,500 or more.

SMITH, F. Hopkinson. *American Illustrators.* New York, 1892. Folio, 5 parts, printed wraps in printed board folder. One of 1,000. $250.

SMITH, F. Hopkinson. *Colonel Carter of Cartersville.* Boston, 1891. Olive green cloth. With apostrophe in "Carter'sville" on spine, and vignette of staircase on page (i). $125. Later, without apostrophe, in blue-gray cloth and vignette moved to page 3. $75.

SMITH, F. Hopkinson. *Old Lines in New Black.* Boston, 1885. Author's first book. $125.

SMITH, F. Hopkinson. *Venice of Today.* New York, 1896. 21 colored plates, 12 plain plates. Half morocco. $150. One of 118 on handmade paper. $300. New York, 1902. Half morocco. $250.

SMITH, Frank Meriweather (editor). *San Francisco Vigilance Committee of '56.* San Francisco, 1883. 83 pages, wraps. $300.

SMITH, Garden C. *The World of Golf.* London, 1898. $400.

SMITH, Harry B. *A Sentimental Library . . .* (No-place) 1914. Issued in dustwrapper and slipcase. $375.

SMITH, J. Calvin. *A New Guide for Travelers Through the United States.* New York, 1846. Folding map in color. Cloth, or leather. $300. New York, 1848. $250.

SMITH, J. Calvin. *The Western Tourist and Emigrant's Guide . . .* New York, 1839. Colored folding map. In original cloth, or leather. $300. New York, 1845. $200.

SMITH, James E. *A Famous Battery and Its Campaigns, 1861–64.* Washington, 1892. $100.

SMITH, James F. *The Cherokee Land Lottery . . .* New York, 1838. $350.

SMITH, John Thomas. *Antiquities of Westminster.* London, 1807–(09). Illustrated, including color plates. 2 vols. $600.

SMITH, John Thomas. *Cries of London, Exhibiting Several of the Itinerant Traders of Ancient and Modern Times.* London, 1839. Portrait and 30 hand-colored etchings. In original half leather and cloth. $750. Large paper. $850.

SMITH, Johnston. *Maggie: A Girl of the Streets.* (New York, 1893.) (By Stephen Crane, his first book.) Yellow printed wraps. (For the second edition, see the entry under Crane, Stephen.) $15,000.

SMITH, Joseph, Jr. See *A Book of Commandments.*

SMITH, Joseph, Jr. *The Book of Mormon.* Palmyra, N.Y., 1830. In original leather. Author's first book. First edition, first issue, with 2-page preface and testimonial leaf at end and without index. $9,000. Second issue, without testimonials, etc. $6,000. Kirtland, Ohio, 1837. Second edition. $3,500. Nauvoo, Ill. (actually Cincinnati), 1840. Third edition. $1,000. Liverpool, 1841. Leather. First English edition. $2,500. Nauvoo, Ill., 1842. Fourth edition. $3,500.

SMITH, Joseph, Jr., et al. (editors). *Doctrine and Covenants of the Church of the Latter Day Saints.* Kirtland, 1835. In original leather. $10,000 or more.

SMITH, Kate Douglas. *The Story of Patsy. A Reminiscence.* San Francisco, 1883. 27 pages, wraps. (By Kate Douglas Wiggin, her first separate publication.) $500.

SMITH, Lee. *The Last Day the Dogbushes Bloomed.* New York (1968). Author's first book. $150.

SMITH, Lillian. *There Are Things to Do.* Clayton, Ga. 1943. Author's first book. Wraps. (16-page off-print, stapled.) $125.

SMITH, Logan Pearsall. *Trivia.* London, 1902. One of 300. $250. Garden City, 1917. Half leather. One of 100. $175.

SMITH, Logan Pearsall. *The Youth of Parnassus and Other Stories.* London, 1895. Blue or red cloth (priority unknown). Author's first book. $150.

SMITH, Lucy. *Biographical Sketches of Joseph Smith the Prophet, and His Progenitors for Many Generations.* Liverpool, 1853. $850.

SMITH, Michael. *A Geographical View, of the Province of Upper Canada, and Promiscuous Remarks upon the Government* . . . Hartford, 1813. 107 pages. $300. New York, 1813. Second edition. $150.

SMITH, Moses. *History of the Adventures and Sufferings of Moses Smith* . . . Brooklyn, N.Y., 1812. 2 plates. $200.

SMITH, Nathan. *A Practical Essay on Typhous Fever.* New York, 1824. $400.

SMITH, Robert W. (editor). *A Complete Guide to Judo: Its Story and Practice.* Tokyo, 1958. Stated first. $75.

SMITH, Robert W. *Chinese Boxing: Masters and Methods.* Tokyo, 1974. Stated first. $40.

SMITH, Mrs. Sarah. *A Journal Kept by Mrs. Sarah Foote Smith While Journeying with Her People from Wellington, Ohio, to Footeville, Town of Nepeuskun, Winnebago County, Wis., April 15 to May 10, 1846.* (Kilbourn, Ohio, 1905.) Boards, paper label. $200.

SMITH, Sidney Lawton. See *Sidney Lawton Smith* . . .

SMITH, Stevie. *Novel on Yellow Paper.* London (1936). Author's first book. $500. New York, 1937. $200.

SMITH, T. Dudley. *Over the Wall.* London, 1943. Author's first book. $150.

SMITH, T. Dudley. *Into the Happy Glade.* London, 1943. $150.

SMITH, Thorne. *Biltmore Oswald: The Diary of a Hapless Recruit.* New York (1918). Pictorial boards. Author's first book. In dustwrapper. $250. Without dustwrapper. $50.

SMITH, Thorne. *Topper: An Improbable Adventure.* New York, 1926. $750. London, 1926. $600.

SMITH, Wallace. *Garden of the Sun: A History of the San Joaquin Valley, 1772–1939.* Los Angeles (1939). $150.

SMITH, William H. *History of Canada.* Quebec, 1815. Folding table. 2 vols. $1,500. Later edition. (Quebec, 1827). 2 vols. $500.

SMITH, William H. *Smith's Canadian Gazetteer...* Toronto, 1846. Large folding map. $300.

SMITH, William Jay. *Poems.* New York, 1947. Author's first book. 500 numbered copies. Issued without dustwrapper. $100.

SMITHWICK, Noah. *The Evolution of a State ...* Austin (1900). $750. One of 10 signed. $1,500.

SMOLLETT, Tobias. *The Expedition of Humphrey Clinker.* London, 1671 (1771). 3 vols., with vol. 1 misdated. $2,000.

SMOLLETT, Tobias. *The Adventures of Roderick Random.* London, 1748. Author's first book. 2 vols. $1,000.

SMYTH, Henry de Wolf. *Atomic Energy for Military Purposes (The).* Princeton, 1945. First commercial edition, possibly preceding GPO edition. First 3 printings are indistinguishable. Cloth in dustwrapper. $300. Wraps. $100.

SMYTH, Henry de Wolf. *A General Account of the Development of Methods of Using Energy for Military Purposes . . .* (Washington, 1945.) 193 pages in stapled wraps. Text printed by lithoprint. Issued with broadside headed: "FUTURE RELEASE . . ." laid in. $2,000. One of 4 (?) copies in spiral binding with name of recipient printed on front wrapper. $3,250. Superintendent of Documents, Washington, 1945. Stiff printed wraps. 182 pages with "1945" at foot of last page. First public edition, printed by GPO. $750.

SMYTHE, Henry. *Historical Sketch of Parker County and Weatherford, Texas.* St. Louis, 1877. $650.

SNARLEYYOW, or The Dog Fiend. London, 1837. 3 vols., in original boards. (By Frederick Marryat.) $350. Philadelphia, 1837. 2 vols., in original cloth. First American edition. (Published with byline "F. Marryat.") $250.

SNELLING, William J. See Bell, Solomon; see also *Tales of the Northwest.*

SNELLING, William J. *The Polar Regions of the Western Continent Explored.* Boston, 1831. $250.

SNODGRASS, W. D. *Heart's Needle.* New York, 1959. Author's first book. $175. (Hessle, England, 1960.) First English edition. Adds an addendum. $100.

SNOW, C. P. *Death Under Sail.* London (1932). Author's first book. $300.

SNOW, Lorenzo. *The Voice of Joseph.* Liverpool & London, 1852. First U.K. edition. $200.

SNYDER, Gary. *The Back Country.* London (1967). One of 100 signed. In dustwrapper. $200. Trade. $50.

SNYDER, Gary. *The Blue Sky.* New York, 1969. Oblong, wraps. One of 126 signed. $175.

SNYDER, Gary. *Myths and Texts.* New York (1960). Illustrated. Decorated wraps. $200.

SNYDER, Gary. *Riprap.* Origin Press. (Ashland, Mass.), 1959. Japanese-style blue-and-white wraps. Author's first book. $350.

SNYDER, Gary. *Six Sections from Mountains and Rivers Without End.* (San Francisco), 1965. Wraps. $75. Fulcrum Press. London (1967). Green cloth. First English edition. One of 100 signed. In dustwrapper. $200. Trade. $50.

SNYDER, Gary (translator). *The Wooden Fish: Basic Sutras & Gathas of Rinzai Zen.* (Kyoto, Japan), 1961. Prepared by Kanetsuki Gutesu and Gary Snyder. Wraps. First edition, with errata slip laid in. $450.

SOMBRERO (The). Quarter-Centennial Number. Yearbook of the Class of 1895. University of Nebraska. Lincoln, Neb. (1894). White and red cloth. $750. (Contains Willa Cather and Dorothy Canfield's prize story "The Fear That Walks by Noonday.")

SOME Antiquarian Notes. Naples, 1907. 56 pages, red wraps. (By Norman Douglas.) One of 250. $250.

SOME Papers Hand Made by John Mason. 100 numbered copies signed by John Mason. Enclosed in carboard box. $350.

SOMEBODY Had to Do Something. Los Angeles, 1939. Wraps. (Contains tributes to James P. Lardner, killed in the Spanish Civil War, including material by Ernest Hemingway and Ring Lardner, Jr.) $200.

SONN, Albert H. *Early American Wrought Iron.* New York, 1928. 3 vols. In dustwrappers. $600.

SOTHEBY, Samuel Leigh. *Principia Typographica.* London, 1858. 3 vols. 128 plates. One of 215 copies. $475.

SOULE, Frank, GIHON, Frank, and NISBET, James. *The Annals of San Francisco.* New York, 1855. 6 plates, 2 maps. Leather. $500.

SOUTAR, Daniel C. *Australian Golfer.* Sydney, 1906. $300.

SOUTH Carolina Jockey Club (The). Charleston, 1857. (By John B. Irving.) $250.

SOUTHERN, Terry. *Flash & Filigree.* (London, 1958). Author's first book. $150. New York (1958). In full cloth with dustwrapper price of "$3.50." $75.

SOUTHEY, Robert. See Bion and Moschus.

SOUTHEY, Robert. *All for Love; and The Pilgrim to Compostella.* London, 1829. $200.

SOUTHEY, Robert. *History of Brazil*... London, 1810–19. 3 vols., with folding map. $600.

SOUTHEY, Robert. *Poems* . . . (With Robert Lovell.) Bath, 1795. $2,000. Boston, 1799. $400.

SOUTHSPRING Ranch (The). Colorado Springs (1902?). Illustrated. 28 pages., wraps. $150.

SOUTH-WEST (The). By a Yankee. New York, 1835. (By Joseph Holt Ingraham, his first book.) 2 vols., in original cloth, paper labels. $500.

SOUTHWARD, John. *Artistic Printing.* London, 1892. Four plates (2 in color). $125.

SOUTHWARD, John. *The Principles and Progress of Printing Machinery.* London (no-date) (circa 1889). $125.

SOUTHWARD, John. *Progress in Printing and the Graphic Arts During the Victorian Era.* London, 1897. Stiff paper wraps. $175.

SOWELL, A. J. *Early Settlers and Indian Fighters of Southwest Texas.* Austin, 1900. 12 plates. $400.

SOWELL, A. J. *Rangers and Pioneers of Texas.* San Antonio, 1884. Illustrated. Pictorial cloth. $650.

SPALDING, C. C. *Annals of the City of Kansas.* Kansas City, 1858. 7 plates. $2,250.

SPARAGO, John. *Anthony Haswell: Printer, Patriot, Balladist.* Rutland, Vt., 1925. 300 signed and numbered copies. 35 facsimiles. $150.

SPARAGO, John. *The Potters and Potteries of Bennington.* Boston, 1926. Boards. Issued without dustwrapper. One of 800. $150.

SPARK, Muriel. See Camberg, Muriel.

SPARK, Muriel. *Child of Light.* Essex (1951). $150.

SPARK, Muriel. *The Fanfarlo . . .* Kent, 1952. Wraps. First issue, wraps printed in red. $100.

SPARK, Muriel. *Not to Disturb.* London, 1971. Illustrated. Boards and cloth. One of 500 signed, with an original etching by Michael Ayrton. In glassine dustwrapper. $300.

SPARK, Muriel. *The Prime of Miss Jean Brodie.* London, 1961. $175.

SPARKS, T. *Sunday Under Three Heads.* London, 1836. (By Charles Dickens). In original drab wraps. With the title at the beginning of chapter III on page 35 and "hair" spelled correctly in line 15 on page 7. $3,000.

SPARLING, H. Halliday. *The Kelmscott Press and William Morris, Master Craftsman.* London, 1924. 16 plates and portrait frontispiece of Morris. $150.

SPARROW, Walter Shaw. *A Book of Sporting Painters.* London (1931). 138 illustrations, some in color. Buckram. $200. One of 125 with 2 extra plates. $350.

SPARROW, Walter Shaw. *British Sporting Artists, from Barlow to Herring.* London (1922). 27 color plates, other illustrations. $250. Limited issue in buckram. One of 95 signed. $450.

SPAULDING, Thomas M., and KARPINSKY, Louis C. *Early Military Books in the University of Michigan Libraries.* Ann Arbor, 1941. $150.

SPEARMAN, Frank. *Nan of Music Mountain.* New York, 1916. In dustwrapper. $250.

SPEARMAN, Frank. *Whispering Smith.* New York, 1906. In dustwrapper. $300.

SPEARS, John R. *Illustrated Sketches of Death Valley and Other Borax Deserts of the Pacific Coast.* Chicago, 1892. Printed wraps. $300. Cloth. $200.

"SPEC." *Line Etchings.* St. Louis, 1875. (Pseudonym of Beverly R. Keim and William Weston.) $600.

SPECIMENS. (Canyon City, Ore. 1868.) 54 pp., pink wraps, stitched. (By Joaquin Miller—preface signed "C. H. Miller.") Author's first book, suppressed by him. $3,000.

SPECIMENS of Woodcuts and Engravings, A Portfolio of Original Leaves . . . (New York, 1926.) 15 folders each containing a leaf, enclosed in case. One of 120 copies. $550.

SPEER, Emory. *The Banks County Ku-Klux.* Atlanta, 1883. 60 pp., wraps. $200.

SPENCER, Elizabeth. *Fire in the Morning.* New York, 1948. Author's first novel. $400.

SPENCER, Elizabeth. *This Crooked Way.* New York (1952). $150. London, 1953. $100.

SPENCER, Mrs. George E. *Calamity Jane: A Story of the Black Hills.* New York (about 1887). (By William L. Spencer.) Frontispiece. Wraps. $250.

SPENCER, Herbert. *Education: Intellectual, Moral, and Physical.* New York, 1861. $150.

SPENCER, Herbert. *The Principles of Biology.* 2 vols. London, 1864–67. $300.

SPENCER, Herbert. *The Proper Sphere of Government.* London, 1843. Author's first book. $200.

SPENCER, Herbert. *Social Statics.* London, 1851. $200.

SPENCER, J. W. *Reminiscences of Pioneer Life in the Mississippi Valley.* Davenport, Iowa, 1872. Portrait. $125.

SPENCER, O. M. *Indian Captivity: A True Narrative of the Capture of . . .* Washington, Pa., 1835. In original gray wraps. First edition (?). $750. New York, 1835. $500. New York, 1836. Third edition. $150.

SPENDER, Stephen. See S., S. H.

SPENDER, Stephen. *Poems.* London (1933). $200. New York, 1934. $150.

SPENDER, Stephen. *Returning to Vienna 1947.* Banyan Press. (London, 1947.) Wraps. One of 500 signed. $150.

SPENDER, Stephen. *Twenty Poems.* Oxford (1930). Wraps. Signed copies (75 of 135). $750. Unsigned. $400.

SPENDER, Stephen. *Vienna.* London, 1934. $125.

SPENSER, Edmund. *Minor Poems.* Ashendene Press. London, 1925. One of 200 on paper. $1,500.

SPENSER, Edmund. *The Shepheardes Calender.* London, 1579. $70,000 at auction in 1990. Kelmscott Press. London, 1896. 12 woodcuts. Boards and linen. One of 225. $1,000. One of 6 on vellum, specially bound. $8,000. Cresset Press. London, 1930. Boards, vellum spine. One of 350. In dustwrapper and slipcase. $500.

SPEYER, Leonora. *Holy Night: A Yuletide Masque.* New York, 1919. Designs by Eric Gill. Stiff blue decorated wraps. Author's first book. One of 500. $75.

SPICER, A. Dykes. *The Paper Trade* . . . London (1907). $125.

SPICER, Jack. *After Lorca.* (San Francisco, 1957.) Wraps. Author's first separate book. 26 signed and lettered copies. $350. One of 474 copies. $150.

SPICER, Jack. *Correlation Methods of Comapring Idolects* . . . Author's first book with David W. Reed. (Offprint of "Language" 1952.) Wraps. (Fewer than 100 copies.) $1,250.

SPICER, Jack. *Lament for the Makers.* (Oakland, 1962.) Wraps. One of 100. $300.

SPIELMANN, M. H., and LAYARD, G. S. *Kate Greenaway.* London, 1905. 53 colored plates, other illustrations. White cloth. One of 500 with an original pencil sketch by Kate Greenaway inserted. $1,500. With sketch foxed. $800. Trade. Purple cloth. $300.

SPIELMANN, M. H., and JERROLD, Walter. *Hugh Thomson, His Art, His Letters, His Humour and His Charm.* London, 1931. 13 plates in color. $125.

SPILLANE, Mickey. *I, the Jury.* New York, 1947. Author's first book. $350.

SPILLANE, Mickey. *Kiss Me Deadly.* New York, 1952. $200.

SPILLANE, Mickey. *My Gun Is Quick.* New York, 1950. $275.

SPILLER, Robert E. *The Philobiblon Club of Philadelphia; The First Eighty Years, 1893–1973.* (North Hills), 1973. 275 numbered copies. $175.

SPILLER, Robert E., and BLACKBURN, Philip C. *A Descriptive Bibliography of the Writings of James Fenimore Cooper.* New York, 1934. One of 500 copies. $125.

SPIRIT of the Age (The). London, 1825. (By William Hazlitt.) $200.

SPORTSMAN'S Portfolio of American Field Sports (The). Boston, 1855. 20 full-page wood engravings, title page vignette, illustration at end. Oblong wraps. $2,500.

SPOTTS, David L. *Campaigning with Custer* . . . Los Angeles, 1928. Map, 13 plates. One of 800 (All but about 300 burned—Howes.) $200.

SPRAGUE, John T. *The Treachery in Texas.* New York, 1862. 35 pp., wraps. $125.

SPRINGARN, J. E. *A History of Literary Criticism in the Renaissance* . . . New York, 1899. Author's first book. $200.

SPRING, Agnes Wright. *The Cheyenne and Black Hills Stage and Express Routes.* Glendale, Calif., 1949. Map, 17 plates. Cloth. Issued without dustwrapper. $150.

SPRINGS, Elliot White. *Nocturne Militaire.* New York (1927). Author's first book. $250.

SPRINGS, Elliot White. *War Birds* . . . New York, 1926. Edited by Springs. His first publication. One of 210 signed copies. $400. Trade. $300.

SPY (The): A Tale of the Neutral Ground. New York, 1821. By the Author of *Precaution,* (James Fenimore Cooper.) 2 vols. $10,000. Limited Editions Club, New York, 1963. Cloth. In slipcase. $50.

SPYRI, Johanna. *Heidi.* Boston, 1885. Translated by Louise Brooks. First American edition. $450. Philadelphia, 1922. Illustrated by Jessie Wilcox. $200.

SQUIER, E. G., and DAVIS, E. H. *Ancient Monuments of the Mississippi Valley.* Washington, 1848. Map, 48 plates. Folio, cloth. $400. New York, 1848. Second issue. $350.

SQUIRE, J. C. *Socialism and Art.* London (1907). Author's first book. $150.

STACTON, David. *An Unfamiliar Country.* (Swinsford, 1953). Author's first book. Wraps. $250.

STAFFORD, Jean. *Boston Adventure.* New York (1944). Author's first book. $100.

STAFFORD, William E. *Down in My Heart.* Elgin, Ill. (1947). Green cloth. Author's first book. $850.

STAFFORD, William E. *Traveling Through the Dark.* New York (1962). $250.

STAFFORD, William E. *Weather.* Mt. Horeb, Wis. (1969). Wraps. One of 207. In dustwrapper. $150.

STAFFORD, William E. *West of Your City.* Los Gatos, 1960. $500. Wraps. $300.

STANFORD, Ann. *In Narrow Bound.* Gunnison (1943). Author's first book. Wraps. $125.

STANFORD, Don. *New England Earth...* San Francisco (1941). Author's first book. Wraps. $125.

STANLEY, David S. *Diary of a March from Fort Smith, Ark., to San Diego, Calif., Made in 1853.* No-place, no-date. 37 pp., multigraphed. In cloth case. $150.

STANLEY, F. *The Grant That Maxwell Bought.* (Denver, 1952.) Map, 15 plates. Cloth. (By Father Stanley Crocchiola.) One of 250 signed. $300.

STANSBERY, Lon R. *The Passing of 3D Ranch.* (Tulsa, 1930.) $300.

STANSBURY, Howard. *Exploration and Survey of the Valley of the Great Salt Lake of Utah...* Philadelphia, 1852. 57 plates (some folding). 3 folding maps with the 2 large maps bound in separate portfolio. $400.

STANSBURY, P. *A Pedestrian Tour of 2,300 Miles, in North America...* New York, 1822. 9 plates. $350.

STANTON, Schuyler. *Daughters of Destiny.* Chicago (1906). Red cloth. (By L. Frank Baum.) $250.

STAPLEDON, Olaf. *Darkness and the Light.* London (1942). $200.

STAPLEDON, Olaf. *Last and First Men...* London (1930). $500.

STAPLEDON, Olaf. *Latter-Day Psalms.* Liverpool, 1914. Author's first book. $150.

STAPLEDON, Olaf. *Star Maker.* London (1937). $350.

STAPLEDON, Olaf. *Walking World.* London (1934). $250.

STAPP, William P. *The Prisoners of Perote.* Philadelphia, 1845. Wraps. $1,000. Cloth. $750.

STAR City of the West (The): Pueblo and Its Advantages. Pueblo, Colo., 1889. 24 pp., folded. $150.

STARBUCK, Alexander. *History of the American Whale Fishery . . .* Waltham, Mass., 1878. 6 plates. $350. New York, 1964. 2 vols., half leather. Slipcase. One of 50. $300. Trade edition. 2 vols. Slipcase. $100.

STARK, Freya. *Baghdad Sketches.* Baghdad, 1932. Author's first book. $150.

STARKEY, James. *Reminiscences of Indian Depredations.* St. Paul, 1891. 25 pp., wraps. $150.

STARR, Julian. *The Disagreeable Woman.* New York, 1895. (By Horatio Alger, Jr.) $1,750 or more.

STARRETT, Vincent. *All About Mother Goose.* (Glen Rock, Pa.), 1930. One of 275. In glassine jacket. $150.

STARRETT, Vincent. *Arthur Machen: A Novelist of Ecstasy and Sin.* Chicago, 1918. Boards and cloth. Author's first book. One of 250. $200.

STARRETT, Vincent. *The Private Life of Sherlock Holmes.* New York, 1933. $250.

STARRETT, Vincent. *221B: Studies in Sherlock Holmes.* New York, 1940. $250.

STARRETT, Vincent. *The Unique Hamlet.* Chicago, 1920. Boards. One of 250. Issued without dustwrapper. $1,500.

STARRETT, Vincent (editor). *In Praise of Stevenson.* Chicago, 1919. One of 300. $150.

STATE of Indiana Delineated (The). New York, 1838. Boards, leather spine. (Published by J. H. Colton to accompany his separately published map, which is inserted in some copies.) With the map, $1,000. Without the map, $400.

STATEMENT Respecting the Earl of Selkirk's Settlement of Kildonan, upon the Red River, in North America. London (about 1817). (By John Halkett.) Folding map. 125 pp. $1,000. London, 1817. Second (enlarged) edition. 194 pp., boards. With title altered to *Statement Respecting the Earl of Selkirk's Settlement upon the Red River, in North America.* $750.

STATIONERS Catalogue, Tags and Specialties. South Framingham, 1910. $225.

STATIONERS' Hand-Book; and Guide to the Paper Trade. London, 1870. Fifth edition, revised and enlarged. $125.

STEAD, Christina. *The Salzburg Tales.* London (1934). Author's first book. $200. New York, 1934. $125.

STEADMAN, Ralph. *Still Life With Raspberry . . .* London, 1969. Author's first book. (50 signed copies with original drawings.) $350.

STEAM-BOAT (The). Edinburgh, 1822. (By John Galt.) $250.

STEARNS, Samuel. *The American Herbal or Materia Medica.* Walpole, N.H., 1801. $850.

STEDMAN, Charles. *The History of the Origin, Progress, and Termination of the American War . . .* London, 1794. 2 vols. 15 maps and plans (11 folding). $4,000.

STEDMAN, Edmund C. *Poems, Lyrical and Idyllic.* New York, 1860. Author's first book. $100.

STEDMAN, John G. *Narrative of a Five Years' Expedition Against the Revolted Negroes of Surinam in Guiana on the Wild Coast of America.* London, 1796. 2 vols. $1,250. London, 1813. 80 full-page colored engravings, 3 maps, and 1 folding plate. 2 vols. Third edition. $1,000.

STEEDMAN, Charles J. *Bucking the Sagebrush.* New York, 1904. 3 portraits, folding map, 9 Charles M. Russell plates. Pictorial cloth. $400.

STEEL, Flora A. (editor). *English Fairy Tales.* London, 1918. 16 color plates by Arthur Rackham. Vellum. One of 500 signed by Rackham. $1,000. Trade. Cloth. $200. New York, 1918. Half cloth. $200.

STEELE, James W. *The Klondike.* Chicago, 1897. Illustrated, 2 maps. 80 pp., pictorial gray wraps. $200.

STEELE, John. *Across the Plains in 1850.* Caxton Club. Chicago, 1930. 7 plates. Issued without dustwrapper. $125.

STEELE, John. *In Camp and Cabin: Mining Life and Adventure, in California . . .* Lodi, Wis., 1901. 81 pp., printed wraps. $450.

STEELE, R. J., and others (compilers). *Directory of the County of Placer.* San Francisco, 1861. Boards and calf. $850.

STEELE, Robert. *The Revival of Printing . . .* (London, 1912.) 350 numbered copies. $125.

STEELE, Zadock. *The Indian Captive.* Montpelier, Vt., 1818. $200.

STEFANSSON, Vilhjalmur. *My Life with the Eskimo.* New York, 1913. Author's first book. $175. London, 1913. (U.S. sheets.) $125.

STEFANSSON, Vilhjalmur. *Ultima Thule: Further Mysteries of the Arctic.* New York, 1940. Maps, illustrated. One of 100 signed. Issued without dustwrapper. $350.

STEFFENS, Lincoln. *John Reed Under the Kremlin.* Chicago, 1922. Introduction by Clarence Darrow. Wraps. One of 235. $300.

STEFFENS, Lincoln. *The Shame of the Cities.* New York, 1904. Author's first book. $150.

STEGNER, Wallace. *The Big Rock Candy Mountain.* New York, 1943. $150.

STEGNER, Wallace. *Clarence Edward Dutton: An Appraisal.* Salt Lake City (1935?). Author's first book. Wraps. $350.

STEGNER, Wallace. *Remembering Laughter.* Boston, 1937. $150.

STEIN, Gertrude. See Toklas, Alice B.

STEIN, Gertrude. *An Acquaintance with Description.* Seizin Press. London, 1929. Oyster white linen. One of 225 signed. In glassine dustwrapper. $400.

STEIN, Gertrude. *Before the Flowers of Friendship Faded Friendship Faded.* Paris (1931). Wraps. One of 118 signed (of an edition of 120). In glassine dustwrapper. $1,500.

STEIN, Gertrude. *Blood on the Dining Room Floor.* Banyan Press. (Pawlet, Vt., 1948.) Half buckram and boards. One of 26. In glassine dustwrapper and slipcase. $500. One of 600 in glassine dustwrapper and slipcase. $300.

STEIN, Gertrude. *A Book Concluding with as a Wife Has a Cow: A Love Story.* Paris (1926). 4 lithographs (one in color) by Juan Gris. Wraps. One of 102 signed. In glassine dustwrapper. $3,500. One of 10 on Japan vellum, signed. $7,500.

STEIN, Gertrude. *Composition as Explanation.* Hogarth Press. London, 1926. Green boards. Issued without dustwrapper. $250.

STEIN, Gertrude. *Dix Portraits.* Paris (1930). Translated by G. Hugnet and Virgil Thomson. Illustrated by Picasso and others. Decorated wraps. One of 10 on Japan vellum, signed, and with an autograph page of text by Stein. In glassine jacket. $3,500. One of 25 on Holland paper, signed by author and translators. In glassine dustwrapper. $1,500. One of 65 on Velin d'Arches paper, signed. In dustwrapper. $1,250. One of 402 on Alfa paper without illustrations. In printed dustwrapper plus glassine jacket. $450.

STEIN, Gertrude. *An Elucidation.* (Cover title.) (Paris) 1927. Wraps. (Issued as a supplement to *Transition* magazine after having been printed there with errors.) $200.

STEIN, Gertrude. *The Geographical History of America or The Relation of Human Nature to the Human Mind.* (New York, 1936.) Black and white cloth. $1,250.

STEIN, Gertrude. *Geography and Plays.* Boston (1922). Foreword by Sherwood Anderson. First binding, with lettering on front cover. $500. Second binding, cover unlettered. $350.

STEIN, Gertrude. *Have They Attacked Mary. He Giggled.* (West Chester, Pa., 1917.) Woodcut. Printed red wraps. One of 200. $850.

STEIN, Gertrude. *How to Write.* Paris (1931). Boards, paper labels on spine. One of 1,000. (Issued without dustwrapper.) $250.

STEIN, Gertrude. *Lucy Church Amiably.* Paris, 1930. Boards. In plain brown paper dustwrapper. $350.

STEIN, Gertrude. *The Making of Americans.* (Dijon, 1925.) Wraps. One of 500 (but only a portion released). $2,500. One of 5 on vellum, with a letter by Stein inserted. $10,000. New York, 1926. First American issue (bound up from French sheets). Issued without dustwrapper. $1,000.

STEIN, Gertrude. *Matisse Picasso and Gertrude Stein, with Two Shorter Stories.* Paris (1933). Wraps. In glassine dustwrapper and slipcase. $400.

STEIN, Gertrude. *Narration: Four Lectures.* Chicago (1935). Introduction by Thornton Wilder. Blue, black and gilt cloth. One of 120 signed by Stein and Wilder. In slipcase. $850. Trade (unsigned). Orange cloth. $250.

STEIN, Gertrude. *Operas and Plays.* Paris (1932). Wraps. In slipcase. $600.

STEIN, Gertrude. *Picasso.* Paris, 1938. Illustrated. Pictorial wraps. $300. London (1938). Rose-colored cloth. First English edition. $200. (New York), 1939. $175.

STEIN, Gertrude. *Portrait of Mabel Dodge at the Villa Curonia.* (Florence, 1912.) Stitched wraps. With imprint at foot of last page. $1,500.

STEIN, Gertrude. *Portraits and Prayers.* New York (1934). Pictorial cloth. In cellophane dustwrapper. $250.

STEIN, Gertrude. *Tender Buttons. Objects. Food. Rooms.* New York, 1914. Boards, paper label. (Issued without dustwrapper.) $500.

STEIN, Gertrude. *Three Lives.* New York, 1909. Author's first book. Blue cloth. (1,000 printed; issued without dustwrapper.) $1,250. New York and London, 1915. First English issue (300 from American sheets, with new title page). $1,000. London, 1920. First English trade edition in dustwrapper. $350.

STEIN, Gertrude. *Useful Knowledge.* New York (1928). $250. London (1928). First English edition. $200.

STEIN, Gertrude. *A Village Are You Ready Yet Not Yet.* Paris (1928). Illustrated by Elie Lascaux. Wraps. One of 102 signed. In glassine dustwrapper. $1,750. One of 10 on Japan vellum, signed. $4,500.

STEIN, Gertrude. *What Are Masterpieces?* (Los Angeles, 1940.) Portrait frontispiece. Blue cloth. $200. One of 50 or so signed. $750.

STEIN, Gertrude. *The World Is Round.* New York (1939). Illustrated by Clement Hurd. Boards. One of 350 signed. In slipcase. $600. Trade. $200. London (1939). First English edition. $150.

STEINBECK, John. See *El Gabilan.*

STEINBECK, John. *Bombs Away.* New York, 1942. (Note: "Second Printing" on bottom of rear panel of dustwrapper of that later printing.) $175.

STEINBECK, John. *Cannery Row.* New York, 1945. Light buff cloth. $150. Second issue in yellow cloth. $100. London/Toronto (1945). Strong orange-yellow cloth (variants: brilliant orange-yellow and deep orange cloth). $150.

STEINBECK, John. *Cup of Gold: A Life of Henry Morgan, Buccaneer.* McBride. New York, 1929. Author's first book. First issue, top edges stained blue and "First Published August, 1929" on copyright page. $4,000. Second issue, Covici-Friede. New York (1936). Maroon cloth, spine stamped in gilt: using McBride sheets. $450. Second printing, New York (1936). blue cloth. $150. London/Toronto (1937). Blue cloth, spine stamped in gilt. $1,250.

STEINBECK, John. *East of Eden.* New York, 1952. 1,500 signed copies (750 for private distribution). Issued in glassine dustwrapper and slipcase. $1,000. Trade. $200. London (1952). $125.

STEINBECK, John. *The First Watch.* (Los Angeles), 1947. 60 numbered copies. Buff wraps with hand-ties in envelope. $2,000.

STEINBECK, John. *The Grapes of Wrath.* New York (1939). Dustwrapper states "First Edition" on lower right corner of front flap. $1,500. London/Toronto (1939). $250. Limited Editions Club, New York, 1940. 1,146 copies signed by the illustrator, Thomas Hart Benton. 2 vols. Issued in glassine dustwrapper in slipcase. $600.

STEINBECK, John. *How Edith McGillcuddy Met RLS.* Cleveland, 1943. 152 numbered copies. Issued in plain green dustwrapper. $2,500. Without dustwrapper. $2,250.

STEINBECK, John. *In Dubious Battle.* New York (1936). 99 signed and numbered copies. In tissue dustwrapper and black slipcase with orange paper label printed in black. $3,500. Lettered copies. $5,000. Trade. Top edges stained red. $750. London/ Toronto (1936). $500.

STEINBECK, John. *Foreword to "Between Pacific Tides."* (Stanford) 1948. Wraps. (Estimated at 10 copies in Harvard Library Catalog and at 25 copies by Cohn in a letter to Hersholt.) $6,000.

STEINBECK, John. *The Log from the Sea of Cortez.* New York, 1951. New title of *Sea of Cortez* with narrative portion only "About Ed Ricketts" by Steinbeck. Various cloth colors with maroon being the preferred. $300. London (1958). $150.

STEINBECK, John. *The Long Valley.* New York, 1938. $350. London/Toronto (1939). $250.

STEINBECK, John. *The Moon Is Down.* New York, 1942. Without printer's name on copyright page. Large period between "talk" and "this" on page 112, line 11. $150. "Haddon of Kingsport" on copyright page and period deleted. $75. London/ Toronto (1942). Terra-cotta cloth. $100.

STEINBECK, John. *Of Mice and Men.* First issue/printing. Page 88 has bullet between the *8*s. "and only moved because the heavy hands were pendula," page 9, lines 20–21. $450. Second issue/printing, with line 21 on page 9 reading "loosely." and bullet on page 88 deleted. $150. London/Toronto (1937). Blue cloth, spine stamped in gilt, top edges stained blue, blue dustwrapper printed in black. (Some copies with wraparound band.) (Also a variant with pink top edge and dustwrapper printed in black.) $500. Limited Editions Club, New York, 1970. 1,500 copies signed by the illustrator, Fletcher Martin. Issued in slipcase. $125.

STEINBECK, John. *Of Mice and Men: A Play.* New York (1937). Beige cloth, top edges stained blue. First-issue dustwrapper (reportedly) without reviews on back panel. $500.

STEINBECK, John. *The Pastures of Heaven.* Brewer, Warren & Putnam. New York, 1932. Green cloth, front cover stamped in gilt, top edges stained black. $3,500. Robert O. Ballou imprint on cloth spine, dustwrapper still has Brewer imprint. $1,250. Ballou on book spine and dustwrapper. $1,000. London (1933). Green cloth, spine printed in black. $1,000. Covici-Friede. New York (no-date). $500.

STEINBECK, John. *The Red Pony.* New York, 1937. 699 signed and numbered copies. Flexible beige cloth, clear cellophane dustwrapper, in tan slipcase with limitation number on spine. $850. 52(?) lettered copies (have seen "H" and "QQ" catalogued). $1,750.

STEINBECK, John. *Saint Katy the Virgin.* (New York, 1936.) 199 signed and numbered copies. Issued in decorated boards, gilt cloth spine printed in red, in glassine dustwrapper. $2,000.

STEINBECK, John. *Tortilla Flat.* New York (1935). Tan cloth printed in blue, top edges stained blue. $750. London (1935). Blue cloth stamped in gilt. $750.

STEINBECK, John. *The Wayward Bus.* New York, 1947. Dark reddish orange cloth with blind-stamped bus showing up lighter than rest of binding. $125. London/ Toronto (1947). Coarse red cloth. $75.

STEINBECK, John, and RICKETTS, Edward F. *Sea of Cortez.* New York, 1941. Green cloth, top edges stained orange. $400.

STEPHENS, Mrs. Ann S. *Malaeska: The Indian Wife of the White Hunter.* New York (1860). Printed orange wraps. First issue, with covers 6⅝ by 4½ inches, and without woodcut on cover. $400.

STEPHENS, Ann Sophia. *High Life in New York.* (New York, 1843.) Wraps. Author's first separate book. $150.

STEPHENS, Ann Sophia (editor). *The Portland Sketch Book.* Portland, Me., 1836. In original cloth. Author's first book appearance. $150.

STEPHENS, James. See Esse, James.

STEPHENS, James. *Collected Poems.* London, 1926. Boards and vellum. One of 500 large paper copies, signed. $200.

STEPHENS, James. *The Crock of Gold.* London, 1912. Green cloth. $150. London, 1926. Illustrated. Half vellum. One of 525 signed. In dustwrapper. $400. Limited Editions Club, New York, 1942. In slipcase. $60.

STEPHENS, James. *Green Branches.* Dublin, 1916. Wraps. One of 500. $100. New York, 1916. Half vellum. First American edition. One of 500. $100.

STEPHENS, James. *The Insurrection in Dublin.* London, 1916. $125.

STEPHENS, James. *Insurrections.* Dublin, 1909. Author's first book. In dustwrapper priced "1/-net" and single imprint of Maunsel. $600. In dustwrapper, without price and with both Maunsel and MacMillan on front (second printing). $250. Without dustwrapper. $100.

STEPHENS, James. *Irish Fairy Tales.* London, 1920. Illustrated by Arthur Rackham. Vellum and boards. One of 520 signed by Rackham. $1,000. Trade. $200.

STEPHENS, John L. *Incidents of Travel in Central America, Chiapas and Yucatan.* New York, 1841. Folding map, other maps and plans, plates, other illustrations. 2 vols., cloth. $450.

STEPHENS, Lorenzo Dow. *Life Sketches of a Jayhawker of '49.* (San Jose) 1916. 6 plates. 68 pp., printed wraps. $250.

STERLING, George. *Ode on the Opening of the Panama-Pacific International Exposition . . .* San Francisco, 1915. Boards and cloth. One of 525. $125.

STERLING, George. *The Testimony of the Suns and Other Poems.* San Francisco, 1903. Black cloth. Author's first book. $125. San Francisco, 1927. John Henry Nash printing. Folio, boards. One of 300. (Facsimile of title poem with comments by Ambrose Bierce.) $200.

STERLING, George. *To a Girl Dancing.* Grabhorn Press. (San Francisco, 1921.) Printed boards. Issued without dustwrapper. One of 120. $250.

STERLING, George. *Truth.* Chicago, 1923. One of 285 signed. $200.

STERLING, George, TAGGARD, Genevieve, and RORTY, James. *Continent's End: An Anthology of Contemporary California Poets.* Book Club of California. San Francisco, 1925. Boards, pigskin spine. One of 600.

STERLING Library (The), A Catalogue of the Printed Books... (No-place) 1954. $125.

STERN, James. *The Heartless Land.* London, 1932. Author's first book. (First regular publication.) $200.

STERNE, Laurence. *A Sentimental Journey Through France and Italy.* London, 1768. 2 vols. $2,000. Black Sun Press. Paris, 1929. Illustrated by Polia Chentoff. Wraps. One of 335 on Arches paper. In tissue jacket and slipcase. $400.

STERNE, Laurence. *The Life and Opinions of Tristram Shandy.* London, 1760–67. 9 vols. $4,000. Golden Cockerel Press. Waltham St. Lawrence, 1929–30. Illustrated. 3 vols., cloth. One of 500. $300. Limited Editions Club, New York, 1935. 2 vols. In slipcase. $75.

STEVENS, C. A. *Berdan's United States Sharpshooters in the Army of the Potomac.* St. Paul, 1892. Illustrated. $350.

STEVENS, Henry. *American Books With Tails to 'Em . . .* London, 1873. $100.

STEVENS, Henry. *Recollections of Mr. James Lenox of New York and the Formation of His Library.* London, 1886. Large paper copy on Whatman paper. Three portraits done in proof on India paper. $125.

STEVENS, Henry. *Who Spoils Our New English Books.* London, 1884. $125.

STEVENS, Isaac I. *Campaigns of the Rio Grande and of Mexico.* New York, 1851. 108 pp., wraps. $600.

STEVENS, Isaac I. *A Circular Letter to Emigrants Desirous of Locating in Washington Territory.* Washington, 1858. 21 pp., sewn. $350.

STEVENS, Wallace. See *Harvard Lyrics; Verses from the Harvard Advocate.*

STEVENS, Wallace. *The Auroras of Autumn.* New York, 1950. $175.

STEVENS, Wallace. *The Collected Poems of Wallace Stevens.* New York, 1954. First collected edition. $150.

STEVENS, Wallace. *Esthétique du Mal.* Cummington Press. (Cummington, Mass.), 1945. Illustrated by Wightman Williams. Half leather. One of 40 signed by author and artist. In glassine dustwrapper. $3,000. Ordinary copies (300), unsigned. $1,000.

STEVENS, Wallace. *Harmonium.* New York, 1923. Author's first book. First binding in checkered boards. $1,500. Second binding in striped boards. $750. Third binding: blue cloth. $500. New York, 1931. $300.

STEVENS, Wallace. *Ideas of Order.* (Alcestis Press.) New York, 1935. One of 165 signed. In glassine dustwrapper and slipcase. $1,500. Knopf. New York, 1936. First edition stated. First binding in striped cloth. $600. In rose-colored boards. $500. In yellow boards. $400.

STEVENS, Wallace. *The Man with the Blue Guitar & Other Poems.* New York, 1937. First issue dustwrapper, with "conjunctioning" on front flap. $1,250.

STEVENS, Wallace. *The Necessary Angel.* New York, 1951. $200.

STEVENS, Wallace. *Notes Toward a Supreme Fiction.* Cummington, Mass., 1942. One of 190. In acetate dustwrapper. $500. One of 80 signed. $1,500. Cummington (1943). Boards. Second edition. One of 330. In plain paper jacket. $250.

STEVENS, Wallace. *Owl's Clover.* New York (1936). Wraps. One of 105 signed. $2,500.

STEVENS, Wallace. *Parts of a World.* New York, 1942. $300.

STEVENS, Wallace. *A Primitive Like an Orb.* New York, 1948. Illustrated by Kurt Seligmann. Olive green wraps. One of 500. $350.

STEVENS, Wallace. *Raoul Dufy: A Note.* (New York, 1953.) 4 pp., wraps. One of 200. $750.

STEVENS, Wallace. *Transport to Summer.* New York, 1947. $350.

STEVENSON, R. Randolph, M. D. *The Southern Side: or, Andersonville Prison.* Baltimore, 1876. $175.

STEVENSON, Robert Louis. See *The Pentland Rising.*

STEVENSON, Robert Louis. *Across the Plains.* London, 1892. Cream-colored cloth. One of 100 on large paper. $250. (Hillsborough, Calif., 1950.) Allen Press. Illustrated. Boards. One of 200. $300.

STEVENSON, Robert Louis. *The Black Arrow.* London, 1888. First English edition. Wraps. $400. Cloth. $200. New York, 1916. Illustrated by N. C. Wyeth. $150.

STEVENSON, Robert Louis. *Catriona, A Sequel to "Kidnapped."* London, 1893. $200.

STEVENSON, Robert Louis. *A Child's Garden of Verses.* London, 1885. Blue cloth. $1,000. New York, 1885. $350. London, 1896. Illustrated by Charles Robinson. First illustrated edition. One of 150 large paper copies. $600. Trade. $200. Limited Editions Club, New York, 1944. In slipcase. $125.

STEVENSON, Robert Louis. *Father Damien.* Sydney, Australia, 1890. Wraps, stapled. One of 25. $2,000. Edinburgh, 1890. Unbound sheets in board portfolio. One of 30 on vellum. $400. London, 1890. Wraps. First published edition. $200. San Francisco, 1930. John Henry Nash printing. 2 vols., half vellum. $300.

STEVENSON, Robert Louis. *The Graver & the Pen, or Scenes from Nature with Appropriate Verses.* Edinburgh (1882). Woodcuts. Gray wraps. $750.

STEVENSON, Robert Louis. *An Inland Voyage.* London, 1878. Frontispiece by Walter Crane. Blue cloth. Author's first novel. $600.

STEVENSON, Robert Louis. *Island Nights' Entertainments.* New York, 1893. $250. London, 1893. First English edition, first issue, with price correction in ink in list of Stevenson's works. $250.

STEVENSON, Robert Louis. *Kidnapped.* (London), 1886. Folding frontispiece map. Issued in various colors of cloth. First issue with the reading "business" in line 11 of page 40 and ads dated "5.G. 4.86" and "5.B. 4.86." $1,250. Second printing with the reading "pleasure" on line 11 of page 40. $500. New York, 1913. Illustrated by N. C. Wyeth. $200. Limited Editions Club, New York, 1938. In slipcase. $75.

STEVENSON, Robert Louis. *The Master of Ballantrae*. London, 1889. Red cloth. $250. Limited Editions Club (New York), 1965. In slipcase. $75.

STEVENSON, Robert Louis. *The Merry Men and Other Tales and Fables*. London, 1887. Decorated blue cloth. With 32 pages of ads at end dated September 1886. $300.

STEVENSON, Robert Louis. *New Arabian Nights*. London, 1882. 2 vols., green cloth. First issue, with yellow endpapers in vol. 1. and ads in vol. 2 dated May 1882. $600.

STEVENSON, Robert Louis. *The Silverado Squatters*. London, 1883. Decorated green cloth. First issue, with 32-page catalogue dated October 1883 at back. $500. Grabhorn Press. San Francisco, 1952. Boards and cloth. One of 900. In original plain wrapper. $200.

STEVENSON, Robert Louis. *The Strange Case of Dr. Jekyll and Mr. Hyde*. London, 1886. First issue, in wraps, with the date on front cover altered in ink from 1885 to 1886. $4,000. Cloth. $1,500. New York, 1886. Wraps. $1,200. Cloth. $750. Limited Editions Club, New York, 1952. Marbled boards. In slipcase. $125.

STEVENSON, Robert Louis. *Ticonderoga*. Edinburgh, 1887. Vellum boards. One of 50. $500. (A Thomas J. Wise forgery.)

STEVENSON, Robert Louis. *Travels with a Donkey in the Cevennes*. London, 1879. Frontispiece by Walter Crane. Green cloth. $500. Limited Editions Club, New York, 1957. In slipcase. $75.

STEVENSON, Robert Louis. *Treasure Island*. London, 1883. Green, gray, blue, or rust-colored cloth. First(?) issue, with "rain" for "vain" in last line of page 40, "dead man's chest" on page 2, line 7 not capitalized and ads dated July 1883. $2,500. Boston, 1884. Frontispiece map, illustrated. Pictorial cloth. First American (and first illustrated) edition. $1,000. London, 1885. Illustrated. Red cloth. First English illustrated edition. $500. London, 1927. Illustrated by Edmund Dulac. Vellum. One of 50 signed. $1,000. Trade. Cloth. $200. New York (1927). Dulac illustrations. First American trade edition. $200. Philadelphia, 1930. Illustrated by Lyle Justis. Tan cloth. In dustwrapper and slipcase. $150. Limited Editions Club, New York, 1941. In slipcase. $150. Extra lithograph bound in. $200. London, 1949. Illustrated by Mervyn Peake. In dustwrapper. $300.

STEVENSON, Robert Louis, and OSBOURNE, Lloyd. *The Wrecker*. London, 1892. $200.

STEVENSON, Robert Louis, and VAN DE GRIFT, Fanny. *More New Arabian Nights. The Dynamiter*. London, 1885. Cloth. $250. Green pictorial wraps. $350.

STEWART, James Lindsey (editor). *Golfiania Miscellanea*. London, 1887. $600.

STEWART, Sir William Drummond. See *Altowan*.

STIFF, Edward. *The Texan Emigrant*. Cincinnati, 1840. Folding map in color. Cloth. $1,350.

STILL, James. *Hounds on the Mountain*. New York, 1937. Author's first book. One of 700. $150. One of 50 numbered copies, not for sale. $250.

STILL, James. *River of Earth*. New York, 1940. $125.

STILLMAN, Jacob D. B. B. *The Horse in Motion, as Shown by Instantaneous Photography.* Boston, 1882. 107 plates, 9 in color, by Eadweard Muybridge. $750. London, 1882. $500.

STILLWELL, Margaret Bingham. *Gutenberg and the Catholicon of 1460.* New York, 1936. Folio, cloth. With an original leaf of the *Catholicon* printed by Gutenberg in 1460. In slipcase. $3,000.

STIPP, G. W. (compiler). *The Western Miscellany.* Xenia, Ohio, 1827. $3,500.

STIRLING, James. *Letters from the Slave States.* London, 1857. Map. $300.

STOCKTON, Frank R. *The Floating Prince and Other Fairy Tales.* New York, 1881. $300.

STOCKTON, Frank R. *The Great War Syndicate.* Collier. New York, 1889. Printed wraps. $150.

STOCKTON, Frank R. *The Lady, or the Tiger? and Other Stories.* New York, 1884. Pictorial gray and brown cloth. $250.

STOCKTON, Frank R. *Tales Out of School.* New York, 1876. Illustrated. Pictorial cloth. $150.

STOCKTON, Frank R. *Ting-a-Ling.* New York, 1870. Illustrated. Pictorial purple cloth. Author's first book. $300.

STODDARD, Maj. Amos. *Sketches, Historical and Descriptive of Louisiana.* Philadelphia, 1812. $400.

STODDARD, Herbert L. *The Bob-White Quail . . .* New York, 1931. One of 260 signed, and with an original drawing signed by Frank W. Benson. $600.

STODDARD, Richard Henry. *Footprints.* New York, 1849. Author's first book. Wraps. $1,500.

STOCKER, Bram. *Dracula.* Westminster (London), 1897. Yellow cloth. First issue, without ads. $3,000. Second issue, with ads at back. $2,500. New York, 1899. Pictorial cloth. First American edition. $850. Limited Editions Club, New York, 1965. In slipcase. $150.

STOKER, Bram. *The Lady of the Shroud.* London, 1909. $200.

STOKER, Bram. *Under the Sunset.* London, 1882. $300.

STOKES, I. N. Phelps. *The Iconography of Manhattan Island.* New York, 1915–28. Many plates, some in color. 6 vols. One of 360. In dustwrapper and slipcase. $4,500. One of 42 on Japan vellum. $7,500.

STOKES, I. N. Phelps, and HASKELL, Daniel C. *American Historical Prints: Early Views of American Cities.* New York, 1932. $600. New York, 1933. $500.

STONE, Henry A. *Wrestling Intercollegiate and Olympic.* New York, 1939. $60.

STONE, Herbert Stuart. *First Editions of American Authors.* Cambridge, 1893. $100.

STONE, Irving. *Pageant of Youth.* New York, 1933. Author's first book. $125.

STONE, Robert. *A Hall of Mirrors.* Boston, 1967. Author's first book. $300. London (1968). $150.

STONE, Wilbur Macey. *The Gigantick Histories of Thomas Boreman.* Portland, 1933. 250 signed and numbered copies. $100.

STOPPARD, Tom. *Lord Malquist and Mr. Moon.* London (1966). Author's first book. $150. New York, 1968. $75.

STOREY, David. *This Sporting Life.* (London, 1960.) Author's first book. $125.

STORY, Joseph. *The Power of Solitude.* Boston (1800). Author's first book. $200.

STOUT, Rex. *Fer-de-Lance.* New York, 1934. (First of the Nero Wolfe detective novels.) $3,500. London, 1935. $1,000.

STOUT, Rex. *How Like a God.* New York, 1929. Author's first book. $600.

STOUT, Rex. *The League of Frightened Men.* New York (1935). $2,750. London, 1935. $600.

STOUT, Rex. *Over My Dead Body.* New York (1940). $1,000. London, 1940. $150.

STOUT, Rex. *Some Buried Caesar.* New York (1939). $1,250. London, 1939. $250.

STOUT, Rex. *Too Many Cooks.* New York (1938). $1,500. London, 1938. $350. Also: Same title *American* magazine (no-place), 1938. Consisting of a box shaped like a book, in dustwrapper. Box contains title page and cards laid in as follows: "Important" note from Nero Wolfe, "menu," and 34 menu cards. The dustwrapper is attached to the back of the box. $1,500.

STOWE, Harriet Beecher. See Beecher, Harriet Elizabeth.

STOWE, Harriet Beecher. *Dred: A Tale of the Great Dismal Swamp.* Boston, 1856. 2 vols. $400.

STOWE, Harriet Beecher. *A Key to Uncle Tom's Cabin.* Boston, 1853. Wraps. $200. Cloth. $125.

STOWE, Harriet Beecher. *Uncle Sam's Emancipation.* Philadelphia, 1853. $150.

STOWE, Harriet Beecher. *Uncle Tom's Cabin.* Boston, 1852. Title vignette, 6 plates. 2 vols. First issue, pictorial wraps, with slug of Hobart and Robbins on copyright page. (Later "George C. Rand.") $7,500. First printing, second issue (cloth) binding. $3,500. Also, "Gift" binding of gilt-decorated brown cloth. $5,000. Cassell. London, 1852. Illustrated by George Cruikshank. 13 parts, pictorial wraps. First English edition. $1,000. London, 1852. Cloth. First English book edition, with Cassell imprint. $600. Limited Editions Club, New York, 1938. Marbled boards and leather. In slipcase. $300.

STOWER, Caleb. *The Compositor's and Pressman's Guide to the Art of Printing* . . . London, 1808. $325.

STRACHEY, Lytton. *Books and Characters.* London, 1922. $150.

STRACHEY, Mrs. Richard. *Nursery Lyrics.* London, 1893. Author's first book. $200. (Reissued with new title page and binding—"Lady Strachey.")

STRAHORN, Mrs. Carrie A. *15,000 Miles by Stage* . . . New York, 1911. Numerous illustrations, including 4 in color by Charles M. Russell. $450. New York, 1915. Second edition. $250.

STRAHORN, Robert E. *The Hand-book of Wyoming, and Guide to the Black Hills and Big Horn Regions.* Cheyenne, 1877. 14 plates. 272 pp., printed wraps. $500. Cloth. $300.

STRAHORN, Robert E. *Montana and Yellowstone National Park.* Kansas City, 1881. 191 pp., flexible cloth wraps, plus 14 pp. ads. $300.

STRAHORN, Robert E. *The Resources of Montana Territory.* Helena, 1879. Map. Cloth. $250.

STRAHORN, Robert E. *To the Rockies and Beyond* . . . Omaha, 1878. Folding map. Wraps. $500. Cloth. $350. Omaha, 1879. Cloth. Second edition. $250.

STRAND, Mark. *Sleeping with One Eye Open.* Stone Wall Press. Iowa City, 1963. Author's first book. One of 225. In acetate dustwrapper. $300.

STRANG, William. *The Earth Fiend.* London, 1892. Etchings by the author. Buckram. One of 150 signed. $350.

STRANGE, Edward F. *The Colour-Prints of Hiroshige* . . . London, 1925. 16 colored, 36 plain plates. Buckram. In dustwrapper. $350. Vellum. One of 250. $600.

STRANGER in Lowell (The). Boston, 1845. (By John Greenleaf Whittier.) Wraps. $350. Cloth. (Not in Johnson, but at auction in 1988.) $300.

STRATTON, R. B. *Captivity of the Oatman Girls* . . . San Francisco, 1857. Woodcut portrait and map. 231 pp., printed wraps. Second edition of *Life Among the Indians* (entry following). $1,250. Chicago, 1857. (Reprint.) $600. New York, 1858. 3 plates. Third edition, enlarged. $350.

STRATTON, R. B. *Life Among the Indians.* San Francisco, 1857. Illustrated. 183 pp., wraps. $3,000. Grabhorn Press. San Francisco, 1935. Plates, Half cloth. One of 550. $125. (See preceding entry.)

STRAUB, Peter. *Ishmael.* London (1972). Author's first book. Wraps. One of 100 signed copies in dustwrapper. $300.

STRAUS, Ralph. *The Unspeakable Curll, Being Some Account of Edmund Curll, Bookseller* . . . New York/London, 1928. One of 525 copies. $100.

STRAUSS, David Friedrich. *The Life of Jesus.* London, 1846. 3 vols., blue-green cloth. (Translated by George Eliot [Mary Ann Evans].) First edition in English. George Eliot's first book. $2,500.

STREET, Cecil John Charles. See Rhode, John.

STREET, George Edmund. *Brick and Marble in the Middle Ages.* London, 1855. Author's first book. $500.

STREETER, Floyd Benjamin. *Prairie Trails and Cow Towns.* Boston (1936). 12 plates. $250.

STREETER, Thomas W. See *Americana-Beginnings.*

STREETER, Thomas W. *Bibliography of Texas.* Cambridge, Mass., 1955–56–60. 5 vols. Part I, 2 vols; part II, 1 vol.; part III, 2 vols. One of 600. In dustwrapper. $850.

STREETER, Thomas W. (sale). *The Celebrated Collection of Americana Formed by the Late Thomas Winthrop Streeter.* New York, 1966–69. 8 vols. (including index). $750.

STRIBLING, T. S. *The Cruise of the Dry Dock.* Chicago (1917). 4 color illustrations. Author's first book. $125.

STRICKLAND, William. *Reports on Canals, Railways, Roads, and Other Subjects* . . . Philadelphia, 1826. Plates. $1,000.

STRICTURES on a Voyage to South America, as Indicated by the "Secretary of the (Late) Mission" to La Plata . . . Baltimore, 1820. By a Friend of Truth and Sound Policy. (By H. M. Brackenridge.) $200.

STRONG, L. A. G. *Dallington Rhymes.* Author's first book. (200 copies privately printed, 1919.) $300.

STRONG, L. A. G. *Dublin Days.* Oxford, 1921. Wraps. $75.

STRONG, L. A. G. *The Jealous Ghost.* London, 1930. One of 75 signed. In dustwrapper. $150.

STRONG, Gen. W. E. *A Trip to the Yellowstone National Park in July, August, and September, 1875.* Washington, 1876. 2 folding maps, 7 signed photos, 7 plates. Half morocco. $1,000.

STRUTT, Joseph. *A Biographical Dictionary.* London, 1785, 1786. 2 vols. $600.

STUART, Granville. *Forty Years on the Frontier.* Cleveland, 1925. 15 plates. 2 vols. $400.

STUART, H. *We Have Kept the Faith.* Dublin, 1923. Author's first book. $350.

STUART, Jesse. *Beyond Dark Hills.* New York, 1938. $200. New York (1972). Pictorial cloth. One of 950 signed. In slipcase. $125.

STUART, Jesse. *Harvest of Youth.* Howe, Okla. (1930). 80 pp. Author's first book. Possibly as few as 20 copies according to Stuart. $2,000.

STUART, Jesse. *Head O'W-Hollow.* New York, 1936. $400.

STUART, Jesse. *Man with a Bulls-Tongue Plow.* (New York, 1934.) $400.

STUART, Jesse. *Men of the Mountains.* New York, 1941. $500.

STUART, Jesse. *Taps for Private Tussie.* New York, 1943. First edition stated. $150.

STUART, Joseph A. *My Roving Life.* Auburn, Calif., 1895. 2 vols. $1,250.

STUART, Robert. *The Discovery of the Oregon Trail.* New York, 1935. Edited by Philip Ashton Rollins. $250.

STUDER, Jacob H. *The Birds of North America.* New York, 1888. 119 color plates. Folio, morocco. $750. New York, 1903. Half leather. $350.

STUDER, Jacob H. *Studer's Popular Ornithology: The Birds of North America.* New York and Columbus, (1874–78). 2 vols. $1,250.

STURGEON, Theodore. *More Than Human.* New York (1953). $250. Wraps. $35.

STURGEON, Theodore. *Without Sorcery.* Philadelphia (1948). Author's first book. $125. Red buckram. One of 80 signed. In slipcase. $500.

STURGIS, Thomas. *Common Sense View of the Sioux War.* Cheyenne, 1877. 52 pp., wraps. $350.

STYRON, William. *The Confessions of Nat Turner.* New York (1967). 500 signed and numbered copies. Issued in slipcase. $250. Trade edition with extra leaf signed. $125. Trade. $50. London (1968). $50. Franklin Press, 1976. "Limited" edition (not signed). $50. Franklin Library, 1979. Signed limited edition. $75.

STYRON, William. *Lie Down in Darkness.* Indianapolis (1951). First edition stated. Author's first book. $200. London (1952). $150. Franklin Library. Signed "limited" edition. $75.

STYRON, William. *Sophie's Choice.* New York, 1979. 500 signed and numbered copies. Issued without dustwrapper in slipcase. $150. Trade edition with extra leaf "Advance Presention Edition" bound in. Light blue cloth in tissue dustwrapper. $50. Franklin Library, 1979. "Limited Edition." $40. Trade. Maroon cloth. $30. London, 1979. $40.

SUGDEN, Alan V. *A History, of English Wallpaper, 1509–1914.* New York or London (1925). 70 color plates and 190 half-tone illustrations. Folio, blue buckram. In dustwrapper and slipcase. $600.

SULLIVAN, James. *The History of the District of Maine.* Boston, 1795. Folding frontispiece map. $1,500.

SULLIVAN, Louis H. *A System of Architectural Ornament.* New York, 1924. Illustrated. Folio, half cloth. One of 1,000. $600.

SULLIVAN, Maurice S. *The Travels of Jedediah Smith . . .* Santa Ana, Calif., 1934. With 2 plates and folding map. Pictorial cloth. Issued without dustwrapper. $500.

SULLIVAN, W. John L. *Twelve Years in the Saddle for Law and Order on the Frontiers of Texas.* Austin, 1909. 13 plates. $225.

SULZBERGER, Cyrus. *The Resistentialists.* New York (1962). (Suppressed because of the author's unauthorized use of three Ernest Hemingway letters.) $600.

SUMMERS, Montague. See Scot, Reginald; Sinistrari, Ludovico.

SUMNER, Charles. *'Cross The Plains.* (San Francisco, 1869). Folding map. Wraps. $200.

SUMNER, James. *The Mysterious Marbler.* North Hills, 1976. One of 250 copies. With 11 original marbled samples. $450.

SUNDERLAND, LaRoy. *Mormonism Exposed and Refuted.* New York, 1838. 54 pp., printed wraps. $1,750.

SUPERNATURALISM of New England (The). New York, 1847. (By John Greenleaf Whittier—his name on cover but not on title page.) Printed wraps. $350.

SURTEES, Robert Smith. See *The Analysis of the Hunting Field; "Ask Mama"; Hawbuck Grange; Jorrocks' Jaunts and Jollities; Mr. Facey Romiford's Hounds; Mr. Sponge's Sporting Tour; "Plain or Ringlets?"*

SUTHERLAND, Thomas A. *Howard's Campaign Against the Nez Percé Indians.* Portland, Ore., 1878. 48 pp., wraps. $850.

SUTPHEN, William. *Golfer's Alphabet.* New York, 1898. (Sketches by A.B. Frost.) $400.

SUTPHEN, William. *Golficide and Other Tales of the Fair Green.* New York, 1898. $350.

SUTRO, Adolph. *The Mineral Resources of the United States.* Baltimore, 1868. Folding map, plates. $250.

SUTRO, Adolph. *The Sutro Tunnel and Railway to the Comstock Lode in Nevada.* London, 1873. 2 folding maps. 37 pp., printed wraps. $250.

SUTTER, Johann August. *Diary of Johann August Sutter.* Grabhorn Press. San Francisco, 1932. Edited by Douglas S. Watson. 3 colored plates, 3 facsimiles. Boards. One of 500. $125.

SUTTER, Johann August. *New Helvetia Diary.* Grabhorn Press. San Francisco, 1939. 2 color plates, facsimile, map. Half cloth. One of 950. $100.

SWALLOW Barn, or A Sojourn in the Old Dominion. Philadelphia, 1932. (By John Pendleton Kennedy, his first book.) 2 vols., in original half cloth and boards, paper labels. $600.

SWAN, James G. *The Northwest Coast . . .* New York, 1857. Folding map, plates. $450.

SWASEY, William F. *The Early Days and Men of California.* Oakland (1891). Portrait, 2 plates. Calf. $400.

SWIFT, Graham. *The Sweet Shop Owner.* London, 1980. Author's first book. $175.

SWIFT, Jonathan. *Gulliver's Travels.* London, 1909. 13 color plates by Arthur Rackham. Cloth. One of 750 signed by Rackham. $1,250. Trade. (Only 12 color plates.) $250. New York, 1929. Limited Editions Club. (The first Limited Editions Club book.) $175. London, 1930. Cresset Press. Colored engravings by Rex Whistler. 2 vols., morocco and boards. One of 195. In slipcase. $2,500. (The true first, London 1726, brought $26,000. [in contemporary binding] at auction in 1990.)

SWINBURNE, Algernon Charles. *Atalanta in Calydon: A Tragedy.* London, 1865. White cloth. With only 111 pages of text. (Second printing had 130 pages.) $750. Kelmscott Press. London, 1894. Woodcut title, initials, etc. Vellum, silk ties. One of 250. $1,000. One of 8 on vellum. $5,000.

SWINBURNE, Algernon Charles. *Chastelard: A Tragedy.* Moxon. London, 1865. $200.

SWINBURNE, Algernon Charles. *Erechtheus: A Tragedy.* London, 1876. $150.

SWINBURNE, Algernon Charles. *Laus Veneris.* Golden Cockerel Press. London, 1948. One of 650. $200. One of 100 specially bound. $350.

SWINBURNE, Algernon Charles. *Lucretia Borgia.* Golden Cockerel Press. (London), 1942. Illustrated. Full leather. One of 30 specially bound with manuscript facsimile. $750. One of 320. $300.

SWINBURNE, Algernon Charles. *Poems and Ballads.* E. Moxon. London, 1866. $1,000. J. C. Hotten. London, 1866. Second issue. $250.

SWINBURNE, Algernon Charles. *The Queen-Mother. Rosamond. Two Plays.* London, 1860. Author's first book. Slate gray cloth, white spine label. First issue, with "A. G. Swinburne" on spine and Pickering imprint on integral title page. $3,000. Second issue: The title page is a cancel and the label is corrected to "A.C." $2,000. Third issue has Moxon imprint on title page. $500. Later issued with a Hotten imprint on title page in 1866. $350.

SWINBURNE, Algernon Charles. *A Song of Italy.* London, 1867. Bright blue cloth. $200.

SWINBURNE, Algernon Charles. *Songs Before Sunrise.* London, 1871. Blue-green cloth. $200. Large paper issue in morocco. One of 25. $1,000. Florence Press. London, 1909. Levant morocco extra. One of 12 on vellum. $2,000. One of 600 on paper. $400.

SWINBURNE, Algernon Charles. *The Springtide of Life: Poems of Childhood.* London, 1918. 9 color plates, numerous text illustrations by Arthur Rackham. Half vellum. One of 765 signed by Rackham. $750. Trade. $150.

SWINBURNE, Algernon Charles. *Under the Microscope.* London, 1872. Wraps. With suppressed leaf laid in. $1,000.

SWINBURNE, Algernon Charles. *William Blake: A Critical Essay.* London, 1868. 8 plates. First issue, with the word "Zamiel" below woodcut on title page. $400.

SWISS Family Robinson (The). New York, 1832. 2 vols., in original cloth. (By Johann David Wyss.) First American edition. $750. Limited Editions Club, New York, 1963. In slipcase. $75. Also see *The Family Robinson Crusoe.*

SYMONDS, John Addington. *The Escorial: A Prize Poem.* Oxford, 1860. Wraps. Author's first book. $200.

SYMONDS, John Addington. *In the Key of Blue and Other Prose Essays.* London, 1893. Light blue or cream cloth. First edition, with 15 pages of ads at end. $300. Vellum. One of 50 on large paper. $500.

SYMONDS, John Addington. *The Life of Michael Angelo Buonarotti* . . . London, 1893. 2 vols. $350.

SYMONDS, John Addington. *The Renaissance.* Oxford, 1863. Wraps. $150.

SYMONDS, John Addington. *Walt Whitman: A Study.* London, 1893. 5 plates. $100.

SYMONDS, Mary, and PREECE, Louisa. *Needlework Through the Ages.* London, 1928. 8 color plates, 96 other plates. Half vellum. $600.

SYMONS, A. J. A. *Desmond Flower, Francis Meynell. The Nonesuch Century; An Appraisal* . . . London, 1936. 750 numbered copies. $450.

SYMONS, A. J. A. *The Quest for Corvo.* London, (1934). $150. New York, 1934. $100.

SYMONS, Arthur. *Aubrey Beardsley.* London, 1898. Half cloth. $200. London, 1905. Half vellum. Second edition. One of 150 on large paper. $250. Trade. Boards. $125.

SYMONS, Arthur. *Days and Nights.* London, 1889. $1,500.

SYMONS, Arthur. *An Introduction to the Study of Browning.* London, 1886. Green cloth. Author's first book. With ads dated January 1887. $125.

SYMONS, Arthur. *A Study of Thomas Hardy.* London, 1927. Photogravures of Hardy by Alvin Langdon Coburn. One of 100 signed by Symons and Coburn. $650.

SYMONS, Julian. *Confusions About X.* London (1939). Author's first book. $200.

SYNGE, John M. *The Aran Islands.* Dublin, 1906. Drawings. $300. Dublin, 1907. Illustrated by Jack B. Yeats. $500. One of 150 on large paper, signed by Synge and Yeats. $1,500.

SYNGE, John M. *Deirdre of the Sorrows: A Play.* Cuala Press. Dundrum, Ireland, 1910. Preface by W. B. Yeats. Boards, linen spine. One of 250. $250. New York, 1910. Boards and cloth. One of 50. $3,500. (All except 5 on vellum and 5 on handmade paper were reported destroyed by the publisher, John Quinn.)

SYNGE, John M. *In the Shadow of the Glen.* New York, 1904. Author's first book. Pale gray printed wraps. One of 50 published for copyright purposes. $2,000. (For first English edition, see *The Shadow of the Glen.*)

SYNGE, John M. *The Playboy of the Western World.* Dublin, 1907. Portrait. $450. White linen. One of 25 on handmade paper. $3,500.

SYNGE, John M. *Poems and Translations.* Cuala Press. Dundrum, 1909. Blue boards, tan linen spine, paper label. One of 250. $250. New York, 1909. Boards and cloth. One of 50. $750.

SYNGE, John M. *The Shadow of the Glen, Riders to the Sea.* London, 1905. Synge's first commercially published book. Printed green wraps. $400. (For first edition, see *In the Shadow of the Glen.*) Boston, 1911. Half vellum. $150.

SYNGE, John M. *The Tinker's Wedding.* Dublin, 1907. Rust-colored cloth, beige spine. $150.

SYNGE, John M. *The Well of the Saints.* London, 1905. Wraps. First issue. $300. London, 1905. Boards and cloth. Second issue, with introduction by William Butler Yeats. $200. New York, 1905. One of 50. First American edition. $1,000.

SYNGE, John M. *The Works of John Millington Synge.* Dublin, 1910. Portraits. 4 vols. $500. Boston, 1912. 4 vols. $350.

SYNTAX, Doctor. *The Life of Napoleon: A Hudibrastic Poem in 15 Cantos.* London, 1815. (By William Combe.) 30 color plates by George Cruikshank. $600.

SYNTAX, Doctor. *The Tours . . .* (1st, 2d, and 3d.) (By William Combe.) *The Tour of Doctor Syntax in Search of the Picturesque.* London, 1812. Frontispiece, title page, and 29 colored plates by Thomas Rowlandson. *The Tour of Doctor Syntax in Search of Consolation.* 24 colored plates by Rowlandson. London, 1820. *The Tour of Doctor Syntax in Search of a Wife.* 24 colored plates by Rowlandson. London (1921–22). $1,500.

SZYK, Arthur (artist). *Ink and Blood: A Book of Drawings.* New York, 1946. Text by Struthers Burt. 74 plates. Morocco. One of 1,000 signed by Szyk. In slipcase. $750.

SZYK, Arthur. *The New Order.* New York (1941). $350.

T

TABB, John Banister. *Poems.* (Baltimore, 1882). Author's first book. $400.

TACITUS, C. Cornelius. *De Vita et Moribus Julii Agricolae Liber.* Doves Press. London, 1900. Vellum. One of 225. $600. One of 5 on vellum. In special morocco binding by the Doves Bindery. $3,500. First book printed at the Doves Press.

TAFT, Robert. *Artists and Illustrators of the Old West.* New York, 1953. $250.

TAFT, Robert. *Photography and the American Scene: A Social History, 1839–89.* New York, 1938. $250. New York, 1942. $100.

TAGGARD, Genevieve. *For Eager Lovers.* New York, 1922. Boards, paper labels. $100.

TAGGARD, Genevieve. *The Life and Mind of Emily Dickinson.* New York, 1930. One of 200 on large paper, signed. $200. Trade. $75.

TAGGARD, Genevieve. *Travelling Standing Still.* New York, 1928. One of 110 signed. In dustwrapper and slipcase. $150.

TAGGARD, Genevieve. *What Others Have Said . . .* Berkeley (1919). Author's first book. Wraps. $150.

TAGORE, Rabindranath. *The Post Office: A Play.* Cuala Press. Dundrum, Ireland, 1914. Preface by William Butler Yeats. Boards and cloth. One of 400. $150. New York, 1914. $75.

TAINE, John. *The Purple Sapphire.* New York (1924). Author's first book. $200.

TALBOT, Clare Ryan. *Historic California in Bookplates.* Los Angeles, 1936. No limitation given but obviously limited. $150.

TALES of the Northwest; or, Sketches of Indian Life and Character. By a Resident from Beyond the Frontier. Boston, 1830. (By William J. Snelling.) Author's first book. $500.

TALES of Terror; with an Introductory Dialogue. London, 1801. Engraved half title. (Falsely attributed to Matthew G. Lewis.) $400.

TALES of Travels West of the Mississippi . . . Boston, 1830. Map. (By William J. Snelling.) $600.

TALLACK, William. *Friendly Sketches in America.* London, 1861. $100.

TALLAHASSEE Girl (A). Boston, 1882. (By Maurice Thompson.) $100.

TALLENT, Annie D. *The Black Hills; or The Last Hunting Grounds of the Dakotahs.* St. Louis, 1899. 50 plates. Cloth, or half leather. Either binding: $200.

TAMERLANE and Other Poems. Boston, 1827. By a Bostonian. (By Edgar Allan Poe, his first book.) Printed wraps. $250,000. London, 1884. Vellum. One of 100. $1,500. San Francisco, 1923. 2 vols., boards (folio plus a smaller facsimile volume). One of 150. $300.

TANNER, Henry S. *A New American Atlas . . .* Philadelphia, 1823. 16 double-page and 2 large folding maps. $3,000.

TANNER, J. M. *A Biographical Sketch of James Jensen.* Salt Lake City, 1911. $750.

TANSELLE, G. Thomas. *Guide to the Study of United States Imprints.* Cambridge, Mass. 1971. 2 vols. $125.

TAPLEY, Harriet Silvester. *Salem Imprints 1768–1825.* Salem, 1927. $100.

TARASCON, Louis A., et al. *Petition . . . Praying the Opening of a Wagon Road from the River Missouri, North of the River Kansas, to the River Columbia.* Washington, 1824. 12 pp. $250.

TARBELL, Ida M. *The History of the Standard Oil Company.* New York, 1904. 2 vols. $200.

TARCISSUS: The Boy Martyr of Rome, in the Diocletian Persecution, A.D. CCCIII. (By Baron Corvo [Frederick William Rolfe].) (Essex, England, 1880—actually 1881.) 4 leaves, printed gray wraps. Author's first book. $3,000.

TARG, William (editor). *Bibliophile in the Nursery.* Cleveland, 1957. $125.

TARG, William (editor). *Carrousel for Bibliophiles.* New York, 1947. $75.

TARKINGTON, Booth. *The Gentleman from Indiana.* Pictorial green cloth, top stained green. New York, 1899. Author's first published book. First issue, with "eye" as last word in line 12, page 245; with line 16 reading "so pretty." $125.

TARKINGTON, Booth. *Penrod.* Garden City, 1914. Illustrated by Gordon Grant. In blue mesh cloth. First state, with page viii so numbered and with "sence" for "sense" in third line from bottom of page 19. $250.

TARKINGTON, Booth. *Penrod and Sam.* Garden City, 1916. Illustrated by Worth Brehm. First state in pictorial light green cloth, with imprint at foot of spine stamped in black. $175. Foot of spine stamped in white. $125.

TARKINGTON, Booth. *Penrod Jashber.* Garden City, 1929. $250.

TARKINGTON, Booth. *Seventeen.* New York (1916). With letters "B–Q" on copyright page. $150.

TATE, Allen. *The Fathers.* New York, 1938. $150.

TATE, Allen. *The Golden Mean . . .* (Nashville, 1923.) Author's first book with R. Wills. (200 numbered copies.) $3,500.

TATE, Allen. *The Hovering Fly and Other Essays.* (Cummington, Mass.), 1949. Illustrated. Boards. One of 245. $300.

TATE, Allen. *Jefferson Davis, His Rise and Fall.* New York, 1929. $400.

TATE, Allen. *The Mediterranean and Other Poems.* New York, 1936. Green wraps. One of 165 numbered copies on Strathmore all-rag paper, signed. In tissue jacket and slipcase. $500. One of 12 signed. $1,250. Signed but not numbered (bound up later by Gotham). $300.

TATE, Allen. *Mr. Pope and Other Poems.* New York, 1928. $650.

TATE, Allen. *Poems, 1928–1931.* New York, 1932. In acetate jacket. $300.

TATE, Allen. *Reason in Madness.* New York (1941). $250.

TATE, Allen. *Stonewall Jackson, the Good Soldier: A Narrative.* New York (1928). Author's first separate book. $500.

TATE, Allen. *Two Conceits for the Eye to Sing, If Possible.* (Cummington, Mass.), 1950. Wraps, paper label. One of 300. $175.

TATE, Allen. *The Winter Sea: A Book of Poems.* (Cummington, Mass.), 1944. Decorated cloth. One of 300. In plain paper dustwrapper. $250.

TATE, James. *Cages.* Iowa City, 1966. Wraps. Author's first book. One of 45. $300.

TATE, James. *The Lost Pilot.* New Haven, 1967. $150.

TATTERSALL, C. E. C. *A History of British Carpets.* London (1934). 116 plates (55 in color). Buckram. Issued without dustwrapper. $200.

TATTERSALL, George. *The Pictorial Gallery of English Race Horses.* London, 1844. 90 plates. Cloth. $1,250.

TAUBERT, Sigfred. *Bibliopola, Pictures and Texts About the Book Trade.* Hamburg (1966). In slipcase. $125.

TAUNTON, Thomas Henry. *Portraits of Celebrated Racehorses . . .* London, 1887–88. 463 plates. 4 vols., hall morocco. $1,250.

TAYLOR, Arthur V. *Origines Golfianae.* Woodstock, 1912. Limited to 500 copies. In slipcase. $400.

TAYLOR, Bayard. *Eldorado, or, Adventures in the Path of Empire . . .* New York, 1850. 8 lithograph views. 2 vols. First edition with list of illustrations in vol. 2 giving Mazatlan at page 8 instead of page 80 (VAB). $750. Second edition, with Mazatlan reference corrected. $600. London, 1850. 2 vols. First English edition. $400.

TAYLOR, Bayard. *Ximena and Other Poems.* Philadelphia, 1844. Author's first book. $1,000.

TAYLOR, Elizabeth. *At Mrs. Lippincote's.* London, 1945. Author's first book. $200. New York (1946). $100.

TAYLOR, F. W. *The Principles of Scientific Management.* New York, 1911. 118 pp., green cloth. $750. Later, enlarged issue, red cloth. $250.

TAYLOR, James W. *Northwest British America and Its Relations to the State of Minnesota.* St. Paul, 1860. Map. $2,250.

TAYLOR, James W. *The Sioux War.* St. Paul, 1862. Wraps. $1,000. St. Paul, 1863. Second edition. $600.

TAYLOR, Jane and Ann. *Little Ann and Other Poems.* (London, 1883.) Illustrated in color by Kate Greenaway. Pictorial boards and cloth. $150.

TAYLOR, John Henry. *Golf: My Life's Work.* London, 1943. $150.

TAYLOR, John Henry. *Taylor on Golf.* London, 1902. $600. New York, 1902. $300.

TAYLOR, John W. *Iowa, the "Great Hunting Ground" of the Indian; and the "Beautiful Land" of the White Man.* Dubuque, 1860. 16 pp., printed wraps. $275.

TAYLOR, Joseph Henry. *Beavers—Their Ways and Other Sketches.* Washburn, N.D., 1904. 20 plates. $200.

TAYLOR, Joseph Henry. *Sketches of Frontier and Indian Life . . .* Pottstown, Pa., 1889. 12 plates. Half leather and boards. $500.

TAYLOR, Joseph Henry. *Twenty Years on the Trap Line.* Bismarck, N.D., 1891. 8 plates. 154 pp., boards and calf. $750. Second edition, same place and date. 173 pp., maroon cloth. $400.

TAYLOR, Oliver I. *Directory of Wheeling and Ohio County.* Wheeling, W. Va., 1851. 2 plates, including tinted frontispiece. Half leather. $250.

TAYLOR, Peter. *A Long Fourth and Other Stories.* New York (1948). Author's first book. $250. London, 1949. $250.

TAYLOR, Peter. *A Woman of Means.* New York (1950). $175. London, 1950. $200.

TAYLOR, Philip Meadows. *Confessions of a Thug.* London, 1839. 3 vols., in original boards. Author's first book. $250.

TAYLOR, Phoebe Atwood. *The Cape Cod Mystery.* Indianapolis (1931). Author's first book. $350.

TAYLOR, Thomas U. *The Chisholm Trail and Other Routes.* San Antonio, 1936. $125.

TEASDALE, Sara. *Love Songs.* New York, 1917. In dustwrapper. $250. Without dustwrapper. $50.

TEASDALE, Sara. *Sonnets to Duse and Other Poems.* Boston, 1907. Boards, paper labels. Author's first book. $250.

TEASDALE, Sara. *Stars To-Night.* New York, 1930. Illustrated by Dorothy P. Lathrop. One of 150 signed by author and artist. In dustwrapper. $200.

TEERINK, H. *A Bibliography of the Writings of Jonathan Swift.* Philadelphia (1963). Second edition, revised and corrected. $250.

TEN Thousand a Year. Philadelphia, 1840–41. (By Samuel Warren.) 6 vols., boards, paper labels. First issue, without volume number on title page of vol. 1 (VAB). $1,000. Second issue, with volume number on title page of first volume. $800. Edinburgh and London, 1841. 3 vols., dark brown or plum-colored cloth. First English edition. $400.

TENNANT, Emma. See Ardy, Catherine.

TENNANT, Emma. *The Time of the Crack.* London, 1973. Author's first book under her own name. $125.

TENNYSON, Alfred, Lord. See *In Memoriam; Poems by Two Brothers.*

TENNYSON, Alfred, Lord. *Enoch Arden.* London, 1864. Green cloth. First issue, with ads dated August 1864 (VAB). $250. Boston, 1864. Brown cloth. First American edition. $150.

TENNYSON, Alfred, Lord. *Idylls of the King.* London, 1859. Green cloth. First issue, with verso of title page blank. $350. London, 1868. Illustrations after Gustave Dore. Folio, cloth. $200. London, 1875. 20 mounted photographs by Julia Margaret Cameron. Half leather. $1,000. Limited Editions Club, New York, 1953. Illustrated by Lynd Ward. In slipcase. $60.

TENNYSON, Alfred, Lord. *Maud, and Other Poems.* London, 1855. Green cloth. First edition, with yellow endpapers and 8 pages of ads dated July 1855 and a last leaf advertising Tennyson's books (VAB). $150. (Note: Contains first printing of "The Charge of the Light Brigade.") London, 1905. Essex House. One of 125 on vellum. $450.

TENNYSON, Alfred, Lord. *Poems.* London, 1833. In original boards, white spine label. $1,000. London, 1842. 2 vols., boards. $500.

TENNYSON, Alfred, Lord. *Poems, Chiefly Lyrical.* London, 1830. In original drab or pink boards, white spine label. First issue, with page 91 misnumbered 19. Author's first separate, regularly published book. $1,250.

TENNYSON, Alfred, Lord. *Poems MDCCCXXX. MDCCCXXXIII.* Toronto (London), 1862. Printed wraps. Pirated edition. $450.

TENNYSON, Alfred, Lord. *Seven Poems and Two Translations.* Doves Press. London, 1902. Vellum. One of 325. $350. One of 25 on vellum. Slipcase. $2,500.

TENNYSON, Alfred, Lord. *Timbuctoo.* (Cambridge Prize poem, 1829.) Wraps. $1,500.

TENNYSON, Alfred, Lord. *Tiresias and Other Poems.* London, 1885. $150. Gehenna Press. Northampton, Mass. (1970). Engraved title page. 5 signed etchings, 1 in color, by Leonard Baskin. One of 50 signed. In slipcase. $750.

TENNYSON, Charles. *Sonnets and Fugitive Pieces.* In original boards, or cloth. Cambridge, 1830. $350.

TENNYSON, Frederick. *Days and Hours.* London, 1854. Author's first book. $125.

TENTH MUSE, Lately Sprung Up in America (The). (By Anne Bradstreet.) London, 1650. Author's first book. Perfect copy. $25,000–30,000. (A repaired copy with wear and two pages in skillful facsimile sold for $16,000 in recent years.)

TERHUNE, Albert Payson. *Caleb Conover, Railroader.* New York, 1907. $100.

TERHUNE, Albert Payson. *Lad of Sunnybank.* New York, 1929. $350.

TERHUNE, Albert Payson. *Syria from the Saddle.* New York, 1896. Author's first book. $150.

TERHUNE, Mary Hawes. See Harland, Marion.

TERRITORY of Wyoming (The); Its History, Soil, Climate, Resources, . . . Laramie City, Wyoming Territory, 1874. (By J. K. Jeffrey.) 84 pp., printed wraps. $750.

TEVIS, Walter. *The Hustler.* (New York, 1959.) Author's first book. $150.

TEXAS Almanac (The). Galveston, 1857. (First of this series.) Wraps. $250. Other issues: 1859, $200; 1860, $200; 1861, $200; 1867, $100; 1868, $100; 1870, $75.

TEXAS in 1840, or The Emigrant's Guide to the New Republic. New York, 1840. Colored frontispiece. Cloth. (By A. B. Lawrence and C. J. Stille.) $600.

TEXAS, The Home for the Emigrant from Everywhere. Houston, 1875. (By J. B. Robertson.) Folding map, wraps. $500. St. Louis, 1876. $300.

THACHER, J. B. *Christopher Columbus.* New York, 1903–4. Plates. 3 vols., half vellum. $350. 3 vols. in 6, plus portfolio of facsimiles of published accounts of the voyages of Columbus. $600.

THACHER, J. B. *The Continent of America.* New York, 1896. One of 250. $350.

THACHER, James. *Observations on Hydrophobia* . . . Plymouth, Mass., 1812. Hand-colored plate. $300.

THACKERAY, William Makepeace. See Pendennis, Arthur; Titmarsh, M. A.; Wagstaff, Theophile. See also *The History of Henry Esmond.*

THACKERAY, William Makepeace. *The Adventures of Philip on His Way Through the World.* London, 1862. 3 vols., brown cloth. $500.

THACKERAY, William Makepeace. *The English Humourists of the Eighteenth Century.* London, 1853. $150. New York, 1853. First American edition. $100.

THACKERAY, William Makepeace. *The Four Georges* . . . New York, 1860. $150. London, 1861. First English edition, first issue, with title page reading "Sketches of Manners, Morals, Court, and Town Life." $250.

THACKERAY, William Makepeace. *The Great Hoggarty Diamond.* New York (1848). Vignette on title page. Buff wraps. (Harper's Library . . . No. 122). First issue, with "82 Cliff Street" on title page (later "306 Pearl Street"—VAB.) $3,500.

THACKERAY, William Makepeace. *The History of Samuel Titmarsh and the Great Hoggarty Diamond.* London, 1849. Pictorial glazed white wraps. First English edition. $1,500.

THACKERAY, William Makepeace. *The Orphan of Pimlico, and Other Sketches.* London, 1876. Illustrated by Thackeray. Boards. $500.

THACKERAY, William Makepeace. *Vanity Fair: A Novel Without a Hero.* London, 1847–48. Illustrated by the author. 20 parts in 19, yellow pictorial wraps. $10,000. London, 1848. First issue with engraved title-page date of 1849 (VAB) and made up from the parts with the heading in rustic type on page 1, woodcut of the Marquis of Steyne on page 336 (later omitted), and the reading "Mr. Pitt" on page 453 (later "Sir Pitt"). $2,000. New York, 1848. $750. Limited Editions Club, New York, 1931. 2 vols. In slipcase. $150.

THACKERAY, William Makepeace. *The Virginians: A Tale of the Last Century.* London, 1857–59. 24 parts, printed yellow wraps. $1,000. London, 1858–59. 2 vols. First book edition. $350.

THACKERAY, William Makepeace. *The Yellow Plush Correspondence.* Philadelphia, 1838. $1,500.

THAXTER, Celia. *An Island Garden.* Boston, 1894. Illustrated by Childe Hassam. $500. London, 1894. First English edition. $250. Boston, 1895. $400.

THAXTER, Celia. *Poems.* New York, 1872. Author's first book. $150.

THAYER, William M. *The Pioneer Boy, and How He Became President.* Boston, 1863. $150.

THERION, The Master. *The Book of Thoth.* (London), 1944. (By Aleister Crowley.) 8 color plates. 78 other illustrations. Half morocco. One of 200 signed. $800.

THEROUX, Alexander. *Three Wogs.* Boston, 1972. $100. (London, 1973.) Author's first book. $75.

THEROUX, Paul. *Waldo.* Boston, 1967. Author's first book. (Indeterminate number of dustwrappers printed in red vs. white, priority unknown.) $200. London (1968). $150.

THEROUX, Paul. *Fong and the Indians.* Boston, 1968. $150. London (1976). $75.

THEROUX, Paul. *Murder in Mount Holly.* (London, 1969.) $600.

THEROUX, Paul. *Girls at Play.* Boston, 1969. $125. London (1969). 200.

THIS Is the Preachment on Going to Church. Roycroft. East Aurora, N.Y., 1896. (By George Bernard Shaw.) One of 26 on Japan vellum. $1,000. Half cloth. $125.

THISSELL, G. W. *Crossing the Plains in '49 . . .* Oakland, 1903. 11 plates. $200.

THOM, Adam. *The Claims to the Oregon Territory Considered.* London, 1844. Wraps. $250.

THOMAS, D. M. *Personal and Possessive.* London, 1964. Author's first book. $350.

THOMAS, D. M. *Two Voices.* London, 1968. Cloth. One of 50 signed. In glassine jacket. $250. Trade. wraps in glassine dustwrapper. $75.

THOMAS, David. *Travels Through the Western Country in the Summer of 1816.* Auburn, N.Y., 1819. Folding map. Errata slip. $450.

THOMAS, Dylan. *A Child's Christmas in Wales.* Norfolk (1955). $75. London (1968). $35. New York, 1969. 100 numbered copies signed by the illustrator, Fritz Eichenberg, with portfolio of signed prints. $750. Trade. $35.

THOMAS, Dylan. *Collected Poems 1934–1952.* London (1952). 65 signed and numbered copies. Issued full dark blue morocco and plain cellophane dustwrapper. $2,250. Trade. $125. (New York, 1953.) The word "daughter" misspelled on page 199 (corrected in later printings). $100.

THOMAS, Dylan. *Conversation About Christmas.* (New York), 1954. Wraps. Christmas greeting. 6 leaves stapled. In mailing envelope. $125.

THOMAS, Dylan. *Deaths and Entrances.* London (1946). $200. Gregynog, Newton, Wales, 1984. Issued in slipcase. $300.

THOMAS, Dylan. *18 Poems.* Sunday Referee & Parton Bookshop. London, (1934). Author's first book. Black cloth, flat spine, lacks ad leaf between half-title and title pages, front edge roughly trimmed. $2,000. London (1936). Rounded spine, has ad leaf between half-title and title pages, front edge cut evenly. $300. London (circa 1942). Verso of title page still states "First Published in 1934 . . . ;" red buckram, lettered in gold. $100.

THOMAS, Dylan. *In Country Sleep and Other Poems.* (New York, 1952.) 100 signed and numbered copies. Issued in dark brown slipcase. $1,250. Trade. $150.

THOMAS, Dylan. *The Map of Love: Verse and Prose.* London (1939). First issue in fine grained mauve cloth, an almost silky texture. Title blocked in gold on front cover. Title and author's name in gold on spine. "Dent" blind stamped at foot of spine. Top edge stained dark purple. $300. Second issue bound in coarser and plum-colored cloth, otherwise same as above. $200. Third issue bound in purple cloth intermediate between fine and coarse grained. Blocked in blue (including "Dent" at foot of spine). Top edge stained purple. $100. Fourth issue bound as third issue but top edge unstained. $75.

THOMAS, Dylan. *New Poems.* Norfolk (1943). Paper boards. $200. Wraps. Issued simultaneously. $50.

THOMAS, Dylan. *Portrait of the Artist as a Young Dog.* London (1940). $300. Norfolk (1940). "Printed for New Directions . . . September 1940." $250.

THOMAS, Dylan. *Selected Writings of Dylan Thomas.* (New York, 1946.) (Rolph notes that reprints are identifiable only by the dustwrapper, which has printing number stated on front flap.) $150.

THOMAS, Dylan. *Twenty-five Poems.* London (1936). $400.

THOMAS, Dylan. *Twenty-six Poems.* New Directions. (Norfolk, 1950.) 8 signed and numbered copies on Japanese vellum numbered III–X. Issued in slipcase. $10,000. 87 signed and numbered copies on handmade paper copies numbered 61–147. Issued in slipcase. $2,000. Dent. London (1950). 2 signed and numbered copies on Japanese vellum. Copies numbered I–II. In slipcase. $10,000. 50 signed and numbered copies numbered 11–60. Issued in slipcase. $2,000.

THOMAS, Dylan. *Under Milk Wood.* London (1954). $200. (New York, 1954.) $75.

THOMAS, Dylan. *The World I Breathe.* Norfolk (1939). With one star on either side of author's name on title page and spine (VAB, not in Rolph or Maud.) $600. Five stars on either side of author's name on title page and spine. $300.

THOMAS, Edward. *Selected Poems.* Gregynog Press. Newtown, Wales, 1927. Buckram. One of 275 on vellum. $300.

THOMAS, Edward. *Woodland Life.* London, 1897. Author's first book. $400.

THOMAS, George C., Jr. *Golf Architecture in America.* Los Angeles, 1927. $350.

THOMAS, Henry. *Early Spanish Bookbindings XI–XV Centuries.* London, 1939. 99 plates. $150.

THOMAS, Isaiah. *The History of Printing in America.* Worcester, 1810. 2 plates, 3 facsimiles. 2 vols. $400. Albany, 1874. 2 vols., cloth. Second edition. $125.

THOMAS, Jerry. *The Bar-Tender's Guide.* New York, 1862. $150.

THOMAS, Joseph B. *Hounds and Hunting Through the Ages.* Derrydale Press. New York, 1928. One of 750. $250.

THOMAS, Lowell. *The First World Flight.* Boston, 1925. Illustrated. Half vellum. One of 575 signed by Thomas and the aviators. $600.

THOMAS, P. J. *Founding of the Missions.* San Francisco, 1877. Map, plates. $200.

THOMAS, R. S. *The Stones of the Field.* Carmarthen, 1946. Author's first book. $500.

THOMAS, Robert Bailey. *The Farmer's Almanac No. 1 . . .* Boston (1793). $250.

THOMAS, Ross. *The Singapore Wink.* New York, 1969. $150. London, 1969. $100.

THOMAS, Ross. *The Cold War Swap.* New York, 1965. Author's first book. $300.

THOMAS, Ross. *The Seersucker Whipsaw.* New York, 1967. $200. London, 1968. $150.

THOMAS, Ross. *Spy in the Vodka.* (London, 1967.) U.K. edition of *The Cold War Swap.* Author's first book. $175.

THOMASON, John W. *Fix Bayonets.* New York, 1926. Author's first book. $150.

THOMASON, John W. *Gone to Texas.* New York, 1937. $150.

THOMASON, John W. *Lone Star Preacher.* New York, 1937. $150.

THOMES, William Henry. See *The Gold-Hunter's . . .*

THOMPSON, A. C. *Preludes.* London, 1875. (By Alice Meynell, her first book.) First issue, with brown endpapers. (Republished later under the name Alice Meynell as *Poems.*) $125.

THOMPSON, Daniel Pierce. See *The Adventures of Timothy Peacock, Esquire; The Green Mountain Boys.*

THOMPSON, Daniel Pierce (editor). *The Laws of Vermont, 1824–34, Inclusive.* Montpelier, 1835. In original calf. Author's first book under his name. $350.

THOMPSON, David. *David Thompson's Narrative of His Explorations in Western America: 1784–1812.* Toronto, 1916. 4 large folding maps laid into rear pocket. $1,500.

THOMPSON, David. *History of the Late War, Between Great Britain and the U.S.A.* Niagara, U. C. (Upper Canada), 1832. $275.

THOMPSON, Dorothy. *The Depths of Prosperity.* New York (1925). Author's first book, with P. Bottome. $175.

THOMPSON, Edwin P. *History of the First Kentucky Brigade.* Cincinnati, 1868. 6 plates. Morocco and boards. $350. Cloth. $250.

THOMPSON, Francis. *The Life and Labors of Blessed John Baptist . . .* London (1891). Author's first book. Green wraps. $750.

THOMPSON, Francis. *Poems.* London, 1893. Decorated boards. With ads dated October. One of 500. $350. Vellum. One of 12 signed. $3,500.

THOMPSON, Francis. *Sister-Songs: An Offering to Two Sisters.* London, 1895. Green, gray, or brown cloth. With ads at back dated 1895. (First published edition of *Songs Wing-to-Wing.*) $150.

THOMPSON, Francis. *Songs Wing-to-Wing: An Offering to Two Sisters.* (Cover title.) London (1895). Wraps. First edition (of *Sister-Songs*), with no title page and no dedication leaf. $400.

THOMPSON, Hunter S. *Fear and Loathing in Las Vegas.* New York (1971). $150.

THOMPSON, Hunter S. *Hell's Angels.* New York (1967). Author's first book. $150.

THOMPSON, James Westfall. *The Frankfort Book Fair; The Francofordiense Emporium of Henri Estienne.* Chicago, 1911. One of 300 copies. $175.

THOMPSON, Jim. *Heed the Thunder.* New York, 1946. $750.

THOMPSON, Jim. *Now and on Earth.* New York, 1942. Author's first book. $850.

THOMPSON, Kay. *Eloise.* New York, 1955. Drawings by Hilary Knight. $250.

THOMPSON, Maurice. See *A Tallahassee Girl.*

THOMPSON, Maurice. *Hoosier Mosaics.* New York, 1875. Author's first book. $100.

THOMPSON, Maurice. *The Witchery of Archery.* New York, 1878. $150.

THOMPSON, Peter G. *A Bibliography of the State of Ohio.* Cincinnati, 1880. $150.

THOMPSON, R. A. *Central Sonoma: A Brief Description of the Township and Town of Santa Rosa, Sonoma County, California.* Santa Rosa, Calif., 1884. Printed wraps. $250.

THOMPSON, R. A. *Conquest of California.* Santa Rosa, 1896. Portrait, 3 plates. 33 pp., wraps. $200.

THOMPSON, R. A. *Historical and Descriptive Sketch of Sonoma County, California.* Philadelphia, 1877. Map. Printed wraps. $250.

THOMPSON, R. A. *The Russian Settlement in California Known as Fort Ross . . .* Santa Rosa, 1896. 2 plates, other illustrations. 34 pp., wraps. $200.

THOMPSON, Ruth Plumly. *The Gnome King of Oz.* Chicago (1927). Illustrated. Green cloth. $500.

THOMPSON, Ruth Plumly. *Handy Mandy in Oz.* Chicago (1937). $450.

THOMPSON, Ruth Plumly. *Pirates in Oz.* Chicago (1931). $300.

THOMPSON, Ruth Plumly. *The Wishing Horse of Oz.* Chicago (1935). $350.

THOMSON, James. *The City of Dreadful Night and Other Poems.* London, 1880. One of 40 on large paper. $1,500. Trade. $400.

THOMSON, Virgil. *The State of Music.* New York, 1939. Author's first book. $100.

THOREAU, Henry David. *Autumn: From the Journal of Henry D. Thoreau.* Boston, 1892. $300.

THOREAU, Henry David. *Cape Cod.* Boston, 1865. Purple, green, or brown cloth. $600. Boston, 1896. Colored illustrations by Amelia M. Watson. 2 vols., decorated cloth. $250.

THOREAU, Henry David. *Early Spring in Massachusetts: From the Journal of Henry D. Thoreau.* Boston, 1881. $450.

THOREAU, Henry David. *Excursions.* Boston, 1863. Engraved portrait. Green cloth. $500.

THOREAU, Henry David. *Letters to Various Persons.* Boston, 1865. Cloth, various colors. With "Tickner & Co." on spine. $300. With "James R. Osgood & Co." on spine. $200.

THOREAU, Henry David. *The Maine Woods.* Boston, 1864. Green cloth. First issue, with 1-leaf ad of *Atlantic Monthly* at end reading "The Thirteenth Volume" (Johnson), although Borst notes ads dated April 1864 in some copies. There was another 1864 printing, which may be the same as the first. $500.

THOREAU, Henry David. *Summer: From the Journal of Henry D. Thoreau.* Boston, 1884. Double-page frontispiece map. Green cloth. $300.

THOREAU, Henry David. *Walden or, Life in the Woods.* Boston, 1854. Brown cloth. (Tipped-in ads range from April to October; April ads presumably are earliest.) With April ads: $3,500. With later ads. $3,000. Boston, 1909. 2 vols., half vellum. One of 483. $600. Chicago, 1930. Lakeside Press. Illustrated. Half buckram. One of 1,000. $150. Limited Editions Club, New York, 1936. Illustrated (photos) and signed by Edward Steichen. In slipcase. $600.

THOREAU, Henry David. *A Week on the Concord and Merrimack Rivers.* Boston, 1849. Author's first book. Light brown, brown, or black cloth, yellow endpapers. With 3 lines dropped at bottom of page 396—written in with pencil by Thoreau. $4,000. Not written in. $3,000.

THOREAU, Henry David. *Winter: From the Journal of Henry D. Thoreau.* Boston, 1888. $200.

THOREAU, Henry David. *A Yankee in Canada, with Anti-Slavery and Reform Papers.* Boston, 1866. (Contains "Civil Disobedience.") $600.

THORNTON, Alfred. See *The Adventures of a Post Captain.*

THORNTON, J. Quinn. *Oregon and California in 1848* . . . New York, 1849. Folding map. 2 vols. $600. New York, 1855. 2 vols. $300.

THORNTON, Robert John. *The Temple of Flora* . . . London, 1810. 25 portraits, 31 hand-colored plates. $10,000. London, 1951. In dustwrapper. $250. Also, one of 250 in half morocco. $500.

THORP, N. Howard (Jack). *Songs of the Cowboys.* Estancia, N.M. (1908). Pictorial wraps. $1,500.

THOUGHTS on the Proposed Annexation of Texas to the United States. New York, 1844. (By Theodore Sedgwick.) 55 pp., wraps. $150.

THOUSAND Miles in a Canoe from Denver to Leavenworth (A). Bushnell, Neb., 1880. Wraps. (By W. A. Spencer.) $350.

THREE Monographs. Naples, Italy, 1906. (By Norman Douglas.) 56 pp., light brown printed wraps. One of 250. $300.

THURBER, James. *The Last Flower: A Parable in Pictures.* New York, 1939. Oblong, boards. $175.

THURBER, James. *My Life and Hard Times.* New York, 1933. $250.

THURBER, James. *The Owl in the Attic and Other Perplexities.* New York, 1931. Introduction by E. B. White. $300.

THURBER, James. *The Thirteen Clocks.* New York (1950). Illustrated in color by Marc Simont. Boards and cloth. First edition not stated. $150. (The illustrator's first name, Marc, is misspelled "Mark" on all copies.)

THURBER, James, and WHITE, E. B. *Is Sex Necessary? Or Why You Feel the Way You Do.* New York, 1929. Thurber's first book. $650.

THURBER, James. *The Seal in the Bedroom.* New York, 1932. $350.

THURMAN, Wallace. *The Blacker the Berry: A Novel of Negro Life.* New York, 1929. $500.

THURMAN, Wallace. *Infants of the Spring.* New York (1932). $400.

THURMAN, Wallace. *Negro Life in New York's Harlem.* Little Blue Book #494. Girard, Kans. No date of publication and not certain, but believe it would have preceded *The Blacker the Berry.* If so, author's first book. Wraps. $150.

THWAITES, Reuben Gold. *Historic Waterways: Six Hundred Miles of Canoeing Down the Rock, Fox, and Wisconsin Rivers.* Chicago, 1888. Author's first book. $175.

TIERNEY, Luke. *History of the Gold Discoveries on the South Platte River.* Pacific City, Iowa, 1859. 27 pp., wraps. $15,000 or more.

TIETJENS, Eunice. *Profiles from China.* Chicago, 1917. Author's first book. $125.

TIFFANY, Louis Comfort. *The Art Work of Louis Comfort Tiffany.* Garden City, 1914. One of 492 on Japan vellum. $850.

TILLINGHAST, Arthur W. *Cobble Valley Golf Years & Other Sketches.* Philadelphia (1915). $200.

TILLSON, Christina Holmes. *Reminiscences of Early Life in Illinois by Our Mother.* (Amherst, Mass., 1872). 4 plates. $1,750.

TIMPERLEY, C. H. *A Dictionary of Printers and Printing . . .* London, 1839. With *Manual Containing Instructions to Learners.* London, 1838. The two. $225.

TIMLIN, William M. *The Ship That Sailed to Mars.* London, 1923. 48 mounted color plates. Boards. $1,500. New York (1923). $1,250.

TIMOTHY Crump's Ward; or, The New Year's Loan and What Came of It. Loring Publishing. Boston (1866). (By Horatio Alger, Jr.) Purple cloth, or wraps. Either binding: $3,500.

TINDALE, Thomas Keith, and TINDALE, Harriett Ramsey. *Handmade Papers of Japan.* Rutland, Vt., and Tokyo, 1952. Four booklets bound in Japanese fashion with hand-stenciled wraps enclosed in a protective slipcase. One of 150 copies. $6,500.

TITMARSH, M. A. *Doctor Birch and His Young Friends.* London, 1849. (By William Makepeace Thackeray.) 16 color plates by the author. Wraps. $300.

TITMARSH, M. A. *The Irish Sketch-Book.* London, 1843. (By William Makepeace Thackeray.) Wood engravings. 2 vols., green cloth. $500.

TITMARSH, M. A. *Jeames's Diary; or, Sudden Riches.* New York, 1846. (By William Makepeace Thackeray.) Woodcuts. Wraps. $3,000.

TITMARSH, M. A. *"Our Street."* London, 1848. (By William Makepeace Thackeray.) 16 color plates. Wraps. $400.

TITMARSH, M. A. *The Second Funeral of Napoleon: In Three Letters to Miss Smith, of London, and the Chronicle of the Drum.* London, 1841. (By William Makepeace Thackeray.) Frontispiece, 3 plates, picture of Napoleon on front cover. Wraps. With six lines of shading on the cheek of Napoleon on front cover and inscription on plate opposite title page and page 120. Line 13 has five stars (not four). $750.

TITTSWORTH, W. G. *Outskirt Episodes.* (Avoca, Iowa, 1927.) Portrait (tipped to title page). Red cloth. In dustwrapper. $250.

TOCQUEVILLE, Alexis de. *Democracy in America.* New York, 1838. First American edition. In original cloth. $1,250.

TODD, Frederick P. *Soldiers of the American Army, 1775–1941.* New York, 1941. Frontispiece and 24 hand-colored plates by Fritz Kredel. One of 500 issued without dustwrapper. $150.

TODD, Mabel. *Footprints.* Amherst, 1883. Author's first book. Wraps. $250.

TODD, The Rev. John. *The Lost Sister of Wyoming.* Northampton, Mass., 1842. Frontispiece. $200.

TODD, Ruthven. *Over the Mountain.* London (1939). $125.

TODD, Ruthven. *Laughing Mulatto . . .* London (1939 or 1940?). $125.

TOKLAS, Alice B. *The Autobiography of Alice B. Toklas.* Harcourt Brace. New York (1933). (By Gertrude Stein.) $250. (The Literary Guild also states "First edition," but is not.)

TOLKIEN, J. R. R. *The Adventures of Tom Bombadil.* London (1962). $200. Boston, 1963. $150.

TOLKIEN, J. R. R. *The Devil's Coach-Horses.* London (about 1925). Wraps. $450.

TOLKIEN, J. R. R. *The Father Christmas Letters.* London (1976). "First published in 1976" on page (48). Issued without dustwrapper. $100.

TOLKIEN, J. R. R. *The Fellowship of the Ring.* London, 1953. (First volume in the *Lord of the Rings* trilogy.) $1,500.

TOLKIEN, J. R. R. *Farmer Giles of Ham.* London, 1949. Illustrated, including 2 color plates. Boards. $300. Boston, 1950. $200.

TOLKIEN, J. R. R. *The Hobbit.* London (1937). Illustrated by the author. Green cloth. $4,000. Boston, 1938. $1,500.

TOLKIEN, J. R. R. *The Lord of the Rings.* (3 vols., cloth. *The Fellowship of the Ring,* 1953; *The Two Towers,* 1954; *The Return of the King,* 1955.) $3,000. London, 1966. 3 vols. Second edition revised. $200. Boston, 1967. 3 vols. With a new foreword by the author. First American revised edition. $300.

TOLKIEN, J. R. R. *The Return of the King.* London, 1955. (Third volume in the *Lord of the Rings* trilogy.) $500.

TOLKIEN, J. R. R. *The Silmarillion.* London (1977). Probable first issue/printing, without price on dustwrapper. $125. With price. $100. Boston, 1977. First American edition, probable first issue, with perfect text on lines 27–32 of page 229. $60.

TOLKIEN, J. R. R. *The Two Towers.* London, 1954. (Second volume in the *Lord of the Rings* trilogy.) $1,000.

TOLLER, Ernst. *Masses and Men.* London, 1923. Author's first English translation. $150.

TOLSTOY, Leo. *Anna Karenina.* New York, 1886. First edition in English. $350. Limited Editions Club, New York, 1933. 2 vols. In slipcase. $100. Another issue, 1951. 2 vols. In slipcase. $75.

TOLSTOY, Leo. *Childhood and Youth.* London, 1862. Author's first English translation. $500.

TOLSTOY, Leo. *Resurrection.* New York, 1900. First edition in English. $200.

TOLSTOY, Leo. *War and Peace.* New York, 1886. Translated from the French by Clara Bell. 6 vols., decorated brown cloth. First edition in English. $1,000. Limited Editions Club, New York, 1938. 6 vols. $250.

TOLSTOY, Leo. *Where God Is Love Is.* Ashendene Press. London, 1924. Blue wraps. One of about 200 issued as a Christmas token from St. John and Cicely Hornby. $400.

TOM Brown at Oxford. Cambridge, 1861. 3 vols., blue cloth. (By Thomas Hughes.) $500.

TOM Brown's School Days. Cambridge, 1857. By an Old Boy, Thomas Hughes. Blue cloth. With "nottable" for "notable" in line 15 on page 24. Author's first book. $600.

TOM Cringle's Log. London, 1833. 2 vols., in original cloth. (By Michael Scott, his first book.) $300.

TOMKINSON, G. S. *A Select Bibliography of the Principal Modern Presses . . . in Great Britain and Ireland.* London, 1928. Illustrated. Boards and cloth. $200.

TOMLINSON, Charles. *Relations and Contraries.* (Aldington, Kent, England, 1951.) Wraps. Author's first book. $75.

TOMLINSON, H. M. *The Sea and the Jungle.* London (1912). Frontispiece. Green cloth. Author's first book. $125. London, or New York, 1930. Illustrated by Clare Leighton. One of 515 signed. $250. Trade. $75.

TOMLINSON, H. M. *Thomas Hardy.* New York, 1929. Frontispiece by Zhenya Gay, signed. One of 76 signed by the author. $200.

TOMPKINS, Thomas. *Beauties of Writing . . .* London, 1777. Engraved title page, dedication (numbered "2"), 37 plates (numbered 3–39). $500.

TOOLE, John Kennedy. *A Confederacy of Dunces.* Baton Rouge, 1980. Author's first book. (2,500 copies.) $300. (London, 1981.) (1,500 copies.) $150.

TOOMER, Jean. *Cane.* New York, 1923. Author's first book. $2,000.

TOOMER, Jean. *Essentials.* Chicago, 1931. $750.

TOOMER, Jean. *The Flavor of Man.* Philadelphia (1949). Wraps. $350.

TOPOGRAPHICAL Description of the State of Ohio, Indian Territory, and Louisiana (A). Boston, 1812. (By Jervis Cutler.) 5 woodcut plates, errata slip. $1,350.

TOPONCE, Alexander. *Reminiscences of Alexander Toponce, Pioneer, 1839–1923.* (Ogden, Utah, 1923.) 14 plates. $125.

TOPPING, E. S. *The Chronicles of the Yellowstone.* St. Paul, 1883. Folding map. $200.

TOPSYS & Turveys. New York, 1893. (By Peter Newell, his first book.) 31 leaves with colored illustrations. Oblong folio, pictorial boards. $750.

TORY, Geofroy. *Champ Fleury.* Grolier Club. New York, 1927. Translated by George B. Ives. Vellum and boards. Printed by Bruce Rogers. One of 7 on larger paper (of an edition of 397). $850. Trade. One of 390. In dustwrapper and slipcase. $650.

TOUR on the Prairies (A). London, 1835. By the author of *The Sketch-Book* (Washington Irving). In original boards, or cloth. $600. Philadelphia, 1835. In original blue or green cloth, paper label. Without catalog with sheets bulking 9/16 inch and last line on page 247 reading "Binger of dawn." $600. Second state-printing is 11/16 inch and page 247 reads "Harbinger of dawn."

TOUR Through Part of Virginia in the Summer of 1808 (A). New York, 1809. (By John E. Caldwell.) 31 pp. $350.

TOURGEE, Albion W. See Churton, Henry; see *also A Fool's Errand.*

TOURGEE, Albion. *Book of Forms.* (Raleigh, 1868.) Author's first book. Wraps. $200.

TOWNSEND, George Alfred. *The Real Life of Abraham Lincoln.* New York, 1867. Frontispiece. 15 pp., printed wraps. $200.

TOWNSEND, John K. *Narrative of a Journey Across the Rocky Mountains . . .* Philadelphia, 1839. In original cloth. $750.

TOWNSEND, John K. *Ornithology of the United States . . .* Philadelphia, 1839. Vol. 1 (all published). Wraps. 4 hand-colored plates. $18,000.

TOWNSEND, John K. *Sporting Excursions in the Rocky Mountains . . .* London, 1840. Engraved frontispieces. 2 vols., in original full leather. First English edition of the preceding item, with the author's name spelled "Townshend" instead of "Townsend." $500.

TOYNBEE, Paget. *Journal of the Printing-Office at Strawberry Hill*... London, 1923. One of 650 copies. $100.

TRACY, J. L. *Guide to the Great West.* St. Louis, 1870. 2 maps. $175.

TRAGEDY of Count Alarcos (The). London, 1839. (By Benjamin Disraeli.) In original cloth. $200.

TRAITS of American Indian Life and Character. London, 1853. (Attributed to Peter Skene Ogden.) $2,250.

TRANSITION Stories. New York, 1929. Edited by Eugene Jolas and R. Sage. Pictorial boards and cloth. One of 100. In dustwrapper. $350.

TRAUBEL, Horace L. (editor). *At the Graveside of Walt Whitman: Harleigh, Camden, New Jersey, March 30th, and Sprigs of Lilac.* (Philadelphia), 1892. 37 pp., printed gray wraps. $200.

TRAUBEL, Horace L. (editor). *Camden's Compliment to Walt Whitman*... Philadelphia, 1889. Frontispiece. Red cloth. $150.

TRAVELLER'S Pocket Directory and Stranger's Guide. Schenectady, 1831. 3 folding plates. 32 pages advertisments. $500.

TRAVELS of Capts. Lewis and Clarke (The). Philadelphia, 1809. Folding map and 5 portraits of Indians. (Unauthorized edition. For authentic first edition see entry under Lewis's name.) $750.

TRAVELS in Louisiana and the Floridas, in the Year 1802. New York, 1806. (By Berquin-Duvallon.) Translated from the French by John Davis. First edition in English. $750.

TRAVEN, B. *The Bridge in the Jungle.* New York, 1938. First American edition. $300. London (1940). $200.

TRAVEN, B. *The Death Ship: The Story of an American Sailor.* London, 1934. Author's first book. First edition in English. Translated by Eric Sutton. $450. New York, 1934. First American edition, revised and translated by Traven. $350.

TRAVEN, B. *The General from the Jungle.* London (1954). First edition in English. $150.

TRAVEN, B. *The Rebellion of the Hanged.* London (1952). First edition in English. $175. New York, 1952. First American edition. $100.

TRAVEN, B. *The Treasure of the Sierra Madre.* London, 1934. First edition in English. $2,000. New York, 1935. First American edition. $750.

TRAVER, Robert. *Anatomy of a Fisherman.* New York (1964). (By John Donaldson Voelker.) $125.

TRAVER, Robert. *Troubleshooter.* New York, 1943. (By John Donaldson Voelker, his first book.) $125.

TRAVERS, Jerome David, and CROWELL, James. *The Fifth Estates: 30 Years of Golf.* New York, 1926. $150.

TRAVERS, P. L. *Mary Poppins.* (London, 1934.) Author's first book. Illustrated by Mary Shepard. $400. New York (1934). $250.

TRAVERS, P. L. *Mary Poppins Comes Back.* London, 1935. $350.

TRAVIS, Walter. *Practical Golf.* New York, 1901. $150.

TREATISE of Human Nature (A). (By David Hume.) London, 1739–40. Author's first book. 3 vols. $12,000.

TREATISE on Tennis (A). London, 1822. By a Member of the Tennis Club (Robert Lukin). Folding engraved diagram of court. $1,500.

TREATY Between the United States and the Chasta and Other Tribes of Indians. (Washington, 1855.) (By Joel Palmer.) Wraps. $450.

TREATY Between the United States and the Comanche and Kiowa Tribes of Indians . . . Proclaimed May 26, 1866. (Washington, 1866.) 8 pp., folio. $400.

TREATY Between the United States and the Confederated Tribes of Sacs and Foxes of the Mississippi. (Washington, 1860.) Printed wraps. $175.

TREATY Between the United States and the Creek and Seminole Tribes of Indians . . . Ratified March 6, 1845. (Washington, 1845.) 6 pp., folio. $450.

TREATY Between the United States and the Klamath and Moadoc Tribes and Yahooskin Band of Snake Indians . . . Proclaimed Feb. 17, 1870. (Washington, 1870.) 8 pp., folio. $400.

TREATY Between the United States and the Nez Perce Tribe of Indians . . . Proclaimed April 20, 1867. (Washington, 1867.) 10 pp., folio. $450.

TREATY Between the United States and the Senecas, . . . Washington, 1868. Folio, 20 pp., sewn. $250.

TREE, Iris. *Poems.* Nassau, 1917. Author's first book. Wraps. $400.

TRELAWNY, Edward John. See *The Adventures of a Younger Son.*

TREVOR, Elleston. See Dudley-Smith, T.

TREVOR, William. *A Standard of Behavior.* London, 1958. Author's first book. $350.

TREVOR, William. *The Old Boys.* London (1964). $150.

TRIALS of A. Arbuthnot and R. C. Ambrister (The), Charged with Exciting the Seminole Indians to War Against the United States of America. London, 1819. 80 pp. $450.

TRIBUNE Book of Open Air Sports (The). New York, 1887. Edited by Henry Hall. Illustrated. Pictorial cloth. (Note: This is the first book composed by linotype.) $400.

TRIBUNE Tracts No. 6, Life of Abraham Lincoln. Horace Greeley. (New York), 1860. 32 pp., sewn. (By John Locke Scripps.) $300. (See also *Life of Abraham Lincoln.*) Detroit, 1900. Leather, with Lincoln photograph on heavy porcelain bound in. $300.

TRIBUTES to Brooke Crutchley on His Retirement as University Printer. Cambridge, 1975. One of 650 copies. $125.

TRIGGS, J. H. *History and Directory of Laramie City, Wyoming Territory.* Laramie City, 1875. 91 pp., printed wraps. $850.

TRIGGS, J. H. *History of Cheyenne and Northern Wyoming, etc.* Omaha, 1876. Folding map. 144 pp., printed wraps. $850.

TRIPLETT, Frank. *The Life, Times and Treacherous Death of Jesse James.* Chicago, 1882. Plates. Pictorial cloth. $350.

TRIPP, C. E. *Ace High: The Frisco Detective.* Grabhorn Press. San Francisco, 1948. Introduction by David Magee. Illustrated. Boards and cloth. One of 500. $125.

TRISTRAM, W. Outram. *Coaching Days and Coaching Ways.* London, 1888. Pictorial cloth. Large paper issue. $300. Trade. $150. London, 1893. One of 250. $250. London, 1924. Illustrated. Leather. $500.

TROCCHI, Alexander. See Lengel, Frances.

TROLLOPE, Anthony. See *Nina Balatka; On English Prose Fiction as a Rational Amusement.*

TROLLOPE, Anthony. *The American Senator.* London, 1877. 3 vols. First binding in pinkish ochre cloth. $3,000. In blue, red-brown, or green cloth. $2,000.

TROLLOPE, Anthony. *Australia and New Zealand.* London, 1873. 8 colored maps. 2 vols. First issue, with dark green endpapers. $1,500. With yellow endpapers. $1,000.

TROLLOPE, Anthony. *An Autobiography.* Edinburgh, 1883. Portrait. 2 vols. First issue, with smooth red cloth covers and green endpapers. $1,000. Second issue in ribbed red cloth with green or brown endpapers. $600.

TROLLOPE, Anthony. *Ayala's Angel.* London, 1881. 3 vols., orange cloth. $1,500.

TROLLOPE, Anthony. *Barchester Towers.* London, 1857. 3 vols., cloth. First binding, pale brown cloth with brick red endpapers. Some with ads dated December 1857. $10,000. Second binding, tan cloth (VAB), with 24 pp. of ads dated October 1860. $7,500. Limited Editions Club, New York, 1958. In slipcase. $75.

TROLLOPE, Anthony. *Castle Richmond.* London, 1860. 3 vols., dark purple-gray cloth. First binding, without line under the author's name on spine, 16-page catalog dated February 1860 and "W. Clowes & Sons" on verso of title page. $3,000. Second issue, with line under author's name on spine, 32-page catalog dated May 1860 and "William Clowes & Sons." $1,500.

TROLLOPE, Anthony. *Doctor Thorne.* London, 1858. 3 vols., gray-purple cloth with "Mamma" on page 18, line 15. $11,000 at auction in 1990. Second edition, same date with "Mammon." $1,000.

TROLLOPE, Anthony. *The Eustace Diamonds.* New York, 1872. Printed wraps. $1,500. Cloth. $1,000. London, 1873. 3 vols., brown cloth, spine title in gold. (Later all lettering in black). First English edition. $1,500.

TROLLOPE, Anthony. *The Fixed Period.* Edinburgh, 1882. 2 vols., red cloth. $1,750.

TROLLOPE, Anthony. *Framley Parsonage.* London, 1861. Millais illustrations. 3 vols., gray-purple cloth. With April ads at end of vol. 3. $7,500.

TROLLOPE, Anthony. *He Knew He Was Right.* London, 1868–69. Illustrated by Marcus Stone. 32 parts, gray-green wraps. $2,000. London, 1869. Illustrated. 2 vols., green cloth. First English book edition. $1,250.

TROLLOPE, Anthony. *How the "Mastiffs" Went to Iceland.* London, 1878. Illustrated. Blue cloth. $1,000.

TROLLOPE, Anthony. *Hunting Sketches.* London, 1865. With May ads. $1,000.

TROLLOPE, Anthony. *John Caldigate.* London, 1879. 3 vols. First binding, lilac-gray cloth. $2,500. In dark green cloth. $1,750.

TROLLOPE, Anthony. *The Kellys and the O'Kellys.* London, 1848. 3 vols., boards. $3,500. New York, 1860. First American edition. $750.

TROLLOPE, Anthony. *Kept in the Dark.* London, 1882. Frontispiece by Millais. 2 vols., olive-brown cloth. $1,750.

TROLLOPE, Anthony. *Lady Anna.* London, 1874. 2 vols., bright red-brown cloth. $1,000.

TROLLOPE, Anthony. *The Landleaguers.* London, 1883. 3 vols., green cloth. $2,000.

TROLLOPE, Anthony. *The Last Chronicle of Barset.* London, 1866–67. Illustrated. 32 parts, pictorial wraps. $2,000. London, 1867. 32 plates. 2 vols., blue cloth. First book edition. $5,000. (Note: Both the parts and book issues are complicated books. See Sadleir.)

TROLLOPE, Anthony. *The Macdermots of Ballycloran.* London, 1847. 3 vols., dark brown cloth. Author's first book. $4,500. London, 1848. Second printing (with 1848 title page). $1,500.

TROLLOPE, Anthony. *Marion Fay.* London, 1882. 3 vols., yellow-ochre cloth. $2,000. New York, 1882. Illustrated. Wraps. First American edition. $750.

TROLLOPE, Anthony. *Miss Mackenzie.* London, 1865. 2 vols., dark green cloth. $1,000.

TROLLOPE, Anthony. *North America.* London, 1862. 2 vols., pinkish maroon patterned cloth. With October ads. $1,750. New York, 1862. Gray cloth. First American (pirated Harper) edition. $350. Lippincott. New York, 1862. 2 vols. First authorized American edition. $350.

TROLLOPE, Anthony. *Orley Farm.* London, 1861–62. Illustrated by J. E. Millais. 20 parts, buff wraps. $10,000. London, 1862. 2 vols., purple-brown cloth. (First book edition is a complex book. See Sadleir's bibliography.) $6,000.

TROLLOPE, Anthony. *The Prime Minister.* London, 1876. 8 parts, gray wraps, or brown cloth. $2,000. London, 1876. 4 vols., red-brown cloth. First book edition. $1,500.

TROLLOPE, Anthony. *Rachel Ray.* London, 1863. 2 vols., pinkish red cloth. With volume numbers on spines in roman capitals with serifs (not block) type. $2,000.

TROLLOPE, Anthony. *Sir Harry Hotspur of Humblethwaite.* London, 1871. Scarlet-orange cloth. With "th" for "the" on page 40, line 1, in perfect type and with a period after "iv" at head of page 43 (many others). $1,250. New York, 1871. Cherry red or green cloth. First American edition. $450.

TROLLOPE, Anthony. *The Struggles of Brown, Jones, and Robinson.* New York, 1862. Wraps. $1,500. London, 1870. Illustrated. Brown cloth. First English and first illustrated edition. $750.

TROLLOPE, Anthony. *Tales of All Countries.* London, 1861 and 1863. (First and second series.) 2 vols., blue cloth. $1,250.

TROLLOPE, Anthony. *Thackeray.* London, 1879. In smooth cream cloth, paper label with Church's *Spenser* in ads as "in the press." $750.

TROLLOPE, Anthony. *The Three Clerks.* London, 1858. 3 vols., boards, blue cloth spine, labels. $3,000. Also, variant issue. full cloth. $2,000.

TROLLOPE, Anthony. *Travelling Sketches.* London, 1866. $1,000.

TROLLOPE, Anthony. *The Vicar of Bulhampton.* London, 1869–70. Illustrated. 11 parts, decorated gray-blue wraps. $3,500. London, 1870. Brown cloth. First book edition. $1,000.

TROLLOPE, Anthony. *The Warden.* London, 1855. Pale brown cloth. With 24 pages of ads dated September, 1854. $2,500.

TROLLOPE, Anthony. *Why Frau Frohmann Raised Her Prices, and Other Stories.* London, 1882. 1 vol. $1,000. 2 vols. $1,000.

TROLLOPE, Frances. See *Domestic Manners of the Americans.*

TROLLOPE, Frances. *The Vicar of Wrexhill.* London, 1837. 3 vols., in original boards, paper labels. $600.

TROLLOPE, T. Adolphus. *A Summer in Brittany.* London, 1840. Edited by Frances Trollope. 14 plates, 2 in color. 2 vols., purple cloth. Author's first book. $250.

TROWBRIDGE, John Townsend. See Creyton, Paul.

TROWBRIDGE, John Townsend. *Cudjo's Cave.* Boston, 1864. Pictorial half title. Cloth. Listing "L'Envoy" as beginning on page 503 in table of contents (later, page 501). $250.

TROWBRIDGE, John Townsend. *The South: A Tour of Its Battlefields and Ruined Cities.* Hartford, 1866. $200.

TRUMAN, Maj. Ben. C. *Life, Adventures and Capture of Tiburcio Vasquez, the Great California Bandit and Murderer.* Los Angeles, 1874. Frontispiece map. 44 pp., pictorial wraps. $600. Los Angeles, 1941. Cloth and leather. One of 100. $75.

TRUMAN, Harry S. *Mr. Citizen.* (New York, 1960.) One of 1,000 signed. In slipcase. $600. Trade. $75.

TRUMBO, Dalton. *Eclipse.* London (1935). Author's first book. $1,750.

TRUMBO, Dalton. *How Johnny Got His Gun.* Philadelphia (1939). $200.

TRYPHE. Cinq Petits Dialogues Grecs. (By Natalie C. Barney.) Paris, 1902. Wraps. $250.

TSA TOKE, Monroe. *The Peyote Ritual.* Grabhorn Press. San Francisco, 1957. 15 color plates. Boards and cloth. One of 325. $300.

TUCKER, Beverley. *The Partisan Leader.* Richmond, 1862. Printed wraps. Reprint of the anonymous 1836 novel forecasting the Civil War. $600.

TUCKER, Dr. Joseph C. *To the Golden Goal, and Other Sketches.* San Francisco, 1895. One of 50. $300.

TUCHMAN, Barbara. See Wertheim, Barbara.

TUER, Andrew W. *History of the Horn-Book.* London, 1896. 2 vols with 7 facsimile hornbooks in pockets (3 in first volume and 4 in second volume). $1,250.

TUER, Andrew W. *Pages and Pictures from Forgotten Children's Books.* London, 1898–99. $150.

TUFTS, James. *A Tract Descriptive of Montana Territory.* New York, 1865. Map. 15 pp., unbound folded sheets. $450.

TUFTS, Richard S. *The Principles Behind the Rules of Golf.* Pinehurst, 1960. $75.

TULLIDGE, Edward W. *The History of Salt Lake City and Its Founders.* Salt Lake City, 1886. Third edition, revised and enlarged. $350.

TULLIDGE, Edward W. *Tullidge's Histories, (Volume II). Containing the History of all the Northern, Eastern and Western Counties of Utah . . .* Salt Lake City, 1889. The only volume published. $325.

TULLOCH, W.W. *Life of Tom Morris.* London, 1908. $1,250.

TULLY, Jim. *Emmett Lawler.* New York (1922). Author's first book. $150.

TURBYFILL, Mark. *The Living Frieze.* Evanston (1921). Author's first book. 350 numbered copies. $150.

TURNBULL, Robert J. See Brutus.

TURNER, Frederick Jackson. *The Character and Influence of the Fur Trade . . .* (Madison, Wis., 1889.) Author's first book. Wraps. $500.

TURNER, Frederick Jackson. *The Significance of the Frontier in American History.* Madison, Wis., 1894. 34 pages. $1,500 and up for copies in original wraps.

TURNER, Mary Honeyman Ten Eyck. *These High Plains.* Amarillo, 1941. Portrait and plates. Cloth pictorial label. Issued without dustwrapper. One of 150. $150.

TURNER, Orsamus. *History of the Pioneer Settlement of Phelps and Gorham's Purchase . . .* Rochester, 1851. Boards and leather. $300.

TURNER, T. G. *Gazetteer of the St. Joseph Valley.* Chicago, 1867. Frontispiece and plate. $150.

TURNER, T. G. *Turner's Guide from the Lakes to the Rocky Mountains.* Chicago, 1868. $500.

TURNLEY, Parmenas T. *Reminiscences of Parmenas T. Turnley, from the Cradle to Three-Score and Ten.* Chicago (1892). 6 plates. $250.

TURRILL, H. B. *Historical Reminiscences of the City of Des Moines.* Des Moines, 1857. Double-page frontispiece plate and 7 other plates. 144 pp., printed dark blue wraps. $200.

TUTTLE, J. H. *Wam-dus-ky: A Descriptive Record of a Hunting Trip to North Dakota.* Minneapolis, 1893. Illustrated. $450.

TWAIN, Mark. See Harte, Bret, and Twain, Mark. See also *Date 1601; What Is Man?*

TWAIN, Mark. *Adventures of Huckleberry Finn.* London, 1884. Red cloth. Publisher's catalogue dated October 1884 inserted at back. $1,000. New York, 1885. Issued in blue and in green cloth. Earliest state: title page with copyright notice on verso (1884) tipped in. page (13); "Him and another man" listed incorrectly at page 88; page 57, line 11 up: ". . . with the was . . ."; page 155: Johnson has final 5 in page number same font in various "off-balance" position; page 283: fly outline of trousers a pronounced curve; leaf bound in (seen only in prospectuses and leather bound copies). Portrait frontispiece: cloth under bust visible. "Heliotype" imprint. Blue cloth. $5,000. Green cloth. $2,500. Mixed-state copies would bring less. See Blank, Johnson, McBride, or the *Author Price Guides* for further details. Limited Editions Club, New York, 1933. 1,500 numbered copies. Slipcase. $125. Limited Editions Club, New York, 1942. 1,500 numbered copies signed by the illustrator, Thomas Hart Benton. Slipcase. $350. Pennyroyal Press. West Hatfield, 1985. Illustrated by Barry Moser. Slipcase. $1,000.

TWAIN, Mark. *The Adventures of Tom Sawyer.* London, 1876. $2,500. Toronto, 1876. $1,000. American Publishing Co. Hartford/Chicago/Cincinnati. A. Roman & Co. San Francisco. 1876. First printing is on wove paper. Front matter paged (I)–xvi, fly-title, P.(I). Pp. (II–III) blank. Frontispiece, p.(iv). Collation: (I)–xvi, (17)–(275); blank, p. (276); 4 pp. ads. (Verso of half title and preface blank.) Half morocco (200 copies). $7,500. Calf (1,500 copies). $4,000. Blue cloth, edges gilt. $5,000. Blue cloth, edges plain. $3,500. Limited Editions Club. Cambridge, 1939. 1,500 numbered copies signed by illustrator, Thomas Hart Benton. Slipcase. $250.

TWAIN, Mark. *The American Claimant.* New York, 1892. Gray-green or olive green cloth. $125. London, 1892. $75.

TWAIN, Mark. *The Celebrated Jumping Frog of Calaveras County, and Other Sketches.* New York, 1867. First issue has single leaf of ads on cream-yellow paper before title page; page 66: last line "life" unbroken; page 198: last line "this" unbroken. In various cloth colors. Usually with frog in left corner of front cover, variant has frog in middle. Favored color is plum. $12,500. London, 1867. Wraps. $2,500.

TWAIN, Mark. *A Connecticut Yankee in King Arthur's Court.* New York, 1889. Ads dated June 1889 earliest noted. $300. Toronto (1889). With "s"-like ornament between "The" and "King" on page 59. $300. New York, 1889. Earliest state: page (59) has a small "s"-like ornament between "The" and "King" in the caption. $450.

TWAIN, Mark. *A Curious Dream.* London (1872). Pictorial yellow boards. Earliest printing: endpapers blank; leaf L4 blank; "Bradbury, Evans" imprint on pages (2) and/or page 150. $300.

TWAIN, Mark. *A Double-Barrelled Detective Story.* New York, 1902. Red or maroon cloth. Issued in dustwrapper. $150. London, 1902. $125.

TWAIN, Mark. *Facts for Mark Twain's Memory Builder.* (Cover title.) New York, 1891. Wraps. Designed to accompany "Mark Twain's Memory Builder," a board game (includes board and small box with facts . . . and pins). $400.

TWAIN, Mark. *Following the Equator.* Hartford, 1897. Blue cloth or various leathers (leather-bound copies probably twice as much as the cloth price shown). $150.

TWAIN, Mark. *Life on the Mississippi.* London, 1883. Red cloth. Ads dated March 1883. $500. Boston, 1883. First state: page 441: present is a tailpiece depicting an urn, flames, and head of Twain; page 443: the caption reads "The St. Louis Hotel." (Leather binding probably worth twice as much as cloth prices shown.) $500.

TWAIN, Mark. *The Man That Corrupted Hadleyburg and Other Stories and Essays.* New York, 1900. Earliest state: sheets bulk about $1\frac{1}{16}$ inches; the plate opposite page 2 has, in addition to the caption, the line: "[Page 2." $200. London, 1900. Ads dated June 1900. $200.

TWAIN, Mark. *Mark Twain's (Burlesque) Autobiography and First Romance.* New York (1871). Wraps or cloth. First issue lacks ads for Ball, Black & Co. on copyright page. Wraps. $250. Cloth (in green, terra-cotta or purple cloth). $225. John Camden Hotten. London (no-date). Unauthorized. Cloth. $300. Pictorial wraps. $250. George Routledge & Sons. London (no-date). Wraps. English edition following Hotten's unauthorized edition published two weeks earlier. $175.

TWAIN, Mark. *The £1,000,000 Bank-Note and Other New Stories.* New York, 1893. $150. London, 1893. Ads dated April 1893. $125.

TWAIN, Mark. *Personal Recollections of Joan of Arc.* New York, 1896. Earliest state: page (463): "Some books for the Library The Abbey Shakespeare . . ." The fourth entry is for "Memoirs of Barras" described as in 4 volumes with volumes I–II offered at $3.75 each; volumes III–IV as "just ready." Twain's name on binding but not title page. $200. London, 1896. Ads dated March 1896. $200.

TWAIN, Mark. *The Prince and the Pauper.* London, 1881. Red cloth. Publisher's catalogue dated November 1881 inserted at back. $500. Montreal, 1881. Gray-blue wraps. $1,250. Title page is a cancel with "Author's Canadian Edition . . ." added. Tan cloth stamped in gold and black. $400. Boston, 1882. 6–8 copies printed on China paper, bound in white linen, stamped in gold, inner hinges of blue linen. $15,000. Trade. First state: at front true binder's endpapers of white, or toned white, paper. At back: leaf inch (26)8 used as pastedown. Leaf (26)7 present as a blank. Uppermost rosette on spine ⅛ inch below fillet. Franklin Press imprint on copyright page. Cloth (leather binding probably twice as much). $500. Limited Editions Club. (New York), 1964. 1,500 numbered copies signed by illustrator, Clarke Hutton. Slipcase. $100.

TWAIN, Mark. *Pudd'nhead Wilson: A Tale.* London, 1894. Ads dated September 1894. $250.

TWAIN, Mark. *The Stolen White Elephant.* London, 1882. Presumed first state: list of books on verso of half titles does not list *The White Elephant;* title page has imprint on verso; foot of p. 285 has 1-line imprint. Publisher's catalog dated May 1882. $175. Boston, 1882. Tan cloth. $150.

TWAIN, Mark. *Tom Sawyer Abroad, Tom Sawyer Detective...* New York, 1896. $750.

TWAIN, Mark. *Tom Sawyer, Detective As Told by Huck Finn . . .* London, 1897. Publisher's catalog dated November 1896 inserted at back. First U.K. edition of *Tom Sawyer Abroad, Tom Sawyer Detective . . .* $200.

TWAIN, Mark. *The Tragedy of Pudd'nhead Wilson.* London, 1894. Ads dated September 1894. $250. Hartford, 1894. Earliest state: sheets bulk about 1⅛ inches. The title leaf is clearly joined to the next leaf. Cloth (leather binding probably twice as much). $350. (For English first edition see *Pudd'nhead Wilson.*)

TWAIN, Mark. *A Tramp Abroad.* Hartford/London, 1880. First state: frontispiece captioned "Moses." Priority of other points in BAL not established. Cloth (leather binding probably twice as much). $350.

TWEEDIE, William. *The Arabian Horse: His Country and People.* Edinburgh, 1894. 10 plates, 25 text illustrations, maps and tables. Green decorated cloth. $500. Large paper issue. half morocco. One of 100. $1,000.

TWENTIETH Century History of Southwest Texas (A). Chicago, 1907. Illustrated. Quarto, morocco. $750.

TWENTY Letters to Joseph Conrad. London, 1926. 12 pamphlets, wraps. One of 220 sets. In cloth folder. $400.

TWIN Cities Directory and Business Mirror for the Year 1860, Including the Cities of Davenport, Iowa, Rock Island, Ill., and Moline, Ill. Davenport, 1859. Vol. 1. (E. Coy & Co., publisher.) $250.

TWINING, Elizabeth. *Illustrations of the Natural Order of Plants, Arranged in Groups.* London, 1849–55. 160 colored lithograph plates. 2 vols., tall folio, half morocco. $25,000.

TWISS, Travers. *The Oregon Question, In Respect to Facts and the Law of Nations.* London, 1846. 2 large folding maps and ads. $600.

TWITCHELL, Ralph Emerson. *The Leading Facts of New Mexican History.* Cedar Rapids, Iowa, 1911–12. Folding maps, color frontispiece, other illustrations. 2 vols. One of 1,500. $500. With the 3 additional volumes issued later. $1,000.

TWITCHELL, Ralph Emerson. *Old Santa Fe . . .* (Santa Fe., 1925.) Illustrated. Cloth. One of 1,000. $250.

TWO Admirals (The): A Tale. Philadelphia, 1842. By the Author of *The Pilot.* (James Fenimore Cooper.) 2 vols., purple muslin, paper labels. First American edition. $750. London, 1842. 3 vols., boards and cloth, paper labels. (Issued under Cooper's name.) $600.

TWO Philosophers (The). Boston (1892). (By John Jay Chapman, his first book.) Wraps. $200.

TWO Rivulets. See Whitman, Walt.

TWO Years Before the Mast. A Personal Narrative of Life at Sea. New York, 1840. (By Richard Henry Dana, Jr., his first book.) (Harpers' Family Library No. CVI.) Tan, black, or gray cloth. First issue, with perfect "i" in the word "in," first line of copyright notice. $4,000. Second issue: $1,000. Boston, 1869. With new preface and added chapter. $175. London (1904). Illustrated by Arthur Rackham. $350. Chicago, 1930. Lakeside Press. Illustrated by Edward A. Wilson. Pictorial linen. One of 1,000. In slipcase. $175. New York, 1936. Grabhorn printing. Illustrated. Boards. One of 1,000. In dustwrapper. $200. Limited Editions Club, New York, 1947. In slipcase. $125.

TYLER, Anne. *If Morning Ever Comes.* New York, 1964. Author's first book $1,000. London, 1965. "that" for "than" in quote on front dustwrapper flap. $400.

TYLER, Anne. *The Tin Can Tree.* New York, 1965. $750. London, 1966. $200.

TYLER, Anne. *The Clock Winder.* New York, 1972. $750. London, 1973. $175.

TYLER, Daniel. *A Concise History of the Mormon Battalion in the Mexican War.* (Salt Lake City), 1881. Full leather. $450.

TYLER, Parker. See Ford, Charles.

TYLER, Parker. *The Metaphor in the Jungle and Other Poems.* Prairie City, Ill., 1940. Portrait by Tchelitchew. Cloth. Issued without dustwrapper. $300.

TYLER, Parker (editor). *Modern Things.* New York (1934). Purple and white cloth. $250.

TYNAN, Katherine. *Twenty One Poems.* Dun Emer Press. Dundrum, Ireland, 1907. Selected by W. B. Yeats. Blue boards and linen. One of 200. $200.

TYNAN, Kenneth. *He That Plays the King.* London, 1950. Half leather. Author's first book. One of 50. $250.

TYNDALL, John. *Essays on the Floating-Matter of the Air in Relation to Putrefaction and Infection.* London, 1881. $250.

TYPES and Bookmaking Containing Notes on the Books Printed at the Southworth-Anthoensen Press. Portland, 1943. One of 500 copies. $150.

TYPES of Successful Men in Texas. Austin, Tex., 1890. Red leather. $250.

TYSON, James L., M.D. *Diary of a Physician in California.* New York, 1850. 92 pp., printed wraps. $500.

TYSON, Philip T. *Geology and Industrial Resources of California.* Baltimore, 1851. 3 large folding maps. 9 folding plates. Second edition, following the government document edition of the previous year. $450.

TYSON, Robert A. *History of East St. Louis.* East St. Louis, 1875. Folding map and folding view of stockyards. 152 pp., wraps. $350.

U

UDELL, John. *Incidents of Travel to California, Across the Great Plains.* Jefferson, Ohio, 1856. Portrait, errata leaf. $750.

UDELL, John. *Journal of John Udell, Kept During a Trip Across the Plains.* Jefferson, Ohio, 1868. Vignette portrait. 47 pp., wraps. Second edition. $1,250. Los Angeles, 1946. Edited by Lyle H. Wright. Half morocco. One of 35 signed by Wright. $100. One of 750. $35. (Note: The first edition of Udell's *Journal,* 45 pp., printed wraps, including cover title, appeared in Suisun City, Calif., in 1859 and is known in only 1 surviving copy.) (New Haven, 1952.) Printed wraps. One of 200. $50.

UNDER the Greenwood Tree. London, 1872. 2 vols., green cloth. (By Thomas Hardy.) (Auction records indicate that there is an edition with one pagination for both volumes, whereas most have separate pagination.) $3,000.

UNIFORM and Dress of the Army of the Confederate States. Richmond, 1861. 15 plates by Ernest Crehen. 5 pp., boards, paper label. First edition, first issue, with black-and-white plates. $500. Second issue, same date, with 9 of the 15 plates in color, plus errata slip and tipped-in colored strip illustrating field caps. $2,500.

UNITED States "History" as the Yankee Makes and Takes It. By a Confederate Soldier. Glen Allen, 1900. 99 pp., yellow wraps. (By John Cussons.) $100.

UPDIKE, D. B. (printer). *Vexilla Regis Quotioe.* Boston, 1893. Author's first book. 100 copies. $250.

UPDIKE, John. *The Angels.* Pensacola, 1968. One of 150. Sewn wraps in mailing envelope. $750.

UPDIKE, John. *Assorted Prose.* New York, 1965. With tipped-in leaf signed by Updike. $200. Without signed leaf. $100. (London, 1965.) $75.

UPDIKE, John. *Bath After Sailing.* Stevenson, Conn. (1968). 125 signed copies in stiff wraps. $400.

UPDIKE, John. *The Carpentered Hen and Other Tame Creatures.* New York (1958). Author's first book. In first-state dustwrapper, with "two children" in biographical information $600.

UPDIKE, John. *The Dance of the Solids.* (New York, 1969). Was to be used as a Season's Greeting (along with W. H. Auden's *A New Year Greeting),* both issued in cardboard sleeve. $750.

UPDIKE, John. *Hoping for a Hoopoe.* London, 1959. First U.K. edition of *The Carpentered Hen.* $75.

UPDIKE, John. *Midpoint and Other Poems.* New York, 1969. 350 signed and numbered copies. In dustwrapper and slipcase. (Dustwrapper differs from trade edition.) $175. Trade. $50. (London, 1969.) $50.

UPDIKE, John. *The Music School.* New York, 1966. page 46, line 15 starts "the state . . ." $200. page 46, line 15 states "The King . . ." on tipped-in leaf. $125. page 46, line 15 starts "The King . . ." on integral leaf. $60. (London, 1967.) $60.

UPDIKE, John. *On Meeting Authors.* Newburyport, 1968. 250 numbered copies. Wraps. $600.

UPDIKE, John. *Pigeon Feathers.* New York, 1962. $125. (London, 1962.) $100.

UPDIKE, John. *The Poorhouse Fair.* New York, 1959. (Note: the second-printing dustwrapper has a biographical note as second paragraph on back flap which is not on first-printing dustwrapper.) $200. London, 1959. $150.

UPDIKE, John. *Rabbit Is Rich.* New York, 1981. 350 signed and numbered copies in dustwrapper (which differs from trade edition) and slipcase. $175. Trade. $30. (London, 1982.) $30. Franklin Library, 1984. $50.

UPDIKE, John. *Rabbit Redux.* New York, 1971. 350 signed and numbered copies in acetate dustwrapper and slipcase. $250. Trade. $40. (London, 1972.) $40. Franklin Library, 1979. Signed limited edition. $75.

UPDIKE, John. *Rabbit, Run.* New York, 1960. $250. (London, 1961.) $150. Franklin Library, 1977. Limited signed edition. $75.

UPDIKE, John. *The Same Door.* New York, 1959. $150. (London, 1962.) $125.

UPFIELD, Arthur W. *The House of Cain.* London (1928). Author's first book. $600. New York, 1928. $200.

UPHAM, Samuel C. *Notes of a Voyage to California Via Cape Horn . . .* Philadelphia, 1878. $400.

UPHAM, Samuel C. *Notes from Sunland, on the Manatee River, Gulf Coast of South Florida.* Braidentown, Fla., 1881. Frontispiece. 83 pp., printed wraps. $175. Second edition (so stated), same date. $100.

UPWARD, Edward. *Journey to the Border.* Hogarth Press. London, 1938. Author's first book. $150.

URIS, Leon. *Battle Cry.* New York (1953). Author's first book. $175.

UYENISHI, S. K. *The Text Book of Ju-Jutsu as Practiced in Japan.* London (no-date). $60.

UZANNE, Octave. *The French Bookbinders of the Eighteenth Century.* Chicago, 1904. One of 250 copies. $450.

V

VAIL, Alfred. *Description of the American Electro-Magnetic Telegraph . . .* Philadelphia, 1845. $300.

VAIL, Isaac Newton. *Alaska: Land of the Nugget. Why?* Pasadena, 1897. 68 pp., wraps. $125.

VALENTIA, George, Viscount. *Voyages and Travels to India, Ceylon, the Red Sea, Abyssinia, and Egypt, 1802–6.* London, 1809. 69 engraved views and folding maps. 3 vols. $1,000.

VALÉRY, Paul. See McGreevy, Thomas.

VALPERGA: Or, The Life and Adventures of Castruccio, Prince of Lucca. London, 1823. (By Mary Wollstonecraft Shelley.) 3 vols. Without half titles. $750.

VAN BUREN, A. D. *Jottings of a Year's Sojourn in the South.* Battle Creek, 1859. $375.

VANCE, Jack. *The Dying Earth.* New York (1950.) Author's first book. Wraps. $150.

VANCE, Jack. *Emphyrio.* Garden City, 1969. $250.

VANCE, Jack. *The Language of Pao.* New York (1958). $200.

VANCE, Jack. *To Live Forever.* New York (1956). $600.

VANCE, Jack. *Vandals of the Void.* Philadelphia (1953). $200.

VANCOUVER, George, Capt. *A Voyage of Discovery to the North Pacific Ocean, and Round the World . . .* London, 1798. 3 text volumes, plus 18 plates, plus atlas volume of 16 plates, including 10 folding maps. $12,500.

VANDERBILT, Harold S. *On the Wind's Highway.* New York, 1939. Issued without dustwrapper. In slipcase. $250.

VANDERBILT, William K. *Taking One's Own Ship Around the World.* New York, 1929. 19 color plates. 112 photographs. Half (or full) morocco. One of 200. In slipcase. $400.

VANDERBILT, William K. *To Galapagos on the Ara, 1926.* (New York, 1927.) Boards and leather. One of 900. $250. New York, 1927. One of 500. $450.

VANDERBILT, William K. *West Made East with the Loss of a Day.* New York, 1933. 7 color plates, 13 charts. Cloth. Issued without dustwrapper. In slipcase. One of 800. $250. Half morocco. One of 200 on Rives paper. $400.

VAN DINE, S. S. *The Benson Murder Case.* New York, 1926. (By Willard Huntington Wright, his first book under this name.) $1,000.

VAN DOREN, Carl. *The Life of Thomas Love Peacock.* New York, 1911. Author's first book. $150. London, 1911. $100.

VAN DOREN, Mark. *Henry David Thoreau.* Boston, 1916. Author's first book. $150.

VAN EVERY, Edward. *Muldoon the Solid Man of Sport.* New York, 1929. Stated first. $50.

VAN GULIK, Robert. *The Lore of Chines Lute . . .* Tokyo, 1940. Author's first book. Wraps. $200.

VAN GULIK, Robert. *Dee Goong An.* Tokyo, 1949. One of 1,200 signed. Plain white dustwrapper. $750.

VAN GULIK, Robert. *The Chinese Maze Murders.* The Hague, 1956. $400. London, 1957. $300.

VAN MOE, Emile A. *The Decorated Letter . . .* Paris, 1950. Parchment covers. In dustwrapper. $100.

VAN TRAMP, John C. *Prairie and Rocky Mountain Adventures.* Columbus, Ohio, 1858. 61 plates. $200.

VAN VECHTEN, Carl. *Music After the Great War.* New York, 1915. Purple cloth, paper labels. Author's first book aside from a musical score and a promotional pamphlet. $75.

VAN VECHTEN, Carl. *Nigger Heaven.* New York, 1926. Decorated cloth, printed spine label. One of 205 signed. In slipcase. $200.

VAN VECHTEN, Carl. *Spider Boy: A Scenario for a Moving Picture.* New York, 1928. Half cloth. One of 220. In slipcase. $175. Red vellum. One of 75 on vellum. In slipcase. $600.

VAN VECHTEN, Carl. *The Tattooed Countess.* New York, 1924. Boards and cloth. One of 150 signed in slipcase. $125. Trade. $75.

VAN VECHTEN, Carl. *The Tiger in the House.* New York, 1920. Half cloth. In dustwrapper. $125.

VAN VOGT, A. E. *Slan: A Story of the Future.* Sauk City, Wis., 1946. Author's first regularly published book. $200.

VAN VOGT, A. E. *Tomorrow on the March.* (Los Angeles, 1946.) 14-page stapled, self-wraps. Author's first book. $150.

VAN VOGT, A. E. *The Weapon Makers.* Hadley. Providence (1947). $150.

VAN WINKLE, C. S. *The Printers' Guide . . .* New York, 1818. Foldout frontispiece table, 32-page section entitled "A Specimen of Printing Types . . ." and 22-page section entitled "A Specimen of Printing Types Cast . . ." $4,500.

VAN ZANDT, Nicholas Biddle. *A Full Description of the Soil, Water, Timber, and Prairies of Each Lot, or Quarter Section of the Military Lands Between the Mississippi and Illinois Rivers.* Washington City, 1818. 127 pages, plus separately issued folding map. $3,500. Much less without map.

VARDON, Harry. *My Golfing Life.* London, 1933. $350.

VAUGHN, Robert. *Then and Now, or 36 Years in the Rockies . . .* Minneapolis, 1900. Illustrated. Pictorial cloth. $200.

VEBLEN, Thorstein. *The Theory of the Leisure Class.* London, 1899. Author's first book. $500. New York, 1899. $300.

VEDDER, Elihu. *Miscellaneous Moods In Verve.* Boston, 1914. One of 100. $200.

VEGA CARPIO, Lope Felix de (attributed to). *The Star of Seville.* Gregynog Press. Newtown, Wales, 1935. Translated by Henry Thomas. Half morocco. One of 175. $1,000.

VELASCO, José Francisco. *Sonora: Its Extent, Population, Natural Productions, Indian Tribes, Mines, Mineral Lands . . .* San Francisco, 1861. Translated by William F. Nye. First American edition. $450.

VENABLES, Robert. *The Experienc'd Angler.* London, 1662. $1,750.

VENEGAS, Miguel. *A Natural and Civil History of California.* London, 1759. 2 vols. Folding map and 2 plates. Second volume has 2 plates. $1,250.

VERGA, Giovanni. *Mastro-Don Gesualdo.* New York, 1923. Translated by D. H. Lawrence. $175. London, 1925. $150.

VERNE, Jules. *Adrift in the Pacific.* London, 1889. $350. London/New York, 1889. First American edition. $350.

VERNE, Jules. *An Antarctic Mystery.* London, 1898. $250. Philadelphia, 1899. $175.

VERNE, Jules. *Five Weeks in a Balloon.* New York, 1869. Green cloth. First edition in English. $250. London, 1870. $300.

VERNE, Jules. *From the Earth to the Moon.* London, 1873. First edition in English. $200. New York, 1874. $150.

VERNE, Jules. *The Fur Country; or, Seventy Degrees North Latitude.* London, 1874. 100 full-page illustrations. Pictorial red cloth. First edition in English. $125. Boston, 1874. $100.

VERNE, Jules. *Journey to the Center of the Earth.* London, 1872. $350. New York, 1874. With no ads in book or address under publisher's imprint. $250.

VERNE, Jules. *The Lottery Ticket.* London, 1887. $300.

VERNE, Jules. *Mistress Branican.* New York (1891). First is 15 by 20 cm. (Later 13 by 18 cm.) Illustrated. First edition in English. $150.

VERNE, Jules. *The Mysterious Island Dropped from the Clouds.* London, 1875. First edition in English. $150.

VERNE, Jules. *The Purchase of the North Pole.* London, 1891. First edition in English. $300.

VERSES by Two Undergraduates. (Cambridge, Mass.), 1905. Wraps. (By Van Wyck Brooks and John Hall Wheelock.) First book for both authors. $500.

VERSES from the Harvard Advocate. Cambridge, 1906. (Contains 5 poems by Wallace Stevens.) $150.

VERSES on Various Occasions. London, 1868. (By John Henry, Cardinal Newman.) With text ending on page 340. $350.

VERVLIET, Hendrick D. L. (editor). *The Book Through Five Thousand Years.* London/New York (1972). $375.

VESEY, Paul. *Elfenbein Zahne. (Ivory Tusks).* Heidelberg (1956). Author's first book. English/German text. $300.

VESPUCCI, Amerigo. *Letter of Amerigo Vespucci Describing His Four Voyages to the New World.* San Francisco, 1926. Map in color, illustrations by Valenti Angelo. Vellum. One of 250. In slipcase. $400.

VESTAL, Stanley. *Fandango.* Boston, 1927. (By Walter S. Campbell, his first book.) $150.

VICENTIO, Ludovico. *The Calligraphic Models of Ludovico degli Arrighi, Surnamed Vicentio.* Montagnola (Paris), 1926. Edited by Stanley Morrison. 64 pp., facsimile. One of 300. $850.

VIDAL, Gore. See Box, Edgar.

VIDAL, Gore. *The City and the Pillar.* New York (1948). $250.

VIDAL, Gore. *Dark Green, Bright Red.* New York, 1950. $175.

VIDAL, Gore. *In a Yellow Wood.* New York, 1947. $250.

VIDAL, Gore. *A Search for the King.* New York, 1950. $150.

VIDAL, Gore. *The Season of Comfort.* New York, 1949. $150.

VIDAL, Gore. *Williwaw.* New York, 1946. Author's first book. $350.

VIDOCQ, François Eugene. *Memoirs of Vidocq . . .* London, 1829. Author's first book. 4 vols. $600.

VIGNOLES, Charles. *Observations Upon the Floridas.* New York, 1823. $1,500.

VILLA, Jose Garcia. *Footnote to Youth.* New York, 1933. Author's first book. $100.

VIRGINIA Illustrated . . . New York, 1857. (By David Hunter Strother.) $200.

VISCHER, Edward. *Missions of Upper California.* San Francisco, 1872. 15 plates. Wraps. $350.

VISCHER, Edward. *Sketches of the Washoe Mining Region.* San Francisco, 1862. Cloth portfolio with 29 mounted plates (25 numbered—VAB) and 24 pages of text, wraps. $3,500. (Howes calls for 26 plates.)

VISCHER'S Pictorial of California. San Francisco, 1870. 2 vols. $2,500.

VISIT to Texas (A). New York, 1834. Folding map in color, 4 plates. $750. New York, 1836. Second edition, with plates omitted. $400.

VISSCHER, William Lightfoot. *"Black Mammy": A Song of the Sunny South.* Cheyenne, 1885. Author's first book. $150.

VIVIAN, A. Pendarves. *Wanderings in the Western Land.* London, 1879. Frontispiece, plates (two folding). $200.

VIVIAN, George. *Scenery of Portugal and Spain.* London, 1839. 35 hand-colored plates. In original half morocco. $3,500.

VIVIAN, George. *Spanish Scenery.* London, 1838. Engraved title, 27 other plates. In original half morocco. $2,500.

VIVIAN Grey. London, 1826–27. 5 vols. (By Benjamin Disraeli.) Author's first novel. $300.

VIZETELLY, Henry. *A History of Champagne . . .* London, 1882. $400.

VOLNEY, C. F. *A View of the Soil and Climate of the United States . . .* Philadelphia, 1804. 2 folding plates, 2 folding maps. First American edition. $350.

VOLTAIRE, Jean François Marie Arouet de. *Candide.* New York, 1928. Translated by Richard Aldington. Illustrated by Rockwell Kent and colored by hand. Cloth, leather spine. Limited edition. One of 95 signed. In slipcase. $1,500. Ordinary issue (not hand colored). Buckram. One of 1,470 signed by Kent. $175. (First book published by Random House.)

VON HAGEN, Victor W. *The Aztec and Maya Papermakers.* New York, 1943. Illustrated, including paper samples. One of 220 signed. Issued without dustwrapper.

$600. New York (1944). 39 full-page plates at end and a tipped-in sample on Huun-Paper as the frontispiece. $125.

VONNEGUT, Kurt, Jr. *Canary in a Cat House.* Greenwich, Conn. (1961). Wraps. $125.

VONNEGUT, Kurt, Jr. *Cat's Cradle.* New York (1963). $100. London, 1963. $50.

VONNEGUT, Kurt, Jr. *Mother Night.* Greenwich, Conn. (1962). Wraps. $100. New York (1966). $75. London (1968). $60.

VONNEGUT, Kurt, Jr. *Player Piano.* New York, 1952. Author's first book. Publisher's seal and "A" on copyright page. (There is a Book Club edition which has an "A," but no seal.) $350. London, 1953. $200.

VONNEGUT, Kurt, Jr. *The Sirens of Titan.* (New York, 1959.) Wraps. $75. Boston, 1961. Cloth. $150.

VONNEGUT, Kurt, Jr. *Slapstick.* New York (1976). Trade. $30. 250 signed and numbered copies. Issued without dustwrapper in slipcase. $125. Franklin Library. Limited edition. $50. London (1976). $40.

VONNEGUT, Kurt, Jr. *Slaughterhouse-Five.* (New York, 1969.) $150. London (1970). $75.

VONNEGUT, Kurt, Jr. *Welcome to the Monkey House.* (New York, 1968.) $200. London (1969). $75.

VOORHEES, Luke. *Personal Recollections of Pioneer Life on the Mountains and Plains of the Great West.* (Cheyenne, 1920.) Portrait. 75 pages, cloth. $300.

VOORN, Henk. *Old Ream Wrappers.* North Hills, 1969. 2 copperplate prints of nineteenth-century Dutch ream wrappers. 375 numbered copies. $300.

VOSBURGH, W. S. *Cherished Portraits of Thoroughbred Horses from the Collection of William Woodward.* New York, 1929. Derrydale Press. 70 plates. Full morocco. One of 200. $1,000.

VOYAGE to Mexico and Havanna (A); Including Some General Observations on the United States. New York, 1841. By an Italian (Charles Barinetti). Half calf. $250.

W

W., E. B. *The Lady Is Cold: Poems by E. B. W.* New York, 1929. (By E. B. White.) Author's first book. First issue with Plaza Hotel statue on cover, spine lettered in gold. $350. Second issue with city skyline on cover, spine lettered in green. $300.

WADDINGTON, Miriam. *Green World.* Montreal, 1945. Author's first book. Stiff wraps and dustwrapper. $150.

WADE, Allan. *A Bibliography of the Writings of W.B. Yeats.* (London), 1958. Second edition, revised. $150.

WADE, Henry. *The Verdict of You All.* London, 1926. Author's first book. $125.

WAGNER, Lieut. Col. A. L., and KELLEY, Comdr. J. D. *The United States Army and Navy: Their Histories...* Akron, Ohio, 1899. 43 colored plates. Oblong folio, leatherette. $750.

WAGNER, Henry R. *Bullion to Books, Fifty Years of Business and Pleasure.* Los Angeles, 1962. $100.

WAGNER, Henry R. *The Cartography of the Northwest Coast of America to the Year 1800.* Berkeley, 1937. 2 vols., folio. In dustwrapper and slipcase. $400.

WAGNER, Henry R. *The Plains and the Rockies.* San Francisco 1920. Boards and cloth. First edition (suppressed). With 6-page pamphlet of corrections. $600. San Francisco, 1921. Boards. First published edition. $175. Grabhorn Press. San Francisco, 1937. Revised by C. L. Camp. Second edition. One of 600. $175. Columbus, Ohio, 1953. Third edition. $200. Boards, deluxe edition. One of 75. In slipcase. $500.

WAGNER, Henry R. *Sir Francis Drake's Voyage Around the World...* San Francisco, 1926. Maps, plates. $250. Morocco and cloth, extra illustrated. One of 100 signed. $500.

WAGNER, Henry R. *Spanish Explorations in the Strait of Juan de Fuca.* Santa Ana, Calif., 1933. Maps, illustrations. One of 425. $500. Vellum. One of 25 signed and extra-illustrated. $850.

WAGNER, Henry R. *The Spanish Southwest. 1542–1794.* Berkeley, 1924. Half morocco. One of 100. $1,000. Vellum. One of 20 signed and extra-illustrated. $1,250. Albuquerque, 1937. 2 vols., half vellum. One of 401. $1,250.

WAGNER, Henry R. *The Spanish Voyages to the Northwest Coast of America...* San Francisco, 1929. Maps, plates. $500. Vellum. One of 25 signed and extra-illustrated. $850.

WAGNER, Richard. *The Flying Dutchman.* Corvinus Press. London, 1938. Vellum. One of 130. In slipcase. $200.

WAGNER, Richard. *The Rhinegold & The Valkyrie.* London, 1910. Translated by Margaret Armour. 34 color plates by Arthur Rackham. Vellum. One of 1,150 signed by the artist. $1,000. London, 1910. Cloth. Trade edition. $200. New York, 1910. American trade edition. $150.

WAGSTAFF, Theophile. *Flore et Zephyr: Ballet Mythologique.* London, 1836. (By William Makepeace Thackeray, his first separate publication.) 9 tinted plates (including cover title) by the author. Wraps. $2,000.

WAIN, John. *Mixed Feelings! Nineteen Poems.* Reading, England, 1951. Wraps. Author's first book. One of 120. $250.

WAKEFIELD, H. R. *Gallimaufry.* London (1928). Author's first book. $200.

WAKEFIELD, H. R. *They Return at Evening.* New York, 1928. $175.

WAKEFIELD, John A. *History of the War Between the United States and the Sac and Fox Nations of Indians...* Jacksonville, Ill., 1834. $750.

WAKEMAN, Geoffrey. *Aspects of Victorian Lithography, Anastatic Printing and Photozincography.* Wymondham, 1970. 250 numbered copies. 3 mounted examples inserted. $325.

WAKEMAN, Geoffrey. *English Hand Made Papers Suitable for Bookwork.* (Loughborough), 1972. 75 numbered copies. Contains 41 specimens of paper. $550.

WAKEMAN, Geoffrey. *English Marbled Papers, A Documentary History.* (Loughborough), no-date (1978). 16 specimens of marbled papers. Limited to 112 copies. $400.

WAKEMAN, Geoffrey. *Twentieth Century English Vat Paper Mills.* (Loughborough), 1980. Small pocket at rear containing 5 paper samples. 102 numbered copies. $350.

WAKOSKI, Diane. *Coins and Coffins.* (New York, 1962.) Printed wraps. Author's first regular book. $100.

WAKOSKI, Diane. *The Diamond Merchant.* Cambridge, Mass. (1968). Gray cloth, paper label. One of 99 signed. In dustwrapper. $200.

WAKOSKI, Diane. *Discrepancies and Apparitions.* Garden City, 1966. $125.

WAKOSKI, Diane. *Justice Is Reason Enough.* (Berkeley, private printing), 1959. Author's first book. (50 mimeographed copies.) $500.

WAKOSKI, Diane. *The Magellanic Clouds.* Black Sparrow Press. Los Angeles, 1970. One of 250 signed. In acetate dustwrapper. $125. Wraps. $35.

WAKOSKI, Diane. *Thanking My Mother for Piano Lessons.* Mt. Horeb, Wis., 1969. Wraps. One of 250. $150.

WALCOTT, Derek. *In a Green Night.* London, 1962. Author's first book. (First outside Caribbean.) $200.

WALCOTT, Mary Vaux. *North American Wildflowers.* Washington, 1925–29. 400 color plates. 5 vols., cloth portfolios. One of 500 signed. In portfolios. $750. Trade. $500.

WALDROP, Keith. *Songs from the Decline of the West.* Mt. Horeb (1970). Calf. One of 120. $175.

WALEY, Arthur. See *Chinese Poems.*

WALGAMOTT, Charles S. *Reminiscences of Early Days.* Plates. (Twin Falls, Idaho, 1926–27.) 2 vols., cloth. $150.

WALKER, Alice. *Once.* New York (1968). Author's first book. $450. London, 1986. Wraps. $40.

WALKER, Alice. *The Color Purple.* New York (1982). Cloth. $350. Wraps. (Issued simultaneously.) $35. (London, 1983.) Wraps. $35. (London, 1986.) "This hardcover edition published 1986." $60.

WALKER, Alice. *The Third Life of Grange Copeland.* New York (1970). $250.

WALKER, Charles D. *Biographical Sketches of the Graduates and Eleves of the Virginia Military Institute Who Fell During the War Between the States.* Philadelphia, 1875. $150.

WALKER, Judson E. *Campaigns of General Custer in the North-West, and the Final Surrender of Sitting Bull.* New York, 1881. Illustrated. Wraps. $350.

WALKER, Margaret. *Come Down from Yonder Mountain.* (Toronto, 1962.) $200.

WALKER, Margaret. *For My People.* New York, 1942. Author's first book. $200.

WALL, Oscar G. *Recollections of the Sioux Massacre.* Lake City, Minn., 1909. $175.

WALL, W. G. *Wall's Hudson River Portfolio.* New York (about 1826). 21 color plates. Oblong atlas folio. Last complete set about $75,000 at auction.

WALLACE, Ed. R. *Parson Hanks: 14 Years in the West.* Arlington, Tex. (1906?). Wraps. $175.

WALLACE, Edgar. *The Four Just Men.* London, 1905. Frontispiece. Yellow cloth. First issue, with folding frontispiece plate and "Solution" leaf at end. $250.

WALLACE, Edgar. *The Mission That Failed! A Tale of the Raid and Other Poems.* (Cape Town, 1898.) Wraps. Author's first book. $600.

WALLACE, Edgar. *Writ in Barracks.* London, 1900. $350.

WALLACE, Lew. *Ben Hur: A Tale of the Christ.* New York, 1880. With six-word dedication (which was in first few printings). $300. Limited Editions Club, New York, 1960. In slipcase. $75.

WALLACE, Lew. *The Fair God.* Boston, 1873. Author's first book. First state on thin paper, bound in beveled boards. $100.

WALLANT, Edward Lewis. *The Pawnbroker.* New York (1961). $100.

WALROND, Eric. *Tropic Death.* New York, 1926. Author's first book. $150.

WALTERS, L. D. O. (compiler). *The Year's at the Spring: An Anthology of Recent Poetry.* London or New York, 1920. Illustrated by Harry Clarke. Vellum. One of 250 signed by Clarke. $1,000.

WALTERS, Lorenzo D. *Tombstone's Yesterday.* Tucson, 1928. Illustrated. $200.

WALTON, Izaak (or Isaac), and COTTON, Charles. *The Compleat [or Complete] Angler.* London, 1653. $20,000. New York, 1847. Edited by George W. Bethune. 2 portraits, 2 plates, other illustrations. 2 parts bound in 1 vol., light tan cloth, horizontal red stripes. First American edition. Large paper issue, with proof impressions of plates. $1,500. Trade. $750. London, 1888. "Lea & Dove Edition." Edited by R. B. Marston. Illustrated, including 54 photogravures. 2 vols., full morocco (large paper issue of 250). $2,000. Half morocco (trade issue of 500). $1,250. (The photos are on India paper in the large paper version.) London, 1893. "Tercentenary Edition." Illustrated. 2 vols., half vellum and green cloth. One of 350. $750. London, 1902. "Winchester Edition." Illustrated with etchings by William Strang and D. Y. Cameron. 2 vols., full vellum. One of 150 large paper copies signed by the artists. $650. London, 1927. 16 wood engravings by Eric Fitch Daglish. Half vellum. One of 100 with an extra signed engraving. In slipcase. $500. London (1931). Illustrated by Arthur Rackham. Vellum. One of 775 signed by Rackham. $1,000. Trade. $300.

WALTON, W. M. *Life and Adventures of Ben Thompson, the Famous Texan.* Austin, 1884. 15 plates, 229 pp., pictorial wraps. $2,500.

WANDREI, Donald. *Dark Odyssey.* St. Paul (1931). One of 400. $200.

WANDREI, Donald. *Ecstasy.* Athol, 1928. Author's first book. Issued without dust-wrapper. $500.

WANDREI, Donald. *Poems for Midnight.* Sauk City, Wis., 1964. $125.

WAR in Florida (The). Baltimore, 1836. By a Late Staff Officer (Woodburn Potter). Folding map. 2 plates. In original green cloth. $600.

WAR in Texas (The). Philadelphia, 1836. By a Citizen of the United States (Benjamin Lundy). 57 pp., printed wraps. First edition under this title (but second, enlarged, edition of an earlier Philadelphia pamphlet of the same date, *The Origin and True Causes of the Texas Insurrection*). $750.

WARD, D. B. *Across the Plains in 1853.* (Cover title.) (Seattle, 1911.) Portrait. 55 pp., printed wraps. $350.

WARD, Harry Parker. *Some American College Bookplates.* Columbus, 1915. 500 signed and numbered copies. $100.

WARD, Lynd. *God's Man: A Novel in Woodcuts.* New York (1929). Author's first book. 143 plates, no text. Pictorial boards and cloth. $150. One of 409 signed and numbered copies. In slipcase. $400.

WARD, Lynd. *Prelude to a Million Years: A Book of Wood Engravings.* New York, 1933. One of 920 signed. Issued without dustwrapper. $300.

WARD, Lynd. *Song Without Words, A Book of Engravings on Wood.* (New York, 1936.) 1,250 signed and numbered copies. $250.

WARD, Lynd. *Vertigo: A Novel in Woodcuts.* New York, 1937. Pictorial cloth. In dustwrapper. $250.

WARDER, T. B., and CATLETT, J. M. *Battle of Young's Branch, or, Manassas Plain.* Richmond, 1862. 2 folding maps. Wraps or half leather. $600.

WARDROP, James. *The Script of Humanism, Some Aspects of Humanistic Script, 1460–1560.* Oxford, 1963. $125.

WARE, Eugene. *The Indian War of 1864* . . . Topeka, 1911. Frontispiece. $175.

WARE, Joseph E. *The Emigrants' Guide to California.* St. Louis (1849). Folding map. 56 pp., cloth. $6,000 (with map).

WARHOL, Andy. *Andy Warhol's Index Book.* New York, 1967. One of 365 signed. In half cloth. $3,500. Trade. $200.

WARHOL, Andy. *Love Is a Pink Cake By Corkie & Andy.* (No-place, no-date.) Author's first book. 23 leaves in folder. $1,000.

WARNER, Charles Dudley. *Backlog Studies.* Cambridge, Mass., 1899. Illustrated. Boards. One of 250 signed. $125.

WARNER, Charles Dudley. *The Book of Eloquence.* Cazenovia, New York 1852. Author's first book. $125.

WARNER, Charles Dudley. *My Summer in a Garden.* Boston, 1871. $75.

WARNER, Susan B. See Wetherell, Elizabeth.

WARNER, Sylvia Townsend. *The Espalier.* London, 1925. Author's first book. $250.

WARRE, Henry J. *Sketches in North America and the Oregon Territory.* (London, 1848.) Map, 20 colored views (on 16 sheets). Large folio, boards. $45,000 at auction in 1988.

WARREN, Arthur. *The Charles Whittinghams Printers.* New York, 1896. One of 388 copies. $200.

WARREN, Edward. *An Epitome of Practical Surgery for Field and Hospital.* Richmond, 1863. Boards and cloth. $1,000.

WARREN, G. K. *Explorations in the Dacota Country in the Year 1855.* Washington, 1856. 3 folding maps. $400.

WARREN, John C. *Etherization: With Surgical Remarks.* Boston, 1848. $750.

WARREN, Mercy. *Poems, Dramatic and Miscellaneous.* Boston, 1790. $500.

WARREN, Robert Penn. *All the King's Men.* New York (1946). Dark red (maroon) cloth, spine lettered in gilt. Dustwrapper panel has "What Sinclair Lewis says . . ." Later dustwrappers moved Lewis's statement to the flap and had 2 other reviews on back panel. $1,000. London (1948). Dustwrapper in blue and white. $200. Dustwrapper in red with English reviews. $150. Franklin Library, 1977. Signed limited edition. $100. Limited Editions Club. (New York, 1989.) 600 numbered copies signed by Warren and the photographer, Hark O'Neal. Slipcase. $1,000.

WARREN, Robert Penn. *Blackberry Winter.* (Cummington, Mass.) 1946. 50 signed copies. Numbered in small Roman numerals 1–50. In clear wax-paper and plain white (unprinted) dustwrapper. Signed by Warren and the illustrator, Wightman Williams. $2,000. 280 numbered copies. Numbered 1–280. Issued in clear wax-paper dustwrapper and plain white paper dustwrapper (unprinted). $850.

WARREN, Robert Penn, *Chief Joseph of the Nez Percé.* (no-place, 1982.) A *Georgia Review* offprint in printed white wraps. $125. (Winston-Salem, 1982.) 5 signed and lettered copies. Issued in red quarter leather. $750. 12 signed and numbered copies in quarter leather. $400. New York (1983). 250 signed and numbered copies. Issued without dustwrapper in slipcase. $125. Trade. $15. London (1983). $30.

WARREN, Robert Penn, et al. *For Aaron Copeland.* (Winston-Salem, 1978.) 28 signed and numbered copies (I–XXVIII). Reserved for authors. Broadsides by Warren, James Dickey, and Reynolds Price. Laid-in quarter cloth folio. $450. 50 signed and numbered copies. $250.

WARREN, Robert Penn. *John Brown: The Making of a Martyr.* New York, 1929. Author's first book. $1,000.

WARREN, Robert Penn. *Meet Me in the Green Glen.* New York (1971). 300 signed and numbered copies. Issued in acetate dustwrapper and slipcase. $150. Trade. $40. London (1972). $35.

WARREN, Robert Penn. *Night Rider.* Boston, 1939. Gray cloth with maroon lettering on front and spine. $500. London (1940). $250.

WARREN, Robert Penn. *Selected Poems: New and Old, 1923–1966.* New York (1966). 250 signed and numbered copies. Issued in dustwrapper and slipcase. $225. Trade. $60.

WARREN, Robert Penn. *Thirty-six Poems.* New York, 1935. Wraps. 135 signed and numbered copies. Wraps. Numbered 1–135. Printed on Strathmore permanent all-rag paper. Clear wax-paper dustwrapper. $1,250. (There were also 10 "out-of-series" copies for review and 20 signed and numbered copies [numbers I–XX] on Duca Di Dudena Paper with clear wax-paper dustwrapper.)

WARREN, Robert Penn. *To a Little Girl . . .* (No-place, 1956.) Issued without dustwrapper. $850.

WARREN, Samuel. See *Ten Thousand a Year; Passages from the Diary.*

WASHBURNE, The Reverend Cephas. *Reminiscences of the Indians.* Richmond (1869). $300.

WASHINGTON, Booker T. *Black Belt Diamonds.* New York, 1898. $400.

WASHINGTON, Booker T. *Daily Resolves.* London/New York, 1896. Author's first book. "Booker T. Washington" on title page. $400.

WASHINGTON, Booker T. *The Future of the American Negro.* Boston, 1899. $250.

WASHINGTON, Booker T. *Up from Slavery: An Autobiography.* New York, 1901. $200. Limited Editions Club, New York, 1970. In slipcase. $100.

WASSON, R. Gordon. *The Hall Carbine Affair.* Danbury, Conn., 1971. Illustrated. Half morocco. One of 250. In slipcase. $125.

WASSON, R. Gordon. *Soma: Divine Mushroom of Immortality.* New York, 1968. Illustrated, including color plates. Half morocco. One of 680. In slipcase. $500.

WASSON, Valentina Pavlona, and WASSON, R. Gordon. *Mushrooms, Russia and History.* New York (1957). Color plates, folding maps, and plates. 2 vols., folio, buckram. One of 510. In slipcase. $2,250.

WATER Witch (The), or The Skimmer of the Seas. Dresden, 1830. By the Author of *The Pilot* (James Fenimore Cooper.) 3 vols. $2,500. London, 1830. 3 vols. First English edition. $750. Philadelphia, 1831. First American edition. $750.

WATERS. *Recollections of a Detective Police Officer.* New York, 1852. (By William Russell Waters, his first book.) $300. London, 1856. (Pictorial boards.) $750.

WATERS, Frank. *The Colorado.* New York (1946). $150.

WATERS, Frank. *Fever Pitch.* New York (1930). Author's first book. $400.

WATERS, Frank. *Leon Gaspard.* Flagstaff, Ariz., 1964. Illustrated, including color, by Gaspard. One of 500 signed. In slipcase. $200. Trade. first edition not stated. In dustwrapper. $75. Flagstaff (1981). One of 150 signed. Issued without dustwrapper. In slipcase. $200. Trade in dustwrapper. $60.

WATERS, Frank. *Midas of the Rockies.* New York (1937). $275.

WATERS, Frank. *The Wild Earth's Nobility.* New York, 1935. $300.

WATKINS, C. L. *Photographic Views of the Falls and Valley of Yosemite.* San Francisco, 1863. Map and 53(?) mounted photographs. Folio, morocco. $35,000.

WATKINS, C. L. *Photographs of the Columbia River and Oregon.* San Francisco (about 1873). 51 mounted albumen prints. Elephant folio, morocco with redwood inlay. $50,000 or more depending on condition of prints.

WATKINS, C. L. *Photographs of the Pacific Coast.* San Francisco (about 1873). 49 mounted albumen prints. Elephant folio, morocco with redwood inlay. $50,000 or more, depending on condition of prints.

WATKINS, C. L. *Watkins' New Series Columbia River Scenery, Oregon.* No-place (about 1880). 40 plates. Oblong, leather. $12,500.

WATSON, Douglas S. *West Wind: The Life Story of Joseph Reddeford Walker . . .* Los Angeles, 1934. Plates, folding map. Boards. One of 100. $850. Trade. $250.

WATSON, Douglas S. (editor). *California in the Fifties.* San Francisco, 1936. 50 views. Oblong folio, cloth. One of 850. In dustwrapper. $450.

WATSON, Douglas S. (editor). *The Spanish Occupation of California.* Grabhorn Press. San Francisco, 1934. Illustrated. Boards and cloth. One of 550. $150.

WATSON, Frederick. *Hunting Pie.* Derrydale Press. New York (1938). Illustrated. Boards. One of 750. $175.

WATSON, William. *The Father of the Forest and Other Poems.* London, 1895. Frontispiece portrait. One of 75. $125.

WATSON, William. *Odes and Other Poems.* London, 1894. One of 75. $125.

WATTS, W. J. *Cherokee Citizenship and a Brief History of Internal Affairs in the Cherokee Nation.* (Cover title.) Muldrow, Indian Territory (Okla.), 1895. Portrait. Wraps. $250.

WATTS, W. W. *Old English Silver.* New York, 1924. 307 plates. $200. London, 1924. First English edition. $200. One of 40 in leather binding. $300.

WAUGH, Alec. *The Loom of Youth.* London, 1917. Author's first book. $125. New York (1917). $75.

WAUGH, Evelyn. *Basil Seal Rides Again.* London, 1963. 750 signed and numbered copies. Issued in glassine dustwrapper. $450. Boston (1963). 1,000 signed and numbered copies. Issued in blue buckram and acetate dustwrapper. $350.

WAUGH, Evelyn. *Black Mischief.* London (1932). 250 signed and numbered copies. Issued in dustwrapper. $1,750. Black cloth with variant noted in gray-blue cloth. (Some copies with Book Society wraparound band.) $600. New York (1934). $450.

WAUGH, Evelyn. *Decline and Fall.* London, 1928. "Originally publ . . . September 1928" on copyright page. Pages 168 and 169 have "Martin Gaythorn-Brodie" and "Kevin Saunderson," respectively. $2,500. Second issue with pages 168 and 169 with "The Hon. Miles Malpractice" and "Lord Parakeet," respectively. $2,250. Doubleday, Garden City, 1929. $1,250. Farrar & Rinehart, New York, 1929. Doubleday remainder sheets with Farrar title page tipped in. $850. Franklin Library, 1979. Limited edition. $60.

WAUGH, Evelyn. *A Handful of Dust.* London, 1934. Noted in Book Society wraparound band. $3,000. New York (1934). $500.

WAUGH, Evelyn. *The Holy Places.* London, 1952. 50 numbered copies signed by Waugh and the illustrator, Reynolds Stone. Issued in red niger morocco and dustwrapper. $1,500. 900 numbered copies. Bound in red buckram and numbered 51–950. Issued in plain gray dustwrapper. $250. London/New York, 1953. 50 signed and numbered copies. $1,250. 950 numbered copies. $200.

WAUGH, Evelyn. *Labels: A Mediterranean Journal.* (London) 1930. 110 signed and numbered copies with a page of author's holograph manuscript tipped in. $1,250. London, 1930. $600.

WAUGH, Evelyn. *Love Among the Ruins.* London, 1953. 350 signed and numbered copies. Issued in glassine dustwrapper with printed paper flaps. $450. Trade. $150.

WAUGH, Evelyn. *The Loved One.* Boston, 1948. Also states "Published June 1948." $100. (London, 1948.) 250 numbered copies signed by Waugh and the illustrator, Stuart Boyle. In glassine dustwrapper. $1,000. Trade. $100.

WAUGH, Evelyn. *P.R.B.: An Essay on the PreRaphaelite Brotherhood.* London, 1926. Half cloth. $4,000. (Kent, 1982.) 475 numbered copies. In acetate dustwrapper. $125.

WAUGH, Evelyn. *Remote People.* London, 1931. $750. New York (1932). $600.

WAUGH, Evelyn. *Rossetti His Life and Works.* London, 1928. $1,500. New York, 1928. $1,000.

WAUGH, Evelyn. *Scoop.* London (1938). First issue with "s" in "as" in last line of page 88 and "Daily Beast" logo in black letters on front cover of dustwrapper. $600. Without "s" in "as" on page 88 and without "Daily Beast" on dustwrapper. $450. Boston, 1938. First edition stated, and "Publ . . . July 1938." $300.

WAUGH, Evelyn. *They Were Still Dancing.* Cape & Smith, New York (1932). The U.S. edition of *Remote People.* $650. Farrar & Rinehart, New York (1932). Noted with bottom edge trimmed and untrimmed. $500.

WAUGH, Evelyn. *The World to Come.* (Privately printed), 1916. Author's first book. $7,500.

WAUGH, Frederic J. *The Clan of Munes.* New York, 1916. Author's first book. $400.

WAVERLEY; or, 'Tis Sixty Years Since. Edinburgh, 1814. (By Sir Walter Scott.) 3 vols. First issue, with "our" instead of "your" in first line on page 136 in vol. II. In original boards, washed and recased. $11,000 at auction in 1988. Rebound. $1,000.

WAYLAND, John W. *History of Rockingham County.* Dayton, Va., 1912. Plates. Buckram. $150.

WEALE, W. H. James. *Bookbindings and Rubbings of Bindings in the National Art Library, South Kensington Museum.* London, 1898. 2 vols. bound in 1. $175.

WEARY, Ogdred. *The Beastly Baby.* (New York, 1962.) (By Edward Gorey.) Wraps. $200.

WEATHERLY, Frederick Edward. *Magic Pictures: A Book of Changing Scenes.* London (about 1890). 16 pp. with pull slides to change pictures (a movable book). Pictorial cloth. $350.

WEATHERLY, Frederick Edward. *Pretty Polly: A Novel Book for Children.* London (about 1895). 4 double-page three-dimensional color plates. Half cloth. $250.

WEATHERLY, Frederick Edward. *Punch and Judy and Some of Their Friends.* London (1885). Illustrated by Patty Townsend. Half cloth. $300.

WEBB, Mary. *The Chinese Lion.* London, 1937. Decorated boards, red cloth spine, red label on front cover. One of 350. In slipcase. $150.

WEBB, Mary. *The Golden Arrow.* London, 1916. Author's first book. $175.

WEBB, Mary. *Gone to Earth.* London (1917). Dark red cloth. $150.

WEBB, Mary. *The House in Dormer Forest.* London (1920). In dustwrapper. $200.

WEBB, Mary. *Precious Bane.* London (1924). $250.

WEBB, Walter Prescott. *The Great Plains.* Boston (1931). Illustrated. With error in heading of chapter 2. $200.

WEBB, Walter Prescott. *The Texas Rangers . . .* Boston, 1935. $200. Half leather. One of 200 signed. In slipcase. $750.

WEBBER, C. W. *The Hunter-Naturalist; Romance of Sporting, or Wild Scenes and Wild Hunters.* Philadelphia (1851). Engraved title page and 9 colored lithographs, other illustrations. Cloth, leather spine and corners. $500.

WEBBER, C. W. *Old Hicks the Guide . . .* New York, 1848. $350.

WEBBER, C. W. *Wild Scenes and Song Birds.* New York, 1854. 20 colored plates. Morocco. $400. New York, 1855. $250.

WEBER, Carl J. *Fore-Edge Painting, A Historical Survey of a Curious Art in Book Decoration.* Irvington-on-Hudson, N.Y., 1966. Originally appeared as *A Thousand and One Fore-Edge Paintings.* $150.

WEBER, Carl J. *A Thousand and One Fore-Edge Paintings.* Waterville, Me., 1949. Illustrated. Half cloth. One of 1,000. In dustwrapper. $600.

WEBER, Max. *Cubist Poems.* London, 1914. Author's first book. 100 numbered copies. $300. Blue pictorial cloth. $200. Wraps. $150.

WEBSTER, Jean. *Daddy Long Legs.* New York, 1912. Illustrated by the author. Decorated cloth. $125.

WEBSTER, John White. *A Description of the Island of St. Michael.* Boston, 1821. Author's first book. $200.

WEBSTER, Noah. See Ford, Paul Leicester (for *Webster Genealogy*).

WEBSTER, Noah. *An American Dictionary of the English Language.* New York, 1828. Portrait. 2 vols. $5,000.

WEBSTER, Noah. *A Compendious Dictionary of the English Language.* Hartford, 1806. $1,000.

WEEDOM, J. *Round Text Copies, with a Set of Roman Ciphers for Marking Goods.* London, 1794. Wraps. 15 engraved plates. $250.

WEEGEE. *Naked City.* New York (1945). Author's first book. $200.

WEIDMAN, Jerome. *I Can Get It for You Wholesale.* New York, 1937. Author's first book. $300.

WEINBAUM, Stanley G. *Dawn of Flame and Other Stories.* (Jamaica, New York, 1936.) Author's first book. One of 5 copies with introduction by Palmer. $1,750. With introduction by Keating. (250 copies.) $1,000.

WEITENKAMPF, Frank. *The Etching of Contemporary Life.* Marlborough-on-Hudson, 1916. One of 250 copies (although 270 actually produced). $750.

WEITENKAMPF, Frank. *The Illustrated Book.* Cambridge, 1938. 210 numbered copies. Slipcase. $100.

WEIZMANN, Chaim. *Trial and Error.* New York (1949). 2 vols. One of 500 signed. $150. Trade. $50.

WELBY, Adlard. *A Visit to North America . . .* London, 1821. 14 plates. $1,000.

WELCH, Charles A. *History of the Big Horn Basin With Stories of Early Days . . .* (Salt Lake City), 1940. $150.

WELCH, Denton. *Maiden Voyage.* London, 1943. Frontispiece portrait. Author's first book. $200. New York. $60.

WELCH, Lew. *Wobbly Rock.* (San Francisco), 1960. Wraps. Author's first book. One of 500. $60.

WELD, Isaac, Jr. *Travels Through the States of North America, and the Provinces of Upper and Lower Canada, During the Years 1795, 1796 and 1797.* London, 1799. Ads, 16 maps (1 folding) and plates. $1,250.

WELDON, Fay. *The Fat Woman's Joke.* London, 1967. Author's first book. $100.

WELLMAN, Paul. *Broncho Apache.* New York, 1936. $200.

WELLMAN, Paul. *The Callaghan Yesterday and Today.* Encinal (about 1945). Illustrated, map. Stiff pictorial wraps. $200.

WELLMAN, Paul. *The Iron Mistress.* New York, 1940. $150.

WELLS, H. G. *The Adventures of Tommy.* London (1929). $175.

WELLS, H. G. *The Country of the Blind.* London (1911). First edition not stated. Dark blue cloth. $250. Golden Cockerel Press. London, 1939. Wood engravings. Orange vellum. One of 30 signed. $1,250. Trade. One of 280. $600.

WELLS, H. G. *The Door in the Wall.* New York, 1911. Illustrated with Alvin Langdon Coburn photogravures. Boards. One of 600. $1,250. Many were issued without the photogravures. $300.

WELLS, H. G. *The First Men in the Moon.* London, 1901. Illustrated by Claude Shepperson. First issue dark blue cloth, gilt lettering on cover. $400. Second issue in light blue cloth with black lettering. $300. Indianapolis (1901). $250.

WELLS, H. G. *The Invisible Man.* London, 1897. $500. New York, 1897. First American edition. $250. Limited Editions Club, New York, 1967. Cloth. In slipcase. $75.

WELLS, H. G. *The Island of Doctor Moreau.* London, 1896. First issue with publisher's monogram stamped on back cover. (No priority established on ads.) $600. New York, 1896. Black cloth. (Blue and green cloths were later issues.) $300.

WELLS, H. G. *The Sea Lady.* London, 1902. First issue in red cloth with catalog dated July 1902. $150. New York, 1908. Green cloth. First American edition. $100.

WELLS, H. G. *Select Conversations with an Uncle (Now Extinct) and Two Other Reminiscences.* London, 1895. Wells's first literary work. $350. New York, 1895. $250.

WELLS, H. G. *Tales of Space and Time.* London, 1900 (actually 1899). Olive cloth. $400. New York, 1899. Green cloth. First American edition. $150. (Currey considers the English edition as the first.)

WELLS, H. G. *Text Book of Biology.* London (1893). Author's first book preceded by a doctoral thesis. 2 vols. First binding dark green cloth. $600. Later in brown cloth. $350.

WELLS, H. G. *Thirty Strange Stories.* New York, 1897. Pictorial boards. $400.

WELLS, H. G. *The Time Machine.* New York, 1895. In tan cloth with Wells's name on title page as "H. S. Wells" and 6 pages of ads. $750. London, 1895. First issue in gray cloth stamped in purple and 16 pages of ads. $750. Light blue-gray wraps printed in dark blue, no catalog. $1,000. (See Currey for later bindings.)

WELLS, H. G. *Tono Bungay.* London, 1909. With ads dated "1.09." $150.

WELLS, H. G. *Twelve Stories and a Dream.* London, 1903. $200.

WELLS, H. G. *The War in the Air.* London, 1908. 16 plates. First issue in pictorial blue cloth. With all lettering and decorations in gilt and "George Bell & Son" at base of spine. $400. New York, 1908. Illustrated by Eric Pape. $200.

WELLS, H. G. *The War of the Worlds.* London, 1898. Gray cloth. With 16 pages of ads. (Later 32 pages.) $400.

WELLS, H. G. *When the Sleeper Wakes.* London, 1899. 3 plates. $250. New York, 1899. Green cloth. $200.

WELLS, H. G. *The Wonderful Visit.* London, 1895. Red cloth. With front cover blank is probable first. $350. With red cloth and front cover stamped in gold. $250. New York, 1895. $250.

WELLS, H. G. *The World of William Clissold.* London, 1926. 3 vols. One of 198 signed. $350. Trade. $150.

WELLS, Oliver (editor). See *An Anthology of the Younger Poets.*

WELLS, William, and ONKEN, Otto. *Western Scenery: or, Land and River, Hill and Dale, in the Mississippi Valley.* Cincinnati, 1851. Pictorial title page, 19 full-page lithographic views, 52 pp. of text. Boards and calf. $5,000.

WELLS, William Charles. *An Essay on Dew* . . . London, 1814. $500. Philadelphia, 1838. First American edition. $250.

WELSH, Charles. *A Bookseller of the Last Century* . . . London, 1885. $10.

WELTY, Eudora. *The Bride of the Innisfallen.* New York (1955). Copyright notice of first issue contains only one date: "copyright . . . 1955, by Eudora Welty." Issued in blue-and-green mottled boards, green cloth spine, silver stamping. $500. Second issue copyright contains 5 dates: "copyright . . . 1949, 1951, 1952, 1954, 1955 . . ." Copyright page tipped in. Binding as in first issue. $200. Third issue and second binding: copyright notice with 5 dates, but issued in light grayish brown cloth, blue and gold stamping. $125. London (1955). $125.

WELTY, Eudora. *A Curtain of Green.* Garden City, 1941. Author's first book. Preceded by a prepublicity pamphlet. $1,000. London (1943). $300.

WELTY, Eudora. *Delta Wedding.* New York (1946). $300. London (1947). $200.

WELTY, Eudora. *Eudora Welty: A Note on the Author and Her Work.* (Garden City, 1941). Wraps. A prepublicity pamphlet for *A Curtain of Green* written by Katherine Anne Porter and containing Welty's short story "The Key." Considered to be Welty's first book. $2,000.

WELTY, Eudora. *The Golden Apples.* New York (1949). $175. London (1950). Issued without endpapers. $150.

WELTY, Eudora. *Losing Battles.* New York (1970). 300 signed and numbered copies. Issued in acetate dustwrapper and slipcase. $300. London (1982). $40.

WELTY, Eudora. *Music from Spain.* Greenville, Miss., 1948. 750 signed and numbered copies. Issued in glassine dustwrapper. $750.

WELTY, Eudora. *The Optimist's Daughter.* New York (1972). 225 signed and numbered copies. Approximately 75 copies were destroyed of projected edition of 300 because of defective bindings. Issued without dustwrapper in slipcase. $350. Trade. $50. (London, 1953.) $50. Franklin Library, 1978. Limited edition. $50. Franklin Library, 1980. Signed limited edition. $100.

WELTY, Eudora. *Place in Fiction.* (No-place, no date. Circa 1956.) Printed wraps. About 50 copies. An off-print from the *South Atlantic Quarterly.* $800. New York, 1957. 26 signed and lettered copies. Issued in glassine dustwrapper. $750. 300 signed and numbered copies. Issued in glassine dustwrapper. Part of the edition was destroyed. $450.

WELTY, Eudora. *The Ponder Heart.* New York (1954). $125. London (1954). $100.

WELTY, Eudora. *The Robber Bridegroom.* Garden City, 1942. $500. London (1944). $200. West Hatfield, Mass., 1987. 150 numbered copies signed by Welty and the illustrator, Barry Moser. In full red leather without slipcase. $750. Trade (illustrated by Moser). $30.

WELTY, Eudora. *A Sweet Devouring.* New York, 1969. Wraps. 26 signed and lettered copies. $400. 150 signed and numbered copies. Wraps. $300.

WELTY, Eudora. *Twenty Photographs.* (Winston-Salem, 1980.) 20 signed and numbered copies (Roman). Photographs mounted on heavy rag board in clamshell folio box. Errata slip laid in. 5 of these copies were for the author's use. $2,250. 75 signed and numbered copies. Issued in clamshell box. Errata slip laid in. $1,750.

WELTY, Eudora. *The Wide Net and Other Stories.* New York (1943). $600. London (1945). On reverse of Welty dustwrapper is dustwrapper for F. E. Mills Young's *Unlucky Farm.* $250.

WENDEHACK, Clifford Charles. *Golf and Country Clubs.* New York, 1929. $350.

WENTWORTH, Lady Judith Anne. *The Authentic Arabian Horse and His Descendants.* London (1945). 26 color plates, numerous other illustrations. Blue cloth. In dustwrapper. $600.

WENTWORTH, Lady Judith Anne. *Thoroughbred Racing Stock and Its Ancestors.* London, 1938. 21 color plates. Red buckram. In dustwrapper. $350. London (1960). Second edition. In dustwrapper and slipcase. $200.

WEPT of Wish Ton Wish (The): A Tale. Philadelphia, 1829. By the Author of *The Pioneers.* (By James Fenimore Cooper.) 2 vols. First American edition. $600. (For first edition, see *The Borderers.*)

WERTH, John J. *A Dissertation on the Resources and Policy of California.* Benicia, 1851. 87 pp. $1,500.

WERTHEIM, Barbara. *The Lost British Policy.* London, 1938. (Maiden name of Barbara Tuchman, her first book.) $400.

WERTHER'S Younger Brother . . . (By Michael Fraenkel.) New York/Paris (1931). Author's first book. Stiff wraps. $150.

WESCOTT, Glenway. *The Babe's Bed.* Paris, 1930. One of 375 signed. $250. One of 18 on parchment. $500.

WESCOTT, Glenway. *The Bitterns: A Book of Twelve Poems.* Evanston, Ill. (1920). Author's first book. Black wraps with printed silver design. One of 200 copies. $600.

WESCOTT, Glenway. *A Calendar of Saints for Unbelievers.* Paris, 1932. Illustrated by Pavel Tchelitchew. Half morocco. One of 40 signed. In slipcase. $500. Cloth. One of 695. In glassine dustwrapper and slipcase. $250.

WESCOTT, Glenway. *Goodbye, Wisconsin.* New York, 1928. One of 250 signed. In slipcase. $200. Trade. $75.

WESCOTT, Glenway. *The Grandmothers.* New York, 1927. Cloth-backed boards. One of 250 signed. In slipcase. $200. Trade. $60.

WESCOTT, Glenway. *Natives of Rock, XX Poems: 1921–1922.* New York, 1925. One of 25 on vellum. In slipcase. $500. One of 550 plain copies. In glassine dustwrapper and slipcase. $125.

WEST, Anthony. *Gloucestershire.* London, 1939. Author's first book. $125.

WEST, Anthony. *On a Dark Night.* London, 1951. $75.

WEST, Dorothy. *Living Is Easy.* Boston, 1948. Author's first book. $200.

WEST, John C. *A. Texan in Search of a Fight.* Waco, 1901. 189 pp., wraps. $400. Also in cloth. $300.

WEST, Nathanael. *A Cool Million.* New York (1934). First binding in light tan cloth. $1,000. Also variants in green and rust cloths. $900. London (1954). First English edition. $300.

WEST, Nathanael. *The Day of the Locust.* New York (1939). $750.

WEST, Nathanael. *The Dream Life of Balso Snell.* Paris (1931). Contact Editions. Author's first book. Printed stiff wraps. One of 485. In tissue dustwrapper. $1,500. One of 15 signed and bound in cloth. $7,500.

WEST, Nathanael. *Miss Lonelyhearts.* Liveright. New York (1933). $2,000. Harcourt, Brace. New York (1933). $850. Greenberg. New York (1933). (Remainder imprint.) $300.

WEST, Rebecca. *The Judge.* London (1922). $200.

WEST, Rebecca. *The Return of the Soldier.* New York, 1918. In dustwrapper. $350. Without dustwrapper. $75. London (1918). First English edition. In dustwrapper. $300. Without dustwrapper. $60.

WESTCOTT, Edward Noyes. *David Harum.* Yellow cloth. New York, 1898. Author's first book. First state, with perfect "J" in "Julius" in next-to-last line of page 40. $75.

WESTLAKE, Donald. *The Mercenaries.* New York (1960). Author's first book. $150.

WESTON, Edward (photographer). *California and the West.* (By Charis Wilson Weston and Edward Weston.) New York (1940). Illustrated. $500.

WESTON, Edward (photographer). *Edward Weston.* New York, 1932. 40 plates. Half vellum. One of 550 signed. $1,250.

WESTON, Edward (photographer). *Fifty Photographs.* New York (1947). (By Weston and others.) Half cloth. One of 1,500 initialed by Weston. $850.

WESTON, Edward (photographer). *My Camera on Point Lobos.* Yosemite National Park and Boston, 1950. Illustrated. Folio, spiral binding. In dustwrapper. $500.

WESTON, Patrick. *Desert Dreamers.* London (1914). Author's first book. (250 copies.) $125.

WESTON, Silas. *Four Months in the Mines of California; or, Life in the Mountains.* Providence, 1854. 24 pp., printed wraps. Second edition (of *Life in the Mountains*). $750.

WESTON, Silas. *Life in the Mountains: or Four Months in the Mines of California.* Providence, 1854. 36 pp., printed wraps. $1,000.

WESTROP, M. S. Dudley. *Irish Glass.* London (about 1920). 40 plates. Buckram. Issued without dustwrapper. $250. Philadelphia, 1921. Issued without dustwrapper. $150.

WESTWARD Ho! New York, 1832. 2 vols., in original cloth. (By James Kirke Paulding.) $300.

WESTWOOD, T. *A New Bibliotheca Piscatoria.* London, 1861. With 4-page supplement dated 1869. $100.

WETHERBEE, J., Jr. *A Brief Sketch of Colorado Territory and the Gold Mines of That Region.* Boston, 1863. 24 pp., printed wraps. $2,000.

WETHERED, H. N. and SIMPSON, T. *The Architectural Side of Golf.* London, 1929. One of 50 large paper copies. $1,500. Trade. $700.

WETHERELL, Elizabeth. *The Wide, Wide World.* New York, 1851. 2 vols. (By Susan B. Warner.) First issue, brown cloth. $500. Later, blue cloth. $300. London, 1853. 2 vols., red cloth. $200.

WETMORE, Alphonso (compiler). *Gazetteer of the State of Missouri . . .* St. Louis, 1837. Frontispiece and folding map. In original cloth. $500.

WETMORE, Helen Cody. *Last of the Great Scouts: The Life Story of Col. William F. Cody, "Buffalo Bill."* (Duluth, 1899.) First edition, with 267 pages. $300. Another issue, 296 pages. One of 500 signed by Cody. $450. Trade. $150.

WEYMAN, Stanley J. *The House of the Wolf.* London, 1890. Decorated gray cloth. Author's first book. $125.

WHARTON, Edith. See Jones, Edith Newbold.

WHARTON, Edith. *The Decoration of Houses.* (With O. Codman.) New York, 1897. $350. London, 1898. $250.

WHARTON, Edith. *Ethan Frome.* New York, 1911. Cloth, top edges gilt on early copies. First issue, with perfect type in last line of page 135. $300. New York, 1922. With new introduction. One of 2,000. $150. Limited Editions Club (New York), 1939. Cloth. In slipcase. $60.

WHARTON, Edith. *The Greater Inclination.* New York, 1899. $175.

WHARTON, Edith. *Italian Villas and Their Gardens.* New York, 1904. Illustrated by Maxfield Parrish and others. Pictorial cloth. $400.

WHARTON, Edith. *Twelve Poems.* Medici Society. London, 1926. Buckram and boards. One of 130 signed. In dustwrapper. $600.

WHARTON, Edith (editor). *The Book of the Homeless.* New York, 1916. One of 125 on Van Gelder paper. $400. One of 50 with portfolio of plates and facsimiles. $600. Trade. $200.

WHARTON, J. E. *History of the City of Denver.* Denver, 1866. Printed pink wraps. $1,500.

WHAT Is Man? New York, 1906. (By Samuel Langhorne Clemens.) Gray-blue boards, green-black leather label on spine. First issue, with "thinks about" as last line of page 131. One of 250. $400. Second issue with "thinks about it," $300. (Note: The first English edition identifies Twain as author.)

WHEAT, Carl I. *Books of the California Gold Rush.* San Francisco, 1949. Pictorial boards and cloth. In dustwrapper. One of 500. $400.

WHEAT, Carl I. *Mapping the Trans-Mississippi West.* Grabhorn Press. San Francisco, 1957–63. Illustrated. 5 vols. in 6 vols., folio, buckram, leatherette spine. One of 1,000. $2,750.

WHEAT, Carl I. *The Maps of the California Gold Region 1848–57.* Grabhorn Press. San Francisco, 1942. 26 maps. Folio, cloth. One of 300. $1,750. Three-quarters calf. One of 22 with map by Gibbs added. $2,500.

WHEAT, Carl I. *The Pioneer Press of California.* Oakland, 1948. One of 450. $300.

WHEAT, Marvin T. See Cincinnatus.

WHEATLEY, Dennis. *The Forbidden Territory.* London (1933). Author's first book. $150.

WHEATLEY, Phillis. *Poems on Various Subjects, Religions and Moral.* London, 1773. Author's first book. $5,000. Philadelphia, 1786. $3,500.

WHEELER, Alfred. *Land Titles in San Francisco, and the Laws Affecting the Same* . . . San Francisco, 1852. Tissue map. $1,000.

WHEELER, Ella. *Drops of Water: Poems.* New York, 1872. (By Ella Wheeler Wilcox.) Author's first book. $75.

WHEELOCK, John Hall. See *Verses by Two Undergraduates.*

WHEELOCK, John Hall. *The Human Fantasy.* Boston, 1911. $100.

WHEELWRIGHT, John Brooks. *North Atlantic Passage.* (Florence, Italy, 1924.) Author's first book. $1,000.

WHIGHAM, Henry James. *How to Play Golf.* Chicago, 1897. $150.

WHILLDIN, M. A. *Description of Western Texas.* Galveston, 1876. 28 plates, folding map, 120 pp., pictorial wraps. $750.

WHISTLER, James McNeill. *The Gentle Art of Making Enemies.* London, 1890. One of 250 signed. $600.

WHITE, Antonia. *Frost in May.* London (1933). Author's first book. $200.

WHITE, Diana. *The Descent of Ishtar.* Eragny Press. London, 1903. Frontispiece. Boards, paper label. One of 226. In dustwrapper. $600.

WHITE, E. B. See W. E. B.; Finny, Sterling. See also Thurber, James.

WHITE, E. B. *Charlotte's Web.* New York (1952). Illustrated by Garth Williams. Pictorial cloth. $350.

WHITE, E. B. *Stuart Little.* New York (1945). Illustrated by Garth Williams. Pictorial cloth. $300.

WHITE, The Reverend George. *Statistics of the State of Georgia.* Savannah, 1849. Large hand-colored map. With errata leaf. $450.

WHITE, Gilbert. *The Natural History and Antiquities of Selborne.* London, 1789. With 2 engraved titles and 7 plates. $1,500. Limited Editions Club, Ipswich, 1972. In slipcase. $125.

WHITE, Gilbert. *The Writings of Gilbert White of Selborne.* Nonesuch Press. London, 1938. Wood engravings by Eric Ravilious. 2 vols., gray buckram. One of 850. In slipcase. $650.

WHITE, Gleeson. *English Illustration "The Sixties": 1855–70.* London, 1906. Third printing with minor revision. $150.

WHITE, Grace Miller. *A Child of the Slums.* New York, 1904. Author's first book. Wraps. $200.

WHITE, Owen P. *The Autobiography of a Durable Sinner.* New York (1942). Cloth. First issue, with pages 239–44 intact as part of original binding. $150. Second issue, with pages 239–44 reset and tipped in. $50.

WHITE, Owen P. *Out of the Desert.* El Paso, 1923. Illustrated. $200.

WHITE, Patrick. *The Ploughman . . .* Sydney, 1935. Author's first book. One of 300. $1,750.

WHITE, Patrick. *Happy Valley.* London, 1939. $1,250. New York, 1940. $650.

WHITE, Stewart Edward. *Arizona Nights.* New York, 1907. In dustwrapper. $400.

WHITE, Stewart Edward. *The Birds of Mackinac Island.* New York, 1893. Author's first book. Wraps. $500.

WHITE, Stewart Edward. *The Claim Jumpers.* New York, 1901. Pictorial cloth. $125. Printed wraps. $200. Marbled boards with leather spine. $200.

WHITE, Stewart Edward. *The Forest.* New York, 1903. Illustrated by Thomas Fogarty. Paper label. One of 80 large paper copies signed by the author. $200. Trade. $50.

WHITE, Stewart Edward. *Gold.* New York, 1913. In dustwrapper. $250.

WHITE, Stewart Edward. *The Long Rifle.* New York, 1932. $150.

WHITE, Stewart Edward. *Rules of the Game.* New York, 1910. In dustwrapper. $300.

WHITE, Stewart Edward. *The Gray Dawn.* New York, 1915. In dustwrapper. $200.

WHITE, T. H. See Aston, James.

WHITE, T. H. *England Have My Bones.* London, 1936. $200. New York, 1936. $75.

WHITE, T. H. *Farewell Victoria.* London, 1933. $250. New York, 1934. First binding in orange cloth, paper labels. $175.

WHITE, T. H. *The Green Bay Tree.* (Cambridge, England, 1929.) Wraps. Author's first book. $400.

WHITE, T. H. *Loved Helen and Other Poems.* London (1929). $350.

WHITE, T. H. *The Once and Future King.* London, 1958. $250.

WHITE, T. H. *The Sword in the Stone.* London, 1938. $400.

WHITE, T. H. *The Witch in the Wood.* New York, 1939. $250. London (1940). First English edition. $400.

WHITE, Walter F. *The Fire in the Flint.* New York, 1924. Author's first book. $150.

WHITE, William Allen. *The Court of Boyville.* New York, 1899. Illustrated by Orson Lowell and Gustav Verbeek. Pictorial buckram. $100.

WHITE, William Allen, and PAINE, Albert Bigelow. *Rhymes by Two Friends.* Illustrated. Blue cloth. Fort Scott, Kan. (1893). First book for each author. $125.

WHITEHEAD, Alfred North, and RUSSELL, Bertrand. *Principia Mathematica.* Cambridge, 1910–12–13. 3 vols. $7,500.

WHITEHEAD, Charles E. *Wild Sports in the South.* New York, 1860. $200.

WHITEHEAD, Henry S. *Jumbee and Other Uncanny Tales.* (Sauk City, Wis.) 1944. Author's first book. $200.

WHITELY, Ike. *Rural Life in Texas.* Atlanta, 1891. 82 pp., pictorial wraps. $450.

WHITMAN, Walt. See *Leaves of Grass; Leaves of Grass Imprints.*

WHITMAN, Walt. *After All, Not to Create Only.* (Washington, 1871.) 11 folio numbered sheets, printed on 1 side only, stitched. First edition, first (proof) issue. $1,750. Boston, 1871. Green, maroon, or brown cloth. First book edition. $400. Limp cloth wraps. $500.

WHITMAN, Walt. *As a Strong Bird on Pinions Free, And Other Poems.* Washington, 1872. Green cloth. (Note: Although "Leaves of Grass" appears in small letters above this title, this is not one of the later editions of the book of the same title.) $500.

WHITMAN, Walt. *Calamus: A Series of Letters, Written During the Years 1868–1880 . . . to a Young Friend (Peter Doyle).* Boston, 1897. Cloth. $300. Boards, cloth back, paper label. One of 35 on large paper. $400.

WHITMAN, Walt. *Complete Poems and Prose . . . 1855–1888.* (Philadelphia, 1888–89.) Portrait title page, 1 plate. Half cloth and boards, paper label. One of 600 signed. $1,000.

WHITMAN, Walt. *Democratic Vistas.* See entry under the title *Memoranda: Democratic Vistas;* see also same title entry under Whitman, following.

WHITMAN, Walt. *Franklin Evans; or The Inebriate.* New York, 1842. Whitman's first separately published work priced at 12½ cents. 31 pp., pamphlet without covers. Issued as a supplement to the *New World.* $7,500. Priced at 6½ cents. $4,000.

WHITMAN, Walt. *Goodbye, My Fancy. 2nd Annex to Leaves of Grass.* Philadelphia, 1891. Phototype portrait. Green or maroon cloth. $400. Large paper issue. $600.

WHITMAN, Walt. *The Half Breed and Other Stories.* New York, 1927. Edited by T. O. Mabbott. Illustrated. Half cloth. One of 155. $200. One of 30 with illustrations signed in proof by the artist, Allen Lewis. $450.

WHITMAN, Walt. *Memoranda: Democratic Vistas.* Washington, 1871. Light green wraps. First edition, later printing (the first did not have Whitman's name on title page but only in copyright notice). $600. (For first printing, see the title entry.)

WHITMAN, Walt. *Memoranda During the War.* Camden, N.J., 1875–76. 2 portraits. Red-brown cloth, green endpapers. First printed page beginning "Remembrance Copy" and with space below for autograph (signed). $2,000. Another issue, without the portraits and the leaf headed "Remembrance Copy": $750.

WHITMAN, Walt. *Notes & Fragments.* (London, Ont., Canada), 1899. Edited by Richard Maurice Bucke. Blue pebbled cloth. One of 225 signed by Bucke. $200.

WHITMAN, Walt. *November Boughs.* Philadelphia, 1888. Frontispiece portrait. Maroon or green cloth. $350. Large paper issue. Dark green cloth, or limp red or blue cloth. $500.

WHITMAN, Walt. *Pictures: An Unpublished Poem.* New York, 1927. Boards, paper label. One of 700. $150.

WHITMAN, Walt. *Poems by Walt Whitman.* London, 1868. Edited by William Michael Rossetti. Frontispiece portrait. Ad leaf pasted in. Cloth, gilt panel on cover. First issue, without price on spine (VAB). $350.

WHITMAN, Walt. *Rivulets of Prose.* New York, 1928. Edited by Carolyn Wells and Alfred F. Goldsmith. One of 499. $250.

WHITMAN, Walt. *Specimen Days and Collect.* Philadelphia, 1882–83. First issue, with Rees Welsh & Co. imprint. Light blue wraps. $500. Yellow cloth. $300. Philadelphia, 1883. David McKay imprint. Second issue. $200.

WHITMAN, Walt. *Two Rivulets.* Camden, 1876. Portrait frontispiece, signed "Walt Whitman." Half calf. $1,000. "Centennial Edition." One of 100. $1,250.

WHITMAN, Walt. *Walt Whitman's Diary in Canada.* Boston, 1904. Edited by W. S. Kennedy. Gray boards and vellum. One of 500. $350.

WHITMAN, Walt. *Walt Whitman's Drum-Taps.* New York, 1865. Brown cloth. First issue, with only 72 pages. $750. New York, 1865–66. Second issue, with 24 more pages adding "Sequel." $400.

WHITMAN, Walt. *When Lilacs Last in the Dooryard Bloomed.* Essex House Press. London, 1900. Vellum. One of 125. $1,250.

WHITNEY, Asa. *Memorial of A. Whitney, Praying a Grant of Public Land to Enable Him to Construct a Railroad . . .* (Washington, 1846). Folding map. $175.

WHITNEY, J. D. *The Yosemite Book.* New York, 1868. 28 photographic plates, 2 maps. Half leather. (250 printed.) $4,000 or more. Second edition: Cambridge, 1869. (Retitled *The Yosemite Guide Book.*) $1,000.

WHITTIER, John Greenleaf. See *Justice and Expediency; Moll Pitcher; The Stranger in Lowell; The Supernaturalism of New England.*

WHITTIER, John Greenleaf. *At Sundown.* Cambridge, 1890. Pea green cloth. One of 250 with facsimile autograph presentation slip. $150.

WHITTIER, John Greenleaf. *The Captain's Well.* Supplement to *New York Ledger,* January 11, 1890. Illustrated by Howard Pyle. 4 pp., in imitation alligator leather binding. $400.

WHITTIER, John Greenleaf. *Legends of New England.* Hartford, 1831. In original boards and cloth, paper label. Author's first book. First state, with last line on page 98 reading "the go" for "they go." $750.

WHITTIER, John Greenleaf. *Mogg Megone: A Poem.* Boston, 1836. In original slate-colored cloth. $300.

WHITTIER, John Greenleaf. *Poems.* Philadelphia, 1838. In original leather. $200. Cloth. $150. Limited Editions Club, New York, 1945. In slipcase. $60.

WHITTIER, John Greenleaf. *Poems Written During the Progress of the Abolition Question in the United States.* Boston, 1837. Frontispiece. In original cloth. First issue, 96 pp. $200. Second issue, 103 pp. $125.

WHITTIER, John Greenleaf. *Snow-Bound.* Boston, 1866. Green, blue, or terra-cotta cloth. With last page of text numbered "52." $300. Limited Editions Club, New York, 1930. Boards and cloth. In slipcase. $75. Also, one of 50 large paper copies. $400.

WHITTOCK, Nathaniel. *The Decorative Painters' and Glazeers' Guide.* London, 1827. Plates, many colored. $500. London, 1828. Second edition. $350.

WHYBREW, Samuel. *The Progressive Printer . . .* Rochester, 1882. Second edition. $125.

WHYTE-MELVILLE, George John. See *Market Harborough.*

WHYTE-MELVILLE, George John. *Digby Grand: An Autobiography.* London, 1853. 2 vols., cloth. Author's first novel. $250.

WHYTE-MELVILLE, George John. *The Queen's Maries: A Romance of Holyrood.* London, 1862. 2 vols. $250.

WICKERSHAM, James. *A Bibliography of Alaskan Literature, 1724–1924.* Cordova, 1927. Vol. 1 of the Miscellaneous Publications. $175.

WIDEMAN, John Edgar. *A Glance Away.* New York (1967). Author's first book. $125.

WIELAND; or, the Transformation . . . New York, 1798. (By Charles Brockden Brown.) $1,250.

WIENER, NORBERT. *Cybernetics.* New York (1948). Author's first book. $450.

WIENERS, John. *Ace of Pentacles.* New York, 1964. Boards. One of 75, signed, with manuscript portion tipped in. In glassine dustwrapper. $150. Leather. One of 12 signed with a poem tipped in. $250. Trade. Wraps. $30.

WIERZBICKI, F. P. *California as It Is and as It May Be.* San Francisco, 1849. 60 pp., glazed lavender wraps. First edition, with errata leaf. (The first book written and published in California.) $15,000 or more. San Francisco, 1849. 76 pp., errata, saffron wraps. Second edition. $7,500 or more. Grabhorn Press. San Francisco, 1933. Boards and cloth. One of 500. In dustwrapper. $175.

WIGGIN, Kate Douglas. See Smith, Kate Douglas.

WIGGIN, Kate Douglas. *Rebecca of Sunnybrook Farm.* Boston, 1903. Green pictorial cloth. First issue, with publisher's imprint on spine in type only $^1/_{16}$ inch high. $250. Later, $^1/_8$ inch high. $150.

WIGWAM and the Cabin (The). First series. New York, 1845. (By William Gilmore Simms.) In original wraps. $2,000. Later with the second series. 2 vols. in one, in original cloth. New York, 1845. $300.

WILBARGER, J. W. *Indian Depredations in Texas.* Austin, 1889. 38 plates (37 listed). Pictorial cloth. $650. Austin, 1890. Second edition. $300.

WILBUR, Homer (editor). *Meliboeus Hipponax. The Biglow Papers.* Cambridge, Mass., 1848. (By James Russell Lowell.) Cloth, or glazed boards. First issue. with George Nichols only as publisher. $350. Later, Putnam's name added to imprint. $250.

WILBUR, Richard. *The Beautiful Changes and Other Poems.* New York (1947). Author's first book. $300.

WILBUR, Richard. *Ceremony and Other Poems.* New York (1950). $175.

WILBUR, Richard. *Seed Leaves: Homage to R. F.* Boston (1974). Illustrated by Charles E. Wadsworth. Wraps, paper label. One of 160 signed by poet and artist. In portfolio wraps. $300.

WILBUR, Richard. *Things of This World.* New York (1956). $125.

WILBUR, Richard (compiler). *A Bestiary.* Illustrated by Alexander Calder. Pictorial buckram. New York (1955). One of 750 signed. In slipcase. $400. Folio, half morocco. One of 50 signed by author and artist and with a signed pen-and-ink drawing by Calder. $1,000.

WILCOX, Ella Wheeler. See Wheeler, Ella.

WILDE, Oscar. See C.3.3.; See also *An Ideal Husband; The Importance of Being Earnest.*

WILDE, Oscar. *The Birthday of the Infants.* Black Sun Press. Paris, 1928. Illustrated by Alastair. Wraps. $600. Also, one of 9 on vellum with an original drawing. $1,250. New York, 1929. Illustrated by Pamela Bianco. Boards. One of 500 signed by the artist. In slipcase. $1,000.

WILDE, Oscar. *De Profundis.* London (1905). Blue buckram. With ads dated February. $200. Later, ads dated March. $125. Large paper issues: white cloth. One of 200 on handmade paper. $500. One of 50 on Japan vellum. $1,500.

WILDE, Oscar. *The Happy Prince and Other Tales.* London, 1888. Illustrated by Walter Crane and Jacomb Hood. Vellum boards. $1,500. One of 75 signed. $4,000. London, 1913. Vellum. Illustrated by Charles Robinson. One of 260. $850.

WILDE, Oscar. *A House of Pomegranates.* London, 1891. 4 plates. White cloth, green cloth spine. $850. London, 1915. Color plates by Jessie M. King. Decorated cloth. $500.

WILDE, Oscar. *The Importance of Being Ernest.* London, 1899. One of 1,000. $450.

WILDE, Oscar. *Intentions.* London, 1891. Moss green cloth. $300.

WILDE, Oscar. *Lady Windermere's Fan: A Play About a Good Woman.* London, 1893. Reddish brown linen. $400. Large paper issue. One of 50. $1,250. Limited Editions Club, New York, 1973. In slipcase. $75.

WILDE, Oscar. *Lord Arthur Savile's Crime & Other Stories.* London, 1891. Salmon-colored boards. $450.

WILDE, Oscar. *Oscariana. Epigrams.* (London), 1895. Printed wraps. $250.

WILDE, Oscar. *The Picture of Dorian Gray.* London (1891). Rough gray beveled boards, vellum spine. First edition, with letter "a" missing from "and" on page 208 in eighth line from the bottom. $1,000. One of 250 signed. (Error corrected.) $4,000. Limited Editions Club, New York, 1957. In slipcase. $125.

WILDE, Oscar. *Poems.* London, 1881. White parchment boards. First edition, first issue, with the word "maid" in line 3, stanza 2, page 136. One of 250. $1,500. London, 1892. Violet cloth. One of 220 signed. $2,500.

WILDE, Oscar. *Ravenna.* Recited in the Theatre. Oxford, June 26, 1878. Oxford, 1878. 16 pp., printed wraps. With Oxford University seal on title page and cover. (The Newdigate Prize Poem.) Author's first book with exception of a collaboration. $750.

WILDE, Oscar. *Salome: Drame en Un Acte.* Paris, 1893. Purple wraps. $850. One of 50 on Van Gelder paper. $1,500. London, 1894. Illustrated by Aubrey Beardsley. Decorated cloth. First English edition. One of 500. $1,500. Large paper issue. One of 100 on vellum. $6,000. Grabhorn Press. San Francisco, 1927. Illustrated. Boards. One of 195. In slipcase. $400. Limited Editions Club, New York, 1938. 2 vols., cloth. In slipcase. $300.

WILDE, Oscar. *The Sphinx.* London, 1894. Decorations by Charles Ricketts. Vellum. One of 200. $5,000. One of 25 on large paper (issued later, with Boston firm of Copeland and Day added to London imprint). $7,500. London, 1920. Illustrated by Alastair. One of 1,000. $500.

WILDE, Oscar. *A Woman of No Importance.* London, 1894. One of 500. $500. Deluxe edition. One of 50 large paper copies. $1,000.

WILDER, Laura Ingalls. *Farmer Boy.* New York, 1933. Illustrated by Helen Sewell. Pictorial cloth. $150.

WILDER, Laura Ingalls. *Little House on the Prairie.* New York, 1935. Illustrated by Helen Sewell. Pictorial cloth. $250.

WILDER, Thornton. *The Angel That Troubled the Waters.* New York, 1928. Blue boards and cloth. One of 775 signed. $300. London, 1928. Blue cloth. First English edition. One of 260 signed. $250.

WILDER, Thornton. *The Bridge of San Luis Rey.* London, 1927. Tan cloth. First edition (preceding American edition by a few days). $200. New York, 1927. First American edition, "preliminary issue," with title page printed only in black. $1,000. Regular trade issue, title page printed in green and black. $300. New York, 1929. Illustrated by Rockwell Kent. Pictorial cloth, leather label. One of 1,100 signed by Wilder and Kent. In slipcase. $400.

WILDER, Thornton. *The Cabala.* New York, 1926. Blue figured cloth or tan figured cloth. Author's first book. First issue, with "conversation" for "conversion" in line 13, page 196 and "explaininn" for "explaining" line 12, page 202. Blue supposedly scarcer than tan. $350.

WILDER, Thornton. *The Ides of March.* New York (1948). One of 750 signed. In dustwrapper. $175. Trade. $50.

WILDER, Thornton. *James Joyce, 1882–1941.* (Aurora, N. Y., 1941.) Wraps. One of 150. $300.

WILDER, Thornton. *The Merchant of Yonkers.* New York, 1939. $175.

WILDER, Thornton. *Our Town.* New York (1938). $250.

WILDER, Thornton. *The Woman of Andros.* New York, 1930. $100. London, 1930. First English edition. One of 260 signed. $300. Trade. $75.

WILKES, Charles. *Narrative of the United States Exploring Expedition, During the Years 1838–42 . . .* Philadelphia, 1845. Illustrated. 6 vols., cloth, including atlas volume. First unofficial edition (after the 1844 set printed for Congress). $2,500.

WILKES, Charles. *Western America, Including California and Oregon . . .* Philadelphia, 1849. 3 folding maps. Printed tan wraps. $1,500.

WILKES, George. *The History of Oregon, Geographical and Political.* New York, 1845. Folding map. 127 pp., printed wraps. $1,750.

WILKESON, Samuel. *Wilkeson's Notes on Puget Sound.* (New York, 1870?) 47 pp., wraps. $250. Second edition, 44 pages. $300. Abridged edition, 32 pages. $150.

WILKINS, Mary E. *Decorative Plaques.* Boston (1883). Author's first book (written with George F. Barnes). $600.

WILKINSON, Gen. James. *Memoirs of My Own Times.* Philadelphia, 1816. 9 folding tables, 3 folding facsimiles. 4 vols. Including atlas of 19 maps and plans. $1,250.

WILLCOX, Joseph. *Ivy Mills, 1729–1866 . . .* Baltimore, 1910. $125.

WILLCOX, R. N. *Reminiscences of California Life.* (Avery, Ohio), 1897. $400.

WILLEFORD, Charles. *Proletarian Laughter.* Yonkers, 1948. Author's first book. Wraps. (1,000 copies.) $125.

WILLETT, Ralph. *A Memoir on the Origin of Printing . . .* New Castle, 1820. Second edition (reprinted from the 1818 edition). $225.

WILLETT, William M. (editor). *A Narrative of the Military Actions of Col. Marinus Willet.* New York, 1831. Portrait, plan, facsimile letter. $500.

WILLEY, S. H. *An Historical Paper Relating to Santa Cruz, California.* San Francisco, 1876. 37 pp., printed wraps. $150.

WILLIAMS, Alpheus F. *The Genesis of the Diamond.* London, 1932. 221 plates, 30 colored. 2 vols., buckram. Issued without dustwrapper. $300.

WILLIAMS, Charles. *Poems of Conformity.* London, 1917. $150.

WILLIAMS, Charles. *The Silver Stair.* London, 1912. Author's first book. $300.

WILLIAMS, Charles. *War in Heaven.* London, 1930. $125.

WILLIAMS, G. T. *Receipts and Shipments of Livestock at Union Stock Yards for 1890.* Chicago, 1891. 40 pp., wraps. $350.

WILLIAMS, Iola A. *Points in Eighteenth-Century Verse, A Bibliographer's and Collector's Scrapbook.* London, 1934. One of 500 copies. Volume 7 of the 10-vol. Bibliographia Series edited by Michael Sadleir. $150.

WILLIAMS, Jesse. *A Description of the United States Lands of Iowa.* New York, 1840. Folding map in color. Green cloth. $750.

WILLIAMS, John A. *Africa: Her History, Lands and People.* New York, 1962. First edition stated. $150.

WILLIAMS, John A. *The Angry Ones.* New York (1960). Pictorial wraps. Author's first book. Ace paperback. $60.

WILLIAMS, John A. *Nightsong.* New York (1961). $100.

WILLIAMS, John Camp. *An Oneida County Printer, William Williams . . .* New York, 1906. One of 180 copies. 29 plates. In dustwrapper. $100.

WILLIAMS, John Lee. *The Territory of Florida.* New York, 1837. Folding map, portrait, 2 plates. $500. New York, 1839. $250.

WILLIAMS, John Lee. *A View of West Florida.* Philadelphia, 1827. Folding map. $500.

WILLIAMS, Joseph. *Narrative of a Tour from the State of Indiana to the Oregon Territory.* Cincinnati, 1843. 48 pp., plain blue wraps. $15,000 or more. New York, 1921. Cloth. One of 250. $100.

WILLIAMS, Jonathan. *Painting & Graphics.* Highlands, 1950. (Exhibition folder.) Author's first book. (Previous pamphlet may exist.) $500.

WILLIAMS, Margery. *The Velveteen Rabbit or How Toys Become Real.* London, 1922. Illustrated by William Nicholson. Pictorial boards. Issued without dustwrapper. $750.

WILLIAMS, Samuel. *The Natural and Civil History of Vermont.* Walpole, 1794. Folding frontispiece map. $1,250.

WILLIAMS, Tennessee. *American Blues.* (New York, 1948.) Printed wraps. Only the first printing had misspelling of "Tennessee" as "Tennesse." Other first-issue points exist but are not necessary to list as this error appears on the front cover/wrapper. $200.

WILLIAMS, Tennessee. *Baby Doll.* (New York, 1956.) First edition not stated. $125. London, 1957. First English edition. $100.

WILLIAMS, Tennessee. *Battle of Angels.* (Murray, Utah, 1945.) Printed wraps (comprising double number, nos. 1 and 2, of *Pharos,* Spring, 1945). Author's first book. $500.

WILLIAMS, Tennessee. *Cat on a Hot Tin Roof.* (Norfolk, Conn., 1955.) Tan cloth. First edition not stated. First printing has no credit on the verso of the title leaf to the *New York Times* for a previous appearance of the foreword. No credit appears at page xii to Jo Mielziner and Lucinda Ballard for scene and costume design as these were inadvertently left off and added to subsequent printings. (Later printings also noted at the bottom of the front dustwrapper flap.) $150.

WILLIAMS, Tennessee. *The Glass Menagerie.* New York, 1945. Rust or blue cloth. $250.

WILLIAMS, Tennessee. *Grand: A Short Story.* New York, 1964. One of 300 signed. In glassine dustwrapper. $300. One of 26 lettered copies, signed. $750.

WILLIAMS, Tennessee. *Hard Candy.* (Norfolk, 1954.) Patterned boards, cloth spine. Limited edition. In slipcase. $150. (Norfolk, 1959.) Black cloth boards lettered down the spine in bronze and silver. "New trade edition" on verso of title leaf. (Later printings are noted on copyright page.) $60.

WILLIAMS, Tennessee. *I Rise in Flames, Cried the Phoenix.* Norfolk (1952). One of 300 signed. In slipcase. $450. One of 10 on Umbria paper, signed. In slipcase. $1,500.

WILLIAMS, Tennessee. *In the Winter of Cities: Poems.* (Norfolk, 1956.) White parchment boards, gilt. One of 100 signed. In slipcase. $600. Trade. Patterned boards and cloth. First edition not stated. $150.

WILLIAMS, Tennessee. *The Kingdom of Earth, with Hard Candy.* (New York, 1954.) New Directions. One of 100 signed, plus 20 for "presentation." $1,000.

WILLIAMS, Tennessee. *The Milk Train Doesn't Stop Here Anymore.* Norfolk, 1964. First issue with pages 19–22 integral and scene two beginning on page 22. $450. Second issue with pages 19–22 tipped in and scene two starting on page 21. $100. Third issue: pages 19–22 are bound in. $40.

WILLIAMS, Tennessee. *One Arm and Other Stories.* (Norfolk, 1949.) Boards, vellum spine. One of 50 signed. In slipcase. $1,250. (New York or Norfolk, 1954.) Trade edition. Boards and cloth in dustwrapper. First edition not stated. $60. (Note: Most of the first-edition copies bear a tipped-in title leaf with the copyright in Williams's name, but about 20 are said to exist with an integral title leaf with an incorrect copyright credit by New Directions. $850.)

WILLIAMS, Tennessee. *The Roman Spring of Mrs. Stone.* (Norfolk, 1950.) Marbled boards, vellum spine. One of 500 signed. In slipcase. $350. Trade. First edition not stated. $100.

WILLIAMS, Tennessee. *The Rose Tattoo.* (New York or Norfolk, 1951.) First edition stated. First binding in rose cloth. $125. Second binding in tan cloth. $75.

WILLIAMS, Tennessee. *A Streetcar Named Desire.* (Norfolk, 1947.) First edition not stated, but in lavendar decorated boards not on later printings. (Extremely vulnerable to fading and edge wear). $600.

WILLIAMS, Tennessee. *Summer and Smoke.* (Norfolk, 1948.) First edition stated. Light blue cloth boards. First-issue dustwrapper lists three Williams plays on inside back flap. $175.

WILLIAMS, Tennessee. *27 Wagons Full of Cotton and Other One-Act Plays.* (Norfolk, 1946.) Bound in beige cloth boards. Dustwrapper in brown. $250. Second edition is in yellow boards with black cloth spine, and adds the essay "Something Wild." Dustwrapper in black. $125. (Norfolk), 1953. Third edition. yellow cloth boards lettered in green down the spine. Dustwrapper in black. (First appearance of two plays, *Something Unspoken* and *Talk to Me Like the Rain.*) $75.

WILLIAMS, Tennessee. *The Two Character Play.* (New York, 1969.) One of 350 signed. In slipcase. $250.

WILLIAMS, Tennessee, and WINDHAM, Donald. *You Touched Me! A Romantic Comedy.* New York (1947). 506 hardcover copies in white pictorial dustwrapper printed in dark green ink. $350. Gray wraps printed in black with 85-cent cover price. (All subsequent wraps editions in bright orange.) $100.

WILLIAMS, Thomas J. C. *A History of Washington County* (Maryland). (Chambersburg, Pa.), 1906. 2 vols. $200.

WILLIAMS, William Carlos. See Ginsberg, Allen; Loy, Mina.

WILLIAMS, William Carlos. *Adam & Eve & The City.* Peru, Vt., 1936. 20 signed copies numbered I-XX. Olive green wraps in green slipcase. $3,500. 135 signed copies numbered 1-135. Wraps and slipcase as above. $2,500.

WILLIAMS, William Carlos. *Al Que Quiere! A Book of Poems.* Boston, 1917. Yellow-orange boards printed in black. $750. Also variant with tan paper boards and author's name misspelled "Willams" on spine. Assume later. $600.

WILLIAMS, William Carlos. *The Broken Span.* Norfolk (1941). First binding: gray paper boards printed in black and fuchsia, front flap of dustwrapper has comments about book, rear flap lists 12 *Poet of the Month* pamphlets. $200. Second binding: blank stiff white paper covers, dustwrapper as above. $100. Yellow paper wraps not attached at spine. $75.

WILLIAMS, William Carlos. *The Clouds . . .* (No-place, 1948.) 60 signed copies numbered I-LX on English handmade paper bound in slate cloth boards in slipcase. $1,750. 250 copies numbered 61-310 on rag paper in similar binding but issued without slipcase. $250.

WILLIAMS, William Carlos. *The Cod Head.* San Francisco, 1932. Wraps. One of 125 signed. $500.

WILLIAMS, William Carlos. *The Collected Later Poems.* (Norfolk, 1950.) "The Rose" section loosely inserted. One of 100 signed. Issued without dustwrapper in slipcase. $1,000. Trade. "The Rose" section loosely inserted. $100. Later binding with "The Rose" correctly bound in. $75. (Norfolk, 1950 [actually 1956].) 52 copies, of which 50 are signed and numbered copies in red. Facing title page "Horace Mann School Editions." Gray slipcase ("The Rose" section bound in). $1,000. Trade. In plain brown dustwrapper with circular cutout to reveal H. Mann School seal. "The Rose" section loosely inserted. $60. London, 1965. $40.

WILLIAMS, William Carlos. *Collected Poems, 1921-1931.* New York, 1934. $400. Also, one of 50 signed. $1,500.

WILLIAMS, William Carlos. *The Desert Music and Other Poems.* New York (1954). 111 copies, of which 100 were signed and numbered. Issued in glassine dustwrapper and slipcase. $1,000. Trade. $100.

WILLIAMS, William Carlos. *The Great American Novel.* Paris, 1923. 300 numbered copies. Some copies have a rectangular slip covering name of the press (on the title page) upon which is printed "Contact Editions, 29 Quai d'Anjou, Paris"—priority unknown. $600.

WILLIAMS, William Carlos. *In the American Grain.* New York, 1925. Original price $3.00, but raised to $3.50 right after publication. $300. Norfolk (1939). Yellow cloth boards, lettered in red. Yellow dustwrapper printed in green and red. $50. (London, 1967.) $40.

WILLIAMS, William Carlos. *In the Money/White Mule.* Norfolk (1940). $250. (London, 1965.) $50.

WILLIAMS, William Carlos. *Kora in Hell: Improvisations.* Boston, 1920. Issued in orange dustwrapper printed in black. (Some copies had glassine dustwrappers.) $750. San Francisco (1957). Wraps. $25.

WILLIAMS, William Carlos. *Paterson (Book One).* (Norfolk, 1946.) One of 1,000 copies. $300.

WILLIAMS, William Carlos. *Paterson (Book Two).* (Norfolk, 1948.) One of 1,000 copies. $250.

WILLIAMS, William Carlos. *Paterson (Book Three).* (Norfolk, 1949.) One of 1,000 copies. $200.

WILLIAMS, William Carlos. *Paterson (Book Four).* (Norfolk, 1951.) One of 1,000 copies. $175.

WILLIAMS, William Carlos. *Paterson (Book Five).* (Norfolk, 1958.) No limitation but 3,000 copies printed. $75.

WILLIAMS, William Carlos. *Paterson . . .* The five volumes (listed above) together. $1,250.

WILLIAMS, William Carlos. *Poems.* (Rutherford, N.J.), 1909. Author's first book. 22 pp., printed brown wraps. First state, with "of youth himself, all rose-y-clad," in line 5 of first poem. (100 copies printed, of which 2 are known.) $30,000. Second state, with "of youth himself all roseyclad." $17,500.

WILLIAMS, William Carlos. *Sour Grapes.* Boston, 1921. Author's name on spine label only. $750.

WILLIAMS, William Carlos. *The Tempers.* London, 1913. In glassine dustwrapper. $900.

WILLIAMS, William Carlos. *White Mule.* Norfolk, 1937. White cloth boards printed in black, or gray cloth printed in crimson on spine. Priority unknown. $200. (London, 1965.) $50.

WILLIAMSON, George C. *The History of Portrait Miniatures.* London, 1904. 107 plates. 2 vols., folio, white cloth. One of 520. $350. One of 50 with hand-colored plates. $750.

WILLIAMSON, Henry. *The Beautiful Years.* London (1921). Author's first book. (750 copies.) $350.

WILLIAMSON, Henry. *The Patriot's Progress.* London (1930). Wood engravings by William Kermode. Half vellum. One of 350 signed. In slipcase. $300.

WILLIAMSON, Henry. *The Star Born.* London, 1933. Vellum. One of 70 signed by author and C. F. Tunnicliffe (illustrator). Issued without dustwrapper. $500.

WILLIAMSON, Henry. *Tarka the Otter* . . . (London), 1927. Vellum. One of 100 signed. $750. Trade. Buckram. Issued without dustwrapper. $350. Another issue/ printing later in the year, cloth in dustwrapper. $250.

WILLIAMSON, Henry. *The Wet Flanders Plain.* London, 1929. Half vellum. Issued without dustwrapper. One of 80. $600. One of 240. Issued without dustwrapper. $250.

WILLIAMSON, Hugh. *The History of North Carolina.* Philadelphia, 1812. 2 vols. Folding frontispiece map. $750.

WILLIAMSON, Jack. *Darker Than You Think.* Reading, Pa., 1948. One of 500. $100. Trade edition: $40.

WILLIAMSON, Jack. *The Legion of Space.* Reading, 1947. One of 500 signed. $100. Trade edition: $50.

WILLIAMSON, James J. *Mosby's Rangers.* New York, 1896. $200.

WILLIAMSON, John. *Fern Etchings.* Louisville, 1879. 65 engraved plates. $500.

WILLIAMSON, Joseph. *A Bibliography of the State of Maine from the Earliest Period to 1891.* Portland, 1896. 2 vols. $250.

WILLINGHAM, Calder. *End As a Man.* New York (1947). Author's first book. First issue dustwrapper with back panel blank. $125.

WILLINGTON, James. *Memoirs of a Protestant.* London, 1758. Author's first book. $2,000.

WILLIS, Nathaniel Parker. *American Scenery.* London, 1840. 117 views by W. H. Bartlett. 2 vols., in original cloth or leather. $1,250.

WILLIS, Nathaniel Parker. *Canadian Scenery.* London, 1842. 2 vols. Illustrated by W. H. Bartlett. With engraved titles, portrait, map and 117 plates. $1,250.

WILLIS, Nathaniel Parker. *Pencillings by the Way.* London, 1835. 3 vols., in original cloth or boards. $300.

WILLIS, Nathaniel Parker. *Sketches.* Boston, 1827. In original glazed boards and cloth, paper label. Author's first book. $300.

WILLIS, William L. *History of Sacramento County.* Los Angeles, 1913. Illustrated. Three-quarters leather. $175.

WILLMOTT, Ellen Ann. *The Genus Rosa.* London (1910)–14. Colored and plain plates. 25 parts, gray wraps. $3,000. London, 1914. 2 vols. $3,000.

WILLOUGHBY, Edwin Elliott. *The Making of the King James Bible.* Los Angeles, 1956. With a leaf from the "She" Bible of 1611 inserted in a specially made folder. One of 290 copies. $350.

WILLYAMS, Cooper. *A Voyage up the Mediterranean in HMS "Swiftsure."* London, 1802. 42 hand-colored plates, folding map. $2,500.

WILSON, Alexander. *American Ornithology* . . . Philadelphia, 1808–14. 9 vols. With 76 hand-colored plates. $7,500. New York/Philadelphia, 1828–29. 4 vols., including atlas. Also, with 76 hand-colored plates. $7,500. Large paper copy. $16,500 at auction in 1989.

WILSON, Angus. *The Wrong Set and Other Stories.* London, 1949. Author's first book. $75.

WILSON, Augusta Jane Evans. See *Inez . . .*

WILSON, Carroll A. *Thirteen Author Collections of the Nineteenth Century and Five Centuries of Familiar Quotations.* New York, 1950. 2 vols. One of 375 copies. Slipcase. $150.

WILSON, Colin. *The Outsider.* London, 1956. Author's first book. $125. Boston, 1956. According to the publisher, the first printing has the date on the title page. $60. There are at least 3 variants that state "First American Edition" but do not have a date on the title page. We assume these are later printings or Book Club editions.

WILSON, Colin. *Tree by Tolkien.* (London, 1973.) 100 signed and numbered copies. $125. Trade in olive cloth. $50. Santa Barbara, 1974. 200 signed and numbered copies. Issued without dustwrapper. $60.

WILSON, Colin. *Voyage to a Beginning.* New York (1969). Blue cloth with black letters. Precedes U.K. edition. $40. London, 1969. 200 signed and numbered copies. $100. Trade. Red cloth. $40.

WILSON, Edmund. *Axel's Castle.* New York, 1931. $450.

WILSON, Edmund. *The Boys in the Back Room.* San Francisco, 1941. 100 signed and numbered copies. Issued in acetate dustwrapper. $750. Trade. $250.

WILSON, Edmund. *Discordant Encounters.* New York, 1926. $500.

WILSON, Edmund. *I Thought of Daisy.* New York, 1929. $350. London, 1929. $150.

WILSON, Edmund, *Memoirs of Hecate County.* Garden City, 1946. $150. London (1952). $75.

WILSON, Edmund. *Note Books of Night.* San Francisco, 1942. Reportedly 100 signed copies were to be sold, but only 10 or so were ever issued. These were in decorated floral boards with cloth spine. $1,250. 21 signed copies in later binding of blue paper boards with a black leather spine stamped in gold. $750. Trade. Inner tissue and outer dustwrappers. $200. London, 1945. $75.

WILSON, Edmund. *This Room & This Gin & These Sandwiches.* New York, 1937. 100 signed and numbered copies. Issued in acetate dustwrapper. $750. Trade. $250.

WILSON, Edmund. *To the Finland Station.* New York, 1940. $250. London, 1940. $150.

WILSON, Edmund. *The Triple Thinkers.* New York, 1938. Noted in dark green cloth, gold lettering and top edge yellow; and medium brown, white lettering and top edge unstained. Priority unknown but latter seems cheaper and may have been a remainder binding. $250. London, 1939. $175.

WILSON, Edmund, and BISHOP, John Peale. *The Undertaker's Garland.* New York, 1922. Wilson's first book. One of 50 copies for "Bookseller Friends." Issued without dustwrapper. $250. Trade. In dustwrapper. $400.

WILSON, Elijah N. *Among the Shoshones.* Salt Lake City (1910). Rigidly suppressed. 222 pages. 8 plates. Pictorial cloth. $500. Second edition, same place and date, 247 pages. (Howes W520: "The 247 page reprint omits account of how he lost his Mormon fiancée [given on pp. 194 to 200 of original edition])." $100.

WILSON, Fred. J. F., and GREY, Douglas. *A Practical Treatise Upon Modern Printing Machinery and Letterpress Printing.* London, 1888. $225.

WILSON, Fred. J. F. *Typographic Printing Machines and Machine Printing . . .* London (1879). $150.

WILSON, Harry Leon. *Merton of the Movies.* Garden City, 1922. $250.

WILSON, Harry Leon. *Ruggles of Red Gap.* Garden City, 1915. In dustwrapper. $200. Without dustwrapper. $60.

WILSON, Harry Leon. *Zigzag Tales from the East to the West.* New York, 1894. Author's first book. Illustrated by C. Jay Taylor. Decorated wraps. $125. Cloth. $100.

WILSON, John Albert. *History of Los Angeles County, California.* Oakland, 1880. Illustrated. Leather and cloth. $600.

WILSON, Sir John. *The Royal Philatelic Collection . . .* London, 1952. Edited by Clarence Winchester. 12 color facsimiles, 48 monochrome plates, other illustrations. Full red morocco. $350.

WILSON, Richard L. *Short Ravelings from a Long Yarn, or Camp and March Sketches of the Santa Fe Trail.* Chicago, 1847. Edited by Benjamin F. Taylor. Illustrated. Printed boards. $6,000. Santa Ana, Calif., 1936. $250.

WILSON, Robert. *The Travels of Robert Wilson: Being a Relation of Facts.* London, 1807. Portrait, plates. Mottled calf. $250.

WILSON, Woodrow. *Congressional Government.* Boston, 1885. Author's first book. First issue, with publisher's monogram on spine. $200.

WILSON, Woodrow. *George Washington.* New York, 1897. $150.

WILTSEE, Ernest A. *Gold Rush Steamers (of the Pacific).* Grabhorn Press. San Francisco, 1938. Illustrated. Cloth. One of 500. Issued without dustwrapper. $250.

WIND, Herbert Warren. *Story of American Golf.* New York, 1948. $100.

WINDELER, B. C. *Elimus.* Three Mountains Press. Paris, 1923. 12 designs by Dorothy Shakespear. Gray boards. One of 300. Issued without dustwrapper. $250.

WINDELER, Bernard. *Sailing Ships and Barges of the Western Mediterranean and the Adriatic Seas.* London, 1926. Map. 17 hand-colored copper plate engravings by Edward Wadsworth. One of 450. In slipcase. $400.

WINDHAM, Donald. *The Hitchhiker.* (Florence, 1950.) Printed wraps. One of 250 signed. $125.

WING and Wing (The). Philadelphia, 1842. By the author of *The Pilot* (James Fenimore Cooper). 2 vols., printed terra-cotta wraps. First American edition (of the novel issued first in London as *The Jack O'Lantern* under Cooper's name). $1,000. Later issue, wraps dated 1843. $600.

WINKLER, A. V. *The Confederate Capital and Hood's Texas Brigade.* Austin, 1894. $350.

WINSHIP, George Parker. *William Caxton.* London, 1909. One of 300 copies on paper. $350. One of 15 on vellum. $2,500.

WINSOR, Justin. *A History of the Town of Duxbury . . .* Boston, 1849. Author's first book. $175.

WINSOR, Justin (editor). *The Memorial History of Boston, Including Suffolk County, Massachusetts, 1630–1880.* Boston (1880). 4 vols. $200.

WINSOR, Kathleen. *Forever Amber.* New York, 1944. Author's first book. $60.

WINTER Ship (A). Edinburgh, 1960. (By Sylvia Plath.) Leaflet. $1,000.

WINTER in the West (A). New York, 1835. By a New Yorker (Charles Fenno Hoffman, his first book). 2 vols., in original cloth. $200.

WINTER, William. *Poems.* Boston, 1855. Author's first book. $150.

WINTERS, Yvor. *Before Disaster.* Tryon, N.C., 1934. Printed green wraps. $200.

WINTERS, Yvor. *Diadems and Fagots.* Santa Fe (1920). Author's first book. (Translated by Winters.) (50 copies.) $500.

WINTERS, Yvor. *The Immobile Wind.* Evanston (1921). Wraps. Author's first book other than the translation. $450.

WINTERS, Yvor. *The Magpie's Shadow.* Chicago, 1922. Printed blue wraps. $400.

WINTERS, Yvor. *The Proof.* New York, 1930. $200.

WIRT, Mrs. E. W. *Flora's Dictionary.* Baltimore (after 1837). 58 hand-colored plates. In original morocco. $2,500 at auction in 1989. Baltimore, 1855. $600.

WISE, George. *Campaigns and Battles of the Army of Northern Virginia.* New York, 1916. 2 portraits. $200.

WISE, John. *A System of Aeronautics . . .* Philadelphia, 1850. Illustrated with portrait and 12 plates. Cloth or half leather. $750.

WISE, Thomas J. *The Ashley Library . . .* London, 1922–36. 11 vols. in the original cream-colored buckram. Top edges gilt. $1,250.

WISLIZENUS, Frederick A. *A Journey to the Rocky Mountains in the Year 1839.* St. Louis, 1912. Folding map. First edition in English, One of 500. $400.

WISLIZENUS, Frederick A. *Memoir of a Tour to Northern Mexico . . .* Washington, 1848. 2 folding maps and a folding profile. Boards. $600.

WISTAR, Caspar. *A System of Anatomy for the Use of Students of Medicine.* Philadelphia, 1811–14. 2 vols. $400.

WISTAR, Isaac Jones. *Autobiography of Isaac Jones Wistar, 1827–1905.* Philadelphia, 1914. Folding map, portrait, plates. 2 vols., boards and cloth, leather spine labels. $300.

WISTER, Owen. *The Lady of the Lake.* (Cambridge), 1881. Author's first book. (Chorus book.) $250.

WISTER, Owen. *Members of the Family.* New York, 1911. In dustwrapper. $250.

WISTER, Owen. *The New Swiss Family Robinson.* (Cambridge, 1882.) $300.

WISTER, Owen. *The Virginian.* New York, 1902. Yellow pictorial cloth. In dustwrapper. $1,000. Without dustwrapper. $300. New York, 1911. Illustrated by Frederick Remington and Charles M. Russell. Boards. One of 100. $1,250. Limited Editions Club, Los Angeles, 1951. In slipcase. $75.

WITHERS, Alexander S. *Chronicles of Border Warfare . . .* Clarksburg, Va., 1831. $400.

WODEHOUSE, P. G. *Big Money.* Garden City, 1931. $450. London (1931). Orange cloth, black letters. $750.

WODEHOUSE, P. G. *Carry On, Jeeves!* London, 1925. 13 titles on half-title verso ending with *The Coming of Bill.* $850. New York (1927). $600.

WODEHOUSE, P. G. *A Gentleman of Leisure.* London, 1910. Royal blue cloth lettered in gold. First U.K. edition of *Intrusion of Jimmy.* $1,200.

WODEHOUSE, P. G. *The Intrusion of Jimmy.* New York (1910). "Published May." Bound in black, lettered in gold with circular color portrait pasted on. $400. For U.K. edition, see *A Gentleman of Leisure.*

WODEHOUSE, P. G. *The Little Nugget.* London (1913). Bound in red cloth. 2 sets of advertisements dated May and Autumn 1913. $1,000. New York (1914). "Published January" beneath copyright notice. $400.

WODEHOUSE, P. G. *Love Among the Chickens.* London (1906). Tan pictorial cloth with frontis and 3 illustrations by H. M. Brock. $1,500. New York, 1909. Some copies have pages tipped in after half title "This Advance Copy No.—" which seems more common than the regular issue (6 copies of this catalogued in recent years vs. one of other). $750. London, 1921. List on half-title verso ends with *Indiscretions of Archie.* "Entirely rewritten . . ." on title page. $1,250.

WODEHOUSE, P. G. *The Man with Two Left Feet.* London (1917). $1,750. A.L. Burt Co. New York, 1933. Burt is a reprint house, but this is the first U.S. edition. "First edition" on copyright page. $1,250.

WODEHOUSE, P. G. *Mike.* London, 1909. Olive green cloth, frontispiece and 11 illustrations by T.M.R. Whitwell. $1,500.

WODEHOUSE, P. G. *The Pothunters.* London, 1902. Author's first book. No ads. Royal blue cloth, silver lettering on spine with silver loving cup on front cover and spine. $2,500. Gray-blue pictorial cloth (runners) and 8 pages ads ending with *Mike.* $600.

WODEHOUSE, P. G. *A Prefect's Uncle.* London, 1903. Red cloth lettered and decorated in gold, black, lavender, and pink. No advertisements. $2,000.

WODEHOUSE, P. G. *Psmith in the City.* London, 1910. Blue cloth. Frontispiece and 11 illustrations by Whitwell. $1,000.

WODEHOUSE, P. G. *Ukridge.* London, 1924. 13 titles on half-title verso ending with *Leave it to Psmith.* $1,000.

WODEHOUSE, P. G. *Uncle Fred in the Springtime.* Garden City, 1939. $300. London (1939). Dark red cloth (reissued in orange cloth). $500.

WODEHOUSE, P. G. *William Tell Told Again.* London, 1904. Off-white cloth lettered in gilt on spine and front cover, top edge gilt, publisher's monogram on title page. $1,250. Second issue: (Phelps) light brown pictorial cloth, gilt on spine only; (McIlvaine) advertisements and gilt on cover. $500. Variant state in buff boards with black lettering without date on title page and publisher's address on title page. $300.

WODEHOUSE, P. G. *Wodehouse on Golf.* New York, 1940. Stated first. $250.

WOLF, Edwin, II, and FLEMING, John. *Rosenbach: A Biography.* Cleveland (1960). One of 250 signed. In slipcase. $300. Trade. $75.

WOLFE, Humbert. *Cursory Rhymes.* London, 1927. Illustrated by Albert Rutherston. One of 500 signed. $150.

WOLFE, Humbert. *The Old Man of Koenigsberg . . .* Holy Well, 1907. Author's first book. $200.

WOLFE, Humbert. *The Uncelestial City.* London, 1930. One of 400 signed. $150.

WOLFE, Richard J. *Jacob Bigelow's American Medical Botany, 1817–1821.* North Hills, 1979. 350 numbered copies. 2 plates (one hand colored, the other uncolored). $350.

WOLFE, Thomas. See Koch, Frederick H.

WOLFE, Thomas. *America.* (San Mateo, Calif., 1942.) Wraps. Published by the Greenwood Press. First separate edition. One of 150. $200.

WOLFE, Thomas. *The Crisis in Industry.* Chapel Hill, N.C., 1919. 14 pp., printed wraps. Author's first book. $7,500.

WOLFE, Thomas. *The Face of a Nation.* New York, 1939. Johnston states the Scribner dummy had an "A" on copyright page and the first edition had "CL," therefore this title did not follow Scribners' normal method of identifying the first with an "A" on the copyright page. $125.

WOLFE, Thomas. *From Death to Morning.* New York, 1935. $175. London (1936). $150.

WOLFE, Thomas. *Gentlemen of the Press.* Chicago (1942). Cloth, paper label. One of 350. Issued without dustwrapper. $200.

WOLFE, Thomas. *The Hills Beyond.* New York (1941). $150.

WOLFE, Thomas. *Look Homeward, Angel.* New York, 1929. Author's first novel. Blue cloth, gilt. In first-state dustwrapper with Wolfe's picture on back. $1,500. Without picture. $750. London (1930). First English edition with a few textual changes. $650.

WOLFE, Thomas. *Mannerhouse: A Play in a Prologue and Three Acts.* New York, 1948. One of 500. In dustwrapper and slipcase. $200. Trade. $100.

WOLFE, Thomas. *A Note on Experts: Dexter Vespasian Joyner.* New York, 1939. One of 300. In glassine dustwrapper. $300.

WOLFE, Thomas. *Of Time and the River.* New York, 1935. $250.

WOLFE, Thomas. *The Story of a Novel.* New York, 1936. $100.

WOLFE, Thomas. *To Rupert Brooke.* (Paris), 1948. 4 leaves, printed wraps. One of 100 used as a Christmas greeting. $300.

WOLFE, Thomas. *The Web and the Rock.* New York, 1939. $150.

WOLFE, Thomas. *You Can't Go Home Again.* New York (1940). $150. London (1947). First English edition. $125.

WOLFE, Tom. *The Kandy-Kolored . . .* New York (1965). Author's first book. $100.

WOLFF, Tobias. *Ugly Rumours.* London, 1975. Author's first book. $175.

WOMAN'S Daring; As Shown by the Testimony of the Rock. *Recorded by an Exultant Woman and a Hughmillerated Man.* (Annisquam, Mass., 1872.) 24 pp., wraps. (Note: Contains a contribution by Thomas A. Janvier, his first book appearance.) $350.

WONDERFUL Stories of FuzBuz the Fly and Mother Grabem the Spider (The). Philadelphia, 1867. (By S. Weir Mitchell.) 9 engraved plates. Half morocco. One of 170 on large paper. $750. Trade. Cloth. $200.

WOOD and the Graver, The Work of Fritz Eichenberg. Barre, 1977. 500 numbered copies signed by the artist. Signed woodcut in pocket mounted on the back inside cover. $125.

WOOD, Arnold. *A Bibliography of "The Complete Angler" of Izaak Walton and Charles Cotton . . .* New York, 1900. 120 numbered copies. $350.

WOOD, Charles Erskine Scott. *Imperialism Versus Democracy.* New York, 1899. Wraps. Author's first book. $100.

WOOD, Harry B. *Golfing Curios and "The Like."* London, 1910. $1,000. One of 150 copies. $1,750.

WOOD, Mrs. Henry (Ellen). *East Lynne.* London, 1861. 3 vols., violet cloth. $2,500.

WOOD, James H. *The War, Stonewall Jackson, His Campaigns and Battles, The Regiment, as I Saw Them.* Cumberland, Md. (about 1910). $200.

WOOD, John. *Journal of John Wood.* Chillicothe, Ohio, 1852. 76 pp., printed wraps. $4,500. Columbus, Ohio, 1871. 112 pp., printed wraps. Second edition. $500.

WOOD, R. E. *Life and Confessions of James Gilbert Jenkins: the Murderer of 18 Men.* Napa City, 1864. Illustrated. 56 pp., wraps. $400.

WOOD, Silas. *A Sketch of the First Settlement of the Several Towns on Long Island.* Brooklyn, 1824. $200.

WOOD, William. *Zoography, or the Beauties of Nature Displayed.* London, 1807. Aquatint plates by William Daniell. 3 vols. $850.

WOODBERRY, George Edward. *History of Wood Engraving.* New York, 1883. $125.

WOODBERRY, George Edward. *The North Shore Watch.* New York, 1883. (200 copies.) $150.

WOODBERRY, George Edward. *The Relations of Pallas Athene to Athens.* Private printing, 1877? Author's first book. Wraps. $250.

WOODMAN, David, Jr. *Guide to Texas Emigrants.* Boston, 1835. Map, plate. $2,500.

WOODRUFF, W. E. *With the Light Guns in '61–'65.* Little Rock, 1903. $275.

WOODS, Daniel B. *Sixteen Months at the Gold Diggings.* New York, 1851. $400.

WOODS, John. *Two Years' Residence . . . on the English Prairie, in the Illinois Country.* London, 1822. 2 maps and plan. $750.

WOOLF, Leonard. See Bunin, I.A.

WOOLF, Leonard. *Stories of the East.* Hogarth Press. Richmond, England, 1921. Buff wraps. $300.

WOOLF, Leonard. *The Village in the Jungle.* London, 1913. Blue cloth. Author's first book. $250. London, 1931. First Hogarth Press edition. $200.

WOOLF Virginia. See Cameron, Julia M.

WOOLF, Virginia. *Beau Brummell.* New York, 1930. Boards and cloth. One of 550 signed. In glassine dustwrapper and slipcase. $600.

WOOLF, Virginia. *Between the Acts.* Hogarth Press. London, 1941. $300. New York (1941). $150.

WOOLF, Virginia. *The Common Reader.* Hogarth Press. London, 1925. White boards and cloth. $400. London, 1932. Second series (same title). $250. New York, 1948. Blue cloth. First and second series in one volume. First American edition thus. $150.

WOOLF, Virginia. *Flush: A Biography.* Hogarth Press. London, 1933. Illustrated by Vanessa Bell. Buff cloth. In dustwrapper. $250. Trade. $150.

WOOLF, Virginia. *Hours in a Library.* New York (1958). Frontispiece. Boards and cloth. $175.

WOOLF, Virginia. *Jacob's Room.* Hogarth Press. Richmond, 1922. Yellow cloth. $3,000. Also, one of about 40 signed, with subscriber's list. $4,000.

WOOLF, Virginia. *Kew Gardens.* Hogarth Press. Richmond, 1919. Woodcut by Vanessa Bell. Wraps. $1,500. "Second edition," $850. London (1927). Hogarth Press. Boards. One of 500. In cellophane dustwrapper. $600.

WOOLF, Virginia. *The Mark on the Wall.* (Cover title, no title page.) Richmond, 1919. White wraps. "Second edition" (actually first separate edition, having previously appeared in *Two Stories,* published jointly with her husband, Leonard Woolf). $2,000.

WOOLF, Virginia. *Mr. Bennett and Mrs. Brown.* Hogarth Press. London, 1924. White wraps. $250.

WOOLF, Virginia. *Mrs. Dalloway.* London, 1925. $750. New York, 1925. $350.

WOOLF, Virginia. *Monday or Tuesday.* Hogarth Press. Richmond, 1921. Woodcuts by Vanessa Bell. Decorated boards and cloth. (Issued without dustwrapper.) $1,500.

WOOLF, Virginia. *Night and Day.* London, 1919. In dustwrapper. $3,000. New York, 1920. In dustwrapper. $2,000.

WOOLF, Virginia. *On Being Ill.* Hogarth Press. (London), 1930: Vellum and cloth. One of 250 signed. In dustwrapper. $1,500.

WOOLF, Virginia. *Orlando: A Biography.* New York, 1928. One of 861 signed. (Issued without dustwrapper.) $600. Half morocco. One of 11 on green paper. In slipcase. $1,000. Hogarth Press. London, 1928. First English edition, presumed first issue, brown cloth. $250. Second issue in orange cloth. $200.

WOOLF, Virginia. *A Room of One's Own.* Fountain Press. New York and Hogarth Press London, 1929. One of 492 signed. Of this edition, 100 were reserved for Great Britain and issued in pink dustwrapper. $1,250. Without dustwrapper. $1,000. Trade. London, 1929. $600.

WOOLF, Virginia. *Street Haunting.* Grabhorn Press. San Francisco, 1930. Boards and blue or green morocco. One of 500 signed. In slipcase. $750.

WOOLF, Virginia. *Three Guineas.* London, 1938. 5 plates. Yellow cloth. $200.

WOOLF, Virginia. *To the Lighthouse.* Hogarth Press. London, 1927. $1,000. New York (1927). $350.

WOOLF, Virginia. *The Voyage Out.* London, 1915. Author's first book. $750. New York, 1920. First American edition with text revised by Woolf. In dustwrapper. $1,000.

WOOLF, Virginia. *The Waves.* Hogarth Press. London, 1931. $500. New York (1931). $200.

WOOLF, Virginia. *The Years.* Hogarth Press. London, 1937. $250.

WOOLF, Virginia, and WOOLF, L. S. *Two Stories.* Hogarth Press. Richmond, 1917. Wraps or paper-backed cloth. First book of the Hogarth Press. $5,000.

WOOLLCOTT, Alexander. *While Rome Burns.* New York, 1934. One of 500 signed. In glassine dustwrapper. $125.

WOOLNOUGH, C. W. *The Whole Art of Marbling as Applied to Paper, Book-Edges, Etc.* London, 1881. Second edition, revised. Contains 39 plates of marbled paper specimens, some with multiple samples. $750.

WOOLRICH, Cornell. *The Bride Wore Black.* New York, 1940. $300.

WOOLRICH, Cornell. *Cover Charge.* New York, 1926. Author's first book. $1,250.

WOOLWORTH, James M. *Nebraska in 1857.* Omaha, 1857. Colored folding map. Printed cloth. $1,000.

WOOTEN, Dudley G. (editor). *A Comprehensive History of Texas, 1865 to 1897.* Dallas, 1898. 23 plates. 2 vols., leather. $350.

WORDSWORTH, William. See *Grace Darling; Kendel and Windermere Railway . . . ; Lyrical Ballads; Ode Performed in the Senate House.*

WORDSWORTH, William. *An Evening Walk.* London, 1793. Author's first book. $35,000 at auction in 1990.

WORDSWORTH, William. *The Excursion, Being a Portion of the Recluse, a Poem.* London, 1814. $450.

WORDSWORTH, William. *A Letter to a Friend of Robert Burns.* London, 1816. $600.

WORDSWORTH, William. *Memorials of a Tour on the Continent, 1820.* London, 1822. $350.

WORDSWORTH, William. *Ode on the Intimations of Immortality . . .* Essex House Press. London, 1903. Colored frontispiece by Walter Crane. Vellum. One of 150 on vellum. $600.

WORDSWORTH, William. *Poems.* London, 1807. 2 vols. First edition, first issue, with period after "Sonnets" on page (103) of vol. 1 and "fnuction" on page 98 of vol. 2. $1,500. London (1902). Vale Press. 6 woodcuts. White buckram. One of 310. $300.

WORDSWORTH, William. *The Prelude, or Growth of a Poet's Mind: An Autobiographical Poem.* London, 1850. Dark red cloth. $300. London, 1915. Doves Press. Vellum. One of 155. $1,500. One of 10 on vellum. $6,000.

WORDSWORTH, William. *The White Doe of Rylstone.* London, 1815. Frontispiece. $600.

WORDSWORTH, William. *Yarrow Revisited, and Other Poems.* London, 1835. In original drab boards, paper label on spine, or cloth. With inserted errata slip. $500.

WORK, John. See Lewis, W. S., and Phillips, P. C.

WOUK, Herman. *Aurora Dawn.* New York, 1947. $125.

WOUK, Herman. *The Caine Mutiny.* Garden City, 1951. $250.

WOUK, Herman. *The Man in the Trench Coat.* New York (1941). Author's first book. Wraps. $750.

WRIGHT, Andrew. *Court Hand Restored; Or, The Student's Assistant in Reading Old Deeds, Charters . . .* London, 1776. 20 engraved plates. $300.

WRIGHT, Austin Tappan. *Islandia.* New York (1942). Beige buckram. In dustwrapper. With Basil Davenport prospectus *An Introduction to Islandia,* in white boards without dustwrapper. Author's first and only book. $300.

WRIGHT, E. W. (editor). *Lewis and Dryden's Marine History of the Pacific Northwest . . .* Portland, 1895. Plates. Morocco. $600. New York, 1961. $200.

WRIGHT, Frank Lloyd. See Gannet(t), William C.

WRIGHT, Frank Lloyd. *An Autobiography.* New York, 1932. In dustwrapper. $400. New York (1943). Oblong. Second edition. In dustwrapper. $250.

WRIGHT, Frank Lloyd. *Buildings, Plans and Designs.* New York (1963). 100 plates, loose in half-cloth portfolio. $1,000.

WRIGHT, Frank Lloyd. *The Disappearing City.* New York (1932). Illustrated. Green cloth, with black map design. First edition, first binding. In dustwrapper. $600. Second binding in blue cloth, map label on cover. $500.

WRIGHT, Frank Lloyd. *Drawings for a Living Architecture.* New York, 1959. 200 drawings by the author (75 colored). Oblong folio, cloth. In dustwrapper. $1,000.

WRIGHT, Frank Lloyd. *The Future of Architecture.* New York, 1953. $150.

WRIGHT, Frank Lloyd. *Genius and the Mobocracy.* New York (1949). Illustrated by Louis H. Sullivan. In dustwrapper. $175.

WRIGHT, Frank Lloyd. *The Japanese Print.* Chicago, 1912. Illustrated. Orange wraps. First edition (suppressed). $2,500 or more. (All except about 50 burned by the publisher when Wright protested the binding.) First published edition. Printed boards. One of 35 on vellum. $2,500. Trade. $1,000.

WRIGHT, Frank Lloyd. *Modern Architecture.* Princeton, 1931. Boards. Issued without dustwrapper. $500.

WRIGHT, Frank Lloyd. *The Natural House.* New York, 1954. $350.

WRIGHT, Frank Lloyd. *Studies and Executed Buildings.* (Berlin, 1910.) 2 vols., oblong folio, cloth. $3,000.

WRIGHT, Harold Bell. *Mine with the Iron Door.* New York, 1923. $125.

WRIGHT, Harold Bell. *When a Man's a Man.* Book Supply Co., Chicago (1916). In dustwrapper. $150.

WRIGHT, Harry. *Harry Wright's Pocket Base Ball Score Book, No. 1.* Boston, 1876. $500.

WRIGHT, Harry. *Short History of Golf in Mexico.* Privately printed, 1938. Signed limited edition. $300.

WRIGHT, James. *The Branch Will Not Break.* Middletown, Conn. (1963). $125.

WRIGHT, James. *The Green Wall.* New Haven, 1957. Foreword by W. H. Auden. Author's first book. $300.

WRIGHT, Joseph (editor). *The English Dialect Dictionary.* London, 1898–1905. 6 vols., half morocco. $250. New York, 1962. 6 vols. Reprint. $150.

WRIGHT, Judith. *The Moving Image.* Melbourne (1946). Author's first book. $100.

WRIGHT, Richard. *How "Bigger" Was Born.* (New York, 1940.) Printed wraps. $125.

WRIGHT, Richard. *Native Son.* New York, 1940. First binding in dark blue cloth, stamped in red. In yellow and green (first) dustwrapper. $250. Second binding, gray cloth. In grayish (second) dustwrapper. $60.

WRIGHT, Richard. *The Outsider.* New York (1953). $100.

WRIGHT, Richard. *12 Million Black Voices: A Folk History of the Negro in the United States.* New York, 1941. Photographs selected by Edwin Rosskam. $250.

WRIGHT, Richard. *Uncle Tom's Children: Four Novellas.* New York, 1938. Author's first book. $1,000.

WRIGHT, Richard. *Uncle Tom's Children: Five Long Stories.* New York (1938). First edition not stated. "G-P" on copyright page. Enlarged edition of first book. $600.

WRIGHT, Robert M. *Dodge City, the Cowboy Capital . . .* (Wichita, 1913.) Colored frontispiece, 40 plates. With 344 pp. $350. Second edition, same place and date, 342 pp., black-and-white portrait. $200.

WRIGHT, S. Fowler. *The Amphibians.* London (1925). Author's first book. $150.

WRIGHT, Willard Huntington. See Van Dine, S. S.

WRIGHT, Willard Huntington. *Songs of Youth.* New York, 1913. Author's first book. $350.

WRIGHT, William. See De Quille, Dan.

WRIGHT, William. *The Oil Regions of Pennsylvania.* New York, 1865. $200.

WROTH, Lawrence C. *The Colonial Printer.* Portland, 1938. Limited to 1,500 copies. Slipcase. $125.

WROTH, Lawrence C. *The Early Cartography of the Pacific.* New York, 1934. Folding facsimile maps. One of 100. Issued without dustwrapper. $150.

WYANDOTTE; or The Hutted Knoll. London, 1843. 3 vols., boards. (By James Fenimore Cooper.) $600. Philadelphia, 1843. 2 vols., wraps. First American edition. $750.

WYATT, M. D. *The Art of Illuminating.* London, 1860. Illustrated. Decorated brown cloth, or morocco. $350.

WYETH, Andrew. *Four Seasons.* New York (1963). Preface by Lloyd Goodrich. 12 reproductions. Folio, cloth. Boxed. $150. One of 500 signed. In portfolio. $750.

WYETH, John A. *Life of Gen. Nathan Bedford Forrest.* New York, 1899. 55 plates, maps. $150.

WYETH, John B. *Oregon; or A Short History of a Long Journey.* Cambridge, Mass., 1833. 87 pp., in original printed wraps. First issue, with half title. $4,000.

WYLIE, Elinor. See *Incidental Numbers.*

WYLIE, Elinor. *Angels and Earthly Creatures: A Sequence of Sonnets.* Henley-on-Thames, 1928. Decorated wraps. One of 51 numbered copies. About half of this edition were signed, the rest left unsigned at the author's death. In dustwrapper signed. $750. Unsigned, $350. New York, 1929. Portrait. Black cloth. First American edition (and first commercially published). One of 200. In slipcase. $200. Trade. $60.

WYLIE, Elinor. *Mr. Hodge & Mr. Hazard.* New York, 1928. One of 145 signed. In slipcase. $250.

WYLIE, Elinor. *Nets to Catch the Wind.* New York, 1921. First issue, on unwatermarked paper. In dustwrapper. (First book under her name.) $300.

WYLIE, Elinor. *The Orphan Angel.* New York, 1926. One of 160 on rag paper, signed. In slipcase. $200. Vellum. One of 30 on vellum signed. In slipcase. $500.

WYLIE, Philip. *Heavy Laden.* New York, 1928. Author's first book. $150.

WYNDHAM, John. See Beynon, John.

WYNDHAM, John. *The Day of the Triffids.* New York, 1951. $300. London (1951). First English edition containing revisions. $350.

WYSS, Johann David. See *The Family Robinson Crusoe; The Swiss Family Robinson.*

X

XENOS, Stefanos. *East and West, A Diplomatic History of the Annexation History of the Annexation of the Ionian Islands to the Kingdom of Greece.* London, 1865. $150.

Y

YABE, Yae K. *A Course of Instruction in Jiu-Jitsu.* London, 1904. $75.

YATES, Edmund Hodgson. *My Haunts and Their Frequenters.* London, 1854. Illustrated. Wraps. Author's first book. $125.

YATES, Richard. *Revolutionary Road.* Boston (1961). Author's first book. $100.

YE Minutes of Ye CLXXVIIth Meeting of Ye Sette of Odd Volumes. Ashendene Press. (London, 1896.) Transcribed by John Todhunter. Printed wraps. One of 154. $600.

YEARY, Mamie. *Reminiscences of the Boys in Gray, 1861–1865.* Dallas, 1912. $750.

YEATS, John Butler. *Early Memories.* Cuala Press. Dundrum, Ireland, 1923. Preface by W. B. Yeats. Boards and linen. Issued without dustwrapper. One of 500. $175.

YEATS, John Butler. *Further Letters.* Cuala Press. Dundrum, 1920. Selected by Lennox Robinson. Boards and linen. Issued without dustwrapper. One of 400. $175.

YEATS, John Butler. *James Flaunty.* London (1901). Author's first book. Wraps. $250.

YEATS, John Butler. *La la Noo.* Cuala Press. Dublin, 1943. Boards and linen. One of 250. In dustwrapper. $250.

YEATS, John Butler. *Passages from the Letters of John Butler Yeats.* Cuala Press. Dundrum, 1917. Selected by Ezra Pound. Boards and linen. One of 400. $300.

YEATS, William Butler. See Allingham, William; Bax, Clifford; Dunsany, Lord; Ganconagh; Gogarty, Oliver St. John.

YEATS, William Butler. *The Bounty of Sweden.* Cuala Press. Dublin, 1925. Boards and linen. One of 400. In glassine dustwrapper. $200.

YEATS, William Butler. *The Cat and the Moon and Certain Poems.* Cuala Press. Dublin, 1924. Boards and linen. One of 500. Issued without dustwrapper. $200.

YEATS, William Butler. *Cathleen ni Houlihan.* Caradoc Press. London, 1902. Vellum, silk ties. One of 8 on Japan vellum. $7,500. First regular edition. Cream-colored boards, leather spine. (300 copies.) $1,000.

YEATS, William Butler. *The Celtic Twilight.* London, 1893. Olive green cloth. First binding, with publisher's name on back in capital letters. $450. Later binding, capitals and lower-case lettering. $300. New York, 1894. First American issue (English sheets). $300.

YEATS, William Butler. *Collected Works.* Portraits. Stratford-on-Avon, 1908. 8 vols., half vellum and cloth. $1,750. Remainder bound in cloth and boards. $850.

YEATS, William Butler. *The Countess Kathleen.* London, 1892. Frontispiece. Japan vellum boards. One of 30 on vellum, signed by the publisher. $2,500. Dark green boards, parchment spine. One of 500. $300. London, 1919. Wraps. Revised edition. $100.

YEATS, William Butler. *The Cutting of an Agate.* New York, 1912. $250. London, 1919. Dark blue cloth. First English edition. $100.

YEATS, William Butler. *Discoveries: A Volume of Essays.* Dun Emer Press. Dundrum, 1907. Blue boards and linen. One of 200. $250.

YEATS, William Butler. *Early Poems and Stories.* New York, 1925. First American edition. One of 250 signed. $350. Trade. $150.

YEATS, William Butler. *Eight Poems.* Morland Press. London (1916). Folio, wraps. One of 8 on Dutch paper. $1,000. One of 70 on Japan vellum. $600. One of 122 on Italian paper. $300.

YEATS, William Butler. *Essays.* London, 1924. $200. New York, 1924. Boards and cloth. One of 250 signed. $500.

YEATS, William Butler. *The Golden Helmet.* New York, 1908. Gray boards. One of 50. $1,250.

YEATS, William Butler. *The Hour Glass.* London, 1903. (12 copies issued for copyright; without covers.) $7,500. New York, 1904. Blue cloth. $200. Parchment. One of 100 on vellum. $850. Cuala Press. (Dublin, 1914.) Gray wraps. (50 copies.) $2,000.

YEATS, William Butler. *Ideas of Good and Evil.* London, 1903. Green boards and cloth. $250. New York, 1903. (English sheets.) $200. Dublin, 1905. Second edition. $150.

YEATS, William Butler. *In the Seven Woods.* Dun Emer Press. Dundrum, 1903. Printed in red and black. Linen. One of 325. $400. (First book from the Dun Emer Press.)

YEATS, William Butler. *John Sherman and Dhoya.* See Ganconagh.

YEATS, William Butler. *The King's Threshold.* New York, 1904. Gray boards. One of 100. $1,250. (Many, but not all, signed. $1,750.)

YEATS, William Butler. *The Land of Heart's Desire.* London, 1894. Wraps. First edition, first state without the two fleurons after the word "Desire" on front cover. $600. Chicago, 1814 (actually 1894). Boards. First American edition. One of 450. $150. Portland, Me., 1903. Boards. One of 100 on Japan paper. $200. One of 10 on vellum, signed by T. B. Mosher as publisher. $1,250.

YEATS, William Butler. *Michael Robartes and the Dancer.* Cuala Press. Dundrum, 1920. Printed in red and black. Boards and linen. One of 400. $250.

YEATS, William Butler. *Modern Poetry.* London, 1936. Bright green wraps. One of 1,000. $150.

YEATS, William Butler. *Mosada. A Dramatic Poem.* Dublin, 1886. Author's first book. Brown wraps. $50,000. Dublin, 1943. Cuala Press. Cream-colored parchment wraps. One of 50. In dustwrapper. $1,750. (Note: This poem was first published in the *Dublin University Review,* June, 1886, Vol. 2, No. 6, original decorated wraps. $1,500.)

YEATS, William Butler. *On the Boiler.* Cuala Press. Dublin (1939). Pictorial blue-green wraps. Second edition. (All but 4 copies of the first edition were destroyed.) $150.

YEATS, William Butler. *A Packet for Ezra Pound.* Cuala Press. Dublin, 1929. Boards and linen. Issued without dustwrapper. One of 425. $300.

YEATS, William Butler. *The Player Queen.* London, 1922. Wraps. $150.

YEATS, William Butler. *Plays and Controversies.* New York, 1924. Boards and cloth. Issued without dustwrapper. One of 250 signed. In slipcase. $300.

YEATS, William Butler. *Plays for an Irish Theatre.* London, 1911. First issue, with dark brown (later white) endpapers. $300.

YEATS, William Butler. *Poems.* London, 1895. Light brown cloth. One of 25 printed on Japan vellum, signed by Yeats. $4,000. Trade. 750 copies. $850. American issue with Boston imprint of Copeland & Day added to title page. $600. London, 1899. Dark blue cloth. Second English edition. $300. London, 1901. Dark blue cloth. Third English edition. $200. London, 1904. Fourth English edition. $150. London, 1908. Cloth. Fifth English edition. $100. London, 1912. Pictorial blue bloth. Sixth English edition. $100. Dublin, 1935. Blue wraps. Cuala Press. One of 30. $1,750. London, 1949. 2 vols., olive green cloth. Definitive edition. One of 375 signed. In slipcase. $1,500.

YEATS, William Butler. *Poems Written in Discouragement, 1912–1913.* Cuala Press. Dundrum, 1913. Dark gray wraps, stitched with red cord. One of 50. $1,500.

YEATS, William Butler. *Responsibilities and Other Poems.* London, 1916. $275. New York, 1916. Gray boards and cloth. $200.

YEATS, William Butler. *Reveries over Childhood and Youth.* Cuala Press. Dundrum, 1915. With a blue board portfolio containing a colored plate and 2 portraits. Gray boards and linen. One of 425. $400. New York, 1916. First American edition. $125. London, 1916. Dark blue cloth. $150.

YEATS, William Butler. *The Secret Rose.* London, 1897. Illustrated by John Butler Yeats. Dark blue cloth. First binding, with "Lawrence & Bullen" on spine. $350. New York, 1897. English sheets. $300. Dublin, 1905. English sheets with cancel title. $300.

YEATS, William Butler. *The Shadowy Waters.* London, 1900. $175. New York, 1901. $125.

YEATS, William Butler. *The Singing Head and the Lady.* (Bryn Mawr, Pa.), 1934. Decorated wraps. One of 2 or 3 signed by Yeats from an edition of 20 on different papers. $3,500. Unsigned. $2,500.

YEATS, William Butler. *Stories of Red Hanrahan.* Dun Emer Press. Dundrum, 1904. Blue boards and linen. One of 500. $250.

YEATS, William Butler. *The Tables of the Law. The Adoration of the Magi.* (London), 1897. Portrait frontispiece. Buckram. One of 110. $1,000. London, 1904. Blue wraps. First unlimited edition. $125. Shakespeare Head Press. Stratford-on-Avon, 1914. Second limited edition. One of 510. $125.

YEATS, William Butler. *The Tower.* London, 1928. Pictorial cloth. $350. New York, 1928. Green cloth. First American edition. $200.

YEATS, William Butler. *The Trembling of the Veil.* London, 1922. Portrait. Blue boards and parchment. One of 1,000 signed. In dustwrapper. $500.

YEATS, William Butler. *The Variorum Edition of the Poems of William Butler Yeats.* New York, 1957. Buckram. One of 825 signed. In slipcase. $600.

YEATS, William Butler. *A Vision.* London, 1925. Blue boards. One of 600 signed. In dustwrapper. $650. London, 1937. (Revised.) $125.

YEATS, William Butler. *The Wanderings of Oisin and Other Poems.* London, 1889. Author's first regularly published hardbound book. First binding in dark blue cloth. One of 500. $2,500.

YEATS, William Butler. *The Wind Among the Reeds.* London, 1899. Dark blue cloth. First issue, without correction slip. $400. Second issue, same date, with correction slip. $300. Deluxe binding (full gilt vellum). $3,500.

YEATS, William Butler. *The Winding Stair.* Fountain Press. New York, 1929. Dark blue cloth. One of 642 signed. In dustwrapper. $500. (Another New York edition of 1929, unpublished, bears the imprint of Crosby Gaige with a limitation of 700 copies on handmade paper and 12 copies on green paper. Sheets of this printing have appeared in the market at various times, signed by Yeats. $3,000.) London, 1933. Olive green cloth. First English edition (with *And Other Poems* added to title). $200. New York, 1933. First American trade edition. $150.

YEATS, William Butler (editor). *Fairy and Folk Tales of the Irish Peasantry.* London, 1888. With errata slip. $400. Later printings drop date from title page.

YEATS, William Butler (editor). *Irish Fairy Tales.* London, 1892. $300.

YEATS, William Butler, and JOHNSON, Lionel. *Poetry and Ireland: Essays.* Cuala Press. Dundrum, 1908. One of 250. $200.

YELLOW BIRD. The Life and Adventures of Joaquin Murieta. San Francisco, 1854. 2 plates. 90 pp., wraps. (By John R. Ridge.) $25,000 or more. (For later editions, see *The Life of Joaquin Murieta.)*

YELLOW Book (The): An Illustrated Quarterly. London, 1894–97. 13 vols., printed and pictorial yellow cloth. $1,250.

YELLOWPLUSH Correspondence (The). Philadelphia 1838. (By William Makepeace Thackeray.) In original boards and cloth, paper label. With text starting at page 13. $1,500.

YEMASSEE (The): A Romance of Carolina. New York, 1835. (By William Gilmore Simms.) 2 vols., in original cloth, paper labels. First issue, with copyright notice pasted in vol. 1. $400.

YERKOW, Charles. *Modern Judo.* Harrisburg, 1942. First edition stated. $50.

YOAKUM, Henderson K. *History of Texas.* New York, 1855. Folding document, 4 maps, 5 plates. 2 vols.. cloth. $1,500. New York, 1856. 2 vols. Second edition. $1,000. Austin, 1935. 2 vols. Facsimile edition. $75.

YOKOYAMA, S. and OSHIMA, E. *Judo.* Tokyo, 1915. $75.

YORE, Clem. *Ranger Bill.* New York, 1931. $150.

YORE, Clem. *Raw Gold.* Garden City, 1926. $125.

YOUNG, Al. *Dancing.* New York (1969). Author's first book. Wraps. 50 signed and numbered copies. $150. Trade. $35.

YOUNG, Andrew W. *History of Chautauqua County, New York.* Buffalo, 1875. Half morocco. $125.

YOUNG, Andrew. *Song of Night.* London (1910). Author's first book. $200.

YOUNG, Ansel. *The Western Reserve Almanac for the Year 1844.* Cleveland (1843). 32 pp., wraps. $250.

YOUNG Duke (The). By the author of *Vivian Grey.* London, 1831. (By Benjamin Disraeli.) 3 vols. in original boards, paper spines with labels. First issue, with half titles to vols. 2 and 3 and advertisement leaf at end of vol. 3 (VAB). $750.

YOUNG, Harry (Sam). *Hard Knocks: A Life Story of the Vanishing West.* Portland, 1915. 25 plates. Boards. $200. Chicago (1915). 18 plates. $75.

YOUNG, John R. *Memoirs.* Salt Lake City, 1920. 4 portraits. $150.

YOUNGBLOOD, Charles L. *Adventures of Chas. L. Youngblood During Ten Years on the Plains.* Boonville, Ind., 1882. Portrait. Cloth. $450.

YOUNGBLOOD, Charles L. *A Mighty Hunter.* Chicago, 1890. (Second edition of *Adventures . . .)* $250.

Z

ZACCARELLI, John. *Zaccarelli's Pictorial Souvenir Book of the Golden Northland.* Dawson (1908). Oblong, wraps. $250.

ZAMORANO 80 (The): A Selection of Distinguished California Books. Los Angeles, 1945. One of 500. In dustwrapper. $175.

ZANGWILL, Israel. *The Bachelor's Club.* London, 1891. Author's first book. $150.

ZANGWILL, Israel. *Children of the Ghetto.* London, 1892. 3 vols., decorated cloth. $300.

ZAPF, Hermann. *Manuale Typographicum . . .* New York, 1968. 975 signed and numbered copies. $450.

ZAPF, Hermann. *Pen and Graver, Alphabets & Pages of Calligraphy.* New York (1952). One of 2,000 copies. $450.

ZAPF, Hermann. *Typographic Variations Designed by Hermann Zapf on Themes in Contemporary Book Design . . .* New York, 1964. 1,000 numbered copies also initialed by Zapf. $400.

ZEITLIN, Jake. *For Whispers and Chants.* San Francisco, 1927. Author's first book. (500 copies.) $150.

ZEITLINGER, Heinrich, and SOTHERAN, Henry Cecil. *Bibliotheca Chemico-Mathematica . . .* London, 1921–1952. 6 vols. (2 vols. of original edition plus the first, second and third supplements [all done].) $375.

ZIMMER, John Todd. *Catalogue of the Edward E. Ayer Ornithological Library.* Chicago, 1926. 2 vols. $350.

ZOGBAUM, Rufus F. *Horse, Foot and Dragoons.* New York, 1888. $250.

ZOUCH, Thomas. *The Life of Isaac Walton.* London, 1823. $200.

ZUKOFSKY, Louis. See Reiser, Anton.

ZUKOFSKY, Louis. *"A" 1–12.* (Ashland, Mass.), 1959. With note by W. C. Williams. One of 200. Errata slip laid in. In glassine dustwrapper. $350.

ZUKOFSKY, Louis. *"A"–14.* (London, 1967.) One of 250 signed. $125. One of 26 lettered copies, signed. $200.

ZUKOFSKY, Louis. *Barely and Widely.* New York, 1958. Oblong, wraps. One of 300 signed. $175.

ZUKOFSKY, Louis. *First Half of "A"–9.* New York (1940). Mimeographed. In manila envelope. Author's first book. "First Edition, Limited to 55 Autographed Copies." $1,500.

ZUKOFSKY, Louis. *Initial.* New York, 1970. Wraps. One of 100 signed. $125.

ZUKOFSKY, Louis. *It Was.* (Kyoto, Japan, 1961.) One of 50 signed. $450. One of 200. $250.

ZUKOFSKY, Louis. *Iyyob.* Turret Books. London (1965). Oblong, wraps. One of 100 signed. $150.

ZUKOFSKY, Louis. *Le Style Apollinaire.* Paris, 1934. Wraps. $4,000.

ZUKOFSKY, Louis. *An Unearthing.* (Cambridge, 1965.) Wraps. One of 77 signed. $200.

ZUKOFSKY, Louis (editor). *An "Objectivists" Anthology.* (Dijon, France), 1932. Wraps. (Contributors include T. S. Eliot, William Carlos Williams.) $300.

SELECTED BIBLIOGRAPHY
OF WORKS CONSULTED

(ABERCROMBIE) Cooper, Jeffrey. *A Bibliography and Notes on the Works of Lascelles Abercrombie*. (London): Archon Books, 1969.

(ACTON) Ritchie, Neil. *A Bibliography of Harold Acton*. Florence 1934.

(ADAMIC) Christian, Henry A. *Louis Adamic: A Checklist*. Kent State University Press (1971).

ADAMS, Ramon F. *The Rampaging Herd*. Cleveland: (Zubal) (1982).

ADAMS, Ramon F. *Six-Guns and Saddle Leather*. (Cleveland): Zubal (1982).

(ADE) Russo, Dorothy Ritter. *A Bibliography of George Ade, 1866–1944*. Indianapolis: Indiana Historical Society, 1947.

AHEARN, Allen. *Book Collecting* . . . New York: G. P. Putnam's Sons (1989).

AHEARN, Allen and Patricia. *Author Price Guides*. Rockville, Md.: 1987–90.

(AIKEN) Bonnell, F. W. and F. C. *Conrad Aiken: A Bibliography (1902–1978)*. San Marino: Huntington Library, 1982.

(ALCOTT) Gulliver, Lucille. *Louisa May Alcott: A Bibliography*. Boston: Little Brown, 1932.

(ALGER) Gardner, Ralph D. *Road to Success: A Bibliography of the Works of Horatio Alger*. Mendota, Illinois: Wayside Press, 1971.

(ALGREN) Bruccoli, Matthew J. *Nelson Algren: A Descriptive Bibliography*. University of Pittsburgh Press, 1985.

AMERICAN Book Prices Current. New York: Bancroft-Parkman, 1981–89.

(AMIS) Gohn, Jack Benoit. *Kingsley Amis A Checklist*. Kent State University Press, (1976).

(ANDERSON) Sheehy, Eugene P. and Kenneth A. Lohf. *Sherwood Anderson: A Bibliography*. Los Gatos: Talisman Press, 1960.

(ANDREWS) Webber, William Hallam. *William Loring Andrews: A Study and Bibliography*. Rockville, Md.: 1980.

(ARNOLD) Smart, Thomas Burnett. *The Bibliography of Matthew Arnold*. London: 1892.

(ASHBERY) Kermani, David K. *John Ashbery: A Comprehensive Bibliography*. New York: Garland Publishing, 1976.

(ATWOOD) Horne, Alan J. *A Preliminary Checklist of Writings by and About Margaret Atwood*. In the *Malahat Review* no. 41. University of Victoria, 1977.

(AUDEN) Bloomfield, B. C. and Mendelson, Edward. *W.H. Auden: A Bibliography, 1924–1969*. Charlottesville: University of Virginia (1972).

(AUSTEN) Keynes, Geoffrey. *Jane Austen: A Bibliography*. London: Nonesuch Press, 1929.

(BARNES) Messeri, Douglas. *Djuna Barnes: A Bibliography*. (New York): David Lewis, 1975.

(BARRIE) Garland, Herbert. *A Bibliography of the Writings of Sir James Matthew Barrie*. London: Bookman's Journal, 1928.

(BARRIE) Cutler, B. D. *Sir James M. Barrie: A Bibliography*. New York, 1931.

(BARTH) Weixlmann, Joseph. *John Barth: A Descriptive . . . Bibliography*. New York: Garland, 1976.

(BARTHELME) Klinkowitz, Jerome, Asa Pieratt and Davis, Robert Murray. *Donald Barthelme: A Comprehensive Bibliography*. Archon Books, 1977.

(BECKETT) Lake, Carlton, et al. *No Symbols Where None Intended*. Austin: Humanities Research Center, University of Texas (1984).

(BEEBE) Berra, Tim. *William Beebe: An Annotated Bibliography*. Archon Books, 1977.

(BEERBOHM) Gallatin, A. E. and Oliver, L. M. *A Bibliography of the Works of Max Beerbohm*. London: Rupert Hart-Davis, 1952.

(BELLOC) Cahill, Patrick. *The English First Editions of Hilaire Belloc*. London, 1953.

(BERRYMAN) Stefanik, Ernest C., Jr. *John Berryman: A Descriptive Bibliography*. University of Pittsburgh, 1974.

(BETJEMAN) Stapleton, Margaret L. *Sir John Betjeman: A Bibliography of Writings By and About Him*. Metuchen, N.J.: Scarecrow Press, 1974.

(BISHOP) MacMahon, Candace. *Elizabeth Bishop: A Bibliography, 1927–1979*. Charlottesville: University of Virginia (1980).

(BLACK SUN) Minkoff, George Robert. *A Bibliography of the Black Sun Press*. Great Neck, 1970.

BLANCK, Jacob. *Bibliography of American Literature*. New Haven: Yale University Press, 1953–73. (7 vols.) (BAL).

BLANCK, Jacob. *Peter Parley to Penrod*. Waltham, Mass.: Mark Press, 1974.

BLEILER, E. F. *The Checklist of Science-Fiction and Supernatural Fiction*. Glen Rock, N.J.: Firebell Books (1978).

(BLOCH) Larson, Randall D. *The Complete Robert Bloch*. Sunnyvale, Calif.: Fandom Unlimited, 1986.

(BLUNDEN) Kirkpatrick, Brownlee. *A Bibliography of Edmund Blunden*. Oxford: Clarendon Press, 1979.

BOOKMAN'S McGrath, Daniel, ed. Price Guide. Vols. 36–40. Detroit: Gale Research (1987–90).

(BORROW) Collie, Michael, and Fraser, Angus. *George Borrow: A Bibliographical Study*. Hampshire: St. Paul's Bibliographies, 1984.

(BOWLES) Miller, Jeffrey. *Paul Bowles: A Descriptive Bibliography*. Santa Barbara: Black Sparrow, 1986.

(BRADBURY) Nolan, William F. *The Ray Bradbury Companion.* Detroit: Bruccoli Clark/Gale Research, 1975.

BRADLEY, Van Allen. *The Book Collector's Handbook of Values, 1982–83.* New York: Putnam & Sons, 1982 (VAB).

(BRAND) Richardson, Darrell C. *Max Brand (Frederick Faust): The Man and His Work.* Los Angeles: Fantasy Publishing (1952).

(BRONTË) Wise, Thomas J. *A Bibliography of the Writings . . . of the Brontë Family.* London: Dawsons of Pall Mall (1917).

(BROOKE) Keynes, Geoffrey. *A Bibliography of the Works of Rupert Brooke.* London: Rupert Hart-Davis, 1964.

(BROWN) Baird, Newton. *A Key to Frederic Brown's Wonderland.* Georgetown, Calif.: Talisman Literary Research, 1981.

(BROWNING) Barnes, Warner. *A Bibliography of Elizabeth Barrett Browning.* (Austin): University of Texas . . . (1967).

(BROWNING) Wise, Thomas J. *A Bibliography of the Writings . . . of Robert Browning.* London: Dawsons of Pall Mall, 1971.

BRUCCOLI, Clark, Layman, Richard, and Franklin, Benjamin (editors). *First Printing of American Authors.* 5 vols. Detroit: Gale Research, 1977–89.

(BUCHAN) Blanchard, Robert G. *The First Editions of John Buchan.* (Hamden, Conn.): Archon Books, 1981.

(BUKOWSKI) Fogel, Al. *Charles Bukowski: A Comprehensive Checklist.* (Miami: 1982).

(BUNTING) Guedalla, Roger. *Basil Bunting: A Bibliography of Works and Criticism.* Norwood, Pa.: Norwood Editions, 1973.

(BURGESS) Wright, Wayne W. *Thornton W. Burgess: A Descriptive Book Bibliography.* Sandwich, Mass.: Burgess Society, 1979.

(BURNS) *The Bibliography of Robert Burns . . .* Kilmarnock (Scotland): James M'Kie, 1881.

(BURROUGHS, E. R.) Heins, Henry Hardy. *A Golden Anniversary Bibliography of Edgar Rice Burroughs.* Revised. West Kingston, R.I.: Donald Grant, 1964.

(BURROUGHS, W.) Maynard, Joe, and Barry, Miles. *William J. Burroughs: A Bibliography, 1953–73.* Charlottesville: University of Virginia Press (1978).

(BYRON) Wise, Thomas J. *A Bibliography of the Writings in Verse and Prose of George Gordon Noel, Lord Byron.* 2 vols. London: Dawsons of Pall Mall, 1972.

(BUTLER) Hoppe, A. J. *A Bibliography of the Writings of Samuel Butler.* New York: Burt Franklin (1968).

(BURTON) Penzer, Norman M. *An Annotated Bibliography of Sir Richard Francis Burton.* New York: Burt Franklin (1970).

(BYRNE) Wetherbee, Winthrop, Jr. *Donn Byrne: A Bibliography.* New York: New York Public Library, 1949.

(CABELL) Brussel I. R. *James Branch Cabell: A Revised Bibliography.* Philadelphia: Centaur Book Shop, 1932.

(CARLYLE) Dyer, Isaac Watson. *A Bibliography of Thomas Carlyle's Writings* . . . New York: Burt Franklin (1968).

(CARROLL) Williams, Sidney Herbert. *A Bibliography of the Writings of Lewis Carroll* (Charles Lutwidge Dodgson). London: Bookman's Journal, 1924.

CASANOVA Booksellers Checklists of Twentieth Century Authors. Second Series, Milwaukee: 1933 (Aldington, Armstrong, Huxley, Joyce and Morley); Third Series, Milwaukee: 1935 (Caldwell, F. Harris, Nathan, Newton and Stein).

(CASTLEMON) Blanck, Jacob. *Harry Castlemon Boy's Own Author.* Waltham, Mass.: Mark Press, 1969.

(CATHER) Crane, Joan. *Willa Cather: A Bibliography.* Lincoln: University of Nebraska Press (1982).

(CHANDLER) Bruccoli, Matthew. *Raymond Chandler: A Descriptive Bibliography.* University of Pittsburgh Press, 1979.

(CHURCHILL) Woods, Frederick. *A Bibliography of the Works of Sir Winston Churchill.* (London): St. Paul's Bibliographies, no. 1 (1975).

(CONRAD) Wise, Thomas J. *A Bibliography of the Writings of Joseph Conrad, (1895–1921).* London: Dawsons of Pall Mall, 1972.

(CONRAD) Cagle, William. *A Bibliography of Joseph Conrad.* Unpublished.

COOK, Ralph T. *The City Lights Pocket Poets Series: A Descriptive Bibliography.* La Jolla, Calif.: Laurence McGilvery/Atticus Books, ca. 1982.

(COPPARD) Fabes, Gilbert H. *The First Editions of A.E. Coppard, A.P. Herbert and Charles Morgan.* London: Myers & Co. (1933).

(COPPARD) Schwartz, Jacob. *The Writings of Alfred Edgar Coppard.* London: The Ulysses Bookshop, 1931.

(CORSO) Wilson, Robert. *A Bibliography of Works by Gregory Corso, 1954–1965.* New York: The Phoenix Book Shop, Inc., 1966.

(CORVO) Woolf, Cecil. *A Bibliography of Frederick Rolfe Baron Corvo.* London: Rupert Hart-Davis, Soho Square, 1957.

(COWLEY) Perkin, M. R. *Abraham Cowley: A Bibliography.* (Kent, England): Dawson, (1977).

(COZZENS) Bruccoli, Matthew. *James Gould Cozzens: A Descriptive Bibliography.* University of Pittsburgh Press, 1981.

(CRANE, H.) Schwartz, Joseph, and Schweik, Robert C. *Hart Crane: A Descriptive Bibliography.* University of Pittsburgh Press (1972).

(CRANE, S.) Williams, Ames W., and Starrett, Vincent. *Stephen Crane: A Bibliography.* Glendale, Calif. John Valentine, Publisher, 1948.

(CREELEY) Novik, Mary. *Robert Creeley: An Inventory, 1945–1970.* Kent State University Press (1973).

(CREWS) Hargraves, Michael. *Harry Crews: A Bibliography.* (Westport, Conn.): Meckler Publishing Corporation (1986).

(CUMMINGS) Firmage, George J. *E. E. Cummings: A Bibliography.* (Middletown, Ct.): Wesleyan University Press (1960).

(CUNNINGHAM) Gullans, Charles. *A Bibliography of the Published Works of J.V. Cunningham.* Los Angeles: University of California Library, 1973.

CURREY, L. W. *Science Fiction and Fantasy Authors A Bibliography of First Printings* . . . Boston: G.K. Hall (1979).

CUTLER, B. D., and STILES, Villa. *Modern British Authors.* New York: Greenberg Publisher (1930).

(DAHLBERG) Billings, Harold. *A Bibliography of Edward Dahlberg.* Austin: University of Texas Press (1971).

(DARWIN) Freeman, R. B. *The Works of Charles Darwin: An Annotated Bibliographical Handlist.* Dawson-Archon Books (1977).

(DAVIS) Quinby, Henry Cole, A. M. *Richard Harding Davis: A Bibliography.* New York: E.P. Dutton & Company (1924).

(DAY-LEWIS) Handley-Taylor, Geoffrey, and Smith, Timothy d'Arch. *C. Day-Lewis, the Poet Laureate: A Bibliography.* Chicago and London: St. James Press, 1968.

(DE CAMP) Laighlin, Charlotte, and Levack, Daniel J. H. *An L. Sprague De Camp Bibliography.* San Francisco and Columbia, Pa.: Underwood/Miller, 1983.

(DEIGHTON) Milward-Oliver, Edward. *Len Deighton: An Annotated Bibliography, 1954–1985.* (Kent, England): The Sammler Press (1985).

(DERLETH) (Derleth, August). *100 Books by August Derleth.* Arkham House, 1962.

(DE VRIES) Bowden, Edwin T. *Peter De Vries: A Bibliography, 1934–1977.* Austin: University of Texas (1978).

(DICK) Levack, Daniel J. H. *PKD: A Philip K. Dick Bibliography.* San Francisco and Columbia, Pa.: Underwood/Miller, 1981.

(DICKENS) Smith, Walter E. *Charles Dickens Part I: The Novels with Sketches by Boz.* In *In the Original Cloth: A Bibliographical Catalogue.* Los Angeles: Heritage Book Shop, 1982.

(DICKENS) Smith, Walter E. *Part II: The Christmas Book and Selected Secondary Novels.* In *Charles Dickens in the Original Cloth: A Bibliographical Catalogue.* Los Angeles: Heritage Book Shop, 1982.

(DICKENS) Eckel, John C. *The First Editions of the Writings of Charles Dickens and Their Values: A Bibliography.* London: Chapman & Hall, Ltd., 1913.

(DICKEY) Bruccoli, Matthew J., and Baughman, Judith S. *James Dickey: A Descriptive Bibliography.* University of Pittsburgh Press, 1990.

(DICKINSON) Myerson, Joel. *Emily Dickinson: A Descriptive Bibliography.* University of Pittsburgh Press, 1984.

(DINESEN) Henriksen, Liselotte. *Isak Dinesen: A Bibliography.* (Viborg, Denmark): Gyldendal (1977).

(DOBIE) McVicker, Mary Louise. *The Writings of J. Frank Dobie: A Bibliography.* Museum of the Great Plains, Lawton, (Okla.) (1968).

(DORN) Streeter, David. *A Bibliography of Ed Dorn.* New York: The Phoenix Bookshop, 1973.

(DOS PASSOS) Sanders, Harvey. *John Dos Passos: A Comprehensive Bibliography.* New York and London: Garland Publishing, Inc., 1987.

(DOUGLAS) McDonald, Edward D. *A Bibliography of the Writings of Norman Douglas.* Philadelphia: The Centaur Book Shop, 1927.

(DOYLE) Green, Richard Lancelyn, and Gibson, John Michael *A Bibliography of A. Conan Doyle.* Oxford: Clarendon Press (1983).

(DREISER) McDonald, Edward D. *A Bibliography of the Writings of Theodore Dreiser.* New York: Burt Franklin (1968).

(DUNCAN) Bertholf, Robert J. *Robert Duncan A Descriptive Bibliography.* Santa Rosa, Calif.: Black Sparrow Press, 1986.

(DURRELL) Fraser, G. S., and Thomas, Alan G. *Lawrence Durrell: A Study.* London: Faber and Faber (1968).

DYKES, Jeff. *Western High Spots.* No-place: Northland Press (1977).

(A. E.) Denson, Alan. *Printed Writings by George W. Russell (A.E.): A Bibliography.* Evanston: Northwestern University Press, 1961.

(EIGNER) Wyatt, Andrea. *A Bibliography of Works by Larry Eigner.* Berkeley: Oyez, 1970.

(ELIOT, G.) Lake, Brian, and Nassau, Janet. *George Eliot in Original Cloth: A Bibliographical Catalogue.* (Bloomsbury): Jarndyce Antiquarian Books (1988).

(ELIOT, T. S.) Gallup, Donald. *T.S. Eliot: A Bibliography.* London: Faber & Faber (1970).

(EMERSON) Myerson, Joel. *Ralph Waldo Emerson A Descriptive Bibliography.* University of Pittsburgh Press, 1982.

(EVERSON) Sipper, Ralph. *William Everson, A Collection of Books & Manuscripts.* Santa Barbara: Joseph the Provider (1987).

(FARRELL) Branch, Edgar. *A Bibliography of James T. Farrell's Writings 1921–1957.* Philadelphia: University of Pennsylvania Press (1959).

(FAULKNER) Petersen, Carl. *Each in Its Ordered Place: A Faulkner Collector's Notebook.* Ann Arbor: Ardis (1975).

(FAULKNER) Massey, Linton R. *"Man Working," 1919–1962 William Faulkner.* Charlottesville: Bibliographical Society of the University of Virginia (1968).

(FIRBANK) Benkovitz, Miriam J. *A Bibliography of Ronald Firbank.* London: Rupert Hart-Davis, 1963.

(FIRBANK) Benkovitz, Miriam J. *Supplement to a Bibliography of Ronald Firbank.* London: Enitharmon Press, 1980.

(FITZGERALD, E.) Prideaux, Colonel W. F. *Notes for a Bibliography of Edward FitzGerald.* New York: Burt Franklin (1968).

(FITZGERALD, F. S.) Bruccoli, Matthew J. *F. Scott Fitzgerald: A Descriptive Bibliography.* University of Pittsburgh Press, 1987.

FLAKE, Chad J. *A Mormon Bibliography, 1830–1930.* Salt Lake City: University of Utah Press, 1978.

(FLEMING) Campbell, Ian. *Ian Fleming: A Catalogue of a Collection.* Liverpool (1978).

(FLETCHER) Morton, Bruce. *John Gould Fletcher: A Bibliography.* Kent State University Press (1979).

(FORD) Harvey, David Dow. *Ford Madox Ford, 1873–1939.* New York: Gordian Press, 1972.

(FORSTER) Kirkpatrick, B. J. *A Bibliography of E.M. Forster.* Oxford: Clarendon Press, 1985.

(FROST) Crane, Joan St. C. *Robert Frost: A Descriptive Catalogue of Books and Manuscripts in the Clifton Waller Barrett Library.* Charlottesville: University Press of Virginia (1974).

(FULLER) Myerson, Joel. *Margaret Fuller: A Descriptive Bibliography.* University of Pittsburgh Press, 1978.

(GALSWORTHY) Fabes, Gilbert H. *John Galsworthy: His First Editions Points and Values.* London: W. and G. Foyle (1932).

(GARDNER) Howell, John M. *John Gardner: A Bibliographical Profile.* Carbondale and Edwardsville: Southern Illinois University Press (1980).

(GARRETT) Wright, Stuart. *George Garrett: A Bibliography, 1947–1988.* (Huntsville, Tex): Texas Review Press, Sam Houston State University, 1989.

(GASCOYNE) Benford, Colin T. *David Gascoyne: A Bibliography of His Works (1929–1985).* Isle of Wight: Heritage Books (no-date).

(GIBBINGS) Kirkus, A. Mary. *Robert Gibbings: A Bibliography.* London: J.M. Dent (1962).

(GILL) Gill, Evan R. *Bibliography of Eric Gill.* Folkeston and London: Rowman and Littlefield, Dawsons of Pall Mall, 1973.

(GINSBERG) Dowden, George. *A Bibliography of Works by Allen Ginsberg.* City Lights Books (San Francisco, 1971).

(GISSING) Collie, Michael. *George Gissing A Bibliography.* (Toronto and Buffalo): Dawson (1975).

(GLASGOW) Kelly, William W. *Ellen Glasgow: A Bibliography.* Charlottesville: The Bibliographical Society of the University of Virginia (1964).

(GOYEN) Wright, Stuart. *William Goyen: A Descriptive Bibliography, 1938–1985.* (Westport, Conn.): Meckler Publishing (1986).

(GRAVES) Higginson, F. H., and Williams, William P. *Robert Graves: A Bibliography.* (Hampshire, England): St. Paul's Bibliographies, 1987.

(GREENE) Wilson, Robert A. *Ben K. Green: A Descriptive Bibliography of Writings by and about Him.* Flagstaff: Northland Press (1977).

(GREENE) Wobbe, R. A. *Graham Greene: A Bibliography and Guide to Research.* New York and London: Garland Publishing, Inc., 1979.

(GREY) Myers, Edward and Judith. *A Bibliographical Check List of the Writings of Zane Grey.* Collinsville, Ct.: Country Lane Books, 1986.

(GUNN) Hagstrom, Jack W. C., and Bixby, George. *Thom Gunn: A Bibliography, 1940–78.* London: Bertram Rota (1979).

(HAGGARD) Scott, J. E. *Sir Henry Rider Haggard, 1856–1925.* Takeley (England): Elkin Mathews Ltd., 1947.

(HAGGARD) McKay, George L. *A Bibliography of the Writings of Sir Rider Haggard.* London: The Bookman's Journal, 1930.

(HAMMETT) Layman, Richard. *Dashiell Hammett: A Descriptive Bibliography.* University of Pittsburgh Press, 1979.

(HANLEY) Gibbs, Linnea. *James Hanley: A Bibliography.* Vancouver: William Hoffer, 1980.

(HARDY) Webb, A. P. *A Bibliography of the Works of Thomas Hardy, 1865–1915.* New York: Burt Franklin (1968).

(HAWTHORNE) Clark, C. E. Frazer, Jr. *Nathaniel Hawthorne: A Descriptive Bibliography.* University of Pittsburgh Press, 1978.

(HEARN) Perkins, P. D. and Ione. *Lafcadio Hearn: A Bibliography of His Writings.* Boston and New York: Houghton Mifflin Company, 1934.

(HEINLEIN) Owings, Mark. *Robert A. Heinlein: A Bibliography.* Baltimore: Croatan House (1973).

(HEMINGWAY) Hanneman, André. *Ernest Hemingway: A Comprehensive Bibliography.* Princeton University Press, 1967.

(HEMINGWAY) Hanneman, André. *Supplement to Ernest Hemingway: A Comprehensive Bibliography.* Princeton University Press, 1975.

(HENTY) Dartt, Robert L. *G.A. Henty: A Bibliography.* Dar-Web, Inc. Cedar Grove (N.J.): John Sherratt, Altricham (1971).

(HERBERT, A. P.) See *Coppard.*

(HERBERT, F.) Levack, Daniel J. H. *Dune Master: A Frank Herbert Bibliography.* (Westport, CT.): Meckler (1988).

(HERBERT, W.) Winkle, William Mitchell Van. *Henry William Herbert [Frank Forester]: A Bibliography of His Writings 1832-1858.* Portland, Ore.: Southworth-Anthoesen Press, 1936.

(HERGESHEIMER) Swire, H. L. R. *A Bibliography of the Works of Joseph Hergesheimer.* Philadelphia: Centaur Book Shop, 1922.

(HILLERMAN) Heib, Louis A. *Tony Hillerman: A Bibliography.* Tucson: Press of the Gigantic Hound, 1990.

(HODGSON) Sweetser, Wesley D. *Ralph Hodgson: A Bibliography.* New York & London: Garland Publishing, Inc., 1980.

(HOGARTH PRESS) Woolmer, J. Howard. *A Checklist of The Hogarth Press, 1917-1946.* Revere, Mass.: Wollmer/Brotherson Ltd., 1986.

(HOLMES) Currier, Thomas Franklin. *A Bibliography of Oliver Wendell Holmes.* New York University Press, 1953.

(HOPKINS) Dunne, Tom. *Gerard Manley Hopkins A Comprehensive Bibliography.* Oxford: Clarendon Press (1978).

(HORGAN) Horgan, Paul. *Approaches to Writing.* Farrar, Straus and Giroux, New York (1973).

(HOUSMAN) Carter, John, and Sparrow, John. *A.E. Housman: A Bibliography.* 2d ed., rev. William White. (Suffolk): St. Paul's Bibliographies, 1982.

(HOUSMAN) Ehrsam, Theodore G. *A Bibliography of Alfred Edward Housman.* Boston: F.W. Faxon Company, 1941.

(HOWARD) Lord, Glenn. *The Last Celt: A Bio-Bibliography of Robert Ervin Howard.* West Kingston (R.I.): Donald M. Grant, 1976.

(HOWELLS) Gibson, William M., and Arms, George. *A Bibliography of William Dean Howells.* New York: New York Public Library (1971).

HOWES, Wright. *U.S. Iana (1650-1950).* New York: Bowker, 1962.

(HUDSON) Payne, John R. *W.H. Hudson: A Bibliography.* (Hamden, Ct.): Archon Books (1977).

(HUGHES) Dickinson, Donald C. *A Bio-bibliography of Langston Hughes: 1902-1967.* (Hamden, Ct.): Archon Books, 1972.

(HUXLEY) Eschelbach, Claire John, and Shober, Joyce Lee. *Aldous Huxley: A Bibliography, 1916-1959.* Berkeley: University of California Press, 1961.

(IRVING) Langfeld, William R. *Washington Irving: A Bibliography.* New York: New York Public Library, 1933.

(JAMES) Edel, Leon, and Laurence, Dan H. *A Bibliography of Henry James.* Oxford: Clarendon Press, 1982.

(JARRELL) Wright, Stuart. *Randall Jarrell: A Descriptive Bibliography, 1929–1983.* Charlottesville: University Press of Virginia (1986).

(JEFFERS) Alberts, S. S. *A Bibliography of the Works of Robinson Jeffers.* Rye, N.Y.: Cultural History Research, 1961.

JOHNSON, Merle. *American First Editions.* Revised and Enlarged by Jacob Blanck. Waltham, Mass.: Mark press, 1969.

(JOYCE) Slocum, John J., and Cahoon, Herbert. *A Bibliography of James Joyce.* Westport, Ct.: Greenwood Press (1953).

(JONES) Dace, Letitia. *LeRoi Jones (Imamu Amiri Baraka): A Checklist of Works by and About Him.* London: Nether Press, 1971.

(KEATS) MacGillivray, J. R. *Keats: A Bibliography and Reference Guide with an Essay on Keats's Reputation.* University of Toronto Press (1949).

(KEROUAC) Charters, Ann. *A Bibliography of Works by Jack Kerouac.* New York: Phoenix Bookshop, 1975.

(KIPLING) Livingston, Flora V. *Bibliography of the Works of Rudyard Kipling.* New York: Burt Franklin (1968).

(KIPLING) Livingston, Flora V. *Supplement to a Bibliography of the Works of Rudyard Kipling.* New York: Burt Franklin (1968).

(KOESTLER) Merrill, Reed, and Frazier, Thomas. *Arthur Koestler: An International Bibliography.* Ann Arbor: Ardis (1979).

(LAMB) Thomson, J. C. *Bibliography of the Writings of Charles and Mary Lamb.* Hull: J.R. Tutin, 1908.

(LARKIN) Bloomfield, B. C. *Philip Larkin: A Bibliography 1933–1976.* London/Boston: Faber and Faber (1979).

(LARDNER) Bruccoli, Matthew J., and Layman, Richard. *Ring W. Lardner: A Descriptive Bibliography.* University of Pittsburgh Press (1976).

(LAWRENCE, D. H.) Roberts, Warren. *A Bibliography of D.H. Lawrence.* 2d ed. Cambridge University Press (1982).

(LAWRENCE, T. E.) O'Brien, Philip M. *T.E. Lawrence: A Bibliography.* Boston: G.K. Hall (1988).

(LEIBER) Morgan, Chris. *Fritz Leiber: A Bibliography 1934–1979.* Birmingham: Morgenstern, Selly Oak, 1979.

(LEGUIN) Cogell, Elizabeth Cummins. *Ursula K. LeGuin: A Primary and Secondary Bibliography.* Boston: G.K. Hall (1983).

(LESSING) Brueck, Eric T. *Doris Lessing: A Bibliography of Her First Editions.* (London): Metropolis (Antiquarian Books) Ltd, 1984.

(LEVERTOV) Wilson, Robert. *A Bibliography of Denise Levertov.* New York: Phoenix Bookshop, 1972.

(LEWIS, C. S.) Christopher, Joe R., and Ostling, Joan K. *C.S. Lewis: An Annotated Checklist of Writings About Him and His Works.* (Rochester): Kent State University Press (no-date).

(LEWIS, W.) Morrow, Bradford, and Lafourcade, Bernard. *A Bibliography of the Writings of Wyndham Lewis.* Santa Barbara: Black Sparrow Press, 1978.

(LONDON) Woodbridge, Hensley C., London, John, and Tweney, George H. *Jack London: A Bibliography.* Georgetown: Talisman Press, 1966.

(LONDON) Sisson, James E. III, and Martens, Robert W. *Jack London First Editions.* Oakland: Star Rover House, 1979.

(LONDON) Walker, Dale L., and Sisson, James E. III. *The Fiction of Jack London: A Chronological Bibliography.* El Paso: Texas Western Press, 1972.

(LONGFELLOW) Livingston, Luther S. *A Bibliography of the First Editions . . . of Henry Wadsworth Longfellow.* New York: Burt Franklin (1968).

(LOVECRAFT) Owings, Mark, with Chalker, Jack L. *The Revised H.P. Lovecraft Bibliography.* Baltimore: Mirage Press, 1973.

(LOWELL) Chamberlain, Jacob Chester, and Livingston, Luther S. *A Bibliography of the First Editions in Book Form of the Writings of James Russell Lowell.* New York: Privately Printed, 1914.

(LOWRY) Woolmer, J. Howard. *Malcolm Lowry: A Bibliography.* Revere, Mass.: Woolmer/Brotherson Ltd., 1983.

(LYTLE) Wright, Stuart. *Andrew Nelson Lytle: A Bibliography 1920–1982.* Sewanee (Tenn.): University of the South, 1982.

(MacDONALD) Shine, Walter and Jean. *A Bibliography of the Published Works of John D. MacDonald.* Gainesville: University of Florida, 1980.

(MacDONALD) Bruccoli, Matthew J. *Ross Macdonald / Kenneth Millar: A Descriptive Bibliography.* University of Pittsburgh Press, 1983.

(MACHEN) Goldstone, Adrian, and Sweetser, Wesley. *A Bibliography of Arthur Machen.* New York: Haskell House, 1973.

(MacLEISH) Mullaly, Edward J. *Archibald MacLeish: A Checklist.* Kent State University Press (1973).

(MacNEICE) Brown, Terence, and Reid, Alec. *Time Was Away: The World of Louis MacNeice.* (Dublin): Dolmen Press (1974).

(MASEFIELD) Handley-Taylor, Geoffrey. *John Masefield, O.M. The Queen's Poet Laureate.* London: Cranbrook Tower Press (1960).

(MAUGHAM) Stott, Raymond Toole. *A Bibliography of the Works of W. Somerset Maugham.* Edmonton: University of Alberta Press, 1973.

(McCARTHY) Goldman, Sherli Evens. *Mary McCarthy: A Bibliography.* Harcourt, New York: Brace & World (1968).

(McCLURE) Clements, Marshall. *A Catalog of Works by Michael McClure, 1956–1965.* New York: Phoenix Bookshop (1965).

(McCULLERS) Shapiro, Adrian M., Bryer, Jackson R., and Field, Kathleen. *Carson McCullers: A Descriptive Listing and Annotated Bibliography of Criticism.* New York and London: Garland Publishing, Inc., 1980.

(McFEE) Babb, James T. *A Bibliography of the Writings of William McFee.* Garden City: Doubleday, Doran & Co., 1931.

(MENCKEN) Fre, Carroll. *A Bibliography of the Writings of H.L. Mencken.* Philadelphia: The Centaur Book Shop, 1924.

(MEREDITH) Collie, Michael. *George Meredith: A Bibliography.* (Toronto and Buffalo): University of Toronto Press (1974).

(MEREDITH) Forman, Maurice Buxton. *A Bibliography of the Writings in Prose and Verse of George Meredith.* New York: Haskell House, 1971.

(MEREDITH) Forman, Maurice Buxton. *Meredithiana: Being a Supplement to the Bibliography of Meredith.* New York: Haskell House, 1971.

(MERTON) Breit, Marquita E. *Thomas Merton: A Comprehensive Bibliography.* New ed. New York and London: Garland Publishing, Inc., 1986.

(MILLAY) Yost, Karl. *A Bibliography of the Works of Edna St. Vincent Millay.* New York and London: Harper & Brothers, 1937.

(MILLER) Porter, Bern. *Henry Miller: A Chronology and Bibliography.* (Baltimore: Waverly Press, 1945).

(MILLER) Moore, Thomas H. *Bibliography of Henry Miller.* (Minneapolis): Henry Miller Literary Society, 1961.

(MOORE, G.) Gilcher, Edwin. *A Bibliography of George Moore.* Dekalb: Northern Illinois University Press (1970).

(MOORE, M.) Abbott, Craig S. *Marianne Moore: A Descriptive Bibliography.* University of Pittsburgh Press, 1977.

(MORGAN, Chas.) See Coppard.

(MORLEY) Lee, Alfred P. *A Bibliography of Christopher Morley.* Garden City: Doubleday, Doran & Company, 1935.

(MORLEY) Lyle, Guy R., and Brown, H. Tatnall, Jr. *A Bibliography of Christopher Morley.* Washington, D.C.: The Scarecrow Press, 1952.

(MUIR) Mellown, Elgin W. *Bibliography of the Writings of Edwin Muir.* University, Ala.: University of Alabama Press (1964).

(MUIR) Kimes, William F., and Maymie, B. *John Muir: A Reading Bibliography.* Fresno: Panorama West Books, 1986.

(MUIR) *P.H. Muir: A Check List of His Published Work.* (No author listed). Blakeney (Norfolk, England): Elkin Mathews, 1983.

(MUMFORD) Newman, Elmer S. *Lewis. Lewis Mumford: A Bibliography 1914–1970.* New York: Harcourt Brace Jovanovic, Inc. (1971).

(MUNDY) Grant, Donald M. *Talbot Mundy: Messenger of Destiny.* West Kingston (R.I.): Donald M. Grant, 1983.

(NABOKOV) Juliar, Michael. *Vladimir Nabokov: A Descriptive Bibliography.* New York and London: Garland Publishing, Inc., 1986.

(NATHAN) Laurence, Dan H. *Robert Nathan: A Bibliography.* New Haven: Yale University Library, 1960.

(NEWTON) (Fleck, Robert). *A. Edward Newton: A Collection of His Work.* (New Castle, Del.): Oak Knoll Books, 1986.

(NIN) Franklin, Benjamin, V. *Anaïs Nin: A Bibliography.* Kent State University Press (1973).

(NORRIS) Lohf, Kenneth A., and Sheehy, Eugene P. *Frank Norris: A Bibliography.* Los Gatos (Calif.): The Talisman Press, 1959.

(OATES) Lercangee, Francine. *Joyce Carol Oates: An Annotated Bibliography.* New York and London: Garland Publishing Inc., 1986.

(O'CASEY) Ayling, Ronald, and Durkan, Michael J. *Sean O'Casey: A Bibliography.* Seattle: University of Washington Press (1978).

(O'CONNOR) Farmer, David. *Flannery O'Connor: A Descriptive Bibliography.* New York and London: Garland Publishing Inc., 1981.

(O'CONNOR) Sheehy, Maurice, and Frank, Michael. *Studies on Frank O'Connor.* Dublin: Gill & Macmillan (1969).

(O'FLAHERTY) Doyle, Paul A. *Liam O'Flaherty: An Annotated Bibliography.* Troy, N.Y.; Whitston Publishing Co., 1972.

(O'HARA) Smith, Alexander Jr. *Frank O'Hara: A Comprehensive Bibliography.* New York and London: Garland Publishing Inc., 1979.

(O'HARA) Bruccoli, Matthew J. *John O'Hara: A Descriptive Bibliography.* University of Pittsburgh Press, 1978.

(OLSON) Butterick, George F., and Glover, Albert. *A Bibliography of Works by Charles Olson.* New York: Phoenix Bookshop, 1967.

(O'NEILL) Atkinson, Jennifer McCabe. *Eugene O'Neill: A Descriptive Bibliography.* University of Pittsburgh Press, 1974.

(OSLER) Golden, Richard L., M.D., and Roland, Charles G., M.D. *Sir William Osler: An Annotated Bibliography with Illustrations.* San Francisco: Norman Publishing, 1988.

(OZ) Greene, Douglas G., and Martin, Dick. *Bibliographia Oziana.* (No-place): International Wizard of Oz Club (1976).

(PATCHEN) Morgan, Richard G. *Kenneth Patchen.* Mamaroneck, N.Y.: Paul P. Appel (1978).

(PERCY) Wright, Stuart. *Walker Percy: A Bibliography: 1930–1984.* (Westport, Ct.): Meckler Publishing, (1986).

(PERCY) Hobson, Linda Whitney. *Walker Percy: A Comprehensive Descriptive Bibliography.* New Orleans: Faust Publishing Co., 1988.

(POE) Robertson, John W., M.D. *Bibliography of the Writings of Edgar A. Poe.* New York: Kraus Reprint Co., 1969.

(PORTER) MacLean, David G. *Gene Stratton-Porter.* Decatur: (Americana Books), 1987.

(PORTER, K. A.) Waldrip, Louise, and Bauer, Shirley Ann. *A Bibliography of the Works of Katherine Anne Porter* and *A Bibliography of the Criticism of the Works of Katherine Anne Porter.* Metuchen, N.J.: Scarecrow Press, 1969.

(PORTER) Clarkson, Paul S. *A Bibliography of William Sydney Porter (O. Henry).* Caldwell (Idaho): Caxton Printers, 1938.

(POTTER) Linder, Leslie. *A History of the Writings of Beatrix Potter.* London/New York: Frederick Warne (1971).

(POUND) Gallup, Donald. *Ezra Pound: A Bibliography.* Charlottesville: University Press of Virginia (1983).

(POWYS) Thomas, Dante. *A Bibliography of the Writings of John Cowper Powys: 1872–1963.* Mamaroneck, N.Y.: Paul P. Appel, 1975.

(PRICE) Wright, Stuart, and West, James L. W. III. *Reynolds Price: A Bibliography, 1949–1984.* Charlottesville: University Press of Virginia (1986).

(PYNCHON) Mead, Clifford. *Thomas Pynchon: A Bibliography of Primary and Secondary Materials.* (Elmwood Park, Ill.): Dalkey Archive Press (1989).

(QUILLER-COUCH) Brittain, F. *Arthur Quiller-Couch: A Biographical Study of Q.* Cambridge and New York: University Press/Macmillan 1948.

(RACKHAM) Latimore, Sarah Briggs, and Haskell, Grace Clark. *Arthur Rackham: A Bibliography.* Jacksonville, Fla.: San Marco Bookstore (1936).

(RANSOM) Young, Thomas Daniel. *John Crowe Ransom: Critical Essays and a Bibliography.* Baton Rouge: Louisiana State University Press (1968).

(REXROTH) Hartzell, James, and Zumwinkle, Richard. *Kenneth Rexroth: A Checklist of His Published Writings.* Los Angeles: Friends of the UCLA Library, 1967.

(RIDING) Wexler, Joyce Piell. *Laura Riding: A Bibliography.* New York and London: Garland Publishing, Inc. 1981.

(RILEY) Russo, Anthony J., and Dorothy R. *A Bibliography of James Whitcomb Riley.* Indianapolis: Indiana Historical Society, 1944.

(ROBERTS) Murphy, P. *Kenneth Lewis Roberts: A Bibliography.* Privately printed (1975).

(ROETHKE) McLeod, James Richard. *Theodore Roethke: A Bibliography.* The Kent State University Press, 1973.

(ROOSEVELT) Wheelock, John Hall. *A Bibliography of Theodore Roosevelt.* New York: Charles Scribner's Sons, 1920.

(RUSKIN) *The Bibliography . . . Arranged in Chronological Order of the Published Writings in Prose and Verse of John Ruskin, M.A. (from 1834 to 1881).* Paternoster Row, London: Eliot Stock.

(RUSSELL) Yost, Karl, and Renner, Frederic G. *A Bibliography of the Published Works of Charles M. Russell.* Lincoln: University of Nebraska Press (1971).

SABIN, Joseph. *A Dictionary of Books Relating to America.*

(SALINGER) Starosciak, Kenneth. *J.D. Salinger: A Thirty-Year Bibliography, 1938–1968.*

(SAROYAN) Kherdian, David. *A Bibliography of William Saroyan 1934–64.* San Francisco: Roger Beacham (1965).

(SAYERS) Gilbert, Colleen B. *A Bibliography of the Works of Dorothy L. Sayers.* Hamden, Connecticut: Archon Books, 1978.

SCHWARTZ, Dr. Jacob. *1100 Obscure Points.* Bristol, (England): Chatford House Press (1931).

(SHIEL) Morse A. Reynolds. *The Works of M. P. Shiel.* Los Angeles: Fantasy Publishing Co., Inc., 1948.

(SILLITOE) Gerard, David. *Alan Sillitoe: A Bibliography.* (London, England): Mansell Publishing Limited, 1988.

(SITWELL) Fifoot, Richard. *A Bibliography of Edith, Osbert, and Sachererell Sitwell.* London: Rupert Hart-Davis, 1963.

(SMITH) Sidney-Fryer, Donald, and Hands, Divers. *Emperor of Dreams, A*

Clark Ashton Smith Bibliography. West Kingston, Rhode Island: Donald M. Grant, Publisher, 1978.

(SNYDER) McNeil, Katherine. *Gary Snyder: A Bibliography.* New York: The Phoenix Bookshop, 1983.

(SNYDER) Kherdian, David. *Gary Snyder: A Biographical Sketch and Descriptive Checklist.* Berkeley: Oyez, 1965.

(STEIN) Wilson, Robert A. *Gertrude Stein: A Bibliography.* New York: The Phoenix Bookshop, 1974.

(STEINBECK) Goldstone, Adrian H., and Payne, John R. *John Steinbeck: A Biographical Catalogue of the Adrian H. Goldstone Collection.* Austin: The University of Texas Press, (1974).

(STEVENS) Edelstein, J. M. *Wallace Stevens: A Descriptive Bibliography.* University of Pittsburgh Press, 1973.

(STEVENSON) Prideaux, Colonel W. F. *A Bibliography of the Works of Robert Louis Stevenson.* New York: Burt Franklin (1968).

(STOUT) Townsend, Guy M. *Rex Stout: An Annotated Primary and Secondary Bibliography.* New York and London: Garland Publishing, Inc., 1980.

(STOWE) Hildreth, Margaret Holbrook. Harriet Beecher Stowe: A Bibliography. (Hamden, Ct.): Archon Books, 1976.

STREETER, Thomas W. *Bibliography of Texas 1795–1845.* Cambridge: Harvard University Press, 1960.

(SWINBURNE) Wise, Thomas J. *A Bibliography of the Writings in Prose and Verse of Algernon Charles Swinburne.* Vols. 1 & 2. London: Dawsons of Pall Mall, 1966.

(SYMONDS) Babington, Percy L. Bibliography of the Writings of John Addington Symonds. New York: Burt Franklin (1968).

(TARKINGTON) Currie, Barton. *Booth Tarkington: A Bibliography.* Garden City, New York: Doubleday, Doran & Company, Inc., 1932.

(TARKINGTON) Russo, Dorothy Ritter, and Sullivan, Thelma L. *A Bibliography of Booth Tarkington, 1869–1946.* Indianapolis: Indiana Historical Society, 1949.

(TATE) Falwell, Marshall Jr. *Allen Tate: A Bibliography.* New York: David Lewis, 1969.

(TAYLOR) Wright, Stuart. *Peter Taylor: A Descriptive Bibliography, 1934–87.* Charlottesville: University Press of Virginia (1988).

(TENNYSON) Tennyson, Charles, and Fall, Christine. *Alfred Tennyson: An Annotated Bibliography.* Athens: University of Georgia Press (1967).

(TENNYSON) *The Bibliography of Tennyson.* New York: Haskell House Publishers Ltd., 1970.

(THACKERAY) Van Duzer, Henry Sayre. *A Thackeray Library.* New York: Burt Franklin (1971).

(THOMAS) Rolph, J. Alexander. *Dylan Thomas: A Bibliography.* New York: New Directions (1956).

(THOREAU) Borst, Raymond R. *Henry David Thoreau: A Descriptive Bibliography.* University of Pittsburgh Press, 1982.

(THURBER) Bowden, Edwin T. *James Thurber: A Bibliography.* Columbus: Ohio State University Press (1968).

(TROLLOPE) Sadleir, Michael. *Trollope: A Bibliography.* (Kent, England): Dawson, 1977.

(TWAIN) Johnson, Merle. *A Bibliography of the Work of Mark Twain.* New York and London: Harper & Brothers Publishers, 1910.

(TWAIN) McBride, William M. *Mark Twain: A Bibliography of the Collections of the Mark Twain Memorial and the Stowe-Day Foundation.* Hartford, Ct: McBride/Publisher (1984).

(VERNE) Myers, Edward and Judith. *Jules Verne: A Bibliography.* New Hartford, Ct. Country Lane Books, 1989.

(VONNEGUT) Pieratt, Asa B., and Klinkowitz, Jerome. *Kurt Vonnegut, Jr.: A Descriptive Bibliography and Annotated Secondary Checklist.* (Hamden, Ct.): Archon Books, 1974.

(VONNEGUT) Pieratt, Asa B., Jr., Huffman-Klinkowitz, Julie, and Klinkowitz, Jerome. *Kurt Vonnegut: A Comprehensive Bibliography.* (Hamden, Ct.): Archon Books, 1987.

WAGNER, Henry R., and Camp, Charles L. *The Plains & the Rockies.* San Francisco: John Howell-Books, 1982.

(WALLACE) Lofts, W.O.G., and Adley, Derek. *The British Bibliography of Edgar Wallace.* London: Howard Baker (1969).

(WALPOLE) Hazen, A. T. *A Bibliography of Horace Walpole.* (Folkstone, England): Dawsons of Pall Mall, 1973.

(WARREN) Grimshaw, James A., Jr. *Robert Penn Warren: A Descriptive Bibliography, 1922–79.* Charlottesville: University Press of Virginia (1981).

(WATERS) Tanner, Terence A. *Frank Waters: A Bibliography.* Glenwood, Illinois: Meyerbooks (1983).

(WAUGH) Davis, Robert Murray, Doyle, Paul A., Gallagher, Donat, Linck, Charles E., and Bogaards, Winifred M. *A Bibliography of Evelyn Waugh.* Troy, N.Y.: Whitston Publishing Company, 1986.

(WELLS) Chappell, Fred A. *Bibliography of H. G. Wells.* Chicago: Covici-McGee Co., 1924.

(WEST) White, William. *Nathanael West: A Comprehensive Bibliography.* The Kent State University Press (1975).

(WHARTON) Melish, Lawson McClung. *A Bibliography of the Collected Writings of Edith Wharton.* New York: The Brick Row Book Shop, Inc., 1927.

(WHITE) Gallix, François. *T. H. White: An Annotated Bibliography.* New York and London: Garland Publishing, Inc., 1986.

(WHITMAN) Shay, Frank. *The Bibliography of Walt Whitman.* New York: Friedmans', 1920.

(WHITMAN) Wells, Carolyn, and Goldsmith, Alfred F. *A Concise Bibliography of the Works of Walt Whitman.* New York: Burt Franklin (1968).

(WILDE) Mason, Stuart. *Bibliography of Oscar Wilde.* London: T. Werner Laurie Ltd. (1914)

(WILLIAMS, C.) Glenn, Lois. *Charles W. S. Williams: A Checklist.* The Kent State University Press (1975).

(WILLIAMS, W.) Wallace, Emily Mitchell. *A Bibliography of William Carlos Williams.* Middletown, Ct.: Wesleyan University Press (1968).

(WILSON) Stanley, Colin. *The Work of Colin Wilson: An Annotated Bibliography & Guide.* San Bernardino: The Borgo Press, 1989.

(WODEHOUSE) Jasen, David A. *A Bibliography and Reader's Guide to the First Editions of P.G. Wodehouse.* (London): Greenhill Books (1970).

(WOLFE) Johnston, Carol. *Thomas Wolfe: A Descriptive Bibliography.* University of Pittsburgh Press, 1989.

(WOLLSTONECRAFT) Windle, J. R. *Mary Wollstonecraft (Godwin): A Bibliography of Her Writings.* Los Angeles: 1988.

(WOOLF) Kirkpatrick, B. J. *A Bibliography of Virginia Woolf.* Oxford: Clarendon Press, 1980.

(YEATS) Wade, Allan. *A Bibliography of the Writings of W. B. Yeats.* London: Rupert Hart-Davis, 1958.

ZEMPLE, Edward N. and Linda A. *First Editions: A Guide to Identification.* 2d ed. (Peoria) Spoon River Press (1989).

(ZUKOFSKY) Zukofsky, Celia. *A Bibliography of Louis Zukofsky.* Los Angeles: Black Sparrow Press, 1969.